Railroads of Nevada and Eastern California

Volume III

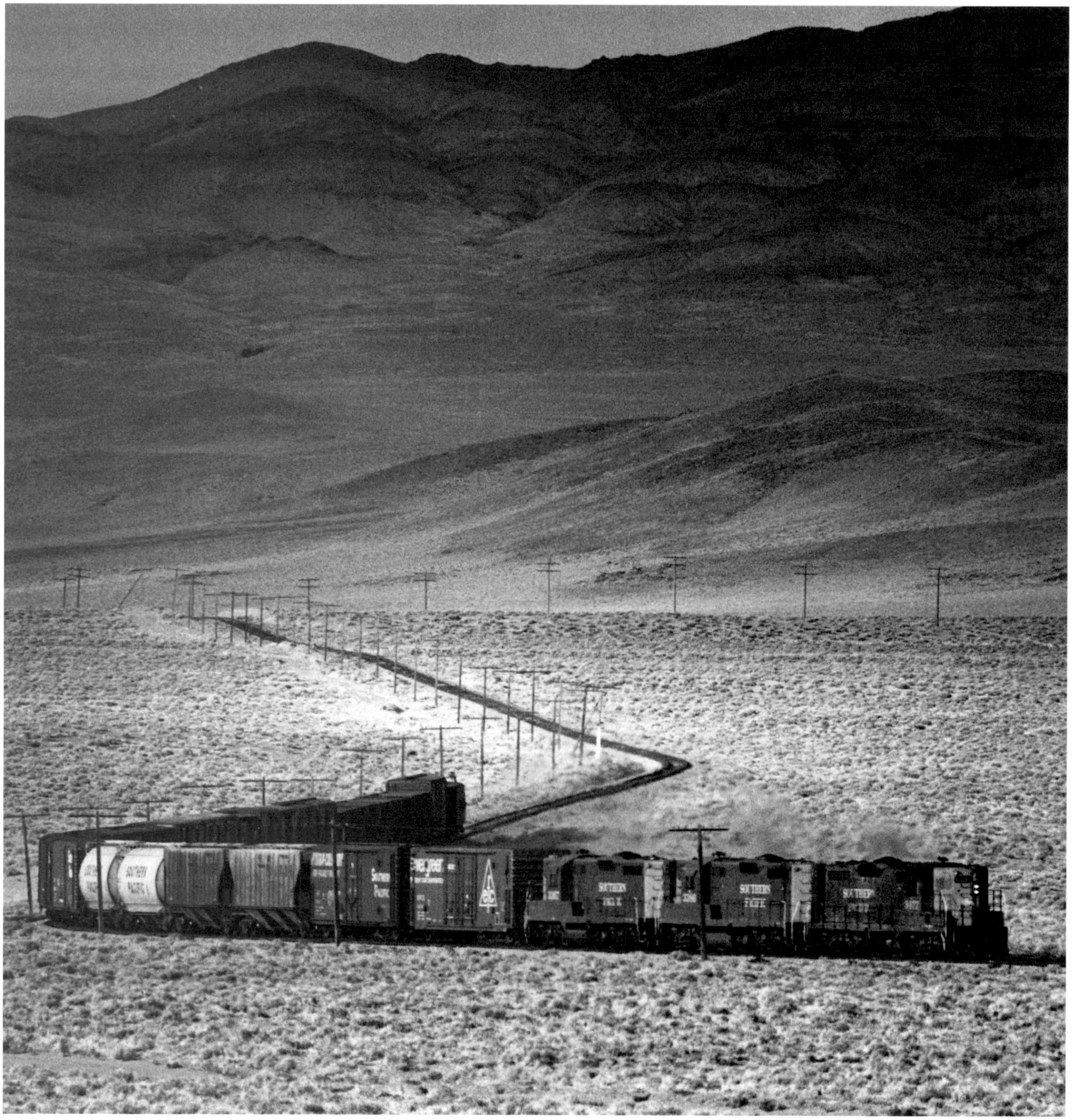

RAILROADS OF NEVADA AND EASTERN CALIFORNIA

Volume III
More on the Northern Roads

DAVID F. MYRICK

University of Nevada Press
Reno & Las Vegas

This book was made possible in part with a grant from Nevada Humanities, a program of the National Endowment for the Humanities.

University of Nevada Press, Reno, Nevada 89557 USA

Manufactured in the United States of America

Layout and composition: David Alcorn, Alcorn Publication Design

Library of Congress Cataloging-in-Publication Data

Myrick, David F.
Railroads of Nevada and eastern California / David F. Myrick
p. cm.
Reprint (vols. 1 and 2), with revisions. Originally published: Berkeley, Calif. : Howell-North Books. 1962–1963.
Includes index.
Contents: v. 1. The northern roads — v. 2. The southern roads — v. 3. More on the northern roads.
ISBN 978-0-87417-193-8 (vol. 1 : alk. paper)
ISBN 978-0-87417-194-5 (vol. 2 : alk. paper)
ISBN 978-0-87417-195-2 (set : alk. paper)
ISBN 978-0-87417-701-5 (vol. 3 : alk. paper)
ISBN 978-0-87417-734-3 (set : alk. paper)
1. Railroads—Nevada—History. 2. Railroads—California—History. I. Title.
HE2771.N3M9 1992
385'.06'5793—dc20 92-21672
CIP

The paper used in this book meets the requirements of American National Standard for Information Sciences—Permanence of Paper for Printed Library Materials, ANSI/NISO Z39.48-1992 (R2002). Binding materials were selected for strength and durability.

16 15 14 13 12 11 10 5 4 3 2

Frontispiece: Three GPs work their train around the undulating landscape north of Schurz on the way to Mina in December 1974. (Ted Benson photograph)

CONTENTS

PREFACE

Since the original volumes of *Railroads of Nevada and Eastern California* appeared over forty years ago, they have been reprinted several times. In these books, I have recorded the stories of the major railroads that traversed the state of Nevada and included photographic and map material for over sixty-five railroads.

After the publication of my books, my interest in the Great Basin continued, and I explored more of the Nevada backcountry. Many people shared my interest and suggested new information or made inquiries about different aspects of the life and times of these railroads, which were scattered across Nevada and eastern California and the communities they served.

With more information coming to the surface, new chapters evolved on the various railroads built during the zenith of railroad construction during the first two decades of the twentieth century. New territories, opened to commerce by the Fernley and Lassen Railway and the Western Pacific Railroad, encouraged the growth of the lumber industry, the expansion of copper mining, and the development of electric power-generating plants. In turn, these activities spawned new railroad lines.

In more recent times, the Nevada railroad scene has changed dramatically. New railroads have blossomed and major corporate changes have ensued, which constitute a chapter in this book titled "Recent Developments in Nevada Railroads." The preservation of old newspaper files, legal proceedings, and corporate records mandated another volume to complete the story of the railroads in this area.

The most exciting development in new historical resources was the discovery of the correspondence of Collis P. Huntington, who along with Leland Stanford, Charles Crocker, and Mark Hopkins—collectively known as the "Big Four"— built the Central Pacific (CP) Railroad and followed that with the Southern Pacific (SP) Railroad. The Huntington letters were found quite by chance. When a descendant, Archer M. Huntington, died, he bequeathed his Hispanic art history collection to Syracuse University in Upstate New York. The collection had been stored in a barn in Westchester County, just north of New York City.

A representative of the library arrived with his van to gather the material, and, after loading his truck, he noticed stacks of boxes in one corner of the barn. Waving his arm in that direction, he asked, "What is in that pile?" "Oh, those are letters that some railroad man wrote. We are going to trash them. Do you want them?" Fortunately, an affirmative answer followed, and the university man relieved the caretaker of his burden as well as saving this historical treasure.

So they went to the university, and the staff of the George Arents Research Library of Special Collections accepted the three-year task of arranging the incoming letters and letter books of Collis P. Huntington.

In the late 1970s, a subsidiary of the *New York Times* investigated the possibility of microfilming the collection. The project hinged on finding ten libraries willing to commit to purchasing the microfilms. Nine libraries agreed to buy the films, whereupon the microfilm company and a western railroad historian heard about each other, so the project was consummated. The result was 115 reels of microfilm. Information and quotations from some of these letters will be found in the Central Pacific and Carson and Colorado Railway chapters.

In addition to the updating of my first two volumes, in July 2006 I published *Western Pacific: The Last Transcontinental Railroad,* which focuses on the construction of the railroad.

ACKNOWLEDGMENTS

Undoubtedly, the greatest reward in researching for a book of this kind is meeting and talking with individuals who share a common interest in this subject. Some are in libraries, some grace historical societies, while others are found in county offices or archives. Some are in the immediate area, while others are in some distant location. Even more personal information comes from people who in past years lived in some community who generously share their recollections with those seeking firsthand information about an event or a business. Over the decades of research necessary to compile this historical record, I have talked with many amiable people whose names form an extended list. I hope that, from my notes, I have them all; for those I have missed, I sincerely apologize.

A number of railroad historians have provided answers to my questions. These include well-known names such as Guy L. Dunscomb, William A. Pennington, Jack Gibson, Lynn D. Farrar, Ted Benson, James H. Harrison, Al C. Phelps, and James Boynton—I climbed the path of the steep incline railway above the Caribou powerhouse with Jim; regrettably, some of these gentlemen are now resting in "the larger world." Others who have helped include James Bryant, S. S. Wheeler, Norman Lamb, Steve VanDenberg, Richard C. Datin, Ken Meeker, Grant S. Allen, Tim Purdy, and Bryce Kimber of Montello.

Over the years, the staff of the Plumas County Museum in Quincy has changed, but their gracious assistance remains at a constantly high level. Currently, this list includes Scott Lawson and Carol Paoli as well as Robert G. Moon and Linda Brennan who are no longer active in the museum. Judy Wells, Pat Nichols, Katherine Williams, and Isabel Andrews of the recorder's office in Quincy have always graciously assisted me in my search for corporate matters.

My thanks also go to Gail Bengard of the Lassen County Historical Society as well as to Cindy O'Rorke of the recorder's office and Robert L. Semon of the district library for important data in the Susanville area.

The Nevada Historical Society in Reno has long been a treasure trove of wonderful material. Here Peter L. Bandurraga, director, and his staff consisting of Lee Brumbough, Eric Moody, Michael Maher, and recently retired Lee Morensen have always been generous in response to my inquiries. Over the years, the Northeastern Nevada Museum in Elko has furnished me with important photographs from its collection, and I particularly thank Toni L. Mendive for scenes of Toano, a ghost town for more than a century.

More distant but equally helpful were John B. Bromley of the Union Pacific Railroad Museum and Cheryl Oakes of the Forest History Society based in Durham, North Carolina. In years past, Alissa Wiener and Ruby J. Shields of the Minnesota Historical Society as well as librarian Andrew F. Johnson of the University of Washington have provided elusive biographical information.

In California, Jim League and George Plantz of the Yuba Feather Historical Society brought to my attention the little-known flume and lumber railroads near Brownsville for which I express my gratitude. David Snyder and Jeff Crawford of the state archives in Sacramento responded well to my challenges for hidden records.

Again and again, it was the cooperative individuals who lived in some remote place who gave me the missing links in a historic record. Some I have mentioned previously, as they have helped in a number of geographic areas. Charles Moran furnished personal information concerning the N-C-O Railway, and Vinton Bowen White, daughter of the proprietor of the Sierra Valleys Railway, provided photographs and gave me great assistance when my research began many years ago. The story of the "Blue Anchor" box factory at Graeagle was assembled from information furnished by Walter Tyndell, Oravale M. Miller, Harvey West Jr., George P. Cotter, and James F. Flanagan. Residents of Chester, many formerly on the Red River Lumber payroll, filled in many gaps in that story. Among them are Murph Kerns, Gordon Purdy, John Sanders and Berti Sanders, Keith Dodge, and Mrs. Richard Lydden. Gene Aldrich guided me along the abandoned railroad grades of the Fruit Growers Supply (FGS) Company, while Jim Bryant and Jim Cooper toured me along the former railroads of the Lassen Lumber and Box Company and the Harvey Mountain area of the Red River Lumber Company. Frances Johnson of the FGS office in southern California worked diligently to arrange to have photos copied for me. Other FGS informants included Fred T. Abbay and James Hart.

The combination of a railroad and an aerial tramway of the Spanish Peak Lumber Company evoked a number of inquiries that were answered by Bill Jacks,

Harold Richards, and Eva Huntington. George McDow and William A. Jones, now Chico residents, added to my knowledge of the lumber industry in Plumas County. Logging operations around Cromberg and Sloat were explained by Stan Johnson, Orville B. Brown, George Penman, Edward C. Brown, and R. M. "Buster" Mason. Calvin Dorithy explored logging railroad grades with me around Portola, while Robert Cooke imparted some of his knowledge concerning Taylorsville. Donald W. Guidici of Vinton gave me important leads, as did Leonard Thayer Jr. and George P. Cotter of Quincy. Jim Johnson, Charles James, and Jim Cooper of the U.S. Forest Service informed me of some of the lumbering history they had researched. With his longtime association of Clover Valley Lumber Company, Clyde Spradling along with Tony DeMartini gave answers to my questions, while Dan Elliott guided me all the way to the site of Camp 14. A. Hunter Land III gave me recollections of his family's connection with the Feather River Railway along with two sterling photographs of the lumber mill. My sincere thanks to all who helped.

Railroads of Nevada and Eastern California

Volume III

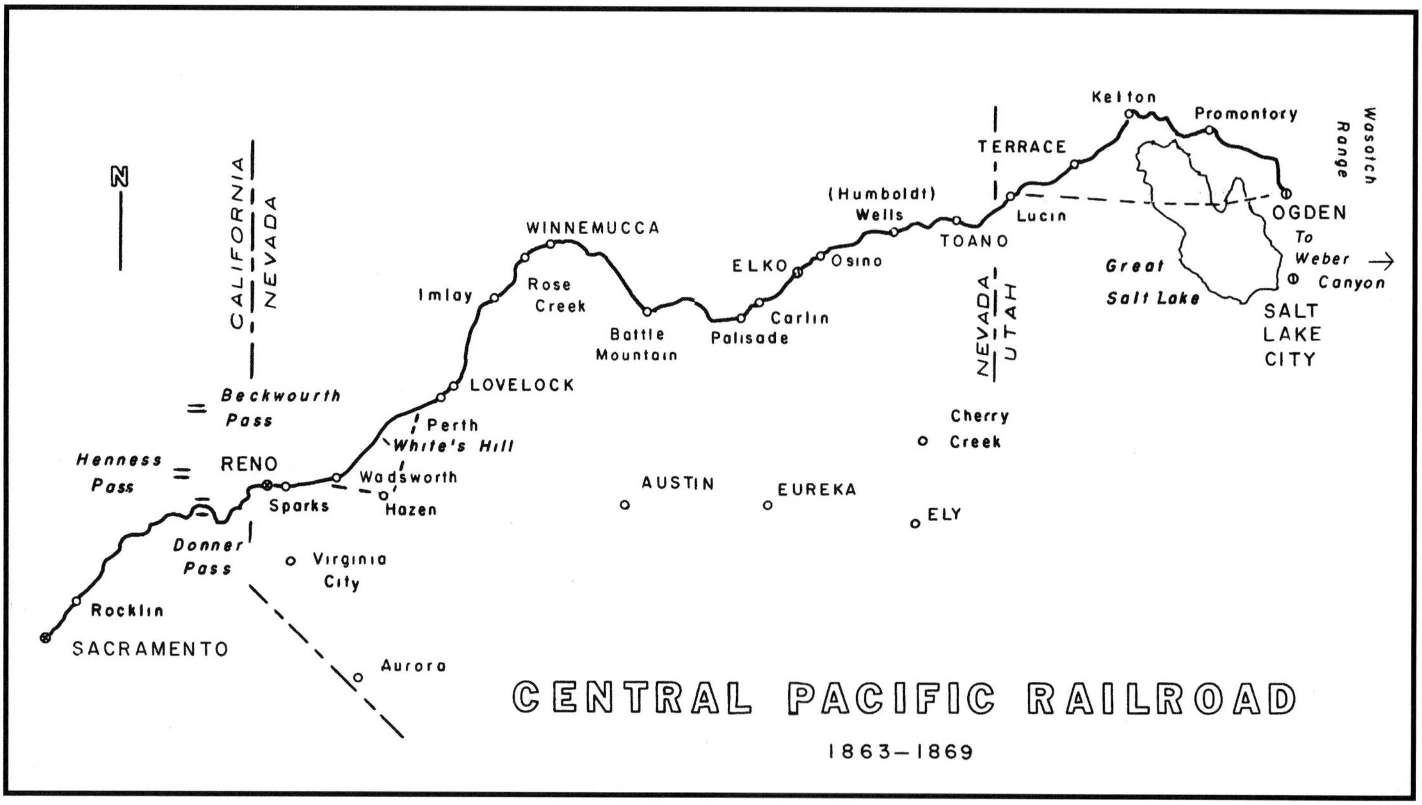

CENTRAL PACIFIC RAILROAD

1863–1869

CENTRAL PACIFIC RAILROAD

Much has been written about the Central Pacific Railroad, yet much of the story has remained untold. In this chapter, some of the lesser-known segments of its history are recorded. A general account of its construction across Nevada will be found in volume 1 of this series.

Small-town newspaper editors in the nineteenth century held fierce determination in promoting their own villages. The management of any prospective railroad, in their opinion, would be held grossly delinquent if the tracks did not reach their communities. For example, outlying newsmen regularly condemned the Central Pacific's Donner Pass route, publicizing any mishap or snow blockade, concluding with the claim that had the railroad been routed through their town, the difficulty would have been avoided.

Donner Pass formed one of the five routes seriously considered, as Theodore Judah, chief engineer of the Central Pacific RR explained in his July 1863 report. With Sacramento as the western terminal, he described barometrical reconnaissance of five routes across the Sierra Nevada as follows:

1. Via Folsom, Greenwood, and Georgetown
2. Via Auburn and Illinoistown, Dutch Flat and Donner Pass
3. Via Nevada [City] and Henness Pass
4. Via Downieville and Yuba Gap
5. Via Oroville, Bidwell's Bar, Middle [Fork of the] Feather River, and Beckwourth's Pass

Perhaps the loudest outcry emanated from newspapermen in Quincy, the county seat of Plumas County, north of Donner Pass. The most logical course, they contended, included a fork of the Feather River and Beckwourth Pass. Judah did not agree.

In his description of the Oroville route, Judah noted that it passed through Bidwell's Bar, then followed the Middle Fork of the Feather River, passing Nelson's Point, Jim Beckwourth's house at the western edge of the Sierra Valley, before surmounting Beckwourth's Pass. From there, it went up Long Valley and Pea Vine Valley to Fuller's Crossing on the Truckee, the present site of Reno and 283 miles from Sacramento. Side excursions permitted observations of the divide between the North and Middle Forks of the Feather River and Spring Garden Ranch. Nothing was said about the North Fork; perhaps its greater length removed it from consideration. Judah recognized, "The advantages of this [last mentioned] route consist in its low grades and a lower altitude of the summit than upon the other routes. But it also presents disadvantages, which render it next to impossible for us to avail ourselves of its advantages in this respect."

Judah estimated the distance to the future site of Reno from Sacramento to be eighty miles longer than via Donner Pass. Perhaps the most negative aspect was that "Bald Rock Canon . . . is a rocky gorge in the [Middle Fork of the] Feather river, rising with smooth granite sides, almost perpendicular, being 3,000 feet high upon the north side, and 2,500 on the South side, the length of this canon being about 1½ miles." Though less severe, the same general condition prevailed for the next fifty miles to Nelson's Point. Judah concluded his remarks on the Feather River passage: "The route is reluctantly placed among the list of those denominated unavailable for Pacific Railroad purposes." The additional 80 miles would have increased the government-bond aid by $3.84 million ($48,000 per mile in mountain territory) and would have invited more criticism.

Turning to the organizers, the usual accounts of the construction center so much on the driving force of Collis P. Huntington, Leland Stanford, Charles Crocker, and Mark Hopkins—conveniently packaged as the "Big Four"—that the contributions of others are brushed aside. Without diminishing the accomplishments of the Big Four, there were others who merit attention. Stanford's brother Charles was an investor, and Crocker's older brother proved a major figure. A. N. Towne was another.

Edwin Bryant Crocker (1818–1875), born in Upstate New York, graduated from Rensselaer Institute. For a short time, he engaged in railway surveying until his parents took him to Indiana in 1836. He read law and practiced in South Bend, and Sacramento after moving there in 1852. Prior to the reorganization of the California Supreme Court in 1863, Edwin Crocker briefly served on this tribunal. Becoming counsel of the Central Pacific, his letters to Huntington in New York provide lucid accounts of construction progress that Collis passed on to eastern investors in the railroad. Huntington leaned on Judge Crocker for answers to problems and new ideas. Responding to an inquiry in January 1867 when the tracks had reached Cisco on the west side of the summit, E. B. Crocker suggested six possible extensions of the railroad. One line would run north of what became Winnemucca to Boise City and the Salmon River in Idaho. From the same starting point, another extension would take a northwesterly course to Eugene City, Oregon, with a connection to Portland. His suggestions included branch lines to mining towns such as Austin and Aurora and the two Virginia Cities, one in Nevada and the other in Montana. The line to Aurora, Nevada, and down California's Owens Valley formed part of a connection with the projected Atlantic and Pacific Railroad around the site of future Needles, and, in the opposite direction, he envisioned a railroad from Sacramento to Clear Lake, terminating at Humboldt Bay.

Again in the summer of 1867, the judge wrote he felt "quite confident that we shall lay a continuous line to the Truckee [River] this year." He noted that the labor force was down from the previous year and that the payroll did not exceed three thousand, excluding teamsters, foremen, and so forth. This number was a far cry, he observed, from the general impression of twelve thousand men tackling the grade. By September, the force was increasing, but the grasp of winter precluded CP rails from reaching the Truckee River until the next spring.

In his own way, Huntington was just as busy in New York as his western associates. Besides the main task of raising money, he also purchased rail, locomotives, and supplies and then arranged for ships to convey these essentials to the Pacific Coast. From time to time, his routine was shattered when he received a hurried call to come to Washington to spur or stem some legislation. Always keeping a wary eye on the Union Pacific (UP) crowd, he was delighted to write the judge that he sold $2 million in CP bonds at 98, while the UP had to sell theirs at 90!

Huntington aimed to meet the Union Pacific in Weber Canyon in Utah, some thirty miles east of Ogden. In his letters written in 1868, he frequently found some way to move from an unrelated topic to the importance of reaching Weber Canyon. In April of that year, shortly before the first locomotive whistled at the site of future Reno, Huntington wrote Judge Crocker, "We all slept too long but will sleep no more until we get to Weber Canon." Two months earlier he had told Stanford that reaching Salt Lake by the end of the year and the Wasatch Range soon thereafter stood as possible goals, "and I am well satisfied we can do it if we make up our minds to do it. *Tell Charlie to let out a link.*" That summer he wrote Charlie, "*So work on as though Heaven was before and Hell behind you.*"

Adding to Huntington's frustrations was the difficulty to secure sufficient iron rail. All of the rail mills were overrun with orders for rail replacements in the spring of 1868, as ten times the normal broken rails had occurred during the cold winter. Technical difficulties at the mills compounded the problem. At the Danville Mill, two weeks were lost when the main shaft broke, while, at another mill, replacing a broken roller suspended operations for ten days. The Spuyten Devil Mill, which had been rolling 75 tons a day for the Central Pacific, suffered a fire in April, closing the plant for two months.

Transportation offered more challenges. A good sailing ship, such as the *Ellen Austin,* could be expected to sail around Cape Horn and arrive in San Francisco in 140 days. When it left in the spring of 1868, it carried 1,932 tons of rail, spikes, and splice bars—twice the load most ships carried. The Panama route provided a costly alternative for shipping rail and locomotives to be used only for meeting urgent needs.

Huntington sought other ways to speed shipments to California. In one case, he instructed Hopkins to pay the master of the *Pactolus* the promised bonus of $250 in currency if the shipload of rails reached San Francisco in 125 days, but the absence of further comment leaves the outcome in doubt. Various causes delayed shipments. The *Helvetia* returned in April 1868 after two weeks with its top masts out and leaking very badly. When repairs took longer than expected, the cargo was transferred to another ship. After losing sails and shipping a heavy sea that stove in bulwarks, the *Calhoun* limped into port at Rio de Janeiro for several weeks of repairs. A second ship also paused at Rio for repairs, but the size of the cargo on the *Calhoun*—2,000 tons of rails and fittings for 20 miles of track—made the delay particularly annoying. Adding to the frustrations was the breaking of the main balance wheel at the Scranton mill and a nine-day strike at other mills. To Huntington these events suggested that "it does seem as though the Devil was amongst our iron."

The rail delivery delays and the many miles of grading necessary to reach Weber Canyon brought the realization to reluctant Central Pacific men that they could not reach the canyon before the Union Pacific. The absence of continued CP railroad ownership to coal resources for locomotive fuel beyond the Wasatch Range also proved a disappointment.

In the later winter months of 1868, two parallel roadbeds marched across northern Utah for some distance. Finally, Promontory (Summit) became the meeting point with the Golden Spike amid appropriate ceremonies on May 10, 1869. Actually, the last spike was fabricated from iron. After difficult negotiations, the Union Pacific sold 72.51 miles of railroad to the CP, bringing the latter's ownership to Union Jct., 5 miles north (railroad-west) of Ogden. The UP leased the intervening 5 miles to the CP for 999 years.

Some Problems in Central Pacific's Early Operations

Though the Big Four worked as a unit, friction ranged among the principals. Crocker and Huntington seemed to be at odds more than once. For example, as the Central Pacific construction approached the finish line, Huntington turned more critical of Charles Crocker's management of the railroad, calling it a "miserable failure." Crocker stood ready to rescind his role; in a letter written shortly after the last spike, Crocker reminded old Collis that he had "frequently expressed a willingness to resign & urged all to use their judgment without regard to me. But as I have failed to notice or hear of any diprecation [*sic*] on the part of Stanford or Hopkins of the sentiments you have so freely expressed." Still, Crocker believed that the two associates were in sympathy with Huntington, and "therefore my position becomes very unpleasant and irksome." Crocker told Huntington that he had given the power of attorney to his brother to sell out completely, if necessary.

Crocker sought a diversion from his labors, and Mrs. Crocker wanted to go shopping in New York. So, on May 24, after having cast aside the mantle of superintendent, the Crocker family including two children departed for the East Coast. While in New York, Crocker conferred with Huntington, which apparently eased the tensions.

Crocker was not alone in his desire to travel; Huntington found himself besieged with requests for passes. Letters would begin with an amiable reference to a California sojourn and close with a request for a pass over the railroad. Members of Congress received favorable consideration, but most others were disappointed.

Although it appeared Huntington had managed to provide necessary funds through the sale of railroad and government-aid bonds, matters turned critical at the end of May 1869. Mark Hopkins, acting as treasurer, telegraphed Huntington for an immediate one hundred thousand dollars, to be followed by three hundred thousand dollars ten days later and still another two hundred thousand on June 15. "I don't see how we can get along with less," Hopkins declared, and then explained that the company had been behind in its payments for the past two months. Not only a lot of "finishing-up work" east of Wadsworth remained to be done, but the Big Four also stood committed to complete the rail link between Sacramento and San Francisco Bay.

The associates had spent five years of stressful work building the Central Pacific Railroad but now were tired. Top management suffered a severe blow when paralysis struck E. B. Crocker's right side while discussing business with Governor Stanford in San Francisco. The judge made some recovery within a week, but Hopkins expressed the thought that the judge's "days of mental labor are over." Although E. B. Crocker now had little to do with railroad operations, improved health enabled him to go to Europe for a prolonged stay the following year. While there he purchased many art objects for his gallery in Sacramento later bearing his name.

The New Superintendent

The associates recognized the need for a superintendent, but, except for Huntington, their isolation on the Pacific Coast made knowledge of other railroad candidates impossible. So the responsibility fell upon Huntington to discover the proper man for the task. Of course, he received unsolicited advice from the others; Hopkins wrote him that the man should have had "more railroad experience than any or all of us and we could well afford to pay a large salary." Stanford concurred, and Crocker told him to "get one as soon as possible."

Hopkins battered Huntington with telegrams seeking money, as payrolls lagged far behind. When funds finally arrived in Sacramento, Hopkins reported that as of July 24, 1869, the remittance would clear up the May payrolls and the "most pressing June bills" but not the June payrolls. When master mechanic E. F. Perkins, formerly of the Vermont Central, advised there was no immediate need for two engines at the builder's plant in Schenectady, New York, Huntington had them sold to garner a little more cash.

In the West, Charles Crocker, assistant general superintendent John Corning, and E. F. Perkins traveled to Promontory by daylight to determine where forces could be reduced. All twenty-seven gravel trains that had been distributing ballast on the track for several months were discontinued at the end of July 1869 with a considerable payroll savings.

Alban Nelson Towne

Huntington's letters, lightly sprinkled with advice that likely candidates for the general superintendent's position were forthcoming, kept his California associates guessing. After many inquiries, he focused on Alban Nelson Towne of Chicago. Towne had grown up in the best of Yankee traditions. Born in 1829 in Charlton (Dresser Hill), Massachusetts, he divided his time between school and work, so at maturity he had developed two trades: shoe making and painting. His first job paid him all of eight dollars a month plus board. An unrewarding venture in a small business caused him to go to Illinois in 1855 and sign up as a freight brakeman for the Chicago, Burlington, and Quincy Railroad.

Except for a brief interim in a supervisory position on the Chicago and Great Eastern Railway (Pennsylvania Railroad), he remained with the Burlington, advancing to assistant superintendent.

Responding to an invitation, Towne visited Huntington in New York on August 5, 1869. Offered the position of general superintendent of the Central Pacific at a modest salary, Towne returned to Chicago and wrote Huntington that he could not "sever my connection with this road to accept the great responsibility at a salary of less than $13,000 per annum." After the rejection of his second offer, Huntington wired Towne on August 17 that he would meet the salary demanded. Rather than replying immediately, Towne kept his prospective new employer dangling until he could confer with his boss, James F. Joy, president of the Burlington. Finally, on August 20, Towne telegraphed Huntington, "Your proposition read and accepted." Four days later, the California partners received Huntington's telegram about the new appointment; at almost the same time, they read the same news in the *Sacramento Union*, plus the additional advice of Towne's $13,000 annual salary.

Spurred on by the publicity of the "exorbitant" salary, the reaction was negative. Crocker refused to consent to the appointment until he knew more about the man. Stanford felt that any one of several assistants "will be about as good as any we can import." Even mild-mannered Mark Hopkins told Huntington, "We concur that he had better not come out here."

Doubts about Towne's experience and the unwanted publicity threatened Towne's acceptance by the associates. After all, the Burlington, consisting of lines to cities in its corporate title plus a few branches, measured only 386 miles, about half the length of the Central Pacific. For those times, the salary proved immense; Towne's superior earned just $10,000, and the president of the Burlington received just a trifle more.

Recognizing the hostile reception confronting his new man, Huntington considered the matter before deciding to introduce Towne personally to his associates. The two men left Chicago on the night of September 6 and, pausing along the way, did not reach Sacramento until two weeks later. One can imagine the hours Huntington devoted to coaching his protégé as their trains rumbled westward. During his California visit of several weeks, Huntington mollified Crocker, Stanford, and Hopkins, and Towne moved into his new assignment.

In his new post, Towne demonstrated that he had a good grasp of his responsibilities. While carefully informing Huntington by letter and telegram, he showed proper deference to the views of the other partners. Reflecting increased confidence in his abilities as the Central Pacific expanded, Towne moved up to the general manager's position three years later. He proved to be a dedicated man with so few vacations during the next twenty-six years that they proved newsworthy. On one occasion, he did take extended leaves for health reasons.

Snow Problems Disrupt Operations

Winter weather sometimes resulted in reduced operating receipts. Mark Hopkins, writing on January 1, 1872, after acknowledging receipt the day before of Huntington's letter, no. 677 of December 16, said, "The delay we suppose is on the Union Pacific. No trains on our road have been behind time." Although Hopkins estimated a revenue loss of $1.5 million, Towne believed it would be much more. Hopkins went on to say:

> After having expended immense sums of money to construct our own road so thoroughly that *every bridge, culvert & embankment* stands the test of the most severe & long continued storm known here for years—and having constructed numbers of the most formidable snow plows known to any Rail Road service & stationed them at all exposed points, with a double supply of locomotives & men under orders to keep the road open at any cost—and having at great cost housed in our track, side tracks, wood & water houses, round houses, repair shops & forges for tempory [*sic*] repairs & provided houses to feed & lodge 250 extra men at each of three different places . . . so as to be prepared for the very worst . . . it is discouraging that . . . our effort is thwarted by the lack of an earnest purpose of the Union Pacific to keep that road open *between Cheyenne and Omaha.*

Hopkins added that the CP ballasted their plows "with several tons of dead weight in the stern & six, seven or eight of the most powerful locomotives behind them." In his opinion, he understood the UP policy was to wait for storms to end before clearing, *"but in no case to put more than two locomotives behind a snow plow."* He wrote, "After being blocked for a week with snow . . . they request that we will send them drawings [of our snowplows]. . . . [W]e sent them complete working plans, & drawings—also photographs."

The difficulties continued. On February 3, 1872, Towne wrote Huntington:

> If I were easily discouraged, I don't know but I would be about ready to give up the ghost.
>
> The Union Pacific blockade is very materially injuring the through business of the line. I have offered to send Mr. Sickels one of our heavy snowplows, which, I am satisfied, would clear

his road of snow. . . . He replied that "they have 25 engines now in the ditch, caused by running them behind snowplows"—which were of a very inferior character, which was the cause of their trouble—very unlike our snow plows.

And when the *New York Herald* corrected an erroneous report in *Harper's Weekly* attributing the snow blockade to the Central Pacific, Towne moved quickly to forward the clipping to Huntington. Still, the CP was not immune to stoppages because of slides; while the Union Pacific was in trouble, a snowslide destroyed part of a snowshed near Emigrant Gap, California, which delayed a passenger train for thirty-six hours.

In 1868, the Big Four began to gain control of the Southern Pacific Railroad, which held congressional authority to build from San Francisco to the southeast corner of California. For some years, the major portion of the SP RR was leased to the Central Pacific; during that period, the SP RR extended its rails from San Francisco to Los Angeles, then across Arizona and New Mexico. Through affiliated companies, the Big Four secured railroads to New Orleans to form the Sunset Route. The CP lease ended in 1885 following the formation of the Southern Pacific Company in 1884 as a holding company of the various railroads constituting the Big Four empire. It also operated the railroads west of El Paso, including the Central Pacific. Its ramifications will unfold later in this text.

In the latter part of October 1873, the CP moved its general offices from Sacramento to San Francisco. In a letter of November 8, 1873, Mark Hopkins, now in San Francisco, wrote Huntington, "After months of delay we are now located in our new office building, corner of Townsend and Fourth Street, San Francisco. The building has cost double what I supposed it would when we resolved to build it. But it is thoroughly built, convenient for our business." (The Southern Pacific Railroad secretary's office was at the corner of Market and New Montgomery Streets at that time.)

A. N. Towne took up quarters at the Palace Hotel, then a practice of a number of businessmen. In November 1888, after the death of Charles Crocker, Towne became vice president of the Southern Pacific Company and also served on its board. About two years later he moved to 1101 California Street, just across the street from the Nob Hill residence of Charles Crocker. Towne's work continued as before until July 16, 1895, when he died of a heart attack.

The San Francisco earthquake and fire of 1906 ravaged an important part of the city without regard to financial or social position. Among the countless structures lost was the SP general office building at Fourth and Townsend as well as the palatial structures on Nob Hill. Of the former Towne house, only the Ionic columns forming the entrance survived. Known as the "Portals of the Past," these columns now stand by Lloyd Lake in San Francisco's Golden Gate Park.

Central Pacific Operating Divisions

Early operating timetables reflected the expansion of the Central Pacific Railroad. With its timetable number 28 of June 16, 1868, the CP opened its line to Reno with a pair of passenger trains. By today's standards, the twenty-three hours required for the 154-mile trip between Sacramento and Reno would scarcely merit the "fast-trip" description, even though it outpaced travel by oxcart.

The operating timetable offered a few instructions such as: "If trains are not met at the regular meeting place, approach sidings carefully, until they are met." At the top of the timetable, "In case of uncertainty, always take the Safe Side," appeared in large letters.

During the construction of the Central Pacific, the line between Winnemucca and Deeth (180 miles) formed the Humboldt Division in February 1869. A month later, the district shortened to Carlin (121 miles) became the Shoshone Division. On May 17, a week after driving the Golden Spike, a pocket Central Pacific timetable appeared. The 742 miles between Sacramento and Ogden were divided into five CP sections and a UP section as follows:

Division	*Termini*	*Mileage*
Sacramento	Sacramento-Wadsworth	189
Truckee	Wadsworth-Winnemucca	135
Shoshone	Winnemucca-Carlin	121
Humboldt	Carlin-Toano	114
Salt Lake	Toano-Terminus (Promontory)	131
Union Pacific RR	Terminus-Ogden	52

With the acquisition of the trackage to Ogden, timetables underwent revisions. The list of stations dated March 1, 1879, showed a different set of divisions:

Division	*Termini*	*Mileage*
Sacramento	Sacramento-Truckee	119
Truckee	Truckee-Winnemucca	205
Humboldt	Winnemucca-Wells	200
Salt Lake	Wells-Ogden	219

Southern Pacific (Pacific System) adopted a new form on July 1, 1892, and each division timetable became number 1. At that time, the number of divisions was further reduced:

Division	*Termini*	*Mileage*
Sacramento	Sacramento-Truckee	119
Truckee	Truckee-Carlin	325
Salt Lake	Carlin-Ogden	299

The list of stations for January 1, 1901, showed only the Sacramento and Salt Lake Divisions, with Wadsworth as the dividing point, and, when the railroad opened Lucin Cutoff, Sparks replaced Wadsworth as the connection between the two divisions. Since then, the former Carson and Colorado Railway and the Nevada-California-Oregon (N-C-O) Railway joined the Salt Lake Division.[1]

Central Pacific placed its motive-power department in Sacramento. A. J. Stevens held the post of general master mechanic in 1879. Roundhouses were located in Rocklin and Truckee, California; Wadsworth, Winnemucca, Carlin, and Wells, Nevada; as well as Terrace and Ogden, Utah. Additionally, machine shops at Wadsworth, Carlin, and Terrace met the needs of the mechanical department.

The term *roundhouse* generously encompasses "engine houses." On the Southern Pacific, only Truckee, Houston, and Algiers (New Orleans) possessed full-circle roundhouses. Although Los Angeles and Sparks workers boasted of their roundhouses, the buildings formed only part of a circle.

Wadsworth, Nevada

Situated at the big bend of the Truckee River where it turns to flow north to Pyramid Lake, the location provided a site for a trading post until the Central Pacific, building across Nevada in 1868–1869, established a division point and named the place Wadsworth. The name is attributed to James Samuel Wadsworth, an army officer killed in an earlier Indian battle.

Railroad shops and a roundhouse soon rose on the east side of the Truckee River to be served by spur tracks from the main line. For almost forty years, engine men and trainmen began or ended their runs at Wadsworth while their engines were serviced at the roundhouses. Many railroad employees lived in the town.

For undisclosed reasons, Central Pacific management in 1882 decided to relocate the roundhouse and shops to the west side of the Truckee River. The decision may have been made during Collis Huntington's visit to California in August. Perhaps the cumbersome single entry for the original facilities dictated a new arrangement with better access. Lengthening locomotives might have been another factor; stalls in the new roundhouse measured twelve feet greater than in the first structure.

The substantial brick structures, built on stone foundations, set a tone of permanence for the long-term needs of the railroad. Operating revenues for 1870, the first full year after completion, totaled $7.4 million but had risen to $25.7 million in 1882, in large measure reflecting contributions of lines leased to the Central Pacific (the SP RR and others).

Major brick structures on the east side of Wadsworth included the twenty-stall roundhouse, machine shop (140 × 80 feet), blacksmith and boiler shop (100 × 60 feet), and car repair shop (150 × 44 feet).

Extensive grading began that fall, and Huntington received a clever, flattering letter from George Gregg, master mechanic of the Truckee Division. The letter explained that the men of the locomotive department had organized a library association for which the company provided tables and chairs and space at one end of the Wadsworth roundhouse. After telling Huntington that he had secured large photos of the other general officers for display in the library, Gregg asked Huntington for his photograph and "also any assistance you may see fit." Huntington's response, if any, vanished over the years.

During 1883, the new engine house and machine shops took form on the west side of the Truckee River at a cost of $96,000, which, with the exception of coal bunkers at Port Costa, represented the largest expenditure made for improvements in that year.

A monumental fire on April 15, 1884, changed everything. Believed to have started in the yardmaster's office in the station in the early afternoon during a time of winds blowing a gale, the flames rapidly enveloped Thomas

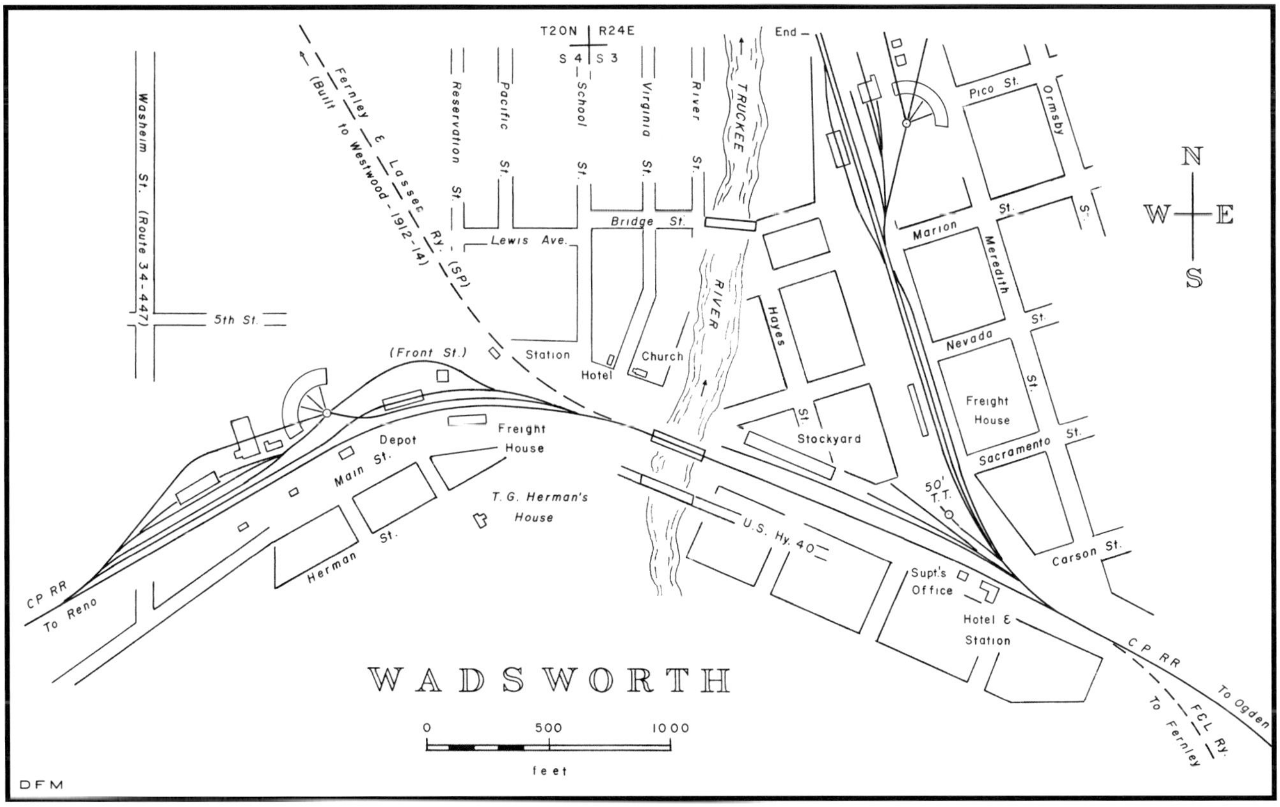

Wadsworth, besides serving the Central Pacific as a division point, also provided a home for helper locomotives assisting trains over White's Hill until the main line was rerouted through Hazen in 1902.

During 1882–1883, the Central Pacific relocated the roundhouse and shops from the east side of the Truckee River to the west side, enlarging them at the same time. This general map of Wadsworth identifies the two locations, with more detail provided on enlarged maps of each facility.

N. Carey's Wadsworth Hotel and Edwin Fowler's news depot. The post office and Wells Fargo Express office soon fed the flames—all before the fire alarm could be sounded. The fire leaped across the street to the business section and consumed every building down to the schoolhouse. E. Griswold lost his store, and both S. Arnstein's and P. Gillespie's stores and dwellings went up in flames, along with John Lee's mercantile house.

Within two hours, it was over. Several men suffered injuries jumping from second-floor hotel windows. Though hampered by limited water supplies, local citizens and railroad employees received high praise for containing the blaze. Thirty-five homeless families found shelter in houses of friends or the roundhouse. Reno citizens, remembering their major fire only a few years earlier, dispatched a special train of supplies to the beleaguered community. Tom Brown, "Oregon Tom," while acting as night watchman in the burned district, fell down an open well. Fortunately, an Indian walking by heard the cries for help and alerted other men. With a bell cord taken from a passenger car standing on a siding, local men pulled Oregon Tom from the well with a broken leg. Fortunately, Dr. Bergman happened to be in town and could set the compound fracture. Brown's awkward situation in the well created comment; had there been more water in the well, it could have broken his fall but he might have drowned before his rescue.

The relocation of the Central Pacific shops and roundhouse to the west side of the Truckee River posed questions in placing rebuilt stores. Two insurance agents promptly arrived from San Francisco to settle losses. Whereas losses totaled $75,000, only $16,000 of insurance was in force. Tom Carey had $7,000 of insurance to meet his $10,000 hotel loss, while John Lee's $5,000 policy covered only one-third of his loss. William Donaldson was even less fortunate, for the policy on his Nevada Hotel had lapsed only a few weeks earlier.

The stouthearted men moved quickly to resume their business activity. Donaldson opened a restaurant in the freight house. Tom Carey gathered three railroad cars

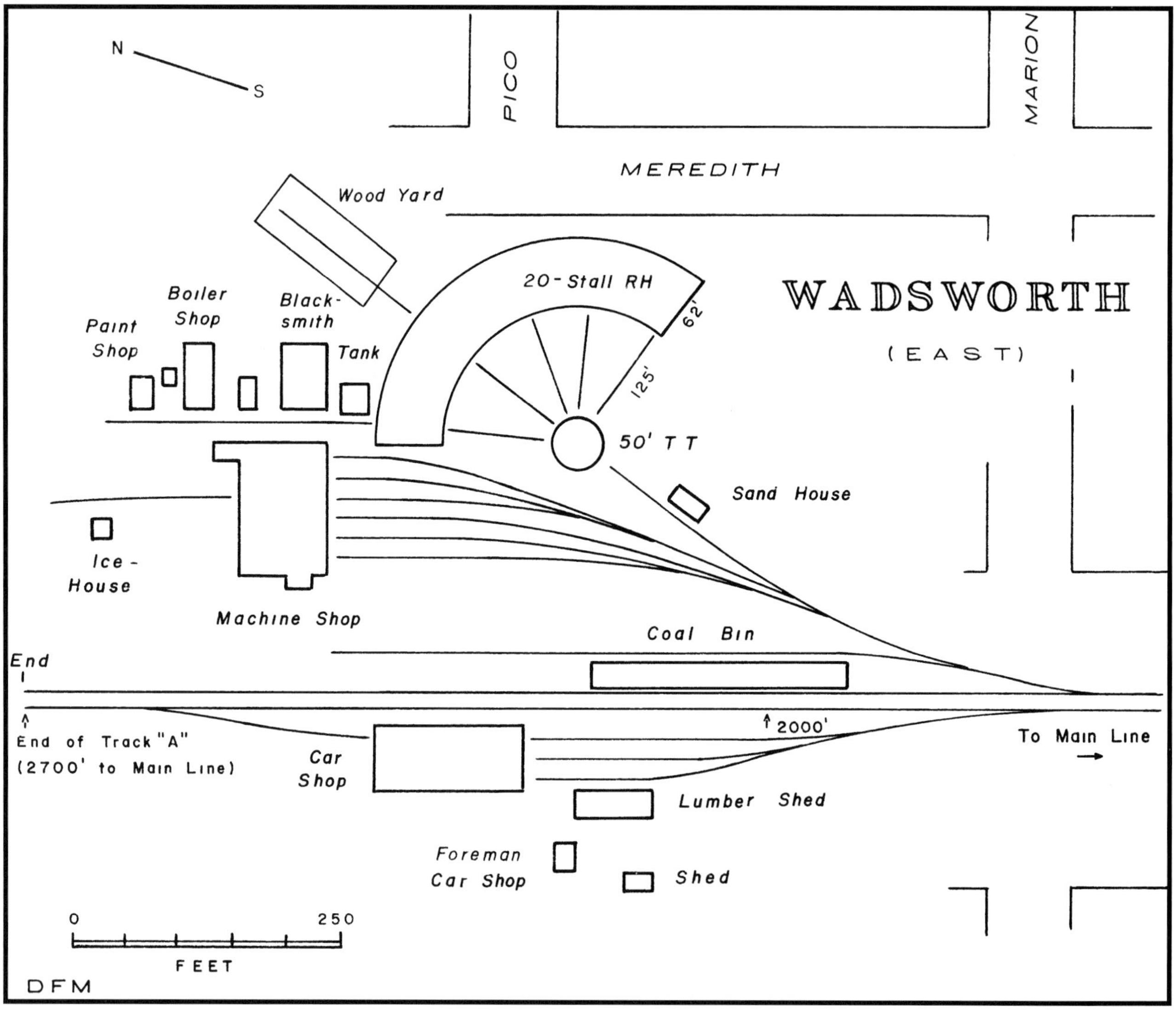

and returned to providing meals. His kitchen occupied a freight car, while the emigrant car served as a diner and a sitting room and an office took over the caboose. Within a week, most of the essential services became available, and most of the residents decided to remain in Wadsworth. Twenty carpenters arrived the next month to erect a new railroad office building and freight station. E. Griswold contemplated a fine brick building for his store, and merchants John Lee and P. Gillespie soon received stacks of lumber for rebuilding their establishments.

Toano, Wells, and Tecoma, Nevada, and Terrace, Utah

By the time the Central Pacific forces reached (Humboldt) Wells in eastern Nevada, the easy grade afforded by following the Humboldt River had ended. Now the railroad faced the formidable Pequop Mountains. Eastbound, the grade begins at Wells and climbs to Moor and continues along the crest of the ridge for the next twenty-four miles to Valley Pass before dropping down to Montello.

Toano stood on the eastern slope of the Pequop Mountains, three miles below Valley Pass. Shortly after the railroad began operations in 1869, Toano, at the western end of the Salt Lake Division, held a key position with a ten-stall roundhouse, 44 × 80–foot machine shop, 32 × 50–foot freight house, telegraph office, section house, and water tank. Besides serving as a division point, Toano also served as the railhead for teams going south to Ely and Pioche or north into Idaho.

A correspondent told of two events in December 1871. Locally, the most important took form as the "Great Toano Gift Festival" planned for Christmas. At this period in time, teamsters departed almost daily for Pioche. When a

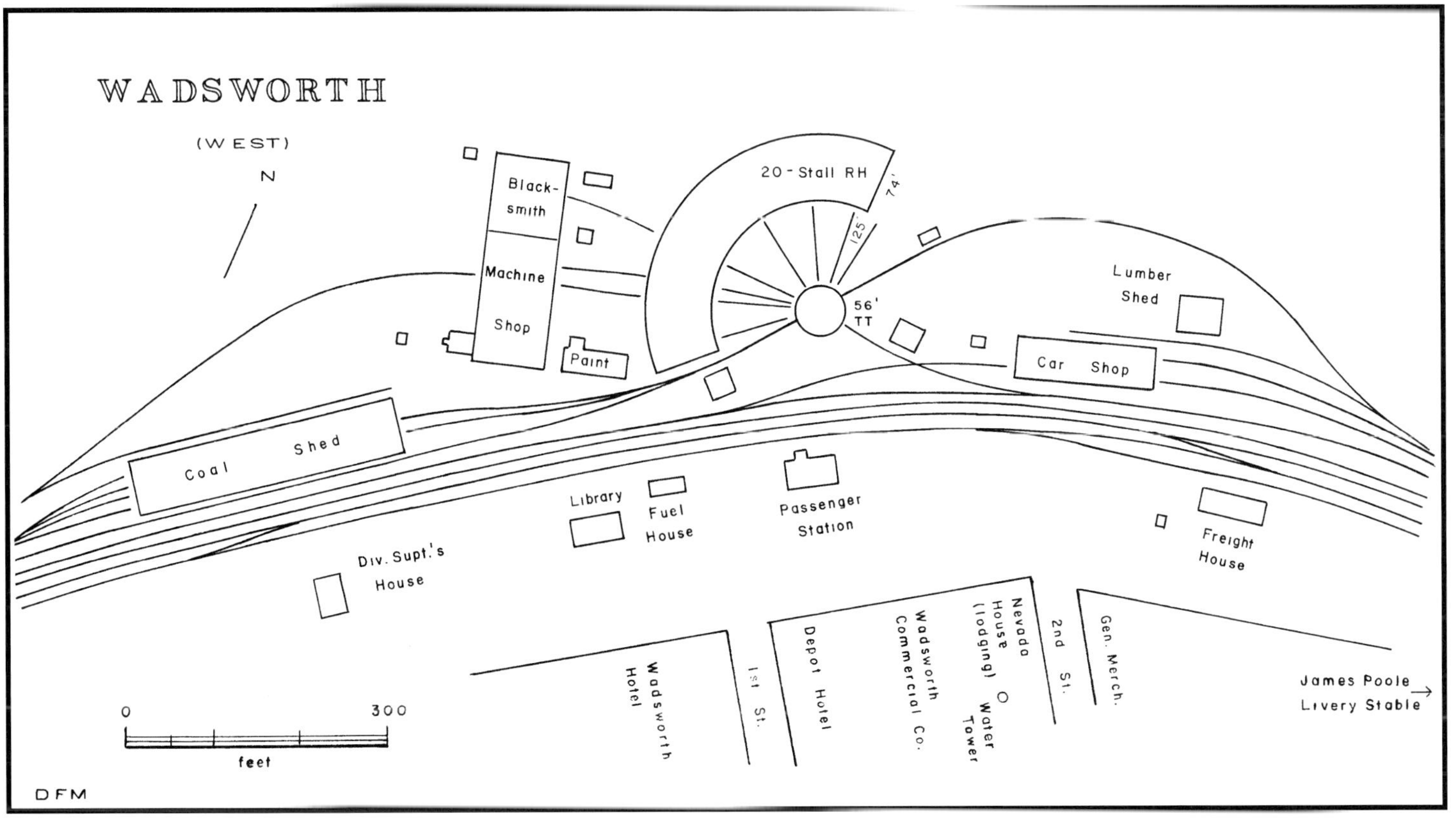

westbound train was caught in a snowdrift, passengers from the eastbound train endured a day in Toano.

The presence of the stalled train augmented receipts for dinners at Mr. Grant's Railroad House kitchen, while "an appreciative throng" filled the adjoining Idaho Saloon, as L. E. Eno dispensed liquid nourishment in "his jolly, noisy and boisterous" manner that often turned compassionate when a poor wayfarer needed shelter and sustenance on a cold winter night.

The cold and miserable weather prevailing in January 1873 left residents with colds, while horses and mules died from something likened to an eastern horse disease. At that moment, with freighting slack, many teams stood idle, waiting for loads to Pioche. Some "honest miners" braved the chill, trying to develop their mines in nearby Silver Zone, and brought four tons of ore for shipment to Winnemucca for reduction.

Those who were in good health played card games spiced with bets in either the Railroad House or the International Hotel and Bar operated by Brinkerhoff and Gray. Dances at the Railroad House drew regular attendance; some sought to make them a weekly affair for the benefit of the flourishing school needing a shelter from the elements.

An early Sunday-morning fire on February 2, 1873, swept through the original Toano roundhouse, reportedly destroying three engines and slightly damaging two others. The new roundhouse was smaller and took the settlement two miles eastward.

Ten days later, an extra freight train left Toano headed for Carlin, as the passenger train pointed in the other direction. The dispatcher ordered the trains to meet at Osino siding; unfortunately, someone overlooked the instructions, and suddenly two locomotives confronted each other on a curve three miles east of Osino. Engine men from both locomotives jumped, with one fireman suffering internal injuries. Seven loaded freight cars derailed, and the front end of the postal car was crushed. Good fortune saved the postal messenger, for he had left the front of the car just before the impact, his second similar experience in recent months. The *Elko Independent* remarked that the clerk "thinks the air in the rear of the car is conducive to his health."

During 1876, the terminal station separating the Humboldt and Salt Lake Divisions was moved from Toano to Wells at the western base of the Pequop Mountains. Most of the population followed the move to Wells. The roundhouse was sold and moved away in July 1882.

Toano continued to serve as the railhead for the nearby ranches for another thirty years. The village store, built of stone, resisted fires, an important consideration, as the community lacked a fire department. A barrel of

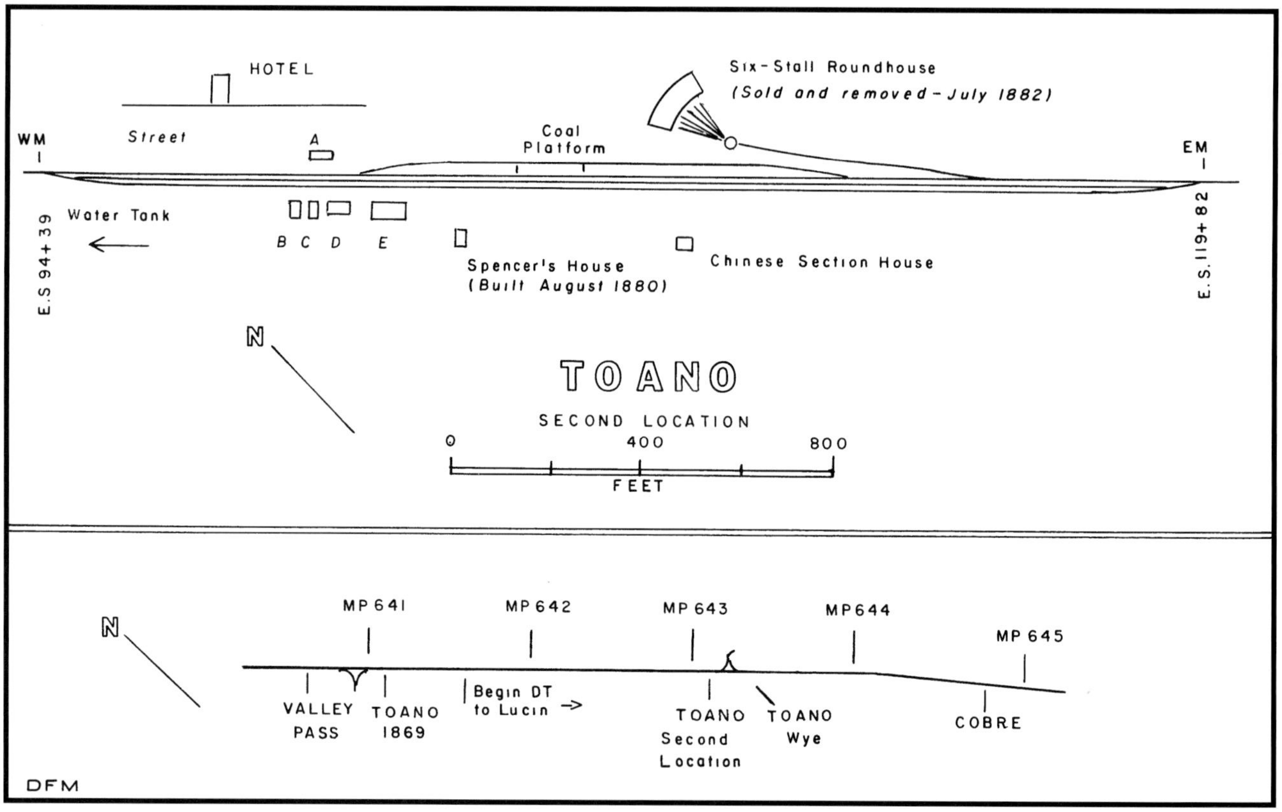

Toano, Nevada, an early Central Pacific division point 559 miles from Sacramento, dates back to 1869. After the Toano fire of 1873 destroyed the ten-stall roundhouse, a smaller replacement rose about two miles eastward. The settlement moved to the second location. An adjustment of operating divisions rendered the second Toano roundhouse superfluous, and it was sold and taken away in July 1882. The lead track to the 50-foot turntable was dismantled in November 1884.

The general map identifies the locations of Toano in relation to the current mileposts, while the detailed map indicates railroad facilities in the early 1880s. The connections of the sidings with the main line are shown with the engineering stations and letters WM and EM, which are 2,543 feet apart. Letters identify the congested structures:

A = Car Inspector's and Wood House
B = Roadmaster's House
C = Section House
D = Spencer and Frank's Warehouse
E = Central Pacific Railroad Freight House

The water tank is 200 feet west of WM and on the north side of the track. The west switch of the Toano wye track, probably installed about 1884, is 700 feet east of EM.

saltwater—salted to retard freezing in the winter—stood on the roof of the freight house to be used in emergencies or a prank. A standard entertainment among ranch hands coming to town involved engaging an eastern dude in conversation, with him standing in just the right place so that an accomplice could dump the contents of the barrel on the unsuspecting victim.

Even without the roundhouse, Toano maintained its importance; in 1901, the station agent could sell tickets or handle freight in any quantity, giving him equal status with agents at Wells and Tecoma. Sheep men brought great bundles of wool to the railroad at Toano, which also served as the headquarters for the Sparks-Harrell ranches. (Sparks was Nevada's governor in later years.)

For many years, H. A. Spencer's teams commanded most of the transport business from Toano to Ely and the Steptoe Valley. Operating his teams from Wells, M. Badt announced in 1905 that he would forward freight to Cherry Creek and Ely at the same rates as Toano, but Mrs. Spencer maintained her service after her husband died.

There were problems with the U.S. mail in August 1905. When the postmaster took a month's vacation without naming a substitute and the undistributed mail piled high, residents petitioned for a new postmaster. Some years before, the postmaster had been a twelve-year-old girl.

The death blow to Toano came in February 1907 when the Nevada Northern Railway began grading its railroad from a new station on the Central Pacific, just two miles southeasterly, first named Omar but soon changed to Cobre. Mrs. Spencer, alerted to the consequences, homesteaded the Cobre town site to be the majordomo there. Besides operating the Pioneer Hotel, store, and post office, she also ran a tent-lodging house, miners' bunkhouse, and amusement hall. When J. W. Kelly of Lane City (near Ely) came along with twenty-five thousand dollars in cash, ownership of Cobre changed hands.

Henry Muller, an assistant engineer on the Nevada Northern survey, met Mrs. Spencer's daughter. The courtship was slow, but after two years, Emma Jane became the bride of Mr. Muller.

In 1869, section houses at Wells, Cedar Pass, Independence, "6 Miles East," Toano, Loray, Montello, and Tecoma accounted for most of the population in that area. Wells, Independence, and Toano possessed more facilities such as telegraph offices, toolhouse and car house, and water tanks. Wells and subsequently Montello had engine houses, with the structure at Wells lasting until 1964 and the advent of diesel power.

As discussed later in this chapter, Huntington's plans to revise the Central Pacific route across Nevada and Utah had to be put aside, pending settlement of the government debt. When Harriman gained control of Southern Pacific in 1901, with it came the Central Pacific, and he was able to carry out these plans in sixteen places, including bypassing the grade on White's Hill by taking a five-mile-longer path through Hazen. The spectacular Lucin Cutoff of 103 miles, partly across Great Salt Lake, captured the public's attention, but the line change over the Pequop Mountains stands out as an important revision. Snowstorms over the Pequops could be expensive. The cost of removing snow during one ten-day period ending February 17, 1944, amounted to $173,000, and the storms completely closed the Overland Route on February 6 and 7 and again on February 14. Actually, that widespread storm extended to the Sierra Nevada and Cascade Range, bringing SP's total bill for snow removal that year to almost $900,000.

Reworking the twenty-seven miles between Moor and Toano, though doing little to moderate the distance, lowered the grade from seventy-nine to twenty-one feet per mile and reduced curvature by one-third. The second main track, covering the eastern and western approaches, was built in 1923, and centralized traffic control filled the single-track gap between Moor and Valley Pass after World War II.

Two line changes between Carlin and Elburz required drilling three tunnels in 1903—the first CP-SP main-line tunnels in Nevada—to shorten the line by more than four miles and reduce both the grade and the curvature. (A fourth tunnel at Palisade, west of Carlin, was opened in 1907.)

Tecoma, a longtime cattle-shipping point, attracted some former residents of Toano. Dances, staged in the local hotel, drew cowboys from nearby ranches when they were not shooting holes in the ceiling of the hotel bar. Tecoma also served a copper mine six miles away for a short period. Before the banking crisis in October 1907, the favorable market price of copper encouraged the Buel Copper Company to employ forty-five men and ship three carloads of 7 percent ore to the smelter each day. SP built a short branch to connect with a tramway constructed by the copper company. In later years, more and more cattle moved to markets over the highway at the expense of the railroads, so in November 1964, SP contemplated dismantling the corral at that point.

Terrace, Utah, lost its importance after 1905 with the opening of the new line across Great Salt Lake. In 1869, the Central Pacific was adding finishing touches to the 80 × 117–foot machine shop, ten-stall roundhouse, 60 × 140–foot car shop, and the important water tanks. Rebuilding and improving the shops came after the 1881 fire. Two years later, CP added an eating house, casting shed, and coal house to the facilities there. Although a telegraph operator was on duty, initially Terrace had no freight house; Kelton and Promontory (then the end of CP ownership) had the only traffic-serving facilities. Terrace stood out as one of the few places where the company established a library.

Winnemucca, Carlin, and Imlay, Nevada

As the headquarters of the Shoshone Division in 1869, Winnemucca boasted its own sixteen-stall roundhouse and machine shop. Other buildings in the inventory included a 14 × 46–foot lodging house, freight house, and roadmaster's office. Contrary to most points, it did not have a section house in the immediate area.

Carlin, 445 miles east of Sacramento and 23 miles west of Elko, possessed the most extensive shop facilities in Nevada other than Wadsworth when the CP began operations. Augmenting the sixteen-stall roundhouse were the 60 × 140–foot car shop, 84 × 120–foot machine shop, and 60 × 62–foot blacksmith shop. There were ten additional structures, including offices, a 16 × 60–foot "sleeping house," and a cottage for the master mechanic. In 1878, the roundhouses in Winnemucca and Carlin were rebuilt with stone foundations and iron roofs. Whereas corrals with water for cattle were found at many points along the system, Carlin and Imlay possessed hog-watering arrangements. Carlin remained as the second-oldest division point on Southern Pacific until replaced by Elko in 1998.

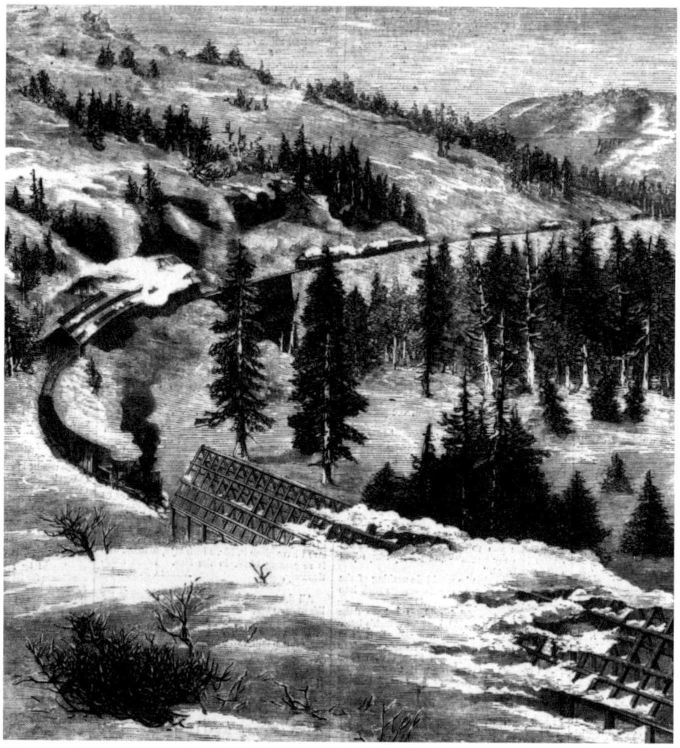

Right: In February 1872, *Harper's Weekly* caught public interest with its story of Central Pacific snowsheds.

Below: In stark contrast with the winter scenes, the snowsheds at Donner Pass are more visible. A turntable is housed in the shed at the far right.

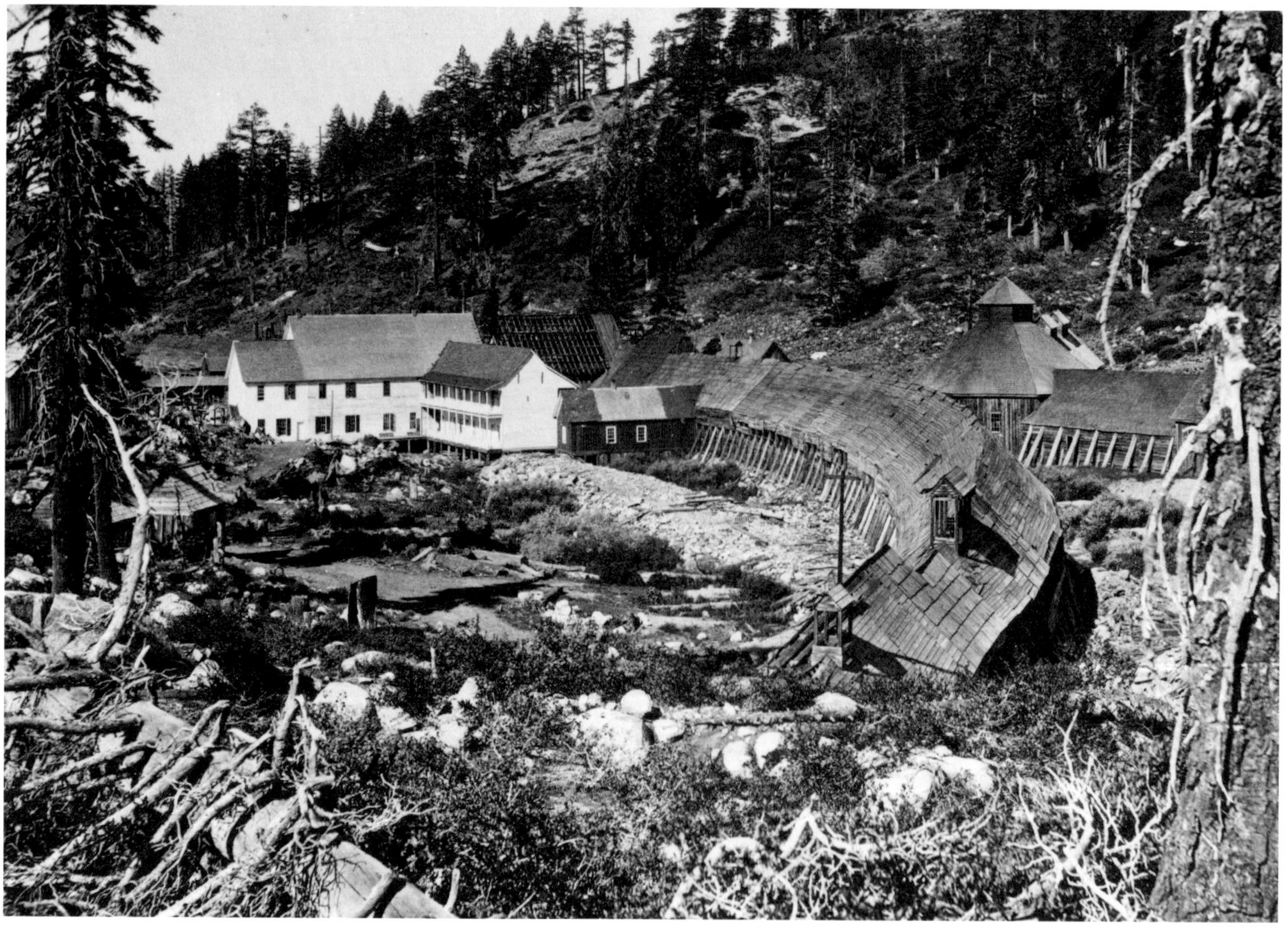

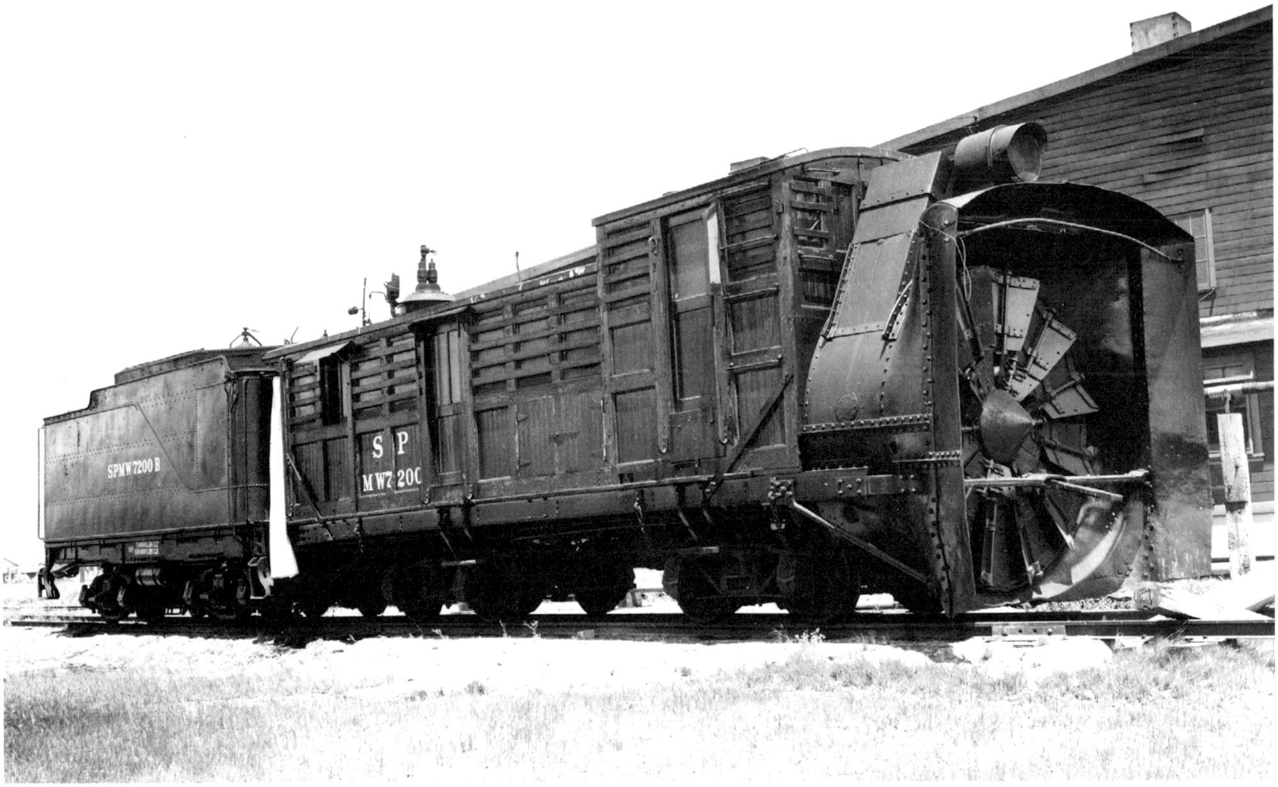

Above: In addition to snowsheds, snowplows were employed. Not only did this rotary snowplow clear the track in the Sierras, but it also performed the same function along the Shasta Route into Oregon. At times, a rotary made the long trip to Fernley, Nevada, to open the line between Susanville and Westwood. (Douglas Richter photograph, Ted Wurm collection)

Below: For more than thirty years, Wadsworth was an important division point. Looking eastward along Main Street, the prominent building on the left, built in 1893, housed the Wadsworth Commercial Company on the ground floor with the Knights of Pythias in the upper level.

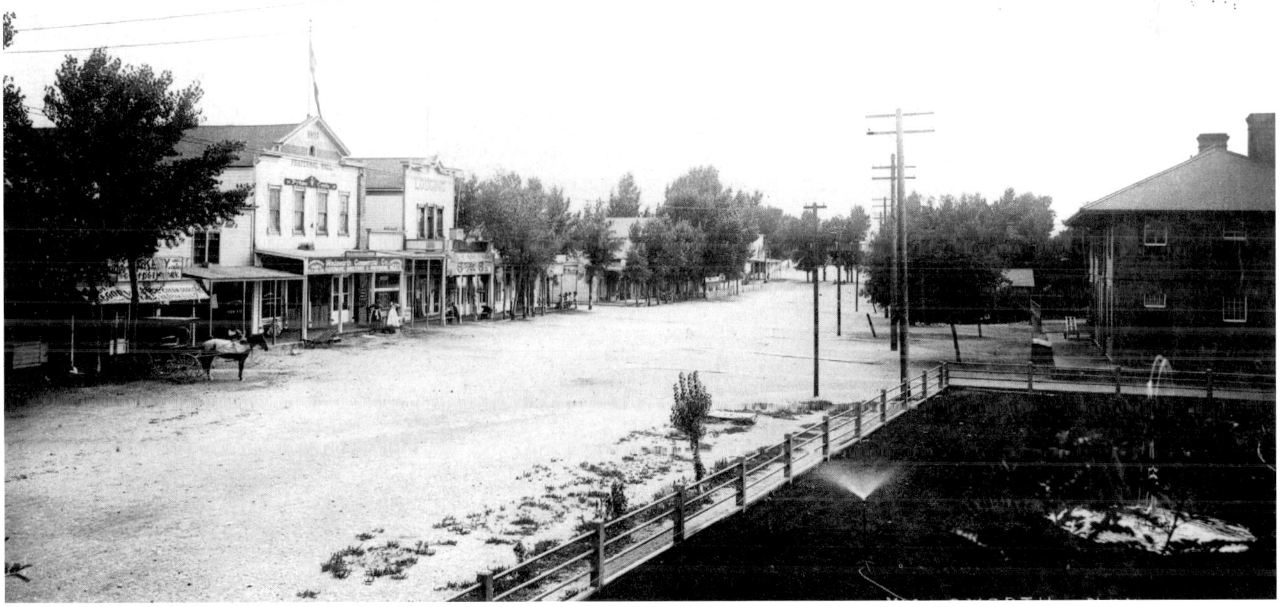

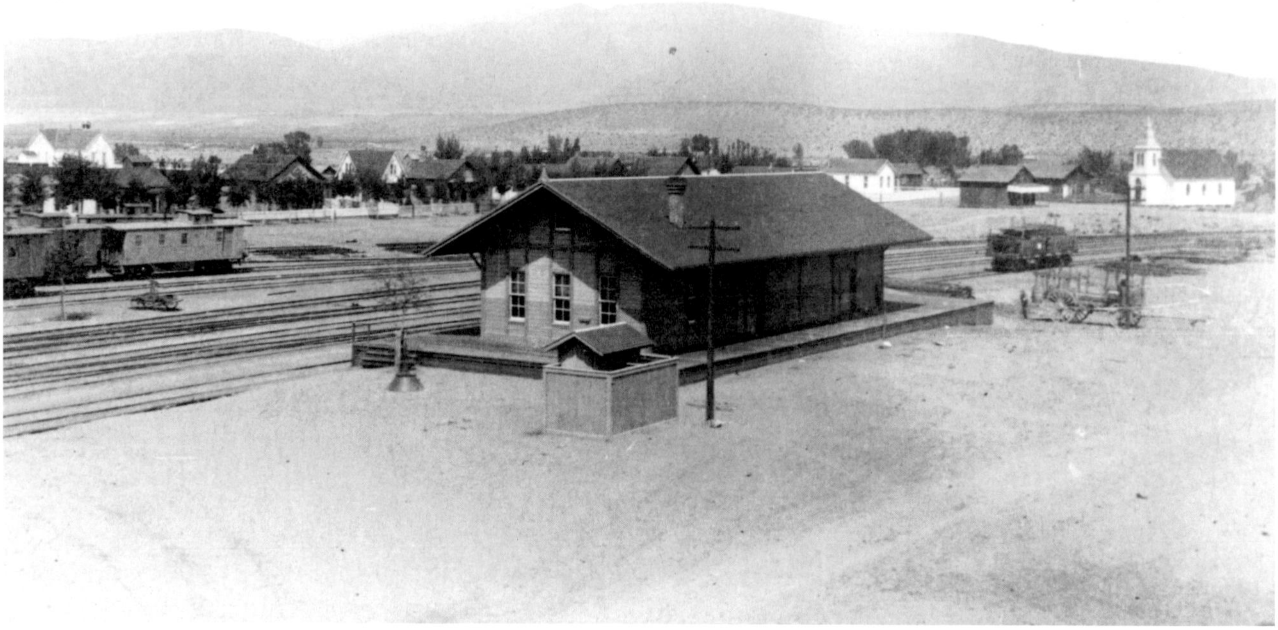

Above: The freight house at Wadsworth with a white church in the background.

Below: An alert photographer caught a switch engine as it moved across the Truckee River at Wadsworth. Built by Cooke in 1878, it was rebuilt as an 0-6-0 switcher in 1897. (Nevada Historical Society)

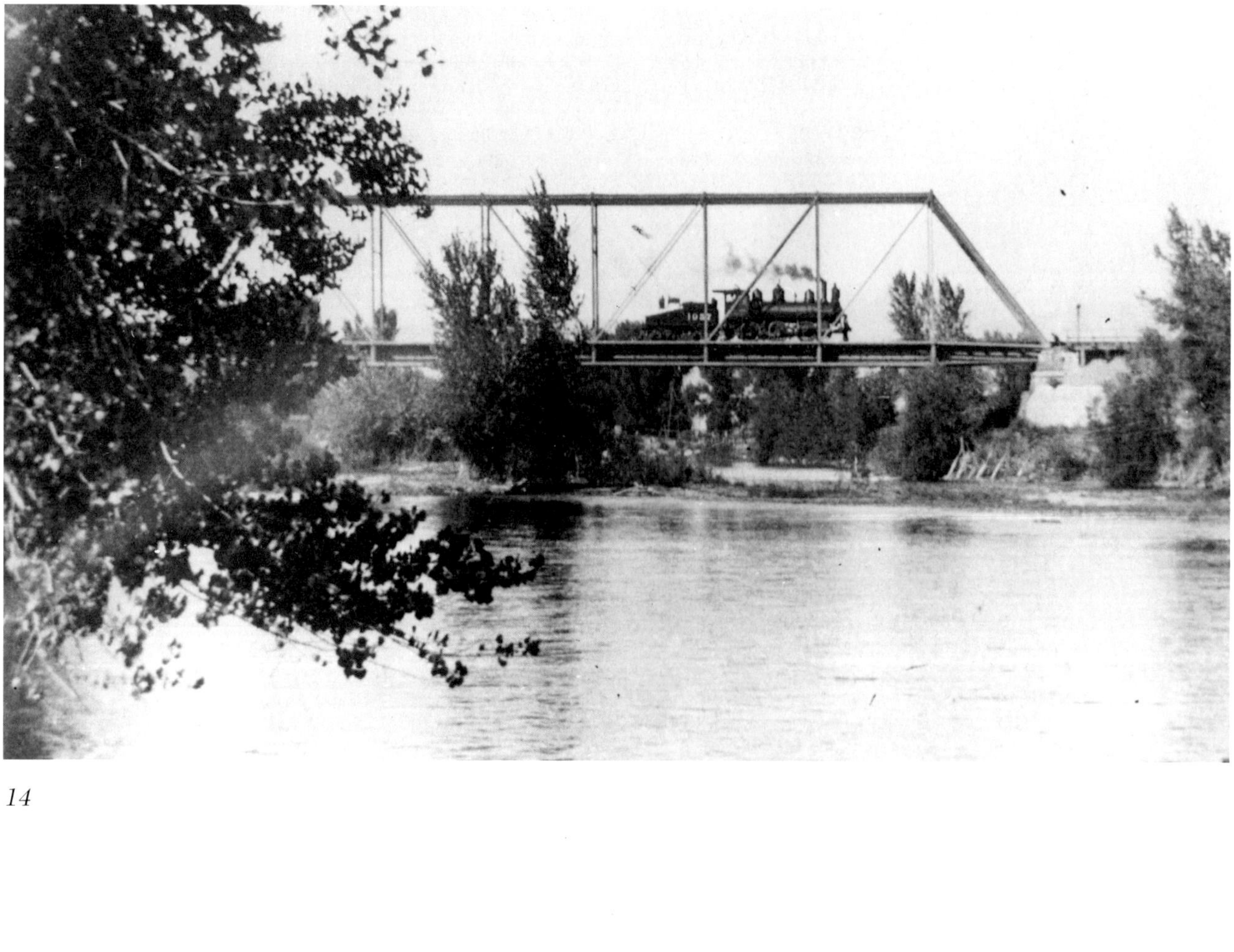

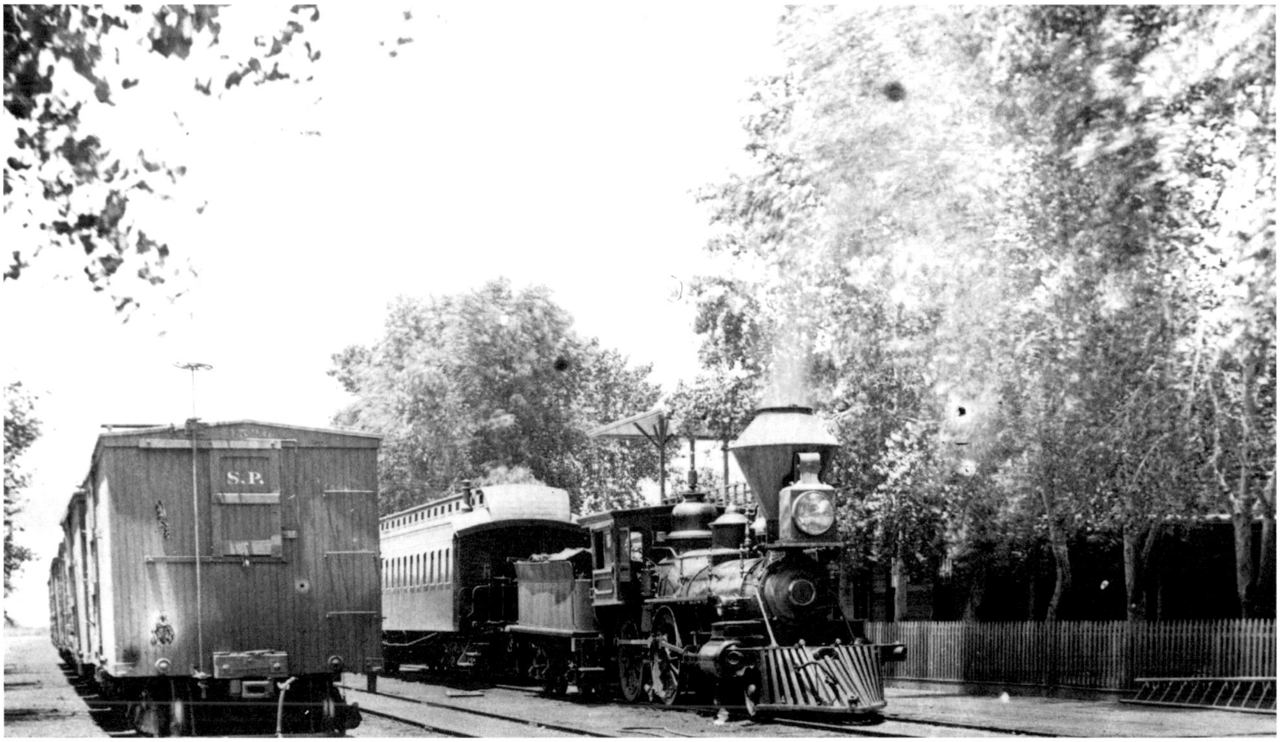

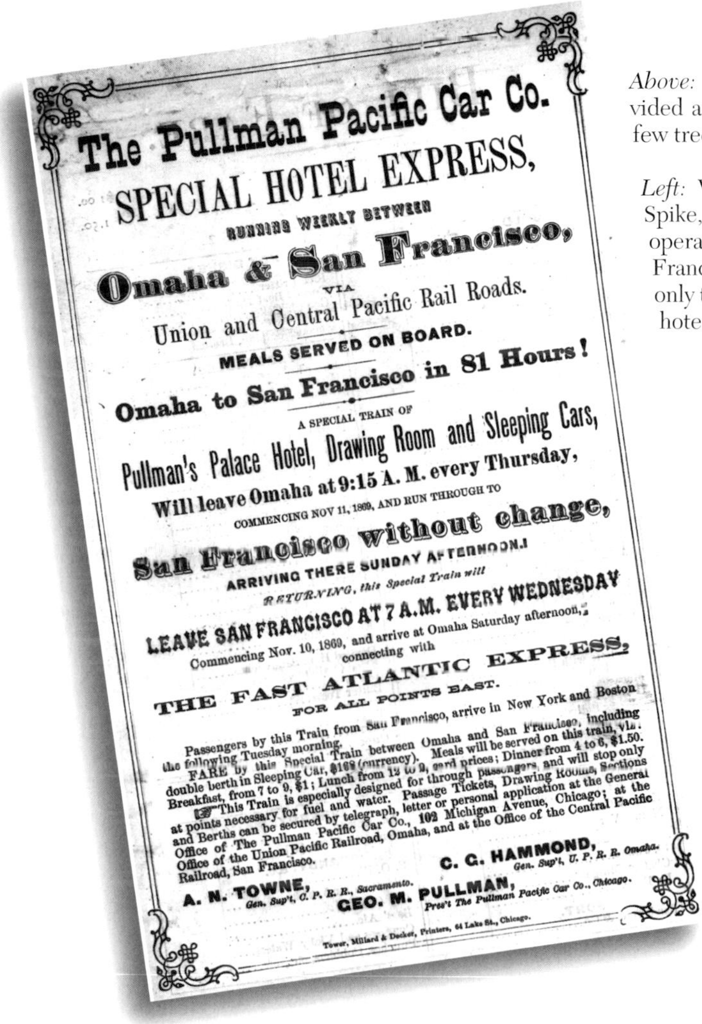

The Pullman Pacific Car Co.

SPECIAL HOTEL EXPRESS,

RUNNING WEEKLY BETWEEN

Omaha & San Francisco,

VIA

Union and Central Pacific Rail Roads.

MEALS SERVED ON BOARD.

Omaha to San Francisco in 81 Hours!

A SPECIAL TRAIN OF

Pullman's Palace Hotel, Drawing Room and Sleeping Cars,

Will leave Omaha at 9:15 A. M. every Thursday,

COMMENCING NOV 11, 1869, AND RUN THROUGH TO

San Francisco without change,

ARRIVING THERE SUNDAY AFTERNOON.

RETURNING, this Special Train will

LEAVE SAN FRANCISCO AT 7 A.M. EVERY WEDNESDAY

Commencing Nov. 10, 1869, and arrive at Omaha Saturday afternoon, connecting with

THE FAST ATLANTIC EXPRESS,

FOR ALL POINTS EAST.

Passengers by this Train from San Francisco, arrive in New York and Boston the following Tuesday morning.

FARE by this Special Train between Omaha and San Francisco, including double berth in Sleeping Car, $168 (currency). Meals will be served on this train, via: Breakfast, from 7 to 9, $1; Lunch from 12 to 2, card prices; Dinner from 4 to 6, $1.50.

☞ This Train is especially designed for through passengers, and will stop only at points necessary for fuel and water. Passage Tickets, Drawing Rooms, Sections and Berths can be secured by telegraph, letter or personal application at the General Office of The Pullman Pacific Car Co., 102 Michigan Avenue, Chicago; at the Office of the Union Pacific Railroad, Omaha, and at the Office of the Central Pacific Railroad, San Francisco.

C. G. HAMMOND,
Gen. Sup't, U. P. R. R. Omaha.

A. N. TOWNE,
Gen. Sup't, C. P. R. R., Sacramento.

GEO. M. PULLMAN,
Pres't The Pullman Pacific Car Co., Chicago.

Tower, Millard & Decker, Printers, 64 Lake St., Chicago.

Above: Humboldt House, 135 miles east of Reno, provided a meal stop in Central Pacific days. Today, only a few trees remain to mark the site.

Left: Within a few months after driving the Golden Spike, the two railroads joined George M. Pullman to operate a deluxe weekly train between Omaha and San Francisco. A. N. Towne had joined the Central Pacific only two months previously. A second weekly "Pullman hotel train" began operations in May 1870.

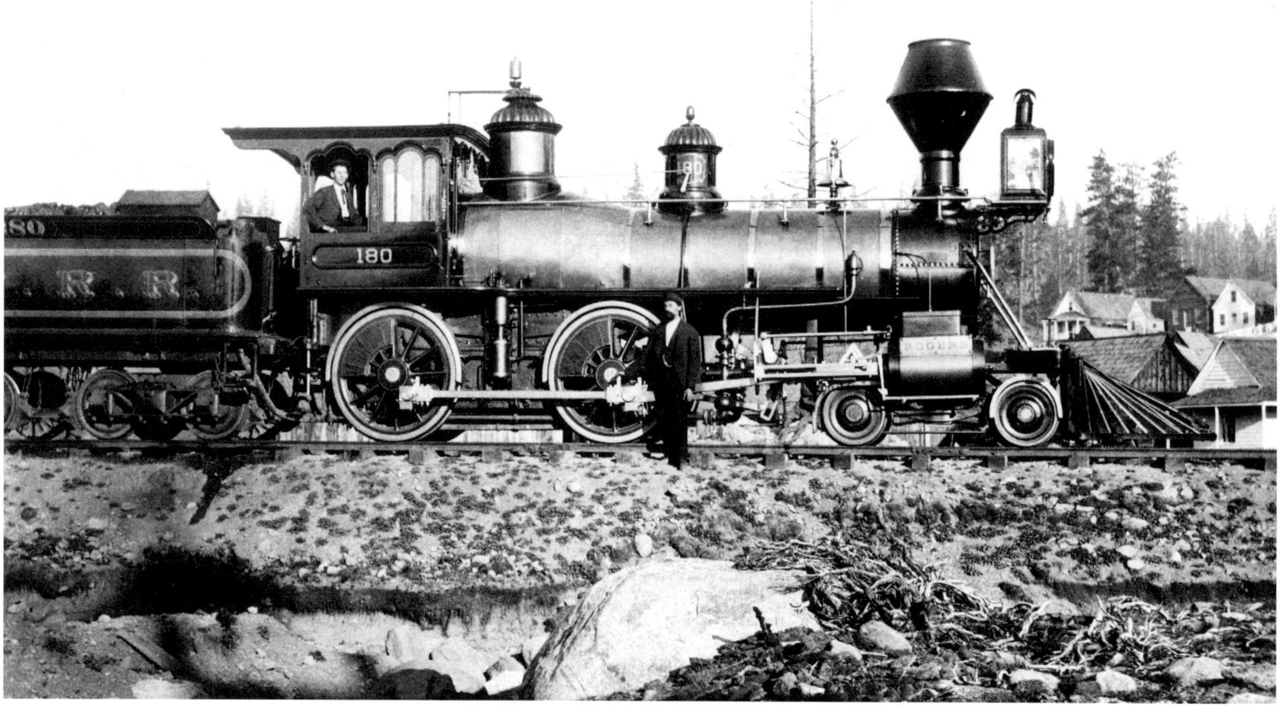

Above: Built by Rogers Works in 1872, the locomotive posed proudly at Truckee. It was sold to the Grants Pass and Eureka Railroad in 1911 to be their No. 1.

Below: Truckee station presented a trim appearance in 1954. Although diesel was replacing venerable steam power, the water spout (*center*) would remain in place a few more years. (J. M. Harder photograph, Harre Demoro collection)

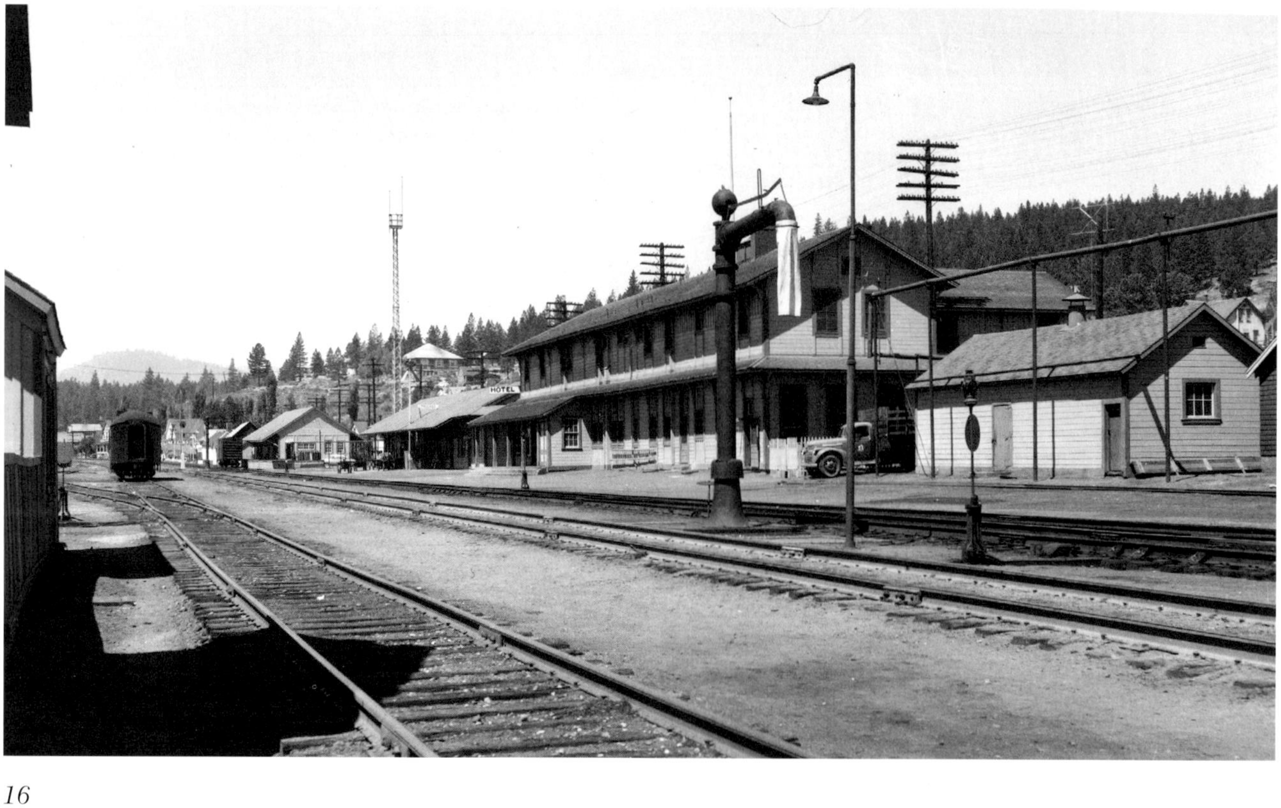

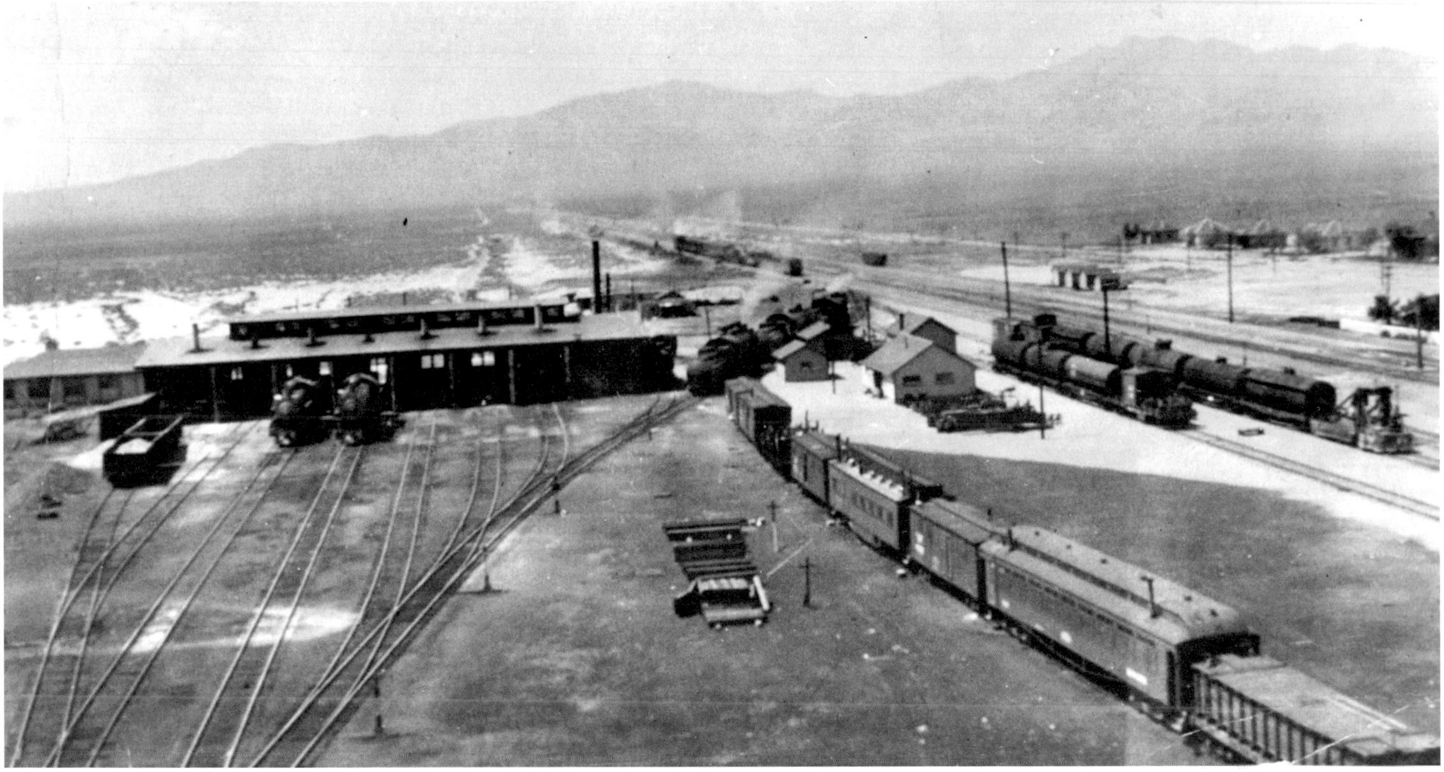

Above: Montello's seven-stall engine house was home for steam locomotives in 1934. (Tom Williamson collection)

Below: The Carlin business district adjoined the railroad in this 1910 scene. The depot is near the right margin of the picture. (Northeastern Nevada Museum)

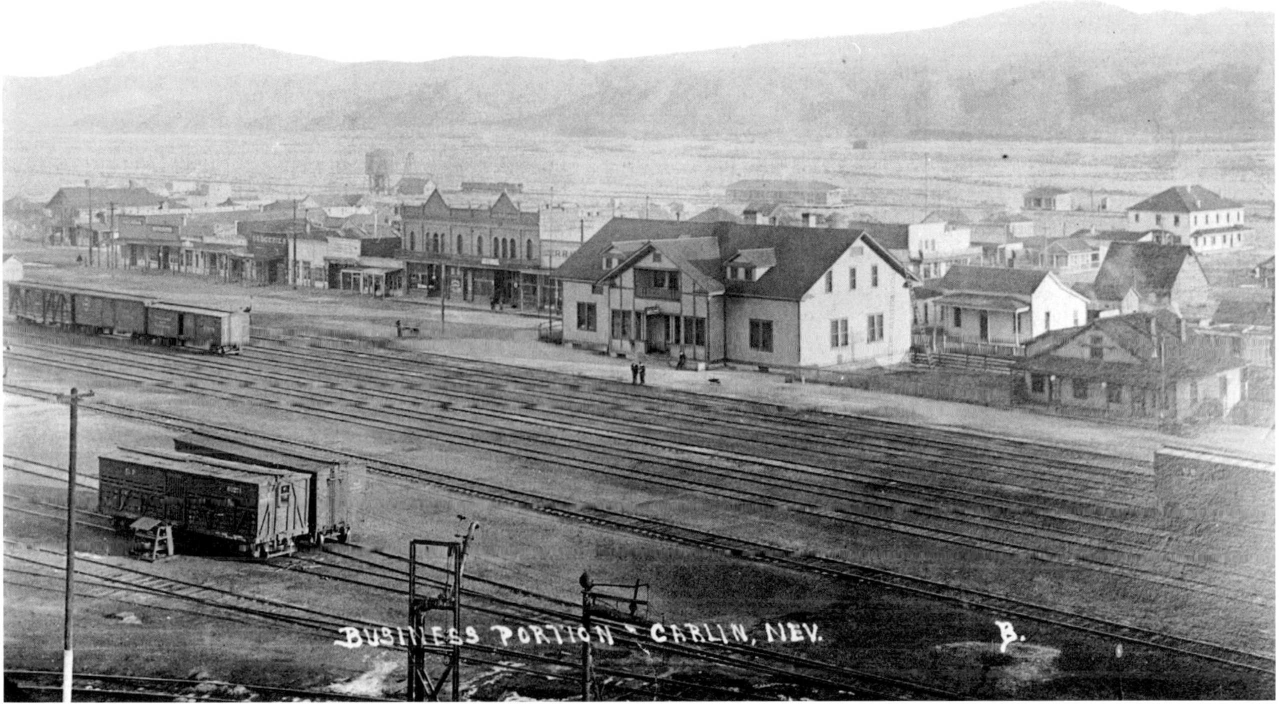

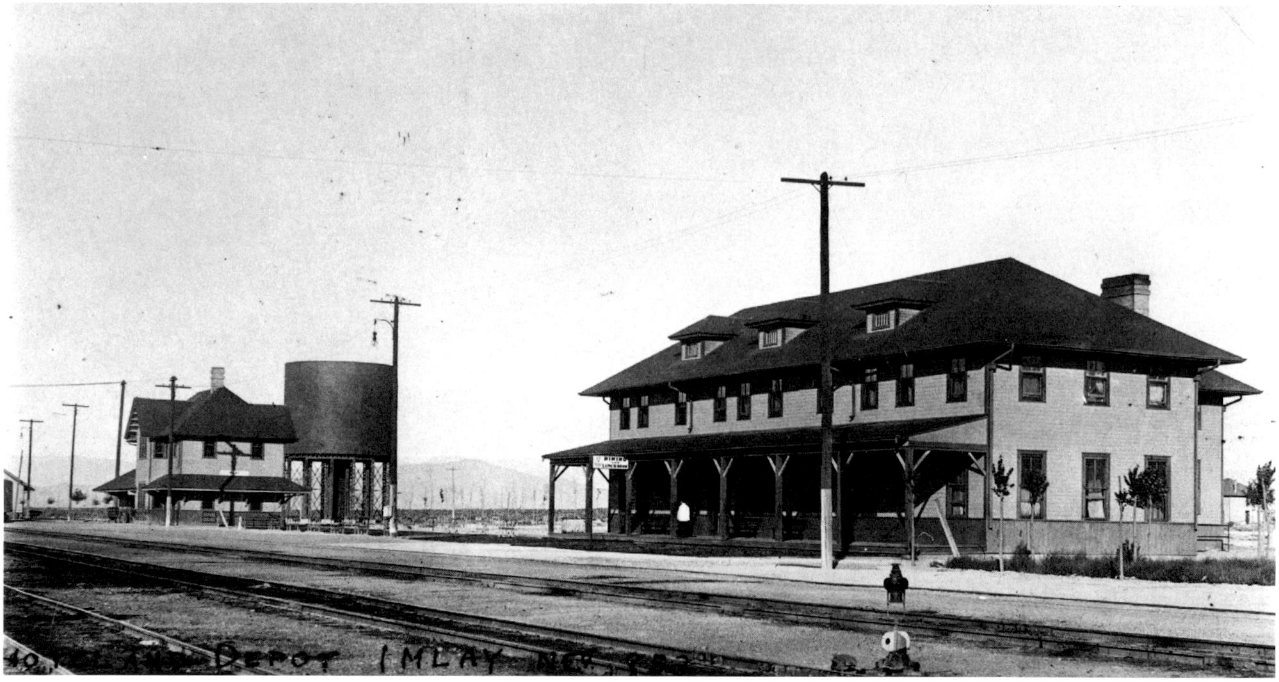

Above: When railroad crews completed their runs at Imlay, they rested in the railroad hotel. The water tank stands adjacent to the depot, and the time is around 1910. (Tom Williamson collection)

Below: In years past, several industries were situated along the Truckee River between Reno and Truckee. The Floriston paper mill provided traffic for the railroad as late as 1922.

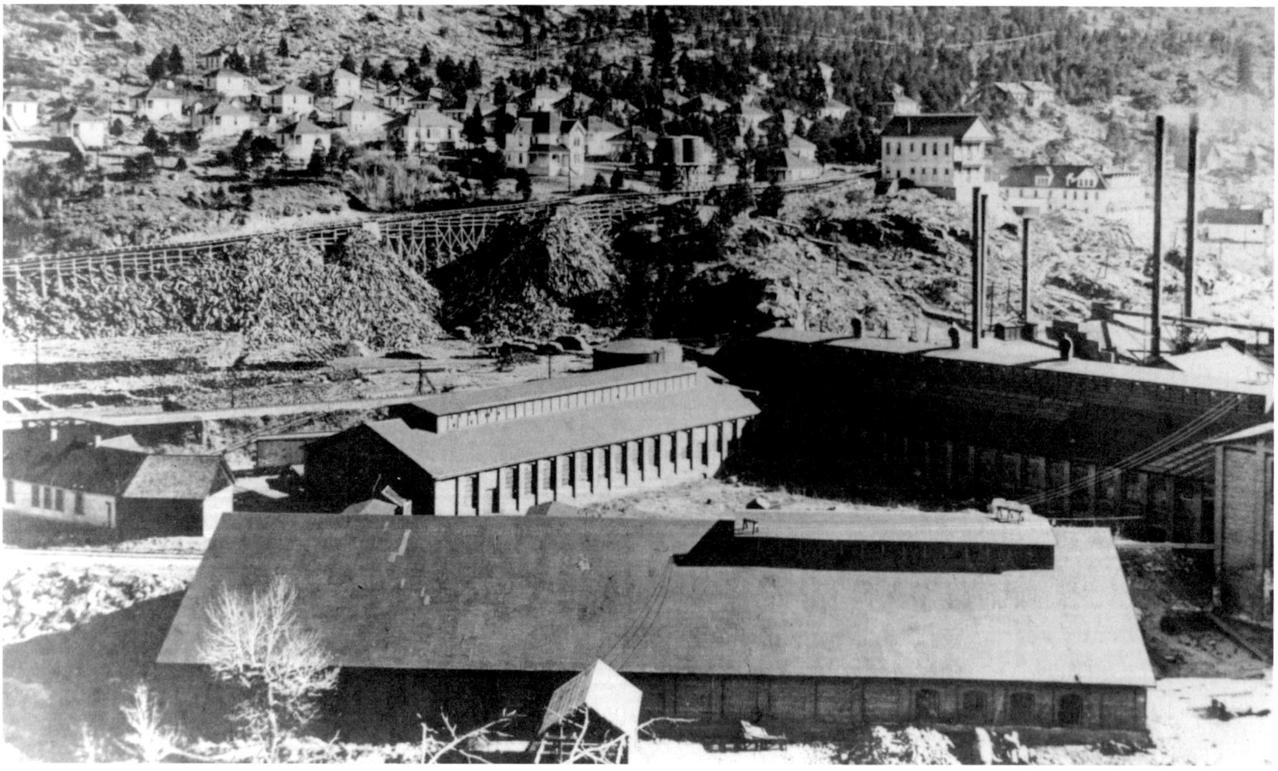

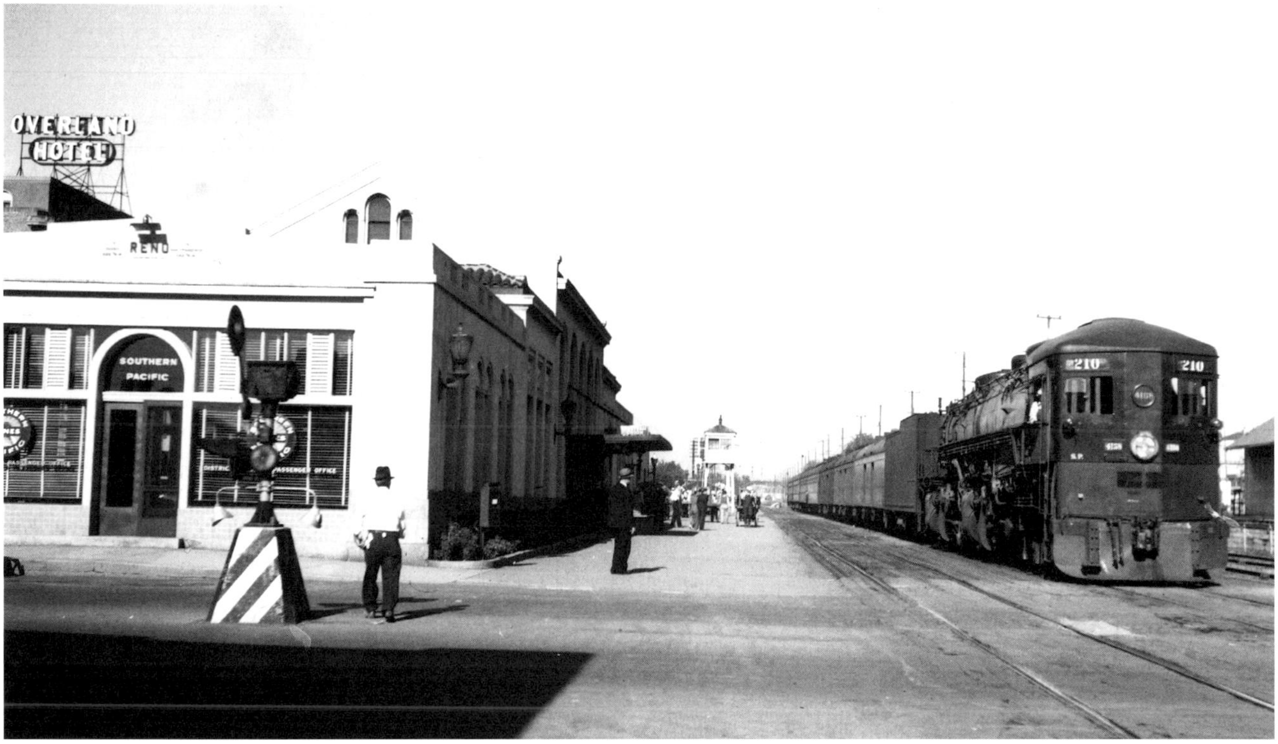

Above: For many years, Southern Pacific operated the Sierra, a convenient overnight passenger train between Oakland Pier and Sparks in 1940. Eastbound it was No. 210, while westbound it was No. 289, except Sundays when operating on a slightly different schedule as No. 295. Baldwin-built No. 4158 paused as passengers arriving from the west disembarked in Reno. (Waldemar Sievers photograph, Harre Demoro collection)

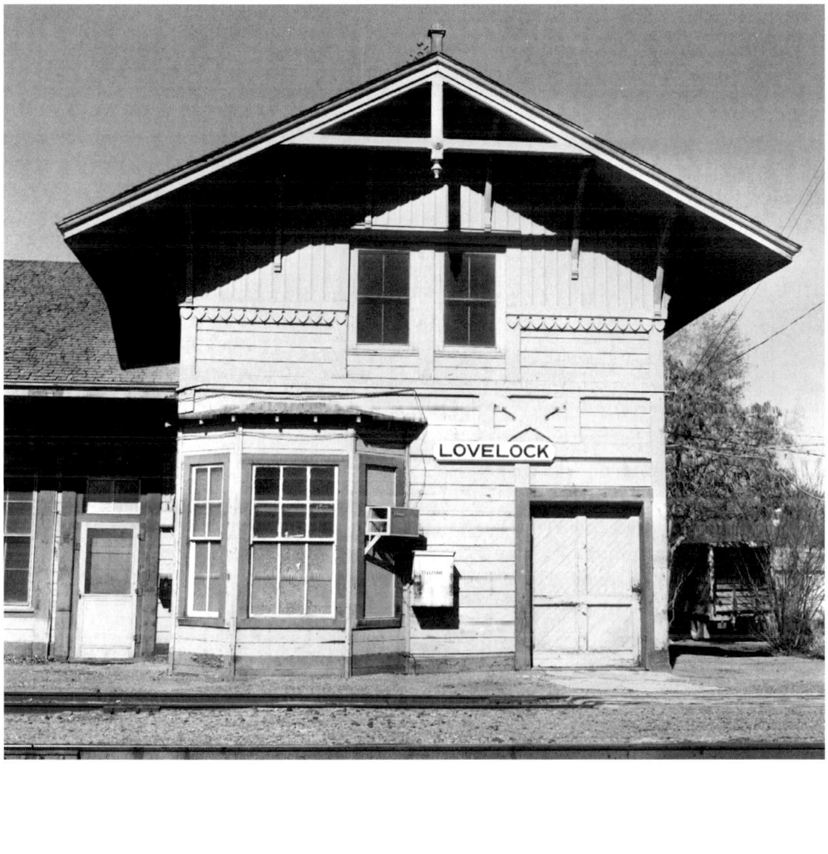

Left: As at many points along the extended Southern Pacific, the agent lived in the upper floor of the Lovelock depot. (Harre Demoro photograph, 1976)

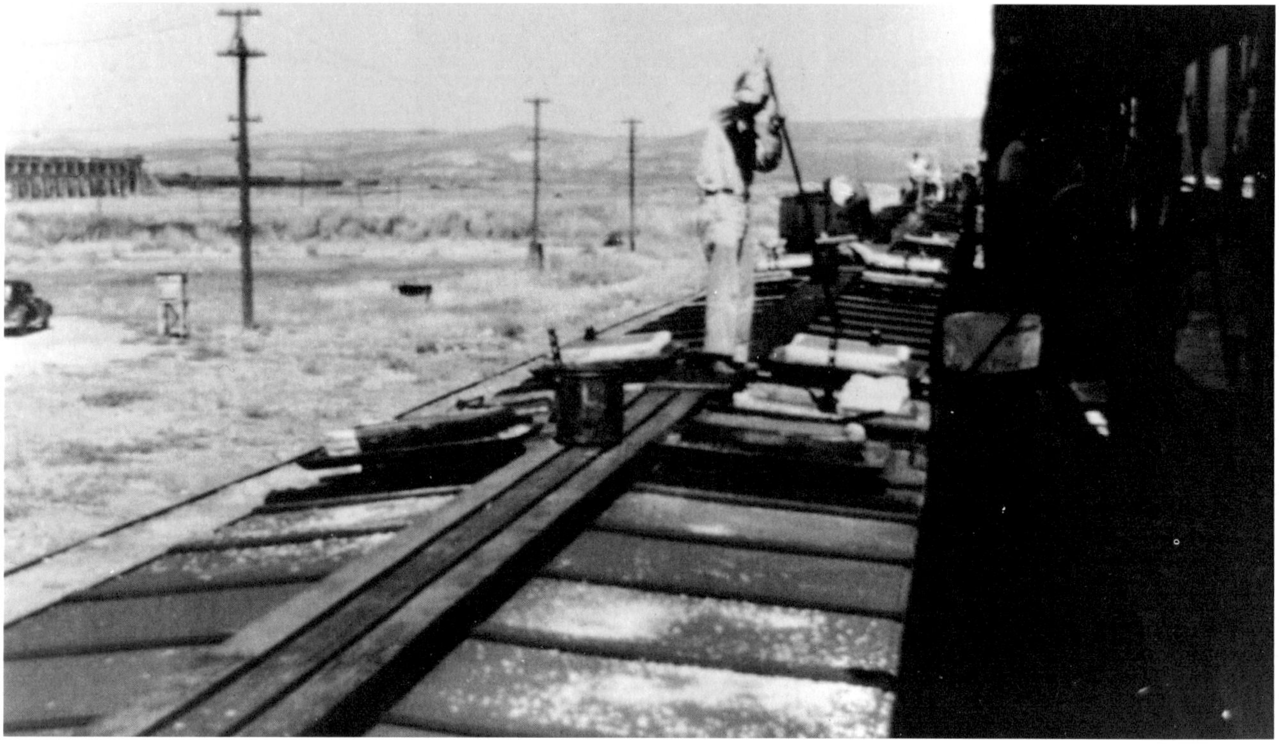

Above: For many decades, shipments of California fruits and vegetables moved to eastern destinations in refrigerator cars. Workers inserted blocks of ice in the top of the car at several points along the line to preserve perishable food. This man is working at the Carlin icing station. (Northeastern Nevada Museum)

Below: Icing decks along the line, such as this one at Carlin, enabled workers to deposit blocks of ice into the refrigerator cars. With the development of reliable mechanical refrigeration, icing decks became history. (Northeastern Nevada Museum)

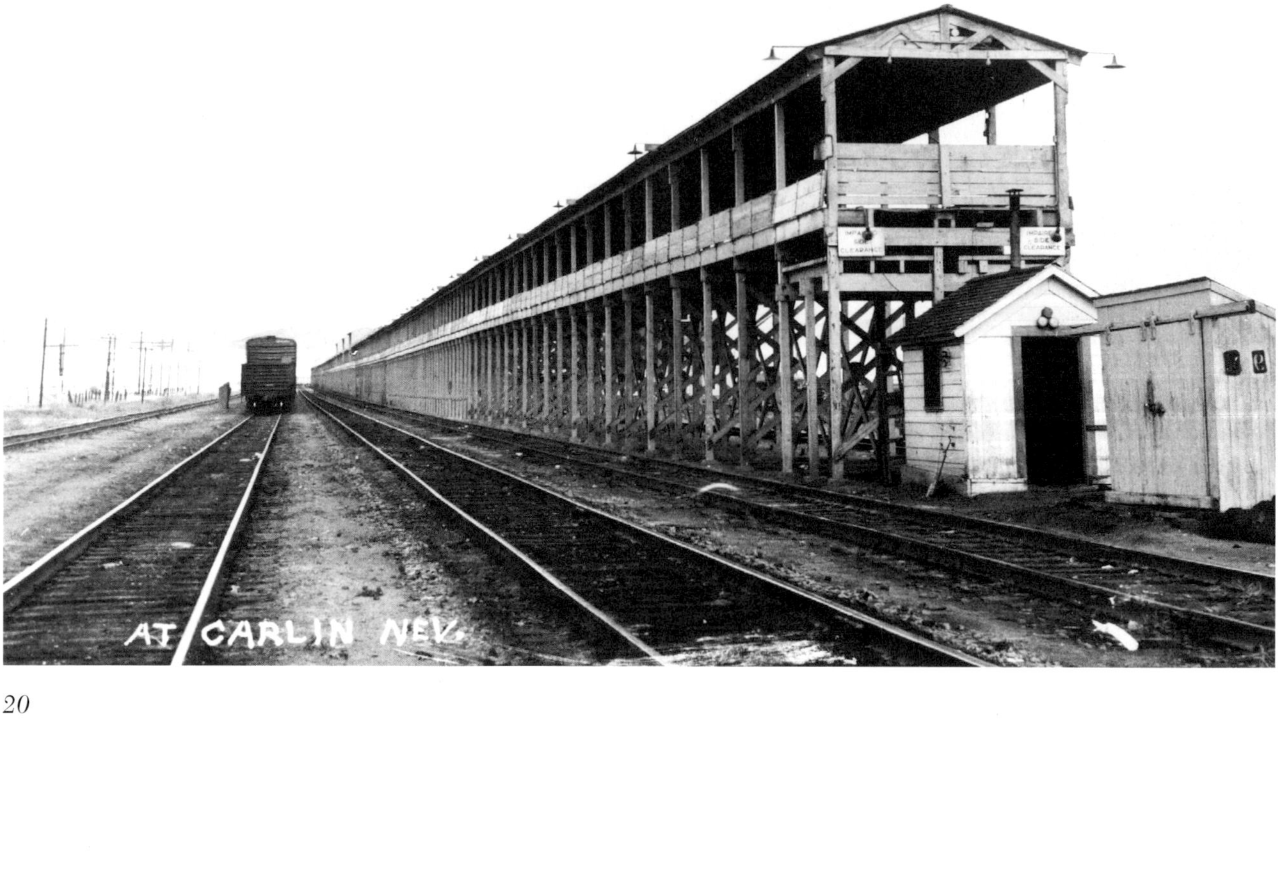

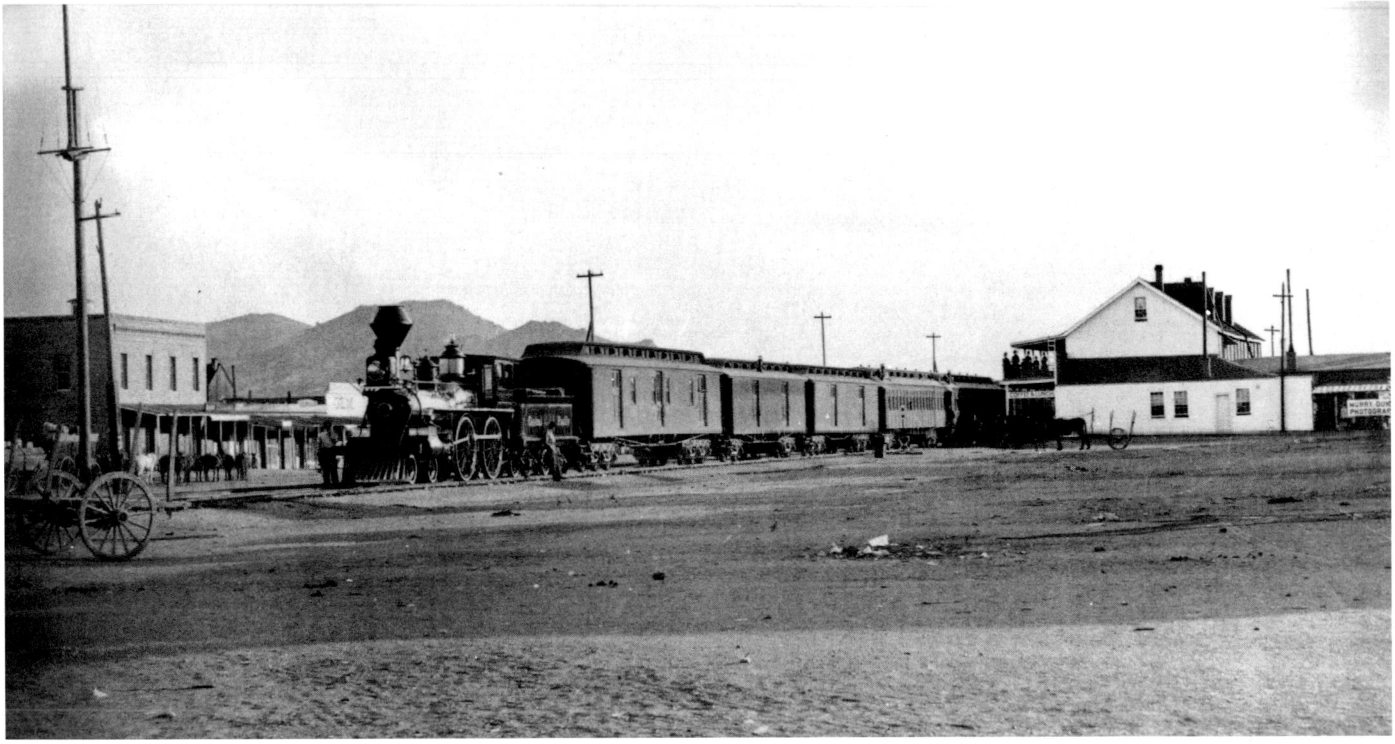

Above: When the train arrived in Elko in 1876, travelers adjourned to the conveniently located Depot Hotel. (Northeastern Nevada Museum)

Below: Many decades later, the second section of the westbound San Francisco Overland Limited was photographed at the Elko station. The milepost indicated the location was 556 miles from San Francisco. (Northeastern Nevada Museum)

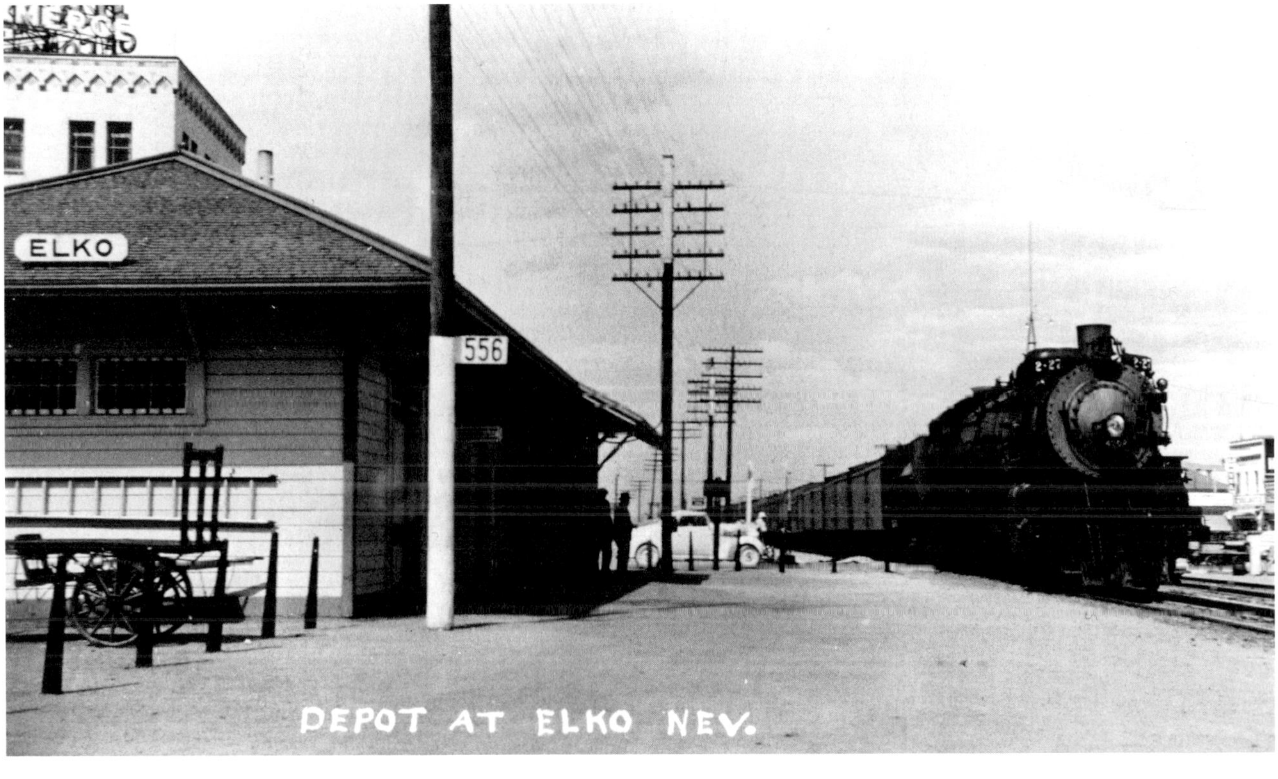

Right: Before the settlement was moved to Cobre, John Casier's hotel in Toano in the late 1800s met the needs of travelers pausing before taking the stage to Ely or Pioche. (Northeastern Nevada Museum)

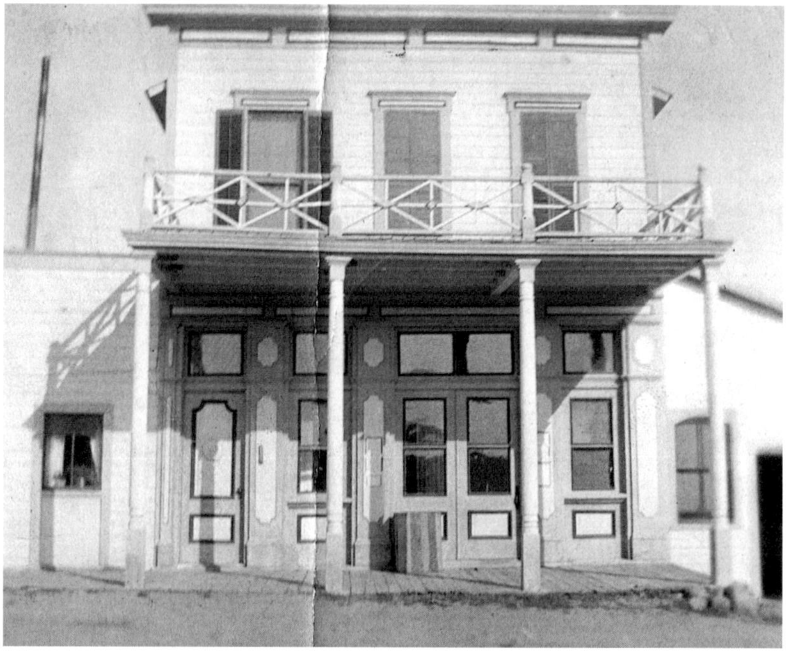

Below: To avoid severe consequences that could result when steam locomotives lacked adequate water, tanks were established at many points along the line. According to a 1940 Salt Lake Division timetable, water for locomotives was available at twenty-two points across Nevada. A fireman climbed aboard the tender to pull the water spout down to fill the tender. (Northeastern Nevada Museum)

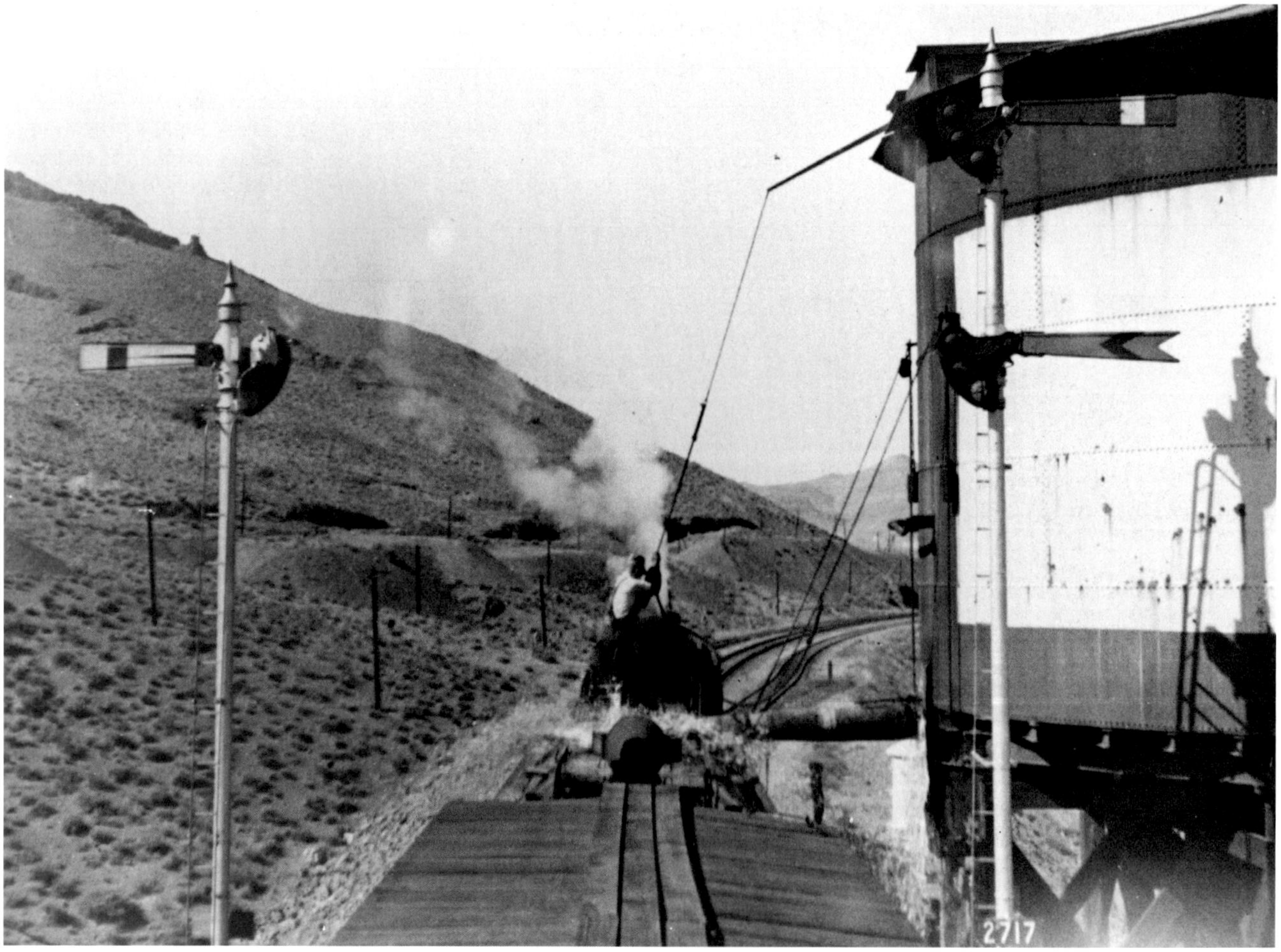

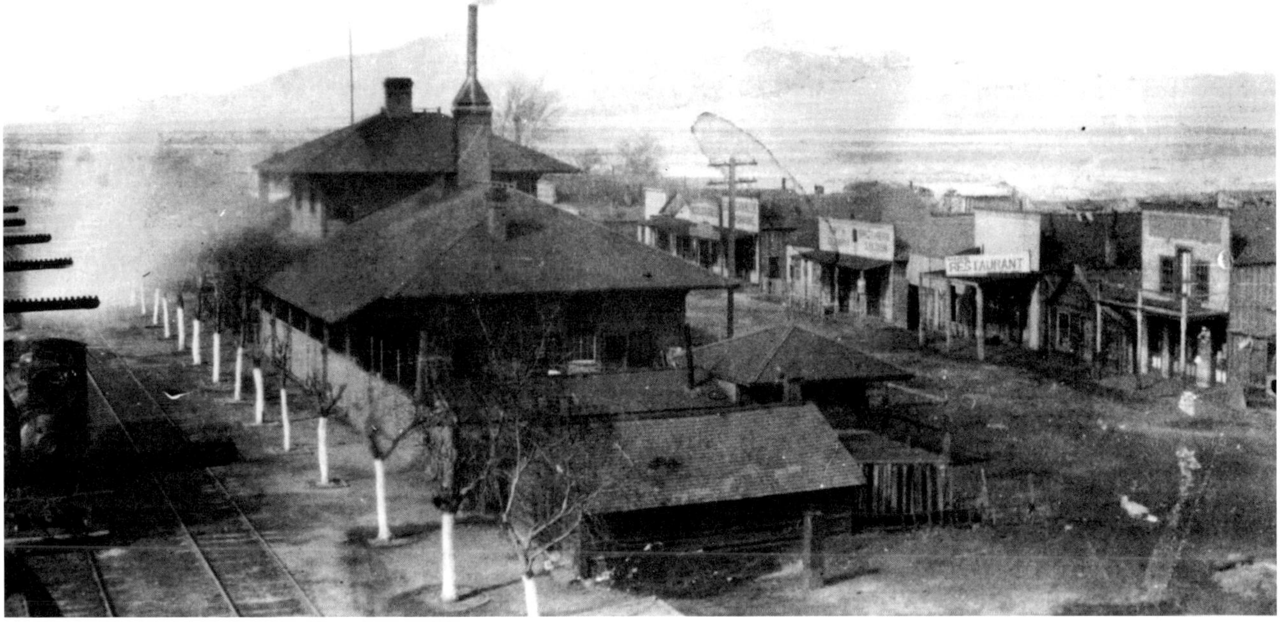

Above: Terrace, Utah, served as an important division point until trains followed the shorter Lucin Cutoff. The scene is about 1880. Though not shown on later Salt Lake Division timetables, it was twenty-one miles east of Lucin. (Tom Williamson collection)

Below: Looking west at Terrace, one would see the depot in the distance on the far right, while the machine shop is almost in the center of the picture. Beyond it was a fifteen-stall roundhouse, while the coaling shed is the large building on the near left. All these facilities vanished a century ago. (Tom Williamson collection)

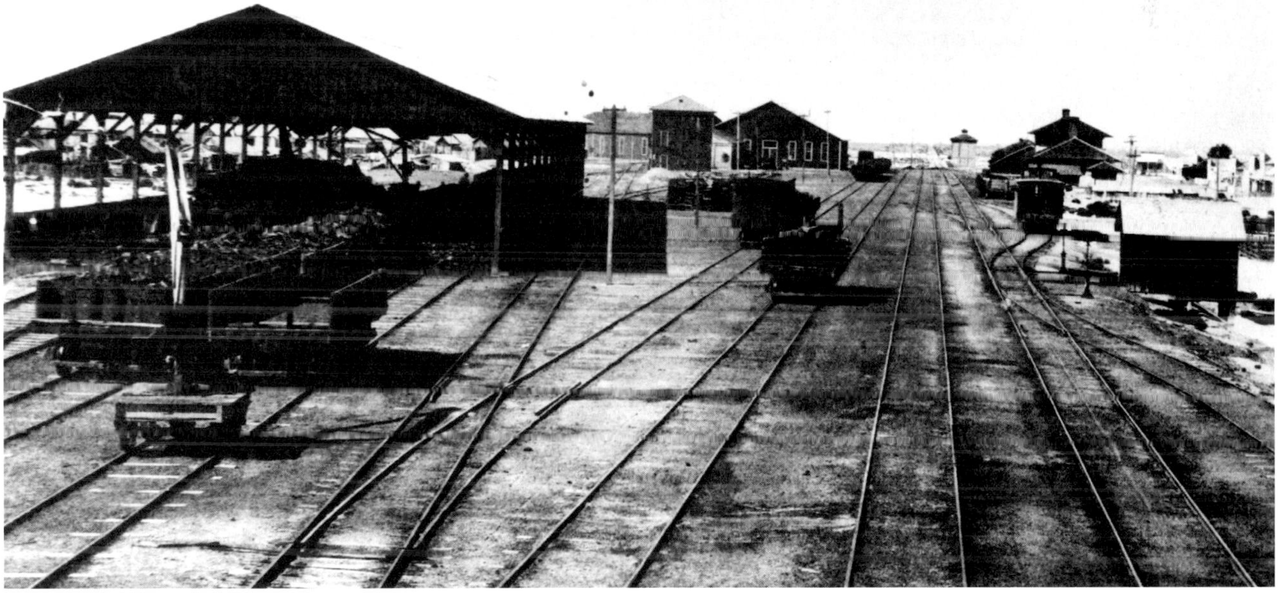

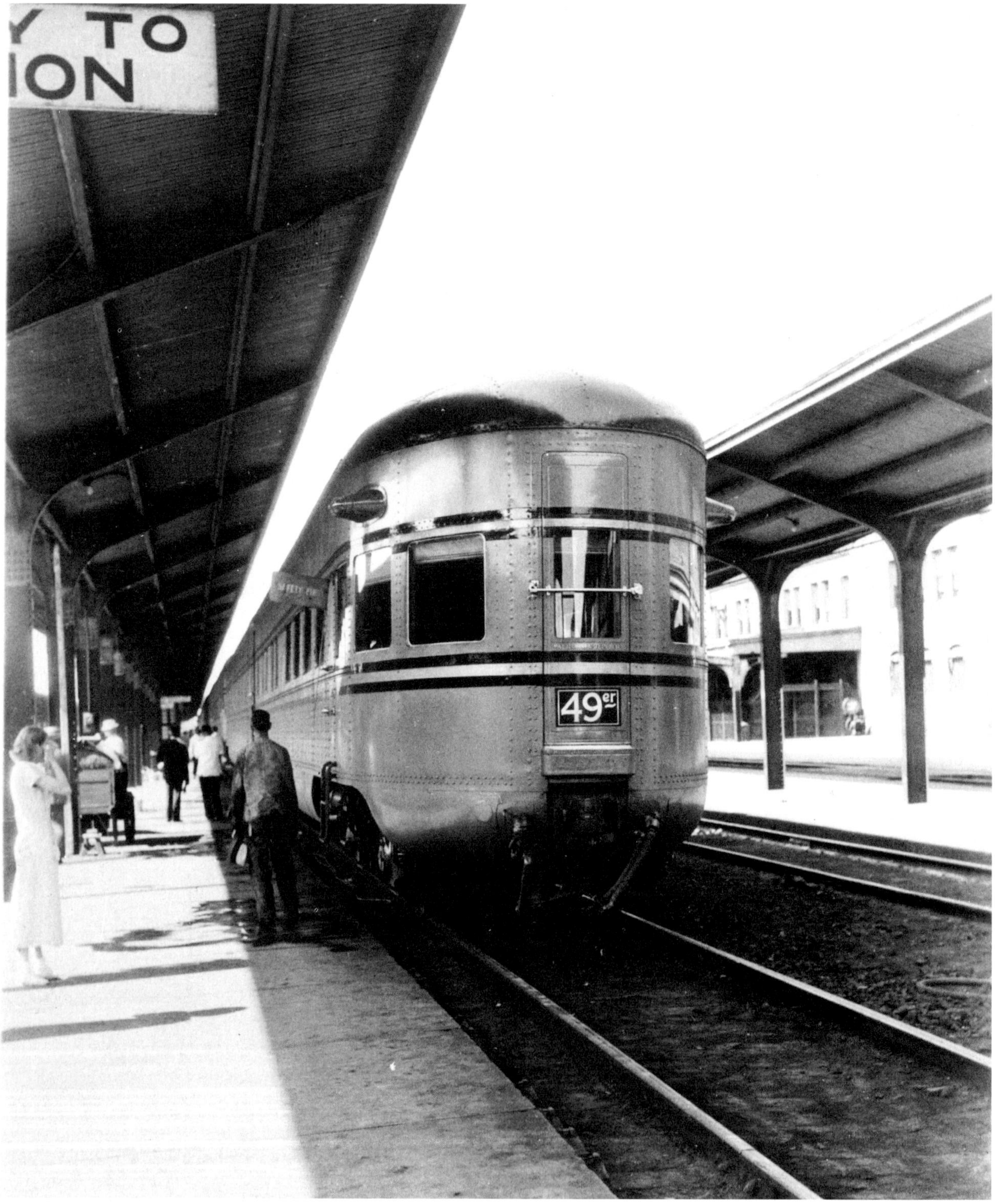

To supplement the five monthly sailings of the City of San Francisco, the '49er was introduced in July 1937. The photographer caught it at the Ogden Union Station. (Tom Williamson collection)

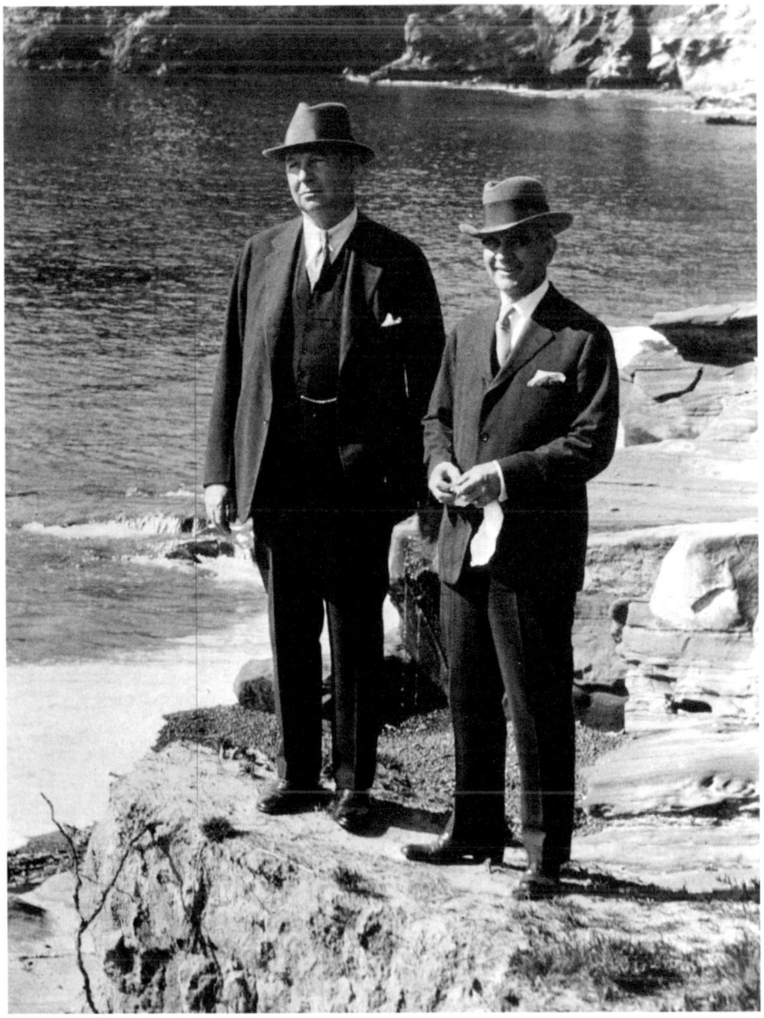

Left: Two SP executives stood in a relaxed moment by the seashore. Hale Holden (a cigar in his right hand) a Harvard Law School graduate, served as president of the Burlington Railroad from 1920 until switching to SP in 1929 as chairman of the executive committee. Paul Shoup, after being president of the subsidiary Pacific Electric for seven years, came to San Francisco and later became SP's president. His slightly older brother, Guy, headed SP's law department.

Below: From 1928 to 1944, Baldwin constructed 195 of these cab-in-front locomotives for Southern Pacific. Although workhorses handling freight trains, these engines had regular passenger runs. The life of No. 4254, built in 1943 and shown here at MP 571 near Ryndon, Nevada, was cut short by the advent of diesel power, for it was scrapped after only twelve years of active employment.

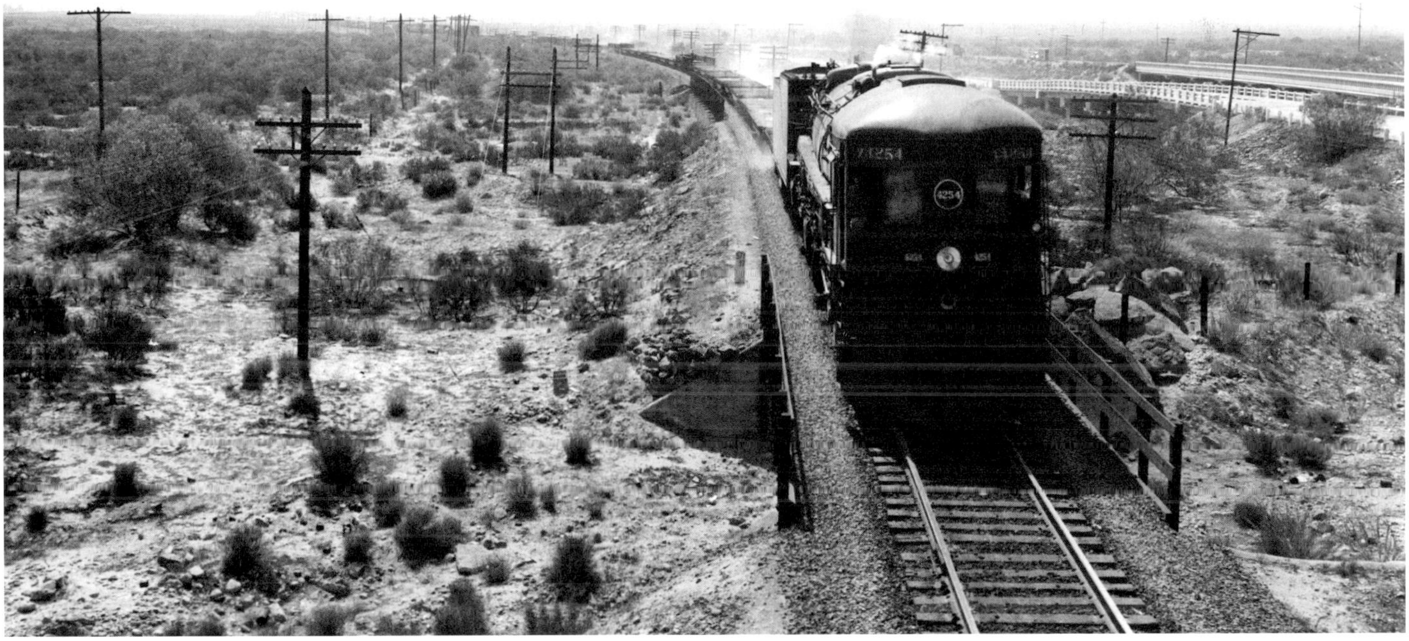

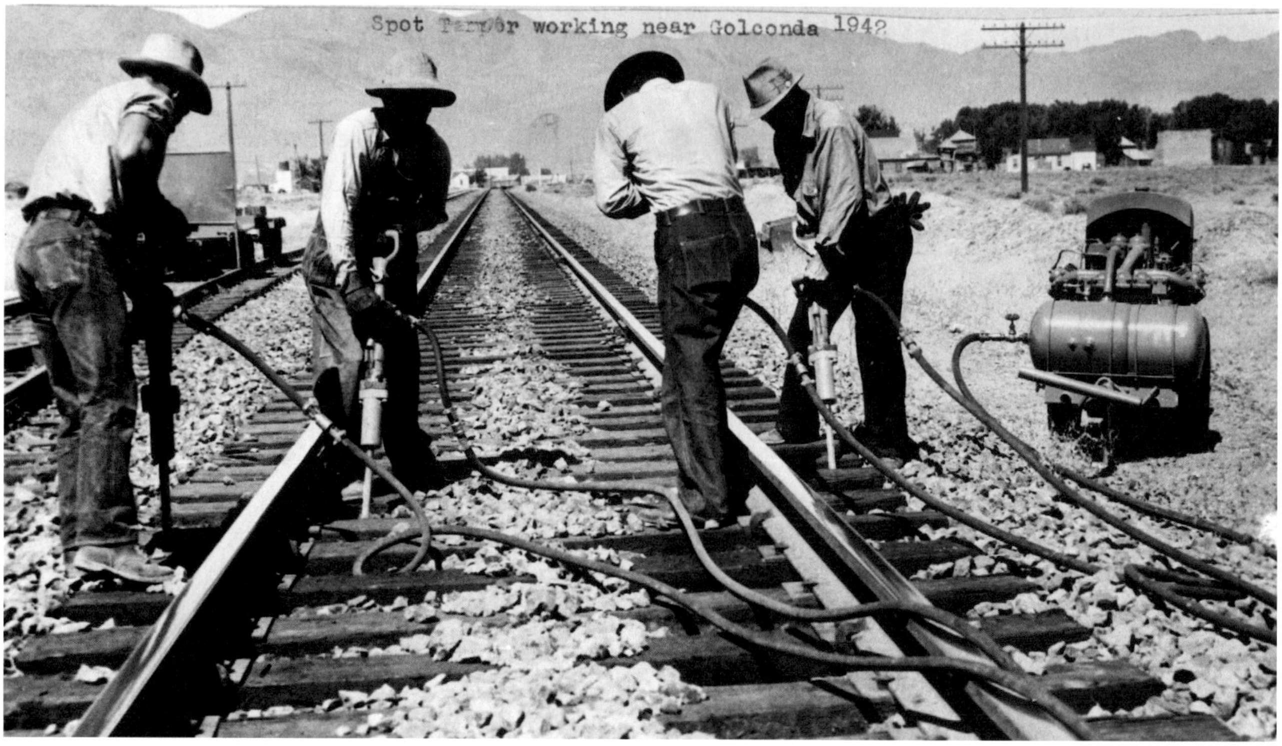

Above: A spot-tamping crew adjusts the roadbed at Golconda to ensure a smooth track. (Tom Williamson collection)

Below: During World War II, women temporarily filled section gangs as the men went into the service. This group was busy near Elko in May 1943. (Tom Williamson photograph)

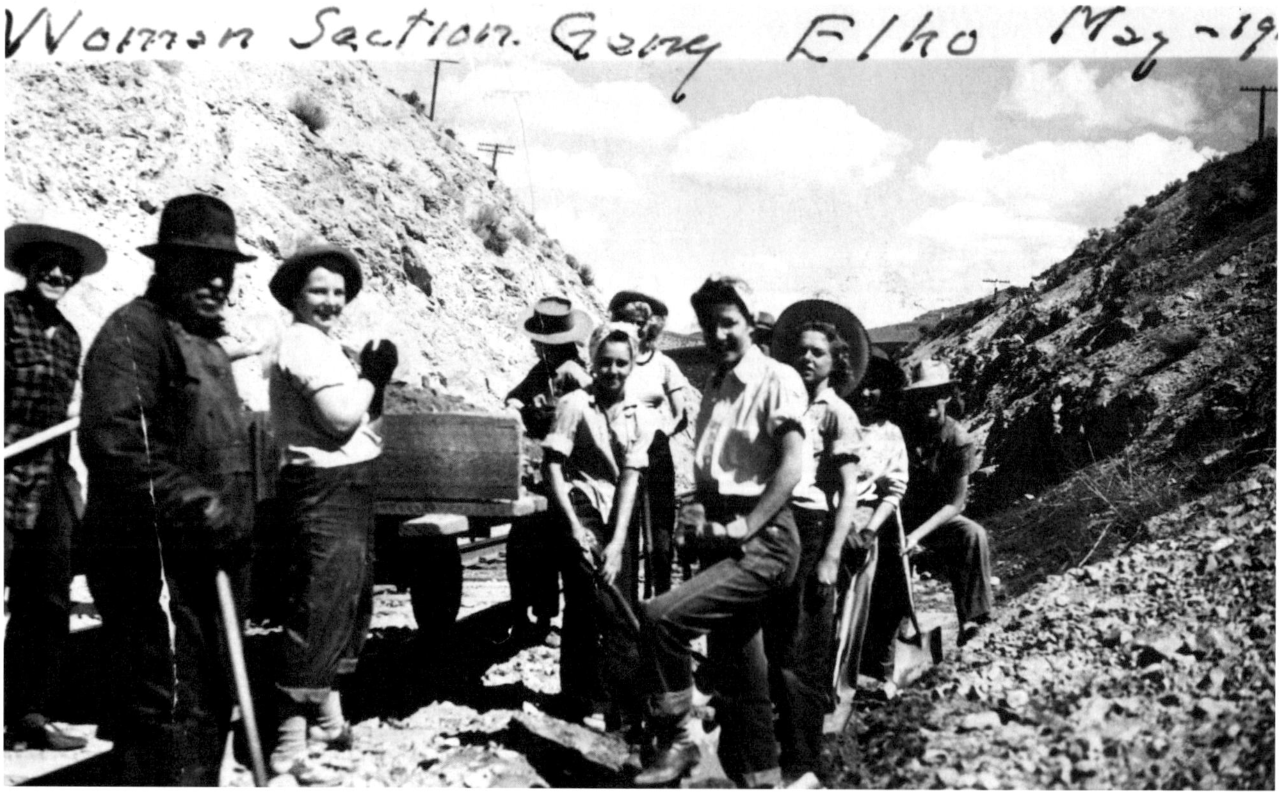

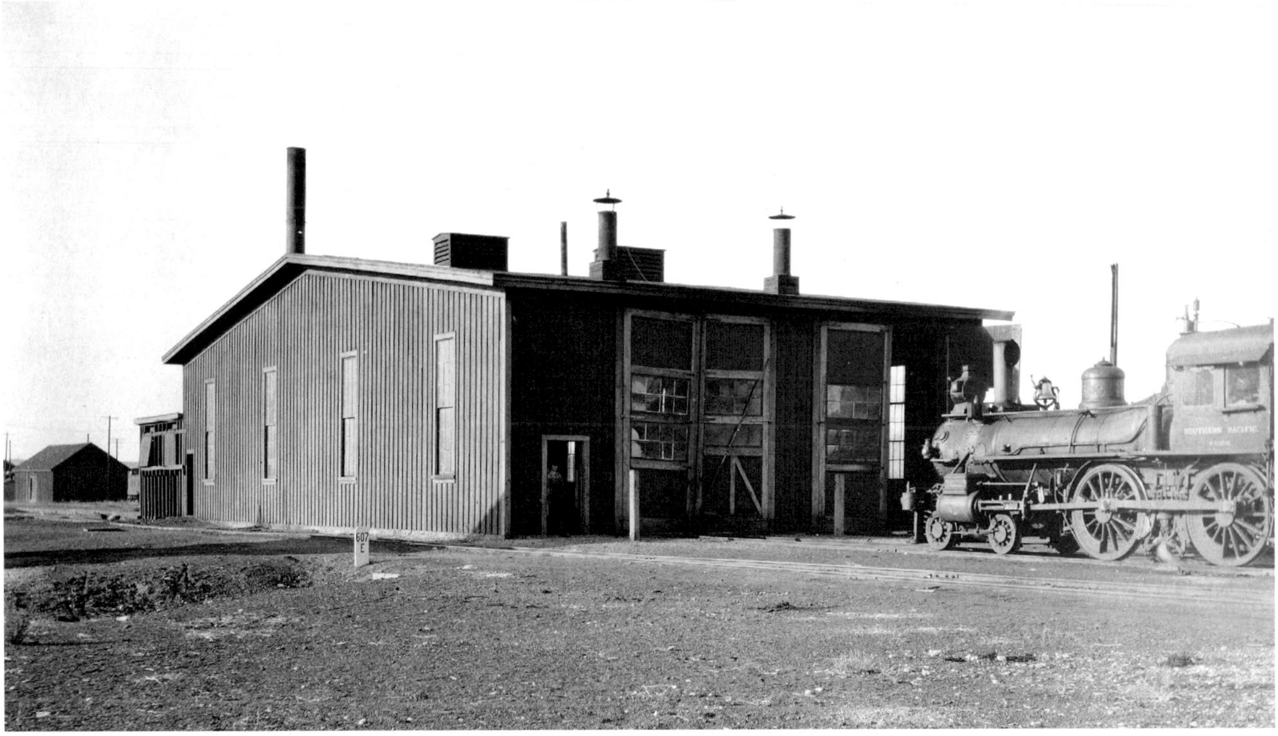

Above: Wells had only a small engine house in 1912, but it was enough to accommodate this 4-4-0 engine seeking shelter. (Ted Wurm collection)

Below: For more than three decades, Central Pacific maintained a major division point at Wadsworth with a roundhouse and machine shop. When the Lucin Cutoff was placed in service in 1904, division points across Nevada were shifted westward and Sparks superseded Wadsworth.

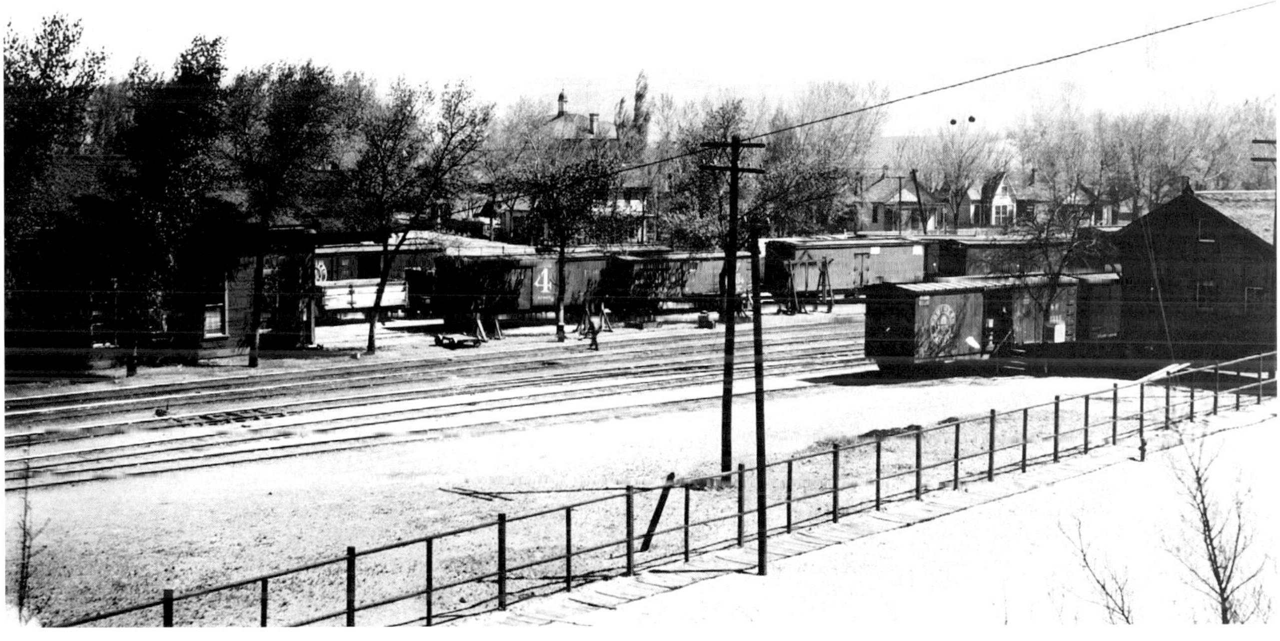

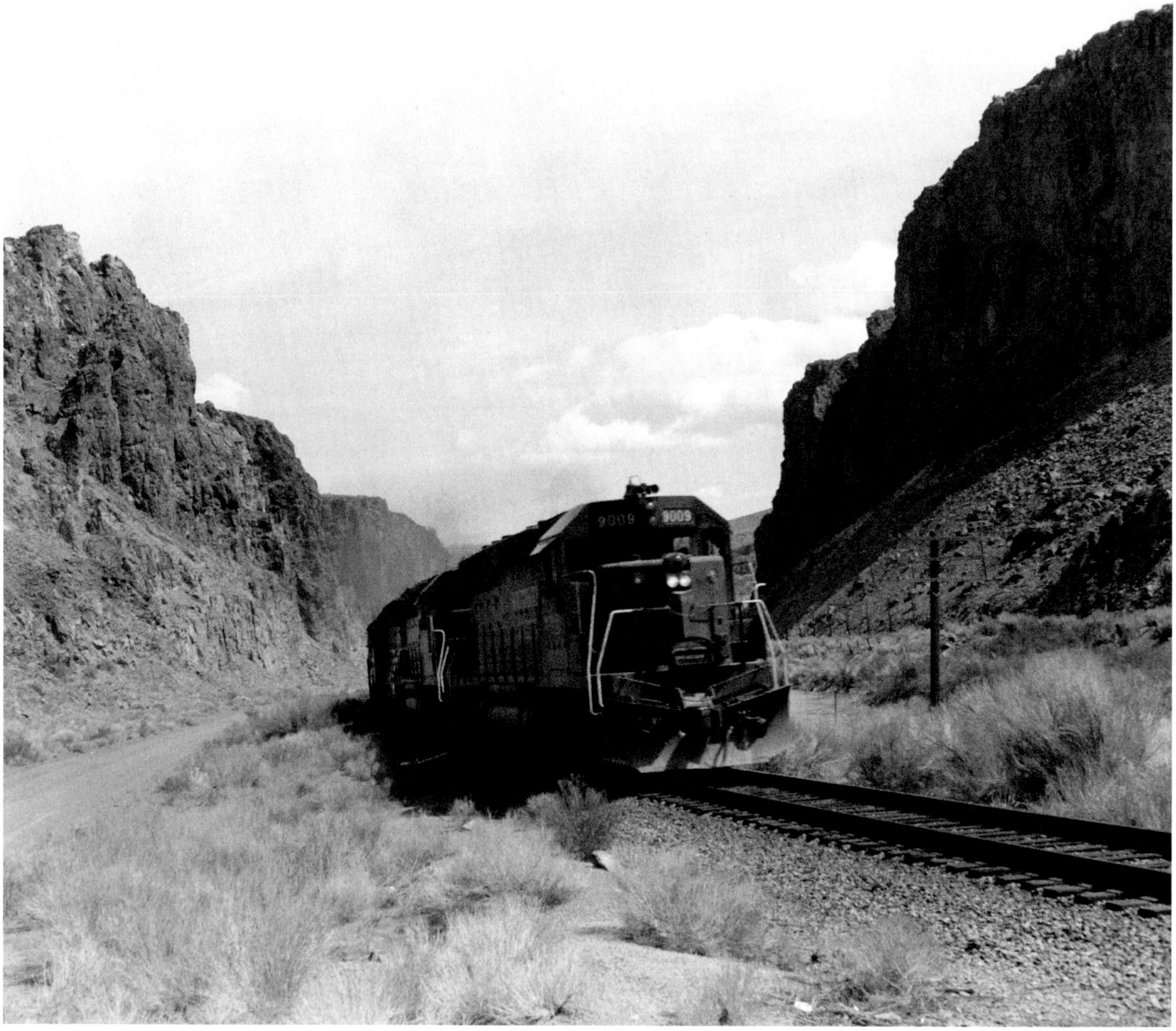

Palisade Canyon remains unchanged, although the trains have a different appearance. (Southern Pacific)

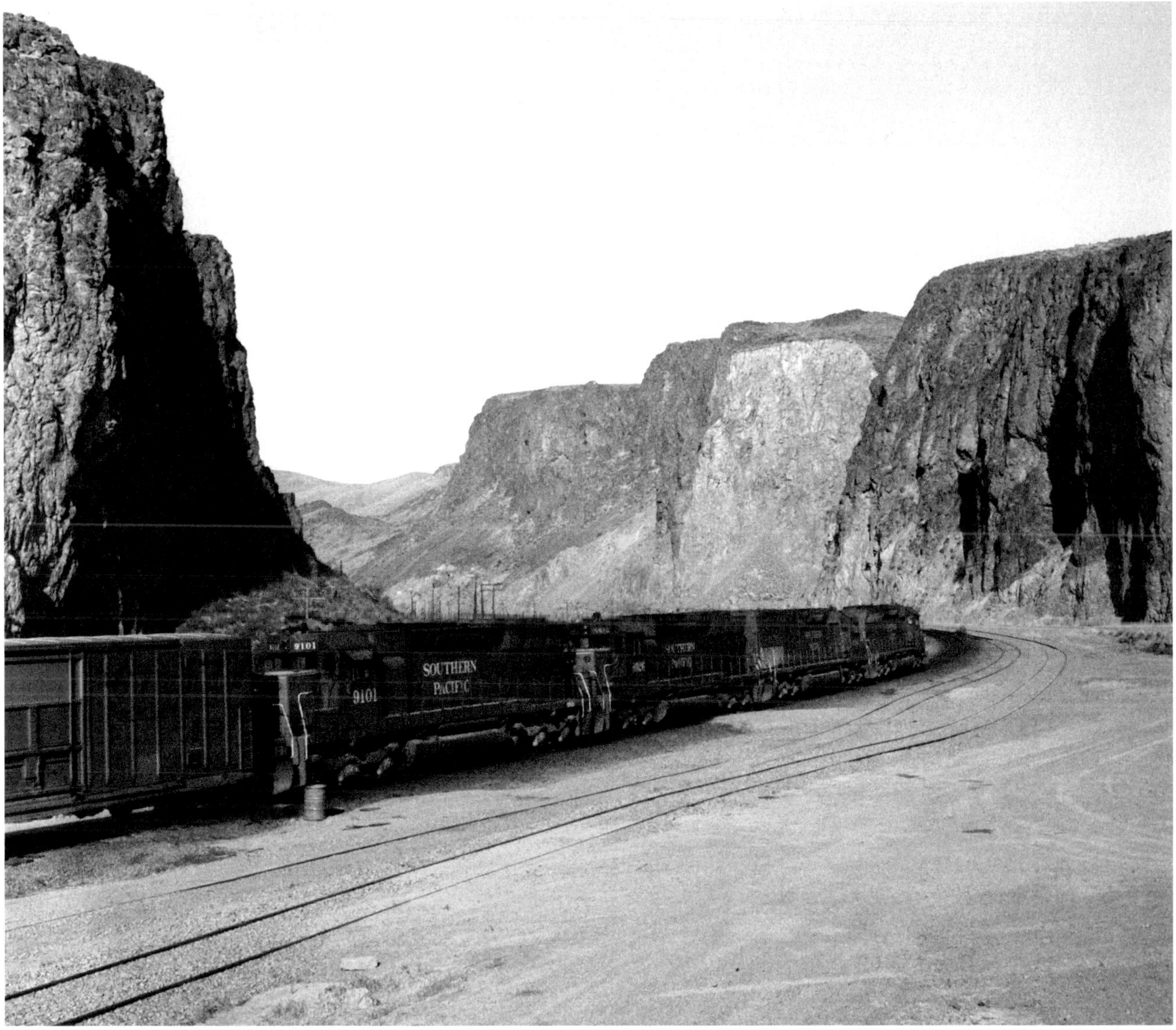

An early morning scene in Palisade Canyon, also in July 1975, found this westbound train with four units on the point (SP 9005, 9185, 8926, and 9101). (Virgil C. Staff photograph)

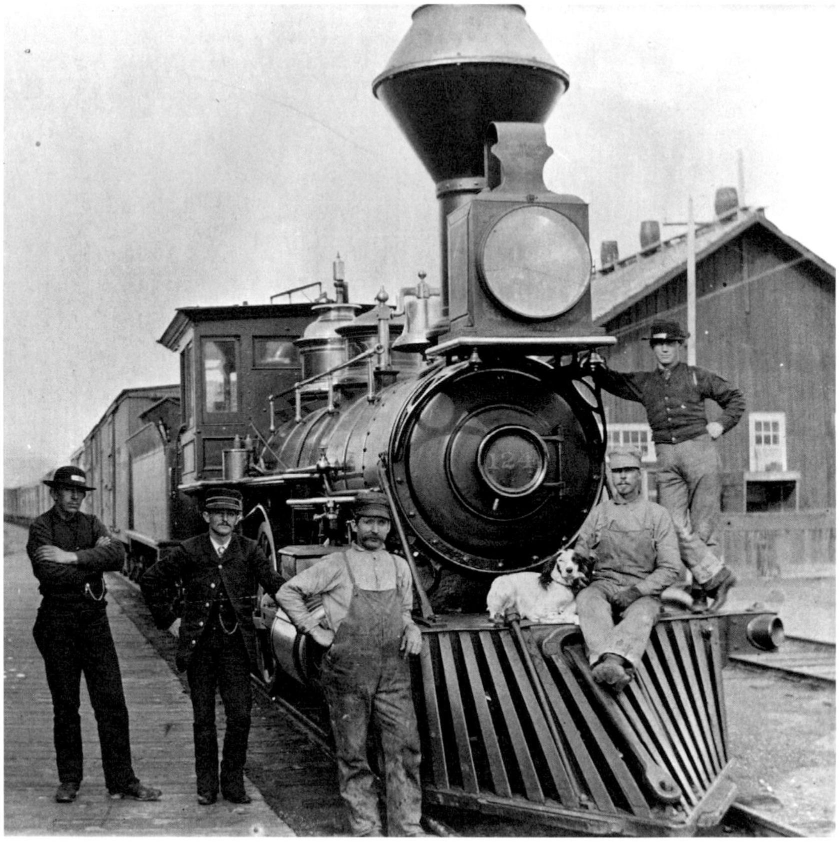

Right: The crew of an emigrant train posed for the camera during a pause at Mill City, Nevada, on the way to San Francisco, then 389 miles ahead.

Below: No. 6446, of EMD manufacture, often called a "covered wagon," was taken from the freight pool to handle train No. 21. Formerly called Pacific Limited, by July 1956 it became a mail train as it passed through Winnemucca. (Al C. Phelps photograph)

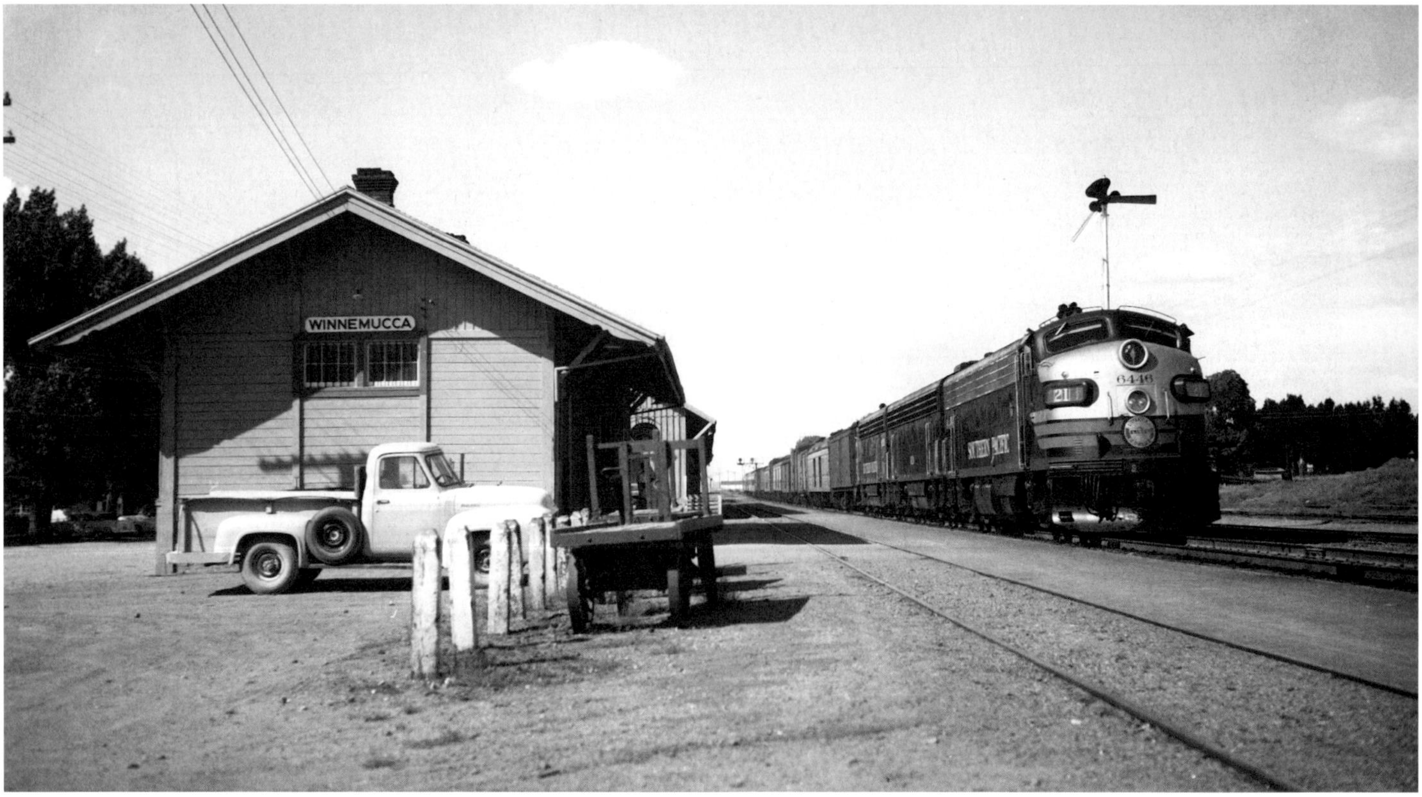

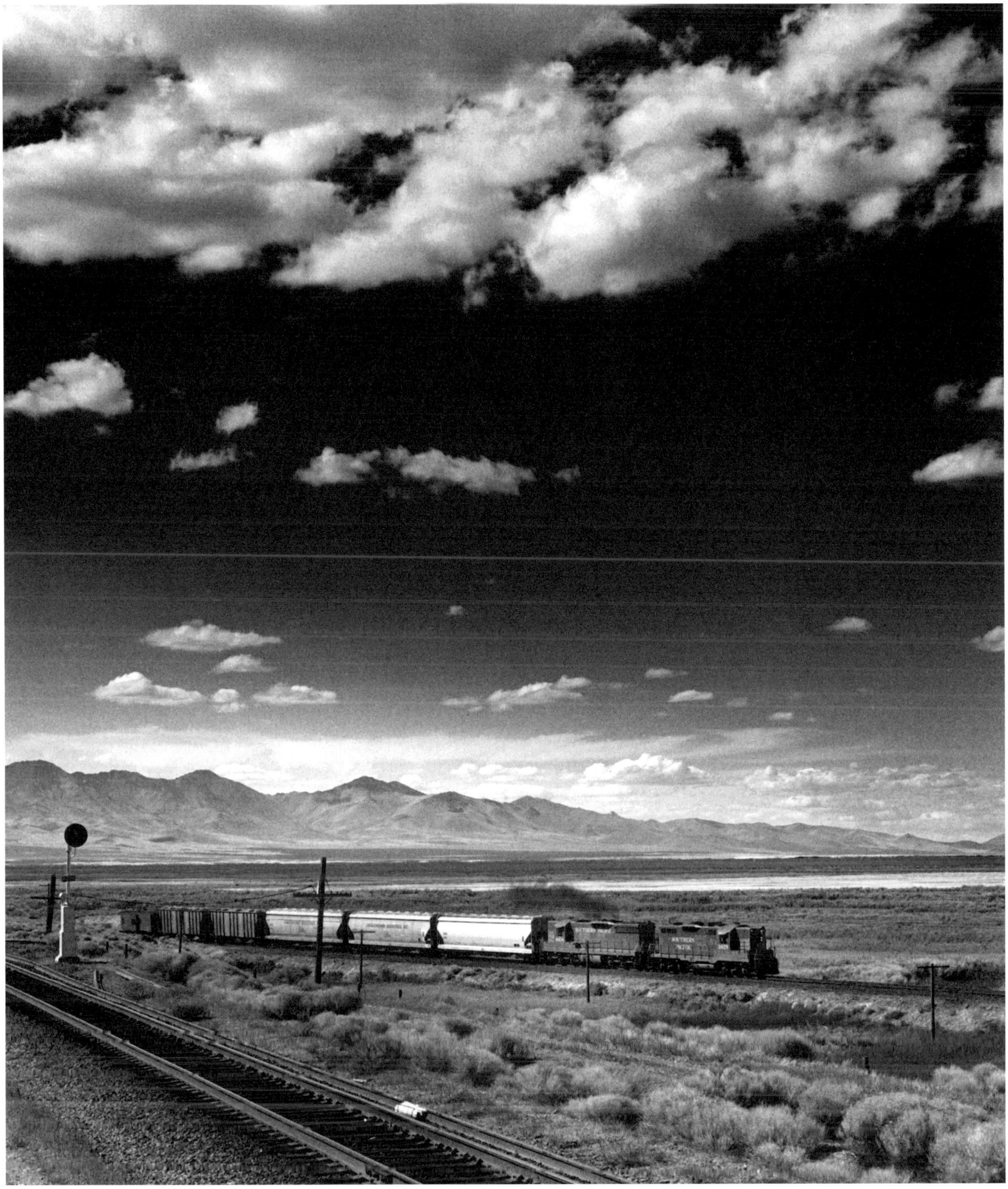

Between Weso and Alazon, Southern Pacific and Western Pacific conducted paired-track operations using WP for eastbound trains and SP for trains in the other direction. SP's Lovelock local, having just entered WP trackage at Weso, accelerates with Carlin as its destination on a sunny afternoon in August 1976. (Ted Benson photograph)

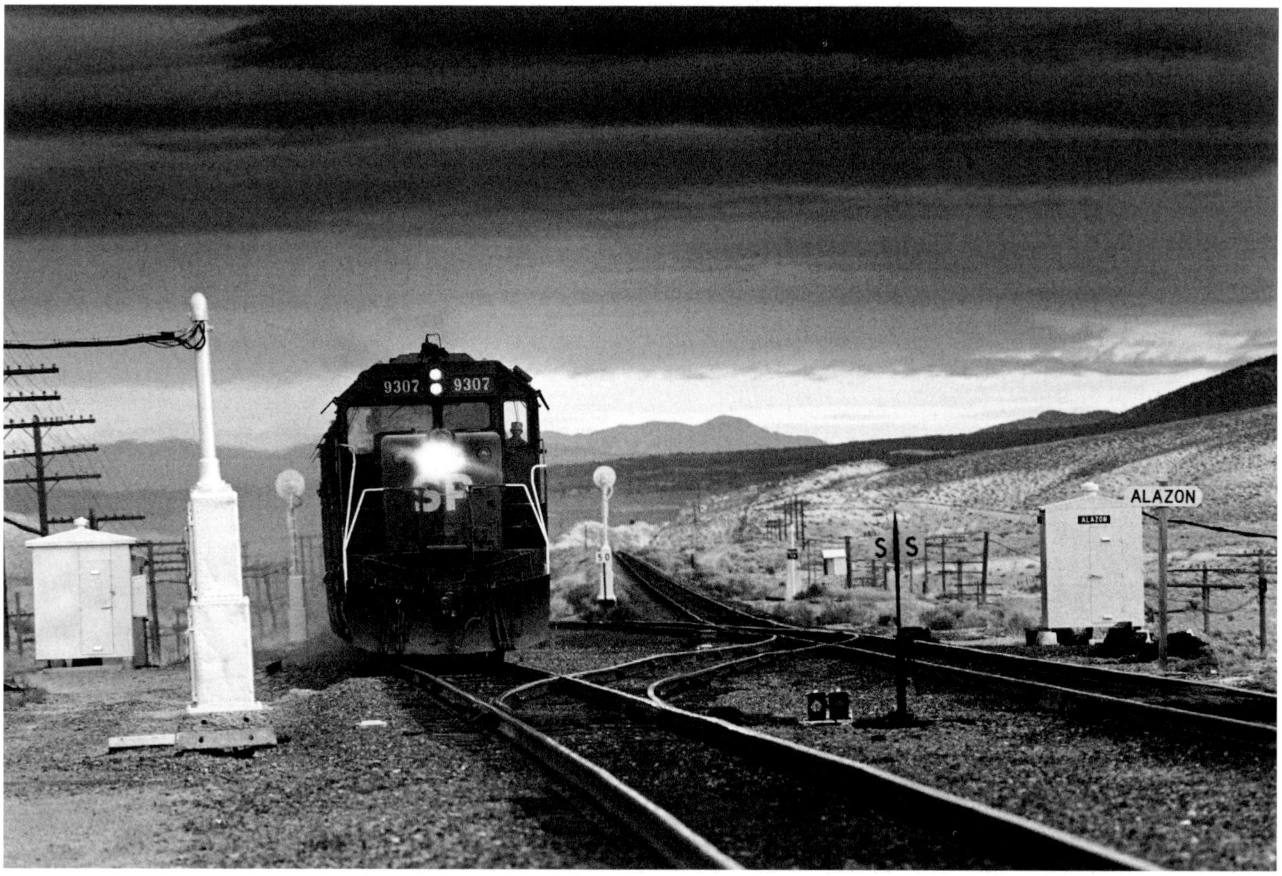

Above: November skies portend precipitation as this westbound SP trailer train moves across Nevada. It has negotiated the Pequop Mountains grades and is now passing Alazon, the eastern end of the paired-track operation. (Ted Benson photograph, 1977)

Below: To battle the Pequops, two helper locomotives temporarily leased from Union Pacific have been called into play to assist the powerful 2-10-2 on the front. A San Francisco rail fan, Dudley Thickens, watches the long train. (Al C. Phelps photograph)

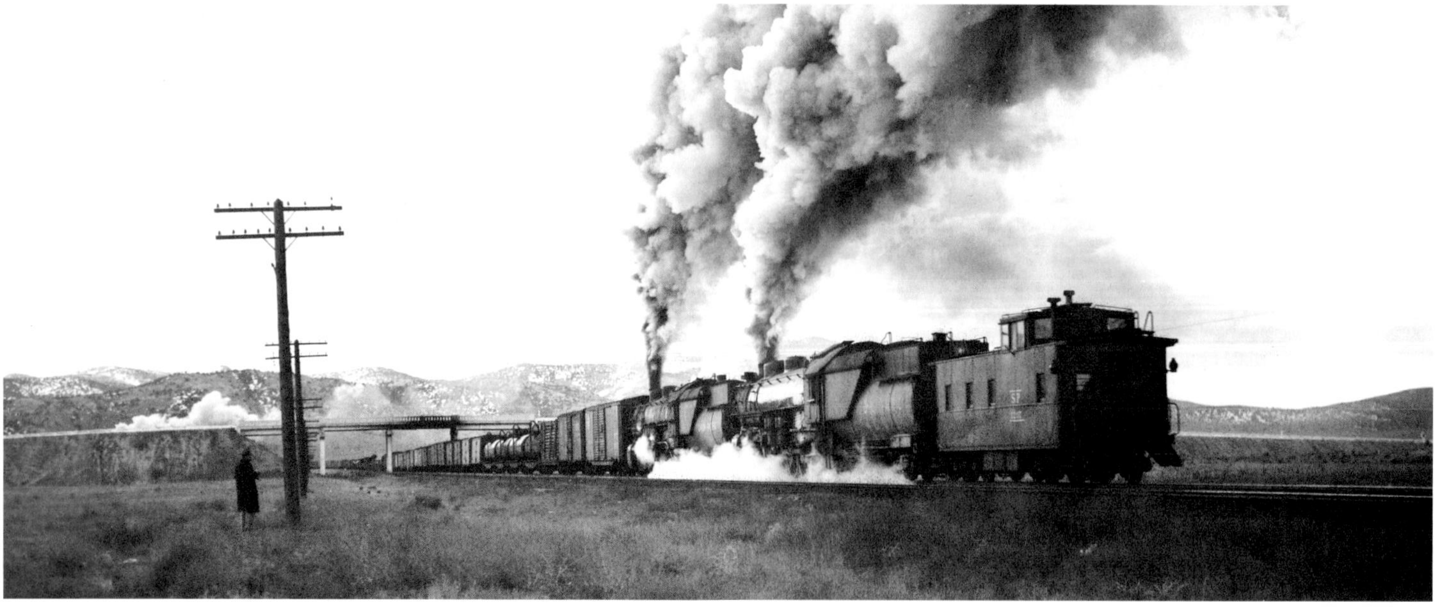

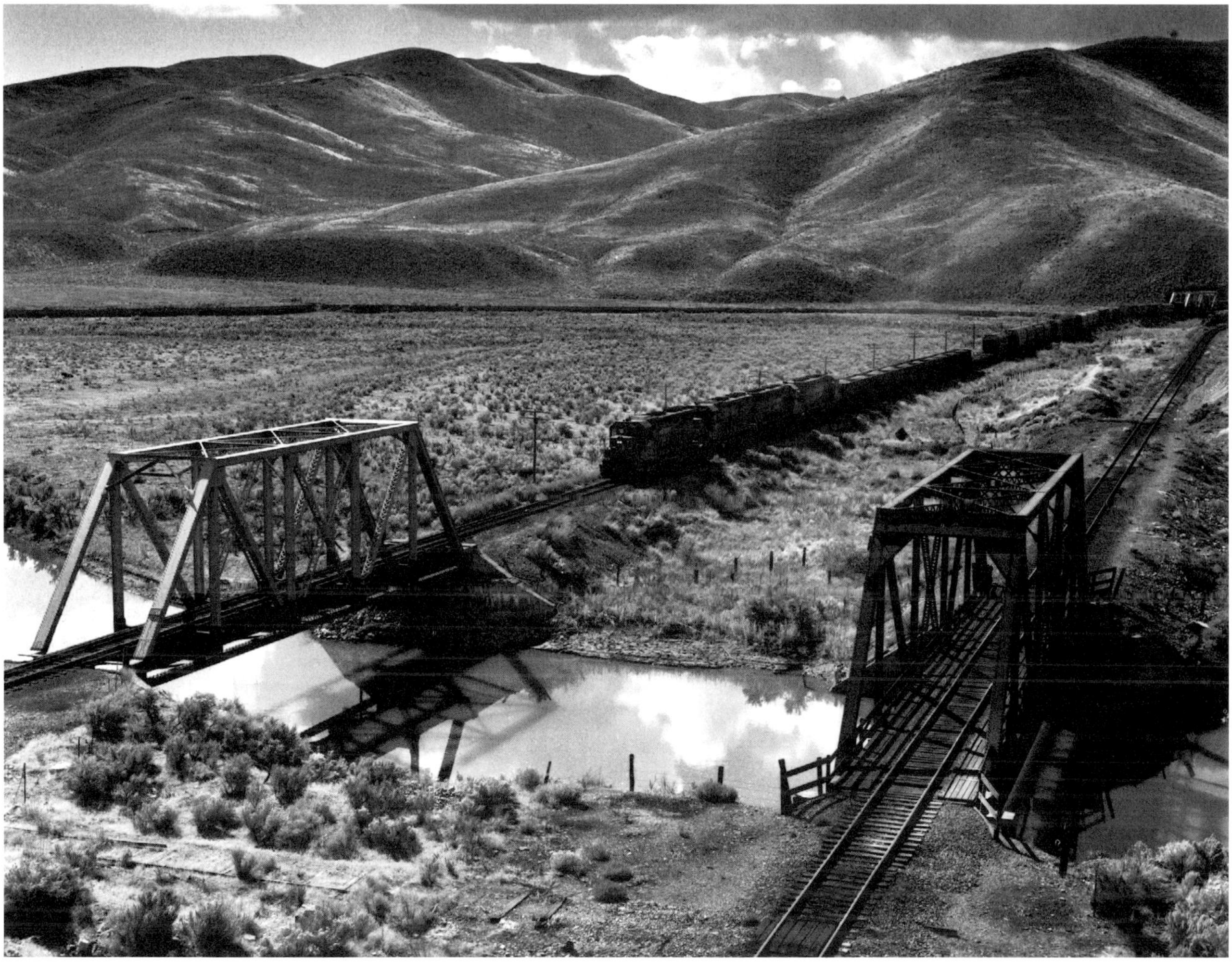

After crossing the Humboldt River, this eastbound Southern Pacific freight train on Western Pacific rails will enter a tunnel before reaching Palisade. Trains on the westbound track (Southern Pacific) also pass through a tunnel at this point. The derelict grade of the former Eureka and Palisade Railroad marks the foreground. (Ted Benson photograph, 1976)

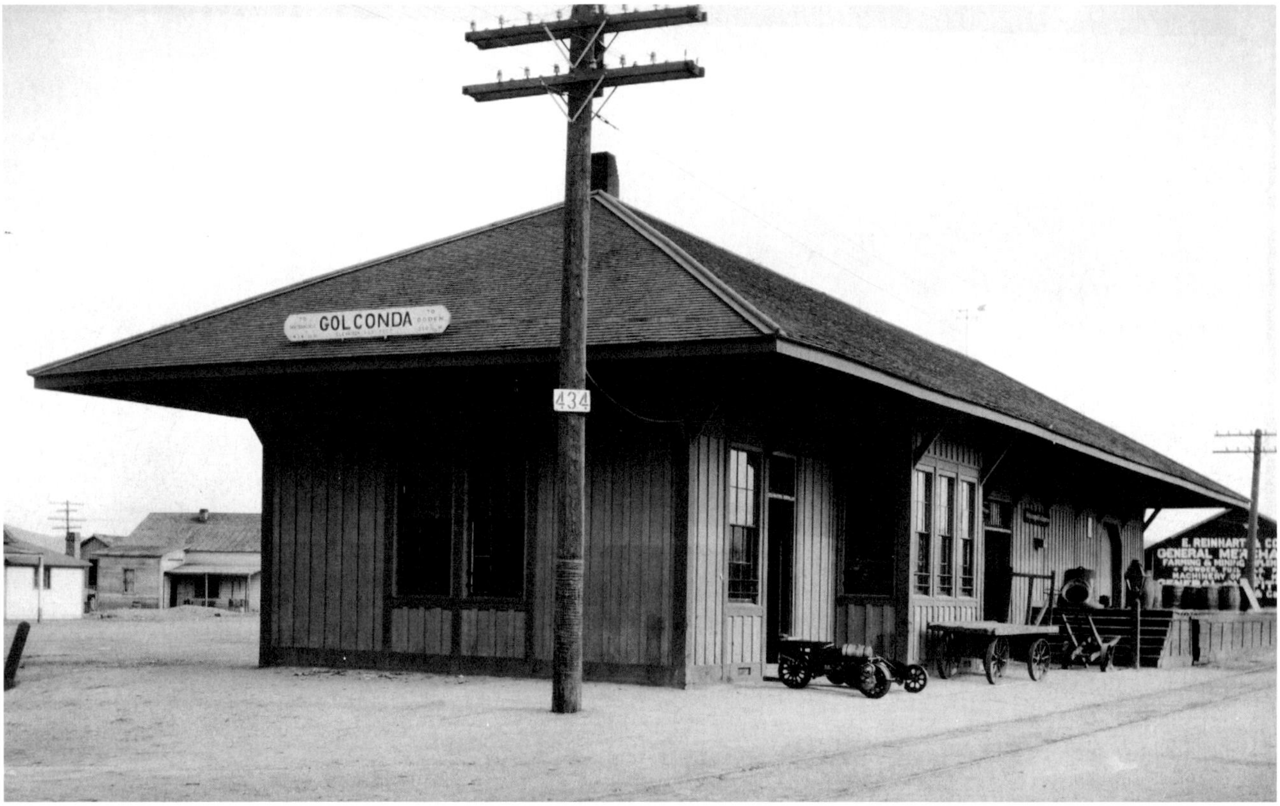

Golconda, the Nevada station with the mythical name, faces reality, with the milepost indicating that it is 434 miles from San Francisco.

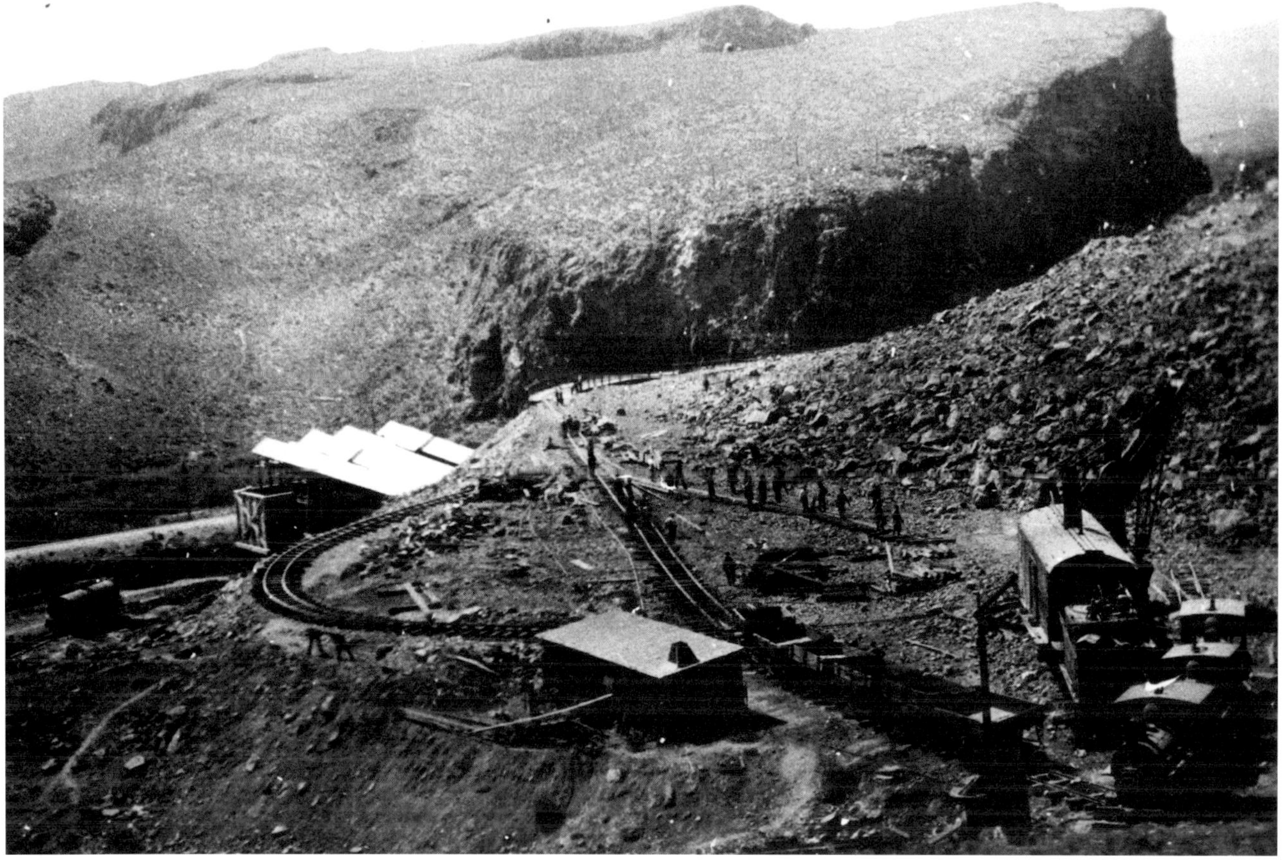

To secure a stable roadbed, ballast, often consisting of crushed rock, was placed under the ties. From its quarry near Palisade, SP used a steam shovel to gather rock that was broken into small pieces in the crusher below the bluff.

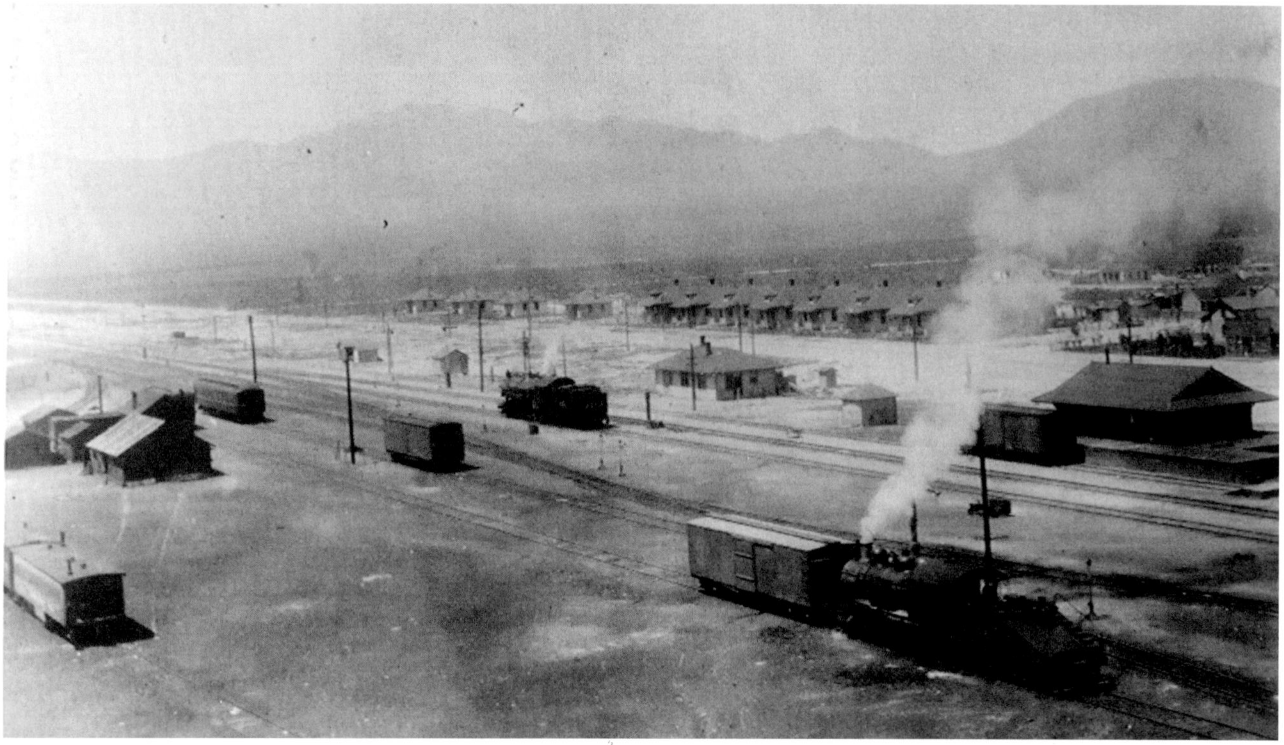

Above: Helper locomotives were based in Montello to assist trains on the stiff grades over the Pequop Mountains in eastern Nevada. This is the yard in July 1914. (Northeastern Nevada Museum)

Below: A 1939 view of the Montello yard and passenger and freight stations. By this time, the town had grown, and the pool hall on the street behind the station offered a diversion for railroad crews between assignments. (Northeastern Nevada Museum)

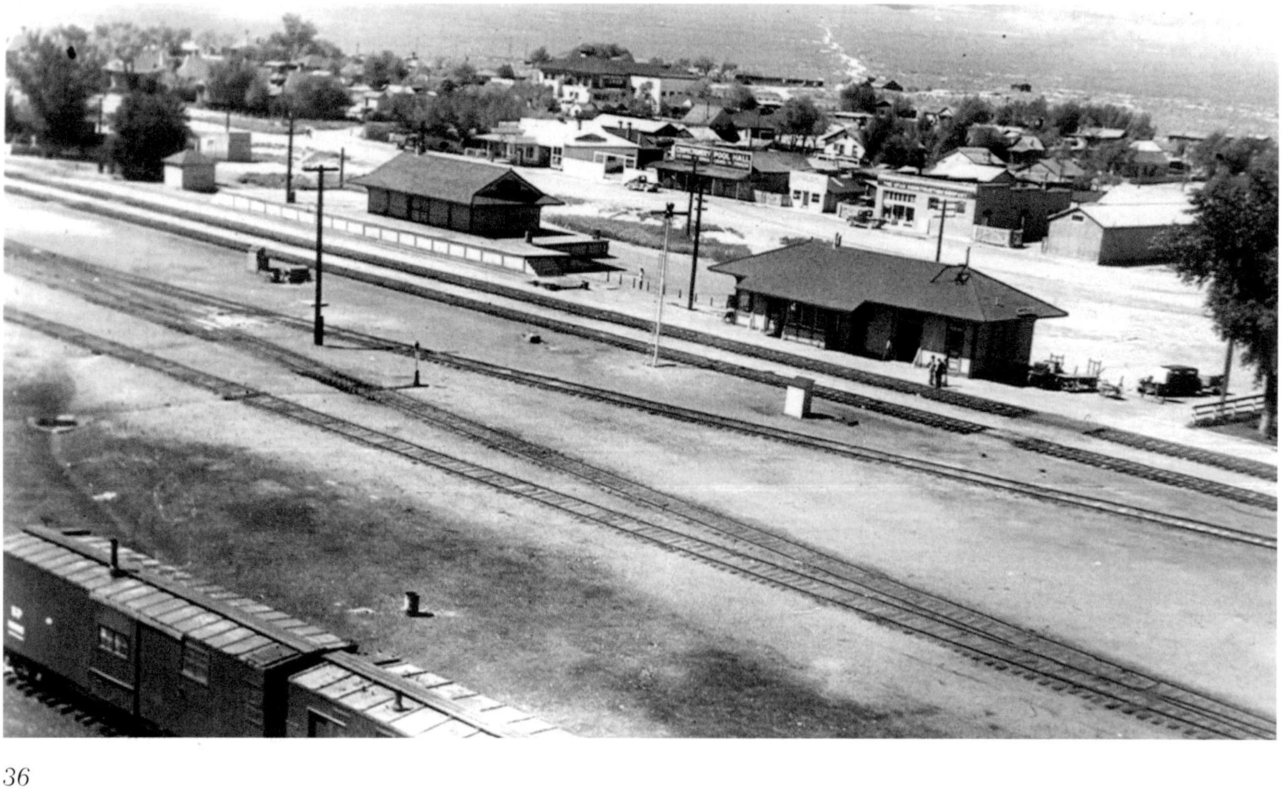

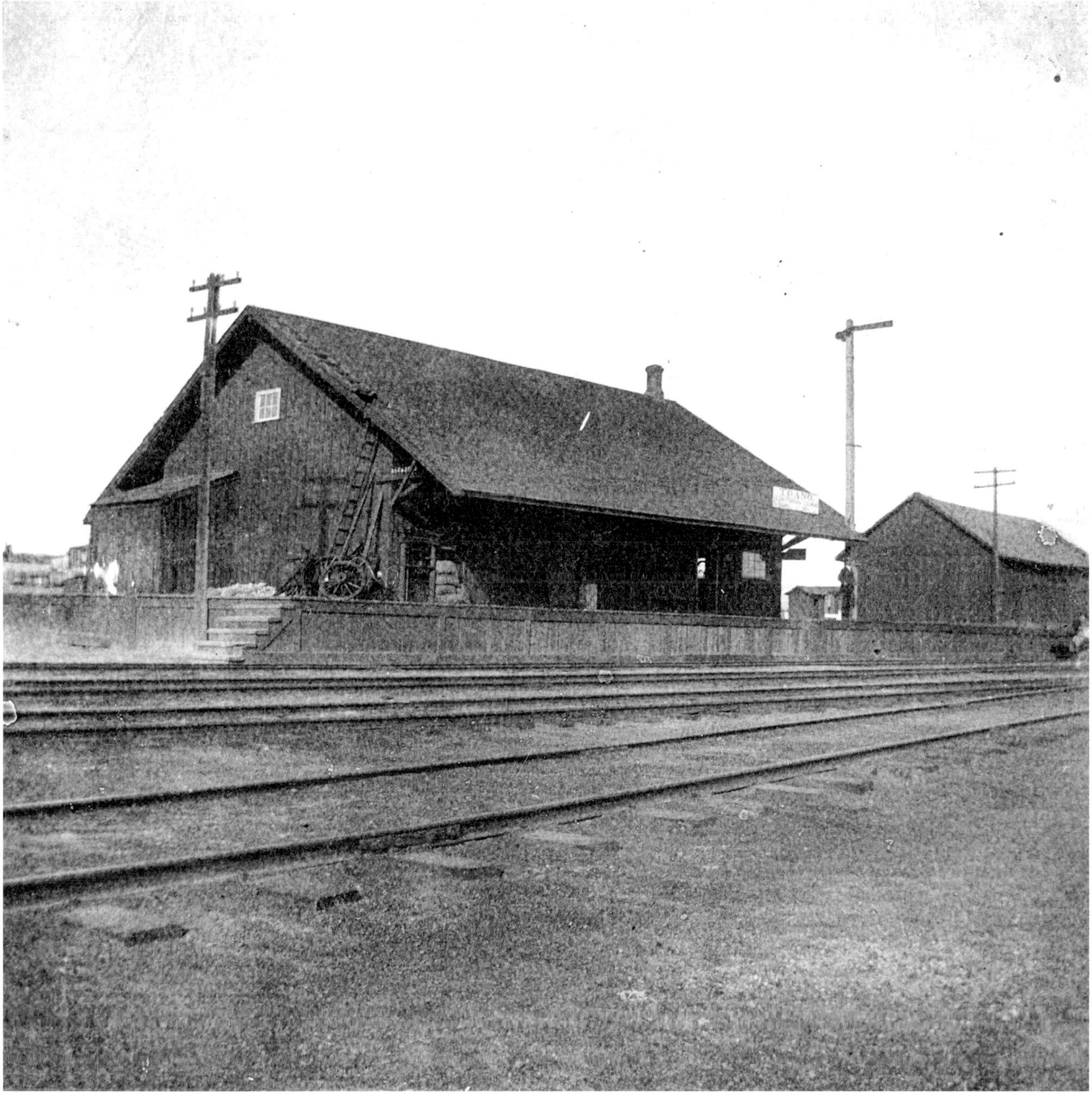

The high platform at the Toano freight station facilitated the transfer of items from Central Pacific boxcars. Spencer and Frank's warehouse is to the right of the station, while the roundhouse stands behind the cameraman. (Nevada Historical Society)

In planning a revision of operations, SP announced in January 1907 that the division point would be changed from Winnemucca to Imlay, 34 miles west. During the next two years, workers erected a twelve-stall roundhouse of brick and concrete at Imlay along with a powerhouse, oil house, and icehouse. As part of the same program, the company added a two-story-frame freight and passenger station, a dozen cottages for employees, a two-story-frame hotel, and an eating house. Water, piped in from a spring six miles away and stored in a steel water tank, met domestic and locomotive needs.

A six-stall brick and concrete engine house with a steel-deck turntable was installed at Hazen together with a yard expansion.

Montello, Nevada, an Offspring of the Lucin Cutoff

When the Lucin Cutoff went into service in 1904, it saved 44 miles of travel and shifted engine districts. The substitution of Sparks for Wadsworth is one example, and the creation of a terminal at Montello in lieu of Terrace is another.

Situated 127 miles east of Carlin and 121 miles west of Ogden, Montello served as a crew-change point and a place to refresh steam locomotives with water and fuel oil. For westbound trains, it marked the start of the 21-mile climb necessary to surmount the Pequop Mountains. For those trains needing an extra push up the 1.35 percent grade, helpful locomotives stood ready to assist.

Montello provided shelter for locomotives in an engine house, variously described as containing five or seven stalls. Old-timers described the machine shop and adjacent boiler shop as possessing the ability to rebuild an entire engine. A good-sized icehouse could supply ice to protect refrigerated perishable shipments if needed. Stock corrals served cattle ranches such as the Utah Construction Company, north of town. This firm also had a major office and a large headquarters store in Montello.

Though diesel locomotives brought many changes to Montello, including the dismantling of the engine house about 1952, the hot-riveted water tank remained almost to the end of the last century. A strong wind made off with the wood roof and shoved the tank to one side, making it hazardous to those walking below, so the county engaged Bryce Kimber, a local resident, to take it down.

A visitor, pausing in town today, would have difficulty picturing the two-story crew dormitory and hotel on the northeastern side of the depot. Railroad forces dismantled the structure and salvaged the fine redwood for use elsewhere. The meal situation expanded from almost nothing to three cafés during World War II, with one "beanery" operated by the Threlkeld Commissary Company under contract with Southern Pacific. In 1939, two sisters ran a dry-goods store, while M. W. "Maine" Johnson who operated the local grocery also found time to be justice of the peace and coroner.

Once a busy terminal teaming with railroad employees, the current Union Pacific payroll consists of just two men: a signal maintainer and a section boss. When needed, a work crew is brought in for the particular assignment. However, Lucy Daz still carries on with her restaurant and bar.

Central Pacific Freight Traffic, 1878–1882

Some data reported to stockholders indicated the type of freight tonnage moving on the railroad during 1878–1882 with some tabulations dating back to 1872. While the tables indicate the commodities moving eastward and westward, no information differentiated between interline traffic and local traffic. Still, the report gives a picture of some of the things transported in those days.

Eastbound shipments of salmon increased seven times in the decade ending in 1882, while the tonnage of wool and tea doubled in the same period. The volume of canned goods increased fivefold, a growth almost matched by wine shipments. Barley surged from 3,500 tons in 1874 to almost 23,000 tons the next year but declined sharply in 1876. Other commodities listed included seal skins, borax, whale bones, lumber, quicksilver, and whale oil. Larger tonnages of westbound commodities—more than double the eastbound categories—ranged from agricultural implements to boots and shoes, hardware, iron, iron pipe, liquors, wagons, and tobacco.

Changes in the Organization

The Central Pacific underwent a number of changes from time to time after the line was opened. The affiliated Western Pacific Railroad soon linked Sacramento with San Jose, and, through connecting short lines, the CP reached the Alameda ferry terminal on San Francisco Bay on September 6, 1869. Trains began serving Oakland on November 8, 1869. Of the total mileage, more than one-half—449 miles—was in Nevada. (Before the corporate life span of the Central Pacific ended on June 30, 1959, the company had been reincorporated four additional times, the first being on June 23, 1870, when it took in the Western Pacific Railroad—no relation to the rival Western Pacific of the next century.)

Expansion in the Central Valley soon followed; from Roseville, a line pointed to Portland, Oregon, and reached Redding, 151 miles away, on September 1, 1872. No further construction ensued until 1884, with the through line completed in late 1887. In the opposite direction, rails extended 146 miles down the San Joaquin Valley, ending at Goshen Jct. in August 1872. With the San Jose branch and local lines around Oakland, the CP RR owned about 1,215 miles, a static figure for many years.

At the close of 1872, A. N. Towne, general superintendent, reported that all of the 184 locomotives were in "excellent condition." During that year, the company purchased ten new locomotives and had received three of an order of ten engines being built in the CP Sacramento shops.

In the same year, the Sacramento shops also built 622 boxcars and 204 platform (flat) cars, bringing the CP boxcar ownership to 1,704 and the flatcar ownership to 1,494. The roster also listed 93 first-class and 54 second-class passenger cars, plus 21 Palace sleeping cars. Westinghouse air brakes were being installed on passenger cars at that time.

In the early years, Nevada residents saw a major portion of the Central Pacific rolling stock moving across their land, but this situation changed as the CP leased and operated the expanding Southern Pacific RR as this road went south, then east in Arizona and New Mexico. Even a portion of the new trackage in west Texas came under the CP leases. Meeting the needs of the leased lines required additional rolling stock, but a segregation is difficult to ascertain. When sail cars first appeared on the roster, the text in the annual stockholders' report offered no explanation for these unusual cars, and their use remains a mystery. Beginning with 24 sail cars in 1879, the number increased to 58 five years later, but by 1886 it had declined to just 19 cars.

Until the SP RR connected with the Santa Fe at Deming, New Mexico, in February 1881, all rail traffic originating or terminating in California, Arizona, and New Mexico passed across Nevada and through the Ogden gateway.

The Change in Management: Huntington to Harriman

With the death of Collis P. Huntington on August 13, 1900, at the age of seventy-eight, a review focusing on his last decade would show that he had successfully worked out an agreement with the federal government in February 1899 to repay in full the principal and interest of the bonds issued to aid in the construction of the railroad. The obligation totaled $59 million (net), and by ten annual payments, it was retired in its entirety by February 1, 1909. The task was not easy. With political and financial hurdles, it moved as a "touch-and-go" proposition. (At the same time, the SP Company purchased CP RR shares from its stockholders.)

During the 1890s, E. H. Harriman revitalized Union Pacific, which then extended generally from Omaha and Kansas City to Portland, Oregon, but San Francisco stood out as his goal. Huntington declined purchase offers from Harriman, but the year after Huntington's death in 1900, Harriman secured a large block of SP stock from his estate. Subsequent purchases boosted Union Pacific ownership to 46 percent, giving it effective control of SP and its many subsidiaries, including Central Pacific.

Some historians fail to recognize that Huntington envisioned many improvements that came to reality during the Harriman decade. Fortunately, the testimony of Julius Kruttschnitt provides some historical background. Kruttschnitt began his Southern Pacific relationship in 1878 as a college-trained civil engineer in his native Louisiana and moved up the ranks to be general manager in 1895 following the death of A. N. Towne. He then became a vice president and in 1904 was named director of maintenance and operations for both Southern Pacific and Union Pacific.[2]

In the Interstate Commerce Commission (ICC) hearings concerned with Southern Pacific control of the Central Pacific (FD 2613), Kruttschnitt discussed the plans and policies of SP before and after Union Pacific acquired control. Under cross-examination, he explained that Huntington had in mind the rehabilitation and rebuilding of Central Pacific. "For years studies have been made by the chief engineer and the principal operating officers, and surveys have been made and were on file in the Southern Pacific offices for the execution of this work. The same applied to the plans and estimates for the building of the Lucin cutoff. That was one of Mr. Huntington's dreams for, I know, at least a period of twenty years."

Harriman sent his chief engineer, John B. Berry, and President Horace G. Burt to San Francisco to look over these plans. Shortly after the men returned, Kruttschnitt received a telegram from Harriman asking him to come to New York with William Hood, chief engineer, and bring all the plans for rehabilitation of Central Pacific. "When I got to New York with Mr. Hood, Mr. Harriman had a short conference, asking in a general way what we had brought along and whether we were prepared to discuss the matter. I told him we were. I was very much surprised not to see Mr. Burt or Mr. Berry there. Mr. Harriman discussed the matter and after a short conference in the afternoon, asked me to come to his house after dinner. I went there about 8 o'clock and spent until midnight going over these improvement plans with Mr. Harriman and explaining them to him."

The next day, after conferring with his executive committee, Harriman instructed Kruttschnitt to go to work. "At the time . . . some little money had been spent [on the Lucin Cutoff] by Mr. Huntington in the way of ordering certain steamshovels and equipment for handling a very large yardage involved in that work. Mr. Harriman looked over those plans and very promptly approved them in their entirety."

The Bayshore Cutoff to San Francisco had been contemplated for many years. A segment had been completed in 1892, and land purchases totaling a million and a half dollars continued to June 30, 1901, before Harriman entered the picture.

In an interesting conversation, Harriman compared SP standards with UP standards. When he asked, "Why don't you use the Union Pacific bridges [standards]?" Kruttschnitt replied, "Mr. Harriman, the Union Pacific bridges for the same duty require 20 per cent more metal than the Southern Pacific designs. Of course, if you wish Union Pacific designs ordered, we will obey your orders." Harriman posed the same kind of question about the width of embankments, and, after an explanation, he said, "Do as you like about it." Southern Pacific standards continued, and when Kruttschnitt served as director of maintenance, these specifications were adopted by Union Pacific.

The Prolonged Effects of Lengthy Litigation

Many published histories of Central Pacific and Southern Pacific evade the subject of litigation, yet it had a pronounced effect on the construction record of both companies. Fortunately, some monographs record the important events. Unlike many areas, the Far West had not been fully developed by railroads as the twentieth century began. In the early 1900s, the Central Pacific proposed a five-mile tunnel under the Sierra Nevada and additional second main tracks along the Ogden route. Probably, the length of the tunnel would have dictated electric locomotives that would have been powered by generators of a subsidiary, Rubicon Power and Light Company. Progress had been made on its Cascade Line in Oregon, and serious attention had been given to building a new cutoff from Basalt, Nevada, to a connection with Central Pacific at Palisade. Several extensions in northeastern California stood in various stages of development; indeed, corporate shells such as Goose Lake and Southern were poised, ready to build.

Harriman's combination of railroads west of the Mississippi bothered President Teddy Roosevelt. The Interstate Commerce Commission began a formal investigation of the "Harriman railroads" in December 1906, and the revelations over the next few months made good news copy, which stirred the U.S. attorney general into filing an antitrust suit in January 1908 to divorce Southern Pacific from Union Pacific control.

The federal district court dismissed the case, whereupon the attorney general appealed to the U.S. Supreme Court, which reversed the lower court by its decision of December 2, 1912 (226 U.S. 61), thus forcing divestiture of UP RR stock control of SP.

Union Pacific endeavored to find some way to gain control of Central Pacific, but, for many reasons, no plan evolved. The government filed another suit on February 11, 1914, in the U.S. District Court (Utah), challenging the relationship between SP and CP. More years went by before the district court found for Southern Pacific and dismissed the government action. Hearings before the U.S. Supreme Court by agreement were suspended during World War I until the government returned the railroads to private ownership on March 1, 1920.

When the litigation was revived, the Supreme Court overturned the lower court, on May 29, 1922, by ruling that the SP-CP relationship was contrary to the antitrust laws. Meanwhile, an important change in transportation law had transpired with the passage of the Esch-Commings Act of 1920 wherein the ICC gained authority to approve of railroad combinations in the public interest even if in violation of the antitrust statute.

On the side, negotiations between SP and UP resulted in an agreement of cooperation in dealing with the Overland Route. SP agreed to maintain passenger service to San Francisco equal to its service between Los Angeles and Chicago. Also, SP agreed to solicit traffic preferentially from a given area in California and Oregon through the Ogden gateway to midwestern destinations. The area, bounded on the north by the Oregon line and Kirk, Oregon, took the name of Santa Margarita Agreement, with Caliente and Santa Margarita, California, forming the southern limits. The commission recognized the adverse effects on both SP and CP and the public if the closely interwoven railroads were separated, and its decision of February 6, 1923 (76 ICC 508), which reflected the terms of the Santa Margarita Agreement, authorized continued Southern Pacific Company control of Central Pacific. The matter ended with the announcement on August 13, 1923, that the government would not appeal the decision.

Nine years of uncertainty adversely affected both Southern Pacific and the public. With its ownership of Central Pacific hanging in suspension, SP made few improvements on that property during these troubled times. After World War I, the proposed 5-mile tunnel had been discarded; in its place, a 10,323-foot tunnel at the summit added to the nearly 18 miles of second main track between Emigrant Gap and Andover, California. The Natron Cutoff in Oregon became a reality in 1926, but the cutoff for Owens Valley never materialized. The delay in construction proved costly, as wage rates rose during the world war, boosting expenditures that in turn resulted in greater long-term borrowings with higher annual interest charges. When traffic revenues fell nearly 60 percent in the early Depression years, enlarged interest costs almost drove Southern Pacific into bankruptcy.

Elko's "Project Lifesaver"

Elko, a creation of Central Pacific when its trains arrived on January 25, 1869, centered around the railroad station, a natural course for the rails that provided the only lifeline to the outside. As the town developed, the tracks stood between Railroad Street and Commercial Street. When the Western Pacific approached the city from the east, it secured a franchise to extend its rails along Silver Street, one block south of Commercial Street.

As the population increased, the two bands of steel severed the community. More auto traffic challenged locomotives at street crossings, often with expensive results. Train speeds, held to fifteen miles per hour on Western Pacific tracks, caused long eastbound freight trains to creep through town like a moving iron curtain, taxing the patience of even the most tolerant residents.

The problem, certainly obvious, defied solution because of its high cost. Finally, a concentrated effort evolved among various Elko residents. Although it is always risky to single out specific individuals, George Gund and Theo Gund were among the early proponents in 1971.

The next summer, Mark Chilton of the engineering firm bearing his name and Mayor Dutch Stenovich journeyed to Washington to plead their case before Nevada senators Alan Bible and Howard Cannon and Congressman David Towell. They also called on the staff of the Federal Highway Administration and the Federal Railway Administration.

Ira Rackley, a member of Chilton's engineering staff and one of the early spokesmen of "Project Lifesaver," put the cost of the relocation of the two railroads at $6 million, "a shot in the dark," according to a quote.

The Federal Highway Trust Fund, dating back to 1956, received larger financial support with almost every session of Congress. One phase of the 1973 bill recognized congestion problems stemming from railroads located in downtown sections of cities. Through the watchdog attention of Nevada's representatives and local citizens, Elko joined the list of a dozen cities participating in demonstration projects. President Nixon signed a new highway bill on August 13, 1973, providing initial funding for railroad relocation pilot projects. Four days later, Elko people staged a "Spike Pulling Party" near the Stockmen's Motor Hotel. Mark Chilton and Bill Nesbit took charge of the celebration in which 104 spikes—one for every year since 1869—were pulled from the Southern Pacific track between Third and Fourth Streets. By a previous arrangement, a railroad crew stood by, ready to replace the pulled spikes.

The celebration—certainly entertaining—did nothing to move the tracks. As the project called for removing tracks of both railroads between Third and Twelfth Streets, eliminating seventeen main-line crossings, and moving the tracks of both railroads south to the Humboldt River was to be largely funded by the U.S. government, the proposal had to work its way through bureaucratic channels. (The government paid 95 percent of the costs, and each railroad paid one-third of the balance along with the local and state agencies.) With inflationary pressures, the cost of the work had risen to $16 million when funded by the Federal Aid Highway Act of 1975. Across the land, active groups in other cities stood ready to sweep up the Elko allotment for their benefit, but again Nevada's representatives stood on guard. A series of contracts were let commencing in August 1978 until December 1982.

The project had many facets. The course of the Humboldt River, instead of normal curves, was straightened, with the railroads running on the north side. Two long bridges carried Twelfth and Fifth Streets over the river and railroad tracks, with a pedestrian crossing at Ninth Street. A number of celebrations marked important work; the Fifth Street crossing was celebrated in October 1981. The Western Pacific yard, located for years on the west side of town, moved to a new site east of the city.

Relocation of the railroads necessitated purchasing eighty-seven parcels held by sixty-four owners. In some cases, the sale price was arrived at by negotiation; in others, property owners as well as lawyers benefited by generous jury awards. In all, the cost of the 547 acres totaled $5.7 million.

The Union Pacific Railroad, which had acquired Western Pacific during the advanced stages of construction, opened its new yard in October 1983. Instead of the roundhouse of steam days, a diesel-locomotive repair shop reflected the new era. On October 8, 1983, a ribbon-cutting ceremony opened the Union Pacific tracks for eastbound trains. The major celebration came the next month. The *Elko Daily Free Press* issued a special fifty-two-page edition replete with current railroad matters and past history. The "Last Train through Town Party" was staged on Saturday, November 12, 1983, commencing with a reception the night before for government officials. This group made an inspection of the new facilities on Saturday morning. A special train, with a UP locomotive engine at one end and an SP engine at the other, manned by volunteer crews, left downtown Elko

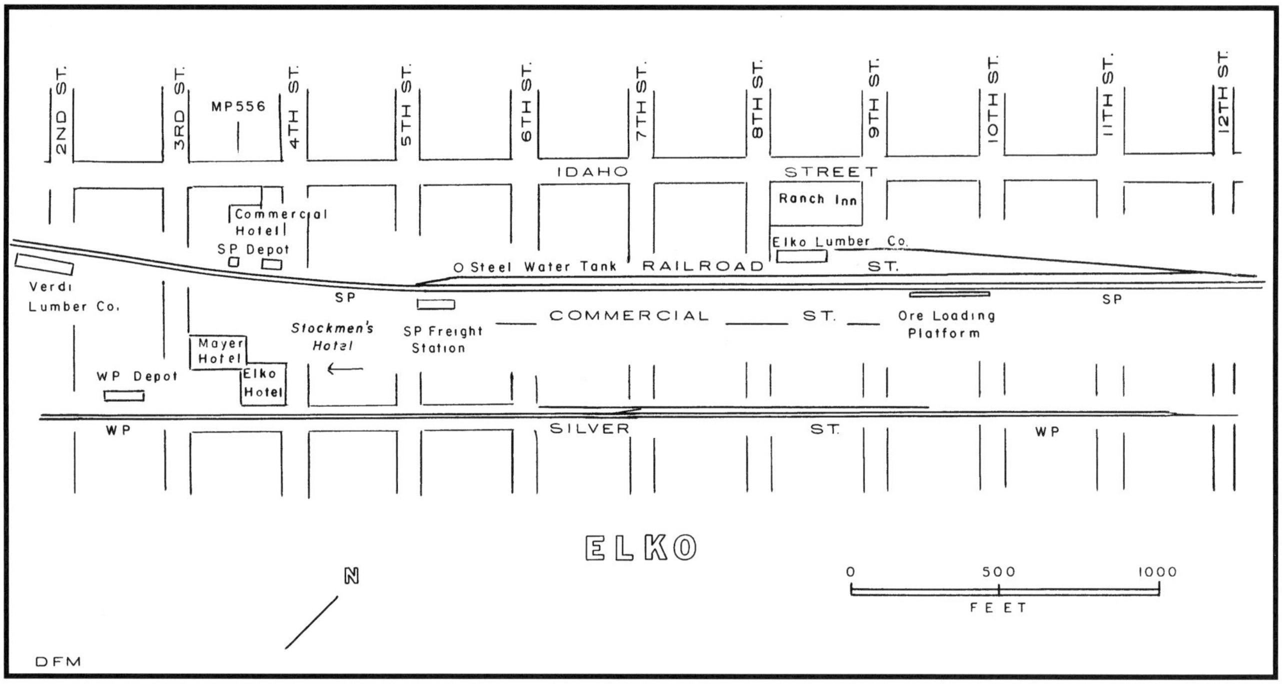

Many changes have occurred since 1916 when a railroad draftsman delineated the tracks in downtown Elko. Among the many changes, the most significant is the absence of the railroads since the close of 1983. All tracks between Third and Twelfth Streets were removed the following year. The Ranch Inn and Stockmen's Hotel have augmented Elko hospitality, with the latter replacing the Mayer and Elko Hotels. From its mill at the far side of Nevada, the Verdi Lumber Company supplied lumber for its outlet in Elko.

at 1:00 P.M. carrying five hundred passengers who had purchased souvenir tickets. Taken first to the new Union Pacific yard, the train continued eastward for another eighteen miles to Elburz. At that point, the train switched to Southern Pacific (westbound) tracks for the return to Elko. When the passengers left the train just west of Fifth Street, they proceeded to a platform in front of the Stockmen's Hotel where various speakers, commencing with Mayor George Corner and continuing with former senator Howard Cannon, sallied forth with the expected praise for the project that had now cost $43.5 million instead of the modest figure contemplated earlier.

Back in the days when the proposal stood in the early stages of wishful thinking, Don Bilbao Jr. of the Stockmen's Motor Hotel casually remarked: "If this project ever gets off the ground, I'll buy champagne for the whole town." True to his word, Bilbao set up six champagne bars in his hotel for two hours of enjoyment. The big celebration closed with a round of fireworks at 5:30.

Contrary to the celebration, westbound trains continued to operate through the city as before, as the new Southern Pacific track work was not completed until December 15, 1983.

A Switch of Double Track

In July 1993, Ed Moyer, former president of the Illinois Central Railroad, was appointed president and chief executive officer of the Southern Pacific Transportation Company. While in charge of Illinois Central, he removed long stretches of second main track to reduce maintenance expenses.

On Southern Pacific he found that the Overland Route traffic had declined 50 percent due to the diversion of Union Pacific traffic to Western Pacific following the acquisition of that railroad in December 1982. A different situation existed on the SP lines in Arizona, largely a single-track operation partly eased by centralized traffic control (CTC). But even CTC has limitations, and the combination of increased traffic and the rugged terrain east of Tucson—locally called "the Stormy"—cried for relief in the form of a second main track.

Southern Pacific's finances, running thin, posed problems, but with traffic down on the former Central Pacific, transferring the now surplus trackage to the southern route provided a solution. In November 1993, 11 miles of second main track were removed between Colfax and Sparks. Specifically, 7 miles commenced at Switch 9 at milepost (MP) 170.9 and ran to MP 177.9. Another 4 miles began east of Norden (at MP 192.2) at the mouth of Tunnel 41 (the long tunnel at Donner

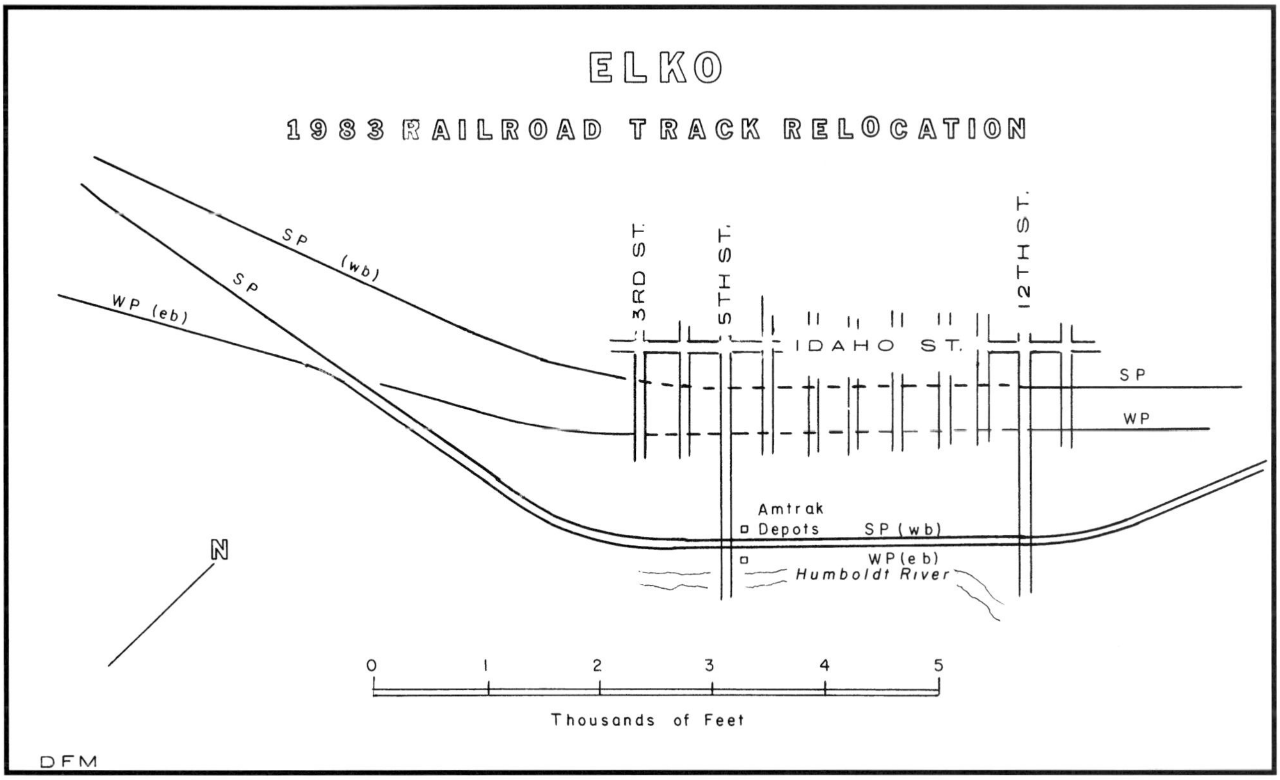

Not surprisingly, Elko citizens chose to develop their city along the railroad. As the town grew, after prolonged efforts, the people secured federal government aid to build a railroad detour. For both Southern Pacific and Western Pacific (the latter being absorbed by Union Pacific during this construction), the bypass measured some four miles. This replaced the railroad tracks between Third and Twelfth Streets in Elko. As part of the project, the Western Pacific yard and roundhouse on the west side of Elko were rebuilt for Union Pacific on the other side of the city. The undulating course of the Humboldt River between Third and Tenth Streets was pushed southward into a new channel. Two overpasses formed part of the project.

Summit opened in 1925) and extended to Shed 46 at MP 196.2. These 4 miles included Tunnels 6 to 12, the latter being the original summit tunnel.

Between Perth and Rose Creek, near Winnemucca, 66 miles, SP had added a second track in 1913 and 1929. Seeking additional track material for Arizona, the second track in this area was pulled up and CTC installed instead.

In Arizona, the former Central Pacific second track was installed at three locations: Fenner to Dragoon (15.5 miles), Mescal to Fenner (11 miles plus 3 miles of sidings), and San Simon, Arizona, to Mondel, New Mexico (16.5 miles plus 3.5 miles of sidings). A second bridge, 310 feet long, over the San Pedro River formed part of the 43-mile project completed in July 1998 at a cost of $41 million.

The Reno Trench

The development of many cities in the West centered around the railroad tracks that with steady growth in more recent decades has caused congestion problems. Elko achieved relief from downtown trains by relocating the rail lines at the southern edge of the city. A Trainway solved a similar problem for El Paso, Texas. The same congestion prevailed around Reno for many decades, exacerbated by the concentration of large casinos near the railroad tracks. Seven attempts to ease the situation had been made between 1938 and 2001 without success.

During the hearings before the Surface Transportation Board—the federal regulatory agency superseding the former Interstate Commerce Commission—when Union Pacific sought authority to acquire Southern Pacific, the State of Nevada and the City of Reno opposed the merger, in part because of their concern about the potential increase in the number of trains passing through Reno, as each train halted pedestrian and vehicle traffic endeavoring to cross the railroad tracks.

To mollify Reno city officials, in its 1996 decision approving the merger, the Surface Transportation Board imposed a condition that before additional trains could be operated through Reno, Union Pacific would have to provide a means to eliminate street crossings. By placing the tracks in a ditch, this task could be accomplished.

Various proposals were brought forth, and the entire subject became controversial. Financing stood as the major hurdle. Finally, a plan evolved using a combination of a local revenue bond issue backed by increases in sales and bed taxes, a special assessment district tax, a federal grant, federal and state loans, and a $60 million contribution from the Union Pacific Railroad.

With authority granted by the Nevada state legislature in 1997, Washoe County was able to increase the sales tax, with part being used to retire the bonded debt. One condition required the City of Reno to present evidence of financial commitments for half of the total cost of the work before imposition of the added sales tax. The action of the Washoe County Board of Commissioners was ratified by the legislature in 1998. The Reno City Council also enacted a special assessment district along the proposed trench.

Although many residents recognized the benefits of the ditch, support was not universal in Reno and the surrounding Washoe County. The city presented evidence at a county hearing on December 8, 1998, that it had met the necessary conditions to impose the sales tax increase. However, the day before the hearing, the proprietors of the Sundowner Hotel and Casino and others sought a preliminary injunction to halt the new tax. Responding to the motion filed by the city and county, the district court ruled that the sales tax ordinance was valid and dismissed the complaint. The Sundowner group appealed the decision to the Nevada Supreme Court, which sustained the lower court decision on February 3, 2000.

Although one threat had been set aside, some Reno people still questioned the project. Jim Galloway of the Washoe County Commission wanted Reno planners to consider alternatives to the ditch. Some suggested street overpasses or underpasses. Mark DeMuth, Reno's environmental consultant, pointed to the cost of dismantling buildings adjoining the proposed structures without a reduction in train noise.

The subject made a major forward step on February 27, 2001, when the city council voted to proceed with the formation of a U-shaped trench with an average depth of 33 feet between Keystone Avenue on the west and Sutro Avenue, 2.2 miles in length, which would eliminate eleven grade crossings.

Some three hundred people, evenly divided between supporters and opponents, crowded the chamber and lobby of city hall to watch the deliberations. Steelworkers, carpenters, and businessmen, including casino owners, favored the project. A contrary view was held by those who indicated that seventy small businesses would be disturbed, while the Downtown Improvement Association, representing seventy-nine firms, supported the proposal.

An alternative proposal placed the tracks along U.S. Interstate 80, but this solution would have upset even more residents. Councilman Dave Aiazzi observed that "people were tired of studies sitting on a shelf." With the expected growth of imports through the Port of Oakland, more trains would aggravate local congestion. With trains running in the ditch, annoying blasting whistles would be only a memory. Part of the plan provided that Virginia Street and the adjoining Center and Sierra Streets would never be closed at the same time during construction.

The Reno City Council voted five to two to pursue the project; two recently elected members cast the negative votes. At that time, the city had spent about $10 million in various studies, including its contract with Nolte Engineering of Sacramento, to determine the estimated cost—$218 million.

On July 11, 2001, the city fathers authorized a design contract with DMJM Harris and Moffat Nichol Engineers, a Long Beach, California, firm. A few weeks later, an attempt to delay the entire work was defeated. More litigation ensued but was settled. Meanwhile, archaeological studies were arranged along with plans to monitor the stability of buildings adjoining the trench, including two structures overreaching the excavation site. Debates continued on the merits of the ditch, now identified as the Reno Transportation Access Corridor, or ReTRAC, and because a final vote in October resulted in a three-to-three tie, the matter was reconsidered on November 6, 2001. At that meeting, Pierre Hascheff, who had been absent in October, observed that there was strong city-wide opposition to the project, but he reminded people that the McCarran Ring Road, unpopular when proposed, was now considered essential. Seventy members of the local carpenters' union staged a rally at city hall, which may have helped to swing the four-to-two vote (one councilman was ill), authorizing the solicitation of construction bids for the Reno Ditch.

In May 2002 three construction firms submitted bids for the ditch, and on July 16, 2002, the city council awarded the contract to the Granite Construction Company for $170,734,640. With headquarters in Watsonville, California, Granite had been engaged in major projects, including highways, tunnels, dams, and mass-transit facilities. Work commenced on September 13, 2002. A month before, Tim Raymond of the Keystone Lounge celebrated the beginning with a block party.

Before removing the existing double-track line, a temporary shoofly was built. On January 4, 2004, Granite started work on a single track parallel and just south of the main line. In some places, an industrial spur could be used, but other segments required temporary tracks along Commercial Row. Many parcels of real estate were acquired, some by eminent domain, and buildings demolished. Thirty-four businesses moved to other sites.

Union Pacific trains commenced running over the shoofly on April 13, 2004. Two weeks later, with the railroad satisfied with the safety of the temporary track, Granite began taking up rails and ties of the long-established main line and donated them to the reconstruction effort of the legendary Virginia and Truckee Railroad.

Lyle Meggerson, a resident of nearby Dayton, holds the honor of turning the first shovelful of earth on May 12, 2004, just east of the Second Street overpass. Rather than using the traditional hand shovel, he operated a Caterpillar shovel with a four-yard scoop when he began excavating.

After removing the top 2.5 feet of earth contaminated with years of oil and grease, the workers dug down 33 feet and poured concrete to form a thick base. In their excavations, men uncovered a pedestrian underpass at Virginia Street. Called the "Reno Subway," it was opened in 1902 but closed twenty-five years later, as too many vagrants congregated there. Also discovered was another ditch near Ralston Street, created in 1865 to convey water from the Truckee River to the English Mill.

The project was not without its problems. Closing streets snarled traffic from time to time, but in an effort to mitigate the effects of disruptions, ReTRAC provided a special telephone service with recorded information advising closures. Kinder Morgan Energy Partners has a gasoline pipeline along the route, and its relocation costs exceeded original estimates. A controversy between the city and the pipeline company ended with a settlement over the allocation of costs.

In September 2005, pools of water appeared at the bottom of the ditch, posing potential problems. Between Ralston Street and a point just east of Evans Avenue, a distance of about three-quarters of a mile, the ditch is below the groundwater table. Responding to the question of responsibility, city officials explained that the contract allowed for a seepage of twenty-five hundred gallons daily and that water would flow to a pump station east of Lake Street. If the flow exceeded that amount during the initial five years, Granite would have to resolve the problem. After that time, it would be the city's responsibility.

Finally, on Friday, November 18, 2005, the great day came. Shortly after the noon hour, a westbound Union Pacific train with a string of covered auto-rack cars inaugurated the use of the ditch. Blasting horns at crossings was no longer necessary, but, for this occasion, the engineer used his horn to salute the crowds lining the overhead crossings. A few Union Pacific officials and Bob Cashell, Reno's current mayor, rode on the front of the diesel locomotive, while Jeff Griffin, mayor during the difficult period of planning, quietly observed the train from the sidelines.

At the base of the 54-foot-wide trench, a maintenance road runs along the south side of the double tracks. Seven of the eleven overhead crossings had been finished by the opening day, with three more to be ready within a matter of weeks.

The lowering of the tracks necessitated a new station for railroad patrons. Following the plan designed by Toby Webb Structural Engineers, a Granite subcontractor, Northern States Construction Inc., commenced work in May 2005 on a new Reno passenger station for Amtrak. The 10,000-square-foot building will rise three stories from its base 24 feet below street level.

The cost of the project totaled $282 million, many times the original cost of the entire Central Pacific Railroad. A few statistics follow. More than 781,000 cubic yards of earth were excavated. Drain pipes measured 42,166 linear feet, while 118,867 board feet of lumber were used during construction. For the shoofly and Reno branch (formerly the WP connection), 310 cars of ballast were needed, while 410 cars were required for the ditch along with 10,281 concrete ties. In January 2006, when the nearby Truckee River flooded part of Reno, the ditch remained comparatively dry.

Distant Palisade, Nevada, once served by three railroads, has not had a station for years. The heirs of John Sexton, the colorful operator of the long-defunct Eureka and Palisade (E&P) Railroad, put up this ghost town for auction in April 2005. Some unidentified individual was the successful bidder and now owns 160 acres of Nevada alongside the Humboldt River, with trains whizzing by every day but no one to wave at the engineer.

NOTES:

1. In a general revision of SP operating of April 10, 1994, the Roseville Division embraced all SP lines from Oakland north to Portland and east to Ogden.

2. In January 1913, following the end of the antitrust litigation, Julius Kruttschnitt became chairman of the board of the Southern Pacific Company. In 1919, he was also a director of the Erie Railroad and Western Union.

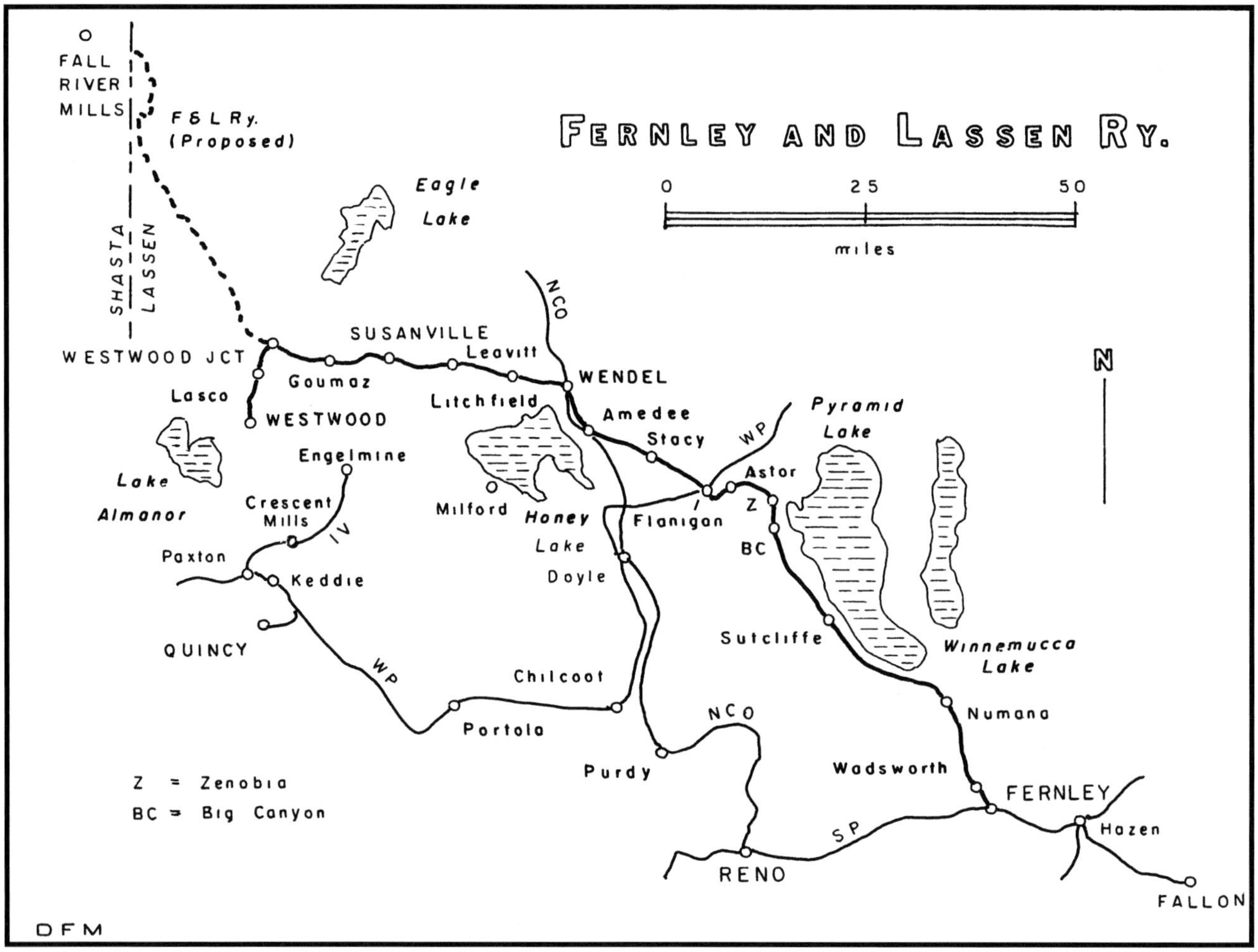
FERNLEY AND LASSEN RY.
0
25
50
miles
FALL RIVER MILLS
F&L Ry. (Proposed)
SHASTA
LASSEN
Eagle Lake
NCO
WESTWOOD JCT
SUSANVILLE
Leavitt
Goumaz
WENDEL
Lasco
WESTWOOD
Litchfield
Amedee
Stacy
WP
Pyramid Lake
Astor
Z
Flanigan
BC
Engelmine
Lake Almanor
Crescent Mills
IV
Milford
Honey Lake
Doyle
Paxton
Keddie
QUINCY
WP
Chilcoot
Portola
Sutcliffe
Winnemucca Lake
Numana
NCO
Purdy
Wadsworth
FERNLEY
Hazen
SP
RENO
FALLON
N
Z = Zenobia
BC = Big Canyon
DFM

FERNLEY AND LASSEN RAILWAY COMPANY

The Fernley and Lassen (F&L) Railway reflected several interests: Southern Pacific's desire for alternate routes, a lumber company's need for transportation to distant markets, and an electric power company's need for a reservoir.

At various times the Big Four of the Central Pacific had discussed construction of a railroad along the east side of the Sierra Nevada and the Cascade Range, but Leland Stanford's vision for a railroad running from Mexico to Canada failed to arouse enthusiasm among the partners. From time to time the subject surfaced; in his letter of January 10, 1882, to A. N. Towne, Huntington considered running a line northerly from Mojave into Nevada. The pressure to keep the major portion of the enterprise afloat while completing the Sunset Route dissuaded further developments in this area for several decades.

T. B. Walker, a highly successful lumberman, foresaw the need for new timber areas to offset his depleted Minnesota forests. In the 1890s he began buying carefully selected timber stands in northern California.

Southern Pacific, including its subsidiary Central Pacific, had been managed by E. H. Harriman since shortly after the death of Collis P. Huntington in August 1900. Though in frail health, "the little giant" sanctioned plans for a railroad along the east flank of the Cascade Range in northern California. A general plan to tap Walker's proposed mill, developed in 1905 and lost in the San Francisco fire the next year, was revived by Julius Kruttschnitt in June 1908. (At that time, as a UP-SP vice president, he directed maintenance and operations.) On October 16, 1909, about a month after Harriman died, Southern Pacific formed the Fernley and Lassen Railway Company to build 135 miles from a connection with the main line in Nevada at Fernley, near Wadsworth and 38 miles east of Reno, to a junction near the site of future Westwood and eventually north to Fall River Mills.

Although steady construction of the F&L did not commence until 1912, press reports indicated that Southern Pacific let a contract to Erickson and Peterson of Ogden in September 1910 for the initial 100 miles of the railroad proposed to link Fernley with Fall River Mills and Klamath Falls. Some grading had been started on the northwest side of Honey Lake according to another dispatch that also reported that a wye track had been installed at Fernley. The next news came just before Christmas, saying that all work had been abruptly halted. However, undermining the merits of this report, a news story a few weeks later had a large force busy grading at Fernley "until the recent storm" (which had also shut down Western Pacific), and it expected SP would be in Susanville by July 1, 1911. All this might indicate the troubles the railroad faced in the tough negotiations with T. B. Walker.

For various reasons Walker delayed committing himself to construction of the mill—Kruttschnitt once remarked, "It has taken us about three years to get T. B. Walker to agree on matters." In March 1911, Julius Kruttschnitt directed Vice President Edgar Calvin to have the country investigated. Accordingly, J. C. Cristy, "one of Mr. Hood's best-equipped engineers and W. H. Snell, a very efficient timber cruiser in our Land Department who has done a great deal of cruising in that region," made a survey and filed their report. Cristy noted that Walker demanded main-line service and a western connection.

At this point in time, the combination of Union Pacific and Southern Pacific was breaking up, and as 1913 began, Kruttschnitt became chairman of the executive committee of Southern Pacific with his office in New York.

Calvin began his railroad service in Indiana at the age of fifteen. Soon thereafter, he joined Union Pacific, advancing sufficiently to be hired by Missouri Pacific as a division superintendent. After twelve years he returned to UP as general superintendent of its Oregon Short Line, and in 1905 Harriman appointed him vice president and general manager of Southern Pacific.

When the Great Western Power (GWP) Company contemplated covering Big Meadows with a man-made lake, its vice president, H. H. Sinclair, approached H. H. Jones, SP's freight traffic manager in San Francisco. The plan Sinclair outlined in April 1911 anticipated flooding two hundred million feet of timber, but the company owned another one hundred million that would be undisturbed. T. B. Walker's adjoining lands contained more than five *billion* feet of timber. In a mutually beneficial move, GWP sold the timber in Big Meadows to Walker to be harvested before full inundation of the area.

The power company faced the problem of delivering fifteen thousand tons of material for the dam (mostly cement), and as wagon hauls would be "practically prohibitive," railroad transportation proved essential.

From the recently opened Western Pacific Railway, a branch line could be built from Keddie or Virgilia, but, if the SP built to Susanville and beyond, a logging railroad constructed by T. B. Walker into the Big Meadows timber could fulfill the needs.

SP sent C. J. Millis, assistant to President William Sproule, into the field. He reported on his return that GWP was anxious to push the project but could not advance its work without railroad service. Millis advised Jones that WP was leaning toward construction of a branch line unless SP built into the area. (Sproule had held various positions in SP's traffic department until 1906, when he began a four-year stint as traffic manager of the American Smelting and Refining Company, which was followed by two years as president of Wells Fargo and Company, the express firm. On September 1, 1911, he went back to the Southern Pacific Company as president.)

Under the name of the Fernley and Lassen Railway, SP contemplated building a line from Fernley as far as the site of Walker's pending lumber mill and included $5,561,000 in its 1911–1912 capital budget. However, the direction of the line remained open, and Kruttschnitt asked Sproule if the Walker mill should be served by a line from Fernley or from the southwest with a slightly more expensive railroad from Vina or Chico in the Sacramento Valley.

With the eastern market expected to take two-thirds of Walker's output, the Fernley connection was chosen—indeed, the first shipment from the Westwood mill went by teams to Susanville on July 19, 1913, and then by rail to Oshkosh, Wisconsin.

Walker told SP traffic men in the summer of 1911 that if the company went forward with the Big Meadows extension to the proposed mill site, he would promptly construct a sawmill with an annual capacity of one hundred million feet, and, for a five-year period from January 1, 1912 (or on completion of the mill), he "would route lumber over your road provided routes and rates are competitive and no higher than Boca, [California]."

In the latter part of 1911, as details were being finalized with the Walkers, some alternatives surfaced. Clinton, one of the sons of T. B. Walker, approached Kruttschnitt and Lewis Spence with a separate proposal. (Spence was about to be promoted to traffic director for the UP-SP system.) His company was considering a logging railroad commencing near Anderson on SP's Portland line and running into Walker timber around Whitmore, about twenty-five miles east of Redding. He wanted SP to loan his firm forty miles of rail and fastenings rent free in exchange for routing future traffic over SP lines. SP could not do it for legal reasons, and the line was not built. When discussions turned to the new sawmill near Big Meadows, T. B. Walker would not commit himself to any construction date until SP committed itself to a date for railroad entry into Susanville.

Alternative Proposals

To shorten the time required for rail access to the Walker mill, SP management considered trackage rights over Western Pacific from Oroville to Keddie and building north from there.

Already John E. Sexton had ideas. A colorful railroad man then operating the Quincy Western Railway, he would later secure attention for his forceful management of the Eureka and Palisade Railway. With H. H. Sinclair of Great Western Power, he organized the California Plumas Railway to link Keddie and the dam site near Big Meadows with a narrow-gauge line.

Supposedly, the Fleischhackers of San Francisco were looking at the proposition, but Edwin Hawley, the former SP traffic official, now the president of GWP and on the WP board, was ostensibly behind this rail project. Organized in December 1911, the California Plumas Railway was expected to be ready nine months later to aid in the construction of the dam. Sexton's link with GWP is a little nebulous; in a letter to Edgar Calvin, he suggested that SP underwrite a healthy portion of the bonds of his railroad.

Conferences between the Walkers and SP officers continued in New York and San Francisco. "T. B. Walker is a hard trader," Sproule mentioned in an internal memo.

Developments were suspended briefly until copies of correspondence could be obtained from San Francisco to replace UP-SP records lost in the January 9, 1912, fire of the Equitable Building in New York. Finally, Walker and Kruttschnitt signed a rail-service agreement on January 29, 1912. Though SP agreed to serve Walker, the contract still included the option of trackage rights over Western Pacific and a connection from Keddie. Robert S. Lovett, chairman of SP, after talking with E. T. Jeffrey, WP's president, reported that Jeffrey would be "glad to enter into negotiations in San Francisco," but WP also proved a tough bargainer and stalled negotiations.

Meanwhile, speculative talk blossomed. In February 1912, a report had Susanville people wanting to talk with Sexton about the rail link he contemplated with the N-C-O near Amedee. Western Pacific executives watched every move with interest but kept their thoughts to themselves. Charles H. Schlacks and T. J. Wyche, vice president and chief engineer, respectively, arrived in Doyle in their private car on May 20, which raised the hopes of Susanville citizens to envision a rail line from Doyle to Susanville, then on to Big Meadows and down to Keddie.

Things really became exciting on June 17 when the *Plumas National-Bulletin* had WP starting work on the new railroad that very day! Of course, neither scheme resulted in actual work.

The editor of Susanville's *Lassen Advocate* echoed the attitude of his readers in February 1912 when he lamented, "If we only had a railroad," for then Honey Lake farmers could send their apples and cherries to distant markets. Railroad prospects came and went over the years, bringing high hopes and deep disappointments; the unrealized Western Pacific dream the editor never forgot.

Yes, at that time auto stages and trucks did link Susanville with Doyle on Western Pacific and the N-C-O at Hot Springs (Amedee). The Northeastern California Transit Company began hauling freight to and from Doyle in a Pope-Hartford motor truck, while another group provided passenger service.

The newly organized Lassen Development League, caught in the whirlwind of railroad rumors, stood ready to hear John Sexton's new proposal for a rail link to start at Doyle. This hope faded away by early March 1912 when SP's President Sproule announced the construction of the Fernley and Lassen Railway. This talk was affirmed when J. E. Pardee, a prominent Susanville attorney then working for SP, requested a right-of-way across county hospital land from the Lassen County supervisors. (Actually, the corporate existence of the Fernley and Lassen Railway had just ended, as a step in corporate simplification, along with seven other railroad satellites into the Central Pacific Railway. However, the early corporate name continued to be used in conversations.)

With pressure from Walker, Kruttschnitt told Sproule to go ahead with the construction of the Fernley-Susanville line, and on May 8, 1912, William Hood, SP's famed chief engineer, signed a grading contract with the Utah Construction Company (UCC). Still, WP sought benefits from SP and continued negotiations through Schlacks, who stopped in New York on his way to Europe to see Lovett. When Sproule learned of this visit, he wrote Lovett, "They think we need the Keddie line so badly that we will trade them other business to secure it."

W. H. Wattis of UCC went over the line with Charles D. Perkins, a subcontractor from Wadsworth. The presence of more subcontractors advanced land prices in Honey Lake Valley.

The most difficult construction stood along the slopes of Pyramid Lake and Davis Hill. Later, when building to Westwood, the hills on the south side of Susanville and the eighteen miles along the upper Susan River proved challenging.

Although location surveys had been made under the direction of E. E. Cooper, an SP civil engineer, William Hood, Al J. Barclay, and George Hackett came to Susanville, had a driver take them up the canyon to Devil's Corral where they dismissed the auto, and walked the eight miles back to Susanville to add refinements to the survey.

News of the forthcoming railroad caught the attention of the Reno Commercial Club, which pushed for the connection to be made at their city. Sproule countered with the advice that starting from Reno would add thirty-three miles to the line with disadvantageous grades.

Construction Begins in June 1912

Prospective construction sparked conflicting rumors. Shortly after Hood's visit, one report had railroad work beginning soon, while another statement postponed construction for another year. In this case, the first report proved correct, as grading began with a flurry in June 1912 after UCC had established a string of fifteen camps northwest of Fernley. Hay and grain for the thousand head of livestock proved scarce and commanded high prices. UCC soon had some working tracks in place to bring the steam shovel to tackle the lakeside hills. At almost the same time, J. H. Maxey began work at Susanville under his subcontract. Using an excavator, his small force began breaking ground on June 26 on the hill back of the Fred A. Cain place on South Weatherlow Street down by the river. During the three months required for this cut, citizens of Susanville took advantage of the opportunity to observe the work firsthand.

J. A. Molina, a labor contractor, attempted to bring fifty Mexican laborers from southern California but arrived with only fifteen, as most departed at stations along the way. Maxey, then working near Susanville, had a little trouble when his Mexican team went on strike for higher wages. They tried to block others from working, at which point Maxey, backed by a deputy sheriff, gave them the ultimatum of going back to work or leaving with their final paycheck. They left. Some walked to Doyle, while others headed west, seeking employment on the GWP dam at Nevis. Replacements soon arrived, and Maxey was directed to move his new force down to Kelley's Swamp.

Small-town fires, though a way of life, occurred too frequently. A midnight summer blaze wiped out the Blue Goose Saloon in Susanville, but heroic efforts and a good water supply saved Charles Emerson's hotel this time. Also saved was the saloon's piano, though considerably damaged in its removal. Frank Watson, the saloon man, recovered some of his nineteen hundred–dollar loss in liquor and cigars through insurance and needed only a few days to get back in business working under a canvas roof at a new site. A few months later, he joined his friends who had previously moved to Rochester, then a new mining camp in Nevada.

Surveyor's stakes took the railroad around the north side of Honey Lake through Amedee, bypassing older settlements on the south side such as Milford and Janesville. In doing do, it invited formation of new towns in Honey Lake Valley; in the summer of 1912, one construction force left Susanville for Standish, which was soon followed by Litchfield, laid out on the old Andy Litch place but later owned by B. F. Gibson. Here the F&L had selected a depot site along a three hundred–foot right-of-way.

The *Lassen Advocate*, watching the advancing track, remarked, "It's a ten-to-one bet that the SP graders will uncover mineral ledges before they get through Susan River Canyon." Apparently, no one took up the wager, and no discoveries came to excite the valley residents.

B. H. "Uncle Ben" Leavitt told reporters around the end of September 1912 that subcontractors had formed a roadbed at the town site bearing his name. Soon, he established a store that occupied most of the time allotted for the last two years of his life.

B. F. Fahey, representing Utah Construction, made an inspection trip in the fall of 1912 and remarked that some subcontractors had finished their assignments. Because of one difficult section along Honey Lake, he cautioned that this segment could not be opened until February 1913. Back at Wadsworth, heavier motive power necessitated remodeling of the 1890 Burr truss bridge over the Truckee River.

The chill of November was of no concern to the railroad builders confronting Davis Hill near Johnstonville. Rock and earth from the major cut there were trundled for a few miles in cars pulled by small locomotives called "dinkeys" and dumped in the swamp on the Kelley place now owned by Dr. Shanks. Maxey's steam shovel, reportedly shipped all the way from Minneapolis, finally arrived at Amedee via the N-C-O. Plans to tackle the cut immediately were thwarted by the absence of certain critical parts, but with that difficulty resolved, Susanville men rode down to Davis Hill to see the iron monster perform.

Casualties on the Job

The construction company formed an enviable record with a minimum number of fatal accidents. One man was run over by a wagon; another slipped into the hot springs near Amedee. He climbed out, limped into the hotel, and called for a glass of water and another of whiskey before being rushed to a hospital in Wadsworth to die a few days later. James Cook, an experienced powder man, succumbed to a blast on Davis Hill. Assigned to light two fuses ahead of the Maxey workers, Cook did so but was seen running with a lantern, perhaps thinking he had forgotten to light the second fuse. In his confusion, he stood over the charge, which then exploded.

Frank Donegan, a Maxey foreman, became ill with pneumonia and though rushed to a hospital in Reno, he died at the age of thirty-seven. Another foreman, Thomas Murphy, after imbibing freely in a Susanville saloon, wandered back to camp in a snowstorm. Near the camp, he fell and remained still until by chance he was found some twelve hours later. As his arms and legs were frozen, it required strong efforts of friends to restore his circulation. Unfortunately, he lost a foot, several toes, and the tips of his fingers. Other workers contracted typhoid fever, which proved fatal in several cases.

A Shipwreck in the Desert

Strong winds ushered in 1913, and during the first few days, a severe storm on Pyramid Lake destroyed the *Dora* and sank several barges used in building the railroad. Fortunately, the crews reached the shore without problems. A week later, the *Utah* was destroyed in a fire following a gasoline explosion. While two men were searching for a leak in the gas line with a lighted match, loose gasoline caught fire. Without waiting for the explosion, the men jumped in the lake and swam ashore without harm.

The *Advocate* editor regularly filled his columns with observations and suggestions. Shortly before Christmas 1912, he stated, "When the railroad gets here, Susanville citizens will know when they can get their freight and how much it will cost them. The days of the I'll-bring-it-when-I-please, charge-what-I-want-to teamster are numbered. His arrogance has not earned him any sympathy."

Meanwhile, work on different sections continued to move forward. In contrast with the forthcoming year, the winter weather, except for the zero temperatures, stood generally conducive to construction. When T. B. Walker called on William Hood on January 3, 1913, he learned that SP still expected to have its rails in Susanville early in May that year. Walker urged Hood to expedite construction to the mill site. Hood had previously explained to Willis J. Walker, another son, that it was "exceedingly difficult to predict labor supply . . . and quite difficult to predict the temper of that class of labor, that is, how continuously they will remain at work." In discussing Walker's latest visit with Edgar Calvin, Hood suggested that some wagon roads be graded to provide advance access to the site of the two tunnels a few miles beyond Susanville.

A shortage of secondhand rail retarded progress, but tracklayers followed graders working along the western shore of Pyramid Lake, passing Sutcliffe, before leaving the lake with a slight rise at Zenobia and then following an almost level profile for some thirty miles to Wendel. On March 18, 1913, F&L rails crossed WP at Flanigan, Nevada, sixty miles from Fernley. Three weeks later graders moved to Litchfield, only fourteen miles from Susanville. To the west, two big cuts ahead stood as challenges, but the addition of a night shift accelerated the work at Davis Hill, while steady work continued just below Susanville. Already plans had been made to haul sugar beets to Fallon from Honey Lake Valley in construction trains.

The *Advocate* editor, still smarting from the tantalizing visit of WP officials in 1904 who had all but promised to put Susanville on their main line, stood ready to poke fun at the railroad whenever it suffered some mishap or storm problems. After slides closed the railroad temporarily in January, he posted this notice: "LOST—A railroad, answers to the name of 'Scenic Route,' strayed from Honey Lake Valley, as it is valued only as a souvenir of Incompetent Management. Last heard of in Feather River Canyon. Send information to Credulous Eastern Shareholders." In contrast, the F&L received more kindly treatment. When the railroad chose the Cain property as the site for the Susanville depot, he wrote: "This is handy enough."

A dozen detonations on Davis Hill, heard in Susanville for the first time in March, left no doubt of the approaching railroad and served to remind the Railroad Day Committee to create an appropriate welcome for the railroad's arrival. Several meetings were held, but lacking a completion date from the contractor, matters drifted along without direction, with the result that, after waiting years for the train, its entry into town went unheralded.

Responding to an invitation, a local reporter visited the tracklayers at the close of March, to find one hundred men strung along the grade. Some were cribbing the gullies pending trestle construction, and a dozen men spread cross ties ahead of the tracklayers who were then just twenty-one miles from Susanville. The reporter noted that the men performed their task without any mechanical contrivances. The superintendent remarked that they laid three miles in one special day when "everything seemed to go just right."

With every effort considered to reach Walker's mill as soon as possible, preliminary work in the canyon of the Susan River above Susanville brought a steady flow of undesirable "blanket men" passing through on their way to work for a grading subcontractor, and remaining just a few days before moving on or heading for a local saloon. One young man at Maxey's camp, after deciding to move along, paused briefly to help himself to his foreman's nice clothes. Sheriff A. C. "Cass" Hunsinger moved quickly by telegraphing his deputy at Doyle to catch the errant traveler. Unfortunately for the thief, the Western Pacific train being just fifteen minutes late enabled Deputy George Greeno to capture him on the station platform and return him to Susanville. Judge Medford R. Arnold levied a thirty-five-dollar fine, but probably lacking funds, the young man spent thirty-five days in jail.

As Walker's mill at Robbers Creek began taking form without waiting for the railroad, it also developed a lot of traffic of men, mules, equipment, and supplies moving through Susanville. Sidewalk observers noted a Red River Lumber Company Caterpillar traction engine climbing its way through town one day in April pulling five wagons of potatoes (36,241 pounds in 316 sacks) from Honey Lake Valley ranches to feed the several hundred workers at the mill.

The Workers' Holiday in Susanville

With the big cut on Davis Hill practically finished in mid-April, Maxey returned his forces to the remaining work in Susanville. Tracklayers made quick work of the intervening 5 miles, spurred on by the promise of a two-day holiday if they reached Susanville on Saturday, April 26, 1913. Without waiting for locals to acknowledge their efforts, the workers met the challenge and then headed for the town saloons for libations.

As May began, SP began running work trains to Susanville, followed by a daily train a few weeks later. May 7 marked the day construction trains delivered the freight to Susanville merchants for the first time and relieved them of the vagaries of teamsters.

SP bosses relaxed momentarily, having met the deadline established with Walker back in January. Though the roadbed needed ballasting and surfacing, 106 miles of track were down, leaving 29 miles to go. More difficult work lay ahead in the canyon of Susan River. Utah Construction prepared for the task by building a corral at Susanville along with a supply warehouse and several yard tracks.

Bums and Blasting

Standing on a hill back of the Cain place, one could witness a plethora of activity. The steam shovel was poking its way into the hill, while whistles of steam engines, signaling instructions to switchmen, shunted cars along the rails approaching from the east.

The railroad brought a new lifestyle to Susanville. Ladies of the Tule Talkers Club, meeting at various homes, enjoyed Mrs. Cain's hospitality for the last time before Fred Cain staged an auction of household furniture, farm implements, and harnesses and took his family to a lower country. A few months later the Susanville Steam Laundry commenced operations at this location.

As mentioned, railroad construction brought a number of "blanket men" to the community, which disturbed citizens. Unable to resist temptations of local saloons, these men and their few dollars soon parted. Stumbling along the streets, these drunken bums soon collapsed and hopefully passed into dreamland. Those who could remain upright hassled men and insulted ladies. One Saturday night was celebrated by twenty-two street fights. Idlers clustered around one shopkeeper's door so thoroughly disgusted him that he stepped outside and proved to be an excellent boxer, for, one by one, he quickly leveled the crowd and then returned to his regular business.

Equally disturbing were the constant explosions necessary to make the deep cuts in (old) Cemetery Hill and by the county hospital. When heavy blasting commenced at the close of May, the concussion, coming before the report, caused people to dash out of shops along Main Street, thinking it was an earthquake. Carving the roadbed through rocky bluffs made blasting noise a regular event that people generally accepted—all but the explosions at three in the morning shattering their dreams.

A "bombardment" late one night in July in the Cemetery Hill cut signaled the ending of that work two weeks later. One blast hurled a seven-pound rock more than a thousand feet, and another broke the stained-glass windows of the Methodist church. UCC responded promptly with a check to cover the damages.

When the workers approached the right-of-way by the county hospital, wiser heads temporarily moved patients to tents in the lower part of town near the old fort to avoid dangers from dynamiting. After four months, midnight explosions around Susanville finally ceased, and city officials adopted a "move-along" policy that cleared the streets of undesirables. Peace reigned once more.

Going back to May 1913, the railroad took steps to become a going concern. C. B. Morton, transferred from Wabuska, Nevada, settled in as agent, with his office in a boxcar near the UCC warehouse. Responding to an inquiry, he said that passengers could leave at 6:20 A.M. but cautioned them of the absence of close connections at Fernley. Miller and Lux, the widespread livestock organization, brought ninety-six cars of cattle from winter range over the F&L and, fortunately for Susanville, unloaded them a few miles distant before driving them to pasture at Mountain Meadows (near Westwood). A trainload of thirty-five hundred sheep on July 19 constituted the first revenue traffic originating in Susanville.

Reacting to hostile government regulations and legislation, SP management had adopted a "wait-and-see" attitude toward new rail lines. Other than the long branch to Marshfield, Oregon, the Fernley and Lassen constituted the only major new construction during 1912–1913. Because of the commitment to Walker, this new line commanded the attention of both division and executive officers.

An informal meeting of Salt Lake Division operating and traffic men in the superior court in Susanville in July proved to be a pleasant gathering. R. F. Pray, manager of the Red River Lumber Company, attended. One man mentioned that, except for a short distance, the F&L still lacked important ballast under the ties.

When President Sproule made a trip to Susanville at the end of August, he told local newsmen that the line would be open October 1. A. J. Barclay of the SP engineering department confirmed that, but for a few minor details, everything would be in good shape by the October date. A respectable structure rose to form the Susanville depot to replace the temporary boxcar depot. (Barclay later served as field engineer on SP's Phoenix main-line project in Arizona.)

With the railroad at its door, some enthusiastic people persuaded the company to stage an excursion to Pyramid Lake on July 13. A few weeks before the excursion, F&L superintendent W. A. McGovern postponed the trip, citing damage from the recent heavy rains and the unstable roadbed. Postponed, the date of the trip was set for October 5 with the adult round-trip fare of $4.15 until the Sunday funeral for an infant son of a popular couple pushed the trip to the next week.

Sunday, October 12, 1913, started as a windy, blustery day when the excursion left Susanville but turned warm and balmy as the train arrived at Pyramid Lake three and one-half hours later. With just two boats available at the lake, only a few people caught a handful of fish. Many people brought their lunches, which probably disappointed Mrs. James Sutcliffe, for she had prepared a nice warm dinner to serve the whole crowd of one hundred people. Although the count was less than expected, the excursion was pronounced a success.

Management of the Fernley-Susanville portion of the line switched from the construction department to the operating department on October 15, 1913. At that time, J. M. Fulton, Reno traffic agent, and T. F. Rowlands, division superintendent, arrived in the business car *Salt Lake* to discuss train schedules. Fulton conceived the idea of a midmorning departure, enabling Bieber patrons to catch the train that would connect with westbound No. 23 at Fernley. The same thought suggested the return trip to arrive about three in the afternoon. An advertisement in the *Advocate* of October 24, 1913, announced a daily train leaving at 10:00 A.M. to connect with No. 23 and arriving in San Francisco at 8:15 the next morning. A standard sleeper left Susanville three days each week and returned from San Francisco on alternate days. Fulton posted a $13.10 fare to San Francisco, but to Reno it was only $5.60. A reduction in freight charges (class rates) would follow shortly.

On to Westwood and the Red River Lumber Company

Whereas the profile from Fernley (elevation 4,157 feet) to Wendel (crossing of the N-C-O Railway) turned gently downward, with the latter point being 145 feet lower than Fernley, the undulations in the topography as the roadbed climbed in and out of washes pushed the ruling grade up to 0.85 percent. Over the next twenty-three miles across Honey Lake Valley to Susanville, the road climbed 203 feet, but the ruling grade was only 0.40 percent. The topography in the next eighteen miles to Pegleg Mountain and Westwood Jct. proved more challenging to locating engineers and subsequently to the operating men. Westwood Jct. (elevation 5,520 feet) stood 2,000 feet higher than Susanville, necessitating a 2.2 percent ruling grade and the use of helper locomotives. The returning grade from Westwood to the summit, though held to 1.5 percent, called for extra power to handle heavy trains bearing the wood products of the Red River Lumber Company.

SP management, fully aware of the agreement with Walker, pushed the work up Susan River months before the trains came to Susanville. Countless men moved through the town to the work site that summer west of Susanville, with the force reported to number fifteen hundred. In February 1913, months before trains whistled in Susanville, the Central Pacific Board of Directors adopted a new location for the initial six miles west of Susanville, replacing the location previously approved on May 19, 1910. Unfortunately, a comparison of the routes is not available. Although the Susan River offered a logical route to Westwood Jct., sharp turns in the river about five miles west of town presented the same problems confronting Western Pacific along the Feather River. Two tunnels, 817 feet and 450 feet in length, in close proximity eased the difficulty. The river had to be crossed twelve times with ten 60 foot deck girder spans and two measuring nearly 200 feet in length. Observing the Boca and Loyalton winding down its operations, its chief engineer, W. F. Sanders, found a place on the F&L as bridge engineer.

Heavy parts of one steam shovel crawled through the streets in a wagon pulled by eighteen animals. This passage followed an earlier move of two dinkey locomotives ordered by subcontractors to work just beyond the hospital cut. Shoppers were startled to witness two 20-ton engines moving up Main Street to Roop Street, where they turned off in the direction of the job site.

Certainly, it was not a speedy process. Each locomotive, under its own power, ran over two lengths of sliding tracks. After leaving one section of track, horses pulled that section forward to the front of the next section, and, after being securely bolted to a connecting plate, the engines moved to the next unit of track.

By repeating this work, the locomotives advanced about one mile each day; fortunately, the distance was relatively short. The same method moved two steam shovels through town the following week. Someone conjured a yarn that the crews of the moving steam shovels had a race between them with a purse of five hundred dollars to the winner.

In July, Isaac Knoch, a local merchant active in a new bank, displayed his interest in the railroad's progress by securing a ride to Devil's Corral and then walking back to Susanville. He reported the tunnel work was going well and that the course of the river was being changed by dumping rock from the tunnels. Somehow, in spite of the precipitous walls of upper Susan River, crews managed to move a smaller shovel to Devil's Corral, but, as the two larger shovels had to move over tracks, they could not be brought up the river until temporary trackage was in place. Doing so in turn depended on the opening of two cuts by the cemetery and county hospital, and that work stood weeks away.

Knoch said the scenery, though not as awe inspiring as WP, stood out beautifully and would make tourists "enthusiastic." With more than one thousand men working along the eight miles to Devil's Corral, and still more beyond, Knoch believed "it is reasonably certain that the road to Walker's mill will be completed this season," and it might have been were it not for the heavy winter.

Troubles along the Line

Although the fear of labor troubles sponsored by the Industrial Workers of the World failed to materialize, it proved difficult to hold men with nomadic leanings on the job. Other problems surfaced in the summer and fall of 1913.

The first cave in at Tunnel No. 1 occurred August 1 in which several men were bruised but not severely, according to Dr. E. S. Drucks, acting UCC physician. Then in the early morning of September 10, a mass of rocks fell from the roof of the same tunnel on J. J. Painter, the civil engineer who had been setting up points for the workmen to drill. Painter died and two other men were seriously injured, while fortunately others escaped injury.

F. A. Schliemann, a local poet, composed a verse titled "Just Beyond" in Painter's memory.

A few days later a fire, perhaps caused by an overturned oil-fired stove, destroyed the Bradshaw hospital. Patients were moved out with great difficulty; Mrs. Lillian M. Coburn, the nurse who assisted in the evacuation and saved lives, was disabled by severe burns, which later necessitated hospital treatment. Local people staged a dance for her benefit the following May, and six months later she received badly needed financial assistance from the Carnegie Hero Fund as well as a medal, with both stemming from the persistence of Mrs. R. W. T. Garner of Susanville and A. J. Barclay, an SP civil engineer. (Mrs. Coburn, a victim of influenza, died in San Francisco in February 1920, four days after the same illness took the life of her son.)

September 1913 was not a good month. At the Smith brothers' camp, James Huston, whose experience as a powder man dated back forty years to his work on Central Pacific and who was "regarded as one of the best in his line of work," died after injuries from an explosion. A week later, a dinkey engine working up the river at a Maxey camp jumped the track. Escaping steam scalded the engineer, Theodore Johnson, when the locomotive turned over and crushed him beneath it.

A mix-up occurred when sixteen laborers recruited by a San Francisco agency could find no jobs on their arrival at the tunnel sites. An investigation confirmed a valid need for the men, but some discouraged men returned to San Francisco before all could be put to work.

A sketchy report in mid-October 1913 stated that grading to Westwood "is practically completed and with fair weather there is no question but that lumber will be shipped over the railroad from the mill by December 1st." Though that projection was repeated in the local press on several occasions, wiser heads disagreed, for at that moment, rails reached only six miles up the canyon, with further work stalled for three weeks pending the opening of Tunnel No. 2. However, efforts to meet the deadline never slackened; six work trains operated out of Susanville, and by the end of November most subcontractors had finished their projects and had departed for milder temperatures. Christianson Brothers stood out as the exception, for an unexpected landslide delayed their departure for about two weeks.

On December 12, 1913, a construction train passed over the bridge at Devil's Corral for the first time; five days later Reno traffic agent J. M. Fulton and Superintendent T. F. Rowlands inspected the track and reported the greater part to be in excellent condition. (This bridge, consisting of two 30-foot deck girders and another 60 feet long, had to be lengthened in 1923 with an additional 60-foot span.) Although Fulton cannot be held personally responsible, light patronage brought the discontinuance of the through Pullman to Oakland; also, the fare was boosted to twenty dollars, which gave the competing auto service to Doyle and the WP to San Francisco an advantage, for its fare remained around twelve dollars each way.

Reports of the progress of the railroad construction between Devil's Corral and Westwood were blanked out by the great snowstorm starting just before Christmas, but echoes of whistles confirmed the movement of trains in the canyon. In Susanville, two feet of snow favored horse-drawn sleighs and discouraged auto traffic.

Beyond Devil's Corral, four feet of snow added to the isolation, and men still on the job found liquid nourishment at Daniel Potter's Mountain Inn a welcome tonic. Potter homesteaded just beyond Devil's Corral, built a house, and operated a lunch counter offering soft drinks and cigars. Back in June 1913, Judge M. R. Arnold fined him one hundred dollars for selling stronger beverages without a license. Potter had his own ideas when he returned to his cabin and paid another hundred-dollar fine just a few weeks later. Somehow, Sheriff Hunsinger suspected that Potter was back to his old tricks, for he raided the Mountain Inn just before Christmas and found gallons of beer and bottles of whiskey. This time Judge Arnold imposed a one thousand–dollar fine pending a trial, but Potter insisted on a change of venue. With the trial transferred to nearby Standish, the jury stood eleven for acquittal and only one for conviction. The civil authorities did not know what to do, but Dan did; he returned to his old trade, only to be arrested in Portola a year later for bootlegging.

Susanville quietly greeted the year 1914, but locomotive whistles sounded as one year followed the other. Warm weather brought rain briefly to raise the Susan River and bring down flotsam, necessitating railroad crews to dislodge accumulations at major bridge crossings.

Though Philip J. Goumaz's ranch was in Honey Lake Valley, the F&L named a station for him thirteen miles west of Susanville. Just beyond this station, a portion of the grade settled greater than anticipated, which required more attention. A few miles beyond, the route ran south of Hog Flat Reservoir and McCoy Flat Reservoir. L. L. McCoy of Red Bluff, after taking his flocks of sheep to Lassen County for forty-one seasons, decided to sell his sheep business and 20,343 acres in the spring of 1913. A year later both reservoirs were modified for the benefit of Honey Lake ranchers.

Cold weather and more storms returned, leaving ten feet of snow at Westwood Jct., the high point on the line.

Rock slides and falling trees brought more problems. In January 1914, slides imprisoned two construction locomotives for several days; dynamite had to come to their rescue. One alert engineer, easing his locomotive down the canyon, spotted a large tree about to topple over, as its roots had been loosened by blasting and river waters. Throwing the Johnson bar into reverse, he brought his engine to a halt, but still the tree crushed the front pilot as it fell.

Even with a short gap in Susanville weather records, it appears that the ninety-three-inch snowfall in January 1914 established a record, far in excess of the sixty-five inches measured in January 1895. Though some part of the last twenty miles of the railroad had been partially graded, the massive blanket of snow crippled the work. As one man remarked, rail laying that winter was at least twenty times more difficult than summer work. With the assistance of a small army of men shoveling the snowbank, the tracklayers reached a point eleven miles from Westwood early in February and finally entered the lumber town on Saturday, February 21, 1914.

Some weeks before, the *Sacramento Bee* carried a story that when the railroad linked Susanville with Westwood in March, the Red River Lumber Company would stage a joint celebration in Westwood, chartering a train at its expense to bring Susanville people to the event at no cost to them. This report proved to be news to residents in Lassen County and all concerned. No celebration occurred, and no special train made the journey.

The Other One Hundred Miles of Railroad

While all efforts concentrated on the battle with the elements to reach Westwood, the newly opened railroad between Fernley and Susanville was not neglected. At Susanville, the new freight house approached its completion and on September 11, 1913, accepted freight for the first time, even if it meant dodging the painters. Two months later, work commenced on the new engine house, initially confined to three stalls, with plans to add four more the next spring. Four stalls proved to be the final decision. Fred T. Abbay, who moved to Susanville in September 1925 to be shop foreman, had a varied career. He signed on at the SP shops in Sparks in 1907 at ten cents an hour. Although that pittance went a lot further in those days, Abbay welcomed his promotion to journeyman four years later at forty-two cents an hour. After 1930, he went into other occupations, eventually heading Lassen Lumber and Box (LL&B) Company Inc. (His father, J. W. Abbay, had been district shop foreman for SP at Carlin, Mina, and Imlay in the 1912–1918 era.)

Stacy, a new town site on the F&L at the crossing of Skedaddle Creek, thirty-seven miles east of Susanville, sprouted in the spring of 1913. Eight months later, trains bearing gravel from the Astor, Nevada, quarry made Stacy their headquarters while ballasting the track. Ballasting, most important in stabilizing the track structure, stood out as a major task. In March 1914, the 150-man ballasting crew settled in Stacy for ten days to spread crushed rock for the third time. Perhaps it marked the era of the peak population for Stacy.

An unseasonably warm spell at the end of 1913, though brief, was enough to melt snow in the Skedaddle Mountains north of Stacy and bring the creek to its highest level ever known. Two days of whirling floodwaters eroded the embankment to threaten the bridge across Skedaddle Creek. J. H. Booth, a special agent of the railroad, wired division headquarters, and within a few hours a train arrived from the Astor pit to dump rock to protect the bridge. Within an hour, the damage had been repaired, so the Fernley local was delayed only a few minutes.

The railroad staked out a corral for livestock shipments in 1915, but the settlement never really blossomed and became only a memory with the passing years.

On the portion of the line to Westwood, people could secure passage on construction trains, commencing in April 1914. By the end of that month, snow had finally melted sufficiently to enable a crew to install sidetracks at Westwood.

Susanville residents remarked on the changed appearance around the depot. The revised schedules of June 1914 created an impressive scene of activity. Each afternoon the Fernley train's arrival began transforming the quiet scene. Soon, the local from Westwood pulled into the station, and passengers transferred to the cars destined for Fernley, which signaled the return trip. Last, the local would climb the hill to Westwood with local patrons as well as travelers arriving on the Fernley train.

Baseball proved to be a popular sport at this time, with teams in Susanville and Westwood. On June 7, 1914, one could purchase a round-trip ticket for $1.50 to witness the game at Westwood, and, in spite of the disagreeable cold and threatening rain, a large contingent from Susanville made the trip to back their team to victory.

Perhaps in an effort to make up for the free excursion to the opening celebration that never happened, Westwood put on a spectacular show for Independence Day in 1914. Though the excursion train required tickets, 502 people boarded eight coaches of the train and after a pleasant ride up the canyon arrived in Westwood to enjoy the parade, followed by a barbecue with many speeches. Another baseball game filled the afternoon, with fireworks and a dance completing the evening program.

A midnight summer blaze a few weeks after the excursion swept the area around the Susanville station. Originating in the Bon Ton restaurant on Weatherlow Street, the fire claimed the restaurant, A. Cameron's store, Hankin's Riverside Hotel, and the old Cain residence before being subdued.

Finally finished, the last section of the railroad was turned over to the operating department on September 1, 1914. A well drilled at Flanigan tapped water, and both Litchfield and Fernley locals could boast of new stations.

Already the railroad recorded its first major derailment. In March 1914, the engine and five cars of cattle left the rails at Zenobia. Some cattle were killed, but about one hundred escaped and took to the hills. Twelve cowboys, recruited in Reno, went out with their horses in a special livestock car to gather the strays.

A sad event occurred at nearby Astor a few weeks later. After twenty years as an SP track walker, Philip Welton reached the age of seventy-three and planned to retire in San Francisco. On what was his last day of work, he failed to hear the warning shouts from the conductor of a train, which backed into his velocipede with fatal consequences.

When some fence posts, scrap iron, and rocks appeared on the track about a mile west of the Leavitt station in July 1914, it brought great concern. Fortunately, a slow-moving train brushed the impediments aside and escaped trouble. Sheriff Hunsinger went to the scene the next morning to find three little Indian boys, ages six to ten, again placing obstructions on the track. The miscreants started to run but were caught and had to endure a severe lecture that discouraged a repetition.

Children living in Susanville and Honey Lake Valley looked forward to May 3, 1916, as the day the A. G. Barnes Circus would arrive in town, only to be disappointed when the advertised mile-long parade and circus had to be canceled. The special circus train ran off a derail switch at the WP crossing in Flanigan, and the locomotive toppled on its side. Engineer K. M. Becker suffered serious injuries as a result. One car left the track but remained upright, and the circus train escaped material damage. To keep his schedule, the circus manager abandoned efforts to reach Susanville and proceeded to the next town.

Bad luck had followed the A. G. Barnes Circus in Nevada. A few days earlier, the train derailed on the Virginia and Truckee Railroad (V&T) north of Carson City, and a baby tiger escaped from his cage in the confusion. The previous year, one of the circus cars caught fire and burned, also near Carson City. In Fallon, a big snowstorm blew down the tent, and trainers had to search for escaping animals.

Another circus arrived safely in November, and half of the Susanville high school students skipped classes to attend.

SP had long experienced deep snows around Donner Pass so was prepared to meet similar conditions around the summit at Westwood Jct. A rotary snowplow generally kept the track open, but a snow blockade closed the line for four days in February 1917. A locomotive derailment and slides hampered work, but a rotary plow pushed by two locomotives managed to clear the line.

Although warmer weather dispatched the snow, another operating problem at Susanville needed attention. As less-than-carload freight was unloaded from the cars on the south side of the depot, boxes, crates, and bundles added to the congestion as they passed through the depot to waiting wagons on the north side. An additional unloading track on the north side of the depot in 1917 solved the problem.

In the fall of that year a visitor reported that Litchfield was one of the liveliest points in Honey Lake Valley. Wheat, hay, and alfalfa were moving out by the trainload. Sugar beets had become an important commodity that year, as was demonstrated by a dozen carloads at Litchfield awaiting shipment to a refining plant such as the one at Fallon, Nevada.

James R. Barnes had transferred from Keeler, at the end of the narrow gauge in California, to be the first SP agent at Litchfield. Jimmy Barnes also represented Wells Fargo and Company and wrote thousands of money orders for people buying from mail-order houses. As the Litchfield Post Office was too small, postal orders were not available, and the distance to Susanville banks discouraged their patronage.

On arrival of the daily passenger train, Barnes sprang into action. With his key, he opened the strongbox in the baggage car, exchanged incoming and outgoing dispatches, then locked the box, and the train went on to Susanville. Both Jimmy and his wife were expert telegraphers, and she handled Western Union messages. An enterprising man, Barnes erected a small hotel in his community and opened it with a dance in April 1922, with some guests coming all the way from Susanville.

After the railroads were returned to private management on March 1, 1920, J. M. Fulton, SP's traffic man in Reno, successfully worked to return the Oakland Pullman car in May 1920 that the government had ordered suspended two years earlier. A dining car became a regular feature in December 1922, and, by a revision the next month, Trains No. 5 and No. 6 began running between Westwood and Oakland Pier.

President William Sproule demonstrated SP's interest in the territory by visits in the summer of 1920 and again three years later. Two weeks after the last visit, Hardy Campbell, SP's dry-farm specialist, spent four days in Lassen County giving lectures on ways to farm in that dry land.

While J. J. Cullen commanded the local depot, William H. Mohler, the "baggage smasher," gained a wider following after the Palmer circus came to town in October 1921. In the sideshow, the circus wrestler promised twenty-five dollars to anyone who could stay in the ring with him for ten minutes. Several men tried and failed until Mohler stepped up and soon had the circus champion on his back and "the money in his pocket." A local man remarked, "Anyone who can 'wrastle' drummers' trunks can put a wrestler down we can very plainly see." Mohler later transferred to Tracy but engaged in exhibition matches, usually ending victorious.

A roadmaster's cottage was erected at Susanville in 1917 when growing traffic warranted that supervision, and O. M. Barlow learned that heavy snowfall around Westwood Jct. offered challenges not found at his former post at Hazen, Nevada.

With more people working in and around Susanville, E. G. Bouchard established a local bus line in June 1923. Between 6:30 A.M. and 9:00 P.M., the bus left Roop and Main Streets every half hour, and for a dime patrons could ride to the SP depot, the two lumber mills, or the Millwood suburb. H. Hancock, the lively manager of the Millwood Variety Store, urged people to "hop on the bus and save" at his store. If purchases totaled one dollar, the store refunded twenty cents for the bus fare.

On the other hand, SP expressed concern that the San Francisco–Susanville-Westwood train of five cars, including an observation-buffet car, lacked sufficient use; on some days, with only three or four patrons, the crew outnumbered the passengers. In a local advertisement, SP explained, "It is needless to say it is an expensive service; but we sincerely hope it will be given sufficient patronage to justify its continuance." In 1927, the passenger train still carried a sleeping car to and from San Francisco as well as a café-observation car with M. J. Richey in charge. He possessed a faculty for remembering the special requests of frequent patrons.

Changes along the Line

The branch line served the lumber trade at both Westwood and Susanville. Besides hauling logs from connecting lumber spurs, Southern Pacific transported finished lumber to distant markets. The thirty miles between Susanville (MP 381.4) and Westwood (MP 411.3) underwent changes from time to time, as demonstrated in the following summary:

MP 385.7, Smith Spur. Two outfit cars, SPMW (maintenance-of-way) 55 and 1158, provided living quarters as late as 1939 for track walkers watching for rock slides.

MP 386. In 1921, a temporary 392-foot spur installed at the east portal of Tunnel No. 1 facilitated a rail-relaying project.

MP 386–87. Heavy rail wear on ten-degree curves necessitated replacing one mile of the original seventy-five-pound and eighty-pound rail with ninety-pound secondhand rail in 1929.

MP 388.9, Fredonia. This nonagency station was abandoned on May 22, 1926.

MP 390.1, Bunnel. During 1920, the McKeen Lumber Company erected a sawmill and planer, but two years later after the property became affiliated with Lassen Lumber and Box Company, SP constructed a spur. Expected daily inbound shipments of five cars of logs coupled with one or two outbound cars of finished lumber justified the installation. Some years later a fire destroyed the mill.

MP 393.3, Salal. SP put in a spur at this point in 1927 to receive logs for shipment to the Bunnel mill then operated by J. B. McAllister. The spur was abandoned on September 17, 1928.

MP 394.8, Goumaz. In July 1917, a car body served as living quarters for section men. The following summer section houses enlarged the settlement and, with the cookhouse, brought the number of railroad-owned structures to seven. Two additional tie houses were added in 1923, and, with growing young families, SP built a fence around the section house for the safety of the small children. In 1957, the buildings were dismantled when larger system-maintenance gangs replaced local section forces. Also, with the change from steam locomotives to diesel power, the water tank, no longer needed, was dismantled. Born in Switzerland in 1844, Philip J. Goumaz came to this country with his parents seven years later. As a young man, he came to California via Nicaragua and in 1865 settled in Lassen County, where he was engaged in farming and stock raising until he retired and moved to Susanville. He died on December 7, 1932.

MP 397, Wheaton. A spur track, unused for some time, was abandoned on January 22, 1921.

MP 399.4, Blair. Established June 5, 1932, this nonagency station was closed on March 10, 1943.

MP 400.1, Westwood Jct. A frame depot, sixteen by twenty-eight feet, formed one of the dozen buildings erected here in 1913. A section house, cookhouse, well, pump house, and water tank made up

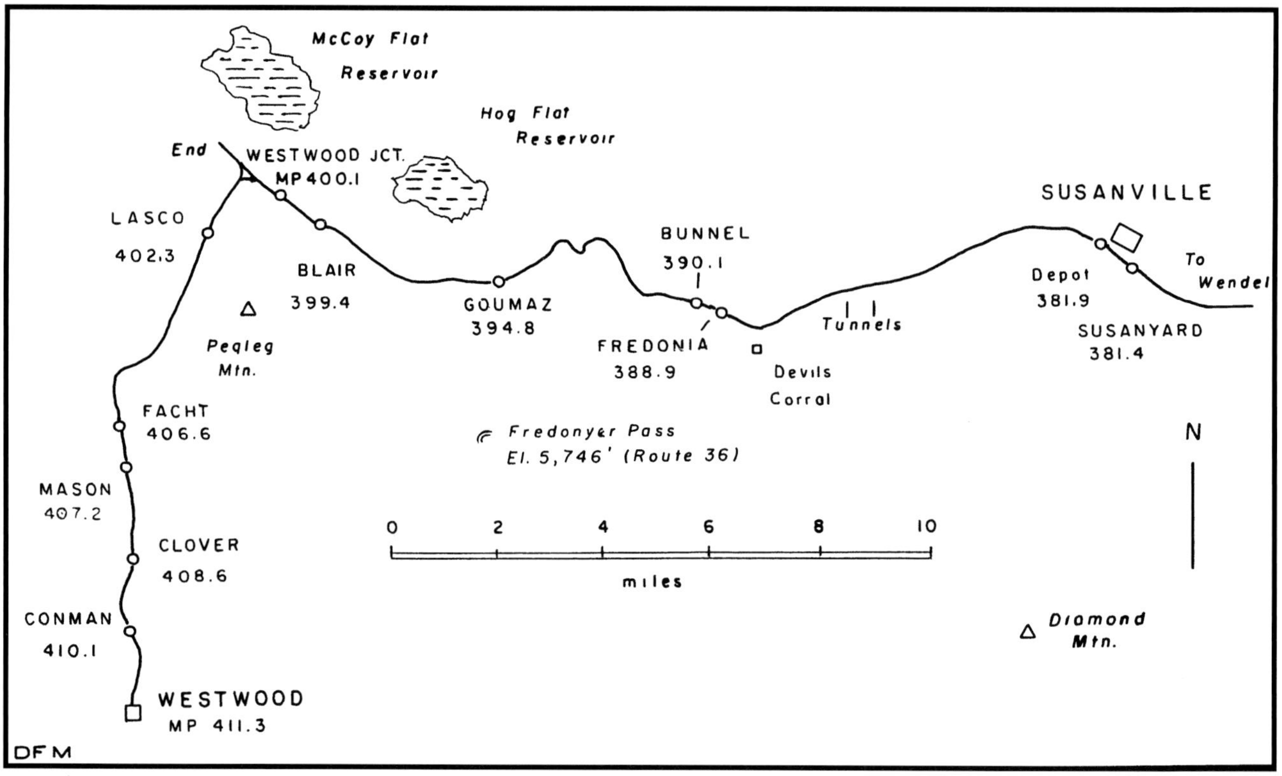

the community. In July 1920, a switch and short spur track were installed to connect with the logging railroad of Fruit Growers Supply and were followed by a modification two years later.

MP 407.2, Mason. Established September 1, 1931, as the northern terminus of Western Pacific trackage rights that commenced at Westwood.

MP 408.6, Clover. Established July 25, 1935. From June 2, 1928, to February 11, 1930, the station of Fir was located around MP 408.

Prior to 1923, the only switches along the line equipped with lamps were the few in the Westwood yard. With the expansion of night-train operations, fifty-eight lamps were installed at ten points between Stacy and Westwood Jct. over a period of six months ending in March 1924.

On September 14, 1927, renovation of the Susanville depot started. Five months later, the job had been finished; it included an addition to accommodate a new ticket office, waiting room, and express office. The older structure, now remodeled, became the baggage room, while the former baggage facility had been rebuilt to serve as the freight station.

The Later Years

Southern Pacific's Shasta Route to Portland, having long contended with heavy competition from coastal steamships, made strong protests when Western Pacific and Great Northern sought authority from the Interstate Commerce Commission to build a new railroad from Keddie to Bieber and on to Klamath Falls, Oregon. The ICC approved construction of the new line, and the driving of the last spike was celebrated at Bieber on November 10, 1931.

As all railroads do, the new line had problems. On December 27, 1931, a soft spot in the roadbed near Greenville necessitated Western Pacific detouring a train over Southern Pacific from Flanigan through Susanville to Westwood, not an unusual practice among neighboring railroads.

The next night, Fred Abbay, SP shop foreman in Susanville, received an emergency call to take an SP snowplow out to Halls Flat, forty-five miles north of Westwood on the new WP line, which was totally unprepared to cope with five feet of snow. The men worked fifty-eight hours in the Bogard section to open the line, and trains stalled at Bieber resumed their journey to Keddie. (It was noted that 1927 was the last time the snowplow left Susanville.)

Several weeks before these incidents, Robert M. Cook, editor and proprietor of the *Lassen Mail*, commenced a series of articles promoting WP's joint use of SP's track between Westwood, Susanville, and Flanigan, Nevada. WP operations over SP tracks to Westwood and then over its own line to San Francisco would shorten the rail distance from Susanville. It would also reduce the distance for WP's shipments between Salt Lake City and Bieber. Cook stirred up enough interest that a committee was formed, and the local chamber of commerce endorsed the proposal, as it cost the merchants nothing.

Charles Elsey, who had just succeeded H. M. Adams as president of Western Pacific, replied to an inquiry that he would be glad to cooperate with Lassen County. From what can be determined, an anticipated meeting with President Elsey never happened, and after six weeks of articles, the whole idea quietly faded into oblivion.

The Last Passenger Train to Susanville

Even before the 1929 stock market crash, sales of lumber had turned downward and grew worse in succeeding years. The decline in lumber shipments and other commodities seriously affected the entire railroad industry. Southern Pacific freight revenues in 1932 were less than half of receipts of 1925–1929 and would drop still more the next year.

In the same five-year period, SP spent large sums to open up markets in Oregon and northeastern California that were largely financed by bond issues. Unfortunately, the newly served domain failed to generate the expected additional traffic and, coupled with increased annual interest payments, placed the entire system in a precarious financial position. SP met the adversities in several ways: by improving service, lowering fares, and curtailing lightly patronized passenger trains.

Starting in 1930, SP offered a store-to-door pickup and delivery service that included Susanville beginning on July 21, 1932, along with a substantial reduction in the first-class freight rate to San Francisco.

To attract more passengers, SP instituted "Dollar Days" as 1933 began, enabling patrons to ride to nearby cities at bargain prices. Rates were lowered on longer distances, the round-trip fare to San Francisco from Susanville costing $7.25; in contrast, the corresponding bus fare of Mt. Lassen Transit to Red Bluff and Greyhound was $15.80. (A special round-trip fare to Westwood was $1.10.) Systemwide, the basic fare was lowered in July from 3.6 cents to 2 cents a mile.

Not withstanding the bargain fares, most branch-line trains ran almost devoid of passengers, which further drained the SP treasury. Early in 1933, when SP proposed to switch to triweekly service, Susanville merchants declared it "extremely detrimental to the community." The matter stood inactive until July when Harry E. Ish, acting district freight and passenger agent in Reno, told a businessmen's lunch gathering that SP had made a contract with Mt. Lassen Transit to handle passengers, mail, and express to Reno. With a more direct route, patrons would arrive in Reno in less than three hours, compared with the existing four-hour train schedule.

Various community meetings ensued and opposed the change. The matter came before the California Railroad Commission at a special two-day hearing in the local courthouse at the end of September. B. V. Currier spoke for the community and expounded various legal theories, but the commission authorized termination of passenger service between Wendel and Westwood. However, if the Reno highway were closed in winter, SP would operate trains until the reopening. (This arrangement concurred with an earlier SP plan.) L. E. Cady, SP agent at Susanville, told the *Lassen Mail* that the last Susanville train would run on November 30, 1933, and the event occurred without public interest.

Heavy snows enveloped a wide area in January 1937 and blocked the highways. Confronted with a closed road to Verdi, Reno motorists shipped their cars by rail, and two V&T locomotives were completely buried in snow between Reno and Carson City. Temperatures fell to minus twenty-three degrees in Susanville, and it was even colder at Westwood Jct. Drifts of snow and sand covered ten miles of the Reno road.

A special train with passenger cars and a combination diner-observation car left Reno for Susanville on February 2. Snowdrifts as high as twenty feet extending a half mile blocked the track near Numana, Nevada, a few miles north of Wadsworth. After a snowplow cleared the track, the train proceeded and arrived in Susanville with twenty-five passengers and two days' mail. The next day, with the road still blocked, SP operated another train to Susanville and return.

In 1940, Southern Pacific operated local freight trains over the Wadsworth Subdivision. Eastward the train left Fernley at 9:00 P.M. for Wendel. At that point, one section continued north to Alturas over the former N-C-O Railway and on to Klamath Falls, while the other turned westward, with Susanville and Westwood as its goal. With another train running in the opposite direction, the two trains met at the Leavitt station, seven miles east of Susanville.

The Red River Lumber Company deeded its Westwood plant to Fruit Growers Supply in December 1944. Eventually, lumber production declined, so the need for SP's Westwood line diminished. The trackage between Mason and Westwood, over which WP had rights, was sold to the latter road in the spring of 1966 for $167,000. Later that year, the Eagle Lake Lumber Company endeavored to acquire the line between Susanville and Westwood, but no purchase could be arranged; perhaps the loss of much of its Susanville plant by fire on June 13, 1955, added difficulties. Since the last train ran in 1957, the twenty-five miles between Susanville and Mason stood idle. When SP filed an abandonment application in June 1976, not unexpectedly local groups filed protests with the ICC. This section was finally abandoned in 1980, and by July 1981, only scattered clumps of ties remained on the part of the railroad that had been so difficult to build. Turning to the remaining link between Susanville and Wendel, the ICC approved abandonment of operations on October 18, 1985, but, effective April 21, 1986, the Quincy Railroad leased these twenty-two miles. One mile of unneeded track at Susanville was abandoned in June 1988.

Previously, after securing operating bridge rights over Western Pacific between Flanigan and Weso, Nevada, in 1962, Southern Pacific abandoned its line between Flanigan and Fernley the next year. The new route to Ogden, Utah, saved fifty-four miles.

In June 2005, the Fernley railroad depot was listed in the National Register of Historic Places. Built in 1914 and used until 1985, it was said to be the last remaining example of a Southern Pacific combination depot with station agent's upstairs living quarters in Nevada. It is now owned by the Fernley Preservation Society.

John M. Fulton

Although the public image of many railroad officials in the formative years of the industry stood less than flattering, John M. Fulton commanded so much respect that Susanville citizens honored him with a banquet on January 18, 1924. Some two hundred people joined together for a dinner at the Story Club of Fruit Growers Supply, and Judge J. E. Pardee delivered the principal address.

Pardee went back forty years when Fulton, then working for the Nevada-California-Oregon Railway, helped farmers to market their potato crop. When the same farmers had a bad year, Fulton secured a special freight rate over Southern Pacific to ease their burden. Near the end of 1924, Fulton turned seventy-five and decided to retire on January 1, 1925; probably, his move stemmed from the loss of his wife a few weeks previously.

Typical of many railroad men of that era, Fulton signed on as a brakeman for the Atlantic and Great Western Railway (forerunner of the Erie Railroad) at the age of eighteen. After serving as a conductor and fireman, he joined Northern Pacific in 1876 as a locomotive engineer. Continuing to move westward, he found similar work on Southern Pacific.

With his mechanical ability, he was appointed master mechanic of the Stockton and Copperopolis Railroad, a short-line SP subsidiary, still maintaining his relations with SP. When A. J. Stevens, head of SP's motive-power department, developed a new type of locomotive, he chose Fulton as its road engineer.

Fulton found himself "loaned" to the fledgling N-C-O Railway in 1884 for a year, which extended to more than a decade in mechanical work but principally as master of transportation. Fulton turned in his time in April 1899 and left railroading briefly to enter the brokerage business before joining the SP traffic department in Reno.

In February 1903, he married Theodora W. Stubbs who had graduated from the University of Nevada in 1895 and then spent another year at Stanford doing graduate work. Her father, Dr. Joseph E. Stubbs, served as president of the university from 1904 to 1914, while her uncle, John C. Stubbs, headed the traffic department of Southern Pacific and then the Union Pacific as well until he retired at the end of 1911. Theodora Stubbs worked as executive secretary of the Nevada Public Health Association and was active in the Trinity Episcopal Church. The couple had one son, John M. Fulton Jr., who was a senior at the university when his mother died.

Robert N. Fulton, John Sr.'s slightly younger brother, worked on several railroads including the SP in the San Joaquin Valley during his early career and is said to have influenced John to come west. From 1879 to 1887 Robert was the proprietor of the *Reno Evening Gazette*. Subsequently, he was a sales agent for the SP Land Company.

John Fulton made regular trips to Susanville during the construction of the Fernley and Lassen Railway as well as during its operations. He was remembered for fighting freight rate schedules he considered inequitable, taking the matter to top officials and often winning his point.

At the announcement of his retirement, the *Nevada State Journal* recognized the contributions Fulton had made to Nevada. "Few citizens of Nevada can point to a record of service equal to that of Mr. Fulton," the paper said. "Mr. Fulton had a hand in nearly every progressive movement that has taken place in the past 25 years." Robert Fulton died in 1920, but his brother John lived another fourteen years.

Bizz Johnson Trail

After SP abandoned the railroad west of Susanville and tracks had been removed, the grade between Susanville and Mason (four miles north of Westwood) became the Bizz Johnson Trail. Harold T. "Bizz" Johnson, a congressman, had been instrumental in the creation of this Rails to Trails project. Measuring twenty-five miles in length, the trail is open to hikers and horseback riders as well as bicycle riders. When winter snow blankets the section between Goumaz and Westwood Jct., cross-country skiers enjoy the trail.

Johnson's congressional district covered twenty counties in eastern and northern California. Before serving in Congress, he had been mayor of Roseville for seven years and also worked for SP's affiliate, the Pacific Fruit Express Company, operating a fleet of refrigerator cars and icing platforms.

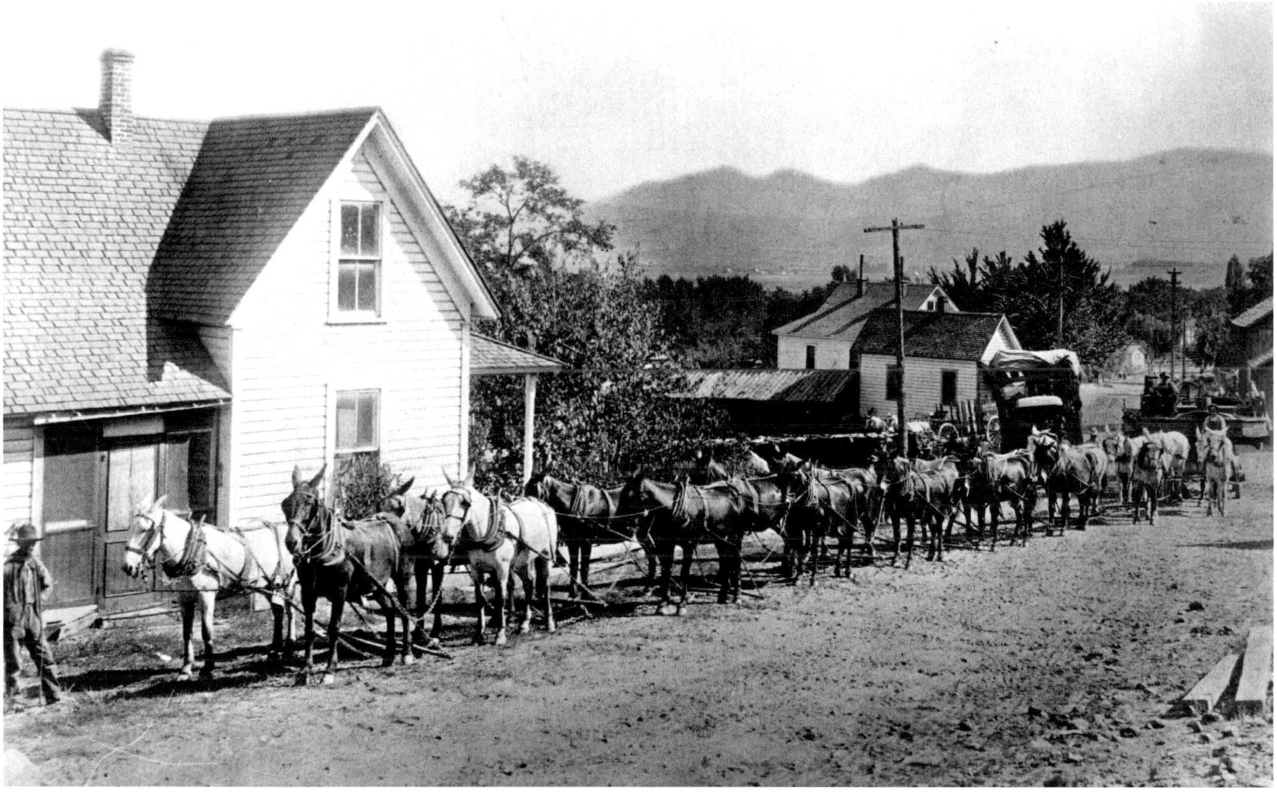

The Fernley and Lassen Railway faced difficult construction problems between Susanville and Westwood Jct. Large steam shovels had to be dismantled in order for teams to deliver them to work sites. This twenty-mule team halted at Susanville for the photographer while the mule skinner stood ready to apply his whip "to encourage" the animals to proceed. (James E. Boynton collection)

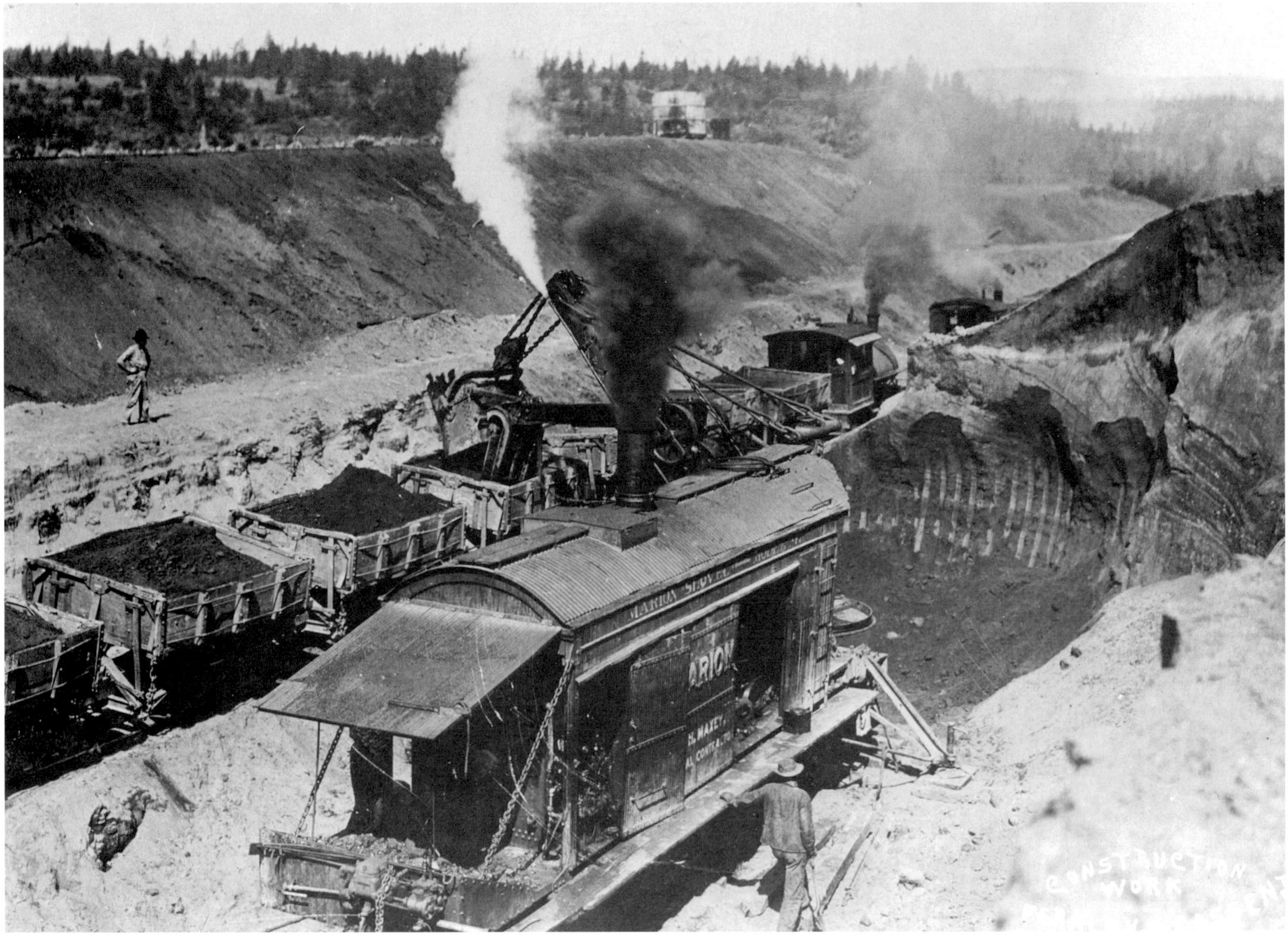

Utah Construction Company, the lead contractor, used a large Marion steam shovel to cut through the hillsides. (Lassen County Historical Society)

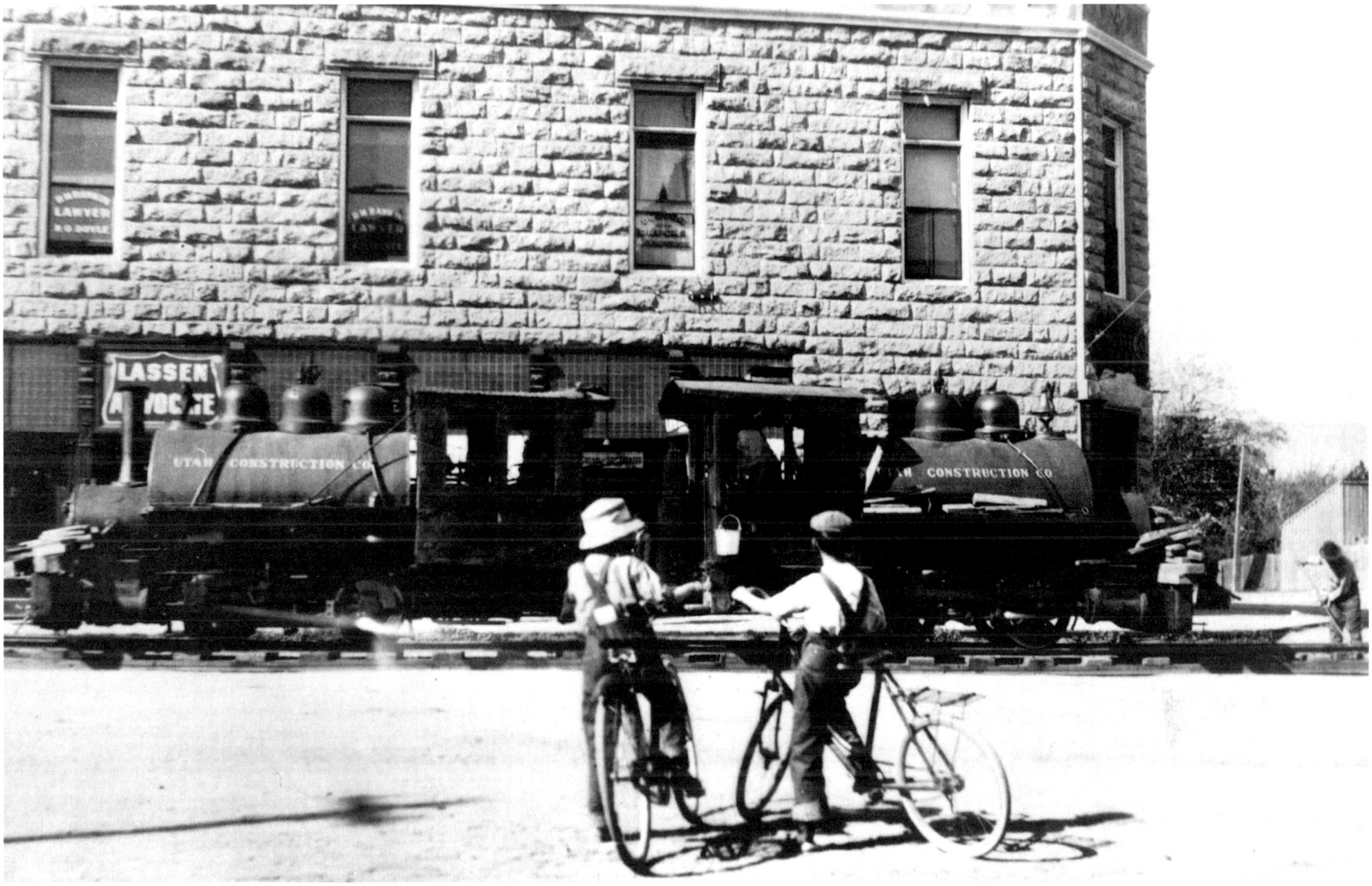

Although Susanville greeted its railroad in April 1913, much work remained to be done in the next eighteen miles to reach the summit at Westwood Jct. At that time, the Utah Construction Company found that the best way to move construction (dinkey) locomotives ahead was to employ track panels and move them slowly up Main Street. George M. McDow snapped this picture. (Lassen County Historical Society)

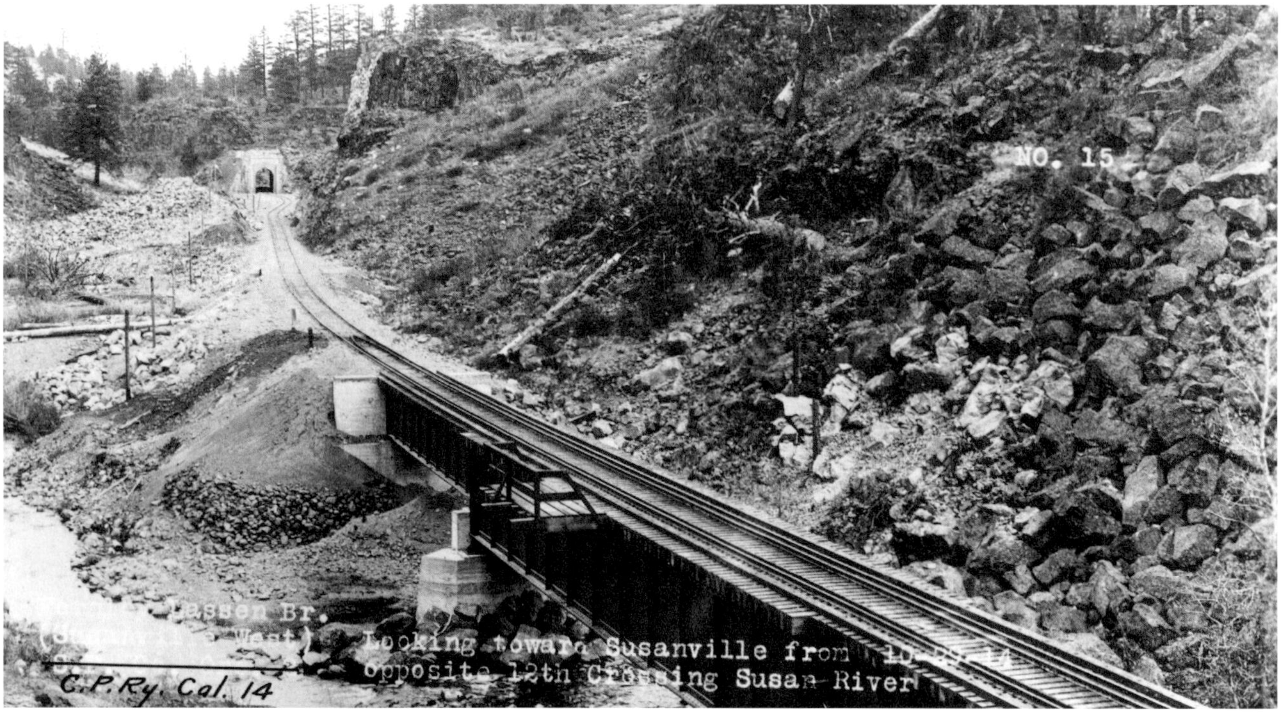

Above: The railroad above Susanville required two tunnels and many bridges as it followed the Susan River. (Southern Pacific)

Below: The wye at Westwood Jct. and Pegleg Mountain as seen in this aerial view of 1929. The railroad has climbed up the river from Susanville (*left*), and the branch to Westwood points south to that lumber town. Had original plans been consummated, the spur on the right would have turned north and continued to Klamath Falls.

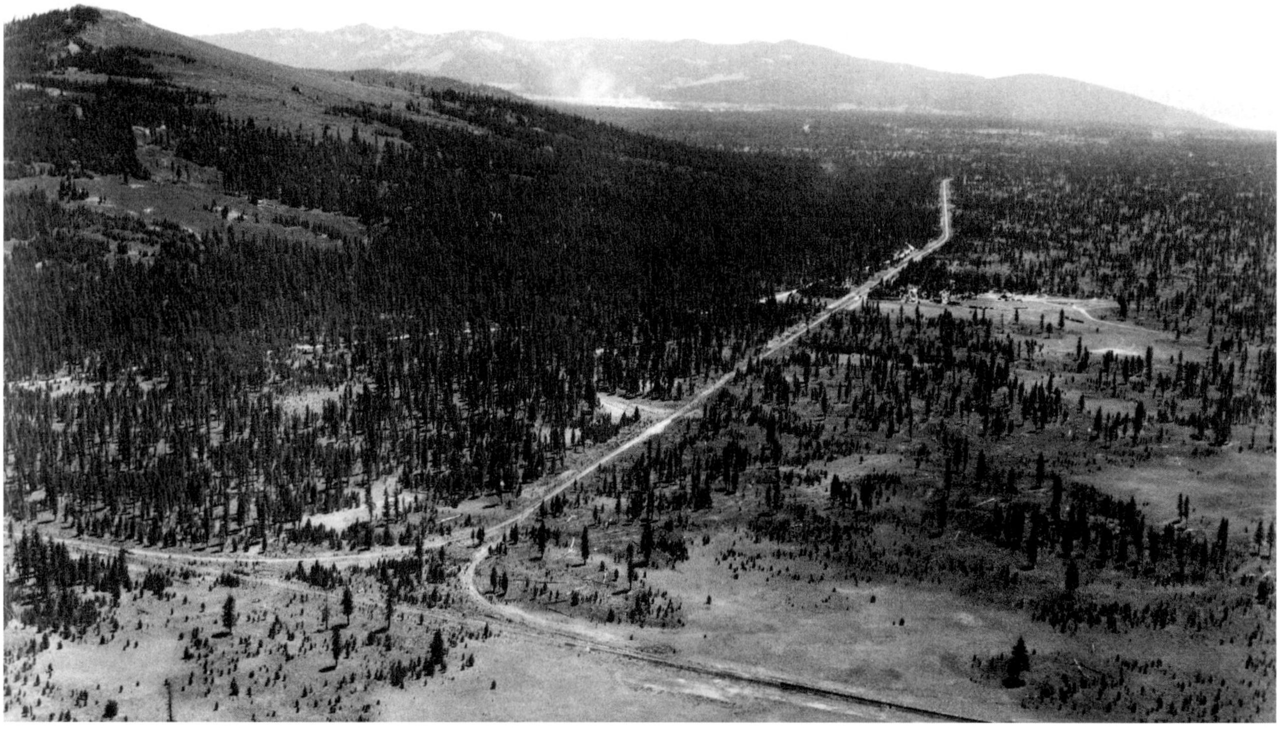

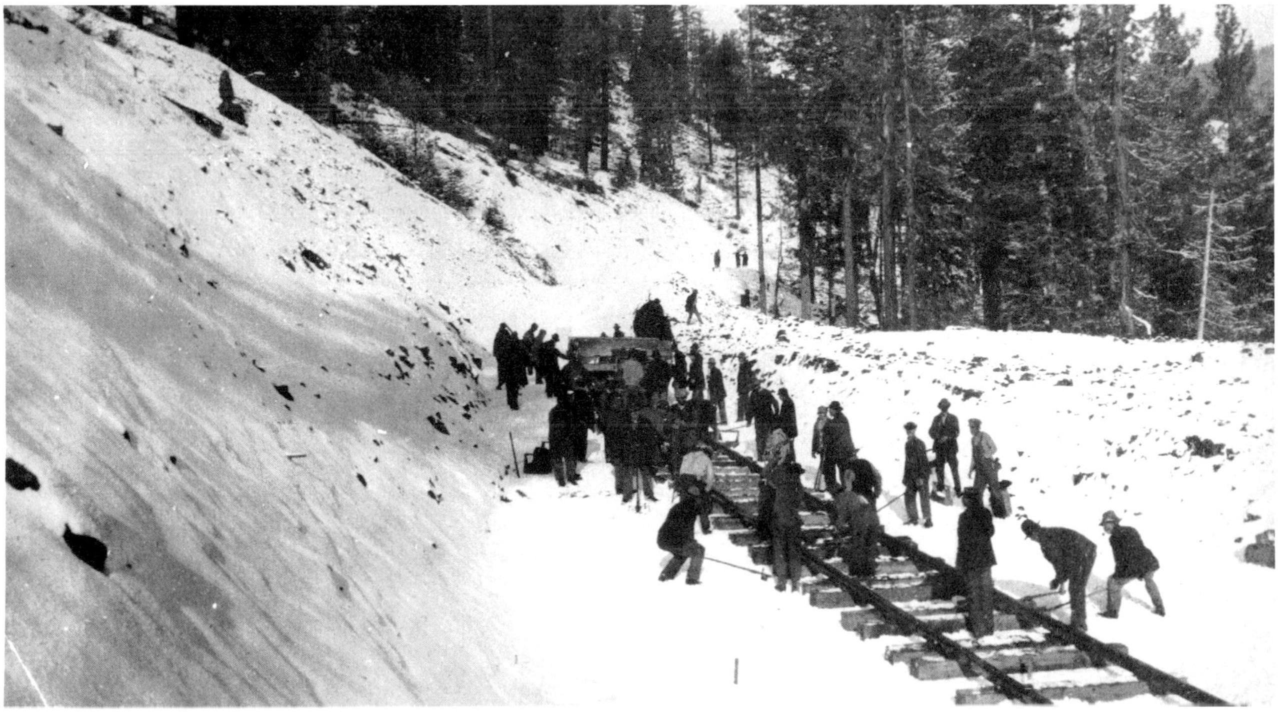

Above: Tracklaying continued under difficult conditions. (Lassen County Historical Society)

Below: A local photographer recorded the height of the snowbank when the railroad began operations. (Tom Williamson collection)

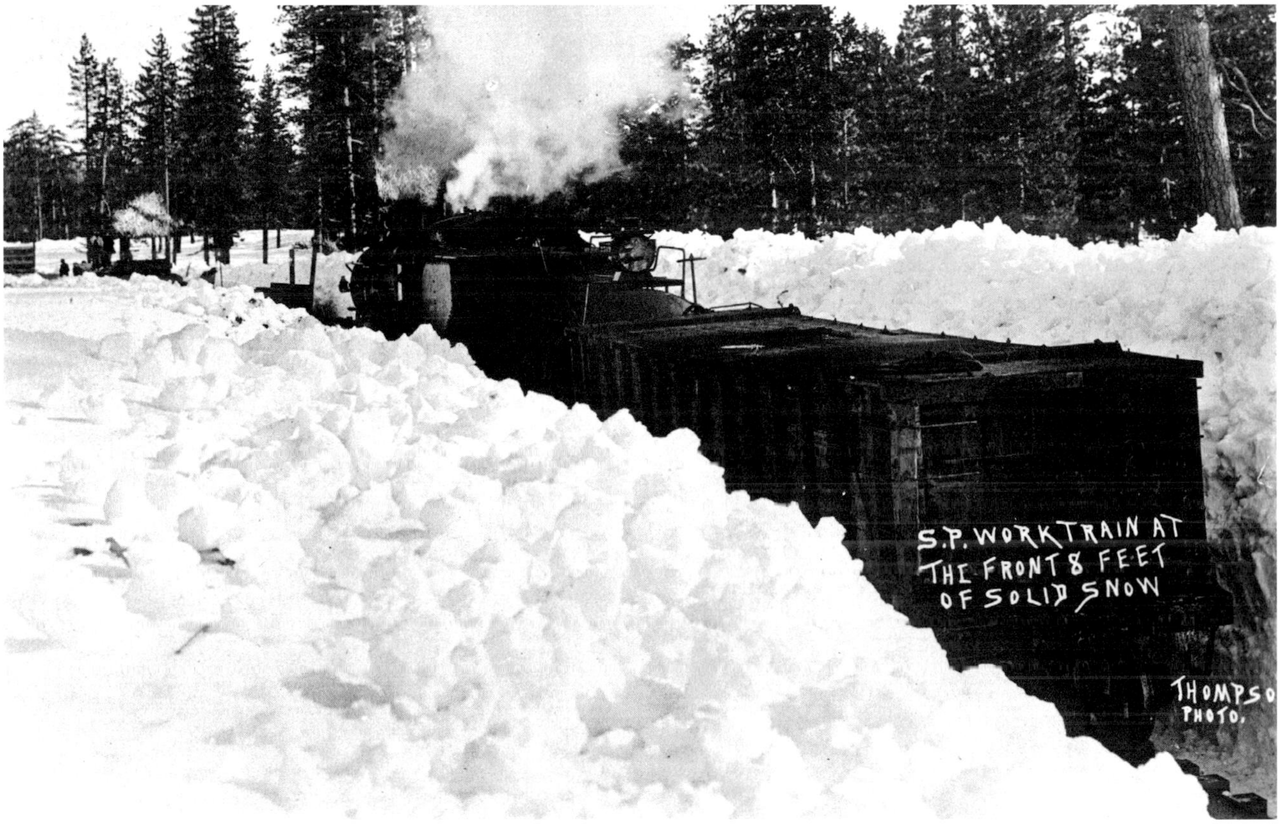

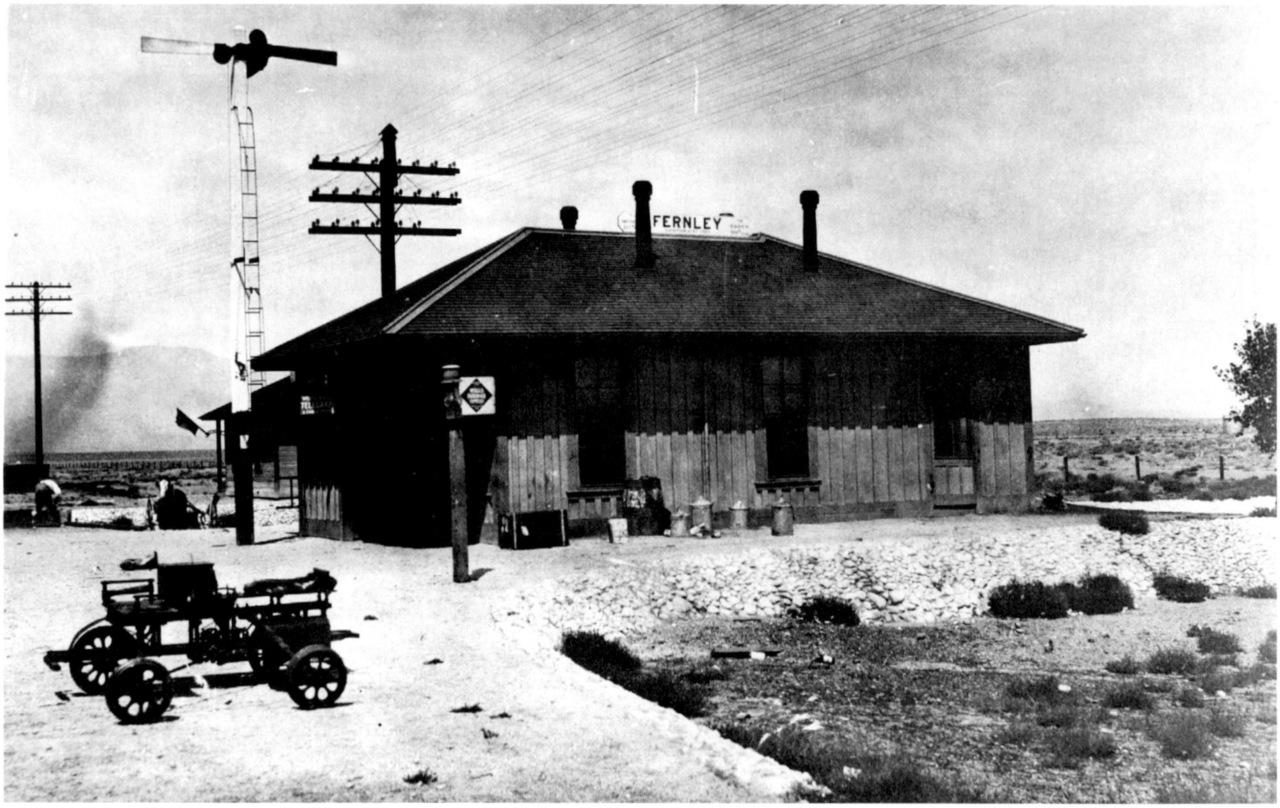

Above: Fernley's history began with the 1904 relocation of Central Pacific around White's Hill. Located just southeast of Wadsworth, it had the standard train-order board signal. With upraised arms, it advised train crews of new instructions telegraphed by the dispatcher. (Tom Williamson collection)

Below: Shortly after entering California, the railroad came to Stacy, a real estate promotion never to be realized, and erected this little shelter in 1913. (Ted Wurm collection)

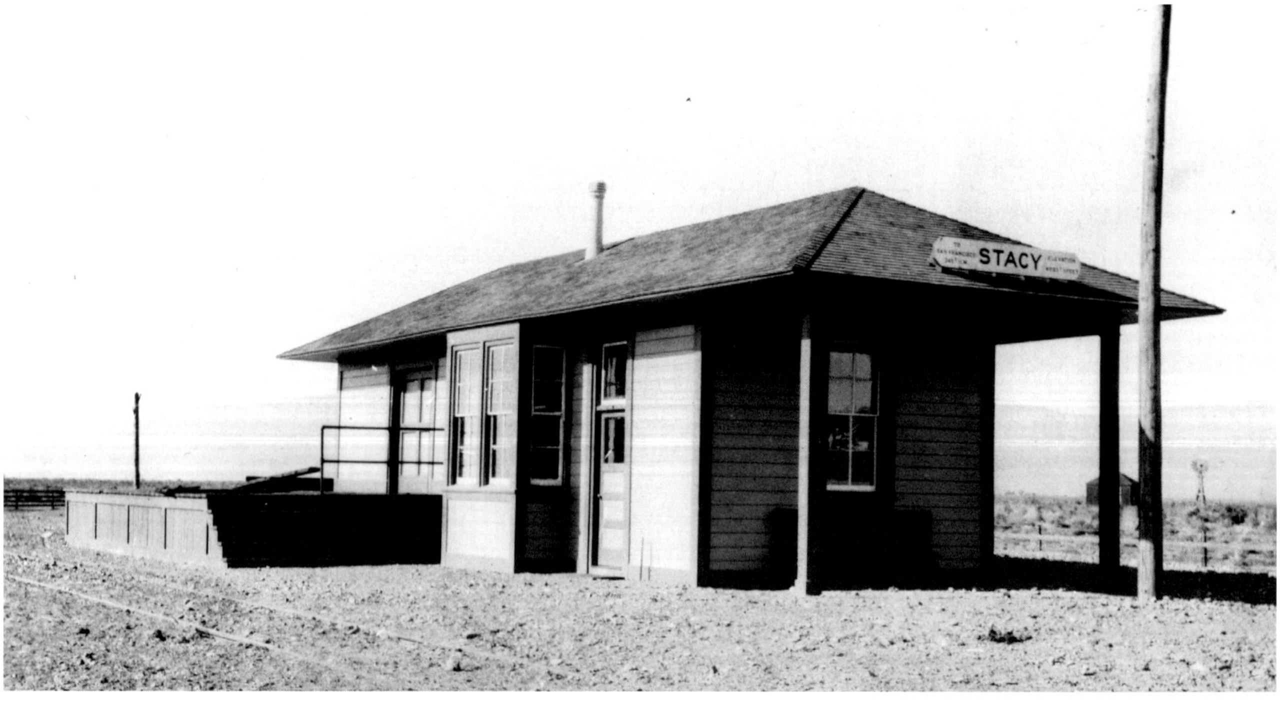

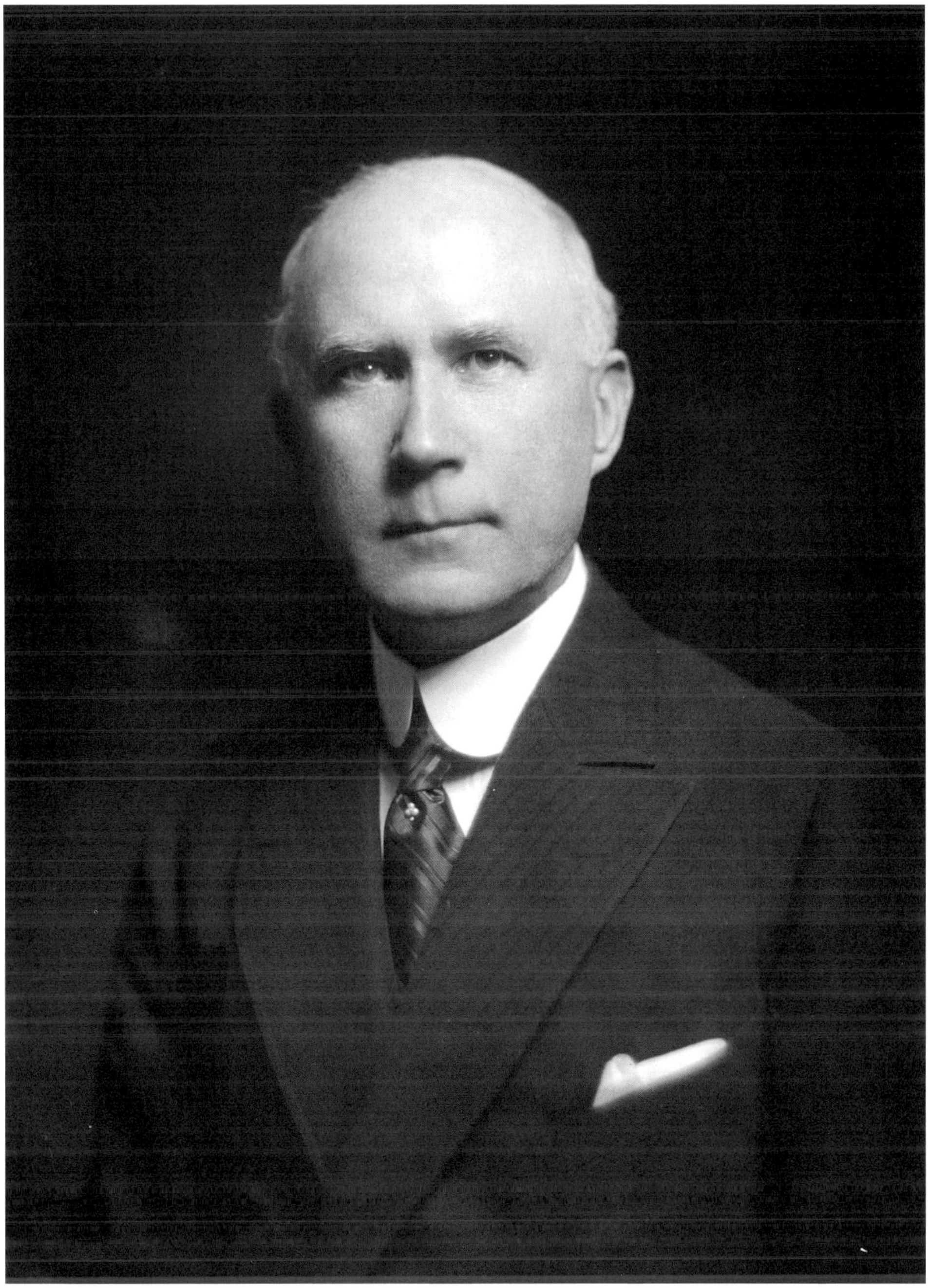

William Sproule, president of Southern Pacific from 1911 through 1928 except for two years during World War I, visited Susanville and Westwood several times on company business.

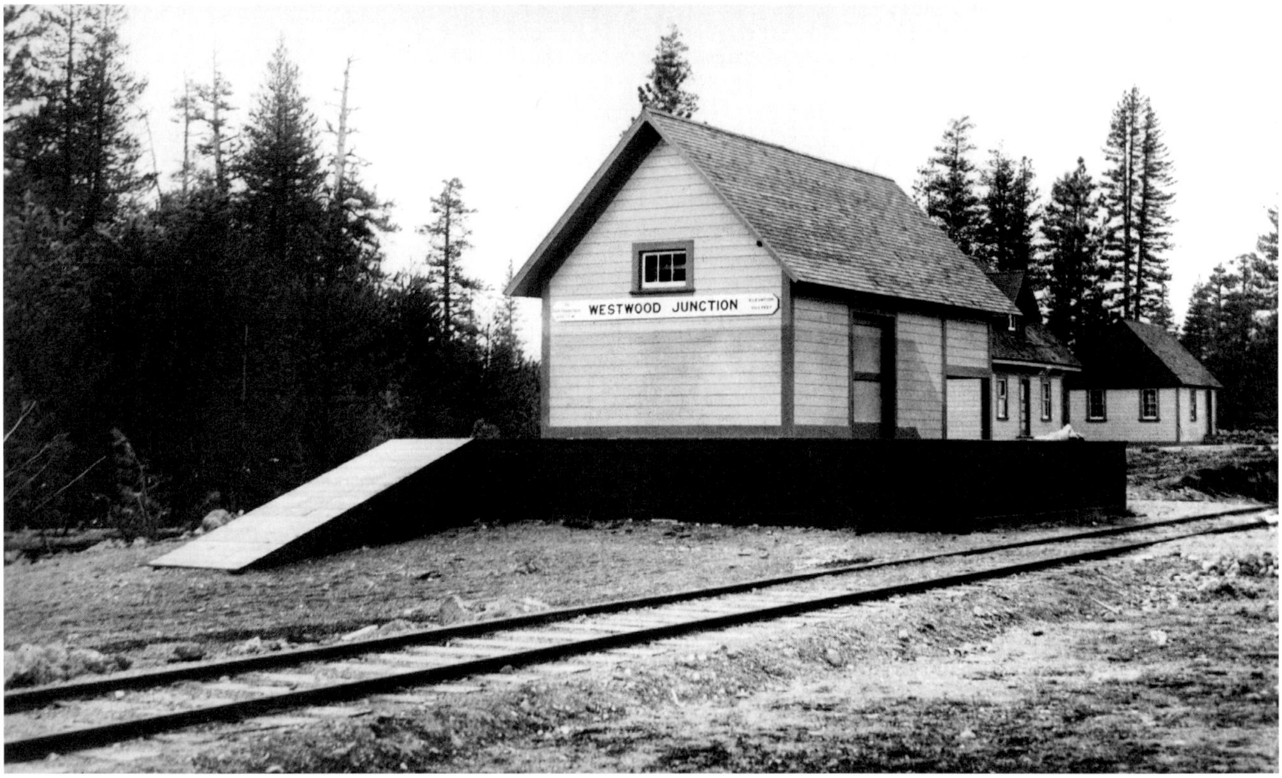

Above: Westwood Jct. had its own station and a house for the agent. Heavy snowfall necessitated steep roofs. (Southern Pacific)

Below: Westwood station marked the end of the SP branch from Fernley. The large Red River Lumber Company mill stood beyond the right margin. (Ted Wurm collection)

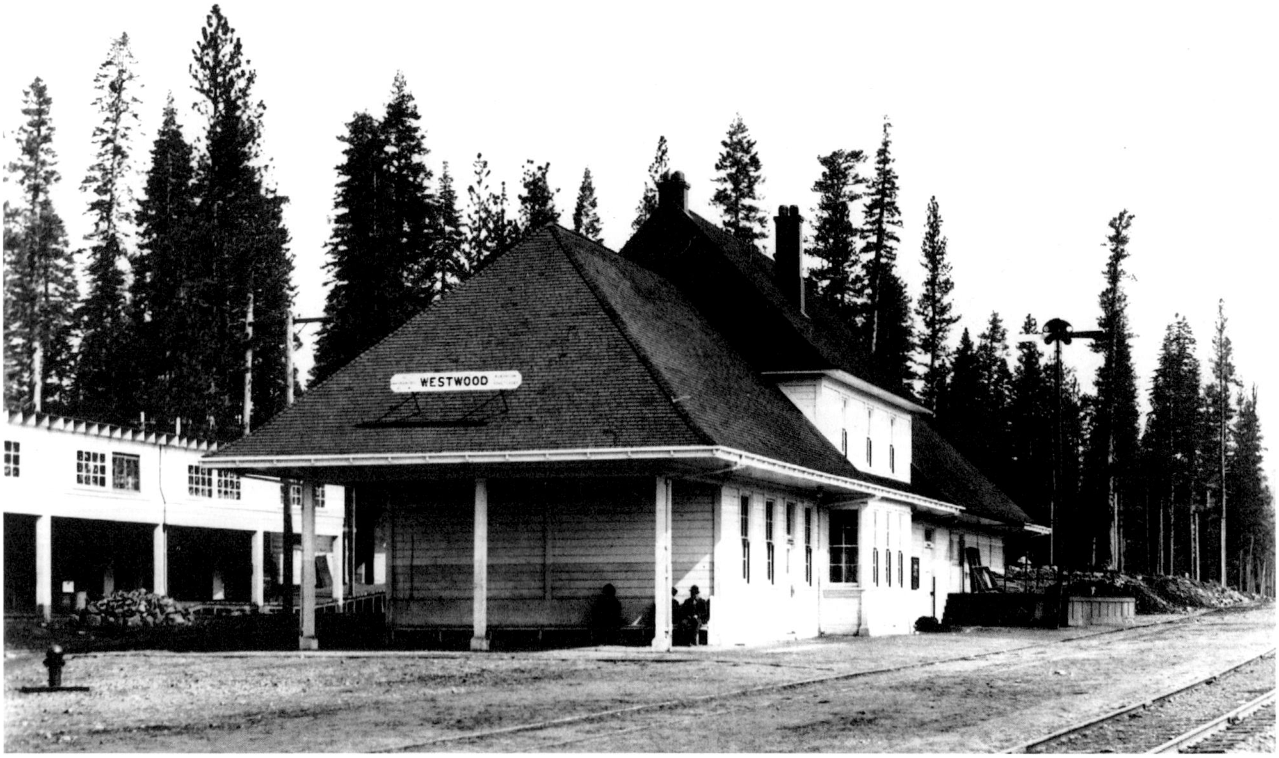

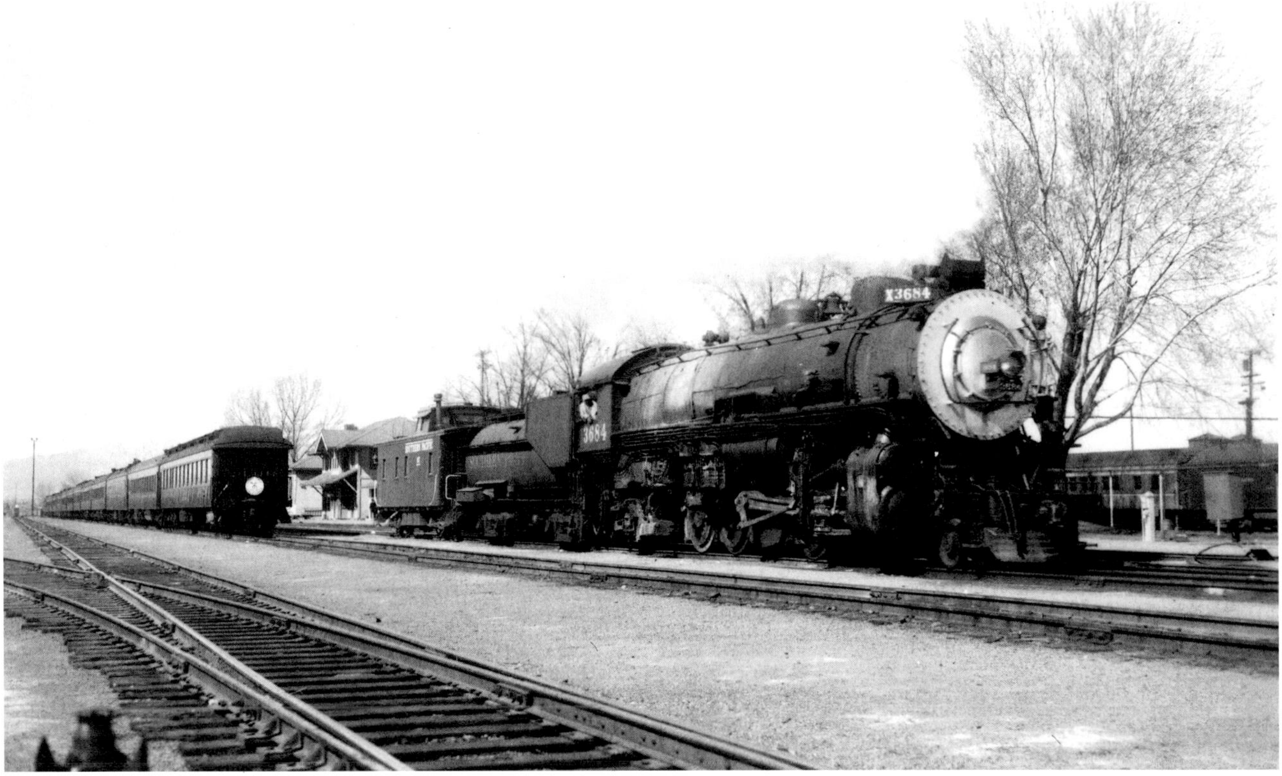

Above: During the era of the heavy eastbound lumber shipments from Oregon, "caboose hops" became necessary to balance motive power. SP 3654 (2-10-2) is about to leave Sparks for the return trip to Fernley and eventually Klamath Falls. A Shriners' special stands on the adjoining track. (Al C. Phelps photograph, 1951)

Below: A locomotive rests quietly in the Wendel yard.

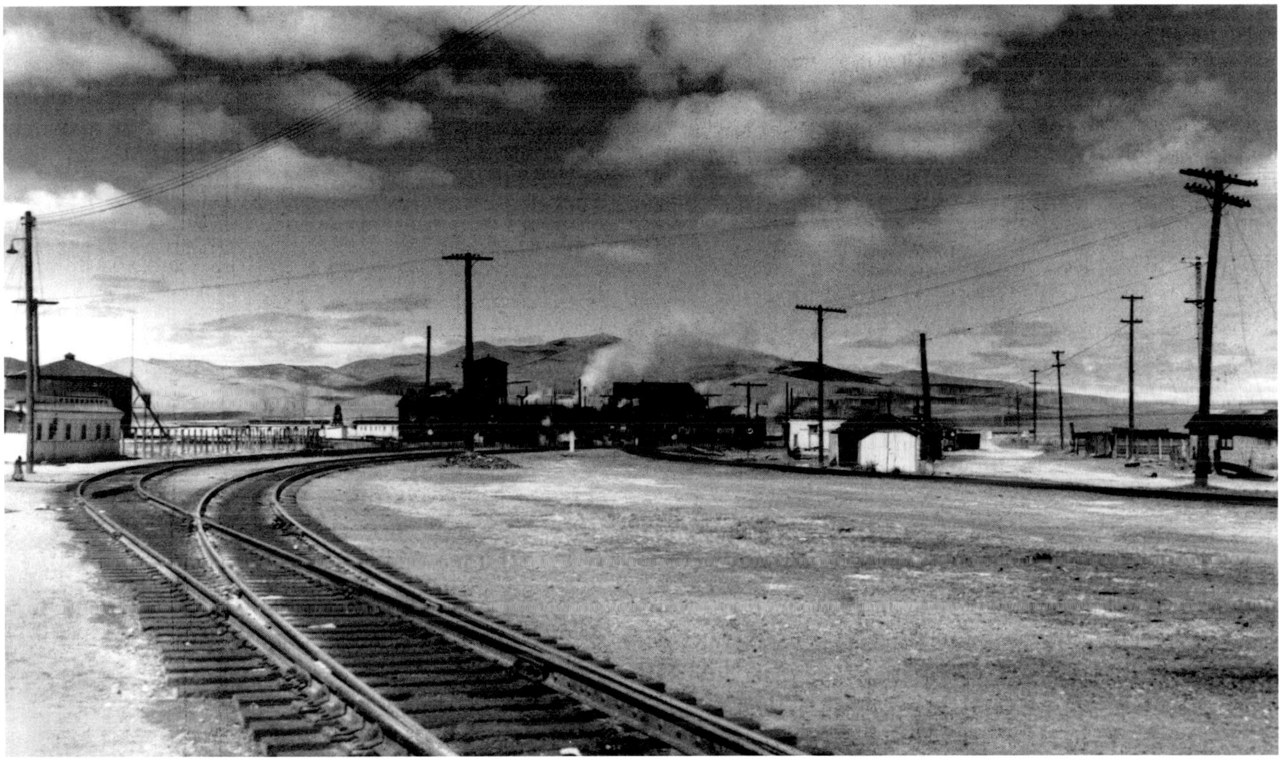

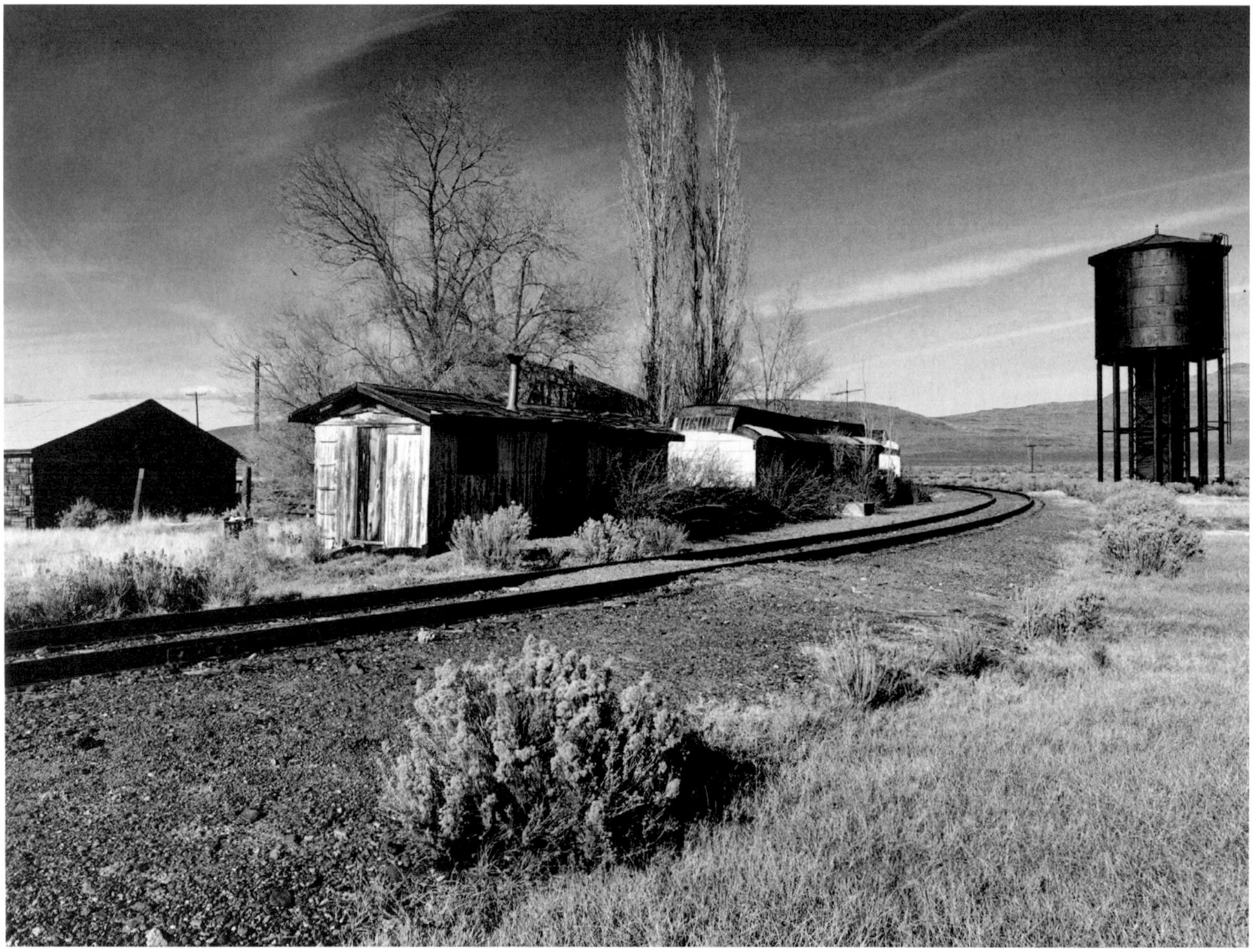

Although diesel power had long replaced steam locomotives in 1977, Southern Pacific retained water tanks at Wendel and many other points along its lines. (Ted Benson photograph)

6

WENDEL SUB-DIVISION

Capacity of Sidings in Car Lengths	EASTWARD — SECOND CLASS		FIRST CLASS	Distance from San Francisco		Time Table No. 42 April 24, 1932	Distance from Wendel	WESTWARD — FIRST CLASS	SECOND CLASS			
	554	552	22					21	555	551	557	553
	Susanville Local Freight	Northwest Special	Passenger					Passenger	Oregon Special	Manifest Freight	Susanville Local Freight	Manifest Freight
	Leave Daily Ex. Saturday	Leave Daily	Leave Daily			STATIONS		Arrive Daily	Arrive Daily	Arrive Daily	Arrive Daily Ex. Sunday	Arrive Daily
Yard PYB	8.50 PM	1.30 AM	★ 7.38 AM	276.1	TO-R	FERNLEY — 2.0 —	82.6	s ★7.55 PM	9.00 AM	7.00 PM	1.05 AM	2.40 AM
11 WP	9.10	1.45	s 7.48	278.1		WADSWORTH — 3.1 —	80.6	s 7.47	8.53	6.40	12.50	2.18
59 YP	9.33	2.03	f 7.54	281.2		DODGE — 9.3 —	77.5	f 7.39	8.43	6.30	12.35	2.03
59 P	9.55	2.23	f 8.09	290.5		NUMANA — 5.0 —	68.2	f 7.24	8.09	6.00	12.05 AM	1.42
17	10.10	2.35	f 8.17	295.5		LIBBY — 3.9 —	63.2	f 7.15			11.45 PM	1.31
61 P	10.25	2.44	f 8.23	299.4		HESLIP — 5.4 —	59.3	f 7.07	7.20	5.30	11.30	1.12
Spur 19			f 8.32	304.8		ROMOLO — 3.4 —	53.9	f 6.57				
59 WP	10.55	3.05	f 8.41	308.2	TO	SUTCLIFFE — 8.4 —	50.5	f 6.50	6.55	5.05	10.55	12.52
62 P	11.20	3.25	f 8.55	316.6		BRISTOL — 5.2 —	42.1	f 6.35	6.35	4.40	10.05	12.32
29 WP	11.50 PM	3.40	f 9.04	321.8		BIG CANYON — 4.3 —	36.9	f 6.24	6.17	4.23	9.45	12.20
59 P	12.10 AM	3.50	f 9.12	326.1		ZENOBIA — 6.7 —	32.6	f 6.17	6.07	4.13	9.17	12.10 AM
60 P	12.35	4.05	f 9.24	332.8		ASTOR — 2.8 —	25.9	f 6.07	5.49	3.56	9.00	11.52 PM
59 P	12.40	4.12	f 9.30	335.6		EASTON — 0.8 —	23.1	f 6.02	5.42	3.50	8.50	11.45
P			f 9.32	336.4		FLANIGAN W. P. Crossing — 8.8 —	22.3	f 6.00				
60 P	1.10	4.33	f 9.47	345.2		STACY — 9.6 —	13.5	f 5.46	5.17	3.30	8.25	11.20
73 P	1.40	4.55	f 10.03	354.8		AMEDEE — 3.9 —	3.9	f 5.32	4.55	3.10	8.00	11.00
POWKY Yard	2.00 AM	5.05 AM	s 10.10 AM	358.7	T-R	WENDEL	0.0	5.25 PM	4.35 AM	3.00 PM	7.45 PM	10.45 PM
	Arrive Daily Ex. Sunday	Arrive Daily	Arrive Daily			82.6		Leave Daily	Leave Daily	Leave Daily	Leave Daily Ex. Saturday	Leave Daily
	(5.10) 15.98	(3.35) 23.05	(2.32) 32.60			........Time over district........ ......Average speed per hour......		(2.30) 33.04	(4.25) 18.70	(4.00) 20.65	(5.20) 15.48	(3.55) 21.08

Westerly end of Wendel sub-division is at west wye switch adjoining Fernley siding.

WENDEL SUB-DIVISION

Capacity of Sidings in Car Lengths	EASTWARD — SECOND CLASS	FIRST CLASS		Distance from San Francisco		Time Table No. 42 April 24, 1932 Westwood Branch	Distance from Wendel	WESTWARD — FIRST CLASS			SECOND CLASS	
	620		34					33				619
	Local Freight		Passenger					Passenger				Local Freight
	Leave Daily Ex. Sunday		Leave Daily			STATIONS		Arrive Daily				Arrive Daily Ex. Sunday
Yard PWKY				411.3	TO-R	WESTWOOD — 4.1 —	52.6					
	12.01 PM		f 3.22 PM	407.2	TO-R	MASON — 0.6 —	48.5	f 12.11 PM				9.17 AM
59	12.10		f 3.23	406.6		FACHT — 4.3 —	47.9	f 12.10 PM				9.15
			f	402.3		LASCO — 2.2 —	43.6	f				
66 YP	12.53		f 3.34	400.1		WESTWOOD JCT. — 5.3 —	41.4	11.57 AM				8.45
57 WP	1.17		f 3.48	394.8		GOUMAZ — 4.7 —	36.1	f 11.42				8.15
84 P	1.37		f 4.00	390.1		BUNNEL — 8.2 —	31.4	f 11.30				7.40
Yard PK	2.10 5.30		s 4.28	381.9	TO-R	SUSANVILLE — 7.0 —	23.2	s 11.09				7.01 4.45
68 P	5.50		f 4.40	374.9		LEAVITT — 7.8 —	16.2	f 10.53				4.25
59 P	6.20		s 4.52	367.1	TO	LITCHFIELD — 8.4 —	8.4	s 10.39				4.05
Yard POWKY	6.50 PM		s 5.05 PM	358.7	TO-R	WENDEL		10.25 AM				3.05 AM
	Arrive Daily Ex. Sunday		Arrive Daily			(48.5)		Leave Daily				Leave Daily Ex. Sunday
	(6.49) 7.11		(1.43) 28.25			......Time over District...... ......Average Speed per Hour......		(1.46) 27.45				(6.12) 7.82

TRAINS BETWEEN WESTWOOD AND MASON GOVERNED BY WESTERN PACIFIC TIME TABLE AND BOOK OF RULES.

RULE S-72. WESTWARD TRAINS ARE SUPERIOR TO TRAINS OF THE SAME CLASS IN THE OPPOSITE DIRECTION.
RULE 83 (B). Nos. 33-34-619-620 may register by ticket at Mason if an operator on duty.
RULE 83 (D). Trains must obtain a clearance before leaving Mason.
RULE 104. Normal position of Junction switch at Mason for Southern Pacific track.

ALTURAS SUB-DIVISION

Capacity Sidings in Car Lengths	EASTWARD — SECOND CLASS	FIRST CLASS	Distance from San Francisco		Time Table No. 42 April 24, 1932	Distance from Alturas Yard	WESTWARD — FIRST CLASS	SECOND CLASS		
	552	22					21	551	553	555
	Northwest Special	Passenger					Passenger	Manifest Freight	Manifest Freight	Oregon Special
	Leave Daily	Leave Daily			STATIONS		Arrive Daily	Arrive Daily	Arrive Daily	Arrive Daily
POWKY Yard	6.20 AM	10.20 AM	358.7	TO-R	WENDEL — 7.0 —	98.2	s 5.10 PM	2.35 PM	10.15 PM	4.15 AM
75 P	6.46	f 10.37	365.7		VIEWLAND — 9.0 —	91.2	f 4.54	2.05	9.48	3.48
64 WP	7.15	s 10.52	374.7		KARLO — 8.9 —	82.2	s 4.35	1.30	9.15	3.13
74 P	8.05	f 11.11	383.6		SECRET — 4.4 —	73.3	f 4.18	1.05	8.50	2.46
Spur 10 P		f 11.21	388.0		HORSE LAKE — 4.5 —	68.9	f 4.09			
65 YP	8.50	f 11.31	392.5	TO	CREST — 5.4 —	64.4	f 4.00	12.25 PM	8.15	2.10
82 WPOYT	9.10	s 11.44	397.9	TO	RAVENDALE — 6.8 —	59.0	s 3.47	11.44 AM	7.30	1.52
Spur 8 P	9.30	s 11.56 AM	404.7		TERMO — 14.2 —	52.2	s 3.34	10.40	6.50	1.30
100 WYP	10.10	s 12.19 PM	418.9	TO	MADELINE — 4.4 —	38.0	s 3.12	10.10	6.20	12.20 AM
71 YP	10.35	f 12.28	423.3		SAGE HEN — 10.7 —	33.6	f 3.03	9.50	6.00	11.50 PM
77 W	11.20	f 12.55	434.0		INDIAN CAMP — 4.7 —	22.9	f 2.36	8.50	5.00	11.00
123 YOWTKP	11.50 AM	s 1.10	438.7	TO	LIKELY — 3.2 —	18.2	s 2.24	8.20	4.30	10.35
Spur 7	12.25 PM	f 1.17	441.9		WIDGEON — 1.7 —	15.0	f 2.15	8.00	4.00	10.15
Spur 12 P	12.35	f 1.21	443.6		BAYLEY — 12.0 —	13.3	f 2.12	7.50	3.45	10.05
6 P	1.15	f 1.45	455.6		PAOLA — 1.3 —	1.3	f 1.54	6.55	3.10	9.10
POWYK Yard	1.30 PM	s 1.50 PM	456.9	TO-R	ALTURAS YARD	0.0	1.50 PM	6.45 AM	3.00 PM	9.00 PM
	Arrive Daily	Arrive Daily			(98.2)		Leave Daily	Leave Daily	Leave Daily	Leave Daily
	(7.10) 13.84	(3.30) 28.05			......Time over District...... ......Average speed per hour......		(3.20) 29.06	(7.50) 12.66	(7.15) 13.68	(7.15) 13.68

SCHEDULE TIME AND TRAIN ORDERS OF TRAINS 21 AND 22 AT ALTURAS YARD APPLY AT JUNCTION SWITCH, LAKEVIEW BRANCH.

★NO. 22 AT FERNLEY WILL HEAD IN ON SIDING AT WEST END, PROCEED ON SIDING TO POINT OPPOSITE STATION, THEN BACK UP ON SIDING TO WEST LEG OF WYE, HEAD OUT THROUGH WEST LEG OF WYE.

★NO. 21 HEAD IN THROUGH WEST LEG OF WYE TO SIDING BACK UP ON SIDING TO POINT OPPOSITE STATION. THEN HEAD OUT THROUGH CROSS OVER WEST OF STATION SECOND PARAGRAPH OF RULE 5 WILL APPLY AT THIS CROSS OVER.

ADDITIONAL STOPS:—NOS. 21 AND 22 WILL STOP ON FLAG AT ARMSTRONG ROAD CROSSING M. P. 448.7.
AT SECTION HEADQUARTERS NEAR M. P. 412.4.
AT PYRAMID POST OFFICE M. P. 319.6.

EASTWARD — MINA SUB-DIVISION — WESTWARD

Capacity of sidings in car lengths	SECOND CLASS		Distance From San Francisco		Time Table No. 42 April 24, 1932 Moundhouse Branch	Distance from Churchill	THIRD CLASS		
		610					609		
		Mixed					Mixed		
		Lv. Tuesday Thursday Saturday			STATIONS		Ar. Monday Wednesday Friday		
Yard BPOT		10.25 AM	342.4	R	MOUND HOUSE — 3.4 —	26.0	s 3.10 PM		
Spur 4			339.0		GOLDY — 2.6 —	22.6			
9 KPW		s 10.55	336.4	TO	DAYTON — 2.3 —	20.0	s 2.35		
Spur 4			334.1		RANDALL — 3.9 —	17.7			
Spur 5		f	330.2		CANTY — 2.8 —	13.8	f		
Spur 1		f	327.4		SPUR A — 2.6 —	11.0	f		
Spur 1		f 11.42 AM	324.8		CLIFTON — 2.5 —	8.4	f 1.40		
Spur 2		f	322.3		LYON — 1.6 —	5.9	f		
Spur 2		f	320.7		TUGELA — 4.3 —	4.3	f		
POY		s 12.19 PM	316.4	R	CHURCHILL	0.0	1.00 PM		
		Arr. Tuesday Thursday Saturday			(26.0)		Lv. Monday Wednesday Friday		
		(1.54) 13.68			......Time over District...... ......Average speed per hour......		(2.10) 12.00		

SP's Alturas Subdivision follows part of the former narrow-gauge Nevada-California-Oregon Railway. The Wendel Subdivision was built by the Fernley and Lassen Railway, an SP subsidiary.

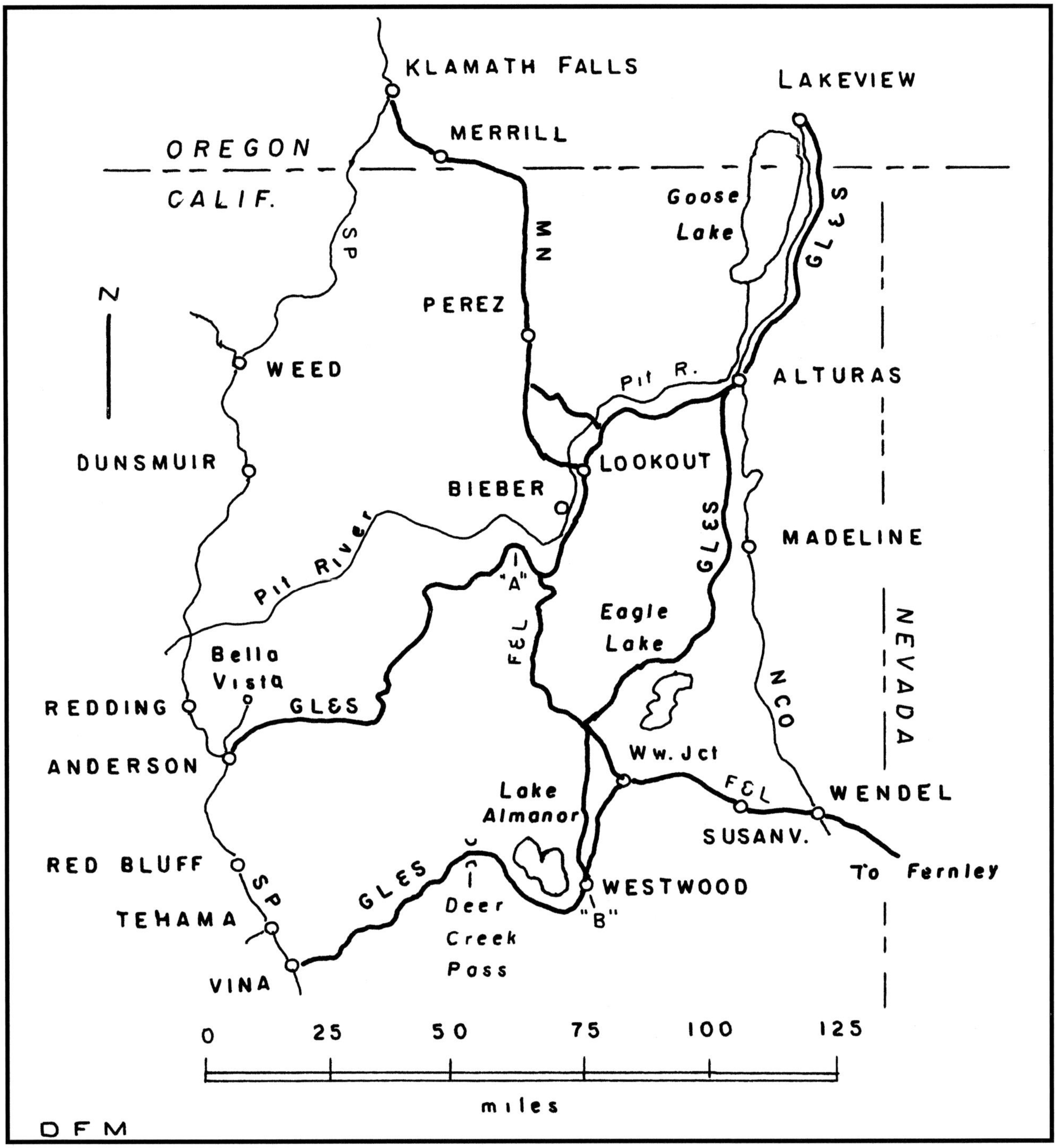

Between 1905 and 1912, Southern Pacific made extensive surveys in northeastern California and formed three railroad companies to build several lines. The Modoc Northern (MN) surveys ran north from Lookout to Klamath Falls, while the Goose Lake and Southern (GL&S) projected railroads from Lakeview to Anderson and from Alturas to Vina as well as Westwood (point B).

The Fernley and Lassen Railway (F&L), beginning at Fernley, Nevada, headed westward to Westwood, California (point B on the map), and reached northerly to a proposed connection with the GL&S at the Lassen-Shasta County lines (point A). The GL&S also made surveys duplicating those of the F&L and also engaged in preliminary surveys in Shasta County on the south side of the Pit River between point A and Bella Vista.

All three corporations were merged into the Central Pacific Railway on February 29, 1912. The Fernley and Lassen Railway was constructed from Fernley to Susanville and Westwood during 1912–1914. Following a slightly different route, the link between Klamath Falls and Alturas opened in 1929.

MODOC NORTHERN RAILWAY AND GOOSE LAKE AND SOUTHERN RAILWAY

The area lying east of the Cascade Range in California, Nevada, and Oregon suffers from the absence of rain found in bountiful quantities on the west side of the mountains. Consequently, few railroad promoters were drawn to the area except those seeking a northern entry into California, or, in the case of Southern Pacific, its officials envisioned a short route across this land for Oregon traffic headed for the Ogden gateway. Still, the Cascades invited promoters to harvest the timber.

In an interview with the *Sacramento Bee* in October 1908, H. V. Gates recounted his hazy recollections of a survey he had made for the Oregon Short Line (Union Pacific) in 1889. Over a period of many months, the survey began at Boise, Idaho, ran west to Ontario, Oregon, and after entering California followed the Pit River to the Sacramento Valley, terminating at Anderson or Red Bluff, both points on SP's Shasta Route. According to Gates, the grade proved so favorable that after spending two days with Jay Gould and S. H. H. Clark, then controlling the destinies of Union Pacific, he gained the impression that Gould would soon authorize its construction. Subsequently, Gould died at the age of fifty-eight, which ended the project.

In July 1901, two parties retraced the early footsteps, but their surveys were shelved until around 1905 when management took another look, only to be set back by the San Francisco earthquake and fire the next year. An economic slump postponed renewed consideration until the spring of 1908 when Southern Pacific proposed a cluster of railroads reaching south from Klamath Falls and Lakeview, Oregon, to Vina and Anderson, California, and Fernley, Nevada. Some projected routes overlapped each other.

The Goose Lake and Southern Railway (GL&S), incorporated April 30, 1908, the first in this series, had extensive plans. Starting at Lakeview, Oregon, its line went to Alturas before heading for two destinations. The first went westerly to Lookout and then followed the Pit River and Cow Creek for some distance before ending near Anderson, in the Sacramento Valley. The second route, commencing at Alturas, paralleled the N-C-O Railway to Madeline before turning southwest for Westwood, and following Deer Creek to Vina it also joined SP's east-side line in the Sacramento Valley. The third projection duplicated the Fernley and Lassen Railway between Fernley, Susanville, Westwood Jct., and Fall River. Had the proposed line from Alturas to Vina been constructed before 1908, it is probable that the N-C-O Railway would not have extended beyond Alturas.

During the years between 1908 and 1912, survey parties of several railroads tramped across northeastern California. At that time, SP and UP were operated together, so cooperation rather than confrontation was the rule. James J. Hill, not satisfied reaching Puget Sound, dreamed of his own rails all the way to San Francisco. Besides survey parties, each company had individual scouts scurrying from one tree to another to observe the work of competing railroads.

SP (GL&S) surveyors, led by E. E. Cooper, began running lines south from Alturas in June 1908 and in September reached Prattville (later under the waters of Lake Almanor). SP's chief engineer, William Hood, directed them to continue over Deer Creek Pass and down Deer Creek to Anderson. That fall, the Goose Lake and Southern Railway filed its location map with the U.S. General Land Office for its projected line between a point near Alturas south to the divide between Grasshopper Valley and Eagle Lake, about 25 miles north of Susanville. One newspaperman raced ahead with the erroneous report that a construction contract had been awarded to the Utah Construction Company.

The Modoc Northern Railway organized July 30, 1908, as the smaller railroad in this series to further SP expansion in northeastern California. At the first meeting, E. E. Calvin, SP's vice president, accepted the presidency of the new railroad, while the post of vice president went to William Hood, SP's chief engineer. The projected route varied from time to time; originally, it extended from Klamath Falls southeast to Alturas, but later plans called for it to link Klamath Falls with two points on the Pit River, one near Lookout and the other close to a connection with the Goose Lake and Southern at an unnamed point on a bend in the Pit River.

Observing that farmers were taking up land around Tule Lake, Calvin obtained authority to spend twenty-one thousand dollars to secure 17.15 miles of right-of-way in that area, which segment would serve the projected line to either Alturas or Lookout.

According to the file relating to the Modoc Northern, matters rested quietly until May 1910 when SP officials learned that James J. Hill, head of the Great Northern Railway, had thoughts about constructing his own railroad around the Klamath Lakes and Medford, Oregon. Both UP and SP management stood well aware of the construction of the Oregon Trunk Railway from the Columbia River southward to Bend, Oregon; indeed, UP and the Oregon Trunk forces had pitched battles in the Deschutes River Canyon. At this time, more than a year would elapse before a locomotive whistled in Bend.

While the Spokane, Seattle, and Portland (SS&P) Railway and its subsidiary, Oregon Trunk, had the backing of Hill, John F. Stevens served as president of these lines for twenty months. Stevens's career followed a peripatetic course as he went from one railroad to another, usually as assistant engineer. In all, he had been on the payroll of ten widely scattered railroads, including a few months as chief engineer and general manager of Great Northern. As head of the SS&P, he arranged for the purchase of the Pacific and Eastern Railroad in September 1909. Starting at Medford, this struggling little line finally pushed its rails into Butte Falls a year after Stevens's acquisition.

As Stevens wanted to run a connection through G. X. Wendling's timberlands near the Klamath Lakes, the two men met in Portland. As a forerunner of later events, Stevens admitted to Wendling that they had investigated a route to central California. SP field men reported that Louis Hill, son of James J. Hill, had spent several days touring the Klamath Lakes region by auto and lake steamer.

Everything seemed to break apart at that point. Stevens resigned his post on May 1, 1911, spent the summer touring Europe, and then set up his own construction company. For the time being, the Modoc Northern had served its purpose as owner of the right-of-way from Klamath Falls to Merrill. In June 1911, the Modoc Northern secured government approval of its line from a point west of Perez southeast to the big bend of the Pit River.

Southern Pacific management continued to be interested in northeastern California through 1912. C. R. Brown led a large surveying party across Big Valley and along the Pit River for almost two years before pausing at Fall River Mills in February 1912 and then retracing his steps, seeking a better grade.

Already the "permanent survey" of the Goose Lake and Southern Railway from the Oregon boundary to Alturas and southwest to Anderson had been completed; indeed, unconfirmed reports stated the GL&S had acquired some right-of-way.

The major surveying program seems to have ended in May 1912 when Brown and his assistant, A. J. Barradas, broke up their outfit at Millville (near Redding). At that time, the Fernley and Lassen Railway had commenced work that commanded a good share of SP's resources.

An important factor casting doubts over the rail project was the Bureau of Reclamation plan to dam the Pit River to store water for Sacramento Valley irrigation. Much of Big Valley, including the settlement of Bieber, would have been inundated by the proposed reservoir. An executive order withdrew lands in 1904, which angered local citizens. Congressman John E. Raker introduced legislation to restore the land to public entry, without success. Little by little the government released its hold, the most important step occurring in June 1915, to the relief of Bieber residents who had suffered four major fires in eighteen months.

Local newspaper editors sought any signs of encouragement pointing to railroad construction in that area, particularly between Westwood Jct. and Klamath Falls. Some speculated that this segment would form part of an important "behind the Sierras" route for Southern Pacific between Los Angeles and the Northwest, offering lower grades and reduced mileage.

Another "black cloud" entered the picture, as the government relentlessly sought to separate Central Pacific from its parent company, Southern Pacific Company, which made it unwise to build new railroads connecting with Central Pacific until this matter was resolved. In September 1916, at a meeting of the Klamath Falls Commercial Club, William Hood, SP's chief engineer, said SP would link that city with Westwood as soon as the lawsuit was settled in favor of SP, which he believed would be done in the fall. But it was not to be, for the litigation extended for almost a decade before SP could look at the situation.

Both Modoc Northern and Goose Lake and Southern never laid a foot of track; they were truly "paper railroads." Along with the Fernley and Lassen, all their rights were absorbed by the Central Pacific Railway on February 29, 1912. The extensive antitrust legislation then enveloping Southern Pacific suspended consideration of all work in this area until after 1923. Southern Pacific absorbed the N-C-O Railway and in 1928 widened its gauge; a year later when building from Klamath Falls to Alturas, the company made use of some of the right-of-way previously located by Modoc Northern. Ironically, much of the route surveyed between Westwood Jct., Bieber, and Klamath Falls formed the Northern California Extension (often called the HiLine) of the Western Pacific Railroad and the Great Northern Railway connection.

CARSON AND COLORADO RAILWAY

Hidden in the desert country behind the Sierra Nevada, the Carson and Colorado (C&C) Railway has long captured the interest of historians because of the remote area it traversed by its narrow-gauge tracks. Much has been written about this line; indeed, it forms an important chapter in the first volume of this series. Some additional facets constitute this chapter.

It was the Comstock wealth augmented by the early successful years of the Virginia and Truckee Railroad that enabled a small group of men to build the C&C, which some called "the narrow gauge to nowhere." After the consolidation of the three divisions in 1892, a private report indicated that D. O. Mills held 19,142.5 shares, or 44 percent of the stock, in the combined railroad. William Sharon had departed from the scene, but Francis G. Newlands, as trustee of his estate, held 11,497.5 shares, or 26 percent of the 43,800 shares outstanding, and eight others held the balance. Of the $2 million First Mortgage Bonds, Mills and the Sharon estate held bonds in the same ratios as their stock holdings. Nicholas Luning, though not a stockholder, held $200,000 par value of the bonds, with other stockholders holding the remainder. The small settlements along the way, such as Sodaville, Mt. Montgomery, and Keeler, generated little traffic. The little railroad proved to be unprofitable, and the shareholders became discouraged with the prospects of their company; probably, they looked for some means to salvage their investment.

Sometime in early 1900, Collis P. Huntington met with D. O. Mills and drafted a carefully worded document to be effective March 1, 1900. Mills confirmed that there was no floating debt (bank loans); that the directors would not declare any dividends, sell property, or borrow money; and that he would arrange for the resignation of the present directors. Mills had gathered 43,720 shares of the railroad and $1.8 million par value of bonds, for which Huntington agreed to pay $1.8 million with $450,000 to be paid March 1, followed by similar payments over the next three years with interest at 4 percent on the unpaid balance with a proportionate amount of bonds to be held as collateral. Of the remaining bonds, George Whittell held $150,000, and Mills agreed to have these transferred to SP at face value with the same deferred payment plan. Whittell had held 80 shares of stock, but the agreement failed to mention this subject.

Mina, Nevada

The first Nevada mining boom ended around 1880. With few exceptions, mining investors diverted their attention away from the state. All this changed with Jim Butler's lucky find shortly after Huntington's acquisition. Jim had trouble getting his samples assayed, as he lacked the necessary funds to pay for the work. It was not until August 27, 1900, that he located his claims. From this discovery, more rich discoveries followed, and as the good news scattered, Nevada entered its second mining boom. From virtually nothing, the towns of Tonopah and Goldfield blossomed, with thousands of people and streets lined with multistory buildings. Traffic on the previously almost idle Carson and Colorado RR soared, and a short connecting railroad soon reached Tonopah and then Goldfield. The boom caused both SP and the Tonopah RR to widen their tracks in the summer of 1905 between Mound House and Tonopah via the junction, and it created the town of Mina as the interchange point between SP and the successor Tonopah and Goldfield Railroad, which involved granting the latter road trackage rights between Mina and Tonopah Jct. It also abruptly brought to Mr. Mills's attention that he had sold the Carson and Colorado Railway too soon and at a bargain price. For several years, the Virginia and Truckee RR enjoyed forming an integral part of the route south of Reno, and when SP tried to buy the V&T, the owners set a high price for their property. SP chose the alternative of bypassing the V&T and opened it own line between Churchill and Hazen on September 1, 1905.

The V&T had added a branch from Carson City to Minden in August 1906, and news leaked out that Thomas Sayers, a railroad contractor who had made a name for himself with the Mexican Central RR as well as the Minden branch, had been engaged by the V&T to examine a route up the Carson River and over the Sierra Nevada to Mokolumne Hill and San Andreas with the goal of connecting with the Santa Fe at Stockton. Wisely, nothing transpired.

At the time of the Tonopah boom, speculators could not resist the opportunity to acquire lands needed for the interchange point, first considered at Tonopah Jct., then Sodaville and New Boston. When the two wells at Mina yielded poor-quality water, SP stretched a pipeline to New Boston Spring to meet its needs. Viewing the site today,

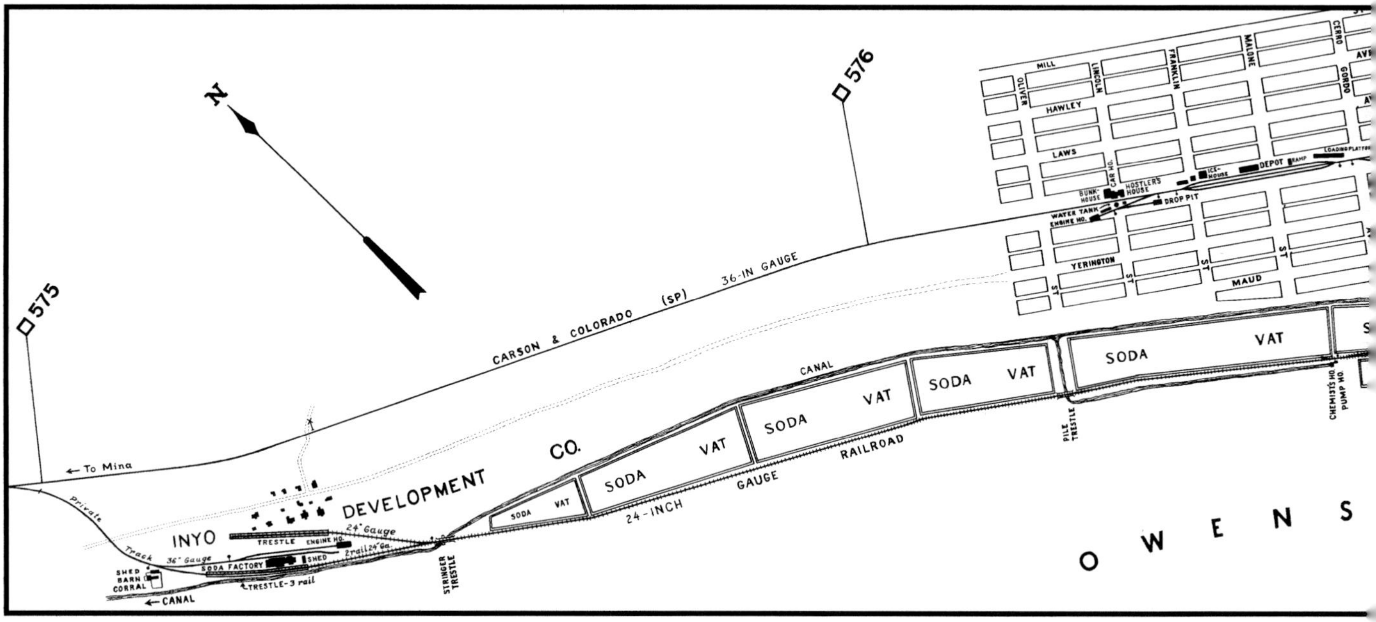

it is hard to believe the number of railroad buildings, painted in the standard ocher-yellow color, that occupied much of the settlement. Besides a passenger station, office building, freight house, and transfer platform, the railroad built fourteen cottages for its employees. An engine house, office, storehouse, pump house, and powerhouse served the mechanical department. An elevated trestle enabled cars of one gauge to dump ores to another car below.

Trackage in the Mina yard consisted of standard-gauge tracks, narrow-gauge tracks, and a combination of both, bringing a switchman's nightmare. Three tracks meant three switch points and three frogs, and all had to be lined up perfectly to avoid derailments. The switch engine assigned to Mina had three couplers at each end, with middle couplers for standard-gauge cars. Depending on the location of the third rail—right or left—one of the narrow-gauge couplers was used. As one can imagine, derailments occurred frequently.

When Tom Williamson moved to Mina in 1918 as roadmaster, his territory extended from Wabuska to Keeler. With the diminished mining activity two years later, not only did his territory expand to reach Hazen and include the Mound House branch, but he also found himself wearing two hats, for now he was also trainmaster.

In the early 1920s, an overnight train from San Francisco (Nos. 23 and 24) carried a through sleeper to Goldfield. A pair of mixed trains (Nos. 189 and 190) served the Mound House branch and part of the main line to the copper smelter at Wabuska. An "extra" local operated between Hazen and Mina. On the narrow-gauge portion, mixed trains (Nos. 191 and 192) ran between Mina and Keeler on a daily schedule, supplemented by Nos. 195 and 196, the locals between Laws and Keeler.

When Williamson was working at Mina, William Sproule made a trip to Tonopah to look over some mining property in which he had invested. As president of the railroad, Sproule wanted a local official to make the return trip to Sparks with him. Superintendent B. A. Campbell, unable to do so, turned the matter over to his assistant, who in turn wired Williamson in Mina to accompany Mr. Sproule.

Tom Williamson recalled that the president was not very garrulous, so there was little or no conversation on the trip except when the special train passed Apache siding. It stirred Sproule to ask, "Are there any Apache Indians in this area?" When Tom gave a negative reply, Sproule turned to his secretary and, telling him to take a wire to B. A. Campbell at Ogden, dictated, "You have a siding on the Mina line called Apache but as there are no Apache Indians in this area suggest name be changed." The next day—August 10, 1920—the name was changed to Appian, although there was no Appian Way either, but Tom surmised that Sproule thought he should do something to earn his pay for that day and to justify the expense of hauling his business car to Tonopah and back.

The Last of the Carson and Colorado Railway

The flow of rich ores from the gold and silver mines of Tonopah and Goldfield diminished to only a trickle, and traffic on the railroad followed a similar decline. The 50 miles between Tonopah Jct. and Benton, California, passed through the hamlets of Filben and Basalt before surmounting Mt. Montgomery Pass with an elevation of

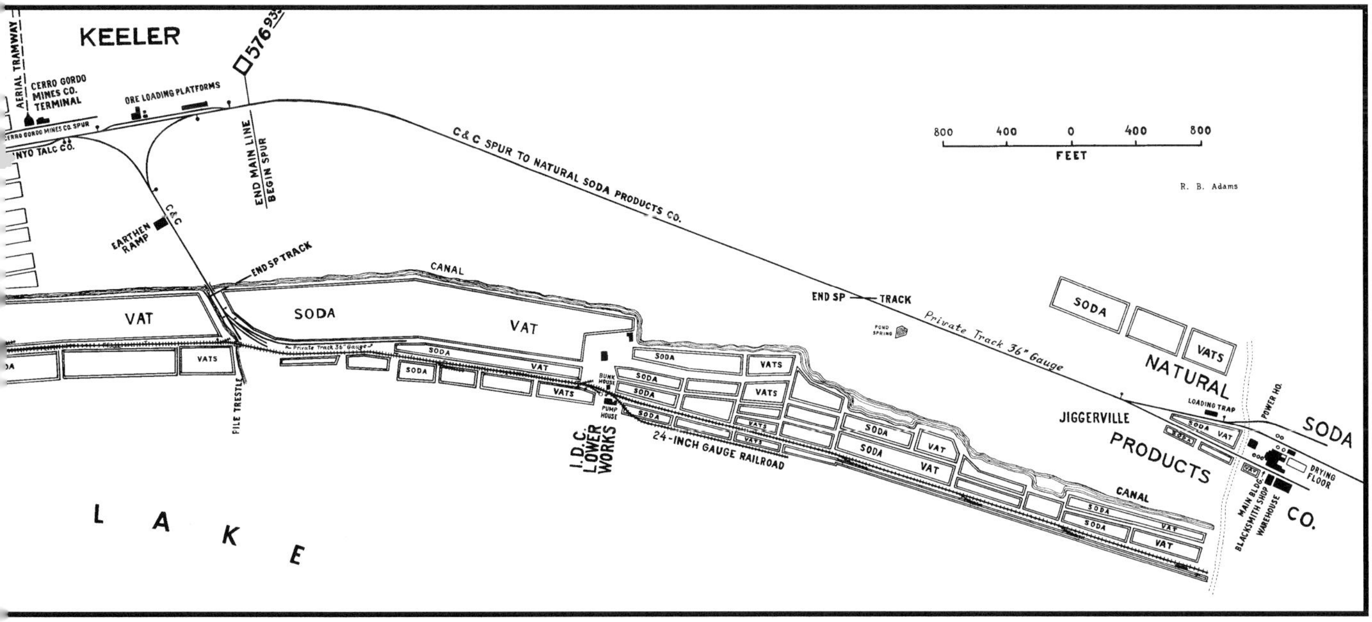

7,141 feet, almost the same as Donner Pass. Passengers on this section of the railroad, which had numbered 497 in 1929, fell to 56 in 1935, reflecting the reduction in service to a weekly train in each direction in March 1933. Even the largest locomotive available could handle no more than six freight cars and one passenger coach without a helper engine; indeed, northbound trains from Benton required additional power three-quarters of the time, and heavy trains sometimes needed three helpers.

Efforts to abandon this section were denied by the ICC in 1934, but the second attempt three years later proved successful, and the last train operated over this section on February 20, 1938. Benton then became the northern end of SP's narrow-gauge lines. (The idle rails remained in place until requisitioned by the U.S. Navy in 1942.) Five years later, railroad service over the 30-mile section between Benton and Laws came to an end. On April 30, 1960, all narrow-gauge operations ceased.

The recent years, reflecting the decline in mining activity around Tonopah and Goldfield, have not been kind to the former Carson and Colorado Railway. Little by little, it had been shrinking; since 1991, only 15 miles of the 292.8 miles of the original main line remain in SP ownership.

The 33 miles between Thorne and Mina were abandoned on September 20, 1989, so the thin populations of Luning and Sodaville no longer saw occasional trains passing by. The section between Wabuska (Lux) and Thorne (52.5 miles) entered litigation because of a long-existing oversight. As the rails of the original narrow gauge approached what became Hawthorne in early 1881, Superintendent H. M. Yerington entered into negotiations with the Paiute Indians for permission to trespass on their reservation along the east shore of Walker Lake. When the Indians sought free passage for all the fish caught in local waters, Yerington envisioned many carloads of fish moving to market without compensation for the railroad. To placate his fears, the Paiutes staged a demonstration to show him that the volume would be minimal. Taking Yerington fishing in Walker Lake, the men used bait fish or even no bait at all. After pulling in three small fish, the Paiutes acted delighted, and to be more convincing of the great catch for the day, they held a dance that night. Yerington went along with the hoax, but few fish appeared in markets. The real problem came when the original railroad owners failed to push the agreement through the U.S. Senate for confirmation.

Attention to this matter lapsed for many decades until the Paiute Tribe sued Southern Pacific and the U.S. government, charging trespass. The court approved a settlement on November 30, 1989, whereby SP and the government paid the tribe $2.2 million for trespassing damages. The Paiutes allowed the U.S. Army to take over the operation of the railroad if the Interior Department granted the right-of-way. With that accomplishment, SP abandoned operation of the line from Lux (4 miles southeast of Wabuska) to Thorne (MP 331.2 to MP 388) under ICC authority as of March 3, 1991. SP then sold the railroad to the U.S. Army on May 7, 1991. With that transaction, SP's ownership of the former narrow gauge stood between Churchill and Lux.

The southern end of the Lone Pine branch, after the 1960 abandonment of the last-operated narrow-gauge

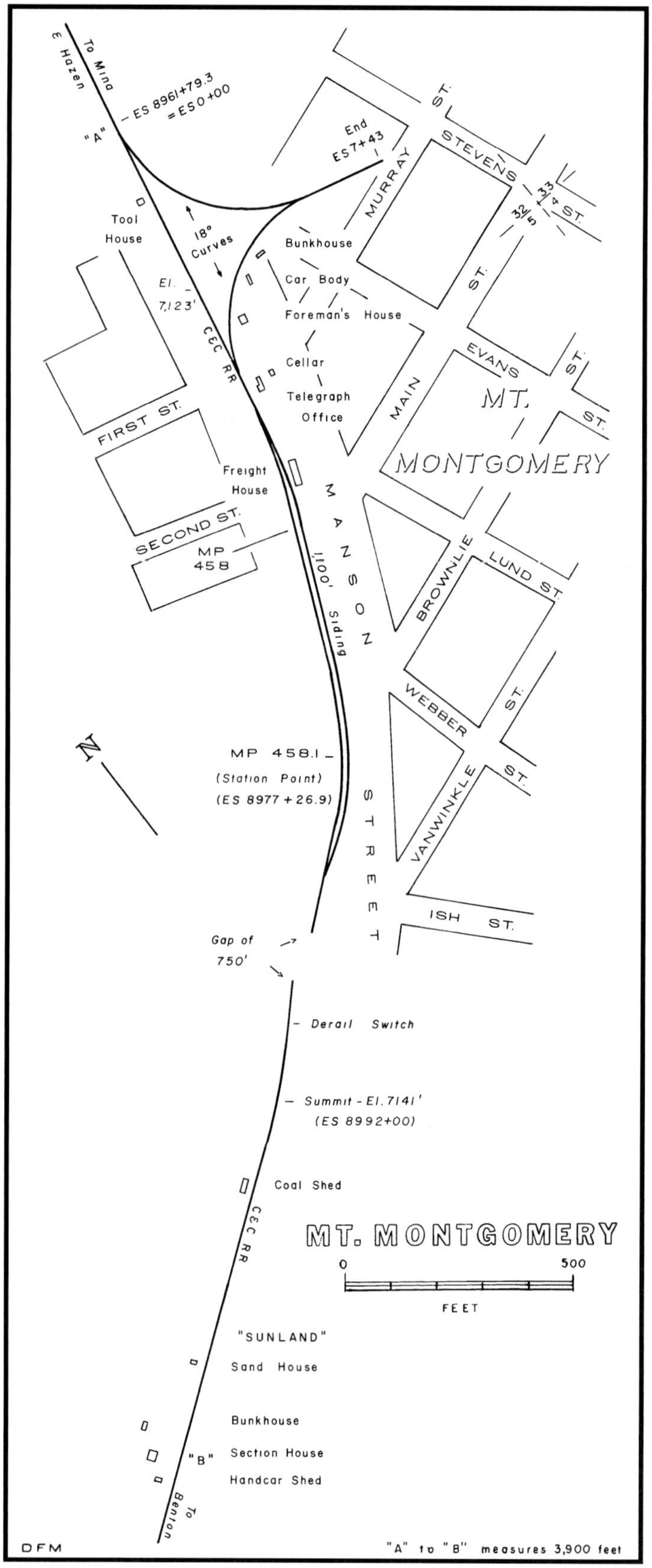

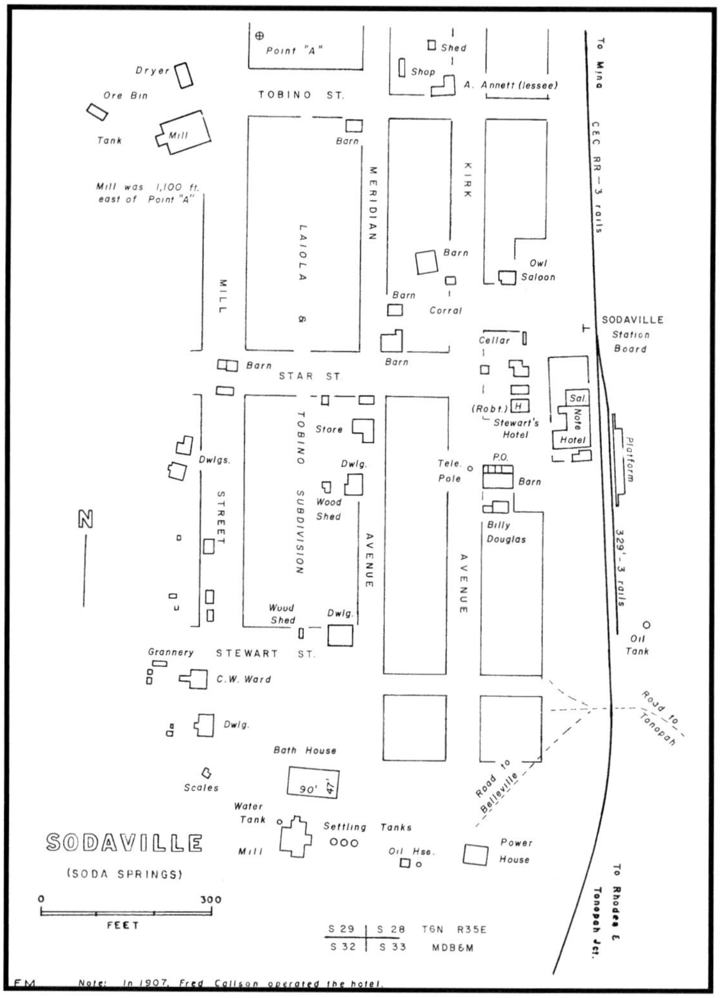

portion of the C&C, proved to be a largely idle railroad between Searles and Lone Pine. Eighty-nine miles of the northern section of the line were discarded in 1982 with ICC authority, but a Canadian mining firm convinced SP to defer dismantling the track in the hope of developing a mineral earth property near Lone Pine. With an annual payment of $10,000, SP agreed to cooperate with the mining venture, and the tracks rested quietly in place along with most of the ties—some had departed during the night to aid in the decoration of suburban gardens.

Around 1992, one firm contemplated shipping calcite from a point near Olancha, but for unspecified reasons it failed to materialize. With prospects of future need vanishing, SP engaged a Texas firm to salvage the rails of the 76 miles of line between Searles and Lone Pine.

Rapid construction necessitated the use of a shoofly track over the summit while workers drilled the 4,340-foot tunnel to reach Searles in 1908 as part of the transportation requirements of the Los Angeles Aqueduct. To reach the potash plant at Trona, the mining company

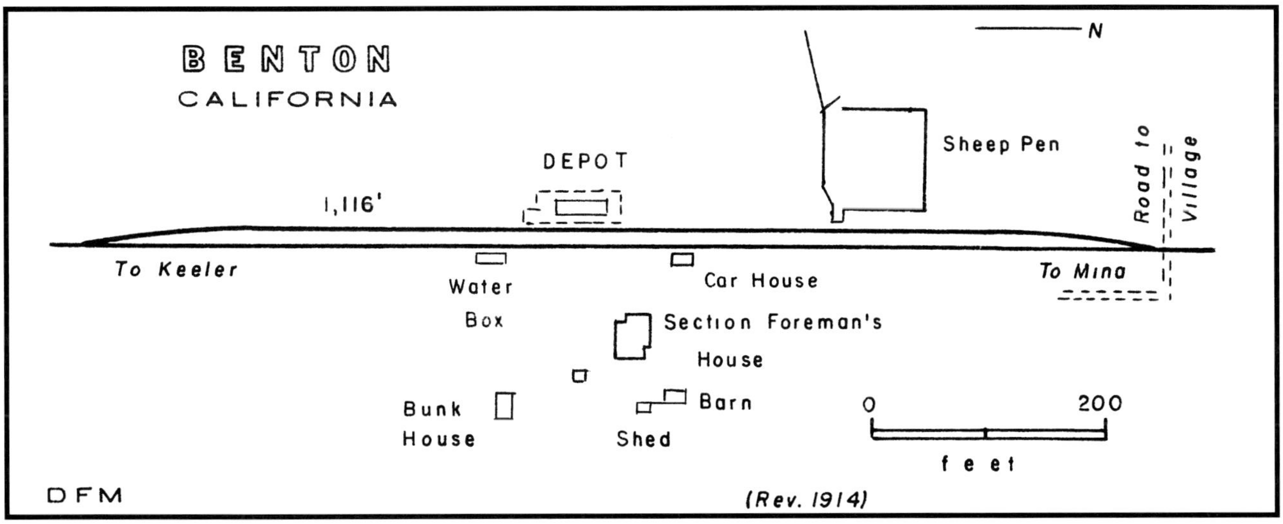

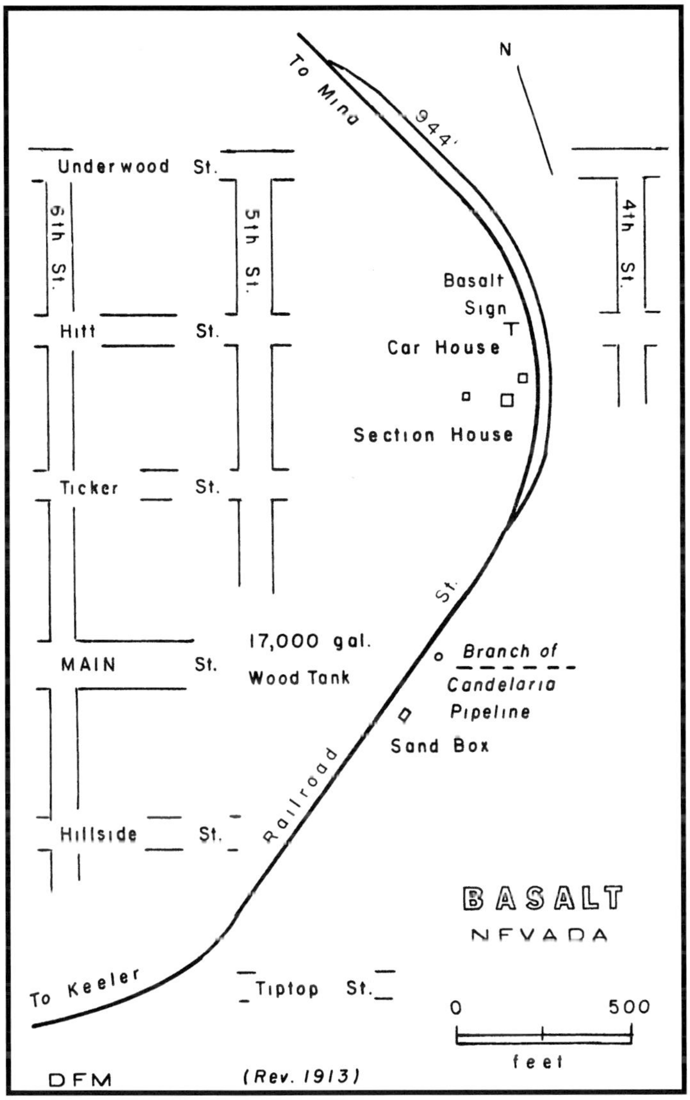

built a connection from Searles in 1913–1914, and for many years cars of potash were interchanged at Trona. On February 21, 1981, a tunnel fire of mysterious origin near Searles suspended shipments until a shoofly could be installed over El Paso summit using the same temporary roadbed of 1908. Considerable time elapsed before the tunnel interior cooled so that SP maintenance-of-way forces could return it to service. Finally, at a cost of almost $3 million, the first train went through the tunnel on July 27, 1982.

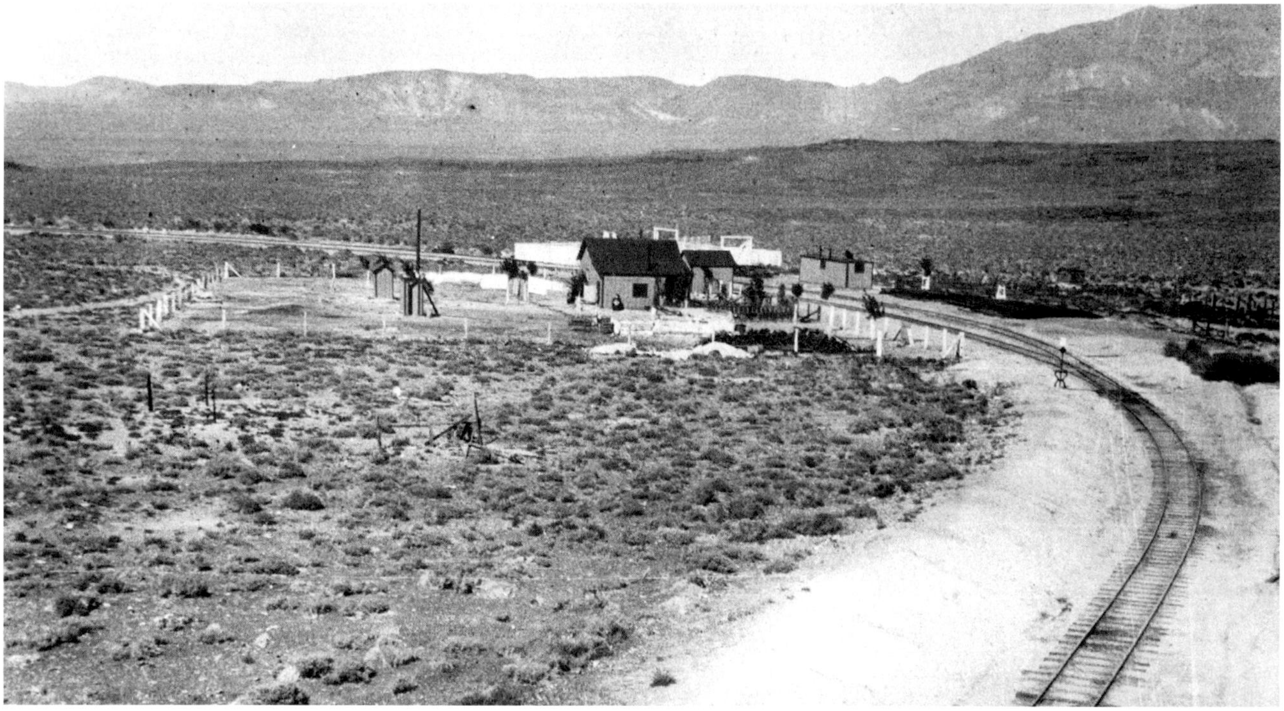

Above: Surveyors laid out Basalt, a Nevada hamlet about eight miles northeast of Mt. Montgomery, into thirty-five blocks on which only a few structures appeared. (Tom Williamson collection)

Below: Behind the station sign, supported by a neat rock base, a car house (*left*) and a section house constituted the principal buildings in Basalt. Following a long-obsolete practice, two posts support an extra rail for emergencies. (Tom Williamson collection)

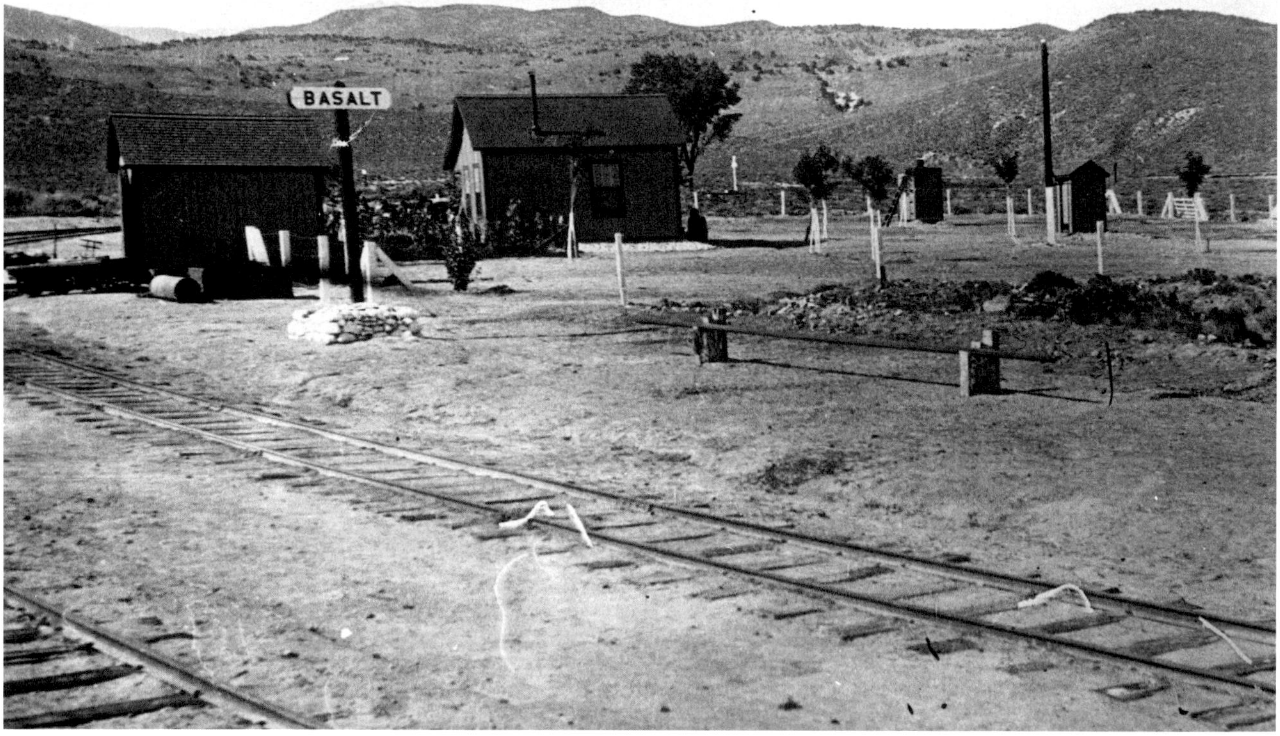

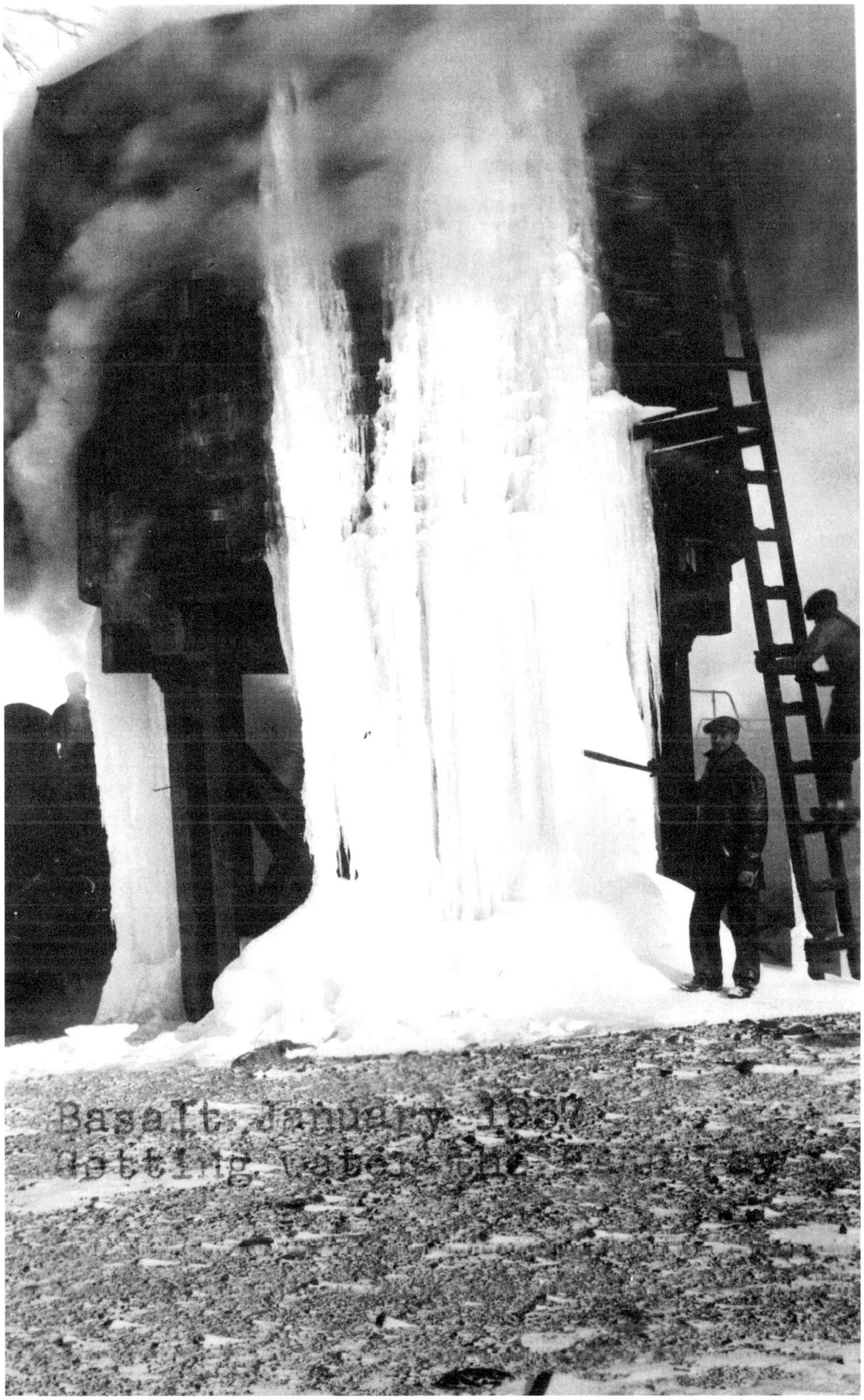

While desert summer temperatures reach three figures, the opposite extreme occurred in winter months, as this ice-covered water tank at Basalt confirms. The time was January 1937, and a year later this portion of the line became silent. (Tom Williamson collection)

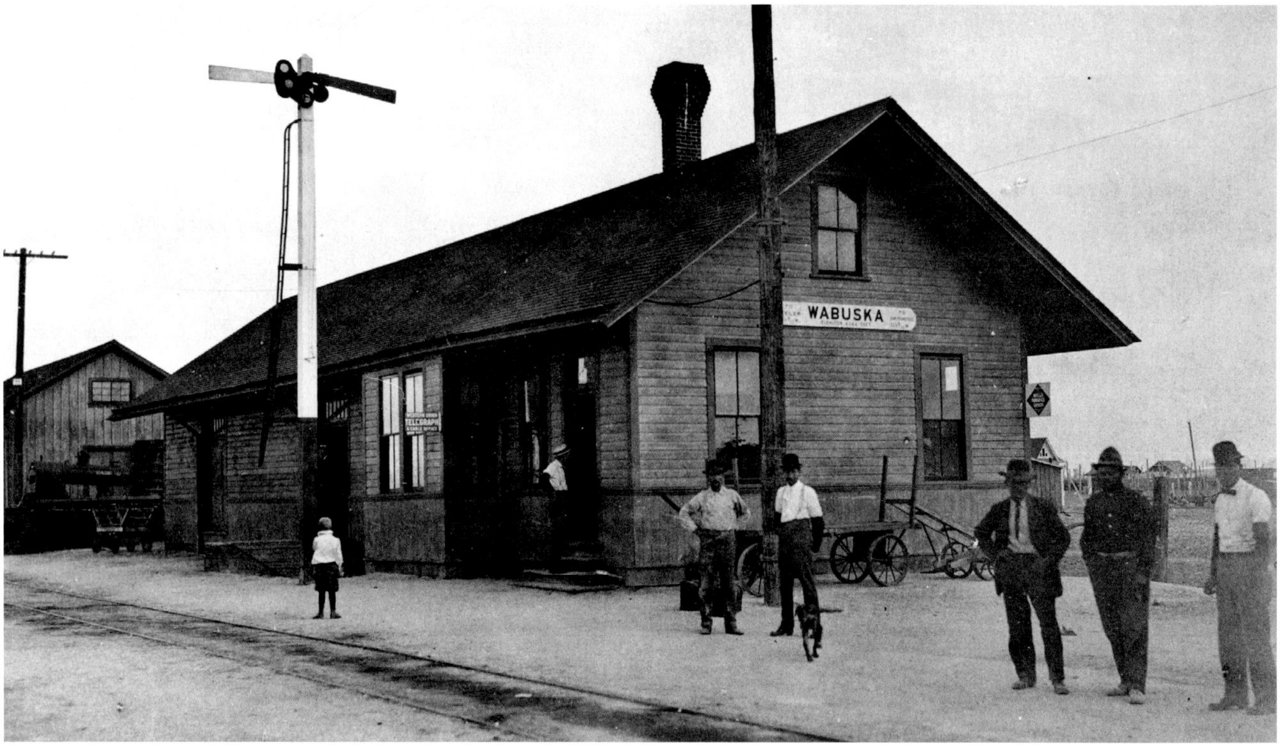

Above: Wabuska warranted a larger station because of tonnage interchanged with the Nevada Copper Belt Railroad. Perhaps these men are waiting for the mixed train between Wabuska and Dayton and Mound House that ran on a leisurely schedule in 1925. (Tom Williamson collection)

Below: When the Carson and Colorado opened its line, the firm erected two engine stalls at Hawthorne. A careful perusal of the photograph indicates a long beam on the inner door of the right-hand shed that, after being moved into the bracket of the opposite door, kept both doors closed.

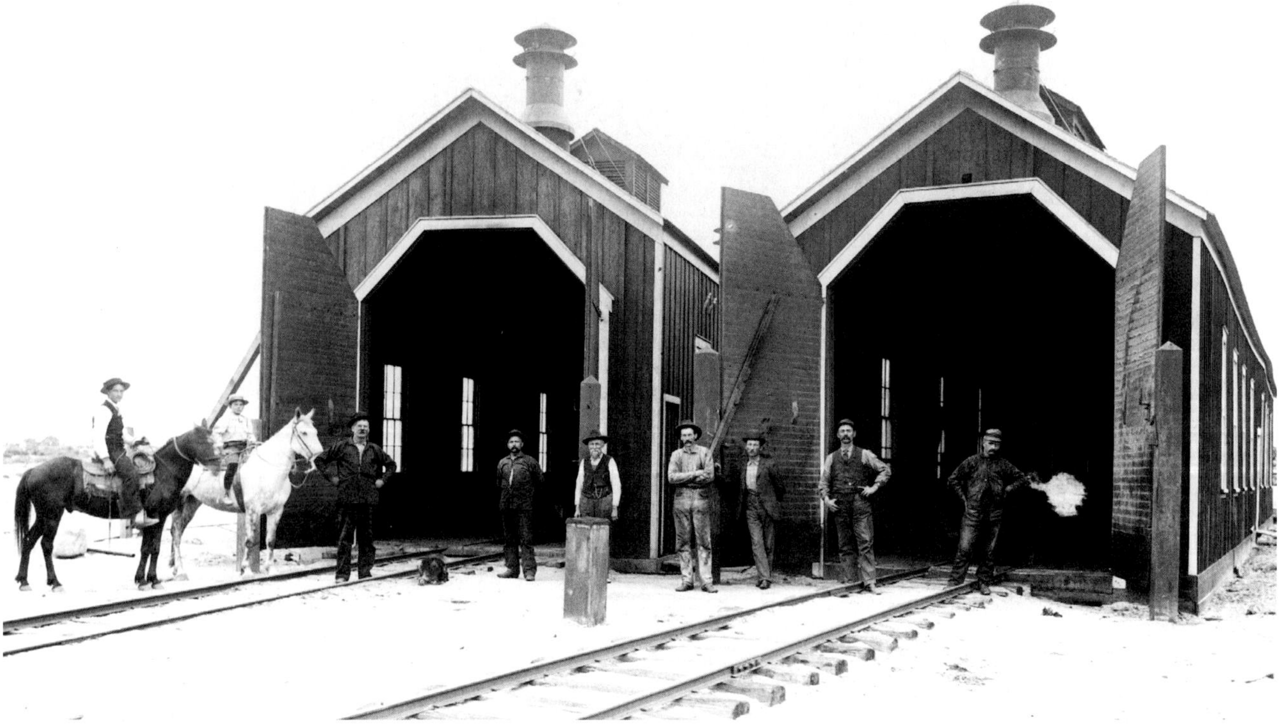

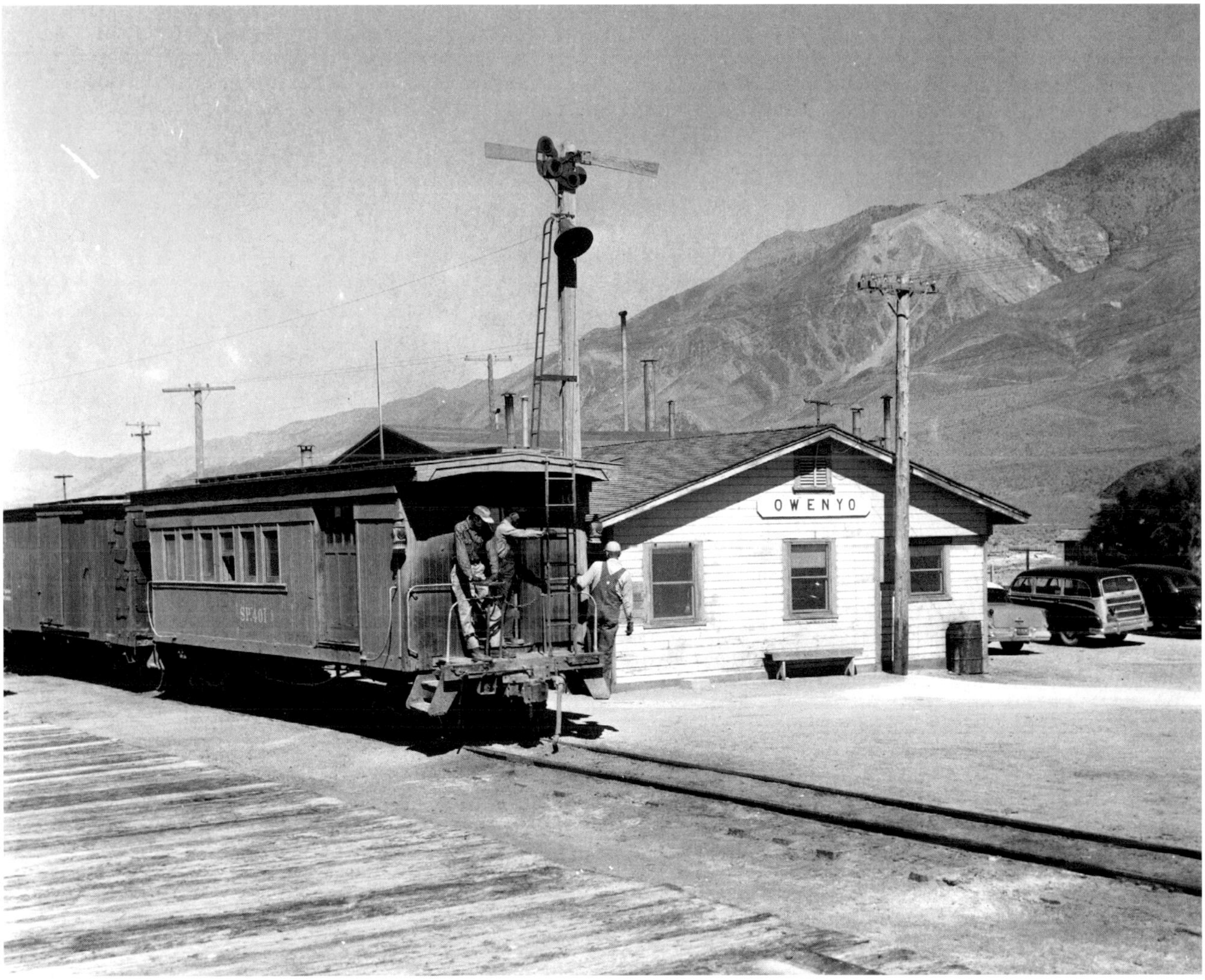

Owenyo marks the connection of the standard-gauge tracks from Mojave with the slim-gauge tracks from Mina. The old combo car found new use as a caboose. During the winter, snow blanketed the White Mountains in the background. (Southern Pacific)

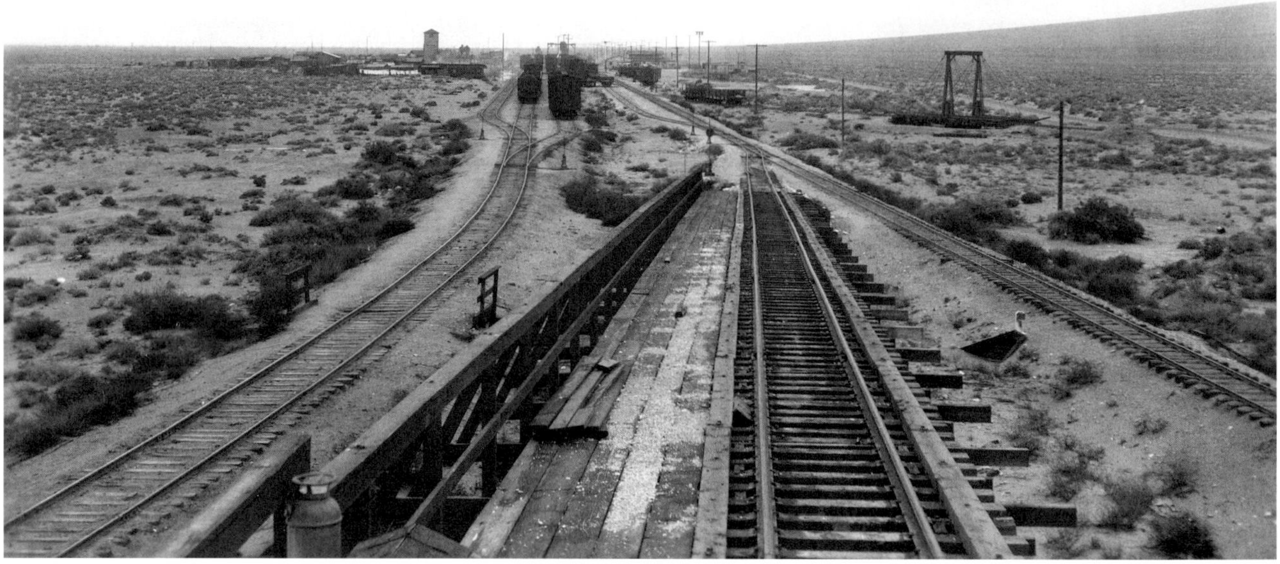

Above: A trestle with narrow-gauge tracks facilitated the transfer of ores from the smaller cars to the standard-gauge cars under the trestle. (Tom Williamson collection)

Below: Well-trained dogs accompanied workers. One held a red flag to warn engineers of unscheduled trains. (Tom Williamson collection)

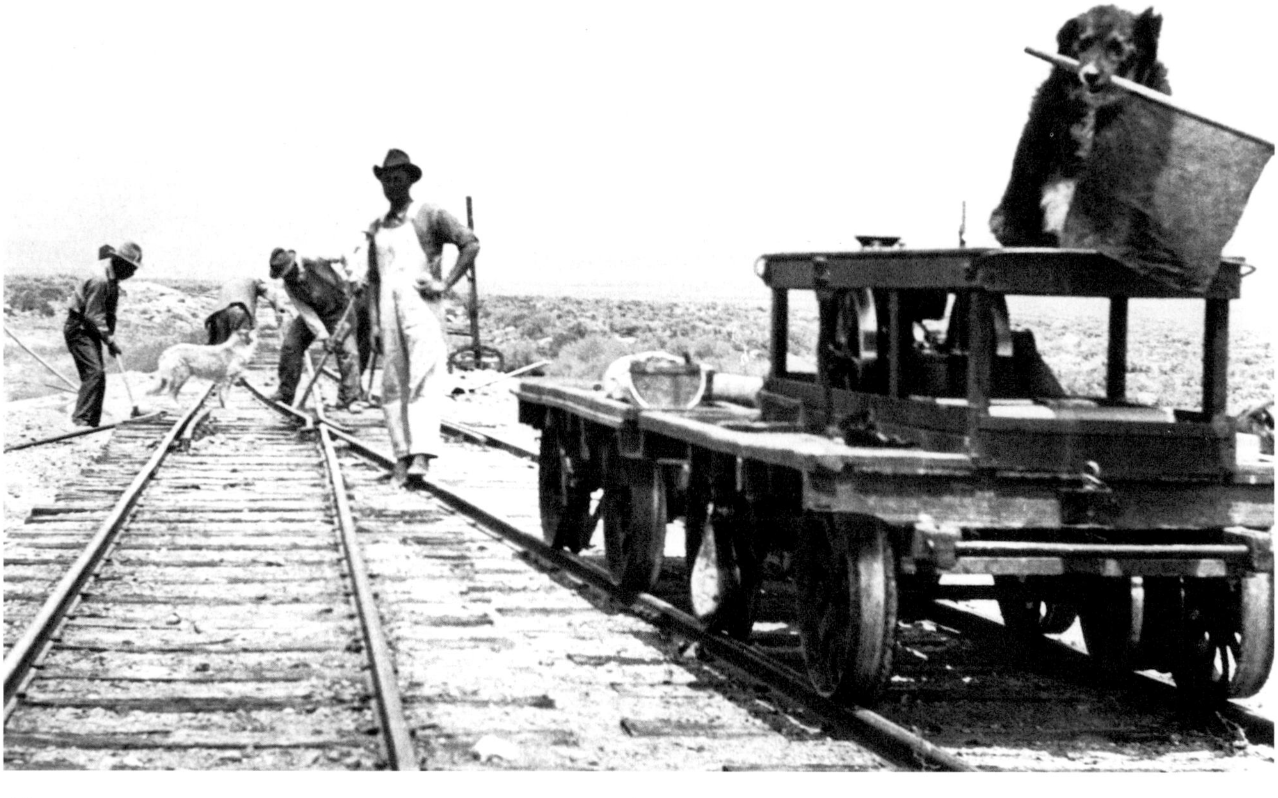

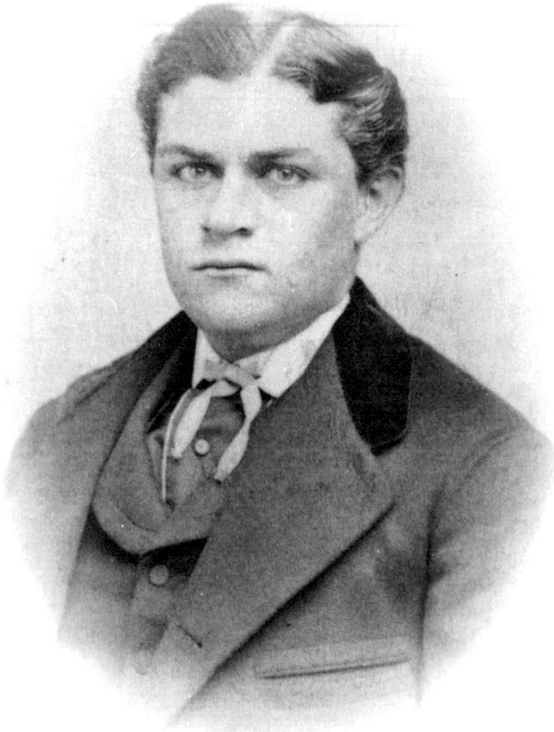

Right: Robert J. Laws, with his long career in railroading, occupies a permanent place in the Owens Valley with the town named for him.

Below: It was a cold winter day in 1921 when Tom Williamson and road engineers rode the motorcars to inspect the railroad.

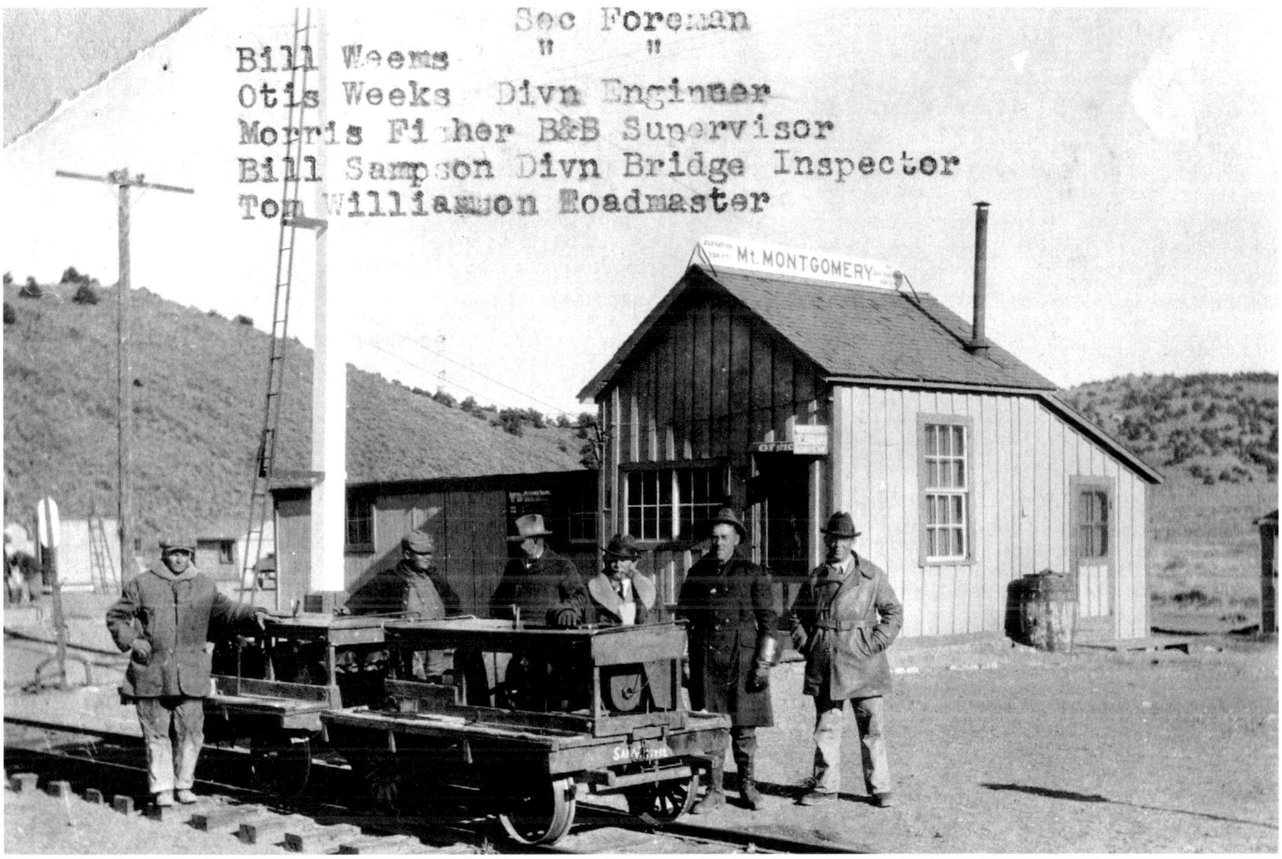

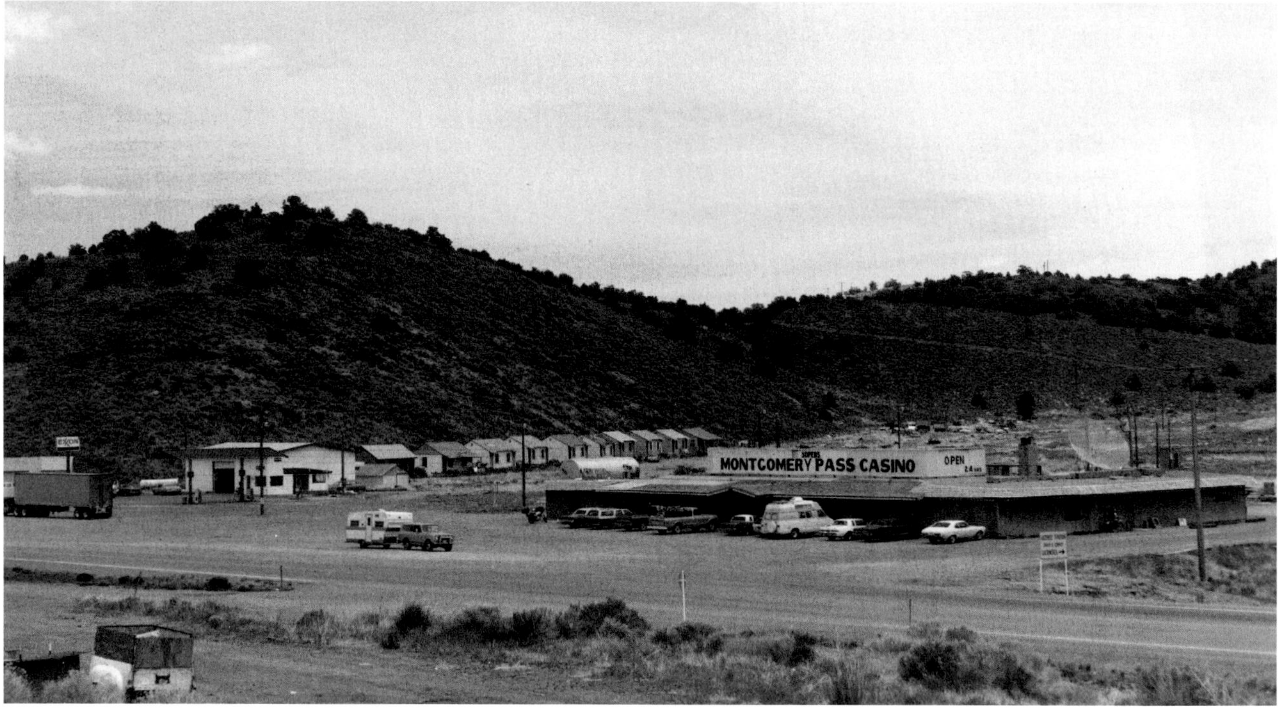

Above: Montgomery Pass had changed considerably by 1982, starting when Bud Soper arrived on the scene some twenty-one years earlier, about the time the new highway was opened. About 1965 Soper purchased the motel and built the casino ten years later.

Below: In the high desert country, Benton was typical of the lonely stations along the Carson and Colorado Railroad. Earlier mining booms had come and gone. The scene confirms D. O. Mills's famous observation: "300 miles too long or 300 years too soon." Until October 1923, patrons could purchase tickets or arrange for freight shipments in this 46 × 20–foot depot. Benton became the northern outpost of the narrow gauge from 1938 until 1942 when the second segment was abandoned. In this 1934 photograph, only the depot remained. (Tom Williamson photograph)

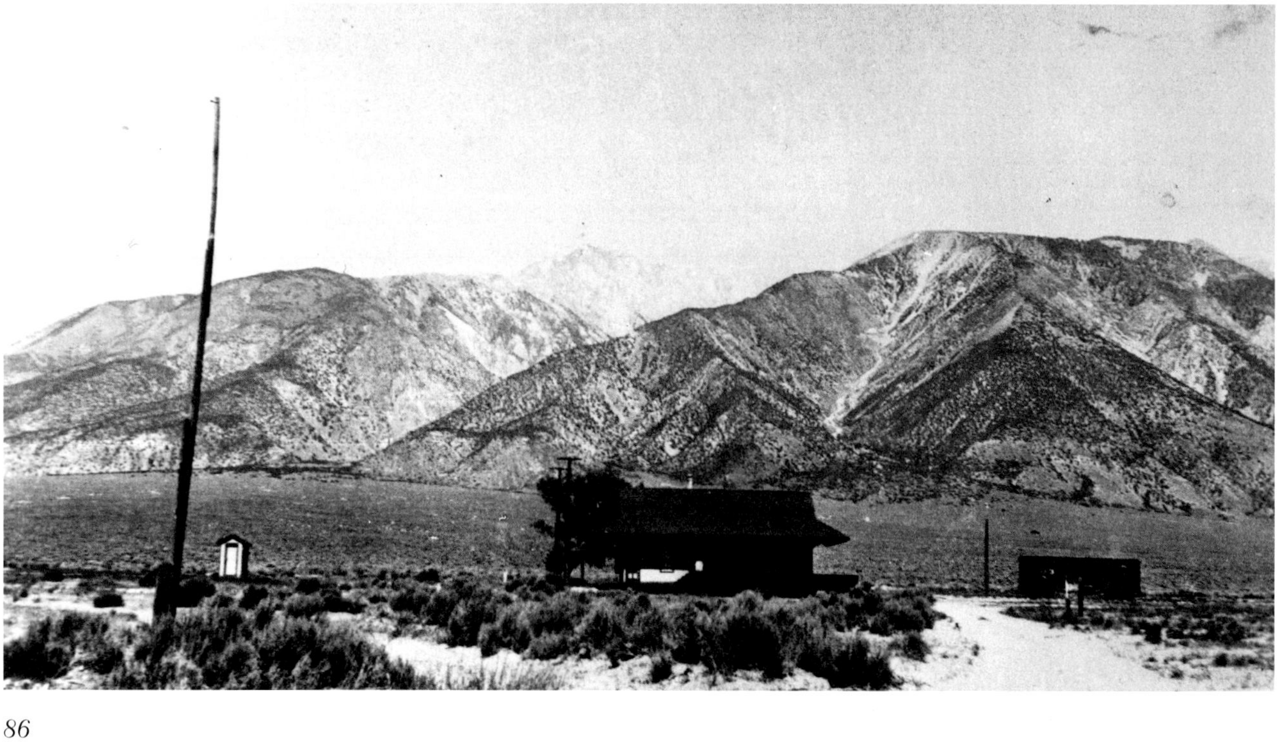

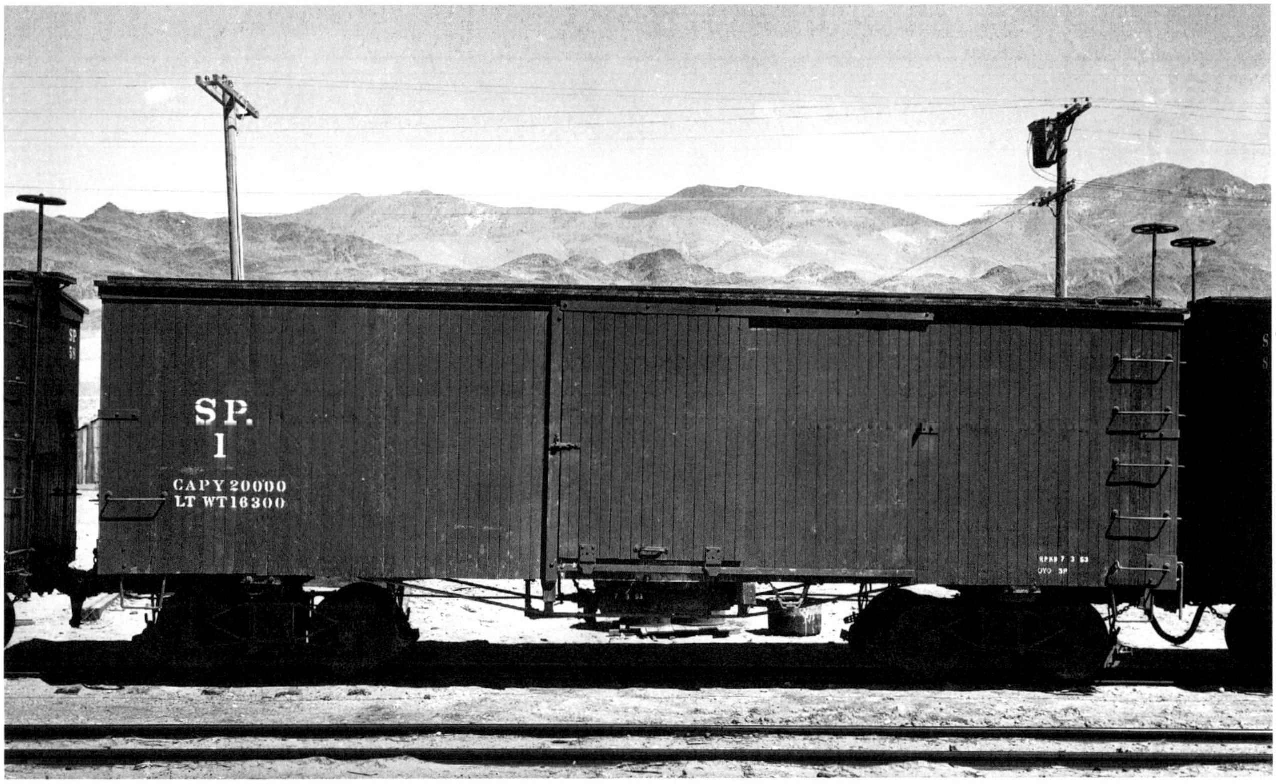

Above: While most Southern Pacific freight cars are identified by five digits, this narrow-gauge boxcar stands as the foremost exception. (Southern Pacific)

Below: A classic photograph of C&C No. 3. Carey Otis Willey is standing, but the identity of the man in the cab has been lost. (Wyoming State Museum, James L. Ehernberger collection)

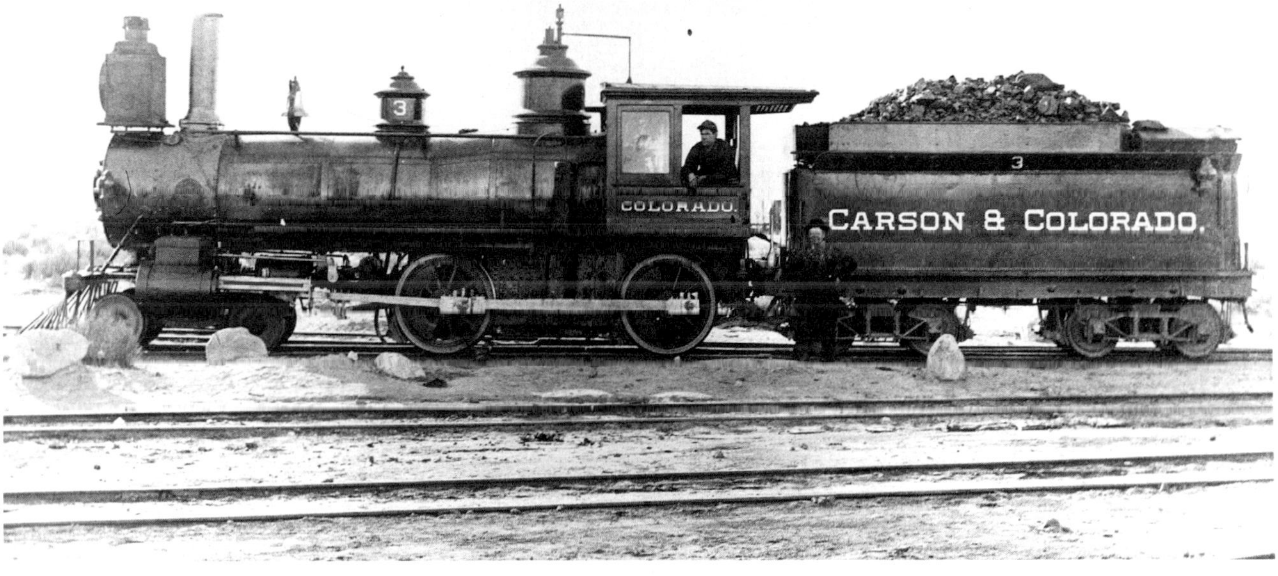

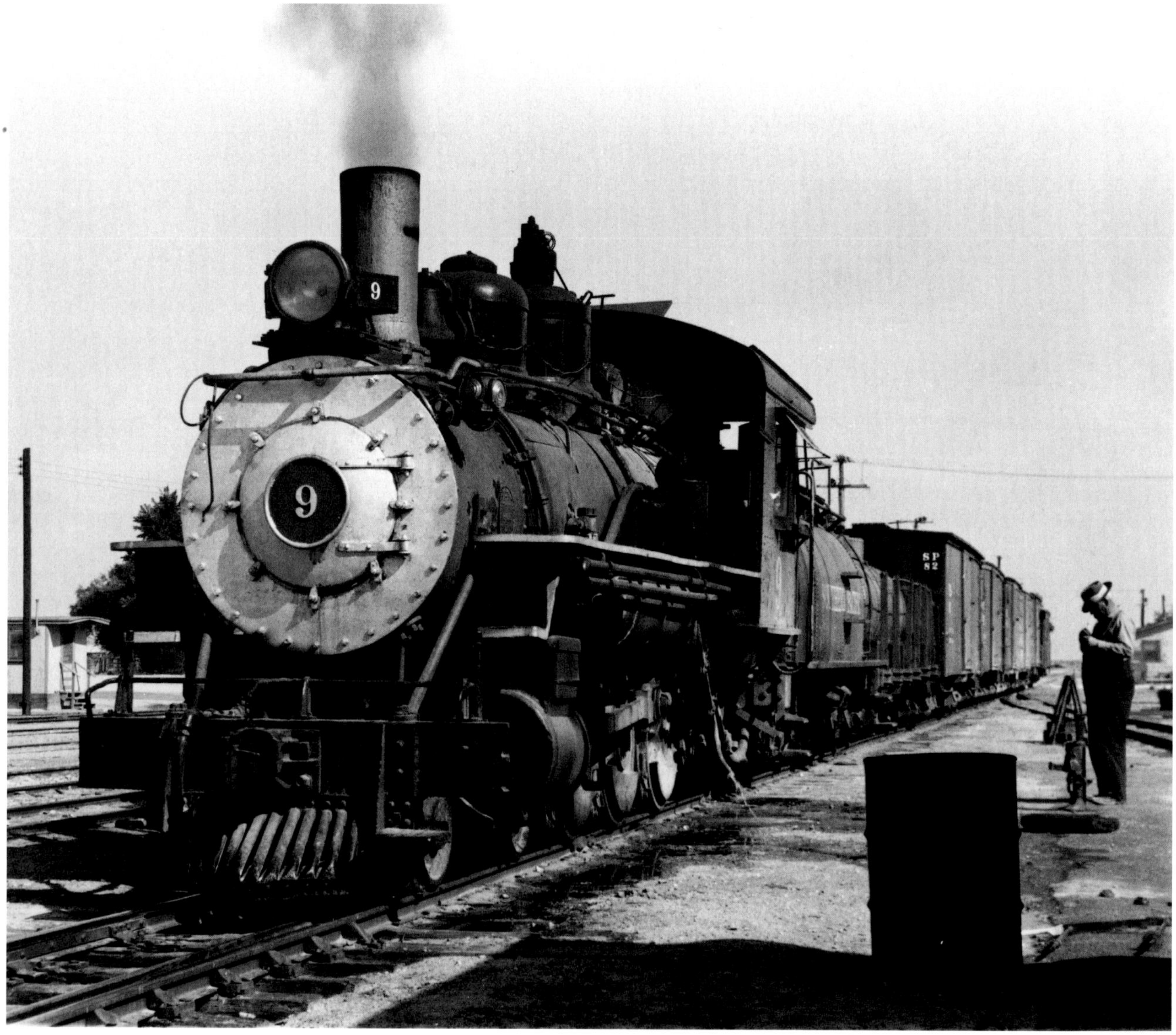

No. 9 with a train at Keeler in 1959 was the last full year of the operation of the narrow gauge. The locomotive now forms part of the Laws Railroad Museum. (R. R. Larson photograph, James E. Boynton collection)

Duplicate

Whereas, THE CARSON AND COLORADO RAILROAD COMPANY, THIRD DIVISION, is justly indebted to D. O. Mills, and his associate contractors, for the building and equipment of the road of said company, in the sum of $450,000, for and on account of the interest due and unpaid on the principal amount payable to said contractors.

And Whereas, said contractors having agreed to accept the bonds of said company, secured by mortgage of its road for the principal amount of their debt free from the interest due, as aforesaid. **And Whereas,** said interest is payable to each of said contractors, in the following sums:

To D. O. Mills, $196,875;	To N. Luning, $45,000;	To E. Mills, $33,750;
To William Sharon, $118,125;	To T. Bell, $33,750;	To H. L. Hill, $11,250;
	To J. B. Randol, $ 11,250.	

Now, Therefore, The said Carson and Colorado Railroad Company, Third Division, acknowledges its indebtedness to *E. Mills*, in the sum of *Thirty three thousand seven hundred and fifty Dollars* payable without interest out of any surplus that may remain of its net income, after paying the interest on its mortgage bonds, and providing for the sinking fund in its said mortgage secured. **And Whereas,** Certificates of indebtedness of like form and effect with the foregoing, are about to be issued and delivered to each of said contractors. **Now,** it is understood, that if the said surplus properly applicable to the payment of said certificates shall not at any time be sufficient for the payment of the whole amount due thereon, then, and in such event, the said surplus shall be payable pro rata among the holders of said certificates, that is to say:

To D. O. Mills, 35-80;	To N. Luning, 8-80;	To T. Bell, 6-80;
To William Sharon, 21-80;	To E. Mills, 6-80;	To H. L. Hill, 2-80;
To J. B. Randol, 2-80.		

Dated San Francisco, July 1st, 1888.

CARSON AND COLORADO RAILROAD COMPANY, THIRD DIVISION,

By *H. M. Yerington* President.

H. Bender Secretary.

The foregoing acknowledgement of indebtedness is hereby accepted subject to and upon the terms and conditions therein set forth.

Dated, San Francisco, Cal., July 1st, 1888. *Edgar Mills*

With ownership vested in just a few names, financing of the Carson and Colorado Railroad is elusive. However, this informative document explains the financing of the Third Division (California-Nevada boundary—projected to Mojave but built only to Keeler).

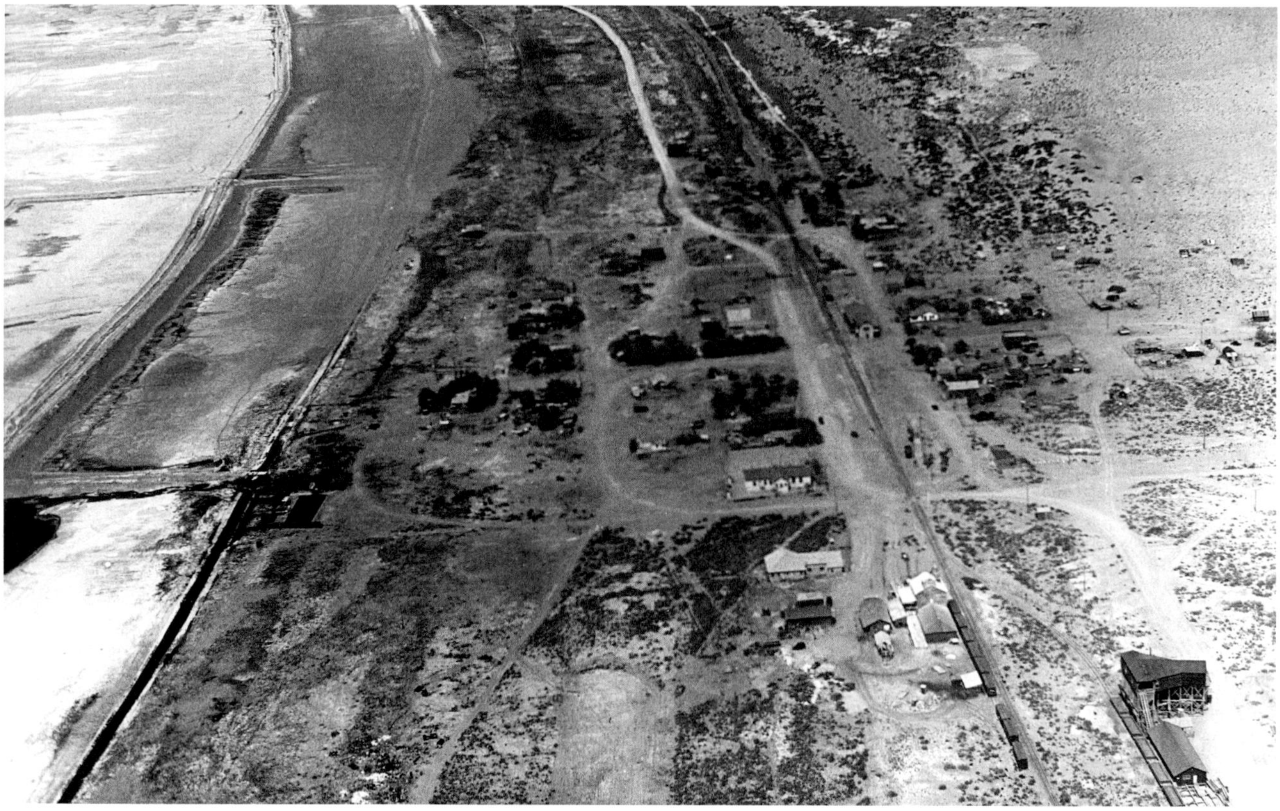

Above: Keeler stretched along the southern end of the narrow-gauge line, as shown in this aerial photograph taken in 1936. Owens Lake is at the left margin, and the terminal of the Cerro Gordo tramway is in the lower right corner. (G. M. Best photograph, R. C. Datin collection)

Below: The station at Schurz presented a fresh appearance in 1952. (Fred L. Hust photograph)

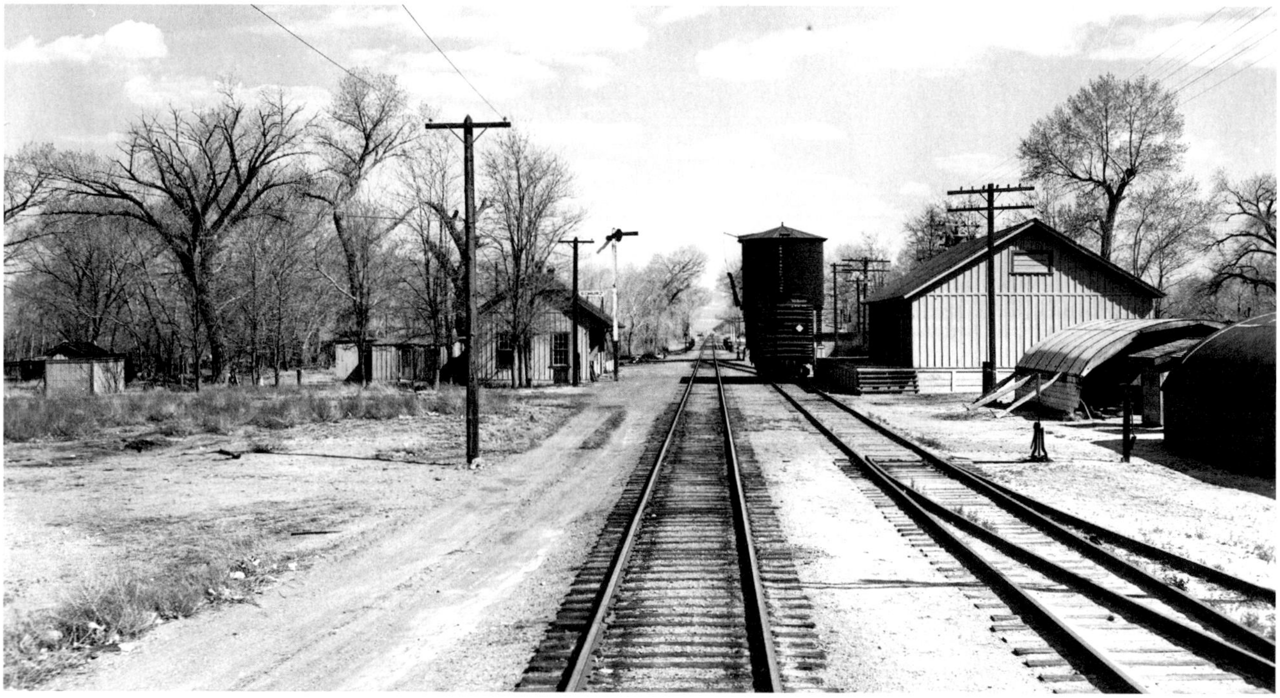

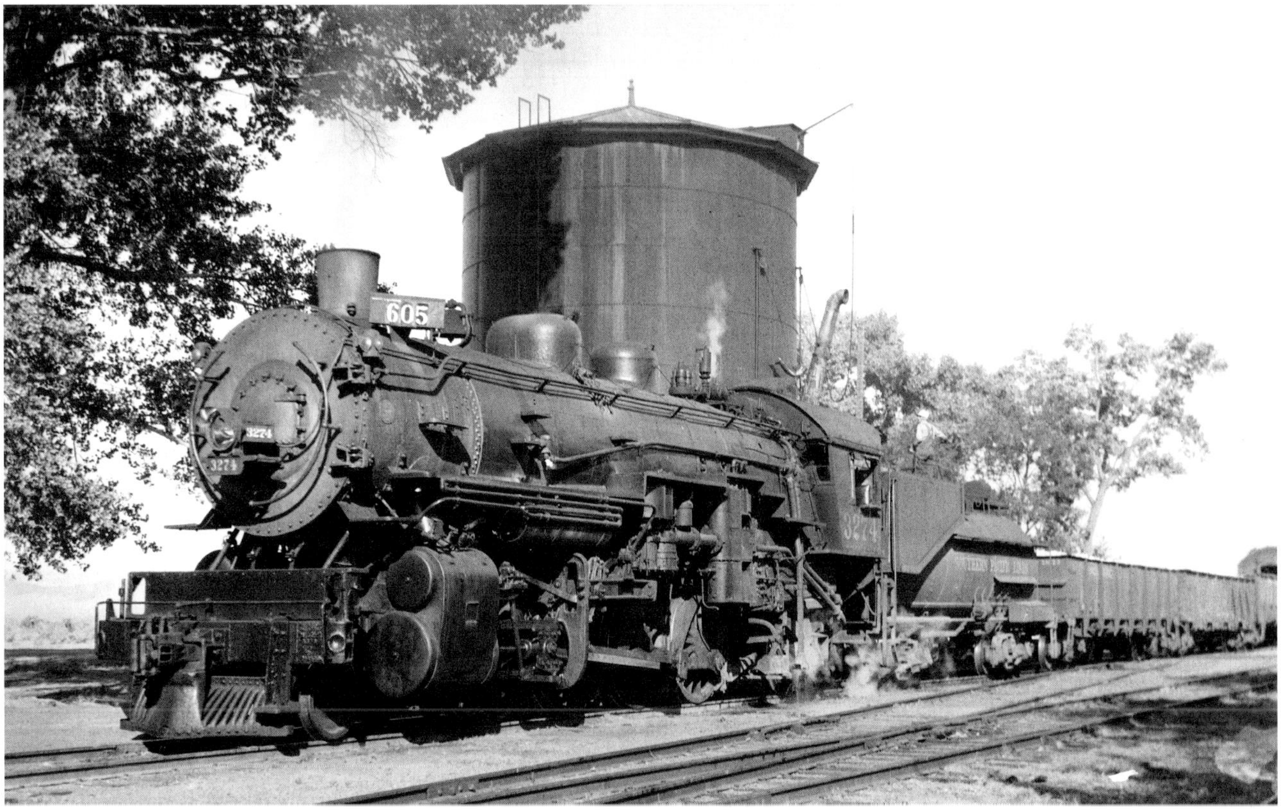

Above: The late Al C. Phelps devoted many days of his vacation to riding and photographing remote SP branch lines. In September 1946, while riding the mixed train to and from Mina, he recorded this locomotive in Wabuska.

Below: When the tunnel under El Paso Mountains, situated a few miles before the connection with the Trona Railway at Searles, caught fire and collapsed in 1981, more than a year went by before it was reopened. In the interim, a shoofly constructed over the roadbed of the original preliminary line, created during the original drilling of the tunnel, enabled operations to continue. (M. D. Isely photograph)

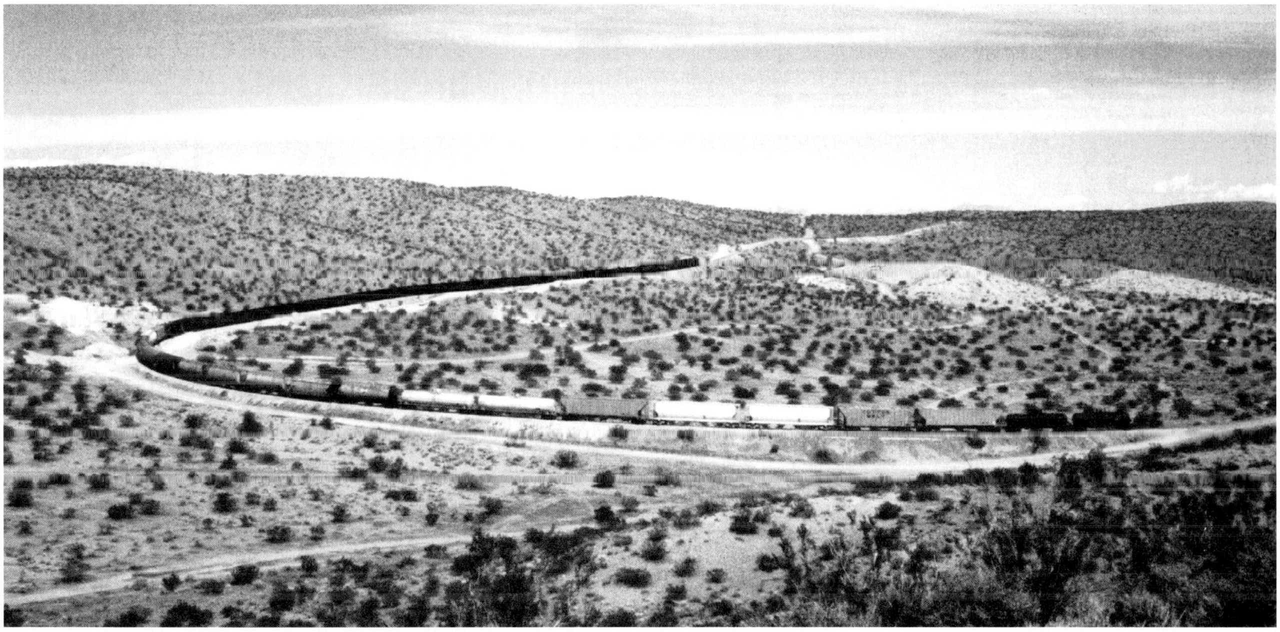

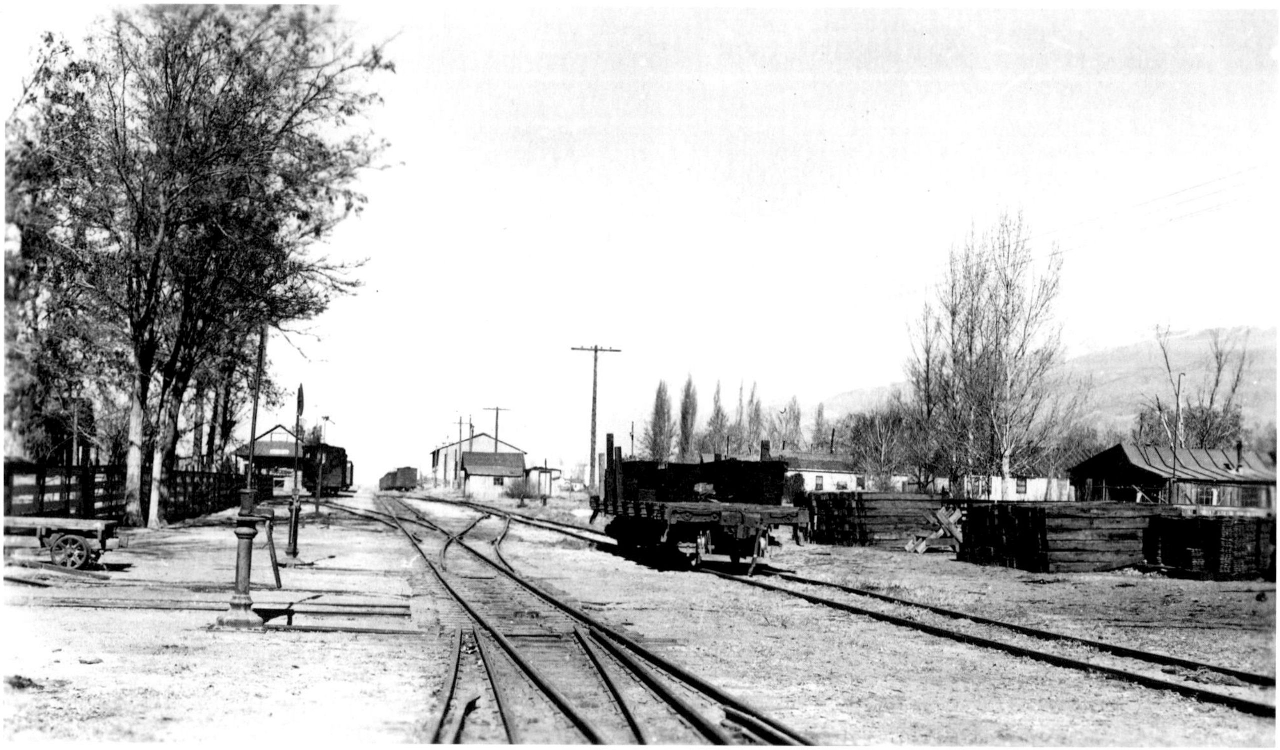

Above: SP's narrow gauge in California's Owens Valley has a steady following. In the last decades of operation, Laws served as the northern terminal, with its depot on the left as it appeared in 1941.

Below: Stairs provide easy access to the cab of SP No. 9 at the Laws Railroad Museum. Built by Baldwin in 1909, it served the N-C-O for twenty years before its transfer to the SP narrow-gauge system.

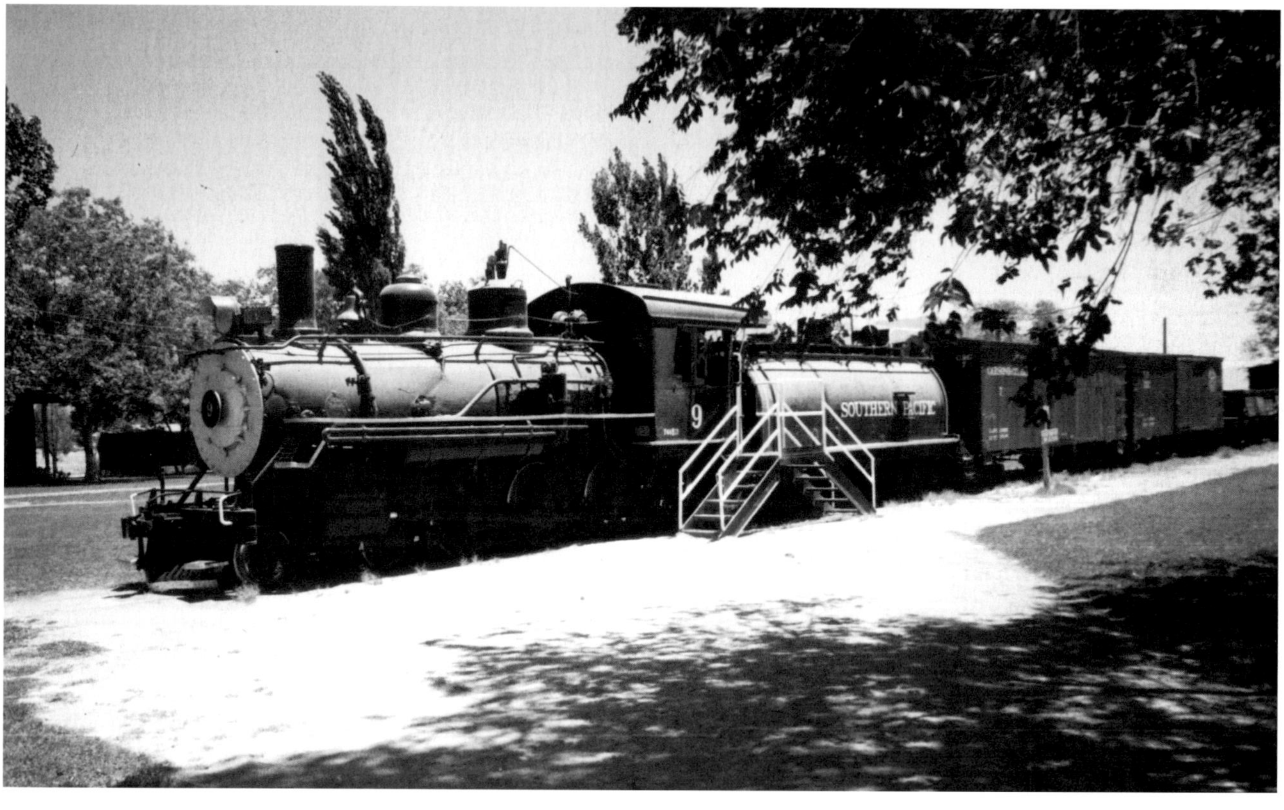

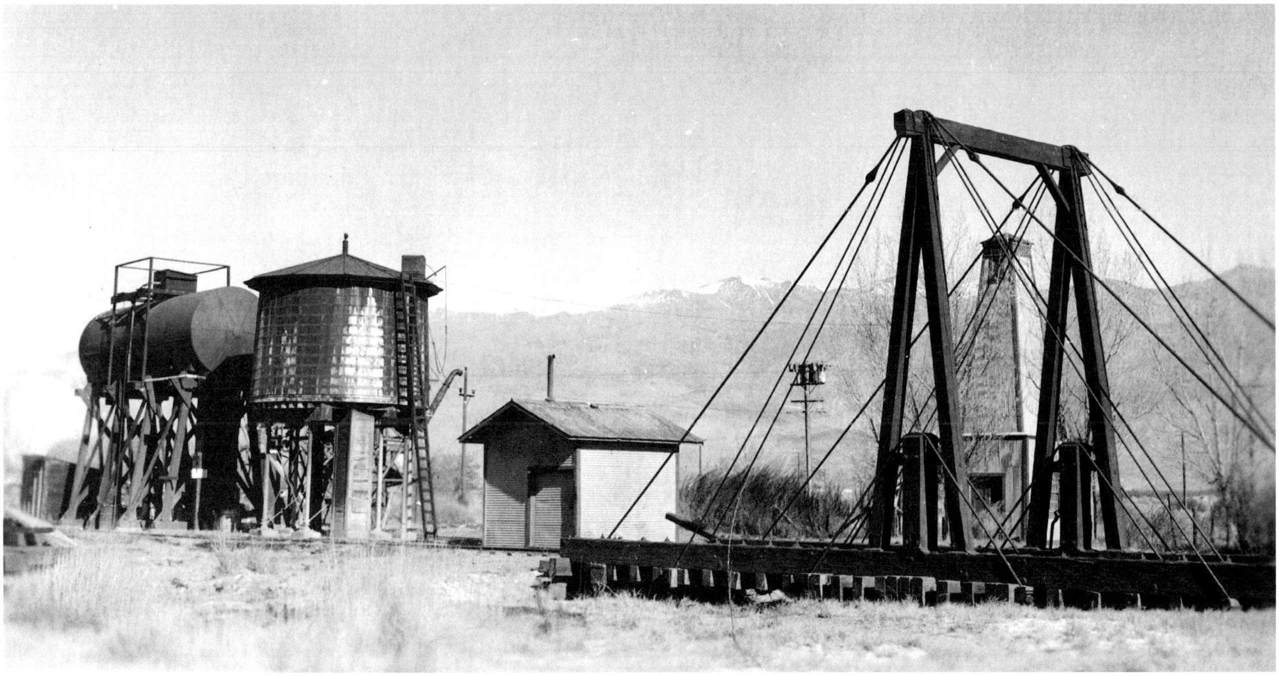

Above: The turntable and oil and water tanks at Laws have changed little in the past sixty years and form part of the museum exhibit.

Below: The Luning depot never looked so much like a movie scene as it did one cold winter evening in December 1974. What the reaction of San Francisco capitalist Nicholas Luning might have been is immaterial, as that portion of the historic Carson and Colorado Railway, which he helped finance, had been abandoned and the building dismantled. (Ted Benson photograph)

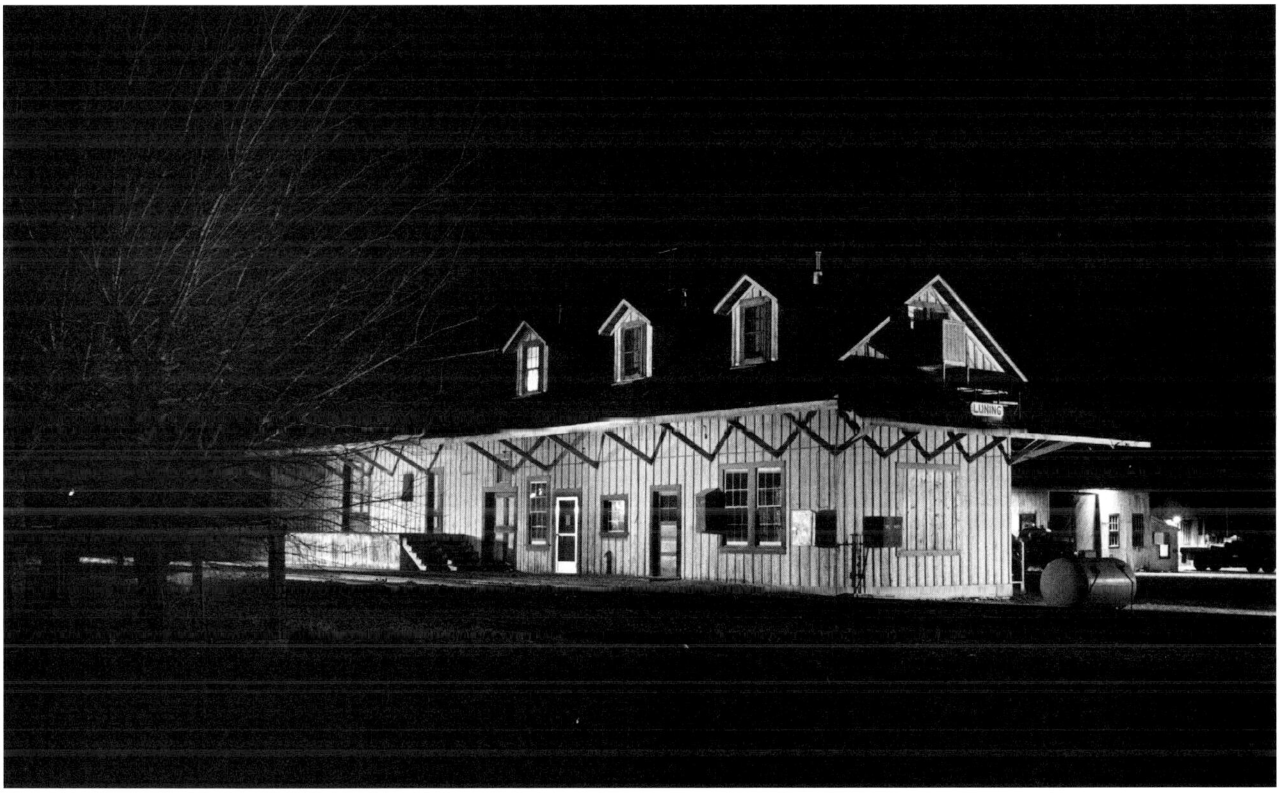

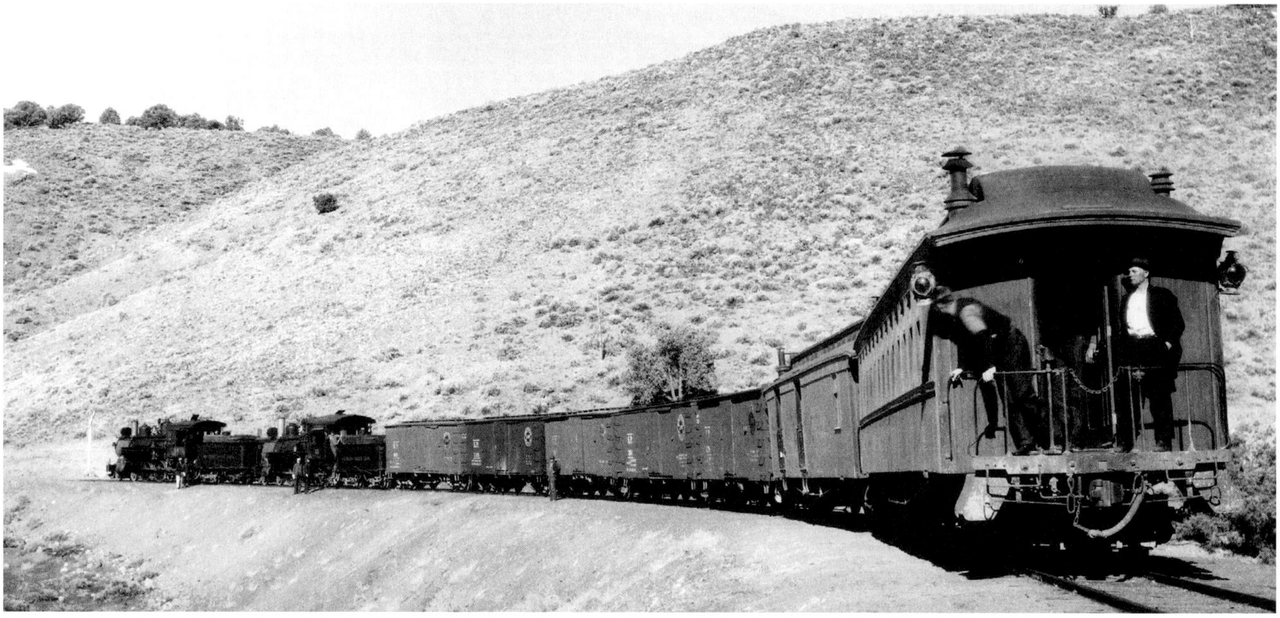

Above: While the engine crews of SP Nos. 15 and 16 (formerly on the South Pacific Coast Railway) conferred, Norman Wallace took a picture of the mixed train on Mt. Montgomery Pass in March 1927. About fifteen years previously, Wallace had been a construction engineer on SP lines in Mexico.

Below: Three GPs work their train around the undulating landscape north of Schurz on the way to Mina in December 1974. (Ted Benson photograph)

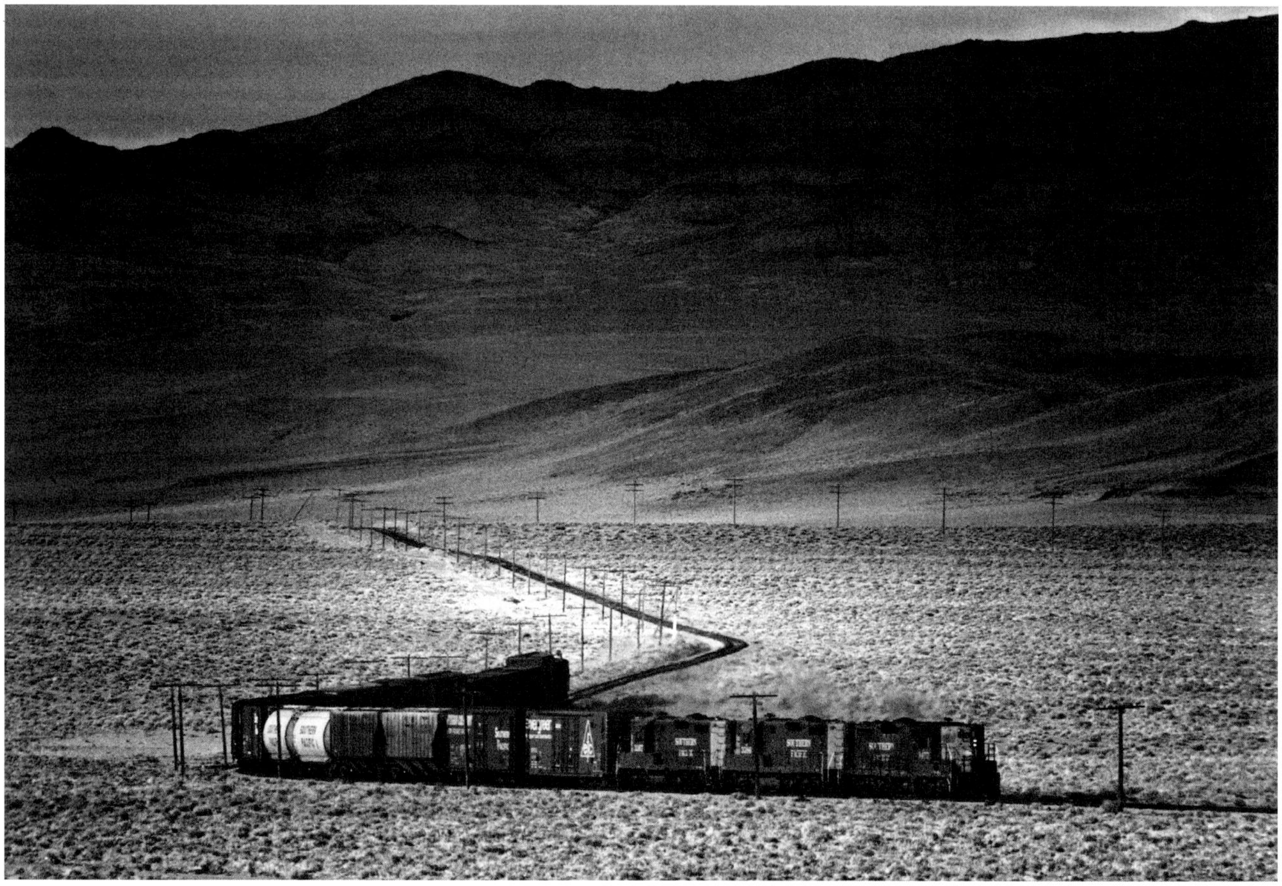

MINA SUB-DIVISION

WESTWARD THIRD CLASS 609 Mixed	607 Mixed
Ar. Monday Wednesday Friday	Ar. Tuesday Thursday Saturday
	s 4.00PM
	f 3.40
	f 3.30
	f 3.17
	f 3.03
	f 2.48
1.00PM	f 2.40
2.35PM	2.15PM
Lv. Monday Wednesday Friday	Lv. Tuesday Thursday Saturday
(0.25) 27.84	(1.45) 22 80

WESTWARD THIRD CLASS 603 Mixed
Arrive Daily
s 4.15PM
f 3.59
f 3.46
f
3.30PM
Leave Daily
(0.45) 21.06

7

EASTWARD (Narrow Gauge) WESTWARD

Capacity of sidings in car lengths	THIRD CLASS 614 Freight		SECOND CLASS 612 Mixed	124 T. & G. Tonopah Express Mixed	Distance from San Francisco	Time Table No. 42 April 24, 1932 Mina Branch STATIONS	Distance from Keeler	SECOND CLASS 123 T. & G. San Francisco Passenger Mixed	611 Mixed		THIRD CLASS 613 Freight
	Leave Daily Ex. Sunday		Lv. Monday Wednesday Friday	Leave Daily				Arrive Daily	Ar. Tuesday Thursday Saturday		Arrive Daily Ex. Sunday
Yard POWYBK			7.00AM	6.20AM	417.0	TO-R MINA (Joint Track Three Rails) 3.5	160.2	s 7.45PM	s 7.40PM		
Spur 4			f 7.10	f 6.30	420.5	SODAVILLE 4.5	156.7	f 7.36	f 7.30		
Spur 4			f	f	425.0	RHODES 1.0	152.2	f	f		
			s 7.30	s 6.45AM	426.0	R TONOPAH JCT. 6.4	151.2	7.20PM	s 7.15		
20 PW			f 7.59		432.4	BELLEVILLE 3.0	144.8		f 6.45		
Y			f 8.11		435.4	FILBEN 3.3	141.8		f		
Spur 2			f		438.7	LITTLE SUMMIT 6.1	138.5		f		
Spur 10			f		444.8	RAYDEL 5.6	132.4		f		
18 PW			s 9.20		450.4	BASALT 7.7	126.8		s 5.25		
24 PY			s 10.00		458.1	TO MT. MONTGOMERY 8.6	119.1		s 4.35		
15 PW			s 10.50		466.7	QUEEN 2.2	110.5		s 3.55		
					468.9	STATE LINE 7.1	108.3				
24 P			s 11.30AM		476.0	BENTON 11.0	101.2		s 3.15		
13 YPW			s 12.05PM		487.0	HAMMIL 2.4	90.2		s 2.35		
12			f		489.4	DEHY 1.9	87.8		f		
4			f 12.15		491.3	SHEALY 7.8	85.9		f 2.15		
14 P			f 12.32		499.1	CHALFANT 2.6	78.1		f 1.55		
12			f		501.7	TOM 5.1	75.5		f		
Yard POTWK			1.05 1.50		506.8	TO-R LAWS 2.8	70.4		1.30 12.45		
			f		509.6	POLITA 2.1	67.6		f		
8			f 2.02		511.7	BIGELOW 4.4	65.5		f 12.30		
8			f 2.13		516.1	BLACK CANYON 6.6	61.1		f 12.20		
14 P			s 2.35		522.7	TO ZURICH 2.8	54.5		s 12.05PM		
9			f 2.42		525.5	MONOLA 1.3	51.7		f 11.51AM		
10 Y			f 2.45		526.8	BENEME 4.1	50.4		f 11.47		
8			f 2.55		530.9	ELNA 6.0	46.3		f 11.36		
20 PW			f 3.10		536.9 536.2	ABERDEEN 14.1	40.8		f 11.20		
14 PW			s 4.00		550.1	TO KEARSARGE 4.9	26.2		s 10.45		
8			f 4.10		555.2	MANZANAR 4.6	21.3		f 10.20		
Yard TPK	11.45AM		s 4.40		559.8	TO-R OWENYO 3.9	16.7		10.10 9.10		9.55AM
14 P	12.05PM		f 4.51		563.7	MT. WHITNEY 5.0	12.8		f 9.01		9.45
Spur 67			f		568.7	ALICO 1.5	7.8		f		
Spur 8			f		570.2	DOLOMITE 1.2	6.3		f		
Spur 39			f		571.4	MOCK 0.8	5.1		f		
6	12.35		f 5.11		572.2	TRAMWAY 4.3	4.3		f 8.43		9.05
Yard WYBK	12.50PM		s 5.25PM		576.5	TO-R KEELER	0.0		8.30AM		8.55AM
	Arrive Daily Ex. Sunday		Ar. Monday Wednesday Friday	Arrive Daily		(160.2)		Leave Daily	Lv. Tuesday Thursday Saturday		Leave Daily Ex. Sunday
	(1.05) 15.41	(3.45) 18.77	(10.25) 15.37	(0.25) 21.00		Time over District / Average speed per hour		(0.25) 21.00	(11.10) 14.34		(1.00) 16.70

The former Carson and Colorado Railroad constituted an interesting part of the Salt Lake Division. Extending almost three hundred miles southerly from Hazen, several gauges of tracks formed the line to Keeler, California. Between Mina and Tonopah Jct., a third rail enabled narrow-gauge (three-feet) train operation to Laws and Keeler. Mixed trains from a connection with the Virginia and Truckee Railroad at Mound House ran daily to Churchill before terminating at Wabuska. Triweekly service between Mina and Laws in 1925 became a "Thursday-only" operation in the 1930s before service over that section was abandoned in 1938. Finally, in 1960, the remaining narrow-gauge section between Laws and Keeler was abandoned. (Robert Kern collection)

THE FINAL YEARS OF THE NEVADA-CALIFORNIA-OREGON RAILWAY

The Nevada-California-Oregon Railway enjoyed only one profitable year after 1913, and operating losses threatened to end the life of the line, leaving Modoc and most of Lassen County without a railroad of any kind.

The major problem confronting the narrow gauge was that, unlike other places in the West, the area did not take on an exuberant growth after the rails reached Lakeview in 1912. Although attempts were made to colonize the area, the new residents stood incapable of generating meaningful traffic. Yes, there was livestock business, particularly sheep. After the European war commenced in 1914, French agents scoured the West for horses for military use, which added a little freight revenue. Villages along the line remained few and far between, and those entrepreneurs brave enough to create a new business usually had only a short stay.

Ravendale, almost midway between Wendel and Alturas, was typical. In October 1912, a week before opening their general store, Mr. and Mrs. Hunt invited all the people on Madeline Plains to a dance. Freezing temperatures kept many at home, but the party ensued anyway. At midnight when the group was enjoying a generous supper, "the lights went out and everyone looked alike." With illumination restored, dancing resumed. How long the Hunts survived is questionable; probably, they went elsewhere before George Marr started his store two years later. In the fall of 1916, the Ravendale Hotel drew a capacity crowd; W. F. Cole, the proprietor, said that travelers filled his rooms every night. The Madeline Hotel, dating back to the days of the colorful promoter J. Noble Jones, after being idle for some time, was torn down in March 1929, with the lumber being salvaged for reuse in Alturas.

The railroad, in addition to lacking sufficient traffic, also faced operating problems. W. H. French, a hostler working for the N-C-O at Likely in October 1912, proceeded to become intoxicated, and, in spite of efforts of the other hostler to stop him, he took a locomotive to Alturas in record time. Thanking his good fortune for not meeting another train, Mr. French celebrated with another drink in an Alturas saloon. His superior took a dim view of this exploit, and the man was arrested. The locomotive made it safely back to its home, while Mr. French spent the next year in the San Quentin penitentiary.

Even with a sober operating force, the N-C-O had trouble keeping trains on the tracks. A wreck along Pit River Canyon in November 1913 tied up the line for two days. A few weeks later, spreading rails at Chat, a mile south of Plumas Jct., postponed the Christmas-night arrival of the train in Reno by twenty-five hours.

The next year, with two narrow-gauge buffet-sleeping cars, the N-C-O ran overnight trains between Reno and Lakeview. Although Alturas patrons applauded the move, some unhappy people complained to the California Railroad Commission, which ordered the railroad to return to a daylight schedule. (The sleeping car, *Alturas*, was retired in 1917.)

A rear-end collision in February 1915 near Horse Lake squashed a passenger car and killed one man. In the summer of 1916, Charles Moran, president of the line, suffered the embarrassment of three wrecks during his California visit. A wreck at Ravendale resulted in scattering escaping mules, and a carload of wool was generally distributed; subsequently, it was stolen. The Termo correspondent of the *Lassen Advocate* took pride in downgrading the N-C-O. He closed his remarks by stating that one wreck "was well in keeping with the established reputation of this railroad of misfortune and procrastination." (Charles Moran succeeded D. Comyn Moran as president in 1914.)

When telling about Moran's trip to Cedarville and the Surprise Valley and the subsequent rumors that N-C-O rails might reach into that region, our Termo scribe remarked: "In passing it might be noted that the N-C-O is prolific as a producer of rumors as wrecks, although the former production is never as actual as the latter."

Stations and New Towns

Suffering from deficit operations, the railroad closed little-used stations. When that transpired at New Pine Creek in March 1913, local residents turned indignant. It was only a few weeks previously that the California Railroad Commission had responded to complaints that the N-C-O, after keeping an agent at Termo on the payroll for ten years, decided to dispense with his services. This dismissal meant that freight, dumped on the ground, was subjected to wandering cattle and the elements. The commission ordered the railroad to provide proper storage for receiving freight for a reasonable time at no extra charge.

A different situation prevailed at Alturas: it had a station but at the wrong location. Again, local people went to the commission, alleging that the station was too far from the center of town. Responding to the commission's order, the N-C-O moved its passenger depot to Rice Street in June 1915, a more convenient location.

The businesspeople of Lassen County shared with the railroad recognition of the need for a greater population. During 1912, the Lassen Development League took an active part in promoting new town sites. In March, shortly before work began on the Fernley and Lassen Railway, F. T. Cromwell envisioned a settlement at the crossing of the N-C-O and WP at Bird Flat. In the N-C-O's sporadic construction pattern, when rails halted at this point years before, the name "Liegan" became a fixture. Nothing spectacular occurred at this station; stage drivers solicited passengers for Susanville when the trains arrived.

Cromwell had great ideas. He contemplated a large hotel, cottages, and a store and sinking a well. Two months later, the Lassen Development League gave its blessing and named the spot Cromwell. The next month, the promoter announced the beginning of construction of a thirty-room hotel costing all of eight thousand dollars. He also hoped to persuade Western Pacific to relocate the Gerlach division point to Cromwell.

From then on, a cloud hung over the embryonic settlement, as needed funds proved impossible to secure, and finally the sheriff auctioned off everything in the town site on February 7, 1914. C. W. McQueen made the winning one hundred–dollar bid and quickly became the owner of the frame of the 40 × 70–foot hotel building together with some loose windows and doors.

In the fall of that year, S. G. Rayl and S. P. Durkee took an interest in the same section. Just before Christmas 1915, the railroad crossing was called Rayl after the new hotel owner at that point. Mention was made of a "union station" and a large corral. The outcome of this venture—the third at the same location—probably duplicated the others. It subsequently became Hackstaff, which boasted a "beanery" for N-C-O engine and train crews. In effect, these efforts were about twenty-five years too soon; had they blossomed at the time of the Sierra Ordnance Depot, undoubtedly the story would have been happier.

Farther north, Russian settlers at Glade, fourteen miles northeast of Ravendale, were earning acceptance by the community in 1914. Farther east in Nevada, the Leonard Creek Mining District was "surely a comer" in November 1914, according to a mining stock salesman, but its career was brief, and today its location is difficult to identify. (The terrible drought of 1916 may have been responsible for the departure of the Russians for a better climate.)

The Time for Abandonment

In part due to the sale of the Plumas branch and the approach to Reno in 1917, next year's N-C-O operating revenues fell to the lowest level in a decade. Lumber tonnage in 1918 fell 88 percent from the earlier year. At the same time, wages rose across the nation, along with higher material prices.

By 1921, the situation became bleak and would have been worse had not Sunday trains been eliminated in May followed by a reduction to triweekly service in September. Two months later, Charles Moran reluctantly filed an application with the Interstate Commerce Commission to abandon operations. Even with reductions in service, 1921 revenues reached an all-time high of $431,000, and coincidentally the company reported the largest loss—$99,000—in its history.

The abandonment proceedings, conducted in Alturas by the California Railroad Commission acting for the ICC, drew expensive legal talent and traffic experts. The railroad described some of its problems: inadequate division of rates, low mail pay, and more. Charles Levey, president of Western Pacific, offered to buy the remaining 171 miles of railroad, widen the tracks, and make several extensions costing several million dollars in addition to the purchase price. Though he considered future development of the territory justified a good railroad, he could not see his way to paying more than $6,500 per mile, or $1,111,500. Moran demanded a higher figure because, after retiring the $975,000 outstanding bonds and other debts, there would be little if anything left for the Moran family holding all the stock. Moran said he would rather scrap the railroad even if he garnered only a fraction of the WP offer. The ICC denied authority to abandon operation but did approve physical abandonment of 16 miles of main line between Hackstaff and Wendel. It also increased the division of rates of interline traffic exchanged with SP.

Although operating revenues were lower than in 1921, by slashing roadway maintenance in half, the company managed to eke out an $18,000 profit the following year, the first since 1913, but that was due to a special payment from the U.S. Railroad Administration.

The Lassen County Chamber of Commerce expressed concern over the 16-mile abandonment, for it no longer had the second connection (Western Pacific) and also slightly reduced county taxes. (N-C-O taxes increased 78 percent between 1918 and 1922.)

Nothing was accomplished by the protest, but a changed attitude took over the Lassen County Chamber of Commerce around the end of 1922. Formation of the Railroad Committee seeking to boost the N-C-O's welfare stemmed from this change. The committee envisioned community benefits if the southern terminal were moved from Wendel to Susanville and set out to promote this change. Old-timers recalled that original surveys carried the N-C-O through Susanville, which the committee hoped to emulate by the N-C-O constructing a new 25-mile link between Susanville and Snowstorm station. Rails from the 16-mile abandonment would cover part of the distance.

Expressing their ideas to Charles Moran in November 1922, the committee received an open-minded reply from him asking for more information. Two civil engineers from Fruit Growers Supply made a preliminary location following part of the early survey to Pete's Valley. The surveyors observed that little grading would be required, and the maximum grade would not exceed 2 percent. Admittedly, the long trestle across Willow Creek offered potential problems.

The Lassen committee found enthusiastic support for the new route in Alturas and Lakeview. A study made for the committee estimated that, by relocating the railroad, traffic of lumber and agricultural products would double. (The foundation for this projection was not revealed.)

During the early months of 1923, further developments ensued. For the first time in years, the *Lassen Advocate* published schedules of N-C-O passenger trains, a practice that continued for five months. The possibility of making Susanville the interchange point with Southern Pacific held the attention of local businessmen. R. D. Baker, president of Lassen Lumber and Box, conferred with Charles Moran in New York City. Though Moran favored the relocation of the terminal, he said he was unable to see how construction of the new link could be financed. As an alternative, he suggested adding a third rail to SP tracks from Wendel. J. E. Pardee, a local attorney on retainer for SP, journeyed to San Francisco to present this proposal to SP traffic men. According to R. D. Baker, Southern Pacific officials gave serious consideration to the proposal, but for undisclosed reasons it never reached maturity.

For the next two years, the N-C-O continued to suffer declining traffic receipts that colored the bottom line in red. Tonnage handled in 1924 and 1925 was about the same, with the increase in lumber in 1925 being offset by a decline in cattle and sheep movements from the year before.

Southern Pacific Enters the Scene

Susanville boosters reacted quickly in September 1925 with the news that SP was considering taking the N-C-O into its family and then widen the tracks. For various reasons, SP had not moved forward with the construction of its proposed line from Westwood Jct. to Klamath Falls. Susanville people rightfully feared that if the SP included the N-C-O in its Modoc Line from Oregon to Wendel and Fernley, it would forever relegate Susanville to branch-line status. Several men hastened to San Francisco in an unsuccessful effort to swing railroad construction their way. (The ICC approved SP's acquisition of the N-C-O on May 3, 1926.)

As a historical footnote, this was not the first time that SP men had considered buying the little railroad. In the spring of 1882, Huntington and Crocker exchanged views about the road's predecessor. On April 23, Huntington wrote Crocker that "the party controlling it has been here several times since I last wrote you on the subject." Six weeks later, Huntington told his associate, "I offered $10,000 a mile in 5 percent bonds and 10,000 in [Central Pacific] stock." Fortunately for Huntington and Crocker, the transaction never transpired, as the little road was soon engaged in extensive litigation over a fraudulent bond issue.

This time Southern Pacific did not choose the route without careful consideration. Two objectives had to be met: first, linking Klamath Falls with Wendel and continuing over existing trackage to Fernley and, second, serving Alturas for the potential lumber traffic in that vicinity.

A study made in July 1925 compared five possible routes between Klamath Falls and Wendel. They ranged in length from 264 miles to 197 miles. Using ninety-pound new rail, the cost ranged from $10,121,000 to $13,600,000, with the inclusion of the N-C-O and Alturas being the most economical. To clarify the basis of the decision, a map on the next page shows the various alternatives.

Commencing at Wendel, SP began widening the tracks of the N-C-O at the end of June 1927, and the first standard-gauge train left Wendel for Alturas on October 24, 1927. Alturas staged a grand Railroad Day on November 11 with a pageant that, in spite of the rain and mud, was pronounced a success.

The Later Years

Changes in the general economy and individuals' lifestyles determine the pattern of railroad operations. The big Pickering mill at Alturas failed to open its doors and stood idle for many years. The through Pullman sleeping car between Portland and Ogden had only a brief existence. The local daily passenger train serving Alturas turned to triweekly as more people enjoyed the

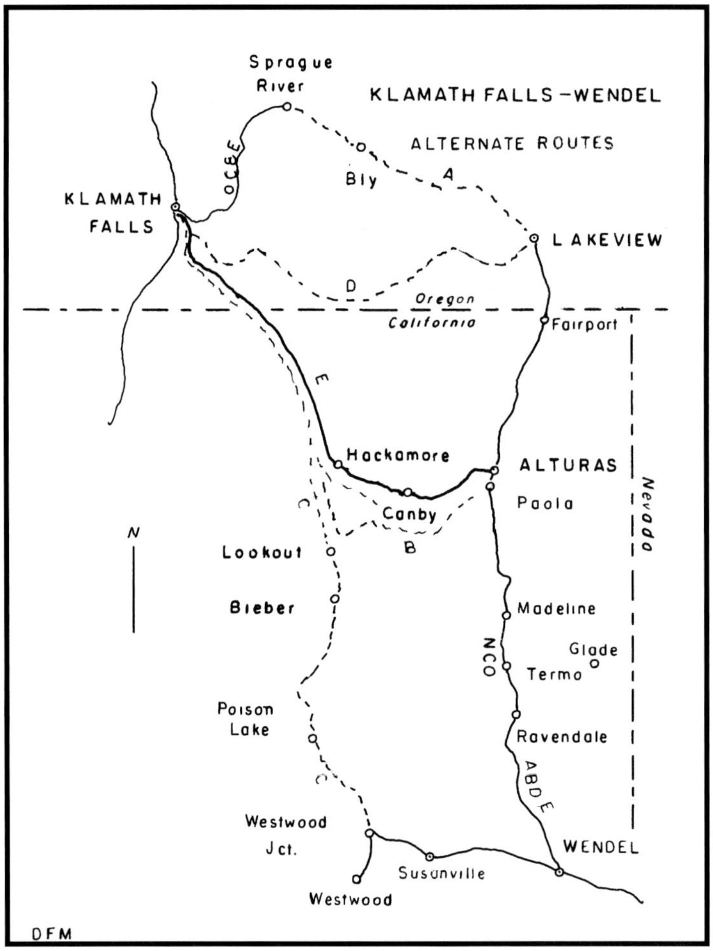

Southern Pacific location engineers offered five different routes between Klamath Falls and Wendel. Initial surveys were made between 1908 and 1912 in the names of the Modoc Northern Railway and the Goose Lake and Southern Railway, as outlined in a previous chapter. Primary objectives were to link Oregon with the Overland Route in Nevada and also to tie Modoc and Lassen Counties in northeastern California with the upper Sacramento Valley as well as to tap the lumber industry around Alturas.

For a number of reasons, prevailing conditions delayed SP construction of a railroad in this area. Matters improved in 1923, and SP moved forward on a series of extensions and route improvements over many sections of its far-fled system. The Oregon-Nevada connection was one of them. Although Klamath Falls had been adopted as the likely northern terminal, additional surveys made in 1926 began at Paunina, seventy-seven miles north of Klamath Falls, and headed southeast to Lakeview via Sycan Jct. and Bly. The route was set aside.

In 1925, the existing common-carrier railroads consisted of SP tracks serving Klamath Falls, the Oregon, California, and Eastern (OC&E) Railway reaching into another timber area east of Klamath Falls. In the southern part of this domain, SP (Fernley and Lassen Railway) tapped Susanville and Westwood, while the Nevada-California-Oregon Railway flanked the eastern border of this area. Four of the five routes included all or part of the N-C-O, which was subsequently purchased by Southern Pacific and widened to standard gauge.

One plan contemplated an extension of the OC&E from Sprague River to Lakeview and the use of the N-C-O to Wendel. Designated as Route A, it proved to be the longest (264.5 miles) and among the most expensive. (The OC&E was later extended to Bly.)

Route D indicates an old Oregon Short Line survey connecting Lakeview by a shorter route. Though shorter (217.3 miles), it too was costly.

Route B used the earlier Modoc Northern Railway surveys almost to Lookout before turning east to pass near Canby on its way to Alturas, where it joined the N-C-O to Wendel.

Route C reflects the work of the surveyors of the Modoc Northern and Goose Lake and Southern Railways between Klamath Falls and Westwood Jct., which had been under active consideration in 1909–1910. Though shorter than the three routes listed above (203.7 miles), it stood out as the most expensive, at $13,600,000. Later, the Western Pacific and Great Northern built the HiLine along this path.

Route E, the adopted line, a combination of part of Routes C and B passing through Canby, necessitated construction of a new railroad between Klamath Falls and Alturas and then following N-C-O trackage to Wendel. With a distance of 197 miles and a cost of $10,171,000, it was the shortest and least expensive of all the routes. (Estimated costs are based on ninety-pound new rail; eighty-five-pound secondhand rail would reduce the cost by 20 percent to 25 percent.) Completion of the Transcontinental Cutoff was celebrated at Hackamore on September 14, 1929, and regular trains began running over the new route the next day.

convenience of their personal automobiles. Scheduled passenger trains to Alturas became only a memory on December 2, 1937. However, in June 1955, the Railway and Locomotive Historical Society ran a three-day, well-attended excursion from Oakland to Reno, north to Alturas and Lakeview, and then to Klamath Falls for the return to Oakland. The local radio station interviewed the rail fans.

The booming Oregon lumber trade of the 1950s almost swamped the Modoc Line; indeed, centralized traffic control received serious consideration for a time. Traffic thinned down, and in January 1973, Alturas ceased to be a terminal point, as train and engine crews ran from Klamath Falls to Wendel where new sleeping cabins were added. It brought back memories of the days when an estimated four hundred railroad men considered Alturas their base. Most men affected by the change found jobs on other parts of the system, while others took early retirement.

Traffic on the Lakeview branch dwindled, and on July 14, 1973, Mrs. Olive Roberts closed the doors of the handsome brick station for the last time, and SP no longer maintained an agent at Lakeview. Following a program of selling branch lines to independent operators, SP sold the Lakeview branch in 1986 for operation by the Great Western Railroad Company of Colorado.

Unfortunately, derailments are not infrequent in railroad operations. A "million-dollar derailment" occurred shortly after midnight on October 27, 1968, when eighty-five cars of a one hundred–car train left the track near Ravendale. To make matters worse, diesel engines in the refrigerator cars with frozen foods caught fire, which consumed twenty cars. Lumber and plywood, also on the train, attracted three men and their lady companions who loaded three trucks with plywood from the wreck, only to be arrested. A Susanville judge fined each man $125 but released the women without charges.

But more troubles would come seven weeks later when a broken 131-pound rail on the high side of a curve a few miles north of Sage Hen dumped the power units on the ground. Two cars close to the engine along with two other cars in the train left the rails and turned over.

Lumber and other traffic moving over the Alturas-Wendel segment in the final years of the twentieth century diminished so greatly that management suspended operations from January 1987 until October 1988. Under Union Pacific ownership, the route proved redundant, as that road had a long-established route from Oregon to its main line east of Ogden. Accordingly, freight tariffs were canceled on March 2, 2003, and all the rails were pulled up between Wendel and Alturas by October 2003, with the exception of a few miles north of Wendel left in place for a storage track for idle freight cars. Aside from the Lakeview branch, the only remaining portion of the N-C-O is part of the former Western Pacific Reno branch. A few miles of the northerly portion have been used as a storage track, with cars being pushed in at the Reno Jct. connection. One rail has been removed at Border Town, Nevada, to capture possible runaways.

Another change along this route came on November 1, 2005, when Union Pacific turned over 107 miles of the former Modoc Line to the Utah Central Railway. With headquarters in Ogden, Utah, the latter organization leased the Alturas–Klamath Falls trackage and with the name Modoc Northern Railroad Company contemplated operating trains twice weekly between Klamath Falls and Alturas and triweekly trains between Copic and Klamath Falls. Two months prior to its operation, it placed an ad in the local paper seeking employees for various positions. Rehabilitation of the Alturas depot formed part of the lessee's plans, while its two General Electric diesel locomotives were to be serviced at its Tule Lake facilities.

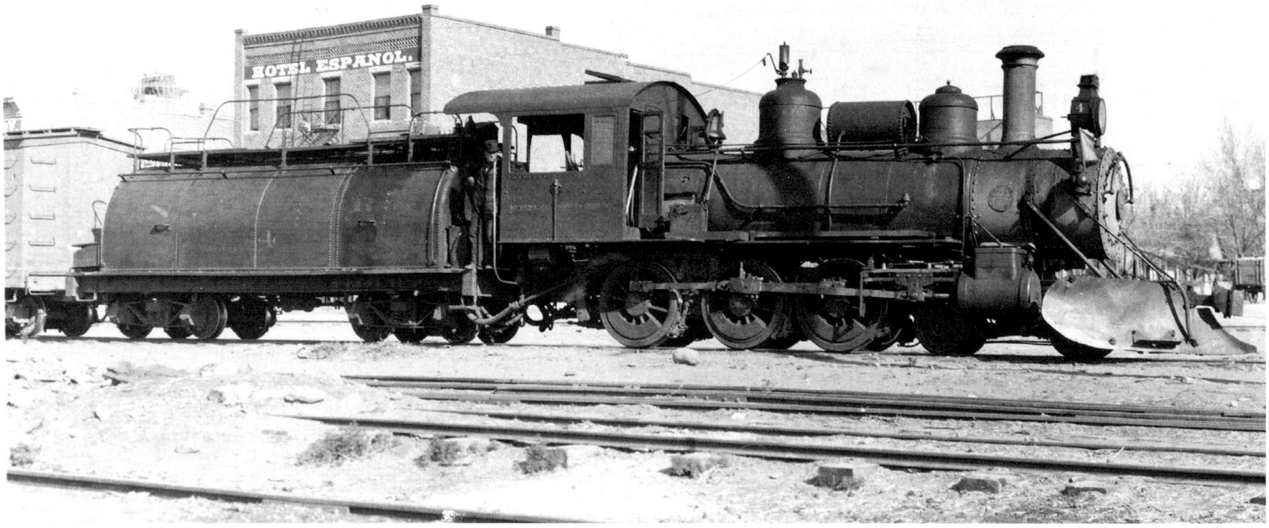

Above: Originally N-C-O No. 6, when released from the Baldwin works in 1899, it became the third N-C-O No. 4 in 1910 in a general reshuffling of road numbers. Fred Jukes, a legendary railroad photographer, caught this locomotive at an idle moment in Reno prepared for winter storms.

Below: Freight wagons with sacks of wool lent activity to this scene at the Hotel Amedee. The sign over the door reads: HOTEL–RESTAURANT–GENERAL MERCHANDISE.

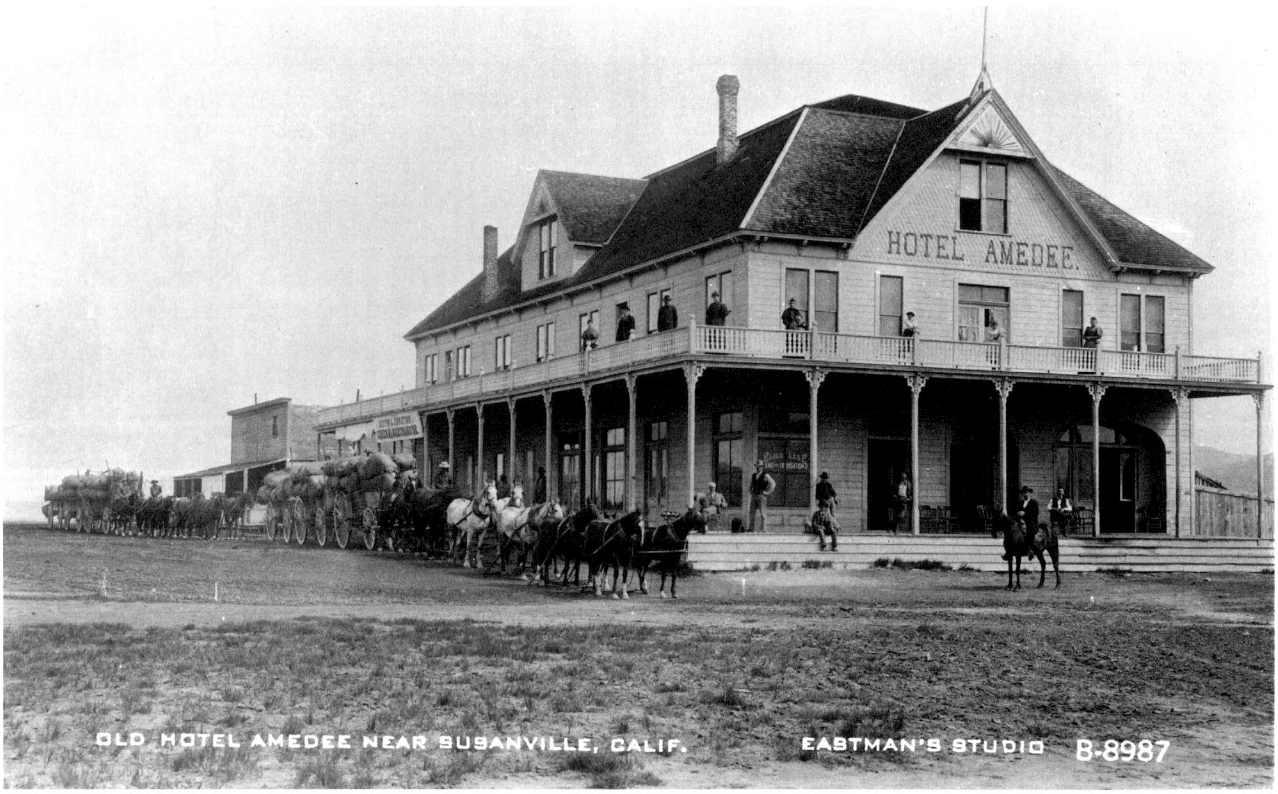

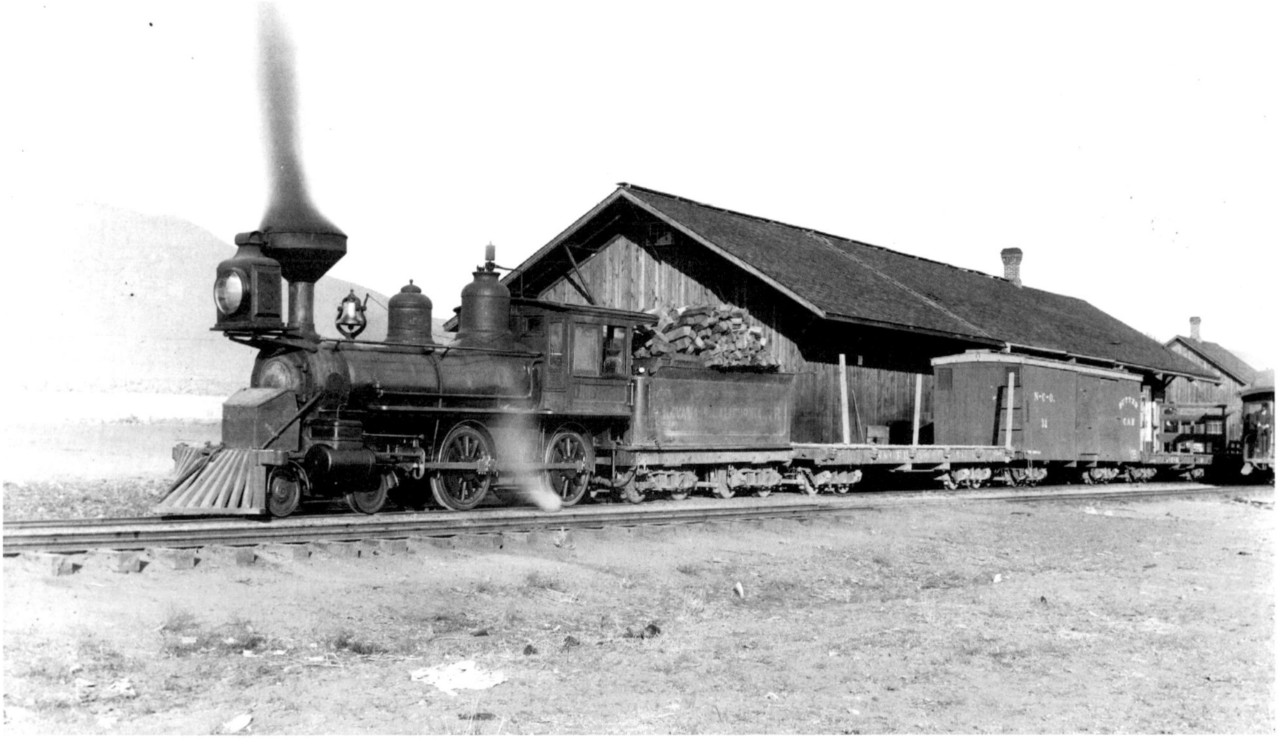

Above: A mixed train posed for the cameraman at some isolated station whose shadow in the foreground serves as his signature. Though the property had been in the name of the Nevada-California-Oregon Railway since 1893, as confirmed by the N-C-O butter car No. 32, the faint lettering on the locomotive tender reads the earlier name of the Nevada and California Railroad.

Below: A party of scientists traveled over the railroad in 1888 to record an eclipse of the sun. N-C-O No. 31, a butter car, was pressed into service.

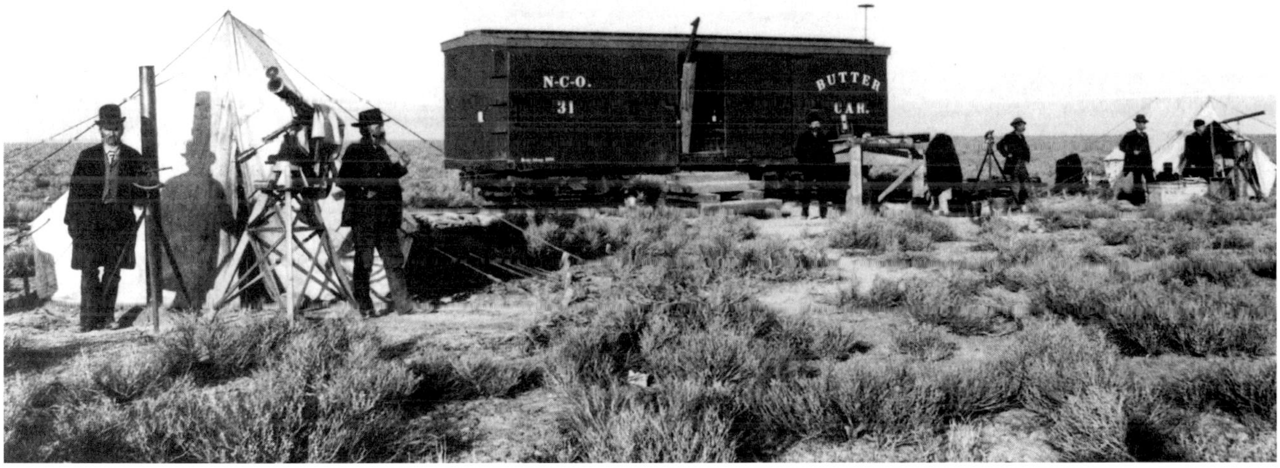

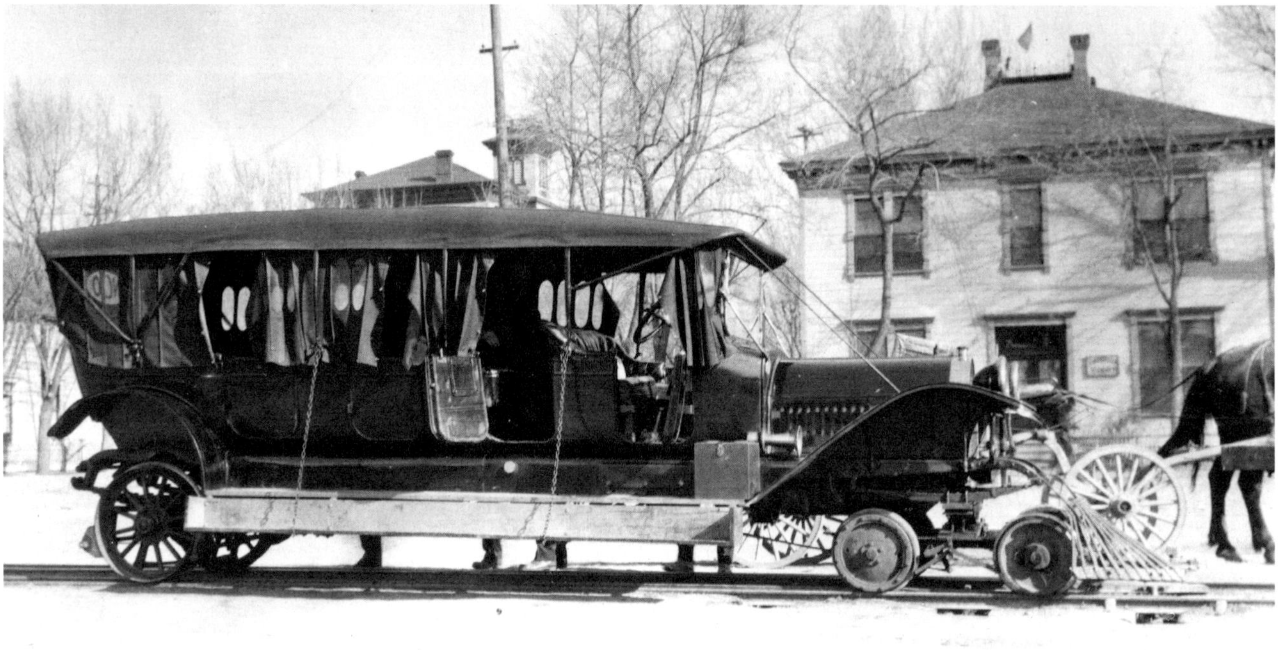

Above: As the N-C-O territory had a scant population, the road carried few passengers on its trains. Fred Jukes photographed this extended auto with flange wheels in Reno that substituted for the more expensive steam train operations. (Robert W. Richardson collection)

Below: A long train brought visitors to the Railroad Day celebration in Lakeview with engine No. 2 in command. (K. Itty collection)

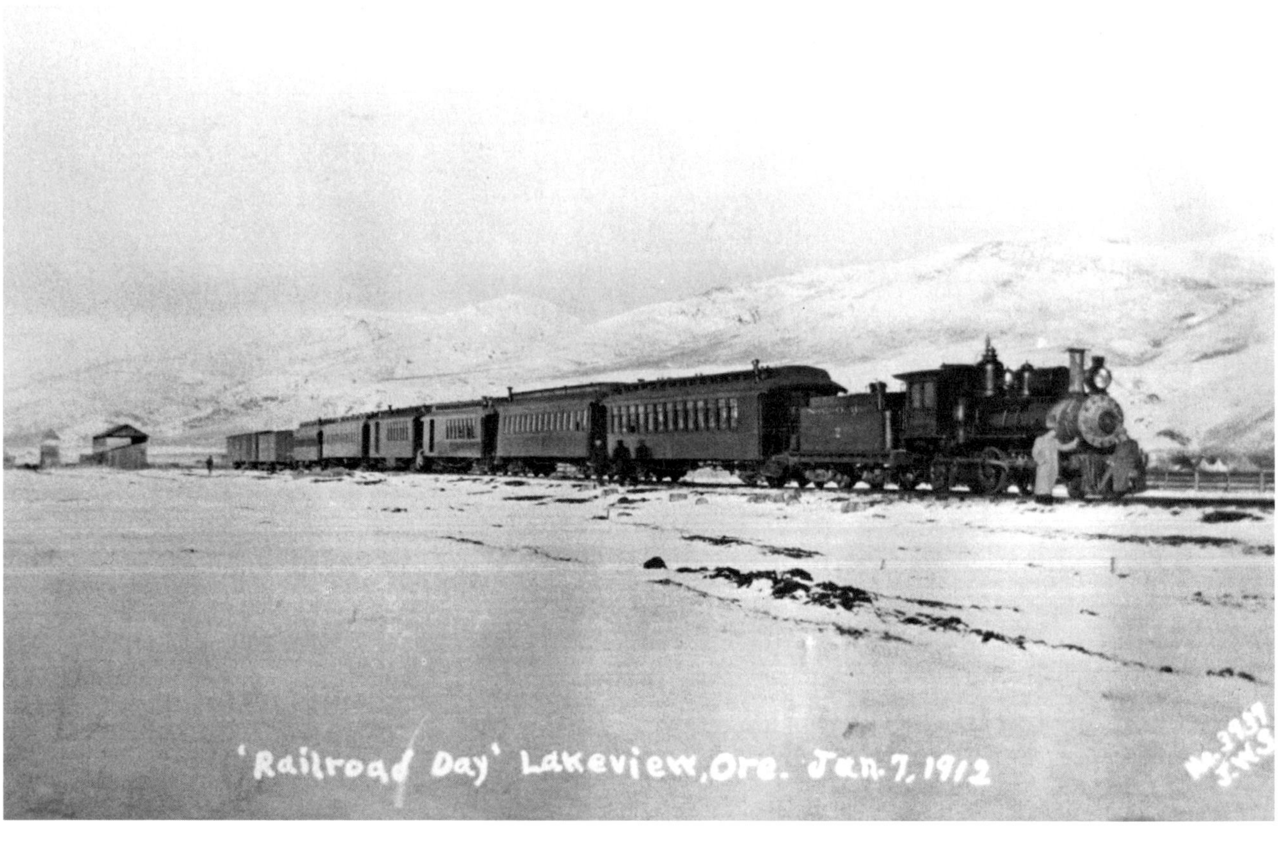

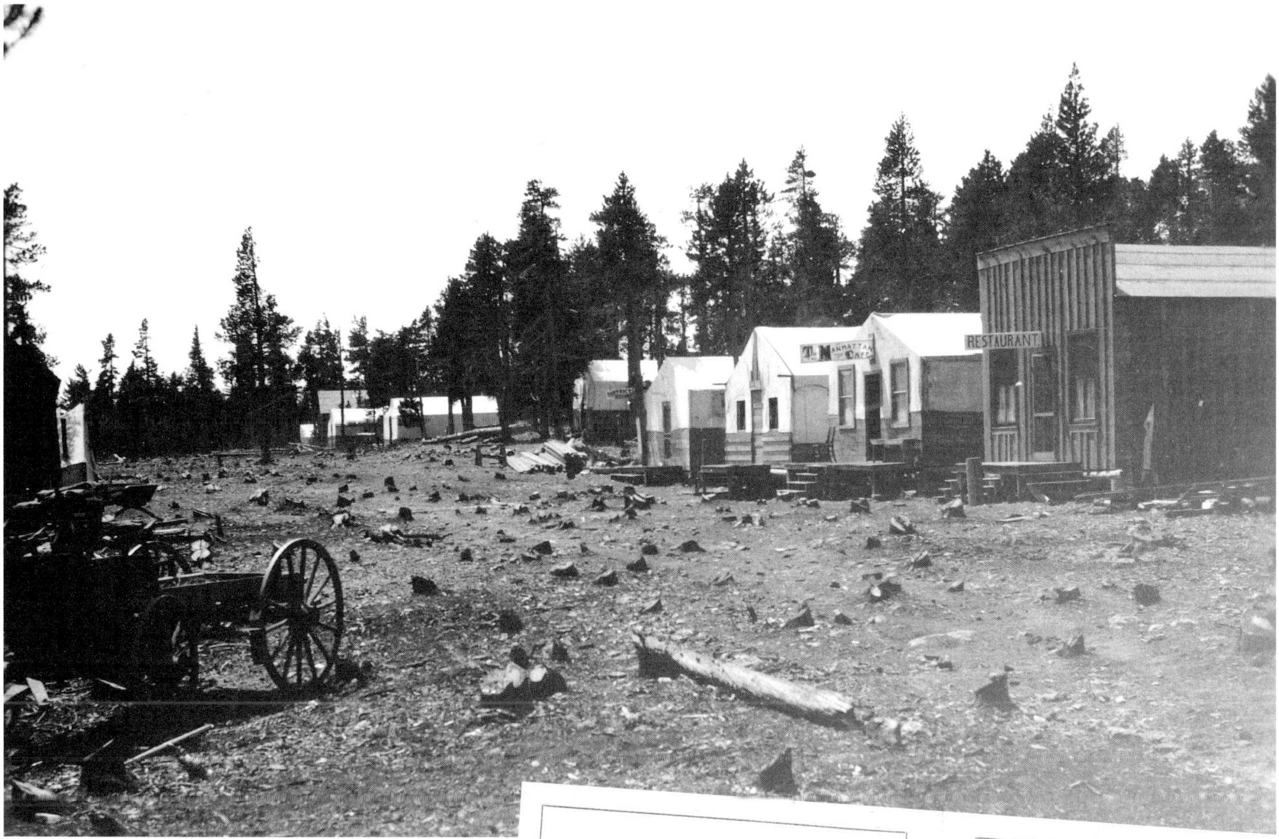

Above: Mining activity at High Grade in the Warner Mountains near the Oregon line held a short-lived promise of additional traffic for the railroad in August 1912. (U.S. Geological Survey)

Right: Southern Pacific invited many guests from Oregon to the September 14, 1929, celebration at Hackamore, California, for the opening of the Klamath Falls–Alturas Transcontinental Line.

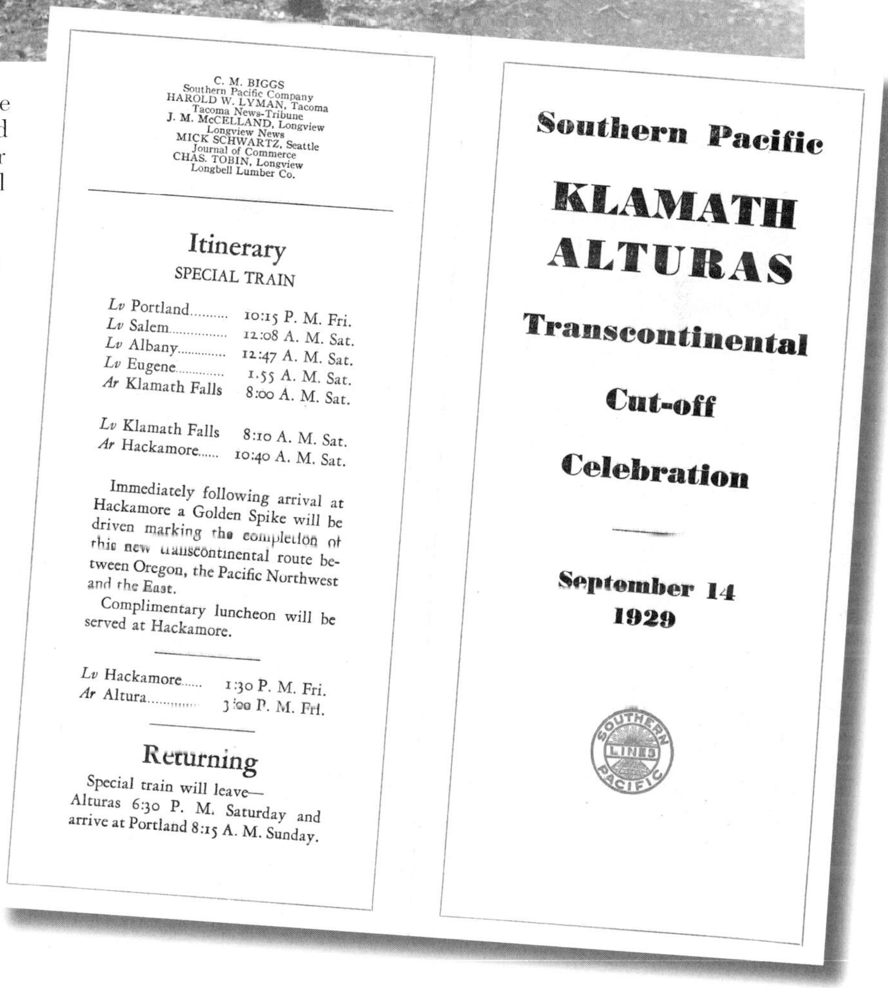

C. M. BIGGS
Southern Pacific Company
HAROLD W. LYMAN, Tacoma
Tacoma News-Tribune
J. M. McCELLAND, Longview
Longview News
MICK SCHWARTZ, Seattle
Journal of Commerce
CHAS. TOBIN, Longview
Longbell Lumber Co.

Itinerary

SPECIAL TRAIN

Lv Portland..........	10:15 P. M. Fri.
Lv Salem................	12:08 A. M. Sat.
Lv Albany.............	12:47 A. M. Sat.
Lv Eugene.............	1.55 A. M. Sat.
Ar Klamath Falls	8:00 A. M. Sat.
Lv Klamath Falls	8:10 A. M. Sat.
Ar Hackamore......	10:40 A. M. Sat.

Immediately following arrival at Hackamore a Golden Spike will be driven marking the completion of this new transcontinental route between Oregon, the Pacific Northwest and the East.

Complimentary luncheon will be served at Hackamore.

Lv Hackamore......	1:30 P. M. Fri.
Ar Altura.............	3:00 P. M. Fri.

Returning

Special train will leave—
Alturas 6:30 P. M. Saturday and arrive at Portland 8:15 A. M. Sunday.

Southern Pacific

KLAMATH ALTURAS

Transcontinental

Cut-off

Celebration

September 14 1929

SOUTHERN PACIFIC LINES

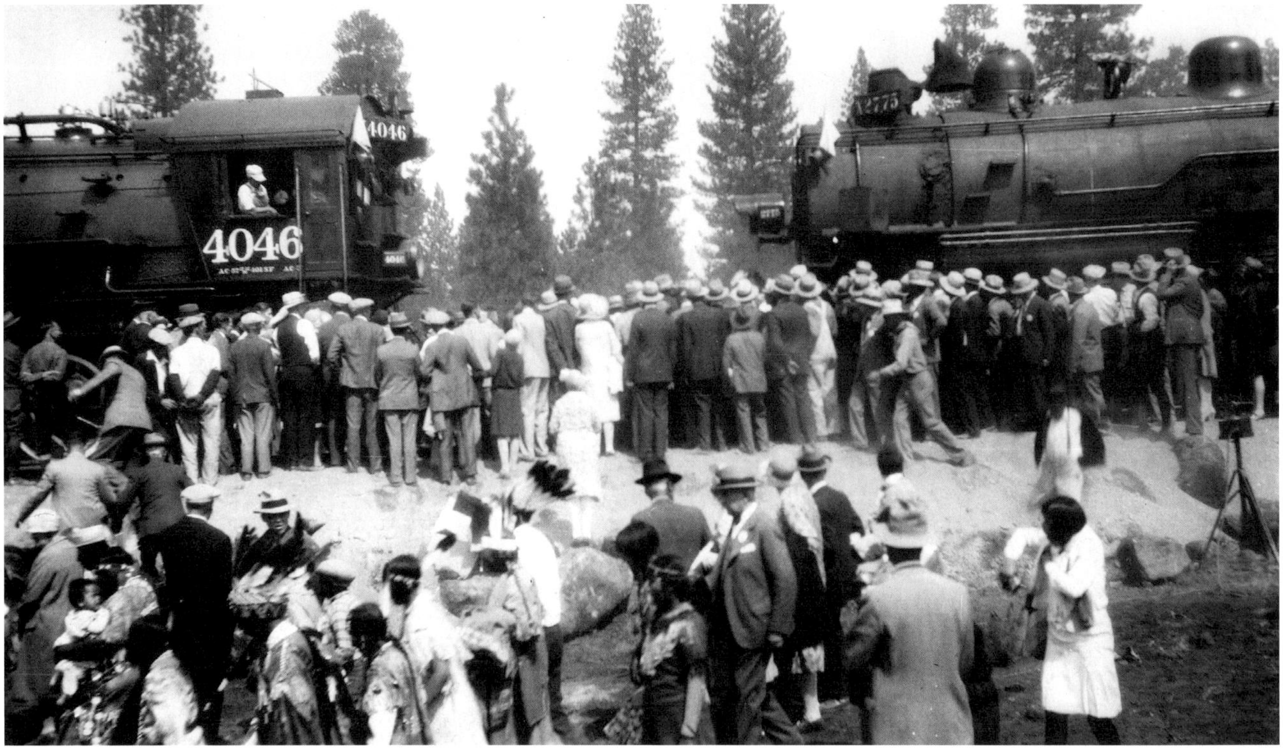

Above: For Southern Pacific, the N-C-O formed part of the Modoc Line that shortened the haul of eastbound Oregon tonnage. At the celebration near Hackamore, two locomotives, Nos. 4046 (2-8-8-2) and 2775 (2-8-0) faced each other as the last spike was pounded home. (J. B. Mathews photograph, Arizona Historical Society collection)

Below: Although the locomotive was still many miles away, Lakeview, Oregon, the eventual end of the line, presented an impressive number of buildings in November 1906. (U.S. Geological Survey)

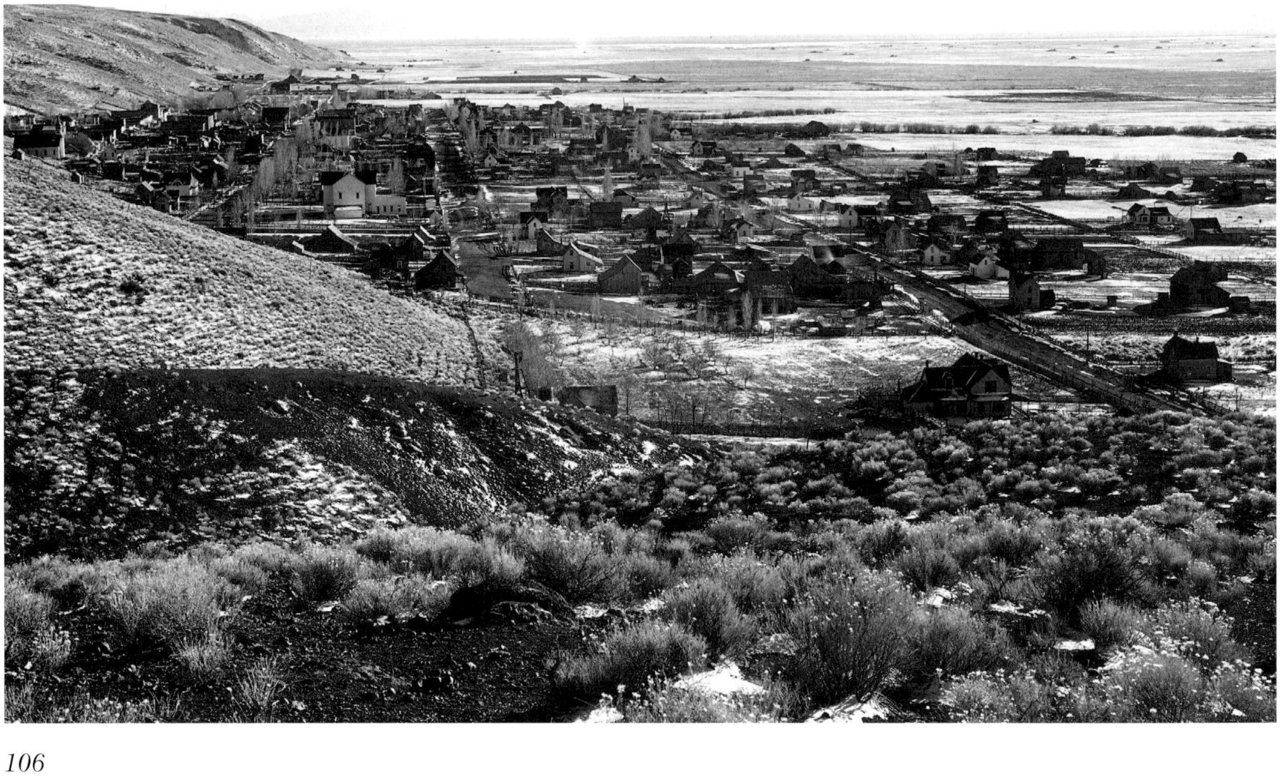

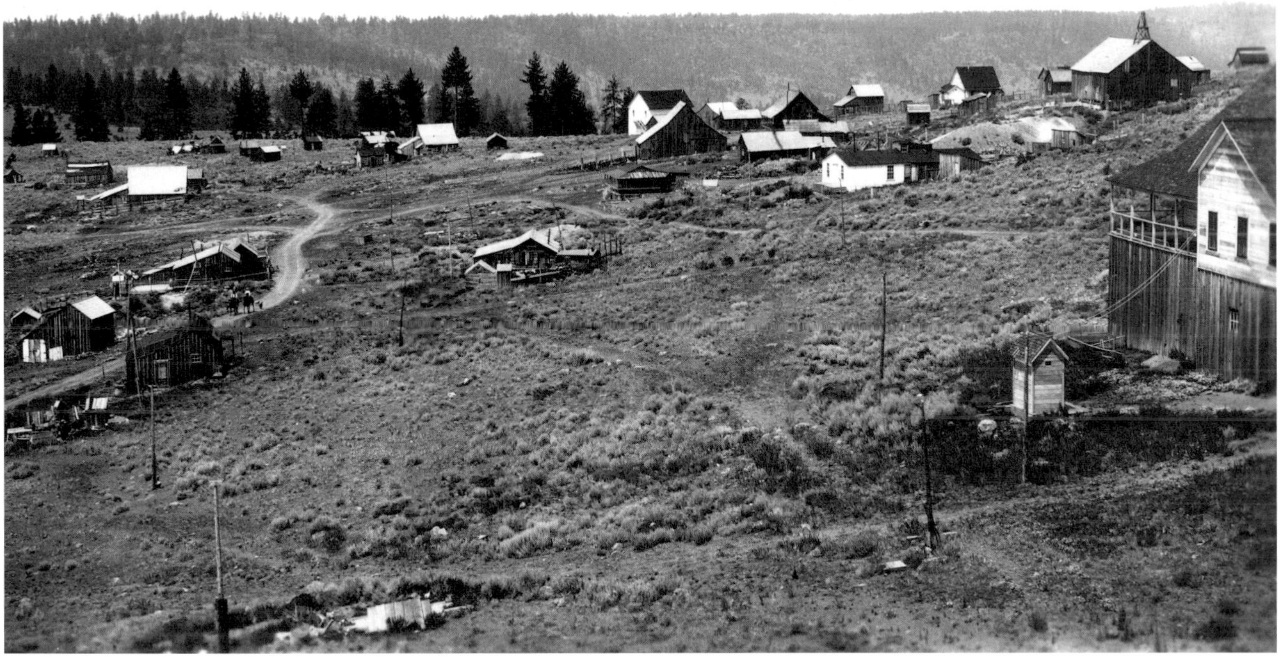

Hayden Hill, though not a station on the railroad, could have been a major source of tonnage had the output of the gold mines reached the figures promised by the promoters. (U.S. Geological Survey)

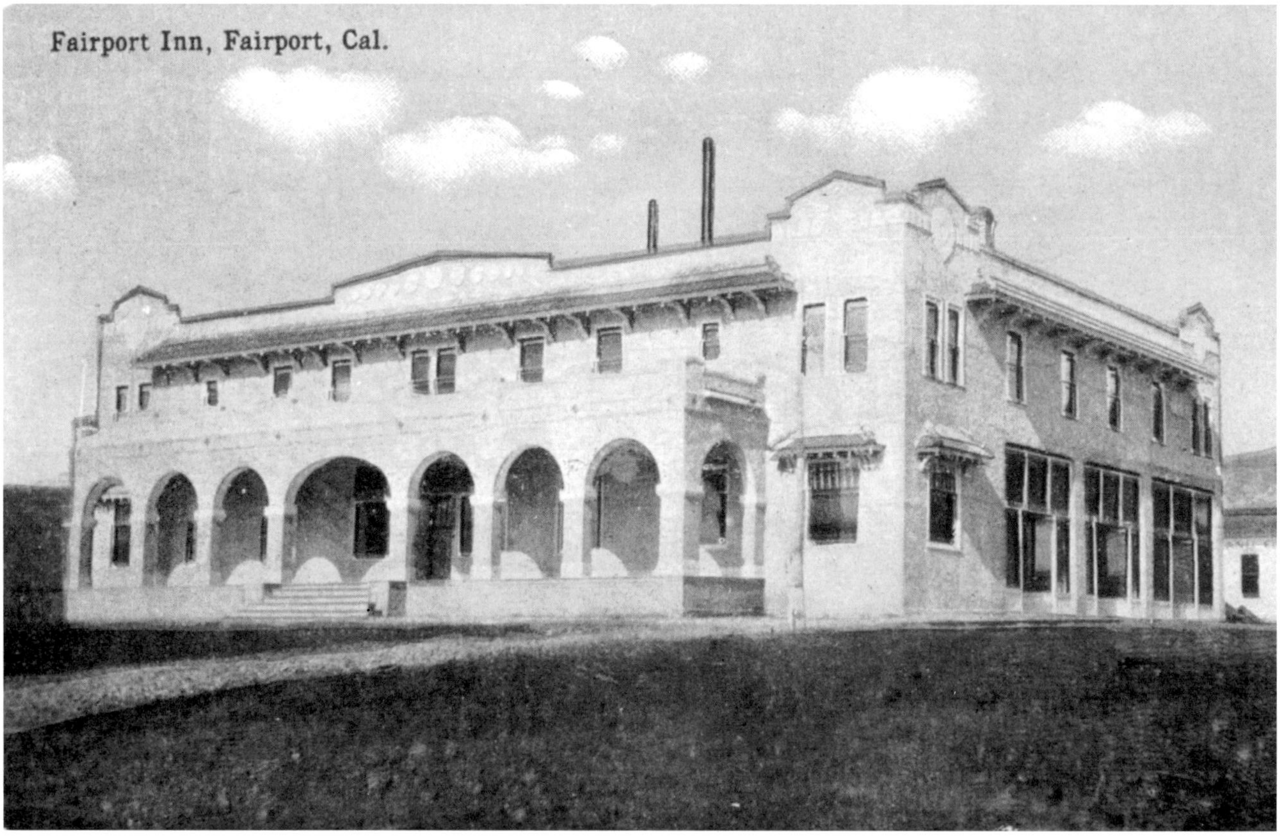

Herbert Green and Felix Green's promotion, Fairport, on the shore of Goose Lake and just below the Oregon border, began in 1909, and, with the mining boom of nearby High Grade, the settlement blossomed with an estimated population of almost one hundred. This postcard depicts the hotel built in 1910. Social activities at Fairport centered around the dance hall and sportfishing in the lake. When the mining boom ended, the town faded. The dance hall burned in 1922, and fire destroyed the neglected hotel eight years later. Today, many nearby residents are not aware that Fairport ever existed. (H. E. Gasaway collection)

Opposite above: When members of the Odd Fellows fraternal organization met in Alturas in 1919, local motorists shared Main Street with the parade. (H. E. Gasaway collection)

Opposite below: New rail for the wide-gauge change necessitated a transfer from SP flatcars to narrow-gauge cars at Wendel. (Vernon Sappers collection)

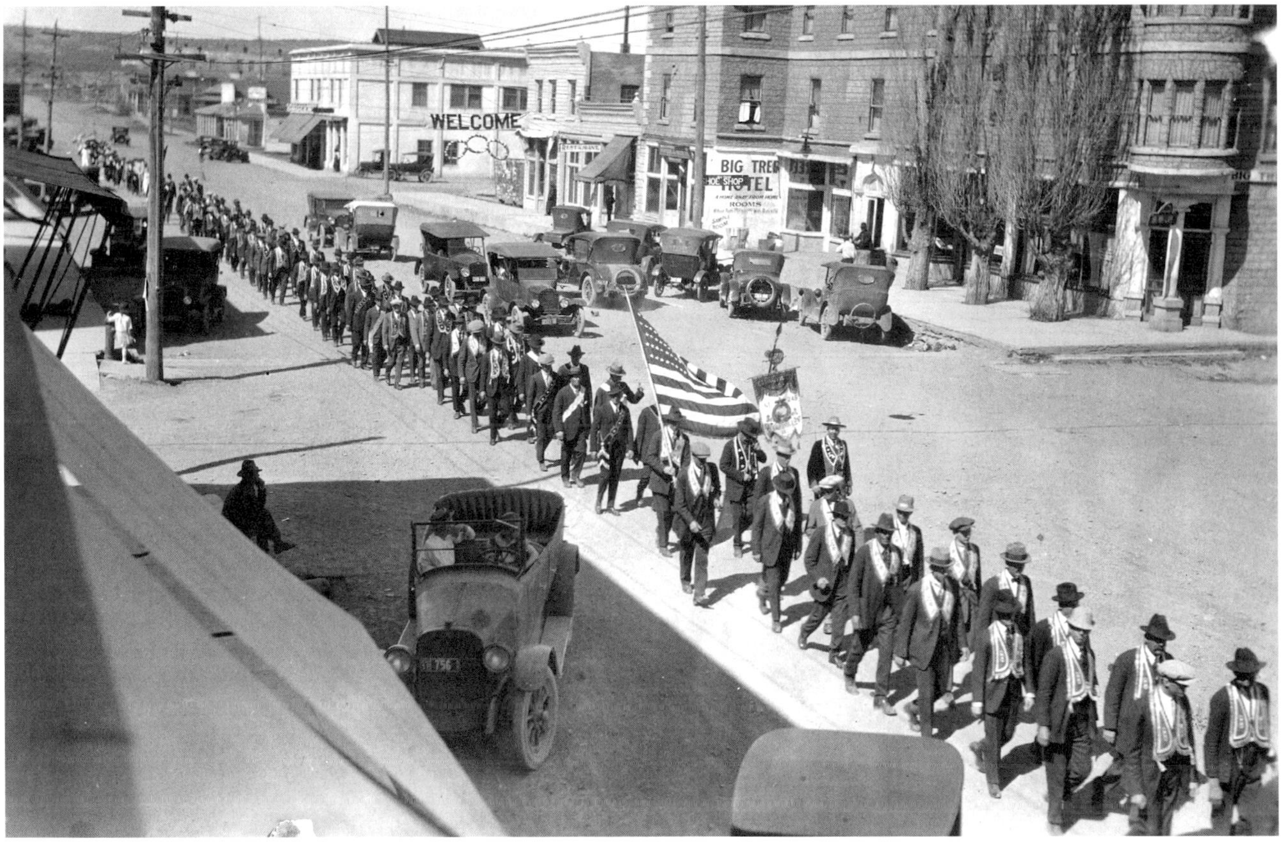
WELCOME
BIG TRE

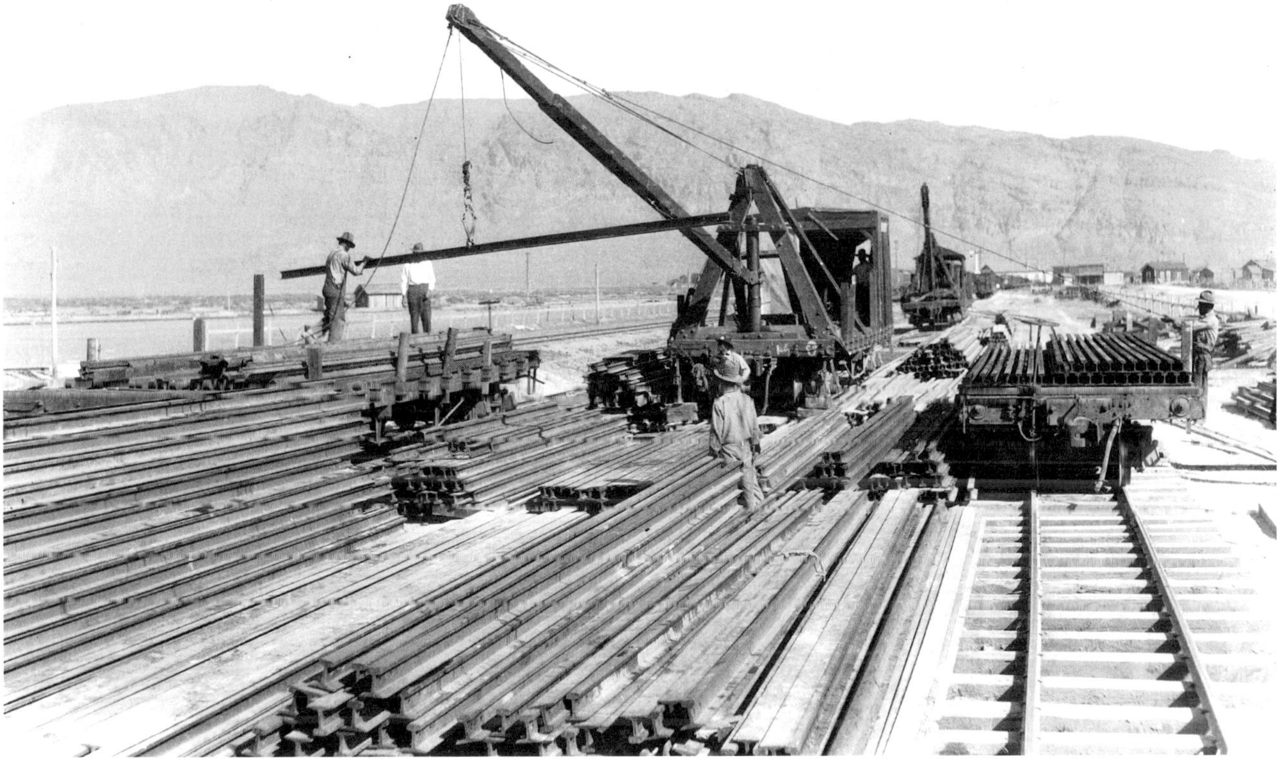

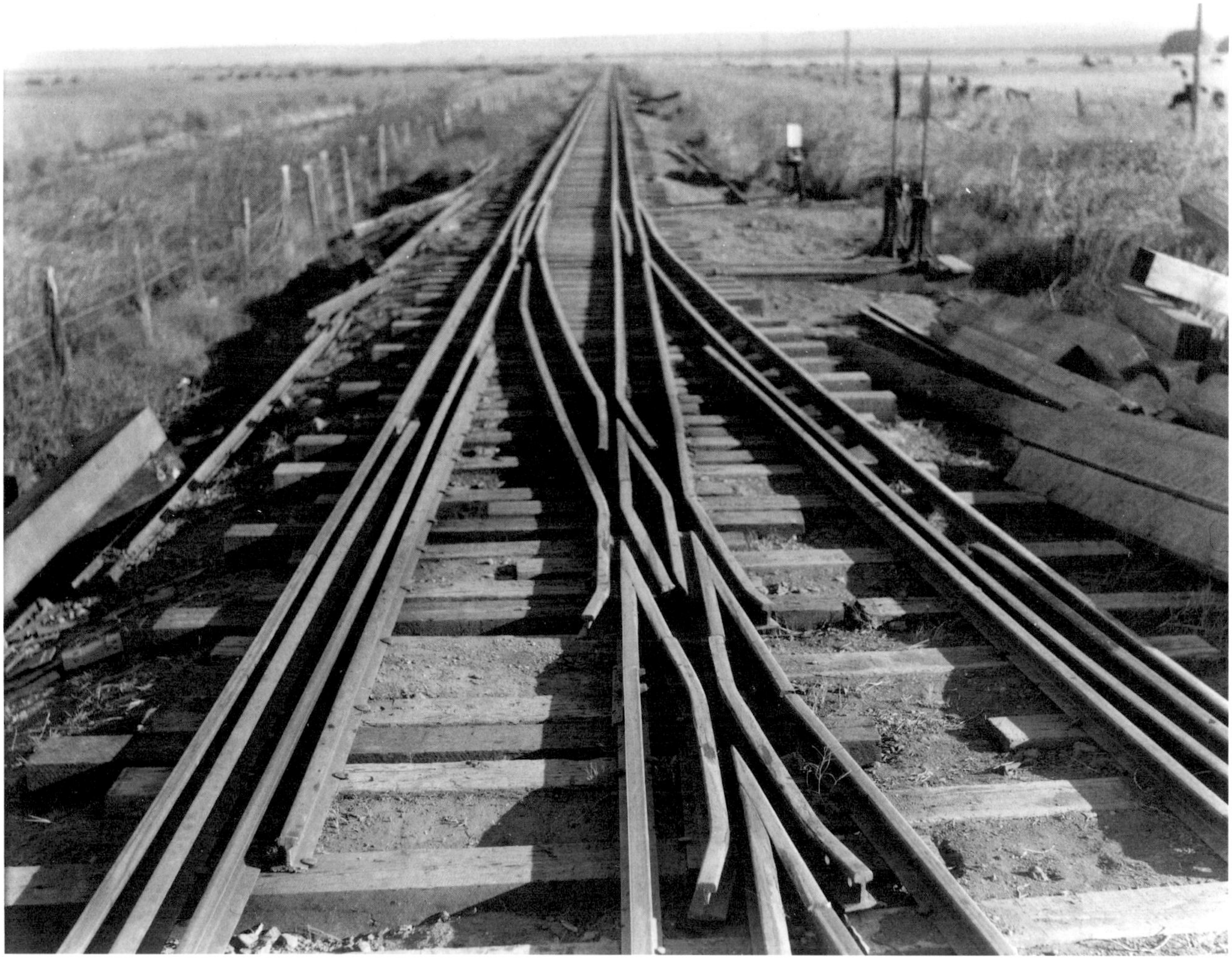

The conversion of the gauge of the railroad, accomplished during regular operations, created this scene of confusion at Bailey's, a few miles south of Alturas in September 1927. (Vernon Sappers collection)

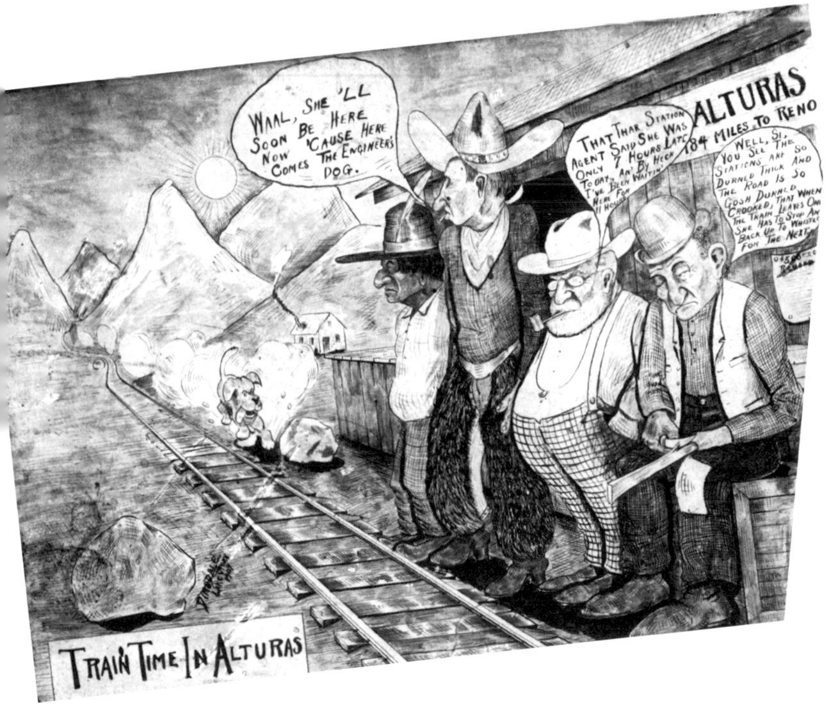

Above: Not everyone in northern California was satisfied with the railroad service. (Patricia Barry collection)

Right: Though it offered different scenery for travelers to and from Portland, the new Pullman service failed to develop sufficient patronage to continue for more than a short period.

Below: A busy construction crew on the Alturas–Klamath Falls segment of the Modoc Line. (Vernon Sappers collection)

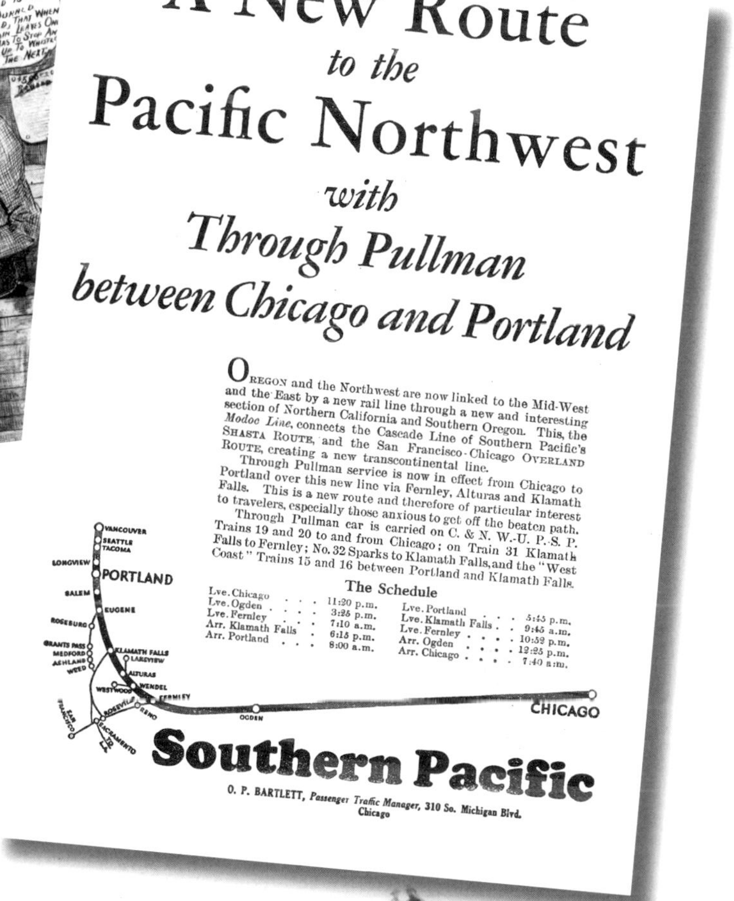

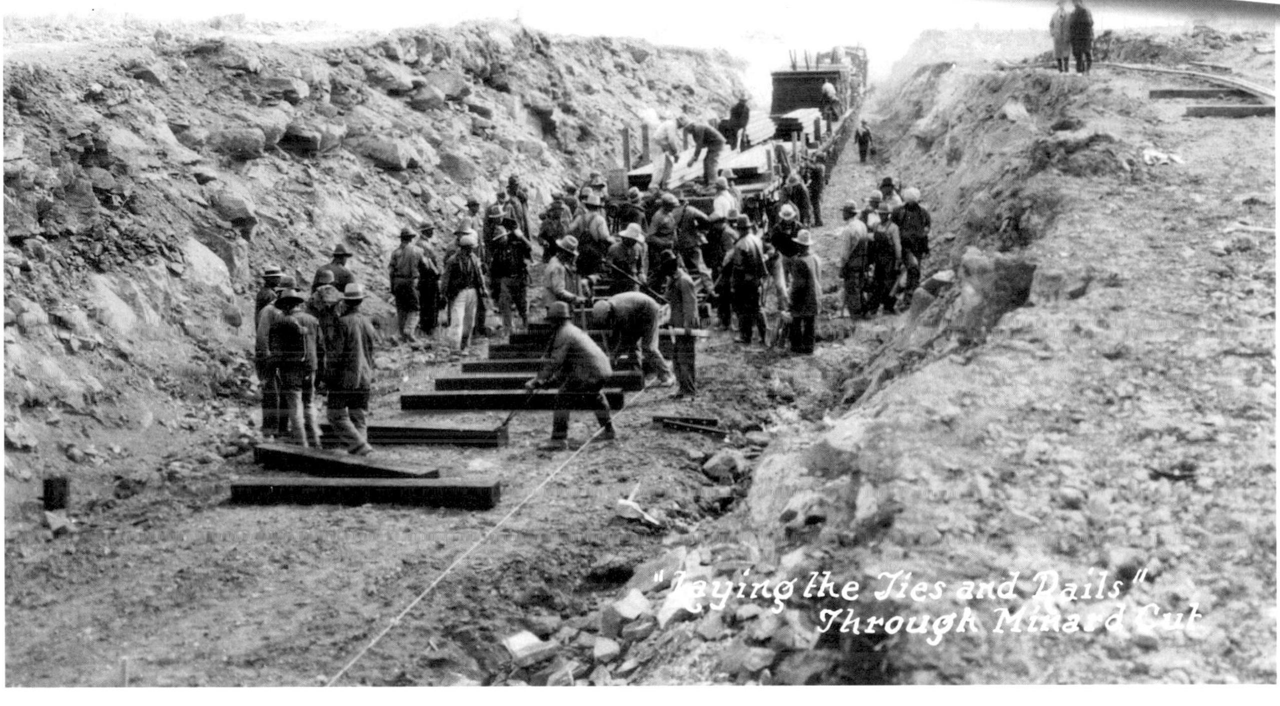

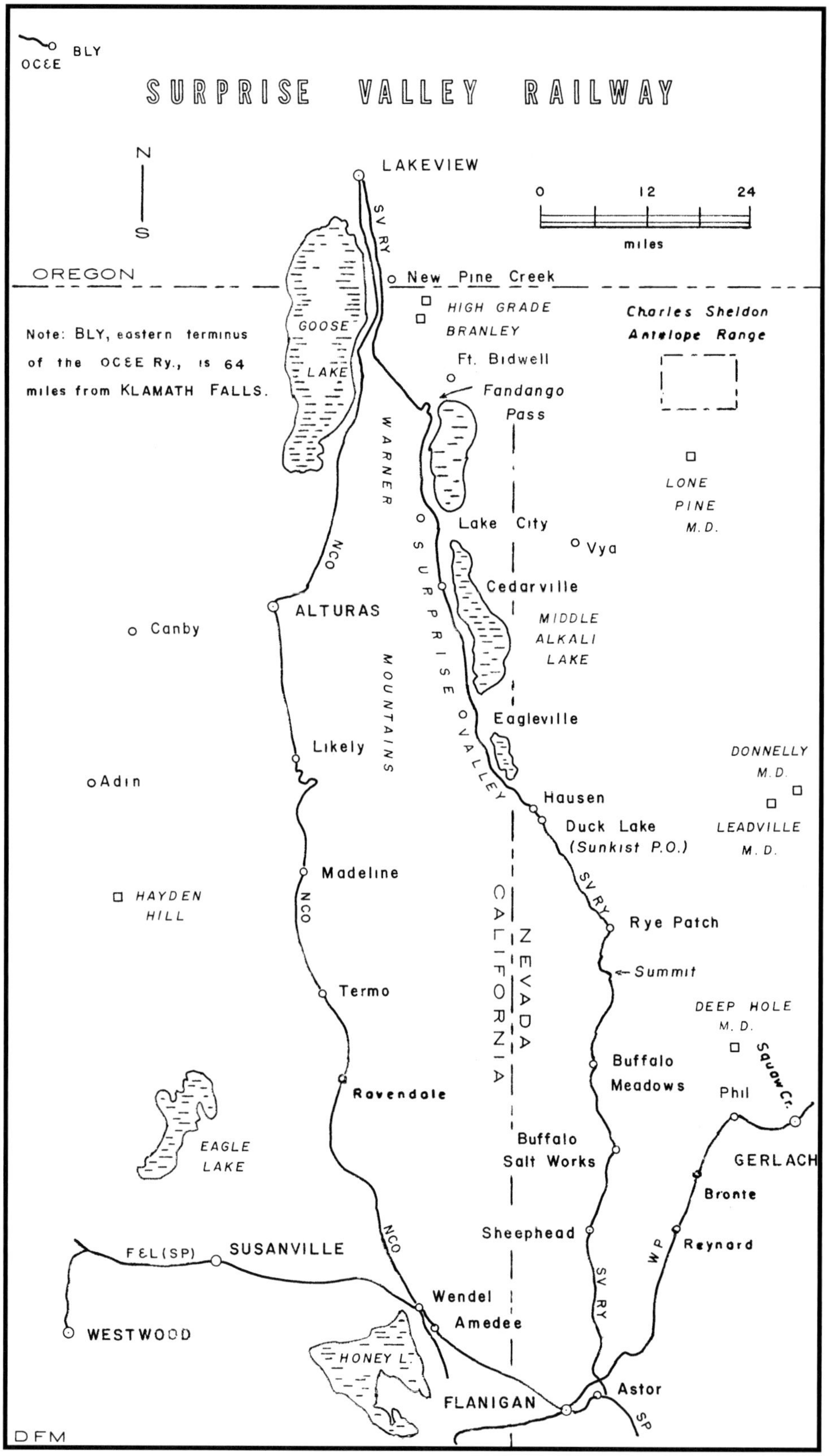

BLY
OC&E
SURPRISE VALLEY RAILWAY
N
S
LAKEVIEW
0
12
24
miles
SV RY
OREGON
New Pine Creek
HIGH GRADE
BRANLEY
Charles Sheldon
Antelope Range
Note: BLY, eastern terminus of the OC&E Ry., is 64 miles from KLAMATH FALLS.
GOOSE
LAKE
Ft. Bidwell
Fandango
Pass
WARNER
LONE
PINE
M.D.
Lake City
Vya
NCO
SURPRISE VALLEY
Cedarville
ALTURAS
Canby
MIDDLE
ALKALI
LAKE
MOUNTAINS
Eagleville
Likely
DONNELLY
M.D.
Adin
Hausen
Duck Lake
(Sunkist P.O.)
LEADVILLE
M.D.
Madeline
SV RY
HAYDEN
HILL
NCO
CALIFORNIA
NEVADA
Rye Patch
Summit
Termo
DEEP HOLE
M.D.
Squaw Cr.
Buffalo
Meadows
Ravendale
Phil
Buffalo
Salt Works
GERLACH
EAGLE
LAKE
Bronte
Sheephead
Reynard
WP
NCO
F&L (SP)
SUSANVILLE
SV RY
Wendel
Amedee
WESTWOOD
HONEY L.
Astor
FLANIGAN
SP
DFM

SURPRISE VALLEY RAILWAY

Three alkali lakes and many ranches share the area known as Surprise Valley lying in the northeast corner of California. The name is attributed to emigrants expressing their delight of the valley after crossing the Black Rock Desert. Settlements include Cedarville and Eagleville. Nearby Fort Bidwell, established as a military base in 1865, was active for almost thirty years.

Although only the Warner Range separated the valley from the N-C-O Railway, the area caught the attention of railroad promoters. In April 1912, Western Pacific, anxious to expand its traffic base, sent a crew to make a reconnaissance survey along Buffalo Creek, opposite Reynard station in Nevada, on the way to Cedarville. Not pleased with their findings, the surveyors moved east to Gerlach and worked up Squaw Creek.

When a prospector learned that his samples from a claim along Squaw Creek assayed two hundred dollars in gold to the ton plus forty ounces of silver, it stimulated interest in the survey for a short time before the matter was set aside. In June 1913, the *Cedarville Record* told its readers that the Surprise Valley Development Company stood poised to promote a rail link with Western Pacific. Encouraging news emanated the next month with the incorporation of a company to construct a railroad to Reynard.

This activity caused ranchers to think in terms of subdivisions, and the editor of the *Bidwell News* insisted that any railroad to the area should be standard gauge, saying that it would be better to have no railroad at all if promoters expected to push a narrow-gauge railroad on his community.

Western Pacific surveyors returned in the fall of 1913 to commence work at Bronte, about eight miles east of Reynard, but that railroad's financial troubles eliminated any chance of mature consideration of the project. J. E. Sexton, busy running the Eureka and Nevada Railroad, announced in March 1914 that he was ready to build a narrow-gauge line from WP to Surprise Valley. "Work to start in ten days" proved to be the last heard about that project. In its place, an enterprising man commenced an auto stage line between Cedarville and Gerlach, subject to suspension in winter months.

Incorporation of the Surprise Valley Railway on October 28, 1915, as an extension of the "Strahorn System" offered new hopes to people in the valley. Robert E. Strahorn's manner fitted comfortably with the lifestyle of the nineteenth century. His peripatetic life spanned from 1852 to 1944, and his occupations ranged from an Indian war correspondent to writing Northwest guide books. It also included working for the Denver and Rio Grande (D&RG) and Union Pacific in the engineering, construction, and operating departments. He took credit for organizing the advertising and publicity department of Union Pacific in 1878. Next he promoted new cities, such as Caldwell, Idaho, and Ontario, Oregon, as well as irrigation projects. He then ventured into developing small railroads and selling them to larger companies.

The Strahorn System, as envisioned by its founder, would have reached out east and north from Klamath Falls to link with other Oregon railroads, including the N-C-O at Lakeview. The Oregon, California, and Eastern Railway (OC&E) stood as the only tangible evidence of his railroad dream.

Seeking another outlet for the Strahorn System, the Surprise Valley Railway proposed to connect with both SP and WP at Flanigan and build north to Cedarville; amended incorporation papers established Lakeview as the northern terminus. Strahorn opened an office in Lakeview in the fall of 1916 and engaged a twenty-man surveying party to locate a 3-mile tunnel under Fandango Pass in the Warner Range.

Strahorn filed definite location maps with the Interior Department for the portion of the line in Nevada and over Fandango Pass. Much of the right-of-way along the western shore of the alkali lakes in Surprise Valley had been secured by deeds in the latter part of 1916.

The railroad encountered three summits in its 154 miles. Sand Pass, about 5 miles north of Flanigan, posed a modest 1 percent grade. A longer climb led the survey from Buffalo Creek over the summit to Cedar Creek and Duck Lake Valley and required a temporary 2.53 percent grade for a short segment on the north side. Instead of the contemplated 3-mile tunnel, a 4,820-foot tunnel conquered Fandango Pass, clipping 766 feet off the 6,130-foot summit. A 2.2 percent grade confronted northbound traffic.

Railroad history in northeastern California might have been quite different had the Surprise Valley Railway been constructed. It would have seriously affected the narrow-gauge N-C-O Railway traffic pattern and caused revision of Southern Pacific's plans for new rail lines. After pocketing $495,000 when he sold the OC&E to SP (Great Northern soon acquired a half-interest), Strahorn and his new wife enjoyed world cruises. The Surprise Valley Railway never entered the construction phases and was quietly abandoned in 1927.

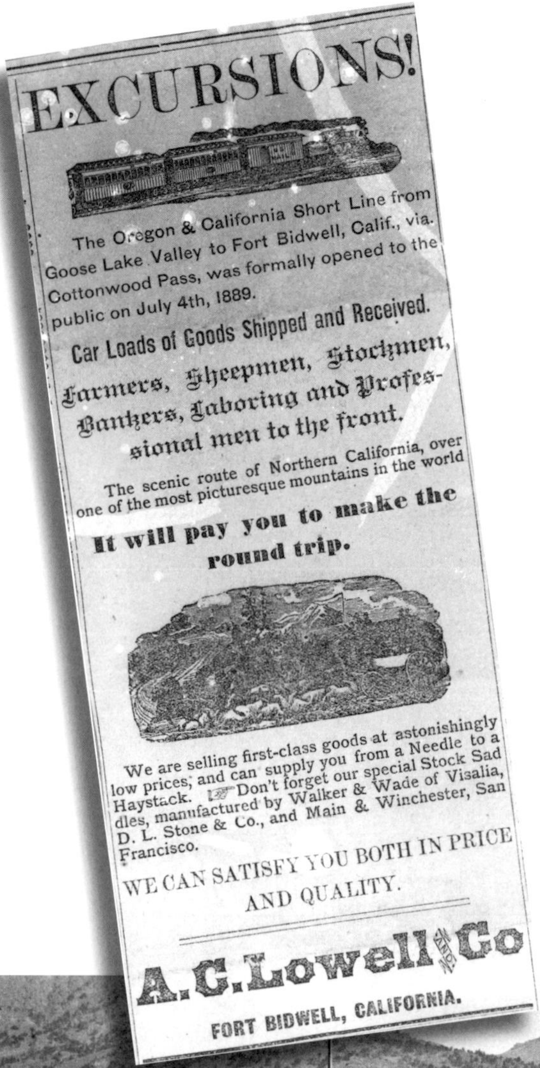

Left: A. C. Lowell, proprietor of a general store in Fort Bidwell at the upper end of Surprise Valley, commenced operations of the Oregon and California Short Line over the Warner Mountains to Goose Lake Valley, north of Alturas, in 1889. Those expecting a comfortable passage on a train, as implied by the advertisement, were disappointed to find it was a rough trip by stage. The claim that the route passed through "one of the most picturesque mountains in the world" could also be questioned.

Below: Cedarville would have been the most important settlement on the proposed Surprise Valley Railway.

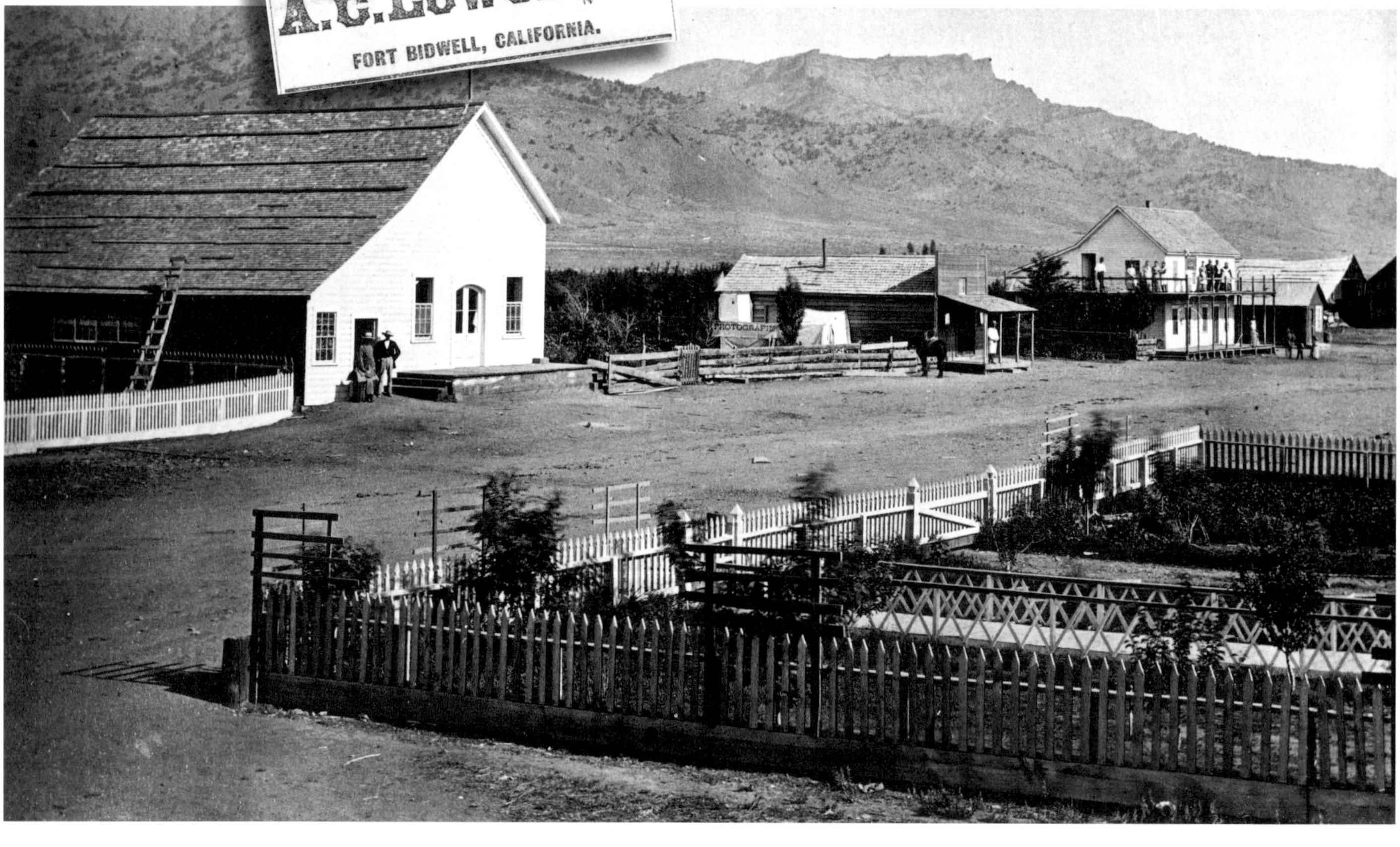

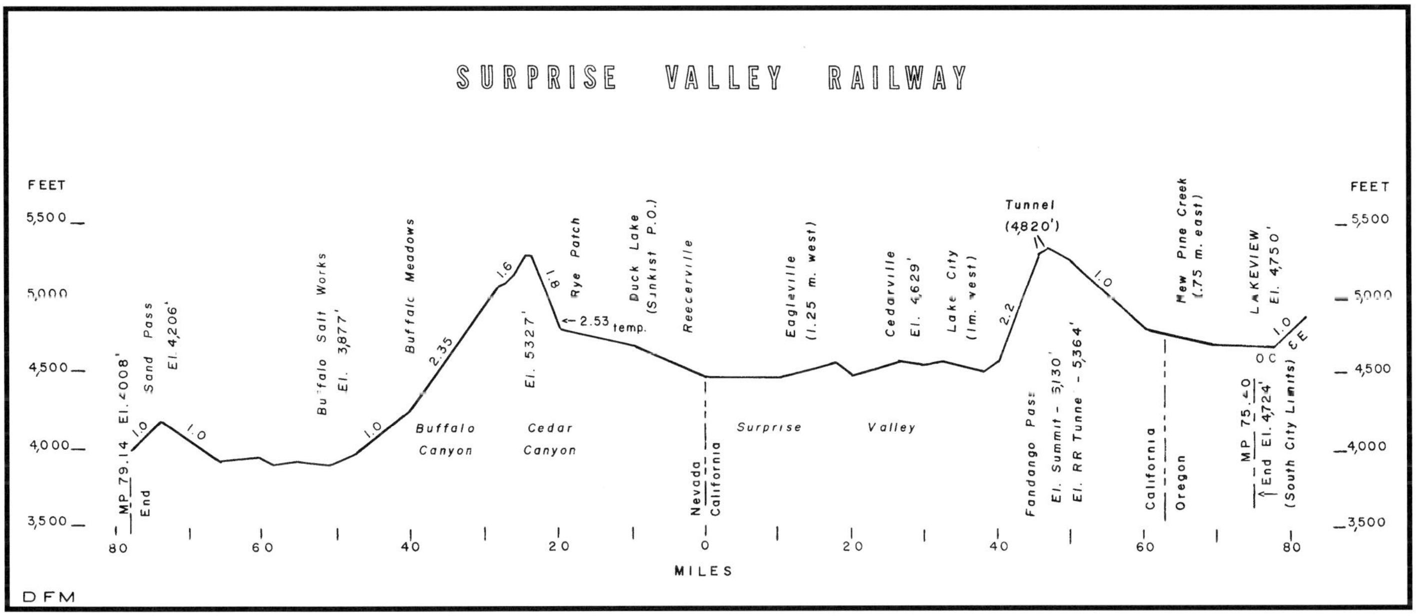
SURPRISE VALLEY RAILWAY
FEET
5,500
5,000
4,500
4,000
3,500
MP 79.14 El. 4008'
End
Sand Pass
El. 4,206'
Buffalo Salt Works
El. 3,877'
Buffalo Meadows
2.35
1.6
1.8
El. 5327'
Rye Patch
2.53 temp.
Duck Lake
(Sunkist P.O.)
Reeceville
Buffalo
Canyon
Cedar
Canyon
Nevada
California
Surprise
Valley
Eagleville
(1.25 m. west)
Cedarville
El. 4,629'
Lake City
(1m. west)
2.2
Tunnel
(4820')
Fandango Pass
El. Summit - 5130'
El. RR Tunnel - 5,364'
California
Oregon
New Pine Creek
(.75 m. east)
LAKEVIEW
El. 4,750'
MP 75.40
End El. 4,724'
(South City Limits)
80
60
40
20
0
MILES
DFM

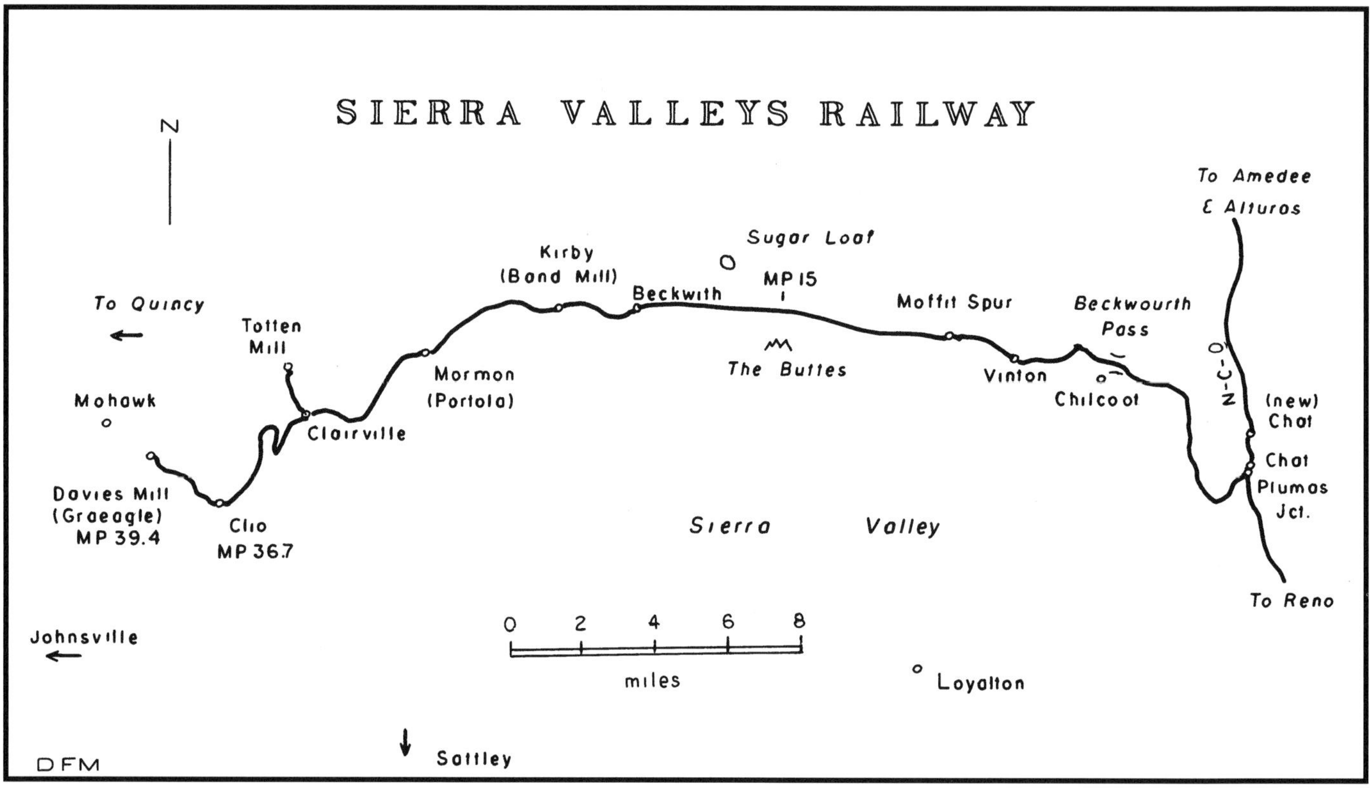
SIERRA VALLEYS RAILWAY
N
To Amedee
& Alturos
Sugar Loaf
Kirby
(Bond Mill)
Beckwith
MP 15
To Quincy
Totten
Mill
Moffit Spur
Beckwourth
Pass
The Buttes
Mormon
(Portola)
Vinton
Chilcoot
N-C-O
Mohawk
Clairville
(new)
Chat
Chat
Plumas
Jct.
Davies Mill
(Graeagle)
MP 39.4
Clio
MP 36.7
Sierra Valley
To Reno
0 2 4 6 8
miles
Johnsville
Loyalton
Sattley
DFM

SIERRA VALLEYS RAILWAY

Plumas County's economic history since the gold rush has been varied, as interest focused on one industry after another. Mining and raising fruits and vegetables together with livestock formed the main occupations in the decades following the excitement of 1849. Sawmilling existed but only to meet local needs. The isolation of Plumas County and lack of transportation prohibited access to a large market.

Drawn by the low elevation of Beckwourth Pass, several railroad enterprises appeared, with surveyors following the grand words of promoters. These projects instilled high hopes among residents in the back country, only to be followed by disappointment when the promoters folded their tents and stole away during the night.

A local railroad proved to be the first to construct a track in Plumas County, but, lacking financial support, it turned idle for about eight years, again causing disappointment in the county. This railroad, a narrow-gauge line called the Sierra Valley and Mohawk Railroad, filed incorporation papers on October 1, 1885, and soon began grading at Chat (later called Plumas Jct.). Tracklayers followed graders up the hillside to Beckwourth Pass and into the broad Sierra Valley. Unpaid bills brought the sheriff on the scene in August 1887 to sell various items convertible into cash. By that time, the Sierra Valley and Mohawk Railroad had laid fourteen miles of track almost to The Buttes (four miles east of Beckwith) and had graded another sixteen miles, extending through Beckwith as far as the Band Mill.[1]

People residing along the several forks of the Feather River and in Quincy insisted that the Central Pacific had made a grievous error in choosing Donner Pass, as it is about two thousand feet higher than Beckwourth Pass. In its initial investigations, CP studied several routes including Beckwourth Pass. What both the critics and the CP engineers failed to recognize was that slides from the decomposed granite walls along the Feather River would continue to cause slides and disrupt operations many times in future years.

The Kennedy survey of 1892 located a line up the North Fork and the Middle Fork of the Feather River with grades not exceeding fifty-two feet to the mile except for forty-eight miles of road where they reached as much as seventy feet per mile.

With Central Pacific confronting the seemingly impossible task of meeting its contract during 1896–1898 to pay its obligation to the U.S. government for the maturing debt and interest, default and bankruptcy appeared inevitable. With bankruptcy, the property would slip out of the Collis P. Huntington domain. Rival ownership of CP would leave Huntington no choice but to build another railroad, and local sages would accept no answer for the route other than the North Fork and Beckwourth Pass. When Collis lent financial support to Henry A. Bowen to purchase the idle narrow-gauge railroad, he had "his foot in the door," if need be. (Bowen considered Huntington a good friend.)

Even before that time, there is some evidence that Huntington speculated about using one of the forks of the Feather River. Back in July 1891, two SP engineers, T. D. Browne and William B. Storey, spent six days working up the North Fork from Oroville to Quincy. Here they paused for two days to write up their notes before going to Nelson Point and making another reconnaissance down the Middle Fork to Oroville. According to the *Oroville Mercury*, the two men considered the Middle Fork entirely practicable for a railroad, although they wanted to find a better route if possible and returned to the mountains. Their final conclusions were lost in time. Storey left Southern Pacific and then joined the Santa Fe where he moved up to the top position of that railroad in 1920.

Bowen had departed from his father's well-established San Francisco grocery firm, Goldberg-Bowen, to purchase the dormant Sierra Valley and Mohawk Railroad. Forming the Sierra Valleys (SV) Railway, Bowen entered into a contract with H. L. W. Knox in October 1894 to push its rails westward. Knox failed to file the contract with the country recorder, an omission that later proved costly to him. Knox's men went to work, and trains began running to Beckwith in June 1895. His forces erected a 36 × 130–foot depot at that point using lumber from Turner's mill near Sattley and continued moving westward. Work was completed on August 8, 1895, when the tracks reached Rock Quarry, a point 900 feet west of Alexander Kerby's (Kirby) mill.

Mining and Lumbering in Eastern Plumas County

Mining had long been the drawing card of the area. Johnsville, four miles southwest of Mohawk, served as the community for the fabled Plumas-Eureka Mine, while farther south the Jamison Mine and the Four Hills Mine were enjoying renewed activity. The Plumas-Eureka, opened in 1852, yielded about four million dollars in gold in the next two decades. Sold to the Sierra Buttes Gold Mining Company Ltd. of England, a four-mile flume brought water from Jamison Lake to power the firm's sixty-stamp mill, by far the largest in the county. The English company continued to produce ore, but when Bowen came on the scene, the mine had been degraded to operations by leasers. The other two mines furnished some welcome inbound traffic, but it proved only transitory.

When Bowen assumed control of the railroad, several moderate-size sawmills dotted the area. J. C. Knickrem dealt in general merchandise in Mohawk when not tending to his sawmill there. Marion C. Bringham, not satisfied as just the proprietor of the Beckwith Hotel, also conducted a lumber operation from which he supplied large bridge timbers for Mr. Bowen's railroad. Bringham erected a water tank on thirty-foot supports at Beckwith just after the first train arrived.

J. G. Totten operated a sawmill at Beckwith, while seven miles to the north, the Horton brothers had been established in Clover Valley since 1891. Instead of horses, the McNair brothers used huge oxen in conveying logs to their mill in the upper stretches of Mohawk Valley. The Band Mill at Kerby (Kirby) station, to the west of Beckwith, was so identified because a continuous band saw, rather than a circular saw, cut logs into boards. The band saw, being thinner, created less sawdust, so more boards came from each log.

How Bowen found J. M. Engle of Pennsylvania is not known, but this man proved invaluable in efforts to solve the new railroad's greatest problem: securing

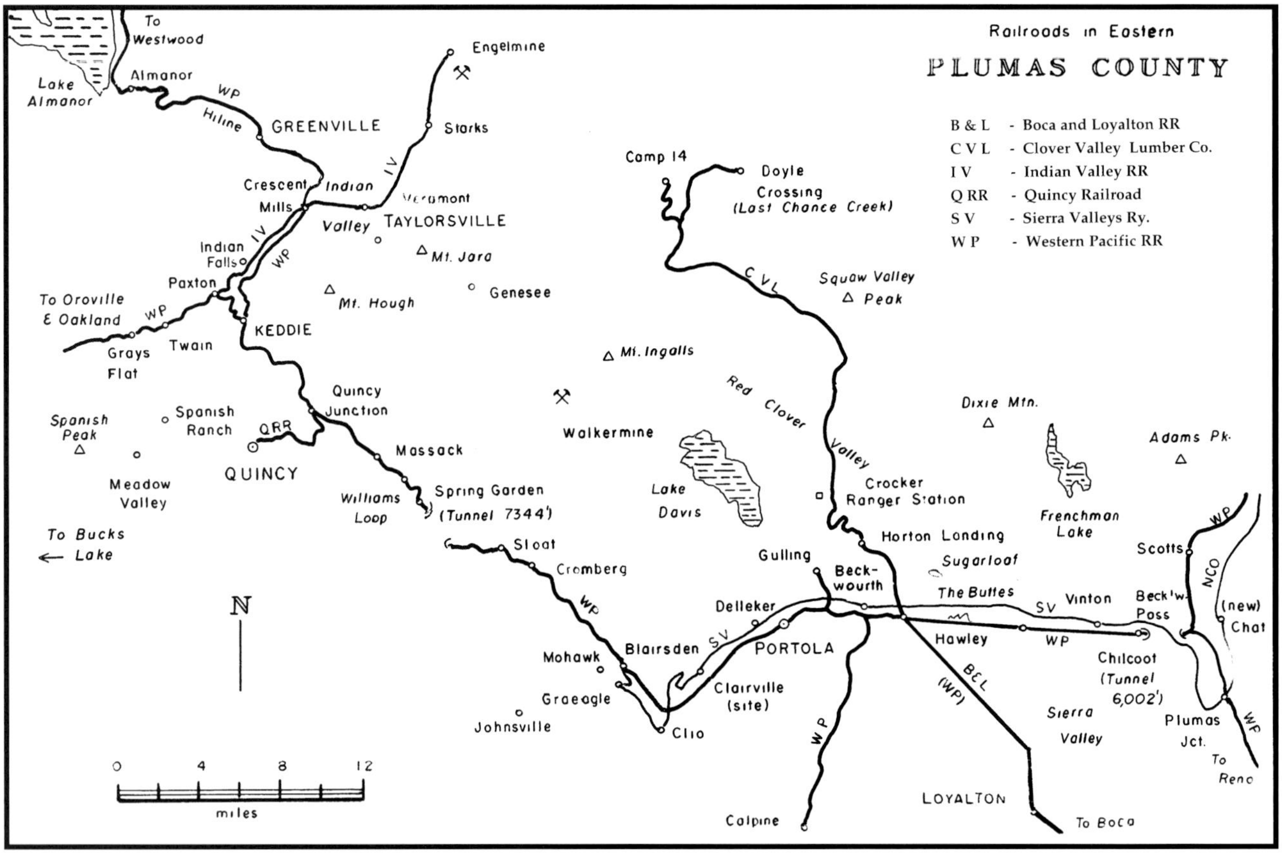

A dozen railroads served eastern Plumas County in the early decades of the twentieth century. The narrow-gauge Sierra Valleys Railway formed the pioneer line, followed by the Boca and Loyalton, which ended in Portola. The opening of the Western Pacific from San Francisco Bay to Salt Lake City in 1909 encouraged a number of industrial railroads, mostly serving the lumber trade, though the Indian Valley Railroad tapped a copper mine and another reached Quincy. Short-line logging railroads were active in the Meadow Valley, at Quincy, Massack, Sloat, Cromberg, Graeagle, and Delleker. The Clover Valley Lumber Company operated its lengthy railroad as far north as Camp 14. One by one, local trackage vanished, and today it forms a segment of the Union Pacific.

adequate traffic. Recognizing mutual benefits to be gained, Engle served primarily as a business developer by encouraging the establishment of lumber mills and then providing a means to ship finished products to distant markets. Lumber was the only available commodity needing transportation in eastern Plumas County. (For a time, Engle managed the railway.)

As the first trains were arriving at Beckwith, Arthur Keddie surveyed a town site ten miles to the west and near Otis Flat that became Clairville. Sol Marble's eight-horse teams hauled two carloads of machinery to the site where W. T. Lloyd's new sawmill took form, and soon Lloyd began cutting ties for the Clairville extension of the Sierra Valleys Railway.

The Extension to Clairville

Reviewing the story of Bowen and his railroad, one will find that he was frequently involved in litigation. One prolonged case came from a dispute over the work of H. L. W. Knox. When it came time to settle accounts, Bowen paid substantially all of the amount due but withheld several thousand dollars, for, in his opinion, Knox still had some work to finish. Knox disagreed, and when Bowen refused to budge, Knox went out on the line east of Beckwith and tore up a dozen rails to get attention. Bowen reacted by telegraphing his Quincy attorneys, J. D. Goodwin and U. S. Webb, to go to Beckwith and arrange for restoration of the railroad. (Webb, then also Plumas County's district attorney, later filled the post of California's attorney general.)

Next Knox turned to litigation to recover $12,611 allegedly due him. Bowen answered the claim, charging Knox with abandoning the work followed by dismantling the track. Bowen then sought $10,000 from Knox. As an important side issue, M. C. Bringham took an interest, for he had supplied seventeen thousand cross ties to Knox at 18 cents each. When Knox was unable to pay more than half the amount due, Bringham filed a lien and sued Knox and the railway. One trial led to another, with decisions reversed by the California Supreme Court; one complaint was directed to be returned to the Plumas Superior Court, which rendered a decision in favor of Bringham five years later. The laborers' lien held by Bringham was finally settled when the entire railroad was sold at a public auction on September 29, 1900. To protect its mortgage on the rolling stock, Southern Pacific bid $2,884 to own the property briefly, and Bringham recovered his money. (The absence of recordation of the Knox-Bowen contract in conformity with the California Code of Civil Procedure rendered it void.)

After leaving Beckwith, much of the westward extension followed the Middle Fork of the Feather River at a safe distance. At a point three miles west of Beckwith, near Alexander Kerby's ranch, the river enters a narrow canyon several miles long. Here Mr. Fitzgerald, a contractor from Stockton, took over the task abandoned by Knox.

With seven miles to go, the new force followed the canyon before crossing the Filippini brothers' ranch, previously owned by Delaney. By the end of October, "The Front" stood just one mile from Clairville, only to be stalled for want of track fittings. Next Bowen and the contractor had a brief hassle over the definition of completed work, but the construction train managed to arrive at the terminus around Christmas 1895. (A completion date of November 15, 1895, will be found in one court decision.) Soon opened to lumber traffic, Bowen would not sanction passengers until the roadbed had been stabilized and the track surfaced. Finally, mixed trains carried passengers over the new section about the end of June 1896; meanwhile, one rumor had Bowen extending the line down to Mohawk Valley, where J. D. Knickrem would start erecting another sawmill. Another rumor had the railroad reaching out as far as Quincy, a dream never to be realized by the narrow gauge. Clairville's civic pride received a boost when the SV Railway completed a 200 × 24–foot depot as passenger service began. An engine house was built six months later. This station constituted the end of the line for some years, with the possible exception of the two-mile spur to Totten's new location along Willow Creek north of Clairville.

The more active Beckwith residents celebrated the last night of 1895 by boarding a special train that took them to a natural skating rink in the Middle Fork of the Feather River about five miles away. Skating ended at eleven, and the train returned the frolickers just before midnight.

At times, interrailroad cooperation enabled shippers to send freight to Reno without transloading at Plumas Jct. Other times, even the best of times, relations turned sour. Quincy people destined to San Francisco endured a longer stage ride to Oroville, where they changed to the steam cars. The more direct route consumed less time than going through Reno.

Lumber tonnage moving over the railroad in 1896 reflected new sawmills. Besides the ones around Clairville, C. J. Lee, a Quincy merchant, erected a new mill at what became Lee Summit (over WP's Spring Garden tunnel) and employed thirty men. Logging was done by an outside contractor using teams until Lee engaged a six ton steam tractor to do the work. Apparently, the enterprise failed to be rewarding, and, after closing his mill, he sold the machinery in August 1900 to W. H. McEwen who took it to his stand of timber on the American River.

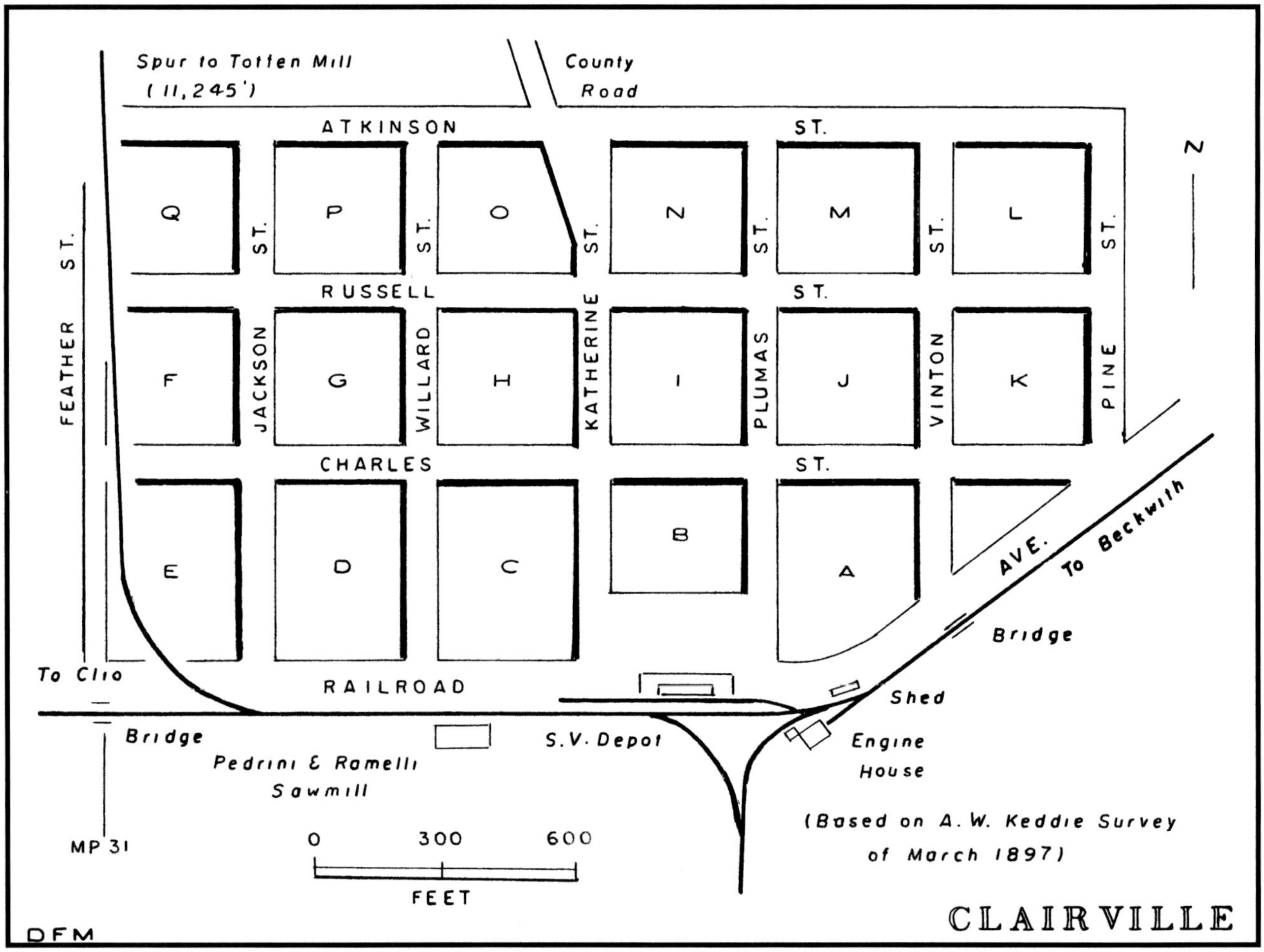

Clairville was established by Henry A. Bowen as a step in the development of the Sierra Valleys Railway. Chat Roberts's hotel occupied the north side of the square opposite the depot. The location of some of the other structures, as recalled many decades later by Vinton Bowen White, Henry Bowen's daughter, was limited to general terms.

Fred Perry, a Plains Indian, was the proprietor of a saloon to the west of the hotel. A substantial barn was situated to the north of the saloon, with Chinatown beyond. One of the important residents of that district was Charlie, the village laundryman, who also diplomatically settled personal grievances without participating in the gunplay that harassed the community.

The village school was in the northeast portion of Clairville, along with the Hayes residence and the home of the Bowens. Until the Bowens' well was deepened, all their water was delivered in whiskey barrels.

In the same year, the Horton brothers established a box factory by their sawmill in Clover Valley. Through J. M. Engle, Henry Bowen sold the Band Mill to C. H. Gardner and with the gold coin in hand returned to San Francisco.

Clairville—Once an Active Community

Only by a careful field examination can the site of Clairville be determined today. The settlement, standing at the end of the Sierra Valleys Railway for seven years, took on an air of importance, for besides the sawmills, it was a transfer point for the stage from Quincy. Stage and train schedules sometimes permitted a 6:00 A.M. departure from Quincy to arrive in Clairville about noon, and, after lunch, one could board the train for Plumas Jct. (Chat) with a Nevada-California-Oregon Railway connection to arrive in Reno late in the afternoon of the same day.

However, this trip was not always possible, as N-C-O train on-time performance at Chat was determined by the arrival of Central Pacific through trains at Reno. At those times, an overnight stay in Clairville became almost mandatory. Chat Roberts, who formerly lived at Chat, envisioned a hotel for those traveling from Quincy to Reno, and engaged carpenters in November 1896 to erect a two-story hotel at Clairville, which he opened at the end of the year.

As colorful characters in the community, Chat Roberts and his family provided much local gossip and entertaining reading in local newspapers. A biography of the family escapades, too long to go into full detail here, could well make an interesting motion picture.

Lloyd's mill, under the name of the Plumas Box and Lumber Company, had suspended operations when his other two partners, Pompey Pedrini and David Ramelli, dissolved the partnership on February 8, 1897, and W. F. Lloyd and Charles Lloyd retired from the firm.

Winter left its mark temporarily in Clairville with thirty inches of snow. Cold weather hampered the Quincy hose company in their efforts to fight a fire, as the hose was blocked with ice; someone had failed to drain the hose after its use the previous July.

The First Clairville Hotel Fire

Starting at 4:20 in the morning of October 21, 1898, everything changed when flames swept through the hotel. Believed to have started in the kitchen, the fire quickly claimed the dining room, sitting room, and hallway. Many escaped through first-floor windows, but Chat Roberts received serious injuries in his jump from the second floor. Five people perished. Pompey Pedrini, who was a partner with David Ramelli in both the dairy and the lumber business, was one of the victims. He had in his possession gold coins to meet the lumber-mill payroll, but the coins were never found in the debris. Though Chat's son, Charles, and his wife escaped through a ground-floor window, her mother and a young daughter of Charles by a previous marriage were among the casualties. The funeral procession, stretched out a full mile, proved to be the longest ever in that part of the county.

The Clairville Hotel formed the center of community life and had drawn a good patronage. Except for the abduction and rescue of two daughters and the arrest of two sons for cattle thievery, the Roberts family might have led a quiet life.

More than two months elapsed while Chat Roberts recovered from his injuries. In spite of his losses, said to be five thousand dollars, and no insurance, Chat was able to replace the hotel, so by June 1899 he accommodated thirty boarders—sawmill workers—as well as transients.

A few weeks later two men engaged in a physical battle in the new hotel. Charles Roberts came out to assist one man by firing two shots at the other. That ended the fight, but that night an unknown person on the outside fired a shot that whizzed by Charles's head with only inches to spare before crashing into the mirror behind the bar. Chat resumed management of the hotel near the end of the year while his son and daughter-in-law moved to Reno.

Just after Christmas 1898, Mrs. J. C. Smith, wife of the superintendent of the Sierra Valleys Railway replacing J. M. Engle, arranged for the construction of a 16 × 24–foot reading room in Clairville. Constructed of stone, the room enjoyed an abundance of light and helped overcome the loneliness of railroad men when away from home. On New Year's night, the railroad men produced a pantomime of a railroad scene complete with a miniature locomotive with steam. True to life, the train was delayed by men repairing the track. After the performance, everyone danced until midnight when they adjourned for supper at the Clairville Hotel. A few days later, Chat Roberts sold the hotel to Jerry Correcco of Reno, only to take it back a year later.

Down at the station, the agent was roused at 11:00 P.M. one night by a man wanting to use the telephone. Once inside, he made his real purpose known by jabbing his revolver in the agent's ribs to force him to open the safe and then walked off with $185. Since some of these funds were in transit in Wells Fargo's care, detective James B. Hume traced the gunman to Sierraville, then Truckee, where he boarded the train and finally arrested him in Oroville. After a trial, he was sent to jail for six years.

Trouble continued to follow Chat. A few weeks after the holdup, one of Roberts's sons used abusive language in the hotel, to which J. W. Webster responded by knocking him to the ground. Recovering, young Roberts attacked Webster, who struck again, but this time Roberts fell against his father, who in turn fell over a chair and broke his leg near the hip. Because of Chat's advanced years, the injury brought concern, but he recovered.

The last episode occurred on August 23, 1903. Chat drove off from his ranch at Plumas Jct. to visit his son, but after a few hours the horse returned minus the harness and buggy. A search soon found Chat lying unconscious by the roadside. Brought back to the ranch, he soon died. There appeared to be no sign of foul play, but the disappearance of the harness and the buggy proved to be an unsolved mystery.

Young Charles had been running the hotel when prosperity returned to Clairville in 1906 due to the construction of the Western Pacific Railway. However, another early-morning fire—the cause attributed to an exploding lamp—destroyed the second Clairville Hotel on May 17, 1909. This time no lives were reported lost, but, as the boom times had passed, no effort was made to rebuild the hotel.

More Problems Confront the Sierra Valleys Railway

The little railroad endured derailments just like its wider-gauge compatriots, but it suffered a longer recovery period.

When the outgoing train derailed near the Delaney ranch on March 30, 1897, Quincy residents had to forgo mail deliveries for a day. Two years later, as a train from Plumas Jct. had struggled up the grade, almost reaching the summit at Chilcoot, a freight car broke loose and raced down the slope for two miles before leaving the track. The car was badly wrecked, and this episode postponed mail deliveries again.

The infamous wreck on June 20, 1899, when a special train hit one of Mr. Humphrey's cows stuck in the trestle 1.5 miles east of Clairville cost the life of Morris J. Chambers, engineer on SV No. 2. Mr. Bowen came up from San Francisco, deeply disturbed by the incident. The coroner's inquiry found Sierra Valleys Railway responsible for the death of Chambers "because the railroad was not fenced." As noted on pages 395 and 397 in the first volume of this series, his widow collected three thousand dollars in damages.

With No. 2 badly damaged and No. 1 already in the shop undergoing major repairs, no trains could operate for about ten days after the accident. No. 2 was finally released in December. Though the sawmills around Clairville were busy cutting ties for the N-C-O Railway extension, benefiting both the mills and Bowen, ominous signs of approaching competition appeared when unidentified surveyors began running lines between the Sierra Valley and Verdi and other points on Central Pacific. One factor instigating the survey was the poor service on the two narrow-gauge railroads as relations became more strained. From this viewpoint, it is difficult to fathom the reasons for the lack of cooperation. Mr. Gest, manager of the N-C-O, refused to interchange cars at Plumas Jct., so freight had to be manually transferred there and again a second time at Reno to the standard-gauge cars. The expansion of the lumber industry around Beckwith and Clairville, reflecting the efforts of J. M. Engle, almost came to naught because of the short car supply. (Mr. Engle had left the railroad shortly before the accident.)

The Sierra Valleys Railway faced the problem common to pioneering railroads where the lack of initial development provided so little traffic that freight rates had to be high for the railroad to survive. Indeed, Beckwith merchants found that the cost of teaming freight from Truckee was less than by rail from Reno. Public relations suffered a blow by the fire that wiped out the town of Beckwith on July 29, 1898, directly attributable to sparks from a passing locomotive that set the depot on fire. The flames spread to the Beckwith Hotel, and, with a lack of firefighting equipment and a brisk wind, the large store of Enscoe and McNeil soon became a mass of flames along with the rest of the town. The church and school escaped—was there a message here?

For one solution, Henry Bowen contemplated building his own line from Plumas Jct. to Reno. In August 1899, his surveyors, having finished several months' work, left a series of alternating little red and white flags to mark the route, reportedly about ten miles shorter than the N-C-O line. Unfortunately, Bowen's limited financial resources prohibited any expenditure beyond the cost of the survey; indeed, he was well behind in paying his property taxes, and it was only by his personal entreaties that he forestalled a sheriff's sale. The family retained a large wall map with the surveyed line to Reno for many decades thereafter. (A projected extension of the SV Railway to Quincy also appears on the map. The map is now in the Plumas County Museum in Quincy.)

As most of the difficulties appeared to originate on the N-C-O, some local sage with a couple of drinks under his belt informed a saloon gathering that a solution had been found. The new yet unnamed embryonic railroad (the Boca and Loyalton [B&L]) would run northerly to Beckwith and form an alliance with the SV Railway, whereby that road would take up its rails between Beckwith and Plumas Jct., widen the remaining tracks, and extend the line westward. Fred Hail of the *Plumas National-Bulletin* in Quincy closed his article with, "Last, but not least, it would deliver the people from the Silurian policy which the N-C-O has been dealing with the traveling public." Of course, the SV track remained undisturbed, but things improved immediately after N-C-O owners replaced the crusty old manager with a more enlightened man.

The strained relations between the N-C-O and the SV ended almost immediately after the Moran brothers installed Thomas F. Dunaway as vice president and general manager on October 16, 1900. (Dunaway had been general superintendent of the Colorado and Southern Railway and its predecessor for six years.) The very next day, a special train originated on the Sierra Valleys Railway and brought fourteen cars of lumber, box shook, and door stock and two cars of Plumas mine concentrates to Reno without a transfer at Plumas Jct., mostly in SV cars.

Down the Hill to Clio

Almost every year since Bowen came on the scene, rumors of construction of the railroad down to the Mohawk Valley circulated until forgotten, only to be revived the next year. It was part of the hopeful intention to push the narrow gauge all the way to Quincy. Its predecessor, the Sierra Valley and Mohawk, had secured a two hundred–foot right-of-way to Clio (Mohawk Valley) from the General Land Office back on March 29, 1887, which became the property of the Sierra Valleys Railway.

Though not ready to make a public declaration, the N-C-O had quietly taken the Sierra Valleys Railway under its wing, and in early 1901, J. H. Bennett served as traffic manager for both lines. Bennett had joined the N-C-O the previous year after a thirty-year career on several railroads; his last connections included the D&RG and the Rio Grande Western. He spoke out of turn in March 1901 when he declared, "I expect the Sierra Valleys Railway to be extended to Mohawk within the next ninety days."

Nothing was to happen immediately, but the N-C-O opened its checkbook to pay $7,435 of unpaid taxes the SV Railway owed since 1896. Next it provided funds to reballast the roadbed, install ten thousand ties, and surface the track. Passenger service improved with through trains to Reno in combination with an early-morning stage ride from Quincy. For a time, another threat of serious competition surfaced when James Conley announced that he would take fourteen passengers from Quincy to Oroville in his new Locomobile in seven hours, five hours less than by stage, and at a tab of five dollars, instead of the seven-dollar stage fare. Like so many other grand ventures, this one appears to have faded away before starting.

Traffic on the railroad picked up; one morning, fifteen cars loaded with lumber stood poised at Clairville for departure to Plumas Jct. and Reno. The Clairville mill, now owned by Noee and Ramelli, resumed operations after the winter lull, and, thanks to a more agreeable interchange with the N-C-O, it expected to ship more lumber that year. Sunday passenger service became a regular pattern along with two daily locals during the week. Cooperation resulted in the issuance of a joint public timetable.

Still, troubles impaired a good operating record. As one train approached a switch at Plumas Jct., a passenger car and a freight car left the track to end on their sides. Passengers were unnerved by the wreck, but no serious injuries resulted.

In spite of Mr. Bennett's ninety-day forecast, some weeks elapsed before surveying began under the watchful eye of Robert M. Hall, N-C-O's chief engineer. The delay in physical work evoked many opinions, one being that the parent railroad, the N-C-O, first wanted to finish grading the section between Termo and Van Loan. Actual grading to Clio began in mid-July with fifty men, ironically fifty-four days after the road was to be finished.

The extension from Clairville to Clio (New Mohawk) measured 5.75 miles in length. Clairville sat on a bluff with an elevation of 4,869 feet, while the terminus stood at 4,411 feet, with the difference of 458 feet presenting engineering problems. As the crow flies, the gap between the two points is about 3 miles, but in order to keep the grade within a tolerable number, the surveyors looped around Willow Creek. A few hundred feet west of Clairville, the survey cut through the timberlands of John B. Otis and Solomon Otis, and, down the line, the railroad crossed more Otis property on both sides of the Willow Creek Bridge.

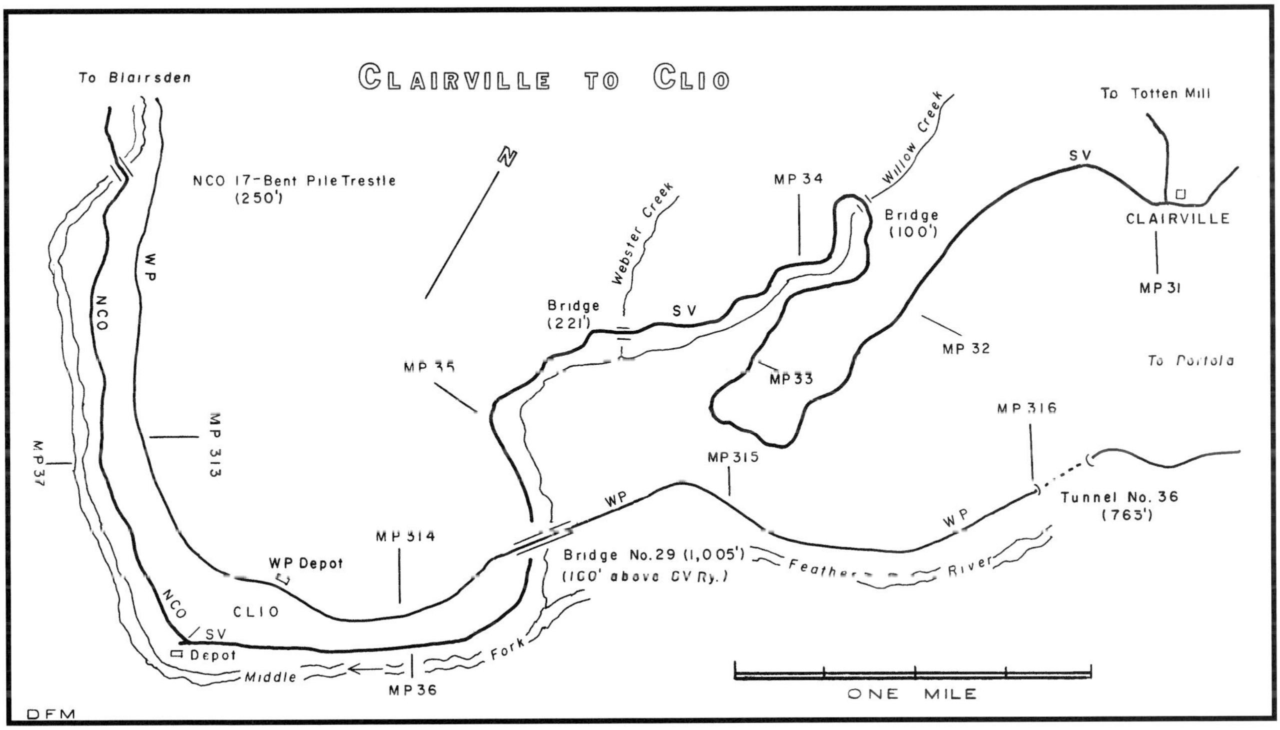

As part of the final survey, engineers estimated the type and scope of excavations to be encountered, dividing the work among solid rock, loose rock, and earth. Most of the solid-rock work extended for more than a mile around Webster Creek, which the railroad crossed on a 221-foot bridge. After Willow Creek, the grade measured 2.6 percent for 1.5 miles as the steepest part of the new line.

Initially, the force, now enlarged to two hundred men, made good progress. At the same time, a Sunday excursion to Clairville drew 350 people from Reno. Another excursion a few weeks later allowed Reno visitors to step off the cars at desirable picnic spots on the way. The balloon ascension and parachute jump at Plumas Jct. the following Sunday drew a local crowd with a fare of one dollar for the round trip.

Adversely to the narrow gauge, the opening of the Boca and Loyalton standard-gauge line to Loyalton in July 1901 drew lumber operators to that terminal. Horton Brothers responded by moving their box factory from Beckwith to Loyalton, which depleted traffic on the Sierra Valleys Railway.

A. D. Moran and Colonel Charles Hamilton, after inspecting the N-C-O extension, met Henry Bowen at Clairville in August 1901, and they went over the new grade, continuing to Mohawk Valley, where they selected a town site (Clio) and a box-factory location. (Hamilton was vice president and general manager of the Texas Central Railroad, a short line in which the Morans held a financial interest.)

The village of Mohawk, four miles northwest of the terminus of the projected SV Railway extension, entered a lively period in comparison with the slow progress of the railroad. N. O. Pauly, having relocated his mercantile business from Nelson Point, wore smiles as his trade thrived. J. C. Knickrem, now manager of the Mohawk Lumber Company, closed the sawmill for the winter after cutting two million board feet during the season and dispatching a shipment of clear lumber to his clients in Australia. With his wife, he also found time to manage the Mohawk Hotel, which had been enlarged and refitted during the summer.

Henry Bowen, near the end of October, found that the grade, weaving through deep cuts and winding around sharp curves, had been finished for four miles. Timbers for the two major bridges were expected the next week, while an inventory of rails and ties waited at Clairville.

In the fall of 1901, J. H. Bennett, traffic manager, announced a new schedule as follows:

No. 1 Pass.	*No. 3 Mixed*		*No. 4 Mixed*	*No. 2 Pass.*
Leave			Arrive	
8:25 A.M.		Reno		6:30 P.M.
10:35 A.M.	5:00 P.M.	Plumas	9:30 A.M.	4:00 P.M.
11:20 A.M.	5:45 P.M.	Vinton	8:40 A.M.	3:15 P.M.
12:05 P.M.	6:30 P.M.	Beckwith	7:55 A.M.	2:30 P.M.
12:55 P.M.	7:20 P.M.	Clairville	7:00 A.M.	1:40 P.M.

Thomas Neal's stage departed daily from Quincy at 6:30 A.M. and arrived at Clairville at 12:30 P.M. Returning an hour later, it pulled into Quincy at 6:30 P.M. The combination fare from Quincy to Reno was six dollars, and for another eight dollars one could ride Southern Pacific all the way to San Francisco.

More Delays on the Road to New Mohawk (Clio)

The approaching winter suspended work on the railroad. Thirty inches of snow blocked trains; in February 1902, no trains ran to Clairville for five days. While neighboring sawmills began a new season in April, a quiet mood hung over the railroad extension until May when sixty men arrived in Clairville to go to work. First they had to restore the damage to the roadbed left by the winter storms, but as June opened they had laid a short stretch of track west of Clairville.

The Band Mill, housed in a three-story structure near Kerby, after passing through several hands, was now owned by the Reno Mill and Lumber Company and managed by Charles E. Gulling. Major stockholders included George Mapes, a rancher and Reno banker; C. T. Bender; and Gulling. Its two steam-powered 75-HP Westinghouse engines provided a capacity of cutting one hundred thousand board feet in twenty-four hours. It was rated as the most complete plant on the east side of the Sierra Nevada. From its seven thousand acres of forest, most of its logs arrived at the mill by a two-mile log chute. With ten to twelve logs chained together, ten big Morgan horses walking down a tow path dragged the logs to the mill. In May 1902, another two-mile chute was nearly ready to deliver logs from Dark Valley. At Clover Valley north of Beckwith, the Horton brothers used both a log chute as well as a steam-traction engine pulling wagons loaded with logs.

The Noee and Ramelli mill made a good run in 1902 that proved to be their last operation in Clairville. The next year they moved their mill about a mile to a point on the Middle Fork to harvest a new timber area on the Delaney ranch, a change that required several months to accomplish. Here they continued business as the Clairville Lumber Company.

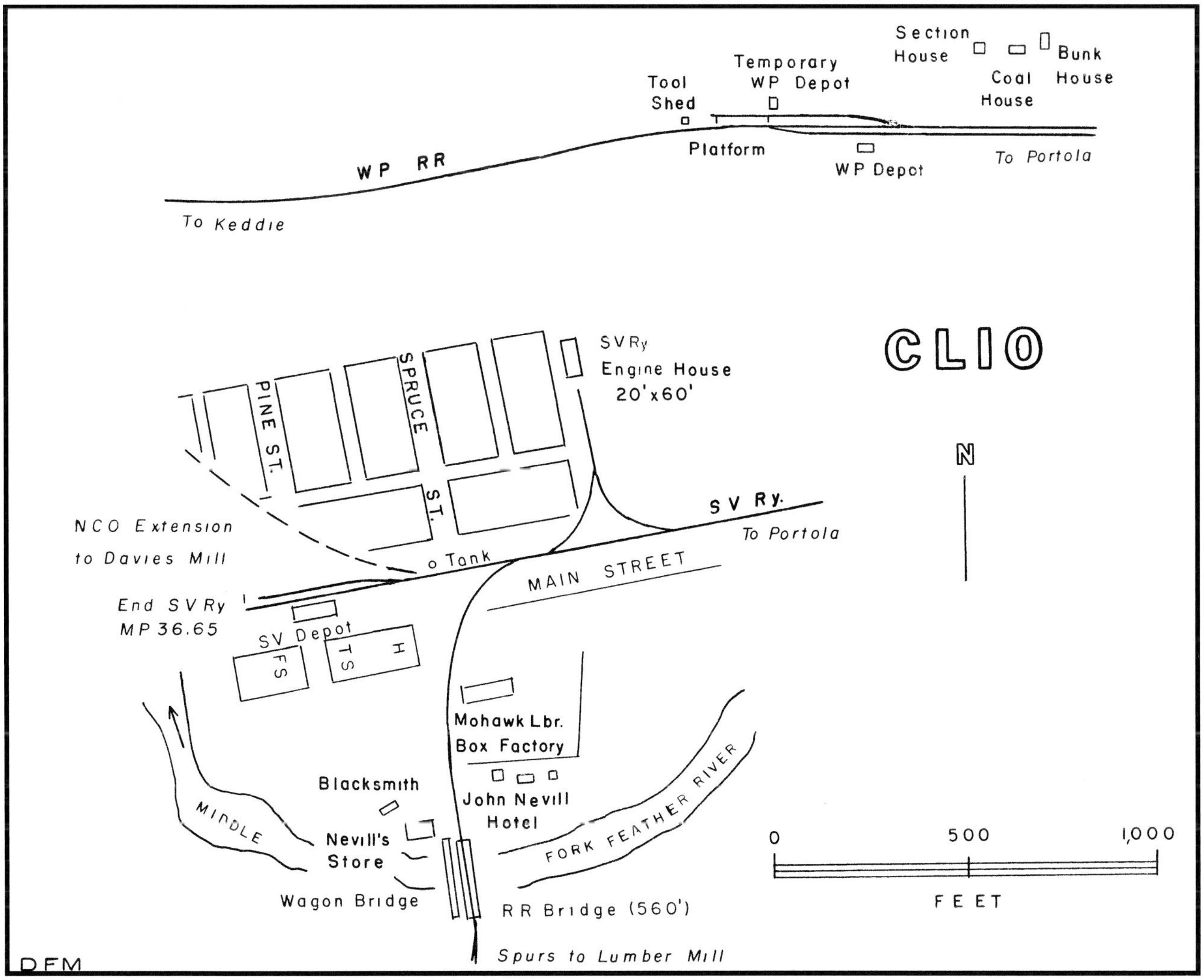

Several business firms occupied buildings among the saloons in Clio on the south side of Main Street. The initials FS indicate the store of A. Farris and his brother. TS marks the location of C. E. Thrall's saloon, while H represents the site of the Western Pacific Hotel of Alden Machomich. For a time in the early 1900s, some promoters tried to change the town's name to New Mohawk. Although the stations of the Western Pacific and Sierra Valleys were separated by less than 2,000 feet, the WP depot on the hillside with an elevation of 4,575 feet stood 164 feet above the Sierra Valleys Railway station (elevation 4,411 feet) on more level land.

After some hesitation, the Reno Mill and Lumber Company joined the other mills in moving to Loyalton in May 1903, which increased traffic revenues for the Boca and Loyalton RR at the expense of the Sierra Valleys Railway.

Considering the short length of the extension—less than six miles—the work moved unduly slowly. Forecast of opening dates stood unreliable from the very beginning. In mid August 1902, J. M. Crowley, an N C O official, said trains would be operating to King's place (Clio) by the middle of September. When October 15 arrived, no trains could be found, but, with one hundred men, the report was that "the grade will soon be completed." Knickrem, anxious to get in the fruit-box-manufacturing trade, could not wait for the railroad, so he started erection of his box factory. Another month went by, and, with tracklaying almost finished, it was reported that "trains are to run in two weeks."

An optimistic advice early in December 1902 claimed the gap between the railhead and the Clio depot site stood less than one mile. Shortage of ties contributed to the delay, which the company met by hewing ties from logs as well as purchasing them from the nearby McKenzie mill.

In accordance with an agreement with the county, the railroad built a bridge across the Middle Fork at Clio. The company laid out the terminal, and soon town lots awaited buyers. H. C. Reed opened a small store in the settlement to serve the few settlers, and all hoped some outsider would build a hotel.

The winter of 1903 ended with unusually heavy rain and snow in the last few days of March. The railroad dedicated the terminus as "New Mohawk," which name could never replace "Clio" in the long run. Knickrem's box factory turned out box shook, while carpenters hammered nails and sawed boards to build the Clio depot that some expected to be "the most commodious of any depot on the line, outside of Reno." Scheduled trains were expected to be operating by the middle of May 1903, two years after work had begun and eight years after first being intimated under the Bowen regime. When trains finally operated to Clio, the Quincy stage made connections there rather than Clairville.

With the line functioning and SV agent J. H. Flynn installed in the new depot, it was time to show off the new railroad to the neighbors. On Sunday, July 19, 1903, an excursion train packed with 450 people departed from Reno. Pausing to pick up the Beckwith baseball team, the train continued to New Mohawk, where the host team triumphed over the visitors by seven to two. Two months later, another excursion brought people from Reno and Virginia City to New Mohawk. The following summer an excursion in the reverse direction took people from Plumas County to Reno to see the new city of Sparks then being developed as a major railroad terminal.

Operations of Bowen's railroad failed to meet expenses and service its debt. In August 1903, the N-C-O went through the formality of foreclosing on the Sierra Valleys Railway—now its subsidiary—because of the default in interest payments on the mortgage.

Sadly, Henry Bowen's financial problems pushed him into bankruptcy in July 1904. With assets of only $200 (household goods) and liabilities of $209,663, he had no choice. The largest indebtedness consisted of a note of $190,474 payable to the N-C-O, which Bowen had signed for both the SV Railway and himself personally. Bowen had given Plumas County its first operating railroad, but the area did not develop sufficient traffic quickly to make his railroad economically viable. Now part of the N-C-O family, the railway reported gross revenues of $24,893 for the twelve months ending in June 1905, but after taxes and interest, there was a net loss of $21,314.

New Mohawk's expansion centered on the saloon business, which was supported by the lumber and box trades. In September 1905, construction commenced on two new hotels, and, with each having its own bar, the number of liquor outlets in the little village rose to six. A new era began with the construction of the Western Pacific Railway, and New Mohawk (Clio) entered a period of great activity.

The intrusion of the Boca and Loyalton in Sierra Valley in 1901 and the opening of Western Pacific nine years later spelled the doom of the little narrow-gauge railroad, which finally gave up the struggle in 1918. However, its contribution to a better way of life in Plumas County when it was the only railroad for six years should always be remembered.

NOTES:

1. When a stage station was established a few miles east of the cabin of mountain man James Beckwourth in 1855, it was incorrectly recorded as "Beckwith," which prevailed until 1932 when the village became "Beckwourth."

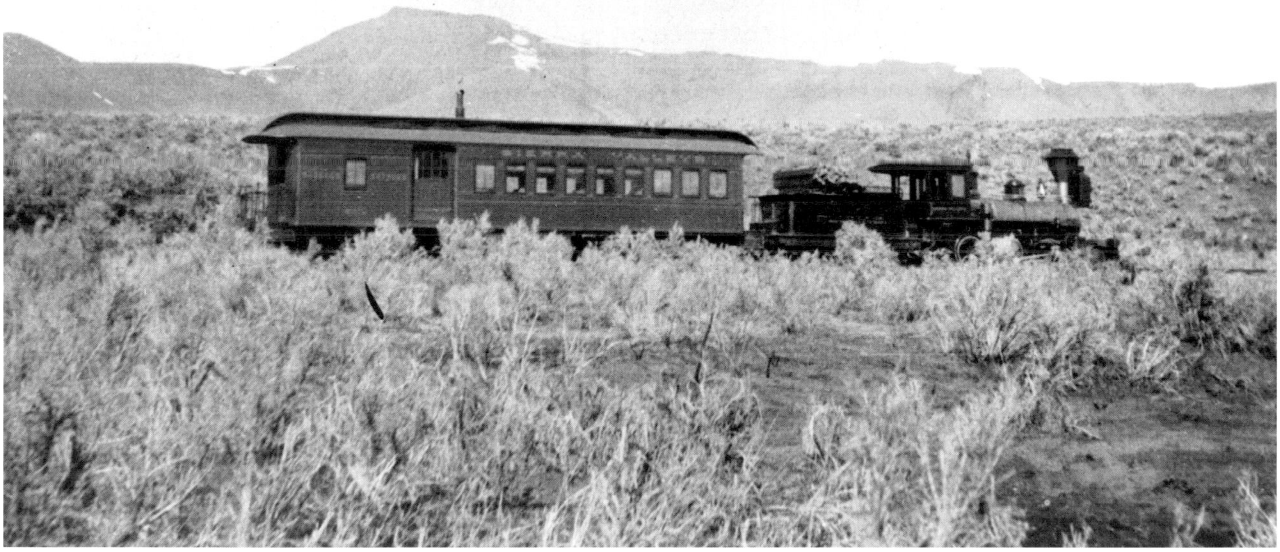

The Sierra Valleys Railway wandered through sagebrush in the Sierra Valley. (Vinton Bowen White collection)

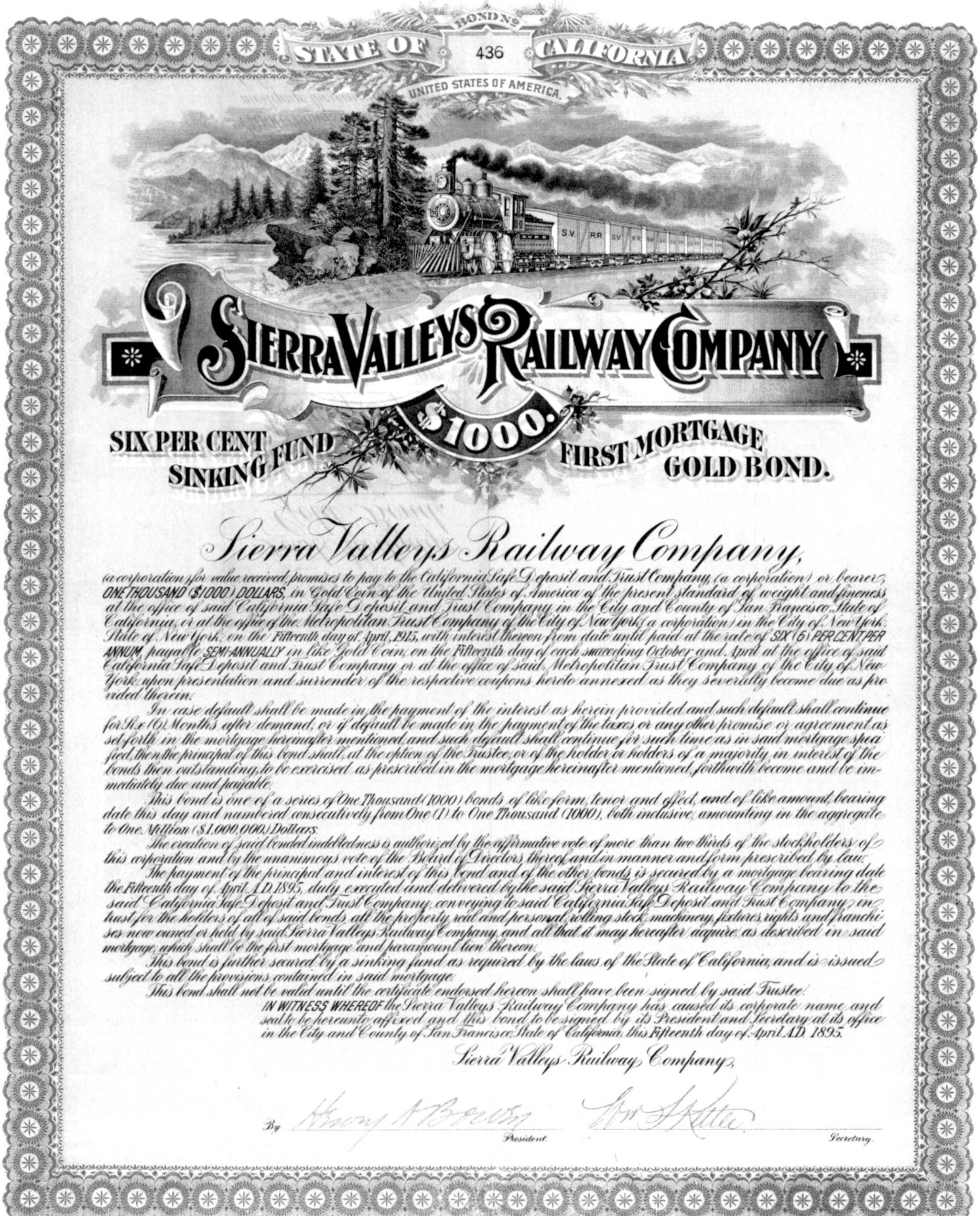

STATE OF CALIFORNIA

BOND No 436

UNITED STATES OF AMERICA.

SIERRA VALLEYS RAILWAY COMPANY

$1000.

SIX PER CENT SINKING FUND FIRST MORTGAGE GOLD BOND.

Sierra Valleys Railway Company, (a corporation) for value received, promises to pay to the California Safe Deposit and Trust Company (a corporation) or bearer, ONE THOUSAND ($1000) DOLLARS, in Gold Coin of the United States of America of the present standard of weight and fineness at the office of said California Safe Deposit and Trust Company in the City and County of San Francisco, State of California, or at the office of the Metropolitan Trust Company of the City of New York (a corporation) in the City of New York, State of New York, on the Fifteenth day of April, 1915, with interest thereon from date until paid at the rate of SIX (6) PER CENT PER ANNUM, payable SEMI-ANNUALLY in like Gold Coin, on the Fifteenth day of each succeeding October and April at the office of said California Safe Deposit and Trust Company or at the office of said Metropolitan Trust Company of the City of New York, upon presentation and surrender of the respective coupons hereto annexed as they severally become due as provided therein.

In case default shall be made in the payment of the interest as herein provided and such default shall continue for Six (6) Months after demand, or if default be made in the payment of the taxes or any other promise or agreement as set forth in the mortgage hereinafter mentioned and such default shall continue for such time as in said mortgage specified, then the principal of this bond shall, at the option of the Trustee, or of the holder or holders of a majority in interest of the bonds then outstanding, to be exercised as prescribed in the mortgage hereinafter mentioned, forthwith become and be immediately due and payable.

This bond is one of a series of One Thousand (1000) bonds of like form, tenor and effect, and of like amount, bearing date this day and numbered consecutively from One (1) to One Thousand (1000), both inclusive, amounting in the aggregate to One Million ($1,000,000) Dollars.

The creation of said bonded indebtedness is authorized by the affirmative vote of more than two thirds of the stockholders of this corporation and by the unanimous vote of the Board of Directors thereof and in manner and form prescribed by law.

The payment of the principal and interest of this bond and of the other bonds is secured by a mortgage bearing date the Fifteenth day of April A.D. 1895, duly executed and delivered by the said Sierra Valleys Railway Company to the said California Safe Deposit and Trust Company, conveying to said California Safe Deposit and Trust Company, in trust for the holders of all of said bonds all the property real and personal, rolling stock, machinery, fixtures, rights and franchises now owned or held by said Sierra Valleys Railway Company, and all that it may hereafter acquire, as described in said mortgage, which shall be the first mortgage and paramount lien thereon.

This bond is further secured by a sinking fund as required by the laws of the State of California, and is issued subject to all the provisions contained in said mortgage.

This bond shall not be valid until the certificate endorsed hereon shall have been signed by said Trustee.

IN WITNESS WHEREOF the Sierra Valleys Railway Company has caused its corporate name and seal to be hereunto affixed and this bond to be signed by its President and Secretary at its office in the City and County of San Francisco, State of California, this Fifteenth day of April A.D. 1895.

Sierra Valleys Railway Company,

By ______ President ______ Secretary.

To finance the extension of his railroad, Henry Bowen created a bonded indebtedness backed by a first mortgage with a maturity twenty years later. Each bond contained coupons enabling the holder to collect semiannual interest on October 15 and April 15. (Vinton Bowen White collection)

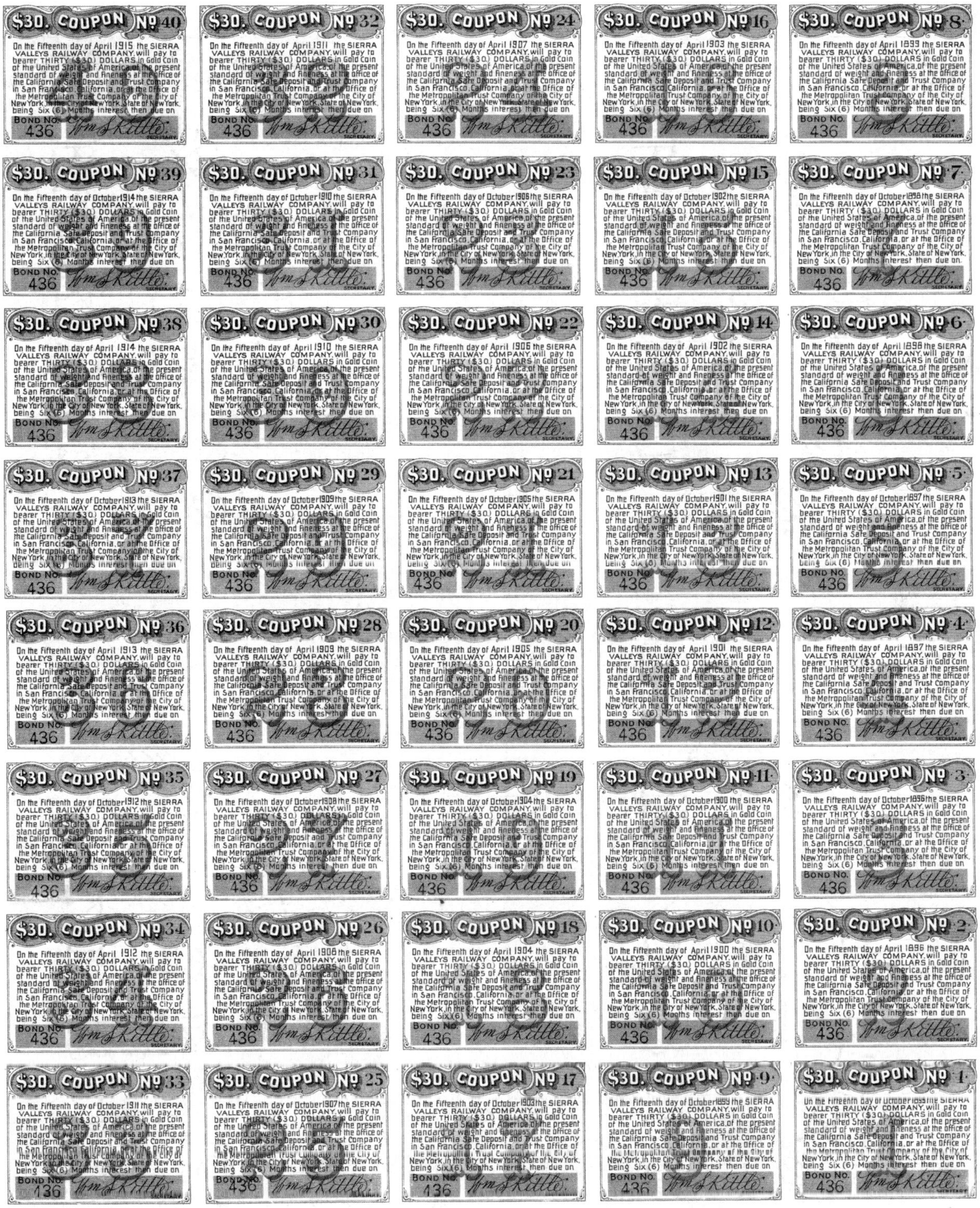

$30. COUPON No 40 — On the Fifteenth day of April 1915 the SIERRA VALLEYS RAILWAY COMPANY, will pay to bearer THIRTY ($30.) DOLLARS in Gold Coin of the United States of America, of the present standard of weight and fineness at the office of the California Safe Deposit and Trust Company in San Francisco, California, or at the Office of the Metropolitan Trust Company of the City of New York, in the City of New York, State of New York, being Six (6) Months interest then due on BOND No. 436 Wm J Kittle. SECRETARY

$30. COUPON No 32 — On the Fifteenth day of April 1911 (text as above) BOND No. 436

$30. COUPON No 24 — On the Fifteenth day of April 1907 (text as above) BOND No. 436

$30. COUPON No 16 — On the Fifteenth day of April 1903 (text as above) BOND No. 436

$30. COUPON No 8 — On the Fifteenth day of April 1899 (text as above) BOND No. 436

$30. COUPON No 39 — On the Fifteenth day of October 1914 · No 31 — October 1910 · No 23 — October 1906 · No 15 — October 1902 · No 7 — October 1898

$30. COUPON No 38 — April 1914 · No 30 — April 1910 · No 22 — April 1906 · No 14 — April 1902 · No 6 — April 1898

$30. COUPON No 37 — October 1913 · No 29 — October 1909 · No 21 — October 1905 · No 13 — October 1901 · No 5 — October 1897

$30. COUPON No 36 — April 1913 · No 28 — April 1909 · No 20 — April 1905 · No 12 — April 1901 · No 4 — April 1897

$30. COUPON No 35 — October 1912 · No 27 — October 1908 · No 19 — October 1904 · No 11 — October 1900 · No 3 — October 1896

$30. COUPON No 34 — April 1912 · No 26 — April 1908 · No 18 — April 1904 · No 10 — April 1900 · No 2 — April 1896

$30. COUPON No 33 — October 1911 · No 25 — October 1907 · No 17 — October 1903 · No 9 — October 1899 · No 1 — October 1895

Commencing October 15, 1895, and continuing until 1915, holders clipping coupons were entitled to receive thirty dollars for each coupon presented. (Vinton Bowen White collection)

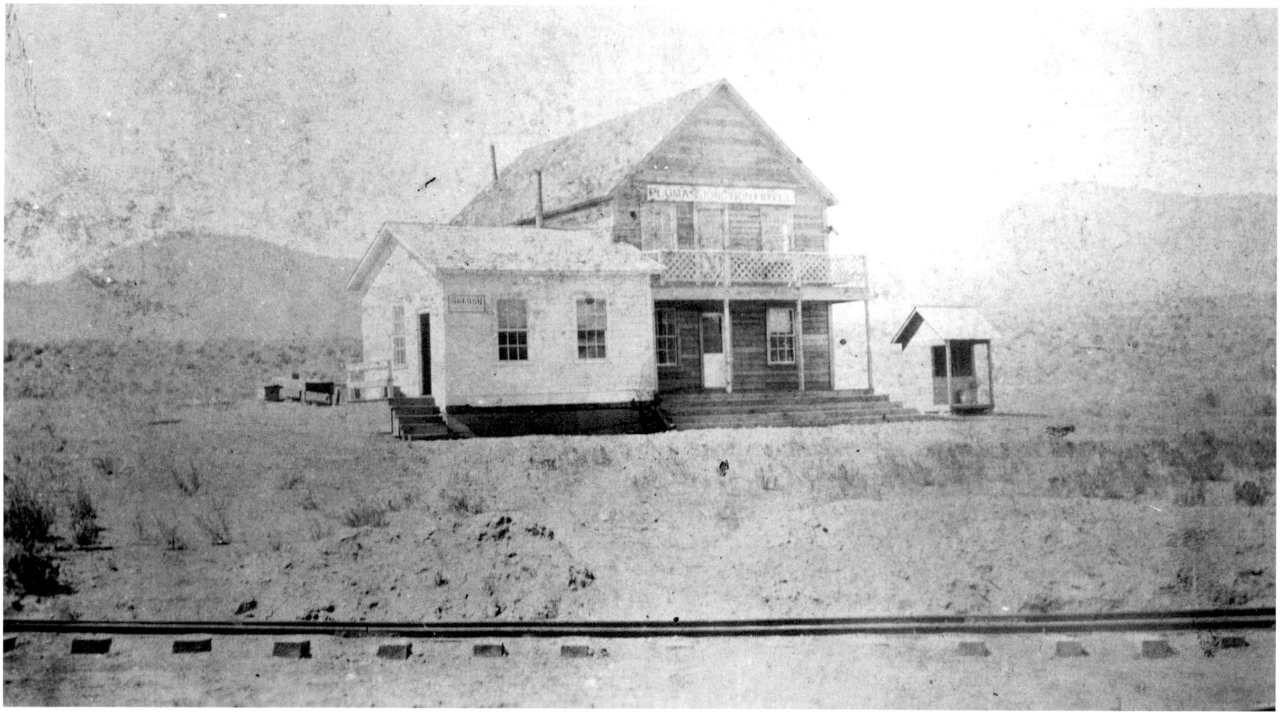

Above: The Plumas Junction Hotel offered limited accommodations for travelers making connections between the Sierra Valleys Railway and the N-C-O Railway. (Vinton Bowen White collection)

Below: A group of well-dressed gentlemen celebrated an excursion to Clairville. The head of conductor Holman peeks through the crowd (*third man from the left*). With a glass of champagne in his hand, Henry A. Bowen stands at the right edge of the table. (Vinton Bowen White collection)

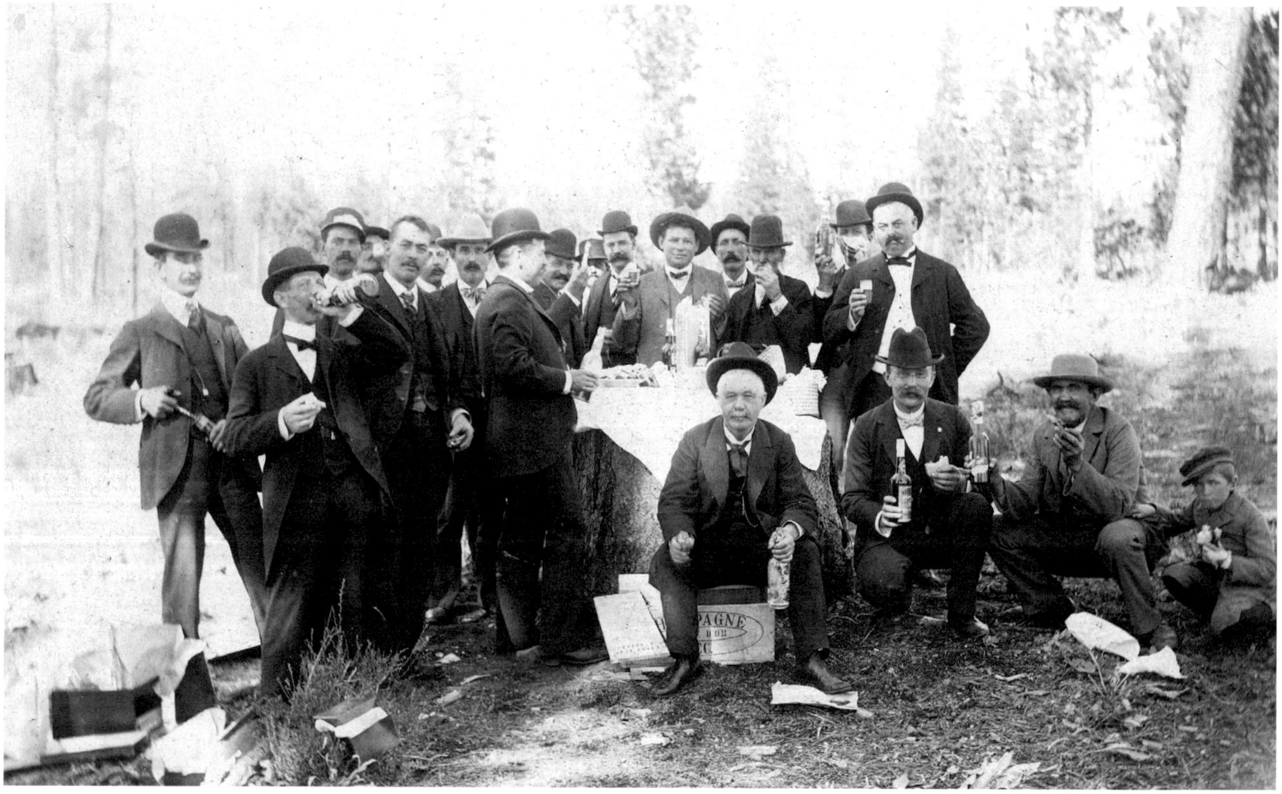

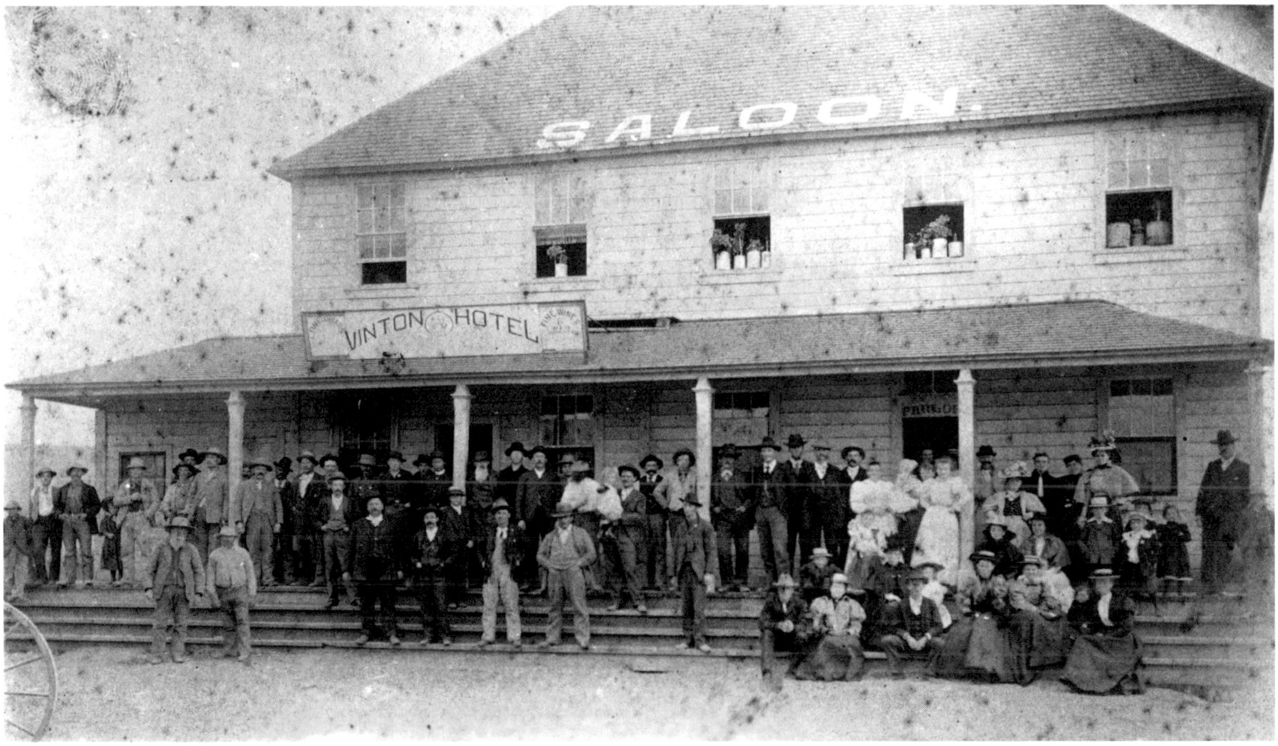

G. Canonica, proprietor of the Vinton Hotel, recognized the importance of saloon receipts by painting large lettering on the roof offering solace to the thirsty. An excursion, ending at the hotel, included prominent local men. Marion Bringham is at the far right. Pompey Pedrini, in the gray suit with hands in his pockets, stands on the lower step in the exact middle of the porch. (He died in the Clairville hotel fire.) The third man to his left, also on the lower step, is J. M. Engle, one-time superintendent of the railroad. (Vinton Bowen White collection)

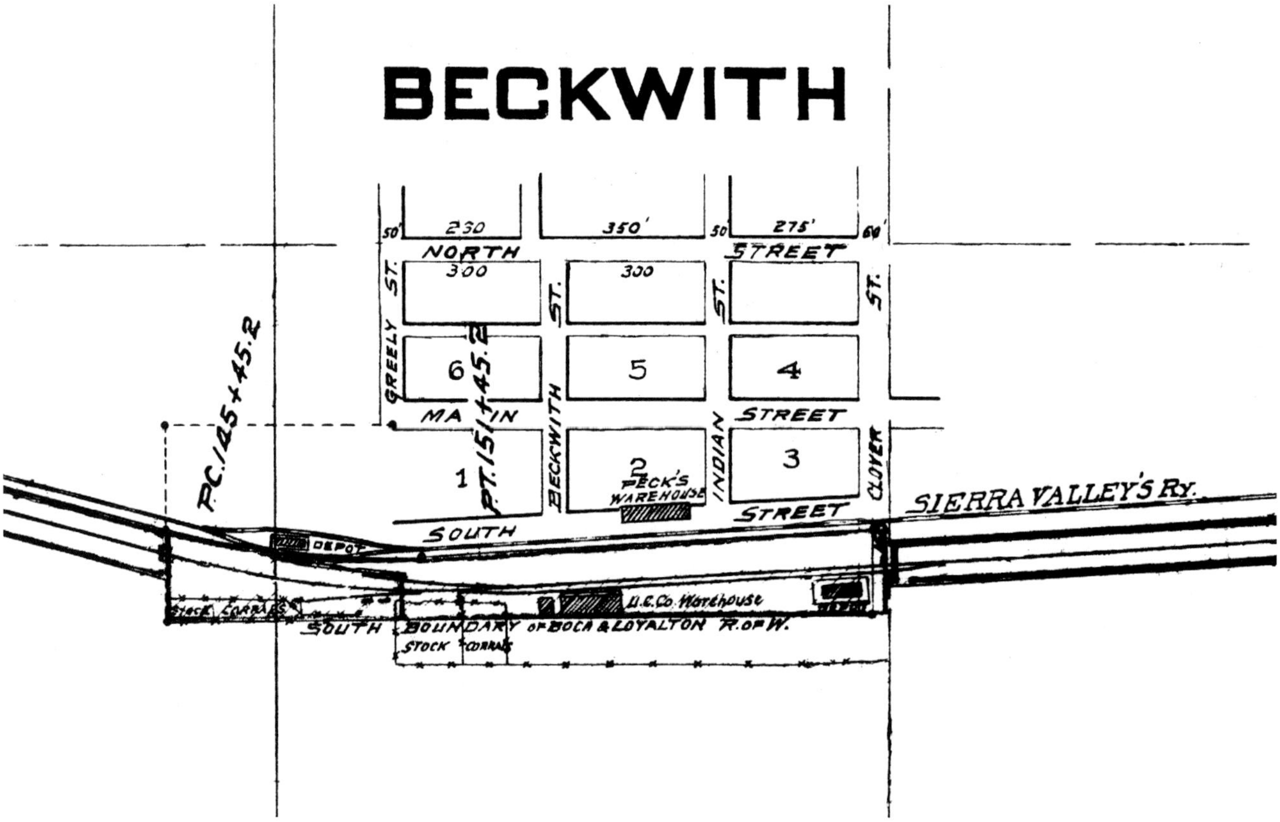

From this map prepared by the Sierra Valleys Railway, both stations are indicated with the SV Railway at the west side of town and the Boca and Loyalton depot at the other side. The Utah Construction Company warehouse was used in the building of Western Pacific.

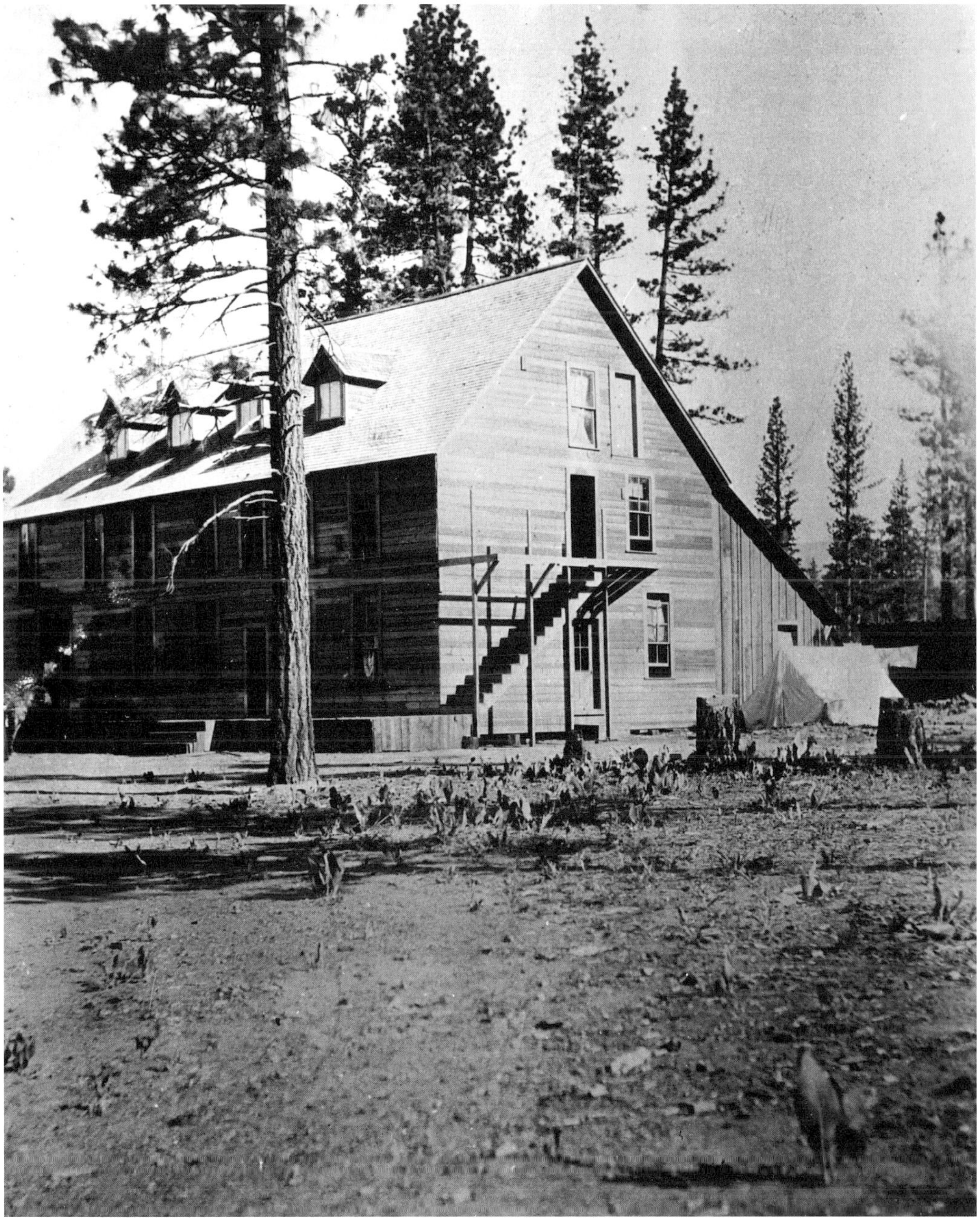

After the Clairville Hotel burned in 1898, Chat Roberts rebuilt the hotel, this time with dormer windows on the third floor. The new hotel suffered the same fate in 1909, when flames consumed the structure. (Vinton Bowen White collection)

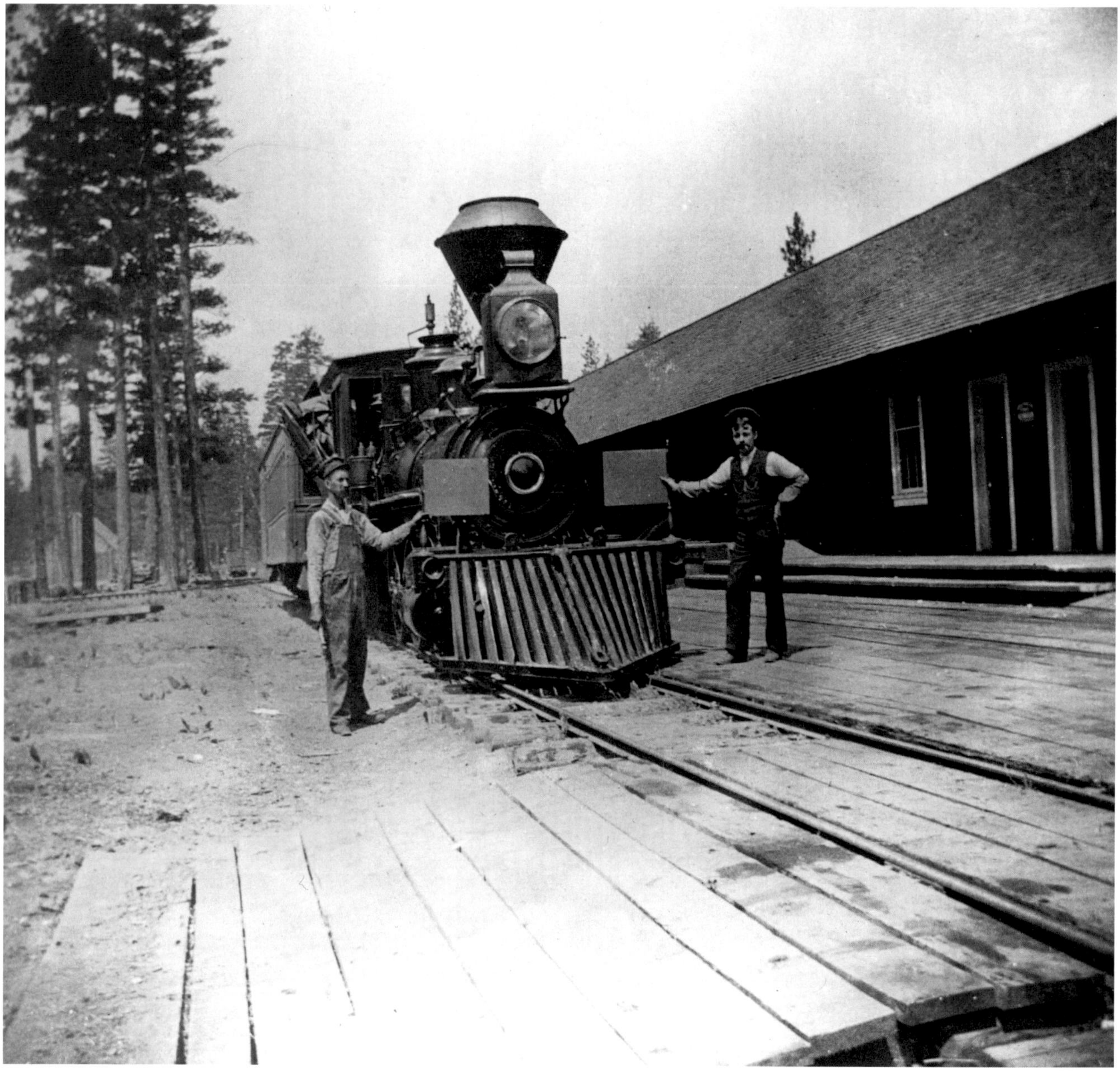

A Sierra Valleys locomotive at Clairville. Undoubtedly, the two men are participating in an undisclosed test of some kind that color photography, had it been available then, might have provided a clue. (Plumas County Museum)

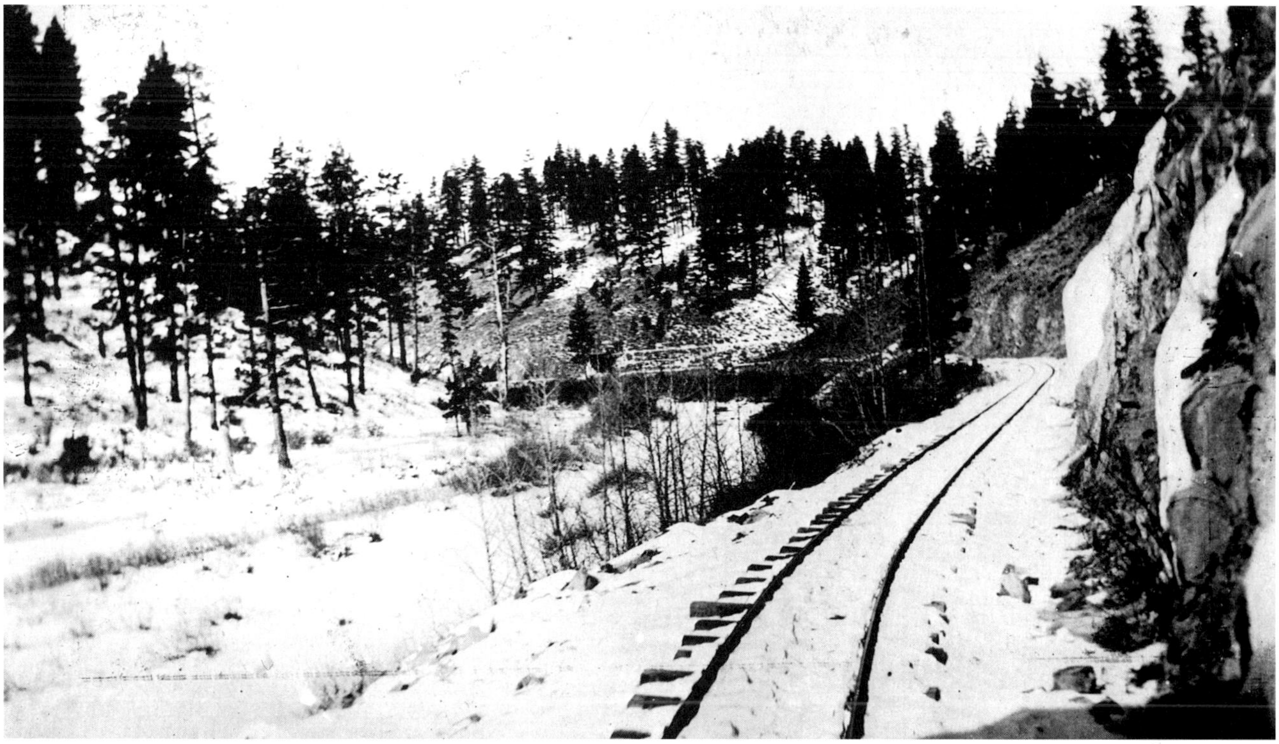

Above: From the back of a train soon to arrive at Portola (Mormon), this photograph shows the Sierra Valleys Railway on the north side of Kirby Canyon after a winter storm. On the far side of the Middle Fork of the Feather River, the Boca and Loyalton built its railroad, which was later absorbed by Western Pacific. (Vinton Bowen White photograph)

Below: The Sierra Valleys Railway commenced at Plumas Jct., near the two-story hotel, and wound its way up the hillside and over Beckwourth Pass. (Plumas County Museum)

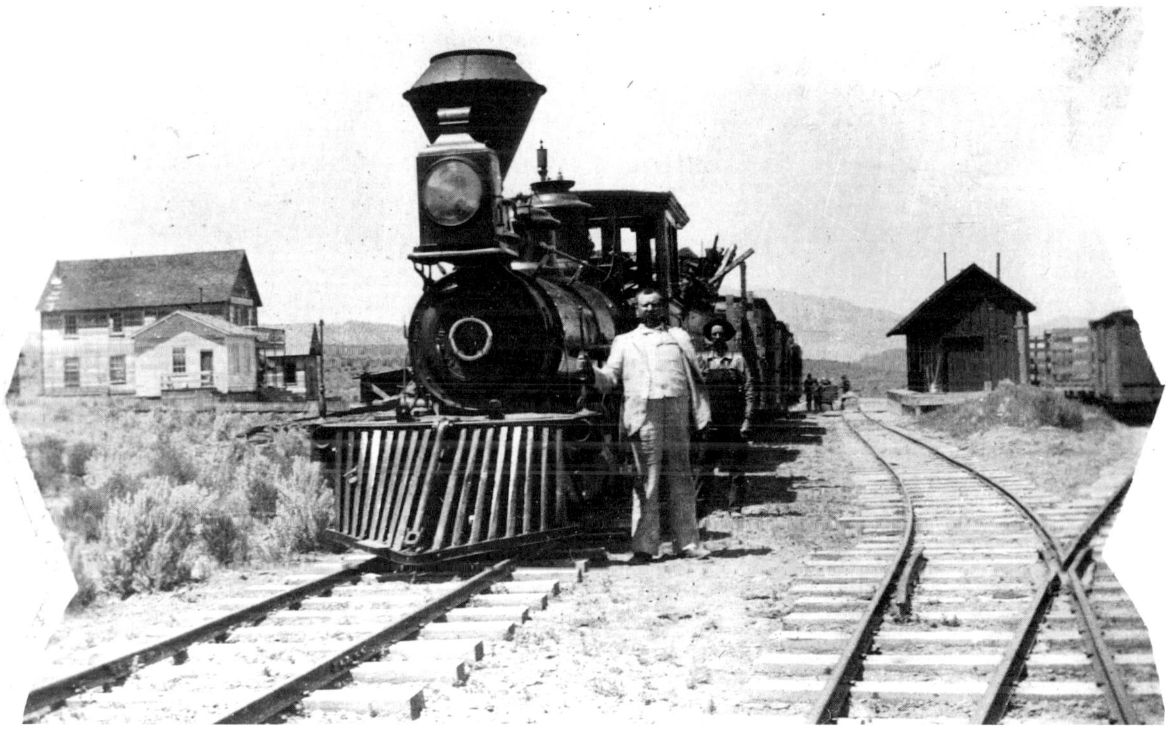

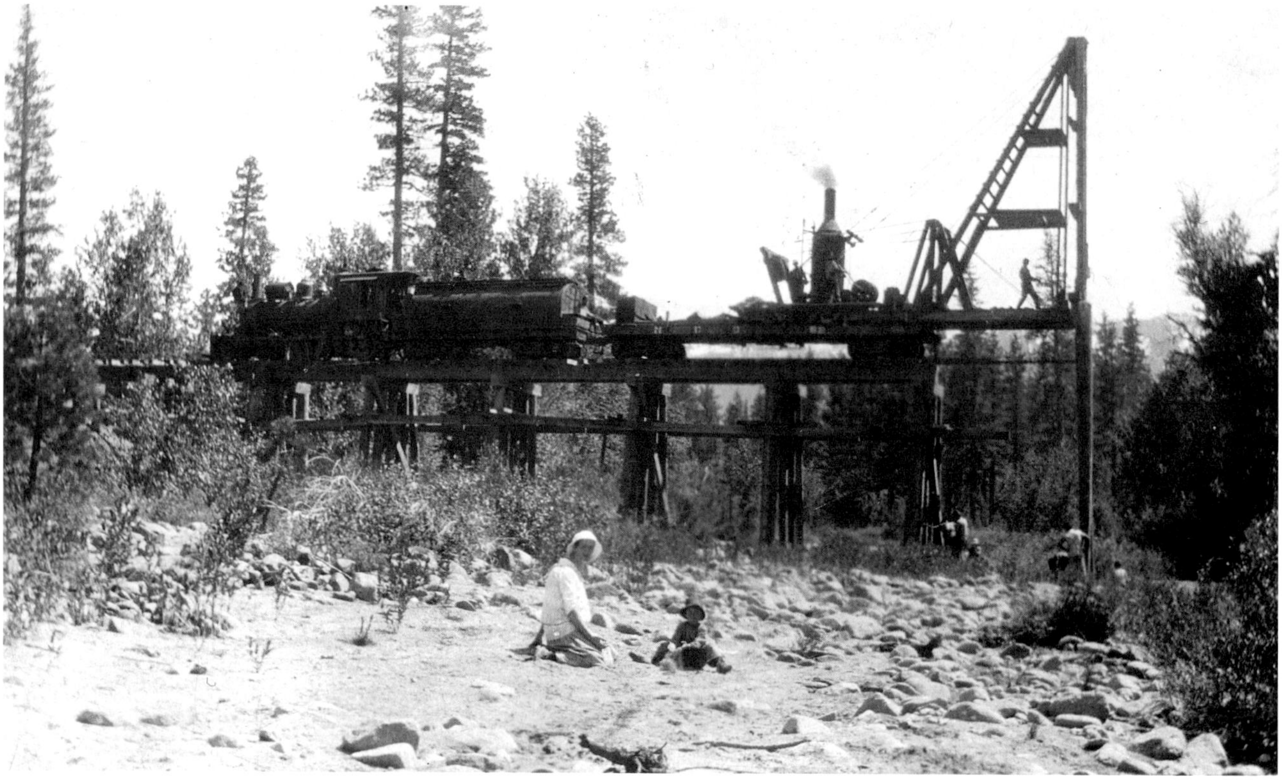

Above: The extension from Clio to Davies Mill required crossing the Feather River. Now part of the N-C-O, Sam Boney, engineer of No. 3, moved the pile driver to the crossing. While H. E. Gasaway watched the work, his sister-in-law and nephew, Raymond Gasaway, enjoyed a picnic. (H. E. Gasaway collection)

Below: The Clairville Lumber Company provided a major source of traffic for the railway.

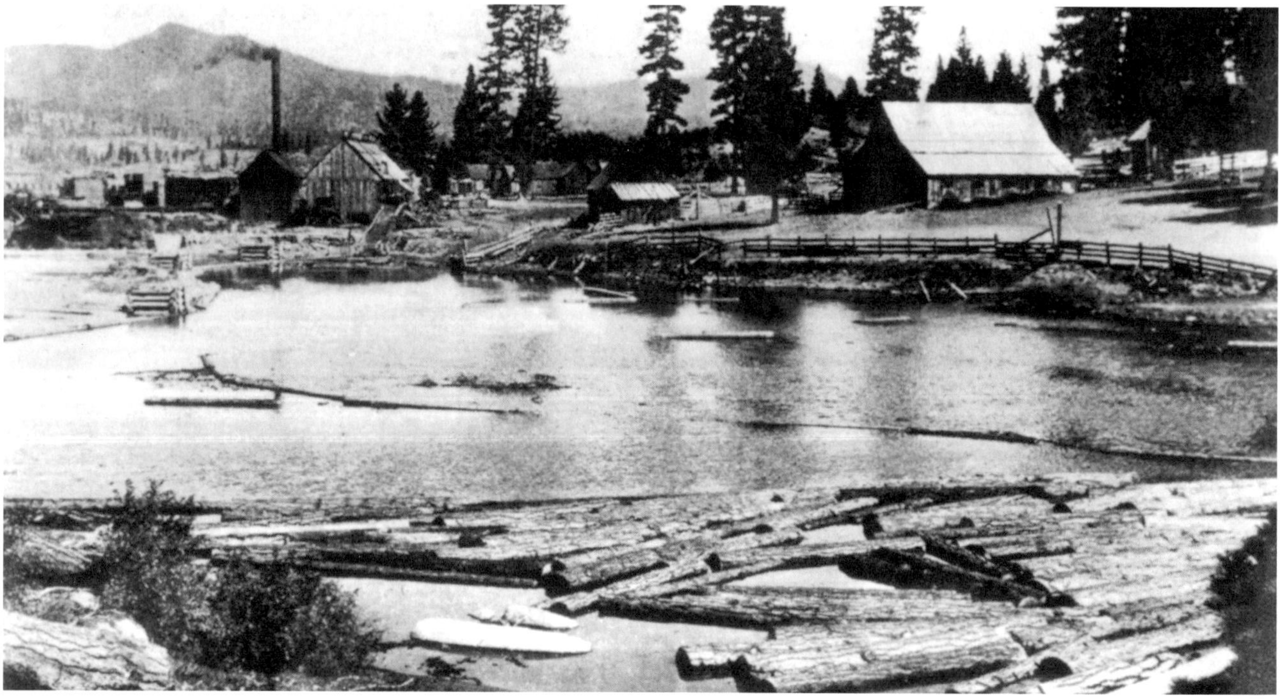

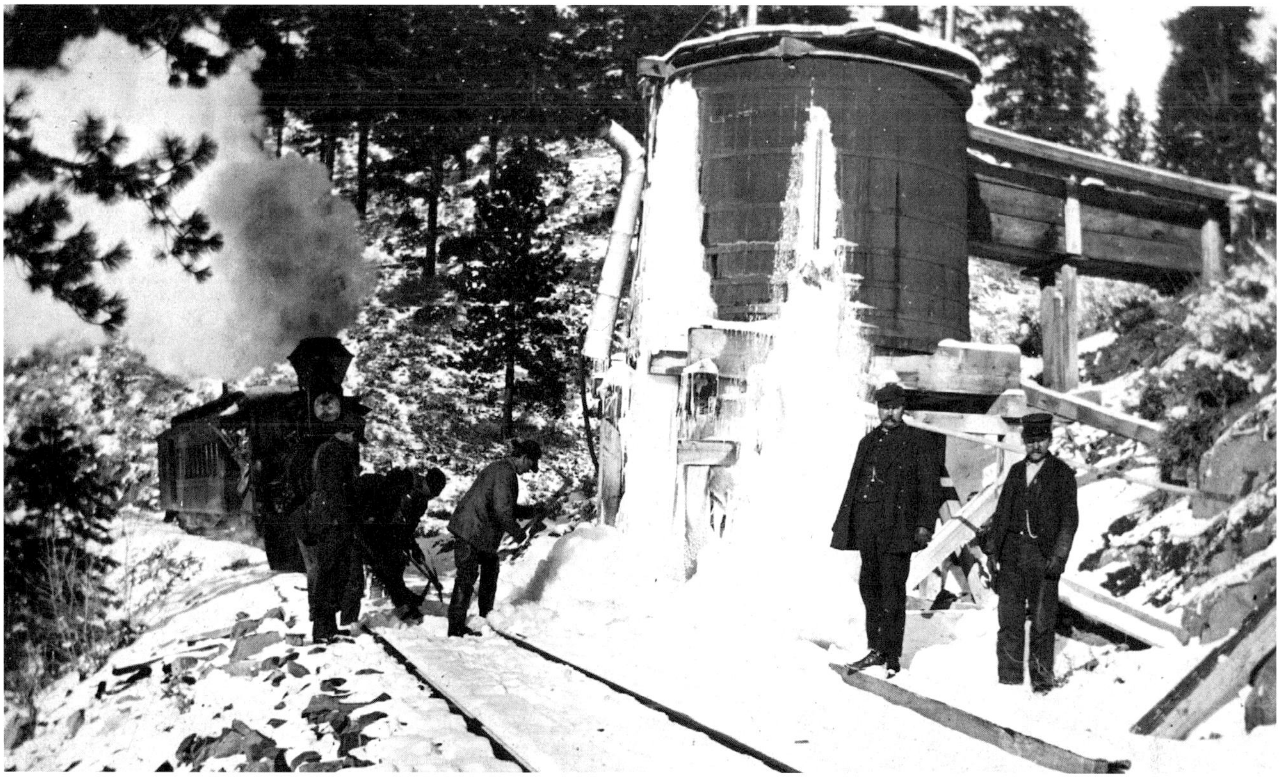

Above: Cold temperatures could disrupt train schedules. Clearing ice around this water tank was necessary before the fireman could fill the locomotive tender.

Below: In the final days of the operation of this branch when the SV Railway was absorbed by the N-C-O, a substantial fireproof freight warehouse was erected at Beckwith.

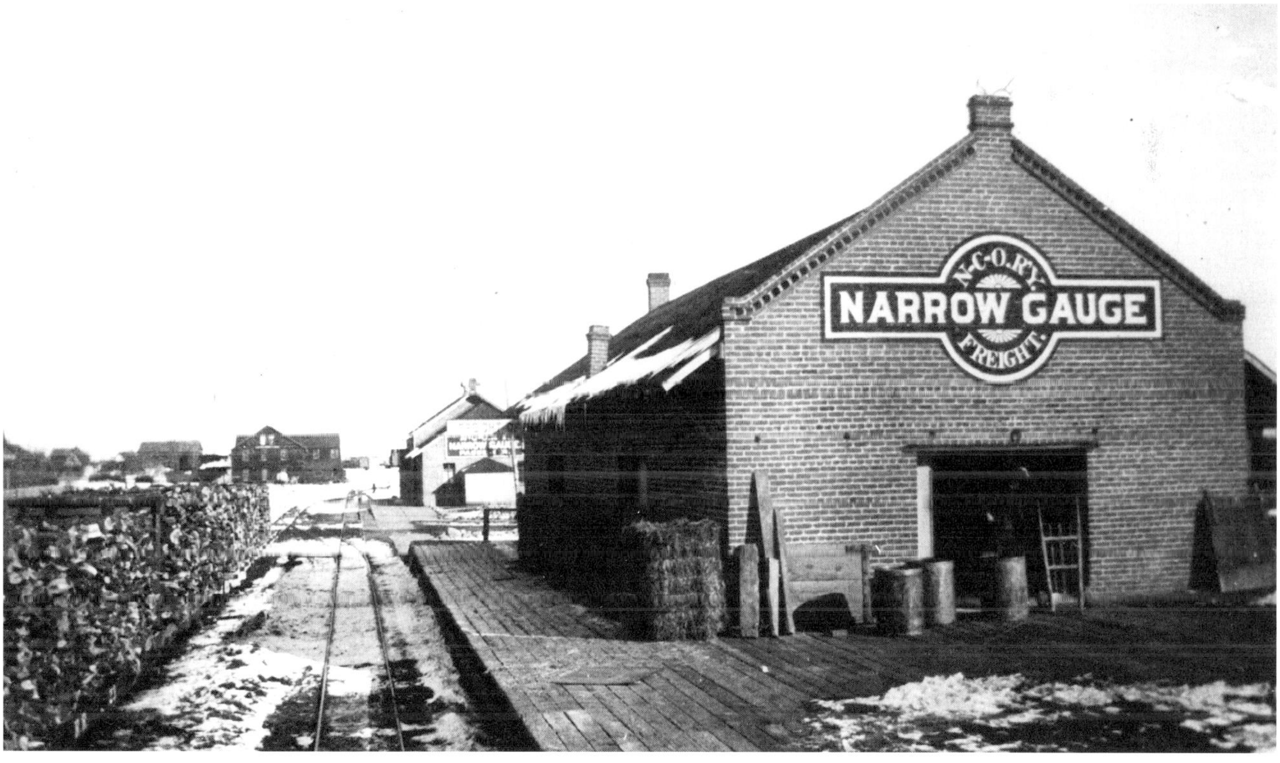

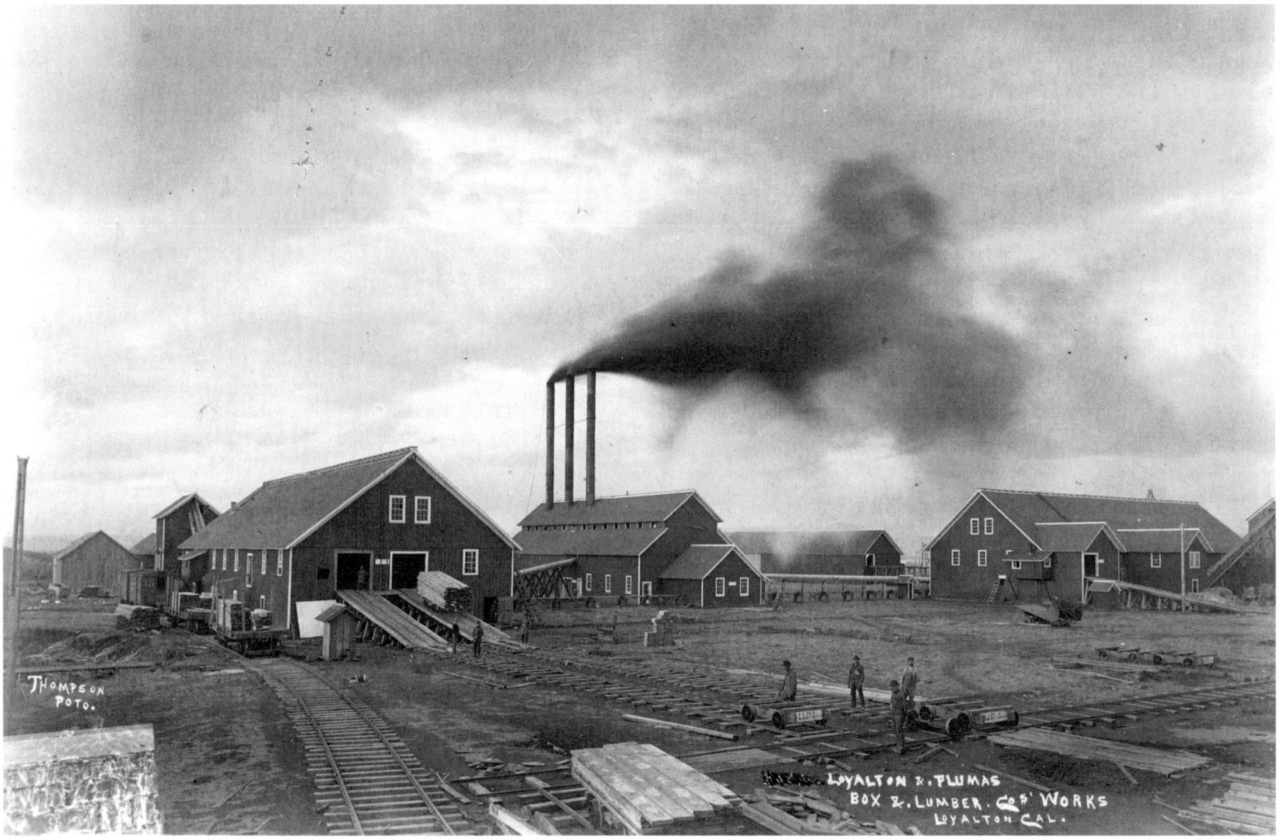

In the early days of the twentieth century, Loyalton was the home of a number of mills and box factories, this one being the plant of the Plumas Box and Lumber Company.

BOCA AND LOYALTON RAILROAD

The Lewis brothers' mill, eight miles up Smithneck Creek, just south of Loyalton in northeastern California, used steam-traction engines to haul lumber to Truckee in 1895. The following spring the Lewis brothers were fortunate that their Loyalton Lumber Company had three million feet of logs ready for their sawmill. A generous blanket of snow facilitated logging on sleds during the winter.

A late-summer visitor in 1897 noted eighty men employed in the mill and box factory. A steam-traction engine, pulling wagons with ten thousand to twelve thousand feet of logs on each trip, supplied timber for the sawmill. One boardinghouse at the mill and another at the logging camp provided meals for the husky men. An added attraction at the box factory was the seven young ladies on that payroll.

Shipments of cut lumber to market began with one of the two Doan steam tractors pulling wagons ten miles to Folk's Summit. From there ten-horse teams continued over the remaining six miles to Verdi, mostly downhill.

People took a mild interest in reports of surveyors locating a wagon road to Verdi and other points on Central Pacific in June 1899, but, on learning that the grades were limited to 2 percent, most suspected that a railroad stood in the wings. They were partly correct, for a year later W. S. Lewis agreed that a railroad was imminent, but, instead of a link to Verdi, it would be limited to a two-mile logging railroad tapping a timber stand two miles north of the Lewis mill.

Two "queer-looking" little locomotives—one with its cab and tender combined—came on their own wheels from Chicago to Truckee, where they would pause until the road was dry before going to the mill.

Proposed Electric Railroad

During the spring of 1900, Plumas County became popular with railroad builders. Besides the railroad at the Lewis Mill, D. M. DeLong contemplated an electric railroad from Oroville up the Feather River and on to Beckwourth Pass to gain access to placer claims commencing near the future site of Pulga and stretching along the North Fork for eight miles. Several generating plants along the river would supply electric power. DeLong, whose background consisted of marine engineering and professional diving, began work in the summer of 1898 and formed the North Feather River Mining Company for this purpose. William E. Colby, then a young San Francisco mining attorney, made several visits to resolve legal matters for DeLong. (Colby, later prominent in mining law, also served as secretary of the Sierra Club for decades.)

An ambitious person, DeLong also proposed to provide electric lighting for the town of Quincy and secured county franchises for both projects on November 6, 1899. His Quincy Electric Light Company had a rocky start when it began furnishing electricity in March 1900 until new equipment arrived. Though fully occupied with the opening of the Quincy plant, DeLong "declared in positive terms that the electric railroad would be built [and that] plenty of capital is ready."

A cash crunch caused DeLong to sell his Quincy operation. Nothing more came about the railroad, except DeLong demonstrated a lack of reality when, after making many trips along the North Fork, he declared that the cost of grading a standard-gauge railroad would not be much more expensive than a wagon road. For him, things went from bad to worse when his mining equipment was foreclosed in January 1901.

The end of summer found the grade from the Lewis mill finished to within three miles of Boca and, in the opposite direction, four miles north of the mill.

Contrary to standard procedures wherein promoters created railroad corporations prior to beginning physical work, these promoters delayed this step until September 25, 1900. Incorporators of the Boca and Loyalton Railroad included Captain John H. Roberts, a California river steamboat man who also amassed a comfortable fortune in mining ventures, who subscribed to $123,900 of the stock in the railroad. William S. Lewis subscribed to $119,010 of the stock, while the balance (six shares, par $15) was taken by Richard H. Lewis; P. J. Harney, general manager of Roberts's Sacramento Transportation Company (riverboats); and attorney George Bates. The delineated route extended from Boca, on Central Pacific, to Beckwith, then westward to Mormon (Portola), 45.2 miles, plus five branches totaling 11.29 miles.

Rail laying in the fall of 1900 culminated with the installation of three-quarters of a mile of track on a cold and miserable day and the driving of the "golden spike" on Saturday, January 5, 1901. Lewis Mill and Boca were now linked with bands of steel.

The job was not entirely finished. Early in March 1901, Lewis had 50 men ballasting the track, while others put in passing tracks. When the ground would become dry—a condition expected in two or three weeks—work would get under way on the extension to Loyalton.

In contrast with the electric railroad dream, Lewis's railroad took on tangible form. With financial support from Captain Roberts, Lewis placed 230 men grading a connection with Boca and the Southern Pacific Railroad, which now operated Central Pacific.

The Timber Rush

Promises of improved transportation for Sierra Valley caused a "timber rush" in eastern Plumas County. J. M. Engle, instead of encouraging lumbermen to boost their production in order to provide traffic on the Sierra Valleys Railway, had left the company to devote his full time to dealing in timber properties, and his efforts turned meaningful. For example, in May 1901, Captain Roberts paid $26,000 for the 4,000-acre Stratton tract near Beckwith and $30,000 for 3,926 acres of McNair timberland at the upper end of Mohawk Valley; Engle had a hand in both transactions.

A general feeling of excitement developed at this time. Fred Langhorst of Cromberg said he had daily inquiries for timberland, which topped with fifteen calls in one special day! Local Quincy residents filed on neighboring government timberland, and the local paper carried as many as a dozen filing notices in some issues. Often the applicants consisted of wives and daughters, with the Keddie family being well represented.

As the days of the June 1901 calendar marched by, graders closed the six-mile gap to Loyalton, with the tracklayers in close pursuit. During these times, small towns vied for the honor of hosting Independence Day celebrations. Usually, people in Plumas County congregated in the town that had arranged programs months in advance with announcements in the local press. Loyalton seized the opportunity with the announcement of a "Celebration at Loyalton—July 4, 1901—Independence Day and Completion of the Railway to Loyalton and Beginning of the Extension to Plumas." The newspaper advertisement stated that Captain J. H. Roberts of Sacramento would drive the last spike.

The Celebration at Loyalton

It was a long day. An excursion to Boca departed at 4:30 A.M., with the unseemly hour partly offset by complimentary passage on the railroad. The Quincy Band joined the crowd, and several open observation cars—probably flatcars with benches and railings—were added at Lewis Mill.

After rounding 174 curves, the special train arrived at Boca about eight to be met by Captain J. H. Roberts standing on the platform. After an hour for breakfast and sightseeing—the immense ice-packing warehouses proved to be the most interesting subjects—the train began its return to Loyalton with a lot of flag waving and band playing. Along the way, the train paused to pick up more celebrants, and a large crowd greeted the train at Loyalton. The Quincy Band led the parade of visitors to the large pavilion that soon would serve as the Lewis brothers' box factory.

Judge Stanley A. Smith of Downieville gave brief remarks focusing on the advantages of the railroad. District Attorney U. S. Webb, orator of the day, also praised the railroad. Luncheon came next, to be followed by four baseball games.

Confusion marred the celebration due to the absence of every member of the Committee of Arrangements. The lack of shelter and some food-serving difficulties proved annoying, but the worst omission was that no one called on Captain Roberts, "in reality the hero of the day," for a speech; apparently, the last-spike event was overlooked. But for many others, it did not matter, for the day was long remembered for its bacchanalian orgy. Loyalton, ostensibly a "dry town," forgot all the regulations that day.

As expected, B&L graders pointed in a northwest tangent toward Beckwith. Grading moved at a moderate pace, for the steel mills could not deliver rails until fall. Some right-of-way came by donation; in other cases, condemnation proved necessary. During August, Beckwith had a little excitement. When some Indians battled among themselves on the streets, citizens held little interest, but when lightning struck a guy wire of a stovepipe of the Beckwith Hotel and ran through the structure to end up in the barroom and knock down several men, it evoked considerable conversation.

Beckwith welcomed its second railroad in early November 1901 when B&L rails came to town. William Sanders, chief engineer, guided his surveyors as they staked out a line as they passed near the Band Mill of the Reno Mill and Lumber Company west of Beckwith, paralleling the Sierra Valleys Railway the entire distance. Ordinarily, this mill cut forty thousand board feet every day, but a critical broken wheel caused a six-week work suspension. Most of the company's output went to its retail yard in Reno, while one-fourth ended at the Plumas Box and Lumber Company in Loyalton, jointly owned by the Horton brothers and the Reno Mill.

Manager Patrick Henry foresaw cutting timber in the Stratton tract up Grizzly Creek that would require a short spur of the B&L. The Horton brothers' production encountered delays due to the conversion of the circular saw to a band mill. Two steam-traction engines conveyed their output to Beckwith, where it was placed on B&L cars to the box factory in Loyalton.

The completion of the Boca and Loyalton Railroad, first to Loyalton, then to Beckwith, had a tremendous effect on the area, as it encouraged expanded lumber operations in the hills around Sierra Valley. With this standard-gauge railroad, carloads of lumber could travel almost anywhere in the country without being physically transferred at railroad connections. The narrow-gauge system stood at a disadvantage in competing with the standard-gauge B&L, but before two decades elapsed most of these two railroads would have vanished.

C. E. Horton remarked that the strong demand for lumber brought orders from as far away as New York. Whereas M. J. Noee's Clairville sawmill catered to a local market, the B&L extension benefited him, as one-third of its output went to the Plumas Box Factory in Loyalton.

Changes in Loyalton lumber mills occurred during the first few years of the new century. Captain Roberts, already owning extensive stands of timber at Spring Garden and other places, formed the Roberts Lumber Company on January 12, 1903, and carefully included the Lewis brothers in his new firm. The same pattern continued with the incorporation of the Lewis Bros. Company on February 2, 1906, with both Roberts and Lewis sharing ownership. In the interim, the partners had sold the property of their

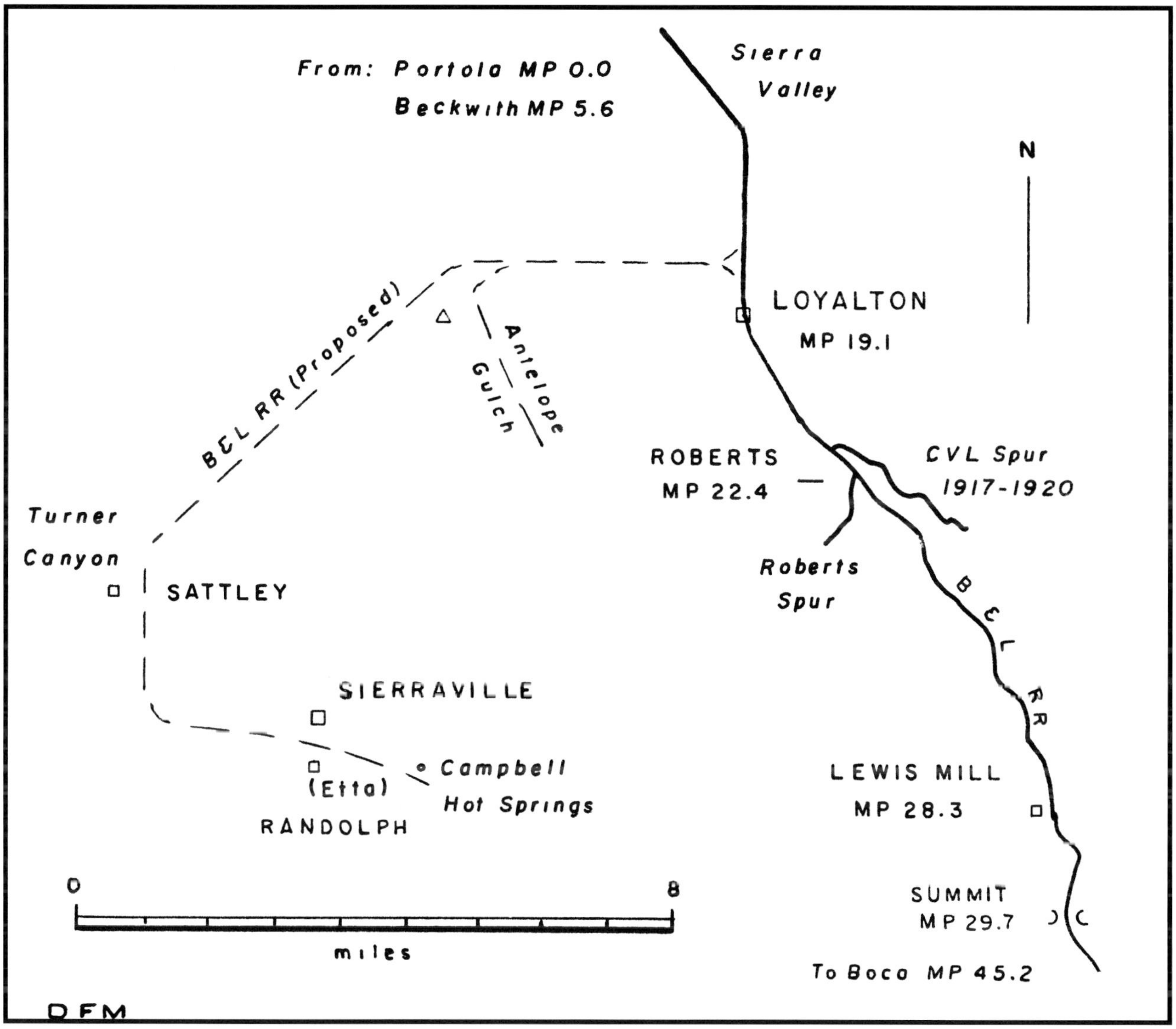

Loyalton Lumber Company to the Kelley brothers in July 1905, referred to as the "lumber kings of Minnesota."

As 1903 began, the B&L flexed its muscles and amended the incorporation papers, whereby Quincy became its western objective, which would have reached Captain Roberts's timber stand near Spring Garden, eight miles east of Quincy.

The Grizzly spur, though it extended only 1.58 miles, had more than its share of right-of-way troubles considering its short length. Unable to reach an agreement with Alfonse Ramelli, litigation proved necessary, with the result that the railroad wrote a check for almost twenty-eight hundred dollars for the land, damages, and court expenses.

At the beginning of the summer of 1903, the B&L received two additional locomotives, building the roster to five, and fifteen cars of rail for the main-line extension west of Beckwith. A few months later, graders neared the Hawks Ranch, later the site of Delleker and just west of Portola. In February 1904, when William S. Lewis was in Quincy, he spoke with authority when he said his road "intends to extend at least to Spring Garden in the very near future" where eastern investors expected to build a sawmill. He added a note of caution about B&L construction, saying that if Western Pacific—then still making surveys—built along that route, the sawmill would be constructed but served by WP.

In April 1905, B&L maintenance-of-way forces laid steel for a short distance to extend the main line west of Beckwith to Mormon (Portola) and then applied their efforts to grading in Turner Canyon, just west of Sattley and Sierraville and about a dozen miles southwest of Loyalton. Actual tracklaying for that long extension is doubtful, for the operated mileage of the Boca and Loyalton Railroad, according to their report as of June 30, 1908, does not mention trackage in this area. This report included the following tabulations:

Main Line	
Boca-Loyalton	26.10 miles
Loyalton-Beckwith	13.50 miles
Beckwith-Mormon [Portola]	5.60 miles
Spurs	
Davies Mill Spur	1.50 miles
Roberts Spur	1.85 miles
Grizzly Spur	1.88 miles
Fay No. 2 Spur (Portola)	2.89 miles
Horton Spur	3.17 miles
Total =	56.49 miles

Snow Blockades

Although the Boca and Loyalton ran its trains over a wider-gauge track, it proved to be no less vulnerable to the fury of winter snows than the Sierra Valleys Railway. Every few years the accumulation of snow at the summit between Boca and Loyalton would close the railroad for a week or more.

One major blockade began on Friday, January 12, 1906, when snow piled up five to eight feet at the summit. That night, B&L locomotive No. 3 left Boca to clear the track and returned the following morning from Loyalton with its crew reporting reasonable conditions. The dispatcher in Boca sent out the passenger train with Nos. 3 and 5 on the point. Inadequately serviced at Boca, No. 3 ran out of fuel and water at the summit, and snowdrifts flirted with the stalled train for the rest of the day.

A section hand bravely walked back to Boca on Saturday night with a note seeking help. In response, No. 4 and the big snowplow departed from Boca at nine o'clock that evening and returned Sunday afternoon with seven passengers from the snow-captured train.

It snowed all day Sunday, but a train powered by three locomotives started out from Loyalton on Monday morning with the objective of clearing the railroad between the summit and Boca. The mission proved unsuccessful, and the train returned to Loyalton later that morning to make another attempt that afternoon. This time the men reached No. 3 but pulled a pin, so they brought the engine back to Loyalton that afternoon. Working through the night, Loyalton shop forces repaired the ailing locomotive. During this period, torrential rains replaced the snowstorms.

Taking the plow out on Tuesday, the crews on Nos. 3 and 4 made some progress until both the plow and No. 4 jumped the rails. With disgust, the force clustered aboard No. 3 and returned to Loyalton in time for lunch. In the afternoon, the engine returned to the derailment, and, by working into the darkness, the men rerailed No. 4 and both engines came back to Loyalton.

Would four days of challenging weather keep the railroad closed? Not without a redoubled effort. After gathering all the snow shovelers to be found in Loyalton, the train left Wednesday morning. Getting over the summit proved difficult, but with a large force of men busy shoveling, they had the line open by the time they pulled into Boca at 8:00 P.M. After a short rest, the gang returned to Loyalton, arriving at 10:30 P.M. "Every whistle was blowing on the engines and the factory whistles chimed in."

In spite of twenty-four hours of heavy rainfall that converted Loyalton streets to flowing rivers, the B&L train went out Thursday morning, though some had doubts that it would reach its destination. Although the outcome stood unreported, the B&L ran a special train to Beckwith so the stranded drummers, or traveling salesmen, could take the N-C-O to Reno.

The life of a railroad man can be full of surprises. Shortly after the B&L resumed regular service, one Loyalton man rode up to the engine house and tied his horse to a locomotive. Just after he had climbed into the cab and set the engine in motion, the night watchman put a stop to this nonsense, but not before the intoxicated pilot had managed to damage the locomotive and a couple of barn doors.

Three years later, heavy snow blocked trains again and delayed mails for several days. In the absence of a rotary plow, the crew employed the customary bucking procedure. As the snow was unusually wet, the crew found themselves captive each time they bucked the wet snow.

The big storm of January 1911 that suspended Western Pacific operations also affected neighboring railroads. When a B&L train succumbed to snowdrifts in the broad Sierra Valley, a rescue mission set out to retrieve the train. Unfortunately, the active locomotive derailed three miles from Loyalton, injuring the engineer and fireman. Not until the big WP rotary arrived from Deeth in eastern Nevada was the track cleared. A short time later, more snow tied up the B&L for another week.

During the construction of Western Pacific, its parent, the Denver and Rio Grande, expended $797,362 to acquire a controlling interest in the Boca and Loyalton Railroad. As the narrow canyon occupied by the Middle Fork of the Feather River from a point west of Beckwith to Portola already accommodated two separate railroads and a wagon road, squeezing in a third railroad would have been impractical. WP found the solution by purchasing and upgrading the portion of the B&L between

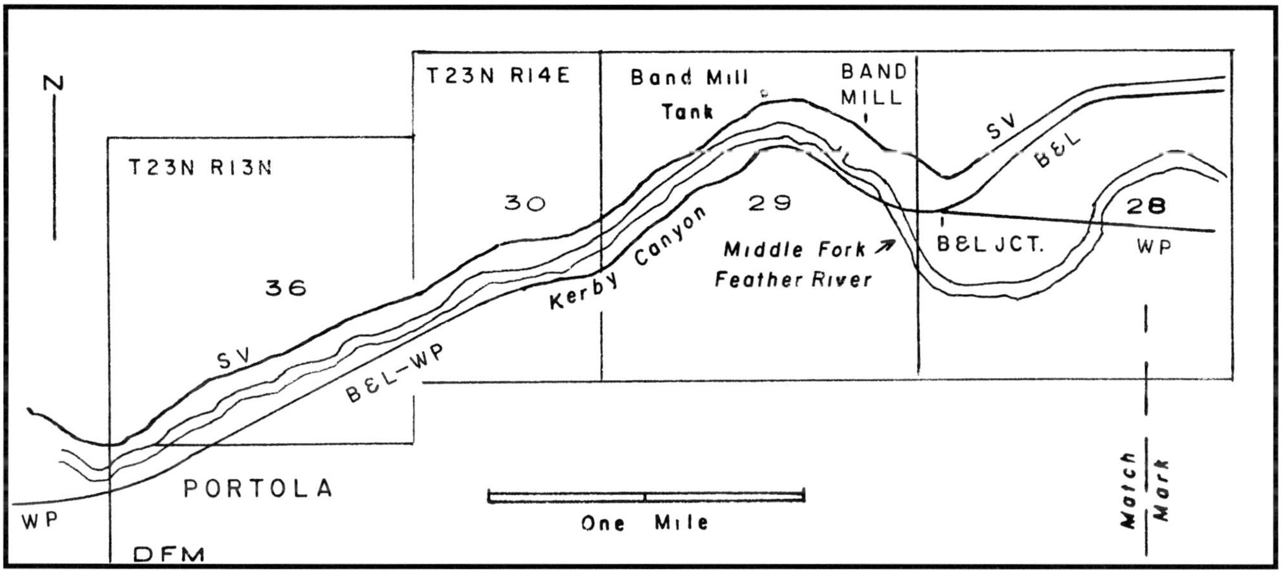

There are a few places in rural California where three independent railroads operated in such close proximity, as in the Sierra Valley in Plumas County. The first railroad surmounted Beckwourth Pass and operated trains to Beckwith in June 1895 (the post office was changed to Beckwourth in 1932). Before a year had elapsed, rails of the Sierra Valleys Railway dodged the hills west of Beckwith before entering Kerby [*sic*] Canyon on their way to Clairville.

After linking the two settlements in its title, the Boca and Loyalton Railroad continued northwest to Beckwith in 1901. Four years later, this standard-gauge railroad had pushed its tracks around the same hills as the Sierra Valleys Railway—parts of the parallel grades are still visible today—to run along the south side of the Middle Fork of the river through the narrow canyon and end at Mormon (Portola).

A critical portion of the Western Pacific route followed the same Middle Fork and Kerby Canyon already occupied by a railroad on either side of the river. By purchasing the Boca and Loyalton, Western Pacific gained access to the segment between B&L Jct. and Portola, which was jointly operated by the two affiliated railroads.

After Western Pacific opened its line to Salt Lake City in 1910, the two smaller railroads struggled for six years to hold traffic on their lines. The end came in 1916 when WP purchased the B&L at a bankruptcy sale and acquired the former Sierra Valleys Railway from the N-C-O the following year. The redundant parallel lines were soon dismantled, leaving WP as the only railroad along the Middle Fork of the Feather River. The magnificent Portola roundhouse of the Western Pacific is now only a distant memory, but the Portola Railroad Museum is a worthy attraction for those interested in railroad history.

Portola and B&L Jct. By a deed signed December 24, 1908, J. H. Roberts conveyed twenty-eight parcels and strips of land, owned by the Roberts Lumber Company and the B&L, to Western Pacific that formed a continuous line between Grizzly Creek (B&L Jct.) and Portola, with scattered parcels extending as far west as Spring Garden. After the sale, B&L and WP conducted joint operations over this segment.

California White Pine Lumber Company

Captain Roberts had envisioned an extension of the B&L to his timberlands near Spring Garden to convey logs to the mill in Loyalton. However, it was not to be. Instead, Los Angeles men formed the California White Pine Lumber (CWPL) Company on June 18, 1902, and within two years the new company acquired the Loyalton sawmill and box factory from the Roberts Lumber Company, along with its timberlands.

In its early years, CWPL fed its Loyalton mill and box factory with logs harvested from its timber around Camp Molloy, a few miles west of Beckwith. Subsequently, it moved its operations west to Cromberg and then to Spring Garden.

CWPL boosted its initial force of twenty-five men in February 1912 to one hundred men to grade a two-mile logging spur commencing near the west portal of WP's Spring Garden. The spur headed northeasterly as it followed Estray Creek, passing through Joe Gill's timberlands to end near the point where the old wagon road passed over the summit.

A description of the motive power servicing this short line escaped recording, along with the life span of the operation. Probably, logging activity ended with the close of World War I, as the corporation ceased to function after 1921.

Passenger Service on the Boca and Loyalton Railroad

Passenger service on the B&L proved to be inconsistent; usually, mixed trains were the rule. After its rails reached Beckwith, the B&L ran a train from Loyalton to Beckwith and then returned to Loyalton, continuing to Boca. Trains in the reverse direction, originating at Boca, went as far as Beckwith before tying up at Loyalton. Sometimes scheduled trains ran only between Boca and Loyalton, but a new timetable in November 1911 showed trains running from Boca all the way to Portola and returning.

Encouraged by an upswing in traffic, the B&L reballasted the railroad during 1912, rebuilt two bridges at the summit, and repaired other bridges. The brighter outlook dimmed in the next year, as several Loyalton mills remained shuttered during the spring because a citrus freeze in southern California reduced demand for packing boxes. The B&L met this adversity by cutting expenses. As of July 1, with the closing of the Loyalton shops, all but one locomotive went into storage, and only a single daily train served patrons between Boca and Portola. Even the crew on that train took on the task of switching cars at various spurs.

The year 1914 started badly. Heavy snowfall suspended B&L service from January 12 to February 18. Three engines proved inadequate to push the ninety-eight-ton WP snowplow through twelve feet of snow at the summit. With heavier motive power, crews finally cleared the railroad, only to have a new snowstorm close the line again for a few days.

With the unrelenting downward trend in lumber traffic as one mill after another closed in Loyalton, Superintendent A. J. Borie resigned his position in March 1914, to be replaced by Oliver G. Hopkins. Since the first of the year, daily service except on Sunday between Portola and Loyalton continued, with a schedule of slightly more than one hour necessary to travel the nineteen miles. South of Loyalton, trains operated only Tuesday and Friday.

The situation worsened in 1915, with the railroad going into receivership in June. A triweekly mixed train alternated with a motorcar from Loyalton to Portola. Confronted with continuing losses, the receivers sought court authority to cease operations at the close of the year, which not unexpectedly raised a howl in Loyalton. The court approved suspension of train service until May 1916, but the California Railroad Commission insisted on a weekly train between Loyalton and Portola through February, followed by two weekly trains in March and April.

Citizens of Loyalton, who boasted having thirteen mills or box factories, saw them fold and drift away so that only a single mill remained. What little tonnage remained, Western Pacific moved over its main line rather than send it to Boca and give the long haul to Southern Pacific.

Western Pacific bought the property at the receiver's sale at Beckwith in September 1916. The new owner abandoned the portion of the B&L south of Loyalton, and title to the remaining property was conveyed to Western Pacific on December 1, 1916. Soon, the only physical evidence consisted of the track across Sierra Valley leading to the timbered areas of Clover Valley.

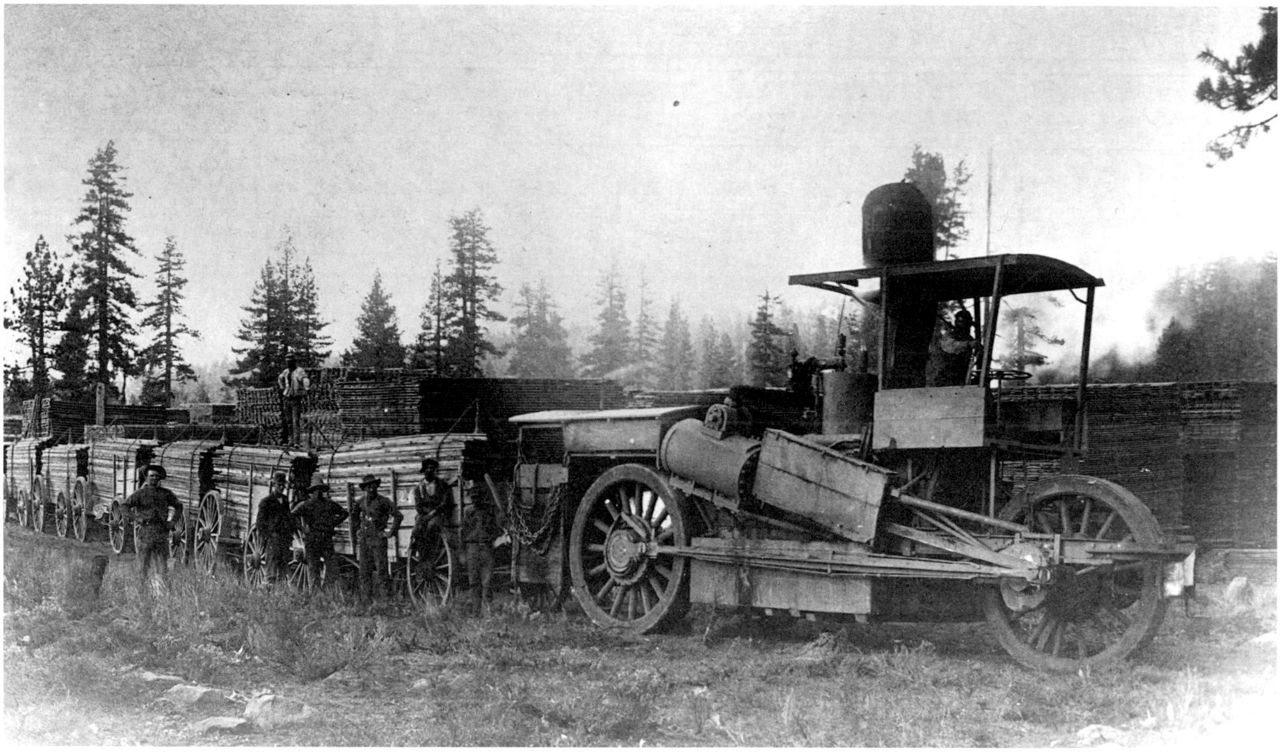

Above: Before the railroad, the Lewis brothers employed this steam-traction engine to deliver lumber from their mill to the Central Pacific at Verdi. (Henry Hanken photograph)

Below: Hauling logs to the lumber mills was an important function of the Boca and Loyalton Railroad. (Louis Stein collection)

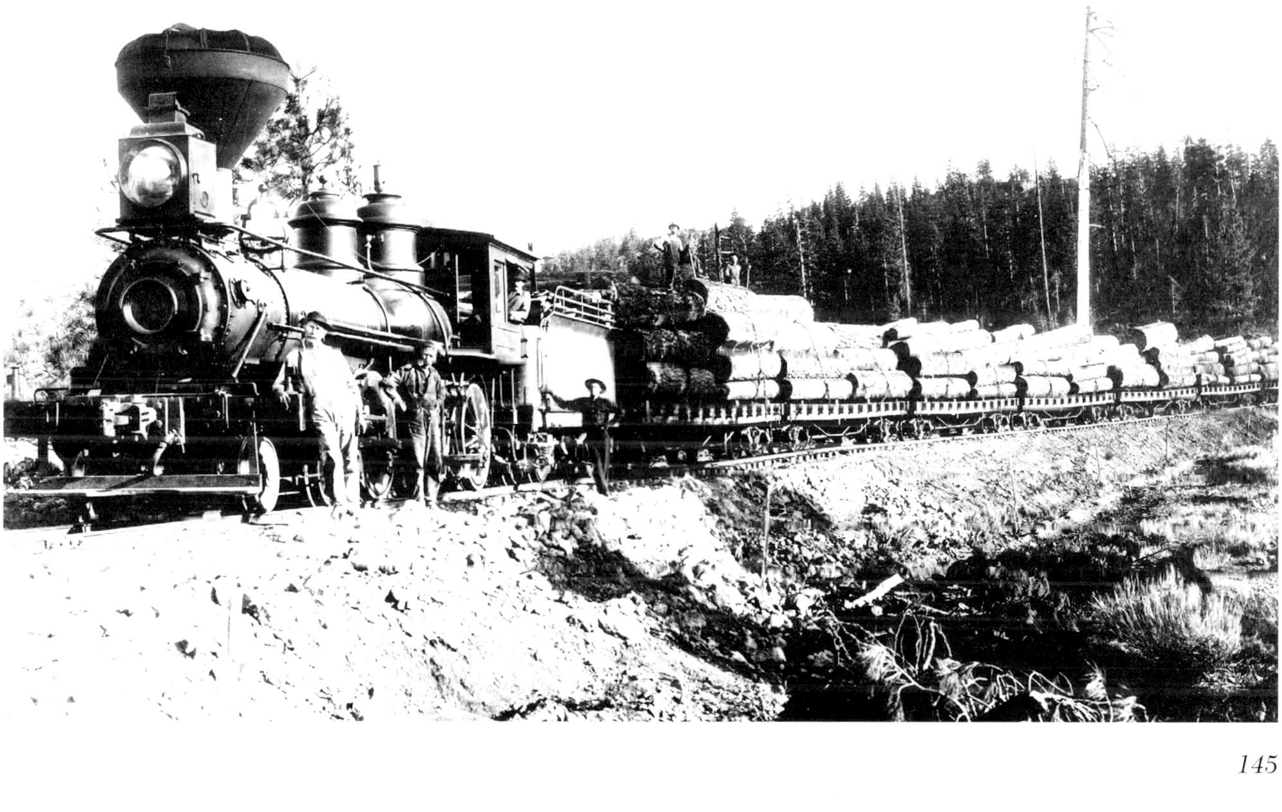

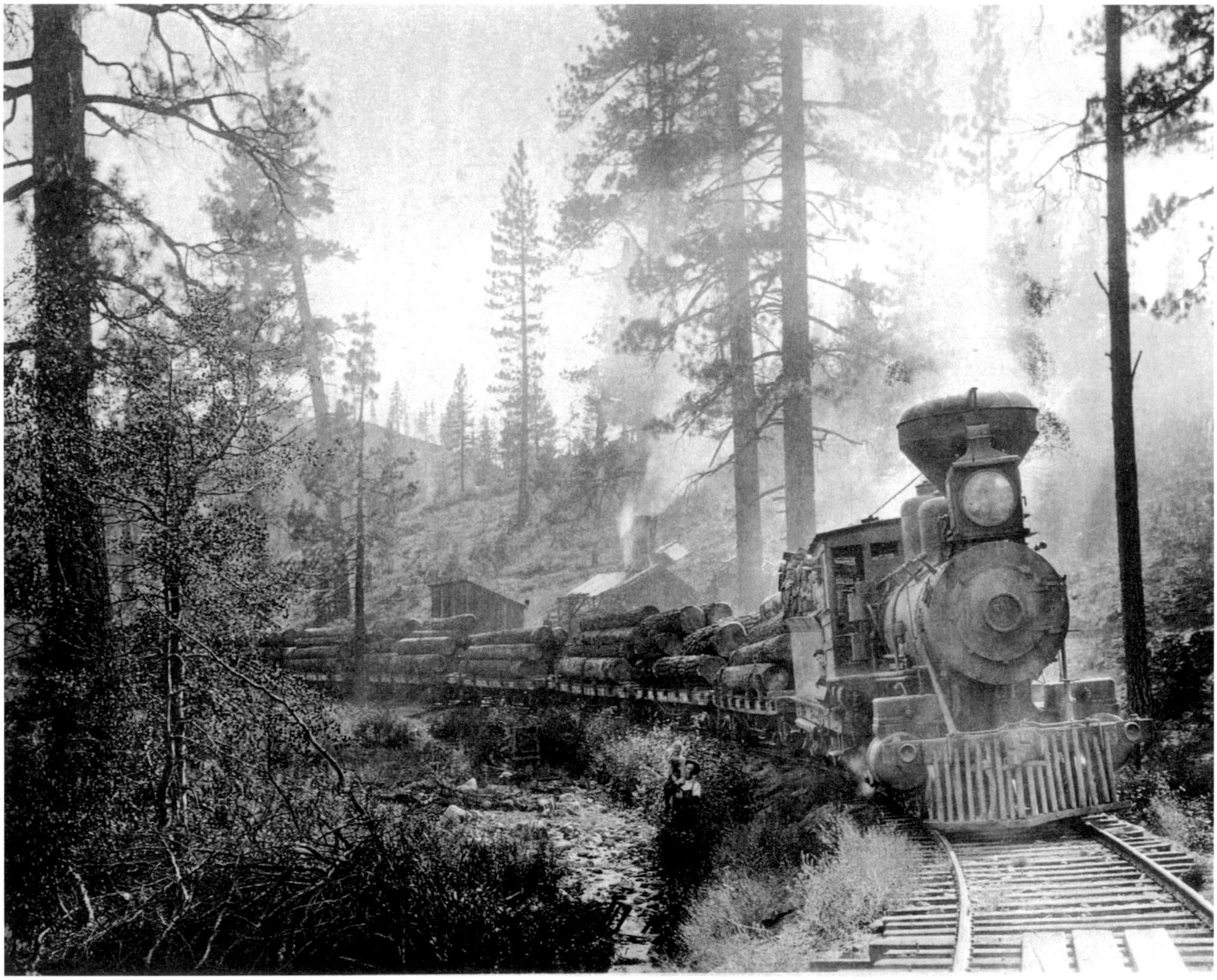

A trainload of logs is ready to leave for a sawmill in Loyalton. The engineer peers around the cab while waiting for instructions. (Plumas County Museum)

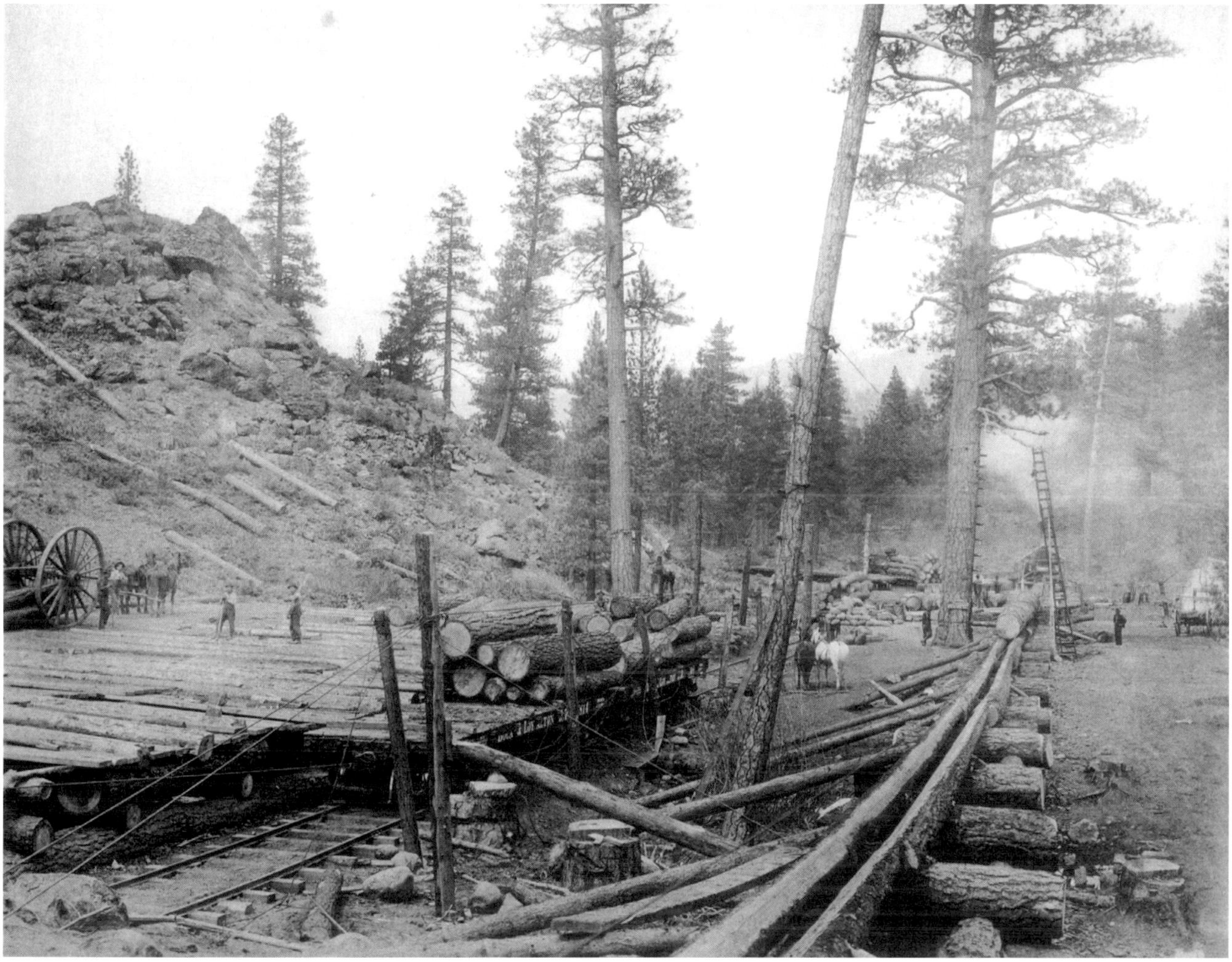

A partially loaded B&L flatcar and log chute stand in the foreground in this loading area. In the distance (*right center*), a locomotive approaches the camp. (Plumas County Museum)

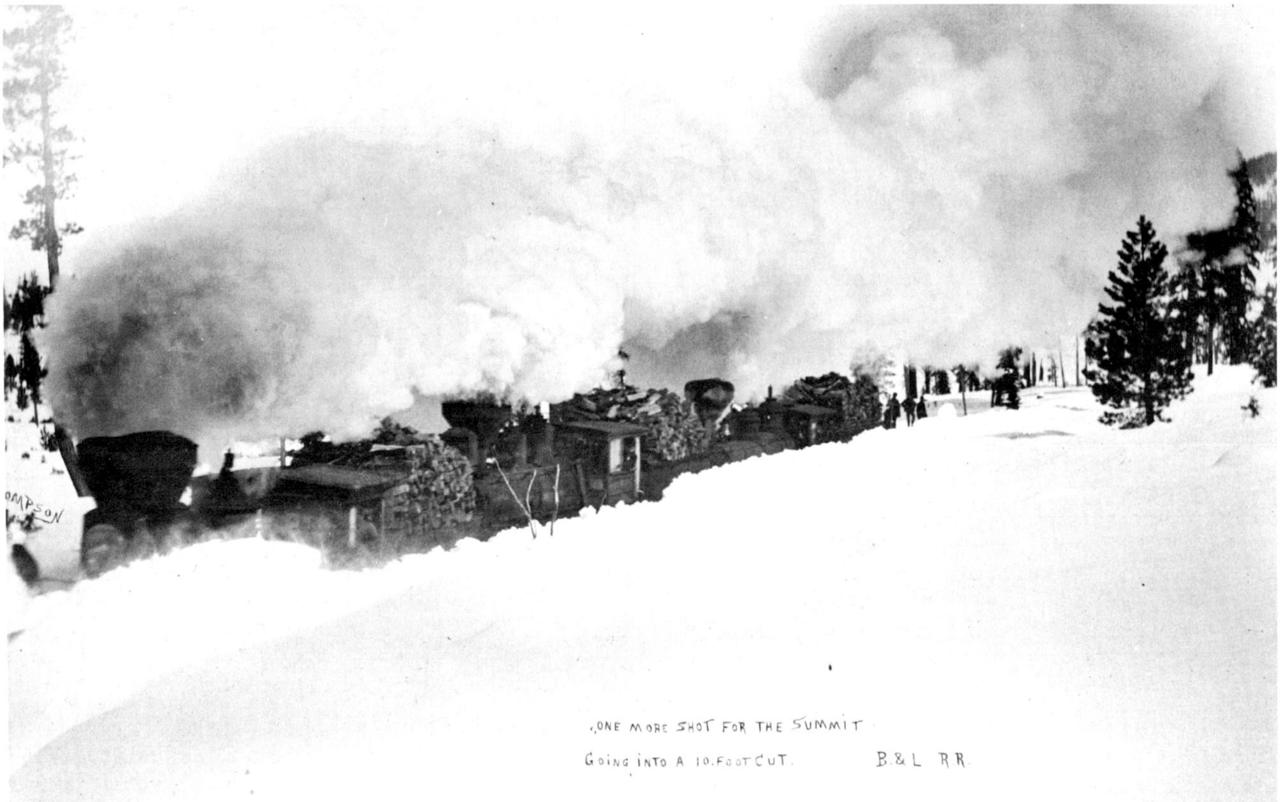

Above: Heavy snows in January 1911 choked the railroad until it could borrow a rotary snowplow from the Western Pacific Railroad.

Below: Until snow shovelers cleared the way, the train could not leave Loyalton.

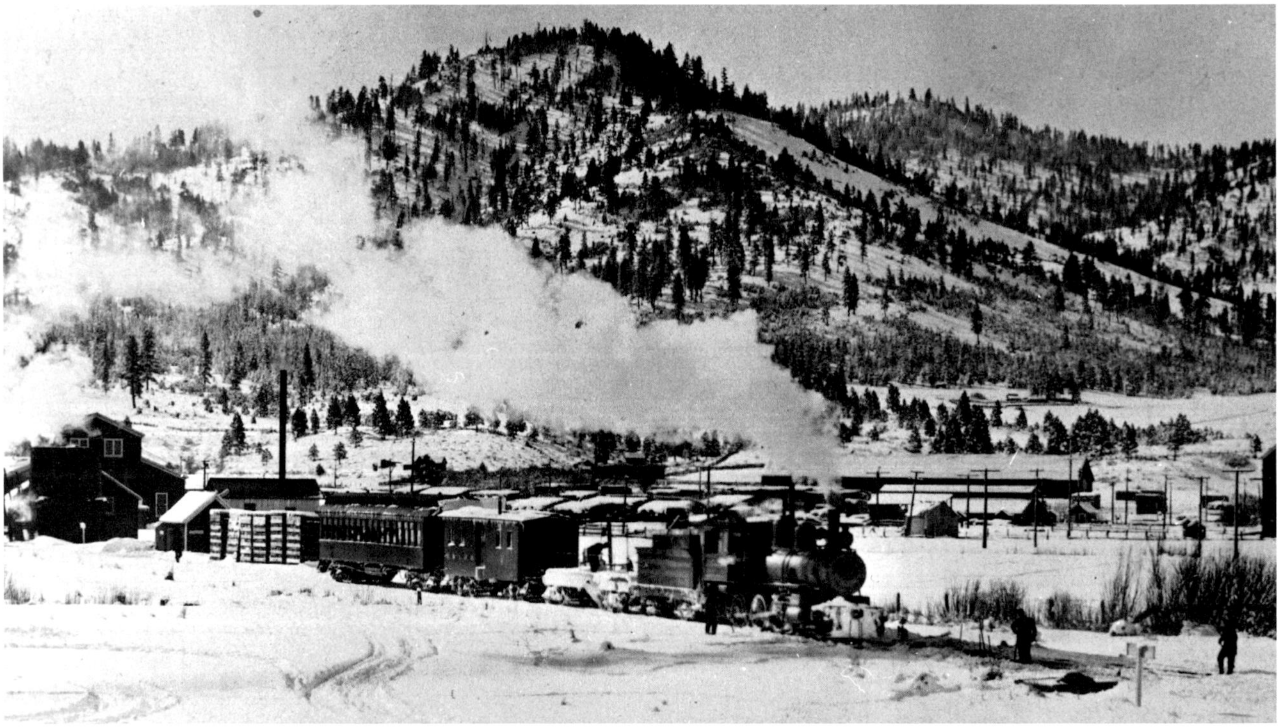

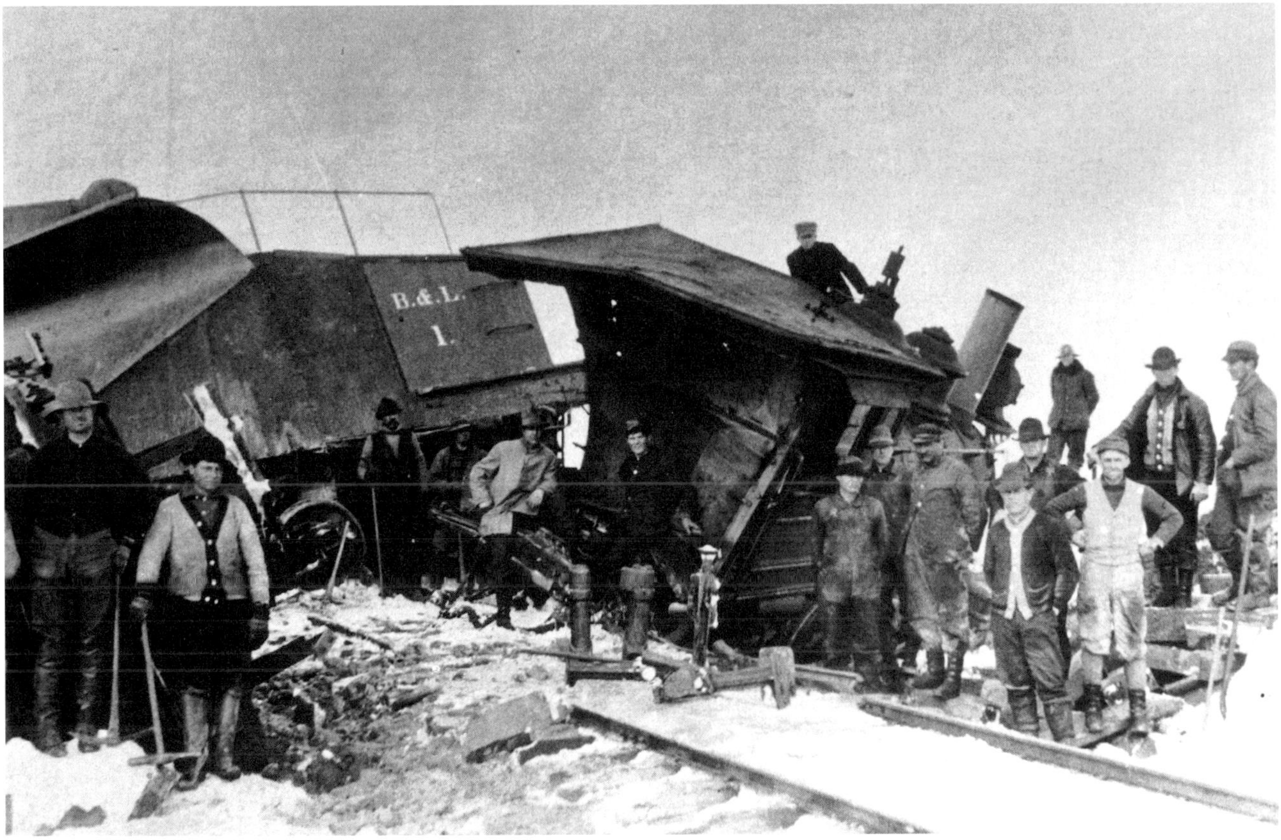

Workers, clearing the derailment of B&L locomotive No. 4 and flanger No. 1, paused momentarily for the photographer. The locomotive, a 2-6-0 built by Baldwin in 1876, served several railroads in its fifty-four-year life. After working on the Virginia and Truckee Railroad as No. 24, the Merrimac, it next hauled logs for the Verdi Lumber Company, and when the bankrupt B&L was sold to Western Pacific in 1916, it joined another roster until finally scrapped in 1930. (James E. Boynton collection)

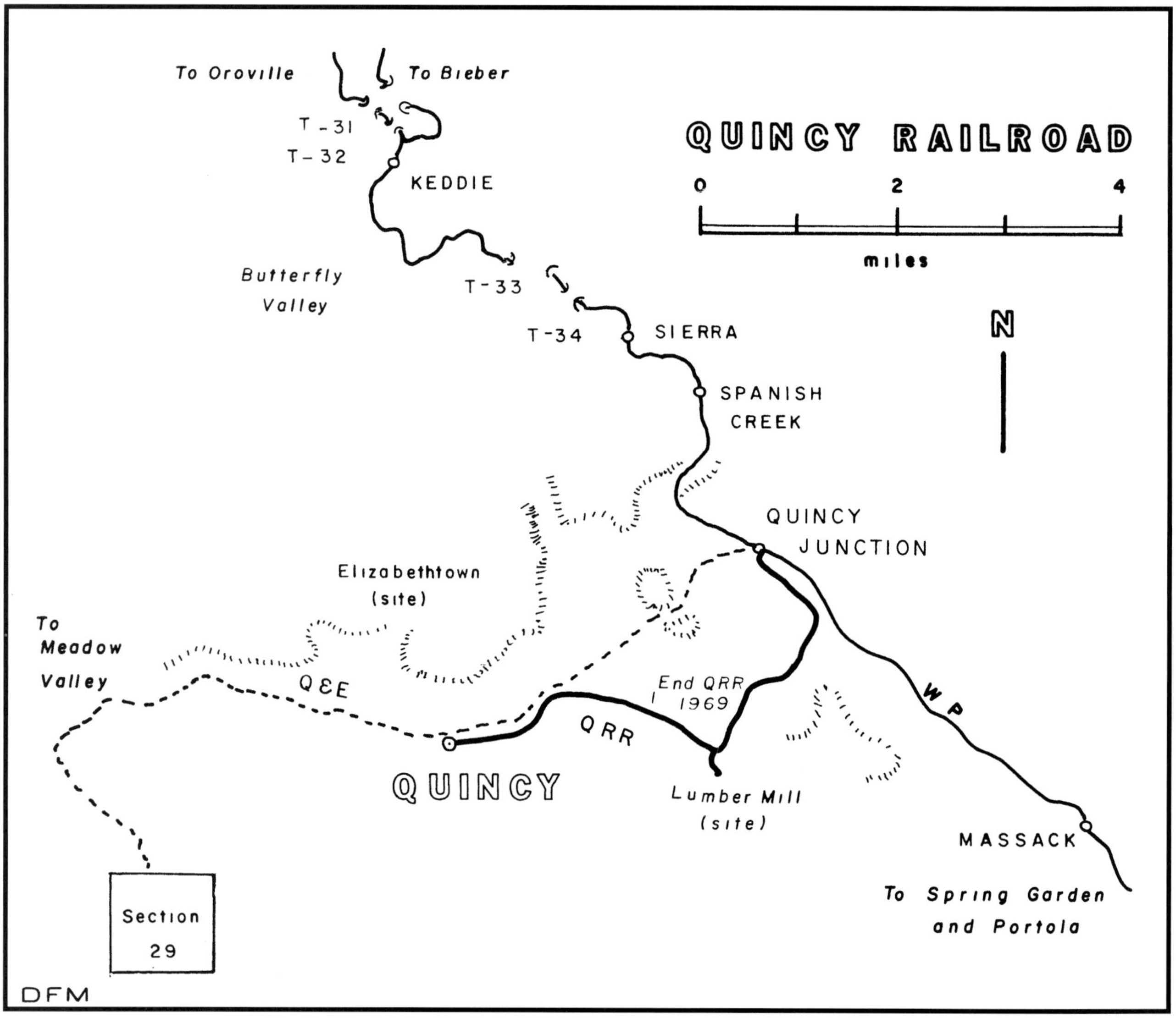
QUINCY RAILROAD
0
2
4
miles
N
To Oroville
To Bieber
T-31
T-32
KEDDIE
Butterfly
Valley
T-33
T-34
SIERRA
SPANISH
CREEK
QUINCY
JUNCTION
Elizabethtown
(site)
To
Meadow
Valley
Q&E
End QRR
1969
QRR
WP
QUINCY
Lumber Mill
(site)
MASSACK
To Spring Garden
and Portola
Section
29
DFM

QUINCY AND EASTERN RAILROAD COMPANY
QUINCY WESTERN RAILWAY COMPANY
QUINCY RAILROAD COMPANY

"So near, yet so far," one resident of Quincy lamented when observing the Western Pacific Railway trains climbing the grade along the eastern edge of the American Valley, five miles away.

The American Valley in northeastern California, stretching about seven miles in an east-west direction, is severed by Spanish Creek and its tributary, Greenhorn (Spring Garden) Creek, on its way to the North Fork of the Feather River. After WP surveyors ran three locations across the American Valley only to find all unsatisfactory, Virgil Bogue, chief engineer, entered the scene in January 1905. With George L. Dillman, he worked out a route in the foothills, about one hundred feet above B. F. Chandler's home, and saved five miles of construction. It also closed the door on any possibility of the WP main line passing through Quincy, even though it was the county seat.

The Bogue locations conformed with the terms of the initial mortgage holding the grade to 1 percent. Western Pacific management failed to be stirred by the wishes of Quincy residents for direct rail service, leaving it to local citizens to arrange for themselves.

Within weeks, Western Pacific secured a right-of-way from L. B. Hartwell and E. H. Hartwell (later the site of Quincy Jct.) and also from B. F. Chandler. Changes occurred in Quincy with the demolition of old structures constituting Chinatown and the creation of Dewsberry Park, "a charming summer retreat."

A San Francisco cigar manufacturer, Nathan Meyer, visited Quincy in March 1905 and foresaw a future for the community. Although the beginning of construction of WP was still months away, he suggested an electric railroad to link the town with the future railroad. While he stood ready to invest in the project, he expected most of the stock to be taken by local residents.

Local stock subscriptions reached some twelve thousand dollars before this first effort faltered. With WP trains still years away, the need for immediate action dissolved, and people's attention returned to their daily tasks.

In July 1908, J. J. Rutledge and G. W. Baker successfully petitioned the Plumas County Board of Supervisors for a railroad franchise from "some available point in Quincy in an easterly direction . . . to the Western Pacific." True to their petition, the promoters secured pledges for stock in the new railroad, and on August 28, 1908, Rutledge with two Oakland friends and two Quincy bankers, E. Huskinson and H. C. Flournoy, incorporated the Quincy and Eastern Railroad Company. The projected route started southwesterly from WP's Hartwell station and followed today's county road between two hills to enter Quincy along Lawrence Street. From there the railroad would continue west along Spanish Creek to the center of Section 18, T24N R9E, and then enter the canyon of Slate Creek and extend south for two miles to end at the north line of Section 29, ten miles from Hartwell.

Rutledge took on the project with great enthusiasm and convinced local citizens to pledge sums in the form of personal notes that were deposited with H. C. Flournoy, cashier of the Plumas County Bank, and guarded by a local committee. When Rutledge demanded these pledges, Flournoy refused to release them until he had ample evidence of sufficient outside funding to complete the railroad. As Rutledge was unable to find the needed funds, the project paused on dead center until after January 1909 when Rutledge and his Oakland friends resigned from the board and returned the corporate books.

With the Western Pacific tracks moving closer—the rails reached nearby Clio from the east on April 3, 1909—renewed interest in Quincy ensued, resulting in a meeting in the Odd Fellows Hall on the evening of April 21. With the resignations of the Oakland men, the five-man board now consisted of Arthur Keddie, William Watson, and C. J. Lee as well as Huskinson and Flournoy.

Various proposals surfaced, such as the community construction of the road, but the star of the evening was John E. Sexton who declared that for thirty thousand dollars, Quincy would have its railroad. Just how Sexton learned of the meeting is unexplained, but the man, born in California in 1866, had been a boomer since his first job on the Market Street Cable Railroad when he was eighteen. He had held a variety of positions, from a green eye-shield clerk to running locomotives on different railroads. He is best known for his colorful management style with the Eureka and Nevada Railroad commencing in 1911.

Railroad prospects grew brighter at the next town meeting several weeks later. William Watson, county surveyor, told the audience that if Quincy people could raise twenty thousand dollars, he had promises of thirty thousand from undisclosed San Francisco parties who turned out to be S. A. Moss and W. P. Hammon, two successful gold-dredging operators.

In June 1909, Watson directed three surveys, and when sixty-five stockholders of the Quincy and Eastern RR pledged fifty-four thousand dollars, the railroad seemed "assured," a frequently abused term of hopeful newspaper editors.

During the summer, Watson and Sexton engaged in the necessary planning, but Sexton did take a few days off for his honeymoon. Southern Pacific agreed to deliver secondhand fifty-pound rail at Marysville at thirty-two dollars per ton. George E. Maurer, awarded the cross-tie contract, purchased a portable sawmill to cut timber on Harvey Johnson's land.

For reasons not revealed, the corporate structure of the Quincy and Eastern Railroad was discarded and replaced by the Quincy Western (QW) Railway Company, organized September 30, 1909. Probably drafted by L. N. Peter, a local attorney and a member of the board of the new company, the lengthy statement of purposes permitted the new company to engage in a widespread variety of activities. The Quincy Western Railway was limited to construction between the Western Pacific Railway and the town of Quincy, about six miles. Instead of the initial southwesterly direction adopted by the previous group, the first mile of this survey pointed *southeast* and went around a marsh before heading for Quincy.

Western Pacific, holding to its steady climb to the west portal of Spring Garden Tunnel, carved a roadbed on the hillside about one hundred feet above the flat American Valley. Watson carefully chose the longer route descending from the connection to the valley. Even so, much of the first mile of the Quincy Western RR to Chandler Creek required a grade in excess of 2 percent; in one place it reached 2.77 percent. (This factor helps explain why Western Pacific found it impractical to swing across the valley and pass through the town of Quincy.)

A public notice advised stockholders of the Quincy Western to meet their stock subscriptions with a 25 percent payment on November 15, a similar amount on December 1, and the balance at the first of the new year.

An additional benefit rose when Western Pacific drove its last spike on November 1, 1909, for now construction materials could come by rail rather by expensive teaming. Soon, timbers for Spanish Creek Crossing began arriving. The longest pile trestle on the new railroad, it would have eight 12-foot spans.

First Steps in Construction

Early in December, John Sexton had a few laborers clearing brush from the right-of-way. Their pay of twenty-six cents per hour would be unreasonable today, but then the cost of living was many times less.

Two unsettling matters surfaced at this time. All the right-of-way had been obtained except for a twenty-five hundred–foot strip near milepost 4 across the Wheeler Ranch. Mr. O. Wheeler wanted one thousand dollars for this right-of-way and other acreage, and the matter was resolved by a purchase in January for an undisclosed figure. The other problem, higher than anticipated preliminary organization expenses, portended financial difficulties in future years.

John Sexton tried to persuade WP to operate a mixed train from Portola to his connection at Hartwell, but a ride in the private car with Superintendent R. M. Ogilvie and T. J. Wyche convinced him that roadbed conditions precluded such service for the time being. When William Watson, Quincy Western president, came up from Oakland to Hartwell, it required two days' riding in a caboose. He reported that the roadbed was generally good, but troublesome slides and settling fills could bring derailments.

Sexton and his crew stood ready to tackle the grade as 1910 began, but Mother Nature had other ideas. Very cold weather encompassed the American Valley, with thermometers reading twelve below zero and even lower in Beckwith. Sexton suspended all work and with his wife joined Arthur Keddie on a train trip to San Francisco after gaining special permission. Fortunately, they departed a week before a snowfall leaving three and one-half feet at Quincy, the heaviest since the monumental winter of 1889–1890.

Rains followed, but the weather did improve, and Western Pacific delivered a new forty-foot passenger coach for the Quincy Western as January 1910 closed. John Sexton and his wife occupied the car from Sacramento. Gray paint covered the outside of the car, while natural wood coloring was used inside the elaborately decorated car.

Around the middle of March, construction activity stirred around Hartwell. Sexton had twenty-five men digging cuts in the first mile; the profile chart marked six cuts and seven fills in the first mile, which, except for the first four hundred feet proceeding to a slight rise, pointed downhill. The challenge of the first cut near

Hartwell, the largest on the entire line, necessitated doubling of the workforce, and when that failed to meet expectations, a night shift was added.

By the end of March, Sexton learned that their locomotive stood at Marysville and that one hundred tons of rail were on their way. Meanwhile, the coming of the railroad invited improvements in Quincy. Bernard Schneider, one of the five board members of the railroad and new proprietor of the Plumas House, had a force engaged in renovating the old hotel.

Now that its roadbed had increased stability, WP offered communication with the outside world by establishing local trains leaving Portola and Oroville at 6:00 in the morning. After departure, the schedule was indefinite; it simply did not exist, but that failed to deter George H. Stevens from meeting trains at Hartwell and conveying passengers to Quincy in his three-seated conveyance.

The arrival of the locomotive spurred construction during April, and when the editor of the *Plumas National* made a short trip on the new railroad on May 11, he wrote that rails had been laid to the crossing of Spring Garden (Greenhorn) Creek, which proved to be a significant point in the construction of this line, for workers could look back with pride on the last of the fills they had made.

From this crossing the railroad eased upward 48 feet in the next 2 miles to the high point at MP 2.75 (near Mill Creek), with a rise not exceeding 1 percent. This profile continued to be reflected in the declining grade for the next 2 miles, but trains from Quincy had to overcome a 1.17 percent rise in this area. Nearly all of the last 1.25 miles—mostly over B. F. Chandler's land—was level or almost level.

The construction policy of the Quincy Western called for rails and ties to be laid on the roadbed and then

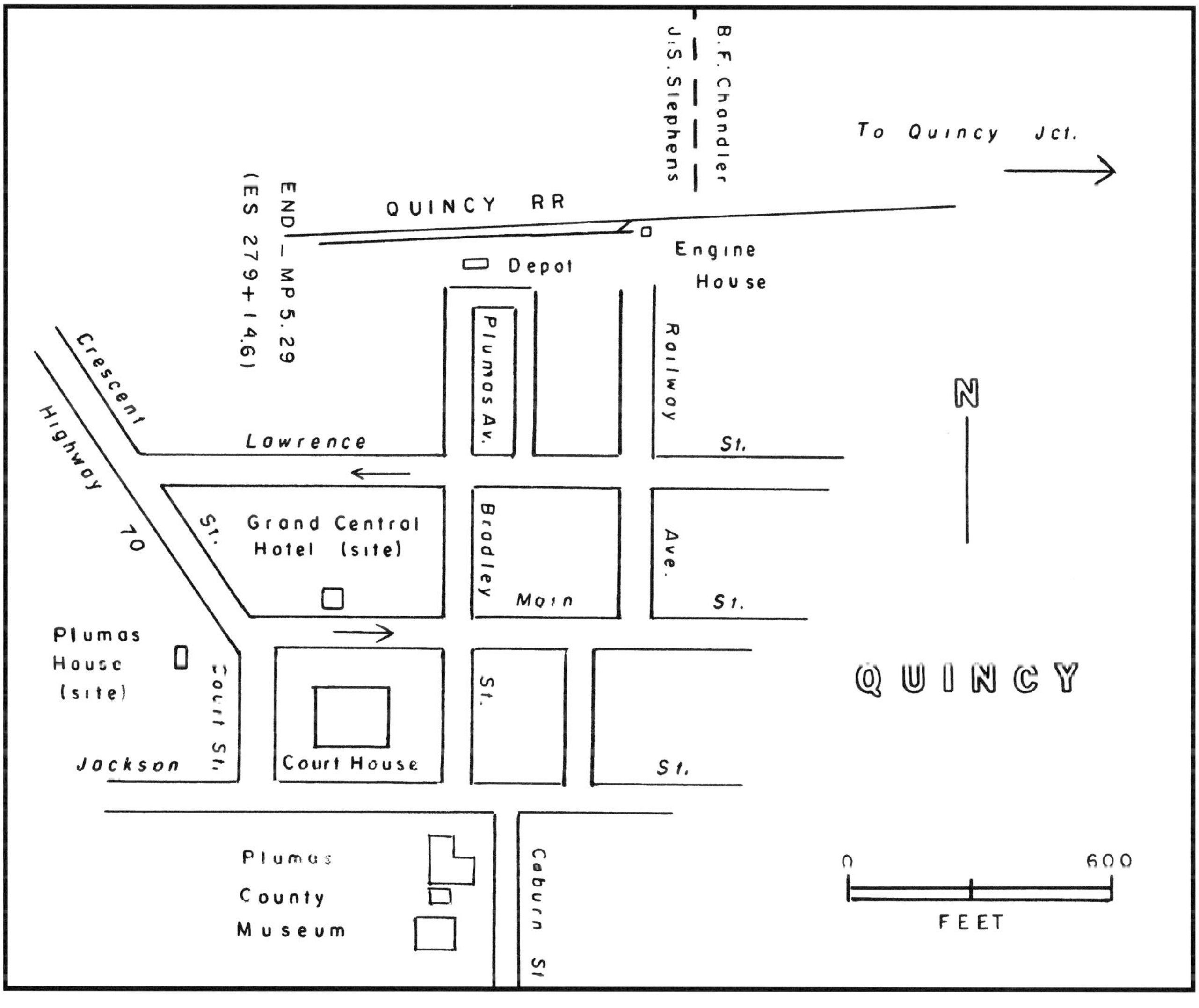

leveled as ballast was inserted under the ties. A week after the editor's trip, completion of the trestles enabled track workers to push "The Front" forward until they exhausted the rail inventory. While waiting for the next shipment, these men cleared brush along the remainder of the 5.28 miles to Quincy.

The delay in the expected shipment of rail plus the soft ground difficulties near Chinatown Point thwarted completion in May; instead, it occurred on June 2, 1910, just one day after the date predicted on March 17.

Primed by the whistle of the locomotive, courthouse bells at 11:00 A.M. alerted one and all of the last-spike celebration. The Quincy Band brightened the day with its music, and Superintendent Sexton played his part by arranging for his men to tie down the last rail except for the final spike. L. N. Peter, local attorney and vice president of the little railroad, drove the last spike, and though the spike was not made of a precious metal, the crowd cheered loudly, in keeping with this important local event.

Peter climbed aboard a flatcar and, after congratulating the citizens for the completion of the railroad, promised everyone a free ride with the commencement of passenger service. Arthur Keddie responded to the request for a few remarks, and the laborers, given a few hours off, enjoyed the complimentary lunch hastily prepared by the local ladies.

With rails spanning the distance between Hartwell and Quincy, construction continued. Most important was the ballast rock supplied from the gravel bed southeast of Rockwell Park. Depots at each terminal proved essential. The right-of-way cost more than anticipated, as only a few owners donated their land.

Supplementing the stock subscriptions, the company secured loans from the Anglo and London Paris National Bank in San Francisco and the Plumas County Bank in Quincy. Even though the loans had been reduced to thirteen thousand dollars and seventy-five hundred dollars, respectively, the bank officers felt uneasy about the fiscal future of the railroad and demanded repayment in August 1911. S. A. Moss, recognizing that his stock investment would vanish in the event of default, met this crisis by advancing nineteen thousand dollars through his Calaveras Gold Dredging Company operating at Jenny Lind (he was president), and Harley C. Flournoy and friends put up twenty-five hundred dollars. In exchange, the railroad issued three-year notes at 6 percent.

Early Operations

On Sunday, June 12, the management offered a free excursion from Quincy to Hartwell and return on one of the five trains operating that special day. People were "invited to make *one* round-trip *only*" and were advised of limited seating capacity.

Probably everyone in Quincy turned out for the free rides. The largest crowd of 214 filled the 1:30 P.M. train, and the count for the day totaled 614. With the road unballasted, the fastest trip was just seventeen minutes behind the locomotive decorated under the direction of Francis Sexton. P. J. O'Neill served as conductor, assisted by John McNulty. John McCartney occupied the right side of the engine cab, with Henry S. Sexton named mechanic. Everything went well that day without derailments or troubles.

With only limited freight traffic, the road existed on passengers. For a while local patrons enjoyed Sunday train rides; on July 17, three Sunday trains and low round-trip rates drew patronage. Near Hartwell, Sexton uncovered a delightful area with a mineral spring and a rivulet of pure cold water that he planned to develop into a picnic area. Time off for recovering from a track motorcar accident delayed implementation of his plans.

Once the novelty of local train rides had run its course, the Quincy Western looked to Western Pacific to bring in visitors from outlying points. So when WP operated its first through train, the event commanded considerable local attention. Patrons of the first train, arriving at Hartwell about one in the afternoon on Sunday, August 21, 1910, found the Quincy Band and a crowd of about four hundred waiting to welcome them. (The Quincy Western had brought the assemblage in its train of one coach and three flatcars.) Congressman Julius Kahn of San Francisco, a passenger on the train, felt compelled to make a short address.

The WP station board at Hartwell carried the arrival times of its trains as follows:

No. 3	Westbound Passenger	11:15 P.M.
No. 4	Eastbound Passenger	6:02 A.M.
No. 64	Eastbound Freight	11:15 P.M.
No. 65	Westbound Freight	8:55 A.M.
No. 94	Eastbound Mixed	2:30 P.M.
No. 95	Westbound Mixed	11:05 A.M.

Freight trains Nos. 64 and 65 did not stop at Hartwell.

Quincy Western patronage, dependent on WP schedules, departed from Quincy thirty-five minutes before WP trains arrived at Hartwell.

A flow of special trains introduced Sacramento Valley people to the picturesque American Valley. Some 250 Oroville residents chose California's Admission Day to venture up the Feather River to Quincy, only to be followed by another large group from Marysville. With its small contribution to the trip's mileage, revenue earned by the Quincy Western proved equally slim. A local comment at this time held patronage as "reasonably good" with daily receipts of thirty-five dollars, but the sum failed to cover operating expenses. Nonetheless, the Quincy Western moved ahead in the fall of 1910 to complete the railroad. The solitary locomotive secured a home of its own when carpenters raced to erect a shelter ahead of the winter storms. The company also finished the freight house at Quincy but delayed the passenger station until the next year. The arrival of a nine-passenger track inspection car on September 17 enabled the railroad to reduce running expenses by alternating the car with steam trains. With the rearrangement of the Quincy yard tracks and completion of the ballasting program, the little railroad stood poised for the winter.

WP passenger trains served Hartwell at unattractively late or early hours that could create inconveniences. When the westbound passenger train arrived at 2:00 A.M. on October 17, 1910—almost three hours late—ten passengers destined for Quincy stood dismayed, finding no local train ready to finish their journeys, as the little railroad's crew, tired of waiting, simply went home. The ten passengers, including eight attending the Teachers' Institute, had to walk to Quincy and arrived after three in the morning, worn out. The railroad management, recognizing the problem, adopted a formal schedule along with a policy of waiting at Hartwell as much as ninety minutes for delayed trains.

Plumas County in 1910 recorded a population of only 5,689, slightly more than 1900, but the census taker found only 884 in Quincy and the American Valley, certainly not enough to support a meaningful trading center. Until 1913 when the first large lumber mill began operations, Quincy lacked a traffic-generating source. For the first fiscal year ending June 30, 1911, QW Railway revenues totaled $7,938, of which freight provided $3,272, passengers $3,858, with mail and express making up the remainder. After deducting operating expenses of $15,800, the road reported a net loss of $7,862. Necessarily, small salaries prevailed; the five officers shared $1,200 for the year, and eight others received $5,780. The passenger count for that year totaled 11,850, with the average revenue per passenger of just 32 cents. Certainly, after all of the struggle to build the connecting link, the little railroad proved disappointing to its shareholders.

With these adverse conditions, shareholders convened at the first annual meeting in October 1910 and elected William Watson, M. A. Boyle, B. Schneider, L. W. Clough, and H. P. Macbeth to the board of directors. Although the group was said to be "harmonious" as President Watson read his statement, it declined to adopt it and adjourned the meeting to November 14. Because the proceedings of the November meeting were not reported in the local press, one might interpret their absence to reflect the editor's wish not to inflame what may have been an unpleasant gathering with controversial attitudes. However, a reduction of forces followed, a difficult task because of the already small staff.

The Big Snowstorms of 1911

The biggest snowfall in years added to the difficulties of the infant railroad early in January 1911 when it left four feet of snow on Quincy streets. The Quincy Western made a gallant effort to reach Hartwell but had to recede at G. E. Droege's place, about a mile outside of town. More snow added two feet to the clogged streets and collapsed barns around Quincy. Mrs. Robert Erwin lost six of her fourteen milk cows when heavy snow crushed the barn.

No trains could move on either the WP or the Quincy Western for several weeks. Near the end of January, two athletes, H. C. Flournoy and H. B. Wolfe, responded to Superintendent Sexton's call for volunteers to dig trenches along each rail, and each man dug fifty feet. Warm weather finally melted the snow but left so much water by the Droege place (MP 2–3) that Sexton had to wait until February 5 before his little locomotive managed to reach Hartwell.

In the middle of the weather problem, the board of directors convened a special meeting on January 17 to accept the resignation of William Watson as president and director.

Spring eventually arrived, enabling the Quincy Western to resume Sunday excursions; sometimes the Quincy Band went along to entertain the group. The *Plumas National* praised the condition of the short line and repeated its congratulations after the Sacramento excursion brought nearly two hundred people for an overnight stay in Quincy. The *Sacramento Bee* also recognized the performance of the young railroad with its unique record of no accidents and no employee injuries. It also noted that the railroad handled an average of six cars of freight each week.

In July, as John Sexton showed signs of restlessness, the Quincy Chamber of Commerce adopted a resolution praising Sexton's operation of the railroad. Sexton had several ideas for new railroads, including the Susan Valley Railroad from Doyle on Western Pacific westward along the south shore of Honey Lake on its way to Susanville. In August, he agreed to prepare an estimate of the cost of restoring service to the Eureka and Palisade Railway in Nevada that had been out of service following severe washouts two years earlier. Next he was promoting an electric railway from Twain on WP across

Indian Valley and north to Nevis and also had plans for a railroad to Surprise Valley (as mentioned in Chapter 6). In November 1911, he signed a contract to rebuild the E&P Railway, which commanded his attention for many years.

Motive-Power Problems

Sexton's departure coincided with motive-power problems. Relying on a solitary locomotive of ancient vintage left the road no alternative but to close down when the engine headed for the shops. In October 1911, the locomotive's failure required the skill of a boilermaker from Sacramento. During the hiatus, no one failed to notice the empty fuel oil tank, and after ordering a tank car, only to have it inadvertently appropriated by Western Pacific, no trains operated for a week.

WP made up for its error when it issued a travel folder describing Quincy as the "Queen of the Sierras" and discussed QW Railway plans for extensions to Meadow Valley and Nelson Point, which never materialized.

The locomotive debacle repeated itself a month later. Attempts to run the motorcar failed, and, with no one locally with authority, confusion reigned. With a leased engine from the Boca and Loyalton RR, trains could run again. The following spring, another failure required the QW Railway to rent a substitute for forty-four days at eight dollars a day.

At the end of November 1911, F. A. Autinreith began his association with the Quincy Western as superintendent and, to curb expenses, also served as a conductor. Born and raised in Yreka, he had managed the Yreka Railroad several years previously.

Recognizing the need for something to draw tourists—and their money—to their town, Quincy business leaders built a fifteen hundred–foot toboggan slide at the end of Buchanan Street. B. Schneider, proprietor of the Plumas House, added a skating rink on his premises, and WP cooperated with a round-trip fare from San Francisco of about eleven dollars and also issued a second folder, this time praising Quincy as "Queen of the Winter World." Though willing hands quickly prepared the toboggan slide and installed night lighting, the venture failed to draw the tourist crowd. The absence of snow in January 1912, unlike the previous winter, canceled one excursion.

By this time the errant locomotive had been repaired, but the cost and rental payment exceeded twelve hundred dollars, a heavy toll on the slim budget. Economic realities forced the diminutive railroad to seek authority for a fare increase from the California Railroad Commission in May 1912. With the disadvantage of being less than six miles long, fares exceeded the usual two or three cents–per-mile charge. One-way fare from Quincy to Rockwell, Pioneer (school), Greenhorn, and Hartwell (soon to be changed to Marston) stood at fifteen, twenty-five, thirty-five, and forty-five cents, respectively, while an added nickel or a dime covered the round-trip fare. At its hearing with San Francisco attorney Max Thelen present, the commission heard the case and several weeks later granted a nickel increase in the one-way fare to Hartwell and a round-trip rate of seventy-five cents. Unfortunately from the revenue standpoint, two large excursions—one with more than four hundred people—visited Quincy in the interim.

In 1913, the outlook for the future brightened with plans for the establishment of a lumber company at Quincy by Frank S. Murphy and associates. For a short time, the Towle Estate was delivering twenty-five thousand feet of lumber each day to the depot for shipment elsewhere.

These two events spurred manager Autinreith into action. For Murphy's new lumber mill, he started construction of a half-mile spur commencing near the high school to the mill site, and, by adding a second leg, he created a wye track for turning locomotives. When the Towle Estate, working in Meadow Valley four miles west of Quincy, began making noises about its own line connecting with the WP, the QW made a preliminary survey from the Quincy end of its line. It was unfortunate that the company's finances prohibited construction of an extension into Meadow Valley, for the future Spanish Peak Lumber Company might have been a good source of traffic.

Murphy's lumber company, the first substantial industry in Quincy, would double the railroad's annual revenue to $20,000; meanwhile, the little road struggled on a hand-to-mouth basis. As 1914 began, the company assessed the stockholders $1 per share, which yielded a precious $6,300.

W. J. Miller successfully circulated a petition to change the name of the connection from Marston to Quincy Jct. and forwarded it to Western Pacific, which responded by adopting the new name in its timetable of April 12, 1915.

The finances of the railroad moved under ominous clouds as 1915 progressed. Although the company had raised some $58,000 cash from stock subscriptions in its beginning (another $1,400 par value of stock represented the cost of the last mile of right-of-way from two parties), it faced interest-bearing debt. One $19,000 three-year 6 percent note stood in the hands of the Calaveras Gold Dredging Company, while H. C. Flournoy and others held similar but smaller notes aggregating $2,353. Annual interest had been lowered to $1,281, but with the road usually failing to meet operating expenses, little if any funds remained for ad valorem taxes and interest, which threatened the very existence of the railroad. Revenues for 1916 (June 30) climbed to $17,000, of which passengers provided $5,000, down slightly from previous years, so the company reported a net loss of $3,600.

Taking cognizance of the financial strain confronting the Quincy Western Railway, the chamber of commerce scheduled a meeting in January 1916 that came after record snowfall measuring more than one hundred inches fell on Quincy that month. Demonstrating their support of the railroad, twenty citizens with shovels joined the railroad workers to reopen the railroad after a ten-day closure. At the meeting the group rejected a substitute auto line and supported the railroad. In contrast with the criticism previously cast on Autinreith, those assembled gave him a vote of confidence. They also discussed the adverse effect of the jitneys running to Quincy Jct. but took no action.

Shortly after the meeting, another storm blanketed the railroad, and, just as the crew had almost cleared the line, a third snowfall voided their efforts. A frustrated Murphy filed a complaint with the California Railroad Commission, but the railroad had resumed normal operations. The widespread storm affected trains trying to reach Westwood; a week later a Nevada-California-Oregon train steamed into Reno after a twenty-day blockade.

The warmer spring weather received a special welcome in Quincy. The lumber company cut ties for the mile-long track from the Johnson Ranch into the Clough and Lee timber tract at the eastern edge of the American Valley for an expected brief harvest. On the opposite side of the valley, Quincy Lumber Company assigned twelve men to brush out the route for logging chutes feeding the camp at the mouth of Dublin Jack Ravine. As soon as the cutting ended near the Johnson Ranch, a crew pulled up the rails for the new 1.75-mile spur of the Quincy Western Railway.

Passenger traffic held an important position on the QW Railway because proportionately it contributed heavily to the gross earnings, as every filled seat in the passenger coach stalled the road's prospective demise. A number of jitney operators stole passengers from the railroad, often operating without filing the required tariff with the California Railroad Commission.

Matters came to a head at the stockholders' meeting in Quincy on August 29, 1917. Leon L. Clough read a letter to the assemblage from S. A. Moss who, with W. P. Hammon, represented 60 percent of the capital stock. The letter referred to the financial problems over the past two years, and the devastating effect of the jitneys that cut into passenger earnings of $200–$300 a month. Moss foresaw a freight-rate increase terminating Quincy Lumber Company operations. By scrapping the property promptly, about $35,000 could be realized, but delays would cut the figure in half.

Judge J. O. Moncur felt the railroad formed a vital part of the community and that leading citizens should curb the jitney abuses. Holding the opinion that the railroad granted the lumber company a ridiculously low log-hauling rate, he ventured that the lumber company might lease or possibly buy the little railroad.

On September 17, the Quincy Western Railway filed a formal application with the California Railroad Commission to abandon operations and sell the equipment. The company reported the property cost $81,000 and that its operations resulted in cumulative losses of $26,000. The company owed $40,000, of which notes represented about $25,000 plus other indebtedness of $15,000, including unpaid interest.

The commission hearing in Quincy on October 5, 1917, stirred considerable interest and revealed interesting information. As part of the effort to cut expenses, the president, now Charles W. Gardner, received no salary. A. L. Dahl, secretary, though paid $100 per month, turned his salary back to the company. The absence of a superintendent—Autinreith had left in July—also saved a few dollars.

Gardner, in reasoning supporting the abandonment, had been informed that the Quincy Lumber Company would complete harvesting all its remaining timber in two years, and this lumber company provided 84 percent of the freight revenues. The only locomotive required $1,500 in repairs; renting temporary motive power could equal this sum. Proceeds from scrapping would retire most of the indebtedness.

Discussing the April 20, 1916, contract between the lumber company and the railroad for the construction of the spur across the Flournoy-Gansner lands to Dublin Jack Ravine, Gardner explained that the lumber company underwrote the $10,000 cost of the spur and that the railroad would receive $2.50 per car handled, with half to be returned to the lumber company. (The railroad would own the spur.) Gardner admitted a rail motorcar costing $2,500 could match the jitneys.

A. H. Dahl offered the pleasant news that the QW Railway made money in some months. Approached by the Towle Estate to haul their lumber over the proposed spur and on to Quincy Jct., Dahl revealed that under the Flournoy-Gansner right-of-way agreement, only Quincy Lumber Company logs and lumber could be transported over the new spur. (Towle would no longer entertain delivering its lumber to the Quincy depot.)

Representing the opposition, H. B. Wolfe, attorney for the Quincy Lumber Company, confirmed the restrictions in the agreement but protested the abandonment of the railroad, as it would cost his company $25,000 to move and the town would lose a monthly payroll of $7,000 to $8,000. He also maintained that existing timber would sustain his company for ten years rather than two.

R. H. Felt, one of the lumber company owners, stated that his company contemplated increasing its output by 25 percent to 30 percent. On cross-examination, Felt admitted the company could stand a 25 percent increase in freight rates.

Wolfe announced that a group of Quincy businessmen stood ready to buy the railroad for $25,000 or its estimated scrap value as determined by three appraisers. If effected, the immediate crises would be resolved. Within two weeks, title was transferred to the group for $25,000.

Quincy Railroad Company

A new company, incorporated November 10, 1917, simplified the name to Quincy Railroad Company, and other changes ensued. People on Quincy streets heard considerable blasting necessary to build the spur to Dublin Jack Ravine. F. S. Murphy loaned the railroad $5,000 to upgrade the track, and W. Y. Stoddard, also general manager of the Quincy Lumber Company, ordered a rail motorcar from San Francisco for passenger operations.

The condemnation of the eighty-year-old locomotive, which had rendered temperamental service since the railroad began, halted operations for a week until Western Pacific delivered a rental locomotive from Wendover, Utah.

Under the new management, the physical plant reflected the infusion of cash, although the railroad continued to operate at a loss for most years in the next two decades.

The original motorcar, built in 1909, measured only ten feet, and the 15-HP engine restricted its performance. Somewhere along the way, probably after 1914, the railroad discarded it. Stoddard went to San Francisco in February 1918 to pick up the new car but returned without it, as the car would not be ready for several weeks. When the car arrived, the local editor told readers that riding in it "will convince you it is a great improvement." With a "natty appearance," the car seated twenty, and a trailer accommodated baggage.

A winter storm came along shortly after the new car to give the railroad its share of problems. Fortunately, the shed for the motorcar had been erected just in time to shield it from the weather, but the car could not avoid trouble when a broken rail some months later pushed it off the track (there were no injuries).

Superintendent H. J. Hoffman, who succeeded F. A. Autinreith, reportedly complained bitterly when the springs of the car were broken because, according to the newspaper, an overweight person from Oroville was on board. The editor was so unkind as to name the individual.

At the start of 1919, the Quincy Railroad operated four round-trips daily to the junction. Talk circulated that the railroad would extend its track around the Plumas House that Bernard Schneider had recently sold to Phil Blume of Winnemucca. Nothing came of this idea, but the combination freight and passenger station at Quincy (30 × 65 feet) was expanded to provide a better waiting room and more space for the superintendent's office. Besides the 16 × 40–foot engine house, motorcar house, and shed, the railroad had a 2,000-gallon redwood water tank at Quincy and an underground 11,000-gallon oil tank.

F. L. Butterfield relieved motorman Polk on the passenger car. Steve Grondona, the genial conductor, express messenger, mail clerk, baggage man, flagman, and head brakeman, decided to change to a less demanding occupation as soon as a replacement could be found. He chose to raise chickens on the Butterfield farm in the eastern part of the American Valley. Six months with his feathered friends proved disenchanting, and Grondona returned to his old job shortly before Christmas 1919.

During his absence, a fire destroyed the engine house on September 15 and severely damaged the locomotive. Superintendent Hoffman lost no time in renting power from Western Pacific.

Six weeks later, the burned locomotive, "spick and span with a new coat of paint," sported a new cab and was "puffing up and down the main line as proud as a boy with a new pair of red top boots." As the railroad had purchased a Shay locomotive just a few weeks before, the Quincy Railroad for the first time enjoyed a full complement of motive power: two locomotives plus a motorcar.

Litigation enveloped the railroad in the late summer of 1920. The U.S. Forest Service charged the railroad with operating an engine without a spark arrester. Although a matter not to be treated lightly in that timbered land, the jury—out for just ten minutes—rendered a "not guilty" verdict.

The railroad office safe captured the attention of those seeking easy money. In June 1917, when the company struggled desperately for every dollar, a midnight thief broke in, dynamited the safe, and made off with around $300. Five years later, the passenger train conductor reported for work one Sunday morning in an intoxicated condition. After taking his train to Quincy Jct., he simply disappeared. An examination of the office revealed an empty safe. A few days later, Superintendent

Hoffman received a letter from the errant conductor at Marysville advising him that the greater part of the loot could be found hidden in the top of the fuel oil tank. Indeed, the information proved accurate—everything was there but $90 cash, checks, and the mail pouch.

Some months went by before a former Quincy Railroad locomotive engineer appeared unannounced in Quincy one morning. He unpacked his bag, donned overalls, climbed into the locomotive cab, and disappeared in the direction of Quincy Jct. with a string of boxcars trailing behind. When the dust settled, an inquiry indicated that this man, working in a minor job by the Russian River in Sonoma County, California, for the past two years missed his old job and wanted to return. Unfortunately, because of heart trouble, he had to live in a lower altitude.

In 1920 W. F. Butcher and C. Hedden of Westwood built a molding factory in Quincy near the high school, and the railroad built a short spur to the new plant. Their company, B and H Moulding Company, moved to Stockton in November 1927 after purchasing the California Siding Company in that city. The extent of additional traffic probably was not large, but the railroad needed all the new business possible, for 1921 marked the third year of deficits. When Standard Oil (Chevron) established a distribution plant in Quincy the next summer, it added two to four cars of revenue traffic each week. A year later, H. J. Hoffman, superintendent for more than ten years, resigned and went to San Francisco. L. H. Thayer, who had been with Western Pacific for a dozen years, filled his place. Willis King, just graduated from the Plumas County High School, joined the railroad as agent and assistant to Thayer. At the same time, Robert J. Youngblood, who had been agent at the junction for several years, departed for Niles Garden. Charles Gibson came up from Sacramento to hold the position.

In 1926, the railroad concentrated its efforts to improve the roadbed made possible by a $10,000 loan from the new Quincy Lumber Company. Another locomotive joined the short equipment roster that then consisted of a single freight car, a passenger car, a motorcar and trailer, and two steam locomotives.

The net profit of $6,388, recorded in 1928, stood as the highest ever for the firm. That year total revenue totaled $33,000, though down from the $47,000 earned in 1926 when the railroad benefited from the construction of the Bucks Lake project. In 1928, the railroad originated 16,400 tons of traffic, which fell to 9,900 tons two years later and, with the mill closed, only 1,361 tons in 1932. Thayer had expected to suspend operations at the end of 1931 but was able to struggle with just five employees in 1933, the low point for the railroad in that decade.

Traffic began to pick up in 1937, and during 1942, 64,000 tons—nearly all lumber—moved over the railroad. Freight revenue soared to just a shade under $80,000, and 1,660 passengers contributed $829 to the treasury that year. Net profit proved a pleasing $22,653 for the owners of the railroad who often were stockholders in the major lumber company as well.

In the delightful times of the late 1940s and early 1950s, steam engines powered trains of rail-fan excursions on the Quincy Railroad. The excursion sponsored by the Northern California Railroad Club in July 1954 used the Western Pacific Budd car up the river and to the junction where a Quincy Railroad steamer hauled a gondola load of passengers to the town.

Responding to the request of the Di Gorgio Corporation, owner of both the railroad and the lumber mill, the ICC approved abandonment of the last two and one-half miles of the railroad in May 1969. The last revenue train left Quincy on December 15, 1969, and after a maintenance train operated on January 13, 1970, dismantling began, leaving the line in place between Quincy Jct. and the big mill, now part of Sierra Pacific Industries. A diesel locomotive, No. 4, continues to meet the needs of the mill, while the earlier diesel, No. 3, has been retired to the Portola Railroad Museum. In 1968, its operating district expanded when the Quincy Railroad leased the twenty-two miles of the Southern Pacific line between Wendel and Susanville.

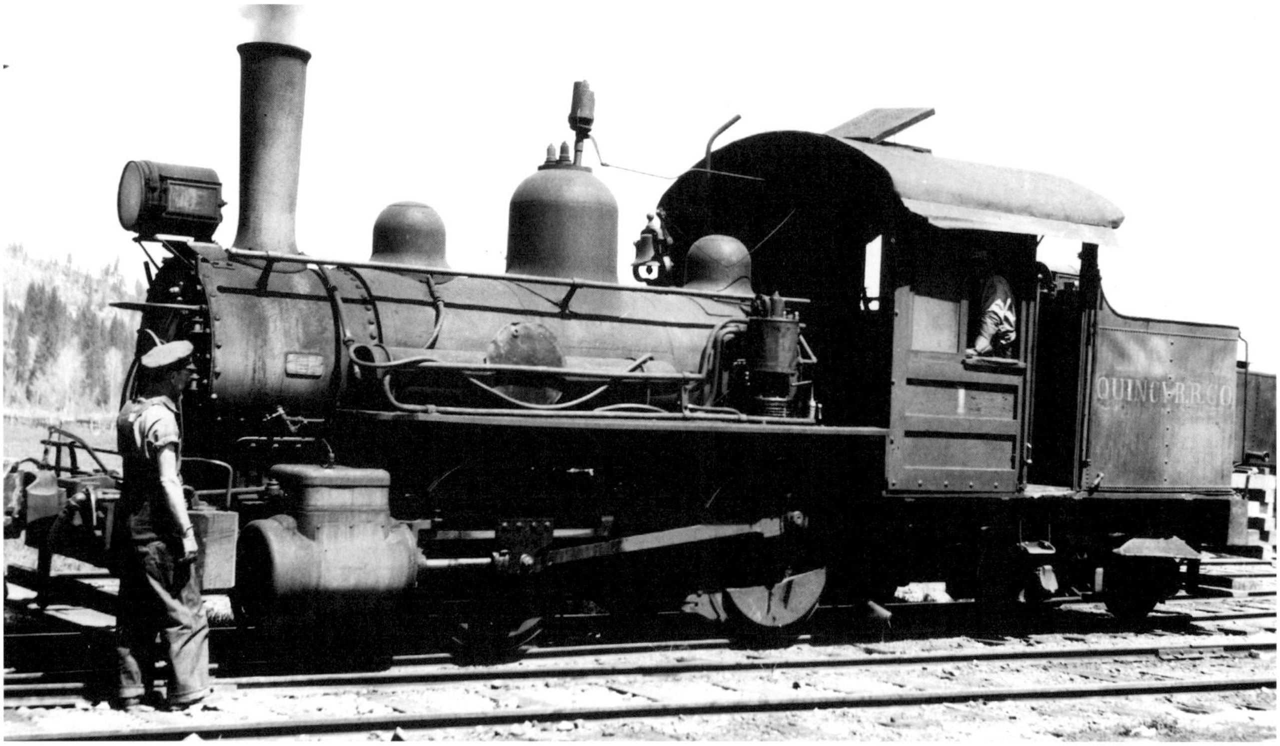

Above: From the Alcoa works at Pittsburgh, the Quincy Western Railroad purchased this 0-4-4T locomotive that was passed along to the successor corporation. Seven years after this 1940 photograph, it was sold to the Essex Cedar Company for stationary boiler service in East Quincy. (James E. Boynton photograph)

Below: Freshly painted, this car carried passengers over the Quincy Western Railway. (California State Library)

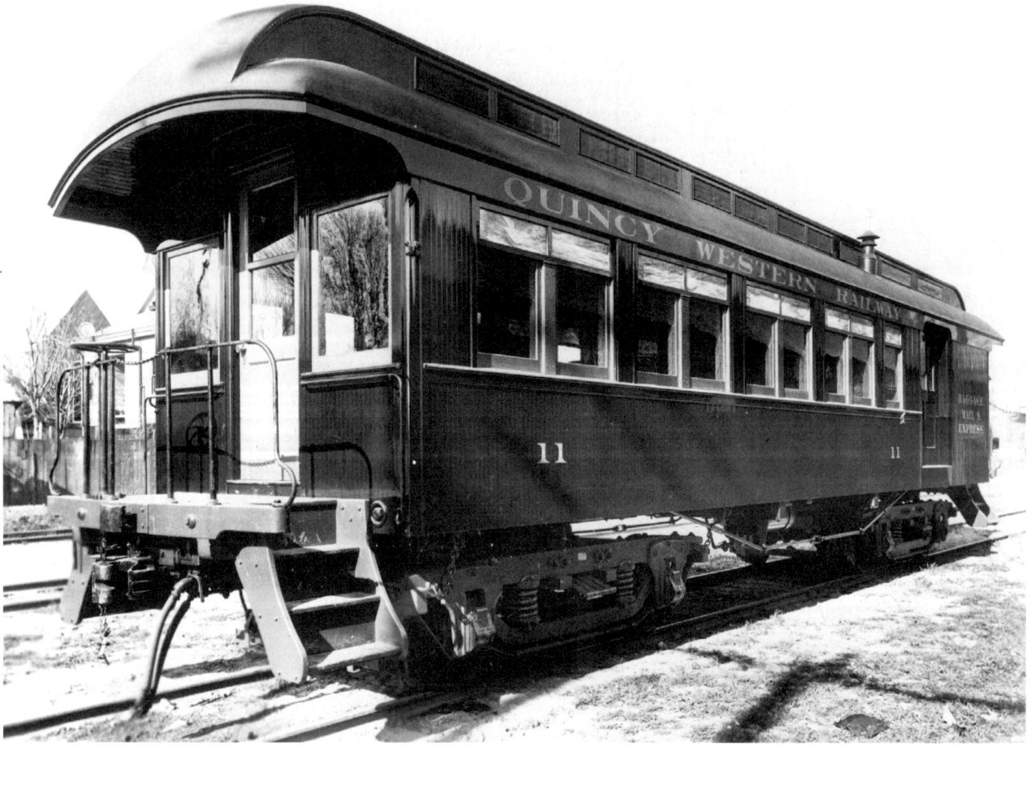

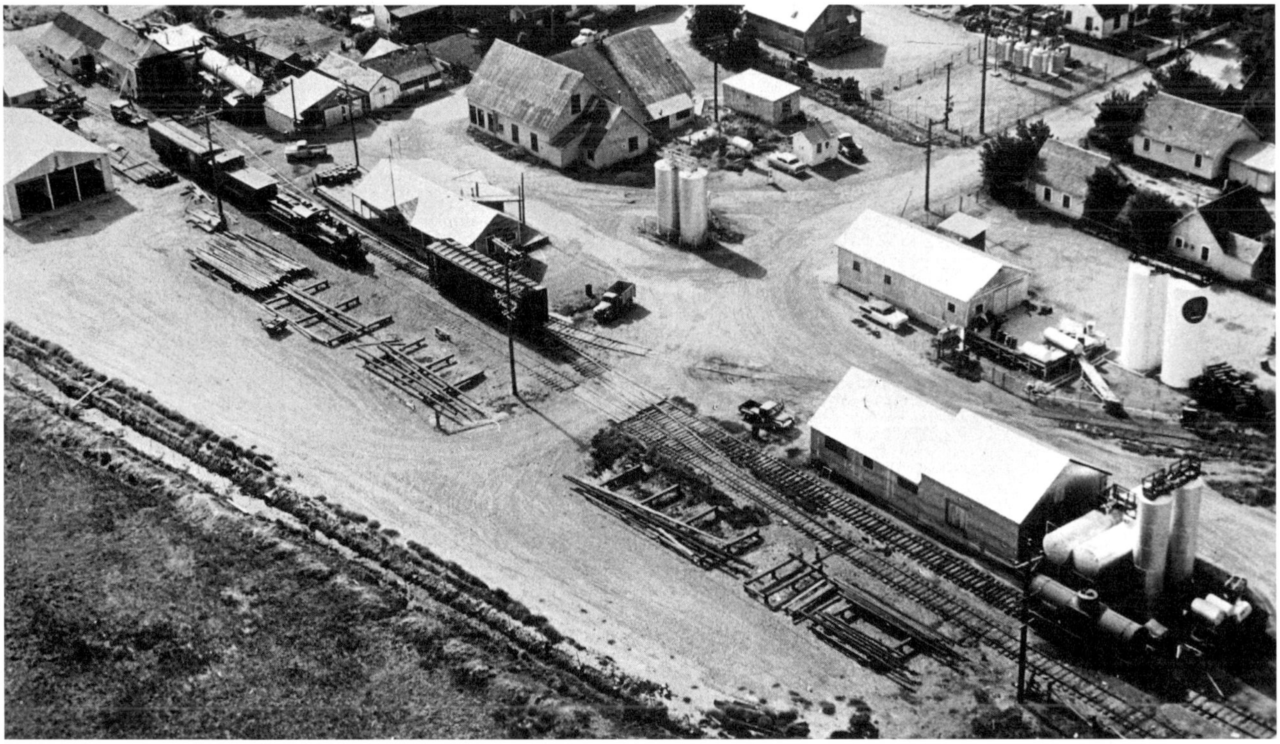

Above: Around 1940, the Quincy terminal contained a varied collection of rolling stock. No. 8 of the Feather River Short Line and caboose rest by the depot. The engine house is in the upper left corner of the picture. In those days, gasoline came by rail to replenish the tanks of oil companies. (Barry Bailey photograph, James E. Boynton collection)

Below; The historic Plumas House began as a log cabin in 1852 but was destroyed by fire eleven years later. This scene represents the first replacement erected in 1866 (dormer windows were added in the 1870s). The Central Stage Company maintained an office in a corner of the building. The new hotel succumbed to a fire in 1923 but was replaced two years later. (Joslyn-Dunscomb collection)

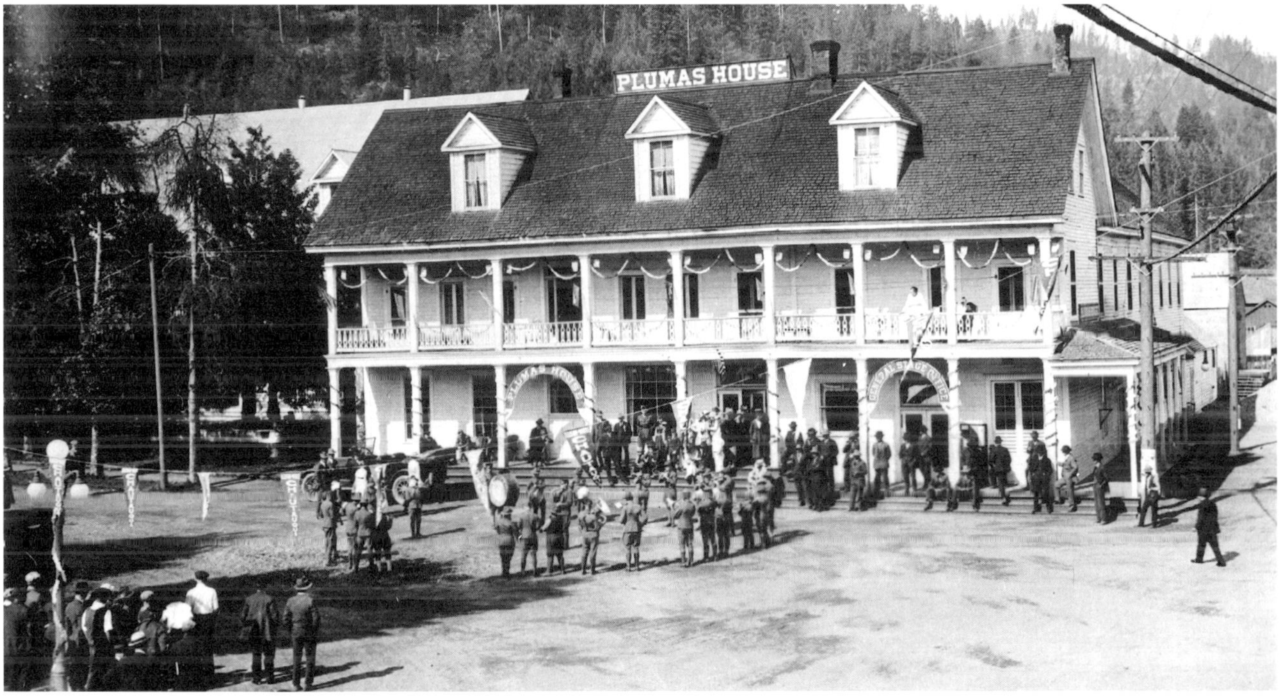

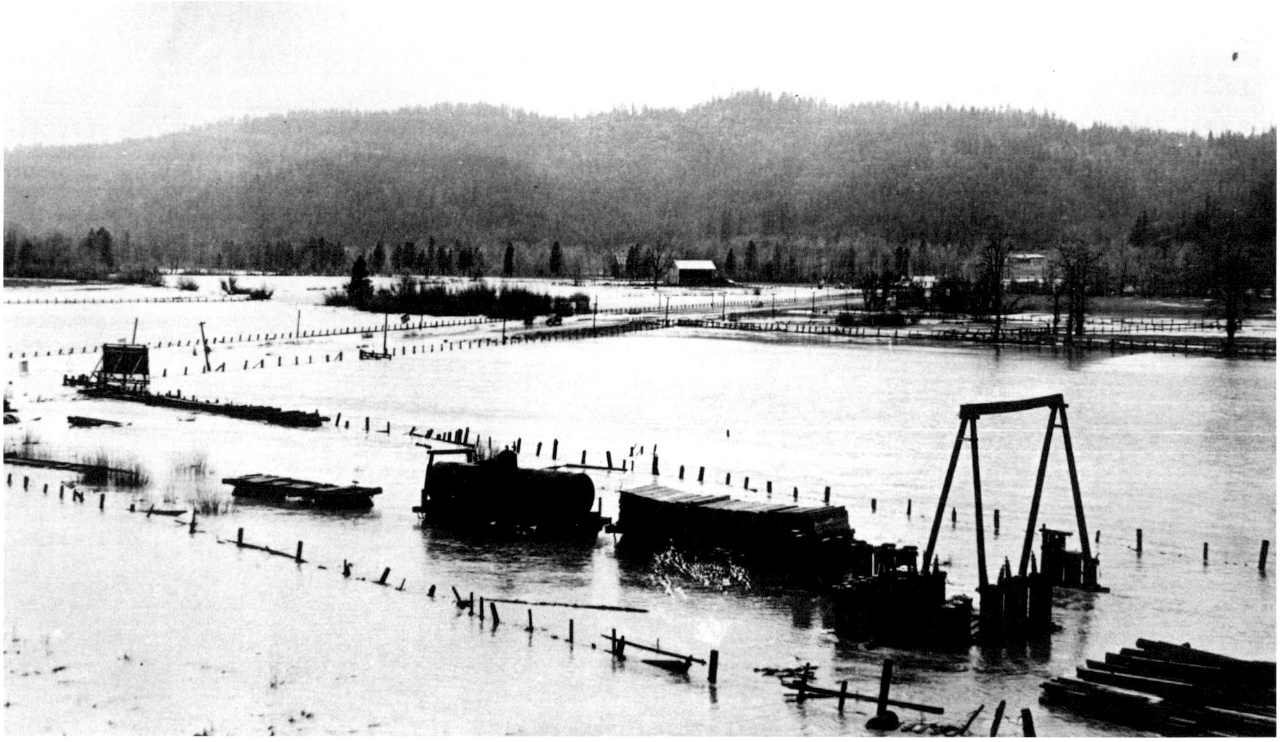

Above: From time to time copious rainfall proved too much for Spanish Creek and covered the railroad yards. The route of the highway leading to the old county hospital (above the gallows frame) can be traced by fence posts across the American Valley. (Leo Thayer Jr.)

Below; Whereas the water tank of Quincy RR No. 1 stood at the rear of the cab, those for the second locomotive were mounted on either side of the boiler. Built in the Schenectady works of Alco in 1924, this 2-6-2T engine was photographed in 1938 by James E. Boynton.

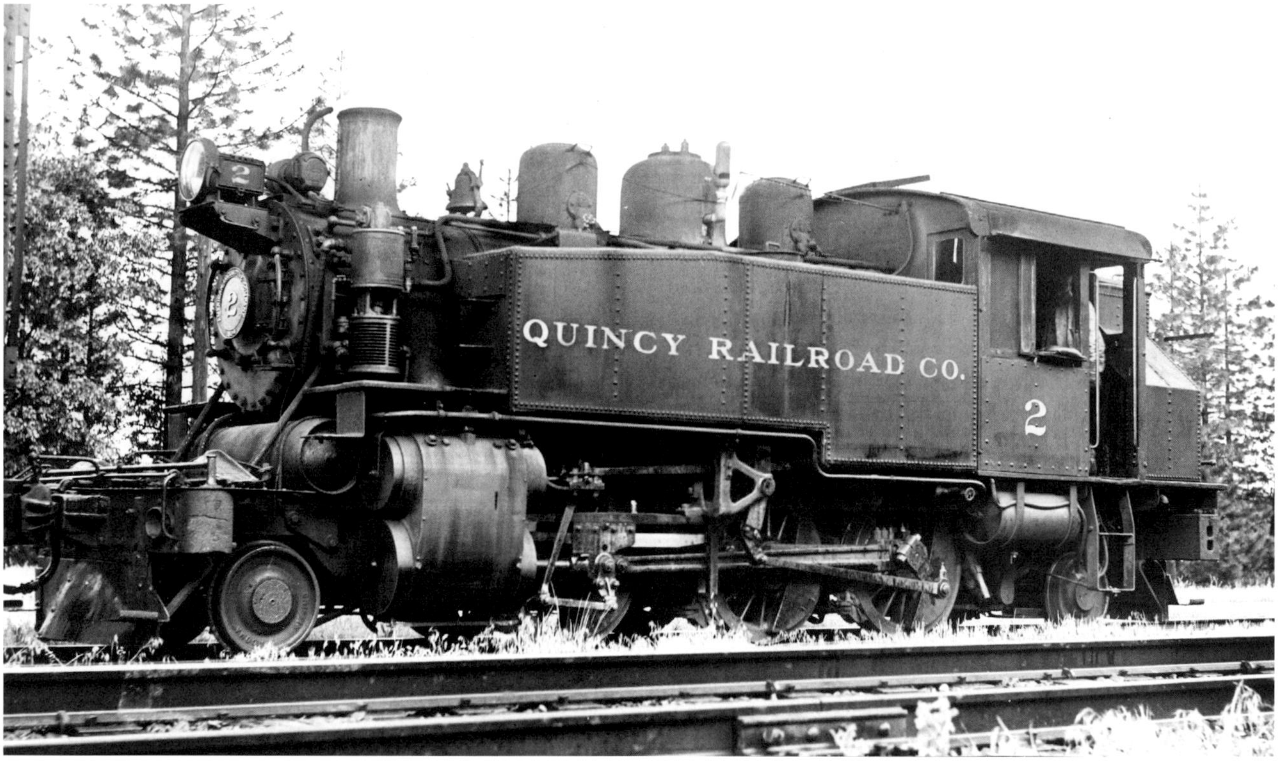

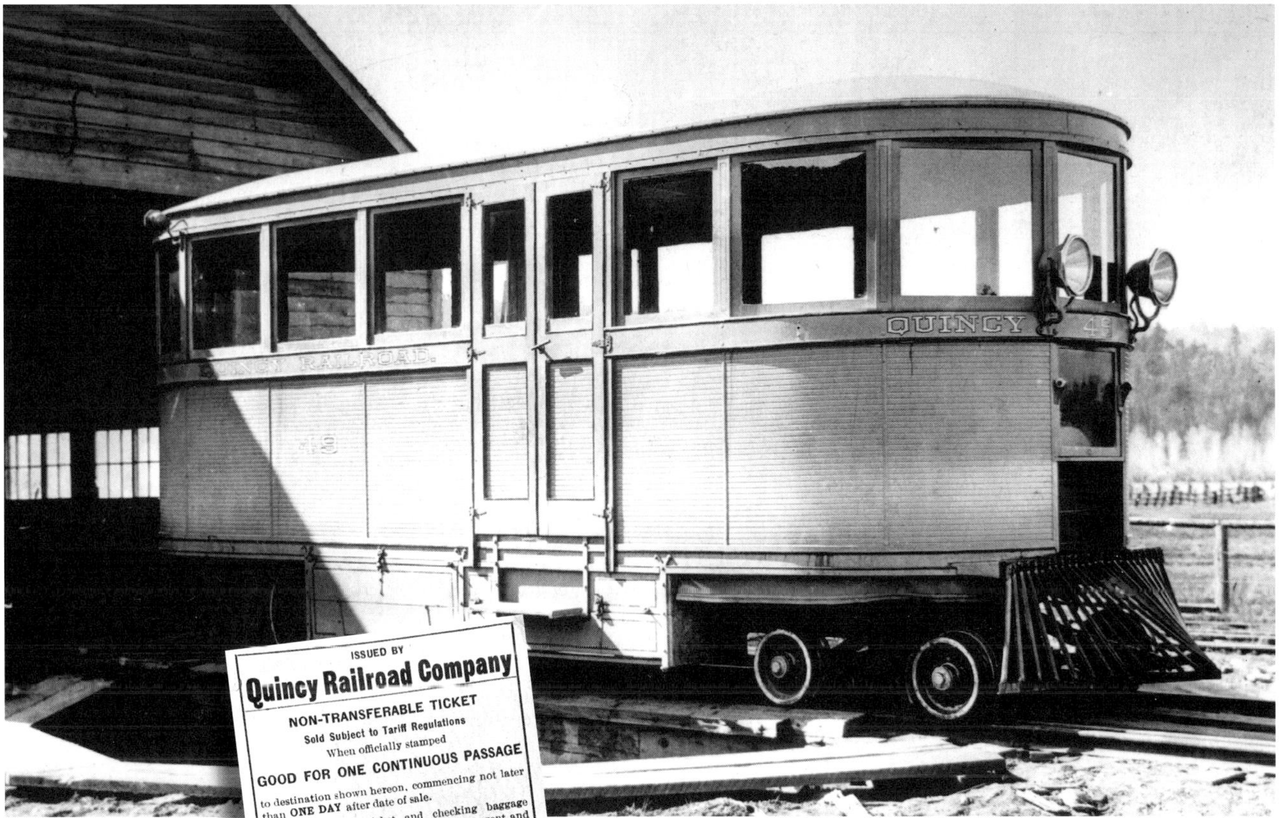

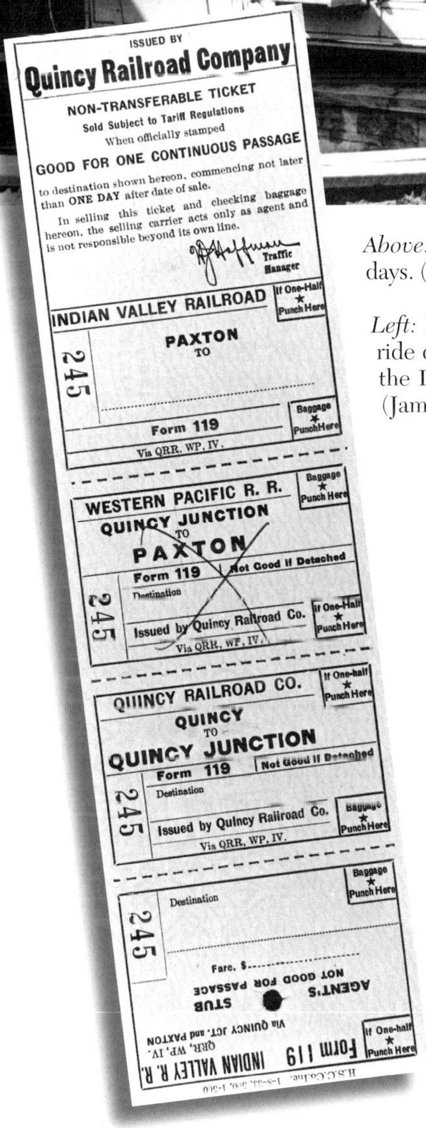
ISSUED BY
Quincy Railroad Company
NON-TRANSFERABLE TICKET
Sold Subject to Tariff Regulations
When officially stamped
GOOD FOR ONE CONTINUOUS PASSAGE
to destination shown hereon, commencing not later than ONE DAY after date of sale.
In selling this ticket and checking baggage hereon, the selling carrier acts only as agent and is not responsible beyond its own line.
Traffic Manager

INDIAN VALLEY RAILROAD
If One-Half ★ Punch Here
245
PAXTON
TO
Form 119
Baggage ★ Punch Here
Via QRR, WP, IV.

WESTERN PACIFIC R. R.
Baggage ★ Punch Here
QUINCY JUNCTION
TO
PAXTON
245
Form 119
Not Good If Detached
Destination
Issued by Quincy Railroad Co.
If One-Half ★ Punch Here
Via QRR, WP, IV.

QUINCY RAILROAD CO.
If One-half ★ Punch Here
QUINCY
TO
QUINCY JUNCTION
245
Form 119
Not Good If Detached
Destination
Issued by Quincy Railroad Co.
Baggage ★ Punch Here
Via QRR, WP, IV.

Baggage ★ Punch Here
245
Destination
Fare, $
NOT GOOD FOR PASSAGE
AGENT'S STUB
INDIAN VALLEY R. R.
Form 119
QRR, WP, IV.
Via QUINCY JCT. and PAXTON
If One-half ★ Punch Here

Above: With limited patronage, motorcar No. 49 proved adequate most days. (Bert Ward photograph)

Left: Properly filled out, this interline ticket would enable a patron to ride over three railroads from Quincy to some designated point along the Indian Valley RR. The ticket stock was pale green with black ink. (James E. Boynton collection)

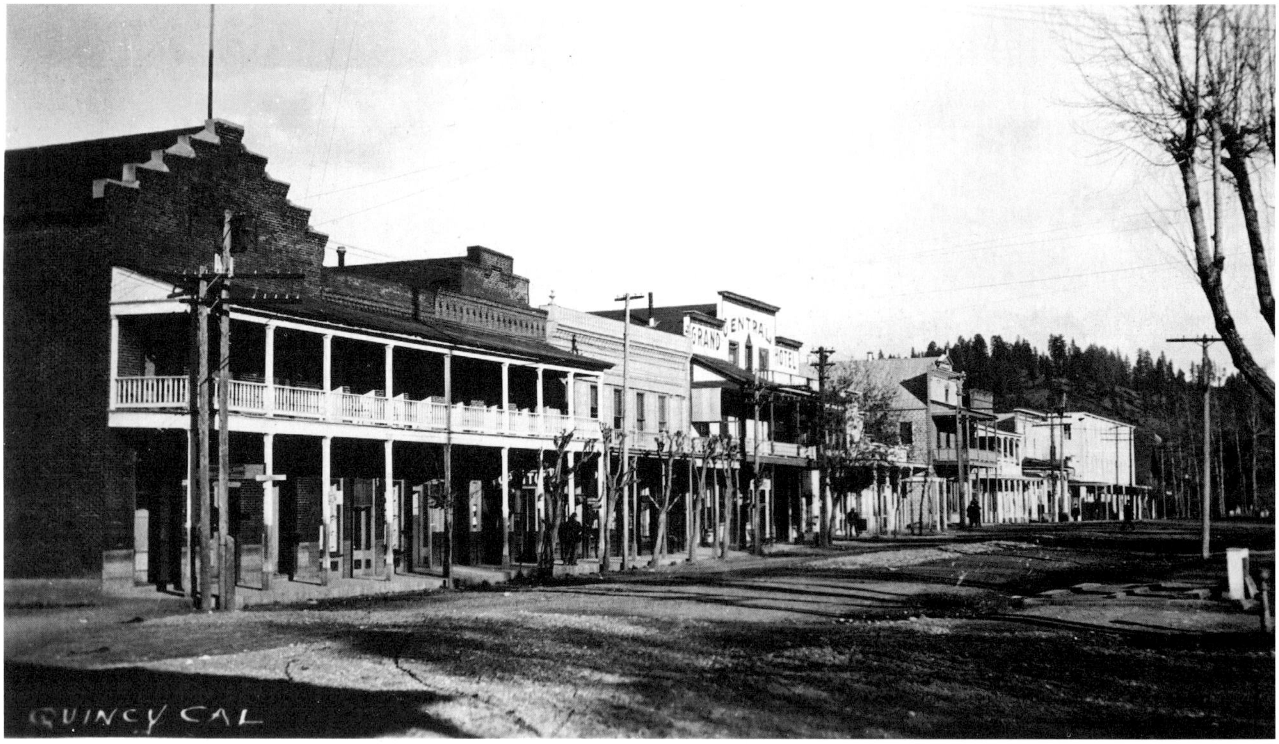

Above: Quincy's Main Street presented a peaceful appearance with the "Huskinson Block" in the foreground. This changed dramatically on August 29, 1934, after a fire, starting in the rear of the Grand Central Hotel, swept through the three-story building and consumed thirty nearby business establishments. Edward Huskinson, an Englishman, came to Quincy in 1869, established the Quincy Drug Company in 1884, and later organized and headed the Plumas County Bank. Currently, Ayoob's clothing store occupies the site of the hotel. (D. L. Joslyn photograph, G. L. Dunscomb collection)

Below: Midway across the American Valley, No. 2 will deliver the cars to Western Pacific at Quincy Jct. The time is June 1940. (Bert Ward photograph)

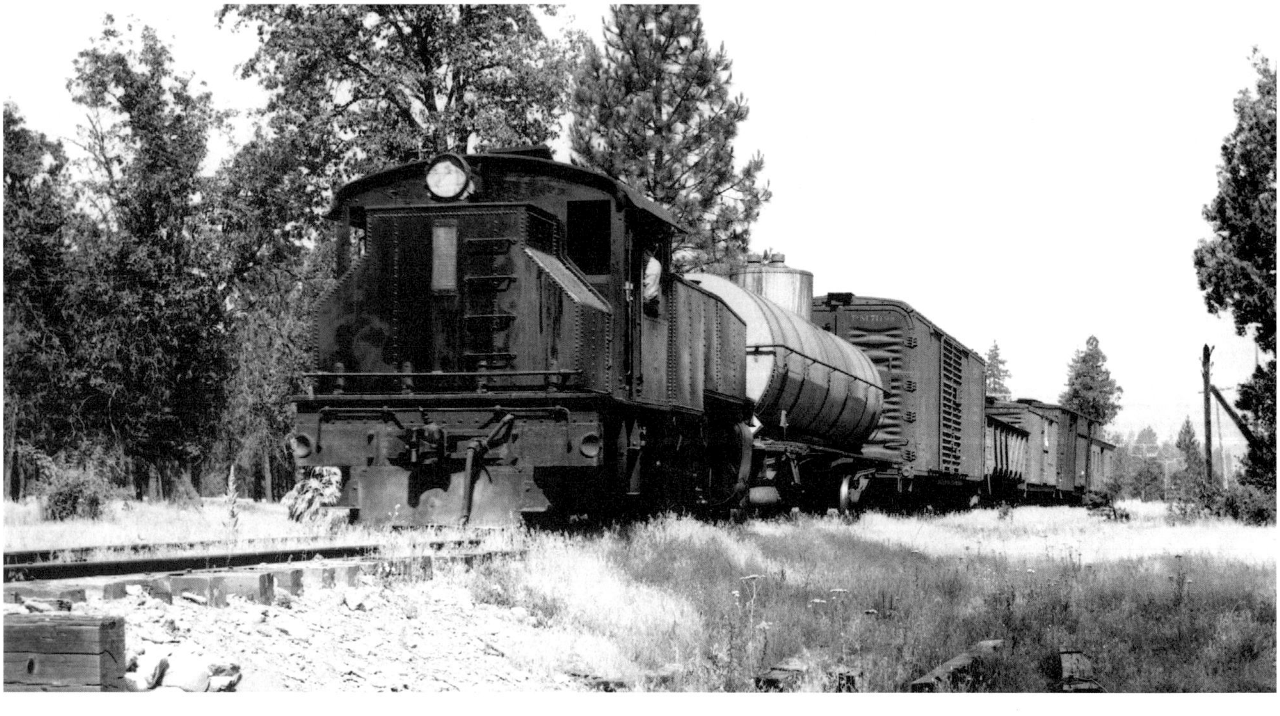

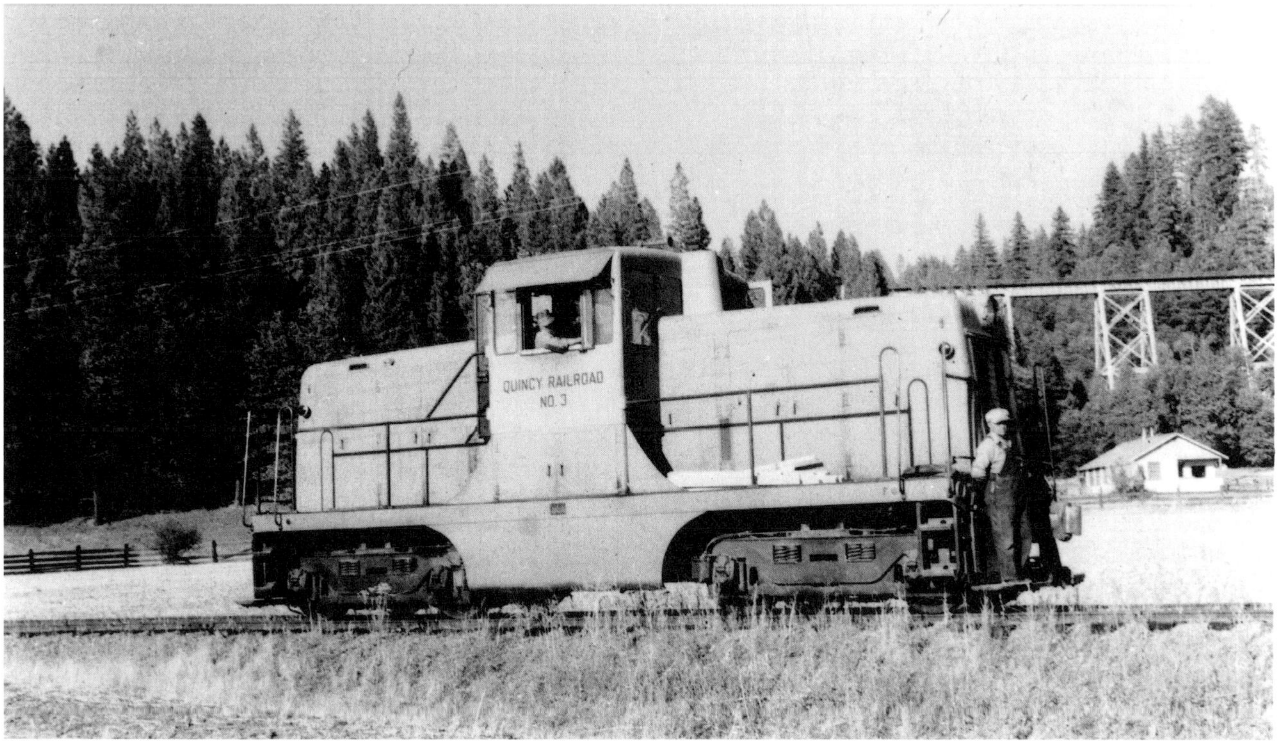

Above: The third locomotive on the Quincy Railroad was a diesel. A Western Pacific viaduct forms the background. (Plumas County Museum)

Below: Quincy RR No. 4 is crossing Chandler Road as it takes a run up the grade to the junction that exceeds 2 percent. (Leo Thayer Jr.)

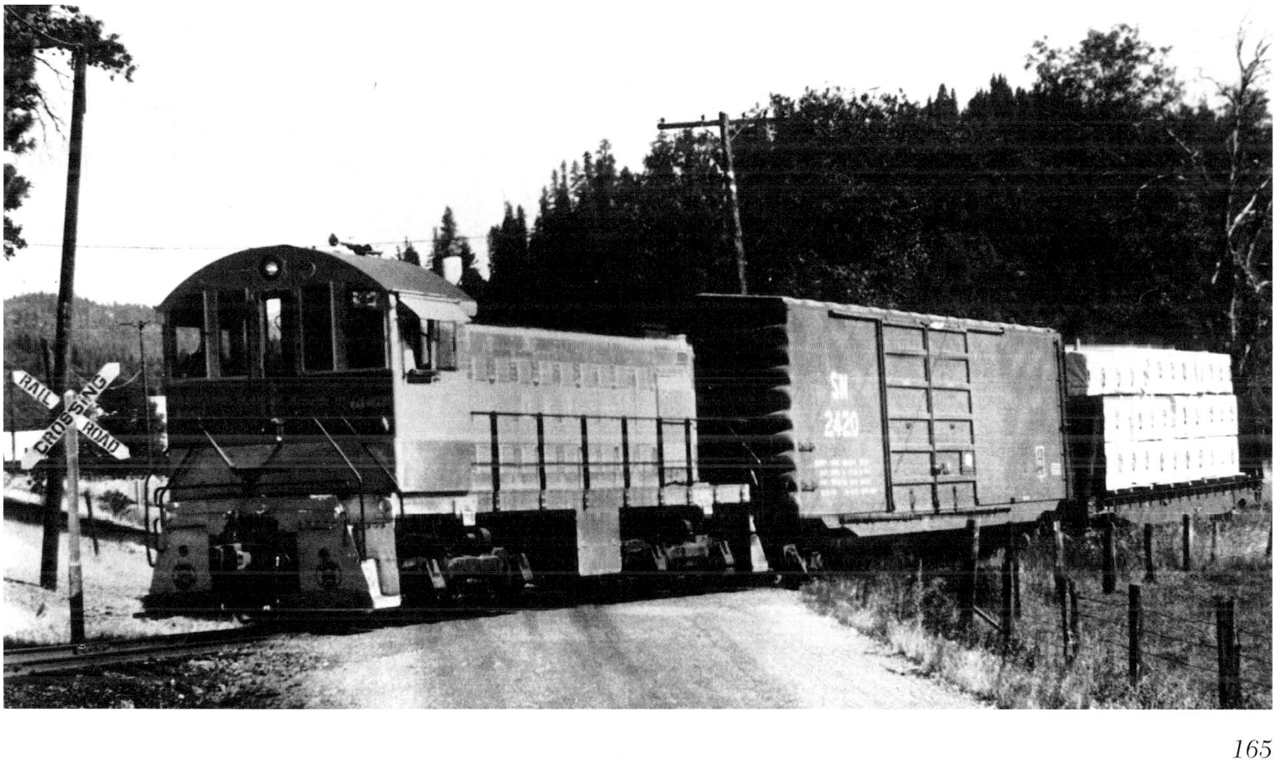

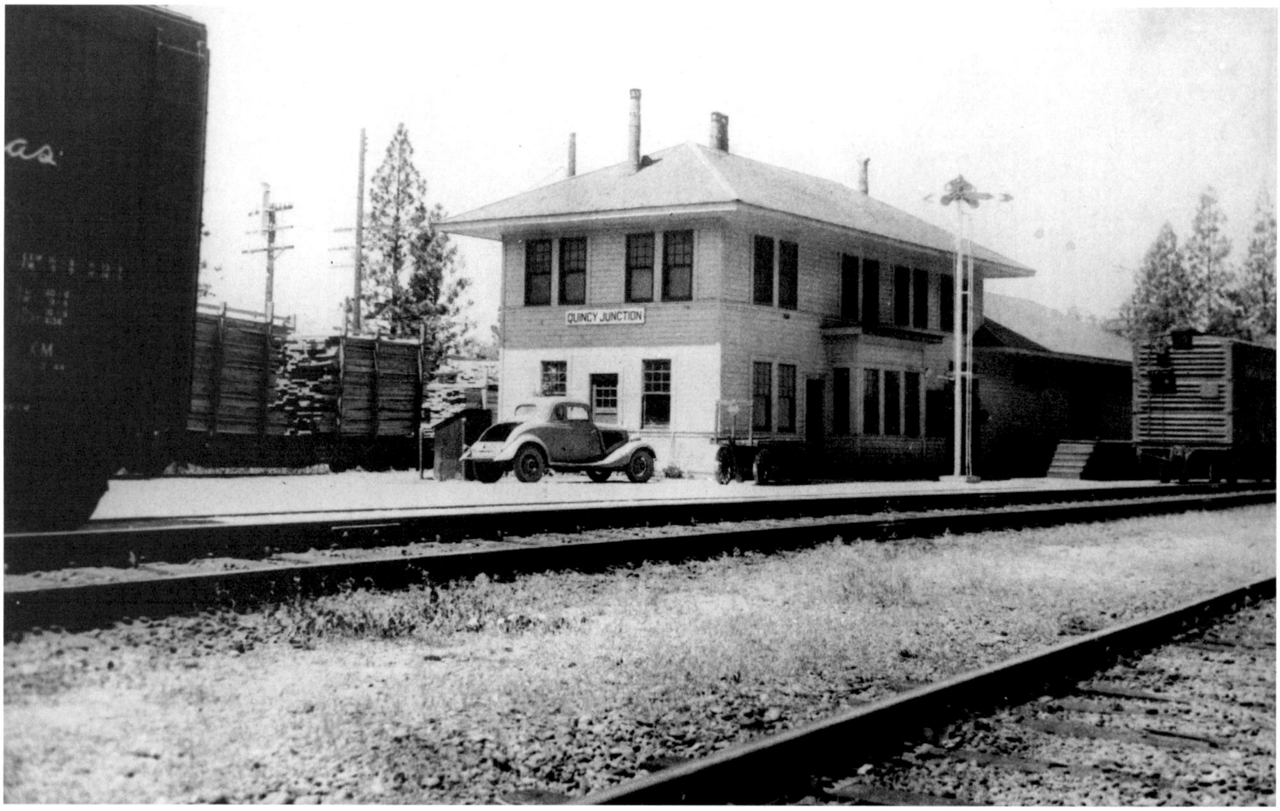

Above: The station at Quincy Jct. provided upstairs living accommodations for the joint agent of the WP RR and Q RR. (Plumas County Museum)

Right: The workday is almost finished, as No. 3 shoves a lonely boxcar into downtown Quincy in June 1968. Subsequently, this portion of the railroad was abandoned, and this forty-four-ton locomotive went to the Portola Railroad Museum. A replacement came from the Sacramento Northern Railway. (Ted Benson photograph)

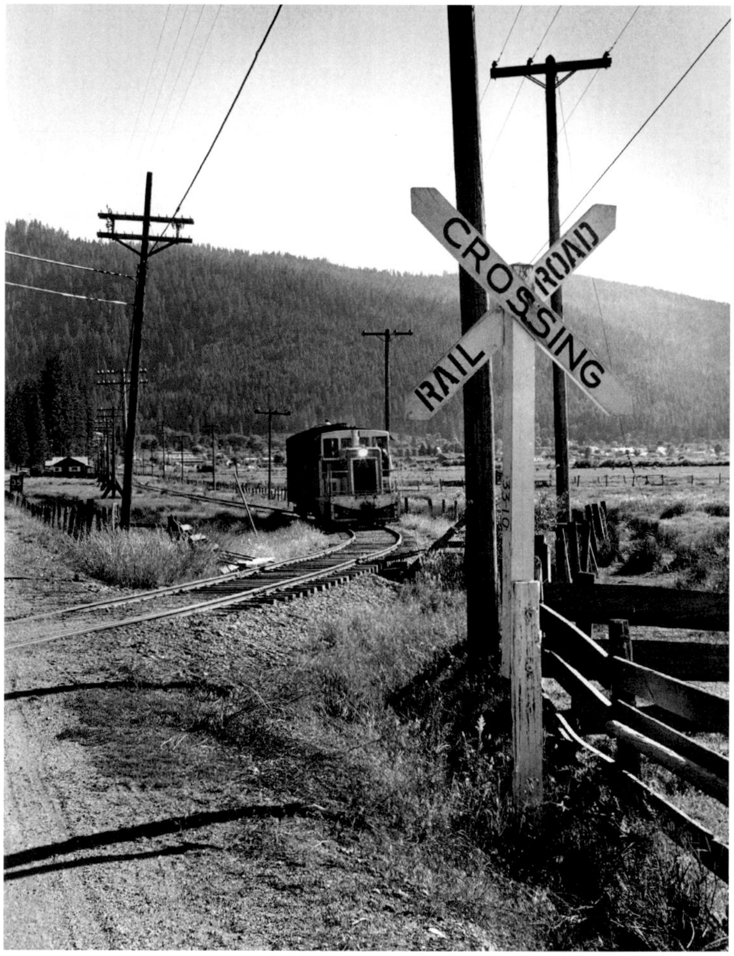

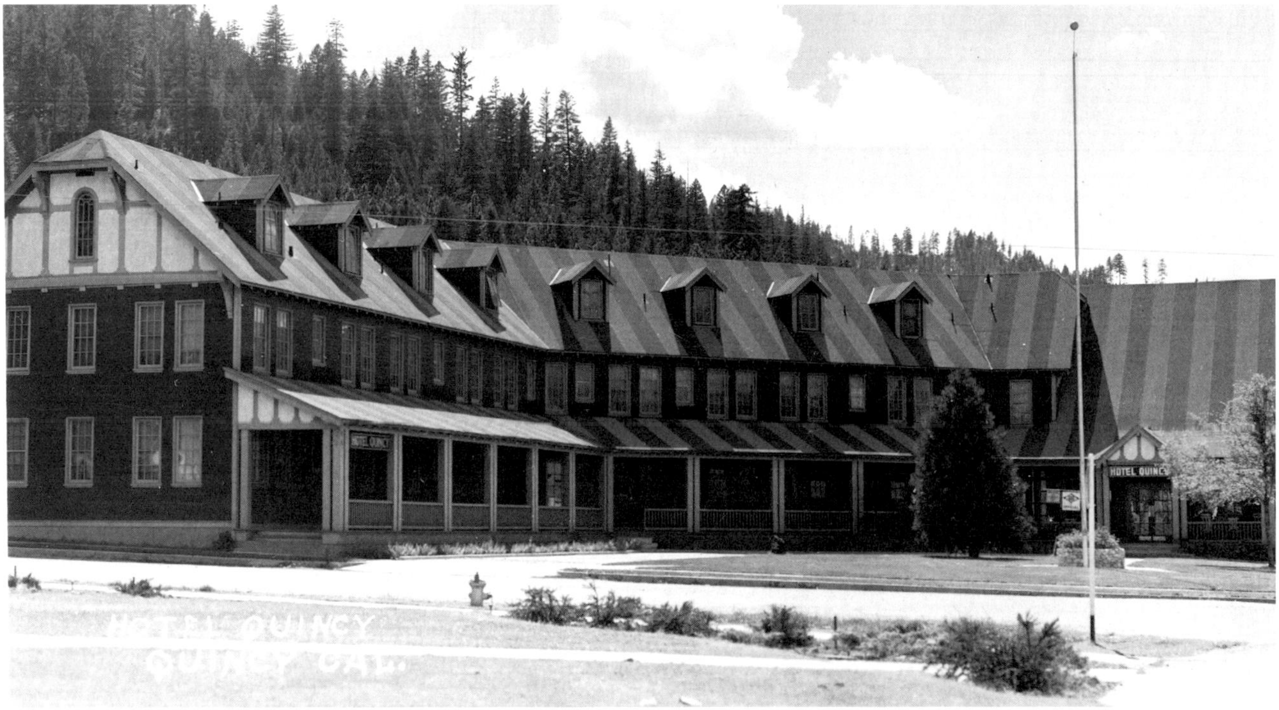

Above: After dedicated effort, sufficient funds were raised to erect a replacement for the Plumas House lost in the June 1923 blaze. Opened with a grand all-night ball in November 1925, Hotel Quincy accommodated many guests in its fifty-four rooms until the fire in 1966. A grass field now occupies the site.

Below: From the southeast, a cameraman secured this view of a part of Quincy and the green American Valley. (Plumas County Museum)

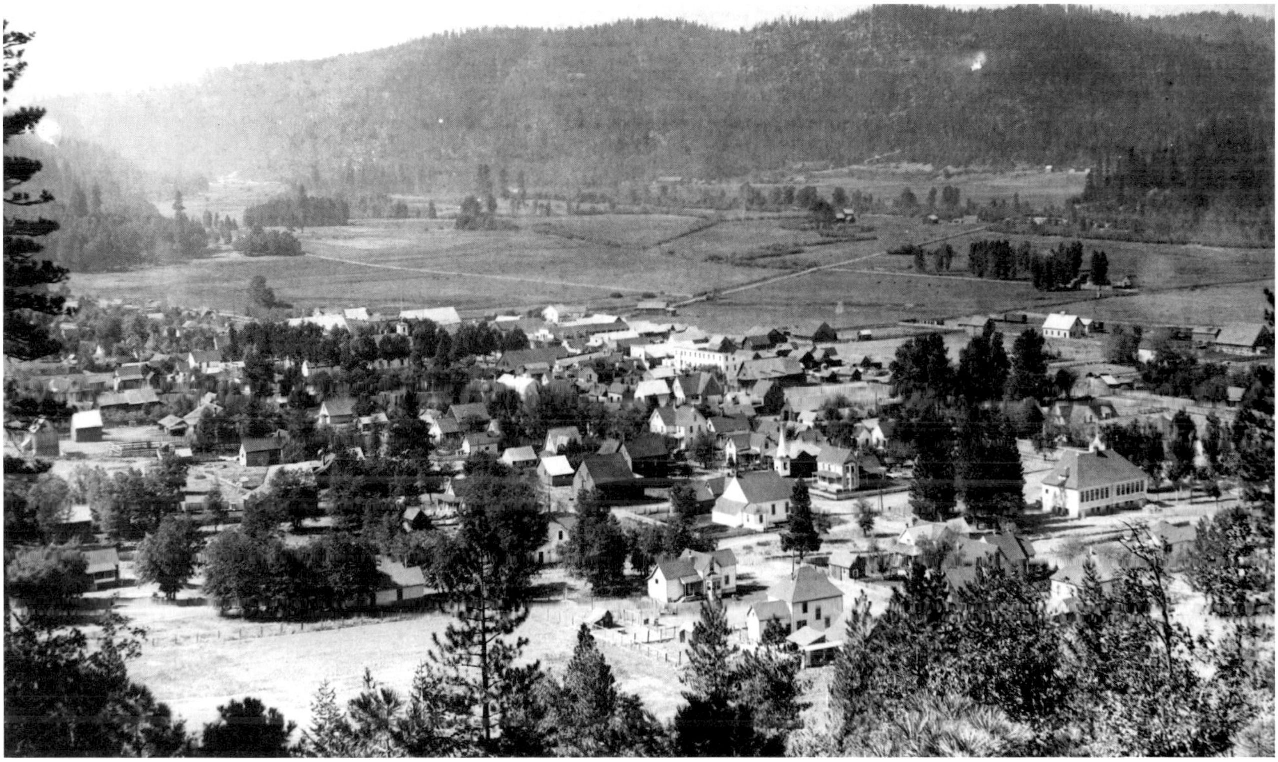

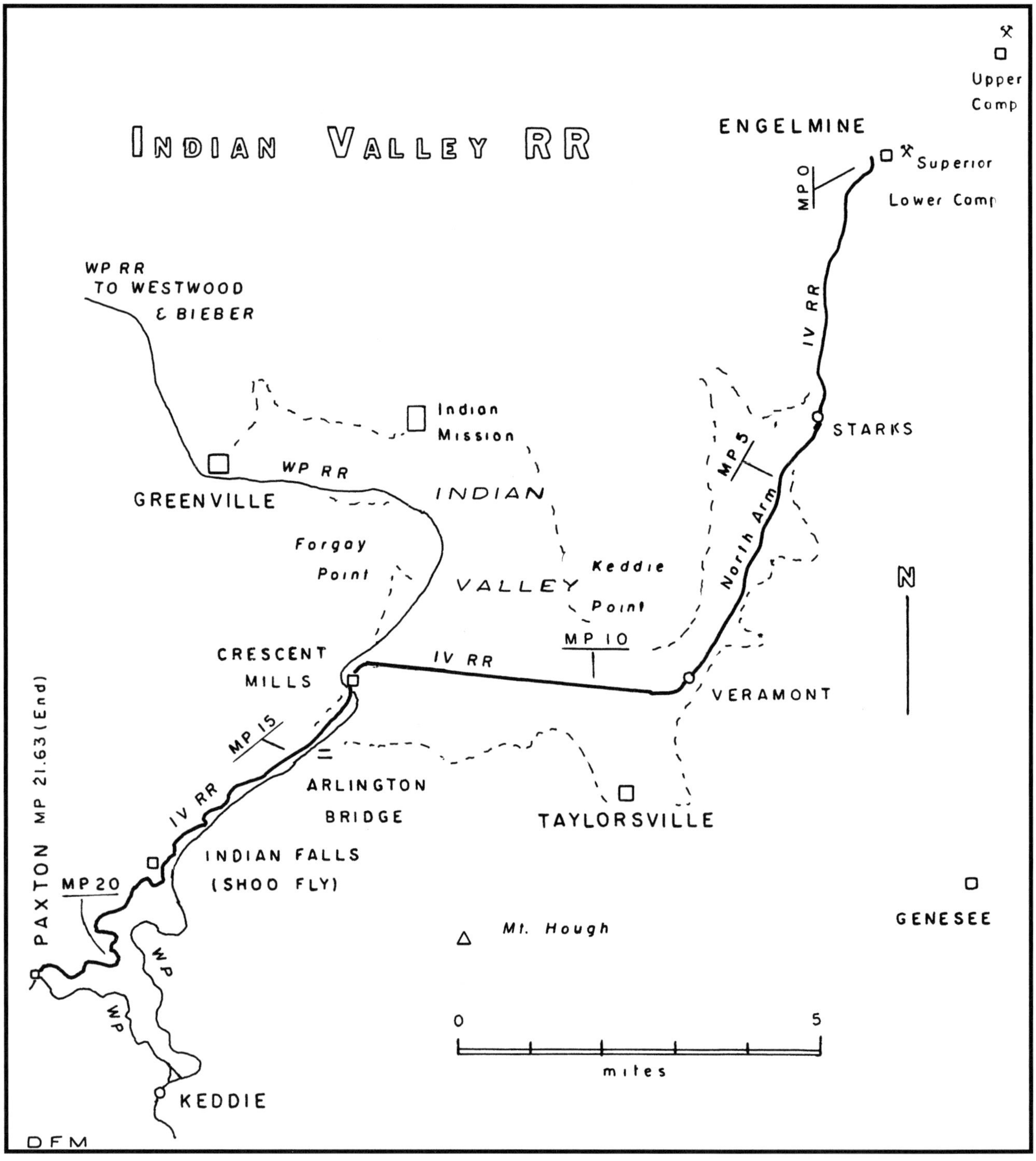
INDIAN VALLEY RR
ENGELMINE
Upper Comp
Superior
Lower Comp
MP 0
IV RR
STARKS
MP 5
North Arm
WP RR
TO WESTWOOD
& BIEBER
Indian Mission
GREENVILLE
WP RR
INDIAN
VALLEY
Forgay Point
Keddie Point
N
MP 10
IV RR
CRESCENT MILLS
VERAMONT
MP 15
ARLINGTON BRIDGE
TAYLORSVILLE
IV RR
PAXTON MP 21.63 (End)
MP 20
INDIAN FALLS (SHOO FLY)
GENESEE
Mt. Hough
WP
WP
0
5
miles
KEDDIE
DFM

INDIAN VALLEY RAILROAD

Although California has never been known as a copper state, this mineral has been found in fifty of its counties. Copper deposits were found as early as 1840, but it was the discoveries at Copperopolis in 1861 that made important contributions to California's general economy. Surprisingly, California's copper production accounted for 27 percent of the nation's output in 1864, with most of it stemming from Copperopolis and other mines in Calaveras County in the Sierra Nevada foothills.

The expanding use of electricity called for more copper wire at the beginning of the twentieth century, which hastened the development of copper mining in the West. Shasta County in northern California became the leading producer in the next fifty years, with Plumas County holding a distant second place and Calaveras County a trailing third. Of the seventy-three copper mines in Plumas County, only three—Engels and the nearby Superior in Lights Canyon and the Walker Mine—proved significant.

Indian Valley, a broad, flat valley in Plumas County, California, is surrounded by Greenville, Crescent Mills, Taylorsville, and Lights Canyon. The hills sometimes answered prospectors' prayers for gold, as did the Bullion Ledge near Greenville. Additional gold mines required stamp mills, which maintained the economic vitality of Crescent Mills. Other men recognized the farming possibilities in the valley; in 1851 famed Peter Lassen erected a cabin and trading post and raised vegetables for sale to miners the following year. John T. Taylor settled on his ranch in 1852 and soon after added a sawmill and gristmill, which attracted others to form the town of Taylorsville.

In his report *Resources of the West* dated November 24, 1866, J. Ross Browne speaks of the Cosmopolitan copper mine discovered in 1862 about five miles from Taylorsville. The high prices of copper prevailing during the Civil War resulted in the formation of a number of companies to work the deposits. John C. Chapman and others purchased a smelter from Bolinger, Blood, and Company at a cost of thirty thousand dollars and enjoyed satisfactory results treating oxide ores. Unfortunately, when sulphide ores replaced oxide ores, the smelter could not handle them, and with copper prices tumbling at the end of the war, operations were suspended.

Depending on the copper market, others stood ready to try their hand in copper mining. General John Bidwell engaged in copper mining there in 1873, but, after paying the cost of shipping ore by teams and trains to the seaport and then by ship to Swansea, Wales, for smelting, the results proved discouraging.

Henry A. Engels, a German immigrant, settled in San Francisco with his sons, Charles, Henry, and William, and two daughters, Elizabeth and Emily. While he was manager of the Pacific Brass and Lock Foundry in San Francisco, he found that, even with rail transportation, copper from the Lake Superior region commanded such a high price that he welcomed an alternative source from the copper deposits in Plumas County. Under various individual names, the Engels family began filing on mineral claims along Lights Creek, the first being on September 2, 1880, followed by six more in October. The next spring and summer they located fifteen claims and an additional eight claims in 1882.

The men endured the loneliness of Lights Canyon as part of their families remained in San Francisco. Potential capitalists shunned the mine because of a continuing trend of low copper prices and the lack of a railroad running across Plumas County. During these lean times, the brothers eked out extra money by making butter firkins (casks) in their little workshop and selling them to ranchers. (Their shop building existed through the active life of the mines.)

By way of clarification, the identity of J. M. Engle should be explained because of the similarity of family names. In the late 1890s, he served Henry A. Bowen as general manager of the Sierra Valleys Railroad. After securing a timber claim, he ventured into selling lumber tracts, subsequently forming the Engle Timber Company and also purchasing a quartz mine on Mill Creek (near Keddie). His career ended with his death in Washington State in 1914.

Engels Copper Mining Company

When the outlook for copper strengthened, the Engels sons moved to establish the Engels Copper Mining Company on June 19, 1901, a few years after the death of their parents.

In the next decade, demand for copper increased, which sparked some mining activity in the general area.

In 1907 Colonel Bannister contemplated an electric generating plant for Genesee, a village five miles east of Taylorsville, with the hope of adding an electric railway. The destinations remained a secret to be lost when the projected railroad wilted. In this decade, the Engels brothers continued development work in their mine, and, notwithstanding two business slumps, they raised funds to underwrite the cost of a local smelter. The announcement of their plans in August 1909 came a week after an election in which the electorate voted 543 to 502 to ban alcoholic beverages in Plumas County. Voters in predominately dry Greenville carried the election.

During the warmer months of 1910, the newly opened Western Pacific Railroad delivered three hundred thousand pounds of material to Keddie for the Engels brothers, which included eighty-four thousand fire bricks for their future smelter. In the fall, thirty men commenced erection of the smelter as well as the seventy-five hundred–foot aerial tramway to bring buckets of copper ore to the smelter.

The project turned out a disaster. Not only did the heavy snows in the early months of 1911 prostrate Western Pacific, but they also halted work on the smelter and tramway. At Engelmine, the deep snow blocked any resumption of work until June, but at the end of July, the Engels brothers expected to complete their work at the end of September.

From a practical viewpoint, it mattered little, as the smelter could never be fired. With its location in a national forest, the rangers obtained an injunction preventing smelter operation, as its fumes would have damaged the surrounding forests. One can imagine the disgusted look on Henry Engels's face when he found that his three hundred thousand–dollar expenditure for the 110-ton smelter had been useless.

For the next several years, the Engels brothers struggled to find a way to curb the obnoxious fumes from their smelter without success. But not all was lost, for a whole new life began in 1914. A. L. Beardsley, who held nearby copper claims, recognized he faced the same potential problems. Conferring with Henry E. Bush, a state employee assigned to find a solution, he learned of a "bubble process" offered by the Minerals Separation American Syndicate with Edward H. Nutter as its San Francisco agent. Beardsley took Nutter to the Engels's mine to explain to William Engels the oil-flotation process for concentrating copper ore.

At the same time, Elmer E. Paxton, said to be "a large sugar man from Hawaii," became interested in the prospects of the Engels mine. With money from Hawaiian associates, perhaps conditioned on his assuming an active part in the management, a 150-ton flotation plant was constructed under the supervision of Henry Bush. Instead of smelting ore at the mine, the flotation process would concentrate the ore so that it would contain about 40 percent copper. On this basis, the material could be sent to smelters in Utah in an economical manner. Higher-grade (smelting) ore could stand the cost of transportation to the Utah smelter without concentration.

Paxton became general manager of the company. With sixty-five men on the payroll in June 1914, Superintendent John Reinmiller opened new ore bodies, although only ten men were extracting copper ore. With three machine drills, they produced enough ore for the first truck hauls to the Western Pacific trains at Keddie on June 23, 1914. Just when things entered a positive mode, the war began in Europe, which dislocated the copper market for several months, causing the Utah smelter to close and the mine to lay off forty men.

The flotation mill, completed late in 1914, stood ready to do its part in copper production as the new year opened with one hundred men working at Engelmine. Winter conditions made roads impassable for the truck, so ten teams and wagons returned to hauling ores and concentrates to Keddie. With other departments operating with increasing efficiency, the twenty-one-mile transportation hurdle still remained. Even with better road conditions in the summer, a round-trip truck haul required six hours.

As a stopgap measure, a Caterpillar tractor pulled wagons between the mine and the "Relay Point," a half mile east of the Arlington Bridge, where teams commenced the last segment of the journey to Keddie.

Plans for a Connecting Railroad

During the late summer of 1915, H. G. Graydon, who had worked on the WP survey, staked out a possible rail line from Engelmine through Taylorsville, to the Arlington Bridge, then along the East Branch of the North Fork of the Feather River to a point opposite Twain. Here the line would cross the river and by a switchback would climb up to a connection with Western Pacific. The Great Western Power Company had just completed its transmission line from Butt Valley to Engelmine, thus relieving the copper mining company of the necessity of caring for its own generating system. With increased output—the force doubled during the year to two hundred employees—the need for the railroad became increasingly imperative. Rising copper prices added a favorable outlook.

At a special meeting of the board of directors of the Engels Copper Mining Company on December 8, 1915, two important issues were resolved. Paxton informed the board of the railroad situation. The survey from the lower camp to Western Pacific near Keddie had been completed. As a possible alternative, the mining company would construct a railroad linking Engelmine with Greenville if Southern Pacific could be persuaded to add the fourteen-mile connection from Westwood. For the mining company, the shorter link with Greenville offered a considerable savings in cost, but the Western Pacific connection had the advantage of a more direct line to San Francisco rather than SP's route through Fernley, Nevada.

Whereas the SP displayed little interest in the Greenville extension—the pending antitrust suit made the expenditure inadvisable—Western Pacific was delighted to add to its traffic base. The cost of a narrow-gauge railroad to Keddie would range from $250,000 to $300,000. Paxton outlined several financing alternatives. After incorporation, shareholders of the mining company would purchase capital stock in the railroad company. Another plan that was adopted called for the railroad company to be a subsidiary of the copper company and be financed by sale of additional mining company stock with the proceeds used to subscribe to the capital stock of the railroad company. Leasing the rail and track fittings from Western Pacific avoided an immediate outlay of $90,000.

A major change occurred in 1916 with the opening of the Superior Mine, about two miles below the Engels mine. In turn, this new mine created "Upper Camp" and "Lower Camp," with the latter becoming more important as the years progressed.

At the June 28, 1916, meeting of the directors at the company's offices in the Mills Building in San Francisco, Paxton reported that he had arranged with President Charles Levey of Western Pacific to lease rails from that road. (When the lease expired in November 1921, the Indian Valley [IV] Railroad purchased the rails and fittings for $84,049 with cash accumulated from earnings.) He also informed the board that both Willis G. Walker of Red River Lumber and Levey frowned on a narrow-gauge line and that one or the other would purchase $75,000 of stock of the railroad at par to cover the extra cost of the wider gauge.

So the Indian Valley Railroad Company gained corporate status on June 30, 1916, with 2,500 shares of its $100 par-value stock held by the mining company and 750 shares by the WP subsidiary, Standard Realty and Development Company, plus a few shares held by officers in the mining company. Paxton received 100 shares for his promotional services. (This Indian Valley RR has no connection with the earlier company with a similar name forming part of the corporate history of Western Pacific.) At the same meeting in June, the board cut a melon by declaring the first dividend of the Engels Copper Mining Company of 1.5 percent, payable in July and to be repeated each month for the rest of the year.

Already J. T. Williams of the WP loop fame and Graydon had moved into the field with twenty-five men to finish the location survey; sometimes they were fortunate to stay at the Indian Falls Inn. The point of the WP interchange moved several times. A point near Twain alternated with Keddie, but Iron Cap (later called Paxton) won the imaginary contest, as it was 130 feet lower than Keddie and also closer to the copper mines. The survey began with MP 0 at Lower Camp and worked toward Paxton. Taylorsville lost the railroad in the final location when the line was shortened slightly to 21.5 miles.

The profile proved challenging, to say the least. Leaving Paxton (elevation 3,057 feet), the railroad "fell downstairs" as it dropped 142 feet in the initial eight-tenths of its first mile, which could be accomplished only with grades as high as 4 percent in places. Crossing the East Branch of the North Fork required two 120-foot-deck Howe truss spans followed by a trestle of 24 bents measuring 360 feet.

The railroad followed Indian Creek, but at MP 19—slightly more than two miles from Paxton—the railroad began another four-mile stiff climb in the opposite direction of 590 feet, eased only with two short level places, again with pitches of 4 percent. After surmounting a crest at MP 15 (H. Terrill's ranch), the line eased downhill as it went by Crescent Mills and continued across Indian Valley with almost no grades. The final 7 miles to Lower Camp (elevation 3,908 feet) consisted largely of a modest grade with short pitches of 2 percent. In either direction, locomotives had difficulty with loaded cars.

Construction of the Indian Valley Railroad

No time was lost in awarding the contract to the Utah Construction Company, and, as in the construction of WP in the previous decade, H. J. Lawler filled the position of superintendent. As the contractor assembled materials at Keddie, quite a number of men who had worked with Lawler previously flocked around him seeking work. Grading got off to a good start on July 31, 1916, and within a few weeks a mile of roadbed around Crescent Mills stood ready to accept ties and rails. It was expected that the railroad would be finished within five months, but it was not to be.

With 150 men, UCC conducted grading in several places. The *Plumas National-Bulletin* of Quincy shared information of the route with its readers. After spanning the Feather River, the grade crossed G. H. Bennett's Flat—by now, Oak Flat—then followed Indian Creek through Indian Falls (the site of Shoofly) to Crescent Mills,

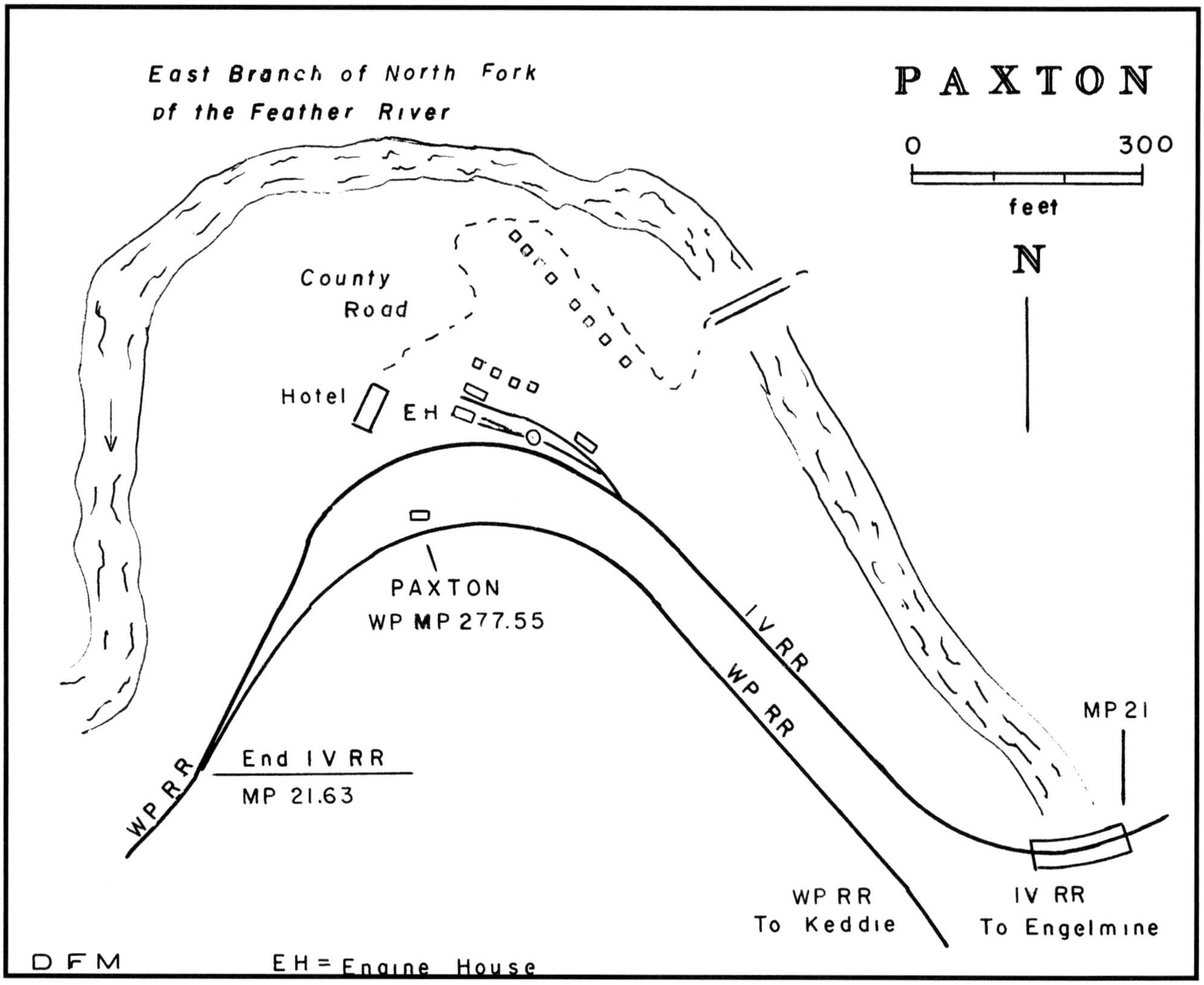

If one climbed the hill on the south side of Paxton and looked north, one could see the work of man and the beauty of nature. Immediately below are the tracks of Western Pacific (now Union Pacific) in their steady 1 percent climb as they wind around the hill. Down below is the hotel, the remaining feature of the terminal of the long-vanished Indian Valley Railroad, and beyond are the rushing waters of the East Branch of the North Fork of the Feather River.

The engineer locating the Indian Valley Railroad faced a difficult problem in making a physical connection with Western Pacific, standing high above the river. Beginning some distance away and continuing over the bridge, the Indian Valley RR climbed some two hundred feet to its junction. In making these connections, grades reached 4 percent, which added difficulties to train operators.

staying below the stage road. Passing the old cyanide plant in Crescent Mills where the IV RR would erect a depot, the railroad soon crossed Indian Creek and followed an easterly tangent for three miles across Indian Valley, almost to Deadfall Lane. Next it would turn up the North Arm, passing G. L. Stark's ranch, and terminate at Lower Camp.

Though most ranchers allowed the railroad a right-of-way, Plumas A. Young and his neighboring rancher, Lloyd A. Hardgrave, resisted. Condemnation proceedings began, a jury was impaneled, but Mr. Young and the railroad reached a settlement without a trial. The decision in Mr. Hardgrave's trial cost the railroad $390 for the land comprising the 1,700 feet of right-of-way and $2,400 for dividing the ranch. Additionally, the court ordered the railroad to pay for fencing at $1.25 per foot.

The litigation in no way impeded the construction; after six weeks, UCC had rounded up 350 men for the job, with 90 working at Iron Bar Camp and 80 at Indian Falls. With many sections of the roadbed ready, efforts concentrated on the spectacular Howe truss bridge rising 90 feet above the Feather River.

November 1 stands out as a sad day in Quincy, for J. T. Williams, who had been directing the engineering

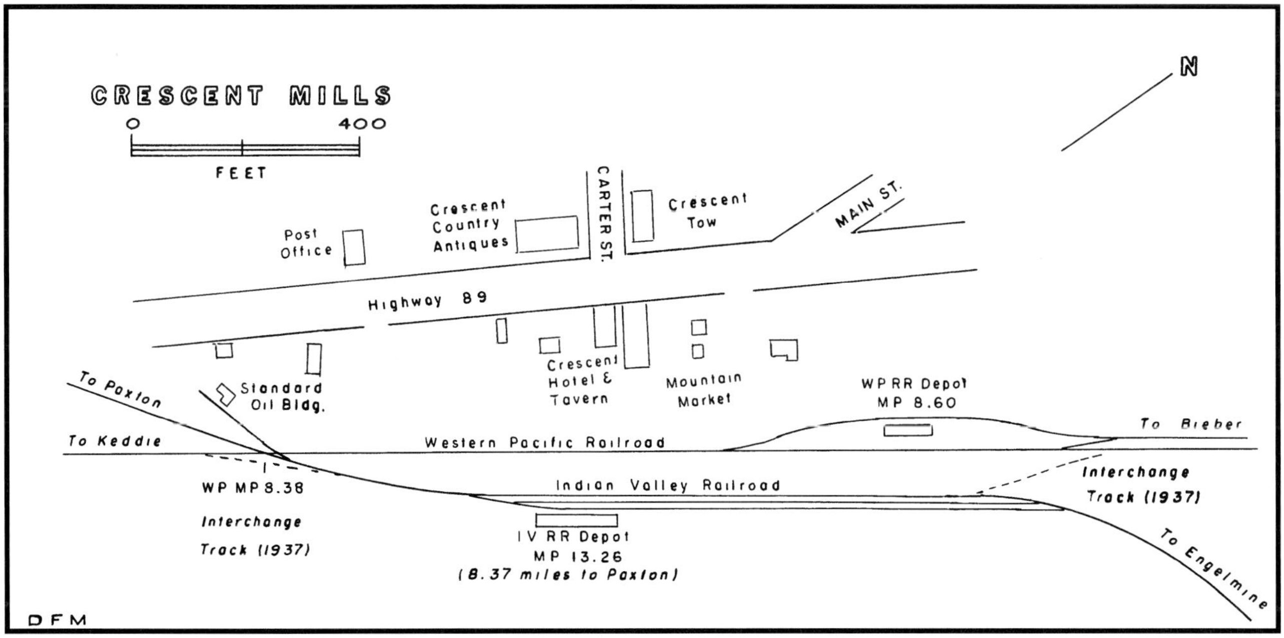

work on the IV RR, suffered a fatal stroke. (Two weeks earlier, Virgil Bogue died on a ship while returning from South America. His engineering career included the Transandean Railroad, Union Pacific, Northern Pacific's Stampede Pass, and the Western Pacific.)

In mid-November 1916, the railroad grade was "practically complete"—a term wiser people accepted with reservations. The Feather River bridge was almost finished, which was just as well, for Engels Copper made plans to double its output. One heavy cut near Indian Falls and some grading across the Hardgrave Ranch remained to be worked, but already a motor truck scattered cross ties along the grade between Crescent Mills and Indian Falls. Dynamiting near the latter place brought some concern, for one large rock struck and damaged the iron stovepipe of the Hafner house, then crashed through an apple tree and a fence, before burying itself in a three-foot hole in the street.

With the end of November, the IV RR track extended one mile out of Paxton, with the hope that the rails could reach Crescent Mills in December. Teams began hauling concentrates to Crescent Mills in anticipation of the railroad. At Engelmine, workers reportedly led by the Industrial Workers of the World went on strike for higher wages. The company closed down for about a week, but after a boost in pay, most of the men soon returned to work.

Tracklaying lagged but eventually reached Indian Falls on December 18, and the workers expected to be in Crescent Mills in a few days, only to be confronted by severe cold weather and a major storm just before Christmas, so more time was lost, which contributed to another problem. The teamsters dumped so many tons of copper concentrates on the platform at Crescent Mills that it collapsed. At that moment, it held little concern for the town as it rejoiced with the news that the Crescent gold mine would reopen after being idle for twenty-five years.

In reporting on conditions on January 17, 1917, Paxton referred to the adverse weather and also that we "have had considerable trouble with small slides in the canyon, and also with the locomotives furnished us by the Western Pacific. Rails are now being laid to Crescent Mills. . . . We now have 170 horses and mules hauling [ores and concentrates] to Crescent Mills."

Paxton pushed tracklaying across Indian Valley "before the ground softens up." Expansion of the works at Engelmine continued, supported by the favorable copper market. Whereas the original concentrator had a 250-ton-per-day capacity, the company moved forward with a 2,000-ton-capacity mill, to be ready in July. Also, a new 1,000-foot tramway began service between the Superior Tunnel and Lower Camp.

In March 1917, the railroad established Veramont station, about halfway to Engels, and taking advantage of the shorter teamster haul, the copper company loaded gondolas at this point. Starks station, almost five miles ahead, marked the beginning of the climb of the last 4 miles to Engels with a steady grade of 1.65 percent and reaching 2.5 percent just before crossing Lights Creek.

The rails reached Engels in April, but no passenger (mixed) service could be operated until better facilities at Paxton became available. The opening had to be postponed for a week pending bridge repairs. When the first train passed through Crescent Mills with its solitary coach on July 12, 1917, the little town responded with a celebration.

Normally, train schedules on short lines are slow, but this one may have established a new record. Two hours and fifteen minutes were required for the 21.5-mile trip from Paxton to Engels, and the return was even worse, as the climb to Paxton necessitated an additional fifteen minutes. (In later years, the elapsed time between Paxton and Engels was shortened by fifteen minutes.)

The Indian Valley Railroad now stood as a going concern. Frederick Klamp, vice president of the copper company, served as president, and the Engels name was conspicuously absent. C. L. Eaton, general superintendent, kept his office in Paxton. Although the copper company provided most of the traffic, Eaton cheered the Noble Electric Steel Company when it leased the manganese mine near Indian Falls and commenced operations in the summer of 1917 with thirty men and shipped the ore to its electric reduction plant at Heroult on the Sacramento Valley and Eastern Railway in Shasta County, California.

Paxton, California

About 1891, placer mining supported the small town of Iron Bar for a brief period, but in 1902, when mining revived, only a run-down log cabin remained. At that time, the Feather River Mining Company erected several buildings, threw a suspension bridge across the river, and dug a half-mile ditch to bring water to power its mill. Heavy rains in the winter of 1904 caused the river to rise and wash out the ditch, at which point the company abandoned operations.

During the construction of the Indian Valley Railroad, the settlement consisted of three canvas tents, one for the workers, one for the dining room, and another for the depot. As work progressed on the new railroad, the tents vanished and a new town, Paxton, was born.

Thinking ahead, Paxton had purchased the site of Iron Bar for the railroad but recognized that accommodations for train crews and transferring passengers stood at dismal levels. After building a roundhouse and station, Paxton secured approval of the Engels board of directors in July to correct the situation. In November 1917, one could count ten 5-room cottages for employees and observe the $15,000 hotel well on its way. As the Feather River Lodge, it opened May 1, 1918, with A. D. Chase as manager.

At Engelmine, both Upper and Lower Camps were going full blast in June 1918 amid full-blown prosperity and a population of six hundred. The July 4 dance sparked social life in the community, boosted by the construction of a large building to be used for a dance hall until another could be erected for that purpose at which time the first building would offer a pool hall and bar-

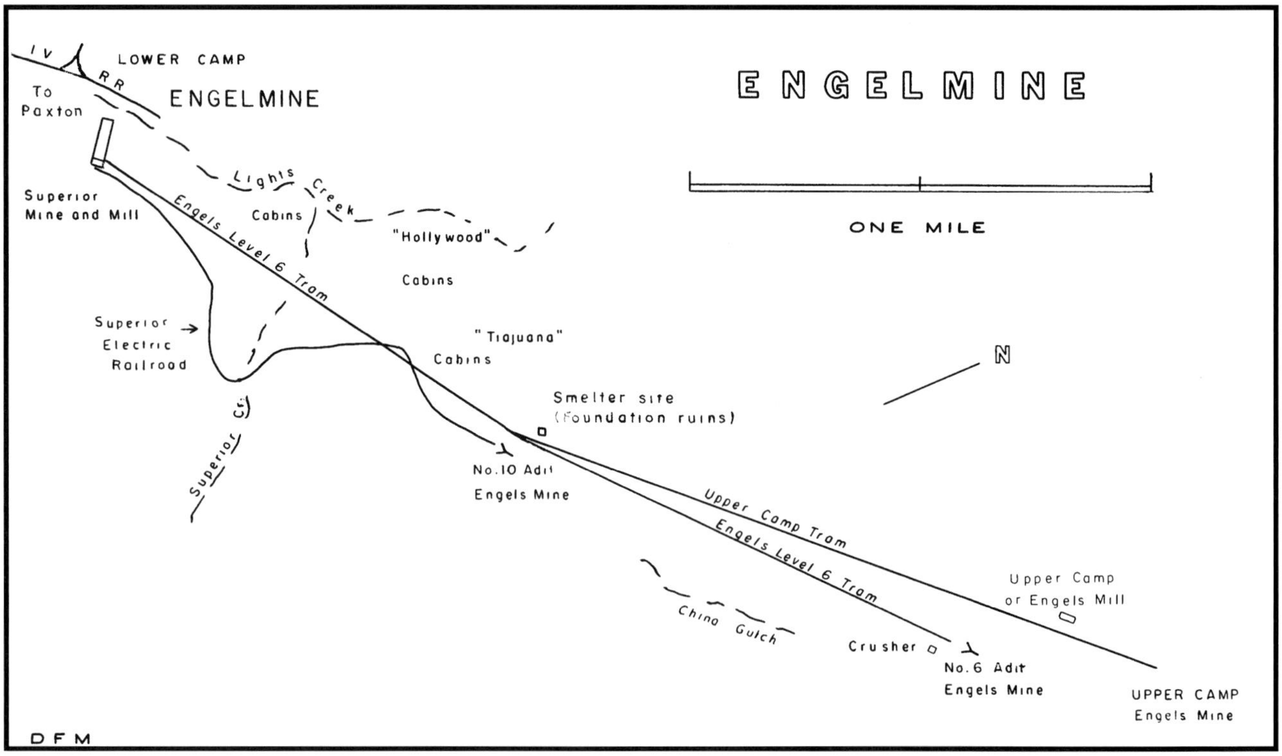

bershop. Carpenters worked quickly to add a large store building to the community as well as a schoolhouse. For employees, housing problems were mitigated with the completion of forty 6-room cottages with electric and water service. A contract had been let for another seventy similar houses.

In February 1918, the new mill at Lower Camp commenced operations, which caused some families to move from Upper to Lower Camp, a trend that would bring the main Engels office to Lower Camp a year later.

Several fires occurred during the year, starting with the loss of the idle Engels sawmill that was rebuilt only to burn again a few years later. Taylorsville lost much of its commercial district, and a fire seriously threatened Indian Falls. On the positive side, there was some excitement centered in Taylorsville and Greenville in January 1918 when surveyors ran lines between those towns for the Indian Valley Electric Railway, a project that never materialized.

The Engels Copper Mining Company reported good results for 1917, with output a third more than the previous year. More than $700,000 was poured into improvements, including $179,000 to finish the railroad. Stockholders received $295,253 in dividends for that year.

In early 1919, the management announced plans for a six-mile extension of the Indian Valley Railroad from Lower Camp to Upper Camp, but nothing transpired for several years. In the preceding years, several independent copper producers tapped the rewards of good copper prices with their own mines in neighboring canyons. To accommodate shipments from the Ruby Mine and Trask and Coffer Mine, the railroad installed a spur and a loading platform at Williams Crossing.

The Indian Valley Railroad cost substantially more than the $300,000 originally estimated, in part due to the housing at Paxton and the rolling stock. Several times, it proved necessary to seek authority for the issuance of more capital stock. From an operating standpoint, the railroad fared well thanks to the favorable interline division of freight rates. In the period of 1918–1921, annual operating revenues ran in excess of $140,000, which qualified it for Class II railroad status. Freight and passenger revenues represented about $115,000 and $20,000, respectively, of the total revenues. Net profit after all charges ranged from $36,000 to $46,000.

With the general business slump across the nation in 1921, the copper company's prosperity vanished. In March the copper company operated at a loss, and a general shutdown appeared necessary. Essential cash stood in short supply, but some borrowing carried the company through the slump. The debt was retired in 1923.

Most of the year 1921 constituted a struggle for Engels Copper Mining Company, but the company managed to avoid a shutdown by improving efficiency and securing a favorable contract with the Garfield Smelting Company in Utah. California's governor, W. D. Stephens, honored the camp with a visit in the fall as he was beginning his second term. Economic conditions brightened during the last quarter, and the payroll listed 470 names. Though the copper company lost $51,116 during 1921, the year ended well with a profitable last quarter. Not only did the production exceed the previous year, but the company substantially boosted its ore reserves. Additionally, with the suspension of mining in the Foothill District, Engels became the top copper producer in California for that year.

In contrast with happier conditions in the copper trade, troubles in the top management surfaced when Henry Engels levied criticism at Paxton for replacing the old concentrating mill and charged him as "directly responsible for the cave-in at the mine some time ago" that lost millions of dollars of ore. Engels solicited proxies for the annual stockholders' meeting on February 13, 1922.

Paxton, after stating that he had no desire to enter into a personal controversy with Engels, denied the accusations. He stated the company had no bonded debt and that the floating debt (bank loans) of $200,000 could be paid with a few months of operations at a fair price for copper. With his Hawaiian connections, Paxton garnered 1,917,622 shares compared with 548,949 shares supporting Engels. Fred Klamp succeeded Engels as president, but the latter remained on the board. (It was about this time that Paxton joined the Western Pacific directorate.)

The troubles slimmed down when the entire area joined in the St. Patrick's Day celebration that year, even with stalled WP and N-C-O trains fighting their way out of snowdrifts. The IV RR ran a special train for the dance leaving Paxton at 6:00 P.M. and hastening to Engelmine in just ninety minutes. The party received high praise as the best masquerade ball ever as the tired dancers boarded the train at 4:45 A.M. for the return trip.

Fires—the Unwelcome Visitor

The Indian Valley Railroad and towns along the way suffered when the fire demon came to call. When agent E. F. Stratton returned to Veramont station after having gone to Taylorsville for lunch on the last day of 1919, he found nothing but smoldering ruins. A boxcar served as the temporary depot until a replacement was finished four months later.

The bunkhouse at Paxton almost suffered the same fate on May 14, 1922, but willing hands extinguished the blaze before great damage had been done. A few weeks later, on July 6, an early-morning mystery blaze consumed the IV RR depot at Engels as well as the connecting freight house. Both were soon replaced.

Terror ran through Engelmine on September 19, 1926, a Sunday morning, when flames threatened to annihilate the entire settlement. Every able-bodied man joined the battle, and they soon had the fire under control.

Crescent Mills had come into the news a few weeks previously when it suffered a major conflagration on September 2, 1926. It started at noon in the Carter Hotel and swept through the store and home of W. P. Kingdon. Schoolchildren were loaded into trucks and driven out of town for safety. Steve Sorolis lost his ice cream parlor and restaurant and thought his cache of Liberty Bonds as well until he learned that a friend had grabbed them just in time. Mrs. J. T. Bacher considered her savings gone, but, after the fire, she dug up the can with five hundred dollars in gold coins she had previously hidden. Backfiring saved the Newhart Lumber Company and railroad depot. A special train brought firefighters from Engelmine who saved a number of homes, but still thirty buildings burned.

J. G. Singleton, owner of the Carter Hotel, was arrested at Paxton while waiting for a Western Pacific train and charged with arson, only to be released for lack of evidence. When his insurance carrier refused to honor his claim because of alleged incendiarism, Singleton took it to court and won, only to have the decision reversed in an appellate court that found for the insurance company.

This fire proved to be the second blaze to threaten Crescent Mills, for back in 1921, a fire closed in on the Indian Valley Railroad station and freight house on the evening of August 21. With hand-carried buckets of water, the flames were subdued after destroying a barn. When the roof of the freight house caught fire in several places, it caused the townspeople to redouble their efforts, knowing of the potential disaster if the fifty barrels of gasoline in the building caught fire.

The Electric Railroad at Engelmine

In lieu of extending the Indian Valley Railroad, as had been considered in 1919, the copper company started construction on an electric railroad in the summer of 1923 for transporting ore from the No. 10 adit (tunnel) to the Superior Mill at Lower Camp, a distance of 6,505 feet. Tracklaying began in October, even while other men continued framing the major trestle. Winter weather, as usual, impeded work, but in early 1924 ore trains moved over the finished part of the line, clinging to the hillside and crossing three trestles, with one being 50 feet high. Local citizens deemed it their "scenic" railway. On Monday, May 20, 1924, the entire electric railroad went into operation financed by five hundred thousand–dollar 7 percent ten-year bonds due in 1934. Three years later, a forest fire threatened to wipe out the trestles, but it was contained until the next day when it broke out again and required the combined efforts of two hundred men who battled four hours before bringing it under control.

In February 1924, school enrollment at Upper Camp came to fourteen; nine months later the place looked like a deserted village, as nearly all the houses and other buildings had been moved to Lower Camp. Upper Camp mines continued to be operated as before, but the men entered No. 10 adit and small cars took them to their workplaces. (The cables of the old tram line came down in 1927.)

The Indian Valley Railroad plugged along as before when Solon Luzzader returned to his engineer's job, while his brother, Ralph, fired the same locomotive. At the mine, management changes came when W. R. Lindsay, general superintendent for the past six years, left for the Grandby Mine in British Columbia in November 1925. W. I. Nelson filled his shoes. Elmer Paxton had been ill for some time, and Lindsay's departure triggered his decision to retire. Henry Engels died October 6, 1928, at the age of seventy-four. The mining company paid monthly dividends in 1916, 1917, and 1918 but none until 1925 and ending with August 1926. After that date, the company lost money every month for sixteen months until profitable operations returned in February 1928.

The little railroad managed to trim fifteen minutes off its run to Engelmine. Some days no trains operated, such as on March 2, 1927, when one hundred feet of fill slipped away, leaving tracks suspended in midair. A year later, a headline read "Six-Day Storm Works Havoc in Plumas County," generally halting railroad operations everywhere. Because the Indian Valley Railroad—a key part in the copper production and distribution—suffered washouts, the company closed the Superior Mine for five days while sending two hundred miners to make emergency repairs to the roadbed. For those passengers who simply had to travel during this period, the speeder—track motorcar—accommodated them. Full restoration of the railroad required more than a month's work by regular forces. The wild weather contributed heavily to a net loss for both the railroad and the mining company in 1928.

During this period, the Red River Lumber Company contemplated rehabilitating part of its logging line along Lake Almanor and extending south under the name of the Northern California Railroad to a connection with the Indian Valley Railroad just east of Crescent Mills. As a part in this venture, Western Pacific secured an option on the IV RR that was dissolved when the ICC denied the application. One can speculate how different railroad history might have been in that area had the Northern California Railroad become a reality!

For its size, Paxton had far more than its share of criminal activity. In May 1922, robbers blew up the safe in the WP depot in a manner that Sheriff L. A. Braden put down as an amateur job. When some men blasted the post office safe a week later, Braden held that it was not the same party. In the same week, two armed men boarded a WP boxcar at Paxton, lined up the twenty-five vagrants inside, and searched them. Only two men had anything; one lost his last few dollars, while the other stuffed his wallet in his shirt and retained his $10 after being searched twice. The two bandits disappeared after leaving the train at Keddie.

Two years passed before two masked men put a gun at the head of W. C. Veyl to persuade him to open the WP safe. Wisely, Mr. Veyl cooperated. Not satisfied with the $110 they had gathered, the men then went through Veyl's pockets. An attempted robbery of the same station in April 1928 proved a failure.

The copper content in the ore had been declining in recent years, from 1.79 percent in 1927 to 1.52 percent in 1929 and only 1.3 percent the next year. Better prices enabled the company to recover in 1929, even though both the copper company and the railroad regularly had heavy charges for depreciation and depletion that resulted in the fortunate increase in cash reserves. The copper company used part of the money to participate in an attempted revival of copper mining in the old town of Copperopolis in the western foothills of the Sierra Nevada. It proved unprofitable and was shut down after a few months.

Lower Copper Prices Close the Mines

Copper prices in 1929 stood at 18 cents, a strong 4 cents over the previous year. One can picture the dismay in corporate headquarters in 1930 as the demand for copper diminished in contrast with rising inventories that deflated market prices severely. At a special meeting on July 5, 1930, President Frederick Klamp confronted the board with the problem of receiving only 11.5 cents a pound of copper that cost the company almost 17 cents to produce. The net result was to dispatch a telegram to Engelmine two days later ordering an immediate closing of the mine. Single men were paid off, while some thirty families remained in their houses.

And so a twenty-year operation came to an end after the Engels Copper Mining Company had produced slightly more than fifty million pounds of copper. Dividends, though paid in only five years, totaled $1,285,971. As will be mentioned in subsequent pages, several attempts came forth to resume mining, but nothing was to transpire for several decades.

The Indian Valley Railroad, even without the mine shipping two or three cars of concentrates each day, managed to survive for another eight years. During 1926 and again in 1928, it declared a 10 percent dividend to its parent owners from accumulated earnings that totaled $97,000.

Standing Alone

Without the tonnage of copper concentrates, the Indian Valley RR found itself standing alone. Comparing annual revenues, the railroad management watched them fall from $135,000 in 1929 to $92,000 the next year and to just $14,000 in 1932. For some reason, operating expenses ran higher in 1930 and, coupled with reduced traffic, swung a $34,000 profit in 1929 to a loss of $17,000 the next year. On the positive side, the railroad had no debt and had $41,000 cash in the bank at the beginning of 1931 that would grow during the year.

More important, the management, represented by the inactive copper company, had a fighting spirit. After the 1928 Northern California RR proposal fell apart, Western Pacific and Great Northern came up with another proposal, this time to build a railroad from Keddie to Bieber and Klamath Falls. Reports of the events are cloudy; some say the Indian Valley RR rejected WP's purchase offer of the Paxton–Crescent Mills portion, while others contend that WP considered the 4 percent grades of the IV RR unsuitable for a main-line railroad. At the ICC hearings in San Francisco relating to this new line, the IV RR joined the protesters, recognizing that WP's parallel line would scoop off its traffic. The ICC gave scant consideration to the future prospects of the IV RR when it approved the application on June 6, 1930, just a few weeks before the end of mining at Engelmine.

Meeting on August 30, 1930, the board of directors of the Engels Copper Mining Company—still owner of 75 percent of the railroad's capital stock—met to review the effect of the parallel railroad. O. H. Bru, treasurer and director, informed the assemblage that he had discussed the damage from the ICC decision with attorney John L. McNab who recommended litigation challenging the ICC decision. McNab believed that "the Indian Valley had more than an even chance of winning its contention and that the . . . decision laid a foundation for such cause of action." The board agreed to retain McNab and John M. Thompson to engage in litigation.

The trial, conducted in the federal district court in San Francisco, with three justices sitting on the bench, ended with approval of the actions of the ICC. Harold Louderbach, who wrote the opinion, discussed several issues, among them finding that the ICC had acted within the Transportation Act of 1920 that "expressly provided for the entry of a competitive carrier into the traffic territory of another carrier" when so required by public convenience and necessity (52 F. (2d 485). With this decision dated August 21, 1931, he dismissed the IV RR claim. The railroad appealed this decision to the U.S. Supreme Court, which on May 14, 1934, affirmed the district-court ruling (292 U.S. 608).

The little railroad limped along for the next several years. By 1933, Charles O. Penfield had moved from assistant to longtime superintendent Eaton to the post of general superintendent. Freight revenue leveled off at $12,000, or about one-tenth of the active years. As mining machinery was sold to parties elsewhere, it went out over the railroad, but more important was the small but steady lumber traffic. Back in 1926, Enhorning and Harrison of Susanville established a sawmill three miles above Engels and used a Caterpillar tractor to bring rough lumber to the railhead. After the WP opened its HiLine in 1931, the Indian Valley Railroad transported most of the output of this sawmill to Crescent Mills, where it was interchanged with WP for delivery to the Red River Lumber Company at Westwood for finishing. Another small sawmill, opposite Moccasin siding on WP, also helped support the railroad. Operated by a Frenchman named Frizzie, the approaching exhaustion of his log supply from an old burn near the Round Valley reservoir portended the mill's closure. Under new arrangements, the Taresch brothers loaded logs at Veramont, and the railroad delivered them to Frizzie's mill for rough cutting followed by shipment to a planing mill at Crescent Mills for finishing. The Standard Oil (Chevron) distribution facility was another source of traffic.

Passenger revenue in 1929, though only a fraction of the earlier figures, still totaled $3,853, equivalent to 2,568 passengers paying $1.50 to ride the mixed train from Paxton to Engels. In 1932, only $8.00 was received from passengers, and in 1934, the year passenger service ended, the revenue totaled only $1.05.

Train operations in 1933 consisted of a roundtrip between Paxton and Crescent Mills on Tuesday, Thursday, and Saturday, with train No. 2 leaving Paxton at 8:00 A.M. and arriving at Crescent Mills forty minutes later. Sixty minutes were required for No. 1 to make the return trip that left Crescent Mills at 9:00 A.M. On Tuesday, the train continued all the way to Engels, but, as it returned to Crescent Mills at 11:35 A.M., it upset the schedule for the normal run to Paxton.

The next superintendent, Grant S. Allen, a railroad boomer who had held twenty-nine jobs on thirteen different railroads, accepted the job on November 1, 1934, with instructions to endeavor to improve the financial results of the railroad. At this time, the California Department of Highways coveted the eight miles of the IV RR grade for an improved highway to Crescent Mills. The earning power or lack of it would play an important part in determining the price of the right-of-way.

The Feather River Villa, the railroad-owned hotel at Paxton, served as the residence of Mr. and Mrs. Allen to meet the insurance carrier's requirement that it be occupied by regular residents. While he performed several tasks for the railroad, she ran the hotel and dining room as needed and also served as postmaster of Paxton. Her two jobs augmented the modest $150 monthly income Grant Allen received as railroad superintendent.

The hotel had only fourteen rooms but a large dining room seating one hundred, the logic being that travelers would step off the overnight train from San Francisco and have breakfast before going on to Engels or Crescent Mills. Returning at the end of the day, the same people needed an evening meal before boarding the night train to San Francisco. The Allens added a bar by the dining room that aided the family finances.

The rolling stock of the Indian Valley Railroad in 1934 consisted of two 2-8-0 locomotives, originally Denver and Rio Grande 661 and 668, which came through Western Pacific to become IV RR Nos. 1 and 2, respectively. Two open-vestibule passenger cars—one a combo—and a flatcar used in roadway maintenance completed the roster.

Allen, acting under his instructions, set out to meet the objective to lower operating expenses. Canceling the triweekly schedules and running trains "on call" as needed was his first act. He then took over the work of the agents at Paxton and Crescent Mills and abolished two jobs. He purchased a Ford station wagon to provide daily express service. His day began with opening Paxton station at 7:00 A.M., helping his wife with the mail, and then taking the station wagon over the highway to Crescent Mills and delivering express packages. After a few hours as railroad agent there, he returned to Paxton for lunch and spent the afternoon as agent and superintendent, with much of the time devoted to preparing the incessant reports demanded by the ICC and the California Railroad Commission.

The post office Star Route was the responsibility of Ira Short, an old-timer dating back to stagecoach days. Checking Railway Express Agency tariffs, Allen found that express rates were lower than parcel-post charges and worked out a cooperative arrangement with Ira Short to solicit express business in Greenville—beyond this railroad—whereby Allen would turn over express matter to Short in Crescent Mills. Greenville merchants appreciated the savings and welcomed the store delivery, and Allen and Short split the standard commission.

The operating force consisted of an engineer, fireman, conductor, and brakeman. Under Allen's regime, many a week went by without the locomotives leaving the two-stall engine house; one supplied steam heat for the hotel. On the days no trains ran, the engine men repaired the locomotives and the trainmen assisted the solitary man maintaining the roadbed.

Timetable No. 18 of March 10, 1935, provided a schedule with a note that trains would be operated "for shipper convenience, when carload shipments require transportation as per schedule, except Sundays." Less-than-carload shipments to Crescent Mills would be handled by truck six days a week.

Allen, who held seniority as a WP brakeman, left the Indian Valley Railroad on September 3, 1935, to rejoin Western Pacific, where he advanced to positions of greater responsibility and spent the last eleven years as superintendent of transportation before ending his fifty-year railroad career.

Carloads continued their generally downward trend. Enhorning and Harrison's lumber traffic was the most importance single source of business, as shown in the table of carload traffic:

	1935 (*cars*)	1936 (*cars*)	1937 (*cars*)
Animals	10	33	14
Enhorning and Harrison	239	178	232
Other lumber	309	138	224
Petroleum products	67	70	61
Miscellaneous	3	2	5
Total	**628**	**421**	**536**

On June 30, 1937, the Indian Valley Railroad applied to the California Railroad Commission to abandon that portion of the railroad from Paxton to Crescent Mills, citing various reasons. Besides the suspension of mining at Engels and the competitive parallel WP line, the railroad sought to curtail operating expenses so that it could restore the balance of the trackage to Engels should the mine reopen, as had been expected. The most important reason stemmed from a pending agreement to sell the right-of-way to Crescent Mills to the California Division of Highways, subject to receiving abandonment approval. The California Railroad Commission approved abandonment on July 31, 1937, as supplemented on February 14, 1938.

A recession commencing in the fall of 1937 that brought lower copper prices and the uncertainty of success in reaching profitable ore at Engelmine canceled any plans to reopen the mine. This decision in turn diminished the usefulness of the 13.23 miles of railroad between Crescent Mills and Engels, so the IV RR returned to the California Railroad Commission requesting abandonment of the remaining portion of the railroad. Matters had become more critical than before, for the cash reserve had dwindled from $25,000 in 1935 to a slim $5,000, notwithstanding the $30,000 received for the right-of-way.

Two important protesters appeared at the hearing in Quincy on September 20, 1938, with suggestions of ways to reduce expenses. When the protesters suggested a general shutdown during the quiet part of the year, the management countered by explaining the difficulties in securing seasonal help, as existing wage levels stood at less than 50 cents an hour. The management explained that the railroad needed annual revenues of $18,000 to $20,000 to survive, which at $18 revenue per car meant one thousand cars per year. With expected shipments in 1938 not expected to exceed two hundred cars, the higher figure seemed unlikely. Even August 1938, an active month, failed to produce sufficient revenues to cover the payroll and fuel costs.

Enhorning and Harrison stated that hauling rough lumber to Crescent Mills by truck would increase their cost of production. The Red River Lumber Company, owning three hundred million feet of timber in the area served by the little railroad, cited increased hauling costs as their concern. An official stated that the company did not plan to start logging in this area until about 1940, and that date was contingent on favorable market conditions. Obviously, this prospective future traffic offered no immediate benefits for the troubled railroad.

After weighing the testimony, the commission on October 3, 1938, authorized the road to abandon operations. Superintendent C. L. Williams announced that after December 5, 1938, the Indian Valley Railroad would no longer cease to be a common carrier but might exist as a private carrier for an unspecified time. As a private carrier, it contributed to the relocation of remaining mining machinery from Engelmine to the Groom Mine in Arizona in early 1939. With that haul completed, Hyman-Michaels Company, by an earlier contract, stood ready to buy 870 tons of steel rails at $12.50 a ton plus another 400 tons of frogs, switches, and so on at $7.50 per ton. The railroad company undertook the dismantling of the track and delivery of the rail's FOB (freight on board) railroad cars at Crescent Mills.

California-Engels Mining Company

The California Copper Company, incorporated July 12, 1922, served as a holding company for the Engels Copper Mining Company, with mostly the same officers. By 1929, it held most of the stock of the Engels Copper Mining Company, which was merged into the holding company on March 3, 1936, to be known as the California-Engels Mining Company.

When Engels closed in July 1930, it used a portion of its substantial cash resources to retire its outstanding debt. Copper prices declined to less than 6 cents a pound in 1932—an all-time low—so no consideration of resuming production occurred until 1936, but nothing transpired then because of limited possibilities. From time to time, the Engels property has been under option, but no production has been resumed. The Feather River Villa passed through several ownerships, and as the Paxton Lodge, its second story was severely damaged by a fire on April 16, 1981, but has since been restored and continues in operation.

The California-Engels Mining Company continues to review possible mining ventures and lately has successfully engaged in a limited timber-harvesting program. On June 17, 1999, the California Tree Farm Committee of the American Tree Farm System accepted the Engels property as the Engelmine Forest, California Tree Farm No. 2611.

The possibility of renewed activity at Engelmine rose with record copper prices in recent years. During 2006, world demand for copper caused prices to range between $3.50 and $4.00 per pound. Based on a drilling program during 1964–1968, Sheffield Resources Ltd. of Vancouver secured an exploration permit in April 2006 with an option to lease and purchase the property of the California-Engels Mining Company. Further development will be determined by the results of the exploration.

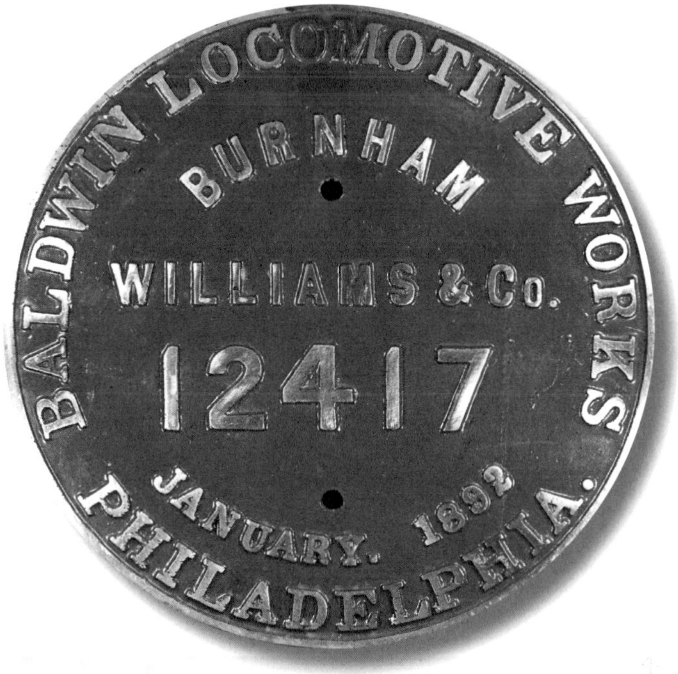

Right: The builder's plate for No. 2 of the Indian Valley Railroad. (James E. Boynton photograph)

Below: For travelers, the Feather River Villa at Paxton provided a convenient stopover on the way to Engelmine. Tracks of the Indian Valley Railroad run across the foreground.

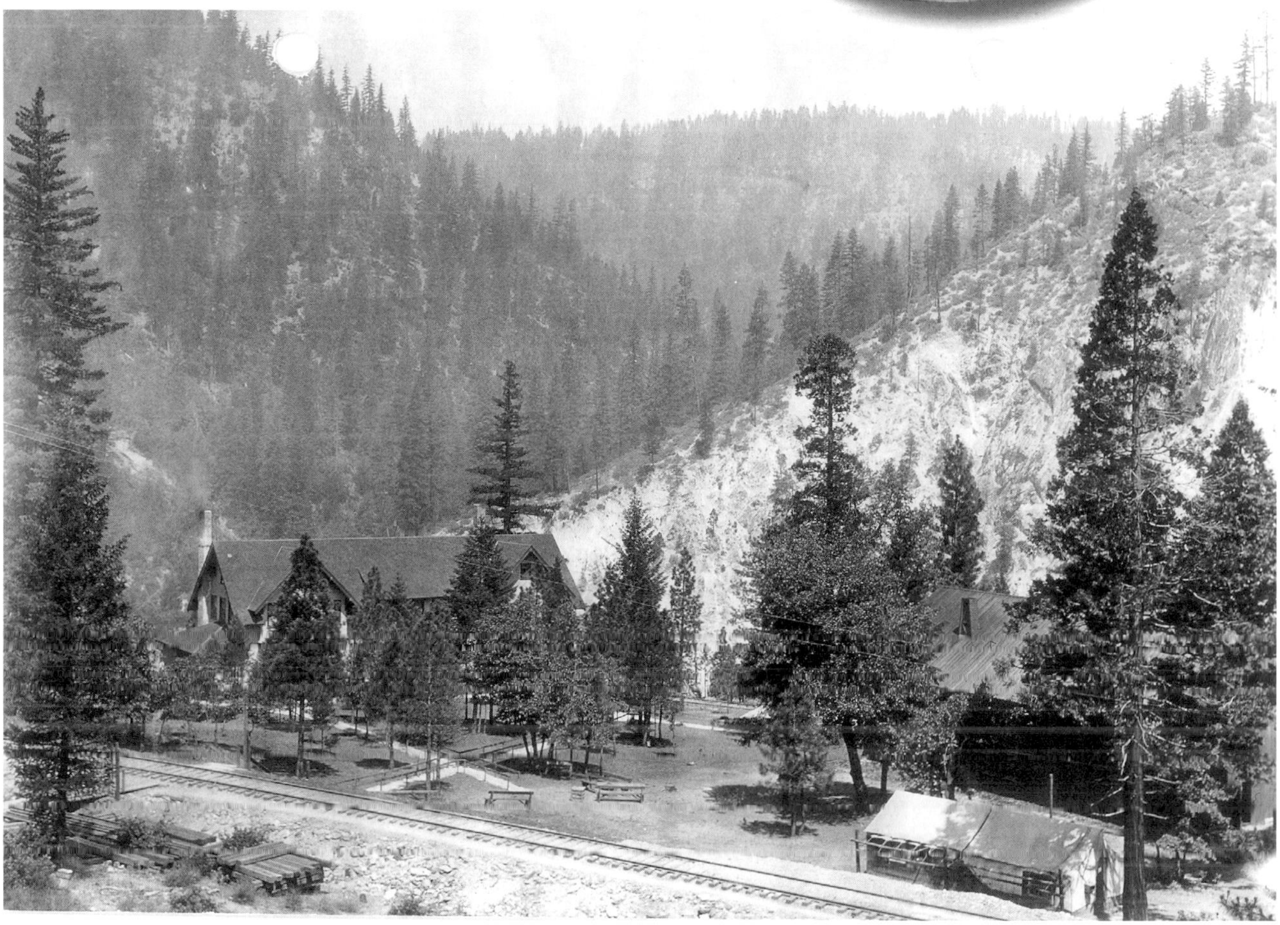

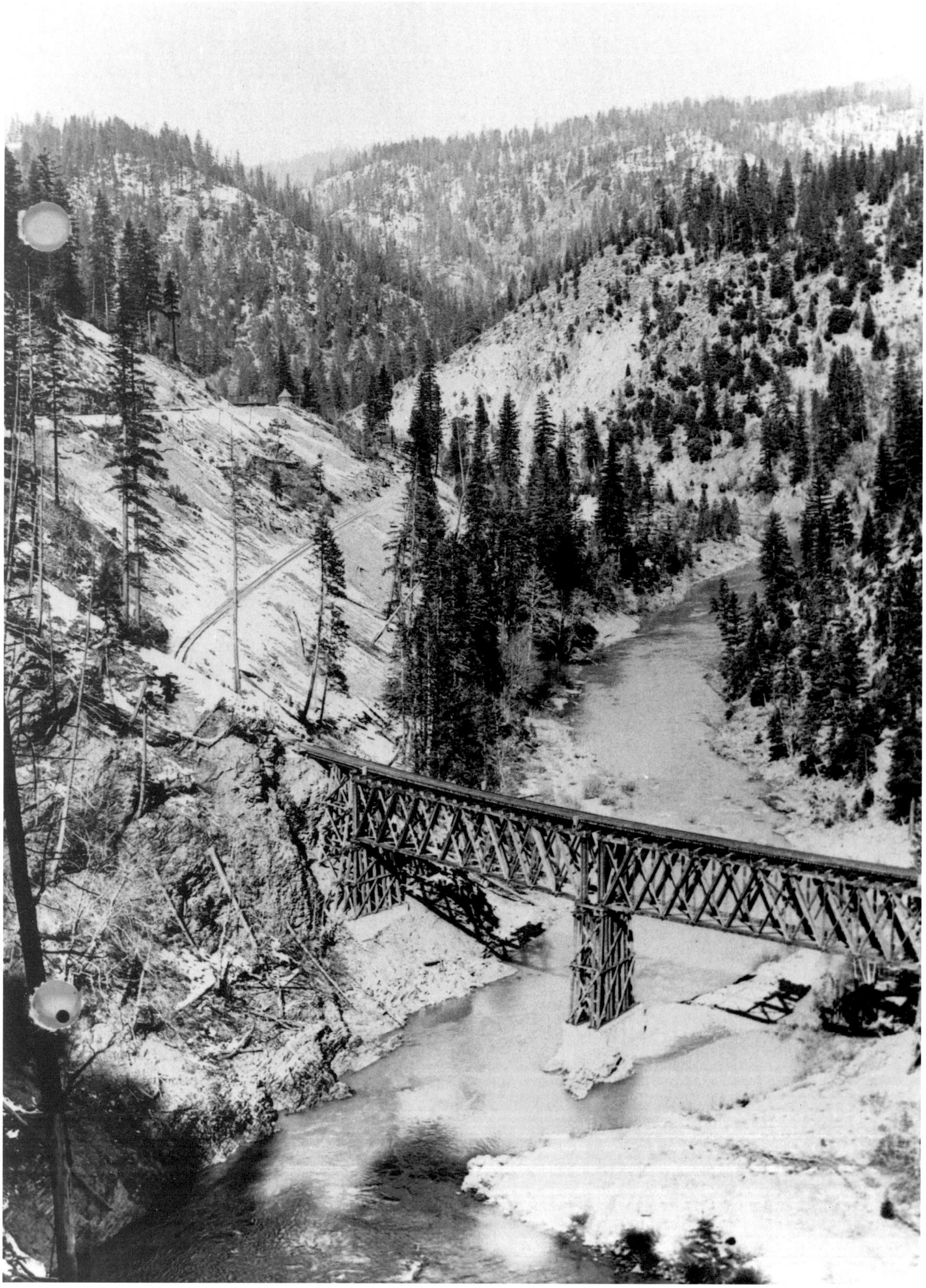

From Paxton and its connection with Western Pacific (*upper left*), the Indian Valley Railroad continued its sharp descent as it crossed the East Branch of the North Fork on two open-deck, 120-foot Howe truss spans forming this timbered bridge. (Plumas County Museum)

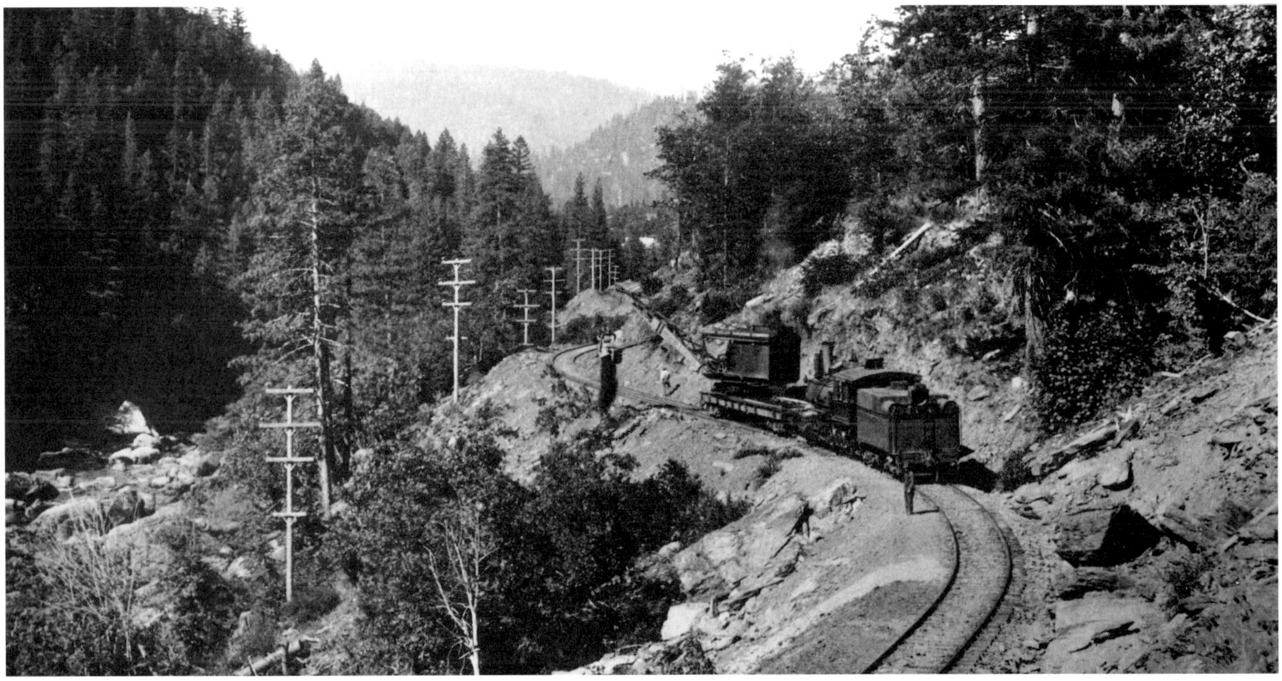

Above: Until this slide was removed near Dixie Canyon, traffic was suspended. (Plumas County Museum)

Below: The crew and agent pose by one of the typically short trains at Engelmine. (Plumas County Museum)

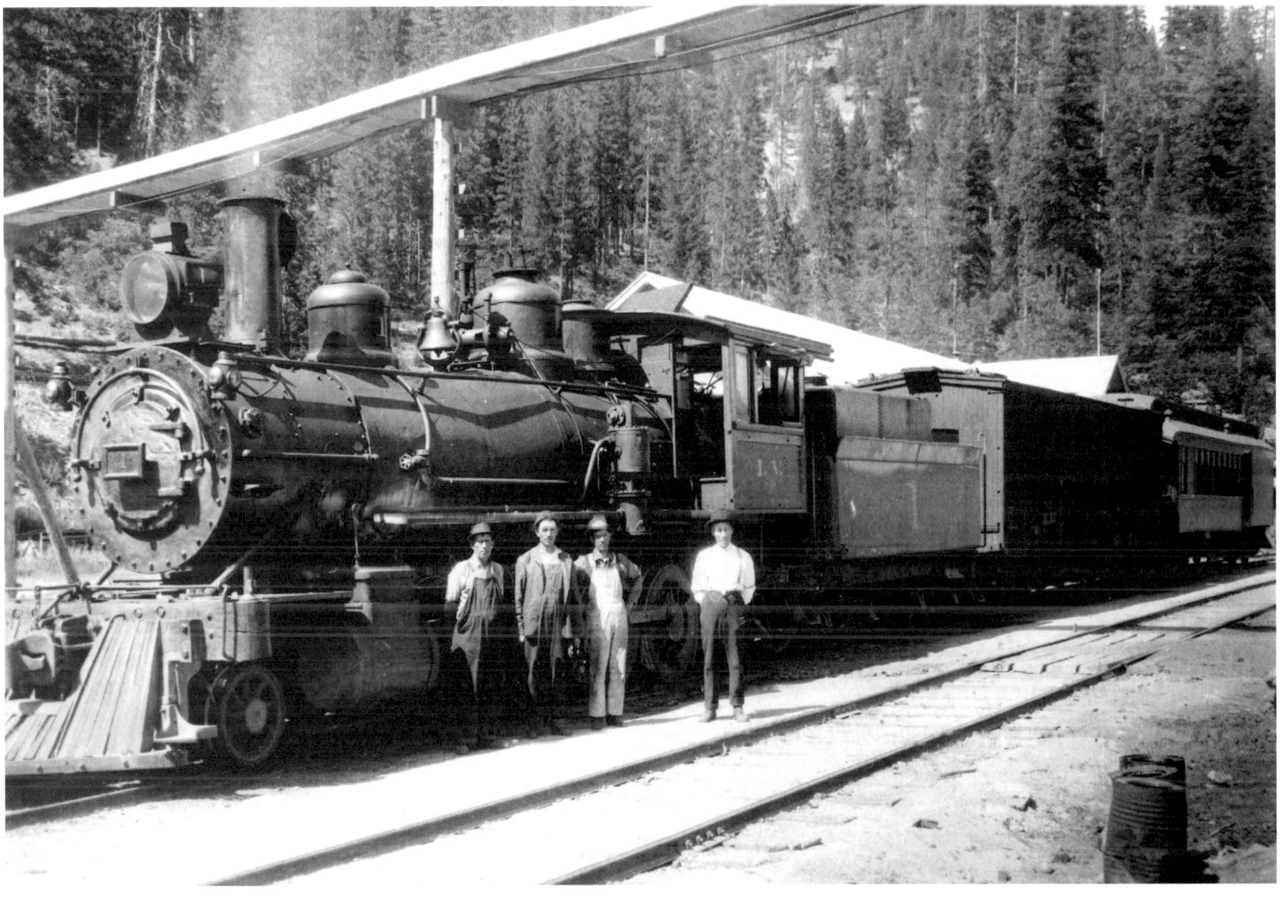

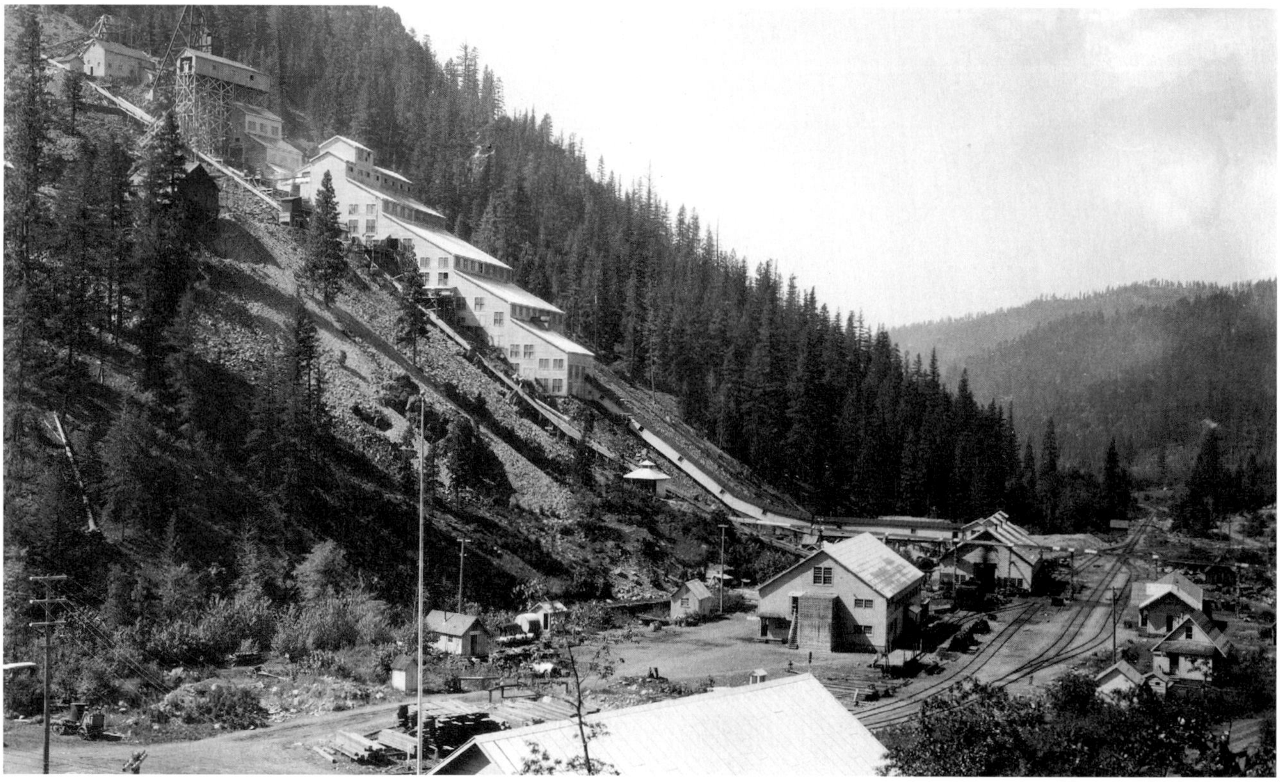

Above: In this 1923 picture, the Superior mill cascades down the hillside. Down below, the powerhouse occupies the large building in the foreground. Beyond stand the warehouse and the smaller machine shop where a locomotive is about to enter for repairs. The Indian Valley RR is opposite the warehouse. (Joe Moir collection)

Below: Lights Creek held a strong fascination for the fireman of this train. (Bob Cooke–Taylorsville Museum)

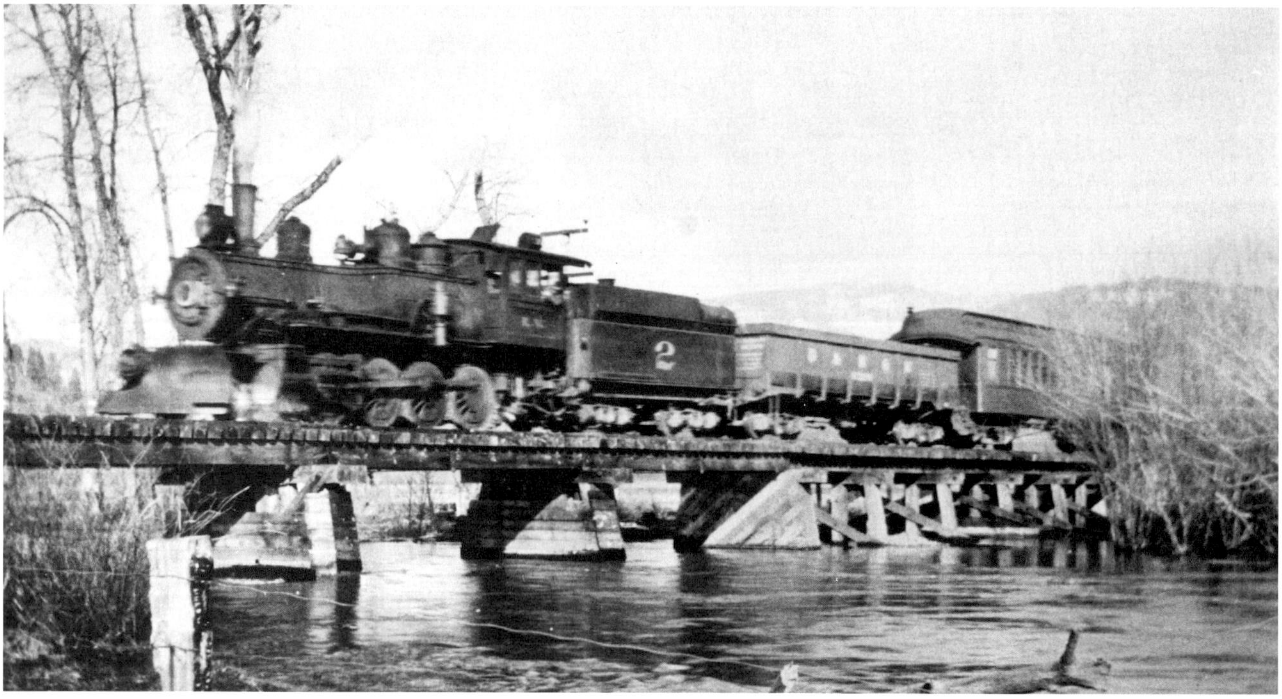

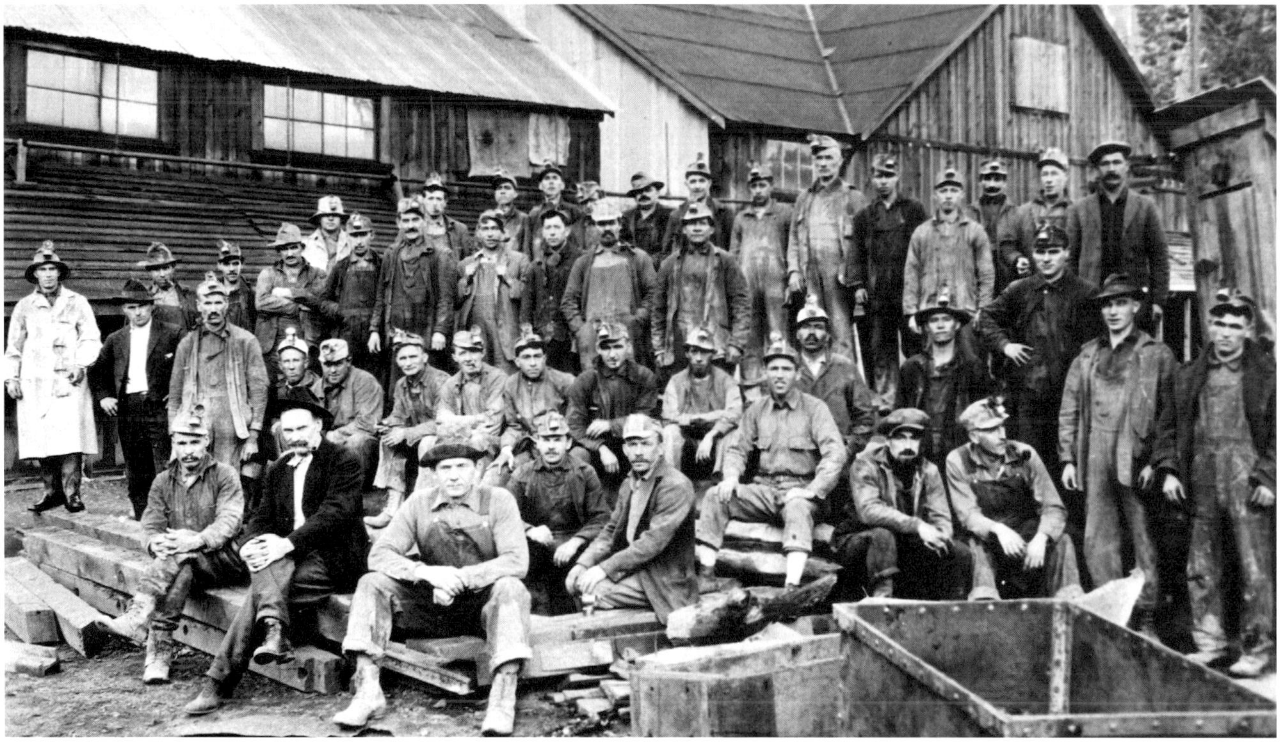

Above: Still wearing their caps with carbine lamps, copper miners assembled for this group picture at Upper Camp. (Edna Fisher–Taylorsville Museum)

Below: The company store and hotel, circa 1923, were located adjacent to Lights Creek at the end of Manzanita Street in Engelmine. The company mercantile department operated the store and hotel as well as the recreation hall, single men's dormitories, and dining hall.

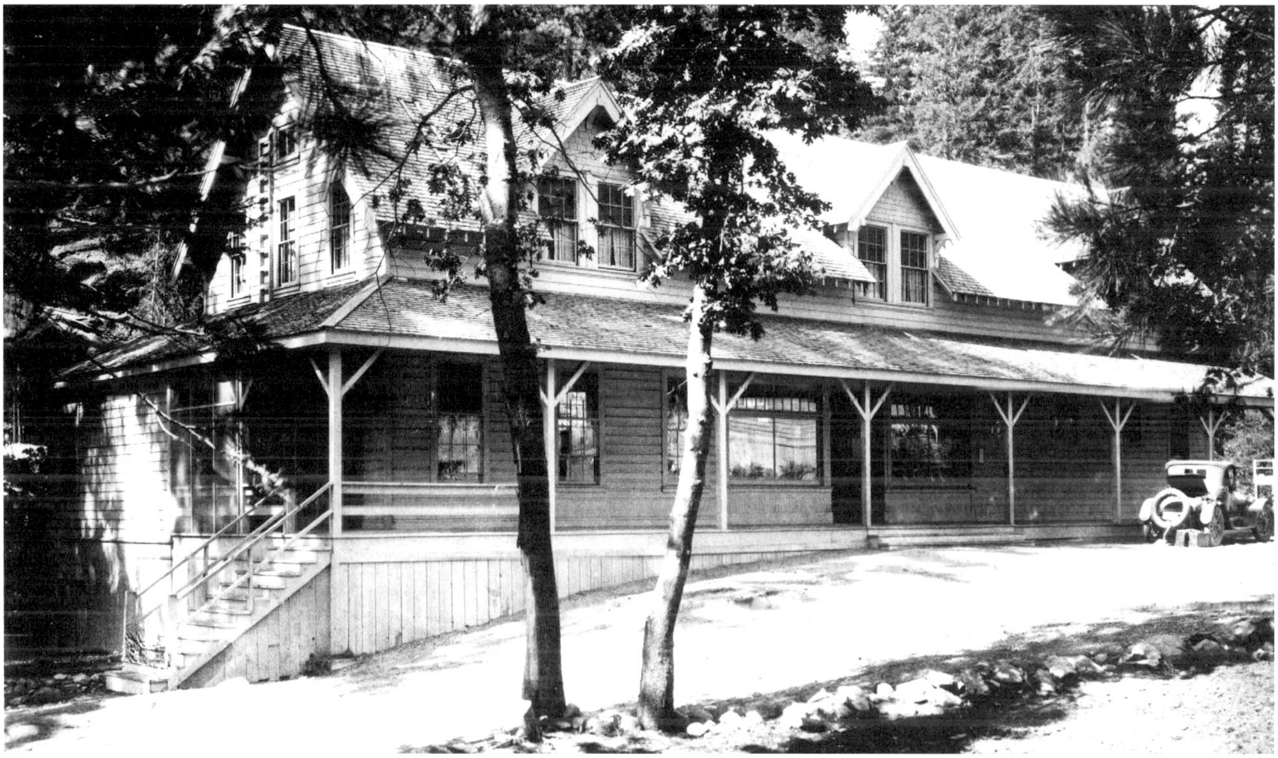

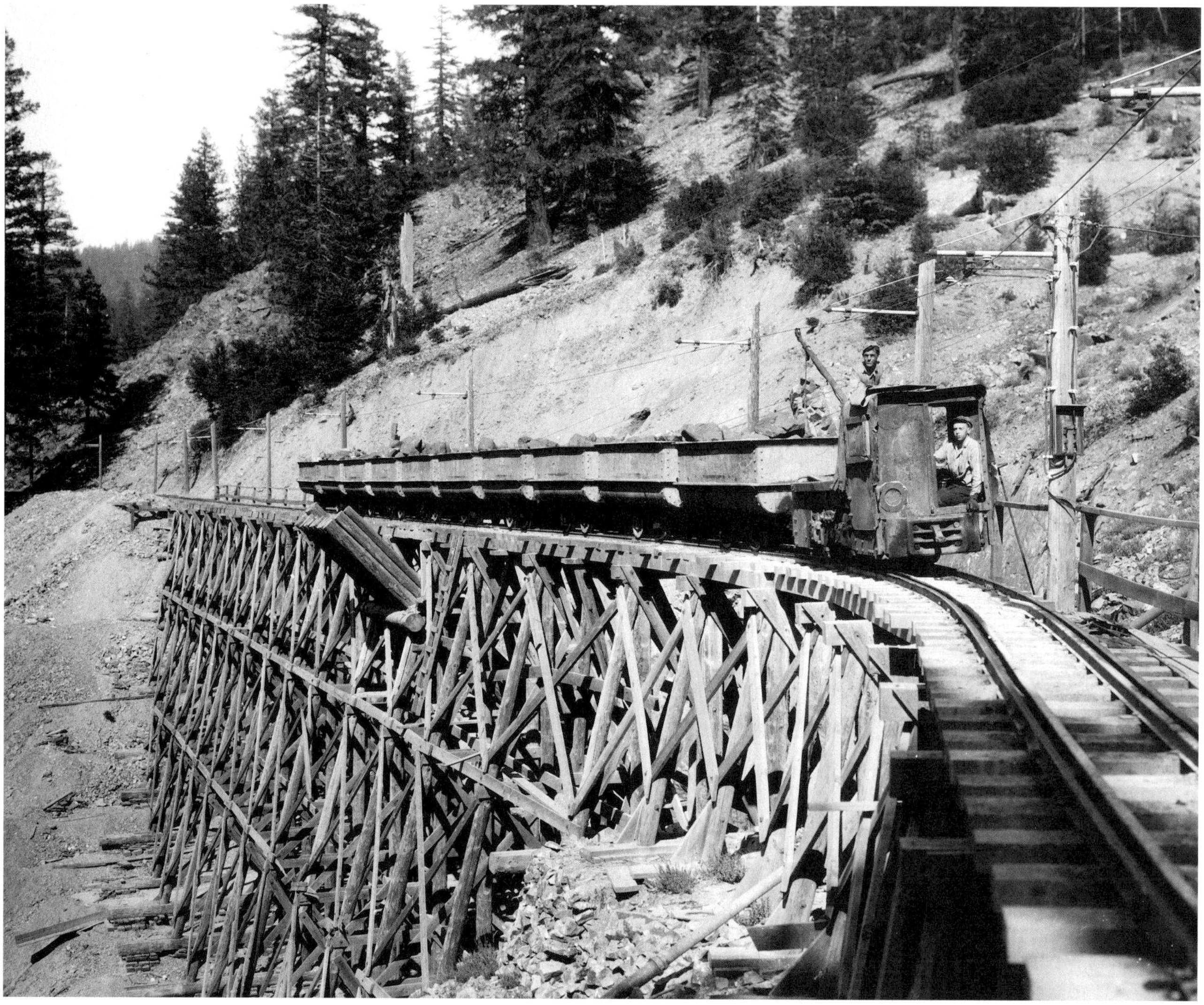

The short electric railroad (6,505 feet) conveyed ore to the mill to the bins at the shaft of the Superior Mine above the mill as it crossed Superior Creek on this trestle. (Joe Moir collection)

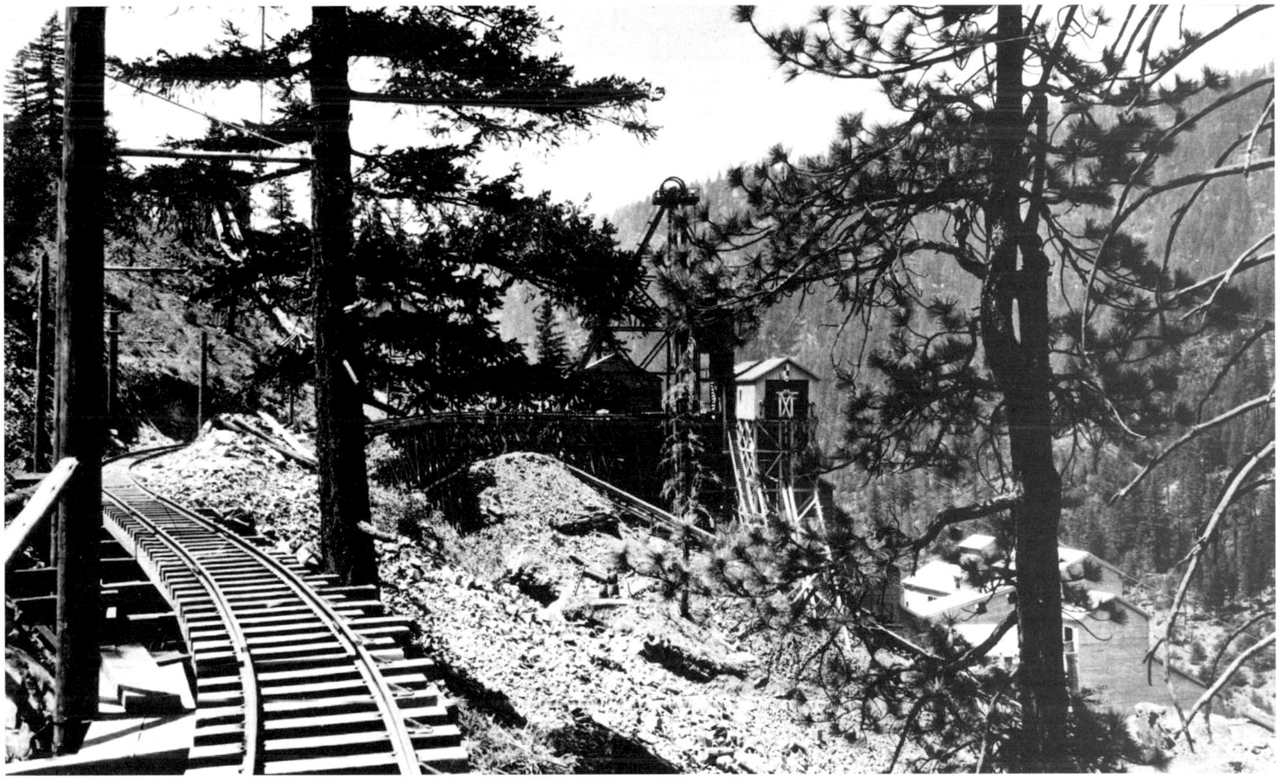

Above: After passing a few gentle curves, the electric train will arrive at the Superior hoist. (Bob Cooke–Taylorsville Museum)

Below: The long trestle of the electric railway ended in a shed at the Superior hoist where ore cars were dumped automatically. (Bob Cooke–Taylorsville Museum)

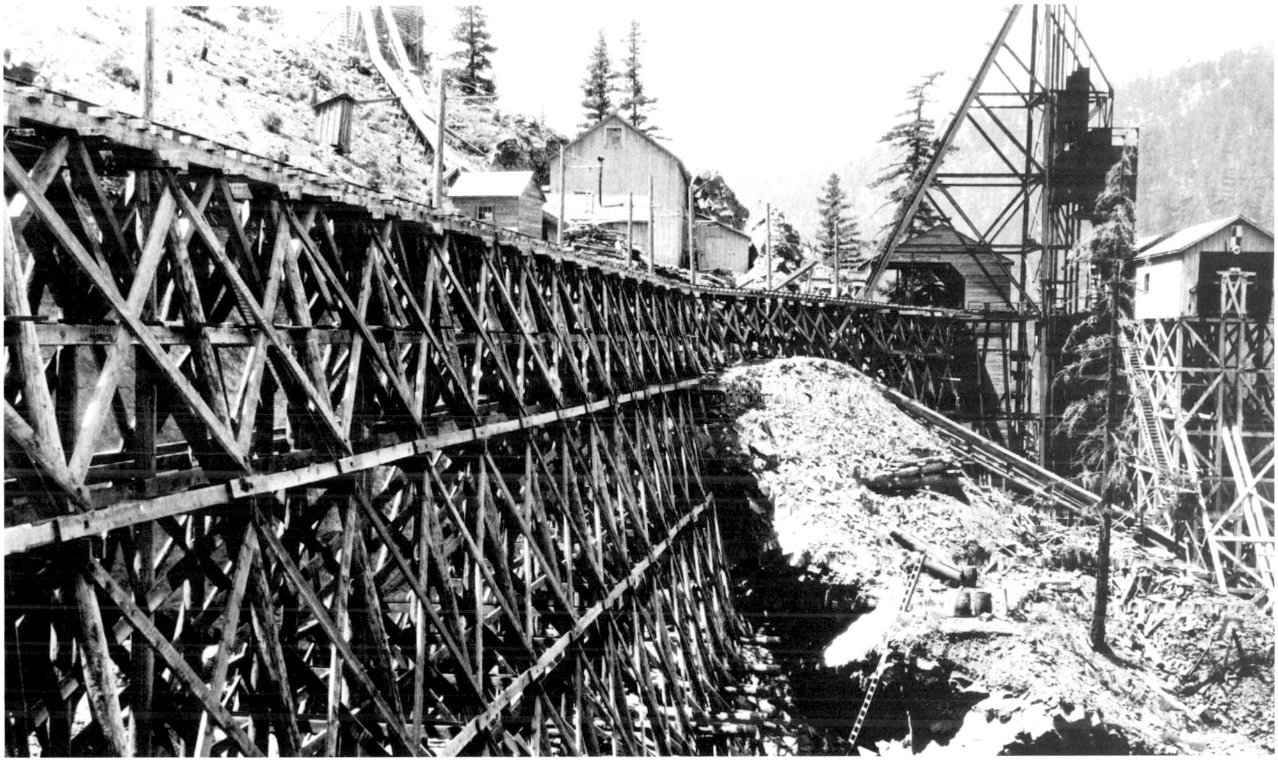

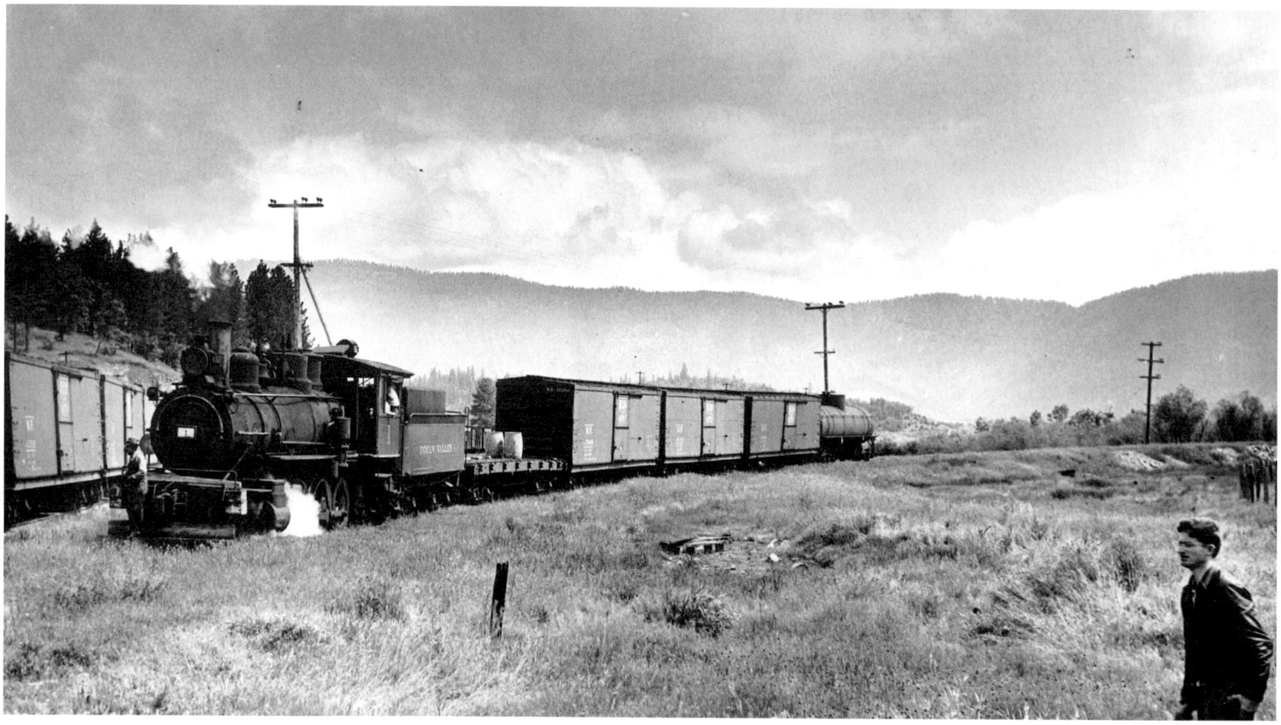

Above: In May 1938, a group of San Francisco rail photographers converged at Crescent Mills, by then the only interchange point with Western Pacific, to record the Indian Valley Railroad on film. A brewing thunderstorm adds a touch of drama to the scene. Will Whittaker, a noted rail photographer, approaches from the right. (James E. Boynton photograph)

Below: When the Veramont station burned, it was replaced by a smaller structure, and when the railroad was abandoned, it became a dwelling at another location.

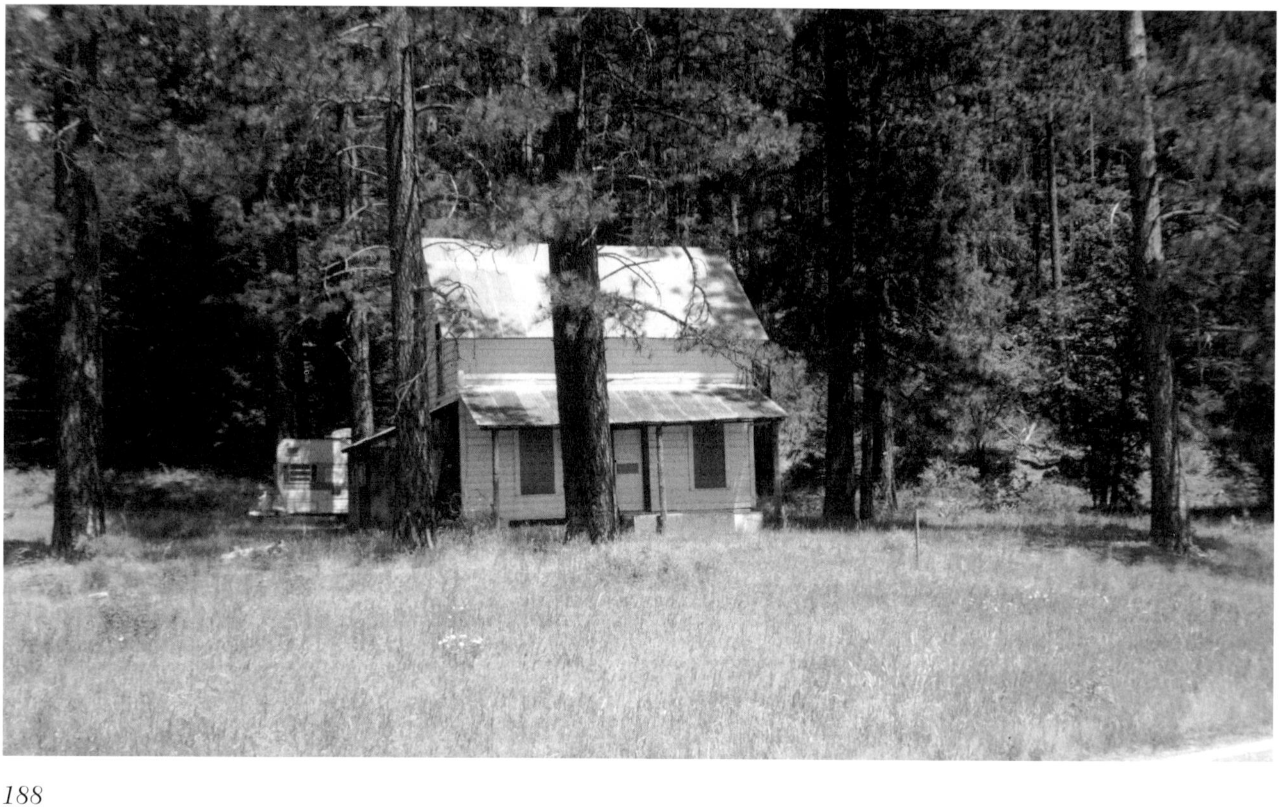

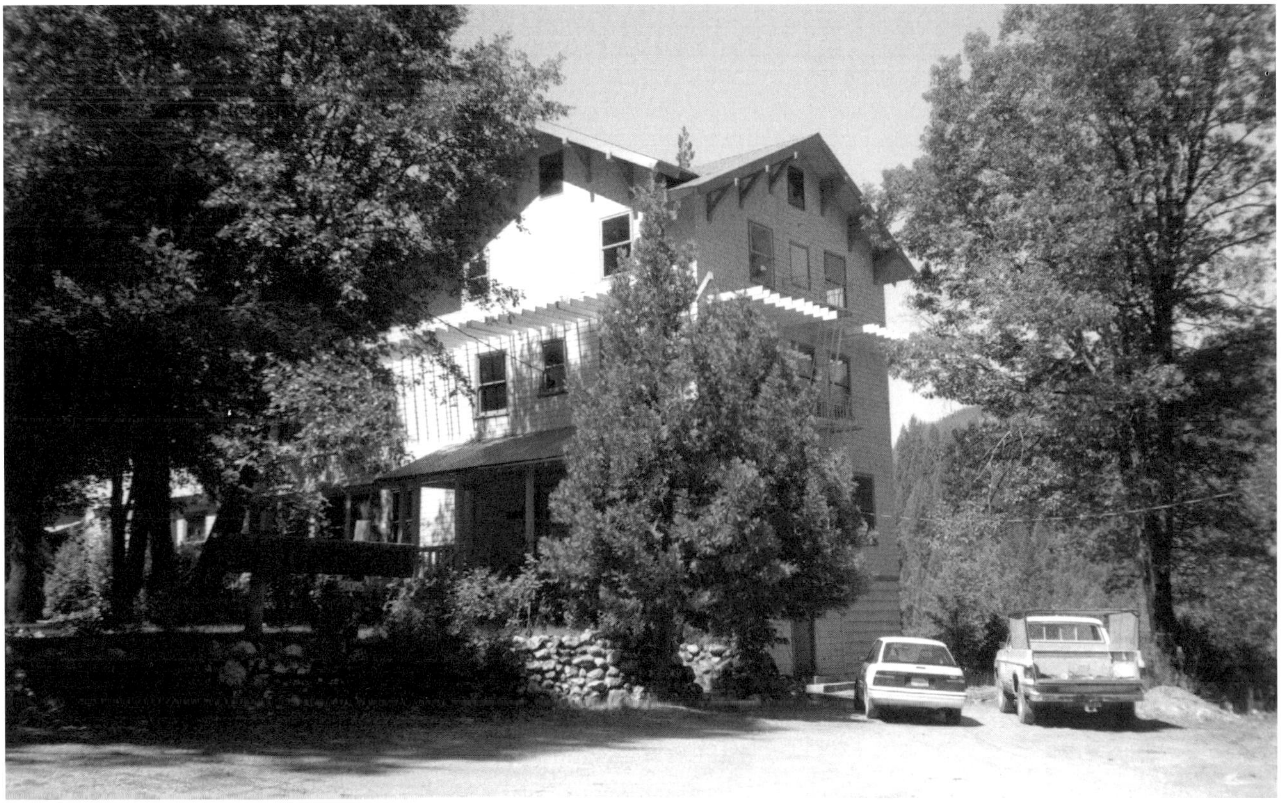

Above: A contemporary view of the hotel at Paxton.

Below: For assistance in handling derailments and roadwork, the railroad made use of this crane. (Bert Ward collection)

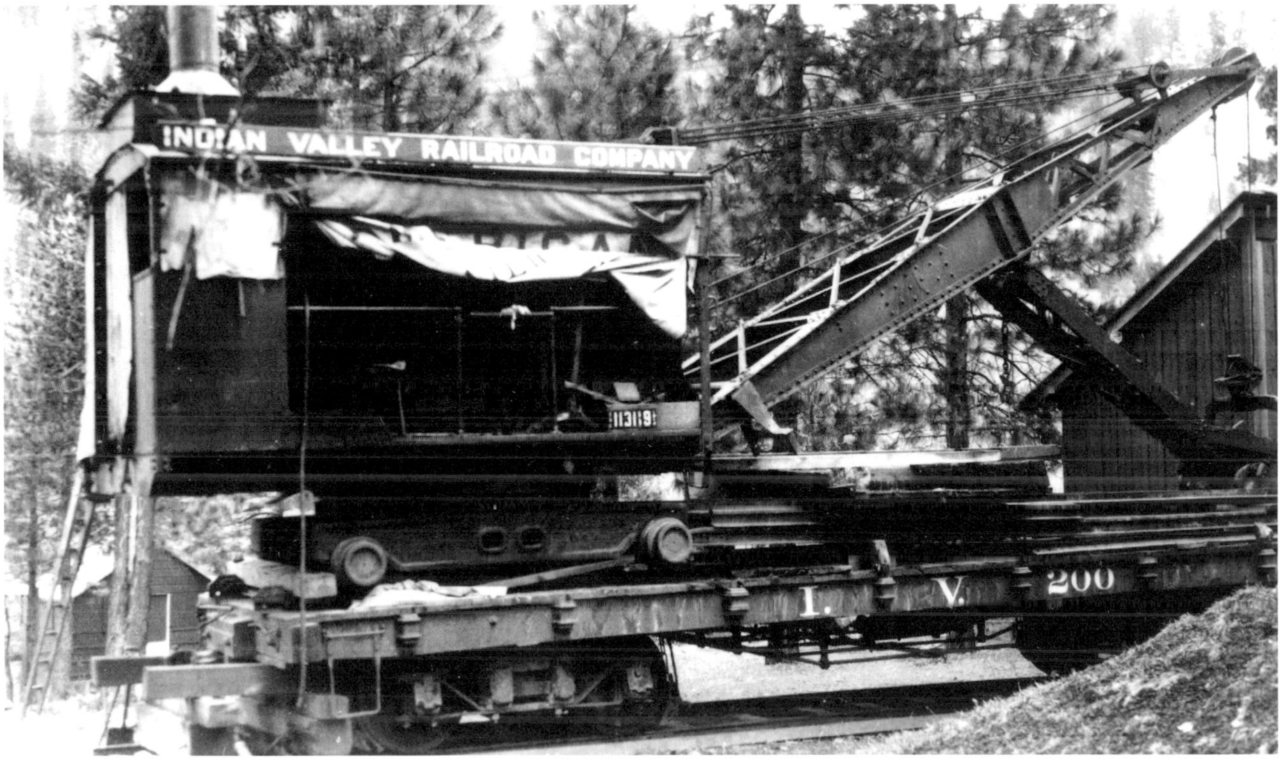

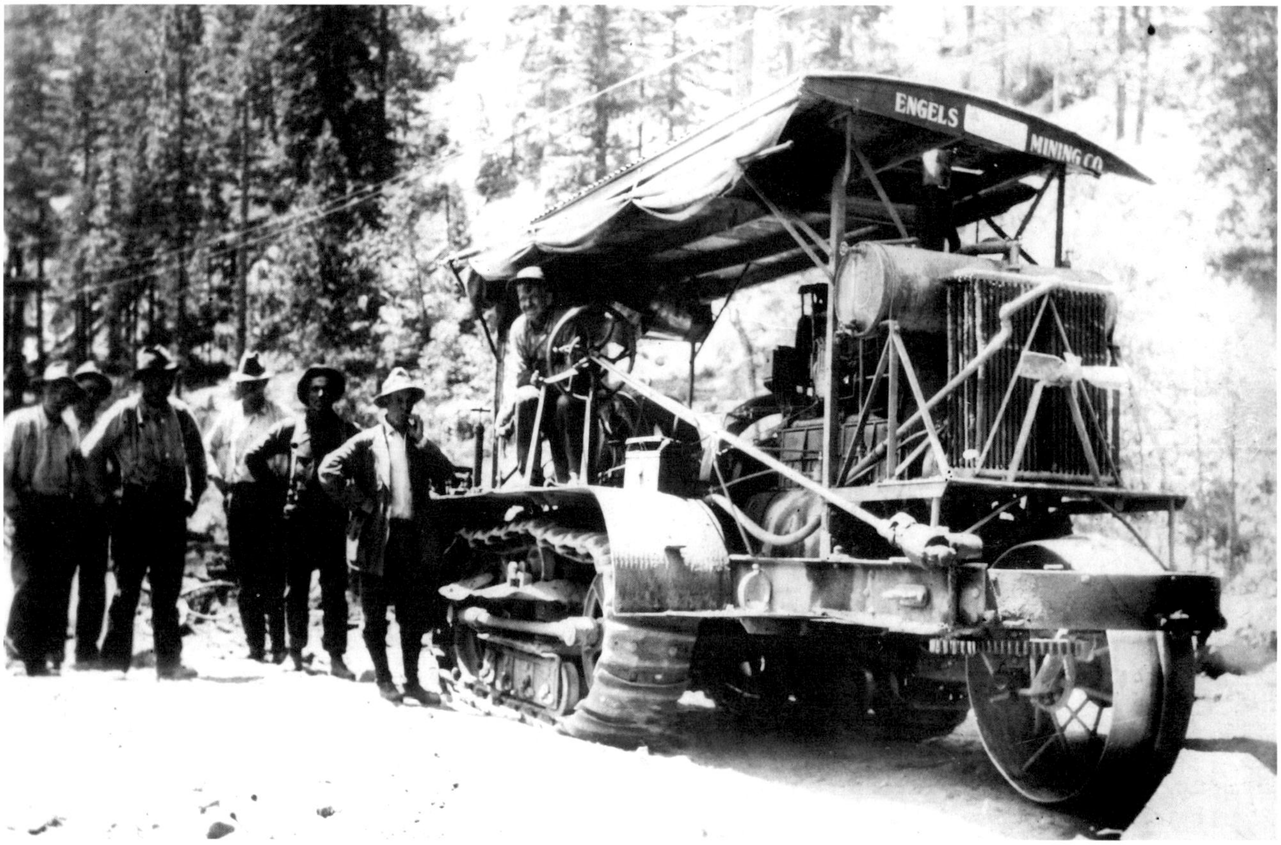

Above: Moving copper ore and concentrates from Engelmine to the Western Pacific was done under difficult conditions before the railroad to Paxton was built. For a short time, the company used this tractor to haul wagons to a relay point where teams continued the haul to Keddie. (Plumas County Museum)

Below: To simulate the color of copper, this stock certificate was printed with black ink on orange paper. (Norman Lamb collection)

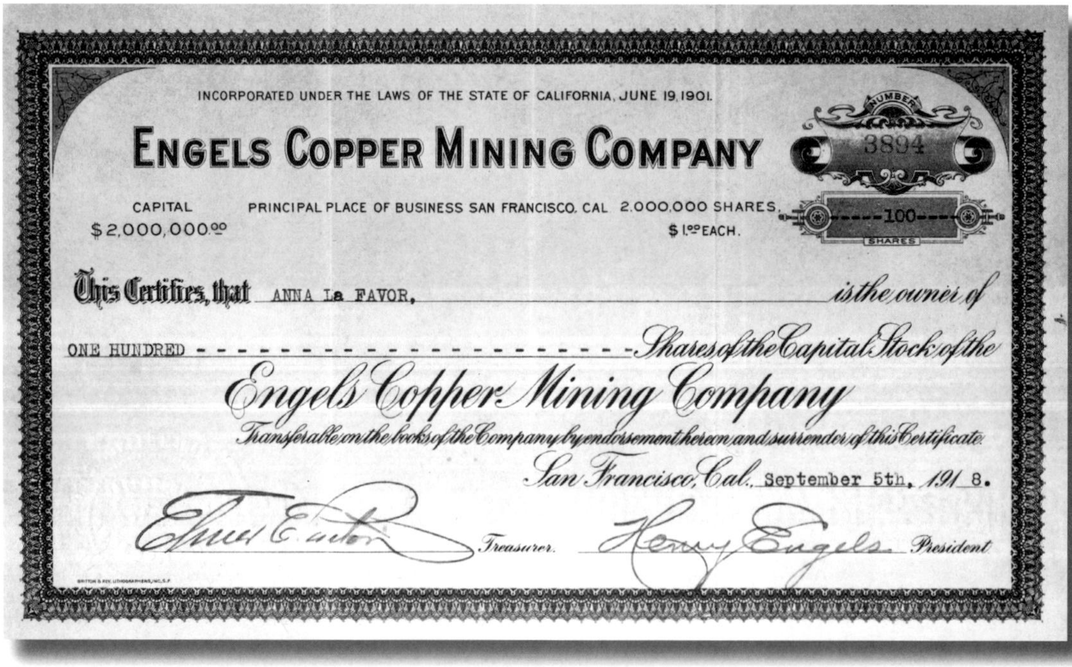

INCORPORATED UNDER THE LAWS OF THE STATE OF CALIFORNIA, JUNE 19, 1901.

ENGELS COPPER MINING COMPANY

NUMBER 3894

CAPITAL $2,000,000.00 — PRINCIPAL PLACE OF BUSINESS SAN FRANCISCO, CAL — 2,000,000 SHARES, $1.00 EACH.

SHARES 100

This Certifies, that ANNA La FAVOR, is the owner of ONE HUNDRED Shares of the Capital Stock of the

Engels Copper Mining Company

Transferable on the books of the Company by endorsement hereon and surrender of this Certificate.

San Francisco, Cal., September 5th, 1918.

Treasurer. Henry Engels President

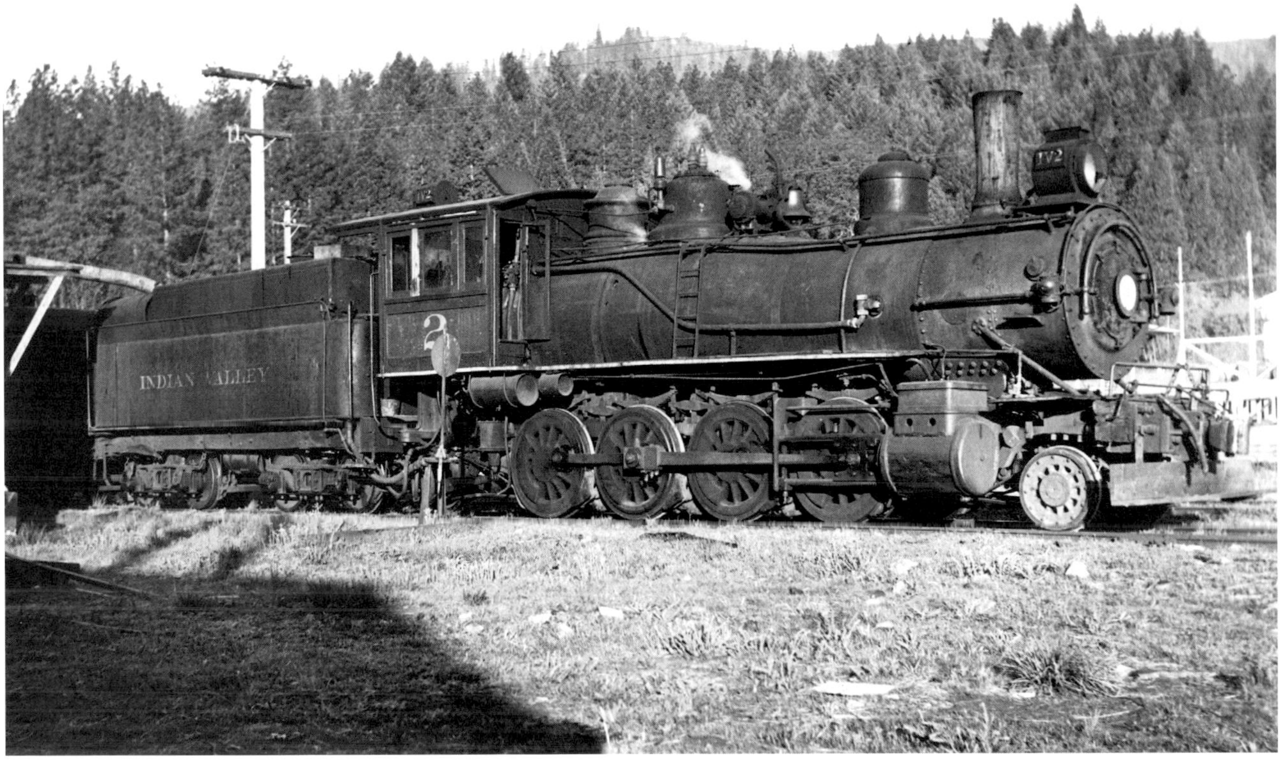

In May 1939, No. 2 was performing the last rites for the Indian Valley Railroad as it participated in the track removal. Jack Gibson photographed it at Crescent Mills as the tender took on water. (James E. Boynton collection)

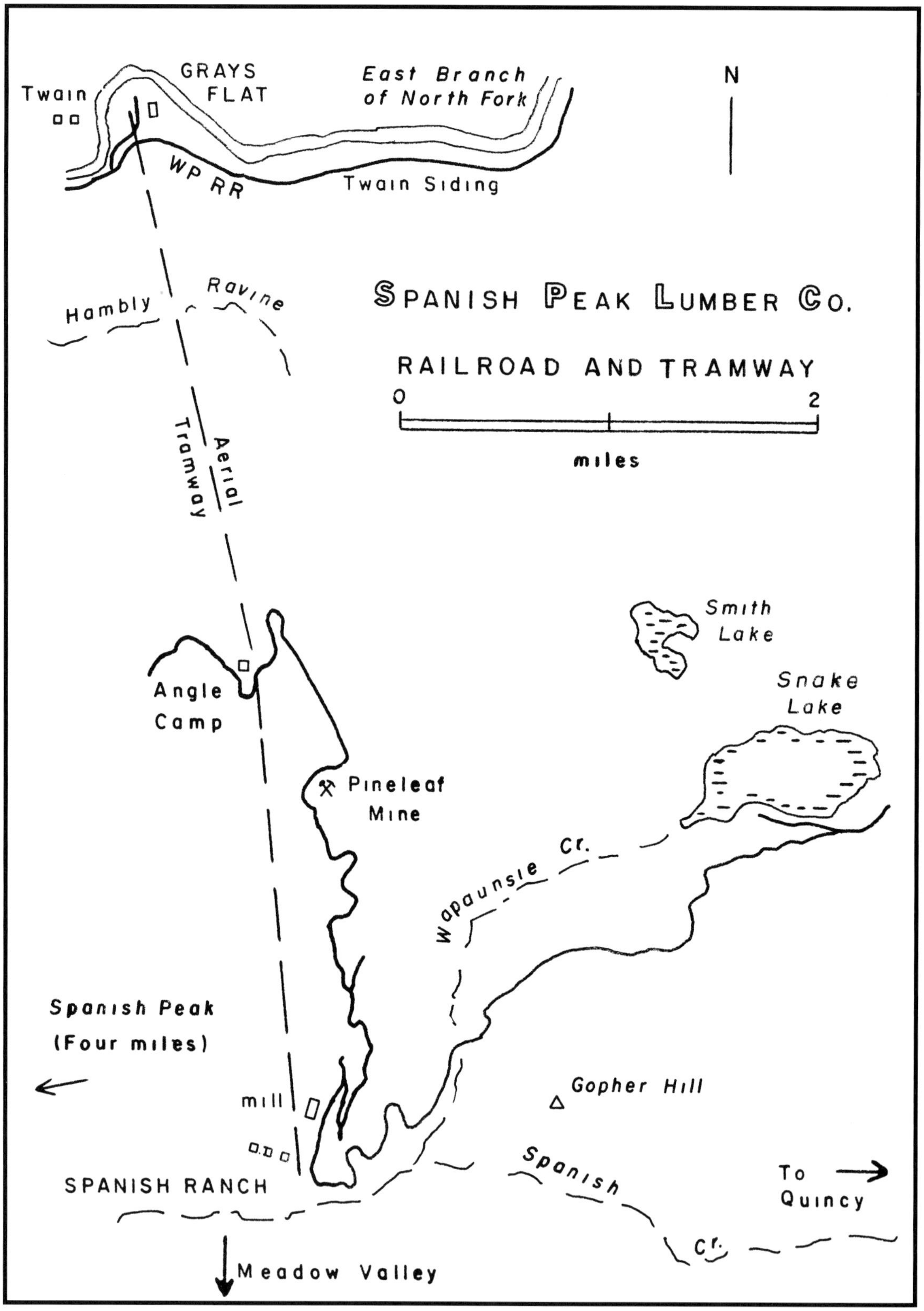
Spanish Peak Lumber Co.
Railroad and Tramway
0
2
miles
N
Twain
GRAYS FLAT
East Branch of North Fork
WP RR
Twain Siding
Hambly Ravine
Aerial Tramway
Smith Lake
Snake Lake
Angle Camp
Pineleaf Mine
Wapaunsie Cr.
Spanish Peak (Four miles)
Gopher Hill
mill
SPANISH RANCH
Spanish Cr.
To Quincy
Meadow Valley

SPANISH PEAK LUMBER COMPANY

Spanish Peak, rising to a lofty 7,107 feet, stands foremost in the mountain barrier standing on the west side of Meadow Valley, which in turn embraces a pleasant alpine land six miles west of Quincy, California. Actually two communities, Spanish Ranch and Meadow Valley, two miles south, became blended into one. Spanish Creek drains the area; nearby, this creek is bridged by Western Pacific where the last spike was driven in 1909.

Spanish Ranch had its beginnings in the summer of 1850 when two Mexicans took on the care of horses and mules belonging to busy gold miners. As a sideline, the two men also raised cattle, selling beef to the hungry men. A community blossomed the next year with a store, three hotels, and, of course, three saloons.

Meadow Valley residents boasted about their post office, the first in the valley when established in 1855. Six years later this service moved to Spanish Ranch, and whatever smug expressions prevailed after this event diminished three years later after restoration of the post office at Meadow Valley. Within two decades, the latter community's economic base afforded a blacksmith, a shoemaker, a sawmill, and the Meadow Valley Inn. Prior to its loss in a fire on December 6, 1923, the inn had been owned by Leslie J. Stratton since 1906 when he arrived from Santa Cruz. The inn was rebuilt.

Placer mining and later hydraulic mining supported the area for many years, and numerous rock ditches carried water long distances. On Gopher and Shores Hills, the Quincy Mining and Water Company conducted hydraulic operations in the mid-1890s, tapping Wapaunsie Creek. On the other side of Spanish Ranch, the Silver Star hydraulic mine drew its water from Silver Creek, two miles away.

Hydraulic mining in California came under the control of the California Debris Commission in 1893. As deputy debris commissioner, William B. Storey spent several weeks at Spanish Ranch checking the debris dams. Returning to railroad work in 1895, he served as chief engineer, first on a Santa Fe subsidiary and then on the Santa Fe system before becoming president in 1920.

Towle Brothers

Allen Towle had arrived in California from Vermont in 1851; five years later he set up a sawmill at Dutch Flat and was joined by his brothers, George W. and Edwin. Not far from Dutch Flat, Central Pacific established Towle station. The Towle brothers' business prospered, and by 1882 their narrow-gauge logging railroad extended seventeen miles into Bear Canyon. Later it measured thirty-five miles into timberlands.

The opening of Western Pacific invited major lumber entrepreneurs to Plumas and Lassen Counties. In June 1912, George W. Towle purchased the Hazzard holdings consisting of eleven hundred acres of excellent timber (Plumas Imperial Mining Tract) along with placer ditches and a dam in Dean's Valley, some four miles south of Spanish Ranch. Towle hired W. W. Lane to construct a sawmill, which cut the first logs in May 1914. C. W. Blakesley's four-horse team hauled finished lumber to Quincy and provided welcome revenue to the struggling short-line railroad. Indicative of changing transportation methods, Towle also used a gasoline-powered truck that carried three times as much lumber as the teams on its trips to the Quincy Western Railway depot. Towle's activity in this area was relatively brief, as he died two years later.

Residents in the Quincy area sensed a coming development the next spring when O. C. Haslett of Alameda on San Francisco Bay and Duane L. Bliss Jr. spent several days tramping around Meadow Valley. Bliss, a member of the Glenbrook lumbering family, managed the Truckee Lumber Company. Even as the Spanish Peak Lumber Company (SPLC) was incorporated on July 17, 1915, Bliss had twenty men doing preliminary work for the large sawmill. Bliss headed the new company; besides Haslett, the board of directors included Wendell P. Hammon, a mining entrepreneur, and two San Francisco attorneys.

The Connection to Western Pacific

Transportation to Western Pacific would take the form of a five-mile aerial tramway from the sawmill to Gray's Flat (Twain) where Bliss purchased 120 acres of land for the tramway terminal and planing mill. This acquisition closed the chances of extending the Quincy Western Railway to Meadow Valley.

The new company issued stock to Hammon and S. A. Moss to acquire timberland and also purchased other lands from a Mr. Stokes. W. C. Robinson of Tollgate (about three miles west of Meadow Valley on the Bucks Ranch road) commenced sawing timber at his small plant for the Spanish Peak sawmill.

William Watson and his son Arthur made the final survey for the tramway, and Bliss signed a contract with U.S. Steel Products Company in early October 1915 by which the steel company furnished necessary materials at $35,536, payable in four installments. A Pelton waterwheel powered the operation because Gray's Flat stood about six hundred feet lower than Spanish Ranch; the downward movement "encouraged" lumber to flow to the planing mill. When crossing five hundred feet over Hambly Ravine, the distance between towers measured twenty-eight hundred feet.

Construction activity at Spanish Ranch occupied the temperate months of 1916. J. E. Sibley of Oroville did everything in his power to complete the building to house the big saw by April 1. Water from Silver Lake flowed down Silver Creek and a ditch patrolled by Philip McElroy. Machinery began arriving in Quincy via the connecting line, but, even before the mill started operations, three men were injured when the driver of a company truck, going too fast, went off the road at Limekiln pitch.

The log pond began filling with timber, and by the middle of August the sawmill's cut totaled sixty thousand to seventy thousand board feet each day. At this time, WP installed a spur at Gray's Flat, and Bliss dispatched lumber by team to the Quincy Western Railway, which turned the cars of lumber over to WP for the haul to the planing mill at Gray's Flat (Twain).

Tramway construction proceeded slowly. By the summer when the sawmill began work, some of the towers rose in Meadow Valley, and the foundations were ready near Gray's Flat. Finally, on Saturday, the last day of September 1916, workers finished the tramway, and it promptly met its purpose. Gathered together in bundles of five hundred board feet, transit for the bundles to reach Twain required one hour. The weather that year enabled timber operations to continue as late as early December before closing for the winter.

Seasonal operations followed a general pattern of most members of the Feather River Pine Association (formed June 4, 1917). Weather conditions dictated the time logging began and ended; in normal years, the snow had vanished by April and did not return until October or November. Lumber prices as well as demand for fruit-packing boxes or home construction also influenced the time spent working in the forests.

E. D. Baldwin, who stepped in as general manager after Bliss left in 1921 to enter the hardware business in San Francisco, faced a terrible fire season in 1923, the worst in the Plumas area since 1917. Lumber production was seriously curtailed as loggers switched to fighting fires—one each day for nine days. Fire lookouts reported seven fires on one Sunday. Another hardworking crew built a concrete dry kiln near the mill that lasted longer than any of the other structures. One observer noted the absence of sawdust piles and stacks of lumber, the reasons being that sawdust was fed to the boilers and that all sawn lumber went over the tramway to the planing mill at Twain.

The vision of lumber flying in the sky attracted widespread attention. After reading articles in trade magazines, Arizona lumbermen arrived in the spring of 1922 and again in August the following year to inspect the tramway. They returned to build a somewhat similar line on the north side of Mt. Graham, near Pima, Arizona, and also enticed several local men to go with them. The fact that the cable broke without warning and snapped to injure the head of a worker between their visits failed to dampen their interest.

The Logging Railroad

Since 1920, the logging contractor for the Spanish Peak Lumber Company used three large Fageol trucks to haul logs to the sawmill. Another truck handled lumber. In the early spring of 1925, Bob Nicholson rounded up a crew to clear wagon roads for logging, which was soon followed by surveys for a railroad commencing in May. In taking this step, SPLC joined neighboring companies building logging railroads for the first time in the 1920s. Beginning at the mill, the railroad ran north and west for 4.5 miles to Camp 4. Without physical connections with other lines, the logging trucks took on added responsibilities. After hauling logs during the day, they transported rail from Quincy to the site during night hours. Jim Ryan, in charge of the woods crew, had a good portion working on a Sunday in June hauling material and equipment to the new railroad. Jim's direction proved effective, and at the time of the seasonal shutdown in mid-November, the grading stood almost finished and part of the track was in place.

Completed the next spring, with one Whitcomb gas engine on hand and another on order, the railroad was ready for business. The first train came down Pineleaf Canyon on April 30, 1926, with Oliver C. Haslett arriving that morning to witness the new operation. The happy day was marred when Floyd "Bud" Poindexter, log loader at Camp 4, was crushed between a large log and a flatcar. Painfully bruised, last reports had Bud getting along well at the Plumas Industrial Hospital. A week later, Jim Ryan was telling friends in Quincy that logs were moving over the railroad "without a hitch."

Frank Henspeter, a tramway operator, remained unaffected by the new railroad, even though new towers and tramline repairs took place. On the other hand, with logging of the McElroy property coming to an end, Camp 3 was gradually vacated as the men moved on to Camp 4. E. I. Lane purchased some of the idle camp buildings to house his workers at Bucks Meadow engaged in clearing the site for Bucks Lake. After one week as locomotive engineer, Nick Biever stepped aside in favor of A. A. Rogers, but for several days it made little difference, as a broken part and delay in securing a replacement from Stockton kept the engine housed in its shelter. The second Whitcomb gas engine was received about this time.

Locally, guests were crowding the rebuilt Meadow Valley Inn, and domestic troubles complicated the personal life of the female caretaker of the cemetery.

After washout damage had been repaired, the railroad began hauling logs to the sawmill in mid-April 1927. The blast of the mill whistle lent confidence to the workers and neighbors. In spite of the heavy rains that closed other mills, both Spanish Peak Lumber and Quincy Lumber extended the cutting season into the late fall. With timber around Camp 4 depleted, SPLC turned its attention to Snake Lake, which resulted in the relocation of the logging railroad.

The date of the opening of the new five-mile line is uncertain. One report had the mill closed for three days in October 1928 because of railroad construction to Camp 5 at Snake Lake, but this account may represent a construction milestone rather than completion.

The initial (1926) railroad running north from Spanish Ranch required a switchback immediately after passing the mill, and this grade remained visible for many years. A track continued a short distance south of the mill to the railroad shop. The logging shop, formerly at the fork of the road about a mile west of the mill, was not served by this railroad.

The new Snake Lake line ran around the hill to the west side of the small canyon formed by Wapaunsie Creek and crossed to the east side of the creek near the junction of the auto road to Whitlock Ridge. At first the railroad tapped lumber on the north side of the lake but later moved to the south side, from whence it continued to the upper part of Whitlock Ridge. In July 1929, the boys at Camp 5 were reported to be moving farther out to a new log landing, and harvesting continued late into the fall.

After the last of the kiln-dried lumber of the 1929 season moved over the tramway to Twain, foreman A. A. McElroy and his crew made necessary repairs to the tramway. The Caterpillar tractors were shopped for the 1930 season, which was shortened because of the slackened demand for lumber. A contributing factor to the October closing may have been the illness that struck O. C. Haslett while at Twain. First taken to a local hospital, he recovered sufficiently to be moved to his home in Alameda.

With the darkening economic clouds in the fall of 1930, the mill underwent its usual cleaning, and a crew built a new trestle for the railroad near Camp 5. The Sierra Box Company at Twain (Gray's Flat)—an important customer of the mill—felt the pinch too and closed down for three weeks around Christmas because of an absence of orders.

Logging operations commenced later than usual in 1931 with smaller crews and reduced wages. The tram cable had to be replaced, and this work involved splicing. In August, Kenneth Jacks was grading an extension to the railroad beyond Camp 5. How much of this extension was used is questionable because when the Spanish Peak Lumber Company resumed operations on a curtailed basis on May 16, 1932, the railroad remained shut down along with the camp at Snake Lake. Logging was confined to the area close to the sawmill, and after the usual repairs were made, timber went to Twain by tramway.

Bankruptcy in 1935

Things went from bad to worse. The mill remained closed for the next two years. Back in 1924, the company had issued $150,000 in bonds to finance property improvements. With the mill shut down, there was no income to cover the interest on this debt, on which the company defaulted on January 12, 1935. Accordingly, the property was sold at public auction on the courthouse steps in San Francisco to the Reliance Securities Company for fifty-five thousand dollars. Payment was made with ten thousand in cash and forty-five thousand dollars' principal amount of the defaulted bonds.

Reliance Securities Company (the name was changed to Meadow Valley Lumber Company on June 28, 1935) had the backing of prominent California people such as C. C. Young, former governor; Louis Breuner, an Oakland furniture dealer; Earl L. Miller, vice president of the Golden State Company, a milk company; Jack Atthowe, operator of the Berkeley Transportation Company; and Will F. Morrish, former head of the Bank of America who became the initial president of the new lumber company.

The Meadow Valley Lumber Company acquired the timberlands of the former Spanish Peak Lumber Company, the lumber mill, the narrow-gauge railroad, and the famed aerial tramway. Also included in the sale were mining claims and reservoirs along Rock and Slate Creeks that had been purchased from the Towle Estate Company on December 26, 1922. These properties included the Orr

(Dean Valley) Reservoir and the three-mile Orr ditch to the Quigley Ravine claim and the shorter Rock Creek ditch, both previously serving long-forgotten mining claims.

The railroad, probably not used after the 1931 logging season, was scrapped by the Sterling Silver Company about 1935, with the material being hauled out over Bucks Lake road, then the only western outlet. The aerial tram, becoming proportionately more expensive to operate, ceased operating with the end of the 1939 season. Trucks of the Atthowe Transportation Company provided substitute service to Twain.

In 1941, the Meadow Valley Lumber Company bought a site from W. W. Bell, a rancher, in what is now East Quincy and erected a planing mill, dry kiln, and box factory. Opened in 1942, Meadow Valley trucks brought sawn timber from Spanish Ranch to the mill. Ray C. Smith, general manager since 1939 and president and general manager from 1953 until his retirement eleven years later, had long urged moving the sawmill machinery to East Quincy. Finally, an announcement appeared in November 1963 that the relocation would be made. On April 14, 1964, an old thirty-five-inch cedar log, used as a pond-barrier boom, had the honor of being the last log cut at the Spanish Ranch mill, now almost fifty years old. The time was 11:20 A.M., and the men cleaned up and then left at noon. After lunch, only eight men returned to begin the task of dismantling the machinery, preparatory to moving it to East Quincy.

On August 25, about four months later, two test logs rolled through the East Quincy sawmill, and regular production began the following week. The benefits of modernization became evident as twenty men in the new plant could saw 25 percent more lumber than the old mill at Spanish Ranch did with thirty-two men.

Late Friday night, June 25, 1965, flames suddenly enveloped the old three-story, two hundred–foot-long structure at Spanish Ranch and created a glow visible for twenty miles. The end had come at last.

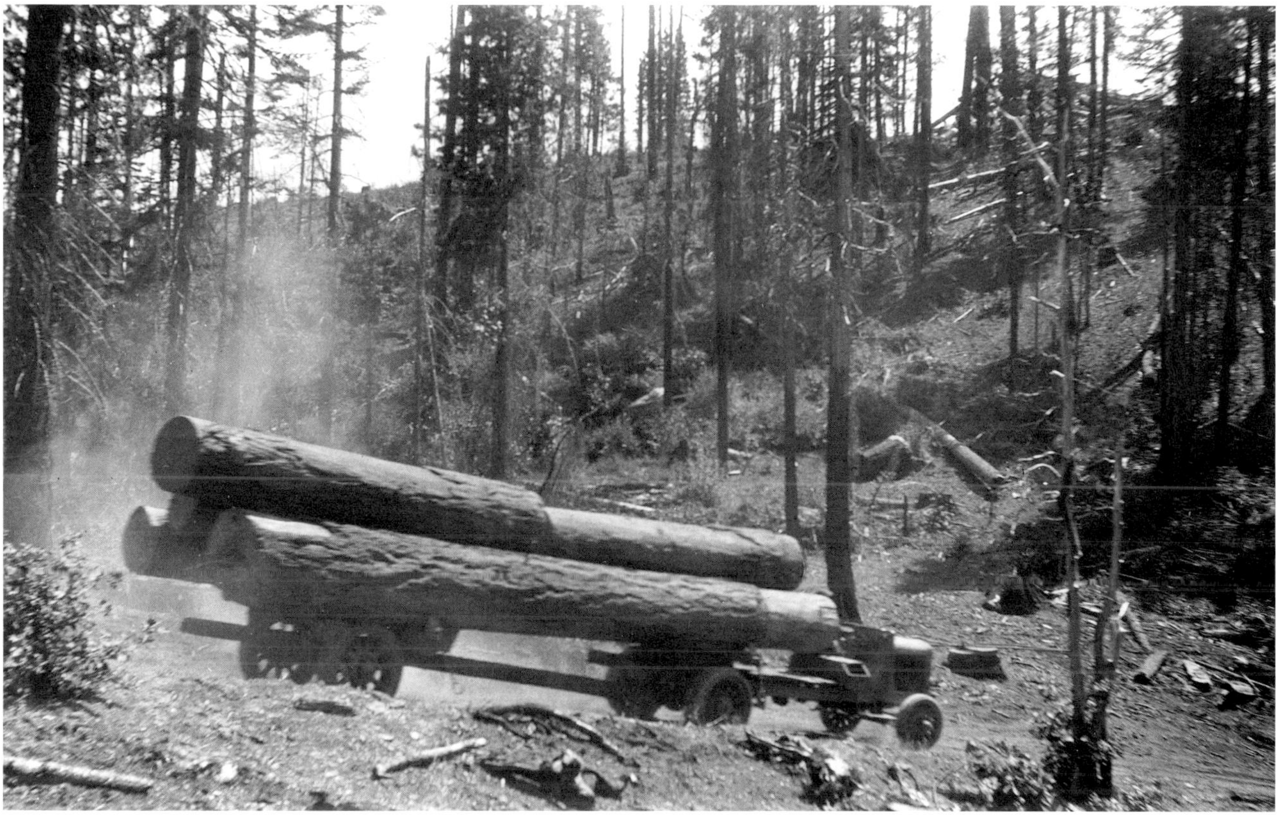

As late as 1925, the Spanish Peak Lumber Company relied on Mack trucks to bring logs to the sawmill. (R. C. Bryant photograph, Ted Wurm collection)

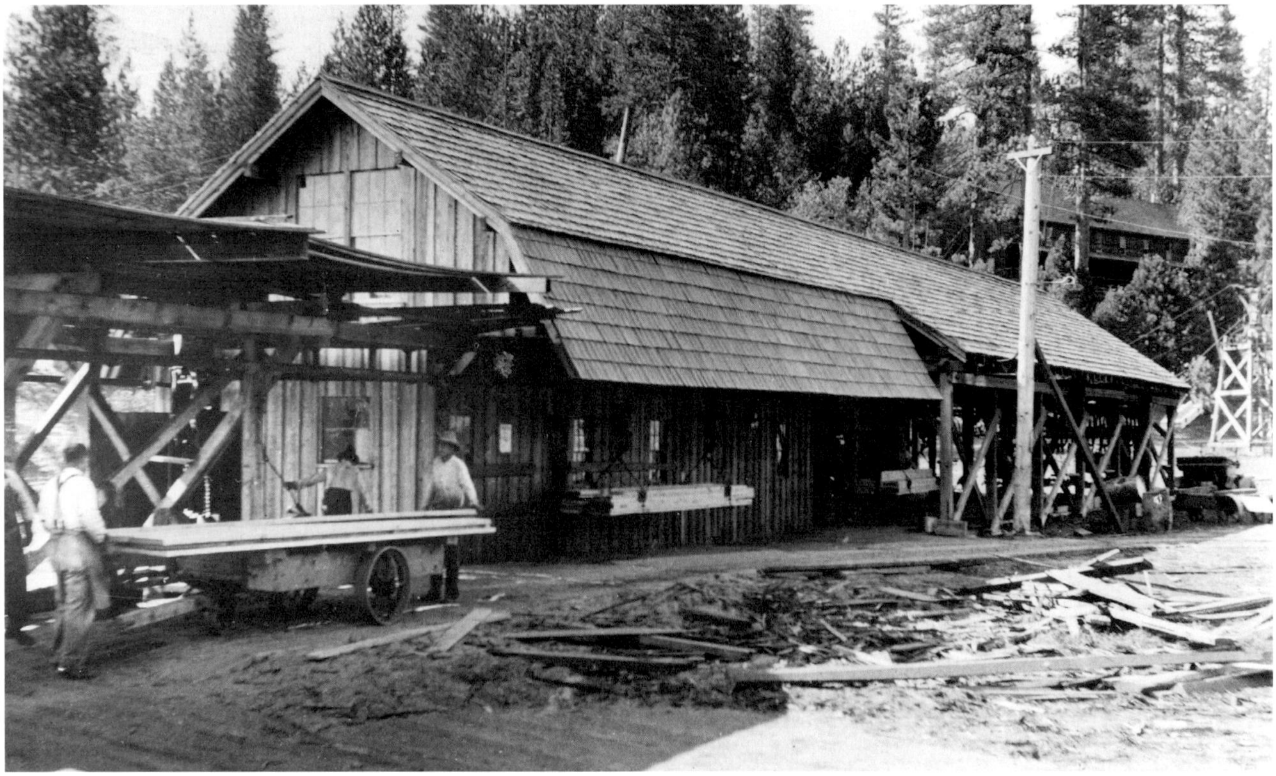

At the terminal, men bundled the lumber into a "package" (*center*) and sent it on its way. The aerial tramway continued to transport lumber for nearly two decades. (Ted Wurm collection)

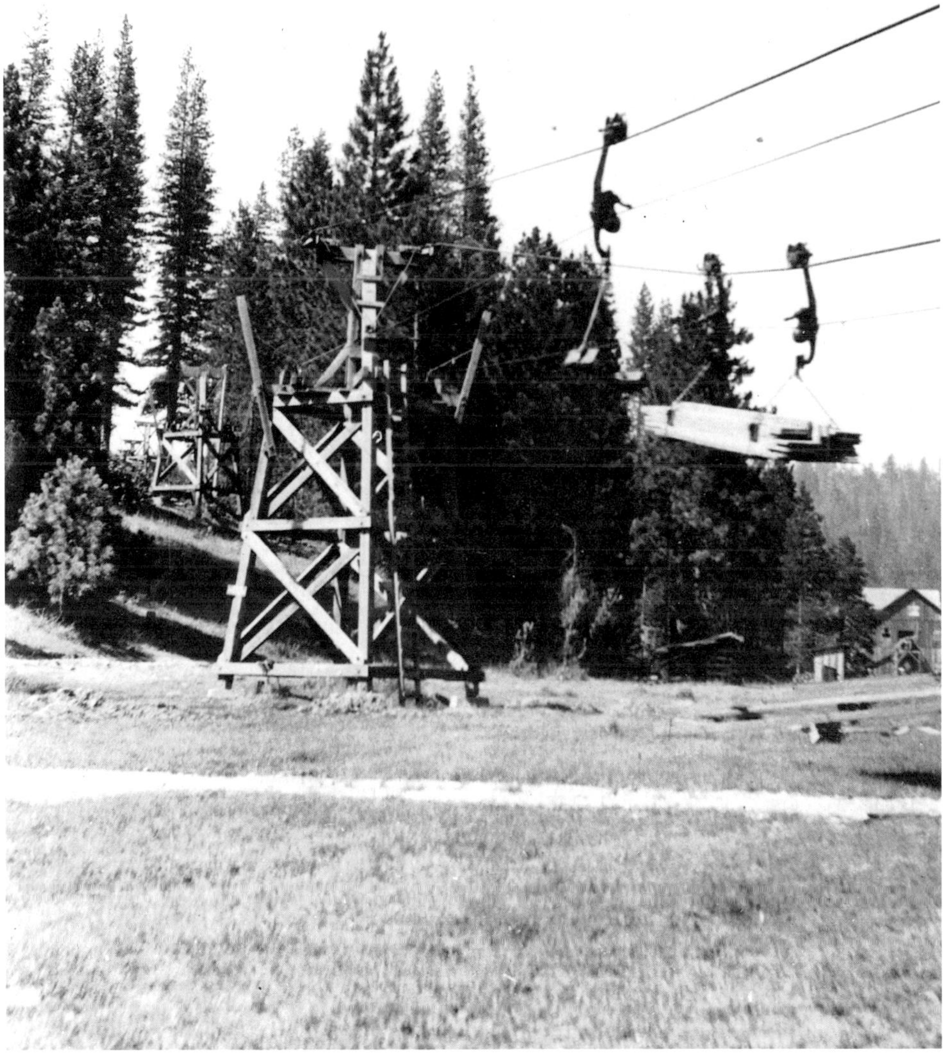

Sturdy wood towers supported the cables conveying lumber through the woods. (Ted Wurm collection)

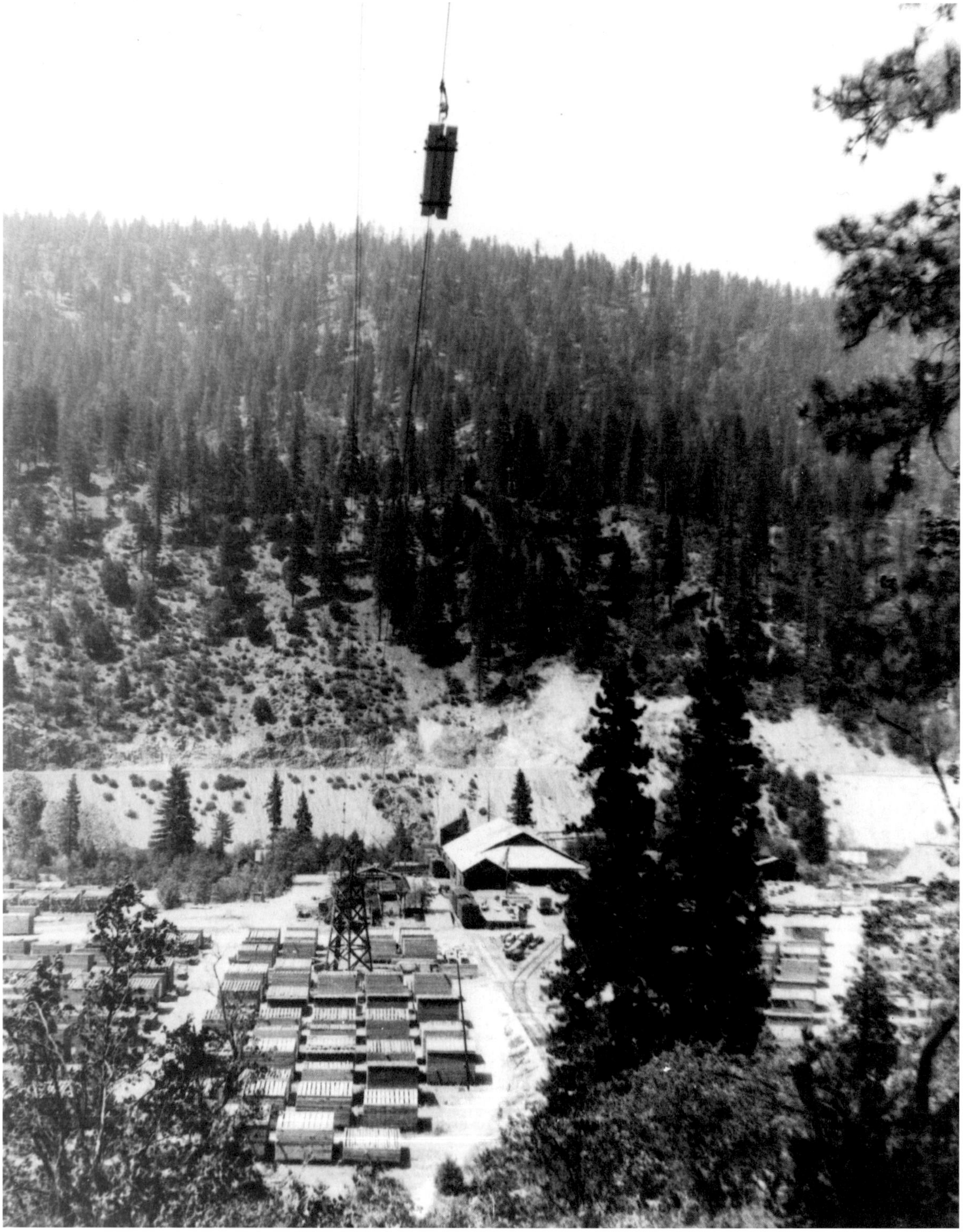

After surmounting the ridge, loads descended to the planing mill and storage yard of the Spanish Peak Lumber Company at Gray's Flat along the East Branch of the North Fork of the Feather River. (Plumas County Museum)

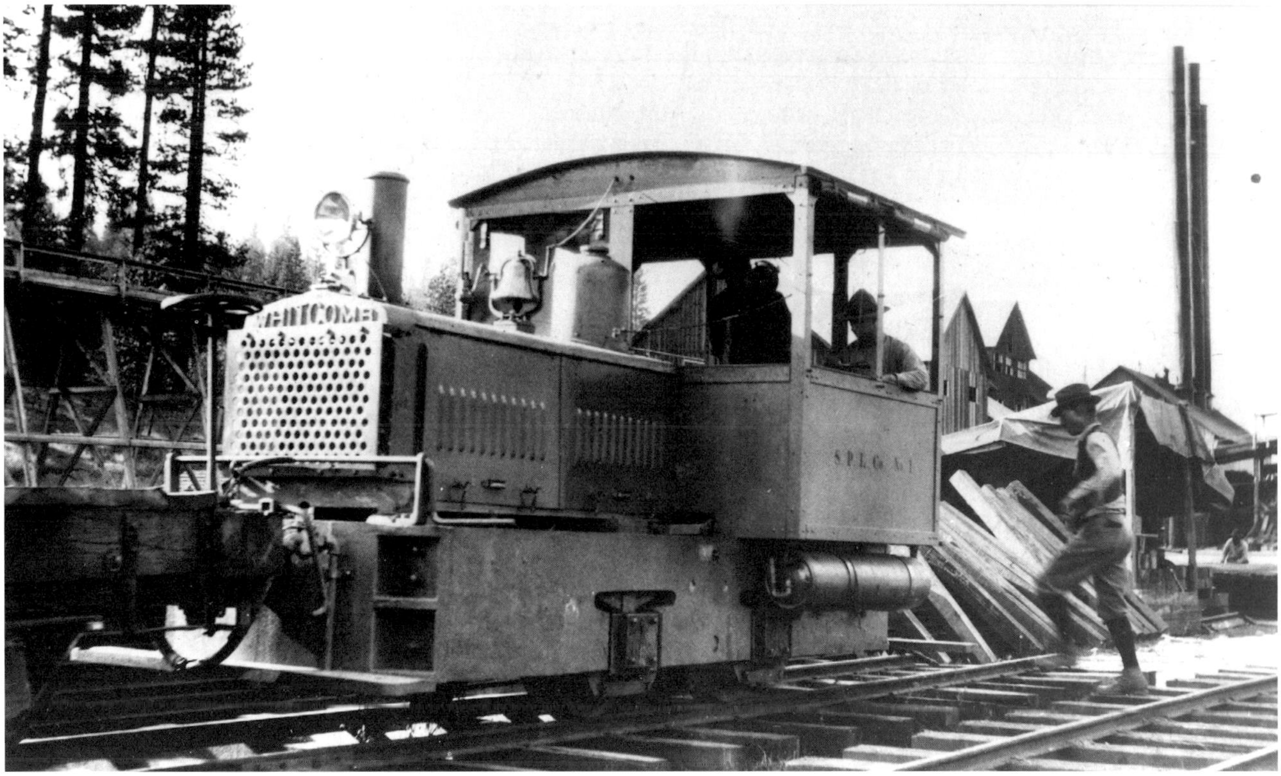

Above: A gasoline locomotive shunted cars around the mill. (Ted Wurm collection)

Below: The logging railroad went by the log pond as it headed for the woods. (Plumas County Museum)

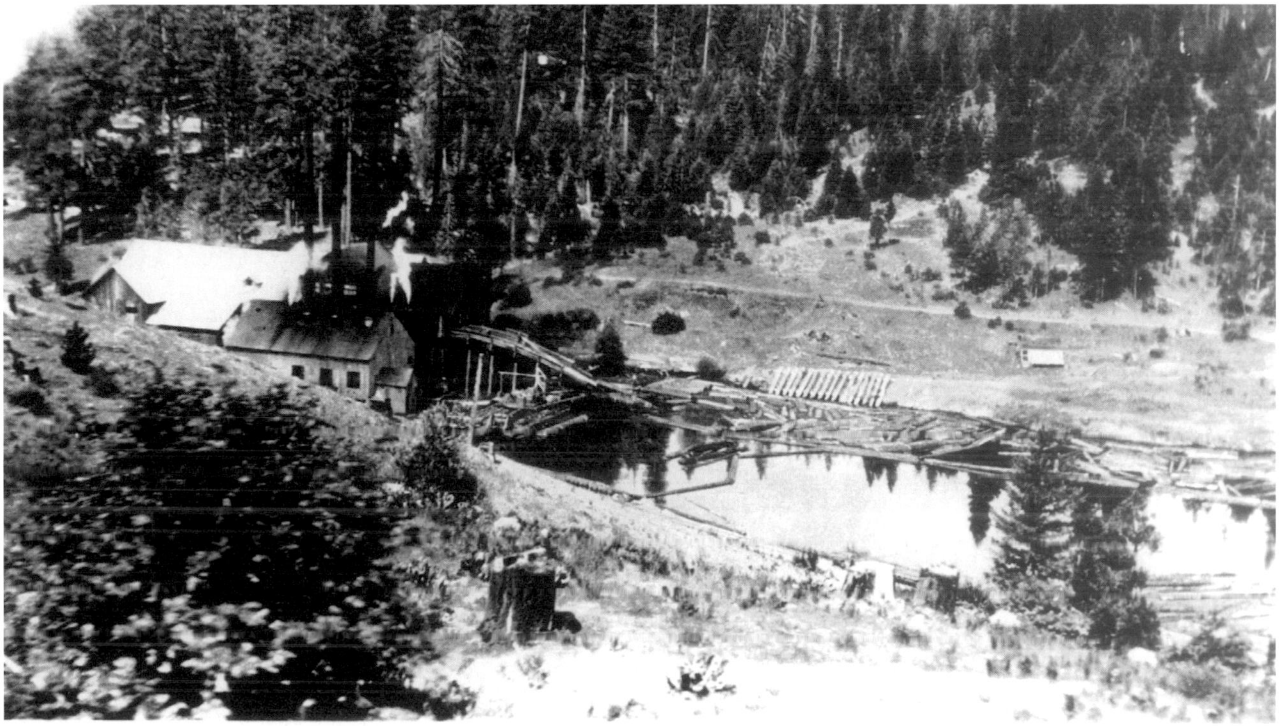

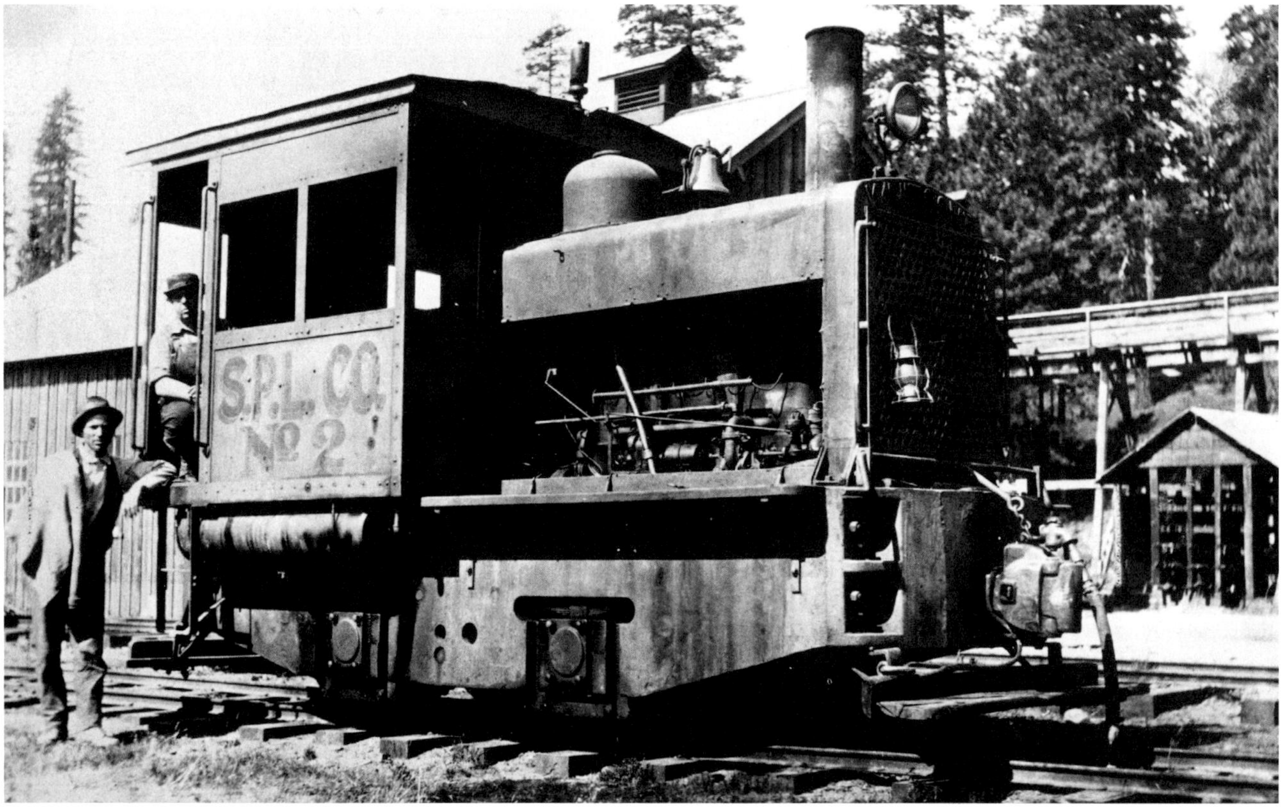

A second gas locomotive, this time with an enclosed cab, replaced the original motive power. In later ownership, the locomotive was converted to standard gauge with this off-center appearance when it operated at the Alameda Naval Stores at Dublin, California. In 2001, this locomotive was returned to Quincy where volunteers are working to restore the appearance. (Ted Wurm collection)

QUINCY LUMBER COMPANY
F. S. MURPHY LUMBER COMPANY

Although lumbermen had harvested timber around the American Valley since early times, primarily this lumber served local needs for houses, barns, and stores. During the winter of 1852–1853, D. R. Cate, J. S. Boyington, and D. W. Judkins established a small mill on what became Mill Creek. Two years later Cate and Judkins erected a mill on their New England Ranch. About a mile west of Quincy, Florin Gansner built a mill in 1878.

The opening of the Western Pacific Railroad in 1910, along with the connecting Quincy Western Railway, encouraged larger lumber operations, as railroads widely expanded their markets.

Frank S. Murphy of Salt Lake City headed the Quincy Lumber Company, which he incorporated in Utah on August 9, 1913, with modest capital of fifty thousand dollars. Other Salt Lake City men in the firm included Charles W. Nibley (vice president), Seth W. Morrison (treasurer), Charles E. Murphy, and James Ingebretson (secretary). Nibley (1849–1925), born in Scotland, served the Church of Jesus Christ of Latter-day Saints as a prominent official for most of his life and also invested in sugar, lumber, and railroads. Morrison came to Utah from Wisconsin in 1890, dealt in wholesale lumber, and took an active part in local politics. Charles Murphy and Frank Murphy were brothers and managed the Utah Lumber Company. Ingebretson's career included a law partnership with Joel Nibley, a relative of C. W. Nibley.

Down the North Fork, Clark Staniford, after selling the Chino Mill to H. H. Yard in 1903, continued to manage it for a time. Subsequently, he created Camp Enjoyment as a summer home subdivision that was followed by the formation of the Butte County Land and Lumber Company. He erected a mill and, similar to the adjoining Swayne Lumber Company, also built a tramway to Blinzig, a station on Western Pacific twenty-three miles above Oroville, and reached his timberlands using a steam-traction engine. Things did not go well, and in 1913 Staniford lost his mill in a foreclosure sale. Murphy took advantage of the distressed sale and purchased the sawmill machinery. A month later the machinery rested at Marston (later Quincy Jct.), pending completion of a spur from the Quincy Western Railway to the mill site near the present Quincy High School.

In the weeks that followed, the two-story structure, 132 x 30 feet, took form and housed the sawing machinery. Murphy arrived to guide the construction of a log chute reaching up from the mill into Hangman's Ravine for a half mile. Two tall iron stacks confirmed the location of the boiler house, and, in recognition of the first test log to run through the mill, the company planned a banquet for its employees at the Plumas House.

With the mill ready for work in December, men commenced logging, but winter storms negated steady work. Good news came after the start of the new year (1914) when the mill received a substantial order for railroad cross ties. The first shipment of three thousand ties to Nevada in March boosted the slim revenues of the QW Railway. Payday soon followed, but the celebration ended in a general brawl at the Grand Central Saloon in which one of the intoxicated men landed in the hospital with a fractured skull.

In the spring, the lumber company added a box factory and a planing mill and, in spite of the sluggish market, enjoyed a strong backlog of orders. The box factory proved to be a major factor in Quincy's economy in 1915, as the company sought more men for both the planing mill and the box factory. During August, by putting the men on overtime, the company boosted its production and shipped forty cars, a boon for the Quincy Western. Railroad ties continued to be in demand.

The following year Quincy Lumber purchased 480 acres from H. C. Flournoy and others in Dublin Jack Meadows, about two miles west of town. At the same time, Quincy Lumber tapped a new cutting area near the H. T. Johnson Ranch in the American Valley. Taking off from the Quincy Western about four miles east of town, the lumber company's one-mile spur was expected to carry about thirty thousand feet of logs every day for a short period.

That summer, the lumber company took steps to tap the forest in Dublin Jack Meadows with a crew of twelve men commencing work on the log chutes in the area. Meanwhile, QW Railway workers prepared the roadbed for the new rail extension of one and a half miles. In November, with the suspension of the timber harvest by the Thompson Ranch, crews pulled the rails and relaid them on the line to Dublin Jack Meadows. A donkey engine followed the rails to the new location.

Murphy found himself more involved in the railroad business when the Quincy Western Railway threatened to cease operations. As it provided the vital initial portion of the outlet to distant markets for his lumber, Murphy acquired it on November 5, 1917.

F. S. Murphy Lumber Company

Murphy engaged in a major expansion as 1918 began when he formed the F. S. Murphy Lumber Company on February 13. The capital of six hundred thousand dollars enabled the new firm to acquire the Quincy Lumber Company, the Sloat Lumber Company, and the White Pine Lumber Company. William Y. Stoddard and his brother Merrill Y. Stoddard, both Quincy lumbermen, participated in the new organization along with Henry M. Feiss, brother-in-law of Harry A. Turner of Sloat.

During 1919, the Murphy company began using trucks in its logging work, and when one loaded truck turned over it claimed the life of one worker. However, this accident did not deter the continued use of trucks in some operations.

In the same year, the company returned to the Thompson Ranch area as its source of lumber. This time the company created a camp with a bunkhouse, cookhouse, and small cottages for family men.

Late in 1920, C. J. Lee sold six million feet of timber in Butterfly Valley adjoining the existing eighteen hundred acres of Murphy land. Surveys followed, but several years went by before any railroad construction began.

As always, logging remained subject to the vagaries of the seasons. When woods boss Claude Maynard opened the 1922 season in early April, snowdrifts retarded his work. Still, the company continued to expand its facilities by adding a dry kiln. A test run indicated the kiln could dry logs in five days versus eight weeks using former methods.

In July 1924, after successfully combating a major fire near the Thompson Ranch, the Murphy company opened a new timber tract on Peppard Flat. Again a spur from the Quincy Railroad started near the Pioneer School in East Quincy and pointed south along Mill Creek. Reaching the timber at the top of the mountain challenged the

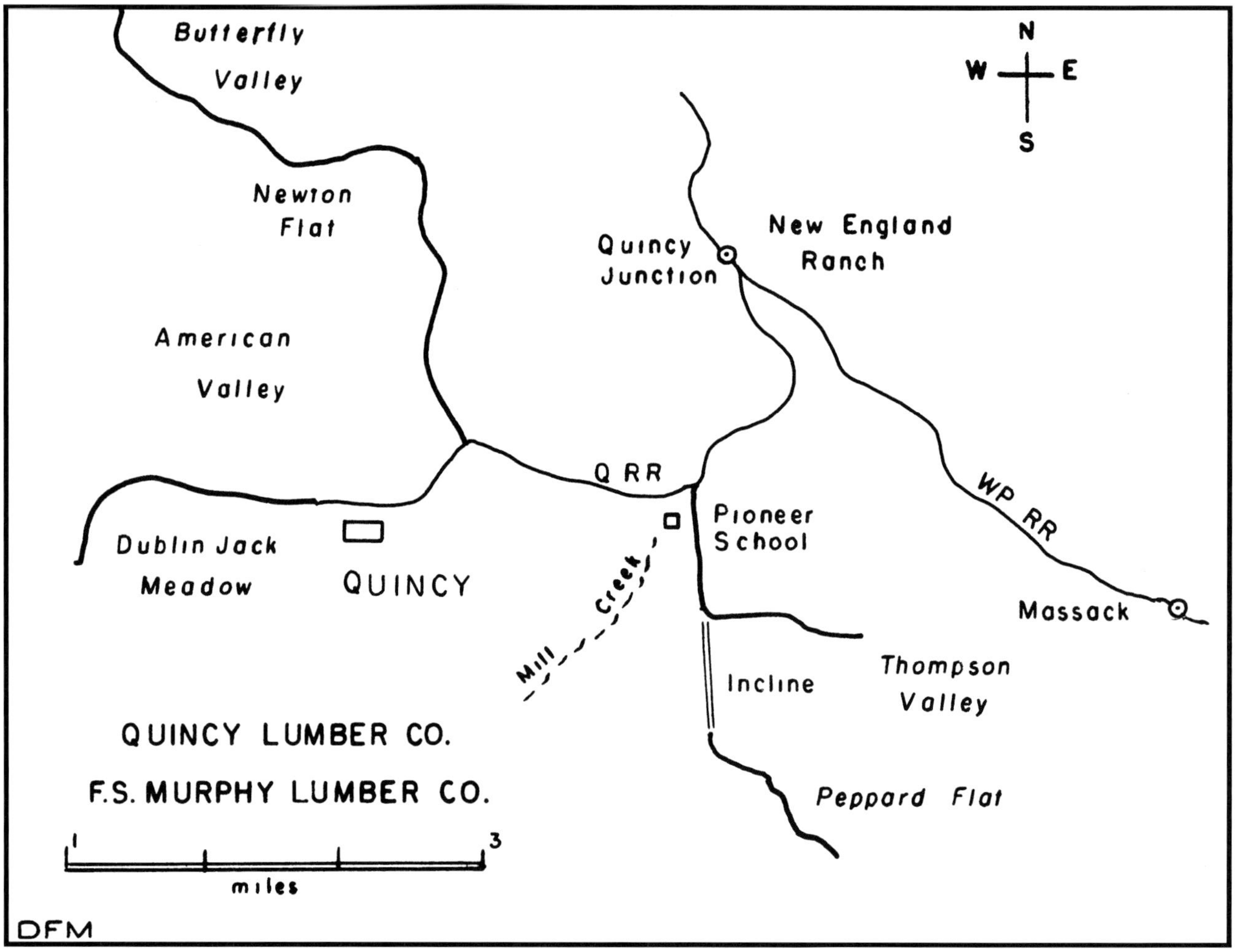

engineers, but it was solved by building a forty-eight hundred–foot inclined cable railway up the steep grade. Manufactured by the Washington Iron Works, which also built the incline for Nibley-Stoddard, the maximum load topped at eighty-four thousand pounds. A lowering donkey engine of the Washington type controlled the down-going cars on the incline.

During August, men worked diligently laying the fifty-two-pound rail on the incline, and the first load of logs came down on September 8. Though the approaching winter ended logging, other forces erected buildings on the crest of Thompson Hill. This included a boardinghouse, sleeping quarters, various storage sheds, an icehouse, and a saw-filing shed. Plans called for bringing in a donkey engine and railroad spurs from the incline into the woods. A Shay locomotive operated on trackage at the top of the incline. All went well with the resumption of logging in March 1925 except for a minor incident when a car derailed near the foot of the incline.

Quincy Lumber Company—Again

F. S. Murphy's death resulted in a change of ownership at the lumber company. For undisclosed reasons, his son Maurice, working in the San Francisco sales office, did not follow in his father's footsteps, and the stockholders sold the entire property, including the Sloat mill and Quincy Railroad, to a group of Louisiana men who took charge on November 15, 1926. W. P. Weber of Lake Charles, the new president, had engaged in wholesale merchandising, rice growing, and lumbering. George M. King, also from Lake Charles, and two Texas men, John C. Saner and M. J. Ragley, completed the combination. Ragley, holding a quarter interest, served as general manager. Initially, supervisors from the old regime stood undisturbed; William Y. Stoddard and Harold Mortensen, mill superintendents at Quincy and Sloat, respectively, retained their posts. R. L. MacArthur moved his accounting work from San Francisco to Quincy along with the sales office.

The Louisiana men returned the corporate name to the Quincy Lumber Company early the next year. They also enlarged the storage pond to accommodate a larger inventory of logs that enabled the mill to run longer during winter months when snow closed down logging. At that time, the Quincy mill cut sixty thousand board feet daily, while the Sloat output reached seventy-five thousand feet. (For 1928, the two mills cut twenty-six million board feet.)

Seeking to boost the output, the new owners had forty men overhauling the Quincy mill during the early winter months of 1928. The nippy Christmas temperatures had frozen the log pond, much to the delight of the active young crowd who enjoyed ice skating. However, the weather made a severe change in March when a six-day storm dropped nearly ten inches of rain and flooded the American Valley, which "presented a remarkable maritime aspect," with one man rowing his boat to Quincy Jct. Considered the worst storm since the ones of 1890 and 1907, it caused the worst tie-up on Western Pacific since its first operating year. With five freight trains stranded in the canyon, passenger trains detoured on other routes. The Quincy Railroad lost its bridge over Greenhorn Creek (MP 1), but Superintendent L. H. Thayer and his crew restored it almost in time to coordinate with the resumption of service on the WP. Even Mt. Lassen Stages suspended operations. High water overflowed the millpond and extinguished the flames under the boilers of the Quincy Lumber Company as well as damaging its "high power dynamo."

Commencing in 1927, the lumber company undertook construction of a six-mile standard-gauge railroad to Butterfly Valley, northwest of Quincy. The route required several bridges; in January 1928, foreman James Patrick and his men finished the pile bridge across the swamp near the Clinch place.

By April, rails reached past Bustiman Summit, and surveyors were locating an extension from Pendelton Pass to the Perry Maxwell place. At the same time, the 7:00 A.M. Monday-morning whistle announced that the Quincy mill stood ready to begin a new day with its newly installed boilers.

Quincy Lumber Company ran into more problems in June. Previously, the company had signed a purchase contract with the U.S. Forest Service for 1.75 million feet of timber in the Butterfly Valley area. Bud Smith and Louis Smith, holding three mining claims in the same area, granted the lumber company a right-of-way over its claims. According to reports, when the company went on the ground to remove timber, the Smith brothers threatened them with violence and allegedly fired several shots at them. Quincy Lumber suspended operations at the location until the dispute could be resolved.

Soon, more trouble rose in Butterfly Valley when a fire, traced to a defective company Caterpillar tractor, swept across two thousand acres. That seemed to be the end of major difficulties until Thanksgiving Day 1929, which would be long remembered by sawyers in the mill. The fifteen-foot flywheel suddenly broke loose and hurled steel remnants all over the room to injure three men, one seriously. Five months later, when the restored mill opened after repairs, the millpond had enough supply for several weeks, even with logging suspended. Of more concern was the plentiful labor supply and the scarcity of lumber sales, the result of an economic downturn.

Mill orders ran sporadically in the early 1930s; at times the planer at Quincy would be operated one week, and the next week Sloat men ran their planer. At the time work commenced on the Western Pacific line from Keddie to Bieber in August 1930, Quincy Lumber sent several "Cats," trucks, and a grader to harvest timber at Cromberg.

A month later the company made news when it felled a "monstrous" sugar pine in Butterfly Valley. As it measured ten feet across at the butt end, the first five or six cuts had to be split before the railroad could take it to the mill. A. C. Ahrens, the six-foot sales manager, posed by the fallen tree for M. J. Ragley, who snapped the picture.

When the company received new orders in January 1931, the *Plumas National-Bulletin* dutifully reported it. WP contractors secured lumber from the Quincy Lumber Company for trestles and the Keddie engine house as well as for concrete forms.

However, work proved so scarce that when the planer started a ten-day run in May 1932, "the sound of the machinery sent a thrill through town, as the mill has been idle most of the time for nearly two years." Of course, with the mill down, timber was not harvested and the railroad stood idle.

John Kenneth "Ken" Metzker

Born in Cedarville, in an isolated part of Modoc County where his father had been a logger, Ken grew up in Lakeview and attended Oregon State College. After working for the Chevrolet plant in East Oakland for about a year, Metzker moved to Winnemucca as a salesman for Standard Oil (now Chevron) for ten years. In 1934, he became a distributor for Associated Oil at Quincy, and while there he extended credit to a gypo logger to find himself owner of two log trucks when the man went bankrupt. In partnership with A. C. "Dell" Dellinger who operated a Quincy garage and distributed Oldsmobile and GMC trucks, he purchased three more trucks and went into the log-hauling business serving Diamond Match, Setzer Box Company of Greenville, and others.

Metzker moved into the lumber trade, and before he was through he had bought or built a half-dozen lumber mills. He purchased the machinery for the mill for twenty-five hundred dollars from the Penman Peak Lumber Company, through Herb Rowe, and erected it at Gray's Flat. With his brother-in-law, Louis D. Ohlsen of Dunsmuir, he established a small planing mill and yard at Oroville. Next came the Oroville Lumber Company, as Dant and Russell of Portland joined the two men to build a sawmill.

Under Nevada statutes, they incorporated High Sierra Pine Mills Inc. on October 1, 1946, and Metzker tried to buy old mills for their timber rights. From Dick Barrington, an Indian, he purchased the Sierraville Lumber Company at that town and then the Sloat property of the Quincy Lumber Company. There he set up a new sawmill and shipped green lumber over Western Pacific to Loyalton at a given price per car. Metzker sold his (new) Feather River Lumber Company to the Di Gorgio Corporation as of September 1967. (Previously, Metzker had bought the name from the company at Delleker, which had used it for sixty years.)

Meanwhile, the Meadow Valley Lumber Company, second successor to the Spanish Peak Lumber Company, bought the Quincy Lumber Company and Quincy Railroad in 1955. Ray C. Smith had headed the Meadow Valley Lumber Company for about twenty-five years. In February 1968, Di Gorgio Corporation acquired the company and its plants and installed J. Kenneth Metzker as president and Vern Lindgren as general manager.

Subsequently, the property became part of Sierra Pacific Industries, which in turn had become the property of "Red" Emerson of Eureka, California, in 1976. The abbreviated Quincy Railroad continues to serve the mill, but the logging railroad was dismantled around the 1940s.

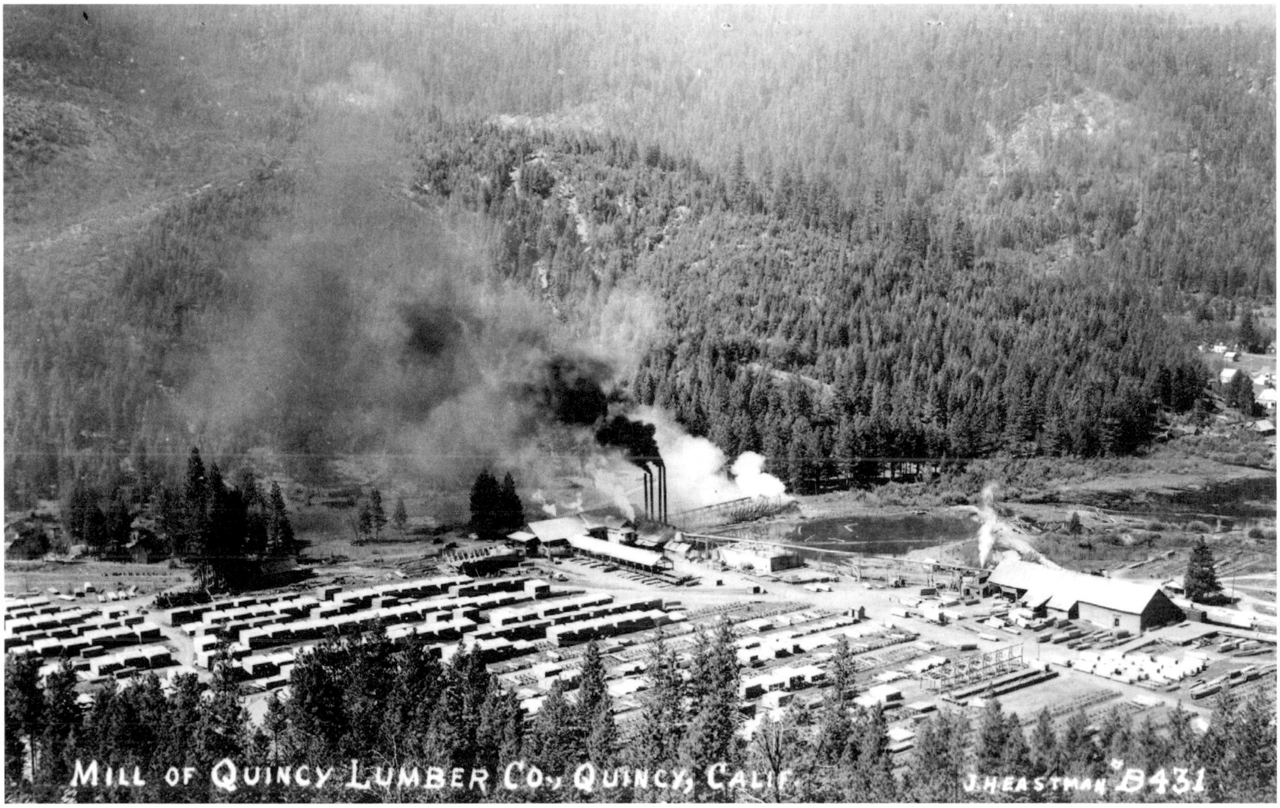

The Quincy Lumber Company provided the principal economic support for the county seat of Plumas County. Located at the site of the present shopping center (near the Quincy high school), it operated as the F. S. Murphy Lumber Company in its early years. (Plumas County Museum)

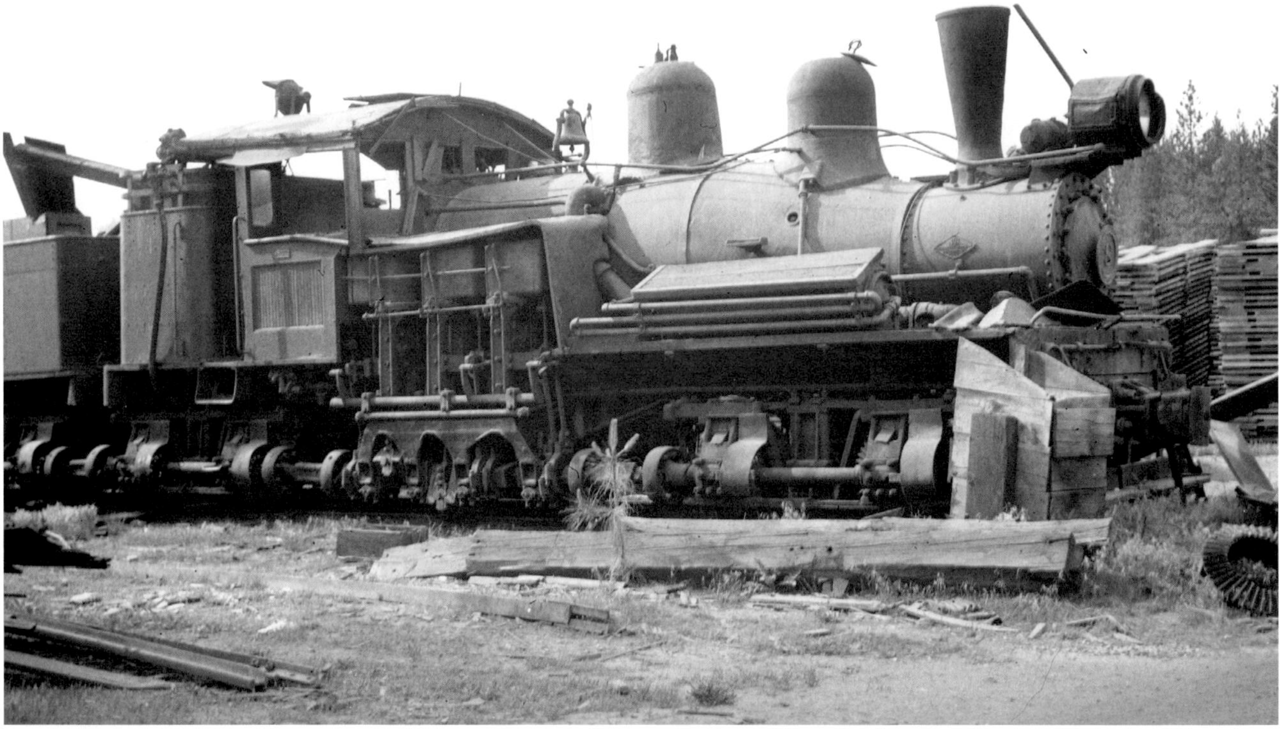

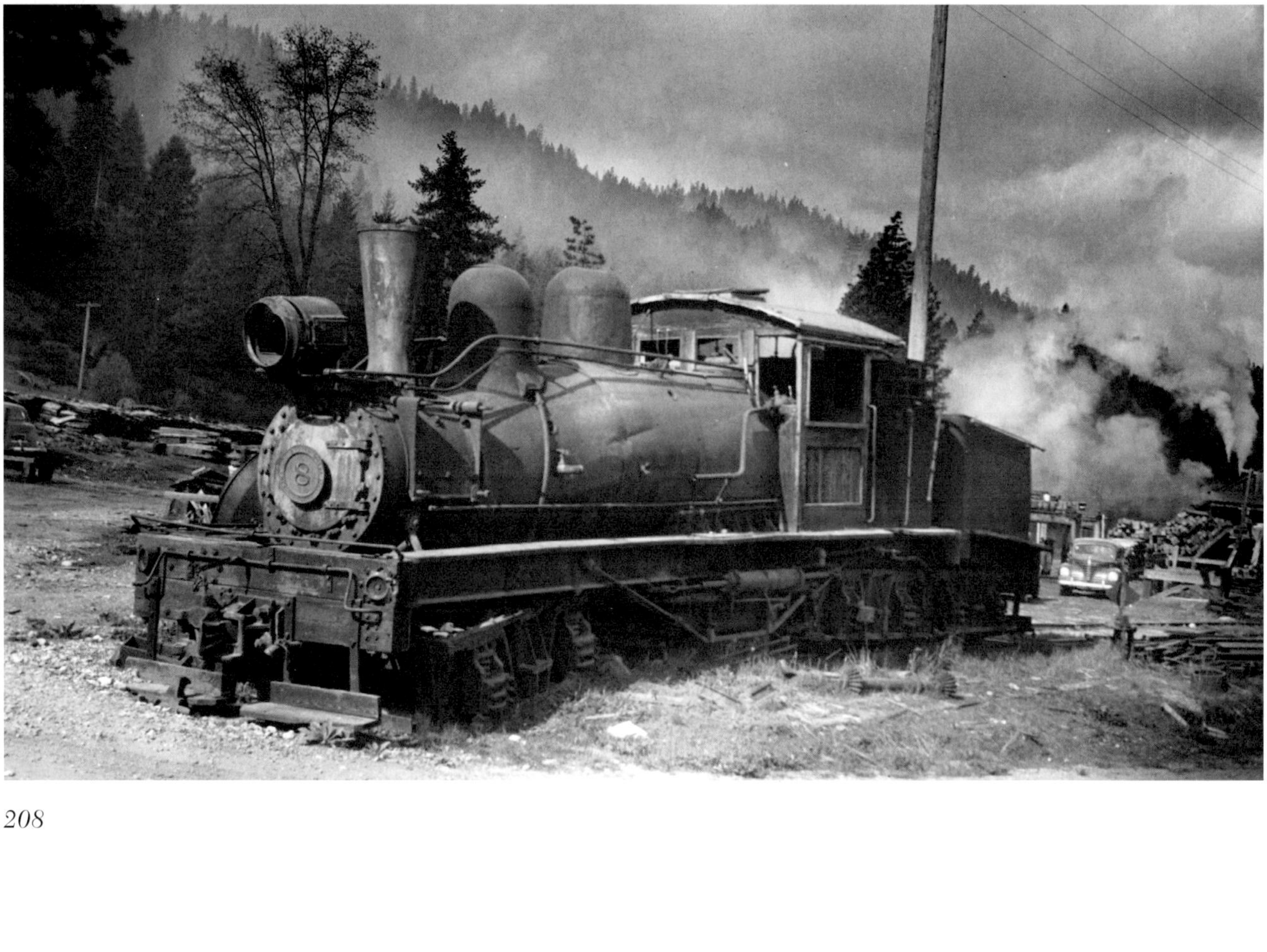

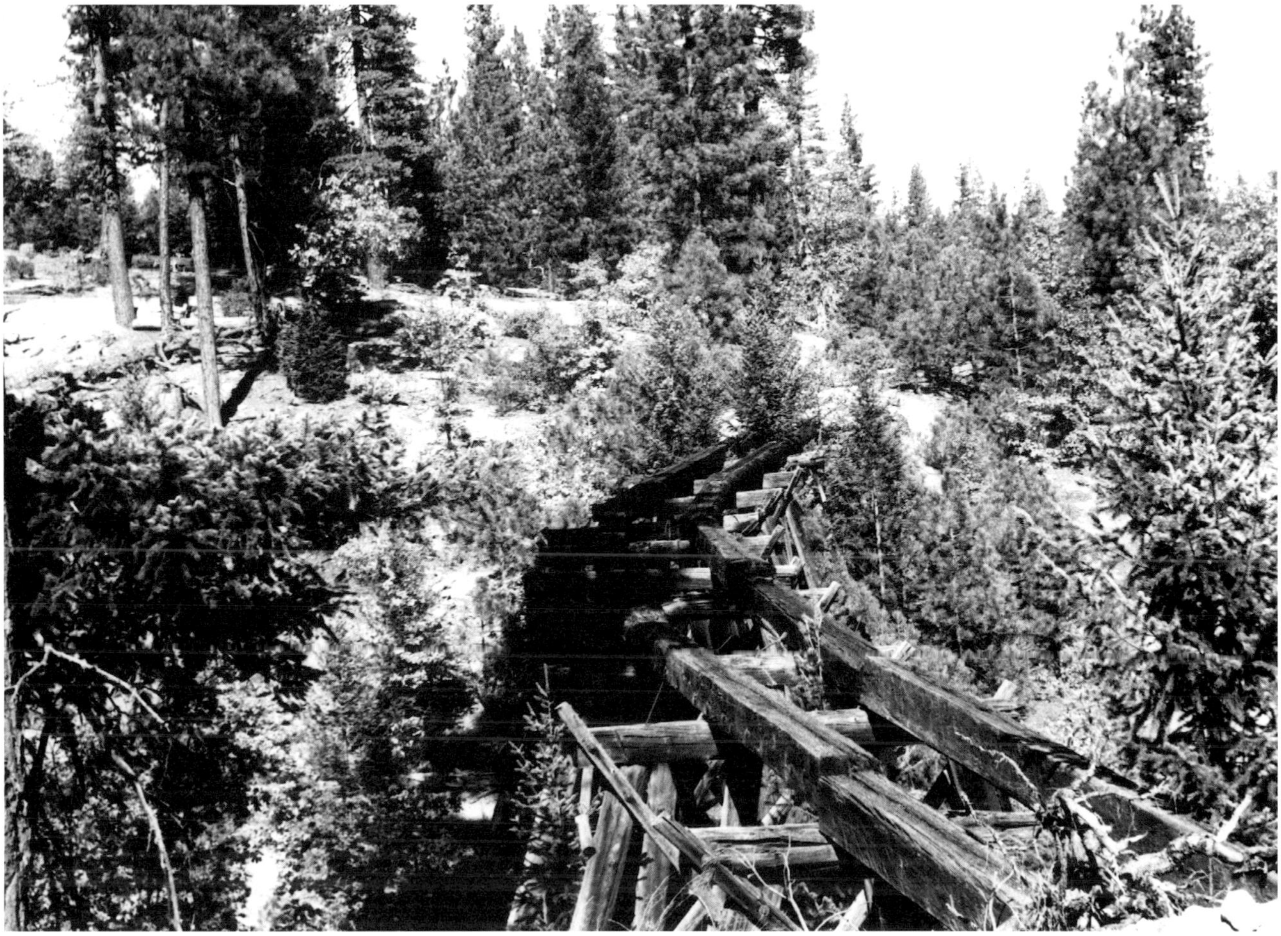

The Butterfly Valley railroad required a number of trestles as it ventured into the woods northwest of Quincy. Though no trains had crossed this bridge in many years, its frame survived the elements, as demonstrated in this 1960 view. (James E. Boynton photograph)

Opposite above: Heavy grades of the Quincy Lumber Company railroad necessitated geared locomotives. Built by Lima in 1920, this three-truck locomotive worked in the Louisiana timber country for the Weber-King Lumber Company before coming to Quincy. No. 8 became the regular motive power assigned to the Butterfly Valley line. (Bert Ward photograph, September 1937)

Opposite below: The left-side view of No. 8 ten years later when Jim Boynton chose a day with a thunderstorm posed over the mountain. The locomotive was scrapped at Quincy in 1955.

MASSACK TIMBER AND LUMBER COMPANY

One of the first lumber companies entering Plumas County after the opening of the Western Pacific Railroad chose Massack Creek for its operations.

Massack (Ravine) Creek, seven miles east of Quincy, passes under the WP tracks just before it joins Greenhorn Creek. In 1895 and again the following years, two Quincy residents, Frank Vere and Henry Luman, engaged in a ground-sluicing process and successfully recovered sufficient gold for a comfortable living.

Years later, with the change in the Plumas economy boosting lumber production, an old California woodsman, Charles Nelson Cox of Truckee, secured timber rights along Massack Creek in the name of the Iceland Wood and Lumber Company. When A. J. Watson, the seasoned Plumas County surveyor, found a site for a spur track, neighbors became aware of the project. The next month, Cox and J. B. Delaney, now operating as the Massack Timber and Lumber Company, put men to work to grade a 900-foot spur linking their mill site with WP as a step in moving the sawmill machinery from near Boca to the new site. Cox, moving cautiously, delayed rail laying until some title difficulties could be resolved. On June 25, 1910, Cox wrote W. J. Shotwell, assistant vice president of WP, advising the new grade would be ready for ties and rails in two days. Cox also requested that the spur be called "Massack," and, because fifty men would be in the camp, he wanted WP to establish a regular stop at that point so men could come and go and supplies could be delivered. With supplies available in Massack, he explained, the men would not have to walk to Spring Garden or Hartwell.

Western Pacific obliged Mr. Cox by establishing the station and completed laying track on the 900-foot spur on July 28, 1910. With the rails in place and the relocation of the Iceland mill to Massack, Cox was able to commence sawing near the end of September at the rate of 40,000 board feet per day.

Next spring, Delaney installed a new steam engine and arranged for a 120-foot extension of the spur track. By 1912, with fifty employees on the payroll, the mill cut 4 million board feet during the active season.

Massack had timber rights on U.S. Forest Service land as well as timberland owned by the Roberts Lumber Company of Loyalton. For a time the company used a steam-traction engine to haul logs to the mill; at another period, logs were skidded down a log chute along Massack Creek. As the 1915 logging season approached, Cox and Delaney stood poised to build their own logging railroad. When August came, the very short and narrow line was ready, with track laid for 1.5 miles with a thirty-six-inch gauge. A Shay engine and ten log cars completed the railroad.

Information concerning the railroad's layout is scarce, but it is understood that trains negotiated a steep climb using a switchback in the canyon before proceeding around the hill, high above the old Johnson Ranch in the American Valley. During the next year, the company pushed its railroad around the mountain and headed for Taylor Creek.

The company achieved annual production of 6.5 million board feet, with a large portion shipped to foreign countries. C. N. Cox and W. C. McNary managed the operation, which was considered "one of the successful mills although medium capacity."

The great fear of lumbermen—a forest fire—came near the sawmill in August 1917. Production was suspended while all the men successfully fought the conflagration.

During 1919, Massack's railroad measured 2.5 miles in length and was expected to be augmented by "at least one-half mile of new track, perhaps more." WP engineers surveyed another extension to a new cutting area 6 miles from the mill. According to one account, the railroad included a section approaching a 10 percent grade, and to avoid more steep climbs, a new truck and new road supplemented railroad operations. With increased employment, camp activities and facilities were enlarged. Dr. A. Rhodes of San Francisco settled in Massack with his wife for the summer to serve as camp physician. Dedication of the new Massack Community Hall on July 29, 1919, with part serving as a school, included a dance sponsored by the school board. The attendance surpassed the wildest dreams of the promoters. Ticket and refreshment sales totaled $204, and, after the cost of the music and groceries, the group had a handsome profit of $20. This event soon brought another dance, and Massack ladies formed a local social group, calling themselves the "Sunshine Club."

But there were unexpected problems. On August 16, the railroad had a "little difficulty." As the heavily loaded log train approached the mill, the cars careened into a ditch. The Shay locomotive, after rocking dangerously on the rails, settled down to good behavior. The brakeman jumped, and no one received injuries. Tearing out a trestle as they sailed into the canyon, all the log cars save one had to be scrapped.

A small blaze erupted in the early fall of 1920 following the passage of a heavy train working up the hill. It may have served as a warning, for the next spring the managers raised the sawmill smokestack thirty-five feet.

With a new roof and other improvements, Massack was heralded as the first operator for the 1922 season when it started work in March. The big change came on July 1, 1922, when Cox and others sold the Massack property to the M. J. Scanlon Lumber Company. Cox agreed to stay on as manager, and Robert L. Scanlon, son of the president, became treasurer at Massack.

October 31, 1922, stands out as the saddest day in the history of Massack. After having lunch, Charles Cox and his wife, Charlotte, proceeded to leave the company dining room when Felipe Bisquera, a twenty-year-old Filipino box-factory worker, suddenly pulled out his revolver and shot Cox is the neck and back. He then turned his gun on Robert Scanlon, who grabbed him and threw him to the ground. Bisquera fought like a wildcat and twice tried to kill Scanlon. With the assistance of two men, he was finally subdued, and Scanlon and another man drove him to Quincy, where Sheriff L. A. Braden incarcerated him.

Cox, who had planned to leave Massack at the end of the season, died thirty minutes later. The following January prison officials at Folsom Prison hung Bisquera. Attempts to close the estate of Charles Cox ran into problems because his last will could not be found. A request for his will appeared in the *Plumas National* in December, but the outcome was not reported.

M. J. Scanlon Lumber Company

This lumber company, conducting operations in many parts of the West, sometimes in a partnership as Brooks-Scanlon, made changes at Massack in the spring of 1923. The firm established a new logging camp on Dry Taylor Creek, about five miles from the mill. For families, the company provided neat little cottages, but single men had only tent-roofed sleeping quarters. Many trees had been left throughout the camp to give shade during the warm summers. H. A. Muller and his daughter, who had worked with Bob Scanlon in British Columbia, managed the kitchen and dining room.

For logging, Scanlon secured a new donkey engine and a forty-two-ton Shay locomotive and double-log railroad cars. After a thorough cleaning, the sawmill was renovated with a new boiler and new twin-band saw. With only a few changes in personnel, the most important being bringing Frank Canzio from Canada because of his special skills as an all-around mechanic, the 1923 season commenced on April 5.

During August of that year, someone attempted to burn the mill one Sunday noon. The traveling road show from Quincy marked a happier event when it entertained people in the community hall, but when three Mexicans appeared for a friendly game of dice, Bob Scanlon confiscated the loaded dice, and others joined him to escort the men out of the camp. M. J. Scanlon, head of the widespread firm, visited his son as he inspected the plant in 1923 and again the next year. In July 1924, a forest fire swept across Lanfear Meadows and came uncomfortably close to the logging camp; before being controlled, it wiped out the old Lanfear house and barn.

The lumber market turned unfavorable in 1924, causing Scanlon to shut down the mill in mid-August, but the box factory continued working. (For the same reason, the big Scanlon mill near Bend, Oregon, was also closed.)

Christmas 1924 offered warmth and cheer. Mrs. Merele McGrath, the local teacher, set up a tree in the school a few days before Christmas. The lumber company not only provided toys and candy for each child but also gave a box of candy to each lady in the camp.

With unsatisfactory markets continuing in 1925, Scanlon did not open Massack that season, with the result that many people moved away. Bob Scanlon remained but decided to dispose of his 1922 Marmon seven-passenger touring car. Though he advertised it "For Sale—Cheap," his success stands unrecorded. J. Victor Jaeger, office manager at Massack, named general manager of the company, moved to Minneapolis in the fall of 1925.

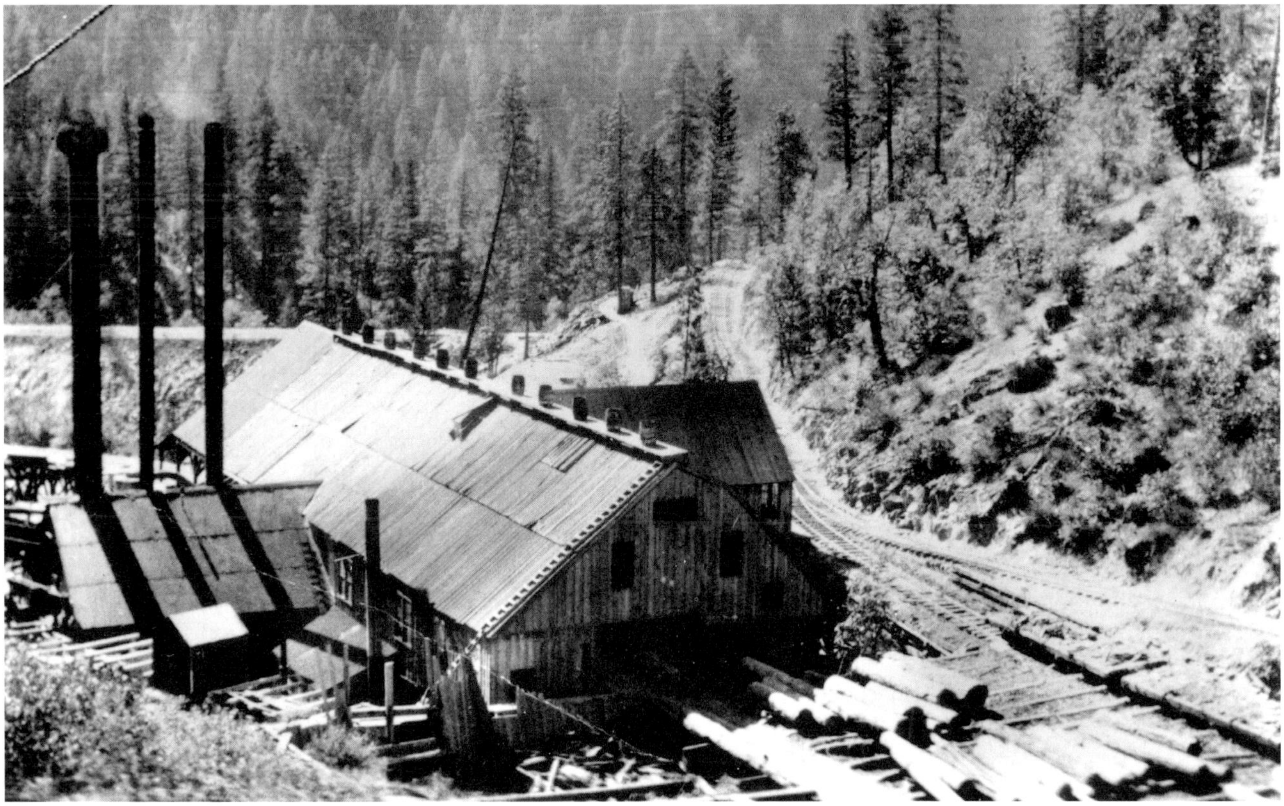

Above: The Massack Timber and Lumber Company, located a few miles east of Quincy, was crammed in a narrow gulch. The railroad climbed up a steep grade to reach the timber. (Plumas County Museum)

Below: Donkey engines found wide acceptance in logging operations; with cables, logs were dragged to railroad loading docks. (Plumas County Museum)

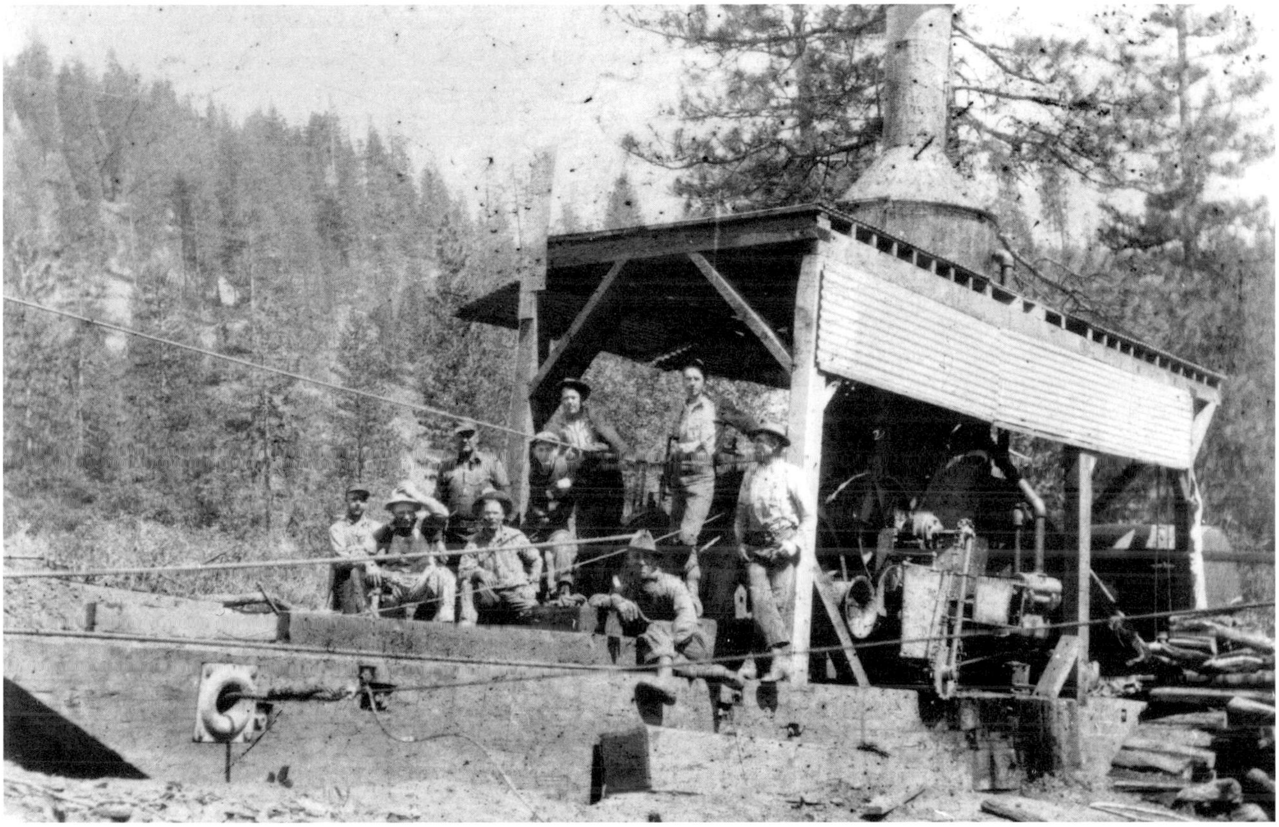

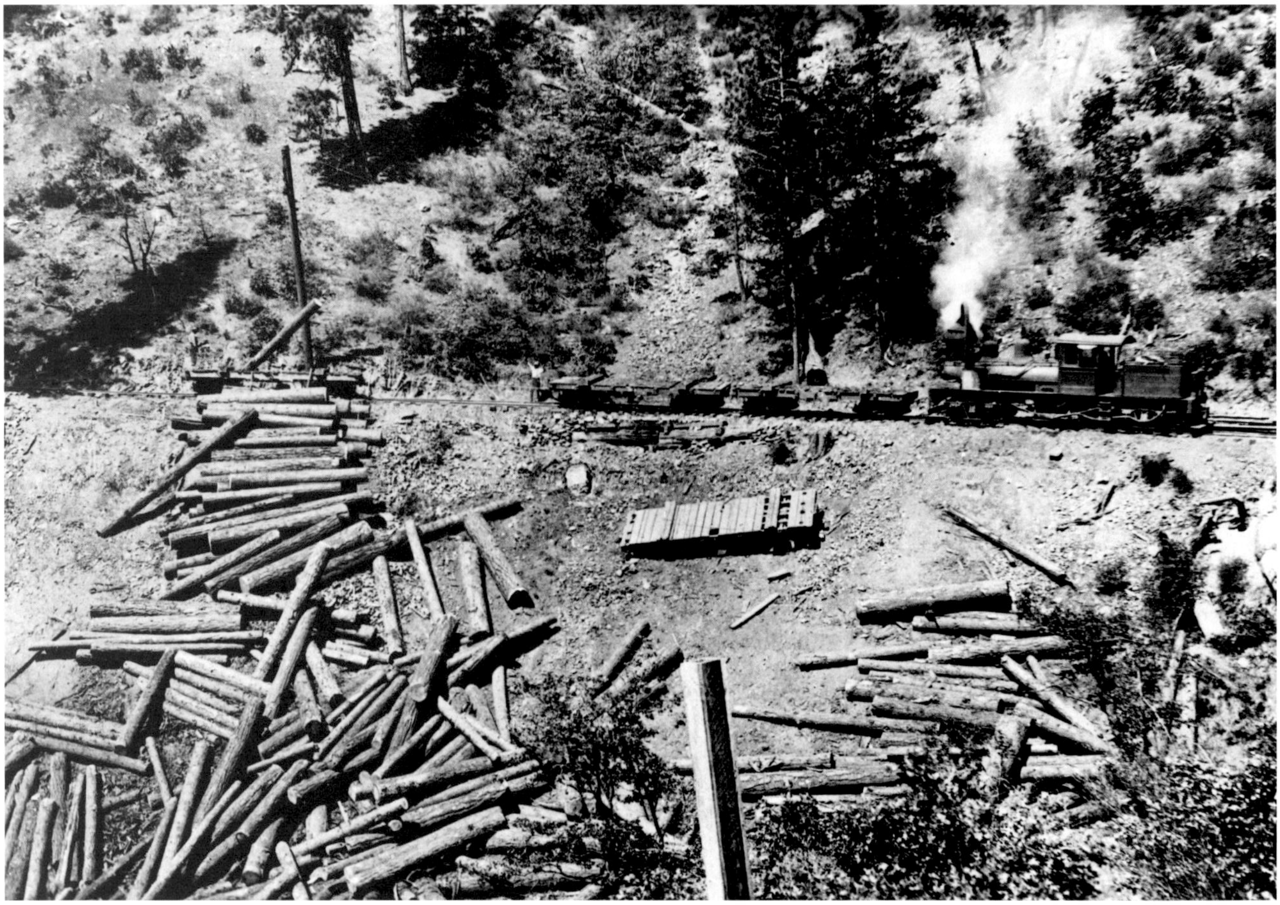

With the steep railroad grades, a Shay locomotive proved essential in Massack operations. In this 1925 view, a gin pole aided by the locomotive is unloading logs for the pond. An old flat car was abandoned after a previous derailment. (Ted Wurm collection)

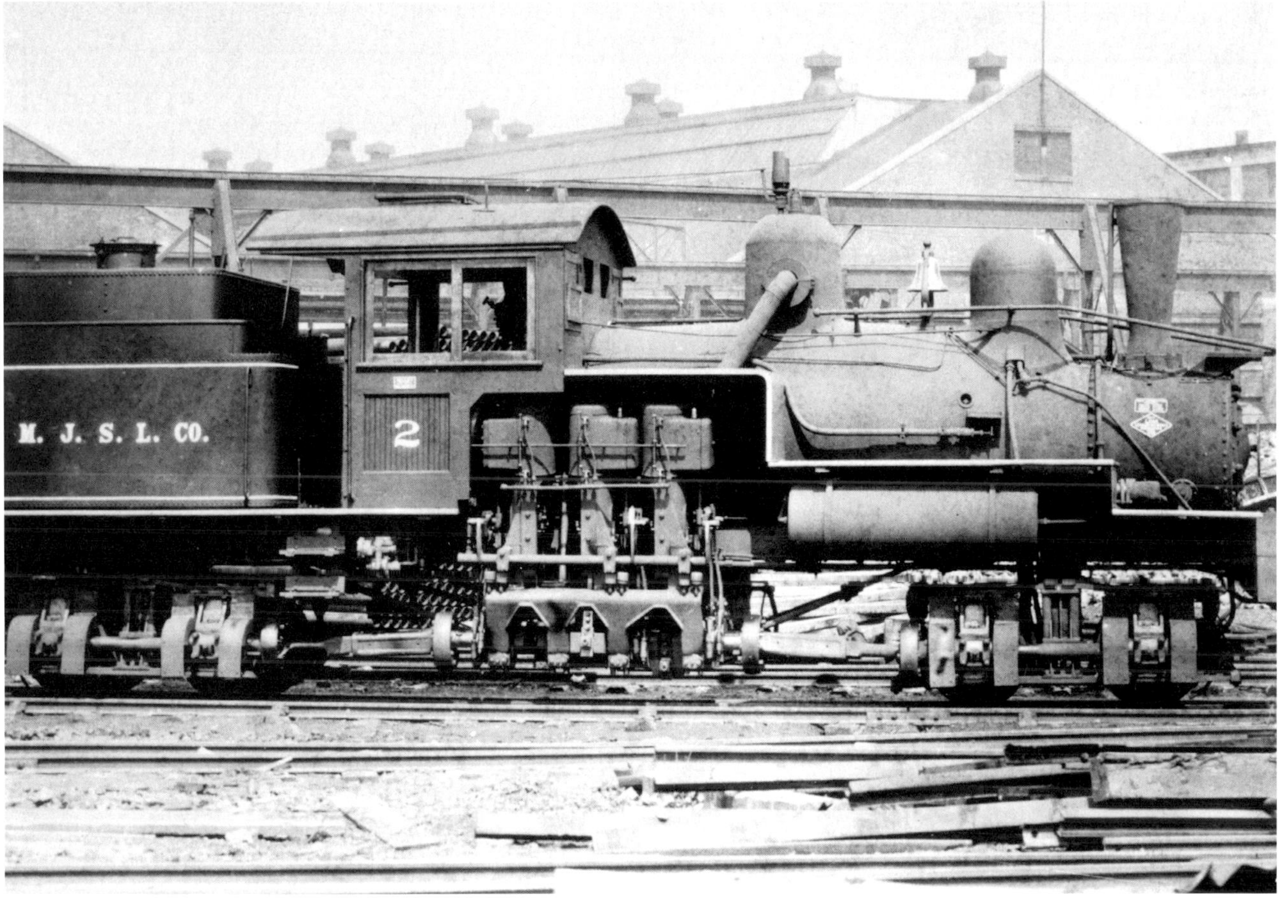

When the M. J. Scanlon Lumber Company took over operations at Massack in 1923, it acquired another Shay locomotive. (Bert Ward collection)

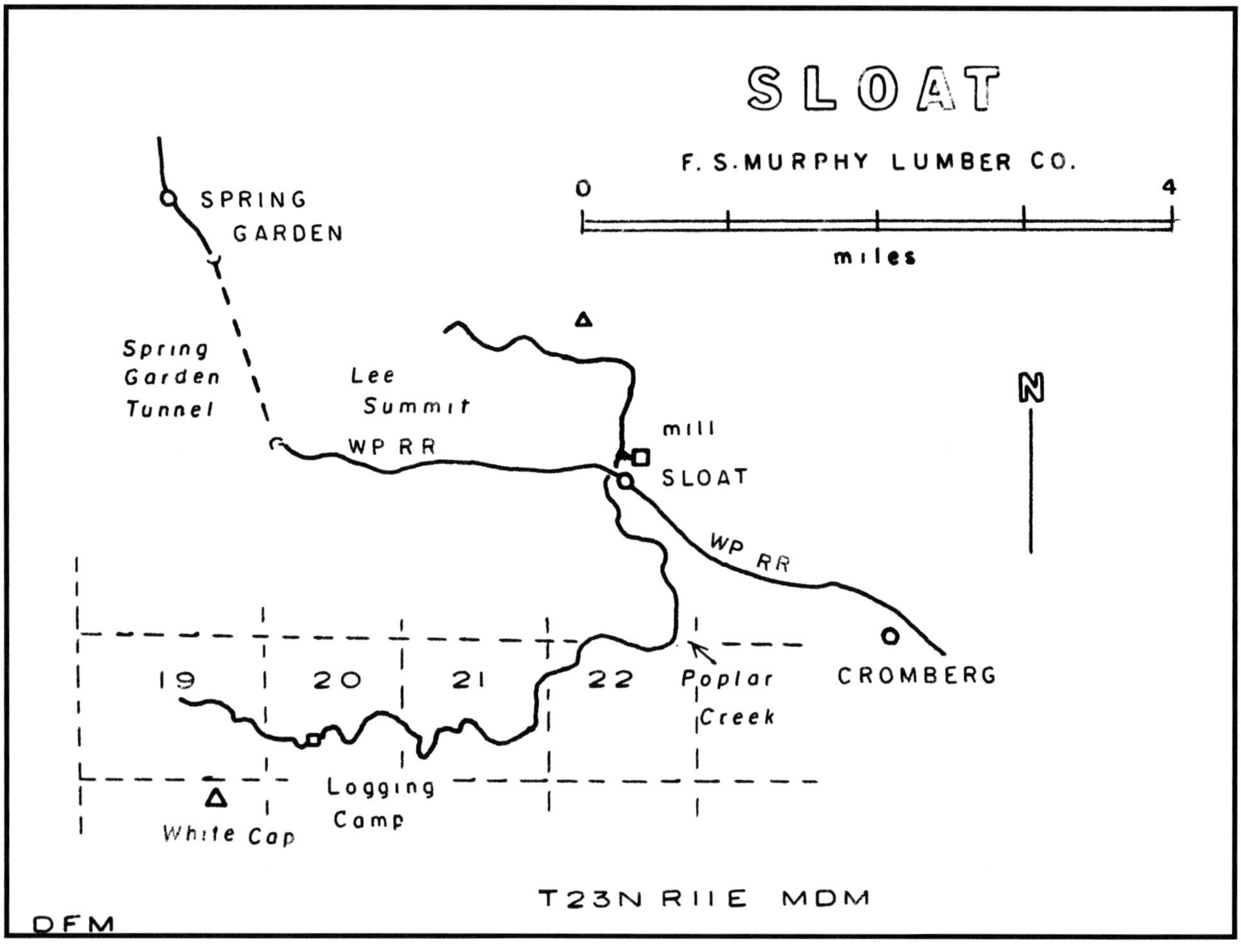
SLOAT
F. S. MURPHY LUMBER CO.
0
4
miles
SPRING
GARDEN
Spring
Garden
Tunnel
Lee
Summit
WP RR
mill
SLOAT
WP RR
N
CROMBERG
19
20
21
22
Poplar
Creek
Logging
Camp
White Cap
T23N R11E MDM
DFM

SLOAT LUMBER COMPANY

Located along the Middle Fork of the Feather River, the settlement of Sloat, named for the California commander in the war with Mexico, is three miles beyond the east portal of the Spring Garden Tunnel of Western Pacific. Here Charles F. Campbell and Frank P. Myers of Beckwourth joined Harry A. Turner, an experienced lumberman, to form the Sloat Lumber Company in March 1912.

At this time, Turner dismantled his Sunset Mill at Sattley, which had been operating for some years, and moved it to Sloat. Three months later, with the sawmill and planing mill in operation, the new company found customers for its finished lumber as far away as Wisconsin in the East and Australia in the West.

Initially, tents provided shelter for the workers until the new mill sawed lumber for the cabins and the boardinghouse. With dense forests nearby, horse-drawn wagons conveyed logs from the Flanigan timber track north of the ranch of Charles Stouky and Ray Stouky. Western Pacific, encouraged by a new source of traffic, erected a small depot at Sloat (MP 301.6), where Joe Fallihee served as agent in 1914. At that time, the lumber company had fifty-five men on the payroll and was feeding forty horses. Subsequently, a Best traction engine was purchased for hauling.

Typically, most lumber mills suspended work during the winter months, but in 1914 Albert J. Maxwell remained in camp, an unfortunate choice for him. While falling trees always constitute a hazard in logging work, this time a heavy wind toppled a large tree that fell across the bunkhouse and killed Maxwell.

The year 1917 proved to be busy. WP built a spur to the yards of the lumber company, and work commenced on three miles of a narrow-gauge logging railroad with a thirty-inch gauge. The railroad extended northwest from Sloat for about three miles to a cutting area near Lee Summit, and the curvature of the railroad necessitated cutting logs in sixteen-foot lengths, half the usual length. (The former roadbed crossed Highway 70 at [highway] mile post 300.)

With the merger of the White Pine Lumber Company, the new firm became the Sloat Lumber Company. (Several years previously, Sloat had purchased timberlands from White Pine.) F. S. Murphy of Salt Lake City took an interest in Plumas sawmills, and with additional financing, extensive changes occurred at Sloat. The old mill vanished, and a larger facility took its place. In the spring of 1918, a Sloat correspondent wrote that "buildings are springing up like mushrooms." During February 1918, Murphy formed the F. S. Murphy Lumber Company to purchase both the Quincy Lumber Company and the Sloat Lumber Company, and all appeared to go well until a mysterious fire in the early hours of June 25, 1918, swept through the mill and left the machinery "hopelessly damaged." At that time the Industrial Workers of the World made unwelcome efforts to organize lumber workers. Rebuffed, some alleged the group as responsible for the fires destroying the mills. Without work, former employees departed, and Sloat took on a lonesome feeling.

With World War I still in progress, new machinery proved impossible to obtain, so Murphy dispatched manager W. Y. Stoddard to New Orleans to acquire secondhand machinery. Murphy replaced the Sloat mill later that year, but a variety of problems plagued his firm. In June 1919, one of the large mill saws flew into pieces; fortunately, the workers dove under benches and escaped with their lives. A few weeks later a near riot almost ensued when Stoddard dismissed a chronic troublemaker who complained about the food. Several other men left with him.

The next year, 1920, Murphy instituted a number of improvements. The enlargement of the planing mill and millpond followed construction of new cottages and renovation of others. F. M. Davis erected an amusement hall for the 110 employees. On the first floor, men could play billiards, read magazines, or suffer with a soft drink (Prohibition had raised its ugly head). The second floor served as a ballroom or movie theater. One scheduled all-night dance had to be postponed because of the inability to find an orchestra.

The motive power for the logging railroad consisted of one Shay and one rod engine, but they were not without problems. Logging operations were slowed in May 1922 after the axle of one engine broke and had to be sent away for repairs.

Attempted logging before the spring months sometimes proved disappointing. Two feet of snow in January

1923 briefly suspended work. Sam Scott, a Sloat locomotive engineer, accepted a temporary assignment at Quincy and then returned to Sloat for a short time until the arrival of F. A. Higby and his son to replace him. When both locomotives broke down, as they did in October 1923, manager Harold Mortensen had no alternative but to suspend logging.

Trucking operations at Sloat lumber began in March 1923 when trucks began serving camps near Lee Summit, bringing logs to the railroad that continued the haul to the mill.

In the fall of 1924, work commenced on a new logging line reaching out south and west from Sloat. Diving under the Western Pacific trestle spanning Long Valley Creek, it continued across the Middle Fork of the Feather River. Four 28-foot spans plus a long trestle made up the 500-foot crossing. Husky Swedes built this railroad largely depending on their picks and shovels; occasionally, a horse-drawn Fresno scrapper joined the scene. After leaving the west side of Sloat, the railroad began its climb as it followed Poplar Creek and, by using two switchbacks separated by some distance, climbed up Eureka Ridge. Grading of the new railroad continued into 1926. The Quincy Lumber Company established a logging camp in the center of Section 20, T32N R11E, while the railroad continued west for another mile to end about six miles from Sloat.

A cluster of driftwood and logs threatened the Middle Fork crossing in February 1927. To alleviate the danger, one Clyde Maynard dynamited the conglomeration under the approving gaze of many spectators.

A month later, reflecting Murphy's sale of both properties sometime previously, C. W. Patterson became manager of the Sloat operation. In the same month, the Shay had a little trouble when spreading narrow-gauge rails put the locomotive on the ground. A few weeks later, more trouble confronted the Shay when a twisted line shaft put it out of service until new parts arrived from Stockton.

Just minutes after August 2, 1927, began, flames devoured the planing mill along with 400,000 feet of stacked lumber plus six freight cars being loaded. Manager Ragley assured workers of the insurance coverage, and the mill soon resumed work. The great Plumas County storm of March 1928 swept away the key bridge across the Middle Fork, and an eighteen-inch snowfall several weeks later closed operations until April 11 when James Patrick of Quincy completed the bridge replacement.

In March 1929, both locomotives encountered problems. Again spreading rails left the Shay stranded in a way that it could not be rerailed easily, so the crew had to walk back to Sloat. A few weeks later, when the rod engine ran into muddy ground, somehow the wheels locked and it crashed into the Shay. The cab and the tender of the rod engine suffered damage, and Jack Murdock, who remained in the cab, making every effort to control the errant iron horse, received painful injuries. (The fireman and brakeman jumped prior to the crash.)

In the spring of 1929, a twisted rail on a small trestle near the blacksmith shop would have dumped the rod engine into the pond had it not been for the quick work of the engineer.

M. H. Grover, superintendent at Quincy and Sloat during the late 1920s, had come from the Fruit Growers Supply at Hilt in northern California. Considered to be an efficiency expert, local workers referred to him as "High Pockets." The blacksmith at Sloat, an old Dutchman, gained a reputation as being very capable in repairing wheels of wagons used around the camp. He also cautiously avoided overexertion, even under Mr. Grover's attention. By carefully knocking a board out of the wall of his shed, he could watch Grover as he approached along the path. This gave him time to pull a piece of hot metal from the forge and starting hammering to give the impression that he was busy. One time he was assigned to repair an old gasoline tank. Given careful instructions to empty the tank, let it dry, and fill it with water before commencing work, the Dutchman would have none of these ridiculous precautions. When he started to weld the tank, the top blew through the roof of the shed; luckily, he was unhurt though thoroughly shaken by the explosion.

Reacting to the need for more logging cars, Grover made a successful trip to Marysville to purchase additional cars, which WP delivered in the spring of 1929. In June, a late storm left two inches of snow to hamper work, and no engines could leave the engine house until the trestle by the log pond had been strengthened. In the woods, an entire crew went on strike for more food and a better cook. With these matters corrected, the men returned to work.

In mid-September 1930, after completing the harvest of timber from a major tract, the logging locomotives went into retirement. From that time on, only trucks brought logs to the mill. The difficult years that followed suspended operations, but, when the economy improved, George Howells logged the south side of Poplar Valley. The Louisiana group continued to control the Sloat property until October 1955 when J. Kenneth Metzker purchased it in the name of the Feather River Lumber Company. In September 1967, he sold the entire company to the Di Gorgio Corporation.

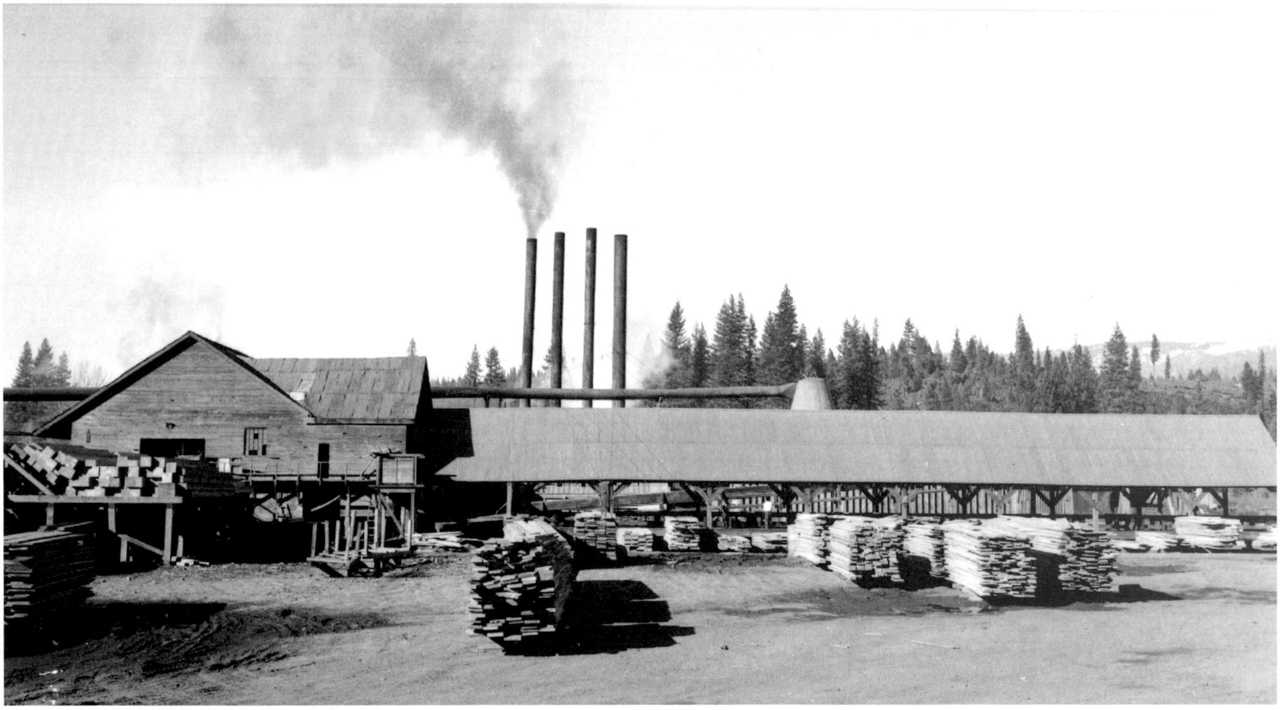

Above: The mill at Sloat in the watershed of the Middle Fork of the Feather River operated under various names such as the Sloat Lumber Companies, F. S. Murphy, and Quincy Lumber Company. The sawmill occupied the long building at the time of this photograph. (Plumas County Museum)

Below: To accommodate the previously owned locomotive, the railroad at Sloat adopted a thirty-inch gauge. (Bill Pennington photograph, Bert Ward collection)

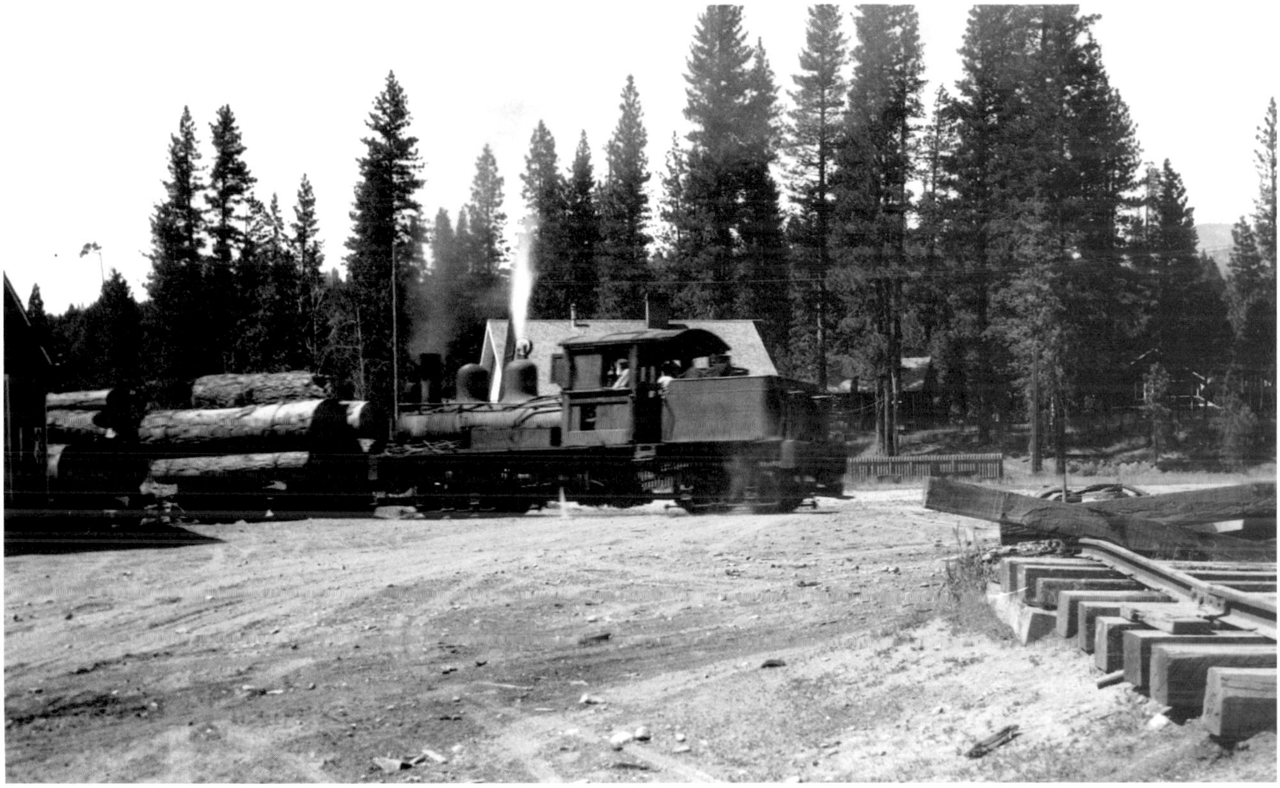

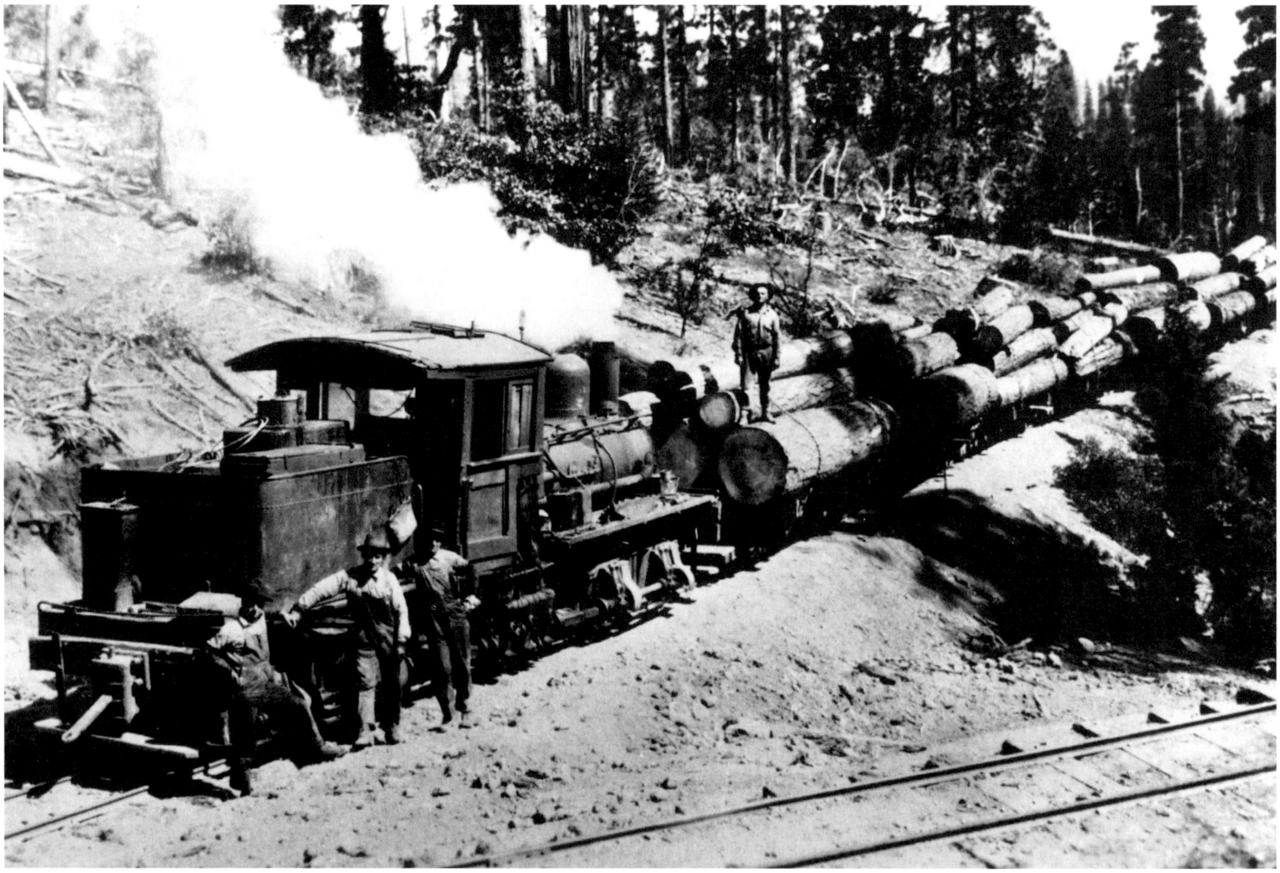

Commencing in 1924, the Sloat company pushed its logging railroad along Poplar Creek on its way to Eureka Ridge. The steep grade required two switchbacks. (James E. Boynton photograph, Bert Ward collection)

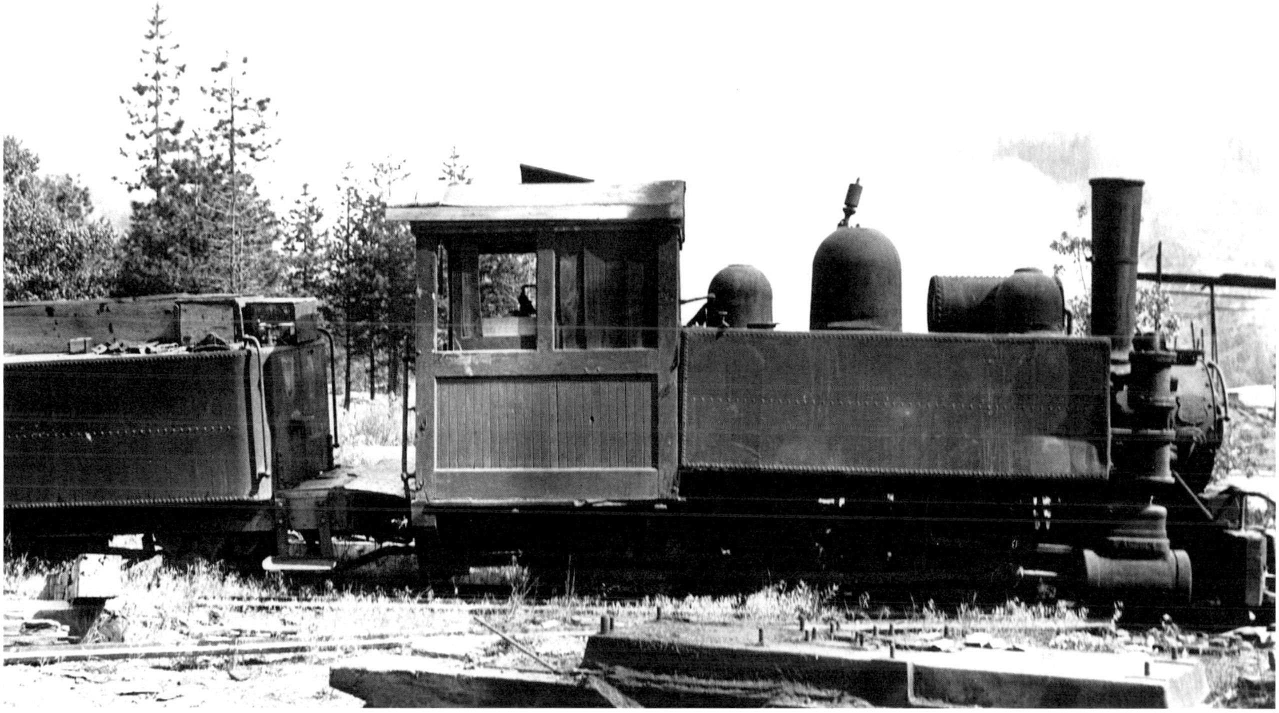

Quincy Lumber Company No. 4, a Porter-built rod 0-4-0T engine, had long been abandoned when photographed in 1938. Ordered by the Yosemite Short Line, it was sent to the Empire City Railway (near Sonora, California), then went to the Standard Lumber Company at Strawberry, California. (Bert Ward photograph)

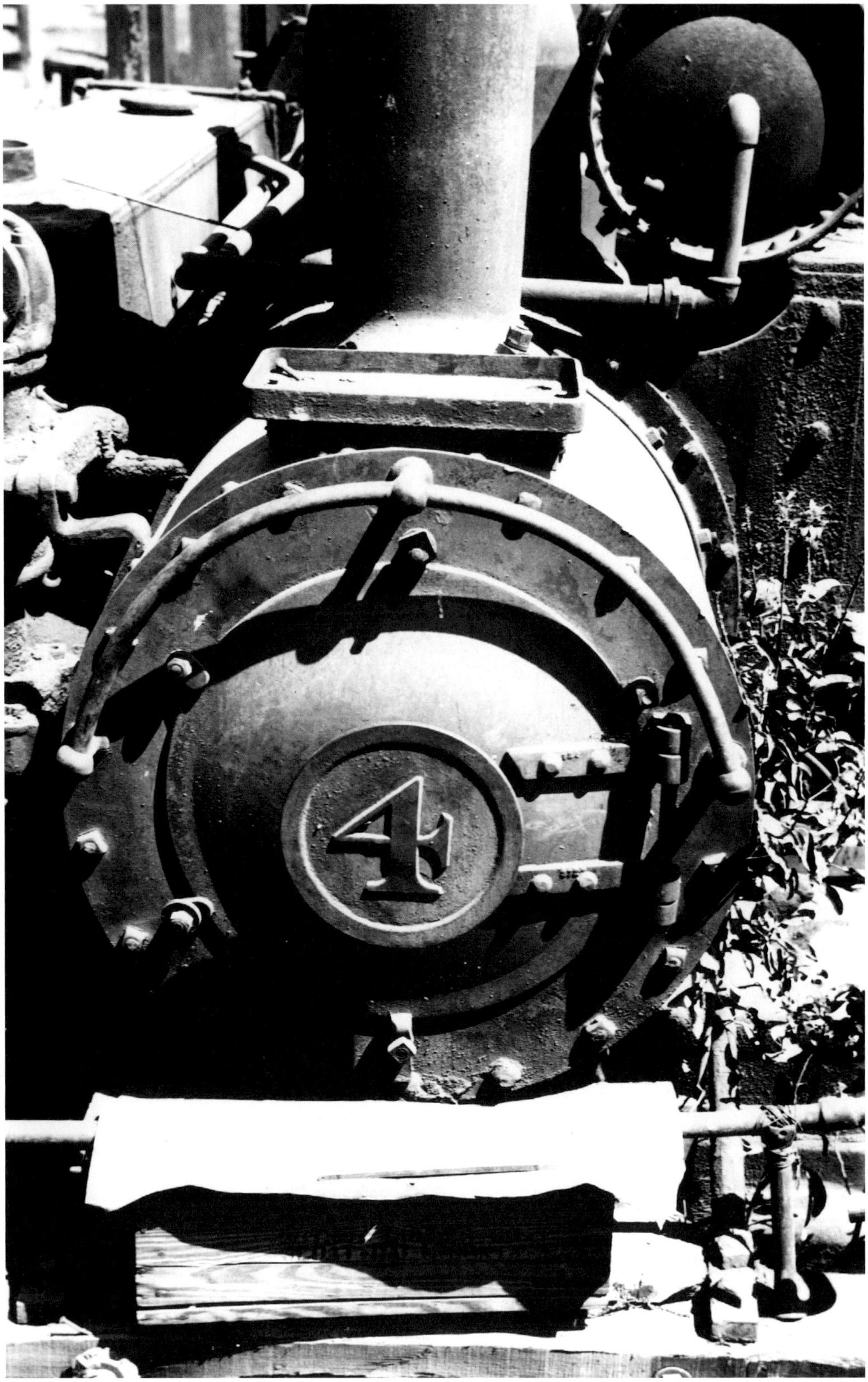

No. 4 stood quietly among the encroaching shrubbery at Sloat when Jim Boynton snapped this picture, September 3, 1939. (Bert Ward collection)

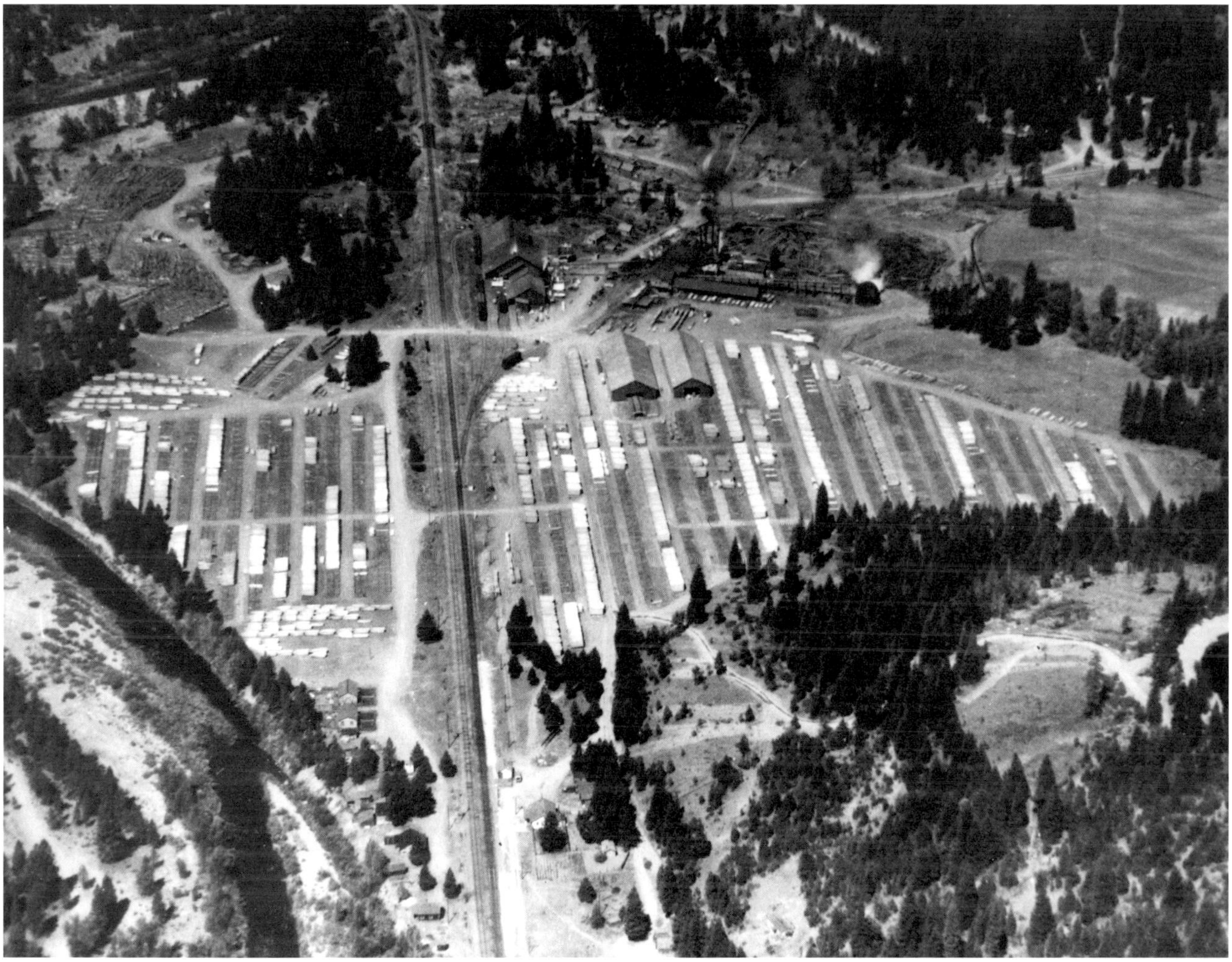

The lumberyards of the Sloat Mill stood on both sides of the Western Pacific main line, while a spur track served the mill. The Middle Fork of the Feather River is in the left corner, but Highway 70 is beyond the right margin of this picture. This photograph represents the activity on October 1, 1949; today, this entire lumber establishment has entirely vanished. (Plumas County Museum)

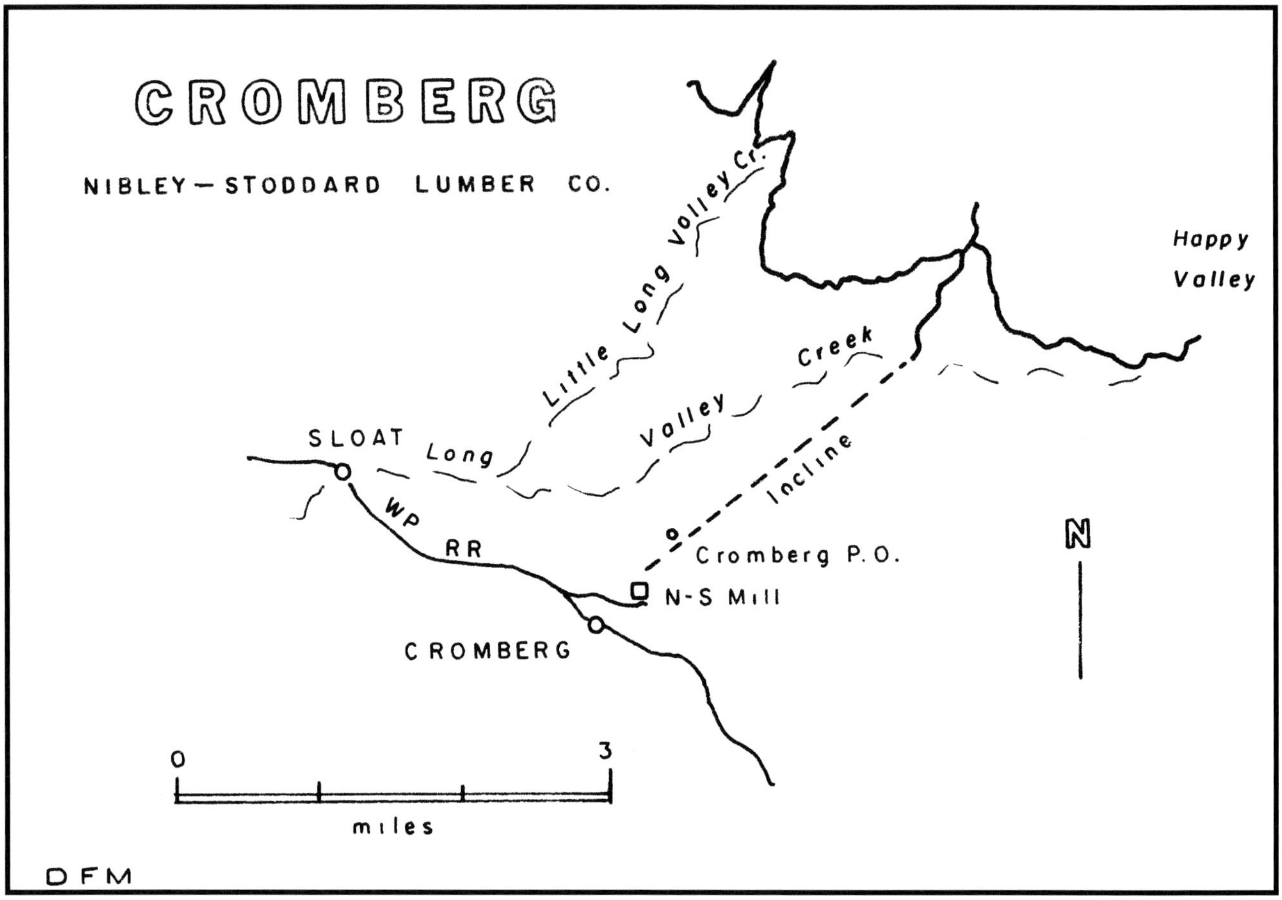
CROMBERG
NIBLEY—STODDARD LUMBER CO.
Little Long Valley Cr.
Happy Valley
Long Valley Creek
SLOAT
Incline
WP RR
Cromberg P.O.
N-S Mill
CROMBERG
N
0
3
miles
DFM

NIBLEY-STODDARD LUMBER COMPANY

Although the Nibley-Stoddard (N-S) Lumber Company was one of the last railroad-oriented lumber companies to be formed in Plumas County, the proprietors were not unfamiliar with the lumber industry.

Charles W. Nibley, born in Scotland in 1849, held prominent positions in the Church of Jesus Christ of Latter-day Saints most of his life. Though he resided in Salt Lake City, he held the top position in the Grande Ronde Lumber Company in Oregon and the San Vincente Lumber Company near Santa Cruz, California, and was vice president of the F. S. Murphy Lumber Company in Quincy. He also served as president of the Utah-Idaho Sugar Company and on the board of the Western Pacific Railroad Company.

Henry H. Stoddard, one of three brothers engaged in the lumber trade, and Nibley met in Quincy in July 1922 to consider establishing a sawmill. Early the next year, Stoddard purchased thirty acres of the old Tefft place near Cromberg for five thousand dollars. This sum included important water rights from nearby Cogswell and Jackson Creeks. The Nibley-Stoddard Lumber Company, organized on March 1, 1923, represented their names in the corporate title plus two men residing in Santa Cruz. On the same day, an announcement revealed that the firm would build a mill on the Tefft place with a daily capacity of ninety thousand board feet, making it one of the larger mills in the area. The company also purchased one hundred million feet of standing timber in the Little Long Valley Unit and also arranged to acquire a similar amount of government timber.

With redwood lumber from Santa Cruz, work commenced on the bunkhouse, cookhouse, and dining hall. Stoddard, as general manager, expected the sawmill to be in full operation by August 1, 1923, but it was not to be. Some delay occurred before WP constructed a short rail link to the mill site that Stoddard needed to bring in a steam shovel to build his own logging railroad. After the initial incline section, the contemplated logging railroad was to reach out ten to twelve miles and be equipped with two Shay locomotives and a number of flatcars.

By October 1923, when construction of the mill began, a "semihotel," kitchen, and two dining halls (one with a poolroom) housed the construction workers. Early the next spring, Stoddard had 85 men on the payroll but no mill. Finally, in July 1924, the mill began sawing sixty thousand feet of logs each day. The steam shovel worked late into the fall, and the company had two miles of logging railroad ready when everything closed for the winter.

The Nibley-Stoddard logging railroad was in several sections. On the plateau, the Shay locomotive brought the cars of logs to the head of the incline. Controlled by a cable, the cars were lowered on an incline to the tracks below for switching as needed to the log pond and mill. Things usually went well, but during August 1925, a cloudburst overtook the area, pushing unmanageable log cars that inflicted damage as they crashed down the incline. The storm also washed out a portion of the nearby WP roadbed.

The mill cut an impressive sixteen million board feet in the 1927 season. Henry Stoddard awarded contracts for five 4-room cottages at Cromberg in the spring of 1928. Though Nibley had died in 1925, things worked well, and the outlook appeared bright—until the unexpected fire. On May 29, 1928, flames suddenly engulfed the whole sawmill at 2 A.M. and moved so fast that the men could do little to halt the fire that consumed the sawmill, engine room, and machine shop. Only the boiler house escaped. Henry Stoddard suffered slightly from burns as he battled the flames, and nearly 125 men were out of work.

With insurance covering much of the plant, Stoddard planned to rebuild the mill and went to Texas to buy machinery. Meanwhile, logging operations enabled the company to survive by sending an average of eleven cars of logs every day over Western Pacific to the Clover Valley Lumber Company mill in Loyalton.

Unable to find sawmill machinery on satisfactory terms, Stoddard began having second thoughts about rebuilding the mill because of the limited amount of timber still available. By April 1929, he announced that he would not rebuild the mill but would continue regular log shipments to the Loyalton mill. WP extended the N-S siding to accommodate the cars.

Two forest fires threatened Cromberg in 1929, but some people considered the Prohibition agent's raid on the nearby still far more disastrous. The following year Nibley-Stoddard crews moved the camp quarters to the plateau above Cromberg.

Responding to an oversupply in the lumber market, N-S laid off 20 men at its logging camps in August 1931. About the same time, the company's name appeared on the tax-delinquent list, and operations ceased.

Cromberg made news on December 14, 1933, when E. C. Rowe of Graeagle dismantled the N-S plant. A freight car went off the incline where it crossed the highway, creating a spectacle when it ended on its side.

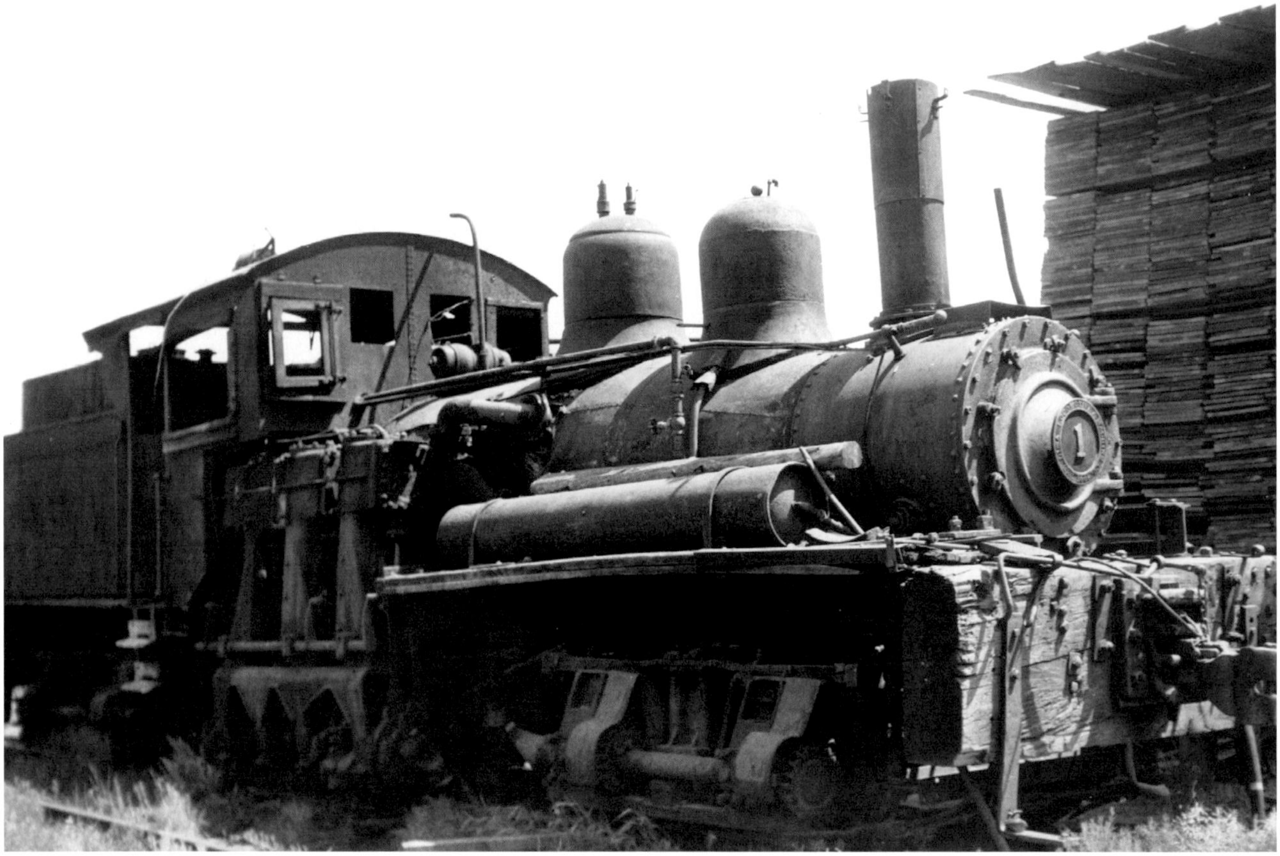

The affiliated San Vicente Lumber Company, near Santa Cruz, California, supplied the first locomotive to haul logs to the top of the incline. After operations ended at Cromberg, the engine was stored at Delleker, where this photograph was taken in 1937, shortly before it was sent to San Francisco for scrapping. (James E. Boynton photograph)

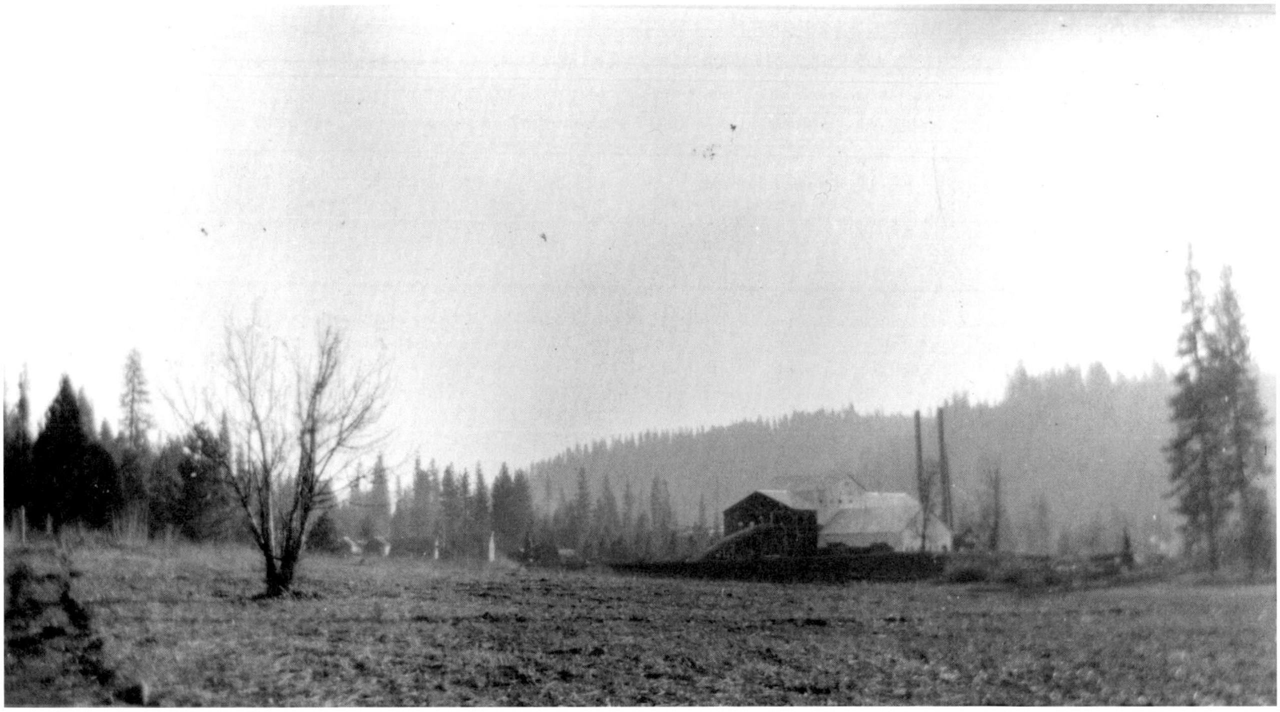

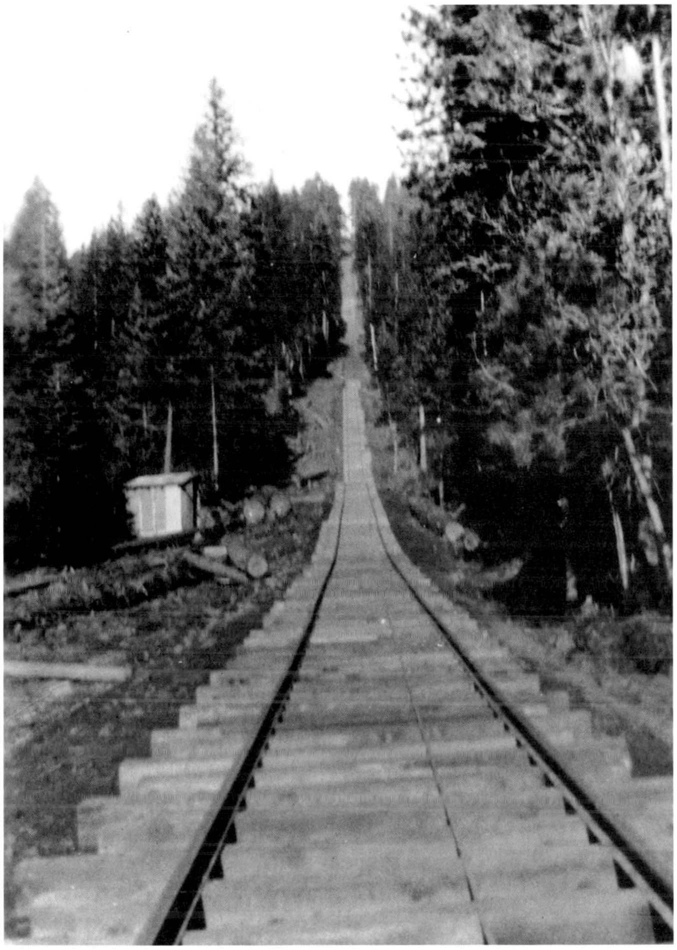

Above: The Nibley-Stoddard mill near Cromberg began operations in 1924. (Plumas County Museum)

Left: The Nibley-Stoddard mill, standing near Western Pacific at the base of a ridge, employed a Shay locomotive and a long incline to secure logs. The Quincy Lumber Company, confronted with a similar problem at East Quincy, resolved it in the same manner. (Plumas County Museum)

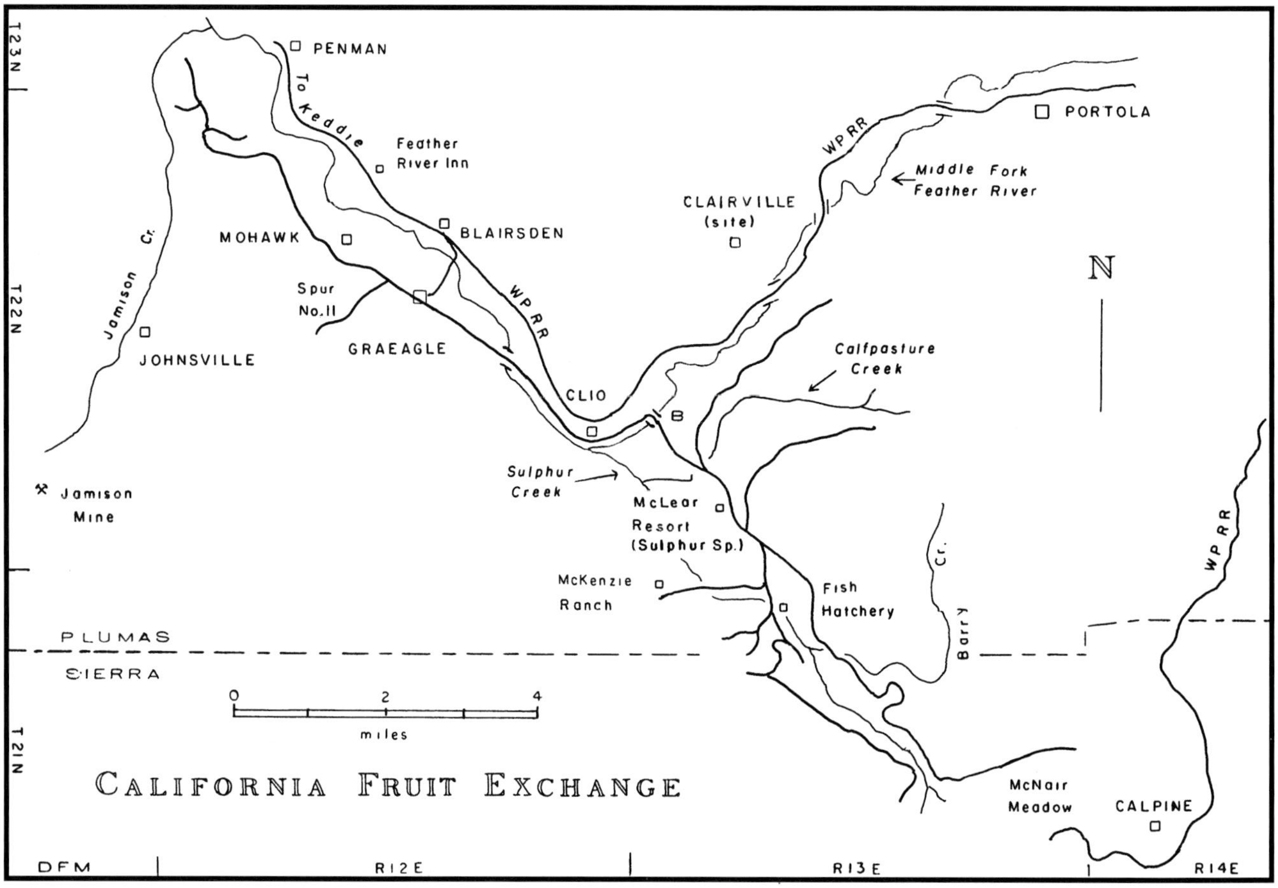

CALIFORNIA FRUIT EXCHANGE

Two years after the California Fruit Exchange constructed a standard-gauge railroad reaching five miles northwest from Graeagle, the company began building another railroad to tap timberlands in the Sulphur Creek watershed. In building the second railroad, the company utilized the former N-C-O Railway roadbed from Graeagle to a mile beyond Clio. Here the logging railroad crossed the Middle Fork of the Feather River on a bridge that collapsed in 1931 (see B on map.) Eventually, the CFE logging railroad extended to McNair Meadow, twelve miles from Graeagle.

This map is based largely on the updated map of James F. Flanagan as well as U.S. Forest Service and U.S. Geological Survey maps. So far, no map of the logging railroad of the Davies-Johnson Lumber Company has been found, but it is believed that this company had several logging spurs along upper Barry Creek linked to the mill at Calpine. The site of the Knickrem mill is slightly west of the end of Spur No. 11 near Graeagle.

DAVIES BOX AND LUMBER COMPANY CALIFORNIA FRUIT EXCHANGE— GRAEAGLE DAVIES-JOHNSON LUMBER COMPANY— CALPINE

Two major problems confronted Arthur Davies as 1915 was drawing to a close. For more than a decade his Davies Box and Lumber Company had run a successful lumber operation in Stampede Valley in Sierra County, California, and had used the wavering services of the Boca and Loyalton Railroad that pulled carloads of lumber from the spur at the Davies Mill for delivery to SP at Boca or WP at Portola.

Now all that was changing. The B&L, rapidly deteriorating along its way to partial abandonment, coupled with an exhausted timber supply, made alternatives imperative. Thirty-five miles to the northwest and many years previously, the Sierra Iron Company acquired several thousand acres of timberland in the Mohawk Valley as part of a grand plan for iron mining including a narrow-gauge railroad. However, after few steps toward the corporate goal, the scheme faltered and became dormant.

For reasons lost in time, Davies conferred with the principals of the Sierra Iron Company and in March 1916 purchased some three thousand acres of its timberland. The cost proved to be a hefty $250,000, but the terms were liberal. Following a down payment of only $26,000, Davies stood committed to monthly payments of $4,000 only during active months—June through December—and 6 percent interest on the unpaid balance. With the agreement signed, Davies moved his mill to the south side of the Middle Fork of the Feather River opposite Blairsden. Houses, after being sawed in half, were loaded on B&L flatcars in Stampede Valley and transferred to N C O narrow gauge cars for delivery at the mill site, and for a long time afterward, the saw cuts remained plainly visible. (Davies leased the land for the box factory and planing mill from J. W. Denten.)

As he had done in Stampede Valley, Davies used teams and steam-traction engines to bring logs to the pond but needed rail service to move box shook and lumber to distant markets. (Box shook is knocked-down boxes, usually packed in bundles of fifty ends, tops, or sides, that are sent to fruit-packing houses.)

Discussions with Western Pacific for a rail spur from Blairsden progressed nicely until the money question rose; WP wanted the box company to provide the necessary cross ties and then furnish $27,000 for construction. Certainly, there was no question that WP needed more traffic, but the company was then in the midst of financial reorganization. Davies threw up his hands and turned to the N-C-O Railway, which, in spite of its shaky finances, responded by building a 2.67-mile extension from Clio to the Davies Mill. (The box company contributed several thousand dollars to the cost of the narrow-gauge connection.) Opened in July 1916, the narrow gauge had a short life; it formed part of the sale of N-C-O Railway trackage to Western Pacific the following year. Subsequently, WP constructed a 6,658-foot standard-gauge connection under undisclosed terms.

Clio had fallen on hard times after WP construction ended, as payroll dollars no longer flooded stores and the thirteen saloons. The early-morning fire of April 5, 1916, would long be remembered as the worst in the history of the town. It all began with the explosion of the hot water tank in the kitchen of Alden Machomich's Western Pacific Hotel and ended with the destruction of the hotel, the Goering Saloon, and an empty store. The top of the boiler, hurled across the street, struck and killed Henry Bedsaul who was walking with two men. The other two, on either side of him, escaped injury. Machomich, formerly proprietor of the Beckwith Saloon and later operator of the Gold Lake (Camp) Lodge, rebuilt his Western Pacific Hotel, which lasted until heavy snow crushed part of the building in 1952, the year Portola people had to dig out of eight feet of snow. (When D. T. Machomich, presumably a relative, died in 1928 at the age of eighty-three, his obituary noted that he had hauled bridge timbers for Central Pacific during its construction in 1868.)

Of course, not everything always went well for Mr. Davies. January 1917 was a cold month; in nearby Quincy, the temperature dropped to zero for ten days, once falling to twelve degrees below zero. A fire in February threatened the entire plant, but fifty employees quickly formed an effective bucket brigade and confined the loss to the two-month-old box factory.

Davies staged a series of community dances at the clubhouse and arranged for a lumber truck to meet the Western Pacific trains at Blairsden. At one dance, Davies was inadvertently stabbed by a man coming to assist him while he was endeavoring to evict a troublesome patron. The errant man received a fifty-day jail sentence that the judge suspended if he found work.

During the years of World War I, prices of almost everything soared. The California Fruit Exchange (CFE), with beginnings in 1901 to assist deciduous fruit growers marketing their crops, heard complaints from its members over the sharply rising costs of wood packing boxes. J. L. Nagle, general manager of the cooperative, unsuccessfully sought cooperation of box manufacturers by modifying prices. In his own words, Nagle recounts his next step: "I broached this subject to a friend in San Francisco who was thoroughly acquainted with conditions surrounding the box shook and lumber industry and when I unfolded my plans, . . . he told me . . . that the plant of the Davies Box and Lumber Company . . . was available and I therefore left that night for Blairsden, arriving at the mill October 19th, 1919. I made as careful a survey of the plant my limited knowledge of the lumber business would permit and decided that the price of $225,000 was about what the plant was worth." The shook situation had become so acute that Nagle gave Davies his personal check for $10,000 to secure an option on the property.

The price included the town site (now known as Graeagle), box factory, sawmill, forty-three dwellings, a herd of dairy cattle, fifteen pedigreed hogs, fourteen head of Percheron horses, and logging equipment. The board of directors of the California Fruit Exchange confirmed Nagle's option and acquired the mill and thirty-eight hundred acres of timberlands for $664,000, with a $156,000 payment in January 1920 followed by five annual payments for the balance. When the cooperative took possession on January 1, it proved to be a quiet day, as many were recovering from the celebration of the previous night. Arthur Davies continued his involvement in the lumber industry at nearby Calpine.

California Fruit Exchange—Lumber Department

During the first year, the Lumber Department under the direction of A. M. Mortenson expanded its timber resources with the acquisition of the McKenzie holdings, renovated cottages, enlarged the sawmill, and established a company store.

Similar to other Plumas lumber firms, Graeagle suspended operations during the winters, but the demon fire had no respect for the season. In December 1922, shortly after midnight, a blaze fanned by high winds took out the store, theater, and clubhouse and damaged the office building. One man, dashing through the village warning people of the fire and wearing only his shoes and a smile, was nearly shot in the confusion.

A few days after the fire, Mortenson left his position to pursue other lumber activities. Herb Rowe, assisted by his brother Edgar "Eggs" Rowe, served as his replacement. Both men, born in Virginia City, moved away in their boyhood, and had worked at Hobart Mills before joining Graeagle. Their sister, Beth, became a marital connection with the Davies family, for Mrs. Arthur Davies's brother, John K. Teeter, became Beth's husband. Beth took the credit for naming both Graeagle and Calpine, a claim contested by others who say that Bell Burns, the daughter of Mrs. Davies by a previous marriage, suggested "Graeagle" in a contest and was rewarded with a bag of groceries from the company store. In any case, the post office recognized the change of name from Davies Mill to Graeagle in May 1920.

While a typical sawmill in the Plumas-Lassen area had a daily capacity of between forty thousand and sixty thousand board feet, Graeagle boasted a one hundred thousand–foot daily output in 1923. In April that year the company received a 7.5-ton truck to bring its logging fleet to five Bulldog Mack chain-drive trucks with solid rubber tires.

A Railroad Becomes Essential

One by one the buildings lost in the 1922 fire were replaced. The new Graeagle Clubhouse opened with a grand ball attended by two hundred people. As the distance between the logging areas and the mill lengthened, it became time to consider a railroad, and, in a major departure from existing practices, California Fruit Exchange began construction of a railroad in July 1924. Even with 1920s prices, the sixty thousand–dollar estimate for a five-mile standard-gauge railroad seems incredibly low, but that was the figure cited in the local press. Starting at the mill, the standard-gauge railroad proceeded northwest to the bluff overlooking Jamison Canyon, passing the site of the old Knickrem mill and going behind the Mohawk Tavern before entering a timbered area. Doubling back, the railroad crossed the county road for a second time as it ventured into a higher elevation. No sooner had work begun than the entire organization shut down so that every man could fight the brush fire on the Mohawk Ranch.

The only locomotive at Graeagle arrived in January 1925. A saddle-tank, oil-burning engine manufactured by Baldwin, it tested satisfactorily on the completed part of the new railroad. A brief setback occurred when a heavy rain damaged the new roadbed, but after repairs, delivery of logs to the mill by rail commenced in April. Two months later, when the board of directors arrived from Sacramento in a special Pullman car, the new engine took over and conveyed it over the last mile to the mill. That summer, the company erected an engine house and shop building. Unusually heavy rains for that season caused suspension of both logging and milling operations.

Arrangements were made for F. J. Zehner to live off-season in a new cottage built under the supervision of Steve Pezolla, who formerly drove the stage to the mining town of Johnsville. During tourist season, Zehner and his wife ran their Gray Eagle Lodge. Plans for extending the railroad in the other direction to Clio and Sulphur Springs surfaced in October 1925 when the company secured a right-of-way through lands of Frank D. Oldham. Meanwhile, sawmill workers deviated from their principal task to cut boards for a minor addition to the Feather River Inn across the river.

The Family Atmosphere in Graeagle

The Graeagle community enjoyed a warm family spirit, as the residents took care of each other when the need arose. Mrs. Herb Rowe is remembered as a "wonderful person" and always among the first to help. The fifty-three cottages in 1930 with three to five rooms rented for ten to fifteen dollars per month, which included water, garbage removal, and electricity. Firewood—mill ends—was sold by the bundle, but still it could be cold enough to break water pipes. Two large rooming houses accommodated the one hundred single men.

As a precaution against nosy Prohibition agents, a trapdoor hidden under a bed or a carpet led to a small wine cellar in the houses. Each year the Sacramento office would send four or five barrels of grapes packed in sawdust for distribution to the Italian workers who made their own wine. When stacking lumber, some men brought water bags with them, while the containers of the Italians held wine, but they never became intoxicated on the job.

Although the company payroll listed no physicians, Dr. Coutler or Dr. McKnight came down from Portola once a week to attend those leaving their names at the office. The medical men went from house to house, always reserving their final call for the house with the best liquor.

Unless one could get to Clio or Portola, the company store was the only provider. Twenty-dollar coupon books, issued to families, were repaid during summer employment. Single men, often drifters but good fighters, departed for cities when winter closed work in the woods. Where possible, family men received alternative employment, but there could be tough times. One family remarked that they existed on canned beans for an entire winter!

Happier times came with steady employment, even with long hours. Sunday diversions included boccie ball games and ice skating on the millpond. Santa Claus (Bert Haywood) assisted by Herb Rowe brought presents for every child, and the company gave each family a Christmas turkey. Dances during the peak season when the payroll reached three hundred plus college students on vacation jobs were particularly welcomed by the ladies, as they received extra attention from the college men. Usually, dances lasted all night long, with a break for a delicious chicken dinner at the cookhouse. With dawn, the men quickly changed into work clothes and boarded the train for a day of logging in the woods.

Railroading in Another Direction

Several Santa Clara College engineering students gained practical experience when they assisted James F. Flanagan, formerly with the SP engineering department in Sacramento, in locating the new logging line reaching up into the Mohawk Valley to the McLear Ranch. The ranch house, built in 1852, came into the possession of George McLear fifteen years later and became a modest resort known as the White Sulphur Springs House. Subsequently, by a series of bequests, it came into the possession of Harry McKenzie whose pioneer grandfather logged in the area.

The former N-C-O roadbed provided a useful course for the new railroad for the 3.83 miles between Graeagle and the bridge site a mile beyond Clio. With a few helpers, Orovale Miller began construction in 1927. Born in Knight's Landing, he joined California Fruit Exchange as a logger in 1922. When the performance of two Caterpillar tractors pleased the company, it acquired several more, and Orovale became the third man entrusted with one of these new machines.

Pulling the narrow-gauge ties constituted the first task to be accomplished by scrapers and Caterpillars. Using a small homemade pile driver, the men built bridges that crossed the Middle Fork of the Feather River and Sulphur Creek near the subsequent golf course. As the railroad lengthened, major trestles spanned Chicken Creek, Barry Creek, and another creek near the McKenzie house. At that time, the rails from the dismantled Jamison Creek line were transferred to the new railroad.

From then on, the annual custom added about a mile of track to keep ahead of the loggers. Generally, railroad building took place in summer months, whereas bridge work occurred during the winter. The rails of the Blue Anchor—the name used by the cooperative in marketing its deciduous fruit—followed the northerly side of

Sulphur Creek most of the way, to end at McNair Meadow, twelve miles from Graeagle. Along the way, the track formed a loop to get around a small stream. At about one thousand–foot intervals, short spurs left the main track to enable engines to push empty cars into the woods for loading. A two-mile spur followed Calfpasture Ravine about two miles east of Clio. Just below the McLear Ranch, a spur crossed Sulphur Creek, and after negotiating switchbacks, trains continued for several miles on the south side of the creek. Perhaps the one-mile Kalamazoo branch acquired its name from a homesick Michigan man. According to unconfirmed reports, a physical connection existed between the Graeagle railroad and the Davies-Johnson logging line starting at Calpine.

Men in the woods worked a ten-hour day, six and sometimes seven days a week. Trains brought them to and from work each day, so, unlike some forestry operations, the men returned home each night. During the day, trains of seven to nine cars conveyed logs to the mill.

The railroad crew included Orren Barton, the engineer who was also Mrs. Ed Rowe's father. Everett Slaughter was the fireman, and his father, Buzz Slaughter, served as conductor. The brakeman's name has been lost, but he is remembered as a big, tall fellow living in Clio.

Unlike some lumber operations, the company did not sponsor railroad picnics, but young boys managed to slip aboard the cars for enticing but unauthorized rides.

Each spring, the railroad roadbed was repaired where necessary, and men inspected the rolling stock. Woods workers sharpened their saws by filing, and, until replaced by Caterpillar tractors after 1925, other men serviced the donkey engines in the field. Additionally, two horses, Tom and Kate, aided the logging crews. A huge horse, Tom knew how to pull a cable and where to take it in logging work. At the end of the day, a man would slap him on the rump and say, "Home, Tom," and the horse always returned. Old Tom died in February 1932, having reached his twenty-second year.

The railroad had its share of mishaps. On May 27, 1930, two heavily loaded runaway cars came down the main spur, jumped a switch into the lumber-loading track, and struck a string of boxcars with such force that they smashed through the wall of the box factory, finally halting on the far side of the interior. Certainly a frightening experience for workers inside, fortunately their guardian angel kept them out of the path of the errant boxcars.

The Spectacular Bridge Failure

Operations commenced in 1931 with shortened hours—eight instead of ten—for both the steel gang and woodsmen. July 23 started as a typical mountain summer day, but at 7:45 A.M. things changed radically when the Feather River bridge collapsed under the morning work train. The rear of the engine and the front of the passenger car dropped ten feet into the riverbed to end up in a V formation.

Of the fifty men on board, thirteen entered the Portola hospital. O. L. Barton, the engineer, stuck to his post and escaped injury, but, in light of the event, he and his wife understandably sought a change of scenery for a few days in San Francisco.

J. J. Brennan and J. L. Nagle, president and general manager of California Fruit Exchange, respectively, arrived to make a personal investigation. According to a neighbor, the braking action of the train bringing in logs the night before pushed the stringers off the caps of the pilings, leaving no support for the next train.

This break came at a busy time, for the box factory was sending out twenty-five cars each week, which called for overtime. By jacks and cables, the locomotive, relatively undamaged, was returned to the rails. The passenger car with its red velvet seats had a different story and was retired. Trucks transported logs to the mill during the time a Western Pacific pile driver was restoring the bridge.

With the exception of Sam Samorovich, the injured men reported for work within a few days. A new passenger car, from an unknown source, arrived in time for the resumption of train operations on August 12, 1931.

According to a 1938 report, the CFE Lumber Department set its locomotive aside, and Western Pacific operated the logging trains under a contract. In 1940, the Lumber Department was transferred to the Graeagle Lumber Company as a CFE subsidiary, and during World War II logging railroad operations ended.

Graeagle Lumber also logged at Spring Garden, using trucks to convey logs to cars on the WP siding where a freight local would take them to the Graeagle mill. The same firm conducted a similar operation from a camp along Last Chance Creek (now covered by Frenchman Lake) and sent logs by rail from Chilcoot.

The sawmill closed down on November 30, 1956, because of depleted timber resources, but the box factory and molding mill continued operations until the next spring. The company, possessing the town of Graeagle and twelve thousand acres of cutover timberland, held the property until a buyer came along. After several months of negotiations, Harvey E. West and his sons acquired the property in early 1958 through the Placerville Lumber Company and subsequently have created an attractive resort around Graeagle and Blairsden.

In 1969, the growers' marketing cooperative underwent a change, creating a parent corporation under the name of Blue Anchor Inc. with the California Fruit Exchange as a subsidiary.

A tabulation of interstate shipments of California deciduous fruits revealed that 5,007 cars were shipped in 1898, with peaches and pears constituting one-half. By 1920 grape shipments made up two-thirds of the 35,430 cars dispatched that year. In the peak years of 1924–1930, after reaching a maximum of 87,389 cars in 1928, shipments steadily declined to 37,026 cars in 1957, with grapes contributing a high proportion of shipments in both years.

Davies-Johnson Lumber Company at Calpine

Just what Arthur Davies had in mind after selling his mill and box factory we shall never know, but only a few months elapsed before he was back in the lumber and box business again in an even larger style.

In March 1920, Davies purchased seventeen thousand acres of timberland about ten miles east of Graeagle that included the Upland and McAlpine tracts. James McAlpine, a Minnesota lumberman, had died in August 1913 in his Duluth home "under mysterious circumstances." A year later, his widow and her sister disputed the share of the estate left to each of them and took the matter to court. Local interest in the matter stemmed from the fact that the sister, Mrs. Mattie B. Titus, had been a resident of nearby Beckwith.

As part of the general plan of development, the Davies Lumber Corporation, formed March 5, 1920, talked of building a ten-mile standard-gauge branch from Western Pacific at a point two and a half miles east of Hawley to a model town and mill on the former Knuthson place. "Calpine" was the name chosen for the new settlement, and on June 21, 1921, the company name became Davies-Johnson Lumber Company to include the name of C. R. Johnson of Alameda.

A. A. Kramm of the WP engineering staff in Sacramento soon began locating the branch line, but ownership had changed before Western Pacific assumed construction. During the next twelve months, the railroad connection became a reality, and in June 1921, T. J. Wyche, then WP's chief engineer, inspected the new line under construction. In the first four miles, the branch climbed almost three hundred feet to a modest summit before entering Folchi Meadows and keeping away from Sierra Valley. Though no explanation of the location was reported, marshes in Sierra Valley may have made the foothill route more desirable and may also have been the reason for moving the connection to a point two miles *west* of Hawley.

Triweekly mixed-train service from Portola began near the end of July 1921, and when the job was pronounced "finished" on August 2, Palmer and McBryde, contractors, closed down, and by noon all hands had gone. When Calpine secured a post office, Davies secured permission to operate a gasoline speeder over the branch to bring in the mail on alternate days.

A heavy accumulation of snow in February 1922 isolated Calpine residents for nine days until a WP snowplow fought its way through sixteen feet of snow at the summit. So delighted were the residents to be rescued from isolation, they held a dance in celebration. Men in the box factory resumed making cantaloupe crates, while others took shovels to dig out two engines caught in the yard.

With the arrival of summer, three camps fed logs to the sawmill, notwithstanding a forest fire consuming valuable timber. Things went well until winter snows brought the closure of the mill on November 7. Some weeks later, another snowfall obliterated the track, so the incoming engineer could not see that the WP rails had been pushed out of line by a falling rock. Consequently, his locomotive derailed and required the assistance of another engine from Portola to get it back on the track.

During the spring of 1923 when Arthur Davies had a prolonged stay in a San Francisco hospital after an operation, the company commenced railroad logging operations with No. 4, a Shay locomotive passed down through four or five previous owners. With better weather and a track extension, trains began delivering logs to the millpond on April 9, 1923. The motive-power fleet expanded that month with the acquisition of a rod engine. Though the correspondent described it as a "new" locomotive, it was new only to that location, for No. 26 had been acquired from the dismantled Ocean Shore Railroad. Perhaps for health reasons, Davies disposed of his interest in the early summer of that year.

During the winter months when operations were suspended, the Calpine locomotives spent time in the WP shops in Portola for general renovations before returning to the forests next spring. In March 1925, Bill Whitlesey served as conductor, while K. W. "Pug" Nicholson bossed the logging crews as they cut trees and brought the logs to the railroad with steam tractors and large wheels.

The plant, besides the logging operations, included a steam-powered sawmill with a capacity of some eighty thousand feet per shift, a box factory, and a planing mill. Frank N. Blagen, the longtime superintendent, satisfied his strong desire for the sea by building his own boat, shipping it to the coast, and sailing it to Hawaii.

Calpine, which had a population of about five hundred when the mill was in full operation, underwent a major change after the mill closed for the last time in 1939. The branch line was abandoned the following year, and new owners sold lots to people desiring second homes.

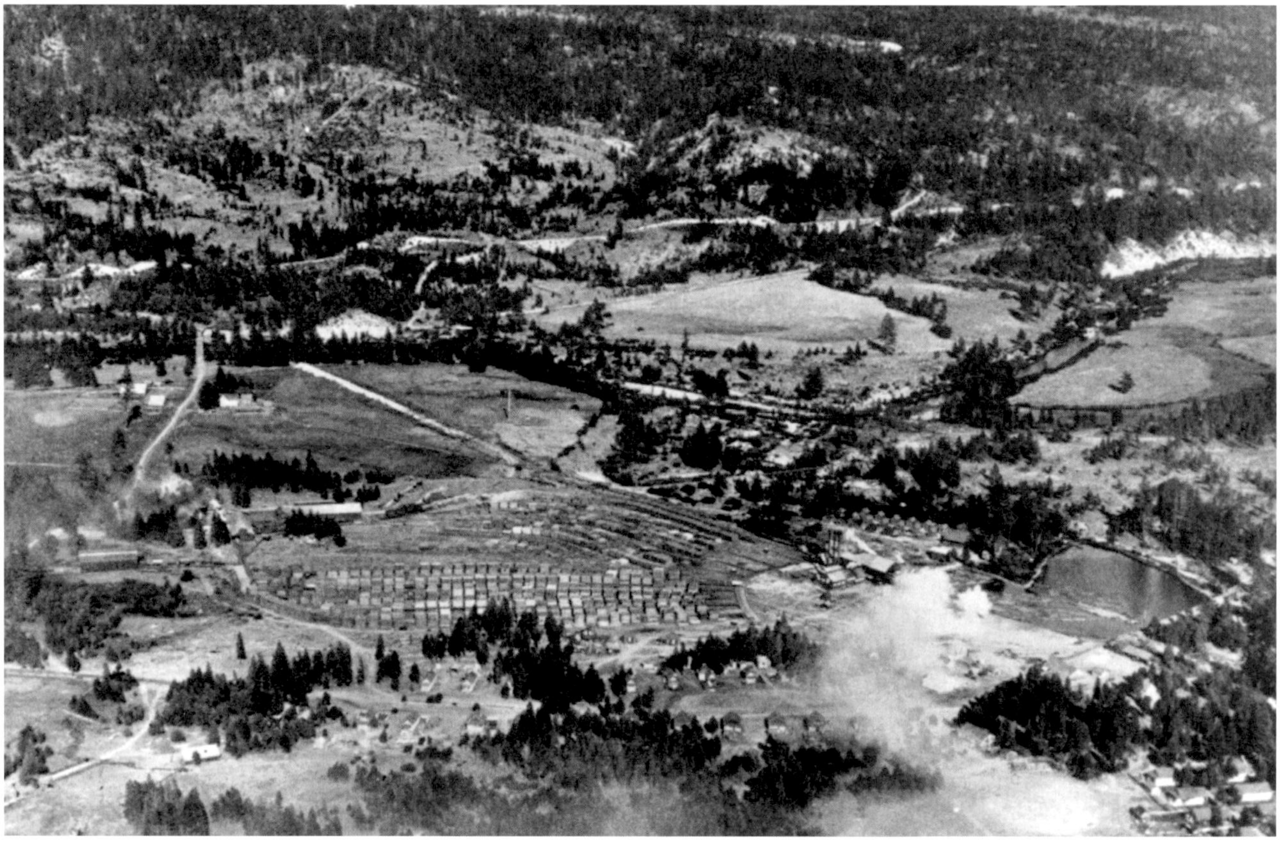

An aerial view of the lumberyards of the California Fruit Exchange at Graeagle.

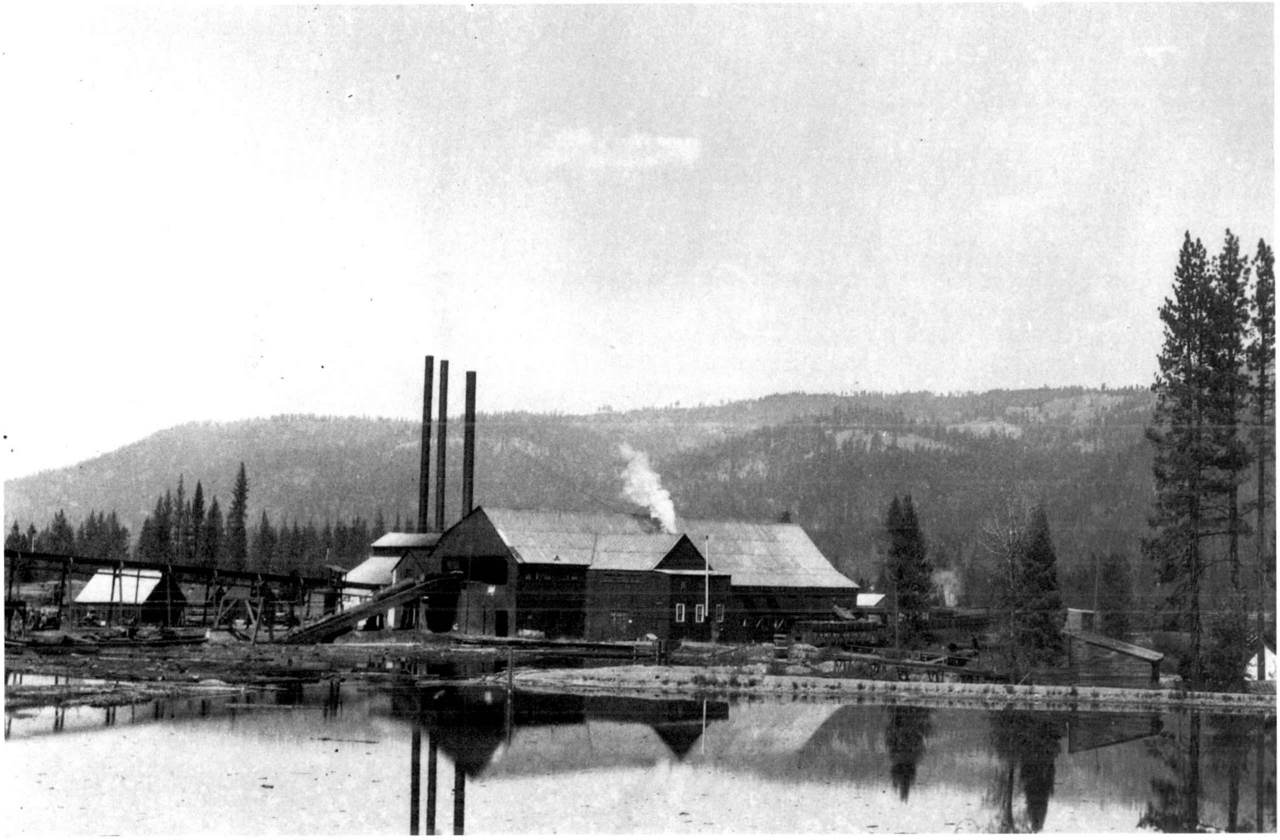

The California Fruit Exchange box factory at Graeagle.

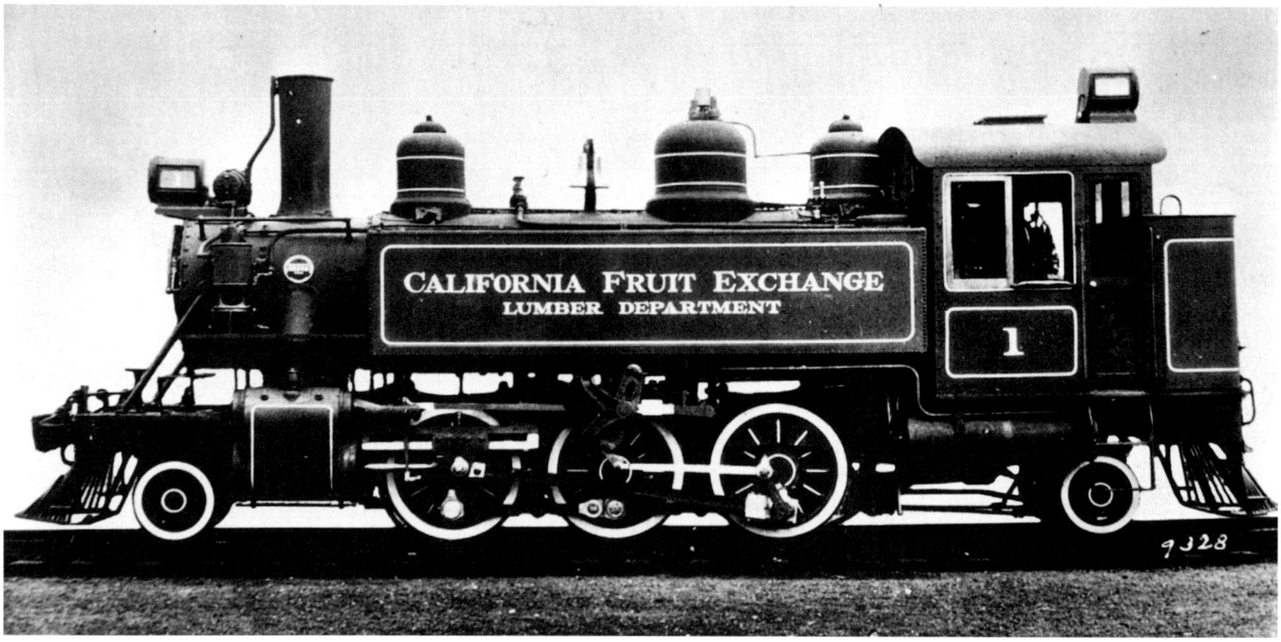

The California Fruit Exchange owned just one locomotive during its operations. Built by Baldwin in 1924, this 2-6-2T engine became No. 14 of the California Western Railroad and Navigation Company when it was sent to Fort Bragg, California, in 1938. (James E. Boynton collection)

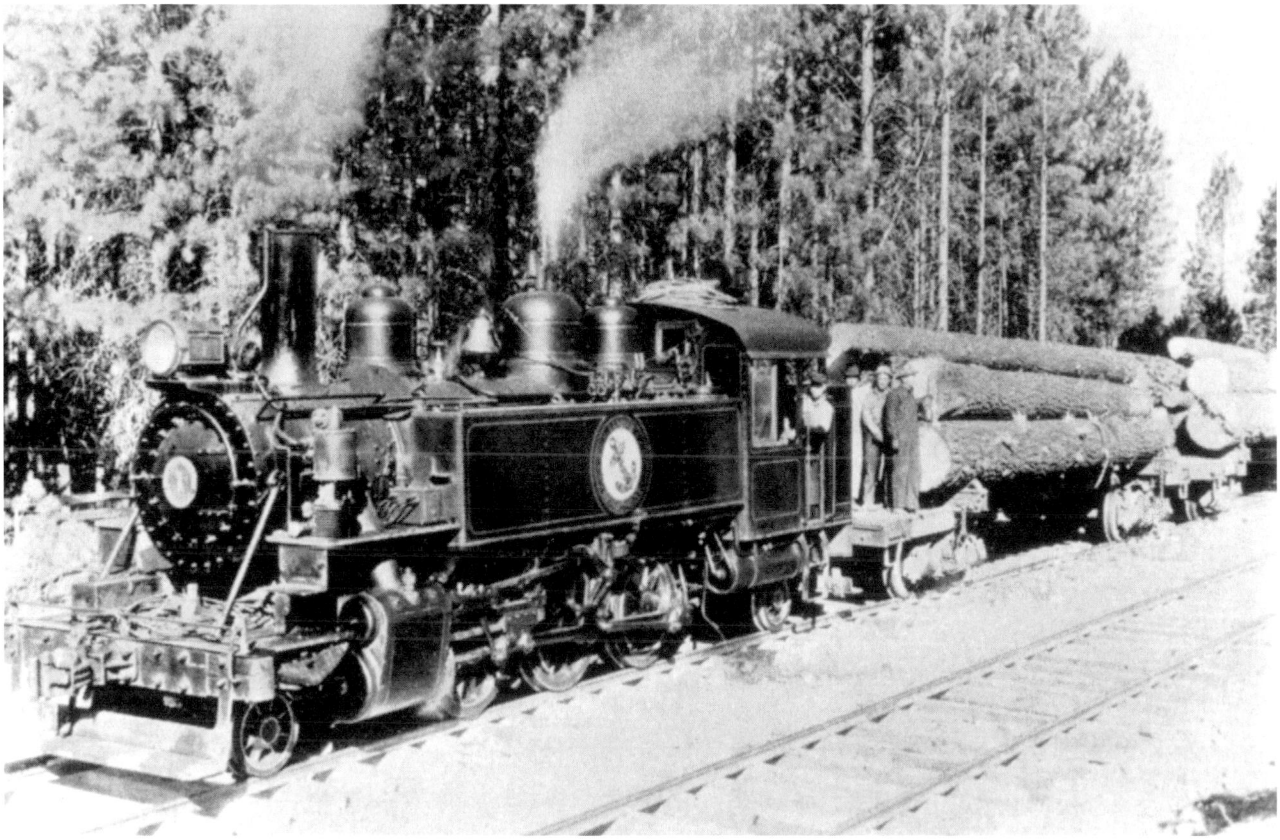

California Fruit Exchange No. 1 kept the box factory supplied with logs. (From *The Blue Anchor,* September 1930)

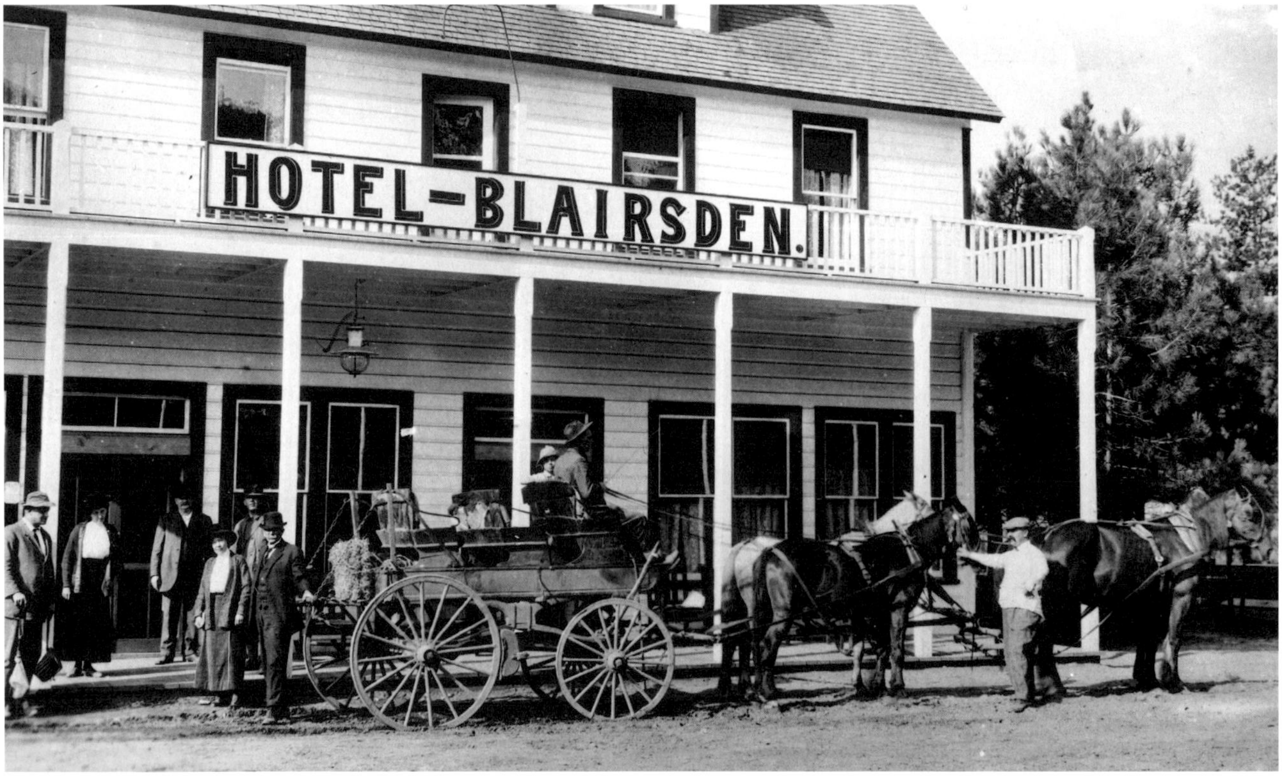

A freight wagon is about to depart from the nearby Hotel Blairsden. (Joslyn-Dunscomb collection)

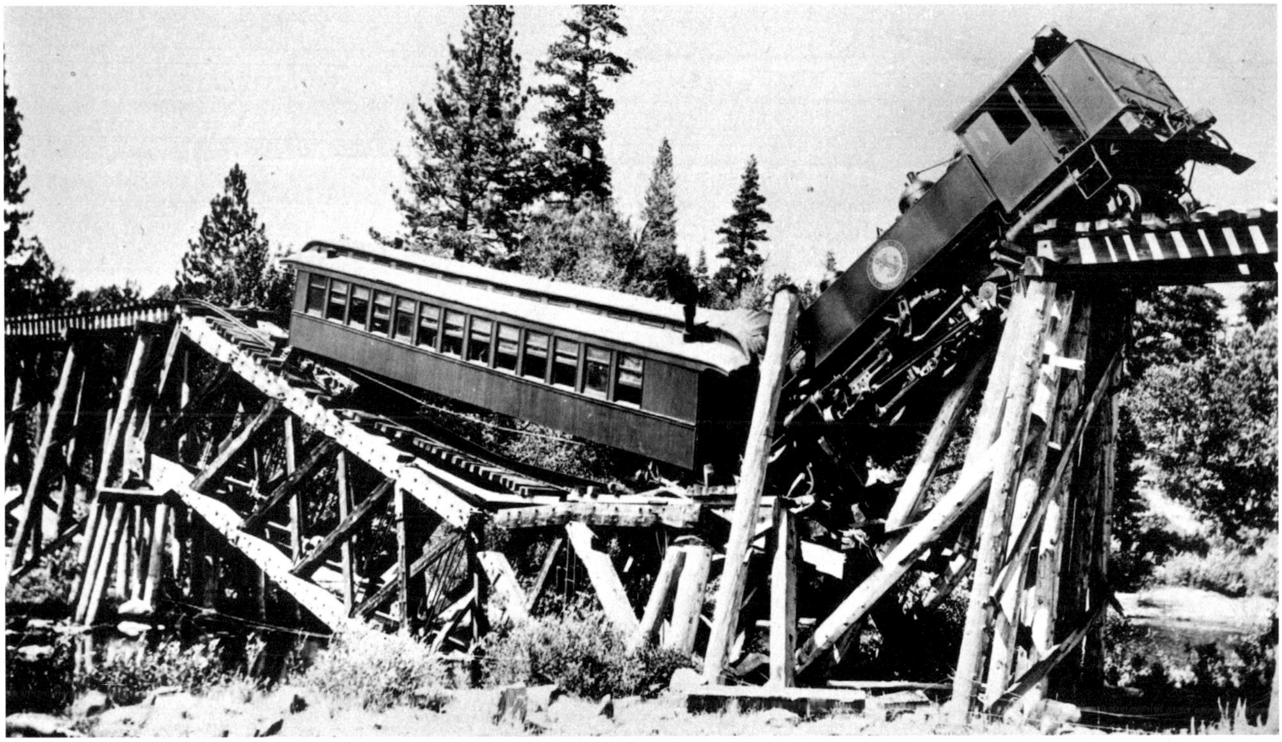

Above: It was a very short train but sufficiently heavy to cause this bridge over the Middle Fork of the Feather River to collapse on July 23, 1931, creating this spectacular scene. Still, most of the forty men going to work in the woods that day escaped injury. (James E. Boynton collection)

Below: The railroad is only a fading memory, but portions of the rebuilt trestle still remain.

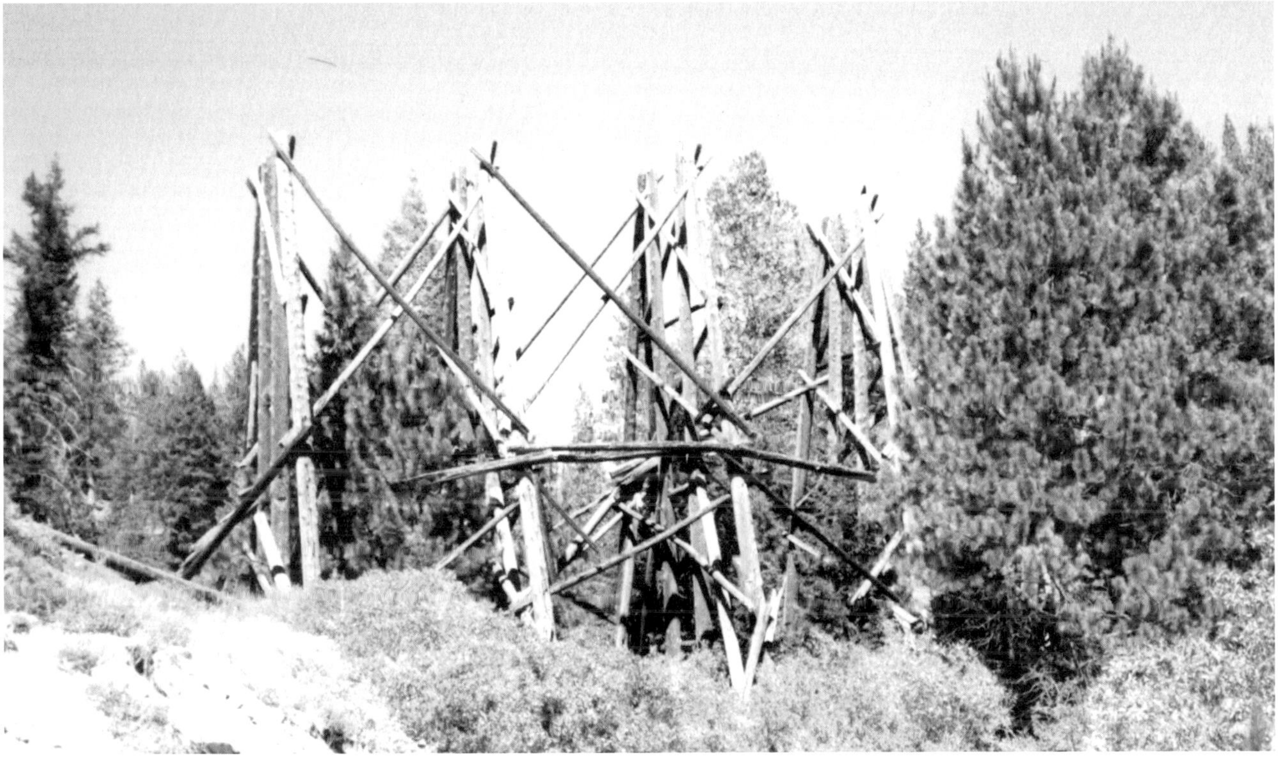

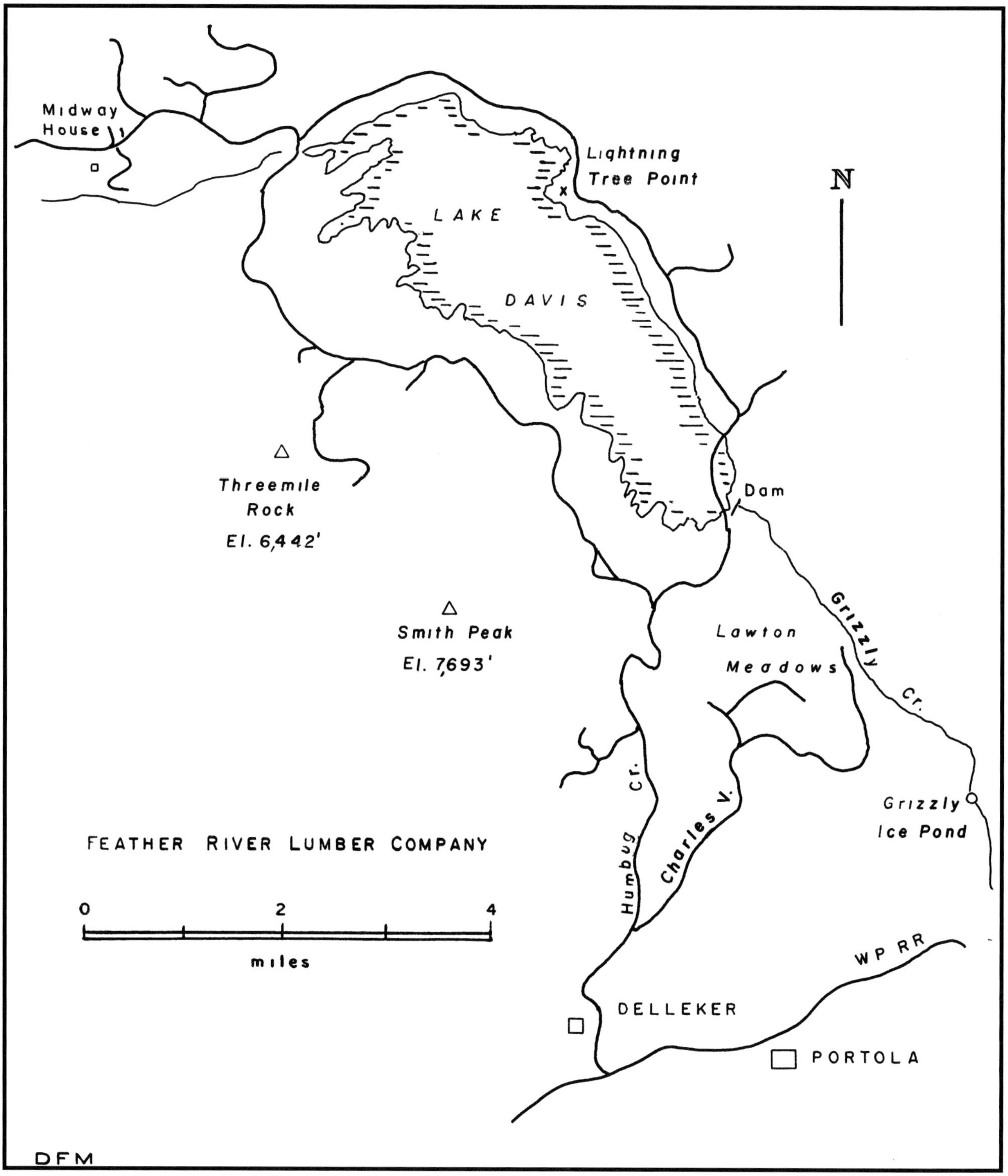
Midway House
Lightning Tree Point
N
LAKE
DAVIS
Threemile Rock
El. 6,442'
Dam
Smith Peak
El. 7,693'
Lawton Meadows
Grizzly Cr.
Grizzly Ice Pond
Humbug Cr.
Charles V.
FEATHER RIVER LUMBER COMPANY
0
2
4
miles
WP RR
DELLEKER
PORTOLA
DFM

FEATHER RIVER LUMBER COMPANY

Several companies with the name Feather River Lumber Company (FRLC) operated in Plumas, Butte, and Sierra Counties in northeastern California. This chapter focuses on the Feather River Lumber Company that operated at Delleker, near Portola, for about thirty-five years. Another company with a similar name, a promotion of H. H. Yard, was located near Blinzig station on the Western Pacific, some ninety-three miles below Portola. Still another had been situated at Prattville in 1892, while after subsequent decades the name was used in the take-over of the Clover Valley Lumber Company with mills in Loyalton.

The Feather River Lumber Company incorporated in Colorado on December 23, 1904, for the stated purpose of conducting business in "Colorado, California or elsewhere." A few weeks later, it filed its papers in California as a "foreign corporation." Principal backers included Theodore A. Schomberg (also involved in northern New Mexico lumbering), George Laws, and William H. Delleker.

The new company purchased several established sawmills, starting in March 1905 with the Totten mill and twenty-four hundred acres of its timberland. Located at the end of a two-mile Sierra Valleys Railway spur from Clairville, it became Feather River Lumber Company Mill No. 1. When J. W. Webster sold his Humbug Valley mill at the future site of Delleker, it was designated as FRLC No. 2 mill. No. 3 mill, just south of Clio, cut timbers from that area.

Initial activity failed to attract much attention; in the summer of 1905, FRLC had fifty loggers at work. The company harvested timber along the Sierra Valleys Railway between Clairville and Clio and then worked around Clairville. Two years later, during the construction of Western Pacific, the company secured a contract to supply seven thousand cross ties.

Farther west in Butte County, the Feather River Lumber Company purchased timberland from H. H. Yard in 1910 as well as a portion of the Pearl Orchard that adjoined Camp Enjoyment. Rather than constructing a logging railroad, plans called for traction road engines to bring logs to the mill, with the finished product going to the WP. In the 1909 dismantling of the old Chino mill, usable timbers were set aside for building the new sawmill. It appears that this mill did not materialize under the Feather River Lumber Company banner.

George Laws established the town of Delleker in 1909 as Western Pacific approached completion. The next year, his company purchased sixty-one hundred acres of timberland in the upper part of Charles Valley from the Reno Mill and Lumber Company. Laws's company also participated in the blossoming town of Portola when it supplied finished lumber to the Superior California Land Improvement Company of Sacramento for building a number of cottages in Portola. Unfortunately, the improvement company failed to pay its bills, so the FRLC took it to court in 1912 and secured a judgment, and the former's home lots were sold at a sheriff's auction.

In 1914, the Feather River Lumber Company carefully entered into logging railroad activity to serve Mill No. 2 at Delleker. From J. L. Humphrey, it secured a right-of-way across his ranch. Probably because of the convenience of the narrow-gauge Sierra Valleys Railway running by its front door and serving all three mills plus the advantage of lower construction costs, the lumber company settled on a narrow-gauge (thirty-six-inch) logging railroad. Through its Colorado connections, it secured two Shay locomotives from the defunct Argentine Central Railway. The promoter of the Colorado railroad contemplated ore shipments and summer tourist traffic for sustenance. That road did not prove to be a financial success—in part because the promoter, also a Methodist minister, refused to operate tourist trains on Sundays—and went into receivership five years after its opening. The Shays, bearing Nos. 5 and 4 on the Argentine Central, became FRLC's Nos. 1 and 2, respectively.

When the two engines arrived from Colorado, it was almost impossible to read the road-ownership lettering, but Stan Johnson, later a longtime Plumas resident, sensed some familiarity with the two hulks that had been stored near his parents' home in Colorado. Recalling that as a boy he had carved his initials in the interior of the wood cabs, he investigated and found his initials had withstood the test of years.

At that time, the Sierra Valleys Railway was approaching its final years as it struggled to compete with the two standard-gauge railroads—WP and B&L—paralleling its tracks. Although the lumber company had talks with the

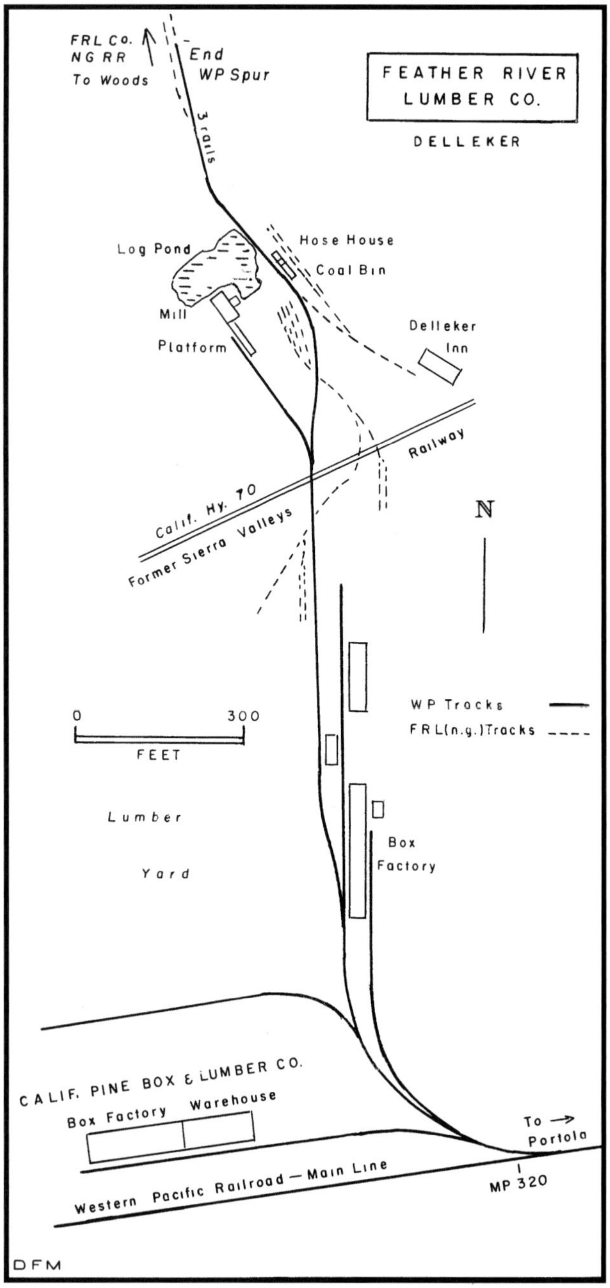

little railroad's management relating to the purchase of some or all of the branch, nothing came of it.

California Pine Box and Lumber Company

Although the California Pine Box and Lumber Company did not have a logging railroad, its proximity to the No. 2 mill of the Feather River Lumber Company warrants recognition. Started by a group of prominent Pacific Coast lumbermen in 1903, its box factory at Loyalton had so many orders two years later that its men worked overtime. It had its share of fires, including one in a boxcar at its lumberyard in Verdi. One hundred men responded, only to find that the fire hose had been cut in three places. Some men found another, and, with an SP fire train from Truckee, the blaze was extinguished.

Under the direction of George X. Wendling, an Oregon lumberman and president of the firm, one of the largest box factories in California was planned to be erected at Delleker with a power plant generating enough electricity to operate the fifteen saws and provide lighting for the plant of the FRLC. Construction problems delayed the opening, scheduled for January 1915, until August, only to be postponed again.

Friday, August 13, 1915, proved to be unlucky, as a fire that started in the lumberyard of the Feather River Lumber Company spread to the neighboring yard of the California Pine Box and Lumber Company and burned fiercely. Though the mills were saved after a ten-hour battle, the blaze consumed twenty-two million feet of cut lumber, to bring the loss to three hundred thousand dollars. A sixteen hundred–foot spur serving the box factory completed six weeks earlier was lost but was subsequently replaced.

The fire started in two places in the FRLC yard, and the night watchman reported seeing a man fleeing from one blaze. The Industrial Workers of the World was suspected, for it had allegedly set fires all over California. The pattern of starting fires after midnight also followed the pattern of several fires in Beckwith. The Western Pacific Hotel, post office, and Capital Saloon in Beckwith burned May 6, and fire destroyed the Plumas Commercial Hall and two saloons some weeks later.

The Logging Railroad and More Fires

The Feather River Lumber Company's logging railroad at Delleker began with a single mile in 1916 but increased to six miles the following year as it reached into Lawton Meadows. A year later a summer fire around Clio destroyed two miles of FRLC log chutes as well as three donkey engines. Fires were part of the life of sawmills everywhere, and 1919 confirmed that image. In January a local blaze threatened the entire Delleker plant, but strong efforts limited the destruction to the planing mill. A WP switch engine hurried over from Portola, pulled two boxcars, but could not rescue a flatcar. In July a more extensive fire destroyed the mill buildings. A month later a forest fire threatened Mill No. 1 near Clairville, but after every male from Camp Layman and the Plumas Lumber Company was called in, the danger eased.

Woods operations commenced earlier than usual when Joseph Arnell, woods superintendent, took a force out to begin logging in February 1920. William Proctor, locomotive engineer, brought logs to the mill as late as November to end an unusually long season. Arnell, after resigning from his position, returned the next year to pilot the first log train as the season opened on April 11. Already the woods camp had been established, with Mr. Longwell in charge while Guy Shipton served as woods superintendent.

The Delleker 1922 program started at the middle of April with the full intention of milling between ninety thousand and one hundred thousand board feet each day, making it one of the larger lumber producers in that area. A derailment retarded this ambitious schedule for a few days in April when rails spread as two Shay engines were bucking well-packed snow. Both engines overturned; luckily, no injuries resulted.

Things turned out differently in another derailment a few weeks later to end in a tragedy. Four young men who had come to work in the box factory climbed aboard a locomotive for a Sunday ride into the woods. Rounding a curve, the engine hit a soft spot in the roadbed that caused it to tip, then hesitate, and finally fall on its side, trapping two men under the heavy Shay. Delmar Brown, nineteen, of Lindsay in Tulare County was killed, while his chum Edward Niels stood at death's door for some time.

Joe Arnell, after explaining that "woods work no longer attracted him and that he proposed to stay as far away from actual logging operations as he conveniently could," left the Feather River Lumber Company. His next job was driving a jitney to the Walker copper mine.

The Industrial Workers of the World plagued many industries in the second and third decades of the twentieth century, and Plumas lumber operators stood among its targets. Twice in 1923 it shut down the Feather River firm, but the company managed to resume logging and sawing.

By 1925, the company's railroad measured twenty miles. A relocation to the west side of Grizzly Creek replaced the original route on the east side. Eventually, the line extended into Grizzly Valley, terminating two miles west of "Midway House." At various times, railroad spurs poked their way into small canyons, the tracks following Cow Creek to the foot of Threemile Rock being an example. The company also commenced using Caterpillar tractors to haul logs to the railroad about this time.

In 1926, George W. Laws, president and general manager of the Feather River Lumber Company, suffered a dizzy spell and fell on a stove in his office. A week later his condition had sufficiently improved so he could be taken to Reno in an ambulance with a nurse and Dr. John Decker. From there, he went by train to Denver accompanied by Dr. Decker.

In October that year, Delleker took on a scene of great activity as MGM filmed *The Trail of '98*, starring Karl Dane and Polly Moran. Though the story was centered in Alaska, MGM found that the Feather River logging train and log pond met its needs, except one Sunday when an engine derailment suspended filming for three hours. No difficulties stood in the way of securing movie "extras," as 130 locals were delighted to take part in the production. This was not the first time the movie people used Delleker; filmed the previous fall, *The Rowdy*, a movie about a frontier lumber camp, included scenes around Delleker and Graeagle. The forest fire scene was at the site of the old Knickrem mill, not far from Graeagle.

As his health improved, Laws was able to return to his desk in June 1930 to begin the struggle of survival common to most lumber operators in the 1930s.

A revival in housing construction improved lumber markets, which caused the company to acquire another Shay engine in 1935, this one being a three-truck model from the Madera Sugar Pine Company. (Over the years, its roster included five Shays.)

Burton Mason fired one of the remaining Shays in 1936 and recalled the challenge offered by the five switchbacks in sixteen miles. Each one had a short tail track that necessitated breaking trains into two sections and tying them down carefully with hand brakes after sections of the train had negotiated each switchback.

In 1937, the engineer, a colorful character from Tuolumne sporting a black bar-handled mustache, proved to be the unfortunate engineer of a runaway train that never made a curve, resulting in several fatalities.

In June 1939, another train bringing down twelve cars of logs left the rails four miles north of Delleker, resulting in the death of the engineer and serious injuries to other crew members. A few weeks later, six million feet of dry lumber suffered the indignity of being reduced to ashes by a fire that also destroyed the plant tramway linking the sawmill to the box factory and planing mill, the dry shed, car repair shop, and yard office. Additionally, several thousand feet of steel rails had to be replaced. Brighter news came the following week when Harold G. Laws, general manager, announced that the repairs had been made so that the 350 men could return to work.

Trucks had entered the scene in the late 1920s and finally took over all transportation requirements, which ended railroad operations in 1943 during the company's period of peak production when some forty-five million feet of timber went through the sawmill annually.

Three years later, Tarter, Webster, and Johnson, a subsidiary of the American Forest Products Corporation, became the owner of the firm. Lacking available timber resources, the company closed down in 1958 when it failed to win a bid for U.S. Forest Service timber. The next year, the sawmill and even the town were sold at an auction, and Delleker, which long supported a payroll of 250 names, vanished from the scene.

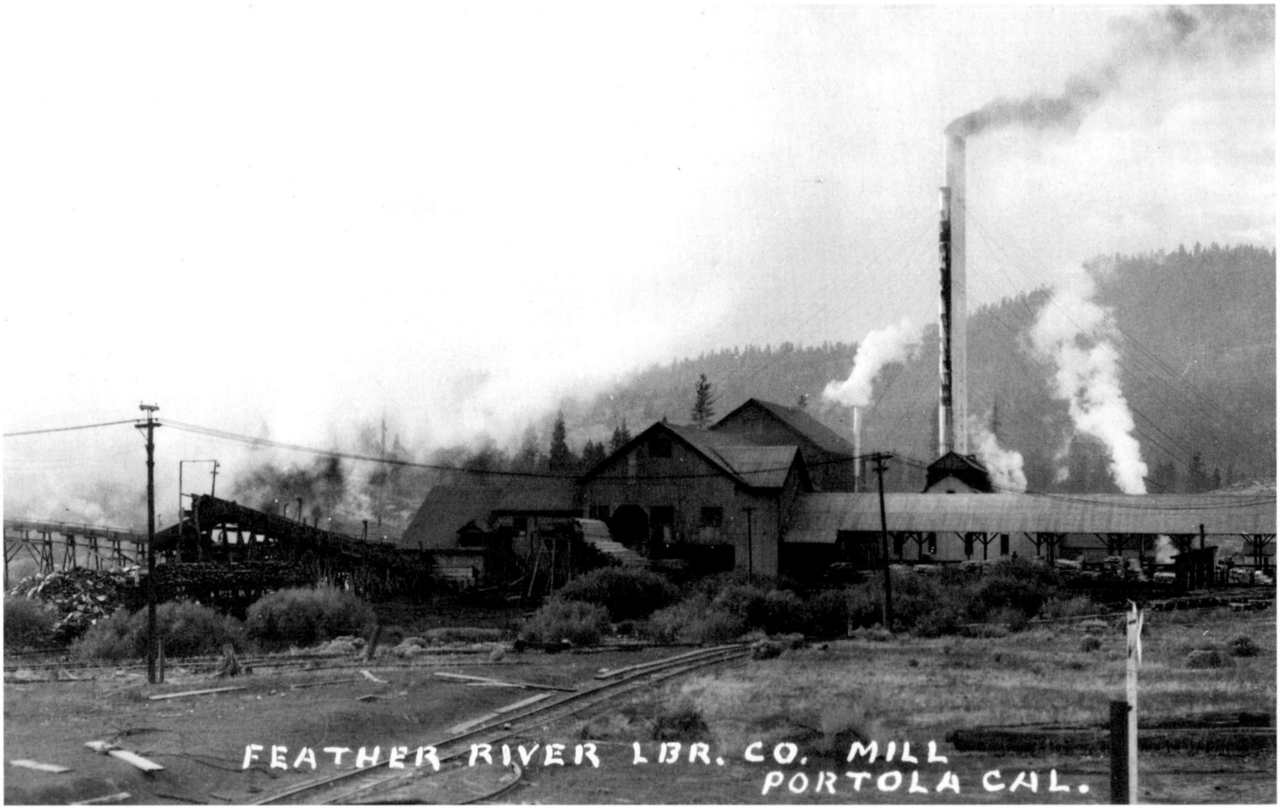

The Feather River Lumber Company operated three mills in Plumas County. No. 2 mill, located at Delleker, a suburb of Portola, was established several years before the Western Pacific Railroad opened in 1909.

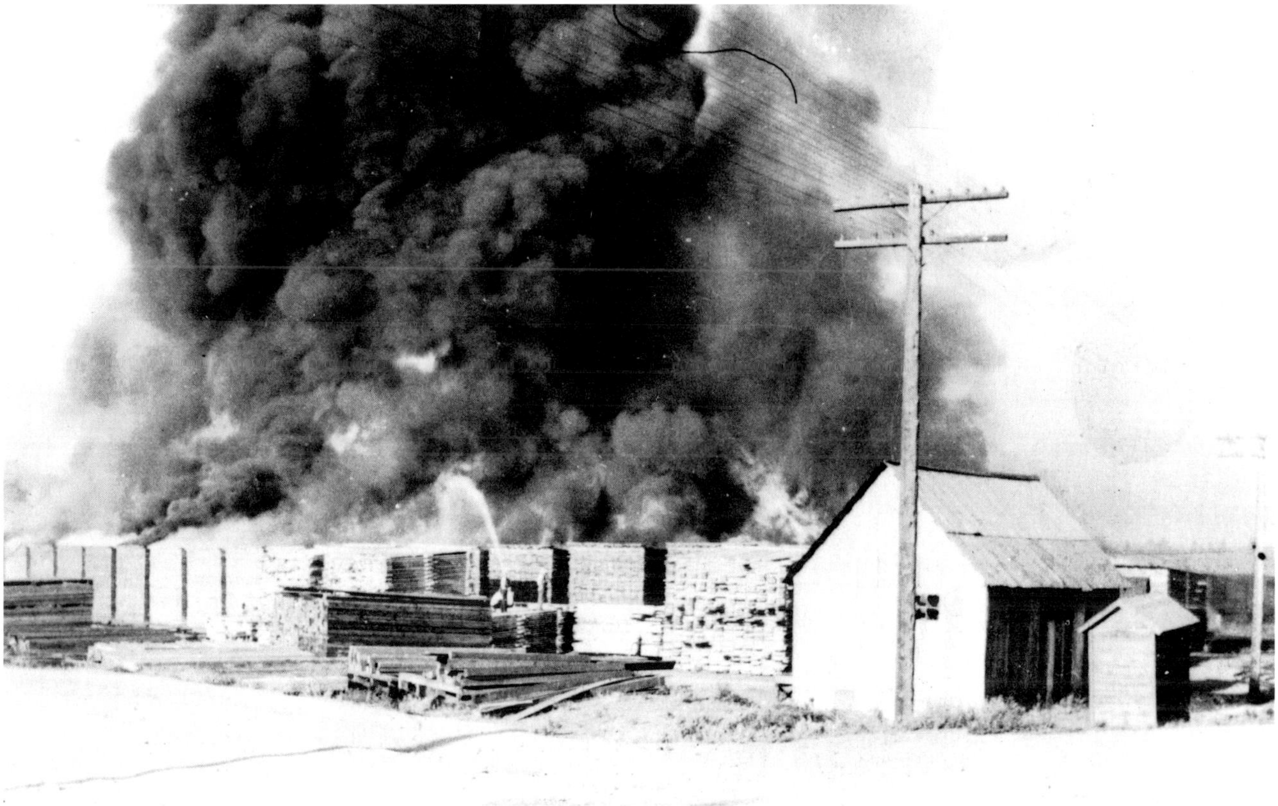

Devastating fires frequently occurred at lumber mills. The Delleker mill suffered major fires in 1909, 1915, and 1919. (Plumas County Museum)

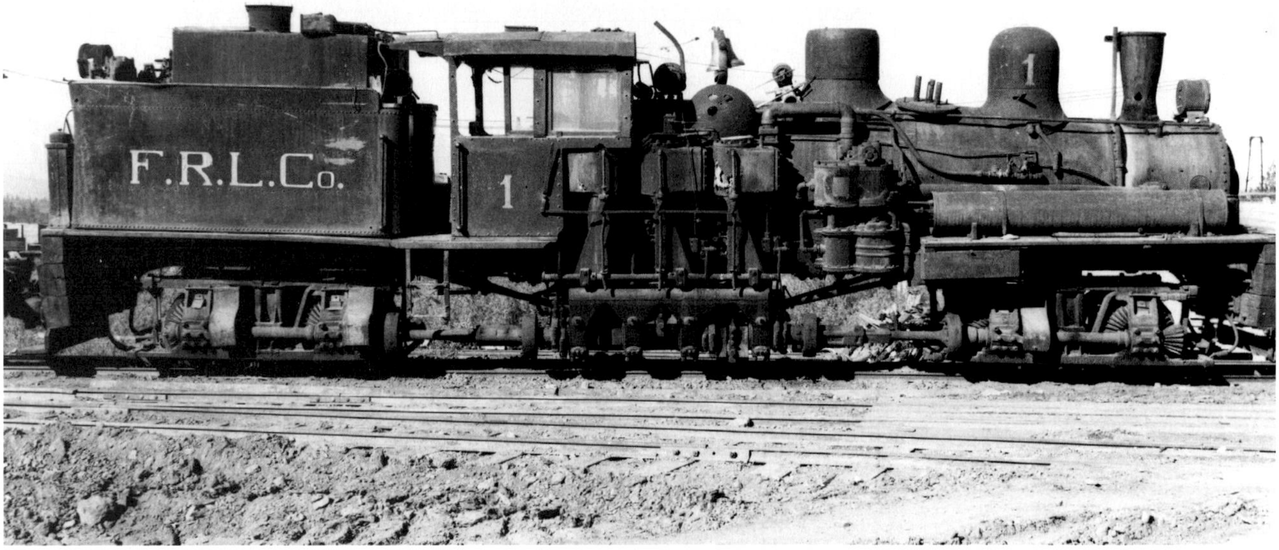

In 1916, the Feather River Lumber Company initiated construction of its narrow-gauge (thirty-six inches) logging railroad. With steep grades, geared locomotives were absolute necessities, and the first two Shay engines were rescued from the Argentine Central Railroad in Colorado. A few years after this 1938 photograph, this engine was destroyed in a wreck six miles from Delleker after a train ran away. (Bert Ward photograph)

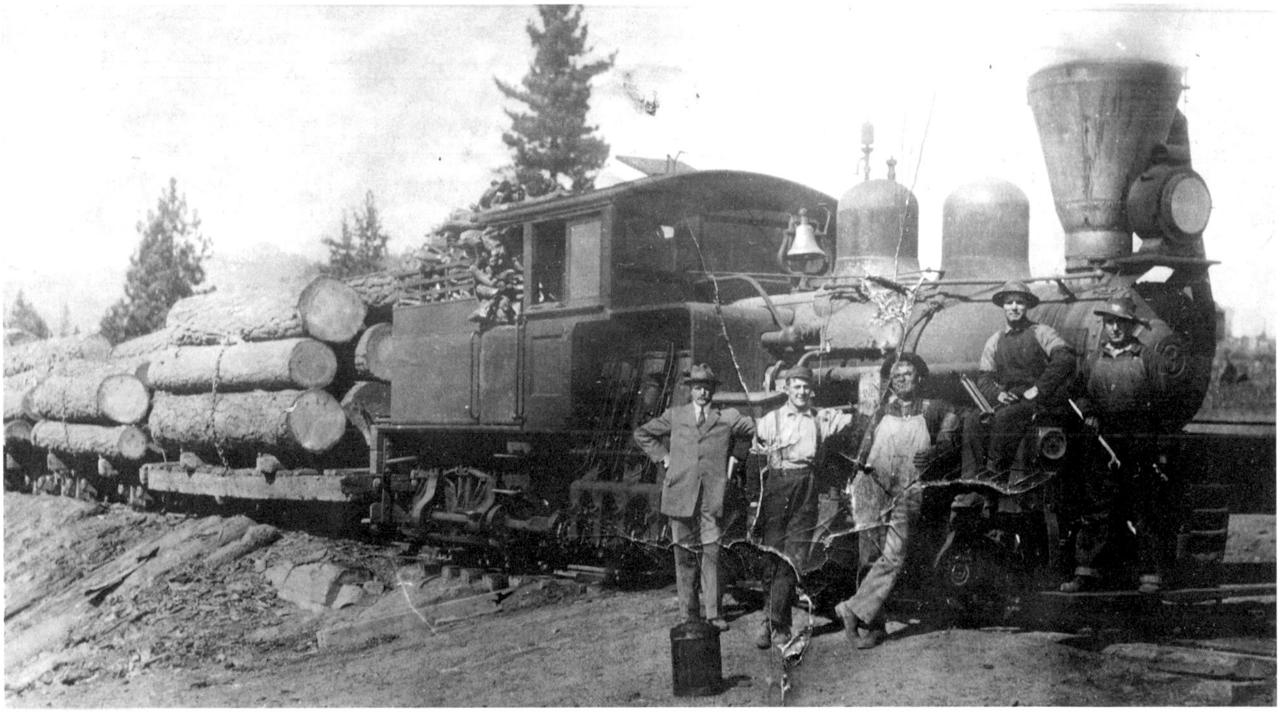

Above: The crew of No. 3, after arriving with a load of logs, posed for the camera with George Laws, superintendent of the Delleker mill, easily recognized by his business suit. This engine began its work life at the Marsh Lumber Company and served a number of lumber railroads. Massack became its next home after leaving Delleker. Later, it went to the Michigan-California Lumber Company at Camino, California, for parts and was scrapped in 1948.

Below: A Holt tractor participated in logging operations. (Ted Wurm collection)

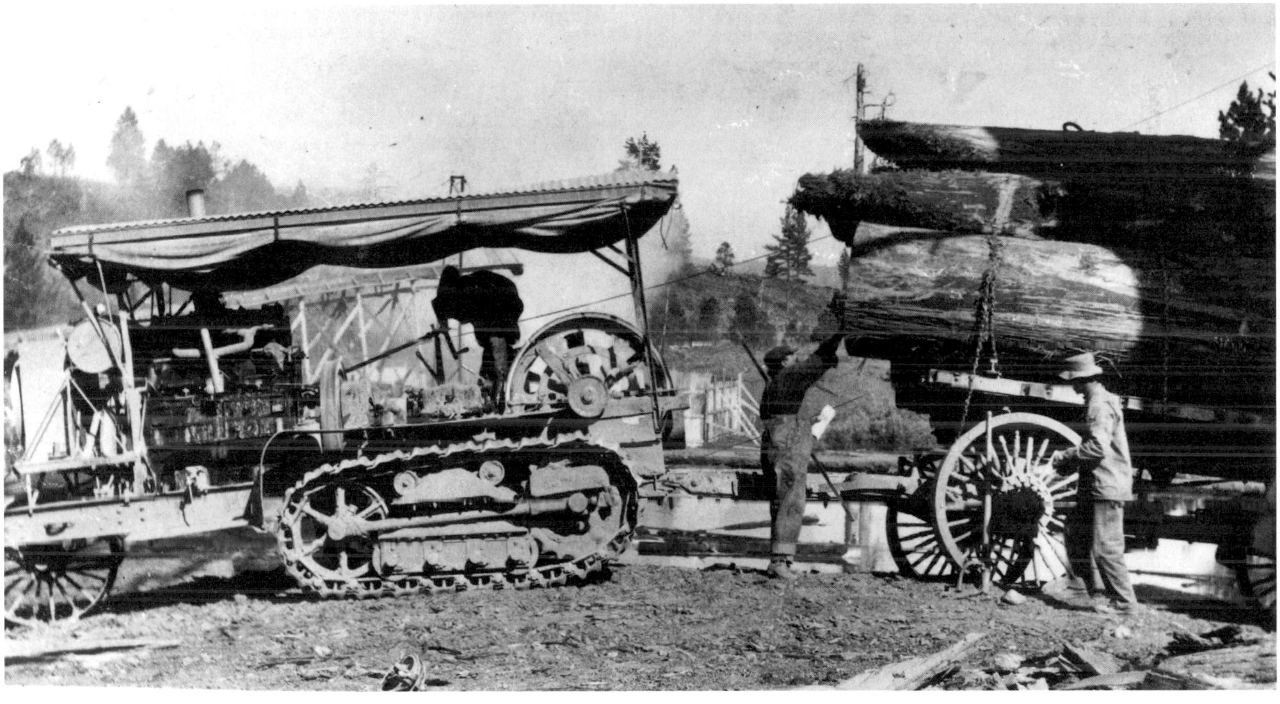

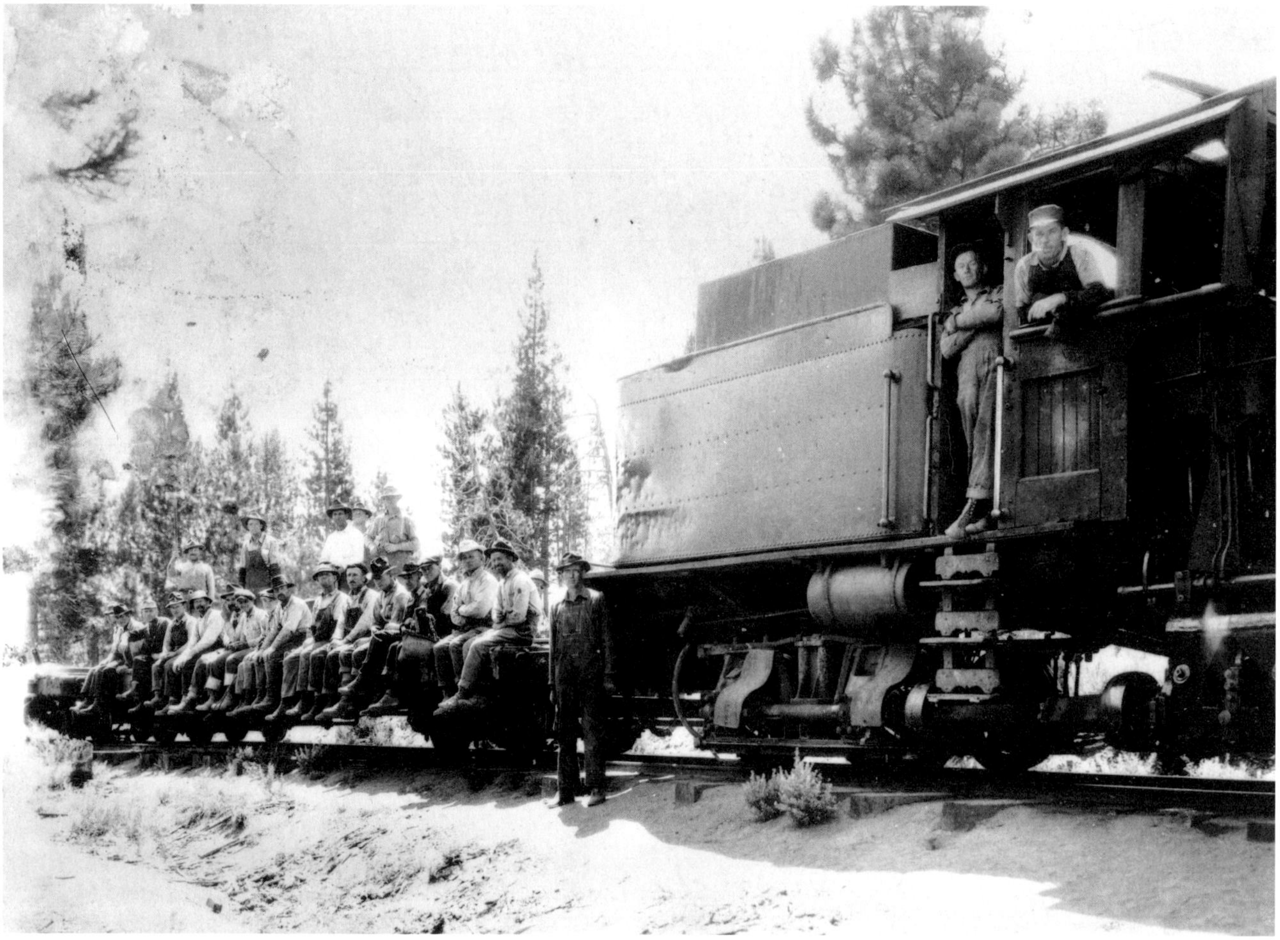

A Delleker logging crew climbed aboard a flatcar for this group picture. (Plumas County Museum)

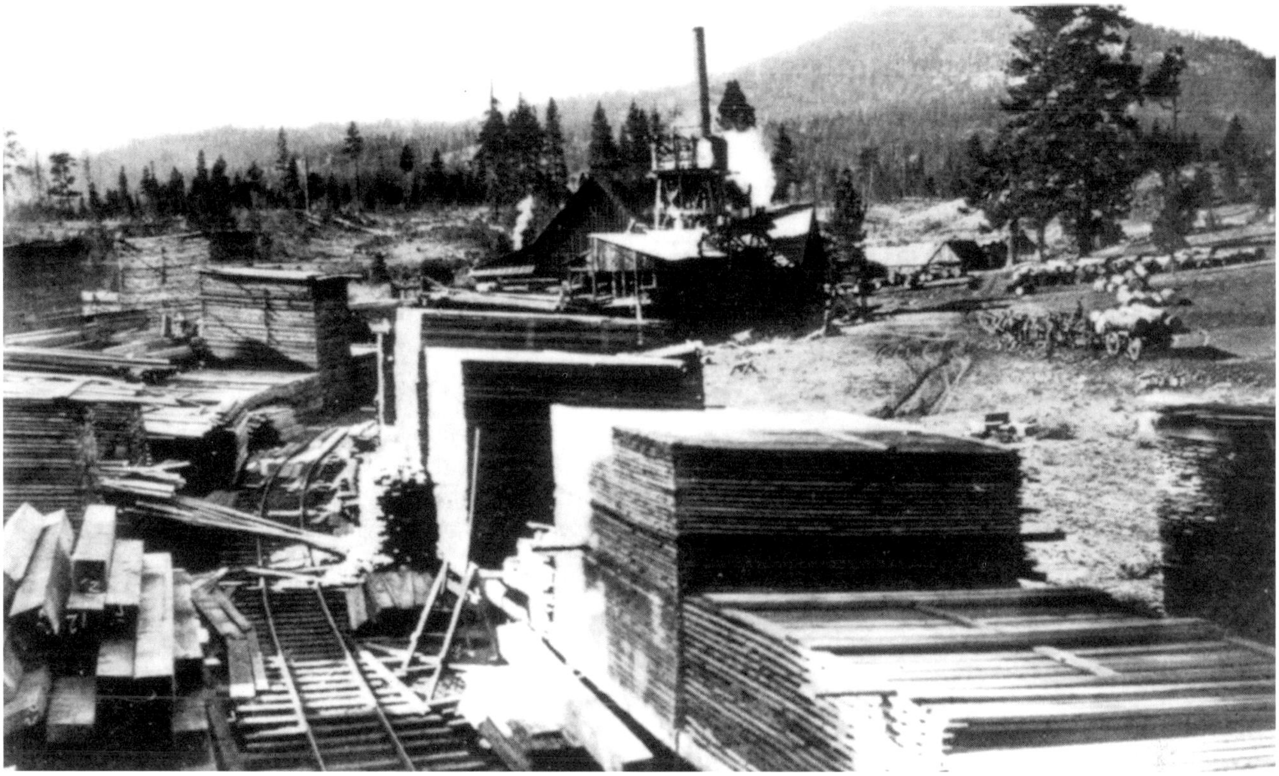

Above: An early view of the lumberyard at Delleker.

Below: The Delleker Inn, on the east side of the mill, provided housing for the unmarried workmen of the Feather River Lumber Company.

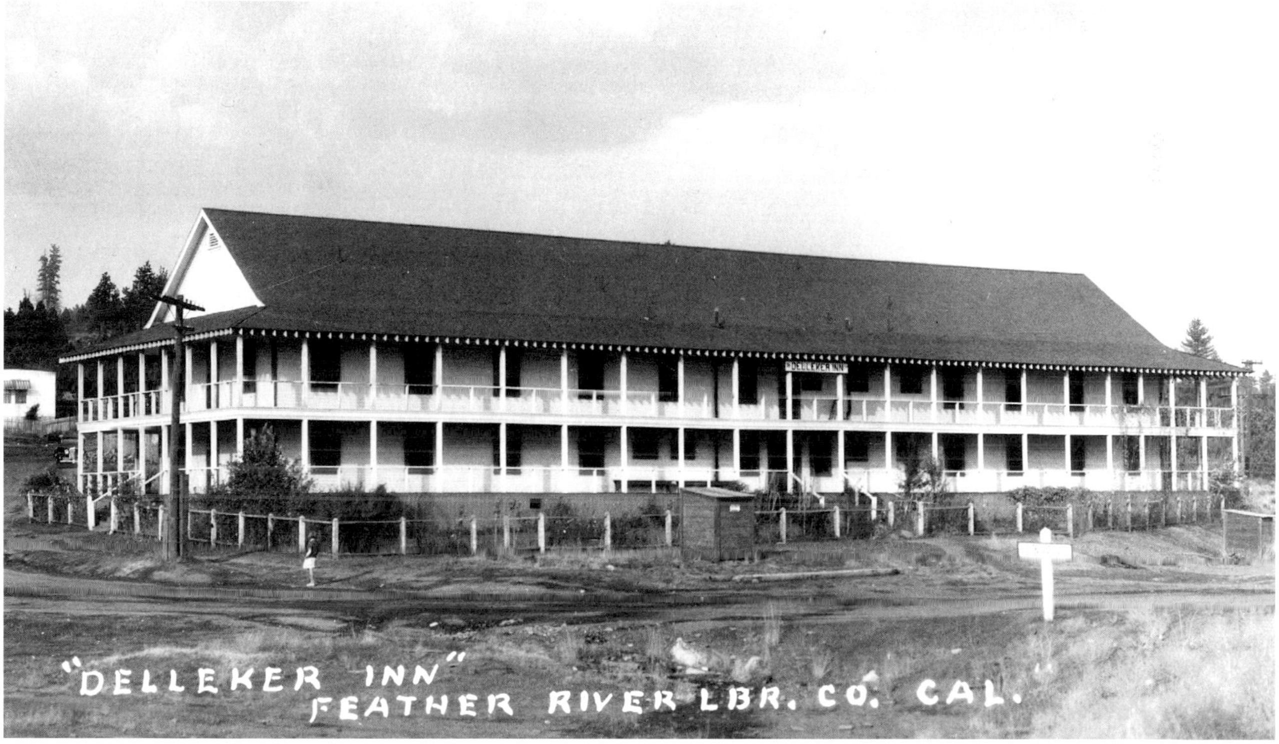

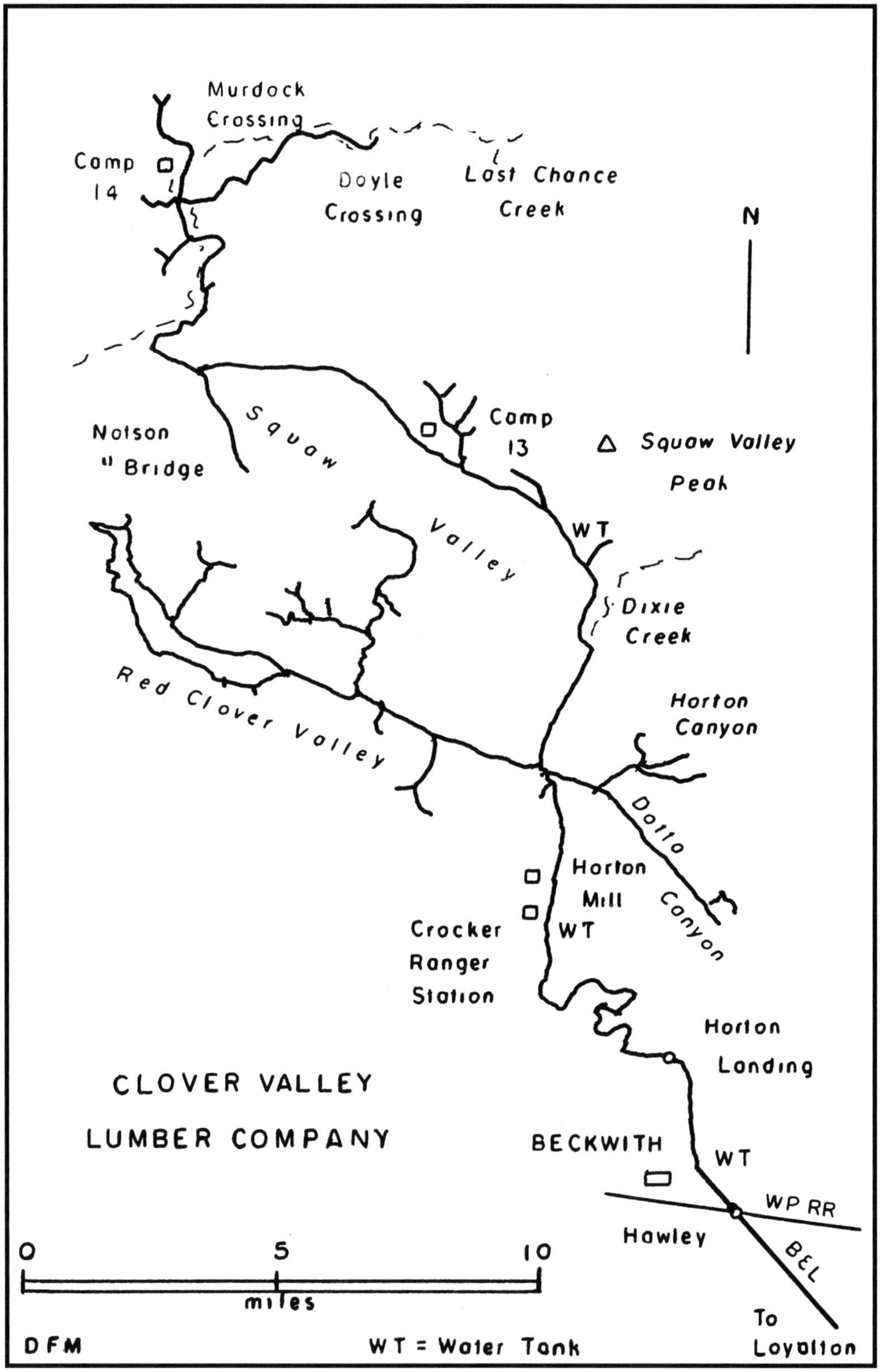
Murdock Crossing
Camp 14
Doyle Crossing
Lost Chance Creek
N
Notson Bridge
Squaw
Camp 13
Squaw Valley Peak
Valley
WT
Dixie Creek
Red Clover Valley
Horton Canyon
Dotta Canyon
Horton Mill
WT
Crocker Ranger Station
Horton Landing
CLOVER VALLEY
LUMBER COMPANY
BECKWITH
WT
WP RR
Hawley
B&L
0
5
10
miles
To Loyalton
DFM
WT = Water Tank

CLOVER VALLEY LUMBER COMPANY

The term *Clover Valley* generally applies to an area north of Portola, California, and is divided into Red Clover Valley, about seven to nine miles northwest of Beckwith, and Squaw (Queen) Valley, six miles farther north, followed by Last Chance Creek. Timbering was conducted on hills surrounded by extensive meadowlands alternating with sagebrush in some places.

Horton Brothers Lumber Company

The first important timber operation commenced after two brothers, Arthur H. Horton and Charles E. Horton, engaged teams in February 1891 to lug machinery up Mapes Canyon, over the summit, for a sawmill along Crocker Creek in Red Clover Valley. With deep snow that year retarding construction of their mill, the brothers were unable to commence lumbering before summer began, but by the end of the season, they managed to cut a half-million board feet.

A year later, now established as Horton Bros., the firm manufactured all grades of rough lumber, but the absence of an operating railroad in Plumas County limited distribution of their product. The message in their advertisement ending with a statement that their "Mill [was] Seven Miles from Beckwith in Clover Valley, over a Good Road," suggests that buyers had to make their own arrangements for deliveries.

In 1896, the firm added a small box factory, but winters suspended operations, and the Charles Horton family found living in Reno more desirable. The next summer the payroll consisted of fourteen names, in part reflecting the addition of two planers at the mill. With the Sierra Valleys Railway in operation, the company shipped five carloads of box lumber to California points and three cars of ordinary lumber to Salt Lake City.

In 1900 Horton Bros. purchased a steam-traction engine capable of hauling twenty-five thousand pounds of lumber to the railroad at Beckwith. The company prospered and acquired more timberland, including the former C. J. Lee holdings on Spring Garden summit, near Quincy. Ownership expanded, and in 1903 the assessor listed fourteen scattered parcels owned by the firm. Many parcels consisted of only forty acres.

The Boca and Loyalton RR pushed its standard-gauge tracks to Beckwith in the fall of 1901 and in November installed James Otis as its agent. Horton Bros., using its steam-traction engine, hauled lumber to the "wide-gauge line" to the detriment of the traffic-starved Sierra Valleys Railway.

Amended articles of incorporation of the Boca and Loyalton Railroad provided for a 35-mile branch starting at the main line near Beckwith and extending northerly into Red Clover Valley and ending above the present Antelope Lake. Actual B&L ownership of this proposed branch was limited to the southerly 3.17 miles, with lumber companies' rails continuing to the woods. Initial grading work, begun in the fall of 1902 and suspended in December, was resumed the following May when men formed a grade across Humphrey's field and then laid rails and ties on this separate segment.

The B&L, lacking a physical connection with its trackage near Beckwith, could not make use of the track until a crossing over the Sierra Valleys Railway had been arranged. When the narrow gauge demanded five thousand dollars—a princely sum in those days—Captain Roberts said, "No way," and B&L forces slipped in a crossing frog on May 30, 1903, a Saturday evening, and then ran a train up the new branch. The SV Railway responded by installing a second track and blocked the B&L spur by parking several boxcars and men to guard them.

When the SV Railway secured an injunction, the B&L gathered four hundred men—most of the male population of Loyalton—to back its contention, but the expected confrontation turned disappointing, as men from Reno failed to attend the meeting.

From there the scenario continued off and on for four years marked by field encounters and courtroom battles. On one occasion, a judge sided with the SV Railway, while another jurist supported the B&L; another time the California Supreme Court ordered a Lassen County judge to refrain from issuing court orders.

In the summer of 1905, W. F. Sanders, B&L chief engineer, directed a force pushing the spur up lower Mapes Canyon, and, after the crossing dispute had been settled, he returned in October 1908 to complete construction of the 3.17-mile branch to Horton Landing. Here Horton Bros.' steam-traction engines, after climbing the summit, delivered finished lumber to the rail connection, but, after the relocation of their new mill at Loyalton in June 1903, the traction engines delivered logs to the B&L to be transported to the Loyalton mill.

Some historians credit Horton Bros. with its own railroad, but this appears unlikely. True, when the partnership became a corporation on April 4, 1902, the articles of the Horton Brothers Lumber Company included authority to "build, equip and run logging railroads," but the *Plumas National-Bulletin,* while making frequent references to the steam-traction engines of the company, never spoke of a railroad. Additionally, the Plumas County Assessor's Records for 1901, 1903, and 1907 list company-owned lands, sawmills, and traction engines for the Hortons but make no mention of a railroad of any kind for this company. Possibly, the delay in the B&L arranging for crossing the Sierra Valleys Railway may have discouraged the Hortons from building their own logging railroad. Meanwhile, the mill underwent a change of ownership.

The Marsh Lumber Company

Headed by W. E. Marsh of New York City, the Marsh Lumber Company was incorporated on October 11, 1906, under New York laws. About a year later, Marsh purchased the stock of the Horton Brothers Lumber Company. The acquisition included timberlands and the Loyalton sawmill, surrounded by twenty-four acres. Marsh, now president of the Horton company, transferred the property to his firm on July 20, 1908. Louis W. Conklin served as general manager for many years.

For a time, Marsh Lumber continued operations with a traction engine, but during 1910 it acquired some relay rail. When the company refinanced its 1908 loan with the Washoe County Bank of Reno in October 1912, property pledged included seven miles of narrow-gauge railroad with thirty-five-pound steel rail "extending from Horton's spur of the Boca and Loyalton Railroad to a point in the Southeast Quarter of the Northwest Quarter in Section 33, T24N, R14E," which would take it to the former Horton sawmill. Along the way, Marsh had three timber spurs on the south side of the climb as well as several more along the approach to the old sawmill. The railroad surmounted the summit by a steep climb as it passed the former Mapes Ranch. Equipment pledged under this mortgage consisted of one Shay locomotive, two Baldwin locomotives, and twelve logging cars.

Financially, the company did not do too well, so in October 1917 it conveyed its property to the Washoe County Bank and settled its indebtedness. Only the two Baldwins were listed along with seventeen logging cars. The two-truck Shay, No. 50, purchased by the Clover Valley Lumber (CVL) Company, had come from the Argentine and Gray's Peak Railway and was converted to a standard-gauge locomotive. It was one of the four Shays on the CVL roster.

The beginnings of the Clover Valley Lumber Company came with its incorporation on June 29, 1917, by A. Revert, C. D. Terwilliger, and W. T. Virgin who had operated the Verdi Lumber Company in California west of Reno. Once organized, the group lost no time preparing for business; only a matter of weeks elapsed before it purchased fifteen million feet of Tahoe National Forest timber in Badenough Canyon.

Loyalton, California, previously the home of numerous sawmills and box factories, now had only the mill of the Plumas Lumber Company in operation. When the report surfaced that Clover Valley had purchased the old Marsh Lumber Company sawmill, it offered hope to the few merchants left serving the dwindling number of residents.

Commencing at a point on its railroad about three-fourths of a mile southeast of Loyalton, the Boca and Loyalton built a spur to the timber stand in Badenough Canyon. Known as the "Clover Valley Lumber Co.'s Spur," it climbed about 600 feet from its beginning, which necessitated a 2.6-mile track to maintain a reasonable grade. Consequently, much of the spur was parallel and only a short distance east of the B&L main line. Construction engineers declared the CVL spur completed as of November 30, 1917. Along this spur several sidetracks provided for car storage. (At B&L MP 22.2, another 6,464-foot spur turned southwest as it poked its way into lower Bear Valley, meeting the needs of the Roberts Lumber Company. In earlier times, it had extended another 3,000 feet. B&L mileposts began with MP 0.0 at Portola.)

Though cutting timber in lower Badenough Canyon met the initial requirements of the company, the partners had the larger timber stands in the Clover Valley area north of Beckwith as their goal. For undisclosed reasons, A. Revert sold his interest to the other two partners and departed from the scene.

Even before the 1920 logging season began, CVL's prospective logging railroad perked interest in Loyalton. The company secured operating rights over the Western Pacific branch (former the Boca and Loyalton RR) from Loyalton to Beckwith and into the hills by paying the owner a flat charge for each car moved. In March, several carpenters made repairs to the mill, and the company announced its prospective employment figures. Sixty men would work in the mill and lumberyards, with another 40 in the box factory. Logging operations would require some 150 men, and more would be needed for railroad construction.

Early in April 1920, Virgin and Terwilliger went to Beckwith to witness the first work on their railroad. The exact location is blurred, but it appears that CVL used the 3.17-mile Horton spur of the B&L and commenced work at the ice pond before passing through the old Mapes Ranch.

In June, the force of 25 Greeks had finished three miles of new grade. One observer described them as "a fine set of fellows." Contemplating extensive use of the new railroad, the CVL managers engaged T. K. Stewart, a Reno civil engineer, and his helper, Scott Hall, to examine the route and to suggest minor changes as they thought necessary. The next month, George R. Worn, CVL superintendent, moved the grading force to the site of the old Marsh camp above the Mapes Ranch.

At the end of September, Worn's crew, having reached timber as well as the old Marsh Lumber Company roadbed, had rebuilt the old line by widening fills and shortening or replacing trestles with fills. A local scribe attributed the policy of "safety first" to Worn before it came into general use. Removing old ties some distance from the roadbed to lessen the threat of fire made up one example.

Taking advantage of favorable fall weather, CVL continued to push "The Front" northward, as did Western Pacific working in the opposite direction to Calpine. When operations in Badenough Canyon finally terminated, the company made a lasting impression on Sierra Valley ranchers when a train of flatcars moved across the valley on November 12, 1920, carrying eight cabins, donkey engines, and a mass of logging machinery. During the next two or three weeks, CVL expected to pick up remaining logs and bring them to the Loyalton mill.

Soon after this significant move, a Beckwith newspaper correspondent, in speaking of the railroad construction, remarked that "the logging outfit has pulled the Arab stunt on us" when it folded its tents and silently stole away. Actually, with the first section of the railroad finished in December, the departure was in order.

The new railroad formed only part of the CVL improvements made that year, for the company also completed a large box factory as well as a water tank on a high tower in Loyalton to aid in fighting fires.

Because of weak demand and lower market prices—wholesale prices stood below 1917 figures—eight Feather River lumber mills did not operate in the 1921 season. The Western Lumber Company, with its Antelope mill served by a steam traction engine, ended its five-year run in September with the exhaustion of timber resources. During July, an axle on the traction engine broke to block the road for several days, and only with great difficulty could autos get by.

CVL stood out as the only lumber company operating in Loyalton and even then on a reduced scale. L. W. Conklin became superintendent soon after 1921 began. While preparations for logging in Clover Valley were under way, the company, through a subsidiary, Sierra Valley Lumber Company, cut timber in Last Chance Canyon and hauled logs seven miles to WP at Chilcoot for transport to Loyalton. The new Clover Valley railroad commenced running to the logging camp but returned empty each time for a couple of weeks until May 13, 1921, when conductor Tom McNaughton arrived at the Loyalton mill late that night with the first logs (seven cars) from the new camp.

During the summer, trains grew longer, and two locomotives were necessary to bring in fifteen to twenty cars each day. When its engines were undergoing repairs, No. 124 of the former B&L RR provided substitute service. A local scribe referred to the logging train as the "Sagebrush Limited," transferring the nickname from the former train of the now-abandoned Sierra Valleys Railway.

The mill closed down in November, and the force moved the log camp to a new site for the next season. During winter months, the men were assigned to other work around the mill; a new machine shop and a roundhouse demonstrated their activities during the winter. Other men engaged in a quick moneymaking venture in October by robbing the local bank of $22,037.39, but, having worked in Loyalton for some time before their hasty departure, their identification posed no problems. One robber settled his bill at the Golden West Hotel only to return later that evening to borrow $5 from one lady proprietor. They were later apprehended in Redding, but the history of the small loan was not recorded.

Deep Snows of 1922 Blanket the Area

Great storms in February 1922—said to be the worst since 1890—isolated many communities in the area. For a week, Loyalton residents had to shuffle through four feet of snow. When a train attempted to reach the town, it stalled two miles south of Hawley but managed to extricate itself and crawl back to Portola. Two days later, another attempt proved successful. Only after some Quincy men with shovels worked two days at Lee Summit was the road opened to Portola on May 1, six weeks later than the previous year.

As spring approached, a worker wearing snowshoes visited the log camp to find it buried in seven feet of snow that flattened two large cookhouses. The starting date for logging, scheduled for May 15, had to be put off several weeks because of snow and soft ground.

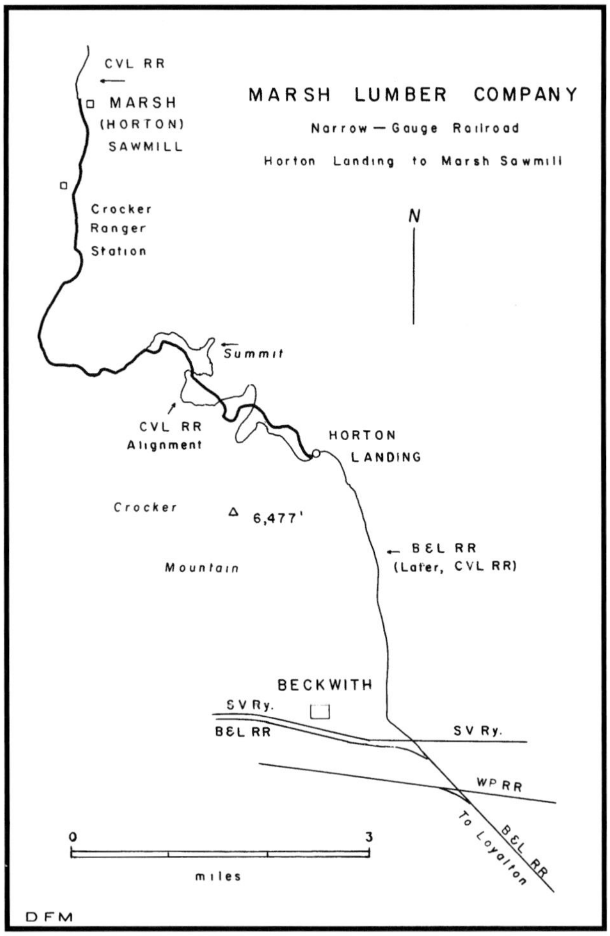

While waiting for better conditions, the little train took Loyalton workers out each day to rebuild the cookhouses and prepare the camp. Oscar Swanson, who managed the log camp, was usually referred to as "the Judge," though the reason is lacking.

While the Marsh Lumber Company's logging railroad extended almost to Angelo Dotta's ranch, nine miles north of Beckwith (in Section 16, T24N R14E), the new lumber company secured a fifty-foot right-of-way from Lucia D. Andrea and her husband in August as the railroad moved northward into Red Clover Valley.

Several events captured local attention in November 1922. When the section boss of the track force was missing for several days, gossip had him hiding, for his moonlighting as a bootlegger was responsible for several Mexicans' weeklong spree. More serious was a wreck on November 6 that followed a runaway train. As the train was descending the heavy grade near the Mapes Ranch, the brakes proved unable to hold the train on the wet track. The caboose and eight of the nine log cars in the train left the track to end huddled in a pile of junk. Three men jumped when the cars became unsteady; Ross McKenzie, brakeman, was killed instantly. Conductor Roy Frost and Charles Willis, the other brakeman, were badly injured and spent time in a Reno hospital. Jack Decker and Hugh Conners, engineer and fireman, respectively, plus four others riding on the first car escaped injury. Frost and Willis had not fully recovered when logging ended in mid-December.

Grizzly Creek Ice Company

Clover Valley Lumber Company diversified its business when it acquired the Grizzly Creek Ice Company late in 1922. The company, formed in 1912 by Nevada men associated with the Reno Mill and Lumber Company, constructed several dams on Grizzly Creek to harvest winter ice and for storage in insulated warehouses for summer use. One important use was for railroad refrigerator cars. (It also secured nearby timber rights from the U.S. Forest Service.) Forty carloads of sawdust from Loyalton mills provided the necessary insulation. It was served by a spur from the B&L Beckwith-Portola section only after another crossing battle. This branch, though measuring only 1.58 miles, was part of a line projected northwesterly for 18 miles.

The first dam failed when tested in April 1912. The replacement, higher but reinforced with steel bars, went out with a loud roar late in the night of April 10, 1914. (The dam had been inspected earlier that day.) The surge of water swept away a government water gauge, fish ladder, and sixteen hundred feet of the railroad spur. No houses were affected, although much of the embankment by the new icehouse had vanished.

Initially, the B&L RR refused to rebuild the branch but then relented, and three months later a new dam, six hundred feet down the canyon, formed a sixteen-acre lake, slightly larger than the previous pond. A cold snap in December created tons of ice that was added to the seven thousand–ton inventory carried over from the previous year, as it could not be shipped during the summer because the spur stood in disrepair.

Expected ice formation could prove disappointing with uneven weather, such as the rain and snow occurring in February 1916, forcing the crop to be abandoned for that year. Adding to the misery, heavy snow collapsed part of the icehouse roof.

J. F. Hoke remained in charge, and the following March he directed men loading ice in the boxcars.

Lumbering in 1923 was slightly disrupted in April when the Shay locomotive blew a cylinder head; fortunately, no injuries resulted. More disruptions came a few weeks later when the company found itself a participant in an industry-wide strike organized by the Industrial

Workers of the World. Oscar Johnson, log foreman, said that of the 164 men on the payroll, 47 drew their time. Many workers subsequently returned to their jobs.

A Partial Change of Ownership

Ownership changed at the annual meeting of shareholders on September 15, 1923, when New Orleans men took an interest in the company and secured control. As part of a plan to expand production, additional stock was issued so that R. H. Downman and his family held almost half of the stock. H. B. Hewes, the new president, held about one-sixth of the stock, as did each of Terwilliger and Virgin. So instead of holding most of the stock between themselves, they now held one-third. The two founders remained with the company: Virgin became vice president, and Terwilliger held the posts of secretary and treasurer as well as general manager.

With renewed vigor, the Clover Valley Lumber Company entered 1924 making a number of additions, all leading toward increased production irrespective of the generally poor lumber market. The company purchased from the U.S. Forest Service a large stand in the Last Chance district in northern Plumas County.

Last Chance Creek took its name from an event during the gold rush. Intrigued by one Stoddard's tale of a lake of gold he had seen previously, a swarm of men followed him up a fork of the Feather River to share in his discovery. After wandering around and unable to locate the bonanza, the angry miners gave him one last chance before hanging him. Stoddard slipped away in the night, eventually settling in Tuttletown where he lived for some years before his natural death.

Last Chance Creek originates near Sugarloaf Mountain (about six miles west of Doyle) to flow west for some forty miles to its confluence with Indian Valley Creek. Confusion stems from a second creek with the same name starting near the same point as the first and running south to join the Middle Fork of the Feather River near Chilcoot. In more recent times, it has been differentiated as Little Last Chance Creek, and Frenchman Lake Dam stores its waters.

Another move, though not as dramatic as the Stoddard tale, caught the attention of Loyalton residents: the delivery of a large 2-6-6-2T locomotive. Manufactured by the Baldwin Locomotive Works in March 1924, the size of this mallet-mogul engine overwhelmed the existing motive power of the company, though its tractive effort was but a fraction of the articulated mallet locomotives of Southern Pacific. Only a few California lumber companies had locomotives of this type.

That summer, E. H. McKibben, superintendent of construction of the logging railroad, worked with A. Kiser who held the contract for extending the railroad into new cutting areas. Leslie A. Flynn and his crew erected trestles along the route; unfortunately, Flynn made a misstep during construction and fell thirty-five feet to his death.

With the mill running at full capacity sawing two hundred thousand board feet daily, its output ranked among the top producers in Plumas County. To achieve this capacity, an adequate supply of logs was essential, and logging continued during that winter with logs decked by the track, waiting for the resumption of train service in the spring.

Early in March 1925, Bob Thompson took a locomotive out to inspect the railroad as far as Camp 8 at the western end of Clover Valley. Returning, he told his boss that while the roadbed was soft, it could handle trains. With this report, the management decided to open the camp in two weeks and dispatched Oscar Swanson and his helpers to prepare the camp for habitation.

The reopening of the camp proved a little premature, for an unexpected heavy snowfall blanketed the area a few weeks later. Warmer weather melted the snow, which softened the roadbed, causing the rails to spread under a train of logs. The wreck took two days to clear up and temporarily closed the mill.

CVL No. 4, the big mallet-mogul, was put to work that summer making two trips across Sierra Valley each day to bring fifty cars of logs to the mill. The same engine became involved in a fish story when Bob Thompson and Billy Washoe discovered a twelve-inch trout happily swimming in the water tank of the locomotive.

As the Clover Valley railroad crossed the Western Pacific main line at Hawley, the big railroad questioned the easygoing operating style of the lumber road. In a policy change, CVL instructed its crews to learn and abide by the rules of WP, which required the men to go to Portola to take the standard tests. Charles Willis, former brakeman and now fireman, was among those tested.

With the distance between the cutting areas and the Loyalton mill growing longer, the lumber company established woods camps. Ben Hover, head carpenter, and his crew assembled twenty cabins that year. F. J. Wilkens took charge of Camp 8, the home for eight families, while Martin Conklin, perhaps a relative of a former manager, held a logging contract at Camp 10.

J. R. Downward, "the guardian of motive power," convinced the management to improve the roundhouse with the addition of a concrete floor. One hopes it improved the safety there.

Mishaps occur in milling as well as in railroading. One Saturday afternoon in November 1924, the main sidehead pulley of the planer broke and scattered metal in all directions. Fortunately, no one was injured, and, as planned, the mill closed that night for the season.

A little more than a year elapsed before the planer caused trouble again. This time, it proved to be the source of a major fire that consumed the planer mill, box factory, and two warehouses. Luckily, a light but steady snowfall prevented flying embers from spreading, but it still required nearly seven hours to control the blaze. A WP wrecking crane came up from Portola the next day to gather the remains of two boxcars and also to remove some of the damaged machinery. Lumber-mill fires are the way of life in the industry, but, with adequate insurance, they are taken in stride. So it was with the Loyalton plant in spite of interruptions.

A week's rainstorm—the heaviest in years—transformed Loyalton streets into rivers and flooded the roundhouse, dry kiln, and engine house. After drying out, the mill saws began cutting in early March 1927, and the rebuilt box factory and planing mill resumed work a few weeks later with new electrically powered machinery.

The manager sent an engineer in a locomotive with a plow ready to tackle drifts, only to find less than a foot of snow covered the rails. With spring in the air, rain and snow surprised everyone as they fell across the land to block roads. When sunshine returned, a correspondent eloquently described a force of "about forty respectable-looking young men assembled at Beckwith on Sunday with two truck-loads of baggage, boarded the logging train Monday morning and, with hats and handkerchiefs waving 'good-byes,' were off for the season's work." One hopes their destination was not Camp 10, for another storm left that camp in deep snow.

Personnel changes put Pat McKabe in the fireman's seat on engine No. 4, while Billy Washoe took his place as roundhouse hostler. Uninvited excitement soon followed. Whatever plans the train crew had in mind for Saturday night, July 23, were forcibly changed when a log train proved too much for the braking power and ran away. Details are lacking, but some cars left the track, the conductor and brakeman jumped (broke his ankle), and somehow the engineer kept ahead of the log cars chasing him most of the way into Loyalton. In that same summer, the final closing of the Verdi Lumber Company released two Shay locomotives, Nos. 3 and 11, which were acquired by the Clover Valley Lumber Company.

Railroad operations were disrupted in May 1928 when fire damaged several trestles along the line. A modification in operations followed the burning of the Nibley-Stoddard mill at Cromberg. Clover Valley purchased its first million feet of logs from the fire-stricken company, and Western Pacific delivered the cars to the mill in Loyalton. This arrangement continued for several years.

Railroad construction continued in 1929 with a crew of twenty-five men based in Camp 9. Loyalton took on an improved appearance in the summer of 1929 after WP had rehabilitated its depot, and the lumber company not only remodeled and repainted houses along Railroad Avenue but planted trees as well.

The general business slump of the 1930s slowed lumber activity everywhere, including Loyalton. A major forest fire north of Beckwith challenged men for more than a week.

The years also took their toll on pioneers. William T. Virgin, born in Genoa, Nevada, in 1871 as the son of an early Nevada lawyer, began his career in the Goldfield branch of the Tonopah Lumber Company. After acquiring an interest in the Verdi Lumber Company in 1904, he subsequently cofounded the Clover Valley Lumber Company of which he was vice president at his death in April 1930. He left most of his shares to his sister and to two former employees. He is buried in Genoa.

His death was preceded by several months by the death of Frank E. Walker, secretary-treasurer, who was killed by a logging train in a snowstorm. Born in Prescott, Arizona, his prior experience included the Tonopah Lumber Company and the Verdi Lumber Company.

L. W. Conklin died in September 1931 after a long illness. Coming to Loyalton in 1904, he managed the Clover Valley Lumber Company for a number of years. The mill, school, and stores were closed during his funeral.

Longer periods of inactivity at the mill and in the forests reflected the diminished demand for lumber in the 1930s. However, the company negotiated with the U.S. Forest Service for the purchase of fire-damaged timber in Clover Valley and resumed work in April 1932. Near the end of the following year, the log train operated only as far as Dotta's Neck.

The Troublesome Thirties

Clyde Sprading's name became a fixture in Loyalton and in the Clover Valley Lumber Company. Moving from Fort Smith, Arkansas, to Carson City, Nevada, with his parents while still a small boy, he grew up in Nevada. Perhaps the connection with George Wingfield encouraged this move, for Clyde's aunt was the mother of the banker. Clyde's brother served as Wingfield's executive secretary and held important positions in a number of Wingfield's mining enterprises. Accordingly, each month he received a handful of paychecks.

Employment was scarce in 1932 when young Clyde sought a position with the Sierra Valley Bank. During his interview, he was asked if he knew anything about banking. "No, sir," was his honest answer. "Good. Report to work Monday morning; if you had experience we would not have hired you!"

The drive from Reno went smoothly until after passing Vinton, when he had a flat tire. Changing the tire, he resumed his trip only to have another flat tire, and, as if he had not already had more than his share, he had a third flat tire before reaching Loyalton. After working for the bank a short time, he joined the Clover Valley Lumber Company.

To finance its development, the company had issued $1 million of 6 percent Serial Sinking Fund Gold Bonds in 1927. Unfortunately, as it turned out later, the indenture specified that the company would retire $50,000 of bonds each May 1, starting in 1933, and end with a balloon payment of $650,000 in 1940. With minimal cash receipts, the company could not meet these obligations. After developing a plan of reorganization to eliminate the burdensome sinking fund and bond interest, CVL formally filed for bankruptcy on September 16, 1935. When the company emerged reorganized in February 1936, each $1,000 bondholder received twelve shares of Class A Convertible, Par $100, Preference Stock, while the equity of existing shareholders was greatly reduced. (In September 1948, when the Preference Stock was called at $125 a share, many holders chose to convert their stock into common shares on a one-for-one basis and then received handsome dividends for some years thereafter.)

Almost no one had any spare cash to jump-start the business until Baker Fentress took a hand and helped to restore the viability of the company. Fentress owned eighteen sawmills along with thirty-nine corporate subsidiaries. Jack Bedford was brought in from the Saginaw and Manistee Lumber Company, a subsidiary in Williams, Arizona, to manage the Clover Valley Lumber Company.

Joel Conklin Sr., son of the former manager, became assistant manager in 1939 when he was promoted from woods superintendent. In 1947, when he moved up to the manager's position replacing Bedford, Alvin C. "Ole" Olsen took his former job, and, when Conklin retired in 1952, Olsen took over the manager's office. Olsen, from Minnesota, had moved west and had worked for Fruit Growers Supply at Hilt, California, after college in Oregon. A brief stay with Swayne Lumber ended in 1936 when he joined Clover Valley Lumber as a logging engineer to locate railroad lines and truck roads. He retired in 1957.

The Railroad and the Many Logging Camps

The Clover Valley Lumber Company operated the largest logging railroad system in Plumas County. Unfortunately, there is a paucity of information about the railroad and logging camps for several reasons. The 180-page handwritten history carefully compiled by Clyde Spradling in 1965 was lost in transit on its way to Chico State University. A subsequent manager directed his staff to "get rid of all that old stuff," and they had no choice but to comply, so basic records are nonexistent. However, some of the story has been gathered from public records, field trips, and recollections of former employees.

The company owned very little timberland and relied on timber purchases from the U.S. Forest Service to meet about 70 percent of its needs. It also bought timber from various ranchers, such as Frank Carmichael who owned the former Mapes Ranch. John Poeo, a Dixie Valley sheep man, pocketed fifty cents every time the mill cut (net) one thousand feet. The ranch of Rees T. Jenkins, a cattleman in the Diamond Mountain area, was another source of timber.

In the timber industry, logging camps and railroad lines led a transitory existence, moving from one timber-cutting area to another. As previously noted, the lumber company shared use of the Western Pacific 12.7-mile Loyalton branch to Hawley, where the company-owned trackage began. After climbing the grade in Mapes Canyon to the summit, the railroad then followed Crocker Creek for about 3 miles to a point north of the ranger station with the same name to enter Red Clover Valley and crept westward to end at Meadow Creek and the Notson Ranch. This 10-mile line served the company from 1921 to 1929. Before reaching the ranger station, CVL constructed two spurs for logging on the north side of the summit. At the crossing of Red Clover Creek, a 4-mile spur reached into Dotta Canyon, and another tapped Horton Canyon.

With the business recovery in 1935, men from the CVL railroad camp salvaged existing rails and resumed construction in Squaw Valley (not to be confused with the ski resort near Lake Tahoe). Two years later, rails reached Last Chance Creek at the west end of Squaw Valley. Subsequently, the railroad was extended north to Camp 14 and, under forces led by Al Maunders, on to Murdock Crossing. A 3-mile connection ended at Doyle Crossing.

Camp 13, which had been established about 1935, reached the end of its useful life with the exhaustion of nearby timber resources, and in the late summer of 1938 the whole community moved to Camp 14. (The new location had been prepared in advance, including a new cookhouse and dining hall.) A tractor pulled the workers' cabins up a ramp to load them on flatcars one at a time and reversed the process at the new site. The whole camp was moved in one day; residents drove their cars to the new camp.

Locomotives could obtain water at tanks located at Carmichael, Summit, Crocker, and Prairie. A sidetrack at the summit above the Crocker station accommodated half of the train when heavy loads made doubling necessary.

Billed as "The Trip of a Lifetime," the California-Nevada Railroad Historical Society staged a grand excursion on May 12–14, 1950. Leaving Oakland Pier on a special Western Pacific train, the group arrived in Portola early the next morning. Powered by WP No. 94, the venerable historic locomotive, a train of mostly open gondolas went to Loyalton over the former B&L tracks. Here the train direction was reversed, and with the Clover Valley Lumber Company No. 4, the 2-6-6-2 tank locomotive on the point, the train retraced its steps to Hawley, then over the summit, continuing all the way to Camp 14. After a box lunch, the group returned to Loyalton and Portola. The next day, the group made a side trip to Quincy and returned overnight to Oakland. The tab for the trip was all of twenty-five dollars, plus seven dollars for a Pullman berth. (Efforts to make a similar run in September 1955 were unsuccessful.)

In 1955, the Clover Valley Lumber Company operated fifty-four miles of railroad with three locomotives. A fleet of thirty-eight trucks operating over eighty-five miles of logging roads extended cutting operations far beyond the rail lines.

Sharl Reece, the senior engineer, piloted No. 4, the largest locomotive. Ordinarily, he departed from Loyalton at 4:00 A.M. (3:00 A.M. if the locomotive had to double the hill) to arrive at Camp 13, about a dozen miles north of the Crocker Ranger Station, around 8:30 or 9:00 A.M. Here, the train and engine crew would deliver empty cars and return with loads. A wye track a half mile south of Camp 13 enabled locomotives to reverse their direction.

Engine No. 8, purchased from Hobart Mills in 1935 for five thousand dollars, was the only other rod locomotive on the roster. The company also had a Plymouth gas engine, formerly used at the Hoover Dam project. Acquired for five hundred dollars, it was converted to use diesel fuel and primarily switched cars around the plant at Loyalton. Tony DeMartini said it "ran up the hill" about eight times. DeMartini started working in the CVL shops in 1942; three years later he began his eight-year stint as a brakeman on the railroad. When he learned that the railroad's days were numbered, he returned to the shop as a welder.

The railroad maintenance workers had their own camp above the former Mapes Ranch, about a half mile south of the summit. For many years Pete Velos bossed the camp of about two dozen men. In later years, George Pappas held the same position.

Camp 9 was on Dixie Creek, while Camp 14, the largest camp, was situated on a spur track north of Last Chance Creek. DeMartini's description of the camp, "I hope to tell you it was a little town," is indeed appropriate, as it housed 350 to 400 workers. Some older loggers said it had the best location of any camp since they had started working for the company.

Another Change in Ownership

J. K. Metzker bought and sold lumber companies during his career (see Chapter 12). He built a new sawmill at Sloat under the name of the Feather River Lumber Company after purchasing that corporate name. Working out a carload rate with Western Pacific, he was able to ship green lumber to the planer at Loyalton. Next he purchased the property of the Clover Valley Lumber Company from the Baker Fentress group as of January 1, 1957, and subsequently received the capital stock.

He came into possession of a double-band sawmill at Loyalton with a daily capacity of 160,000 feet and a railroad. He planned to operate the property, now called the Feather River Lumber Company, for ten years and then sell it. The first few years were tough financially. For years, the railroad had managed to limp along with minimum tie renewals, and, much to his surprise, Metzker learned that thousands of ties cried out for immediate replacement. Looking at the payroll, he counted eighty names in the railroad department, and these two factors together with a tight money situation caused him to cease logging by railroad and expand truck operations. The dismantling of the logging railroad above Hawley in 1958 established a milestone in Plumas County history. Not only had it been the longest logging line in the county, but it also had the longest tenure, and its departure marked the end of rail logging in Plumas County.

Metzker followed his plan to sell the (new) Feather River Lumber Company property after holding it for ten years, but when Di Gorgio became the new owner, Metzker continued to manage the property for several years. In 1972, the name became Di Gorgio Shelter Products, and four years later the plant was acquired by Sierra Pacific Industries.

Happily, No. 4, the great 2-6-6-2T locomotive, is still with us. In 1957, before the logging railroad was dismantled, its lettering read "Feather River Lumber Co." for a brief period. Later that year, the Tahoe Lumber Company bought it for stationary boiler purposes in Reno. Donated to the Pacific Locomotive Association in July 1973, it went to Point Castro, California, and it moved along with the museum in 1986 when relocated to Fremont and Niles Canyon, California.

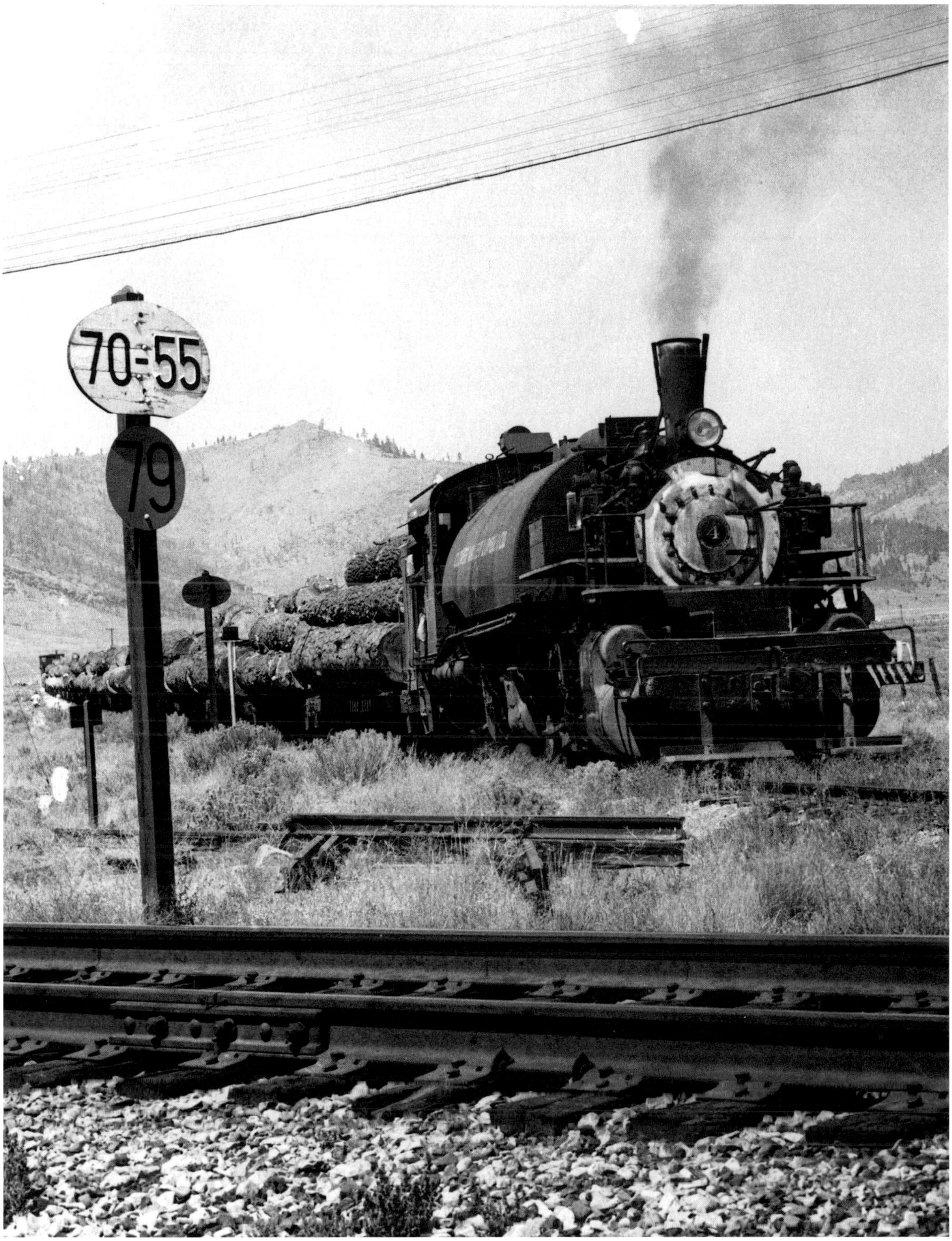

A train of logs is about to cross the Western Pacific main line at Hawley in August 1955. The WP speed board holds passenger trains to seventy miles per hour and freight trains to fifty-five miles per hour, with the exception of the Zephyr, which could travel at seventy-nine miles per hour in the flat area of Sierra Valley. (Harre Demoro photograph)

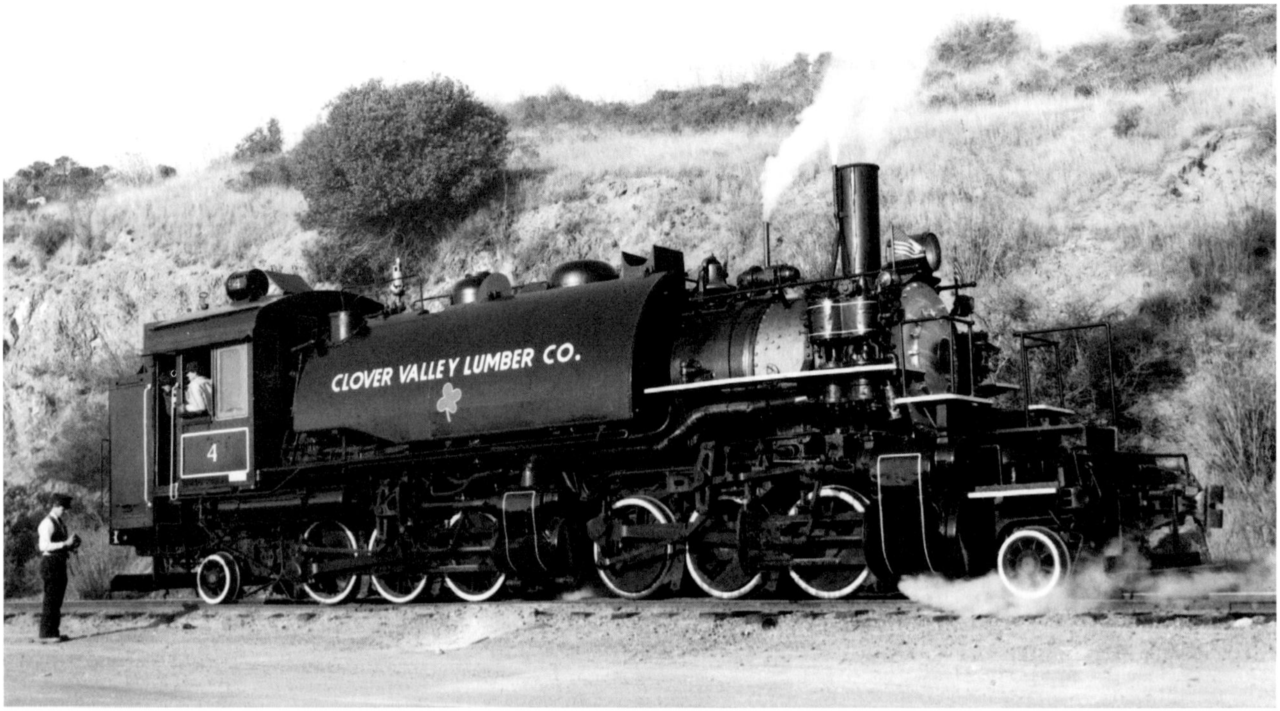

Above: After the Clover Valley Lumber Company railroad ended operations in 1957, this handsome locomotive went to Reno to serve as a stationary boiler. Subsequently, it was donated to the Pacific Locomotive Association, then at Castro Point, on San Francisco Bay. By June 1983 when Douglas Richter took this picture, the engine had been restored to its original glory. (Bert Ward collection)

Below: As most logging trains rarely consisted of more than a handful of cars, cabooses were not part of the scene. The Clover Valley Lumber Company sometimes used this caboose that rested quietly at Loyalton in August 1955. (Harre Demoro photograph)

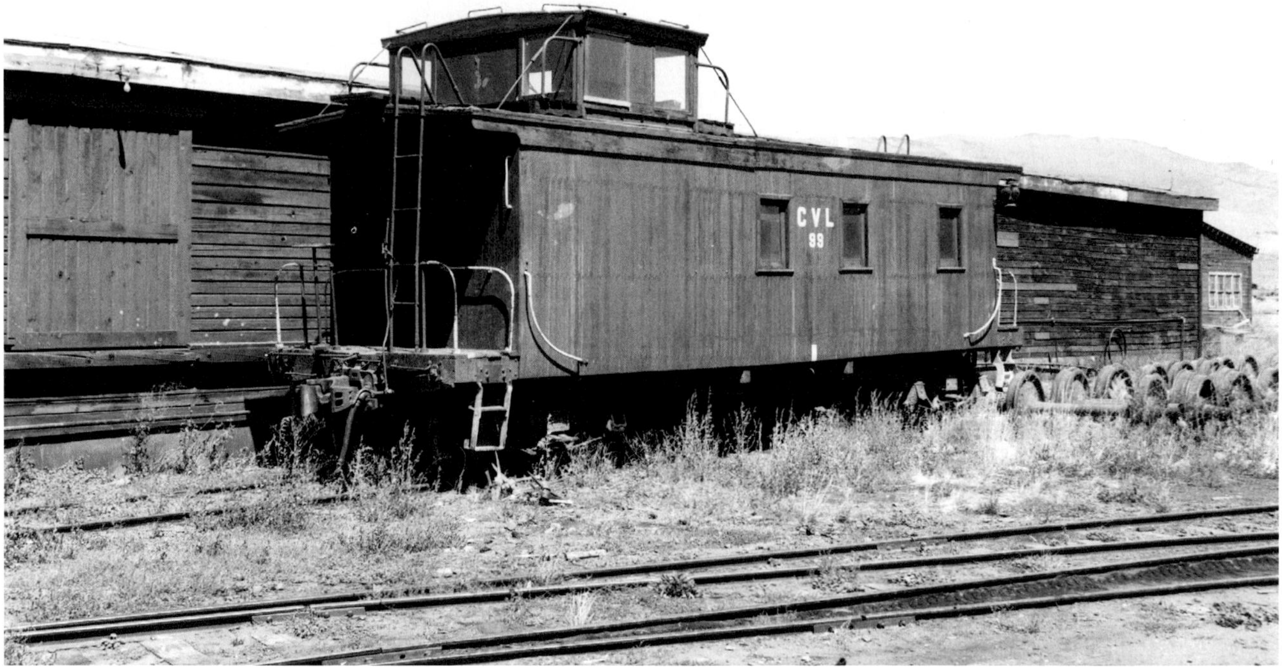

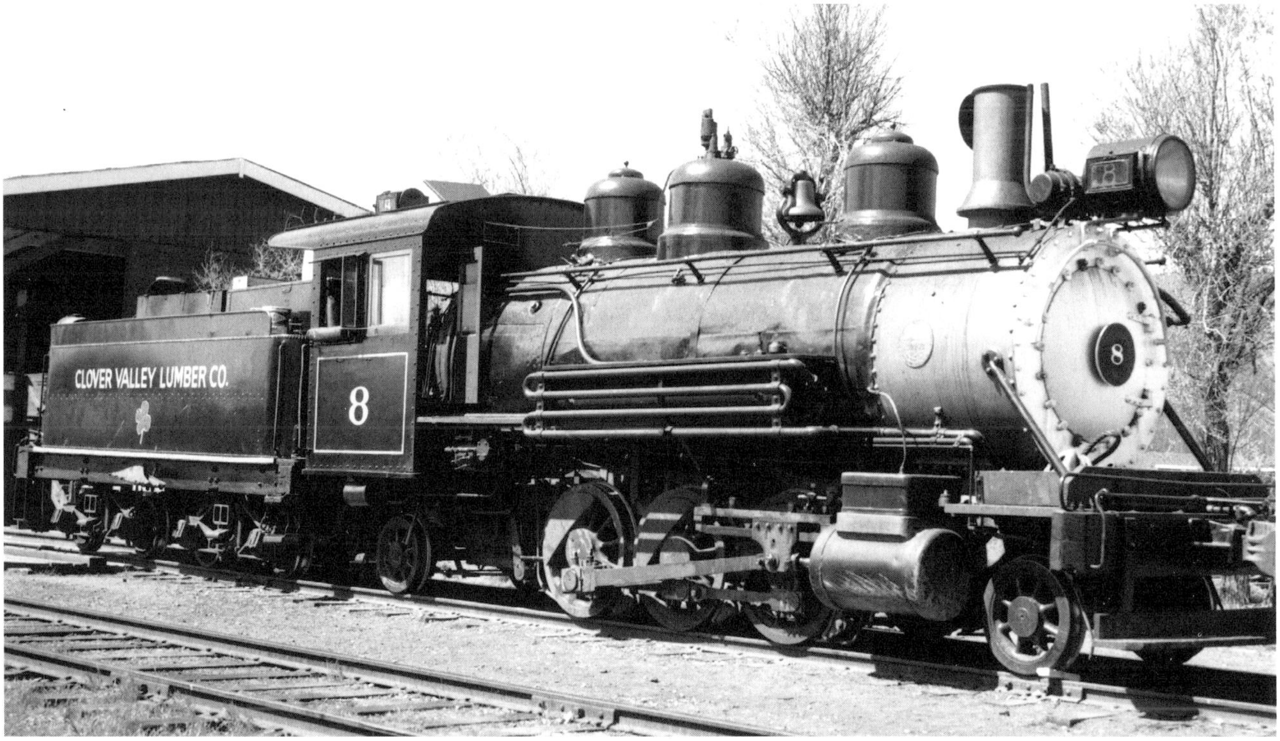

Above: Stiff grades north of Beckwourth often demanded the use of geared locomotives. CVL had only two rod engines. No. 8 was purchased from Hobart Mills in 1935. (Bert Ward photograph)

Below: CVL was the ninth owner of this Shay engine built in 1904. After serving a Kentucky coal operator, it paused briefly in Nevada, where it pulled trains up the hill from Wadsworth to Olinghouse for the short-lived Nevada Railroad. Passed from one logging line to another, it came to the Clover Valley Lumber Company in 1920. When Bert Ward took this picture at Loyalton in September 1937, the engine had been laid aside, as its crown sheet had dropped to the bottom of the firebox.

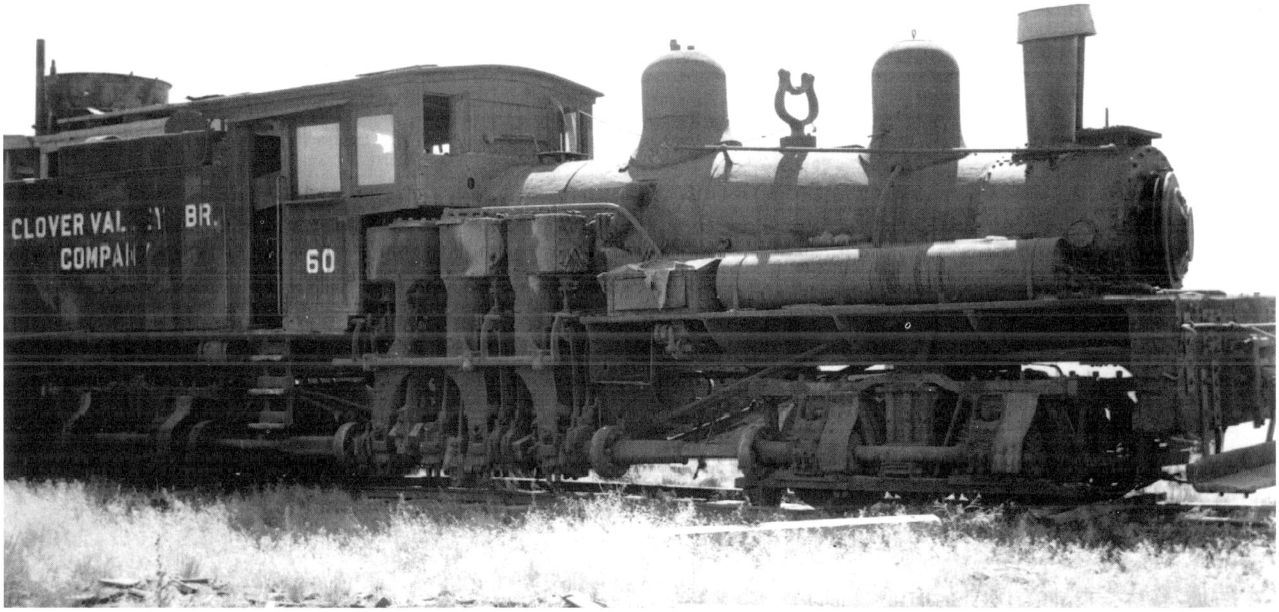

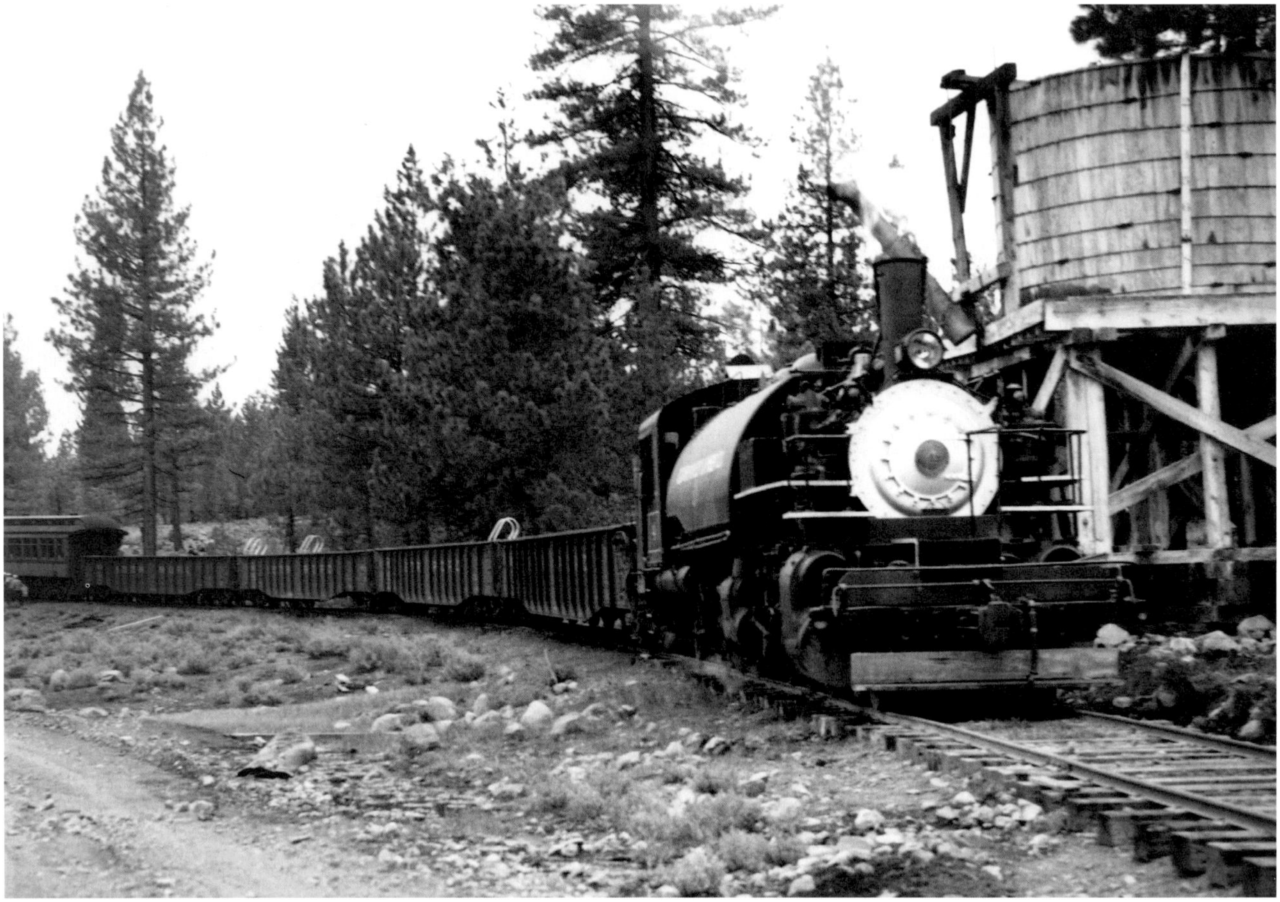

In May 1950, the California-Nevada Railroad Historical Society staged an excursion. For this run-by photograph, rail photographers had left their benches in the gondolas, as No. 4 led the train by a water tank. (Bert Ward photograph)

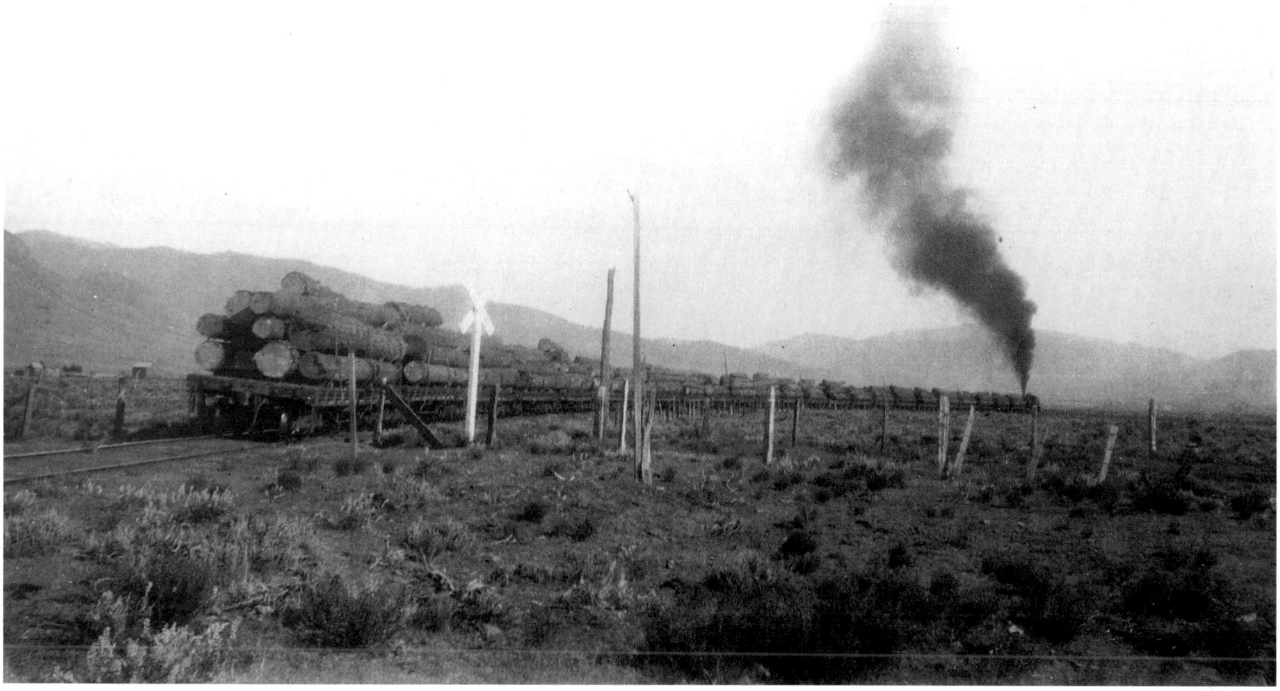

Above: Having crossed Western Pacific at Hawley, a CVL log train of twenty cars continues across Sierra Valley to the mill at Loyalton, located at the far right by the smoke from the steam boilers.

Below: Taking advantage of the cold winters, the Clover Valley Lumber Company also had an ice business on Grizzly Creek. The ice is being prepared for cutting into blocks.

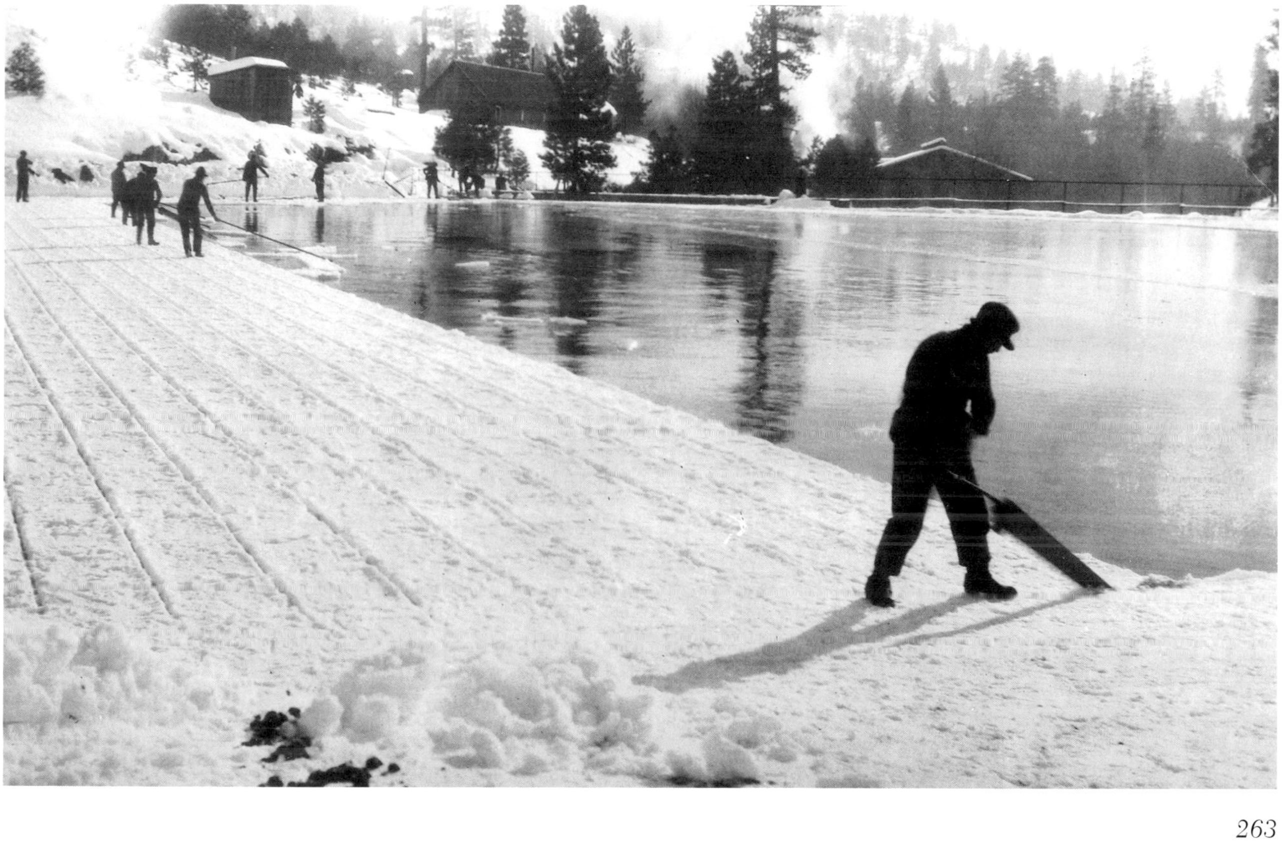

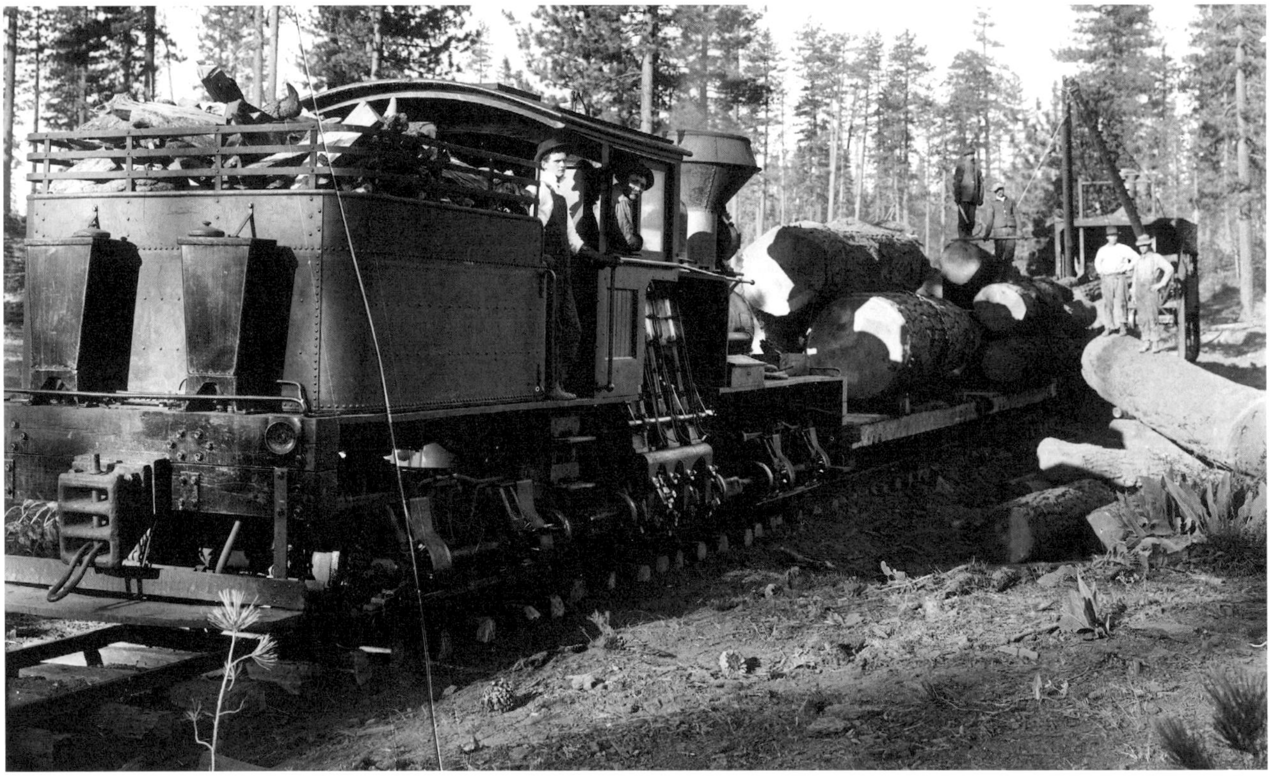

The Horton brothers, pioneer lumbermen in Clover Valley, sold their sawmill to the Marsh Lumber Company in 1907. A few years later, the narrow gauge of the new company went over the pass to link the sawmill with a spur of the Boca and Loyalton RR at Horton Landing. The Shay locomotive could handle heavier trains than a rod engine. (James E. Boynton collection)

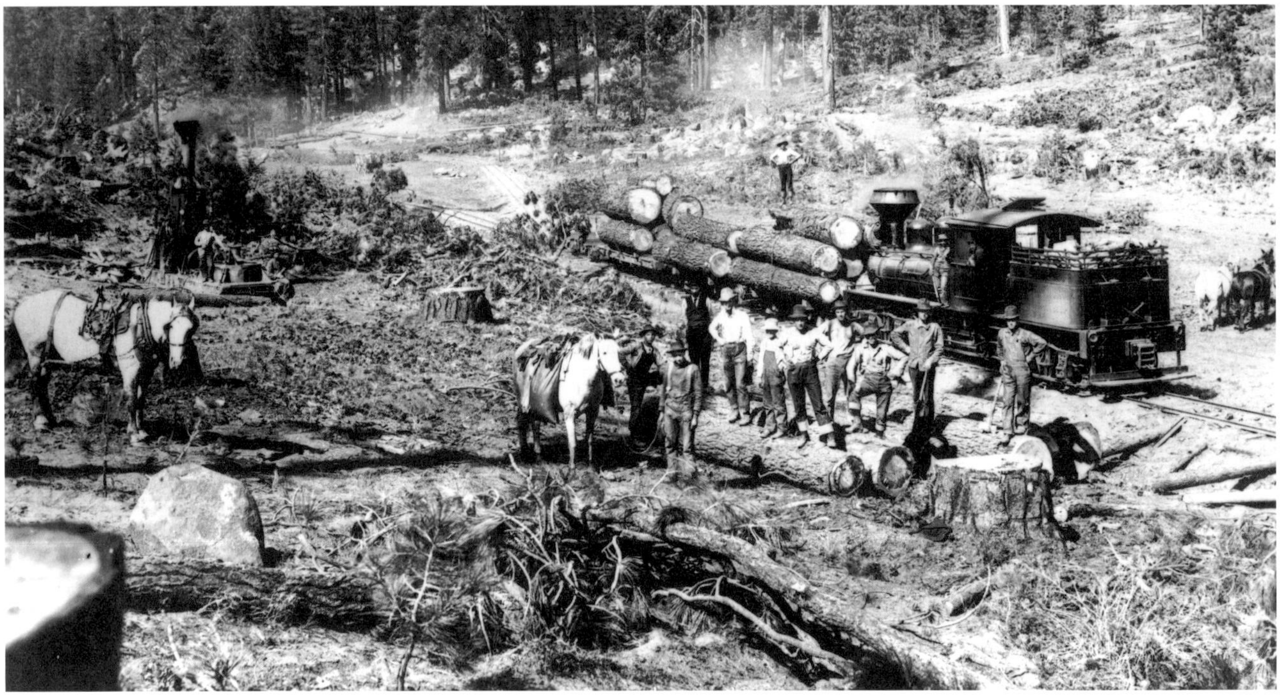

After clearing the timber and loading the cars, the crew posed by the Shay engine before the train departed for Horton Landing. (Plumas County Museum)

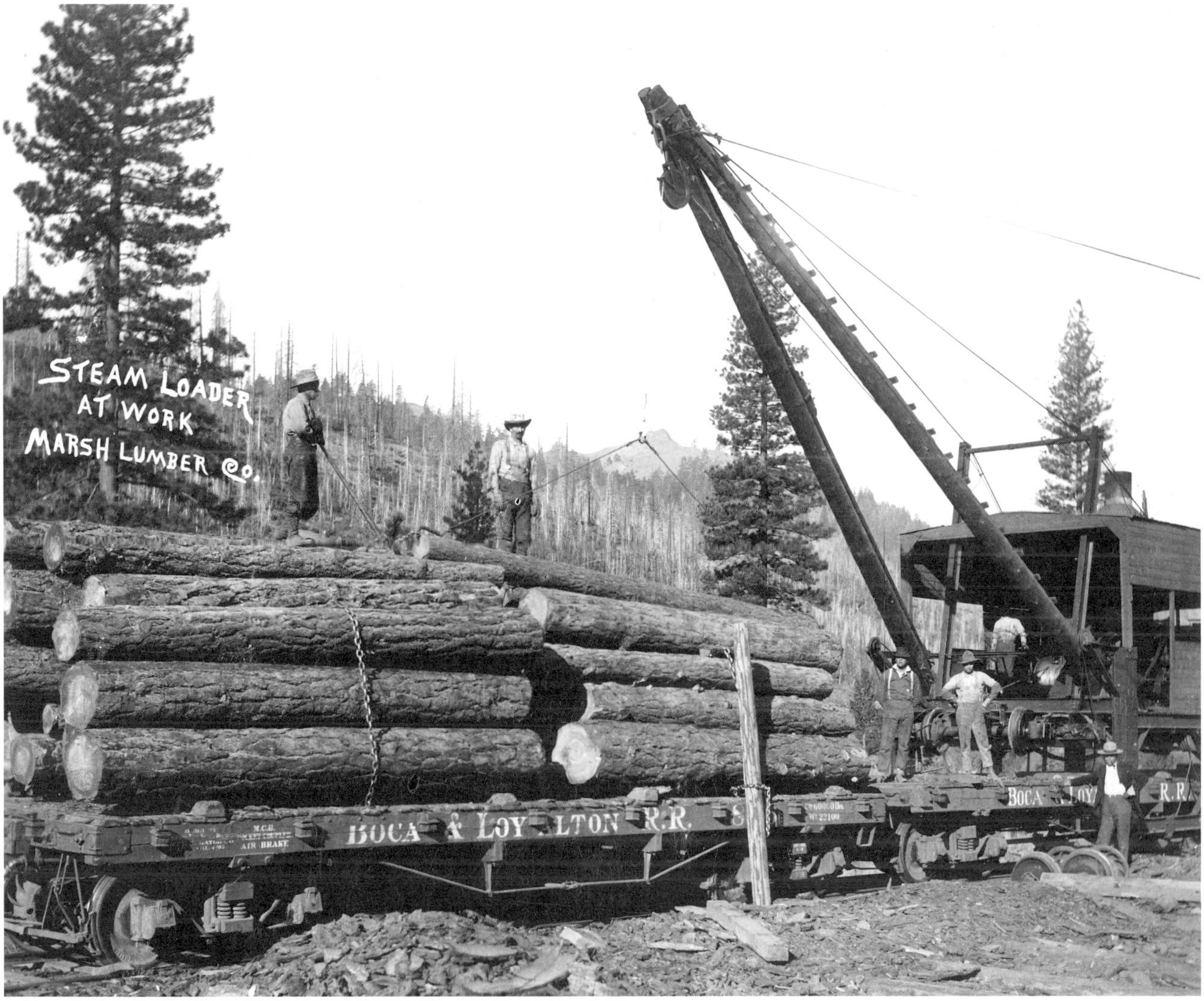

At Horton Landing, the Boca and Loyalton RR used a steam loader to transfer logs to the standard gauge cars. Peter B. Thompson, the photographer of this activity, took many pictures in the area before his death in 1920.

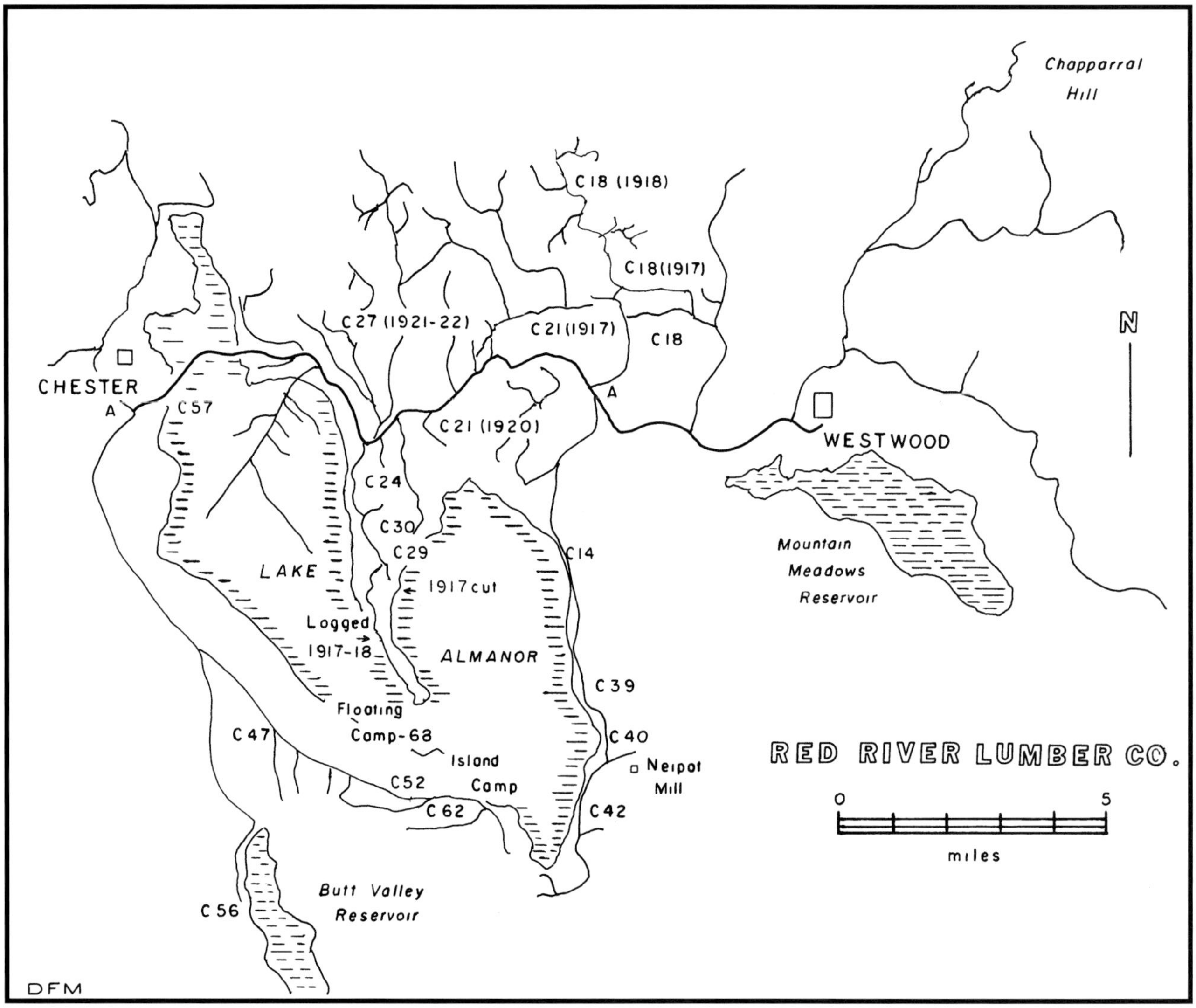

The Red River Lumber Company built temporary railroad spurs to reach its timberlands around Lake Almanor. Among the first areas the company logged were the timber stands that were later flooded at the northwest corner of the lake.

Logging camps are indicated by the letter C and a number, with date where known. During 1926, the company harvested timber around Camp 62.

The electrified trackage stood between Westwood and Chester. Later, the company sold that section of the formerly electrified railroad between the two A letters to the Collins Pine Company, which formed the Almanor Railroad in 1941.

RED RIVER LUMBER COMPANY

When Thomas Barlow Walker saw his source of Minnesota timber diminishing, he made plans to move from Akeley, Minnesota, where he had operated for many years, to California. Within a few years his Westwood plant stood among the largest sawmills in that state.

As the story of this lumber company has been well told in the book *Red River*, by Robert M. Hanft, thus eliminating the need for detailed reporting, this chapter focuses on an outline of the railroad activities.

Through one of his sons, Clinton B., Walker began acquiring California timberlands around 1902. Much acreage was purchased from other companies, including the Santa Fe Pacific Railroad and the Aztec Land and Cattle Company who chose lands in California to replace their Arizona lands taken by the government.

By 1907, T. B. Walker had become the largest taxpayer in Shasta County, as he owned 183,277 acres of timberland assessed at the low value of eight dollars an acre. Serious consideration was given to building a railroad to tap his prospective lumber mills, either by his own logging railroad or some extension from the proposed Goose Lake and Southern of the SP family. Nothing transpired. Late in 1907, there was talk of a railroad from Fall River to Red Bluff where the finished lumber would be barged down the Sacramento River to tidewater.

As 1910 began, Walker focused his attention on his timberlands in Lassen and Plumas Counties, including Big Meadows where stood a luxurious growth of timber. One man who cruised the area in 1905 praised the trees, citing the presence of twenty-seven sugar pines with trunks at least seven feet in diameter.

Special circumstances surrounded the timber in Big Meadows. The Great Western Power Company contemplated damming the North Fork of the Feather River at a gorge near the south end of Big Meadows to form a reservoir as part of its plan to ensure a dependable flow of water for its electrical generating plant at the Big Bend farther down the same river. As the proposed reservoir—later known as Lake Almanor—would flood the forest on Big Meadows, Mortimer Fleischhacker, head of Great Western Power, and T. B. Walker negotiated a contract during 1912 providing for the Red River Lumber (RRL) Company to harvest the trees as the lake began to form. Residents of Big Meadows, when advised of the plan, purchased lots in Chester and moved their houses to the town.

At that time, the Western Pacific station at Doyle, California, stood as the closest railhead, so sawmill machinery dispatched from Minnesota was transferred at that point to teams for the haul to the mill site. The selection of the mill site continued elusive; Susanville held attractions in spite of a collection of saloons, some of which Clinton Walker purchased and closed. The family soon realized that new ones would appear as fast as others shuttered their doors, so they decided to locate their settlement in a pristine area along Robbers Creek about eighteen miles west of Susanville. As owners of the entire settlement, they permitted no saloons, but liquor vendors could never be entirely eliminated.

Initially known as Walker's Camp, then Westwood, the firm drew workers from Greenville and Crescent Mills, and, with a temporary sawmill harvesting local timber, Red River began to create a town and build a major sawmill.

Workers laid the first foundation on July 2, 1913; seven months later the town had grown so much that the store had to be doubled in size. Cottages for workers sprouted along the new streets with monthly rents held to low figures. Five dollars would provide a three-room cottage, and a fourth room would add two dollars to the monthly rent. For a larger family, an eight-room cottage commanded twenty dollars each month.

Life in the bustling town never stood still in the early days of Westwood, with the sound of carpenters casting an irregular beat each day. On the flip side, the unusually heavy snowfall that year and winds could be devastating. During January 1914, strong winds toppled one hundred trees in Westwood to demolish some houses. A carpenter named Moulton, observing a tree about to fall on his cottage, dashed outside just in time, only to be pinned to the ground by the limbs of a falling tree.

Southern Pacific, through its Fernley and Lassen Railway, struggled through deep snowbanks in its effort to reach Westwood. As described in another chapter, trains finally arrived in March 1914.

The big mill took form, machinery was installed, and the first log passed through the saw at 1:00 P.M.,

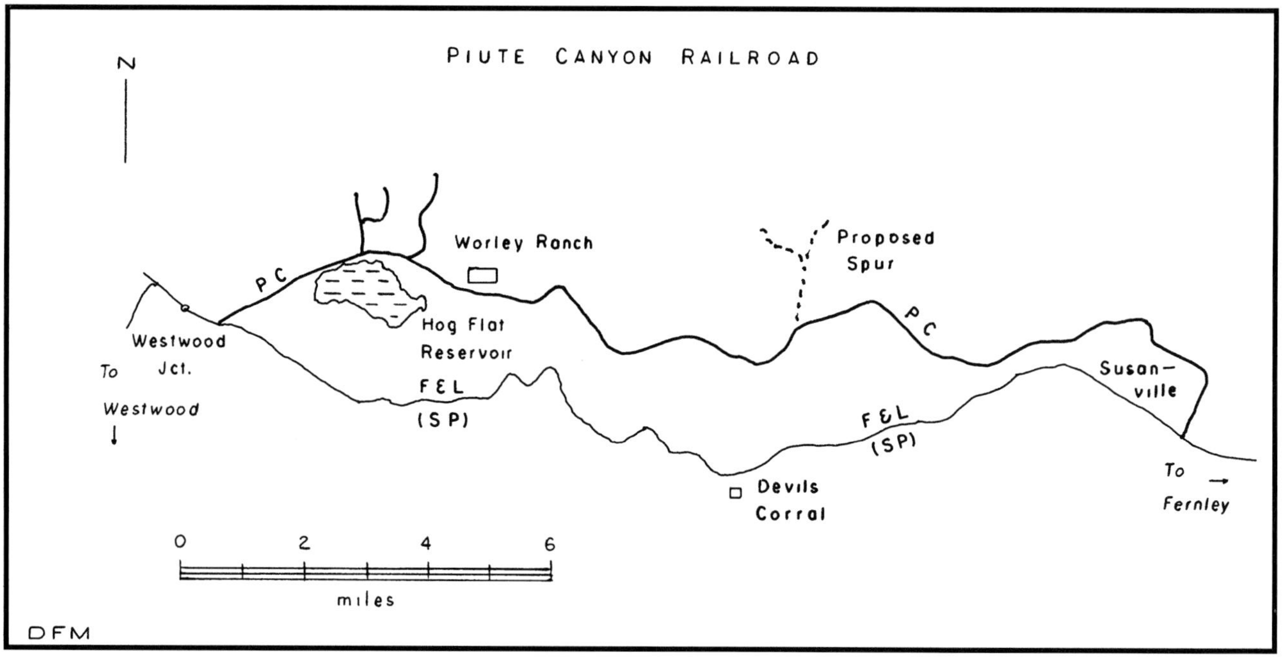

August 1, 1914. The timing proved appropriate, for just six weeks later, a fire consumed the original mill.

Going back to February 1914, loggers plodded through the deep snow to fell great trees in the area to be flooded by the Big Meadows reservoir. To move the logs from Big Meadows to the Westwood mill necessitated efficient planning. After cutting and trimming the logs and floating them in the new lake, a launch gathered and delivered them to the Becraft place on the shore where the Hamilton Branch emptied into the lake.

Surveyors had already set stakes for a nine-mile standard-gauge railroad to bring the logs to the mill from the lake. (Camp 14 was located at this point.) Under T. R. Wilson, construction superintendent, 275 men and 159 teams went to work in the late spring of 1914 to build the first four miles of the railroad to the crossing of the Feather River. The Money brothers took a contract to grade the next five miles. By mid-July, grading had been completed, with the track in place as far as the North Fork of the Feather River bridge. Only a short time elapsed before the entire nine miles stood ready for operation.

Probably the first motive power came from the Tonopah and Goldfield (T&G) Railroad when the lumber company took delivery of T&G Nos. 100–102, consolidation-type (2-8-0) locomotives. On the way, the three locomotives paused in SP's Sparks shops for mechanical work as necessary. All of Red River's steam locomotives came from other carriers and retained the same road numbers as the previous owners. A switch engine joined the roster in the autumn.

Before winter set in, Red River began construction of its first railroad branch. At a point on the original (main) line four and one-half miles from Westwood, tracks reached out to tap a lumber area known as the Falager Ranch. The company continued to grow and celebrated Christmas 1914 with 1,200 names on the payroll. The next year Red River purchased 1,400 acres of timber in Plumas County from the Sierra Lumber Company for $32,900.

Heavy snows in January 1916 blocked efforts to open twelve miles of new railroad northwest of Westwood. The same gathering of snow proved too much for the sawmill, causing the collapse of part of the roof. That failed to halt expansion, for a few months later the mill had four band saws in operation.

In June 1917, the railroad system counted two main lines with 80-pound steel rail, with one measuring nine miles and the other seven miles. Approximately twenty-five miles of branch lines completed the system. In addition to the three consolidation-type locomotives, two 80-ton Shays found places on the roster. One Shay, unusually large, had come from the El Paso and Southwestern Railroad, perhaps for the Cloudcroft branch where steep grades offered access to Sacramento Mountain timber.

Three months later a major fire terrorized the community. Believed to be the work of an incendiary, it began at 3:00 A.M. and consumed two-thirds of the lumber inventory before being brought under control. Train crews responded nobly by rushing into the yard and rescuing thirty-five carloads of lumber. With the flames approaching the big plant, the manager took a decisive step by using fifty boxes of dynamite to level a section of the lumberyard. The bold move proved effective; the mill survived.

During 1916–1917, RRL conducted logging operations west and north of Westwood as far as the base of Brush Hill. At the same time, it continued logging around Lake Almanor, with one phase centering on the Almanor Peninsula where harvested logs, after being floated across part of the lake to Camp 14, continued their way to the mill on the company railroad.

Expansion and Innovation

Expansion and innovation marked operations during the 1920s. Starting at a point later designated as Clear Creek Jct. on the line to Camp 14 and on to the southeast end of Lake Almanor, Red River pushed rails in a generally westward direction beyond Rock Creek. The line catered to the topography, with more curves than an uninformed person might consider necessary. Camp 21, just northeast of Almanor Peninsula, served as logging headquarters in 1920. The next year, workers took their saws farther west and in 1922–1923 extended the rails to Chester where residents for the first time heard a locomotive whistling at their front door. A trestle with a slight curve attracted photographers until it burned and was replaced by a less picturesque fill.

Fletcher Walker, son of T. B. and manager, is recalled as a "friendly man." He also possessed a creative mind from which several mechanical inventions flowed. With this background, it is not surprising that the Red River Lumber Company purchased a 600-HP diesel-electric freight locomotive in 1926, a decade ahead of most railroads. Three companies combined efforts to create this engine, numbered 502. A year later, the seventeen miles of railroad between Westwood and Chester came under electrification; two 800-HP locomotives of Baldwin-Westinghouse manufacture served this line. According to a 1929 company timetable, trains shuttled back and forth to and from Chester, making seven 40-minute trips six days a week.

The combination of the temporary nature of logging spurs and even key lines and the loss of maps leaves the location and timing of Red River Lumber spurs largely undetermined. However, from newspaper accounts and recollections of old timers, some general data have been preserved.

The "Deer Creek Main Line" left Chester and followed Red River loggers to the boundary of Mt. Lassen Park. Following a southwesterly direction, another principal line entered Humbug Valley to the west of Lake Almanor. Logging on the east side of Butt Valley in the 1930s faced the handicap of working on a steep hillside, so logs were tossed into the lake, then gathered by an eighteen-foot tug that towed them to a rail spur on the west side.

Piute Canyon Railroad

For some years, Red River Lumber management contemplated a railroad through its timberlands from Westwood Jct. to Susanville. Surveys, undertaken in 1928, placed the line parallel and north of Southern Pacific's railroad. Starting out with a brisk pace, the company assembled construction equipment at Devil's Corral the next year, but before actual construction began, dark clouds shrouded the economic climate, putting the entire project "on hold."

In the late spring of 1932, the company opened a tract of fifty million board feet north of Westwood. To serve this area, it constructed a four-mile spur starting on the SP about a mile east of Westwood Jct.

Three years later, with a brighter lumber market prevailing, Red River Lumber announced that the railroad would be constructed, but the work appears to have been done in the name of the Waland Lumber Company, reportedly an affiliate. Incorporated in Minnesota in 1911, Waland was not active in California until 1928. In March 1935, company representatives appeared before the board of supervisors of Lassen County and obtained permission to build its railroad across eighteen roads and streets, with half being in Susanville.

By incorporating part of the 1932 spur, the so-called Piute Railroad ran along the north side of Hog Flat Reservoir, past the Worley ranch, and then along Piute Creek on its way to Susanville. Swinging around the north side of town, it crossed the Millwood tract and ended with a connection again with SP's Westwood branch by the mill of the Fruit Growers Supply Company.

Heavy April rains caused a major flood in Big Valley (Bieber) and slowed progress on the new railroad, but grading was soon followed by tracklaying. In June, workers tackled the month-long job of building the Susan River bridge, and Red River Lumber workers enjoyed a wage increase.

On August 23, 1935, the *Lassen Mail*, in an article headed "New Choo Choo," announced that the railroad had been completed that day and that it would soon deliver logs to the lumber mills. In the meantime, work commenced on a new mill for the Springfield Cedar Company of Oakland, California, as a part of an RRL Company program to diversify lumber production in the area. On September 10, 1935, two trains left Camp 8 and brought the first logs over the new line to the Fruit Growers Supply millpond.

For various reasons, never fully quantified, log shipments failed to materialize, and the railroad soon became idle.

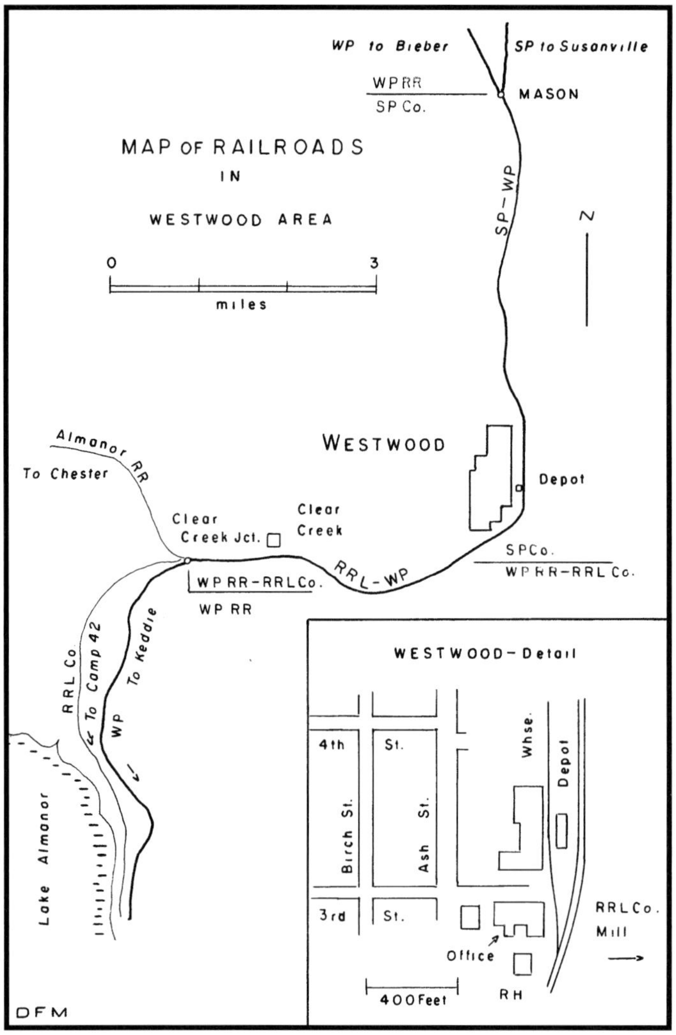

Southern Pacific, after combating an unusually heavy winter snowfall, finally opened its line to Westwood in February 1914 to serve the Red River Lumber Company. Besides building many logging spurs into the woods, the lumber company constructed a "main line" to Chester over which it operated electric trains.

When the Western Pacific Railroad built its line from Keddie to Bieber, it purchased a portion of the Red River Lumber Company's line between what became Clear Creek Jct. and Southern Pacific tracks in Westwood. (On survey maps, the connection was at the south line of Section 7, T28N, R9E.) Red River Lumber continued to have the right to operate over this section after the sale.

From the connection north to the new station of Mason, WP secured trackage rights over Southern Pacific and purchased this trackage in 1966 when SP abandoned its railroad to Susanville. When Red River sold its railroad from Clear Creek Jct. to Chester to the Collins Pine Company in 1941, the new owner transferred this property to the Almanor Railroad.

When George McDow Jr. began his employment with Red River in May 1942, the dismantling was still in progress. Subsequently, the former railroad grade served as a private road for logging trucks.

Around the middle 1930s, the Walkers constructed a short spur to a timbered flat east of Westwood. In the later years of the life of the Red River Lumber Company, logging activity moved north to Halls Flat and around Poison Lake. Taking the name from Paul Bunyan, the mythical lumberman with great accomplishments featured in Red River sales promotion, the company established Camp Bunyan in 1940 at Halls Flat, a station on the Western Pacific Northern California Extension, thirty-seven miles north of Westwood. Operations began a year later, and logging followed on both sides of the railroad as the company built eastward through the Blacks Mountain Game Preserve. Tracks ran around the northern slope of Mt. Harvey where another camp met the basic needs of the workers. Each bunkhouse accommodated four men, and being portable they were often moved during working hours with little notice, which left loggers wondering, "Where am I sleeping tonight?" Rails extended eastward as far as Five Troughs, where trucks delivered more logs from Gooch Valley.

During that time, Red River had some thirty or forty men installing and removing lumber spurs as needed. Finis M. Sanders, usually called "Chief" because of his partial Cherokee ancestry, held the responsibility for removing logging spurs no longer needed. In doing so, he sometimes encountered unauthorized scrap dealers engaged in the same work. This discovery called for firm negotiations in positive terms, always successful with the county sheriff present.

Although WP's Northern California Extension offered no regular passenger service, each weekend a train made a round-trip, taking the men out of the woods for a little R&R in Westwood. Using former interurban cars of the Sacramento Northern Railway, Western Pacific crews or Red River Lumber crews, with a WP pilot, took charge of the trains.

The Poison Lake area came into prominence in 1944 when the RRL built a log spur connecting with Western Pacific at Poison Lake and extending south, passing the gravel quarry and going along the west side of Poison Lake for about seven miles before turning west and continuing for about the same distance almost to Butte Creek. The men lived at Camp Bunyan, and a daily train—with a WP pilot—transported the logging crews to work each day.

The Walker family, like so many other families in similar situations, lost leaders capable of carrying forward the empire created by grandfathers. While convincing reasons for the sale of the company property to Fruit Growers Supply in December 1944 have not been made public, it transpired and closed a major California business enterprise.

Almanor Railroad Company

The Collins Pine Company had its beginnings in 1855 at East Hickory, Pennsylvania, when Truman Collins, Joseph Collins, and others purchased a sawmill along the Allegheny River. While the men continued to be active in Pennsylvania, they also acquired timberlands in Washington, Oregon, and California. The Collins Almanor Forest was secured in 1902.

Around 1940, under the name of Collins Pine Company, Truman Collins, grandson of one of the founders, contemplated a sawmill at Chester near the company's timber. By that time, Red River Lumber Company's logging activity was primarily around Harvey Mountain, which reduced the use of the electrified railroad between Westwood and Chester.

Collins purchased the railroad from Red River Jct. (later called Clear Creek Jct.) to Chester, 13.7 miles, and transferred ownership to the Almanor Railroad Company, a subsidiary incorporated on September 15, 1941. The wires were removed, and Finis "Chief" Sanders moved

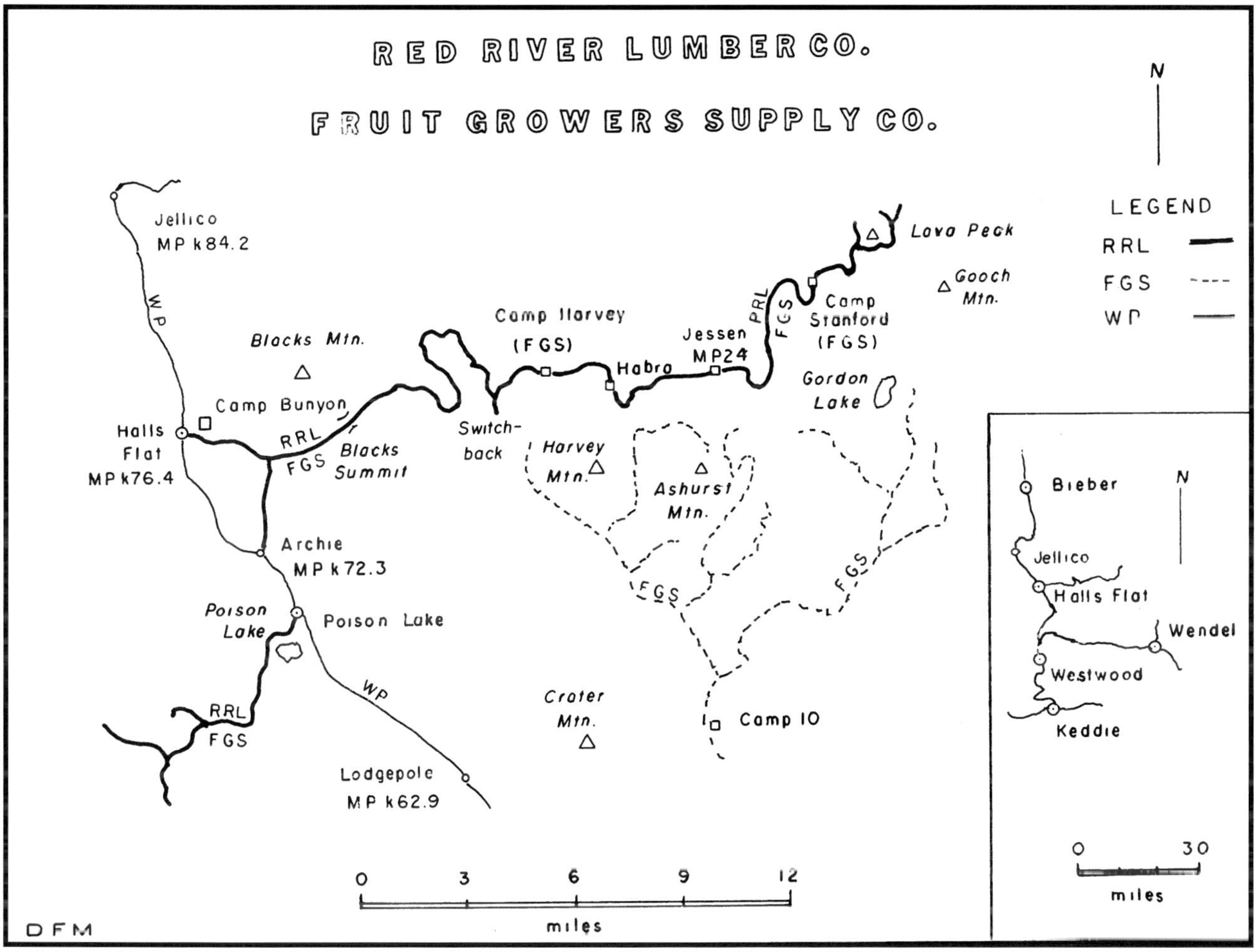

Fruit Growers Supply harvested lumber for fruit packing boxes in an area stretching twenty miles north of Westwood Jct. from 1920 to 1952. From a map drawn by James Bryant after diligent research, this map has been prepared to show the timber railroads of the Fruit Growers Supply Company. To avoid congestion, not all the spurs have been included, and the map represents the location of the various lines operated over the years but not existing at the same time. After a tract of timber had been cut, the tracks were physically transferred to a new cutting area.

Initially, timber was harvested along the line to Antelope Mountain. In 1923, a new "main line" reached out along the west side of Campbell Mountain, continuing northward to Camp 10 in 1929. From Camp 10, logging spurs extended as far north as Harvey Mountain and Gordon Lake, some thirty miles from Westwood Jct.

the railroad's tracks away from the highway on the causeway across the north bay of Lake Almanor. The two electric locomotives began their long journey. After being stored, the Central California Traction Company placed them in switching service in Stockton. After a short time, they were transferred to the Pacific Electric Railway in southern California and finally ended up in Argentina.

Though the main purpose of the Almanor Railroad was to serve the Collins Pine Company, it became a common carrier in May 1942, and the mill began working the next year.

A Heisler geared locomotive, formerly running on the tracks of the Grande Ronde Pine Company as No. 104, arrived to be the first locomotive on the new railroad and continued with the same road number. For a time it was replaced by No. 106, a forty-four-ton diesel engine, but subsequently ownership of the locomotive No. 166 has been vested in the Collins Pine Company. The little railroad interchanges cars with Union Pacific at Clear Creek Jct. Until its final operation in the summer of 2004, this line stood out as the last remnant of the logging railroad in Plumas and Lassen Counties.

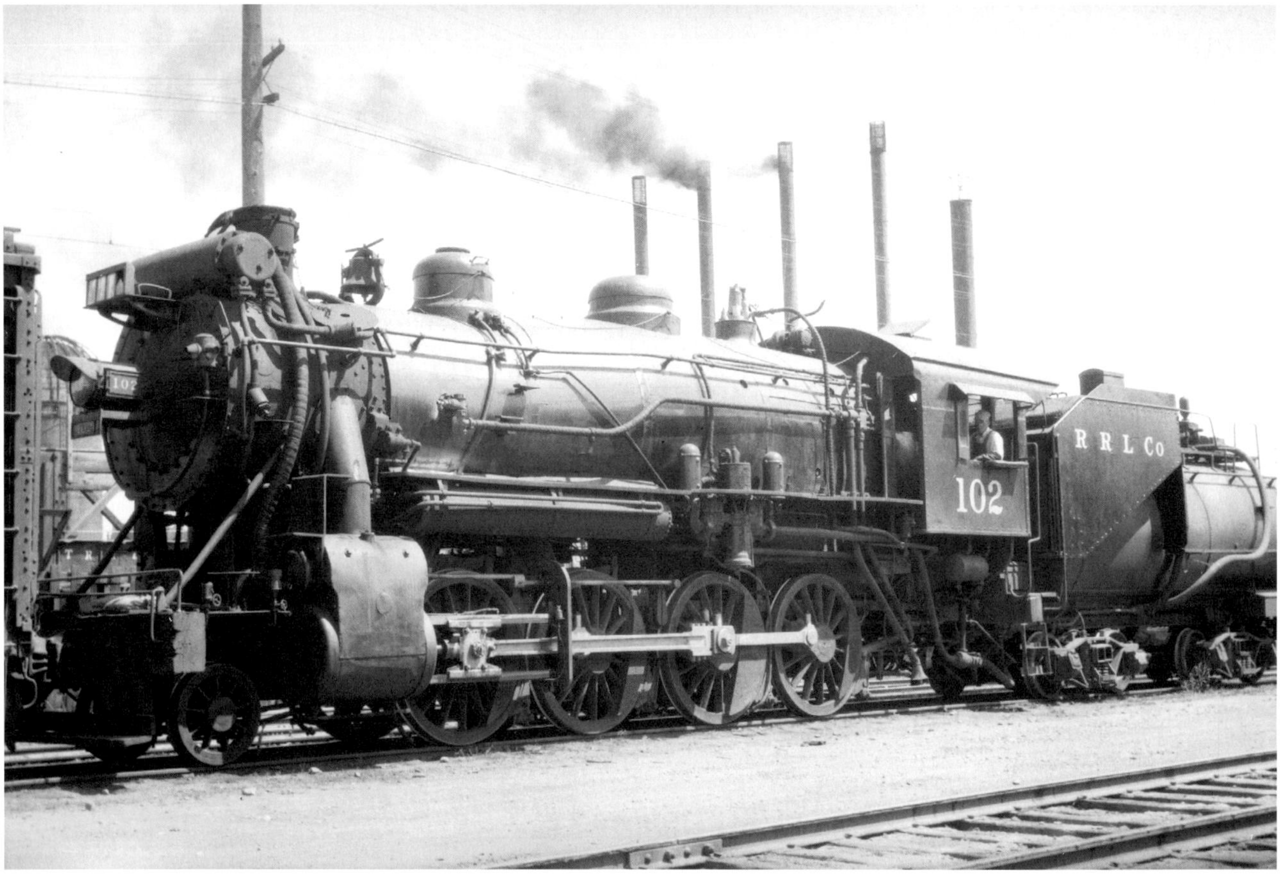

As Red River was pushing its rails into the woods, the Tonopah and Goldfield Railroad was disposing of its excess motive power. When three consolidation-type engines joined the Red River roster in 1914, road numbers remained the same. (Bert Ward photograph)

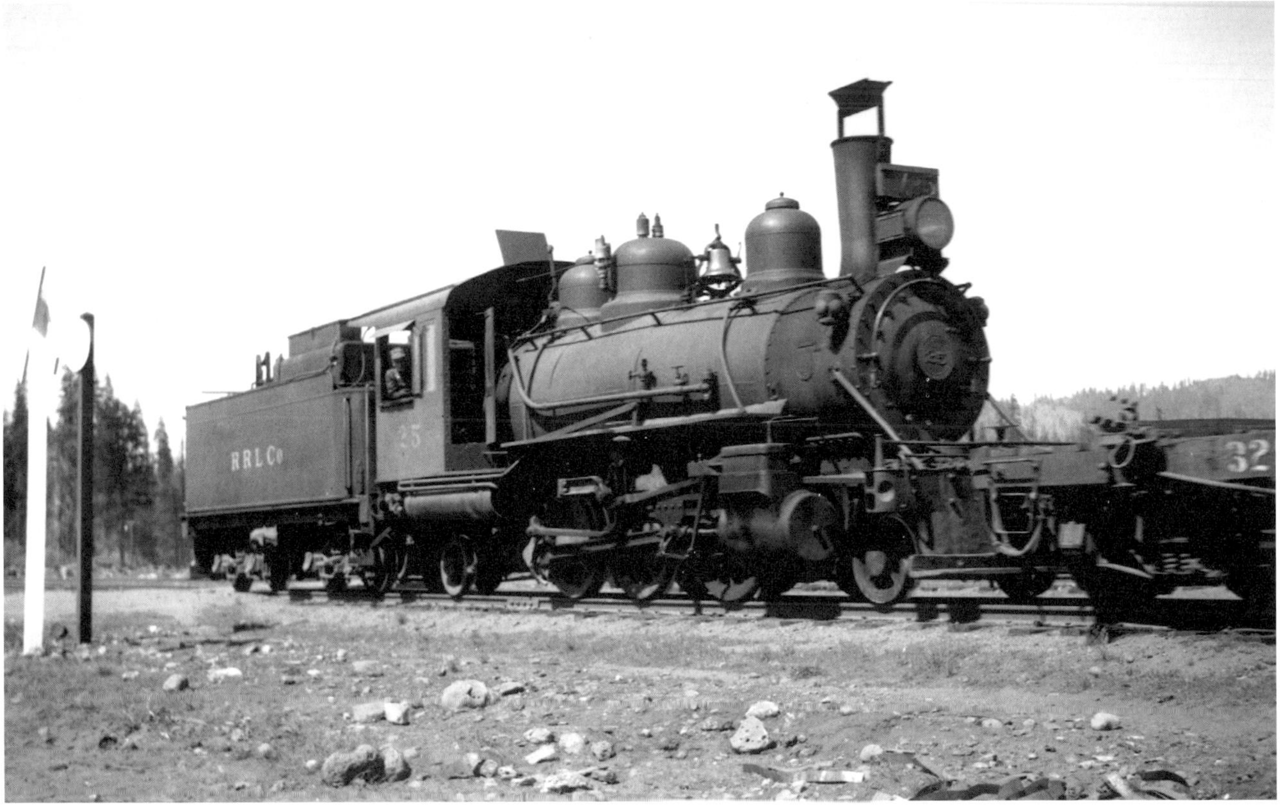

Above: Red River Lumber Company No. 25 at Chester in 1937. The next year No. 25 was working for the Modesto and Empire Traction Company. (Douglas Richter photograph, Bert Ward collection)

Below: Formerly SP 1349, Red River kept the same road number. It is about to couple a tank car at Westwood. (Harre Demoro collection)

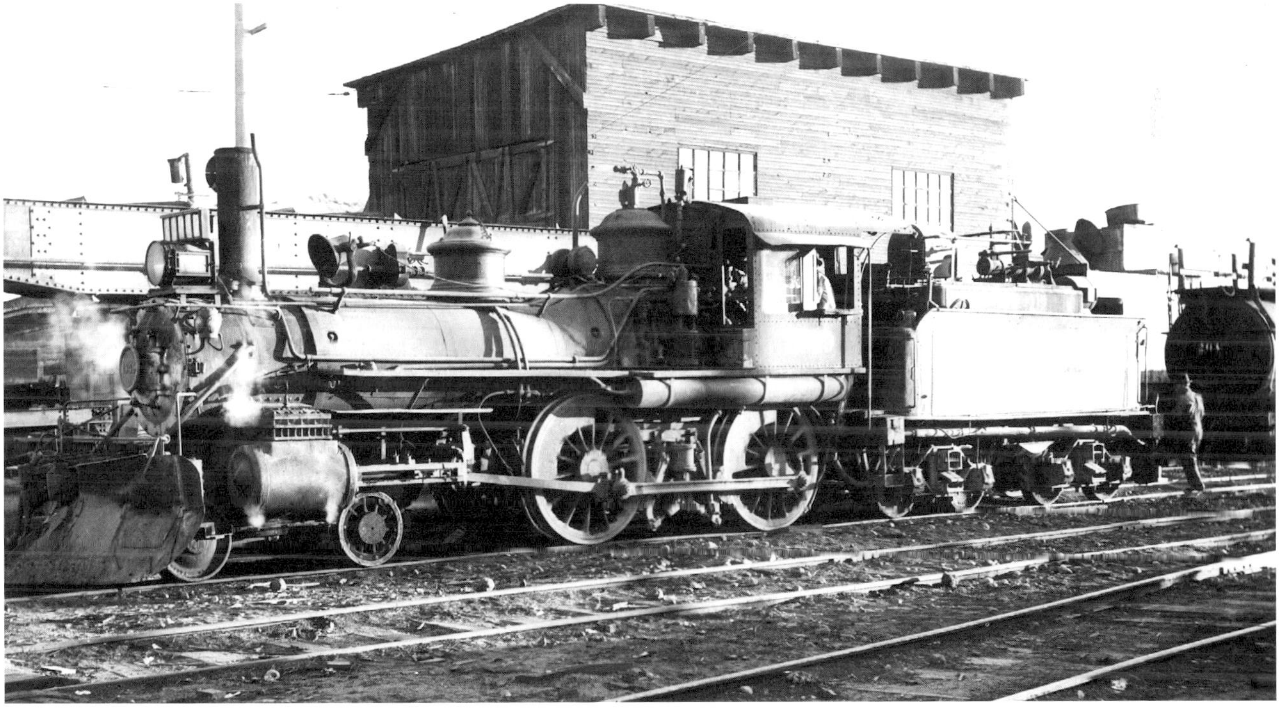

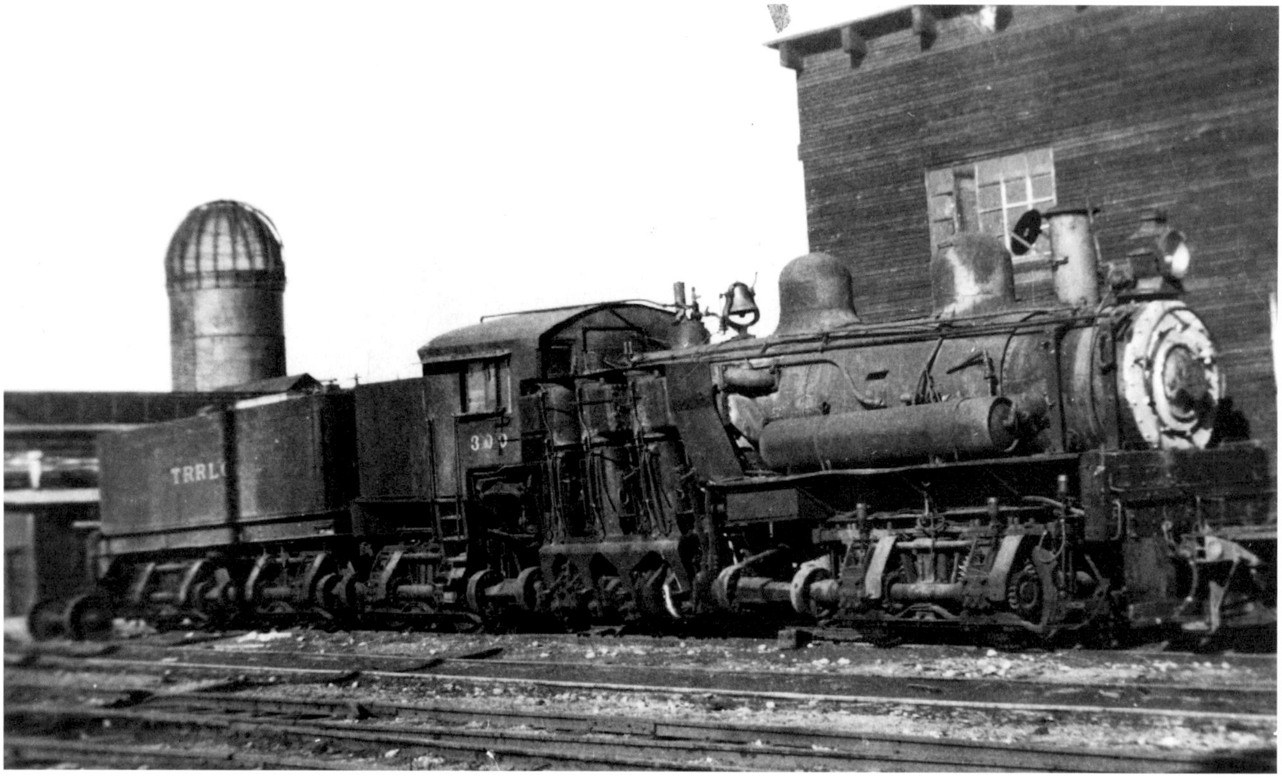

Above: Some logging spurs necessitated a geared locomotive. Built by Lima in 1907, this Shay was photographed twenty-nine years later at Westwood by Jim Harrison. (Bert Ward collection)

Below: In 1926, long before diesel-electric locomotives undermined steam rosters on major railroads, Red River purchased a 600-HP engine manufactured by General Electric–Alco and Ingersoll-Rand. Painted orange, it carried No. 502 as its road number. In 1940, it was sent to Armco Steel in Ohio. (Bert Ward collection)

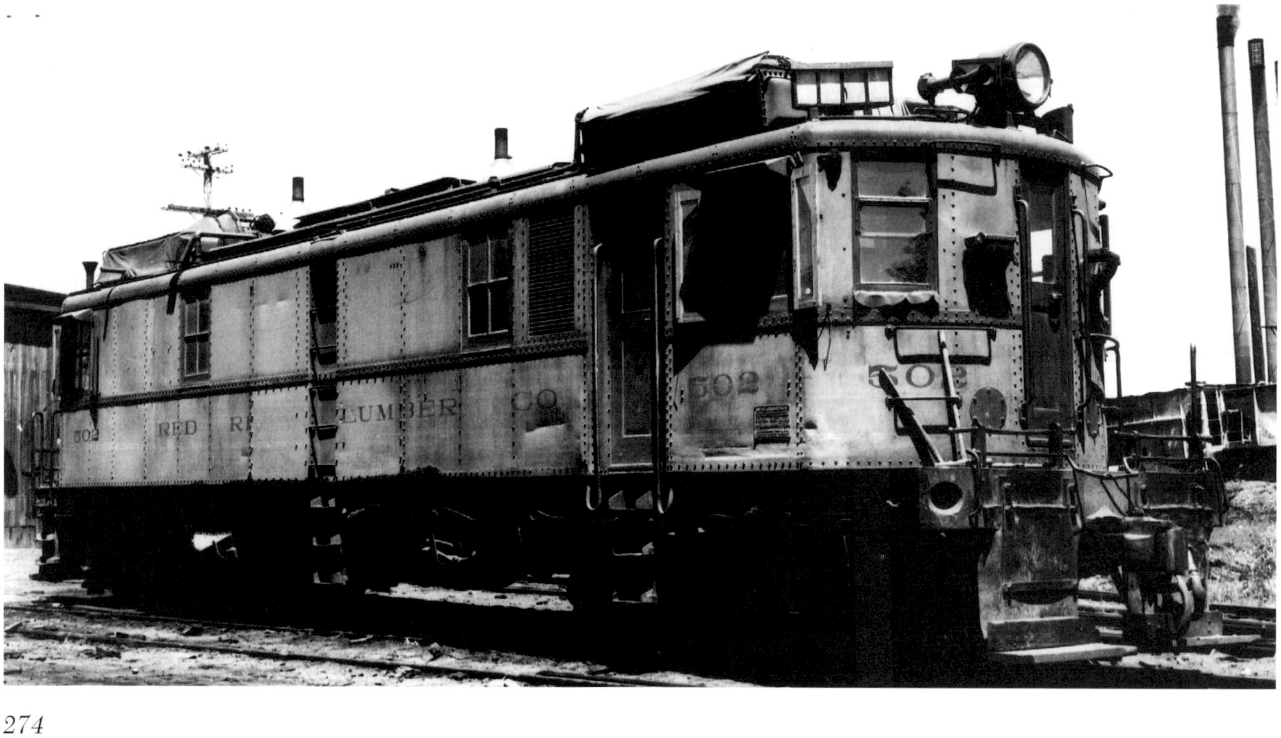

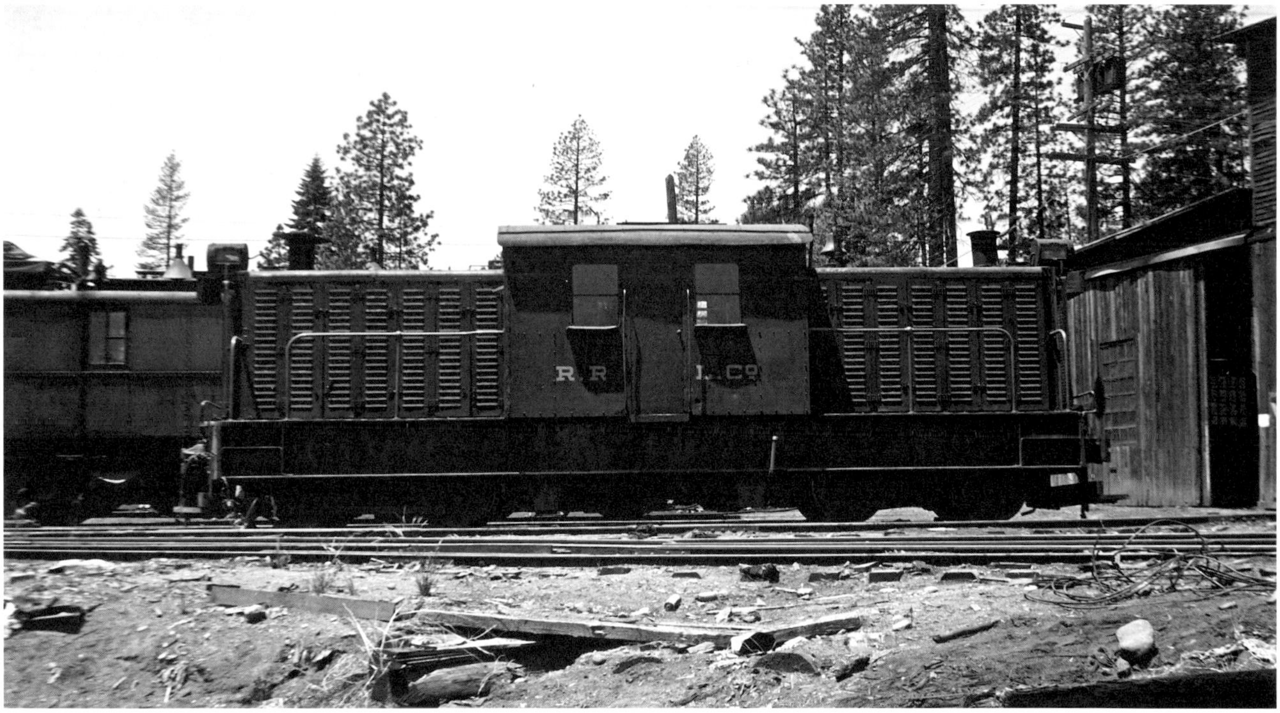

Above: A more modern diesel-electric joined the roster in 1938 as No. 21. (Earl Fancher photograph, Harre Demoro collection)

Below: In 1927, Red River electrified the portion of its railroad from Westwood to Chester and purchased two locomotives manufactured by Baldwin-Westinghouse. The engineer of No. 203 exchanges hand signals with his counterpart of No. 204. (Vernon Sappers collection)

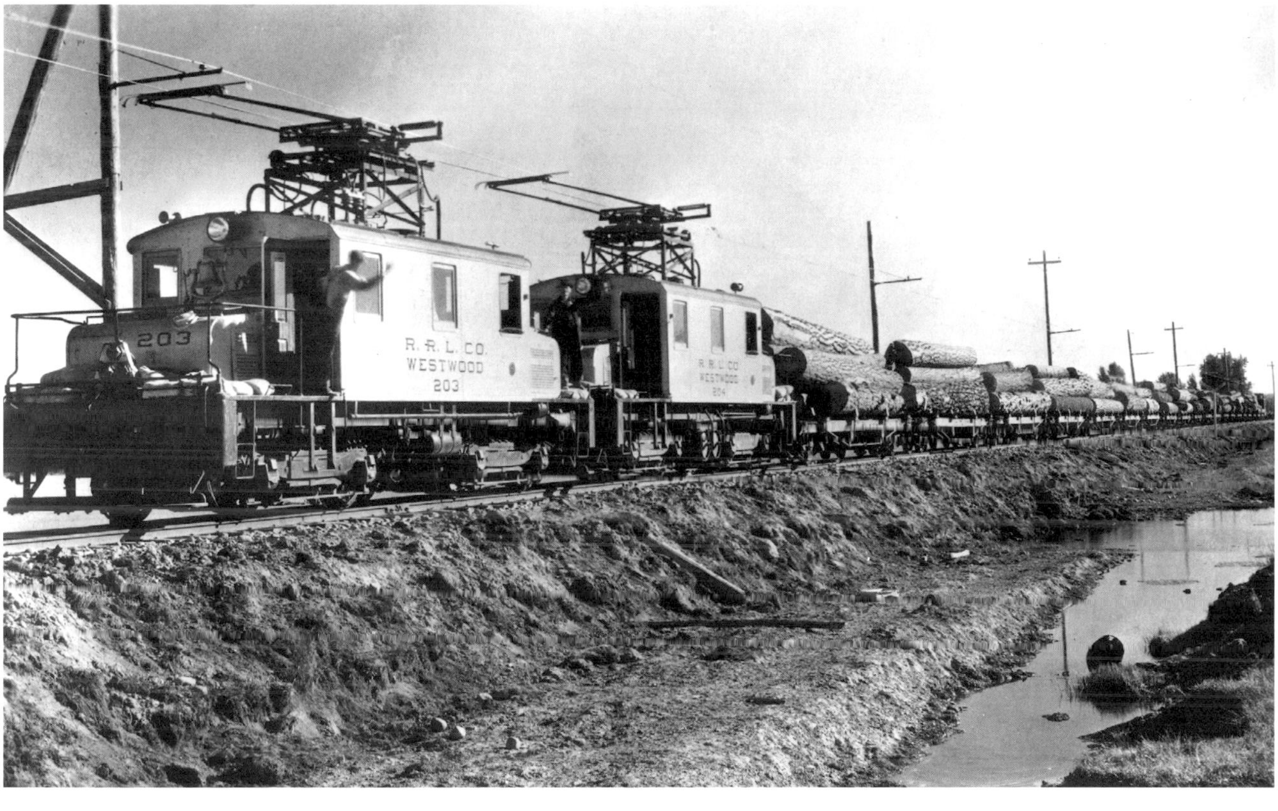

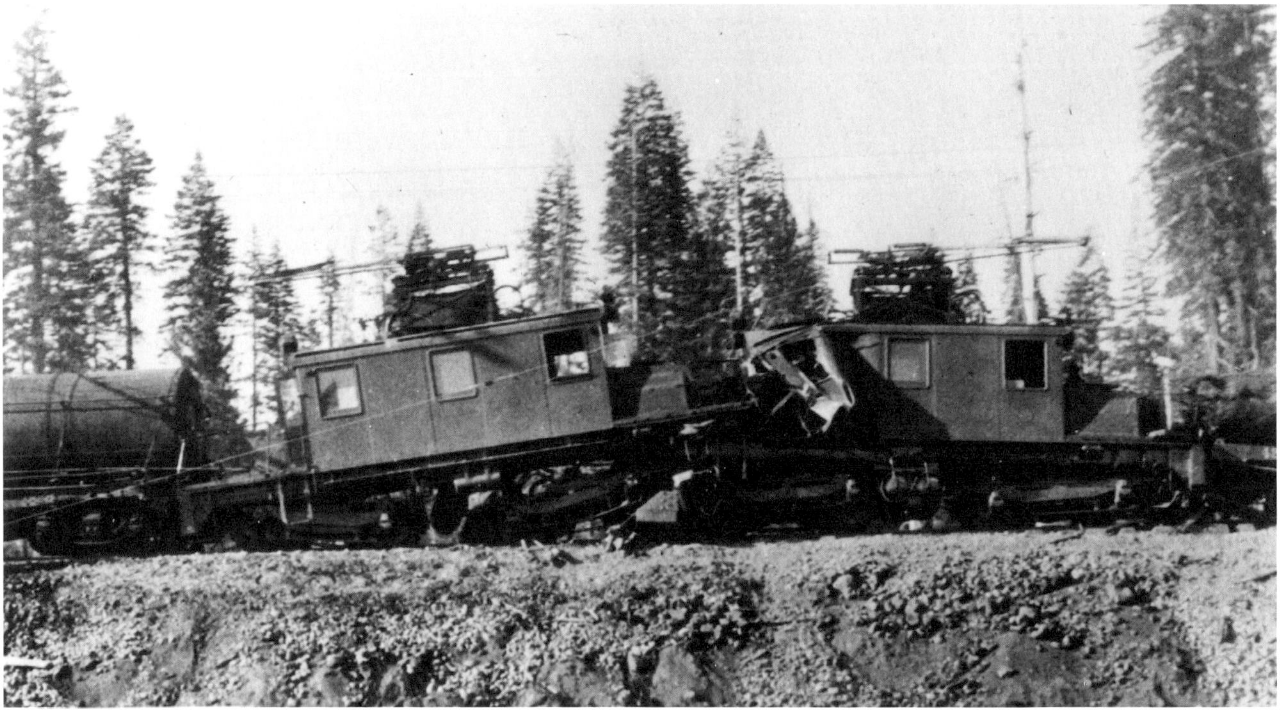

Above: Although usually operated together, the two locomotives were assigned to separate trains on June 30, 1930. Late that afternoon, the trains collided at Rock Creek fill, near Chester. Unlike the wreck of a runaway train the year before that took three lives, the crews involved in this mishap escaped with only minor injuries.

Below: According to the 1929 operating timetable, train No. 27 was scheduled to leave Chester at 10:25 A.M. and arrive in Westwood at 11:40 A.M.

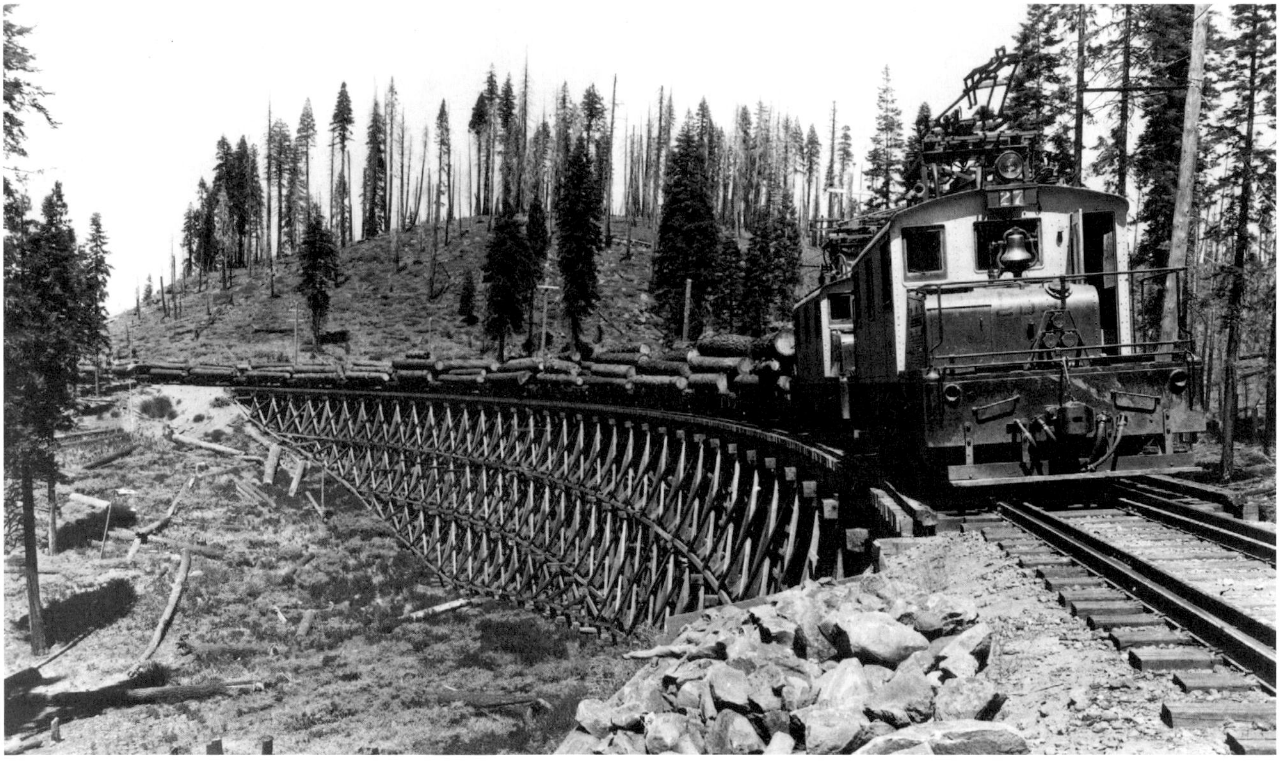

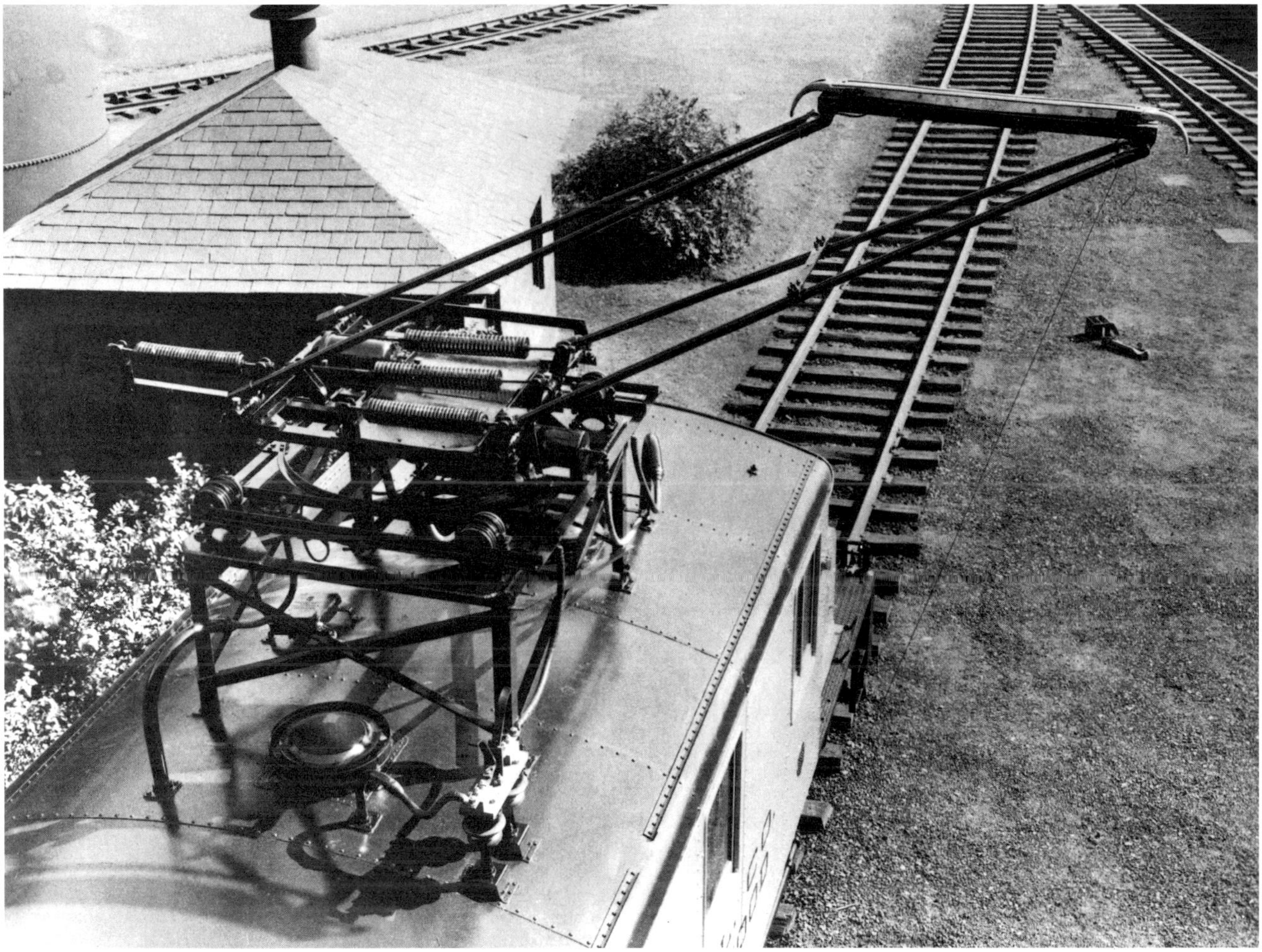

The pantograph was a complicated structure. (Vernon Sappers collection)

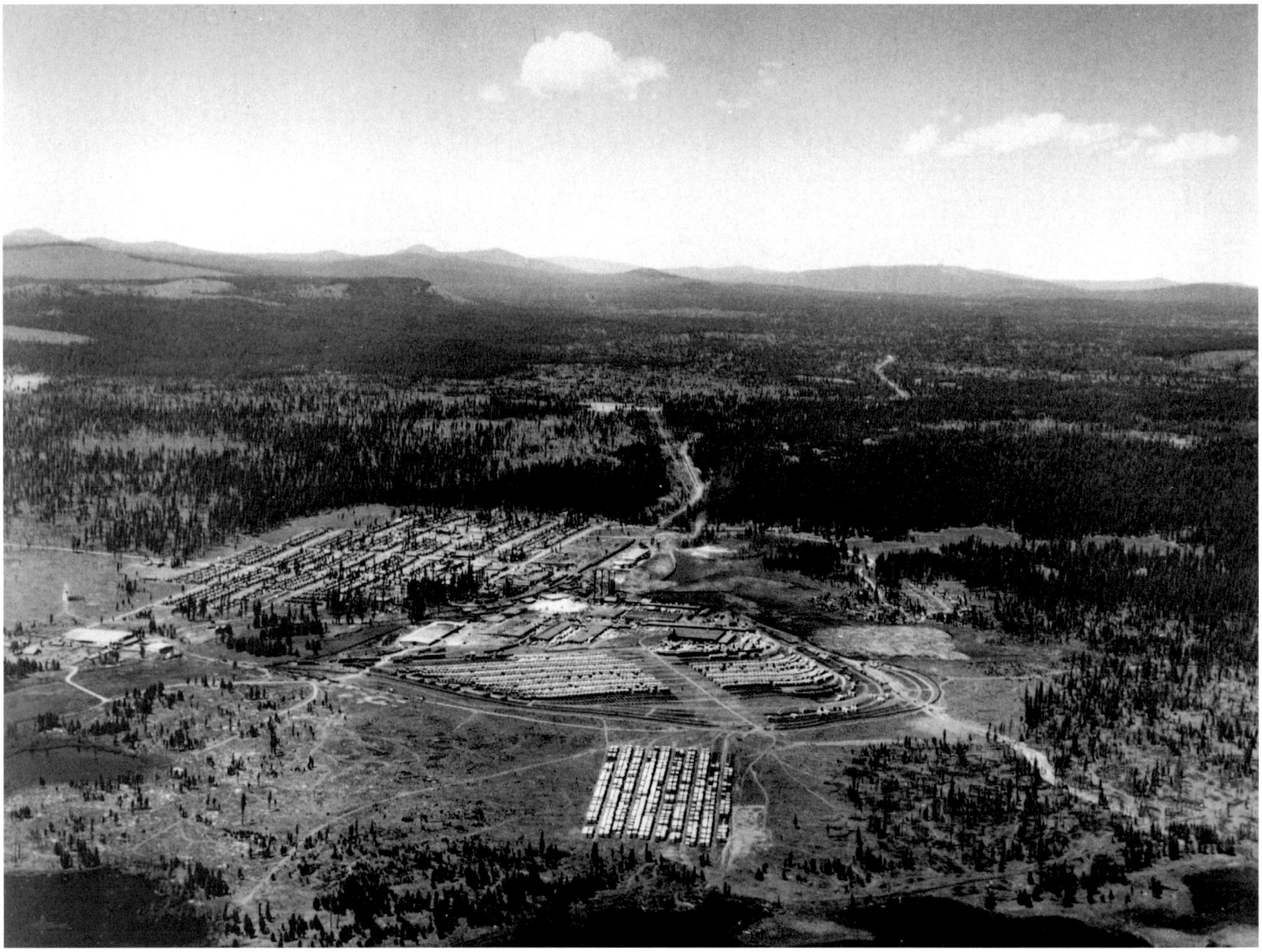

The town of Westwood with the lumber mill. Fernley and Lassen Railway (Southern Pacific, *center*) entered from the north. (Fruit Growers Supply)

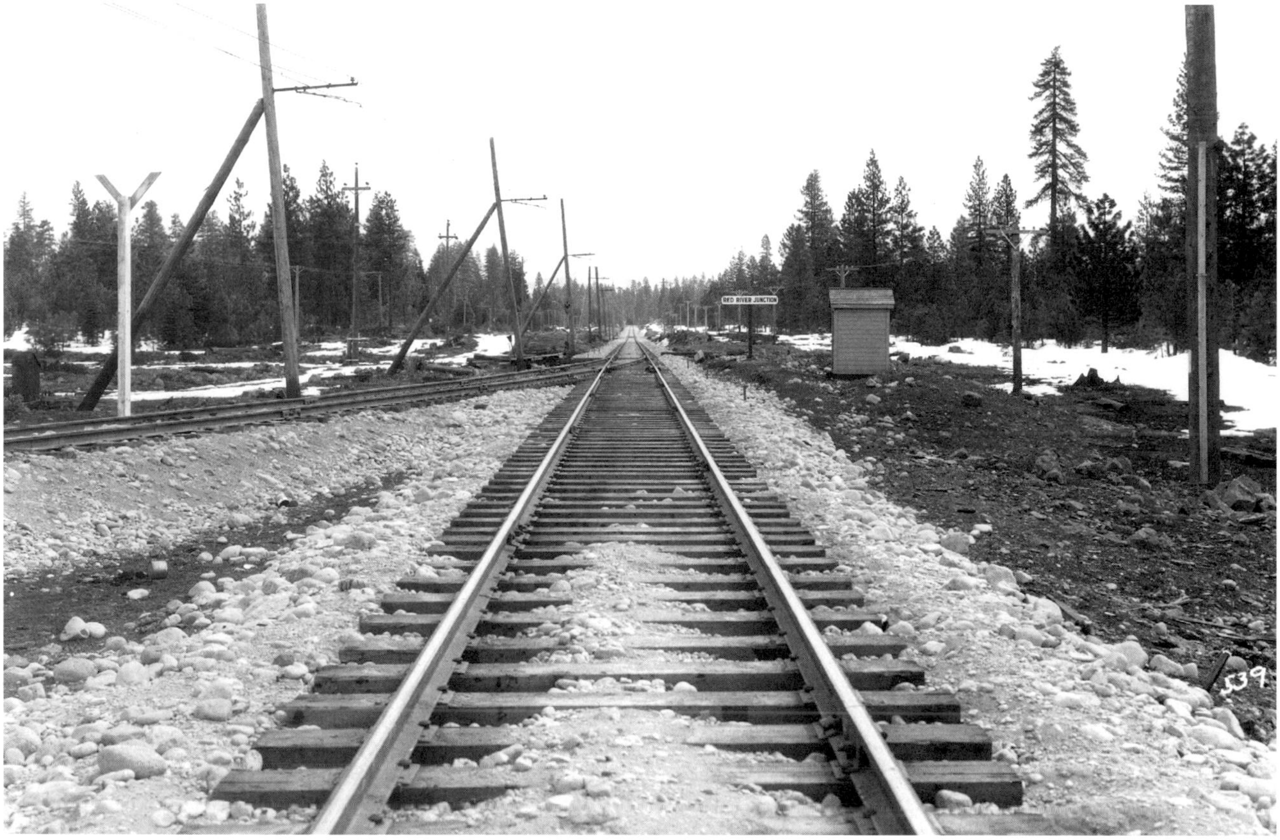

Above and Below: Incorporated in 1941, the Almanor Railroad purchased the portion of the former Red River Lumber electrified line between Red River Jct. (later called Clear Creek Jct.) and Chester, 13.7 miles.

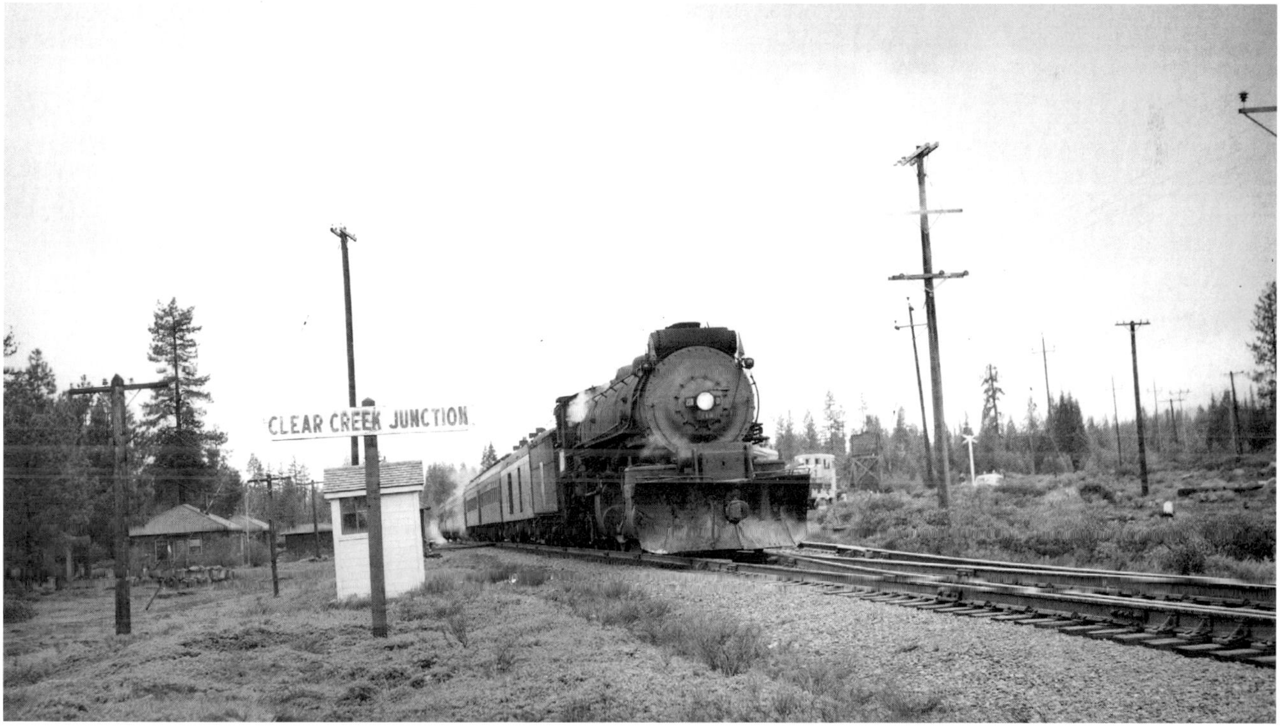

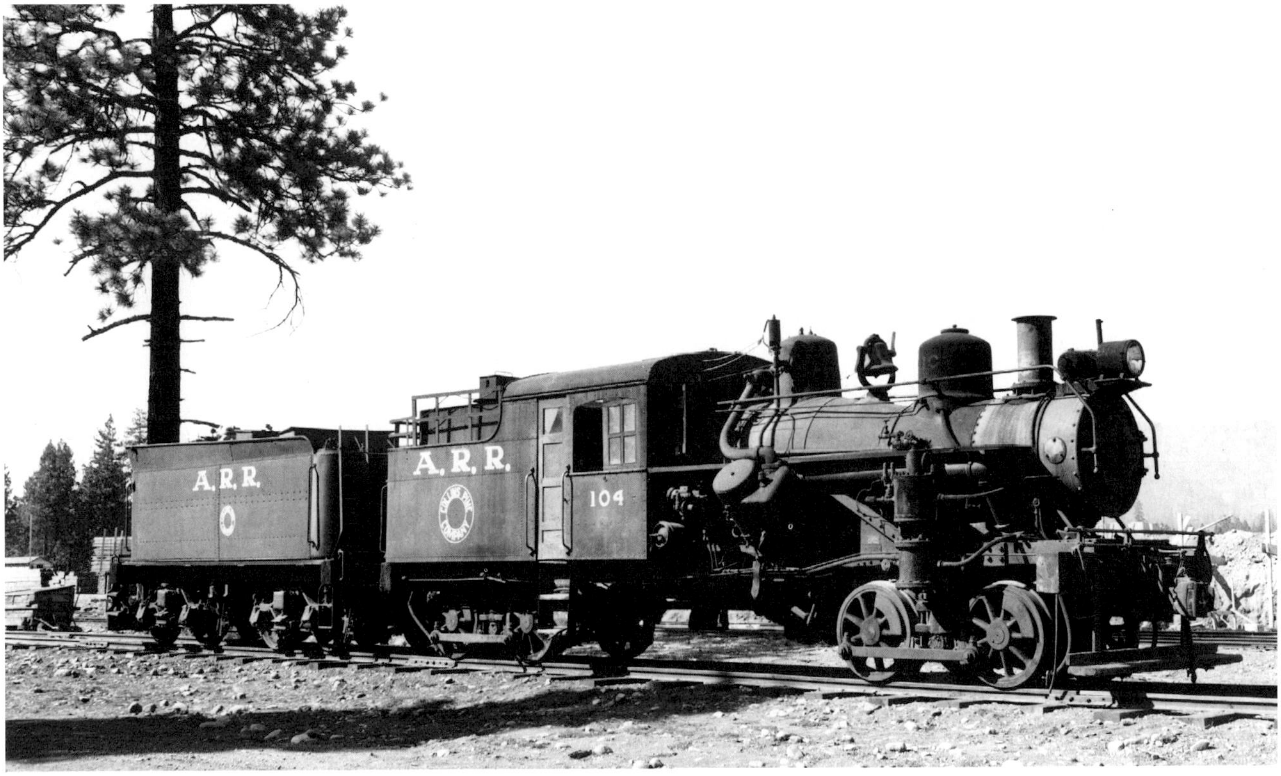

With electric operations discontinued and wires removed, the Almanor Railroad used a geared locomotive of Heisler manufacture. (Ted Wurm photograph, 1947)

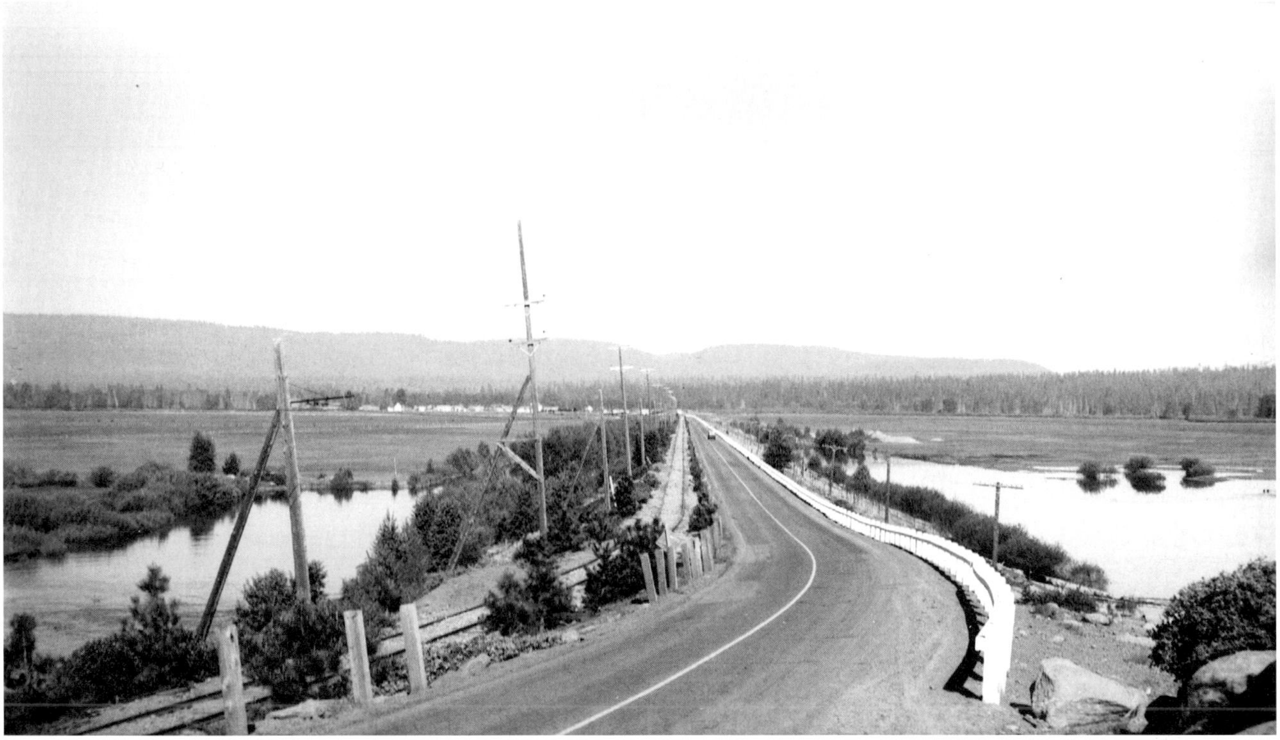

Above: The Chester line of the Red River Lumber Company and the successor Almanor Railroad crossed the north arm of Lake Almanor. In May 1940, when Bert Ward took this photograph, the electric power line of Red River Lumber was still in place.

Below: A rail-fan excursion over the Almanor Railroad in May 1951 proved to be a pleasant event despite the cool weather. (Ted Wurm photograph)

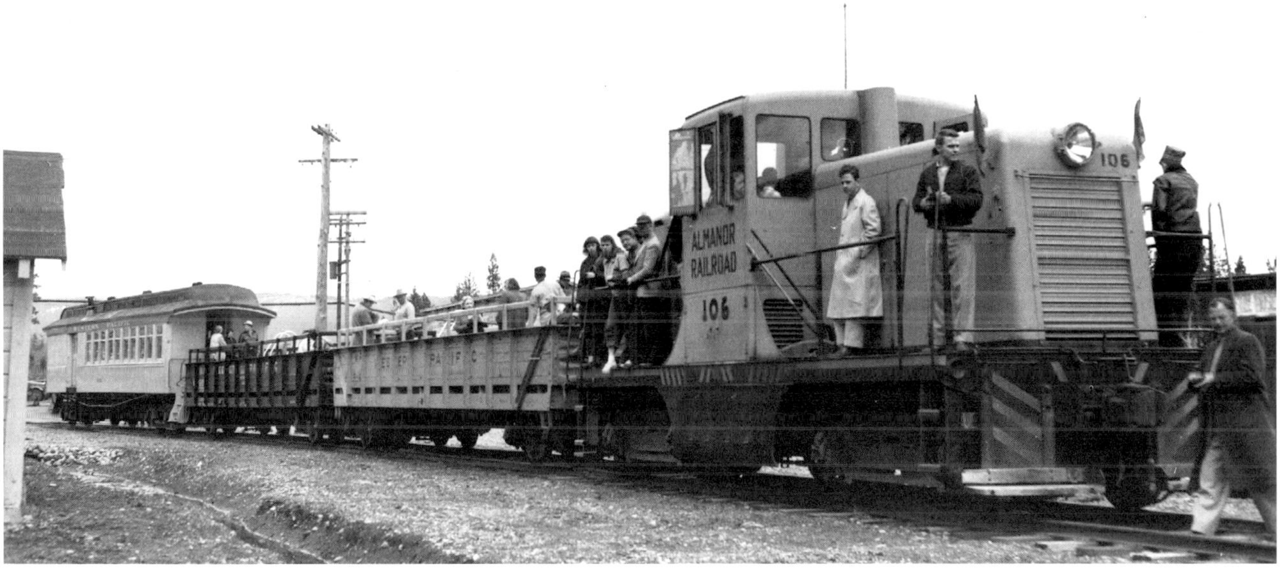

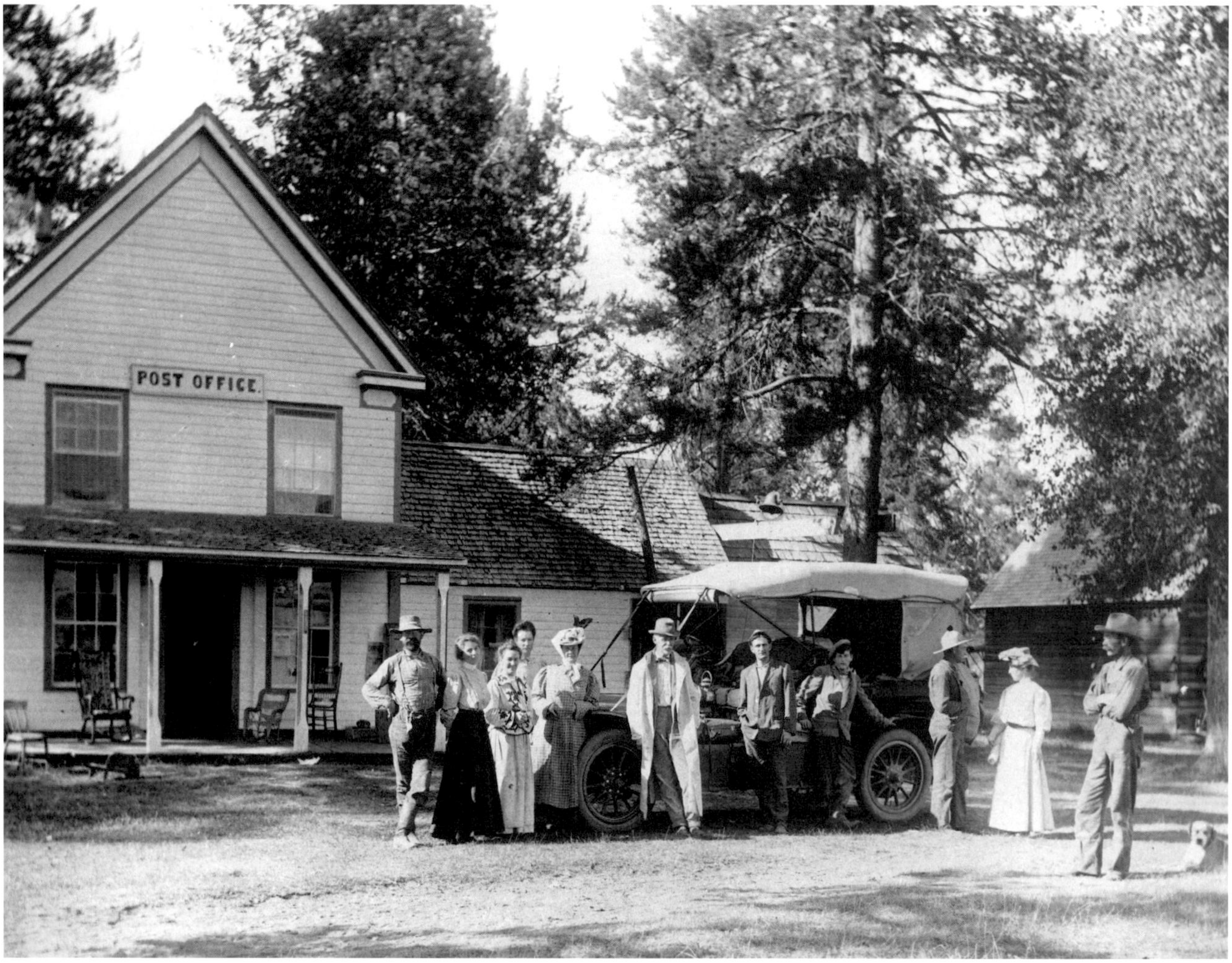

An auto, which now would be sought by collectors of vintage cars, with people in Chester, California.

NORTHERN CALIFORNIA RAILROAD COMPANY

Southern Pacific's line linked San Francisco, California, with Portland, Oregon, with the driving of the last spike at Ashland, Oregon, in December 1887. The line, serving a largely undeveloped timber territory, generated only a modest amount of traffic, a condition that continued until lumber traffic soared after World War II. Although SP was the only railroad between the two states, heavy competition from coastal steamships depressed rail rates and limited earnings from this route.

Even with these conditions, other railroads made surveys into this region, hoping to fulfill their dreams of expansion. James J. Hill of the Great Northern Railway had long coveted California with lines reaching down from his road in Montana, or Washington. The Oregon Trunk Railroad proved a tangible part of his dream. As time went by, the commercial development of the West caused other parties to consider paralleling Southern Pacific's Shasta Route, as it was called.

Southern Pacific's Fernley and Lassen Railway to Westwood, California, enabled the Red River Lumber Company to market its products in the Midwest. Markets in California could be served only by a circuitous route, as cars with lumber first went east to Fernley, thence over Donner Summit on the way to Sacramento.

In combination with the Indian Valley RR, the Western Pacific station at Paxton stood only 39 miles from Westwood and its enticing possible lumber tonnage. WP rates from Paxton measured substantially less than SP rates based on Westwood.

As early as 1916 the Red River Lumber Company management thought about an eventual southern outlet from Westwood. During the summer of 1927, RRL surveyors established a route and made formal entry into the common-carrier railroad business when it organized the Northern California Railroad (NC RR) Company on October 5, 1927. Measuring 31 miles, the new railroad commenced at Westwood and proposed to utilize 14 miles of RRL logging tracks along the east shore of Lake Almanor to a point near Nevis. It would construct 17 miles along Wolf Creek to a connection with the Indian Valley RR just east of Crescent Mills. From there the IV RR would convey the cars to Western Pacific at Paxton.

Recognizing the diversion of traffic that the NC RR would create, Southern Pacific dispatched J. T. Saunders and Joe Dyer, vice presidents of freight traffic and operations, respectively, to meet with Willis Walker, manager of the Red River Lumber Company, owned by his family. In a conversation, he told them that their lumber production in combination with others now exceeded economic requirements to justify the proposed railroad. He mentioned that the need to extend their logging track along Lake Almanor could be fulfilled by this construction and that the WP would give them main-line rates based at Paxton. He further observed that someday WP or northern roads would build to Klamath Falls and that their line would constitute part of the route.

Al J. Barclay, SP division engineer, inspected the logging line proposed to form part of the Northern California Railroad, which resulted in a mixed report. The initial 5 miles from Westwood to Almanor Jct. (recently put under electrification) consisted of well-maintained track of eighty-pound rail supported by eight inches of fair gravel. The ties, cut from soft pine wood, caused problems, as they would not hold the spikes adequately.

Deteriorating conditions prevailed south of the junction, although constructed about ten years after the first section built about 1914–1915. A substantial and well-maintained trestle, 330 feet long and 50 feet high, crossed the Hamilton Branch of the Feather River. At one time, the logging line had continued 15.2 miles southerly from Westwood, but by the time of the inspection 2.7 miles of track had been removed. Several spur tracks as much as 1,000 feet extended into the woods, and a small water tank stood at MP 11.8. The rail weighed from fifty-six to eighty pounds to the yard, and Barclay noted a few tie plates. The maximum grade reached 3 percent, the same figure in the NC RR specifications for northbound traffic. In the opposite direction, the maximum NC RR grade would have been 1.75 percent. (Barclay had been an SP construction engineer on the Phoenix-Welton line in Arizona.)

The ICC arranged for the California Railroad Commission to hear the application in San Francisco in March 1928. Southern Pacific, foreseeing a major diversion of traffic from its Westwood branch, opposed the construction. Joining in opposition were the Public Service Commission of Nevada; City of Alturas; Modoc County; Lions Club of Sparks, Nevada; and others. Western Pacific,

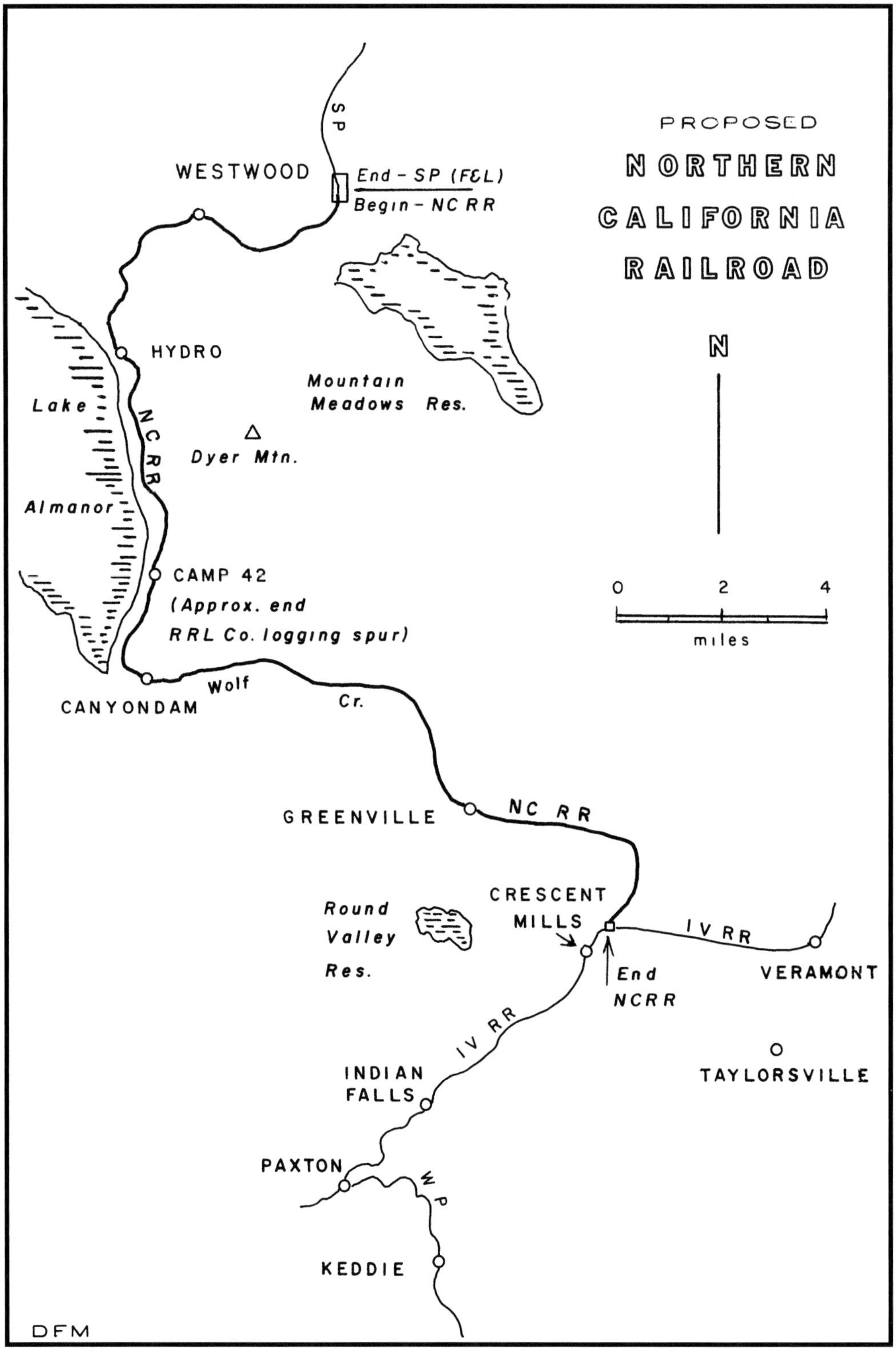
PROPOSED
NORTHERN
CALIFORNIA
RAILROAD
N
0
2
4
miles
SP
WESTWOOD
End - SP (F&L)
Begin - NC RR
HYDRO
Mountain
Meadows Res.
Lake
Almanor
NC RR
Dyer Mtn.
CAMP 42
(Approx. end
RRL Co. logging spur)
CANYONDAM
Wolf
Cr.
GREENVILLE
NC RR
CRESCENT
MILLS
Round
Valley
Res.
IV RR
End
NCRR
VERAMONT
TAYLORSVILLE
IV RR
INDIAN
FALLS
PAXTON
WP
KEDDIE
DFM

various livestock producers, and California chambers of commerce supported the proposed railroad. Both sides entered quite a number of exhibits relating to long-term lumber availability, traffic potential (Red River Lumber anticipated furnishing 90 percent of the traffic), traffic diversion, and construction costs.

Estimated freight revenue for the Northern California Railroad ranged from $177,000 the first year to $214,000 the fifth year. Passenger, mail, and express revenue aggregated about $30,000, and it was assumed that the daily train would carry 7,000 passengers a year between Crescent Mills and Westwood.

Although the shorter route would enable the three carriers to deliver cattle to San Francisco within the thirty-six-hour limit, NC RR expected to handle only 150 cars annually, producing only $1,670. Lower freight rates, envisioned for the shorter route, became non sequitur, as Southern Pacific agreed to match WP rates, thus saving shippers $50,000 annually, conditioned on the denial of application.

William M. Wheeler, head of the Wolf Creek Timber Company, explained that his company's timberlands served as a "deferred reserve." Red River wanted to buy them, "but their bid was so low that it could not be considered." Should the Northern California Railroad occupy Wolf Creek Canyon, it would make it difficult to construct logging spurs at a future date. Though not opposing the NC RR, he thought that "the new road was not needed for the development of its property."

The ICC considered the heavy diversion of tonnage from the Westwood branch and the offer of SP to cut its rates, which it did following the decision. It also took cognizance that the lumber company, owner of the prospective railroad, would control the flow of traffic. "We [ICC] have heretofore found that such conditions do not make for fair and equal competition between the railroads serving the industry." With these conclusions, the ICC denied the application of the Northern California Railroad on June 19, 1929. By then, it proved almost academic, for Western Pacific and Great Northern filed their applications to build between Keddie and Klamath Falls, which followed this route.

Though the ICC denied authority for construction of the new line, the Northern California Railroad formally operated trains over the logging railroad of the Red River Lumber Company along the eastern shore of Lake Almanor. With the filing of freight and passenger tariffs and timetables with the California Railroad Commission on June 2, 1930, the NC RR commenced operations between Westwood and Lake Almanor, the designated name for the station at the end of this railroad, near Camp 42 and 11.5 miles from Westwood. (Canyondam settlement stood three miles beyond.) Intermediate stations included Almanor Jct. (MP 2.1) and Hydro (MP 5.8).

The inaugural train carried company officials and friends riding in the private car *Mizpah* with A. Archibald piloting the diesel locomotive (No. 10) on the point. L. J. Squires stepped away from his dispatching duties to serve as conductor on this trip. Though not a long journey, it was a slow one, with the schedule calling for forty minutes to complete the trip one way.

On Sunday, June 8, the NC RR operated a pair of fishermen's specials. The first left Westwood at 9:25 A.M. and came back to the terminal after depositing anglers along the way. At 4:45 P.M. a second train went down the line to pick up the men, who filled the ears of the crew with stories of their successes or failures as may be.

The span of the daily operation is not known, but it probably lasted only one summer, for Western Pacific opened its HiLine the next year.

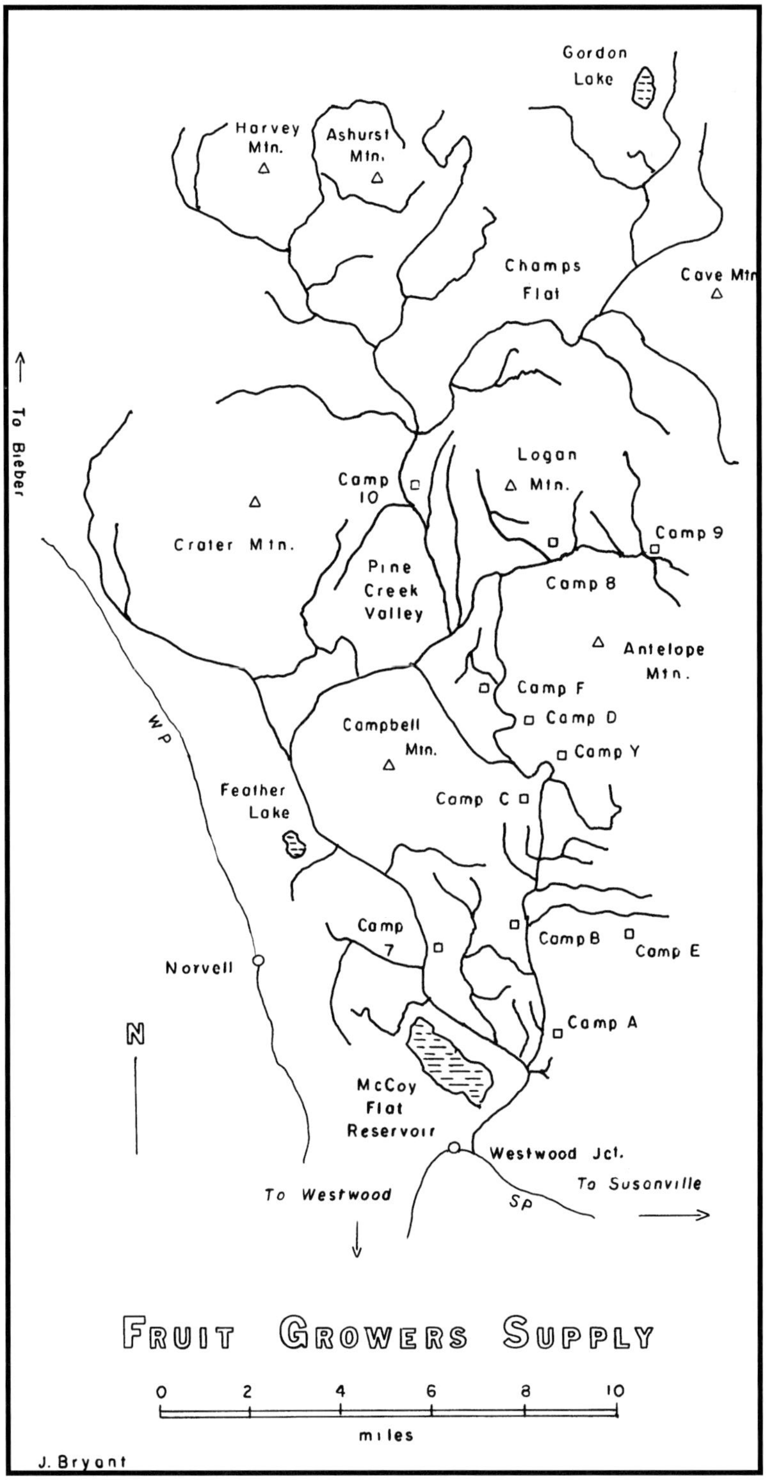
Gordon Lake
Harvey Mtn.
Ashurst Mtn.
Champs Flat
Cave Mtn
To Bieber
Logan Mtn.
Camp 10
Crater Mtn.
Camp 9
Pine Creek Valley
Camp 8
Antelope Mtn.
Camp F
Camp D
Campbell Mtn.
Camp Y
WP
Feather Lake
Camp C
Camp 7
Camp B
Camp E
Norvell
Camp A
N
McCoy Flat Reservoir
Westwood Jct.
To Westwood
To Susanville
SP
FRUIT GROWERS SUPPLY
0 2 4 6 8 10
miles
J. Bryant

FRUIT GROWERS SUPPLY COMPANY

An earthquake and a fire triggered the California Fruit Growers Exchange into the box business. Rebuilding San Francisco after the 1906 disaster demanded so much lumber that the cost of packing boxes soared by 75 percent, causing the Exchange to seek an alternate solution. On October 5, 1907, the Exchange—best known as marketers of Sunkist oranges—formed the Fruit Growers Supply Company to enter into contracts with several lumber mills to supply box shook, including the Northern California Lumber Company at Hilt, California, just below the Oregon border. When financial problems overwhelmed this lumber firm, Fruit Growers Supply acquired the plant and its short railroad in 1910. Over the years, the logging railroad reached almost as far west as Beaver Creek and into Oregon.

The Hilt plant proved beneficial, but expanding citrus shipments called for more lumber for packing crates, necessitating additional sources. The Red River Lumber Company at Westwood and the new plant of the Lassen Lumber and Box Company at Susanville, both served by the Fernley and Lassen Railway (SP), captured management's attention.

When officers and directors of Fruit Growers Supply arrived at Susanville in a special Pullman attached to the regular F&L Railway train, local businessmen took notice. Notwithstanding that the day of arrival was Friday, June 13, 1919, the community leaders held optimistic views as they joined the group for lunch at the St. Francis Hotel before the group departed for an overnight stay at Eagle Lake. From the Pennsylvania Lumber Company, Fruit Growers Supply purchased the Collins tract of lumber in the summer of 1919.

The community learned that other areas coveted this company. Thomas Hill offered FGS a two hundred–acre site gratis at Leavitt with an option for more land if needed. With adequate water (he had augmented the supply with artesian wells), the offer held many natural advantages except that there was no housing available for plant workers.

Another site near Eagle Lake stood available to the company, again at no cost. With the trees almost at the door of the mill, the cost of log deliveries would be minimal. However, the higher elevation, bringing more severe winters, served as a detraction when compared with Susanville.

Though the town had begun turning from an agricultural community to one supported by the lumber industry, thanks to the Lassen Lumber and Box Company factory, Susanville's leading citizens wanted more factories. Now the business leaders faced a dilemma of competing with offers of two free sites. A suitable site in Susanville stood ready but with a price tag of $40,000. The reward of a prospective $150,000 monthly mill payroll held strong appeal, and the company indicated that if the community raised $40,000 to buy the site, FGS would probably settle there. This proposal whipped the civic committee into action. Fund-raising did not go too well, but, realizing that the FGS board of directors was to meet on the next Wednesday, a whirlwind campaign for pledges reached the goal on Monday. H. D. Burroughs, committee leader, then telegraphed general manager F. B. Hutchens the good news and in turn received advice on August 6, 1919, that the board had accepted the offer, subject to confirmation of an adequate water supply.

Under the direction of Superintendent M. H. Grover, work began on the mill foundations the next month. Grading for a railroad spur to serve the mill had been finished, with ties distributed and the rail expected shortly. Construction of a company hotel stood as a top priority that provided a comfortable place for the second company-sponsored dance on the night preceding Thanksgiving 1920.

At the close of that year, resident manager S. M. Bump could look back with pride as his plant approached completion. Saturday, April 16, 1921, stands out as the first day of mill operations, which were celebrated by a banquet giving the directors an opportunity to meet local citizens.

F. B. Hutchens, after an absence managing the McCloud River Lumber Company, returned to his post as general manager of Fruit Growers Supply. He reported that two log camps had been established on the Collins tract, about twenty miles from Susanville, near Westwood Jct., with a spur into the woods. Already rails had reached Camp A and were being extended beyond Camp B, which would become the headquarters camp. With 160 men in the two camps—half the number expected before the end of summer—the loggers began handing twelve to fifteen cars over to the SP each day for transportation to the mill. Some weeks before the mill opened, the California Railroad Commission authorized Louis E. Smith and F. W. Ramsey to run an auto stage twice daily between Susanville and Camp A from May to October 1 so that workers could visit friends in town. (Their operations expanded later.)

Recreation for the workers, which ranked essential with the management, formed the basis of establishing a tent resort at Eagle Lake, appropriately called "Sunkist Lodge."

At the end of September 1921, the box factory had begun operations, and the big sawmill was cutting two hundred thousand board feet per day. Recognizing that more timber would be needed in the future, the company conducted several timber purchases with the U.S. Forest Service in the Lassen National Forest aggregating one billion feet, the largest individual purchase made to that time.

The logging program for 1922 started later than usual. On April 28, A. E. Stonehouse and some workers took FGS locomotive No. 33 up Susan Creek to open the logging railroad. Combining forces with another FGS engine already there, the men plowed a path through the snow to Camp A by nightfall. The same force, working in three feet of snow, opened the railroad to Camp B at the end of the second day. The following day (Sunday), timber spurs were cleared, the camps were opened Monday, and loggers stood ready to begin work the following morning. Actually, it did not quite work out as planned, for a new eight-inch snowfall delayed work for several days but did not deter Mr. Bump's frequent inspection of the camps.

The shipping season for 1922 opened in May when thirteen cars of logs were turned over to SP crews at Westwood Jct. for delivery to the mill, the forerunner of daily moves of twenty-five cars. To be ready for the summer-working college students, the company opened Camp C, and, as August began, a new logging spur stood ready for rails so trains could bring equipment to the new Camp D. Motion pictures in the camps soon became a regular evening diversion.

Plans to apply ballast to the main line in October were quickly thwarted by falling snow that left a four-foot pack. The combination of slightly warmer weather a few days later and a flange-type snowplow applied to FGS engine No. 33 enabled trains to serve the camps. No. 32, one of several locomotives purchased from the defunct Ocean Shore RR, was sent to Susanville for winter shopping.

Stonehouse, who had come to Susanville after several years at Hilt, moved up the corporate ladder to be Mr. Bump's assistant as logging and milling activity increased. In turn, Southern Pacific engaged more train and engine crews to shuttle logging cars between the woods' railroads and the mills.

February 1923 began as a cold month, with temperatures in Susanville at ten degrees below, which construction workers felt as they built fourteen new cottages for mill workers. Breaking a path for trains to gain access to the camps started three months earlier that year, and the men probably remembered working in the low temperatures for many years.

Two locomotives and a crew of 15 started out early one morning for Westwood Jct., and that night the boss telephoned that the locomotive had advanced a mile before returning to the junction. With no formal accommodations available, the men had to rustle to find shelter. The lucky ones took over the engine cab; others occupied the oil house or snowplow cab. Six inches of snow fell that night. More snow—seventeen inches—dropped on the camp, with the next two storms necessitating a snowplow to clear the track to Camp B.

A sign of a subsequent change in transportation methods came that year when a new log landing deck was built at the west end of the millpond to accommodate independent loggers making truck deliveries.

Those men in Camp B witnessed an unexpected event on May 8, 1923, when two gondolas and one flatcar, heavily loaded with steel rail and more, broke away from their moorings to race madly down the track. Fortunately for the men in Camp A, the cars left the track on a sharp curve before the camp and rolled over the embankment. Observing the wreck, men found that a fifty-pound rail had been severed by the impact.

The woods boss called Mr. Bump, who rounded up six automobiles and 40 men who left the mill at 8.30 P.M. Working all night, the track was repaired, and normal operations returned the next morning, with the regular train arriving on time.

Noteworthy events marked logging the next year. S. M. Bump resigned his position in March to go to Seattle as general manager of the Los Angles Products Company. Prior to coming to Susanville as mill construction began, he had worked at Hilt for a year. A shift in management followed. The new Susanville resident manager, B. Birmingham, had held the same position at Hilt, and A. E. Stonehouse became manager of the Hilt division. When the 1924 season was under way, the FGS payroll numbered 550 men in the plant and 450 in the woods.

Locomotive No. 32 was sold to the Red River Lumber Company; in its place Fruit Growers acquired two Shay engines from the McCloud River Railway that received new road numbers, Nos. 4 and 5, to be the only Shays on FGS.

It was almost midnight on June 3, 1924, when the entire complement of Camp C was roused by the impact when one train of sixteen empties being pushed by an engine crashed into another pulled by No. 4, a Shay engine, about one hundred yards from the camp. The conductor riding in the Shay, Charles E. Howard, tried to jump from the cab but was caught and crushed by the Johnson bar and died. A confusion of train orders caused the collision; Howard's train expected to meet the other at Camp C, while the crew of the empty train understood they were to meet at the summit. The Shay was shopped for several weeks for repairs.

Four hundred men from Fruit Growers Supply, plus 50 from Lassen Lumber and Box and 125 from Red River, joined forces to combat a major fire that started at Camp C in August 1924. FGS lost four donkey engines, a water car, and several miles of track. Eight SP logging cars were caught in the blaze. Another train ran away September 8, 1925, when it was returning workers to their camp at the end of the day. When the engineer was unable to control his locomotive on a steep grade, 9 men, fearing the consequences of a wreck, jumped off the train. Some received serious injuries, but good fortune rode with the engineer as he took his chances and stayed with the train until it stopped on level track. An investigation revealed that a brakeman had failed to couple the air hose to the cars.

Lumbering in the Pine Creek Valley

When the company focused its cutting in Pine Creek Valley in 1926, it brought new camp designations. Whereas the camps along the railroad to Antelope Mountain were identified by letters, camps along the new rail line took numbers 7, 8, 9, and 10. When this railroad was constructed, locating engineers carefully placed it on the east side of Pine Creek to avoid soft ground. When winter snows closed Camp 7 before Christmas that year, placing automobiles on flatcars provided the only way to bring nine cars to lower elevations.

The company retained a watchman to guard the camps closed during the winter. A lonely life indeed it was, with long silences broken by occasional telephone calls from the office to determine conditions.

One winter day, after the telephone had been dead for some time, Gene Aldrich and Tom Wahlstrom set out to repair the vital connection. After taking the SP to Westwood Jct., they boarded a logging train as far as it would go. Next it was snowshoes and skis as they followed the wire. When they finally reached the caretaker's cabin between Camps D and E, they were greeted by Mr. Pinneo, who expressed his annoyance at their intrusion. He readily admitted cutting the wire so that he and his new bride would not be disturbed.

Camp 8 suffered a number of mishaps in 1926. One event involving a number of men occurred when a masked bandit held up a poker game one early Sunday morning and relieved the players of $135. Reconstructing the event, it developed that the holdup artist had ridden the logging train almost to the camp to apply for work but told the clerk he had walked the entire distance from Westwood Jct. Instead of working, he entered an unoccupied cabin and, taking pillow and blanket, went into the forest to go to sleep. Somehow he had learned about the traditional Saturday-night poker game, and when he awoke at two in the morning, he went to the cabin, donned the pillowcase for a mask, and relieved the players of their funds. On leaving the camp, he discarded a stolen overcoat lest it impede his departure and successful escape. Two weeks later, an unknown man broke into the commissary and made off with shirts, shoes, and blankets.

Westwood Jct. boasted an unofficial mayor in the 1920s. Joe Owens stood high in popularity with the lumberjacks, for, in spite of the absence of his left arm, he proved to be a well-stocked bootlegger.

The Story Club—named for Francis Q. Story, president of the Exchange in 1904—started 1928 on a happy note with an open house on New Year's Day. The year ended with the closing of Camp 8 and moving all facilities to Camp 10, which became the new headquarters camp. During its active years, Camp 10 had about fifty cabins assigned to families and bunkhouses for 300 to 500 loggers. Besides a switching yard, a shop and oil tanks served the railroad, which was complemented by a general repair shop where much cable-splicing was done (used with donkey engines). In later years, only an old oven indicated the site of the cookhouse with the adjoining mess hall where lumberjacks stacked several porterhouse or T-bone steaks on their plates at each seating.

The 1930s proved to be harsh on the lumber industry, although those engaged in manufacturing packing boxes suffered less. The year 1935 marked a step in the recovery of the California lumber industry, as a number of firms returned to production after being idle during the previous four years. To illustrate the relative size of Lassen lumber companies, Lassen Lumber and Box's output in 1935 measured 29 million board feet, with Fruit Growers (Susanville plant) at 48 million feet and Red River Lumber turning out 132 million feet, the largest figure for any California firm that year. FGS conducted logging around Ashurst Mountain in the late 1930s.

Glancing at logging railroad maps can be deceptive, as they show the all-time locations as opposed to tracks in place at a given point in time. When one cutting program was ending, graders formed a new roadbed and moved tracks to the new site. Main-line relocations were infrequent, but after Camp 10 became the headquarters camp, the line was shifted from McCoy Flat Reservoir to the west side of Campbell Mountain.

In the five years after World War II, FGS men followed the Feather Lake spur to tap timber on Crater Mountain. During the opening days of one season, the crew had great difficulty pushing empty cars up to the jammer because the track was coated with ice. One well-remembered event involved a locomotive creeping up the track with no one in the cab, as the engine crew had joined the others throwing sand under the drivers to gain traction.

Purchase of the Red River Lumber Company in 1944

The RRL company sold its extensive properties to Fruit Growers Supply Company by a series of deeds dated December 15 and 16, 1944. From a lawyer's viewpoint, it was a dream; for inventory clerks, a headache: the deeds filled forty-two pages of Book 31 of *Deeds of Lassen County*.

Both real and personal property were listed in detail. Although the conveyance of the logging railroad formed part of one deed, location descriptions are absent. Red River Lumber Company granted easements for possible future log railroads through 1967 in an area north of existing trackage around Harvey Mountain.

The equipment, particularly automobiles and trucks, comprised a long list of vehicles from various manufacturers. RRL transferred only 7 locomotives to FGS; all were rod engines, as the 4 Shays and electric power had been already scrapped or sold. Along with the 2 steamers purchased from the Tonopah and Goldfield RR in 1914 (Nos. 101 and 102), the other itinerant locomotives, Nos. 32, 33, 103, 104, and 105, moved to the new owner. Among the railroad logging items were 335 log flatcars, 3 cabooses, 5 McGiffert log loaders—often called "jammers"—and 4 passenger train cars (Nos. 17, 18, 19, and 22).

Fruit Growers' acquisitions opened new timber-cutting areas to the firm located north of Harvey Mountain and east of Blacks Mountain. Red River Lumber had already located Camp Bunyan at Halls Flat on Western Pacific and had built a twenty-four-mile railroad extending eastward to Camp Harvey and Camp Stanford. Another short line reached south from WP to serve a timber stand in the Poison Lake area.

Work commenced at the two lumber camps for the 1949 season on May 2. As the cost of feeding the hungry men had soared, FGS contracted with the H. S. Anderson Company to carry out that responsibility. A strike of the culinary workers not only closed the camps on May 17 but also brought the transportation program under review. Trucking had already been established as a means of feeding the logging railroads. When it was determined that economies could be gained by trucking logs from the east side of Blacks Mountain to the FGS railroad serving Camp 10, the year 1949 marked the final days of the Blacks Mountain railroad. Dismantling was authorized the following summer.

In the summer of 1950, Fruit Growers Supply had four locomotives on its roster consisting of one Shay and three rod engines with a simple numbering system: 1, 2, 3 for the rod engines and 4 for the Shay. All were based at Camp 10. Nos. 1 and 3 were former Red River Lumber Company Nos. 34 and 103 (former T&G RR), while No. 2 had been FGS No. 33. The Shay was one of a pair acquired from the McCloud River Lumber Company in 1924. At that time, Nos. 1 and 4 met normal operating needs. No. 2 was held as a spare or for use on work trains, while No. 3 was undergoing heavy repairs but when ready was expected to replace No. 1.

Each morning No. 1 took the previous day's log loadings down to Westwood Jct. where SP picked up the cars and carried them to the Susanville or Westwood mills. For its return trip to Camp 10, the rod engine hauled the empty cars SP crews had spotted at Westwood Jct. This locomotive was rated at twenty-six loads to the junction and thirty-eight empties on the return, unless it brought three water cars in which event the limit was reduced to twenty-five empty log cars. Each trip required about two and one-half hours.

Meanwhile, the Shay, No. 4, had left Camp 10, and after stopping at the water tank out about one and one-half miles, it proceeded to the several jammers before continuing north to Gordon Lake and as far as Gooch Valley. With grades reported at 3.5 percent, the Shay reached its limit with twenty-seven loaded cars as it worked its way back to Camp 10. When serving jammer No. 23, the 4.5 percent grade on the short branch restricted trains to just fourteen loaded cars. No. 1, after finishing its round-trip to Westwood Jct., supplemented the empty-car supply by following the Shay and distributing cars to the jammers.

In October 1950, Baldwin sent out an 800-HP diesel demonstrator, No. 750, to make test runs on the logging railroad. According to the manufacturer's figures, lower fuel costs would have produced substantial savings. However, the FGS management, foreseeing the end of railroad logging in the near future, declined to convert to diesel power.

The End of FGS Railroad Logging

With full conversion to truck logging, the board of directors of Fruit Growers Supply Company in February 1953 authorized abandonment of the "Susanville Railroad" serving Camp 10 and continuing as far north as Gordon Lake. Accordingly, all railroad logging in Lassen County had ended in the 1952 season. For a time, the company had contemplated a railroad from Poison Lake west to Burney in a joint project with the McCloud River Lumber Company; instead, the McCloud River Railroad built a new line southward from Bear Flat, a point near Pondosa, twenty-two miles to Burney, and opened it with a Golden Spike Celebration on July 3, 1955. In that same year, wood fruit-packing boxes were replaced by cardboard cartons.

For those seeking more information about the operations of the company, one should read *Fruit Growers Supply Company: Hilt-Susanville-Westwood-Burney*. Written by Tim L. Purdy, it was published in 2000.

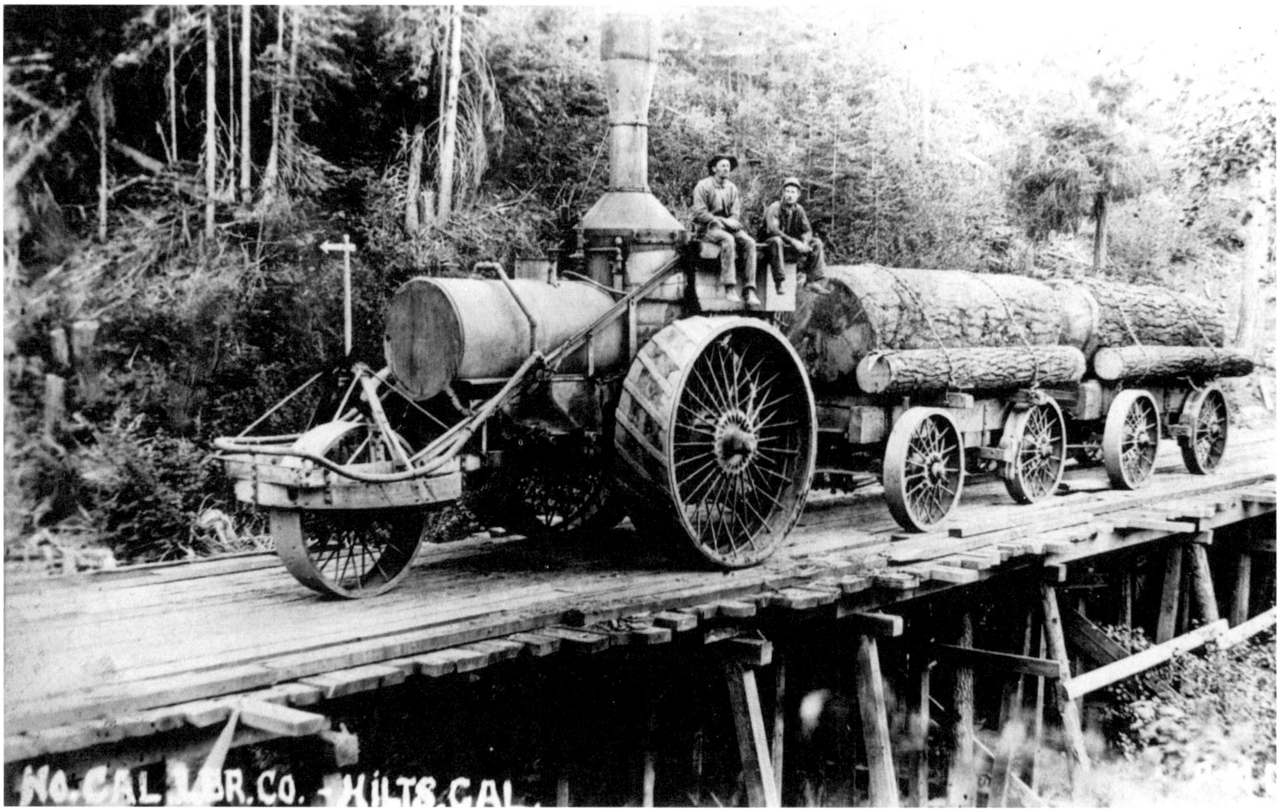

Before Fruit Growers Supply took over lumber operations at Hilt, California, it contracted with the Northern California Lumber Company to supply box shook. (Sunkist Growers)

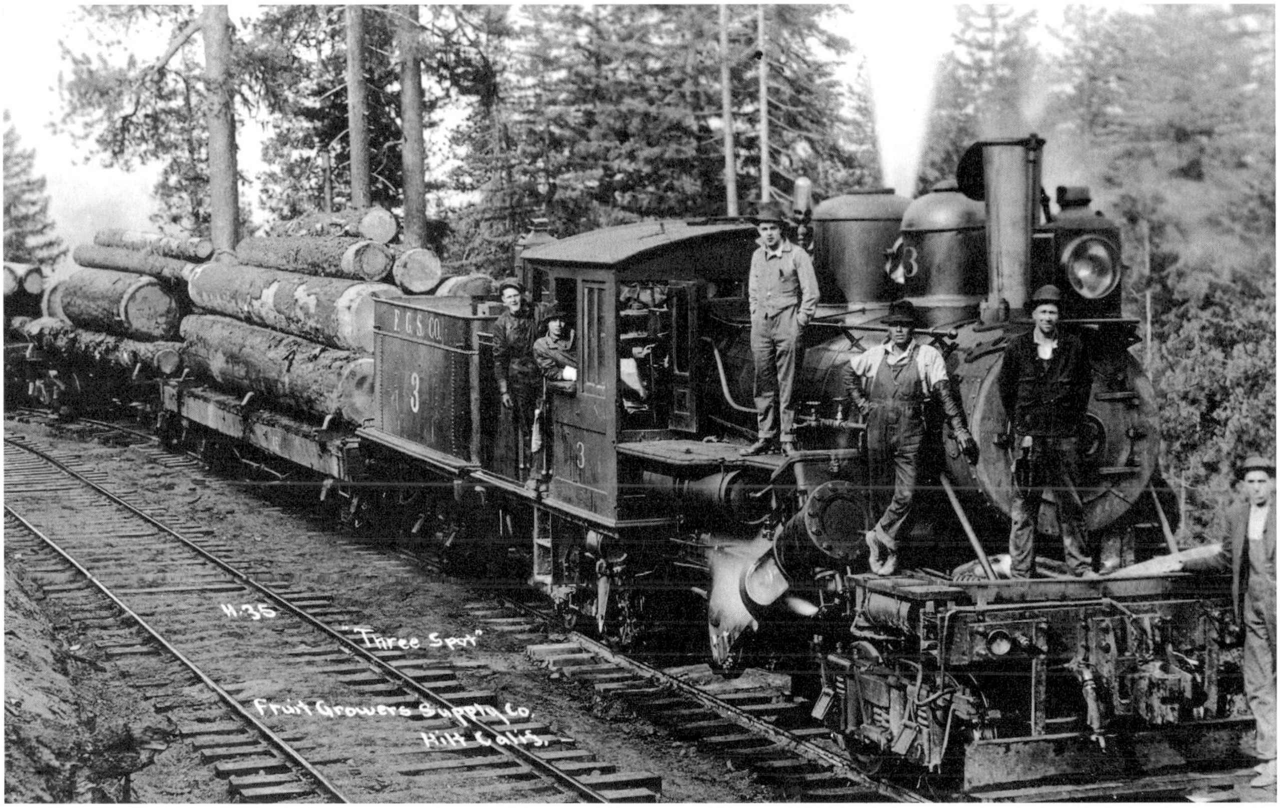

A Climax geared locomotive brings a trainload of logs down to the mill at Hilt. (Sunkist Growers)

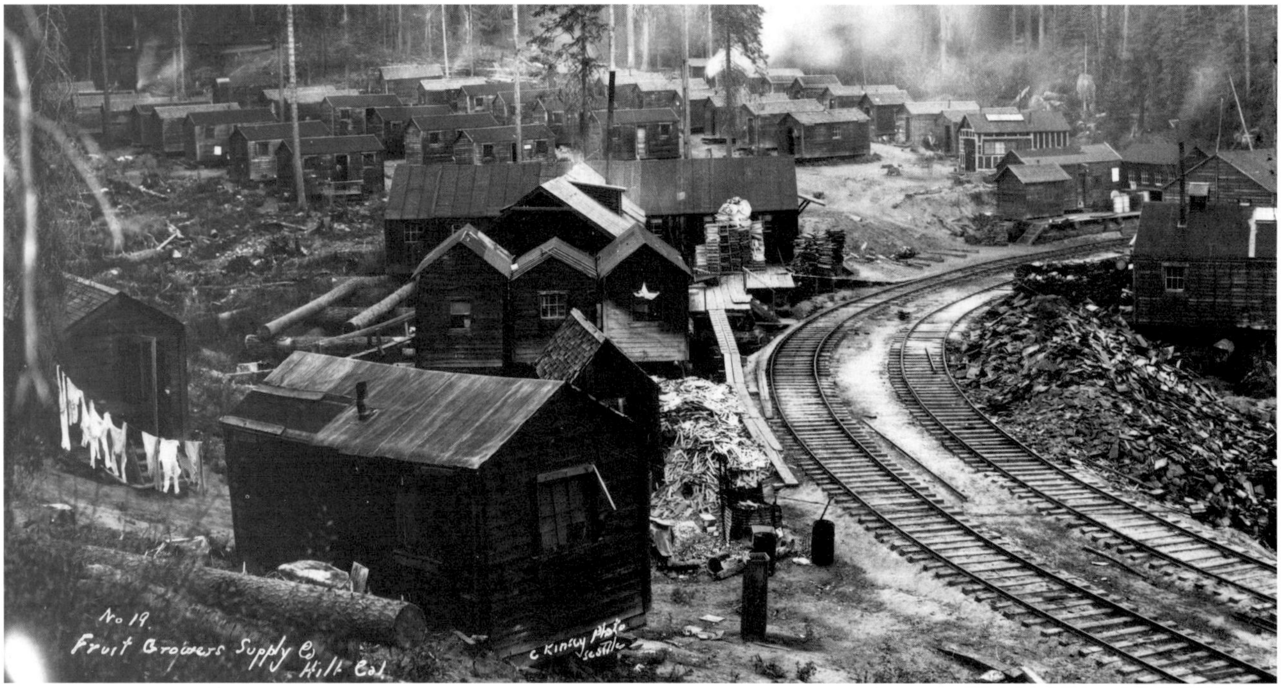

Above: The Fruit Growers Supply camp at Hilt; it is hoped that the steam engine smoke drifted away from the line of laundry. (Sunkist Growers)

Below: When Fruit Growers Supply purchased the Red River Lumber property in 1944, the sale included many locomotives. Fruit Growers retained the same numbers for Nos. 101 and 102, the original numbers of the Tonopah and Goldfield Railroad. (Douglas Richter photograph, Bert Ward collection)

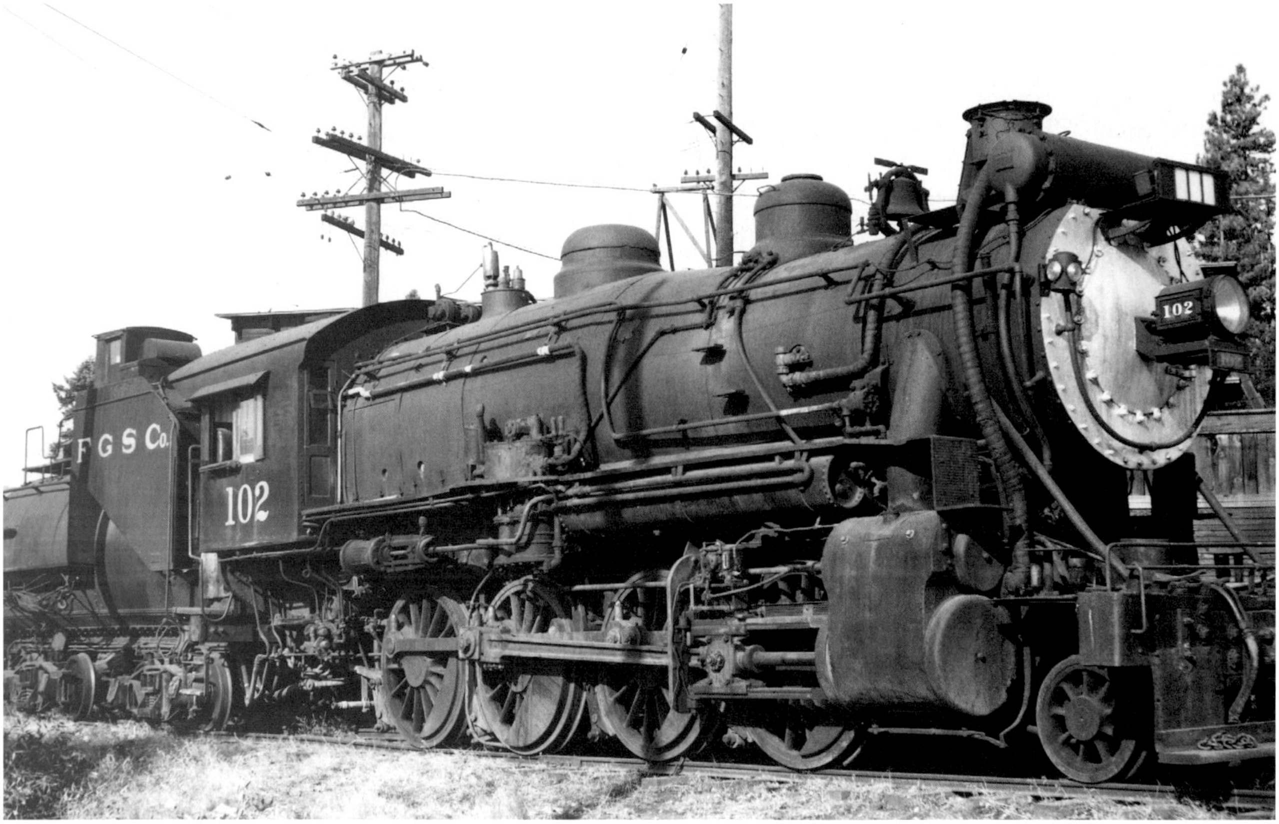

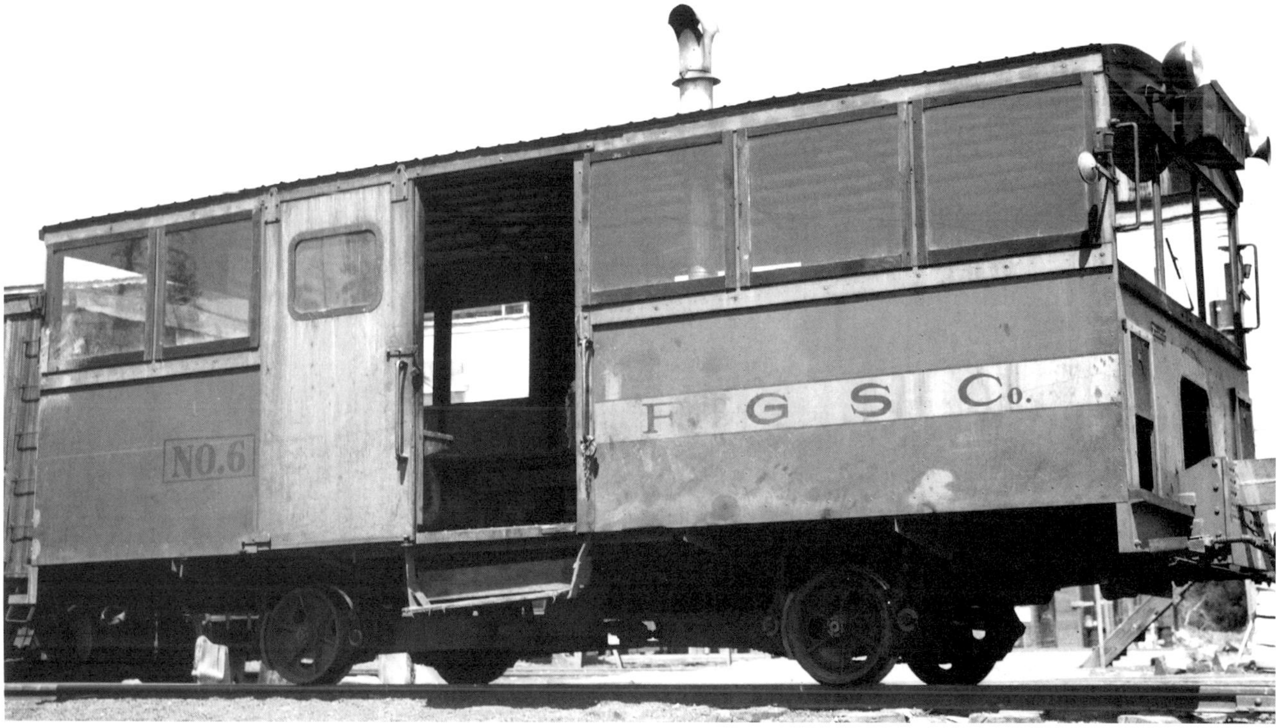

Above: The auto-rail car took men from Camp Harvey to the logging site in this vehicle, 1947. (Douglas Richter photograph, Bert Ward collection)

Below: Caboose No. 908 stood immobile at Halls Flat in 1947. (Douglas Richter photograph, Bert Ward collection)

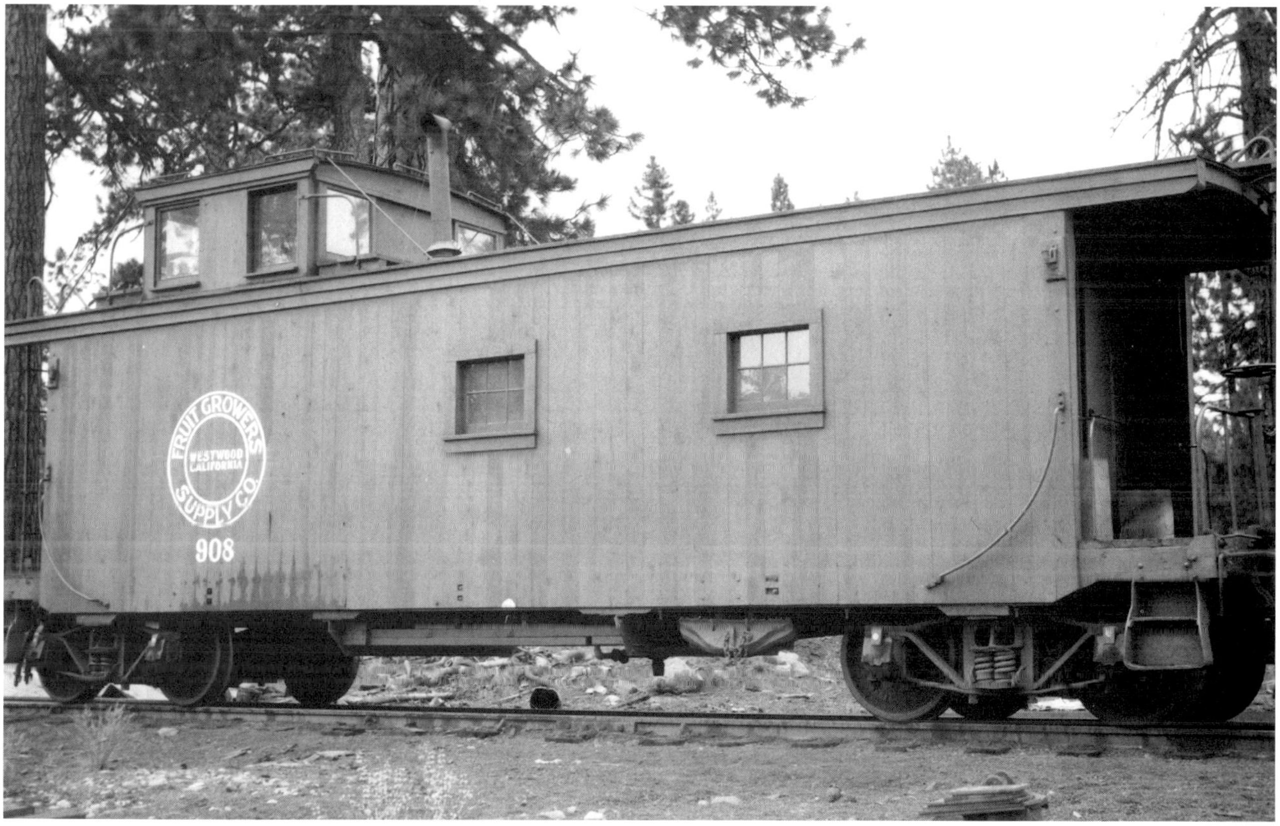

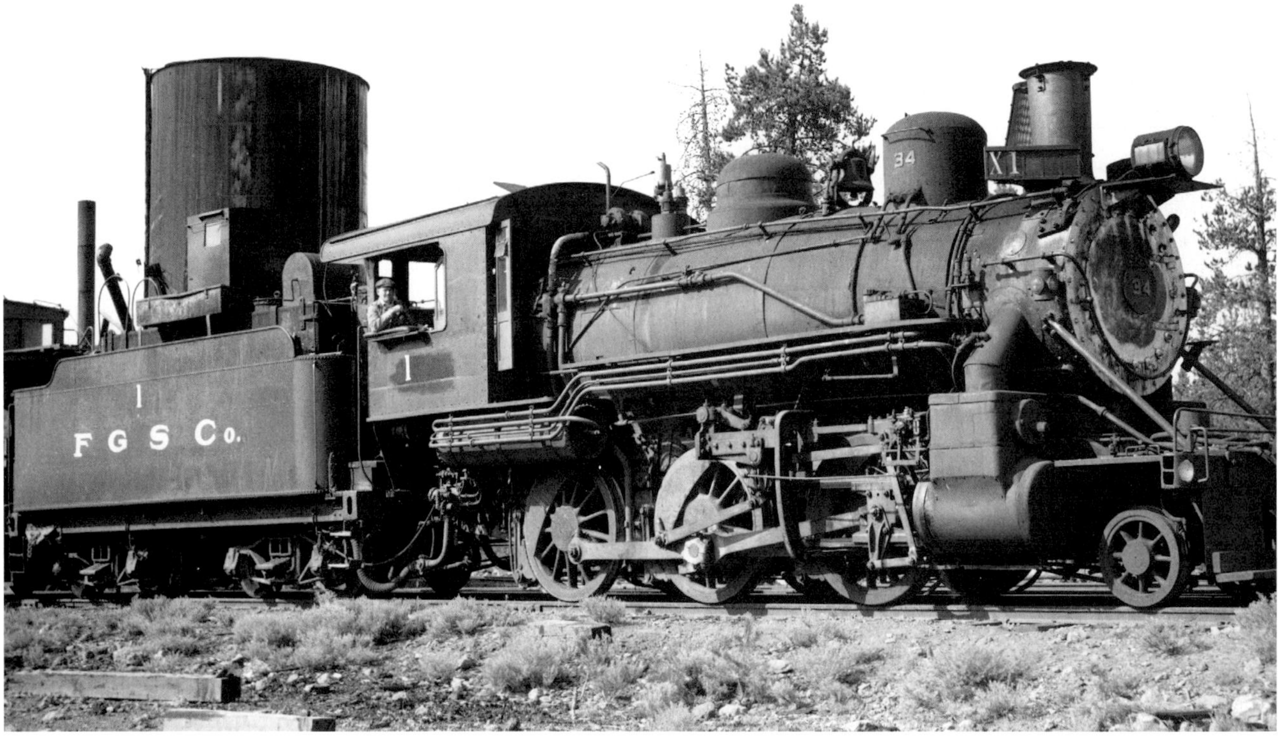

By the time Fruit Growers Supply returned the locomotive to Westwood in 1950, No. 34 became No. 1. (Douglas Richter photograph, Bert Ward collection)

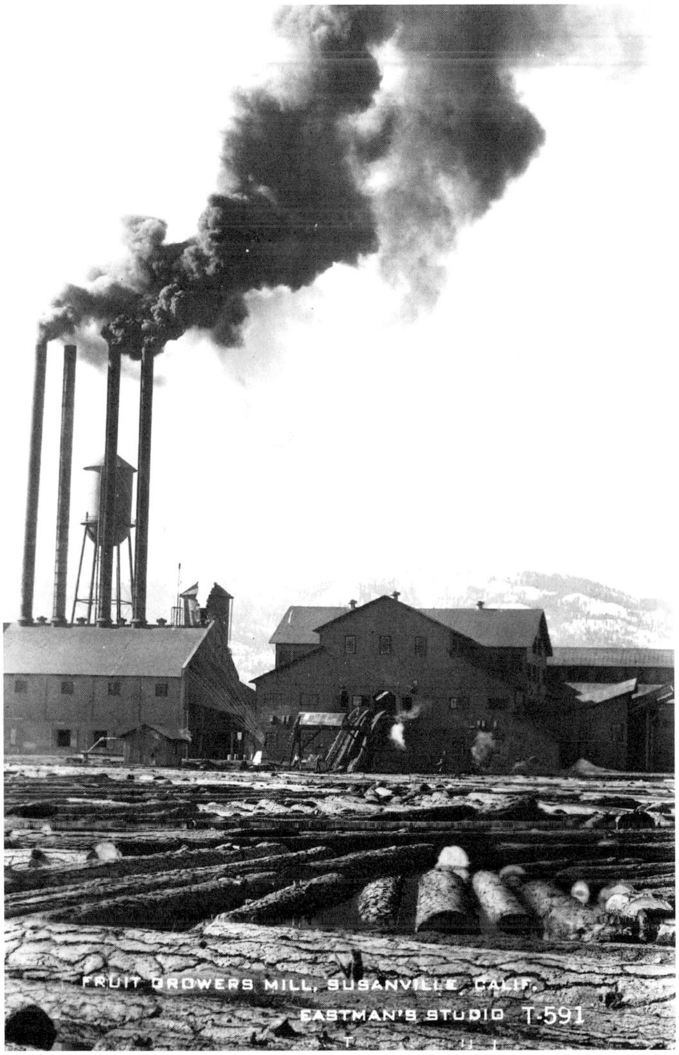

Left: When the smoke from the fires under the boilers filled the sky, it meant prosperous times for Susanville.

Below: Fruit Growers Camp 10, a lively operation in temperate weather, rested quietly under white velvet after a snowstorm. (John Hart)

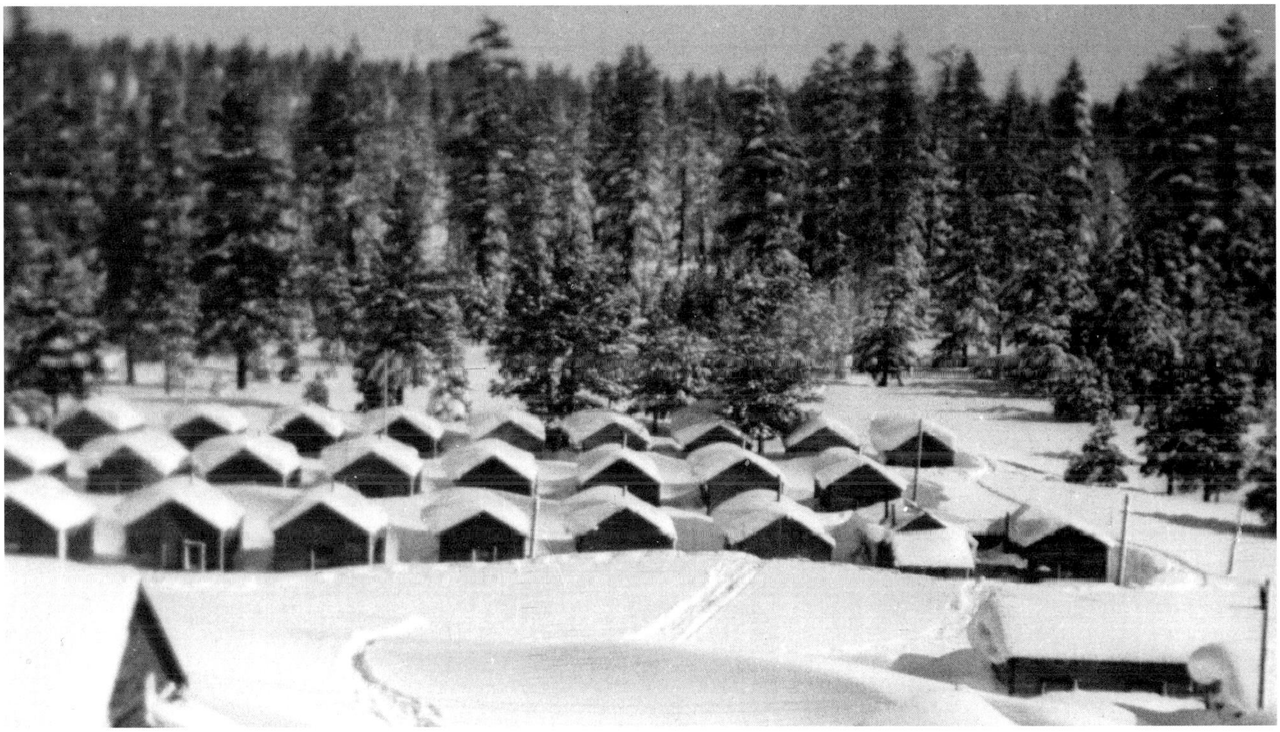

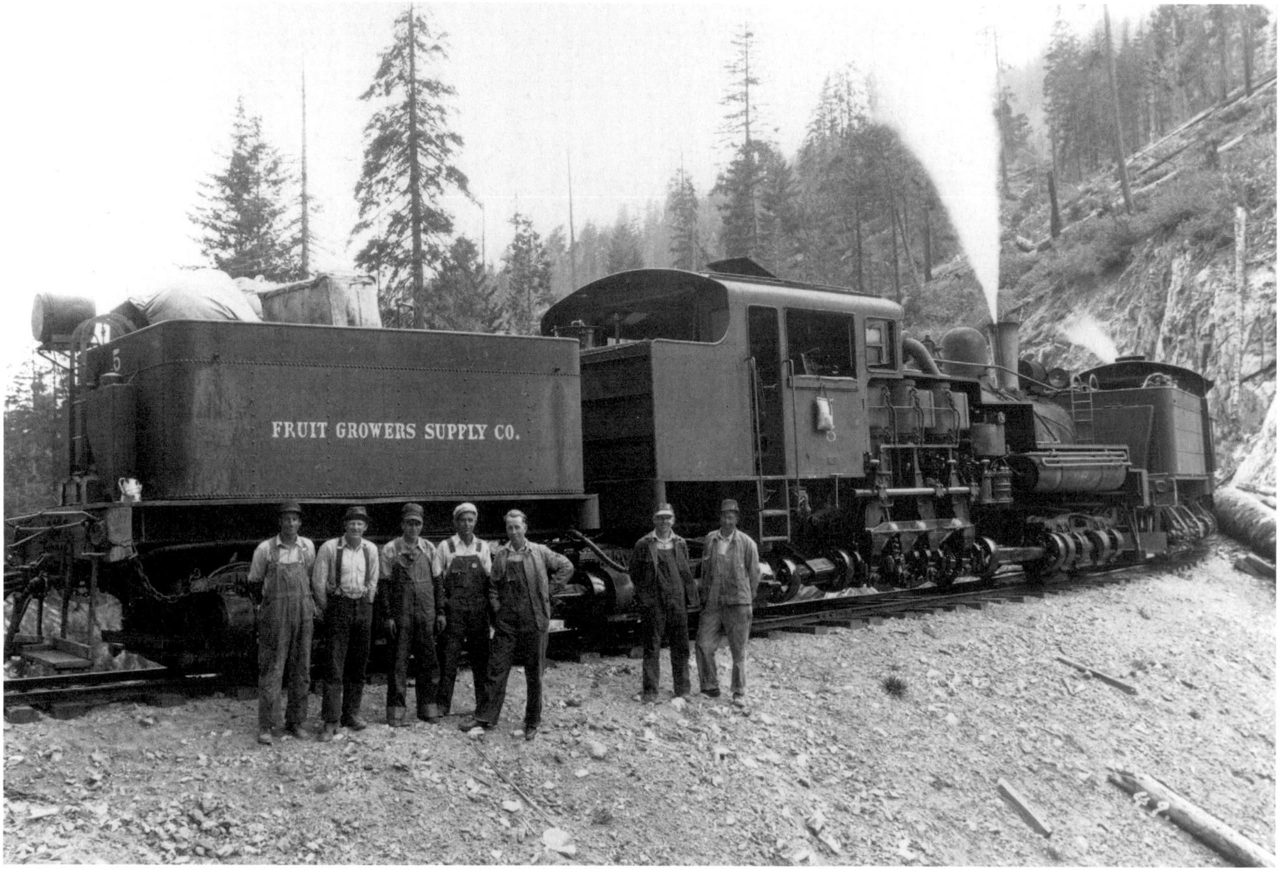

A double-header led by No. 5 (Shay) halted on a downgrade on the way to Hilt. Presumably, the crew had tied the brakes down securely before lining up for the camera. (Fruit Growers Supply)

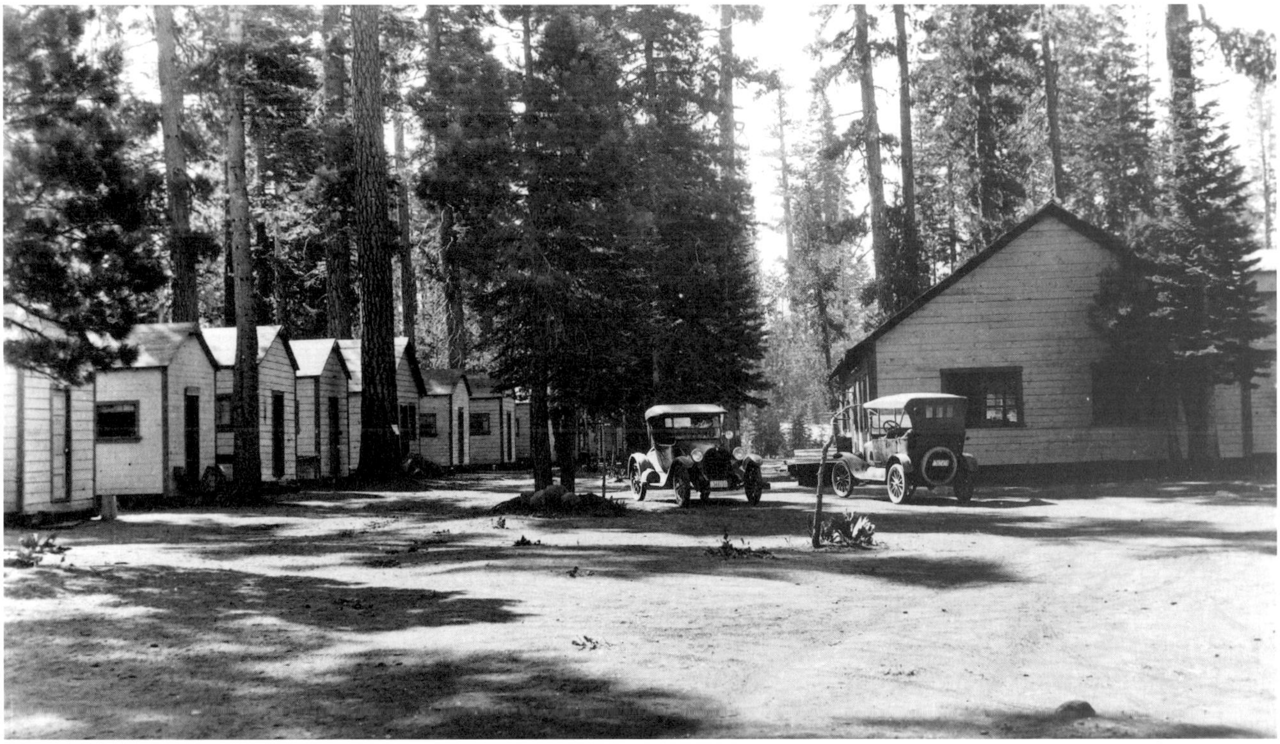

Above: At Camp B, about six miles north of Westwood Jct., the commissary had just been completed in 1922 when the photographer arrived. The cabins are the typical "in-transit type." Mounted on skids, a crane placed them on flatcars when the crew moved to the new campsite. (Fruit Growers Supply)

Below: Men were taken from logging camps to work on this vehicle built by Skagit. During inclement weather, side curtains offered some protection from the rain. The small gas-engine "speeder" took crews out into the field to make emergency repairs when needed. (Fruit Growers Supply)

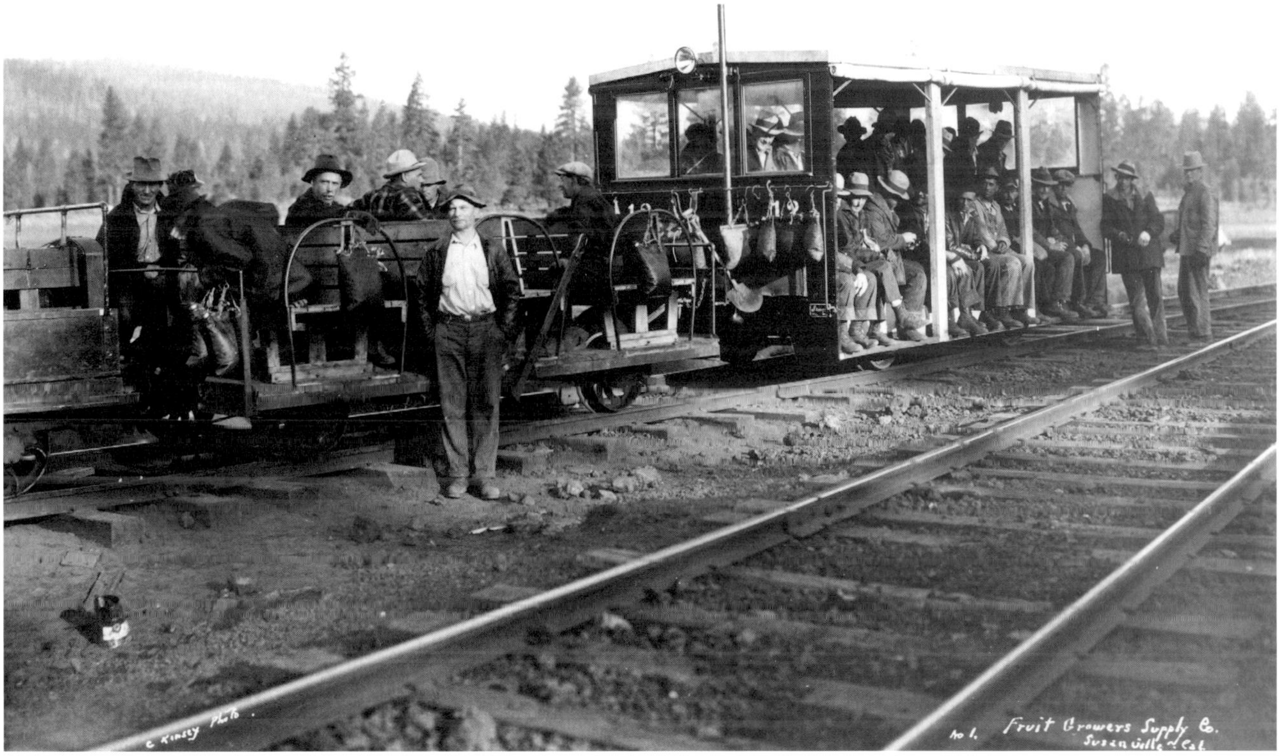

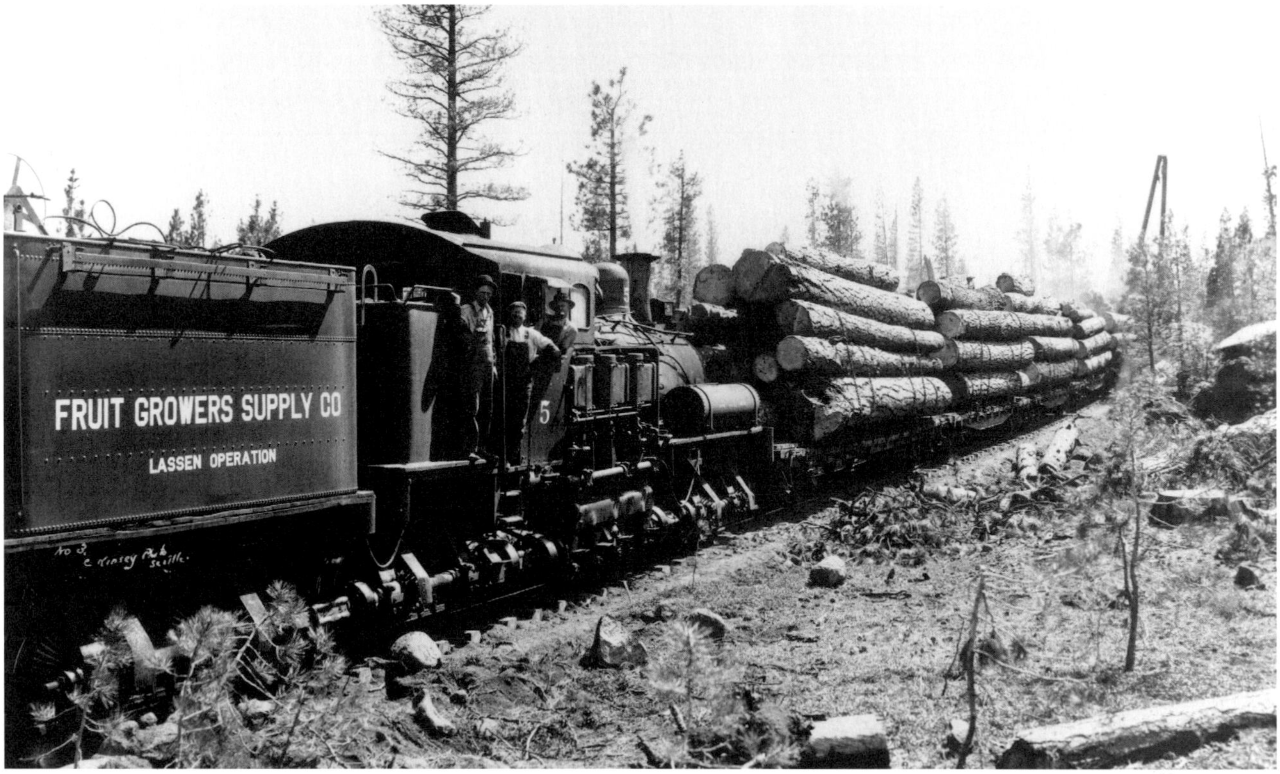

Above: No. 5 brings in a load of logs to the mill. (Fruit Growers Supply)

Below: Locomotive No. 2 with a train in a winter setting. The rod engine has left Camp 10 and is now in Pine Creek Valley. Logan Mountain is in the distance. The maintenance car on the siding carried water and oil for the jammers and cranes. (Fruit Growers Supply)

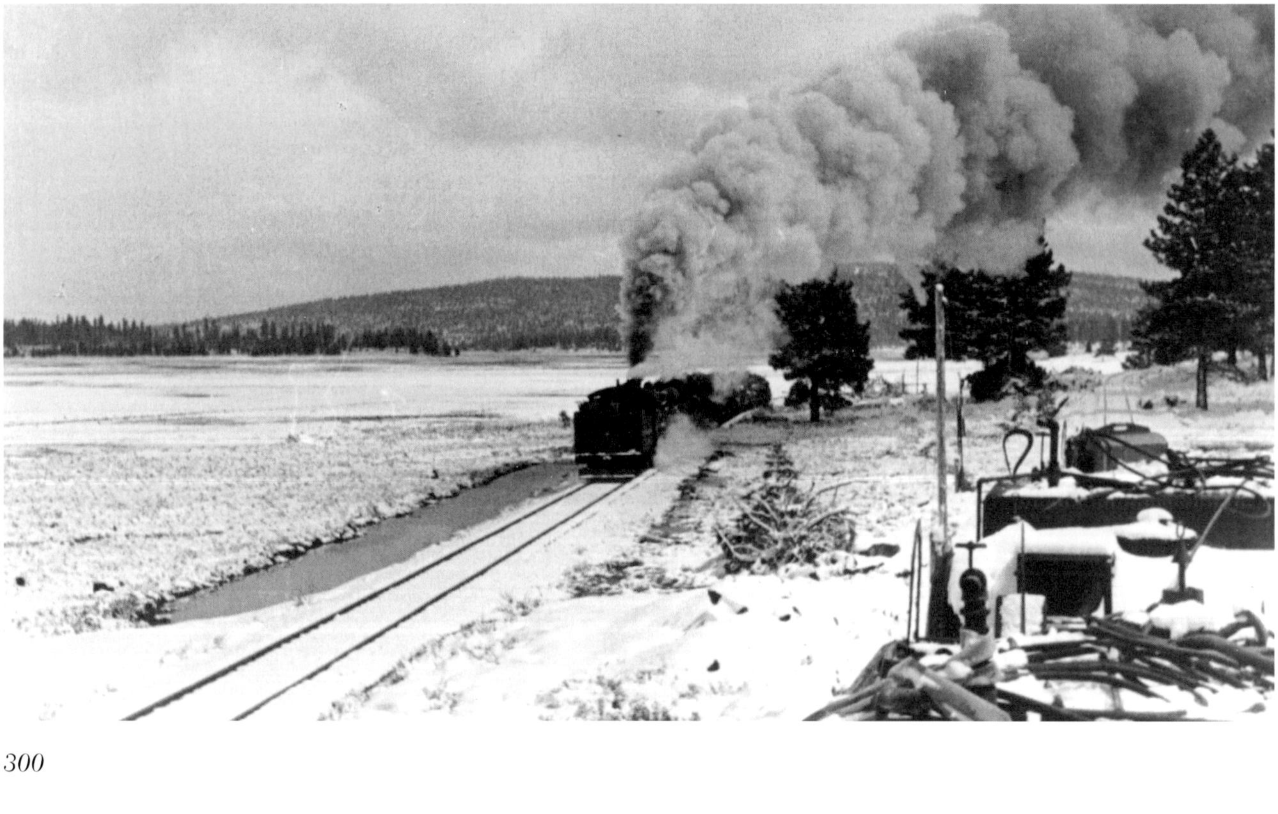

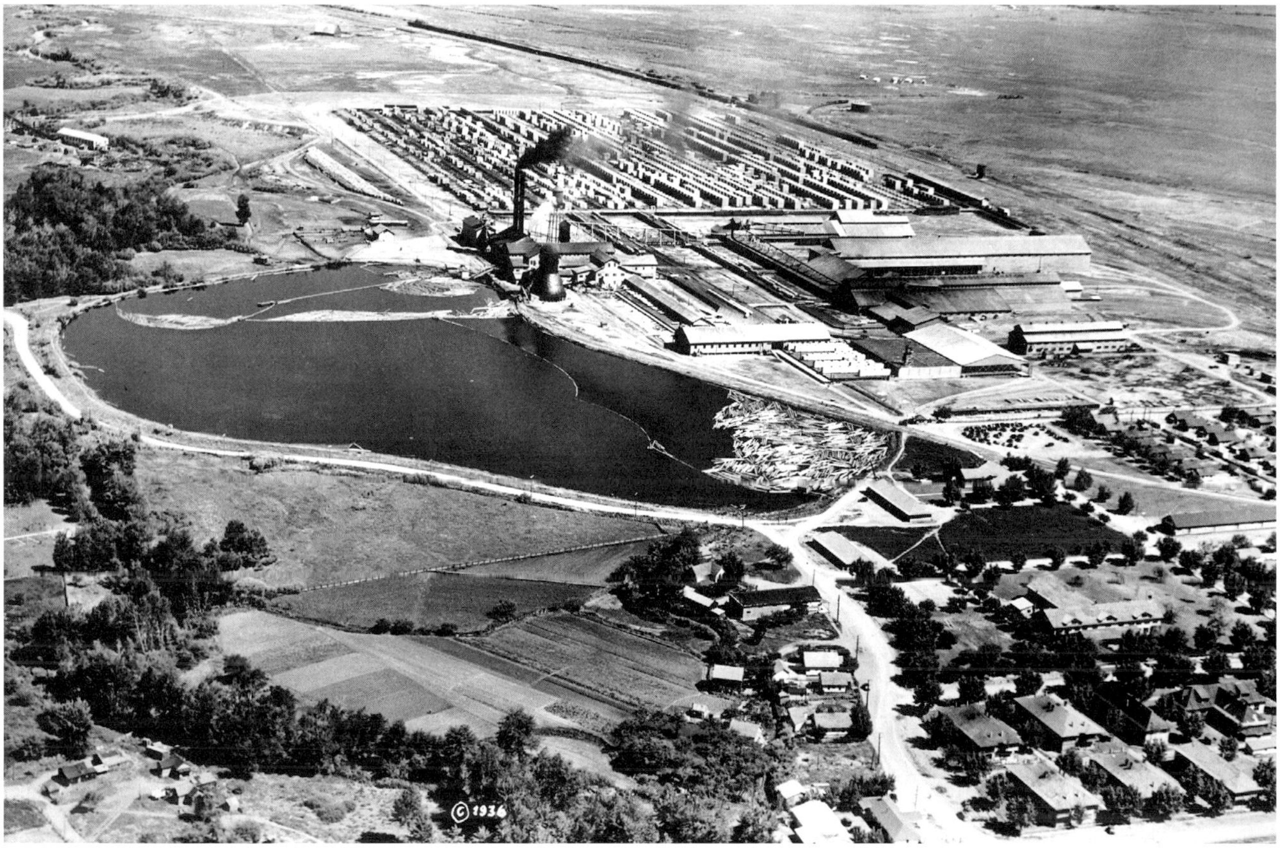

An aerial view of the Fruit Growers Supply's Susanville plant in 1936 included a Southern Pacific train stretched along the background. (Lassen County Historical Society)

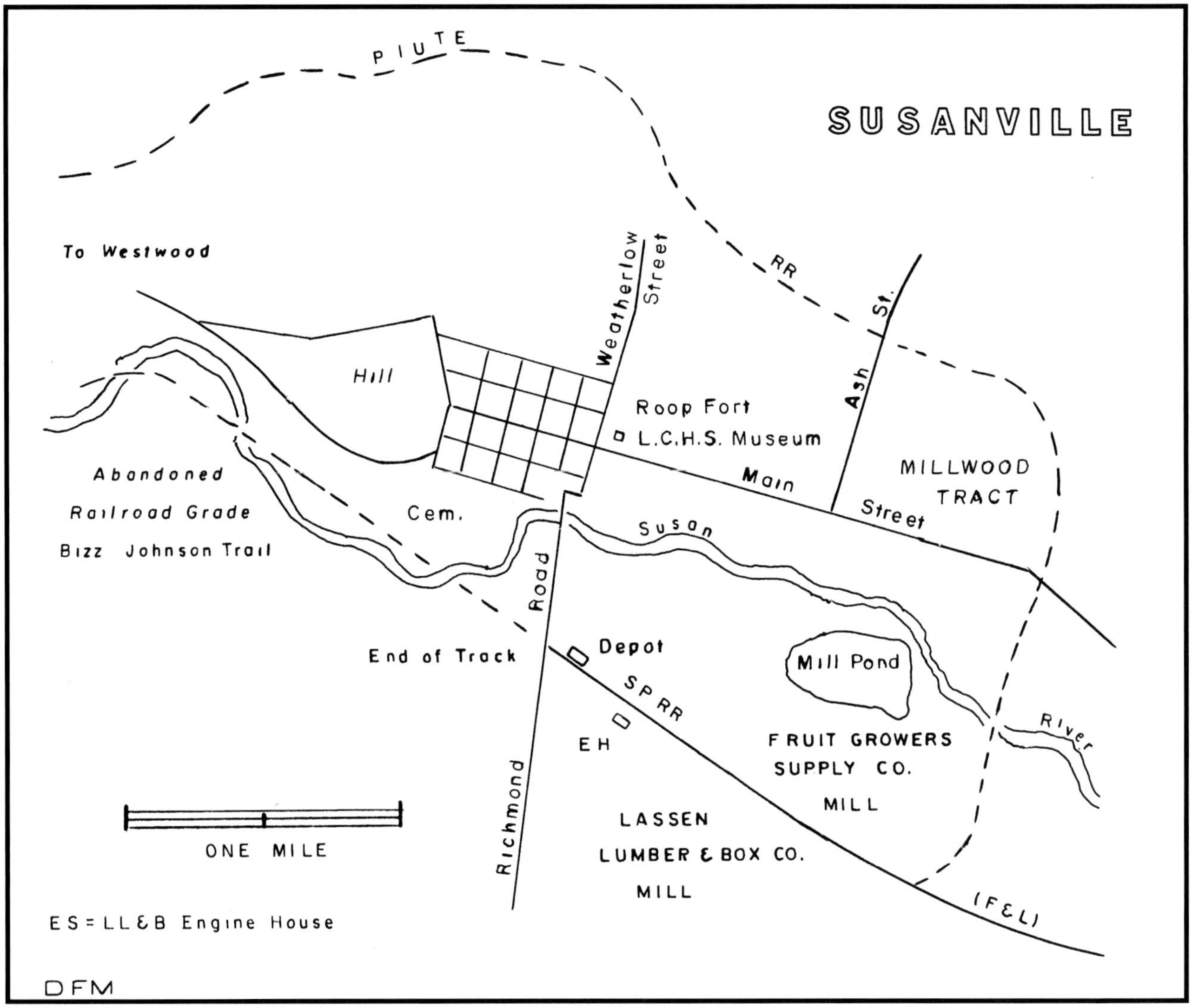
SUSANVILLE
PIUTE
RR
To Westwood
Weatherlow Street
Ash St.
Hill
Roop Fort
L.C.H.S. Museum
Main Street
MILLWOOD TRACT
Abandoned Railroad Grade
Bizz Johnson Trail
Cem.
Susan
Road
Richmond
End of Track
Depot
Mill Pond
SP RR
River
EH
FRUIT GROWERS SUPPLY CO. MILL
LASSEN LUMBER & BOX CO. MILL
ONE MILE
(F&L)
ES=LL&B Engine House
DFM

LASSEN LUMBER AND BOX COMPANY

The ever expanding fruit industry required wood packing crates for shipping its products to markets in distant states. For those in the lumber business, dealing in packing boxes or box shook provided more stable markets than housing construction, which was subject to variations in the general economy. However, devastating cold weather could shrink fruit crops and the need for boxes, as happened after the freezes in southern California in 1913 and 1937.

The impressive operations of the Red River Lumber Company at Westwood plus a number of small neighboring firms attracted lumber people and investors to Lassen County. In the fall of 1916, Susanville residents speculated over the future of their community, hoping to find some industry other than agriculture to support and boost their local economy. With the Fernley and Lassen Railway (SP) running trains with regularity subject to winter snow blockades, industrialists had access to eastern markets.

In November 1916, the U.S. Forest Service advertised a timber sale in Norvell Flat and McCoy Flat. Some weeks later it was reported that the S. H. Chase Company of San Jose had purchased sixty million board feet of timber. The contract called for payment of three dollars per thousand feet of pine but only fifty cents for the fir timber, which constituted only a small part of the forest. The San Jose firm expected to build a mill in Susanville when weather permitted, but plans changed and nothing transpired.

Months went by without any further developments. In October 1917, R. D. Baker of the Empire Lumber Company of Pittsburgh and two men from Klamath Falls, Charles McCowan, formerly with the Ewauna Box Company, and C. E. Cotton, came to Susanville much to the pleasure of local business leaders when they met in the "Rest Room" of the Doyle Building. From the community, the visitors desired the contribution of suitable land for a sawmill and box factory which they committed the firm to erect and operate with a force of two hundred men.

Several sites were offered and options taken. An encouraging step came with the incorporation of the Lassen Lumber and Box Company on February 23, 1918. R. D. Baker served as president, while Charles McGowan was vice president and general manager. Next, the new firm purchased an old sawmill from Doyle and Crowder that has been running in the hills along Little Last Chance Creek west of Constantia since the turn of the century. C. L. Joslyn took the contract to move the machinery and mill frame to Susanville. The task was accomplished in two stages. Before winter storms made mountain roads impassible, moving the machinery to Doyle constituted the first step. Using trucks borrowed from the Red River Lumber Company, Joslyn spent December loading and hauling the material to Susanville.

Lassen Lumber and Box erected two mills on a site at the eastern edge of Susanville. In April 1918, after SP forces laid tracks to the mill site, delivery of building materials commenced. Mill No. 2, using the older machinery, began sawing in July 1918, while No. 1 went into service the following April with the arrival of the new machinery.

Tapping the forest stands that the LL&B had won in November 1917 in a U.S. Forest Service auction was done by independent loggers. Near Facht on the Fernley and Lassen Railway (SP), some four miles south of Westwood Jct., the Lassen Logging Company began cutting timber for LL&B in June 1918. After loading logs on SP logging cars and tying them down with chains, a Shay locomotive led the cars down the track—less than two miles—to the connection at Facht, where the SP crews took the cars to the sawmill in Susanville.

Incorporated in Oregon on June 20, 1918, the Lassen Logging Company was promoted by C. E. Cotton, whom McGowan had known in Klamath Falls. Lost in time is the construction and operating record of this company's four- or five-mile spur appearing on maps of the 1925 era as pointing west from Facht.

J. G. Jellison harvested timber for LL&B from its mill at Buntingville, about seventeen miles from Susanville. Another log contractor was the Diamond Mountain Lumber Company, some six miles away.

LL&B regularly sent out shipments to Facht, and, with a steady and rising volume, SP erected a freight and passenger shed there in July 1920. Measuring ten by twenty feet, Paul Giannini purchased the shed in August 1940.

New machinery boosted the LL&B output in 1920, although the original circular saw was retained for some years. With a larger force and a night shift in the summer of 1921, LL&B production rose, and SP crews picked up three cars of finished lumber or box shook at the mill daily. The *Lassen Advocate,* appreciating the business activity the new firm brought, commented, "The most honorable noise in our Susanville in the first daylight hours is the 6 o'clock whistle at the Lassen Lumber & Box Company."

Heavy accumulations of snow limited lumbering in northern California to seven or eight months of a year, which was partly offset by ten-hour working days. With the mill running night and day, LL&B sent out one hundred cars of finished lumber during July 1921. A. G. Breitwieser, secretary-treasurer of the organization, had made a trip from Pittsburgh in May 1918 to investigate the activities of the new firm, and, pleased with what he saw, he brought his son and three daughters to Susanville, except for the daughter attending college in San Francisco. Entering local politics, he became a trustee of Susanville in 1920 and mayor the following year.

Deep snow closed the logging camp in November 1921, but the box factory operated through the winter as usual. When it came time to open the camp at Facht the following May, the locomotive broke three snowplows trying to clear the track but reached its goal with the fourth attempt. Considering the amount of snow, the camps suffered little; only one roof had caved in. With nearly a million feet of logs decked, the crew loaded six cars that SP delivered in anticipation of starting the mill three days later. Eighty horses were sent to Facht to assist in logging, and soon SP delivered a daily average of twenty cars of logs to the mill.

Recreation was an important matter for the company, which could take pride in its successful baseball team that proved victorious after most games. In 1922, the team held the championship of the Pacific Coast Industrial League.

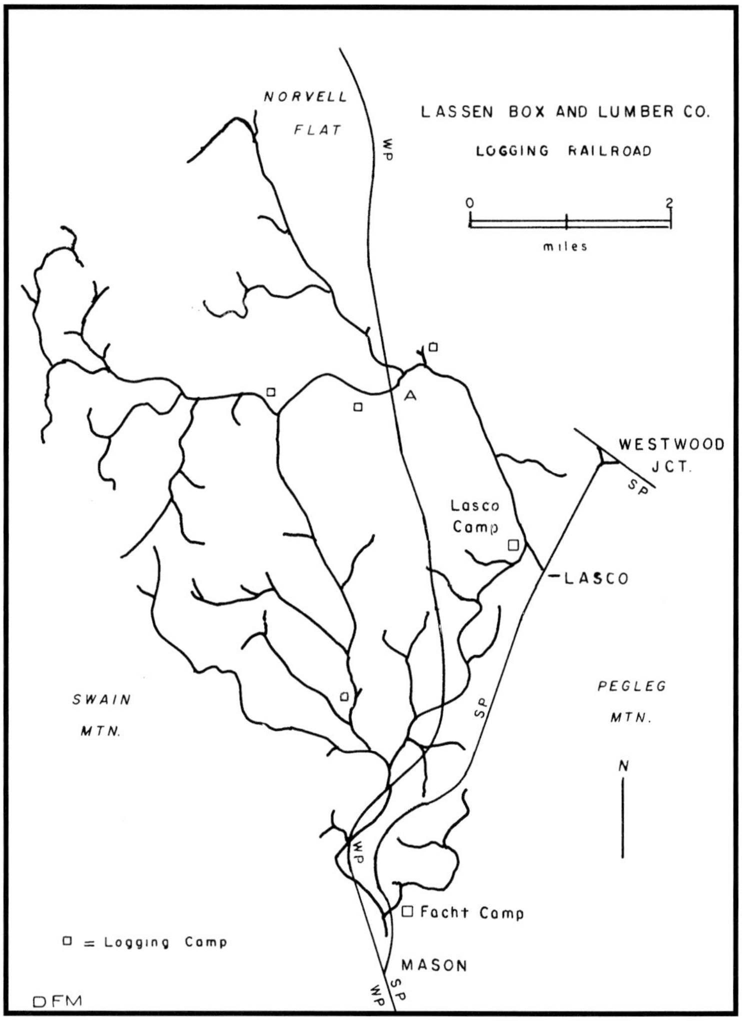

For about ten years, Lassen Lumber and Box Company used a logging railroad in harvesting timber west of Westwood Jct. Initially, tracks were laid into the timber around Facht, but the company soon centered operations around Lasco Camp. Southern Pacific transported the logs from the Facht or Lasco Camp stations to the mill in Susanville. As each timber area was cut over, tracks were moved to another timber location. LL&B ended logging by rail in 1929 but retained a track running northwest from Lasco. In the construction of its Northern California Extension to Bieber, Western Pacific crossed two logging spurs near the point marked A. When rails of the lumber railroad were salvaged a few years later, both crossings vanished.

The New Camp at Lasco

As the logging season ended, the company commenced development of a new camp along SP rails at the foot of Pegleg Mountain, four miles north of Facht. Originally called Juniper, it became Lasco, as headquarters for logging work of the Lassen Lumber and Box Company. Thanks to a less severe winter, 1923 operations began earlier than previous years. McGowan, after denying the purchase of George Wingfield's Meadowbrook Farm in July, confirmed the acquisition of the Nevada banker's ranch the next week. Not only did it provide relaxation and a place to entertain guests, but it also held a fine stand of timber.

With the completion of construction of the Lasco camp in June, it became known as the "Show Logging Camp" of California and paid its way by reduced labor turnover. The company started work on its logging spur into the woods, and a new sixty-ton Baldwin locomotive joined the roster along with two passenger cars, a new twenty-five-ton Brownhoist crane, and a Clyde tracklayer. Installation of a six hundred–barrel fuel-oil tank at Lasco provided for emergencies.

Camille Frizzie, as woods superintendent, managed logging operations at Lasco. Although this position made him a "bull of the woods," he is remembered as "a very fine gentlemen." He graciously staked "winos" in Sacramento during the idle winter months, which they repaid working as summer lumberjacks. Some men never drew their pay until the end of the season, for then they could spend the winter in Sacramento in some comfort.

Operations continued in a generally similar pattern for the next few years. The railroad, divided into two forks several miles west of Lasco, was pushed westerly in the direction of Silver Lake. Unfortunately, both 1924 and 1925 were marked with sad events. In August 1924, a party consisting of office workers joined others at Lasco and took a speeder out for a Sunday in the woods. All went well until the return trip when the velocipede jumped the track and threw its riders into a ditch. Joe Penny, chief accountant, walked two miles to Camp 5 seeking assistance. One man's injuries put him in the Riverside Hospital.

Three months later, Royal Draws, a young conductor, cut a boxcar loose without properly setting the brakes. While he was walking toward the engine, the boxcar quietly rolled down the mild grade. Although Camille Frizzie, uncle of the young man, called to him, he failed to move in time and was crushed by the impact.

In July 1925, eight men suffered injuries when spreading rails dumped a train with a tracklaying machine and a flatcar loaded with rails. It happened shortly after leaving Lasco. The three men most seriously hurt were riding on the car with the rails. One man fell on a saw and ended with deep cuts, while others suffered from a barrage of wrenches, bolts, and heavy tools. Fortunately, the train was moving at ten miles per hour at the time; still, broken shoulders and wrenched backs hospitalized the men.

To honor its employees, LL&B hosted the 1925 Thanksgiving dinner, while Fruit Growers Supply charged each worker forty cents for the same event. As February 1926 was ending, McGowan dispatched a crew to Lasco to work on a cookhouse and dining room on wheels to handle the spring employment, expected to reach 250 that year. Although the snow still measured three feet, it was expected to melt with the warmer weather down to two feet, at which point logging could be started. That summer, a big dance at Lasco drew much attention. Men were allowed to wear their boots but, in deference to the comfort of their partners, had to remove the calks from them.

The first snowfall came in mid-September and melted quickly. The big storm coming later brought four feet of snow and closed the camp. Down at the mill, workers dismantled the original saw, as it had been idle for more than a year. The building was converted to a retail lumber shed.

Spring of 1927 offered a surprise when the anticipated opening date had to be postponed because of a late and heavy snowstorm. With plows, a locomotive cleared the tracks so that work could begin. Starting in July 1927, LL&B harvested timber near Goumaz (east of Westwood Jct.) for three months before returning to Lasco.

After nearly ten years as manager, Charles McGowan chose to leave for Castella to operate a box factory he had purchased in the upper Sacramento Valley. (For some years he had also been president of the Lakeview Lumber and Box Company in Oregon.) A. G. Breitwieser filled his position at Susanville.

Railroad logging operation ceased in 1929, probably because of the shrinking lumber market at that time. The idle tracks remained in place until scrapped in 1934; subsequently, the company utilized trucks in harvesting timber. When Western Pacific opened its Northern California Extension in 1931, its operating timetable noted "L. L. & B. Crossing" in two places about a third of a mile apart. The locomotives—one Shay and three rod engines—were sold to the Red River Lumber Company.

The decade of the 1930s was not a happy one for the lumber industry, and the Lassen Lumber and Box Company shared the misery. To stave off creditors, LL&B secured a Reconstruction Finance Corporation (RFC) (government) loan. Fred T. Abbay, a local businessman, was placed on the board as a watchdog for the RFC. Abbay's career began as an SP machinist in Sparks;

later, he bought the Hallowell Hardware Company in Susanville.

With direction from H. W. Bridgeford, its capable manager, the company struggled through the lean years until better times restored its vitality. Success did not extend to the operation of the golf course, which failed several times.

After World War II, the Pittsburgh management wanted a respite after forty years, and arrangements were made to sell the Lassen Lumber and Box Company to its employees. A new company owned by employees, with a similar name but for one small word, was incorporated on March 20, 1951, as Lassen Lumber and Box Inc. Fred Abbay participated in the new management as president.

As part of a long-established practice, LL&B purchased little privately owned timberland but relied on sales of U.S. Forest Service timber. Shortly after its formation, the new company, by submitting a higher figure than its neighbor, Fruit Growers Supply, won a government stand of timber at Crazy Horse Gulch. This purchase disturbed the latter company's management, and it realized that only by acquiring LL&B would this particular episode not be repeated.

After approaching LL&B management, a proposal was submitted to stockholders who agreed to sell at a figure twice their costs (net after taxes), and by a bill of sale dated November 28, 1952, the trustees of Lassen Lumber and Box Inc. conveyed the property to Fruit Growers Supply.

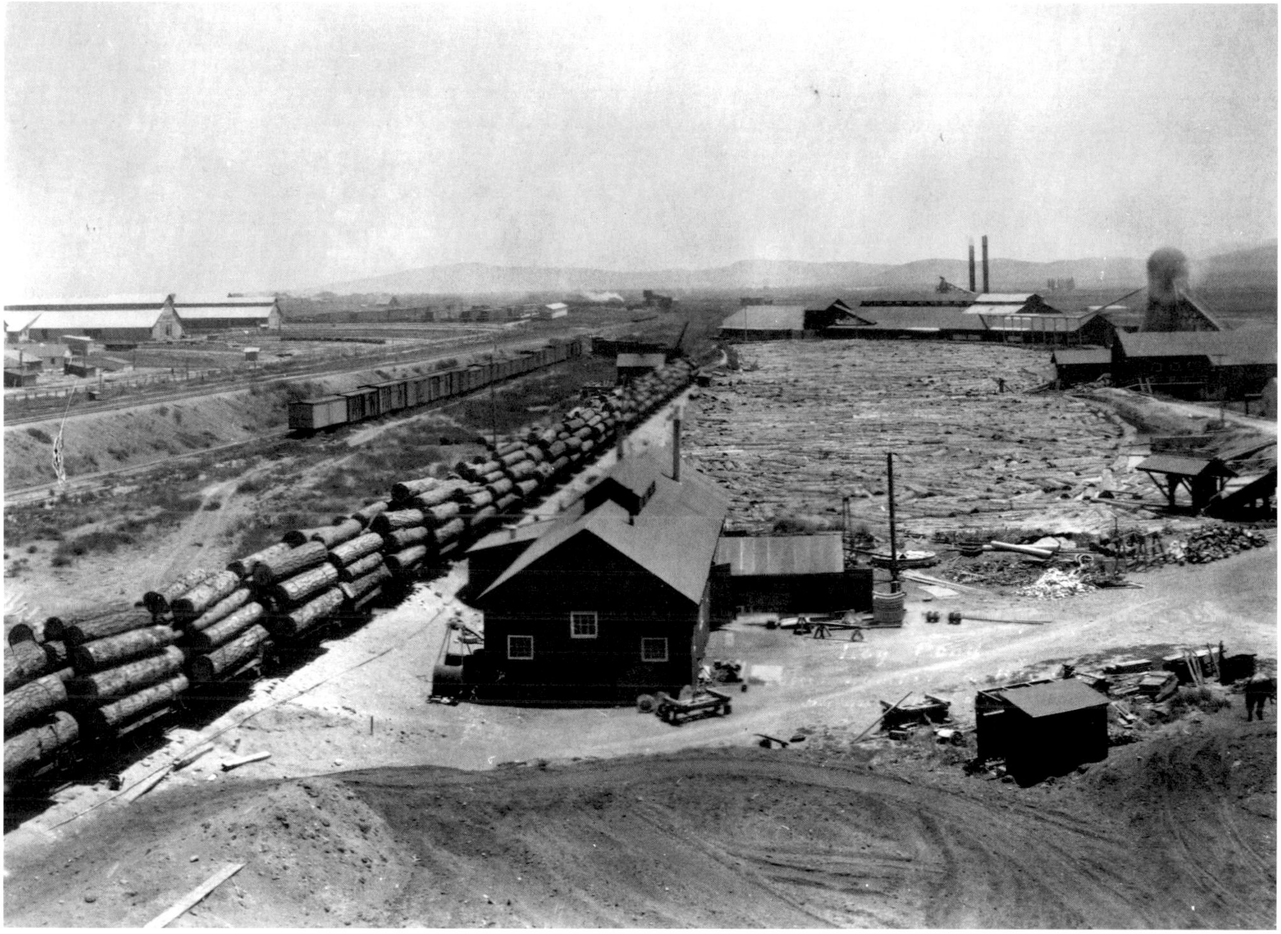

Southern Pacific has just delivered a train of logs from Lasco that will soon be dumped in a log pond of the Lassen Lumber and Box Company. The mill of Fruit Growers Supply Company is on the far side of the railroad grade. (Special Collections, Library, California State University, Chico)

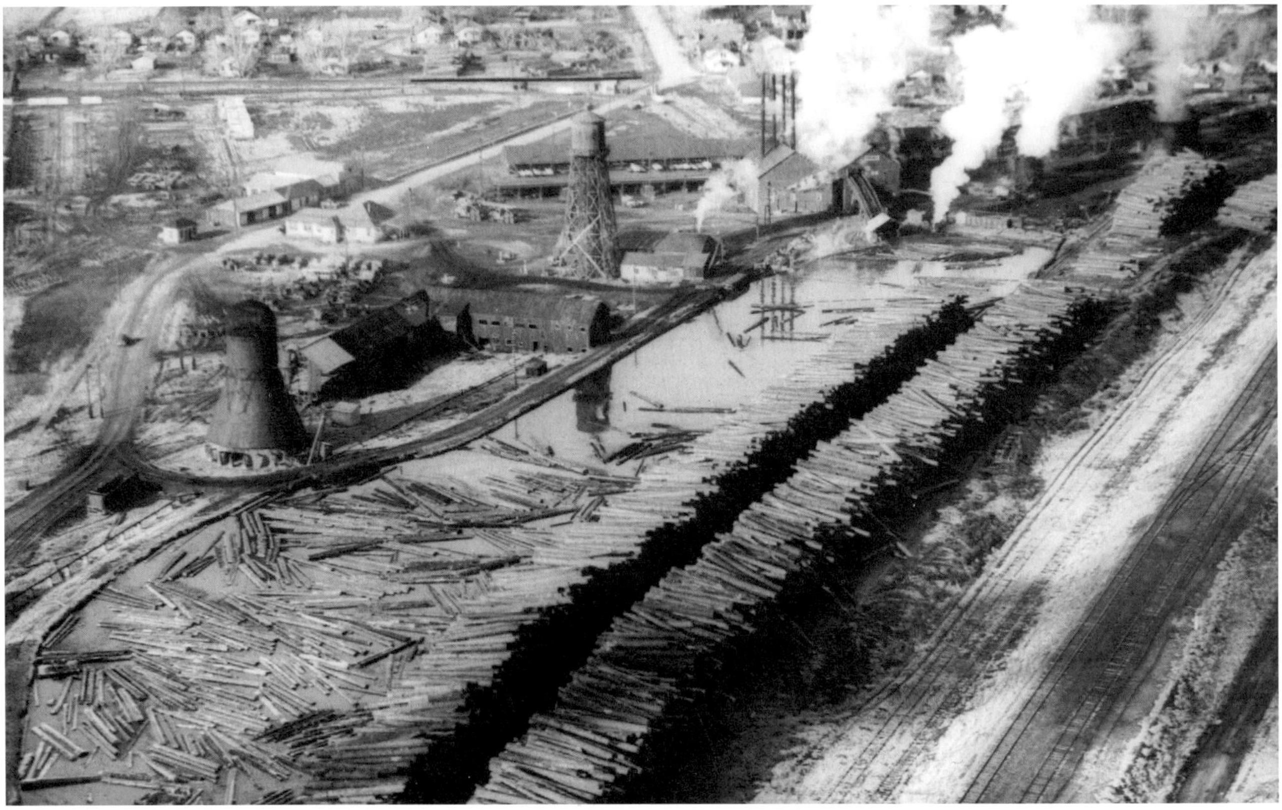

Above: With SP RR tracks adjoining, decked logs are ready for milling at the Lassen Lumber and Box Company. (Special Collections, Library, California State University, Chico)

Below: The office, company store, and dining room at Lasco camp. (Special Collections, Library, California State University, Chico)

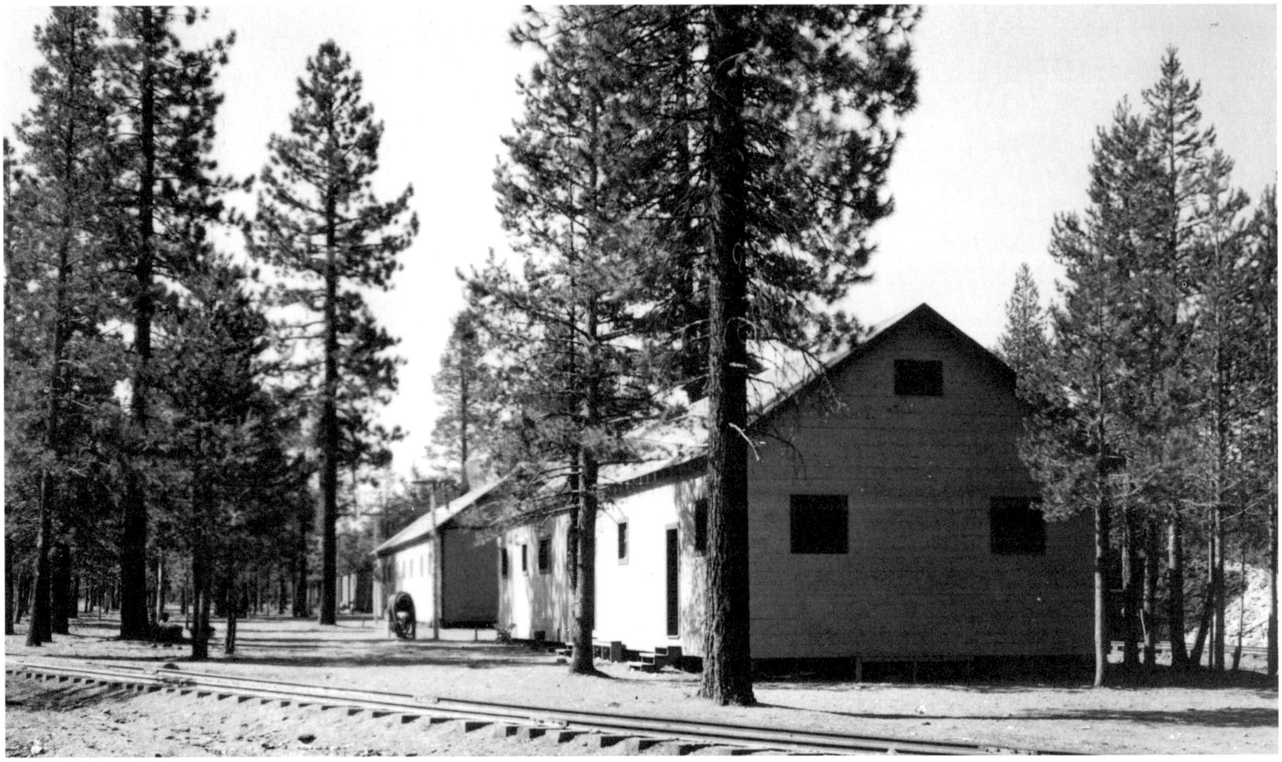

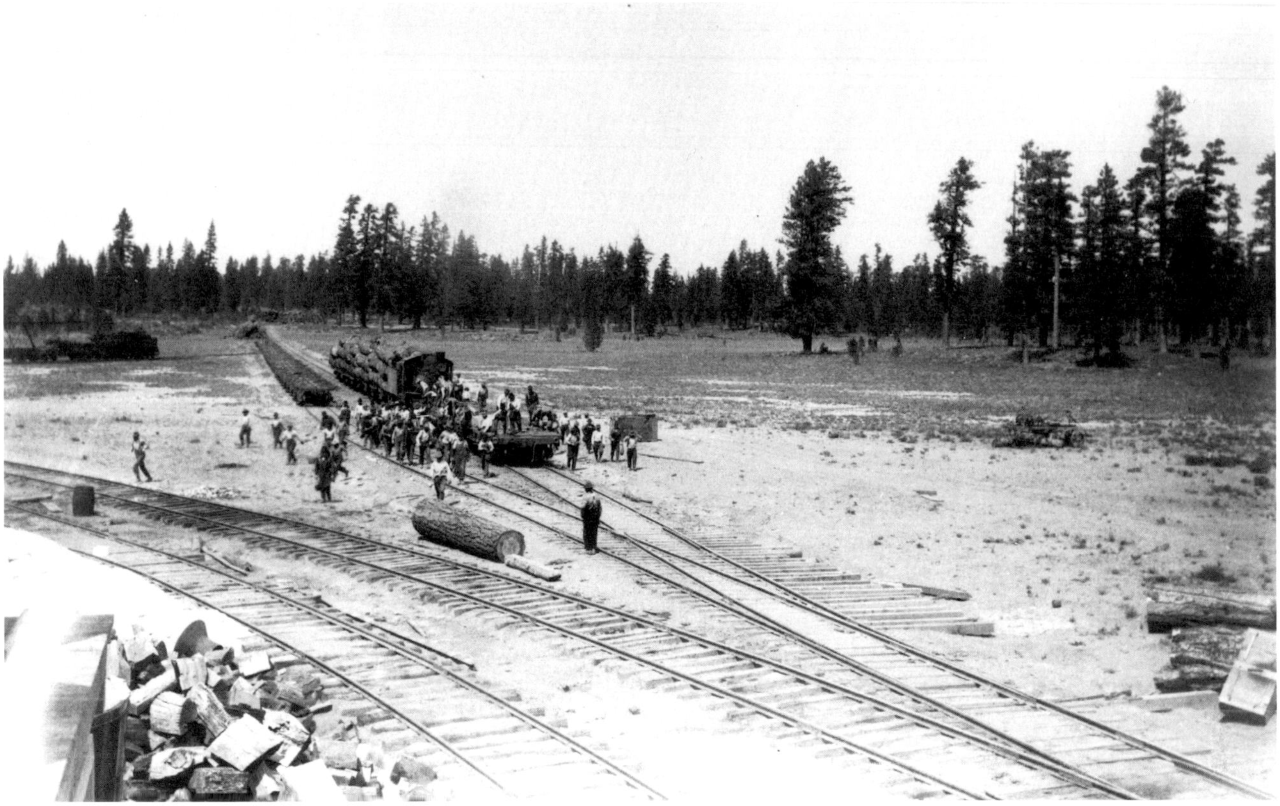

Above: Noon hour at Lasco camp. (Lassen County Historical Society)

Below: Powerhouse and water tanks at Lasco. (Lassen County Historical Society)

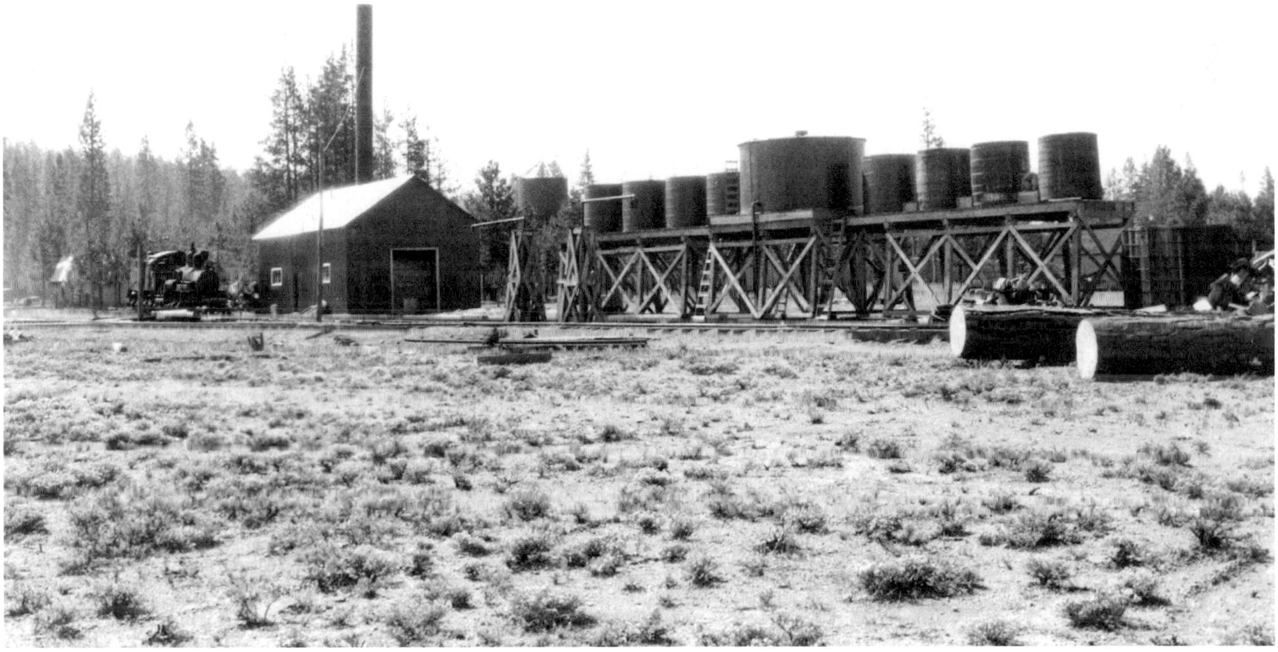

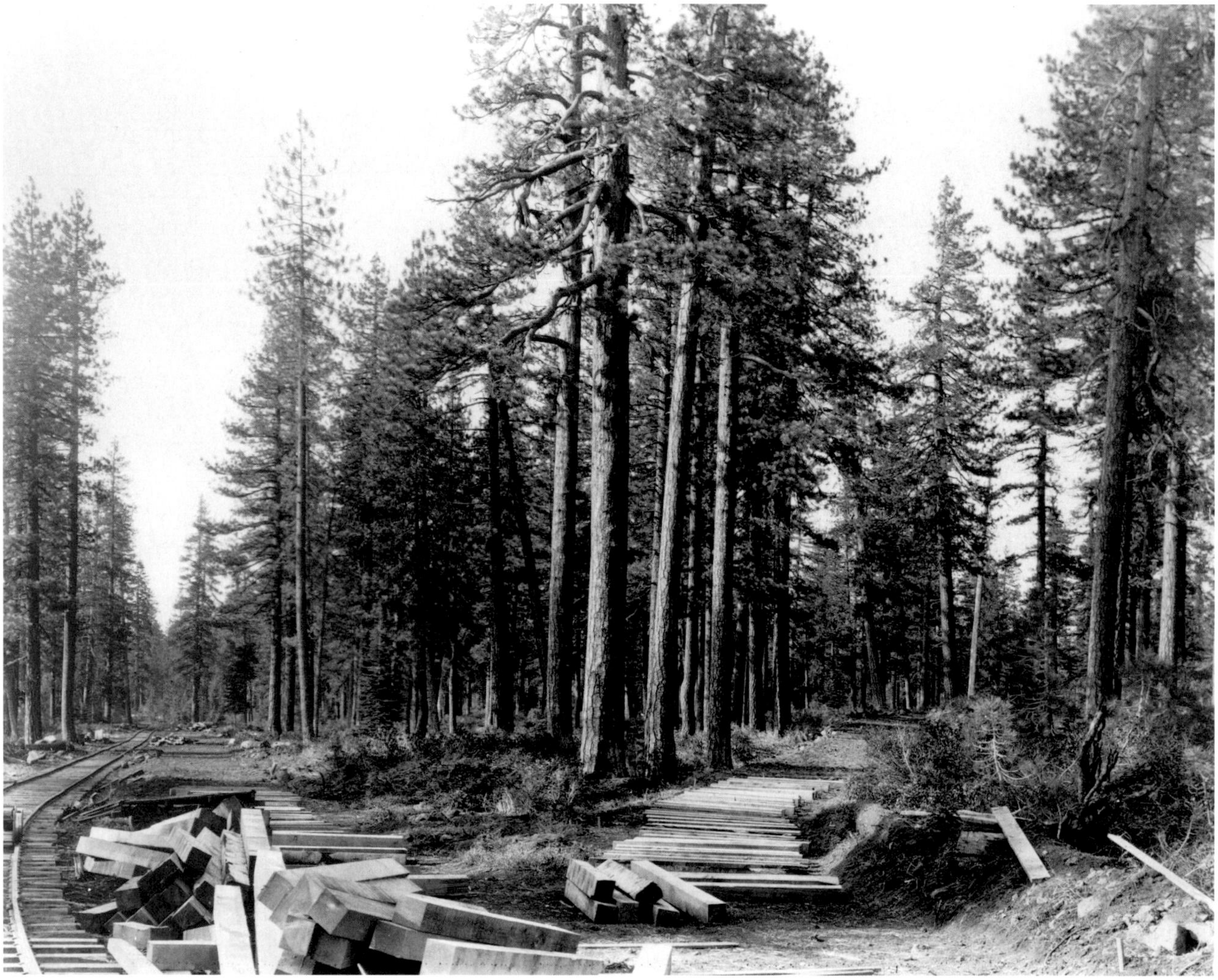

Building a logging spur in the woods. (Special Collections, Library, California State University, Chico)

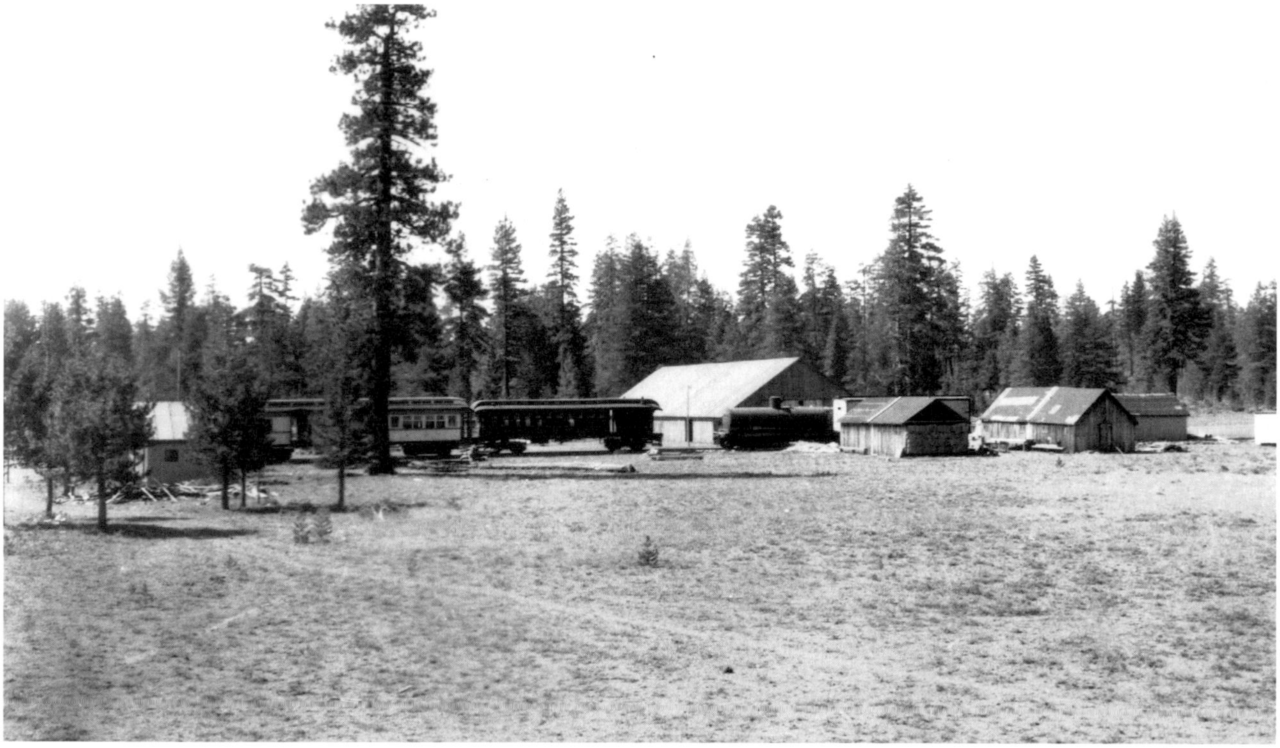

Above: Railroad cars were ready to take workers from Lasco camp into the woods. (Lassen County Historical Society)

Below: No. 23, a 0-6-0 acquired from the Sierra Railway, served the Lassen Lumber and Box Company but ended its days on Red River Lumber Company rails. (Special Collections, Library, California State University, Chico)

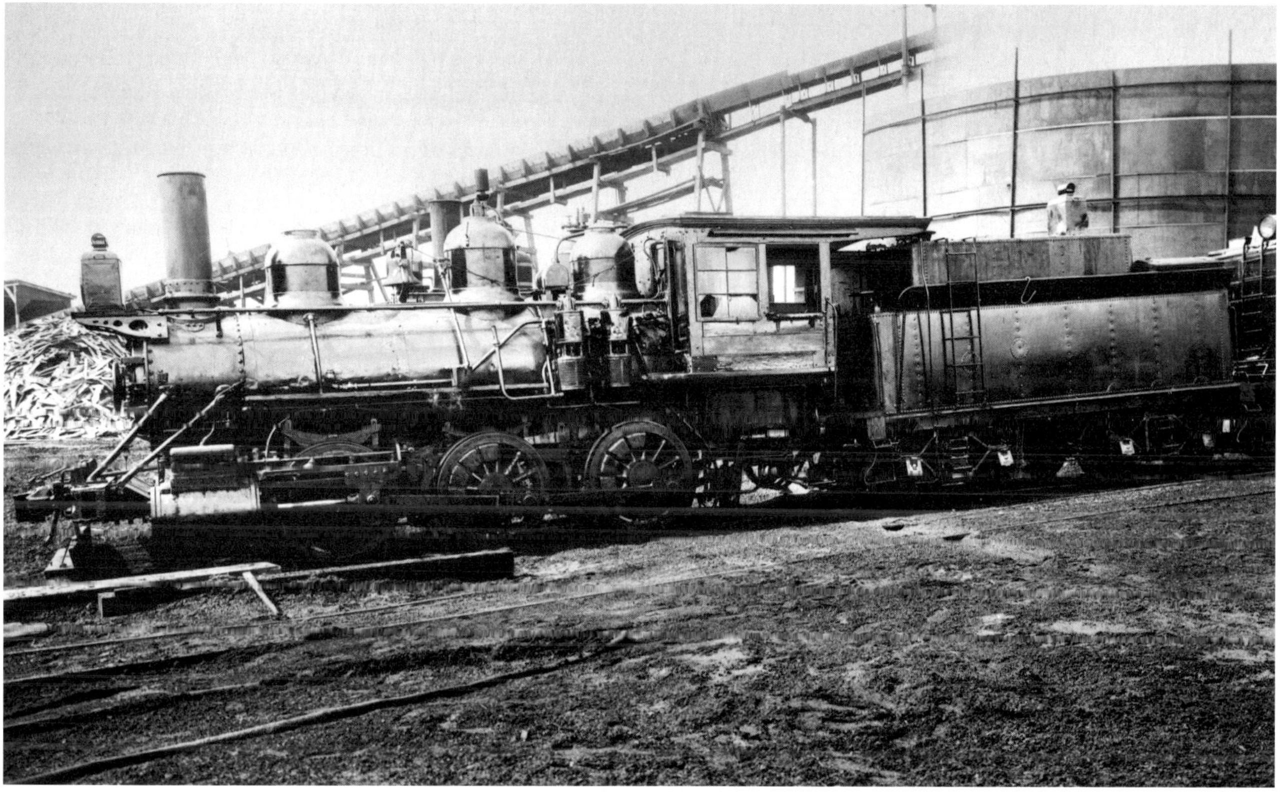

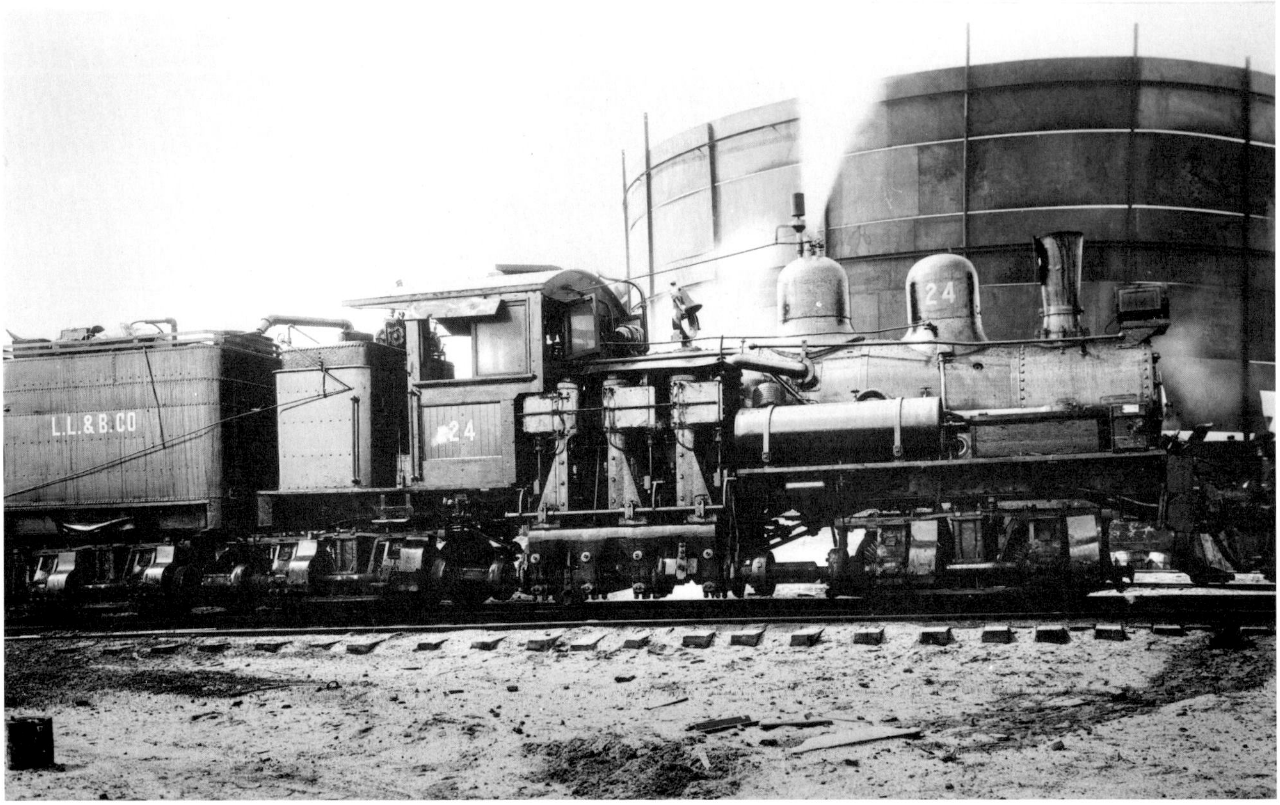

Above: The Lassen Lumber and Box Company's Shay carried the road number 24. (Special Collections, Library, California State University, Chico)

Below: No. 25, manufactured by Baldwin in 1923, was the only engine LL&B purchased from a builder, as all others had previous owners. After Red River bought the three remaining LL&B engines in 1929, it then sold this locomotive to the Modesto and Empire Traction Company six years later. (Special Collections, Library, California State University, Chico)

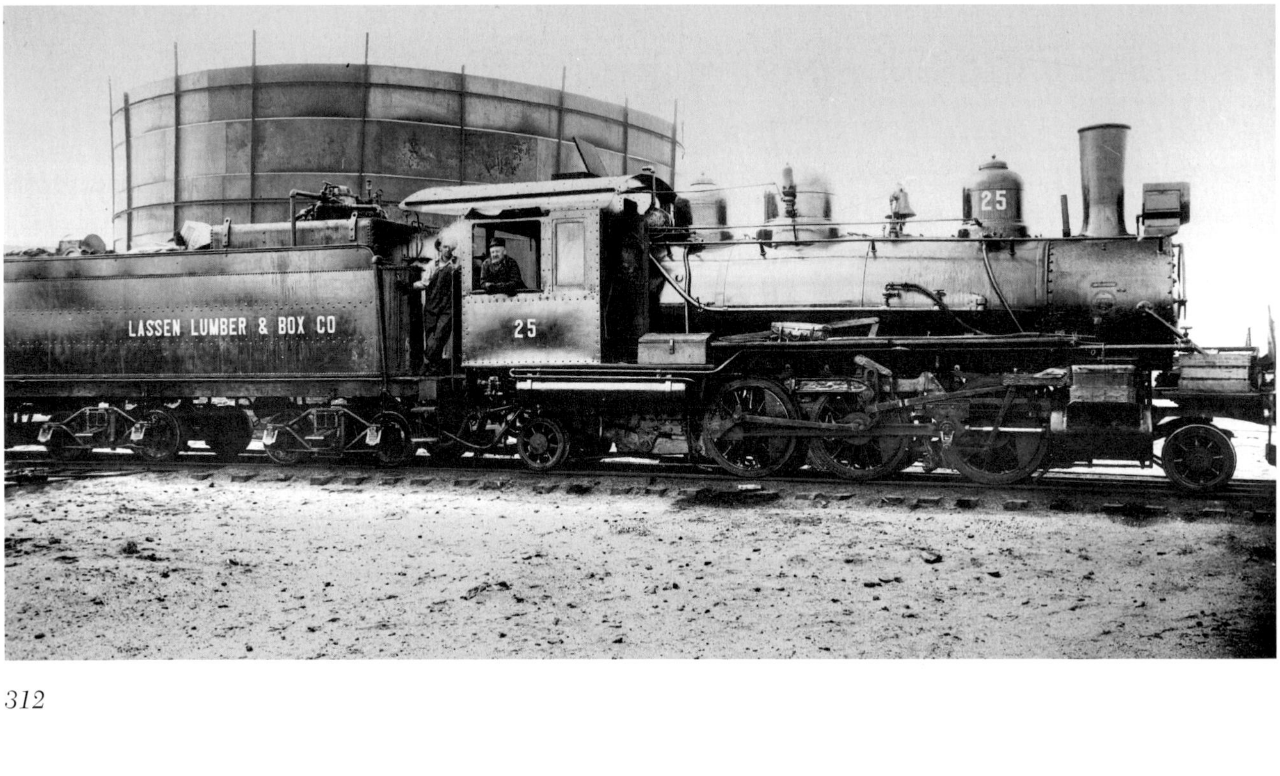

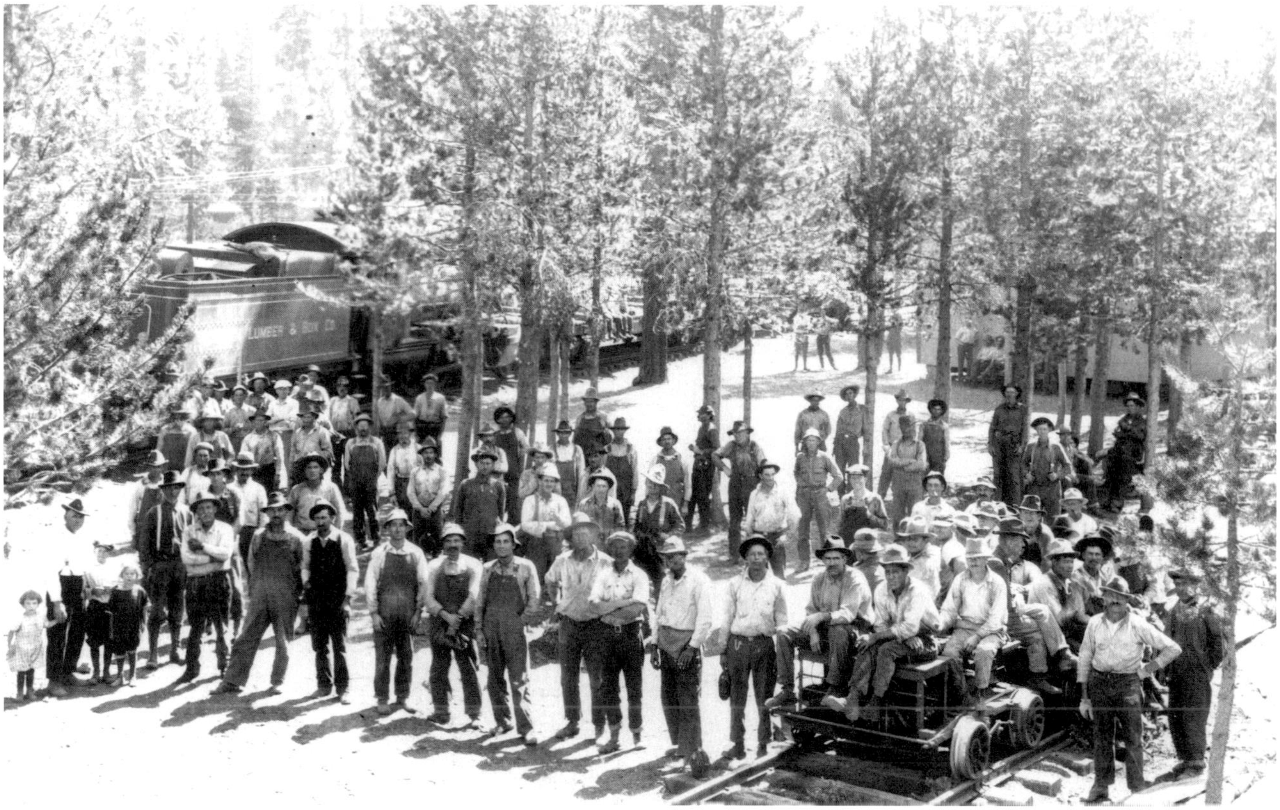

Above: Some of the workers included their children in this group photograph at Lasco. (Lassen County Historical Society)

Below: No. 1 sawmill and workers' cottages at Susanville. (Lassen County Historical Society)

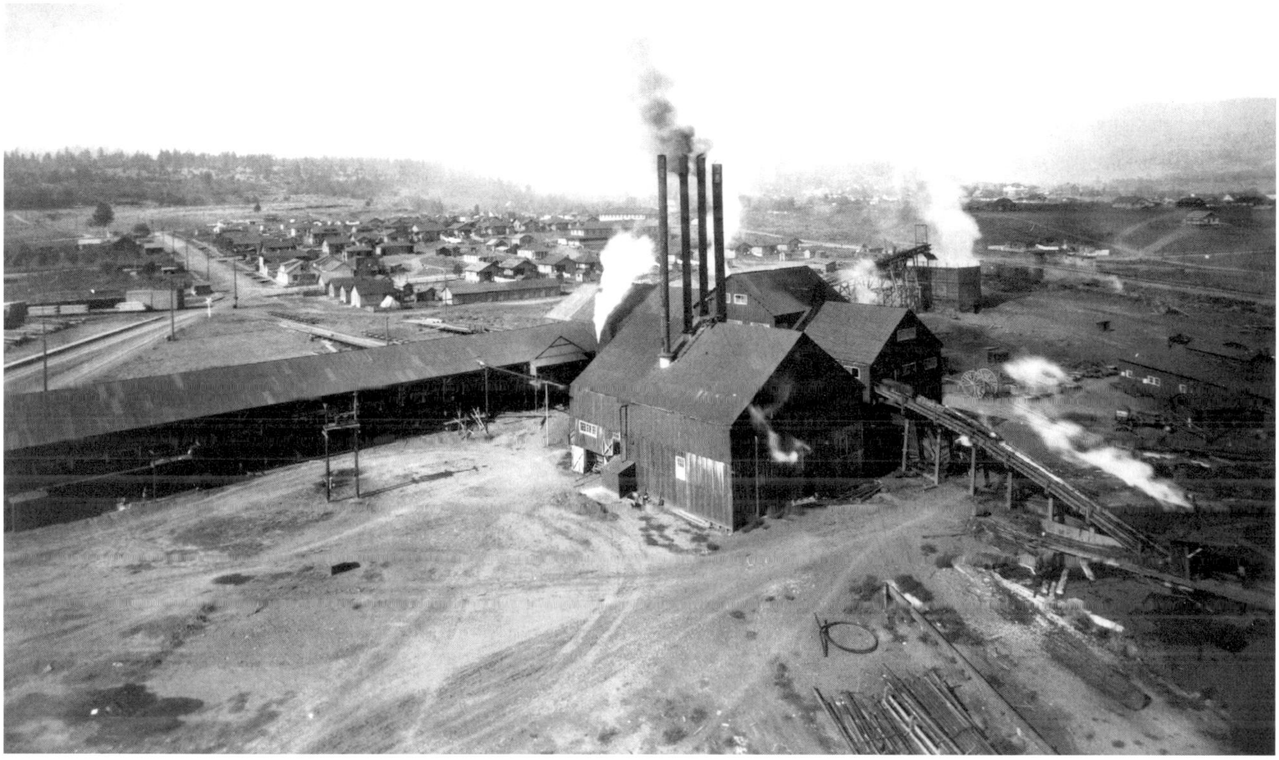

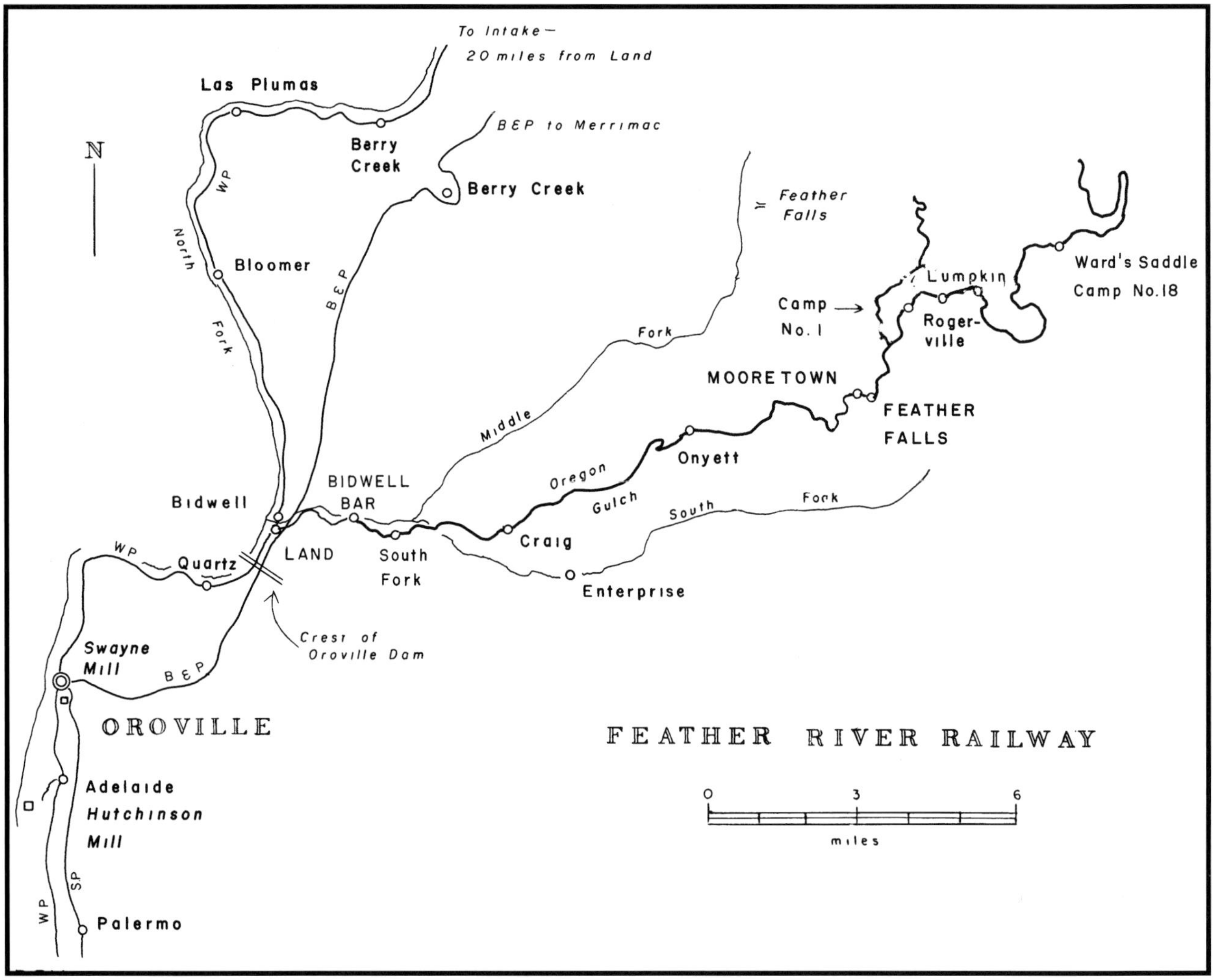

To Intake—
20 miles from Land
Las Plumas
Berry
Creek
BEP to Merrimac
Berry Creek
N
WP
North
Fork
Bloomer
BEP
Feather
Falls
Middle
Fork
Camp
No. 1
Lumpkin
Rogerville
Ward's Saddle
Camp No. 18
MOORETOWN
FEATHER
FALLS
Onyett
Oregon
Gulch
BIDWELL
BAR
Bidwell
LAND
South
Fork
Craig
South
Fork
Enterprise
WP
Quartz
Crest of
Oroville Dam
Swayne
Mill
BEP
OROVILLE
Adelaide
Hutchinson
Mill
WP
SP
Palermo
FEATHER RIVER RAILWAY
0
3
6
miles

FEATHER RIVER RAILWAY

The story of the Feather River Railway began with a Huntington, West Virginia, organization under the name of the Hutchinson Lumber Company incorporated by R. L. Hutchinson on February 3, 1910. Beginning with a small capitalization (fifty thousand dollars), the company operated small mills in the hardwood country, some fifty miles south of Huntington, with timber from Logan and Mingo Counties. A subsidiary, Broad River Lumber Company, harvested both white pine and hardwood near Asheville, North Carolina. Over the years, the authorized stock increased several times to reach two million dollars in 1920.

With the support of John Laing, who headed several coal mining companies near Charleston, and several bankers, including Andrew Hunter Land from Logan who also held coal mines, Hutchinson was able to fulfill his desire to look westward and secure new timber areas in Butte and Plumas Counties, California. Through George L. Hoxie, Hutchinson purchased part of the Wheeler timberland situated between the Middle and South Forks of the Feather River and about a dozen miles or so east of Bidwell Bar.

Already nearby Oroville could boast of the large mill of the Swayne Lumber Company, but William Boucher, the active secretary of the chamber of commerce, persuaded Hutchinson to establish his mill on a large tract south of the Western Pacific Railroad shops. With the chamber of commerce donating half the cost of the land, Hutchinson decided to locate his mill in Oroville.

Some 25 miles stood between the timber and the mill site. The Western Pacific Railroad covered the 7 miles between Oroville and Bidwell, leaving a 17-mile gap to Mooretown, where the timber began. At that time, WP, ready to take reasonable steps to encourage additional traffic, was constructing the 12-mile Calpine branch east of Portola to serve the Davies-Johnson lumber mill.

The tenor of negotiations lacked publicity, but one could imagine that WP had committed to a substantial outlay, for the Calpine branch was not willing to do the same for Hutchinson. Accordingly, WP agreed to build 2.12 miles from Bidwell to Bidwell Bar, leaving most of the distance the responsibility of Hutchinson.

At that moment—January 1921—postwar economic conditions invoked caution among entrepreneurs. After meeting in San Francisco and Oroville, O. C. Griffith and Luther Griffith, vice president and general manager, respectively, concurred with R. L. Hutchinson, president, that work would proceed at a slower pace. With the big Oroville mill scheduled to begin operations in April 1922, the mountain railroad stood essential for log deliveries, but a smaller force would be employed. To link the Oroville mill with WP at Adelaide station, local contractor J. A. Huntington began work on the mile-long industrial lead track. Around the middle of March, one hundred workers, a WP work train, and numerous civil engineers had graded and laid a quarter of a mile of track paralleling Palermo Road. After another week, with ballasting completed, the spur stood ready to receive cars of building materials.

A large steam shovel arrived to dig a log pond, said to be one of the biggest log ponds in northern California. From Oregon sawmills, lumber for the mill structure began arriving over the new spur.

Up in the mountains, engineers located the logging railroad east of Bidwell. In March 1921, WP engaged the Toughy brothers to build its share of the connection to Bidwell Bar. General manager Luther Griffith told a chamber of commerce meeting that mill construction would begin September 1 and operations the following March. Work has already started on the thirty-room boardinghouse. Concurrently, changes occurred at Feather River Falls; the name was shortened to Feather Falls, and this scenic attraction found mention in a new travelogue of the Sacramento Northern Railroad. Some people tried to change the name of the old '49 mining town of Mooretown to Feather Falls. A new hotel, the Feather Falls Inn, rose in Mooretown, but the original village name prevailed for many years.

The Hutchinson Lumber Company standard-gauge railroad followed the south bank of the Middle Fork of the Feather River for about a mile, then turned slightly south to continue along the South Fork for a third of a mile. After crossing to the north side of the river and entering Oregon Gulch, it passed over the land of G. C. Onyett. With Mooretown situated on a ridge rising abruptly some 300 feet, locating engineers pushed north for 8,000 feet before looping back to finish the climb to Mooretown. However, the amended location approached the village from the south side. Mooretown stands about 2,600 feet above Bidwell Bar, thus challenging the locating engineers to accomplish this climb in 17.4 miles. They accepted grades of 5.2 percent in some places, unusually high for railroads.

Before much work had been done, chief engineer T. F. Phillips resigned; S. J. Norris followed him. Previously, Norris had been Oroville city engineer and engineer of the Oroville-Wyandotte Irrigation District. Oroville citizens watched the progress of the new railroad; the local press catered to this interest when reporting that Warren A. Bechtel, after securing the railroad construction contract, approached the work site through the settlement of Enterprise. His plans called for erection of several buildings on the south side of the South Fork.

Responding to the company invitation, Oroville businessmen drove their cars to Bidwell Bar on August 3, 1921, to inspect the progress of the work. They walked and drove their autos over parts of the railroad grade to observe some 350 men utilizing 250 head of livestock pulling scrapers or carts. Three steam shovels were busy cutting away the hillsides.

That the railroad was unusually well designed and built for a lumber road—except for the 5 percent grades—evoked praise from qualified observers, who likened it to a transcontinental line. George W. Mathews, who had been part of the Union Pacific survey team working along the Middle Fork during 1888–1889, remarked that the Hutchinson location almost matched the earlier surveys.

While W. A. Bechtel held most of the contract, J. A. Huntington secured a 4.5-mile subcontract, and Hunt Brothers had a subcontract near Mooretown. It was at the engineers' camp here that the visitors convened for a sumptuous luncheon.

In the fall, foundation work kept 130 men busy at the mill site, while Western Pacific moved a tracklaying machine to Bidwell (Jct.) to lay rail on its portion of the new line. Bechtel purchased six idle passenger cars from the recently abandoned Ocean Shore Railway and brought them to Oroville, where he had one converted to a kitchen dining room and the others into outfit (sleeping) cars. After reaching Bidwell Bar, the tracklaying machine continued to work on the Hutchinson railroad; by December 10, steel rails extended as far as the South Fork. Bechtel suspended work here for three weeks while workers erected a 280-foot wooden bridge 70 feet above the river.

All appeared to be going well on the entire project as the year ended. The 305 x 77–foot mill structure for the three-band sawmill rose rapidly, earning great admiration for Charles B. Sewell for finishing the building just forty-five days after starting work on the foundations. In the mountains, railroad grading to Mooretown neared completion when a massive proposal threatened to make the railroad useless and undermine the entire project.

The Yuba Development Company sought authority from the Federal Power Commission to build a huge dam on the Middle Fork near Bidwell Bar. At the hearings in San Francisco, Hutchinson voiced his objections, explaining that it would submerge the railroad and that an alternate route would add a million dollars to the cost and double operating expenses because of stiffer grades.

C. E. Grunsky, a San Francisco civil engineer appearing for the lumber company, proposed a less obtrusive dam a short distance above the confluence with the South Fork. Details of the proceedings have been lost in bureaucratic files; suffice it to say, no dam was built in either location.

Heavy rains in the weeks following Christmas retarded railroad work, so the eight-mile gap to Mooretown remained. Questioned about a completion date, Bechtel replied that it depended on the weather.

Down at the Oroville plant, machinery began filling the mill buildings, and Great Western Power, after winning a contest with Pacific Gas and Electric, finished installing its power lines to the mill. GWP would also furnish electricity to operate logging equipment in the woods, which reduced the fire danger. At the close of March 1922, Western Pacific officials toured the plant and the railroad. Charles Levey, WP's president, declared the Hutchinson railroad as "one of the most substantial lumber roads he had ever seen."

Some weeks later, J. W. Dawson, reportedly a former railroad president, was now supervising the finishing stages of the work; the last rails to Mooretown were spiked on May 5, 1922. Three days later, a combination of railroads—Hutchinson and WP—delivered the initial five cars of logs to the millpond at Adelaide, just below Oroville.

Oroville Celebrates the New Enterprise

Most stores closed at three o'clock on May 23 so that Oroville people could celebrate the opening of the big mill. After R. L. Hutchinson addressed the crowd, his granddaughter, Kathryn Bird Dickenson, flipped the switch, placing the saws in motion.

When rails reach Mooretown, it marked the second step in railroad work, the WP spur being the first. To provide a good supply of logs, tracks had to be pushed deeper into the timberlands. Rather than rely on outside contractors, Hutchinson recruited workers locally. The following appeared in the *Oroville Daily Register* on May 9, 1922:

Men Wanted

> Experienced track layers, spikers and section men, white, can get steady work at good pay at Bidwell Bar on Orietta Siding, four miles beyond Enterprise.
>
> Take the seven o'clock stage out of Oroville for Mooretown and get off at railroad camp (driver will tell you), or take this notice with you to Bidwell Bar and it will pass you with your bed on construction train to camp, three miles up railroad.

The day after dedicating the mill, President Hutchinson seated eighty guests on three flatcars for a trip on the new railroad. Arriving at Bidwell Bar in their autos, the group boarded the waiting train, first going over the WP spur to Bidwell, then returning and continuing to Logging Camp No. 1 for "an elaborate spread" in the spacious dining room. Those on the excursion included R. L. Hutchinson and W. A. Bechtel and their wives, S. D. Bechtel, S. J. Norris and his family, and other lumber company officials. E. W. Mason, vice president and general manager; J. W. Williams, chief engineer; and Charles Elsey, treasurer, represented Western Pacific.

Physical characteristics of the road called for seventy-five pound rail (eighty-five-pound on the curves) with two Shay locomotives, seventy tons and ninety tons, providing the motive power. Initially, WP provided flatcars for transporting logs. Bechtel told friends that fifteen carloads of dynamite proved necessary to cut a four-mile path for one portion of the railroad.

The guests enjoyed the pleasant spring outing. Ted O'Doul, one Hutchinson man, was so delighted with his day and particularly his meal—prepared by Jay Shannon and Mike O'Leary—that he penned "Ode to the Pines," which later appeared in the local press.

Some management changes came next. O. C. Griffith, general manager, left to take the same position at the North Carolina subsidiary. J. W. Dawson, "director of the railroad," with his work done, believed that he could resign but stayed on as a corporate director. With railroad spurs reaching into the woods, the mill soon received twenty cars of logs daily; subsequently, the number rose to thirty cars.

R. F. Pray resigned his position from the Red River Lumber Company to become the vice president and general manager of the Hutchinson enterprise in January 1923. In doing so, he ended a thirty-year stint with Red River, having been resident manager of the Akeley, Minnesota, plant since 1899 and holding the same position at Westwood since 1913. Before he left, nearly 400 Westwood employees gave a dinner in his honor and presented him with a 156-piece set of silverware. Two days later, as he started his drive to Oroville on January 15, 1923, the local band and a number of friends escorted him to the edge of Westwood.

Shortly after Pray joined the team, the company announced plans to double its output by summer, a move that necessitated more logging and more trains. Accordingly, the company ordered two more Shay locomotives, additional donkey engines, and 104 logging cars.

About this time, the company payroll listed 461 names, divided between milling and logging and the railroad. Even though a good number of dwellings had been added in Oroville, employee housing remained critical, with 38 workers living in tents or shacks and suffering during the winter cold. With the forthcoming expected expansion, the payroll would soar to 1,000, exacerbating the problem. In an effort to alleviate the situation, company officers formed the Oroville Housing Corporation, but their accomplishments went unreported.

The expansion resulted in more camps in the woods. Two were "on wheels," to be moved about to various cutting areas as needed. Of the twenty-eight cars assigned to each camp, the list included two diners, one for cooking, a refrigerator car for food, and a recreation car. The sleeping cars, measuring forty-two by twelve feet, provided beds for each of the eight men assigned to a car. Bed linens were changed weekly. Ventilation received appropriate consideration, and each car possessed a shower. In March 1923, an unidentified Seattle firm was reportedly manufacturing additional cars.

The company established a headquarters camp for men and their families, while a fourth camp housed the railroad-extension crew. During the construction of the main railroad, the engineering force occupied the historic Lumpkin Hotel that the company had purchased from one B. B. Meek. An afternoon fire on March 23, 1923, ended the career of the venerable hotel.

Working in the woods or on the railroad was not without dangers. One conductor lost his life when he fell under a car during a switching move. Another man fell from the top of a sixty-five-foot pole at Camp No. 4. He must have said the right prayers, for angels spared his life; a badly bruised back was his only major injury.

A New Corporate Domicile

In March 1923, the company incorporated a subsidiary with the same name under California laws. A property inventory listed the mill with three saws, dry kilns, a box factory, twenty-one miles of railroad, and 32,401 acres of timberland. The acreage held an estimated 988 million board feet of timber, primarily consisting of sugar pine, white pine, white fir, and red fir. California white (ponderosa) pine and other species made up the balance.

An independent appraiser estimated the value of the property at $4,719,000, of which the logging railroad amounted to $830,000 and the railroad equipment $90,000.

During Pray's regime, mill workers formed their own baseball team. When he was not managing the mill, Pray sat on a side bench watching every match, and his son, Rupert, served as team mascot.

The company bought another 31,000 acres of timberland in May 1923 from the William Wheeler interests and about the same time acquired the works of the Indiana Machine Shop Company in Oroville. Originally set up to repair gold-dredging equipment, the shop commenced repairing lumber machinery after gold dredging became extinct.

Handicapped by lower lumber-market prices, all these improvements failed to yield a satisfactory performance, so the company garnered another million dollars by selling bonds to some of its West Virginia shareholders. In a change in management, R. L. Hutchinson stepped aside, and John Laing became president in November 1923. Born in Glasgow, Scotland, he came to the United States as a small child and began his business career driving a mule team for a coal mine in West Virginia at the age of twelve. Now he headed five operating coal companies as well as a Charleston bank.

R. L. Pray's resignation became effective at the same time, and Andrew Hunter Land, the former banker who had followed the company finances for the past two years while he made his home in Oroville, became vice president with complete control of operations.

A Scourge of Fires

In California, the year 1924 stands out with little rain and many forest fires. In one ten-day period in July, foresters counted 218 forest and brush fires in California, of which 179 were in national forests. Repeatedly, fires threatened villages. Only a change in the wind saved Calpine and Sattley from destruction. Verdi, Nevada, escaped annihilation in August thanks to the presence of fire engines and crews from Reno. On the periphery of Susanville, several houses were taken by the flames.

Hutchinson Lumber received praise for its precautions. A. H. Land reported that a trailer followed each train, watching for incipient fires. The use of electricity for powering donkey engines reduced the fire dangers, and night watchmen patrolled lumber camps.

All these efforts could not stem the losses the company suffered on July 28 and 29. When fire swept through timber one and one-half miles northwest of Lumpkin, it destroyed two electric donkey engines and other logging equipment, a quarter of a mile of railroad track, and several buildings at Camp 4. Flames also consumed about a million board feet of logs cut and waiting to be sent to the mill. With men drawn from Camps 1 and 5, some 350 Hutchinson men fought the blaze.

By the next night, the fire had been brought under control. Camp 5, three and one-half miles northeast of Lumpkin, a "model camp" with fifty buildings, was burned to the ground along with a refrigerator car and cooking, dining, and commissary cars. For a time, 8 firefighters were trapped before managing to escape. This fire, which also wiped out three thousand acres of timber, was believed of incendiary origin, as no one had worked in the area for the previous two weeks where the fire began.

Adding to the woes of the company, the lumber market suffered that year, and Hutchinson, seeking to keep men employed in the mill and woods, followed the action of other lumber companies by trimming wages. The ensuing years failed to improve the fortunes of the company, and it was sold under foreclosure on April 22, 1927.

Feather River Pine Mills Inc.

After managing the Hutchinson Lumber Company for several years, Andrew H. Land bought out his partners and transferred the property to Feather River Pine Mills Inc., which he had incorporated on May 16, 1927. Born in Virginia in 1866, the senior Land, remembered as "the perfect southern gentlemen" by fellow lumbermen, received his education at Virginia Military Institute. Settling in Bluefield, West Virginia, he entered the mercantile business in 1892 and soon became involved in banking and coal mine operations. He also served his community as mayor for two years.

Though the forest fires of 1924 proved costly, the real disaster began in the late afternoon of October 6, 1927, when a fire swept across the Oroville plant, consuming the sawmill, box factory, and fifty million feet of lumber in the yards. Only the office and stable survived the $2 million fire.

As the fire was advancing, records were removed for safety, and with the flames subdued, paychecks were distributed to employees. Questioned about the future, Land replied that he was undecided about rebuilding the mill. After receiving a settlement from the insurance carriers, Land deposited the proceeds in a Detroit bank while formulating plans. Then another blow came: the bank failed, wiping out the depositors.

The enterprise turned idle. The dormant railroad, offered to Western Pacific, failed to interest that company. The general slump in business in the nationwide depression discouraged thoughts of renewing lumbering.

After a decade of inactivity, Land in 1938, feeling that a renewed demand for lumber was approaching, secured an $850,000 loan from the Reconstruction Finance Corporation to build two sawmills, one at Feather Falls (adjoining Mooretown) and a smaller facility at Ward that was leased to an independent operator.

Rather than continuing the railroad as a plant facility, A. H. Land made it a common carrier, for then it could participate in a division of interline freight receipts. He incorporated the Feather River Railway Company on October 13, 1939, and the following January his attorneys filed two applications with the Interstate Commerce Commission. First, they sought authority for the railroad to operate between Land, the name of the connection with Western Pacific, and Ward, 28.43 miles away, under the Interstate Commerce Act.

Next, his attorneys sought ICC permission to issue 605 shares of $100-par common stock. Of this number, 505 shares were to be issued to the parent lumber company in exchange for two Shay engines, one caboose, and two gasoline speeders. The remaining 100 shares were sold to the parent company for $100,000 cash for working capital. No one stepped forward to object, and the ICC granted both applications on May 24, 1940.

The railroad property continued to be carried on the books of the lumber company with a ledger value of $1,529,624, for which Feather River Railway paid an annual rental of $15,000. For the use of the two miles of road between Land and Bidwell Bar, the new railway proposed to pay WP about $2,700 each year. While the new railway maintained several portions of the line, the lumber company assumed the expense of rehabilitation. Already $32,210 had been spent rebuilding the railway between Feather Falls and Ward, but another $19,901 was necessary to repair the remaining section to Bidwell Bar.

In its application to the ICC, the railway estimated the kinds of traffic anticipated. Logs and lumber would make up the major share of the traffic, but for cattle and sheep shipments, the new railway contemplated building a livestock corral at Ward.

No passenger trains ran over the rails except for special excursions. On October 9 10, 1954, a year after Georgia-Pacific had purchased the lumber company from the Land family, the Railway and Locomotive Historical Society joined the California-Nevada Railroad Historical in sponsoring "The Feather Falls Flyer," an all-expenses-paid weekend tour. Leaving San Francisco in the late afternoon on Western Pacific, passengers spent the night in Pullman cars parked at Oroville. Traveling behind a Shay locomotive from Land on a pleasant fall day, the group arrived at Feather Falls and, after lunch, returned to San Francisco that evening. Another local excursion was offered June 1, 1963.

The Oroville Dam Brings the End of the Line

The Feather River Railway, essentially serving only one shipper, moved a weekly average of twenty cars in 1939 and thirty-nine cars in 1961, most destined to points outside California. During that time, careful operation of the railway enabled it to show a small profit. All this was to change in the next few years.

Not only did the Oroville Dam across the Feather River necessitate an extensive relocation of Western Pacific, but a protracted struggle also ended the career of the Feather River Railway. The management of the short line, recognizing that impounding waters would cover the first six miles from Land to Craig, filed a two-part application with the ICC on April 19, 1962. The company sought authority to abandon the portion of the flooded line and replace it with a new railroad between Craig and Quartz, a station on Western Pacific just below the dam. (Later, the proposed connection was moved to Palermo, a station six miles below Oroville.)

The State of California, through the Department of Water Resources, sought to cause abandonment of the entire railway. Feather River Pine Mills, owner of the stock of the railway and practically the sole patron, saw things differently and contended the state should build the new connection between Craig and Palermo. State officials took a dim view of underwriting the line that they estimated would cost between $5 and $8 million.

Confusing legal issues focused on the state's responsibility to provide a new connection for the railroad that it sought to annihilate. In a three-part decision of January 16, 1954, the ICC authorized abandonment of the section from Land to Craig upon commencement of operation of a new line from Craig to Palermo. The decision also "required the acquisition of, or, the operation over, a line to be constructed by the State of California between Craig and Palermo by the Feather River Railway." The order also directed the Feather River Railway to operate over 20.4 miles of the former WP line from Land to Intake (now state owned) until the Palermo trackage became viable. The printed decision, Finance Docket No. 22060 (320 ICC 417), reviewed the economic issues in the area served by the railway.

Matters dragged on in the struggle between the state and Georgia-Pacific. Sleuths from the state found that the railway's twenty-five-year permit to cross federal lands had allegedly expired in 1947, whereupon the Bureau of Land Management notified the railway to vacate within six months.

Meanwhile, the big storm of December 1964 sweeping across northern California flooded the railroad around Land and covered portions of the Land-Intake

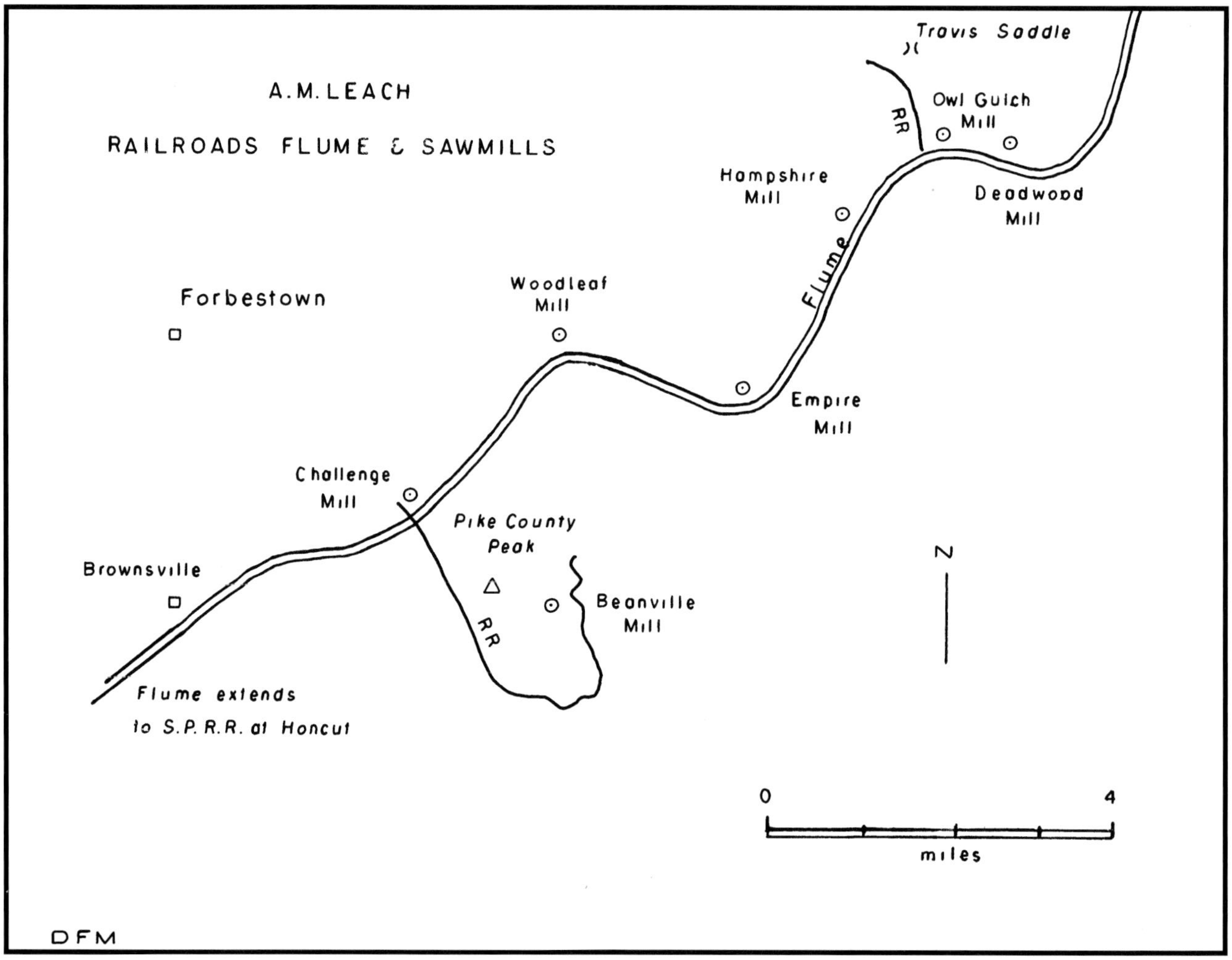

trackage with mud. Some weeks went by before the tracks could be cleared.

On the little railway, two small diesel locomotives supplemented the powerful but slow Shay engines, particularly when moving cars over the former WP line to Intake.

The contest with the state ended with an agreement signed December 9, 1965, wherein the state purchased the six miles of flooded railroad and handed the lumber company a check for $1,322,605, and Georgia-Pacific agreed to end all rail operations by October 1, 1966. After that, the company employed highway carriers to move its logs and lumber.

A. M. Leach Railroads and Flume

One of the lost railroad systems in California complemented a flume to bring lumber from the mills around Challenge, eight miles south of Feather Falls, to Honcut (Moore's Station) on SP's Oroville branch.

While sawmilling commenced at Challenge as early as 1856, the area became more important when A. M. Leach began construction of his flume in 1879. Including ten miles of intake flumes, the total length of the system of flumes measured sixty miles. Most of the flume consisted of a five-foot ditch, except at ravines that it crossed on trestles, some more than one hundred feet high, or when the watercourse flowed through six different tunnels.

Leach operated seven sawmills between Owl Gulch Creek and Challenge. From these mills, he sent rough lumber down the flumes to be finished at his Honcut planing mill. Two short railroads served the mills.

One railroad ran south from Challenge for six miles as it reached around Pike County Peak before turning north to follow Indian Creek in the direction of Woodville. Present maps suggest that part of Peterson Ridge Road runs on the former railroad grade. In the course of time, the mill was moved to the end of the railroad to be closer to timber at Beanville. Instead of hauling logs to Challenge, railroad cars conveyed the rough lumber to the flume at Challenge for the move to Honcut.

A very small locomotive served the second railroad in 1892 that ran up Owl Creek Gulch for about a mile. Leach's lumber and transportation system operated for several decades in spite of problems from snow and rock slides that damaged whole sections of the flume, necessitating expensive repairs. Leach's Honcut planing mill was consumed by a fire in the 1890s.

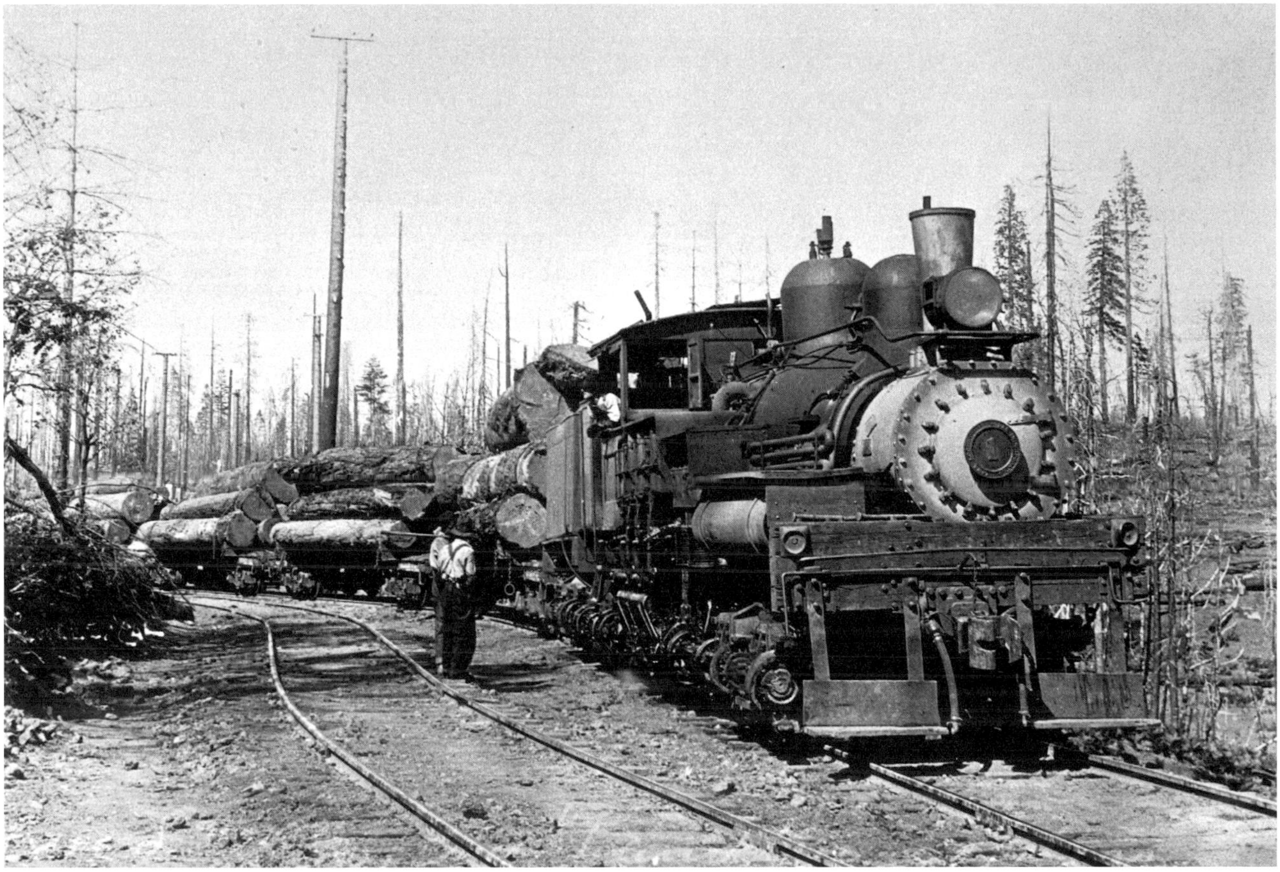

Hutchinson Lumber Company No. 1, a three-truck Shay, was built by Lima in 1921. When Dan McKellips, a legendary short-line locomotive engineer, snapped this picture about 1925, the train was working around a log burn near Feather Falls. As time progressed, the Shay went to the Feather River Pine Mills and to the Feather River Railway in 1939, always retaining its original road number. In 1961, the venerable engine went on display in Oroville. (James E. Boynton collection)

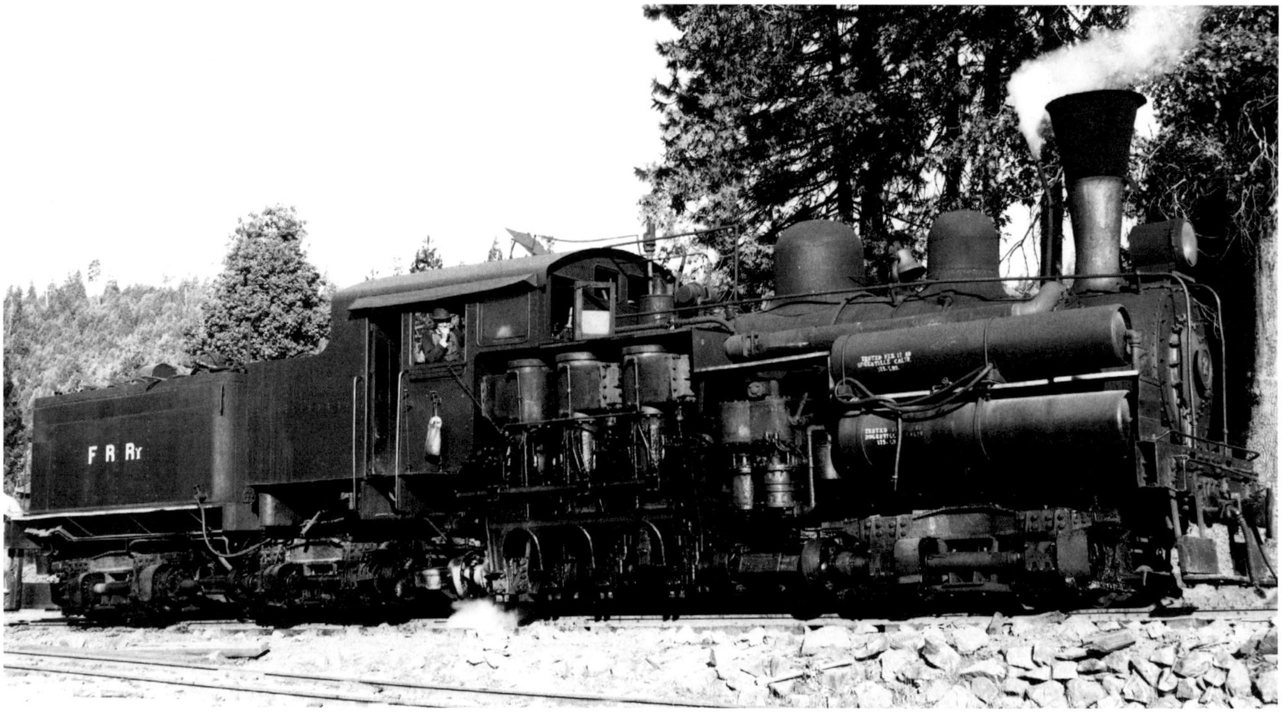

Above: No. 2 formed part of the locomotive roster of the Feather River Railway in 1949. (Ted Wurm photograph)

Below: It was early in the morning when Ted Wurm recorded No. 2 working up the grade near Rogerville.

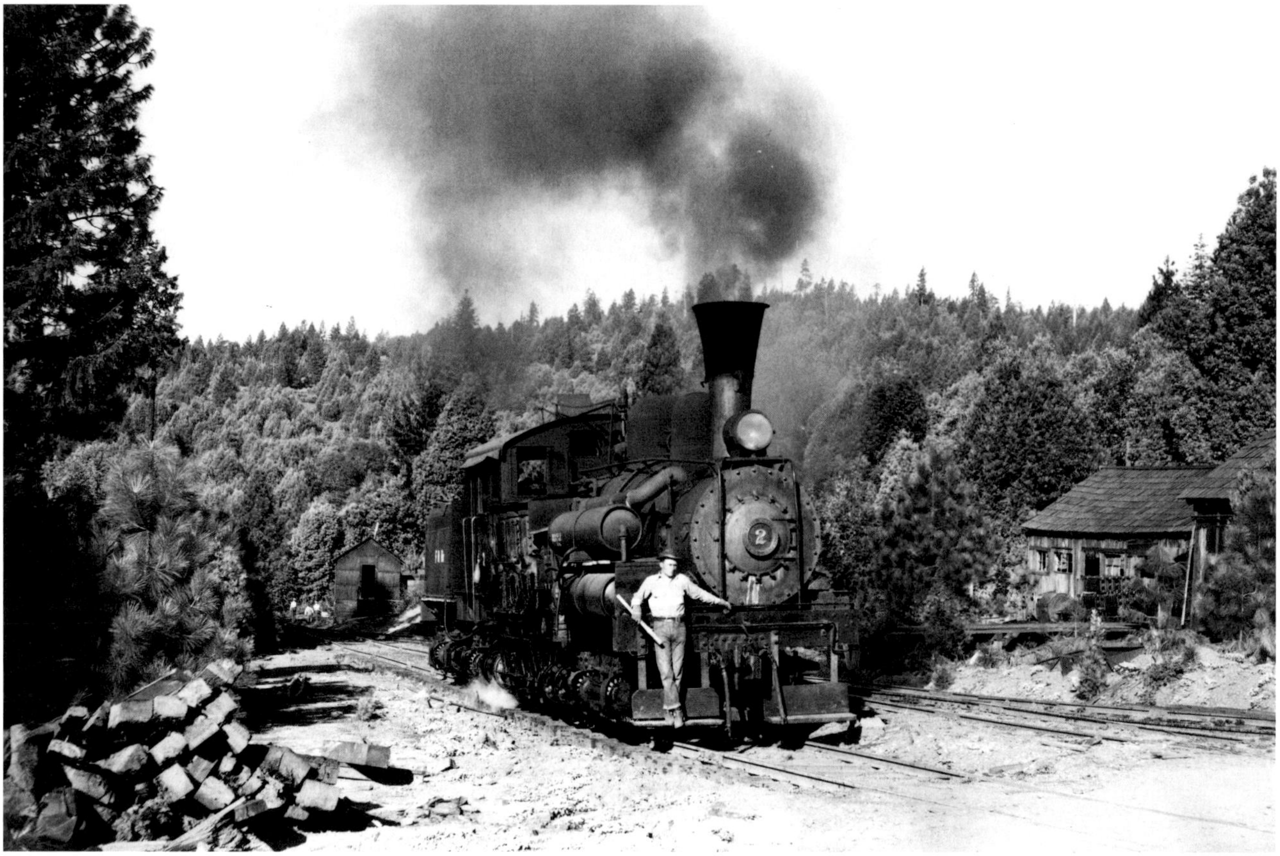

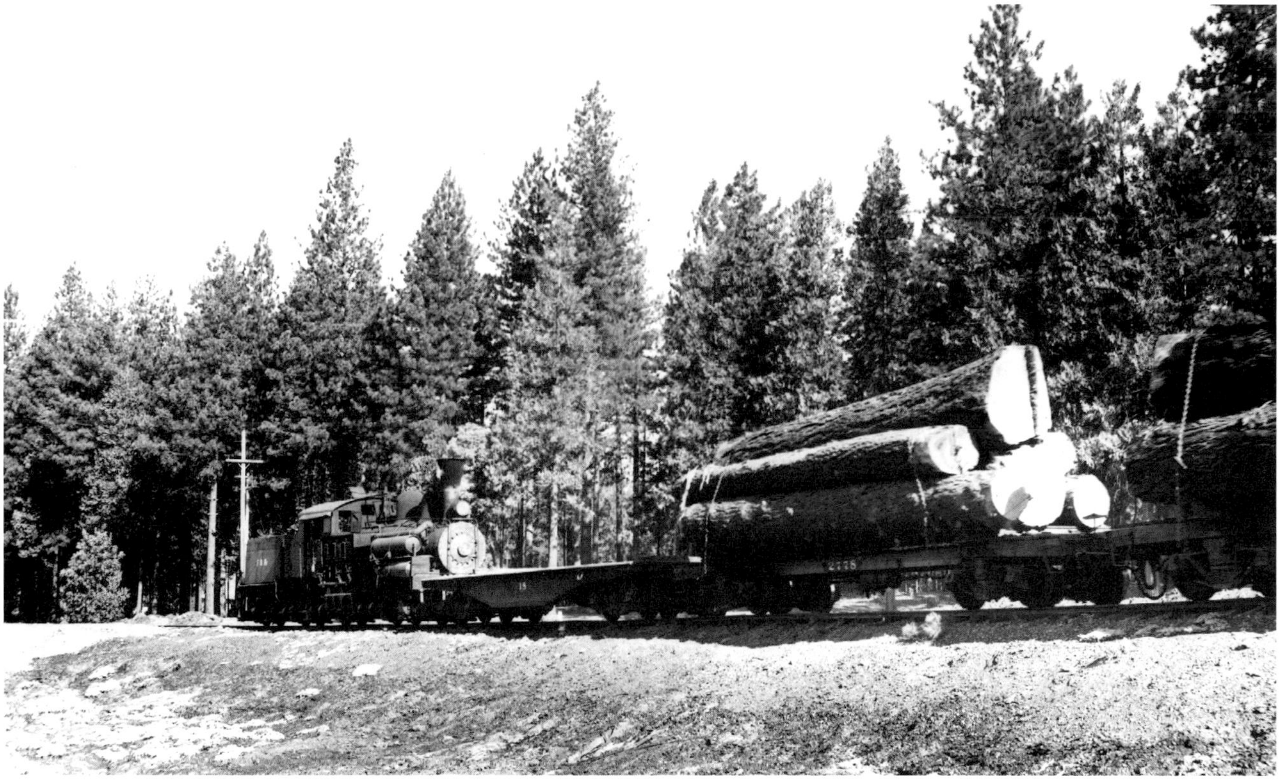

Above: No. 2 is about to push a log train into the yard by the mill at Feather Falls. (Ted Wurm photograph, 1949)

Below: Formerly No. 31 on the Polson Logging Company line, it became No. 91 when serving Rayonier and No. 5 when it operated on the Feather River Railway. (James E. Boynton collection)

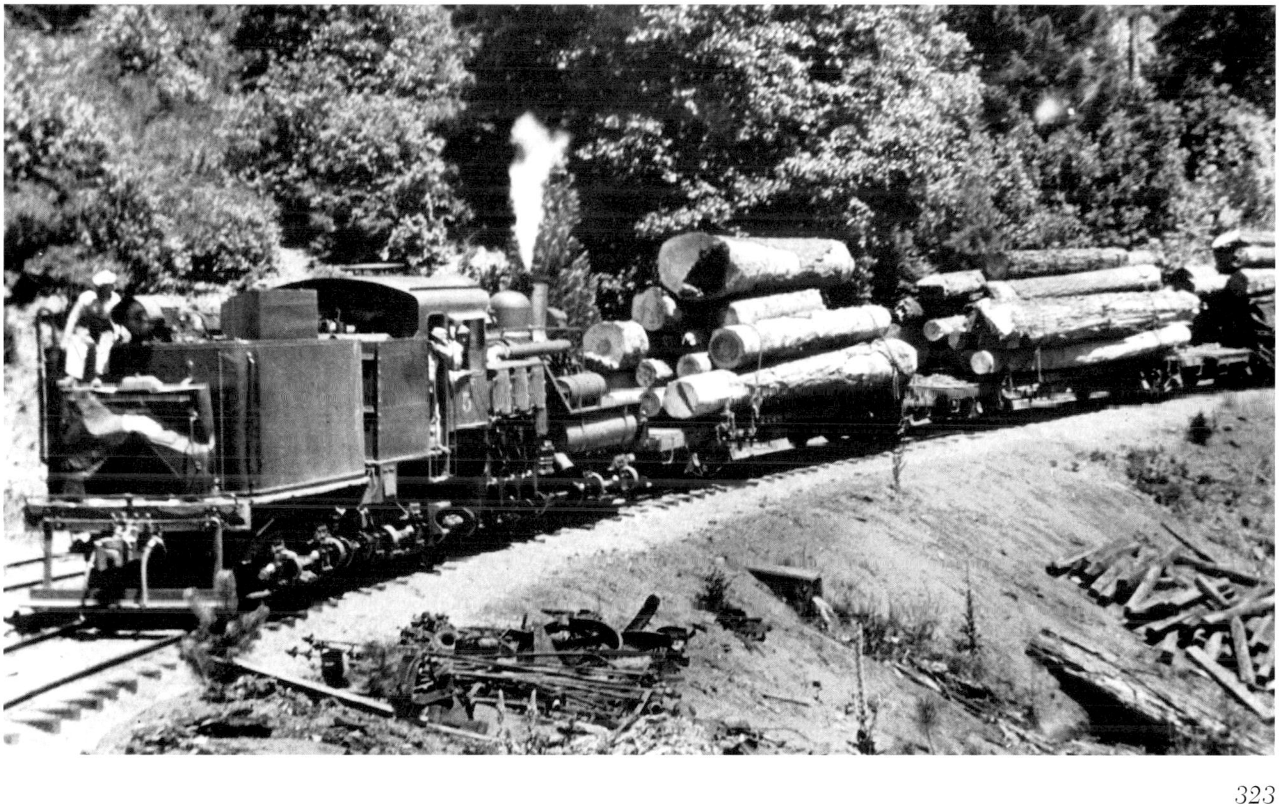

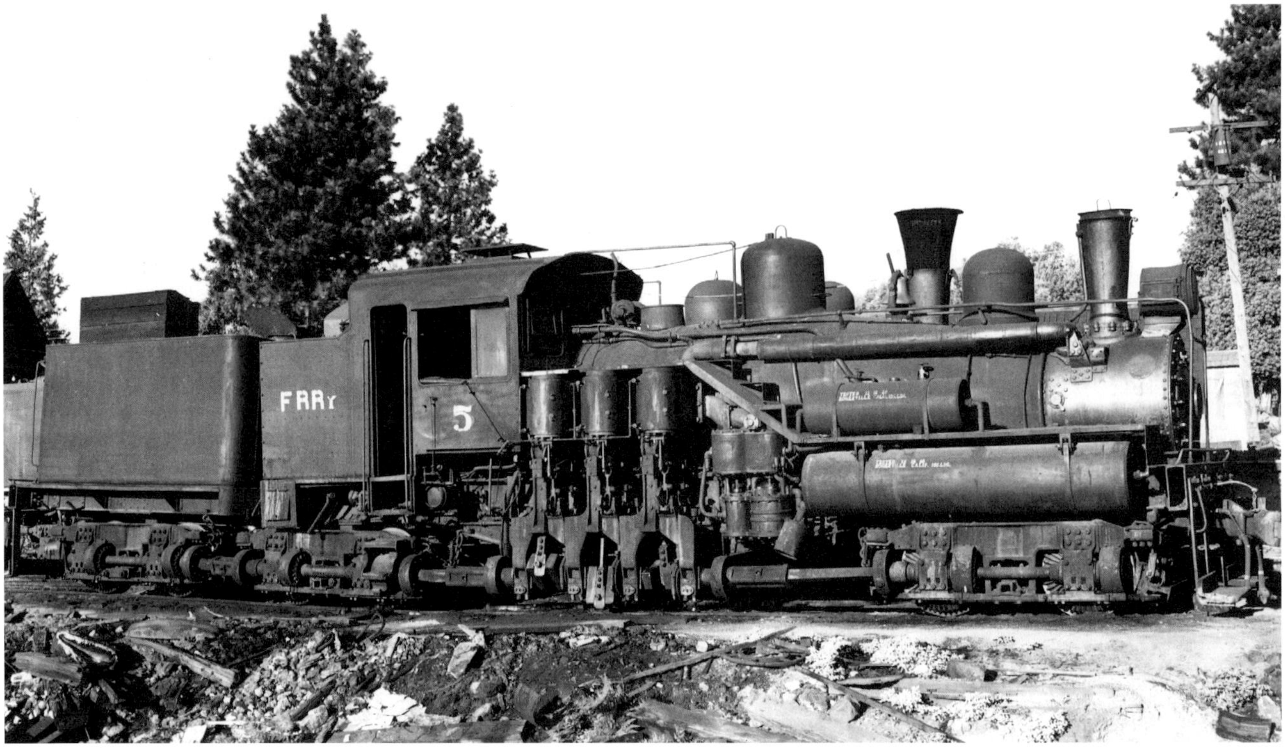

Above: Built by Willamette Iron and Steel Works in Portland, Oregon, in the style of Shay locomotives, No. 5 was one of almost two dozen erected by this firm. (Bert Ward photograph)

Below: To be closer to the timber area than the mill at Feather Falls, locomotives were serviced at the Rogerville shops. The main track leads to the woods, and the log train will be taken down the line to the mill. (Ted Wurm photograph)

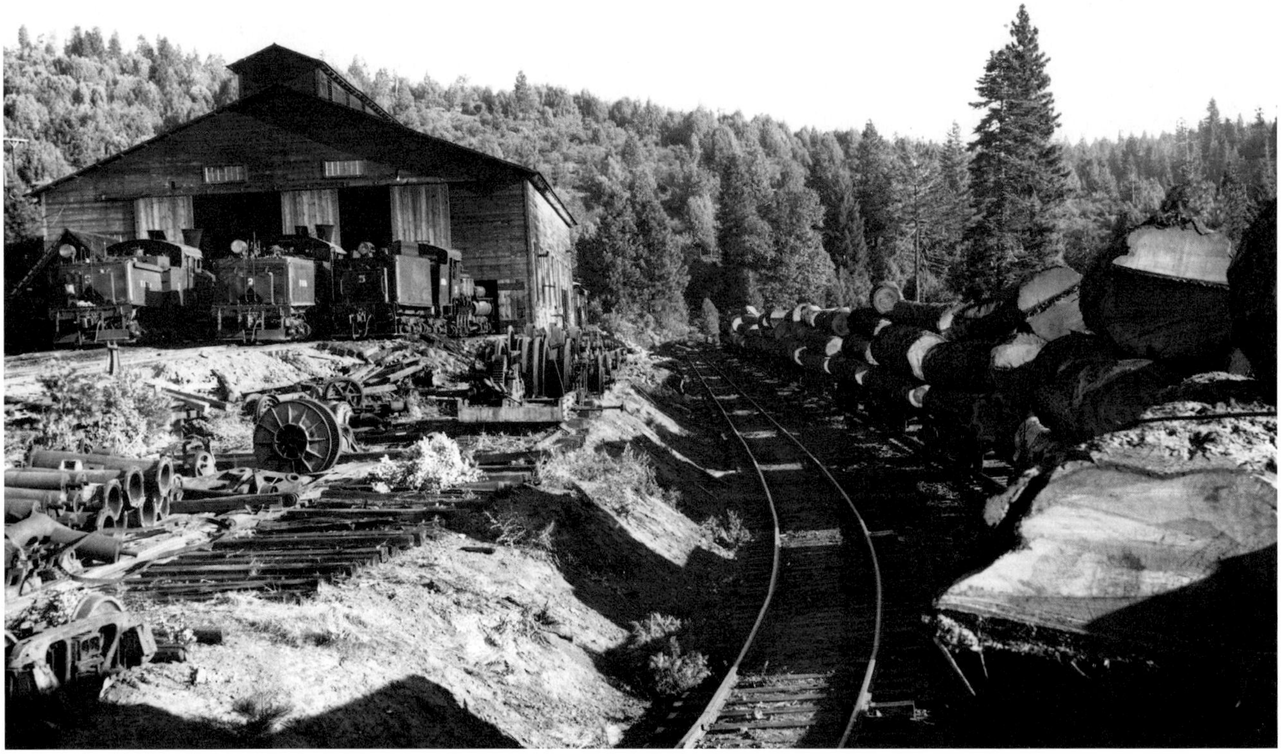

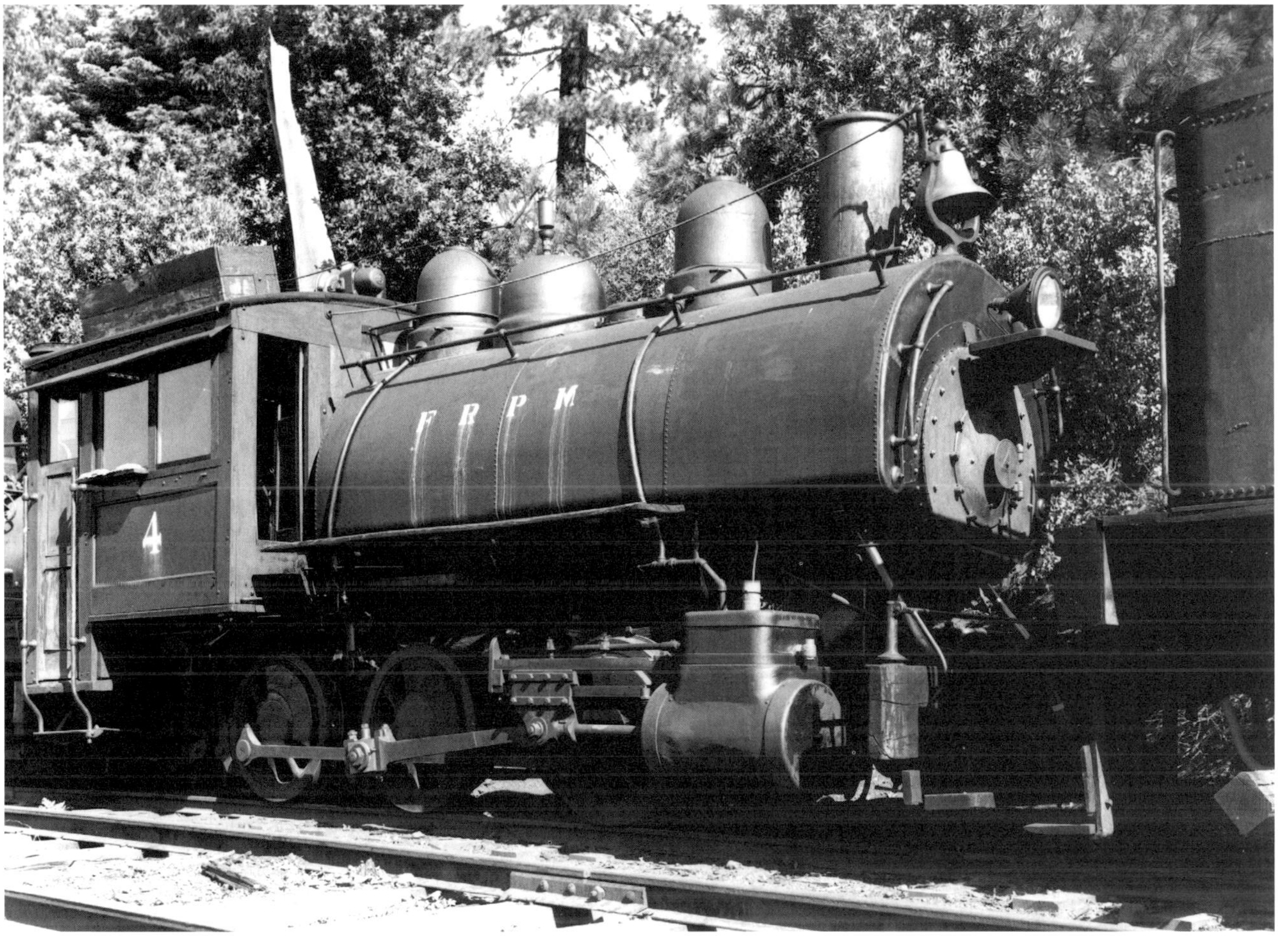

The Feather River Pine Mills saddle-tank locomotive bore the road number 4. The painted initials did not do well in the variable weather. (Bert Ward photograph)

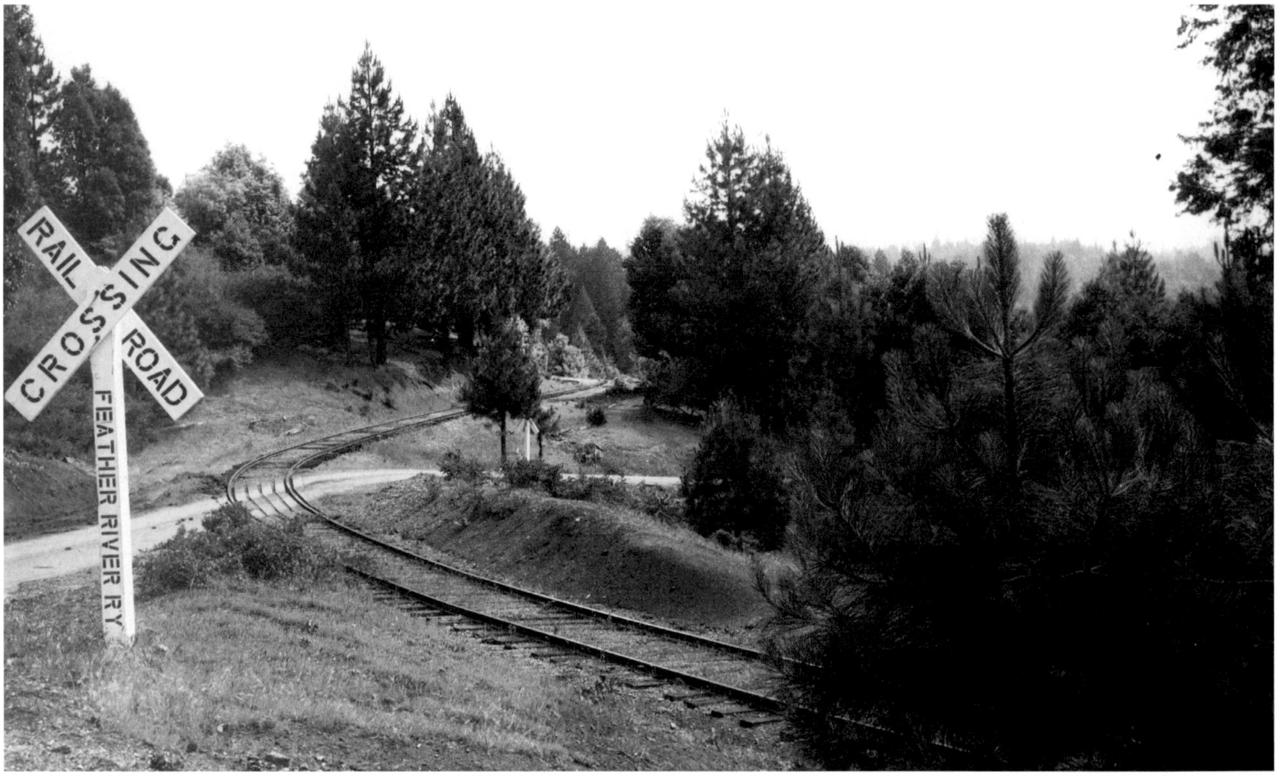

Above: The standard cross-buck reminded motorists of the presence of the railroad above Feather Falls. (Douglas Richter photograph, Ted Wurm collection)

Below: The Feather River Pine Mills at Feather Falls in 1939. (Bert Ward photograph)

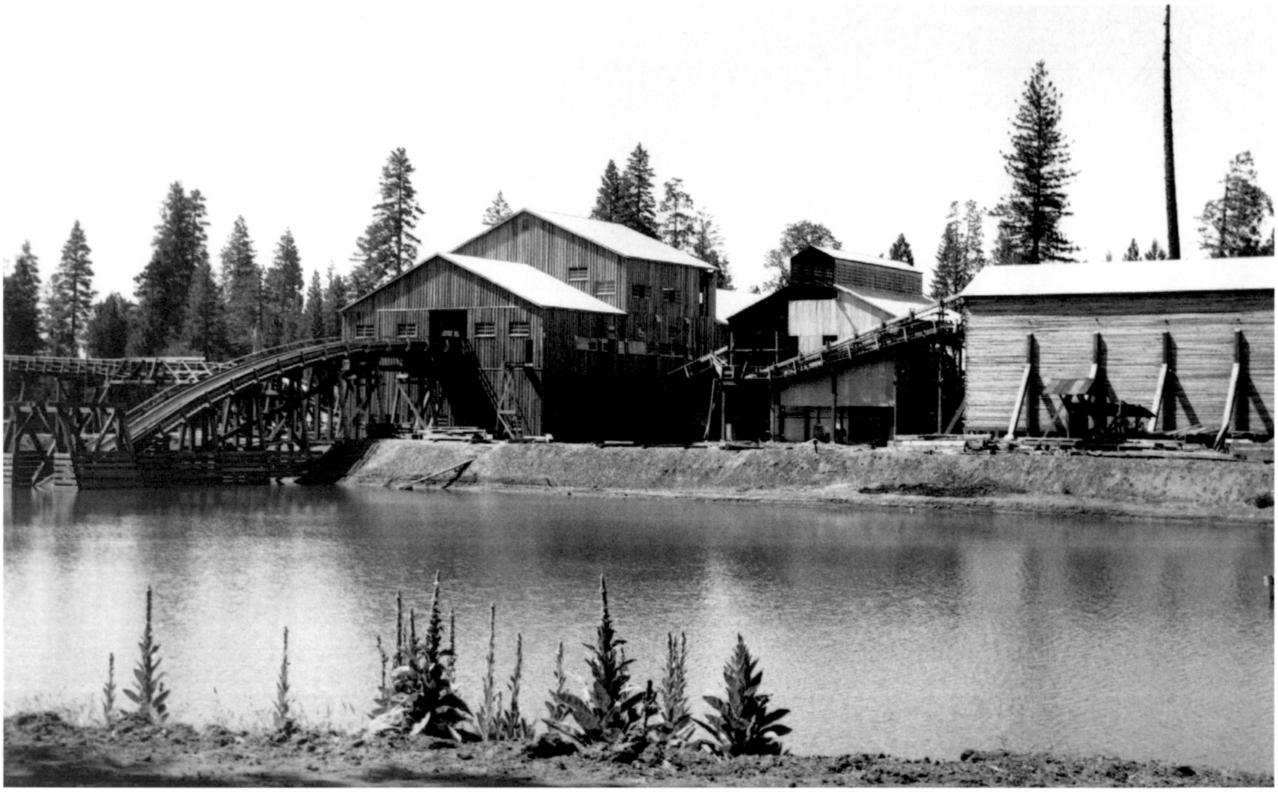

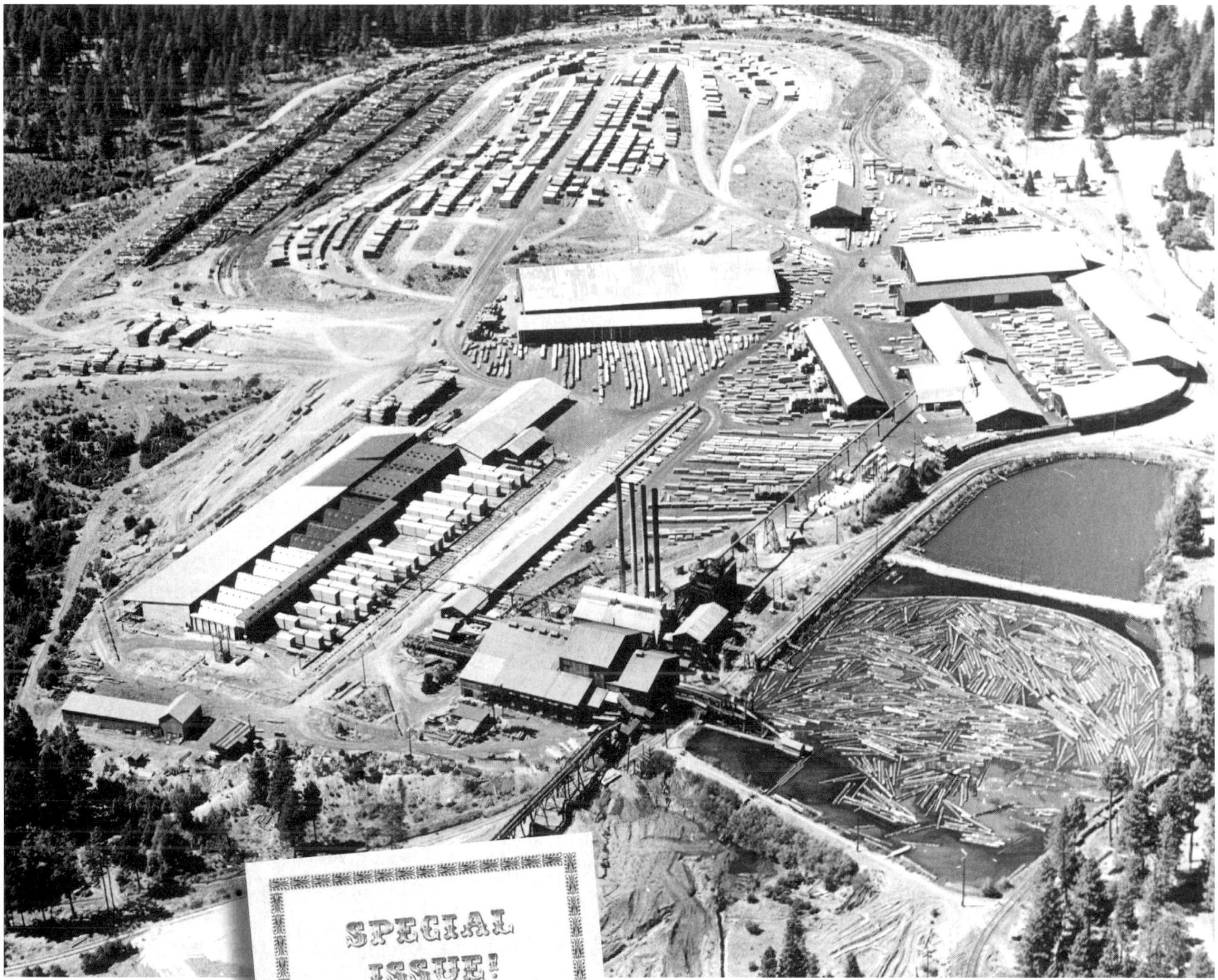

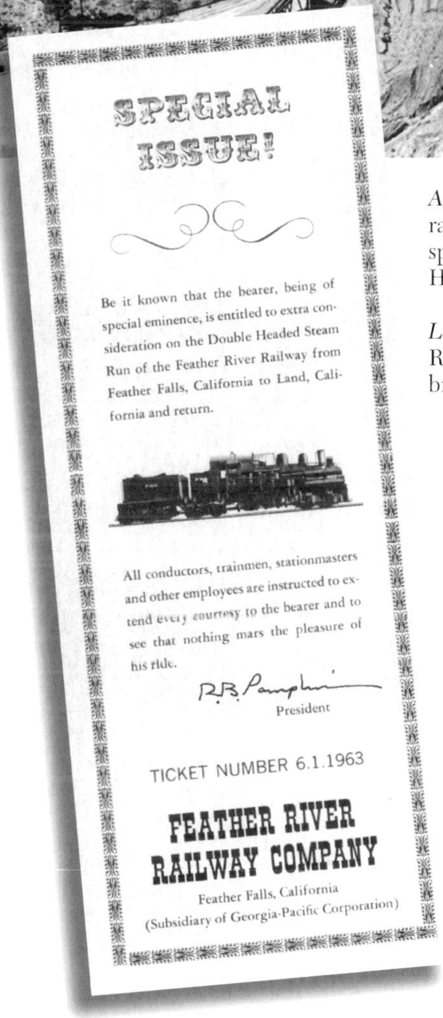

SPECIAL ISSUE!

Be it known that the bearer, being of special eminence, is entitled to extra consideration on the Double Headed Steam Run of the Feather River Railway from Feather Falls, California to Land, California and return.

All conductors, trainmen, stationmasters and other employees are instructed to extend every courtesy to the bearer and to see that nothing mars the pleasure of his ride.

R.B. Pamphlin
President

TICKET NUMBER 6.1.1963

FEATHER RIVER RAILWAY COMPANY

Feather Falls, California
(Subsidiary of Georgia-Pacific Corporation)

Above: An aerial view of the Feather River Pine Mills, with the railroad track skirting along the right edge of the photo. A rail spur swings around the decked logs and stacked timber. (A. Hunter Land III collection)

Left: In June 1963, the management of the Feather River Railway issued a handsome ticket, printed in dark green on brown cardboard, to those on the special excursion.

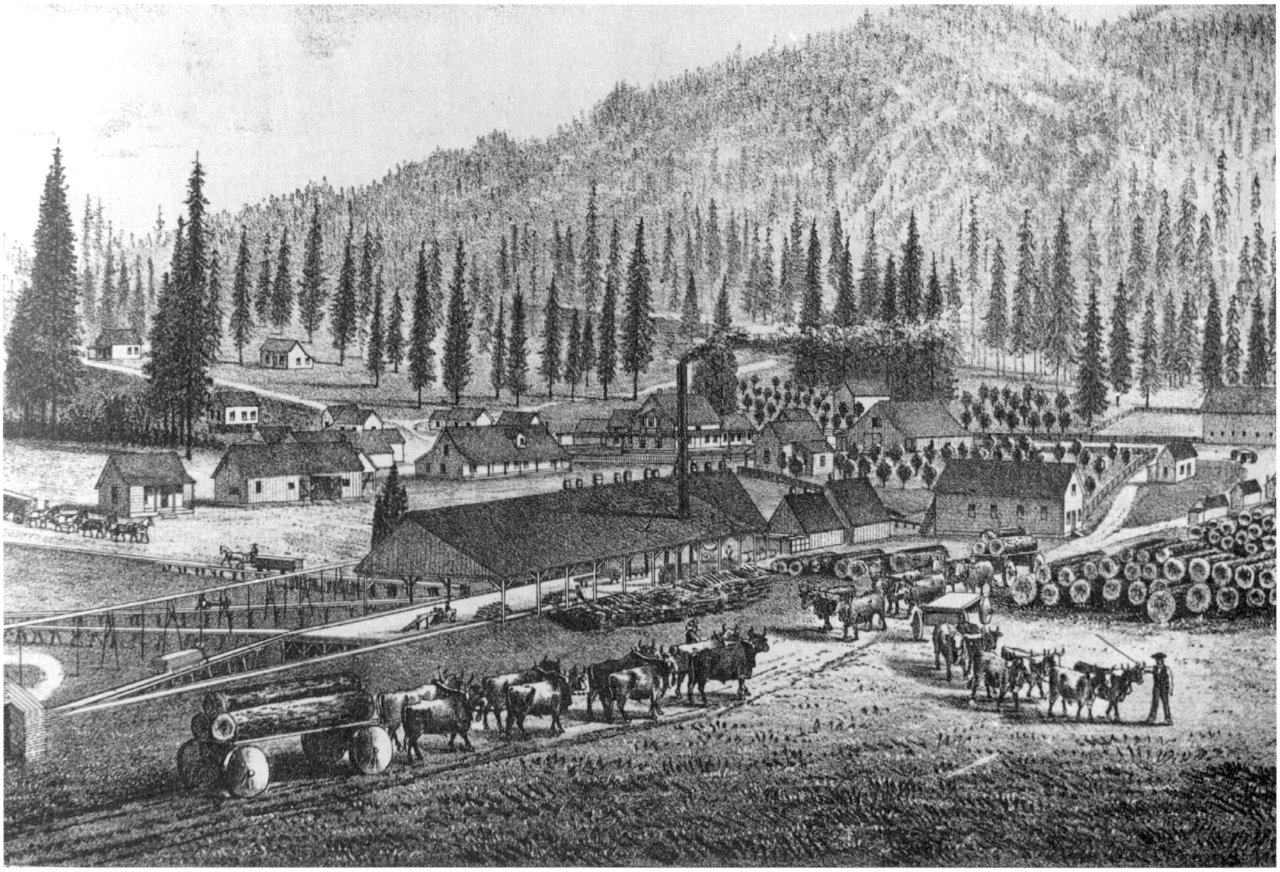

A. M. Leach operated one of the little-known California logging railroads. The artist's conception of the mill with teams bringing in logs probably flattered the establishment. (Yuba Feather Historical Association)

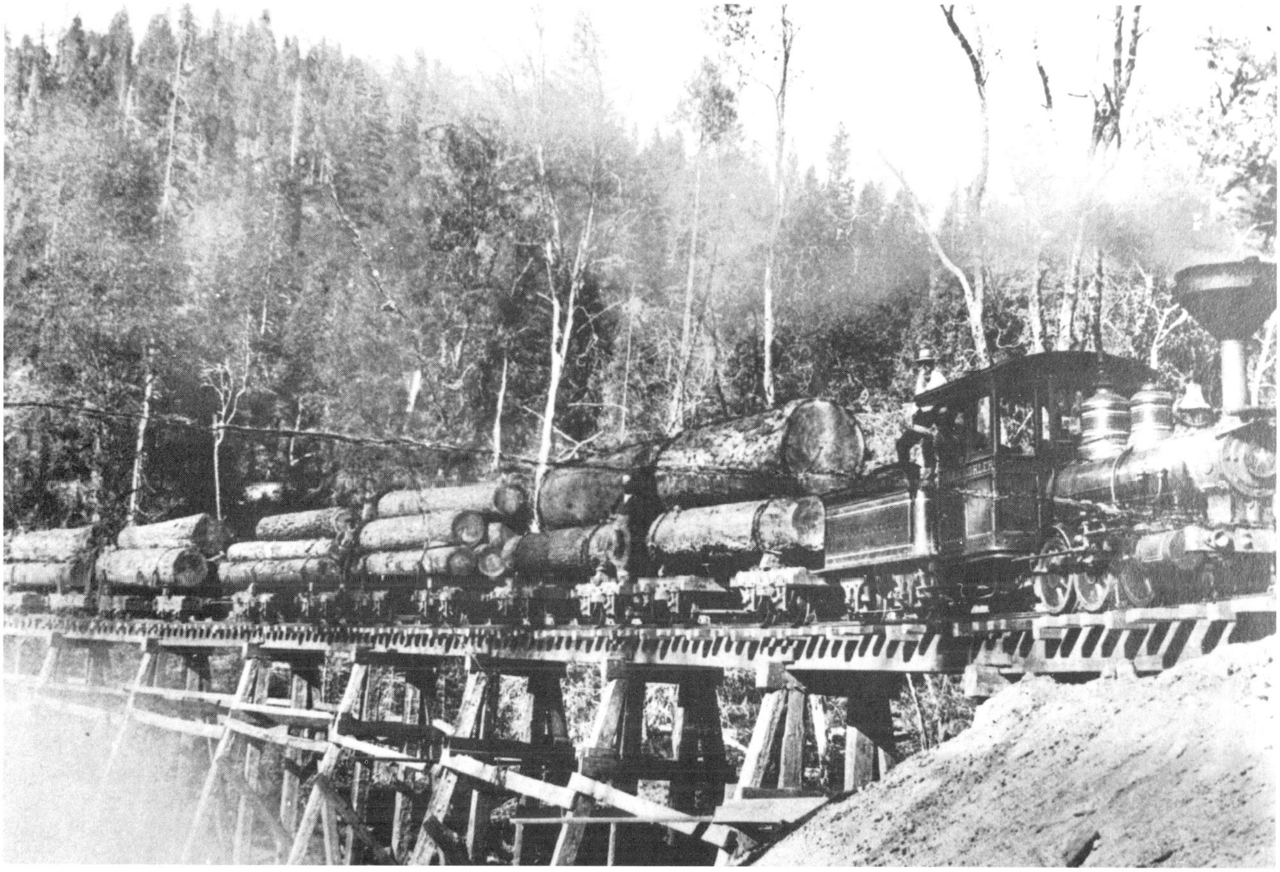

Supplementing his extensive flume system, Leach constructed two short, isolated railroads to bring logs to the flume. According to a legend, this 0-6-0 locomotive spent its final days at McNear's Landing in Marin County, California. (Yuba Feather Historical Association)

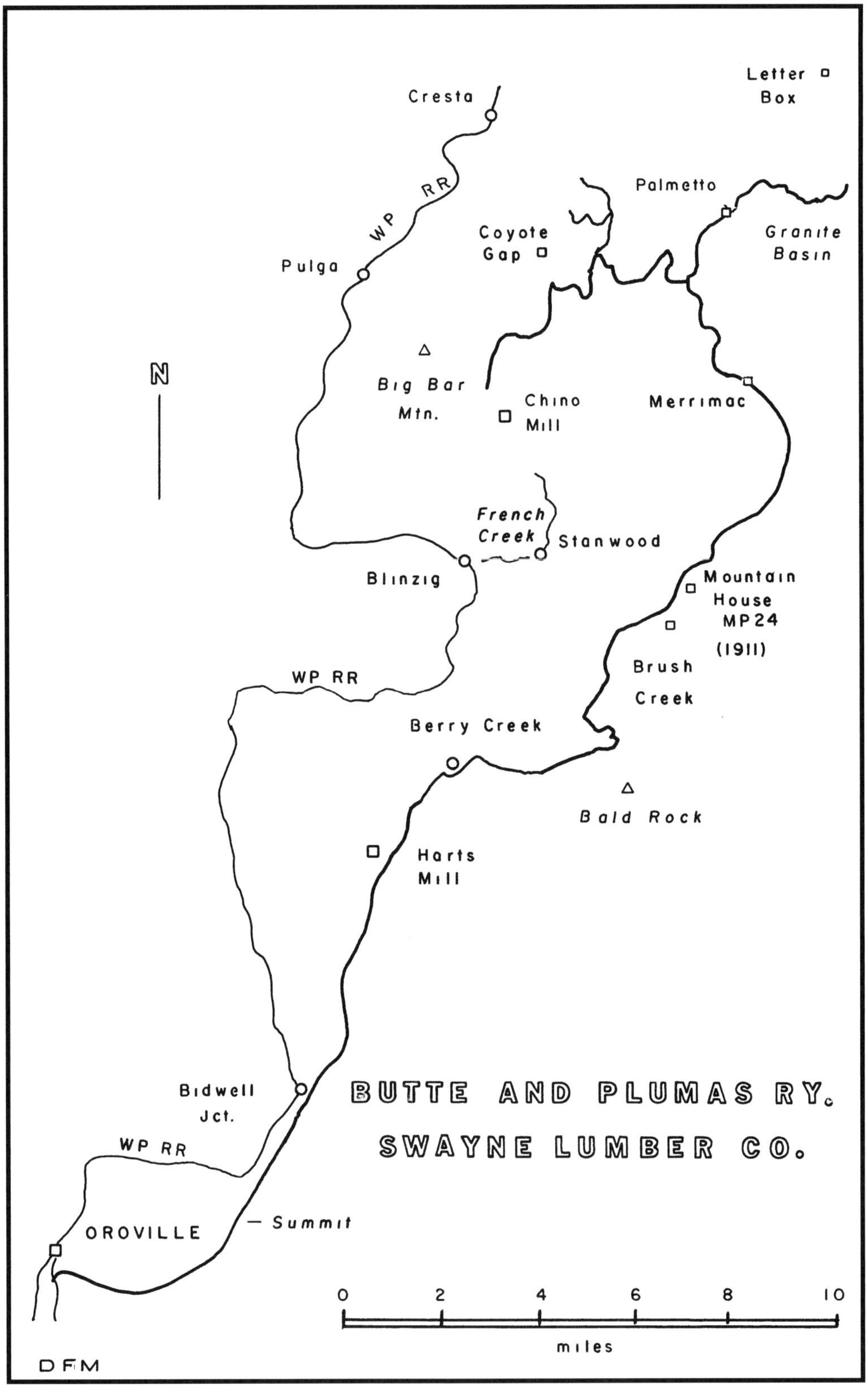
Letter Box
Cresta
Palmetto
WP RR
Coyote Gap
Granite Basin
Pulga
N
Big Bar Mtn.
Chino Mill
Merrimac
French Creek
Stanwood
Blinzig
Mountain House
MP24
(1911)
WP RR
Brush Creek
Berry Creek
Bald Rock
Harts Mill
Bidwell Jct.
BUTTE AND PLUMAS RY.
SWAYNE LUMBER CO.
WP RR
OROVILLE
Summit
0
2
4
6
8
10
miles
DFM

SWAYNE LUMBER COMPANY
BUTTE AND PLUMAS RAILWAY

The Swayne Lumber Company, after a few years of operations on its own near Blinzig, a station on Western Pacific in the Big Bend of the Feather River in northeastern California, became a successor to the Truckee Lumber Company, almost by default.

The Truckee Lumber Company

The Truckee Lumber Company, situated in the town of the same name, had its beginnings in 1867 supplying cross ties and bridge timbers for Central Pacific as well as the affiliated Southern Pacific when it later pushed its track across Arizona.

This lumber company managed to avoid the need of long timber railroads, as logs could be boomed down the Truckee River to the sawmill. In 1883, a short narrow-gauge line worked its way up Washington Creek. An important step in its development came on May 8, 1886, when the Truckee Lumber Company filed incorporation papers, naming W. H. Kruger and others as incorporators along with E. J. Bricknell, who gave Spokane Falls, Washington, as his residence. W. W. Van Arsdale, a member of the group, later joined the McCloud River Railroad as vice president and general manager. Recognizing the importance of fruit shipping boxes for a more continuous market, the company also manufactured packing boxes and, as a further step in diversification, made sashes and doors. After the railroad was opened between Truckee and Lake Tahoe, Truckee Lumber Company extended several spurs from that line into the woods.

With the approach of the twentieth century, the management realized that timber harvesting in their area would soon end. Accordingly, it acquired forestlands northeast of Oroville in the name of the Merrimac Lumber Company, and in the early fall of 1909, when Western Pacific was driving its "last spike" not far from Quincy, Truckee Lumber had a force of men carving a roadbed in the hillside along French Creek, near Blinzig.

Meanwhile, changes occurred in Truckee and Oroville. After forty-one years, the whistle of the big Truckee mill sounded for the last time on November 6, 1909, as a new mill was rising in Oroville.

In March 1910, 350 men with animal support were making good progress on the logging railroad expected to reach Stanwood in June. All looked favorable until Western Pacific informed the management of the Truckee Lumber Company that it would not honor the freight rates quoted verbally by its construction department. One can imagine the consternation this news caused in the offices of the Truckee Lumber Company, as the firm had committed itself to acquiring timberlands and building a large sawmill and a logging railroad, only to find that it could not afford WP's charges to transport logs to the Oroville mill.

Fortunately, an alternative existed, albeit an expensive solution. Instead of a short link to a sidetrack on Western Pacific, the Truckee Lumber Company could build its own railroad for transporting logs to its mill in Oroville. O. C. Haslett incorporated the Butte and Plumas (B&P) Railway Company on June 4, 1910. This created a second railway with the same name, as H. H. Yard on October 24, 1902, had incorporated an earlier Butte and Plumas Railway to secure a right-of-way up the North Fork of the Feather River that he subsequently sold to the Western Pacific Railway. With that transfer accomplished, this early B&P filed for voluntary dissolution, which the Butte County Superior Court approved on September 24, 1906. After this release was filed with the secretary of state on June 18, 1907, the name became available, and Haslett took it.

As Southern Pacific maintained a branch line to Oroville—one of the earliest components of the system—traffic men of that railroad lent a sympathetic ear to the plight of the Truckee Lumber Company. After discussions, Southern Pacific agreed to loan $400,000 to the lumber company to help with the cost of the longer railroad. It also furnished rolling stock valued at $20,210 and took a note of $420,210, dated June 8, 1910, backed by a mortgage on the new Butte and Plumas Railway. With that financing, the B&P built a narrow-gauge line north from Oroville into its timberlands.

The whistle of the Oroville mill blew its first blast on August 14, and the great band saws commenced their work on December 23, 1910, after six cars of logs arrived from the Diamond Match Company. A flag raising and a chorus of whistles saluted the mill as it went into full operation on May 25, 1911.

Over the next few months, the lumber company supported the local economy with a $30,000 monthly payroll divided among 218 employees, with 100 at the mill, 50 building the railroad, and the balance in the woods.

A soft lumber market forced the Truckee Lumber Company to close its mill eight weeks earlier than normal suspension for winter. Things were not going well when the mill shut down in early October 1911; the strike of the construction workers on the railroad added to the problems. Obviously, the management was discouraged by the financial picture and announced that the big sawmill would not reopen the following spring. The company filed a $400,000 lawsuit against WP for failing to honor the freight-rate commitment, but the outcome, unreported, probably was unremunerative.

The narrow-gauge Butte and Plumas Railway commenced at the mill in Oroville, ran east and northeast to surmount a summit about four miles from Oroville, before descending three miles to cross the Middle Fork of the Feather River at Bidwell Jct. After passing Harts Mill, the tracks continued to the Berry Creek settlement and northeast to just beyond Mountain House, where construction halted, twenty-five miles north of Oroville, with the closing of the sawmill. With cash virtually exhausted, everything entered a dormant condition for six years. Except for a little interest paid during the first year, the lumber company failed to meet its debt obligations to Southern Pacific.

Swayne Lumber Company

Swayne, Hoyt, and Company, consisting of Robert Swayne, John G. Hoyt, and Frank L. Hoyt, was a custom-house broker and forwarding agent. The company also operated coastal steamers. Robert Swayne, his son, Warren, and Charles Tilden, a San Francisco attorney also in the warehouse and transfer business, joined the rush to timberlands now that Western Pacific opened a new territory under the banner of Swayne Lumber Company, incorporated on October 7, 1909. Their sawmill stood high above Blinzig siding, which created transportation problems until the firm built a cable tramway. From its mill at Tilden, the company ran several miles of a thirty-six-inch-gauge railroad into the timber area.

Operations commenced in 1910 and generally ran well as a small operator. The company had its share of fires; one in October 1916, starting in the lumberyards, consumed the sawmill and stack of lumber. The loss, reported to be $300,000, was covered by insurance. It proved to be a time for decision.

Not far away, the timberlands of the Truckee Lumber Company stood undisturbed, while the Oroville mill remained silent from 1911 to 1917. The property almost begged to be rescued from idleness. The Truckee Lumber Company, Southern Pacific, and West Side Lumber Company of Tuolumne shared a financial interest in the company and had been unsuccessful in finding a purchaser for the timberland, railroad, and mill. Rather than replace the burned sawmill, the Swayne Lumber Company considered its options and acquired the property. Now major figures in the lumber trade, its managers were confronted with a series of difficulties, including rebuilding much of the railroad.

An agreement dated April 27, 1917, between Swayne Lumber, Butte and Plumas Railway, and Southern Pacific recited conditions at that time. Swayne owned the railroad through stock ownership, and Southern Pacific held a $400,000 mortgage on the property. Under the new agreement, SP reduced the mortgage to $250,000, absorbing the loss, and Swayne promised to pay interest and make annual payments on the debt.

In 1917, George F. McCormick, assistant SP division engineer, joined Warren Swayne on an inspection trip by track motorcar over the line, which had not been used or maintained for about seven years. The men had considerable difficulty keeping the car on the track, especially in cuts where mud covered the rails. Whereas the rail was in "good shape," the ties had decayed.

The lumber company hired P. Lyons, former superintendent of the Diamond Match Company railroad at Stirling City, to serve as roadmaster and set out to restore the narrow-gauge railroad. Bad weather and labor troubles retarded lumber production, and in May 1918 the company stood six months behind in its interest payments. It sought and received a sixty-day extension. Robert Swayne conferred with Southern Pacific from time to time, advising of the progress of the railroad and often seeking concessions on the loan. Usually he conferred with Paul Shoup, vice president of SP. In November 1918, Swayne reported that although they had contemplated using rail from the Tilden trackage to add eight to ten miles to the existing twenty-five miles, they found that the old survey had excessive grades. Also, some nine miles of the upper end of the present road had to be abandoned and relocated, thus leaving only the sixteen miles of the railroad between Oroville and a point near Berry Creek (settlement) undisturbed.

Then it developed that much of the remaining segment stood in poorer condition than had first been believed. Whereas the first seven miles to the crossing of the Middle Fork were in reasonable condition, rail on the next nine miles to near Berry Creek had to be relaid and trestles practically rebuilt. The railroad crossed seventy-eight trestles, but, after replacing the abandoned nine-mile section, the number was reduced to sixty-four.

By the end of the month, Swayne expected to have four more miles graded that would be followed by rails to

Merrimac and well into lands acquired from the Truckee Lumber Company. With that completion, the timber would be connected with the sawmill at Oroville by a railroad, in Swayne's words, "as good as can be built in the mountains with 35-lb. rails, taking into consideration, of course, the large number of trestles on the first 16 miles. . . . The extension has been built without trestles." (Until its railroad could function, Swayne's company continued to buy timber from other parties.) Swayne was proud of his accomplishments, remarking that he had taken up the enterprise two years earlier as war was declared, which had made it difficult to secure workers.

A heavy accumulation of snow greeted F. R. Ferguson, formerly with the Saginaw and Manistee Lumber Company, when he arrived from Williams, Arizona, to be the new general superintendent. In April 1919, when melting snow enabled an SP engineer and Mr. Lyons to make an inspection trip, they reported that thirty-two miles of the main line had been completed and that rail laying was in progress on the last three miles to Merrimac. Embankments were full, with cuts cleared and well drained. The line was properly maintained and the "track well tied"—eighteen ties to a thirty-foot rail.

A labor contractor, Charles D. Virgillio, whose Reno employment agency had supplied many workers for the Western Pacific construction, sued the lumber company for $4,303 allegedly due him for railroad work. The matter went to trial, and several months later, the judge found that Virgillio was not entitled to a $1,800 bonus for his work on the four miles of railroad to Merrimac, as he had not met the specified completion date. Additionally, Swayne had paid him $9,000 more than the work should have cost, and the judge ruled that Virgillio should pay all litigation costs.

Troubles with the Mill in Oroville

Litigation threatened to force removal of the sawmill from Oroville after several olive plants and a fruit-packing concern complained about the soot from the sawmill burners during the summer and fall of 1919. A number of charges were made, but cooler heads arranged for three experts to study the matter, and after their report came out with minor recommendations, the complaint abated.

Warren Swayne wrote to Paul Shoup in December 1919 to explain that because of heavy storms, the extension of the track into timber two miles beyond Merrimac was not placed in full operation until August 26 and that a donkey engine could be put to work. Now the railroad stretched a full thirty-seven miles from Oroville, but it was found wanting in three areas. Warren Swayne contemplated a line change from the summit just north of Oroville to near Bidwell Bar to eliminate a thirty-degree curve and reduce the 3.5 percent grade. This improvement would end the need to "double" log trains. Another four miles on both sides of the trestle at Harts Mill required relocation, as did three miles of railroad north of Berry Creek. All this led up to his request for SP to defer receipt of a debt installment.

Morton Russell, an SP assistant engineer, went over the line in early 1920 and spoke well of the maintenance. He observed that the eight miles beyond MP 18 (near Bald Rock) and the next eleven miles of new construction used a revised survey that reduced the distance to Merrimac by five miles. Down at Oroville, the company had plans to boost the mill output from 120,000 to 140,000 board feet per ten-hour shift. The railroad had closed for the winter on December 1, 1919, but planned to reopen April 1 after repairs had been made in March. For the next year, the company expected to purchase an additional donkey engine and a sixty-ton geared locomotive along with twenty-five logging cars.

Robert Swayne wrote Paul Shoup on February 5, 1920, to explain that the company had expected to start logging at the beginning of 1918 and make the first payment on the debt owed to SP in December; instead, "we are just able to start in the beginning of 1920, or two years late." Shoup replied that SP expected to buy ten thousand ties from Swayne that year.

What started out as a "banner year," with two log trains each day, turned disappointing in the fall, as the lumber business entered "a period of stagnation—we have probably 600 carloads of lumber piled up at Oroville at the present time which we cannot sell." Still, Swayne managed to send SP two checks covering back interest.

An unexpected problem closed the Swayne mill for three days after some unidentified person cut the huge (thirty-five inches wide) leather belt of the main shaft.

With all of the problems confronting the operators, one can sympathize with Robert Swayne in January 1921 when he told Paul Shoup that he had made a mistake in buying the road, getting into a business about which he knew nothing, and he did not appreciate at the time how much money would be required.

The stiff grades along the railroad demanded geared locomotives—usually Shays from Lima—to move the heavy log trains to the mill. To accommodate a sixty-ton, three-truck Shay necessitated three-post construction for trestles. Water barrels were placed at the ends of trestles, and a telephone line paralleled the entire length of the railroad. Each of the seven section foremen had a crew of three men.

In the late afternoon of Friday, June 24, 1921, a fire started at the south end of the lumberyard at Oroville.

A south wind carried the flames forward to consume all seven million board feet of lumber in the yard. The Marysville switch engine, SP 2930, rushed to the scene to pull seven cars to a safer location. A shift in wind direction saved the box factory and lumber mill. Fortunately, the $300,000 loss was insured. That fire marked the start of a series of unfortunate events. The day after the lumberyard burned, sparks from a nearby forest fire ignited into flames to destroy a major trestle between Oroville and Bidwell Jct. By working Sunday, the crew repaired the trestle, so normal operations resumed Monday.

A few days later, shifting logs on cars at Merrimac snuffed out the life of a brakeman. Only two weeks went by before a derailment at Bidwell Jct. hurled men down the embankment along with errant logs, causing the death of one man.

Darkness had settled over the land when James Stephens was riding on an empty car in a Swayne log train. The train stopped en route, and Jim, believing that it had crossed a trestle, jumped off the car. Instead of landing on friendly ground, Jim fell twenty-five feet to the rocks and shrubs below. The initial diagnosis suggested that Jim had broken his hip and several ribs, but a further examination revealed that he had been badly and painfully bruised, which kept him in the hospital several days.

A monster mountain lion, seeking refuge from a cluster of barking dogs in January 1922, climbed a tree, only to by shot by the watchman at Merrimac camp. Soon thereafter, a heavy storm swept across northern California, leaving two feet of snow at Merrimac in March; a month later it stood at ten feet deep. That year, the start of logging work was delayed several weeks into the middle of May, so the following year, the railroad experimented with a small rotary snowplow, but the consequences escaped notice.

In October 1922, Swayne purchased more timber from the U.S. Forest Service, which necessitated extension of the logging railroad.

After R. H. Swayne died in 1924, his brother Lloyd became president and negotiated easier debt terms with SP with a contract of January 5, 1926. For that year, Swayne met all installments by timber sales to SP.

One of the unhappy aspects of Swayne's timber supply stemmed from the fact that more than one-half of its cut was in white fir, which had limited use. In 1928, the company remarked that it had a hard time finding markets for white fir and that revenues approximated the cost of harvesting and milling these trees.

Somehow the company managed to survive through the 1930s. During those years, its production placed it among the medium-size California lumber companies. In 1935, six large California mills produced more than thirty million board feet, while fifteen mills cut between twenty and thirty million feet. Swayne joined the latter group with a cut of twenty-one million feet. In that decade, Swayne added a few miles of track from time to time or moved trackage from a depleted cutting area to new timber stands in Granite Basin, Little North Fork, and west to the Coyote Gap ranger station, then southwest to Big Bar Mountain and beyond.

The end came in the fall of 1938 when the management of Swayne Lumber Company determined not to open the mill and timber the following spring. It had been a long, hard struggle, but finally operations had come to the end of the line. Southern Pacific purchased the Butte and Plumas Railway on October 9, 1939, and proceeded to salvage the line. Some of the Shay locomotives found a new home with the Michigan California Lumber Company at Camino.

Those desiring more information are urged to read the book *The Swayne Lumber Company*, by Paul Beckstrom and David W. Braun, published in 1992.

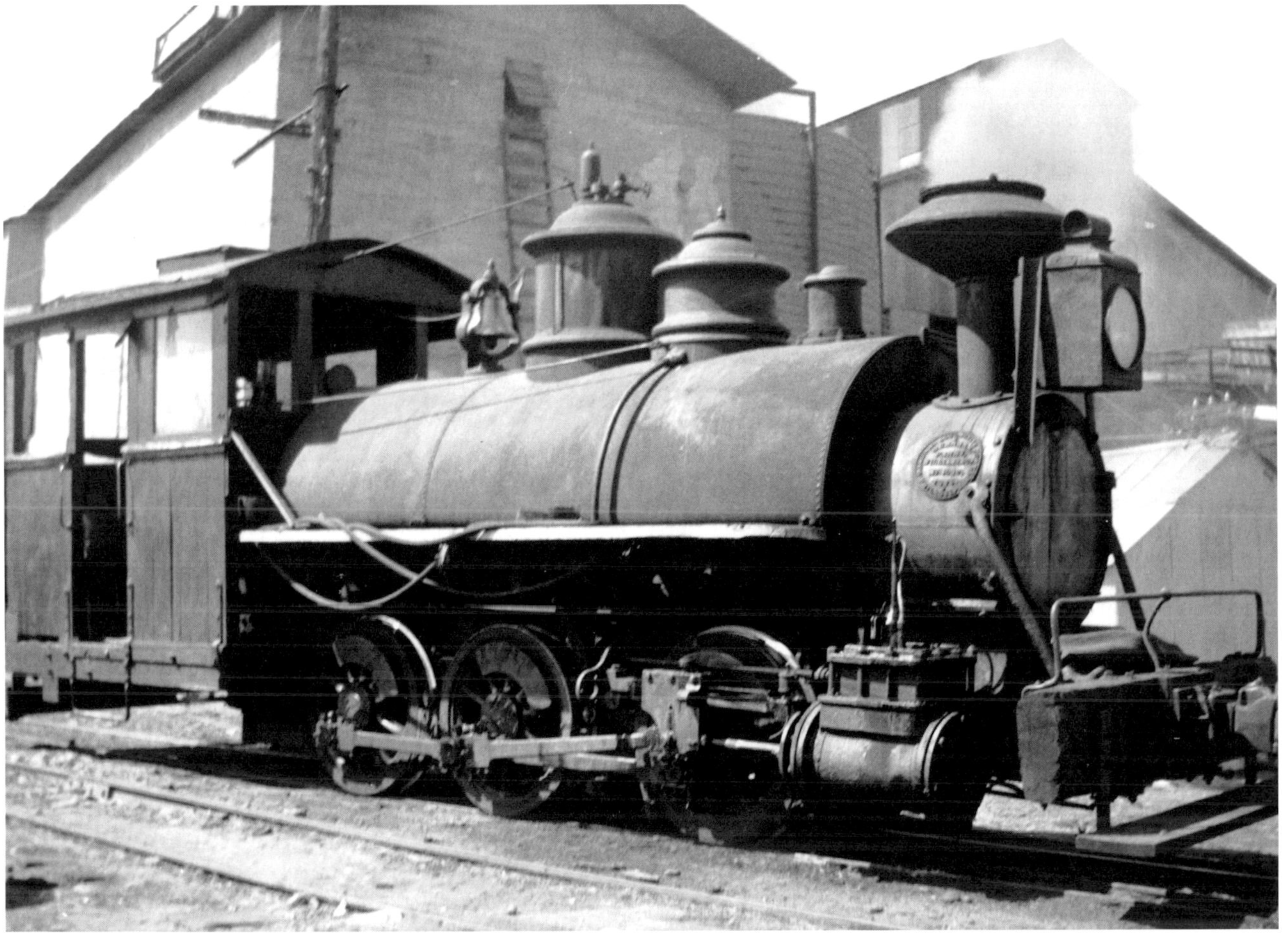

As the Swayne Lumber Company had no road numbers for its two rod engines, rail historians have identified them as A and B. From its shops in 1876, Baldwin delivered this saddle-tank engine to the Ruby Hill Railroad at Eureka, Nevada. Next it went to the Pacific Lumber and Wood Company before going to the nearby Truckee Lumber Company where, designated A, it followed the corporate ownership changes of the Truckee Lumber Company. (L. C. Rowe photograph, 1935; Bert Ward collection)

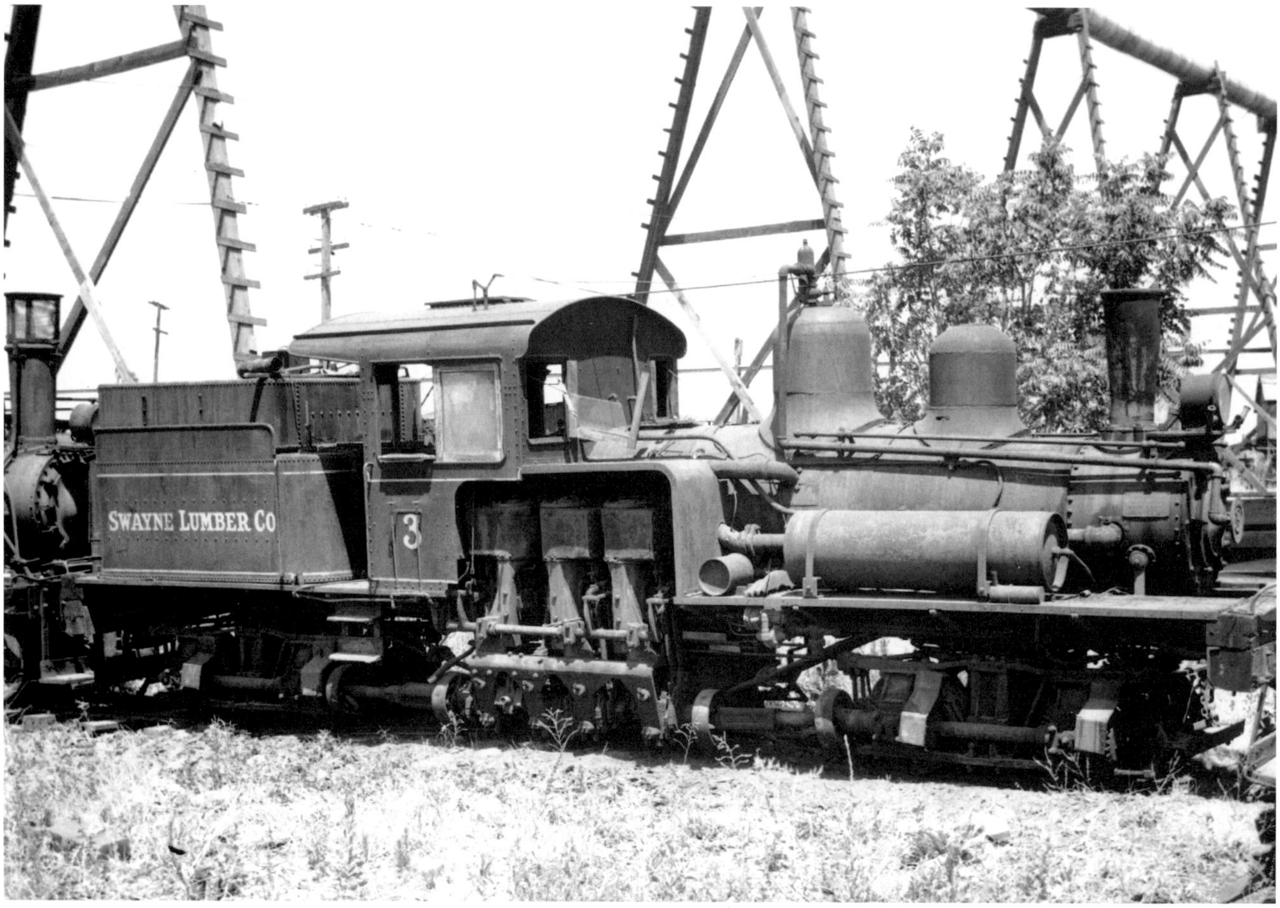

No. 3, another Shay, was photographed at the Oroville mill in 1939, a year after logging operations ended. (Bert Ward photograph)

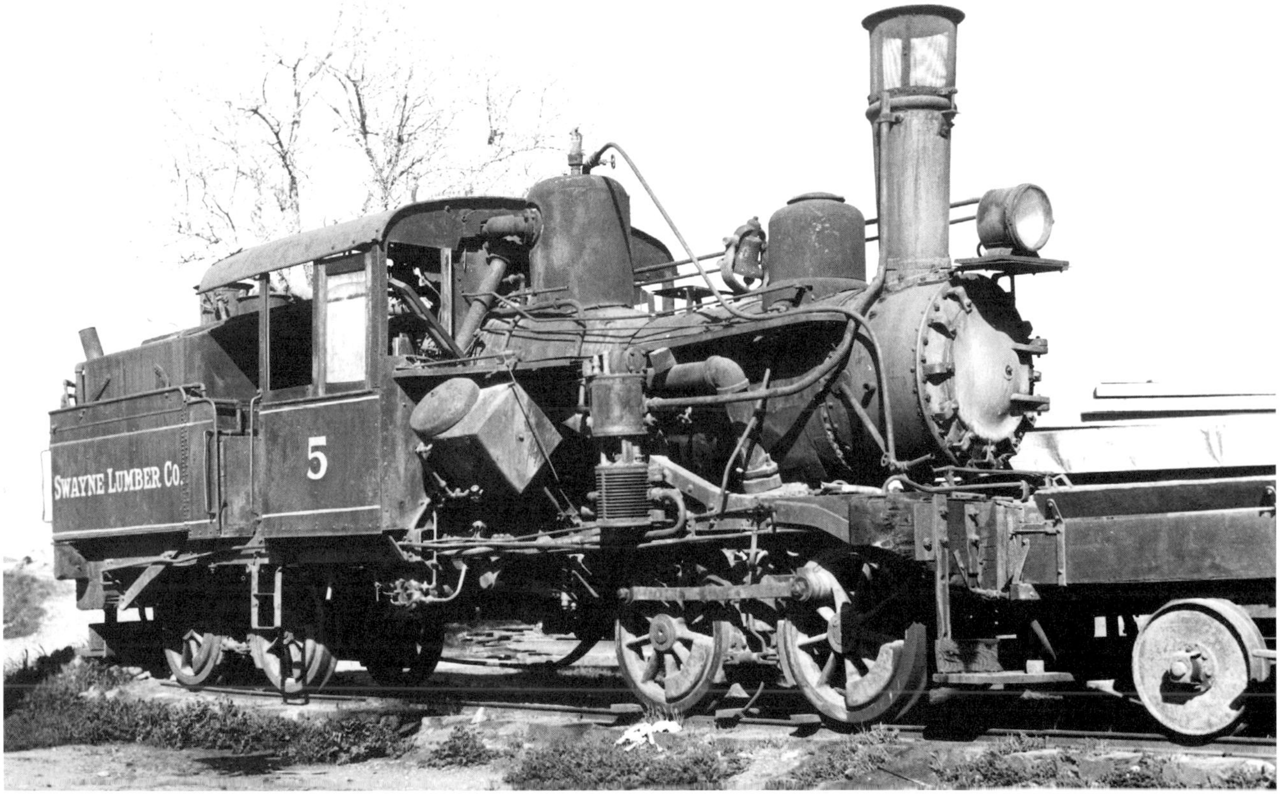

Above: No. 5, a two-truck geared locomotive, came from the Heisler Locomotive Works, a different manufacturer. Before joining the Swayne roster, it had worked on the Hetch Hetchy and Yosemite Valley Railroad and the West Side Lumber Company. It was scrapped in 1940. (James E. Boynton photograph)

Below: No. 6 sported a trim appearance in 1938, the last year Swayne conducted logging operations. Later, it joined the roster of the West Side Lumber Company. (Ted Wurm photograph)

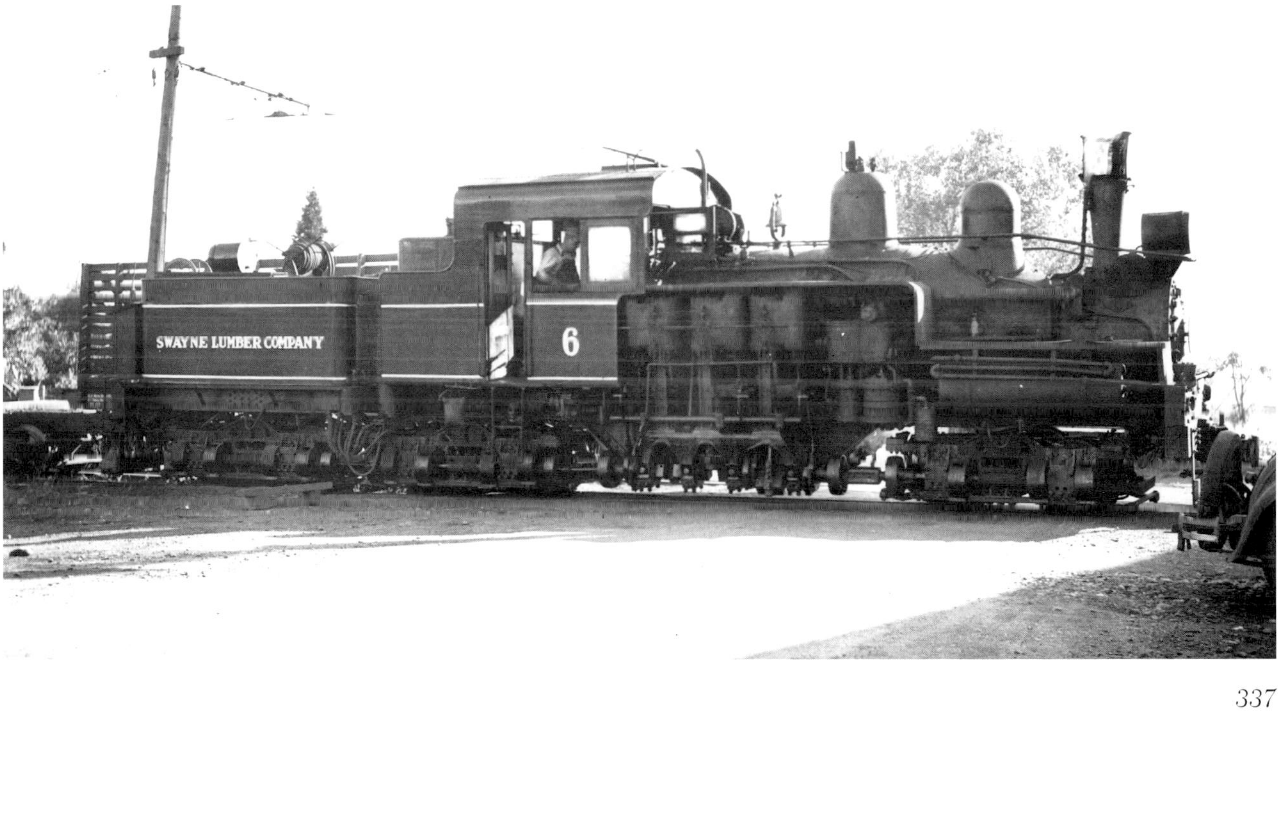

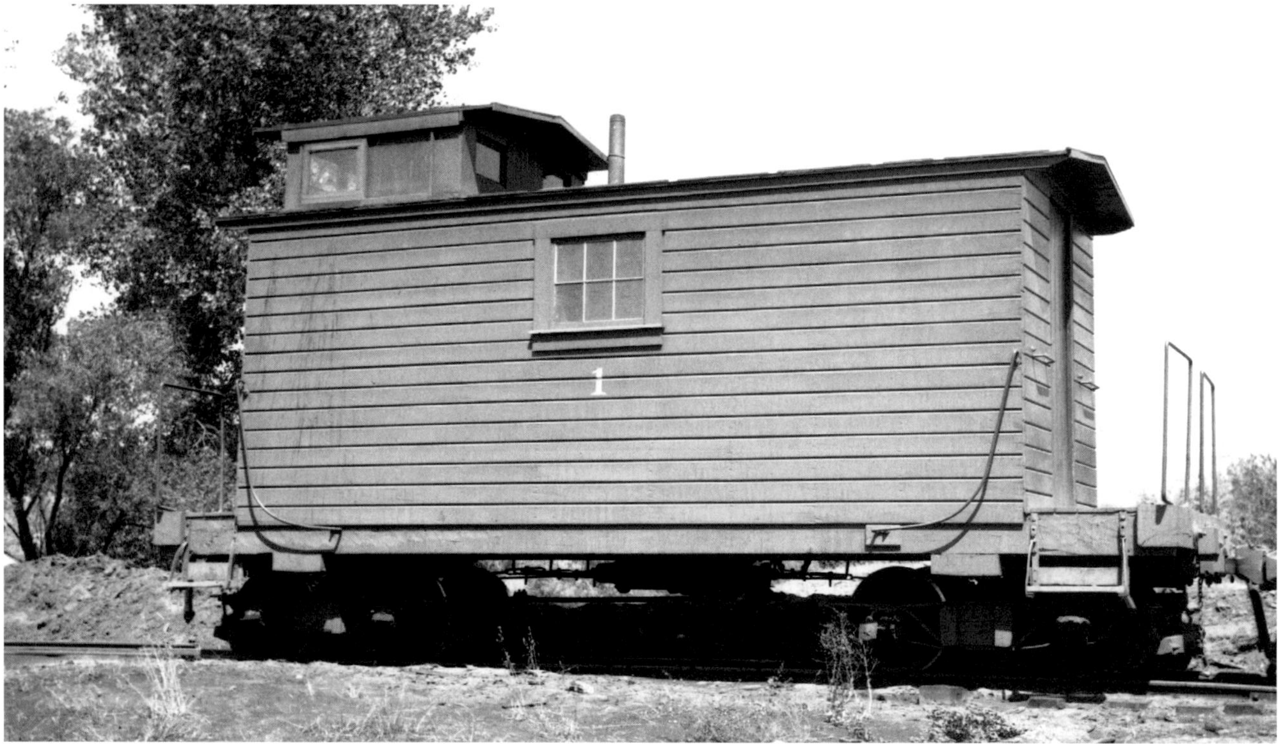

Above: The caboose disdained any embellishments in its design. (Bert Ward photograph)

Below: A homemade rotary snowplow cleared the track each spring in preparation for the opening of the logging camps. (Bert Ward photograph)

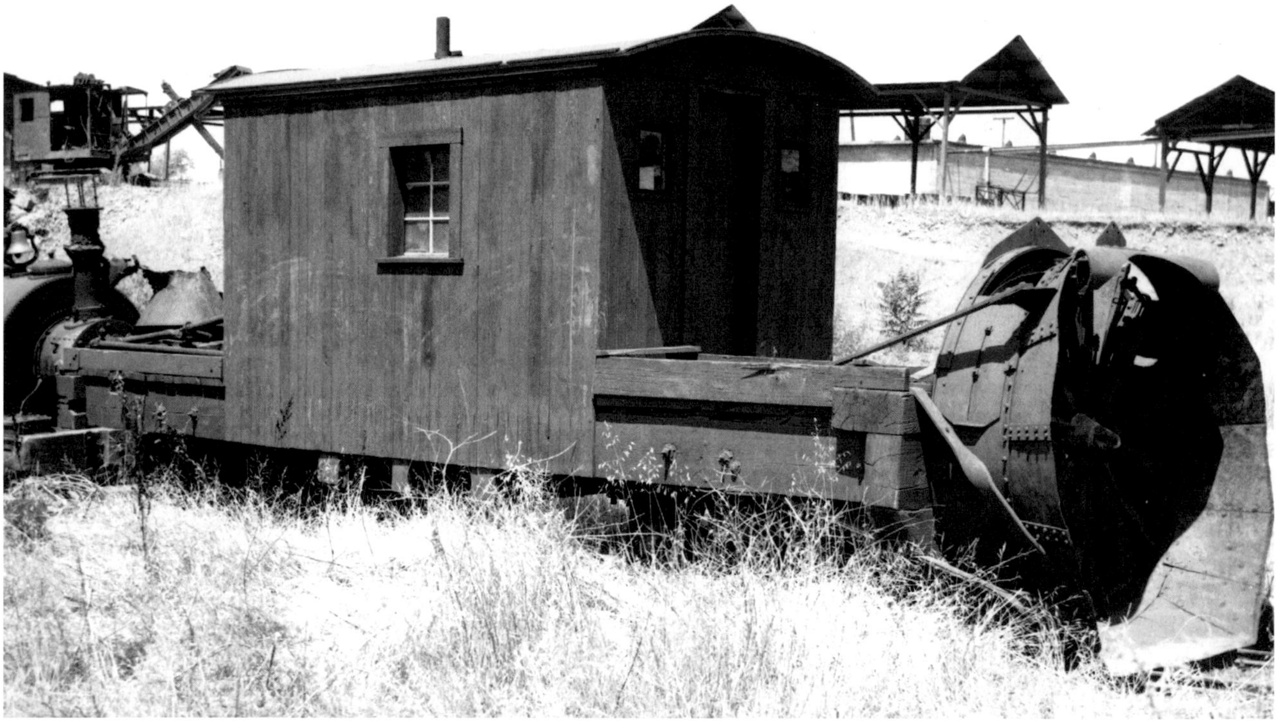

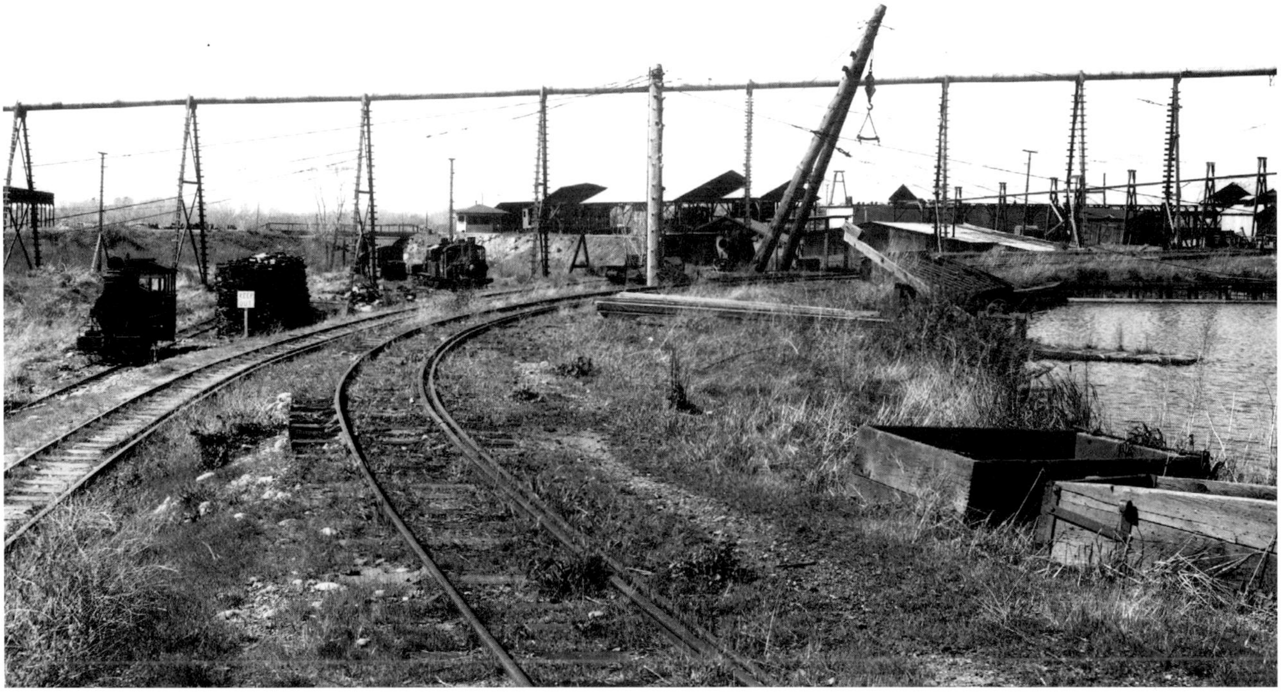

Above: Ted Wurm, a noted railroad historian, captured the idle plant of Swayne Lumber in Oroville in March 1940. At the left, posing on the track leading to the woods, is engine A, followed by Nos. 5, 4, the rotary, and B.

Below: Moving over rusty rails for almost the last time, No. 3 partakes in the dismantling of the railroad. It drags a tank car and boxcar, both assembled in the company shops, followed by a flatcar. (Bert Ward photograph, March 1940)

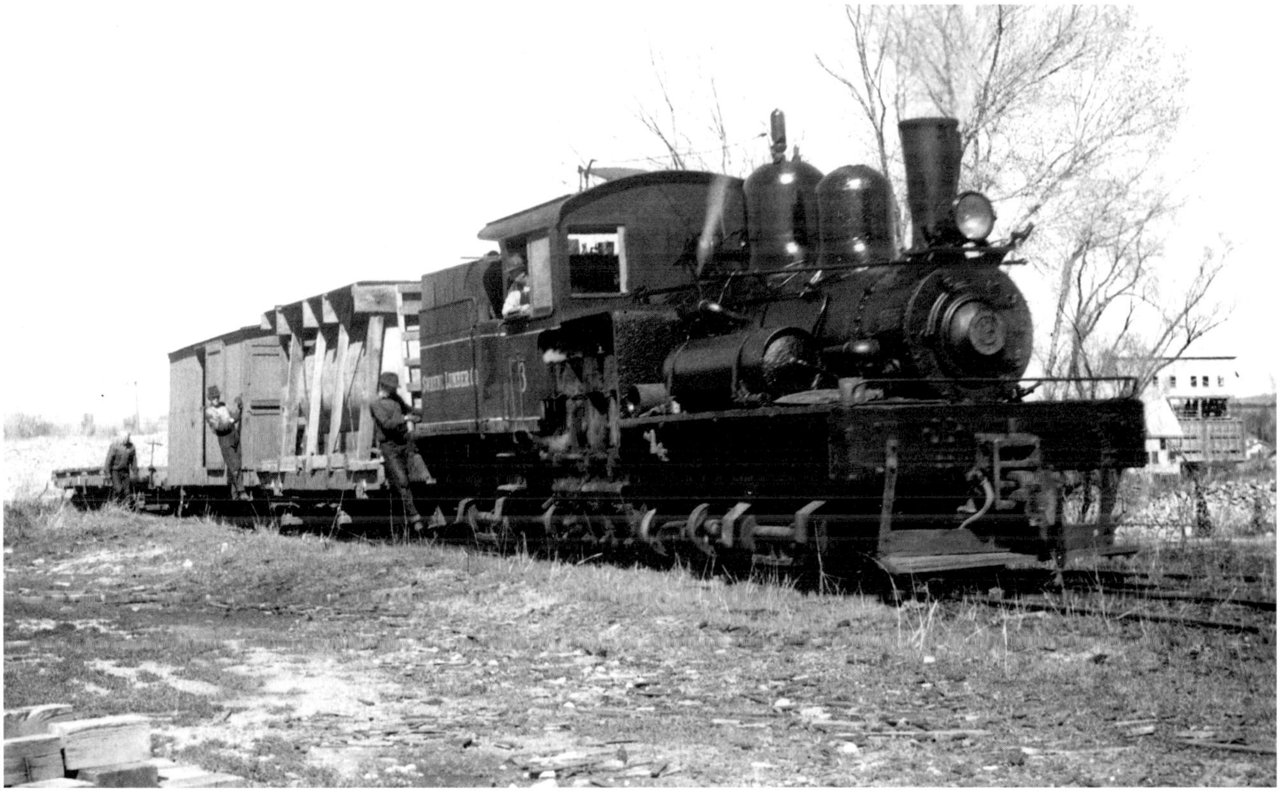

FEATHER RIVER POWER PLANT RAILROADS

The several branches of the Feather River and surrounding lands of Plumas County proved bountiful for California settlers. First, prospectors rushed in to seek fortunes in placer gold mining. Lumbering, which commenced with the first arrivals seeking shelter from the rain and snow, toppled great trees to build houses. A combination of branches of the Feather River—moving from the North Fork to the Middle Fork just east of Quincy—enabled engineers to locate the Western Pacific Railway over the Sierra Nevada with a 1 percent grade.

The same river and its branches were an electrical engineer's dream, inviting utilization of its natural resource—water falling four thousand feet—for electrical generation. (Water from the same river irrigated ranches in the Sacramento Valley.)

The power plant at Las Plumas at the lower end of the Big Bend of the North Fork of the Feather River, sixteen miles above Oroville, built in 1908 formed the first of many projects in this area. When its construction was planned, hydroelectric plants were relatively new in California, the first being the Highgrove Plant in the San Bernardino Mountains in 1887, with the Folsom plant of 1895 among the first in northern California.

Over the years, the construction of dams and aqueducts necessitated special-purpose railroads. One served the needs of Lake Almanor and the Caribou powerhouse, while another served the Bucks Lake project.

Organization of the Western Power Company

Julius M. Howells (1859–1927), a hydraulic engineer whose early experience included a brief stint on the Denver and Rio Grande RR, also served Alexander E. R. Agassiz during 1882–1892 when the noted professor studied the tertiary history of the Sierra Nevada, including Plumas County. Other engineering work occupied his time during the next two decades before moving to Los Angeles in 1901, but the dramatic potential of Big Meadows remained in his mind. Meeting with Edwin T. Earl of Los Angeles, a fruit shipper and "capitalist," as city directories often labeled men in those days, and Guy C. Earl, a brother and an Oakland attorney, he shared his ideas and won their support for forming an artificial lake covering Big Meadows to ensure a reliable source of water for a power plant down the Feather River. The next steps required the quiet acquisition of thousands of acres in Big Meadows and nearby Butt Valley and then securing appropriate water rights.

To move the project forward, these men formed the Western Power Company on March 24, 1902. Several years went by in developing plans for the power company; securing adequate financing stood as a roadblock but turned successful when new faces appeared with the incorporation of the Great Western Power (GWP) Company, a successor company, on September 18, 1906. The additional investors made up an impressive list of names identified with prominent corporations. Henry E. Huntington and William G. Henshaw joined the Earls, and Edwin Hawley, who had recently parted company with E. H. Harriman after a dispute and had thrown his weight to the cause of Western Pacific, became the first president of the new company.

Las Plumas Power House at Big Bend

The group selected the lower end of the great bend in the North Fork as the powerhouse location, taking advantage of a previous mining scheme. Back in 1885–1886, Dr. R. V. Pierce, a successful Buffalo patent medicine man, headed a company that spent more than a million dollars to drill an 11,668-foot tunnel at Big Bend to divert water from the Feather River so that gold could be recovered from the riverbed. A great idea, but it did not work out, so the tunnel lay dormant.

Actually, the lower end of the tunnel halted with an outlet in Piper's Ravine. Howells concluded that by building a short extension from the south portal of Pierce's tunnel, a 400-foot water drop could be obtained—twice that of Niagara Falls.

H. P. Wilson, later vice president of Pacific Gas and Electric, recalled that after two years of negotiations taking them all over the country, the new company purchased the tunnel for five hundred thousand dollars in cash.

To provide a reliable flow of water for the power plant, Great Western Power contemplated reservoirs upstream. One site in Butt Valley covered 1,000 acres, which caused the dismantling the old Mountain View Hotel owned by the Bidwell family that had been idle for several years. Augustus Bidwell, a distant cousin of the California pioneer, represented GWP in that area.

Realizing that the high cost of transporting materials for the dam could be reduced by waiting for the opening of Western Pacific, construction of dams in the upper lands was postponed.

Meanwhile, GWP erected a number of cabins at Hog Flat on the former site of the settlement of Big Bend and opposite Island Bar to house men working on the Big Bend project. In November 1906, 250 men demonstrated good progress in drilling the entrance to the new 3,500-foot tunnel that would link the old tunnel with the powerhouse. Though heavy snows in eastern Plumas County in January 1907 temporarily stalled work on Western Pacific, the Big Bend project with the advantage of a much lower elevation moved ahead under the guidance of Viele, Cooper, and Blackwell, a New York engineering consulting firm. M. A. Viele spent considerable time on the job. At that time, street gossip made GWP an affiliate of Western Pacific as the supplier of electricity to power its trains in the mountains. The presence of Edwin Hawley, with his record of heavy railroad investments, lent credence to the report, which was totally incorrect.

By the fall of 1907, engineers had constructed a five-mile trolley line in the tunnel to transport men and materials where needed. Deliveries of materials and supplies eased after WP tracks poked their way up the canyon to arrive at Island Bar in February 1908. A cable tramway strung across the Feather River carried supplies from the railroad, and the first WP carload shipment in California left Oroville on February 20 for the sixteen-mile haul to Island Bar. By that time, the labor force stood at 1,100 men.

When C. M. Waller, district manager of the GWP, appeared before the board of supervisors of Sacramento County in April 1908 seeking a franchise to run distribution wires along county roads, he whetted their curiosity by describing the Big Bend project, and all accepted his invitation to inspect the plant. Waller chartered a Northern Electric Railway car, No. 224, for the trip to Oroville, where a WP locomotive pulled the car to Island Bar, thus constituting the first WP passenger move in California. At that point the party climbed into the buckets of the aerial tram to cross the river and then boarded the cars of the miniature electric railroad for a trip through the tunnel. All went well, and Waller clinched the franchise.

Not all went well that summer for the residents of Camp 3, as they suffered two major fires. The second blaze on August 7, 1908, spread so rapidly that parents grabbed their children in their arms and ran to safety in the big tunnel. Actually, that big job was nearly finished, and the powerhouse began operating on December 23, 1908. With that task accomplished, Las Plumas Power House performed regular service until all useful machinery was salvaged before the rising water of the Oroville Dam covered the powerhouse.

The Lake Almanor and Caribou powerhouse and Bucks Lake project are discussed in subsequent chapters.

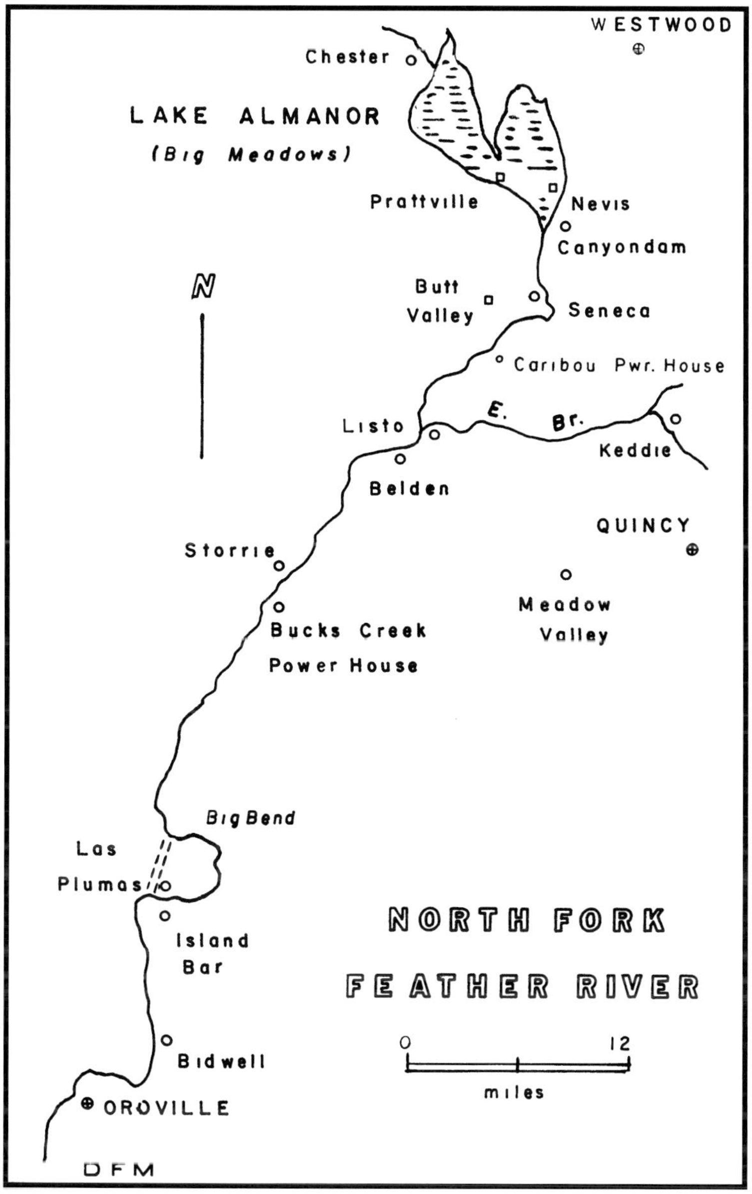

The Feather River in northern California consists of many forks and branches. Starting at the west (*left*) side of the map is the West Branch, which passes Stirling City. Next is the North Fork of the Feather River, which originates around Blue Lake in the most northwesterly corner of Plumas County. Flowing southeast, it now fills Lake Almanor, a reservoir covering Big Meadows. From there it runs south and southwest to join the other branches near Oroville.

The East Branch meets the North Fork near Belden. Tributaries around Sierra Valley form the headwaters of the Middle Fork, which flows westerly to connect with the North Fork near Bidwell. Water stored by the Oroville Dam now covers the lower confluences of the Feather River.

The Western Pacific Railroad chose the North Fork of the Feather River as far as Belden, where it paralleled the East Branch to near Keddie and continued along Spanish Creek. A tunnel under Lee Summit enabled the Western Pacific to change its course to follow the Middle Fork into the Sierra Valley, which ended with a tunnel under Beckwourth Pass.

During the planning stages of the Western Pacific, an alternate route via Deer Creek, Deer Creek Pass, Fredonyer Pass, and Susanville received much consideration. Another alternative continued up the North Fork beyond Belden, with Fredonyer Pass and Susanville as its goal.

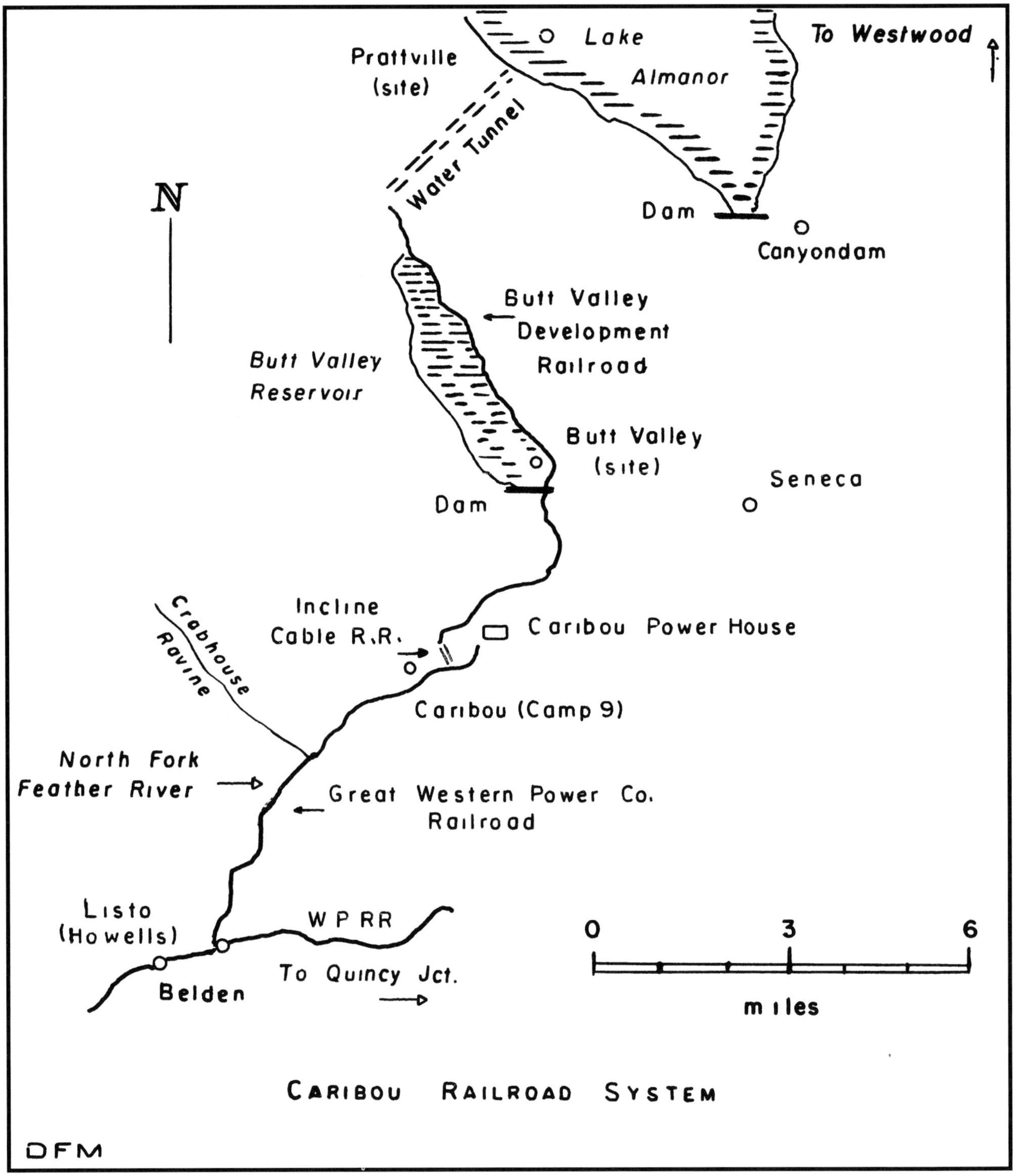

CARIBOU RAILROAD SYSTEM

LAKE ALMANOR AND CARIBOU POWERHOUSE

Big Meadows stood out as a lush green area about twenty by three miles surrounded by a larger valley in northern Plumas County. When immigrants made their way across Nevada and followed the rigorous Lassen Trail into California, they paused here to restore the strength of their livestock.

Dr. Willard Pratt, the son of a Pennsylvania physician, settled in Wisconsin and Iowa before health reasons drew him to Big Meadows in 1867. He soon erected a home for his family and a hotel for visitors. Another early settler, Lute Wellington Bunnell, left Vermont in 1852 to come to California. When in Butt Valley, he divided his time between ranching and merchandising. Moving to Big Meadows in 1869, he married a widow and entered the hotel business. One estimate concluded that two thousand people visited Big Meadows in the summer of 1881, though dairying provided the principal economic support.

Even without a railroad, some ventured into the lumber trade around Big Meadows. Back in 1876, the Watt brothers dug a long canal to bring water to power their sawmill, but this effort proved a failure. High water in May 1890 washed out another channel diverting water for a second mill that A. R. Bidwell bought in 1892, refitted with a Leffel turbine wheel, and added three dams as part of his project. Albert Frazer managed the Feather River Lumber Company near Prattville in 1892, a name similar to a later firm at Delleker.

Mrs. M. McMillan operated the Prattville Hotel under a lease in 1892, and after her only son died, she gave up her lease to the new owner, L. B. Gardner. As 1895 began, W. J. Costar, an Oroville real estate man, listed the Prattville Hotel, a two-and-one-half-story building, together with five hundred acres for sale at a price of seven thousand dollars with terms of four thousand dollars down and the balance at 10 percent interest.

Prattville occupies an area plagued by heavy snows. In February 1895, the large forty-stamp mill and boardinghouse of the Savercool Mine slid down the hill in a big snowslide. Fortunately, the men, sleeping in the bunkhouse some distance away, escaped injury.

Bunnell accepted R. A. Costar as a partner in his various enterprises in the fall of 1895, while Abner Mack offered board and lodging at his Big Spring House not far from Bunnell's place.

When the snows had gone in the late spring, Big Meadows became one of most pleasant valleys in California with a host of attractions. "The hotel at Prattville on the banks of the magnificent spring is one of the grandest in America. Boating and fishing in the stream from the spring cannot be excelled anywhere," the *Oroville Register* boasted in 1896. Even a flock of pelicans discovered the charm of Big Meadows that year as they worked the sloughs and small streams leading to the North Fork of the Feather River.

The popularity of Bunnell's place grew each summer, and in 1903 he also assumed management of the Prattville Hotel. The opening of the branch railroad to Stirling City the following year plus "an up-to-date stage line" improved access and crowded the resorts.

But this situation could not last forever. Great stands of timber—someone counted twenty-seven sugar pines with diameters of at least seven feet—captured the attention of T. B. Walker and his Red River Lumber Company. As previously described, the narrow outlet at the lower end of the valley invited construction of a dam and formation of Lake Almanor as a step of the plan of hydroelectric development by the Great Western Power Company.

As part of its plan to acquire Big Meadows, GWP purchased and closed both the Prattville Hotel and the Bunnell House. Frank Sorseli seized the opportunity to build a twenty-eight-room hotel in Prattville in 1908.

While Prattville citizens and visitors were enjoying a picnic and baseball game on Saturday afternoon, July 3, 1909, someone noticed smoke pouring from the back of Abbott's store. With no water system in town, people stood almost helpless as flames quickly consumed the Sorseli saloon and his new hotel. So intense was the heat that the old Prattville Hotel, across the street and two hundred feet away, also caught fire. Sorseli had only three thousand dollars in a fire insurance policy expiring at noon that day, which pushed his losses to twenty-five thousand dollars. The town slowly rebuilt, and R. A. Costar erected a larger store.

The Nevis Dam Forms Lake Almanor

As chronicled in a previous chapter, Justin Howells envisioned a huge artificial lake at Big Meadows to provide a reliable flow of water for Las Plumas hydroelectric plant.

After quietly buying a good portion of the farms and timberlands of Big Meadows, purchases continued on a more open basis. A number of Big Meadows residents had already moved to Chester after selling their properties. In June 1911, Annie K. Bidwell, widow of pioneer John Bidwell, sold eight hundred acres to Great Western Power for a reported thirty thousand dollars, a transaction including "Robin's Nest," her seventeen-room summer cottage.

Great Western Power established its own sawmill in Butt Valley and, with sixty workers, was cutting sixty thousand board feet each day. At that time the lumber went into the construction of a flume paralleling the old Caribou mining ditch to carry water to a point nine hundred feet above a temporary power plant at Emmons Bar. Electricity from this plant served in the construction of Nevis Dam.

More people sold their property to GWP, recognizing the futility of trying to retain their lands. Frank Sorseli sold his remaining Prattville property in March 1912. The next month, the San Francisco office of GWP, after considering Prattville, dispatched a stern order: "Move the living, raze and burn the town and rebury the dead." Don Moorhead and his crew of twenty-five complied.

In the fall, GWP lawyers filed condemnation suits against twenty-seven individuals and "numerous John Does." Meanwhile, construction of the dam at Nevis, under way since April 1912, kept seven hundred men employed. Many were of Greek origin, which disappointed nearby Greenville saloon keepers, as they were not heavy drinkers.

Twenty-two multiple concrete arches made up the design of the Nevis Dam, but considerable anxiety rose in the fall of 1912 concerning the safety of the structure. With winter approaching, GWP reduced its forces and sold its livestock rather than feeding idle animals. Confusion and doubts grew with the controversy over the project, and the company halted work. Instead, a hydraulic-fill dam was placed upstream, and the earlier construction was abandoned.

Workers convened in May 1913, but the lake began forming before the dam was essentially completed in June 1914. On April 28, a visitor had noted that water covered the old main street of Prattville and had risen to within nine feet of the spillway. All through the winter, loggers from the Red River Lumber Company had been cutting trees below the flood line of 4,450 feet. GWP had a 60-foot steam launch on Lake Almanor—the name coined from selected parts of the names of three daughters of Guy Earl—and the lumber company had another launch under construction. Both were to tow logs to the eastern shore where they would be moved overland to the Westwood mill.

Although building the dam achieved the initial purpose of storing water to provide a steady flow during dry years such as 1915 and 1918, there was more to come to meet the growing demand for electricity.

The hydroelectric system envisioned by Great Western Power constituted a well-coordinated system of power plants. After flooding Big Meadows, water would flow through a tunnel to Butt Creek to be stored by the new Butt Valley Dam. Another tunnel would convey water to the Caribou powerhouse on the North Fork of the Feather River. (In more recent years, the system has been expanded with more tunnels and power plants.)

Delivery of material and supplies, unlike the flow of water, moved in the opposite direction, with a major segment uphill. For this purpose, Stone and Webster (S&W), the general contractor, contemplated an elaborate railroad system. Starting at Western Pacific just east of Belden, a 9.2-mile standard-gauge railroad extended to the site of the Caribou power plant.

The Caribou Railroad System

With the end of World War I and the Armistice signed, it proved the opportune time to carry out plans for further development of the power potential. A shipment of lumber that arrived at Belden for surveyors' use in March 1919 served as a sign of forthcoming activity. A work force grew around Belden, and in July, Stone and Webster concentrated most of the five hundred available men on the construction of the railroad. Though the standard-gauge segment measured just a little more than nine miles, its location challenged civil engineers.

Two miles east of Belden, a new station board and a Western Pacific siding marked the beginning of the Caribou railroad. (The new station of Listo sometimes appears as "Howells" on maps.) From its connection with the WP sidetrack at Listo, the GWP railroad immediately entered a switchback to a lower elevation. In the absence of a convenient hillside, long trestles accommodated the switchback trackage, and, even with short tail tracks (200 feet), one estimated that 1 million board feet of lumber proved necessary. Leaving the last switch point, the new railroad headed for the east side of the North Fork of the Feather River after crossing the East Branch. For some little distance before reaching the East Branch, the GWP railroad ran parallel about 150 feet from the Western Pacific track that continued eastward to Quincy Jct. and beyond without crossing the East Branch.

Continuing along the east side of the North Fork, the Caribou railroad soon passed the site of the old Gansner brewery and then crossed to the west side of the North Fork at Adams Bar. As the railroad bridged Crabhouse Ravine, it went by the site of the early Caribou settlement.

A mile or so beyond, it reached Camp 9, the headquarters camp of Stone and Webster; today, powerhouse-employee cottages replace the construction camp. The present auto road, now using the former railroad grade, offers conclusive evidence that blasting much of the canyon wall in the last mile to the Caribou powerhouse must have been a formidable task.

Transportation needs still loomed ahead. Near the powerhouse, a narrow-gauge, cable-powered railroad reached up a 57 percent grade to a crest 1,400 feet above its base to join more narrow-gauge tracks high above Butt Creek. For the first four miles, the little railroad clung to the hills. Many decades ago, miners had built a flume along this route that the railroad builders found useful as the foundation for several miles of the new roadbed. In the next four miles the railroad depended on long trestles high up on the walls of the canyon before reaching the GWP sawmill camp and finally the south entrance of Tunnel No. 1, eleven miles from the beginning. This tunnel conducted water from Lake Almanor to the powerhouse downstream. (Two additional incline tramways formed adjuncts to the system. One ran uphill from this tunnel entrance, and a shorter one appears to have paralleled the incline down by the powerhouse.)

With all the work required for the Caribou transportation system and other needs involving some two thousand men, Belden buzzed with activity. Its citizens took their responsibilities seriously and stood ready to defend their opinions. One August school-board election ended in a free-for-all after the ballots had been counted.

In August 1919, the first incline railroad went into service, and down below, Stone and Webster forces had the grading moving along nicely. The completion of tracklaying, expected at the end of September, received a setback when the force went on strike.

After enjoying a self-imposed vacation, the S&W crew began drifting back to work, and when William Watson, Plumas County surveyor, returned to Quincy on October 20 after a month in the Stone and Webster Crabhouse Creek camp, he reported that the crew had laid six miles of track and that a large gang was distributing ballast.

When the railroad began operating about January 1920, the local S&W management declared it to be "one of the busiest little roads in the country"—a claim reflecting the pride of accomplishment in spite of many difficulties. Though operations of the Caribou power plant began on May 6, 1921, much work remained to be done that kept the little railroad system busy.

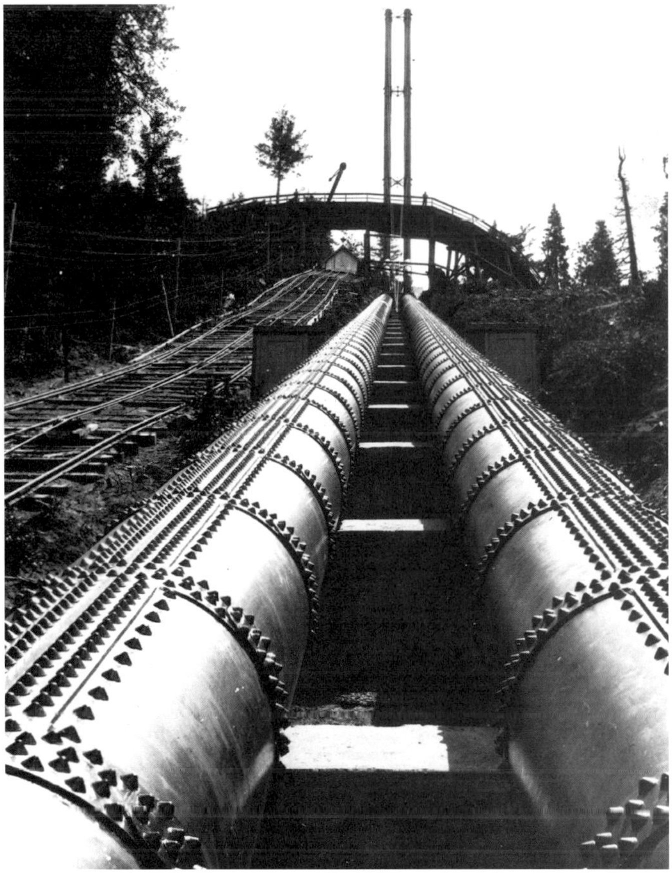

Penstocks and incline trackage.

Expansion and improvements of the power facilities continued over the years, long after the railroad system ceased to exist. Drilling tunnels and building dams disrupted the old trails and roads, but GWP repaired them. A new dam in Butt Valley replaced a smaller dam in 1924, covering a once thriving community. By raising the Nevis Dam several times, Lake Almanor greatly increased in size; in 1926, GWP agreed to build a causeway across the north end of the lake for auto traffic, which also accommodated the tracks of the Red River Lumber Company destined to Chester. Eight years later, the Caribou railroad was abandoned.

In the late 1950s, Pacific Gas and Electric added more generating capacity all over its system. A second plant was built at Caribou, while the company added others at Belden and Butt Valley. In some cases, long tunnels were drilled to connect with penstocks, but this work did not require new railroads.

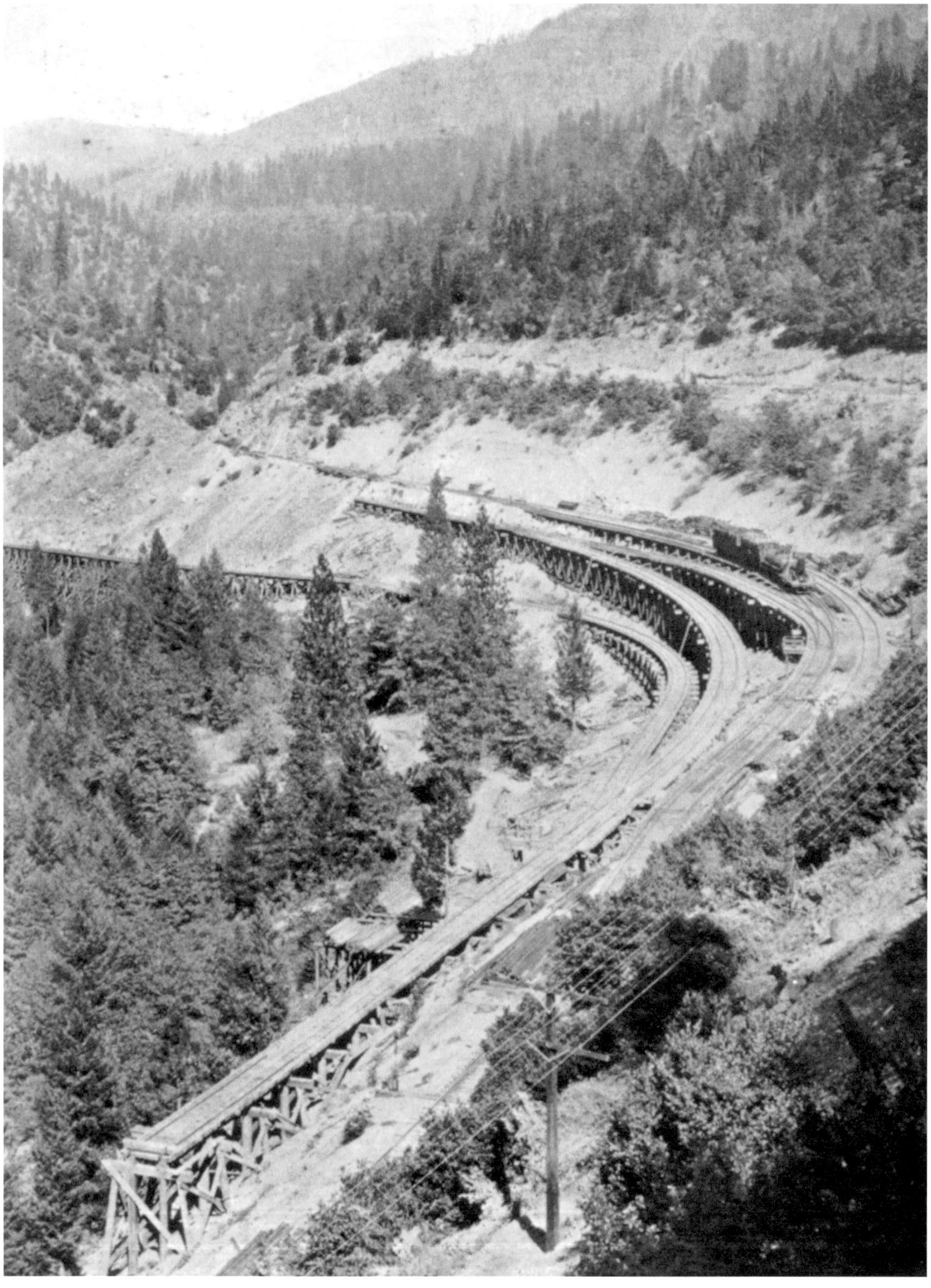

To facilitate the construction of the Caribou power plant and water resources, Great Western Power Company built a system of railroads. This scene, looking northeast from Listo (Howells), shows the connection and the Western Pacific Railroad main line (behind the short train) and the GWP switchback necessary to reach its lower crossing of the East Branch of the North Fork of the Feather River. It then followed the North Fork of the Feather River to the powerhouse. (Stone and Webster)

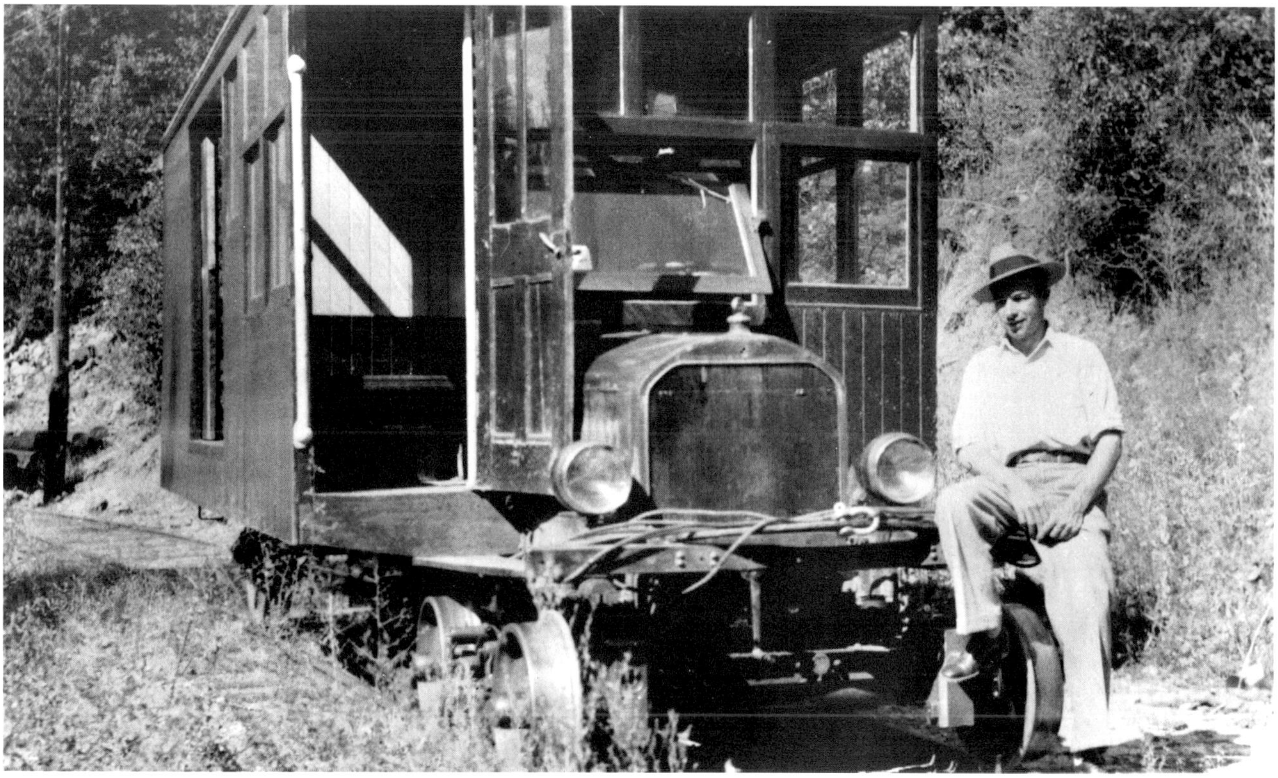

Above: An improvised rail motorcar transported workers to the site of the powerhouse. The "pilot" of this vehicle is unidentified. (James E. Boynton collection)

Below: At Camp 12 (near Listo), the camera recorded WP No. 199 when Stone and Webster borrowed it for local service. This motorcar and its twin served the WP San Jose branch in later years. (James E. Boynton collection).

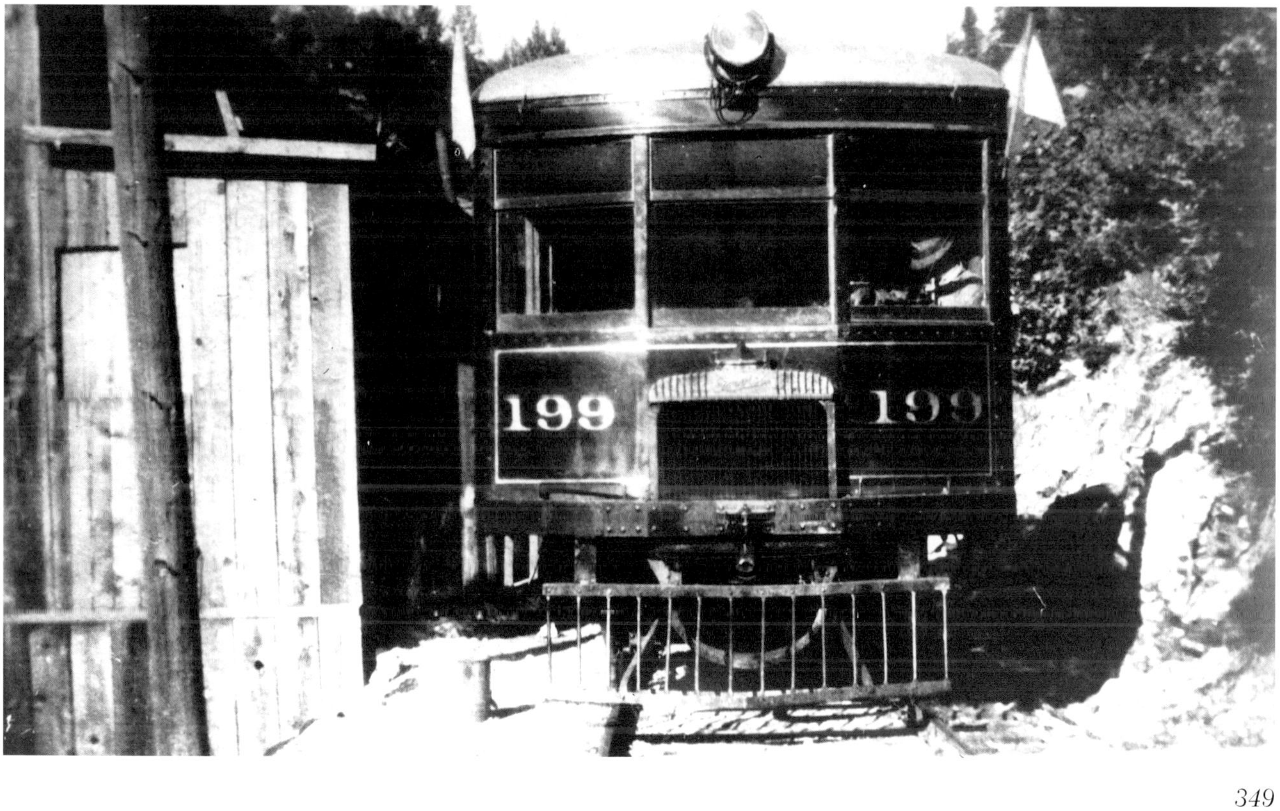

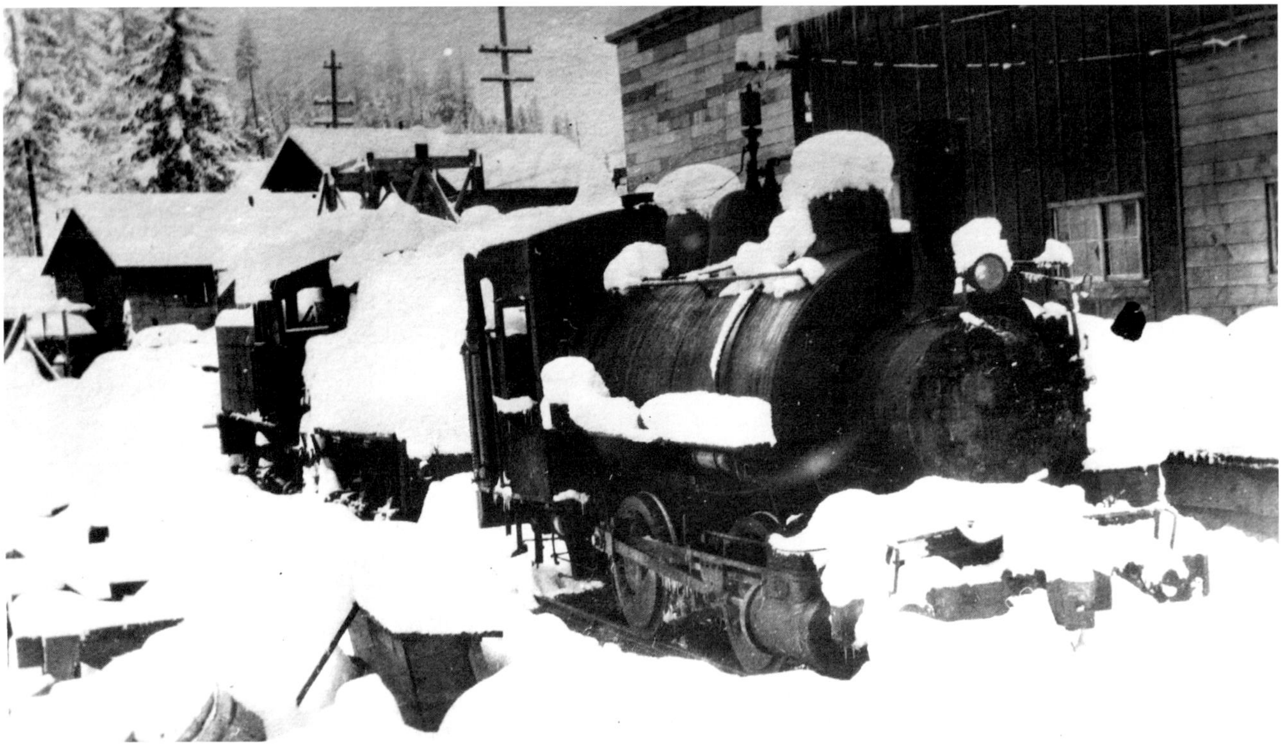

Above: A winter snow idled Stone and Webster engines at Caribou. No. 3 stands at the left, and the locomotive American is on the right. (Vern Richards photograph, James E. Boynton collection)

Below: Though the management desired speedy construction of the hydroelectric plant, nothing was happening, as this locomotive was marooned at Caribou (Camp 9) in ten inches of snow. (James E. Boynton collection)

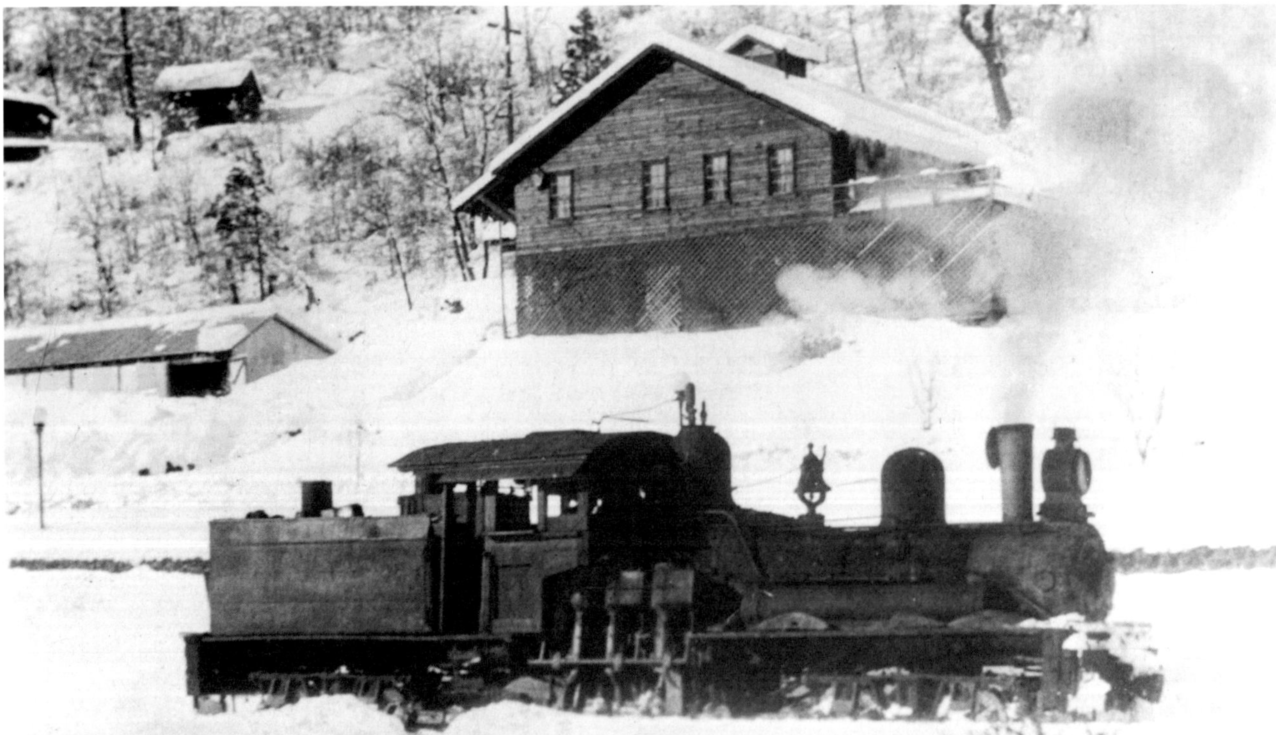

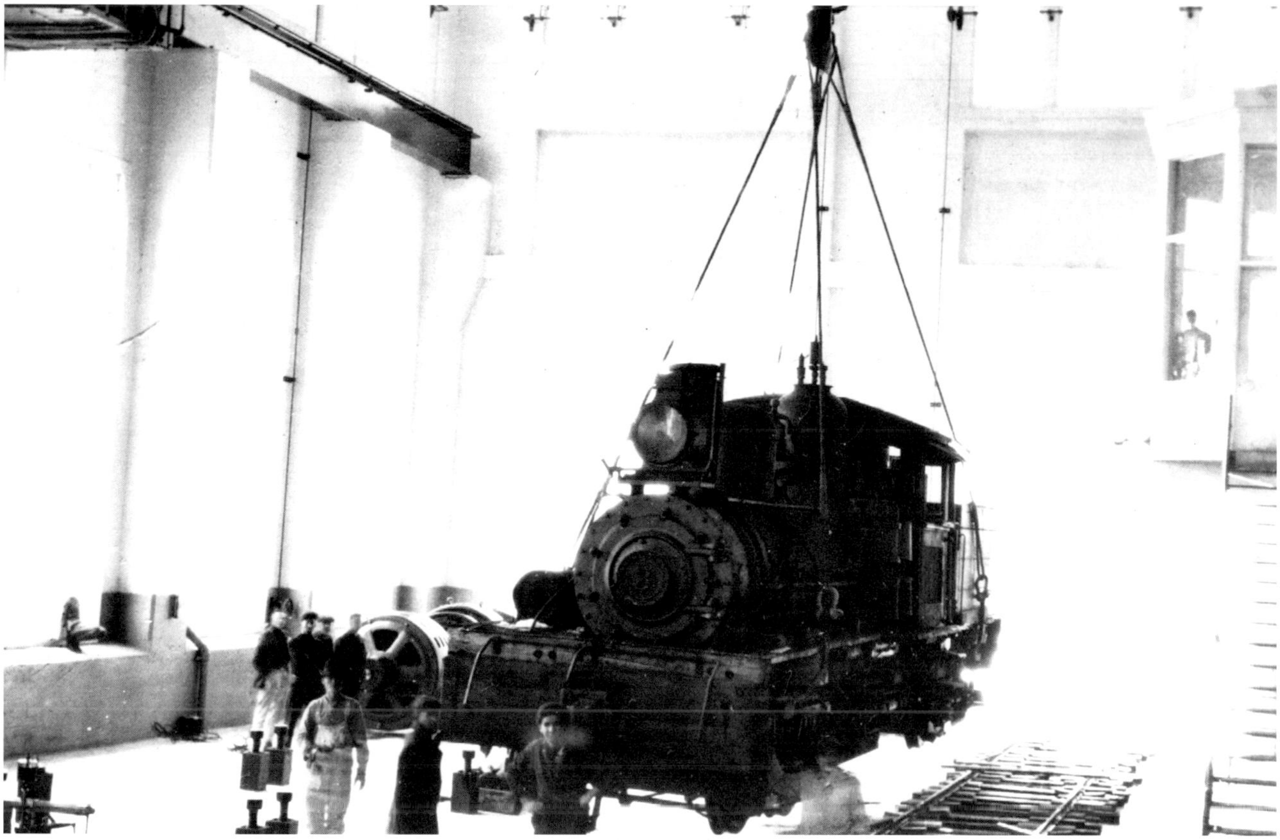

Above: In the absence of a turntable, the hoist in the Caribou powerhouse formed a practical means of reversing the locomotive. (James E. Boynton collection)

Right: After reaching the power plant, an inclined thirty-six-inch-gauge cable railroad constituted the second portion of the GWP railroad system. (Stone and Webster)

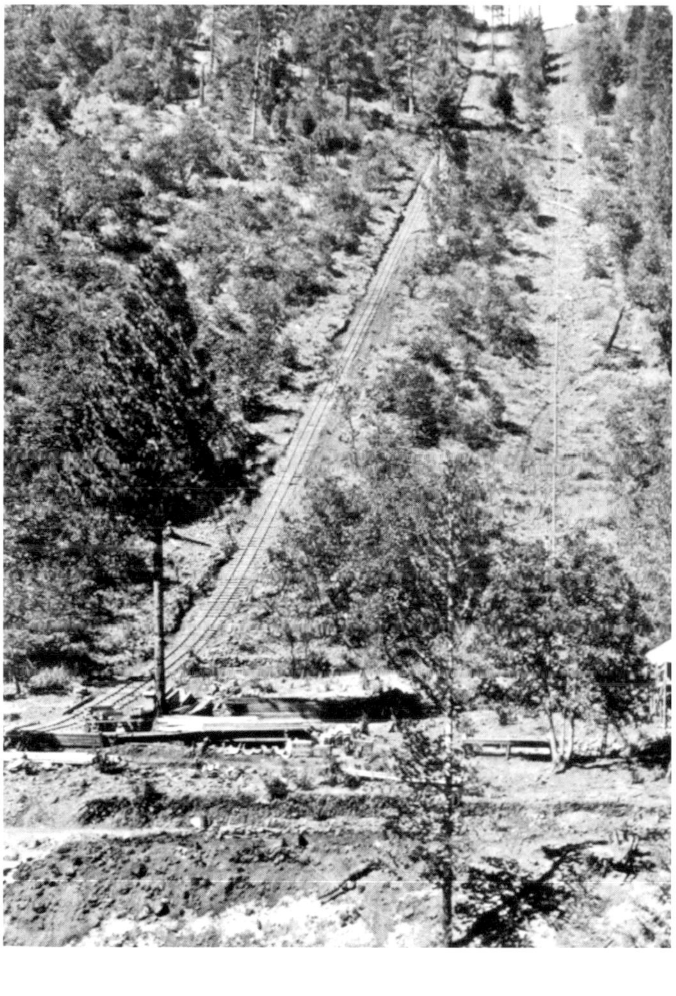

Right: The steep pitch of the hillside created special problems for the branch of the inclined cable railroad. Use of rock ballast was impractical, and only by attaching the track to adjoining rocks by cable could the track be held in place. (James E. Boynton photograph)

Below: To prevent the cable from cutting the ties, cable drums were installed at various points on the line. (James E. Boynton photograph)

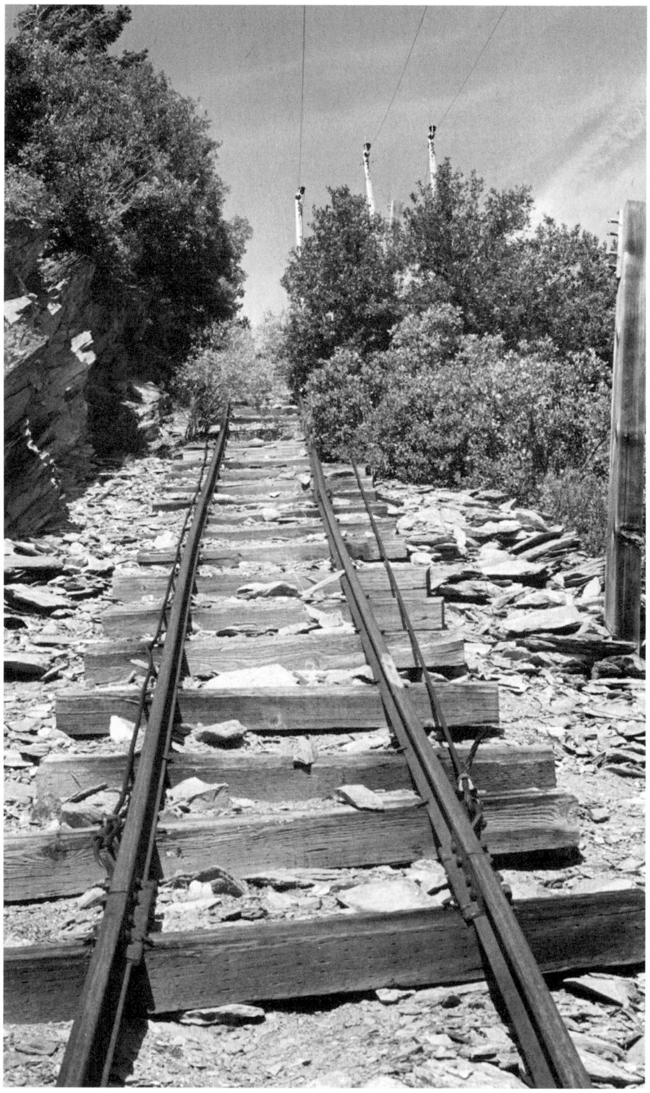

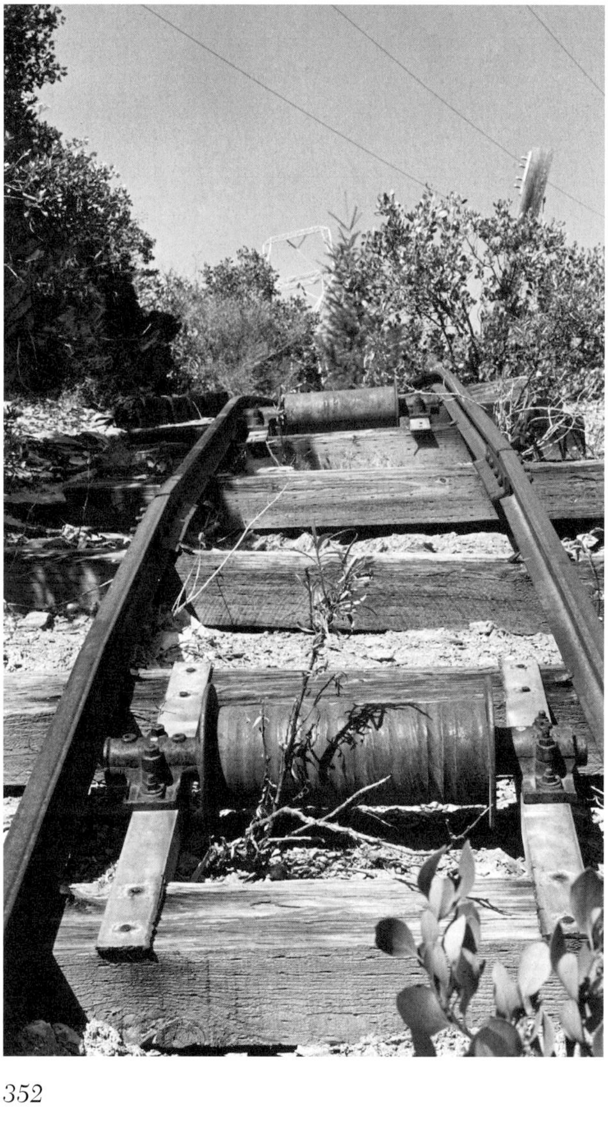

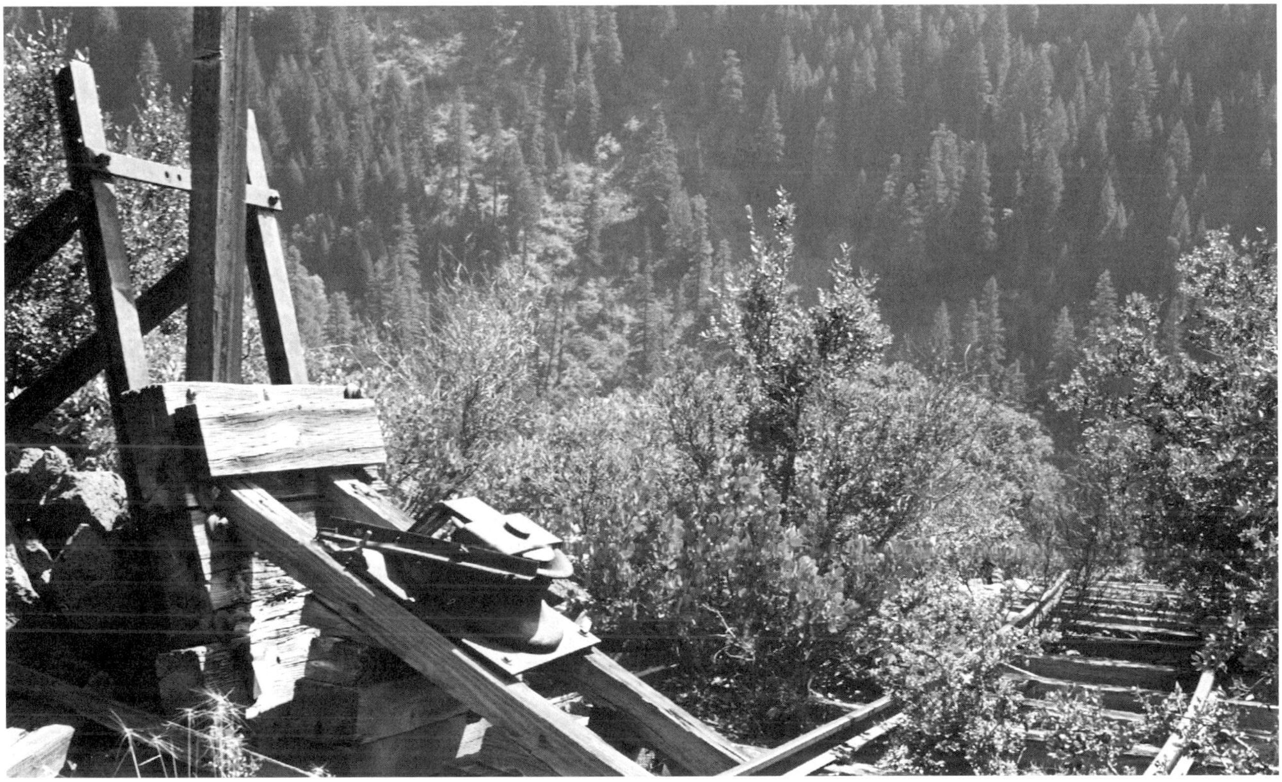

A curve in the track by the surge tank created another challenge for locating engineers, which they solved with this pulley wheel and thus kept the cars on the track. (James E. Boynton photograph)

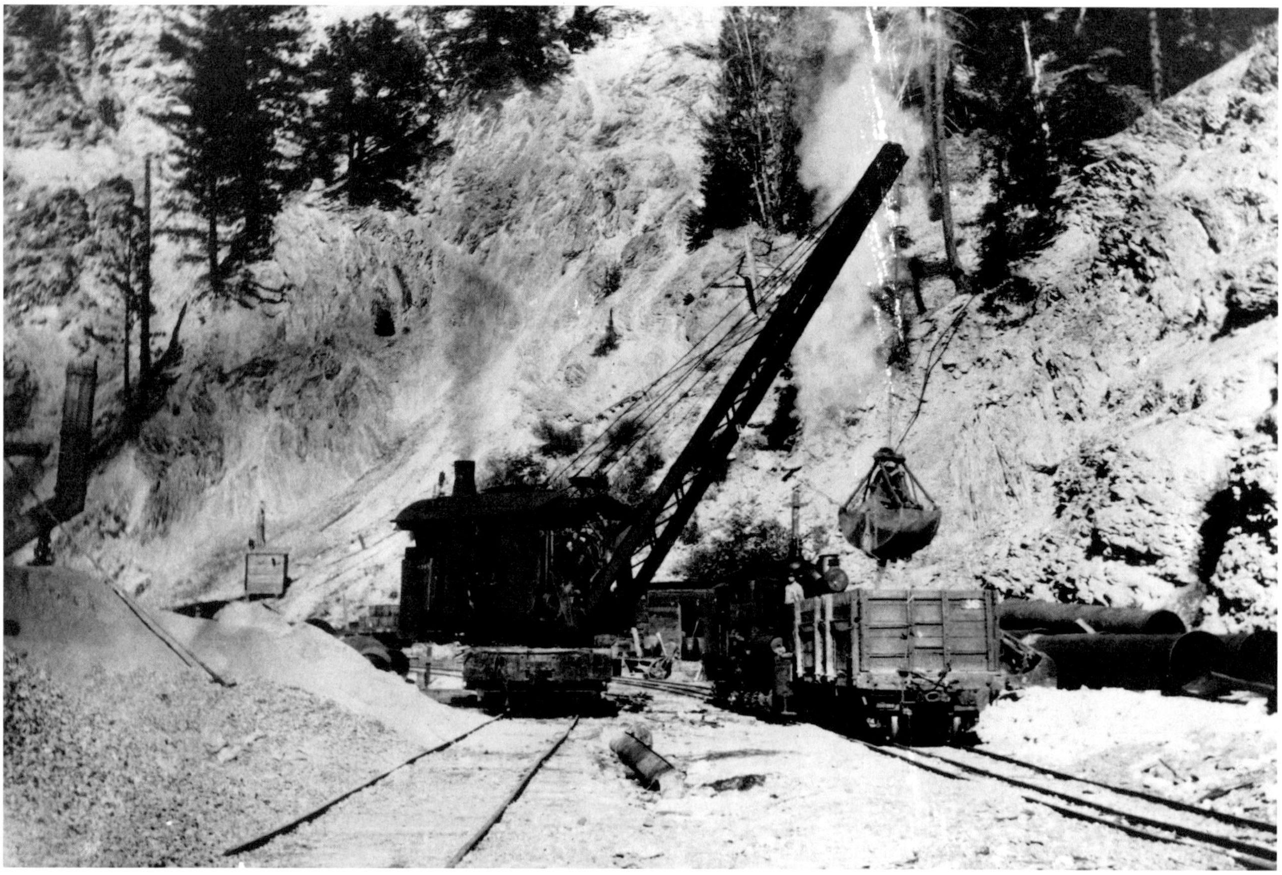

Loading aggregates in the narrow-gauge bucket car. Next it will be pulled up the cable incline. A small Shay engine is partly hidden behind the crane. (James E. Boynton collection)

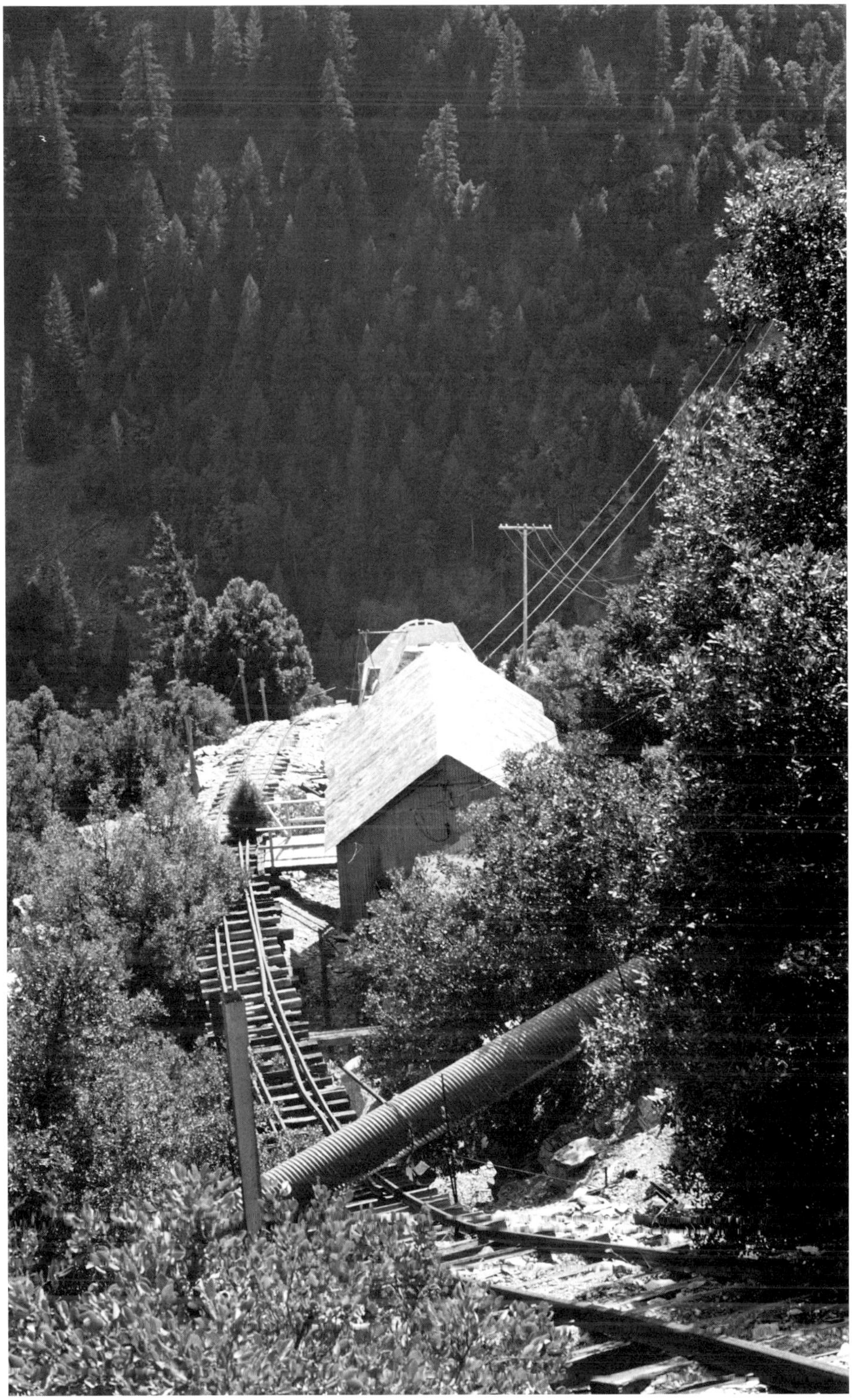

Looking down the branch incline to the control house at the head of the penstock, which carried water to the turbines below in the Caribou powerhouse. (James E. Boynton photograph)

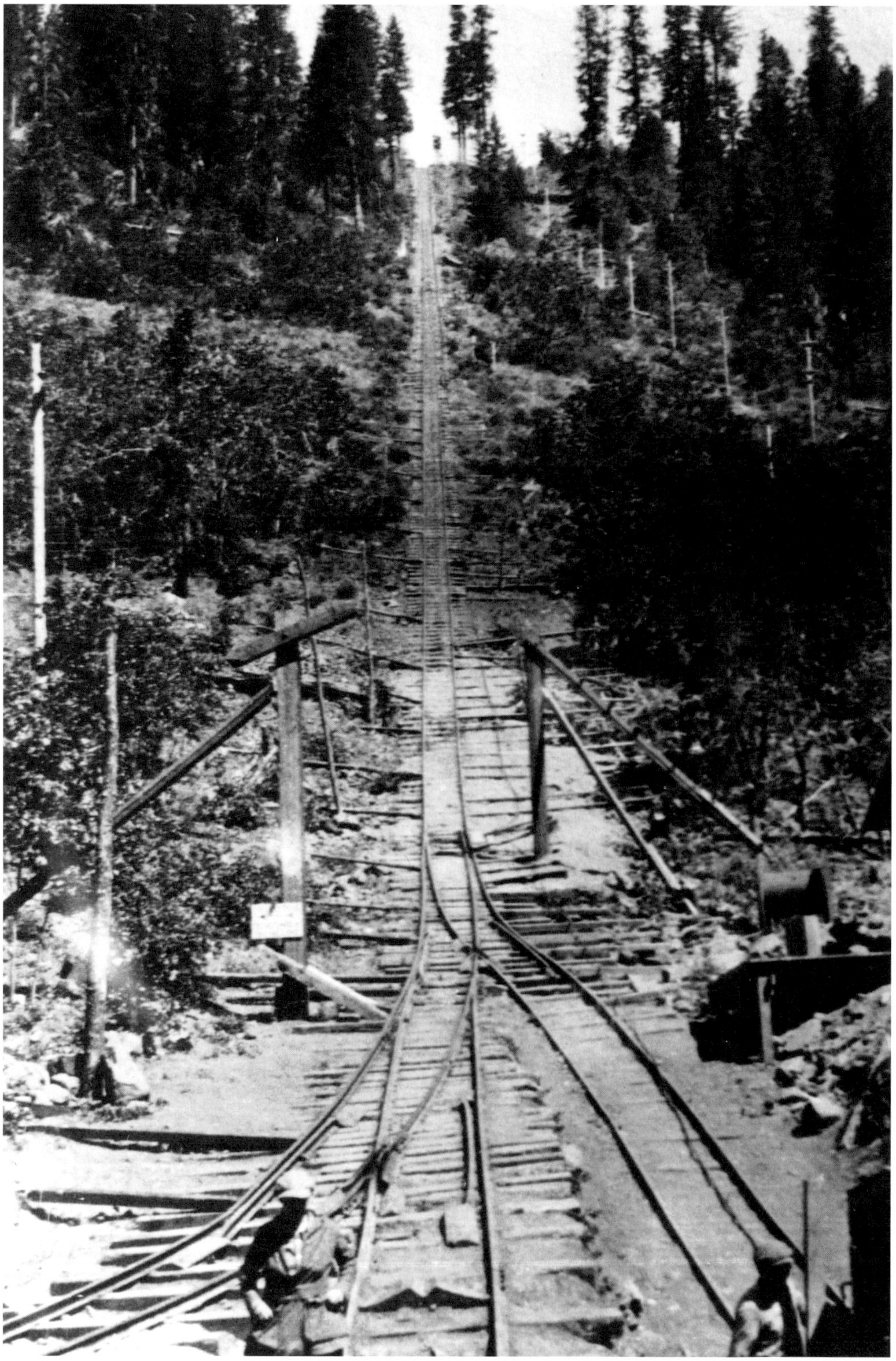

Another incline cable line at the end of the railroad raised cars to the level of Lake Almanor. (James E. Boynton collection)

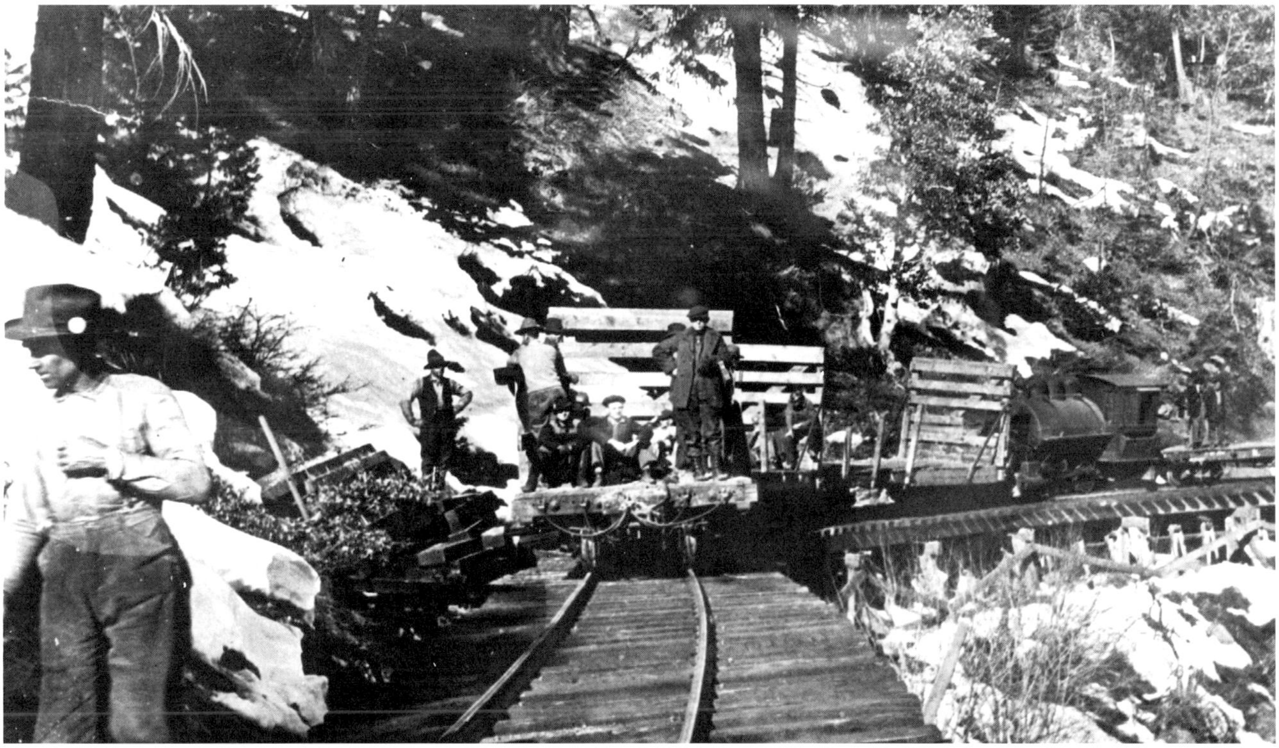

Above: Another scene along the BVD line. The flatcar behind the small engine bears ownership initials of a former narrow-gauge section of the Northwestern Pacific Railroad. (James E. Boynton collection)

Below: The railroad system formed an important part in the construction of the pipelines and tunnels bringing water under high pressure from Lake Almanor to turn the turbines in the Caribou powerhouse. Trains from Listo entered the building at the lower left corner of the structure. (James E. Boynton photograph)

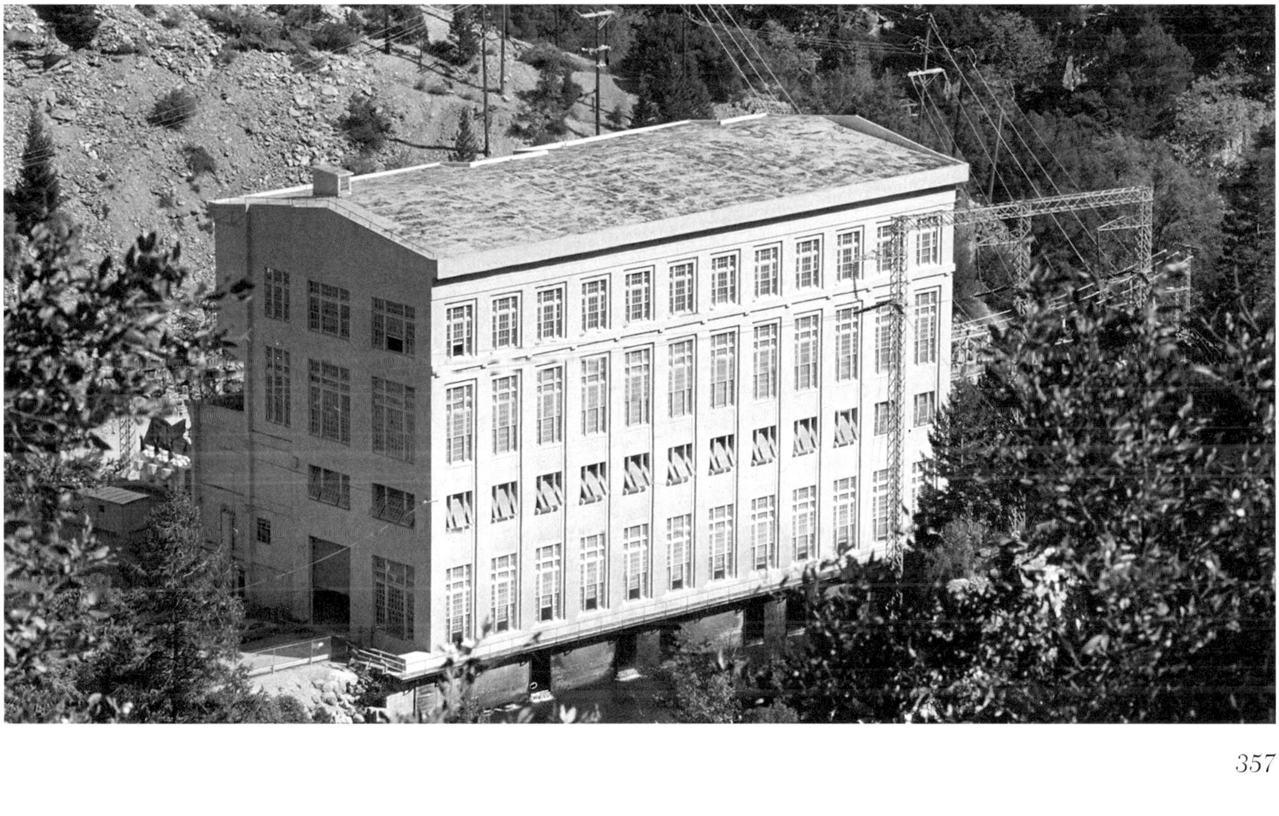

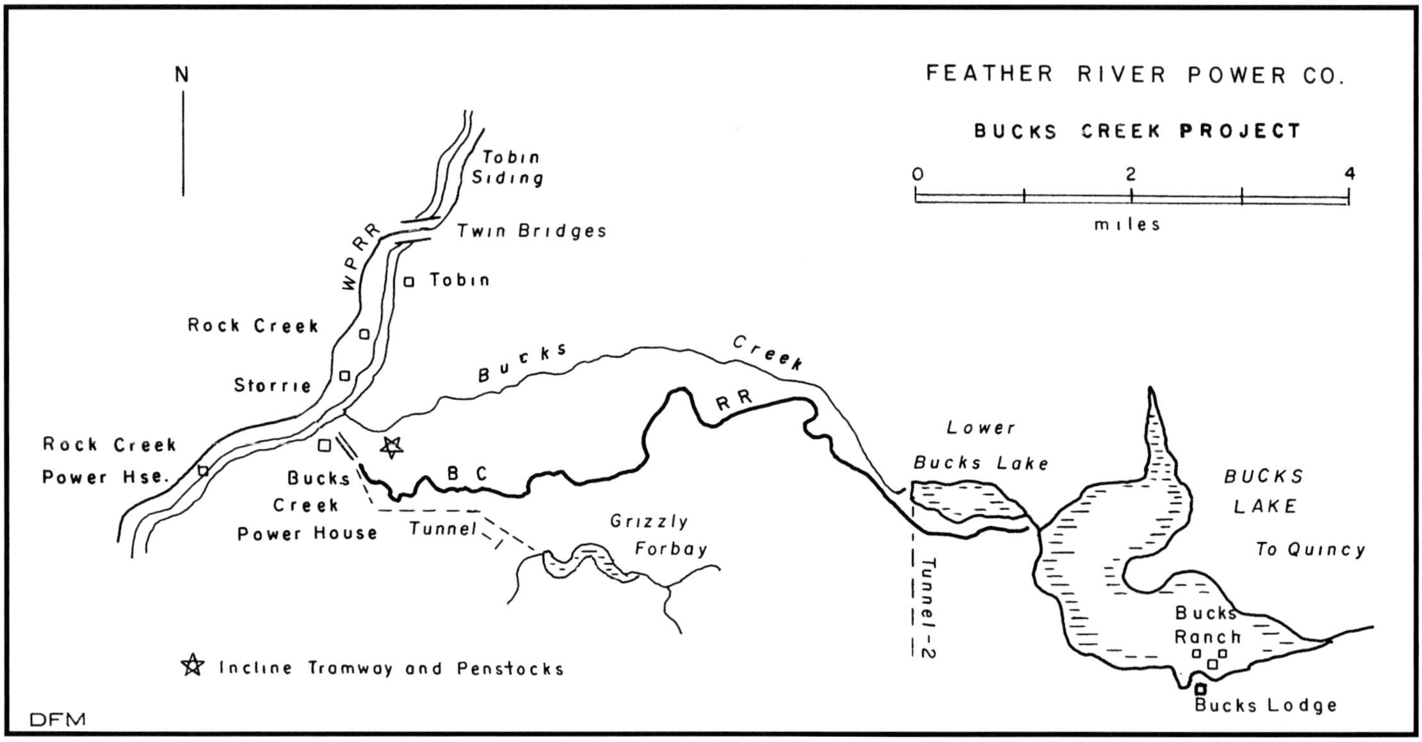
FEATHER RIVER POWER CO.
BUCKS CREEK PROJECT
0
2
4
miles
N
Tobin Siding
Twin Bridges
WPRR
Tobin
Rock Creek
Storrie
Bucks Creek
RR
Rock Creek Power Hse.
Bucks Creek Power House
B C
Tunnel
Grizzly Forbay
Lower Bucks Lake
Tunnel-2
BUCKS LAKE
To Quincy
Bucks Ranch
Bucks Lodge
Incline Tramway and Penstocks
DFM

BUCKS LAKE RAILROAD

California's population and industry growth hastened the development of additional sources of electrical generation. The difference in elevation of water at Bucks Lake and the Feather River at Storrie caught the attention of electrical engineers.

Bucks Ranch (Creek) took its name from Horace Bucklin who arrived on the scene with Francis Walker in 1850. Though the men remained there only a short time, the name suited the stage operators when they established a stop on the road from Oroville to the mountains.

Until the Feather River Highway along the North Fork was opened in 1937, the only practical wagon or auto road from Oroville to Quincy passed through Berry Creek, Mountain House, Letter Box, Bucks Ranch, and Meadow Valley on the way. Heavy accumulations of snow—sometimes as much as fourteen feet at Bucks Lake—kept the road closed from late fall until the following June. Many residents, recognizing the problems, regularly stored their cars in Oroville for the winter.

The power potential of Bucks Creek commanded the attention of various parties, and an intensive review began in the early 1920s. Karl Brehme and Lars R. Jorgenson secured a permit from the Federal Power Commission in 1921 to develop a section of the North Fork of the Feather River and "some upstream storage." Several years later, contractors Robert C. Storrie and Robert B. Muir joined these two men in a partnership in the name of the Feather River Power Company, which became a corporation on June 5, 1925.

Considerable planning followed, and the California Railroad Commission approved the project in 1925 together with the authority to issue stocks and bonds for financing. Months before the Federal Power Commission gave its final approval on April 14, 1926, some preliminary work had begun.

Transportation constituted a key in successful development. Several railroads proved necessary, along with three reservoirs (the largest forming Bucks Lake), two long tunnels, eight miles of conduits, penstocks, a power station, and a transformer yard.

Railroad construction began with a standard-gauge spur leaving the Western Pacific at a new station of Storrie and crossing the North Fork to the powerhouse. An incline tramway paralleled the penstocks up the canyon wall to connect with the narrow-gauge railroad winding along the mountains together with trails and truck roads to the Bucks reservoir. The last of three contracts signed August 5, 1925, expected the eight million–dollar project to be completed by July 1, 1927.

Surveys, continuing through 1925 and early 1926, included a reconnaissance for the narrow-gauge railroad. In November, after consulting with project engineer B. T. Millard, William Watson, a long-established Quincy surveyor, announced that work would "start at once."

Local businesses benefited. The Spanish Peak Lumber Company received an order for one hundred thousand feet of lumber, and G. H. Maurer, a sometime logger, agreed to haul the wood to Bucks Ranch. Traffic volume of the Quincy Railroad rose slightly as the Feather River Power Company used the railroad for part of the haul of the big steam shovel. Most material was unloaded at Storrie on the Western Pacific and taken to the site by the tramway and new railroad.

In February 1926, the company let a subcontract for the two major tunnels where the first of two tragedies struck two months later when falling rocks killed five workers in Tunnel No. 2. Other workers had the incline tramway almost finished by the early summer as the forming of the bridge piers and grading of the spur from Western Pacific was taking place. Another large steam shovel arrived at the Quincy RR dock and inched its way to Bucks Ranch for the preparatory excavation work for the reservoir. Except for three days in August when a forest fire suspended regular work, the contractor made good progress on the dam and Tunnel No. 2.

The location of the standard-gauge spur underwent a change. Original plans contemplated the spur to begin above Tobin where Western Pacific crossed the Feather River and then go down the river for slightly more than two miles to the site of the Bucks Creek powerhouse. As the route finally adopted, the shortened "Storrie Railroad" entered a switchback shortly after leaving WP and crossed the river on a low-level bridge to the powerhouse site.

John Owens ran the switcher for about a year, delivering construction supplies, but decided to move to Sacramento in January 1927. Perhaps the deep snow on

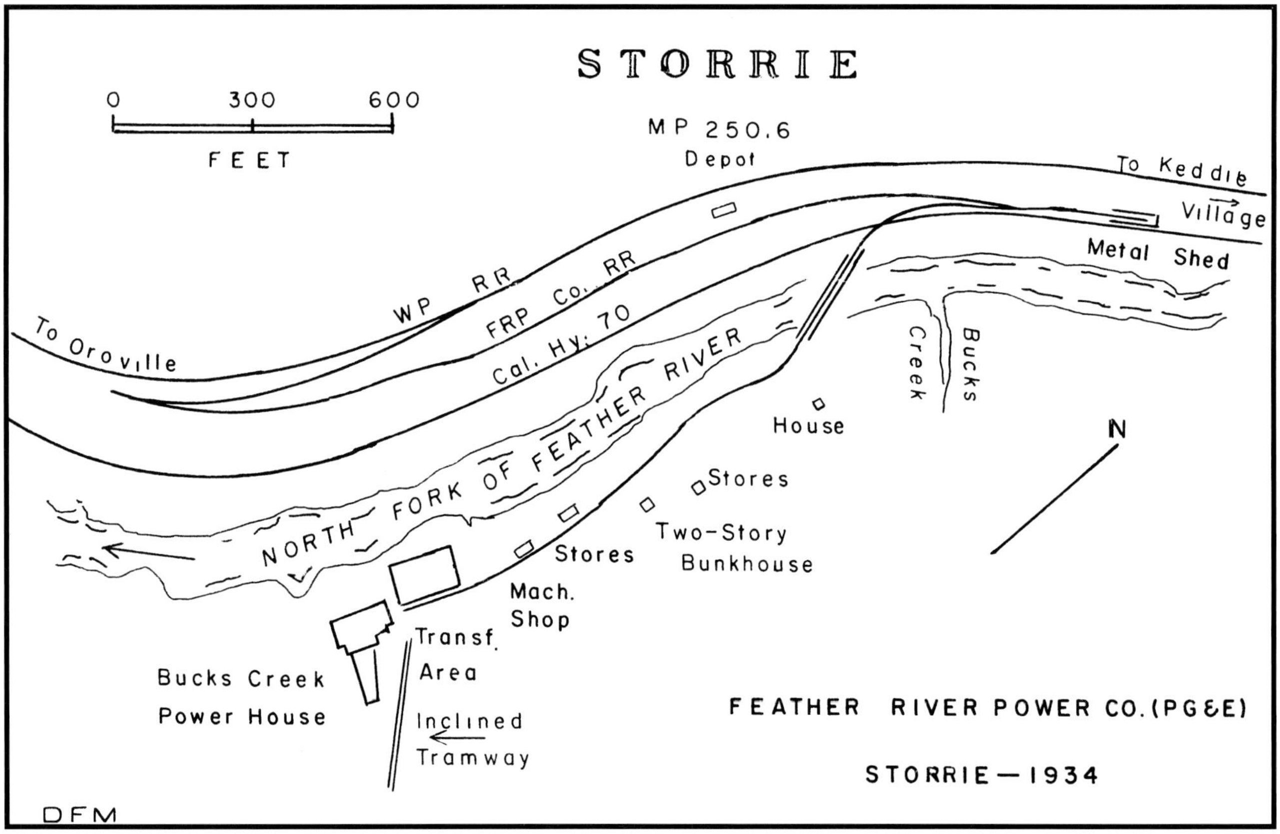

the hills—the heaviest in years—contributed to his decision. Certainly, the contractors faced extreme difficulties getting material to Bucks Ranch. An eight-day storm paralyzed Western Pacific that year. The eastbound passenger train was stalled in the canyon, and a slide of snow and dirt buried the engine of a freight train near Belden. Fortunately, the crew escaped injuries, but no trains ran for several days.

With the storms less intensive, work could be resumed. Perhaps the most personal disturbance occurred in mid-March 1927 when Sheriff L. A. Braden and a full crew of deputies raided the resort of Rae and Henderson in "upper Storrie." Prohibition proved expensive: each proprietor paid a fine of four hundred dollars. Offsetting this loss but in a different way, the company built five modern cottages and a clubhouse on Dead Man's Bar, just east of Storrie.

For WP, the powerhouse construction proved a bonanza; according to local reports, the railroad delivered almost two hundred cars of merchandise and material to Storrie each month.

After watching John C. Rainer's large traveling outfit of fifteen trucks and ten touring cars for construction of the dam, some Quincy people likened the procession to a traveling circus. At Bucks Ranch, where four hundred men worked on the dam forming the lake, thirteen children enrolled in the local school.

The Little Railroad

The route of the little railroad climbed eight hundred feet in the ten miles between the top of the incline railway and Bucks Ranch. As the narrow-gauge railroad wound along the crest of the ridge, initially it was poised some two thousand feet above Bucks Creek. Much of the time, the engine shunted a few cars of material and supplied one of several dams making up the water-collection system. This routine was shattered on November 27, 1927, after the train left its western terminus on the way to the dam, and the new locomotive, refusing to follow a curve, chose to leave the rails and hurtle into the canyon, coming to a rest some two thousand feet below. Sensing the errant behavior, the engineer on the inside of the curve jumped, miraculously escaping injury. Not so fortunate was C. "Con" Sullivan who was riding in the engine. Being on the outside of the curve, he had no chance to jump before the locomotive rolled down the steep mountainside. Thrown out of the cab about seven hundred feet down, he was killed instantly. Ironically, Sullivan had taken the brakeman's assignment just fifteen minutes before the fatal event!

Project engineer B. T. Millard told a reporter of the progress shortly before Christmas 1927. The force totaled about 400 men, with 150 at Bucks Lake, an equal number at Storrie, and 100 at the nearby Grizzly Creek dam. With a greatly reduced force, work was to continue all winter. Millard said the little railroad, not bothered by snow this year, operated regularly. The incline tramway, operating two cars moving in opposite directions on three rails—with a suitable passing track—climbed twenty-five hundred feet with a distance of forty-eight hundred feet.

Water would soon start accumulating behind the dam to form Bucks Lake and flood two ranches. For the past three years, E. L. Lane had operated a store in connection with his auto camp and gasoline filling station. The old Bucks Ranch hotel, built of hand-hewn logs, was to be demolished along with other ranch buildings before the reservoir filled. This destruction proved unnecessary, as the hotel, barn, and shop went up in flames on January 13, 1928 (a Friday), believed to be the work of an arsonist. And over in Portola, the Palace Hotel of Dan Durham burned the next morning. Local citizens placed a plaque near the site of the Bucks Ranch hotel, and appropriately William Watson gave the principal address at the dedication of August 1931.

At the time of the hotel fire, construction neared completion. Already the easterly 1.8 miles of railroad tracks had been removed and the grade converted to an auto road extending to a point near Grizzly Dam. February 23, 1928, marked the date of the first test of the power plant. On March 4, the generating units commenced operating, and four days later, the power company accepted electrical energy. Full operations began on August 1, 1928, and, at that time, the "2,561-foot head" of the Bucks Creek power plant stood as the highest in the United States.

Also in March 1928, Great Western Power acquired the Feather River Power Company, and in June 1930 Great Western Power was merged into the Pacific Gas and Electric Company.

The contractors finished their work in October 1928, and later that month the Storrie Social Club dedicated the clubhouse serving the employees living in five houses and a dormitory. Though the remainder of the little railroad was abandoned—having served its purpose—the location today is marked by a trail. For some years after the project's completion, a little Whitcomb engine pulled an occasional car over the spur to the Bucks Creek powerhouse.

ORO ELECTRIC CORPORATION
PROPOSED RAILROAD TO POWER PLANT ON YELLOW CREEK

Eight months after the Oro Electric Corporation had been incorporated on May 11, 1911, it took over the Oro Water, Light, and Power Company that provided electricity to Oroville. It also had five gold dredges operating near that city. The new company, headed by J. W. Goodwin, president, and R. Leo Van der Naillen, general manager, contemplated bringing similar service to other places, with special emphasis on Stockton. A hydroelectric plant in Humbug Valley called for a dam impounding waters of Yellow Creek. From the reservoir, a thirteen-mile flume would deliver waters to the generating plant on Yellow Creek about a mile above its confluence with the North Fork of the Feather River.

To deliver construction material to the powerhouse site, Oro Electric first proposed a series of tramways but soon discarded them in favor of a standard-gauge spur from Belden, an old gold-mining town and now a station on Western Pacific. As WP stood on the southeast side of the North Fork, the Oro Electric survey took its spur extended along the river for twenty-five hundred feet above Belden before crossing the river at the mouth of Yellow Creek and proceeding up that creek. Even before the survey had been finished, concrete piers were set in the river so that by the end of 1912, the company was ready to move forward.

Belden presented a beehive of activity in February 1913 as an army of workers invaded the quiet village. Houses sprang up, and men were busy unloading the structural steel for the railroad bridge from WP cars. While some forces moved to erect the railroad bridge, Oro Electric had others building a bridge for wagons. The Belden siding became so congested that the company arranged for a six-car storage spur.

Mother Nature stepped in to challenge the work. Twelve inches of snow at the end of February brought a temporary layoff. Four weeks later, more miserable weather idled most of the 300-man force for almost a week, but between storms, the men accomplished some grading on both sides of the river, including a wye track near the bridge. Trestles forming the approaches to the steel bridge took form, but delays ensued when Superintendent M. L. Peppard found it necessary to order a new survey of the section between the WP switch and the bridge, as he recognized the original route to be impractical.

Frustration continued in March after a track had been laid on the steel bridge where the structural joints had not been riveted, an oversight that cost the company several weeks while it hunted for a heavy-duty air compressor.

An unpleasant surprise came at the end of April as the bridge work and the initial grading approached completion. For reasons not obvious to the employees, work came to an abrupt halt, and the 250-man force shrunk to merely 20 men.

Local sages stated the company had trouble marketing its bonds. Equally important, the California Railroad Commission denied the company's application to provide electricity in Stockton and environs, a ruling upheld in the courts.

Another matter, possibly unrelated, stemmed from the diversion dam Oro Electric had built across Butt Creek to add to its water supply. Field men of the Great Western Power Company, confident that their rights to Butt Creek water held, expressed their disapproval by dynamiting the diversion dam, which settled things, at least for that moment.

When Oro Electric suspended its work at Belden, the railroad grade extending from the switch at Belden, across the bridges, and up Yellow Creek stood well along the way toward completion. An important grade would have continued up a hill, but the last forty-five hundred feet to the site of the powerhouse followed an easy pitch. The company had erected a number of small houses at Belden for its employees as well as a small hotel at Longville.

With the various adverse factors, WP removed the switch, and Oro Electric removed its machinery and equipment from the area in the fall of 1914. Fruitless litigation continued for several years until Pacific Gas and Electric bought the remains of the company in 1917.

RECENT DEVELOPMENTS IN NEVADA RAILROADS

In the four decades since the books *Railroads of Nevada and Eastern California* first appeared, there have been a number of changes in the Nevada railroad picture. Some older railroads are being revitalized, and prospects for new railroad construction command attention. Passenger train service is now a federal enterprise rather than a private enterprise. And, with a series of mergers, long-established railroad corporate names have vanished.

With the suspension of copper smelting near Ely in 1983, the Nevada Northern Railway ceased main-line operations except for a brief period. However, the original rails are still in place, and the tracks around Ely serve an active tourist railroad.

To ease street congestion in the major hotel district of Las Vegas, an overhead monorail system has been constructed with the possibility of expansion.

A portion of the Virginia and Truckee Railroad has been catering to tourists successfully for some years, and work commenced in 2005 to rebuild the line from Gold Hill to Carson City.

The U.S. Department of Energy, if its plans to dump radioactive waste at Yucca Mountain materialize, expects to construct a new 319-mile railroad from Caliente in eastern Nevada to Yucca Mountain.

Nevada Northern Railway

Predecessors of the Kennecott Copper Company built Nevada Northern Railway (today, the last of the some forty Nevada short lines) from Cobre to Ely in 1905–1906. Rail extensions to the mines, concentrating mill, and smelter at McGill required another eighteen months to complete.

Subject to the wide swings in world market prices, both the Kennecott mines and railroad generally were busy until the 1970s when the copper company suffered operating losses due to a lower quality of ore and declining market prices. Closure of the Ruth Mine in 1978 was followed by the banking of fires at the McGill smelter on June 20, 1983, after the company's new smelter in Utah commenced operations. On that same day, the last freight train made its way to Cobre, with the motive power returning to Ely the next day. The entire system of mines, smelting, and railroads settled down for three years of inactivity.

Some Ely citizens envisioned using part of the railroad for tourist trains and formed the White Pine Historical Railroad Foundation Inc. to negotiate with Kennecott. In October 1986, the copper company generously donated railroad buildings in East Ely along with thirty-two miles of railroad extending from Keystone Mine to McGill to the foundation. The copper company also gave the foundation rolling stock, shop machinery, and nearly eighty years of operating records.

Commencing in May 1987, the museum began running trains for tourists on weekends during the summer months. The venture proved popular, and over time, more service was added so that several trains are operated each day for an extended season.

During that summer, the Los Angeles Department of Water and Power (DWP) purchased the idle main line as part of its plan to establish a coal-fired electric-generating facility at Cherry Creek.

New life came to Robinson Canyon when a gold mining company began work but soon was acquired by the Magma Copper Company in 1991. With established mining and smelter operations in Arizona including two short railroads, this company considered using railroads to transport copper concentrates from the mines to its smelter at San Manuel, Arizona.

The Los Angeles water agency, after abandoning plans for a power plant, invited proposals to lease and operate its long segment of the Nevada Northern from McGill Jct. to Cobre. Of the sixty respondents, the DWP chose the proposition of Brian Whipple and Tom Stoery, two experienced railroad men who had formed the Northern Nevada Railroad Company in July 1981 for this purpose. Two years elapsed before discussions resulted in the signing of a twenty-five-year lease. The new operators also secured freight trackage rights over the tourist railroad and obtained secondhand rolling stock.

The Northern Nevada Railroad management met with Magma representatives and formed an agreement in late November 1994. The railroad became a common carrier on January 1, 1995. Magma loaned the railroad $1,263,885 for the construction of a new branch to link the Kimberly mines with the new mill at Riepetown, a distance of 3.1 miles. It also loaned the railroad another million dollars to rehabilitate the main line, with repayment for both advances taking the form of a rebate on each revenue car handled. A celebration on November 15, 1995, marked the completion of the new rail line, with local civic leaders and copper men witnessing the driving of the last (copper) spike.

Magma's successful operations drew the attention of Broken Hill Proprietary (BHP) Ltd., an Australian firm with mines around the world. Magma became a segment of BHP a few days after the opening of 1996. On February 6, the Northern Nevada delivered the first car of copper concentrates to Union Pacific at Shafter for the 1,745-mile haul to the San Manuel smelter in Arizona.

In May, BHP officials summoned the Northern Nevada managers to a meeting to tell them that BHP wanted to operate the railroad without Whipple and Stoery. Certainly, this disappointing news troubled the two men who had worked so diligently to return the railroad to operation, but, as a practical matter, they had little choice but to accept a modest cash payment for their work and cancellation of debt owed the copper company. The railroad was turned over to BHP in June 1996, and the Northern Nevada Railroad Company was dissolved. Three years later, BHP, dissatisfied with the results, closed the mine and mill. The last train of concentrates left Riepetown on July 9, 1999.

Two years later, the DWP offered to sell the railroad, and, with funding provided by the Nevada legislature, the White Pine Historical Railroad Foundation stood ready to buy it, only to have a Los Angeles junk dealer secure an injunction suspending the sale, as he wanted to scrap the railroad. Now it is jointly owned by the Foundation and the City of Elko.

In 2004, with the exhaustion of the world copper surplus, the market price of copper began rising and soared to new heights of $1.93 a pound in November 2005 and substantially higher the next year. Quadra Mining Ltd. of Vancouver, British Columbia, purchased the idle property from BHP. The museum formed the Great Basin and Northern Railroad with its plan to resume operations when matters were settled. Unfortunately, the original light rail could not handle heavy carloads of concentrates except at very slow speeds, which made rail movement uneconomical. Accordingly, the new copper company contracted with a highway operator to take the concentrates to Union Pacific at Wendover, Utah, for the shipment to Pacific Coast ports for export.

Future prospects brightened in January 2006 with the news that the Sierra Pacific Power Company planned to erect coal-fired electric-generating plants not far from Ely, for then sustained incoming coal shipments would make financing the installation of heavy rail feasible. Until that time, the museum staff and volunteers continue to restore railroad rolling stock and provide train rides along Robinson Canyon for the enjoyment of tourists.

Virginia and Truckee Railway

Probably the best-known short-line railroad, the V&T Railway became a legend in 1950 after an eighty-year life. Some refused to accept its demise; various groups in the 1960s stepped forward with plans that had little substance other than enthusiasm. Tangible revival began in 1974 when Bob Gray began developing his short railroad that went into operation two years later. His success encouraged him to extend his rails through a tunnel and on to Gold Hill. Still, some factions worked to restore the V&T all the way to Carson City. Affirmative action caused the Nevada legislature to authorize a commission in 1983 to study the possible restoration of the railroad. Eight years later, the Nevada Northern Railway Foundation was formed by the legislature to advance the project. (This group should not be confused with the railroad operating to Ely.)

A four-year, three-phase construction program was announced early in 2005 that moved forward by purchasing a renovated steam locomotive from the McCloud River Railroad for moving trains over the projected railroad.

The rebuilding of the railroad from Gold Hill to a point in American Flat, a distance of 1.4 miles, constituted the first phase. A celebration on April 6, 2005, marked the beginning of physical work. With red-handled shovels, members of the Nevada Commission for the Reconstruction of the Virginia and Truckee Railway dug into the soil as photographers recorded the event. Under the supervision of the Nevada Department of Transportation, a contract was let to the Granite Construction Company—the same firm engaged in the creation of the "Reno Ditch"—which undertook to fill part of the Overman (mine) Pit for the railroad grade. Cross ties were distributed along the course designated by wood stakes with pink bows along the west side of the old Belcher Mine and around the Masonic and Catholic cemeteries. Working under the warm summer sun, tracklayers began driving spikes on July 6 to hold the heavy rails on the creosoted ties. These rails, formerly used by trains running through Reno, were contributed to the cause, and by September tracks covered the first phase of construction.

The second phase, from American Flat to the crossing of U.S. Highway 50 (also the boundary between Lyon and Carson City Counties), will measure 9.3 miles. A steel bridge, formerly serving as an overhead viaduct on the Union Pacific at Las Vegas, has been secured for the same purpose here. This section has its share of problems, particularly with the abandoned 568-foot tunnel, identified as No. 2. It was in this tunnel that the engineer of a passenger train in 1872 was confronted with a fire at one end and, rather than halt his train in the tunnel, charged through successfully. According to local reports, part of the tunnel collapsed immediately after the train escaped the fire.

After the Virginia City section of the railroad had been abandoned in 1938, the management blasted both ends of the tunnel to avoid possible injuries to trespassers. With the rebuilding of the railroad, it is hoped that the tunnel can be safely restored rather than building a new line around the hill.

The third phase, the Carson River Loop, will be the most scenic portion, as it follows the canyon, passing the sites of the stamp mills that treated ore from the Comstock Lode. It will measure 3.7 miles and is expected to be finished in 2008. The final section to Carson City will be about 2.6 miles long, depending on the selection of the site of the terminus.

As the original V&T Carson City depot had been sold and was now used by the local Masonic lodge and much of the right-of-way in that city was now occupied by new structures, a new location had to be found. At this writing, the choice narrowed down to two sites: one near Detroit Lane and the other near Drako Way, on the south side of U.S. Highway 50 below the Eagle Valley Golf Course. Although the Detroit Lane location is closer to the center of the city, it is in a potential flood zone. Drako Way offers more room for auto parking spaces, but trains would have to cross a highway on an overhead structure.

The estimated cost of the completed railroad totals thirty million dollars. Funding will come from several sources. The Nevada legislature provided five hundred thousand dollars, Carson City has taken on the debt of a bond issue—to be repaid by an increased local sales tax—and Storey County, which includes Virginia City, also has instituted an additional sales tax. U.S. Senator Harry Reid was able to insert a provision in the 2005 Highway Construction Bill that will contribute a helpful ten million dollars to the cause. And, of course, it is hoped there will be private donations as well.

Meanwhile, Virginia City citizens erected a steel-frame building for their history center. After considering one of two V&T locomotives from the Nevada Railroad Museum—No. 18 and No. 27—for an exhibit, it chose No. 18, the Dayton, which was trucked to the new site in September 2005.

Las Vegas Monorail

Commencing in 1983, a number of efforts in Las Vegas followed to develop a fixed-guideway transit system. After ten years had elapsed, Bally's Hotel and Casino and the MGM Grand Hotel and Casino concentrated their efforts to build a monorail system between the two hotels, a distance of eight-tenths of a mile. Two idle Mark IV Bombardier monorail trains were purchased from Walt Disney, and operations began in June 1995. In the first year, the monorail carried an average of 13,764 people daily. No fare was charged.

In 1997, the Nevada state legislature enacted a statute enabling cities and counties with large populations to award franchises for fixed-guideway transit systems. In January 1998, Design-Build Equip Contractor submitted a proposal to operate and expand the existing system, which the county subsequently approved.

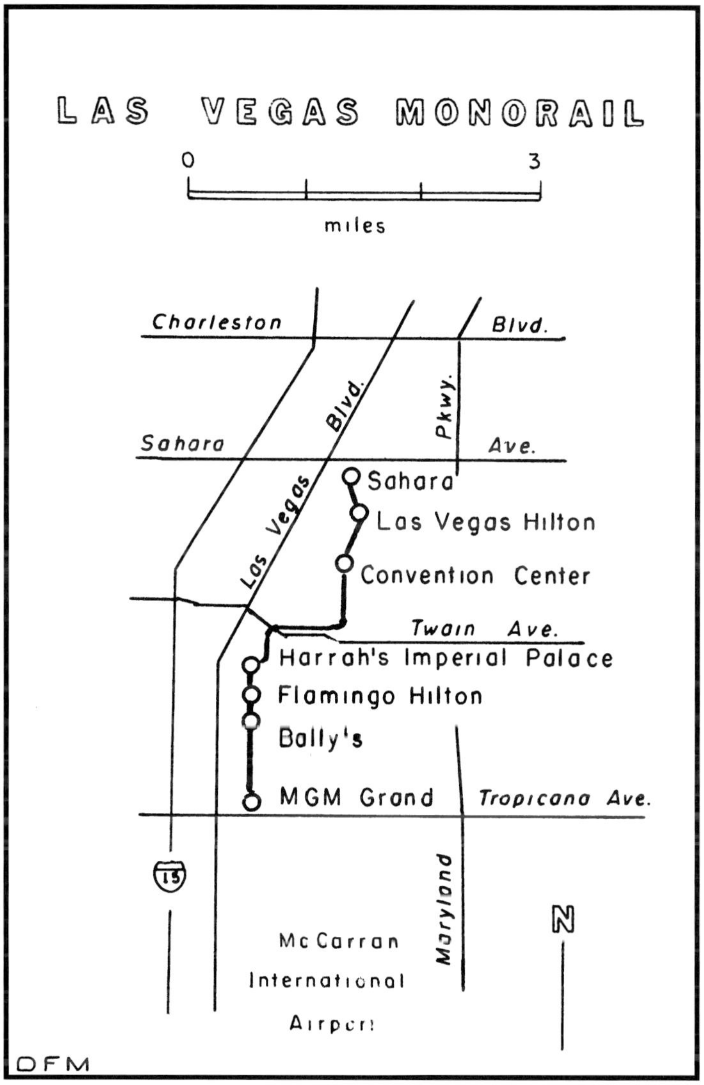

After the formation as a Nevada nonprofit benefit corporation in May 2000, the Las Vegas Monorail Company was to purchase and upgrade the existing monorail between the MGM Hotel and Bally's and extend the line about three miles on the east side of Las Vegas Boulevard to the Sahara Hotel and Casino. The cars were to be newly designed Bombardier M-VI vehicles, a straddle-type monorail riding on top of a narrow concrete guide beam. With automatic controls, the electrically powered cars were to run on pneumatic tires.

A series of revenue bonds was offered by underwriters by a prospectus of September 12, 2000. The 333-page prospectus described the project along with various studies and contracts. With financing arranged, construction commenced, with Granite Construction Company along with Bombardier Transportation holding the major contracts, while Gensler Architects served as the master design firm. At a total cost of $650 million, the Robert N. Broadbent Las Vegas Monorail commenced operations on July 15, 2004, with a civic celebration. Crowds of patrons welcomed the monorail on its opening day; by noon, trains had standing-room patronage as 30,515 patrons paid $98,436 to ride the trains. Broadbent, long a driving force in the monorail project and civic leader, had died the previous August. He had been chairman of the Las Vegas Monorail Company and also a commissioner of the U.S. Bureau of Reclamation from 1981 to 1984.

Nine 4-car trains, with colorfully painted cars, operate on the east side of the Las Vegas Strip from 8:00 A.M. to midnight. A single ticket costs $3, while a twenty-four-hour pass is $10. The trains ride on a monorail twenty to seventy feet aboveground, as the monorail serves eight major hotels and the convention center.

Although the ridership in the fall of 2005 was slightly disappointing, the monorail company celebrated its ten millionth passenger on October 30, 2005.

Currently, studies are under way for extending the present line north to Fremont Street. Also considered is a similar monorail on the west side of Las Vegas Boulevard to serve more hotels as well as an extension to the McCarran Airport. Long taxi lines have created problems there during peak traffic hours; recently U.S. Senator John McCain of Arizona had to wait for almost an hour for a cab at the airport.

Yucca Mountain Railroad (Projected)

The U.S. Department of Energy, as part of its plan to dispose of radioactive waste, chose an area around Yucca Mountain, about 90 miles northwest of Las Vegas. The waste would be gathered from all parts of the country and delivered by truck or railcar. To reach the proposed site, a new railroad would be necessary.

The Energy Department announced plans to construct a railroad extending westward from Caliente, Nevada, a station on the Union Pacific Salt Lake line, across the state to a point near Tonopah, where it would turn south and pass east of Goldfield to end at Yucca Mountain. It would measure about 319 miles in length.

In August 2005, as a beginning step, the department published a statement in the *Federal Register* withholding from encroachment some 300,000 acres of the route of the railroad. It also involved 915 recorded mining claims.

The State of Nevada has strenuously objected to the use of Yucca Mountain as the site for disposition of radioactive waste, and, at this writing, the controversial matter stands suspended.

Corporate Changes

The scene has changed in various ways. Passenger trains, long since departed from branch lines, left the main lines, for the romance of the rails could not hold the necessary patronage. Since May 1, 1971, when the National Railroad Passenger Corporation, better known as Amtrak, took over the passenger service of the industry, it has operated only one train across Nevada. Today,

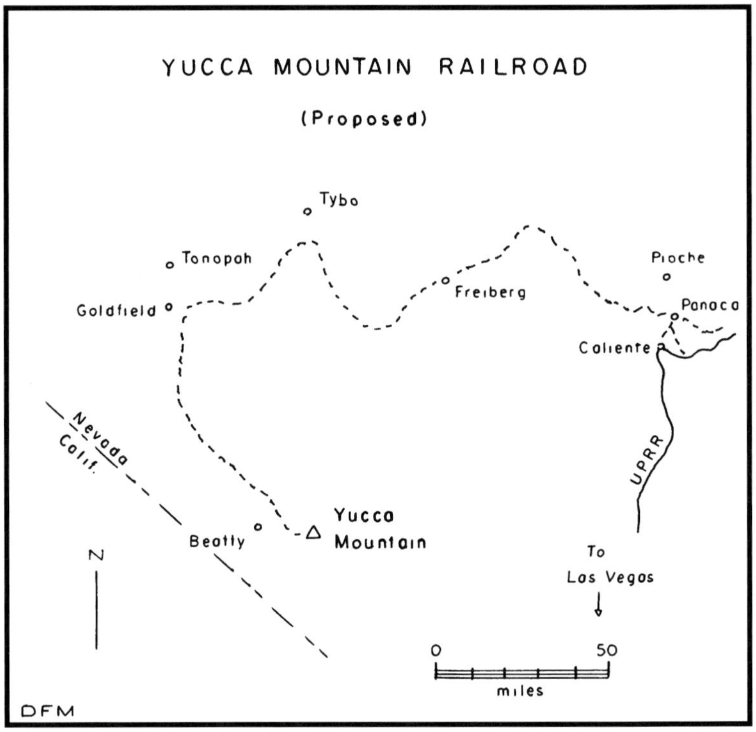

the *California Zephyr*, though developed by the Western Pacific Railroad and its connections, no longer follows the scenic Feather River canyons but uses the shorter Donner Pass route of Southern Pacific.

The railroad corporate structures have undergone many important transformations, the first involving the separation of the railroad and nonrailroad activities. In the West, it began when Santa Fe Industries Inc. became the holding company of the Atchison, Topeka, and Santa Fe Railway Company on August 21, 1968, through an exchange of stock. Ownership of the nonrail assets went to Santa Fe Industries Inc. About a year later, on June 17, 1969, the Union Pacific Corporation was created as a holding company, and the shareholders of the Union Pacific Railroad exchanged their shares for stock in the holding company. Two years later, all the nonrail assets of the railroad company were transferred to the holding company.

On November 26, 1969, a few months after the Golden Spike Centennial celebration, the Southern Pacific Company became a true holding company rather than a holding company as well as an operating company. On that date, all rail properties were transferred to the Southern Pacific Transportation Company (SPTC), while all other subsidiaries, other than the trucking companies, remained with the holding company. The Western Pacific Railroad Company adopted a slightly different approach when its management formed Western Pacific Industries to acquire the stock of the railroad company as of June 17, 1971. This holding company also purchased several industrial companies, and, in a change of policy, it sold the railroad and trucking subsidiaries to the management on April 1, 1979. Previously, in 1978, the management had transferred the corporate home of the railroad to Delaware, using the identical name of the former company incorporated under California laws in 1916 following its first reorganization.

The Time of Railroad Mergers

The era of railroad mergers had just begun when the first volume of *Railroads of Nevada and Eastern California* initially appeared. Both Southern Pacific and the Santa Fe applied to the Interstate Commerce Commission for authority to acquire control of Western Pacific in 1960. The hearing examiner, Paul C. Albus, submitted his report on September 9, 1963, recommending the authorization of Santa Fe control and denying SP's request. The final step came on January 27, 1965, when the ICC denied both applications, as it believed Western Pacific should remain independent. The report, released a few days later, stated that WP was a prosperous carrier and one of the healthiest railroads in the country.

Subsequently, instead of continuing to fight each other, Southern Pacific and the Santa Fe contemplated a merger. Initial talks, terminated in 1980 after only a few months of discussions, were revived three years later, with the proposal partly consummated on December 23, 1983, when the two holding companies, Santa Fe Industries Inc. and Southern Pacific Company, became the Santa Fe Southern Pacific Corporation. ICC authority remained necessary to join the two railroad subsidiaries into the Southern Pacific and Santa Fe Railway Company. Testimony offered at the hearings before the commission failed to convince the ICC, so it denied the application in July 1986.

Three years later the name of the holding company was shortened to Santa Fe Pacific Corporation. In June 1994, the Santa Fe Pacific Corporation and Burlington Northern Inc. signed a merger agreement that the ICC approved to become effective September 22, 1995, as the Burlington Northern Santa Fe Corporation. As 2005 began, the name was shortened again, this time to BN-SF Inc.

During the interim, while the ICC considered the Santa Fe Railway–Southern Pacific Transportation Company proposal, an independent trustee held the stock of SPTC, and the railroad entered a difficult period. Philip F. Anschutz, a successful Denver oilman, acquired complete ownership of Rio Grande Industries Inc., the holding company for the Denver and Rio Grande Western Railroad (D&RGW). He then acquired ownership of the Southern Pacific Transportation Company in October 1988, also through the same holding company. He changed the railroad's name to Southern Pacific Rail Corporation. Subsequently, he merged the D&RGW into Southern Pacific Rail Corporation.

In August 1993, Anschutz and other related shareholders offered a portion of their stock to investors, and for the first time in almost ten years, public ownership of SP stock became possible.

Meanwhile, Union Pacific had been extending its perimeters, beginning with control of the Missouri Pacific and the Western Pacific, which the ICC sanctioned, effective December 22, 1982. This acquisition brought the bright-yellow UP locomotives into northern California and down to Texas and doubled its road mileage. Independent railroad men called the expanding road "the yellow peril," but UP continued its acquisitions. UP purchased the Missouri-Kansas-Texas in August 1988, and, after a five-year effort, the Chicago and Northwestern came into the fold in December 1994.

While the Santa Fe's pending merger with Burlington Northern stood under ICC review, UP officers made overtures to join that road in 1994. After the Santa Fe declined the invitation, Union Pacific focused on the Southern

Pacific Rail Corporation. With other western railroads in agreement on an extensive trackage-rights proposal to preserve competition, the Surface Transportation Board, successor to the Interstate Commerce Commission, accepted the Union Pacific plan, and on September 11, 1996, Southern Pacific became part of the Union Pacific family. Though SP's road mileage had been reduced by the disposition of many branch lines, the inclusion of the former D&RGW in the transaction brought the total route mileage to thirty-six thousand miles, making Union Pacific the longest railroad in the country.

Now, all three Nevada trunk lines are gathered under single ownership. The BN-SF received extensive trackage rights between St. Louis and Texas as well as from Salt Lake City and Ogden to northern California over both the former Western Pacific and Southern Pacific. In more recent years, BN-SF orange-and-green diesel power appears as a regular feature along the Humboldt River, over Donner Pass, and in Feather River canyons.

Nevada has not forgotten the part railroads played in its history. The Nevada Railroad Museum at Carson City with a branch near Boulder City displays an impressive gathering of restored railroad locomotives and cars. Though no train has whistled in its town for almost sixty years, the Beatty (Nevada) Museum and Historical Society celebrated its fourth annual Beatty Railroad Days with a parade and special classic-auto exhibits on June 2–4, 2000.

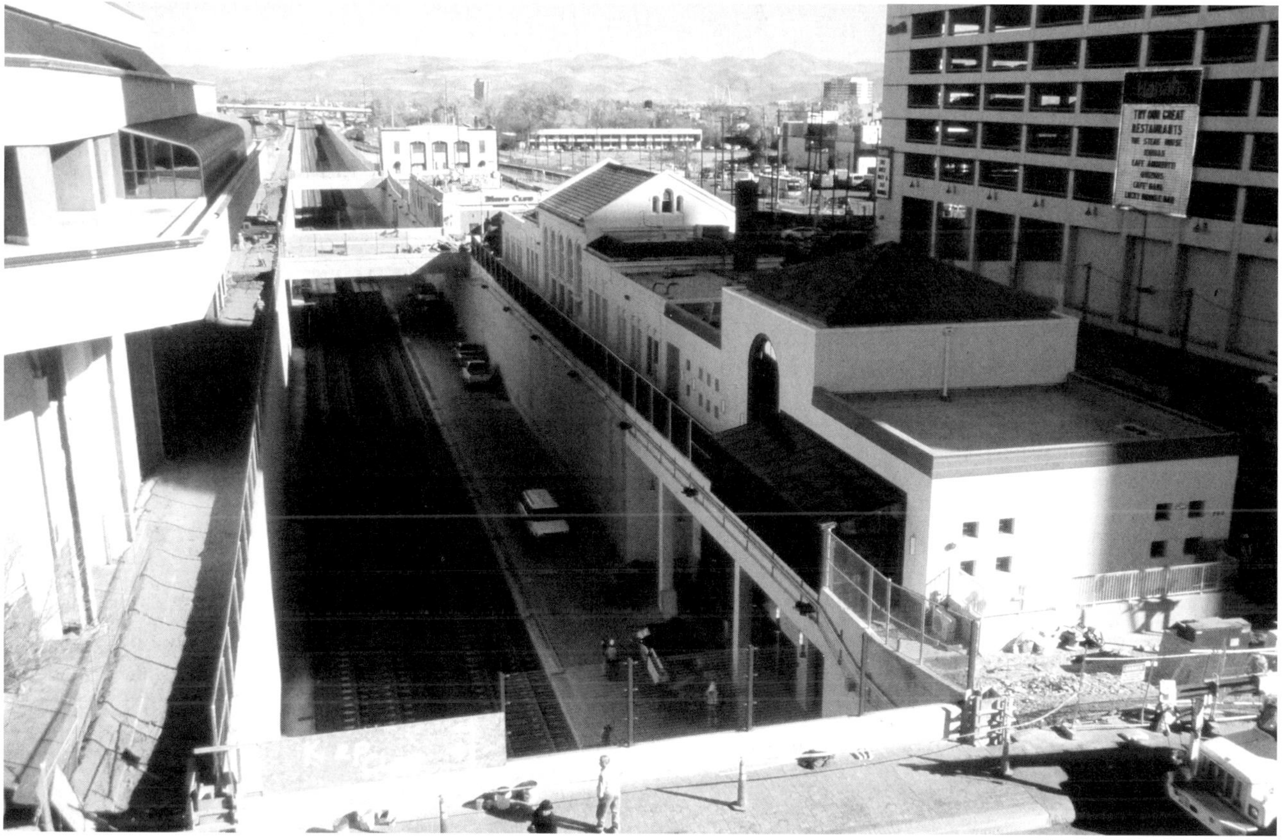

The Reno Trench shortly before its opening (see pages 43–45). The new Amtrak station stands in the right foreground, with the former Amtrak station just beyond. (Steve VanDenburgh photograph)

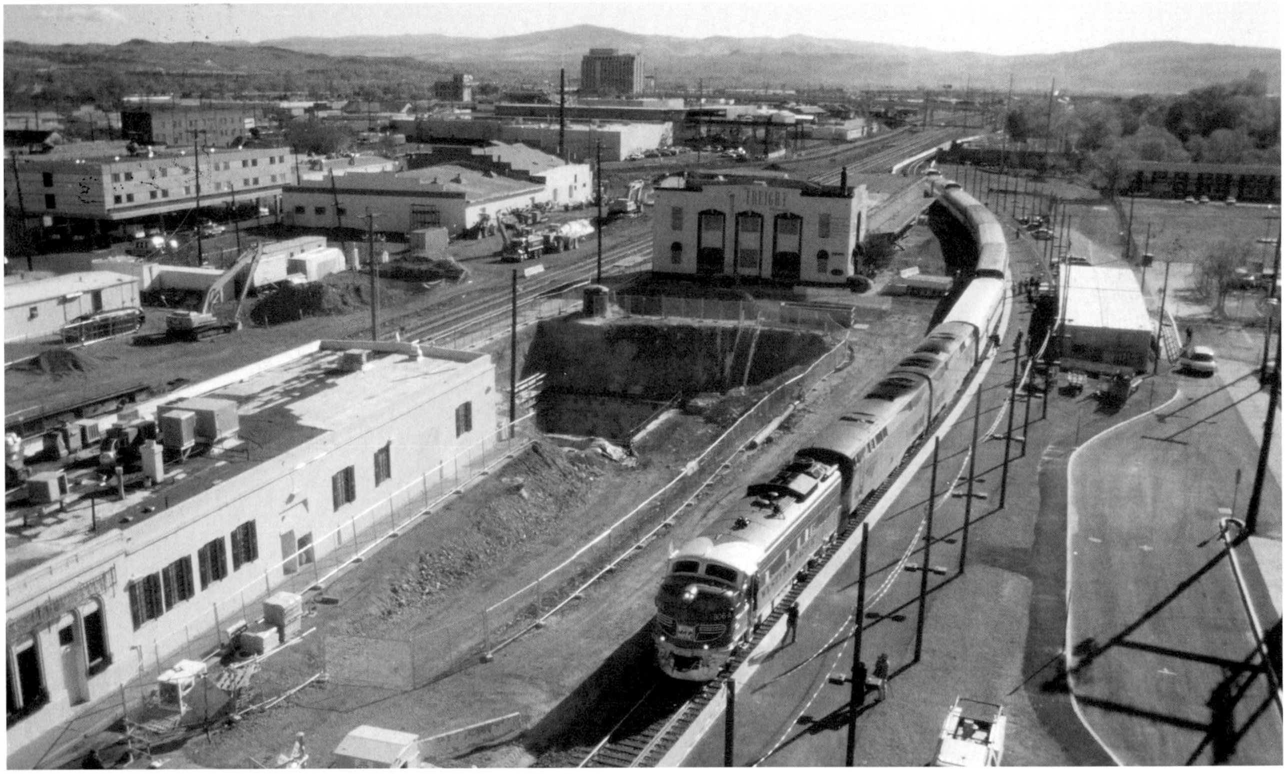

Above: Amtrak's California Zephyr with a Western Pacific diesel locomotive on the point paused on the bypass in April 2004, with the temporary Amtrak station in the right background. The former Southern Pacific freight station stands in the background between the bypass and the former main line. (Steve VanDenburgh photograph)

Below: The west end of the completed Reno Trench, with the bypass track on the right. (Steve VanDenburgh photograph)

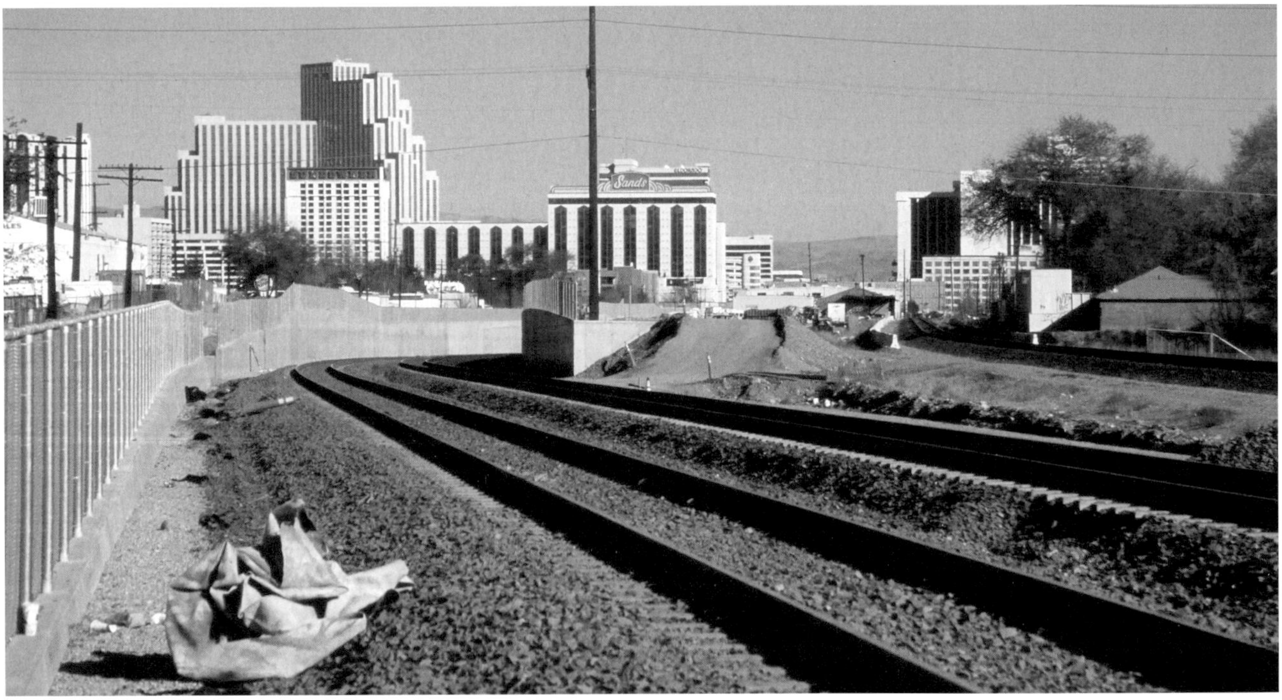

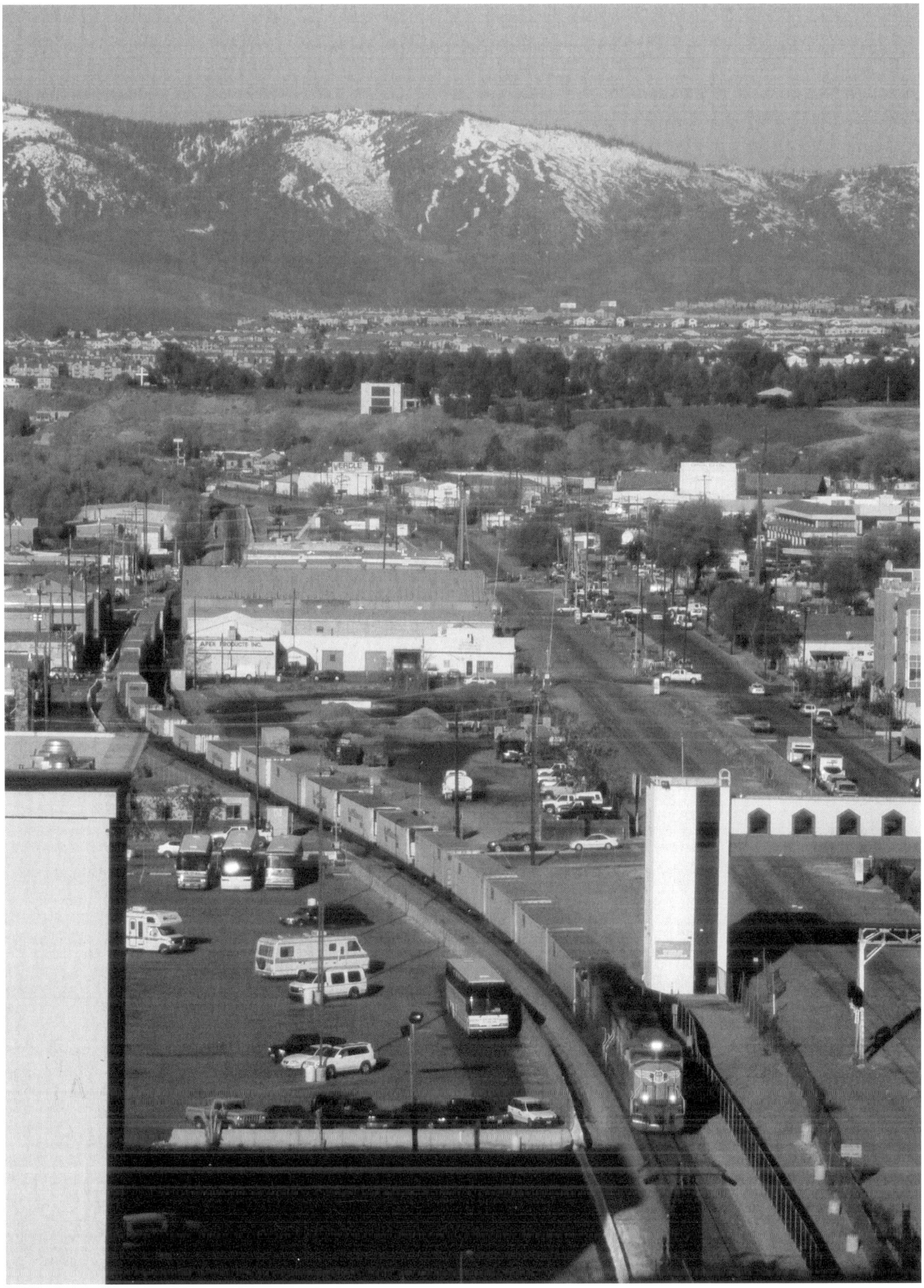

A Union Pacific freight train bearing containers is heading east on the bypass through downtown Reno in April 2004 with the former main line (*right*) and the Sierra Nevada in the background. (Steve VanDenburgh photograph)

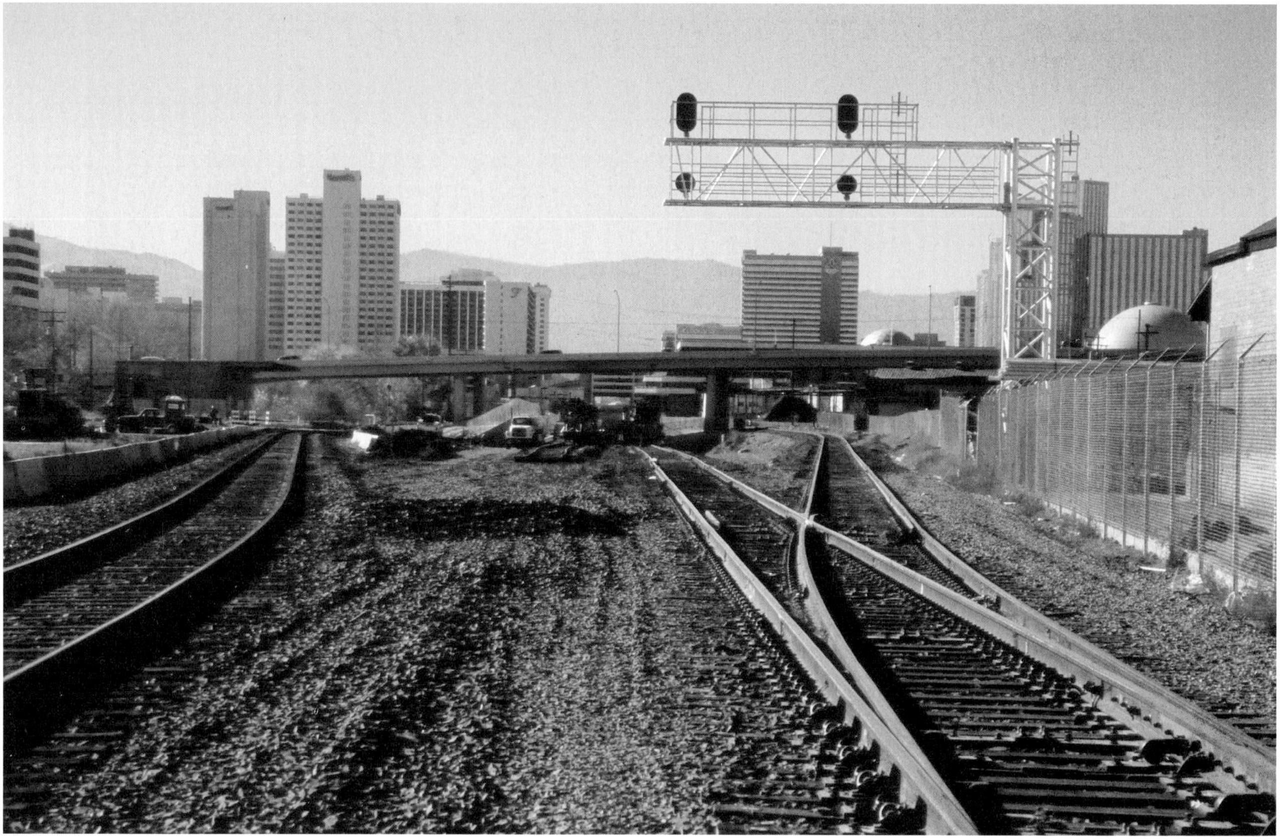

With the target signals looming overhead, this westward view taken at the east end of the bypass (*left*) stands in contrast to the almost completed new main line (*right*) and the connection to the former Western Pacific Reno branch far (*right*). (Steve VanDenburgh photograph)

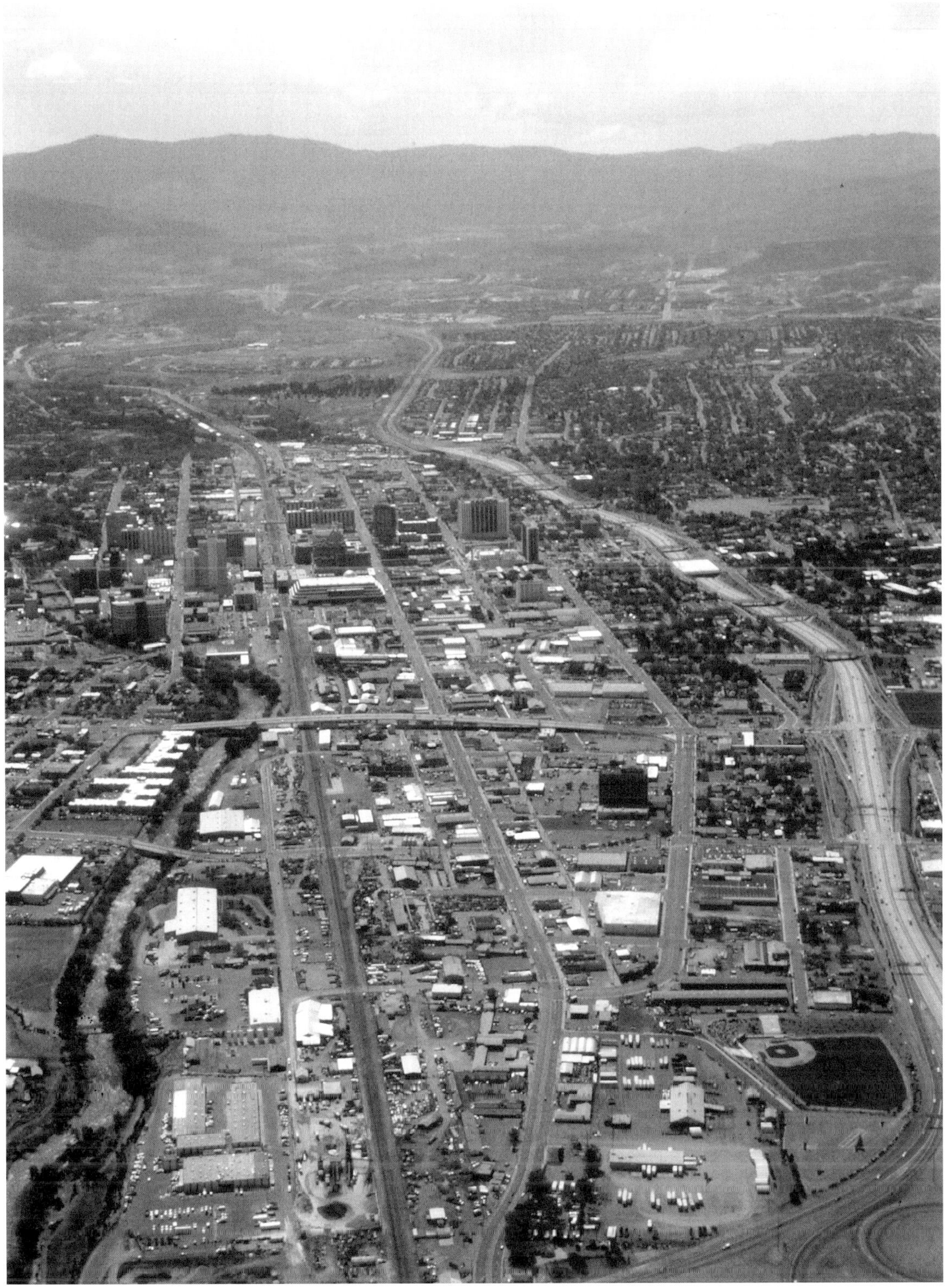

Aerial photograph of Reno. (Steve VanDenburgh photograph)

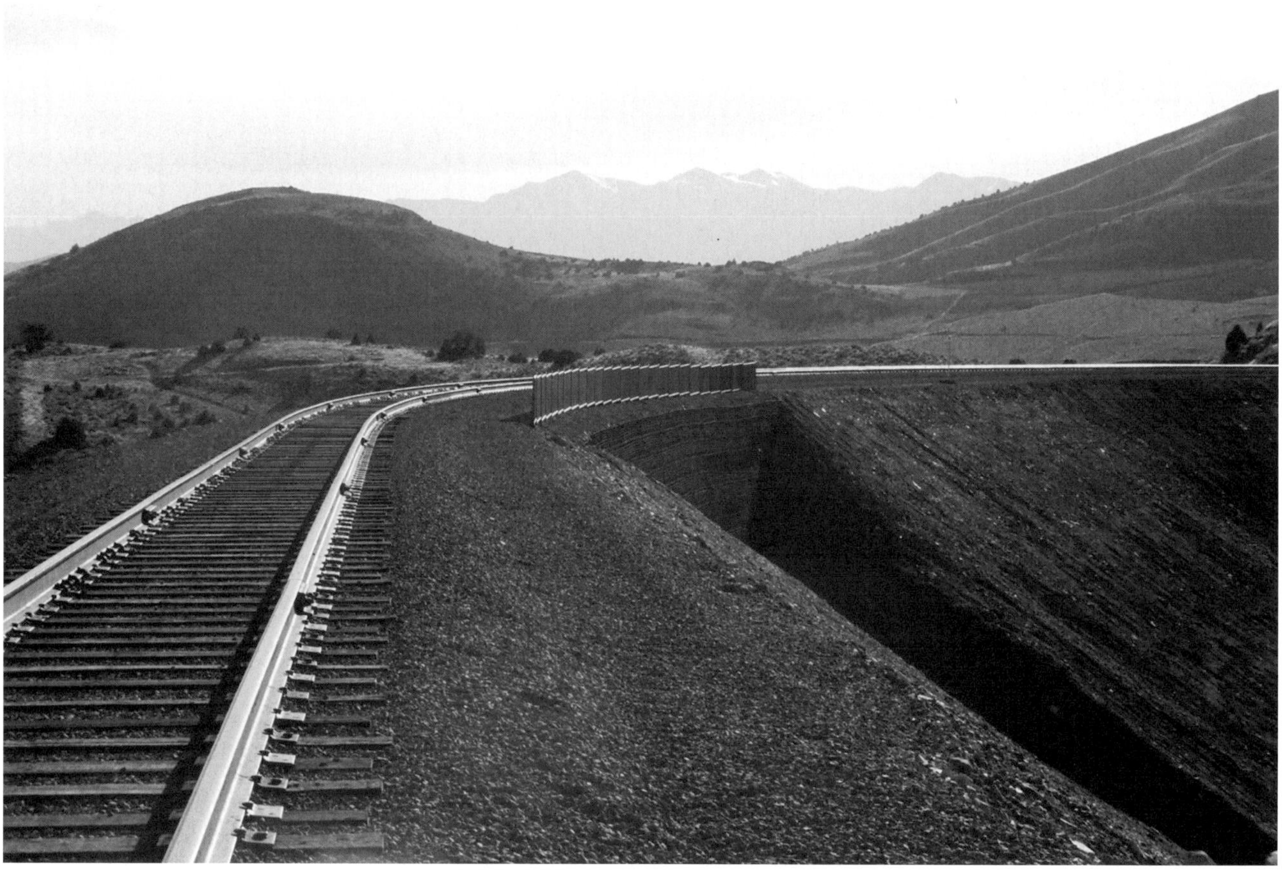

During the summer of 2005, a section of the Virginia and Truckee Railway was rebuilt from Gold Hill to American Flat. Crossing the Overman Pit required a large fill. (Skip Gibson photograph)

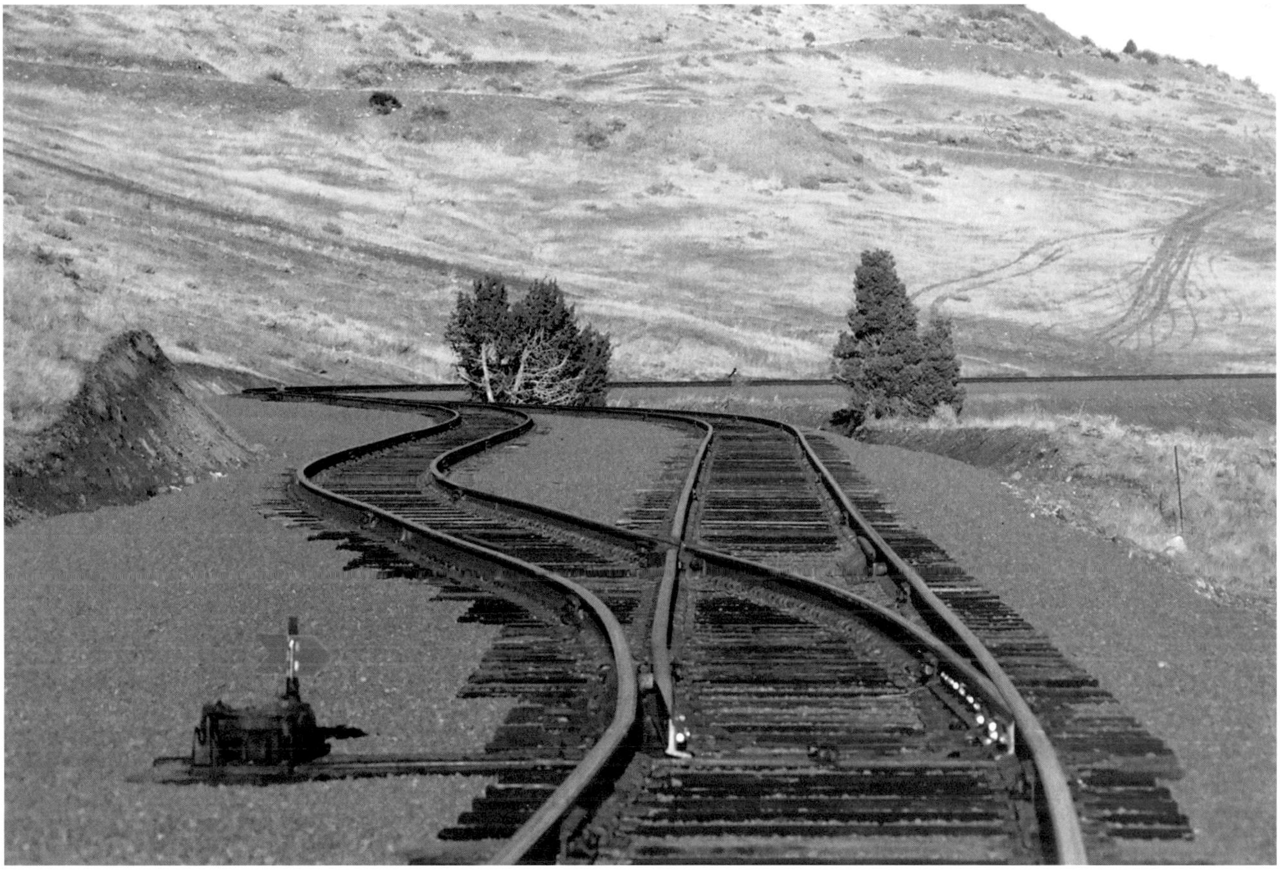

Normal railroad operations require a passing track when trains meet. (Skip Gibson photograph)

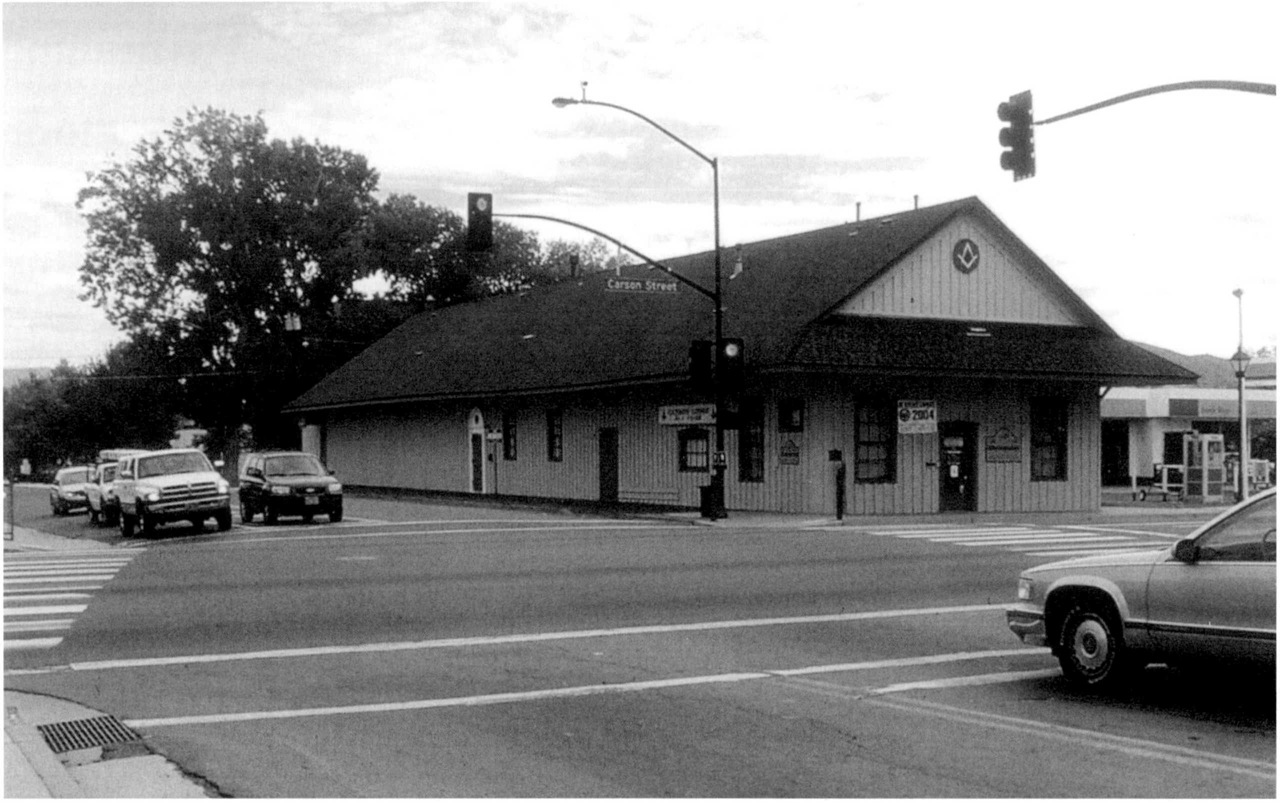

For some time, the former V&T Carson City depot has been occupied by the Masonic order and will not be part of the planned rebuilding of that railroad. Carson Street, in the foreground, forms part of U.S. Highway 395.

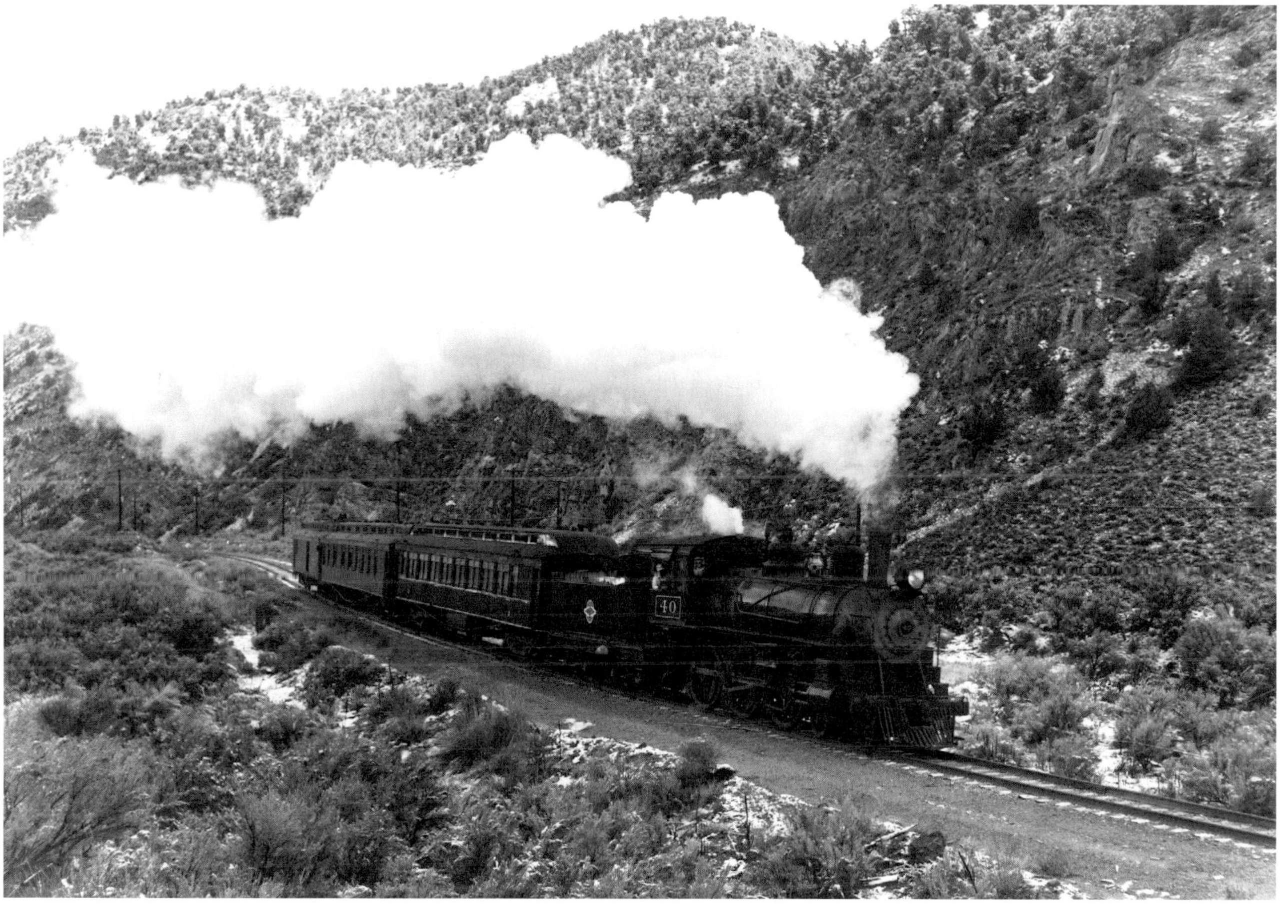

In recent years, trains of the Nevada Northern Railway have provided enjoyment for many visitors. This train is working its way up Robinson Canyon. (Nevada Northern Railway)

INDEX

Italic page numbers refer to photographs and maps.

—D—

—E—

—F—

—G—

—N—

—O—

—P—

—Q—

—T—

—U—

—V—

—W—